EXPOSÉ™

VOLUME 11

Ballistic Publishing

Finest digital art in the known universe

134 Gilbert St | Adelaide SA 5000 | Australia
correspondence: info@BallisticPublishing.com
www.BallisticPublishing.com

First Edition published in Australia 2013 by Ballistic Publishing
Softcover Edition ISBN 978-0-9874036-1-2
Hardcover Edition ISBN 978-1-921828-98-0
Limited Edition ISBN 978-1-921828-97-3

PUBLISHER: Ballistic Publishing
CO-EDITORS: Paul Hellard and Mark Thomas
SENIOR DESIGNER: Mark Thomas
GLOBAL ARTIST LIAISON: Paul Hellard

PRINTING AND BINDING: Everbest Printing (China)
www.everbest.com

PARTNERS: The CGSociety (Computer Graphics Society)
www.CGSociety.org

CGSOCIETY
SOCIETY OF DIGITAL ARTISTS

Visit www.BallisticPublishing.com for our complete range of titles.

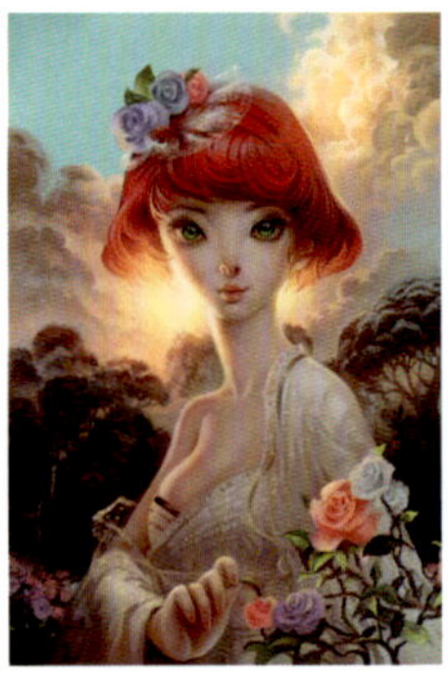

COVER IMAGE CREDITS

Front cover:
EXPOSÉ 11 Softcover
and EXPOSÉ 11 Hardcover

Chaichan Artwichai, THAILAND
page 123

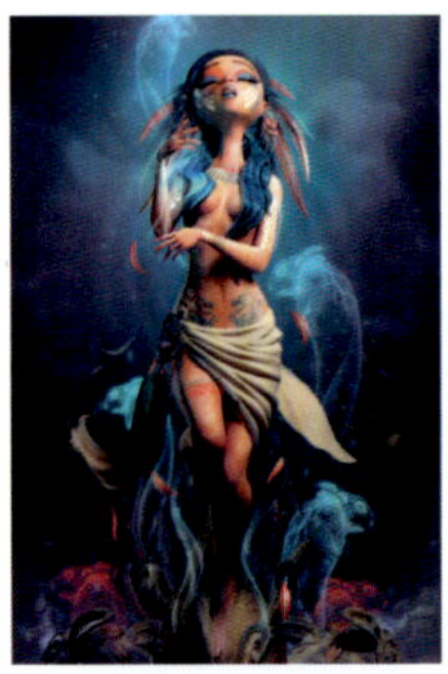

Front cover:
EXPOSÉ 11 Limited Edition

Carlos Ortega Elizalde, MEXICO
page 119

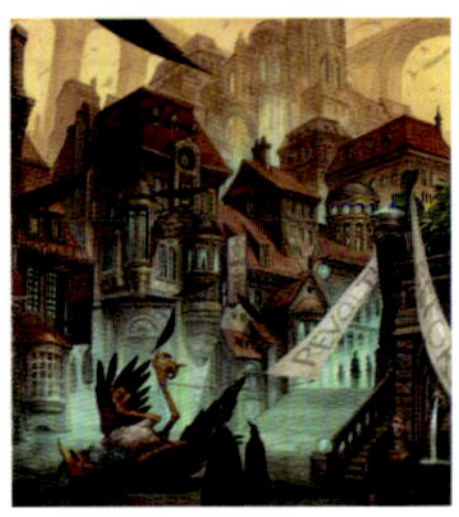

Back cover:
EXPOSÉ 11 Softcover
and EXPOSÉ 11 Hardcover

Sean Andrew Murray, USA
page 274

/BALLISTIC/

EXPOSÉ™

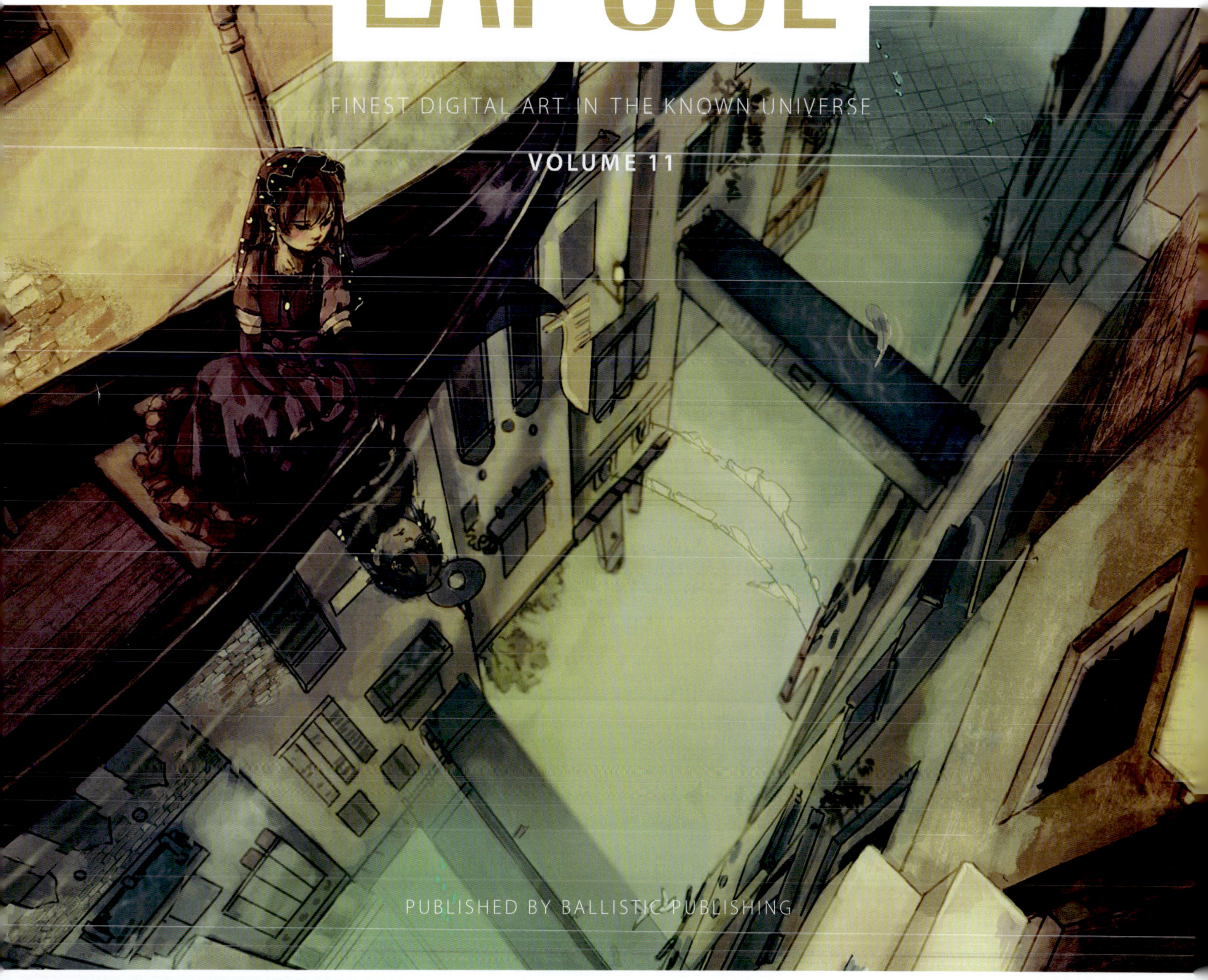

FINEST DIGITAL ART IN THE KNOWN UNIVERSE

VOLUME 11

PUBLISHED BY BALLISTIC PUBLISHING

This world map is a graphic representation of the countries that this year's 406 successful artists are from. It shows the breadth of countries contributing to the global digital arts industry and the world-wide reach of EXPOSÉ. Each country is represented by a single orange dot on their capital city regardless of how many successful artists are from that country.

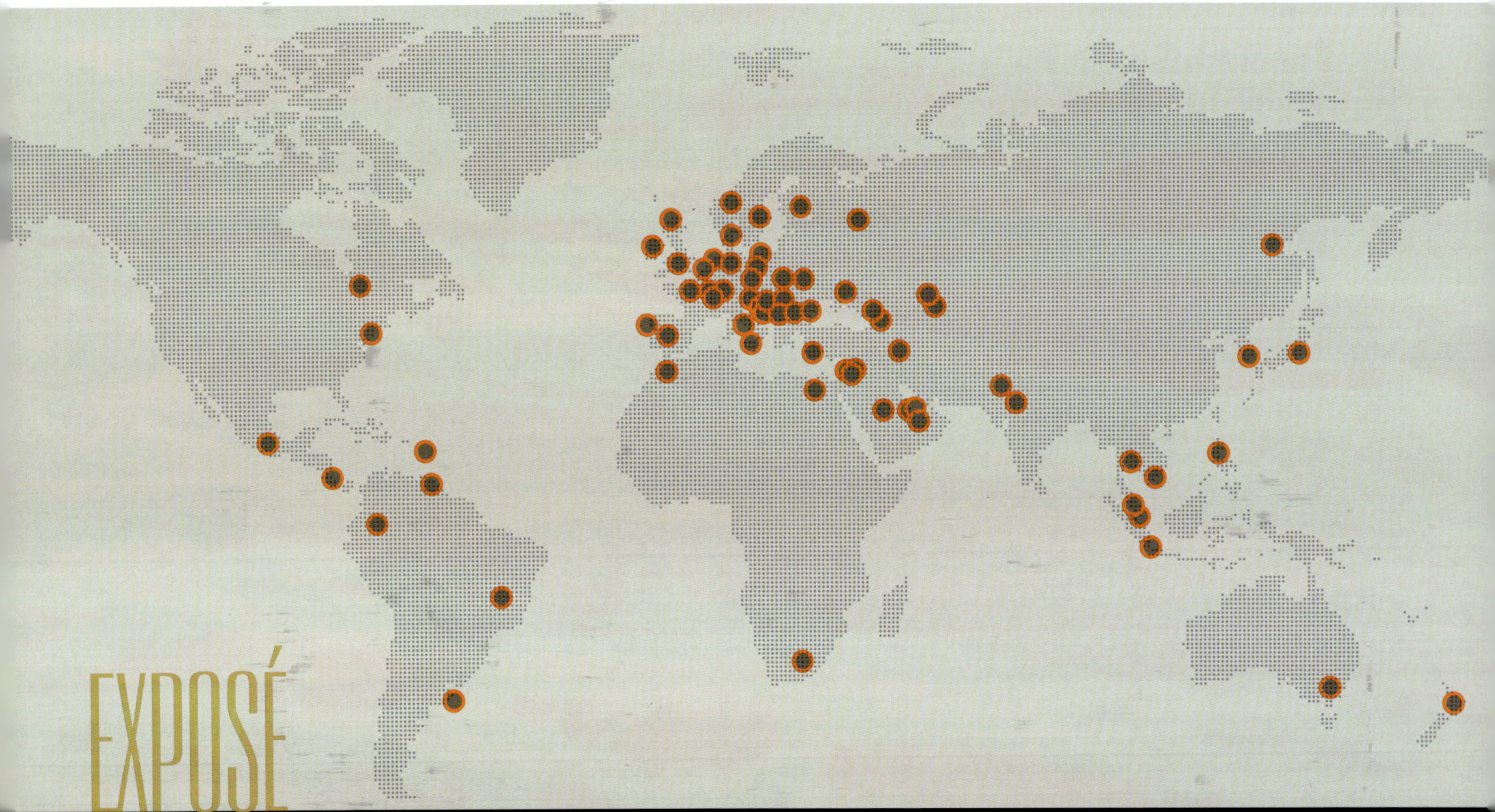

A SNAPSHOT OF THE IMAGES PUBLISHED IN EXPOSÉ 11

HOW MANY ARTISTS INCLUDED 406
HOW MANY ARTISTS NEW TO EXPOSÉ 185
HOW MANY IMAGES INCLUDED 587
HOW MANY COUNTRIES REPRESENTED 58

HOW MANY IMAGES SUBMITTED THIS YEAR 8100
HOW MANY IMAGES SHORTLISTED THIS YEAR 1606

COUNTRY THAT THE GRAND MASTER IS FROM:

GREAT BRITAIN

WHERE THE MASTER AWARD WINNERS ARE FROM:

THE NETHERLANDS, USA, ITALY, TURKEY, CROATIA, UKRAINE, GREAT BRITAIN, MEXICO, UAE, GERMANY, EGYPT, CANADA, CHINA, ESTONIA.

WHERE THE EXCELLENCE AWARD WINNERS ARE FROM:

MEXICO, USA, FRANCE, CHINA, ITALY, GREAT BRITAIN, TAIWAN, SLOVAKIA, AUSTRIA, CANADA, NEW ZEALAND, POLAND, SWITZERLAND, BRAZIL, ARGENTINA, DENMARK, SINGAPORE, JAPAN, NORWAY, THAILAND, FINLAND, SPAIN.

THE TOP TEN COUNTRIES WITH MOST ENTRIES:

SPAIN 16
RUSSIA 17
MEXICO 19
GERMANY 22
GREAT BRITAIN 27
CANADA 31
POLAND 35
CHINA 36
FRANCE 36
USA 136

WELCOME TO EXPOSÉ 11

FROM THE TEAM AT BALLISTIC PUBLISHING AND THE CGSOCIETY

Welcome to a new decade of EXPOSÉ.

Publishing last year's tenth anniversary edition enabled us to reflect on how much the industry has matured in 10 years. Technology has made huge advances, studios have risen and fallen, but great digital art has always prevailed. EXPOSÉ 11, like its predecessors, is in the vanguard of documenting the best of this new era.

We're excited to introduce our new cover design to you. It completes the strong, confident changes to the interior that we began last year. EXPOSÉ is our flagship publication, and this new design will lead us forward into a new decade of EXPOSÉ.

Many of our international judges have returned this year. They are joined by Don Seegmiller, a master artist whose digital and traditional paintings have graced many books and galleries for over 25 years. Together, the judges have selected the Master Award winners and appointed Awards of Excellence in each category. This year sets another record for the number of entries, with just over 8000 images submitted. It's a very demanding task to select just a few winners from the thousands of amazing submissions, and we thank the judges for their dedication to this work.

In selecting images for inclusion in EXPOSÉ, we look for extraordinary technique, originality and pure creative thought – timeless images that tell a compelling story. With artists from 58 countries represented in EXPOSÉ 11, this truly is a global publication. The artwork in EXPOSÉ will always be the defining standard for the digital arts industry worldwide, and both established and emerging artists increase the intensity of the competition for inclusion every year. Every artist whose work appears here is entitled to feel immensely proud of their achievement. They are the best of the best.

We want to extend our congratulations to this year's Grand Master, the internationally recognized British fantasy artist and designer Roger Dean. There was hearty agreement among last year's judges that he should receive the honor this year.

As with a number of our previous Grand Masters, the bulk of Roger's work is not digital. Candidates for Grand Master are considered on a number of broad points: have they had wide influence in this industry; have they been prolific and maintained a consistently high standard; and, amongst other criteria, have they produced a substantial body of well-respected work.

Roger Dean has met all these criteria in abundance, and has helped pave the way for incredible invention, technical mastery and creativity in the digital arts industry. His work still inspires and motivates other artists through its great characters and superb storytelling. You can read more about him on page 6.

Reading through comments on our website's EXPOSÉ 10 'Around the World' page, we are reminded of what a pivotal role the EXPOSÉ series has played in the careers of many artists. The following quote is typical of the responses we receive…

'When I began to illustrate, one of my inspirations was EXPOSÉ, and I always said, "Someday I'll be here in this book." Six years later, my dream comes true and being part of this book with all these talented artists is an honor.'
Rodolfo Velado, EL SALVADOR

We are flattered that so many artists regard inclusion of their work in EXPOSÉ as both a goal and a benchmark in their careers. We are equally proud when we hear that the publication of their work in EXPOSÉ has led to artists in receiving wider recognition and advancement in their careers. After all, assisting artists sits at the core of everthing that Ballistic Publishing and the CGSociety does.

We trust that you will be inspired, challenged and motivated to excellence by the hundreds of exceptionally talented artists on display here. The team at Ballistic Publishing and the CGSociety are very proud to present EXPOSÉ 11 to you.

/ B A L L I S T I C /

CGSOCIETY
SOCIETY OF DIGITAL ARTISTS

Every year the range of work submitted to EXPOSÉ is breathtaking, with many categories consistently overflowing with amazing submissions. Each year we modify our category list in response to the art we receive – deleting some categories and adding others. In this EXPOSÉ, Game Art makes a welcome return, we include a new category called Character, and, for the first time in an EXPOSÉ, we present a Special Feature – digital 'plein air' painting (see page 222).

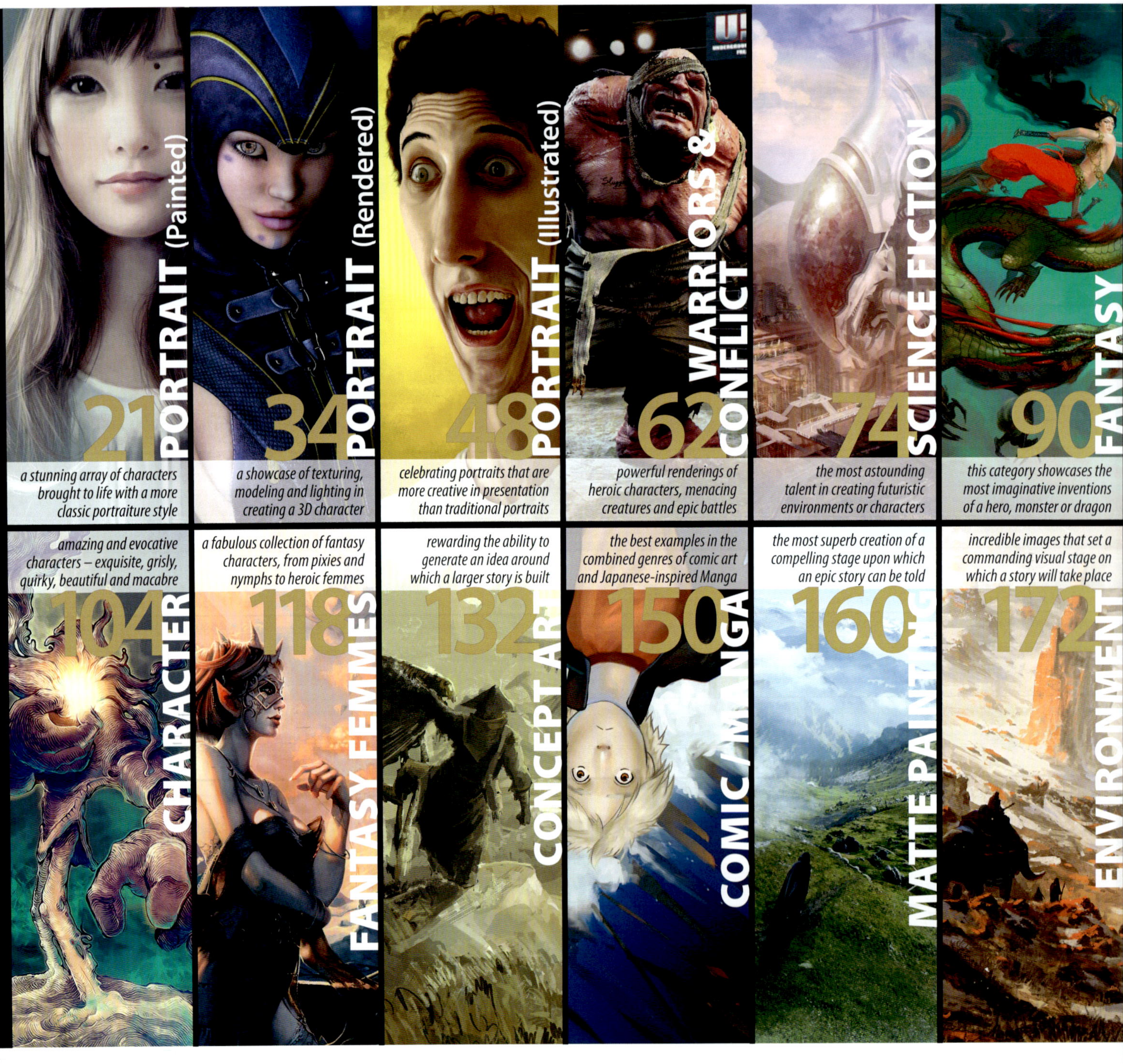

CATEGORIES

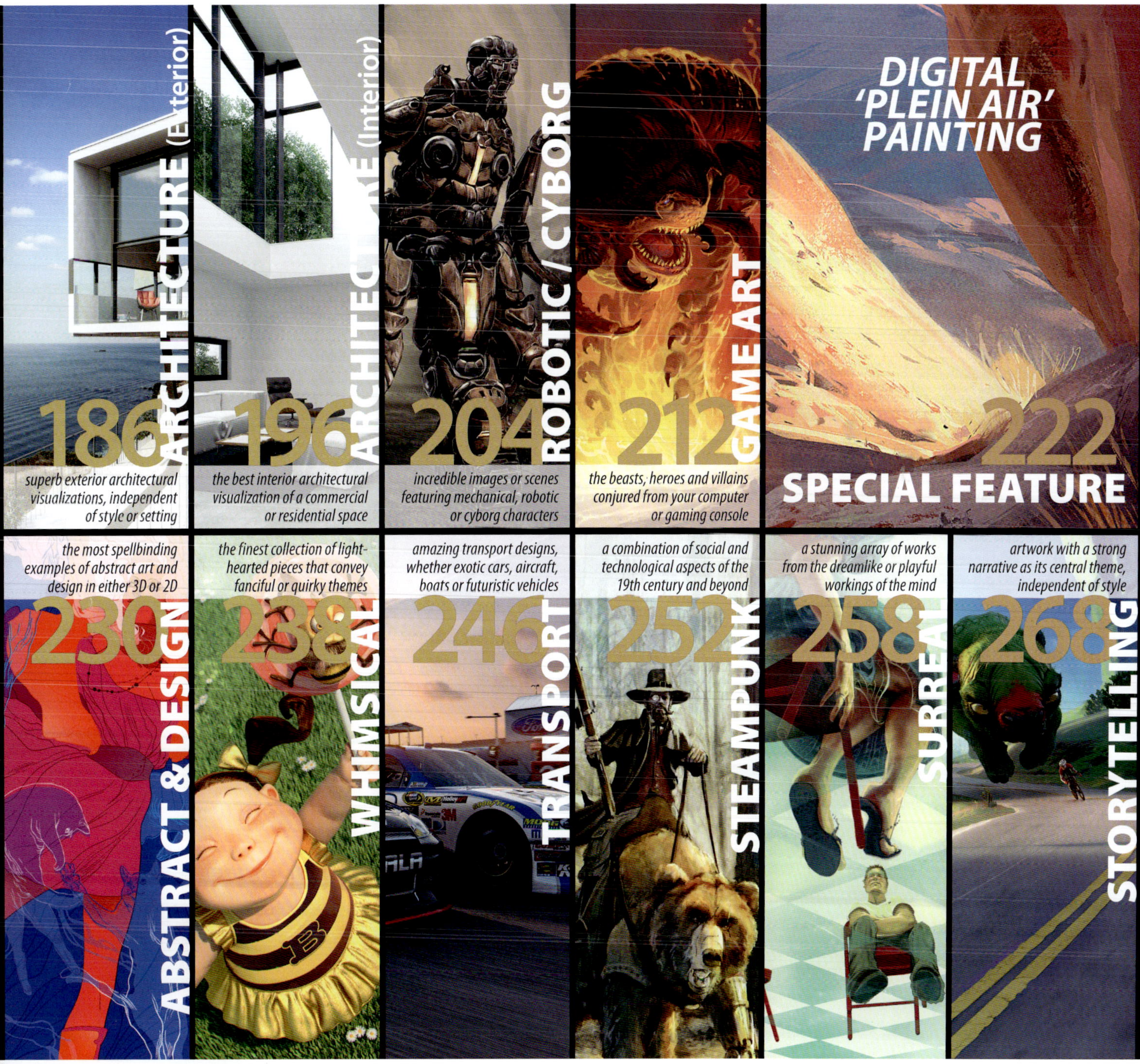

With each edition of EXPOSÉ, we appoint an international panel of judges. They select the Master Award winners in each category, and appoint Awards of Excellence to artists who have created images of outstanding merit. The judges are experts in their fields – either leading artists in their own right, art directors at major studios, or respected editors and reviewers of digital artists and digital content. We have 13 members on our international panel this year. Don Seegmiller was welcomed onto the panel this year, and rounds out an exceptional group.

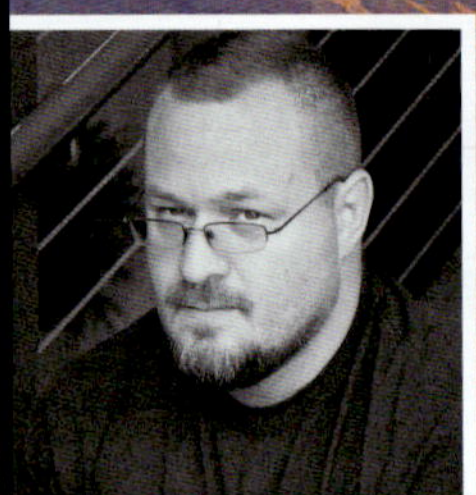

CHRIS PERNA

This Epic Games art director oversees all of the studio's games, from the billion-dollar *Gears of War* franchise to the award-winning *Infinity Blade* series. With more than 15 years in the computer graphics and video game industries, Chris Perna oversees a stable of talented artists/animators at Epic Games' headquarters worldwide subsidiaries.

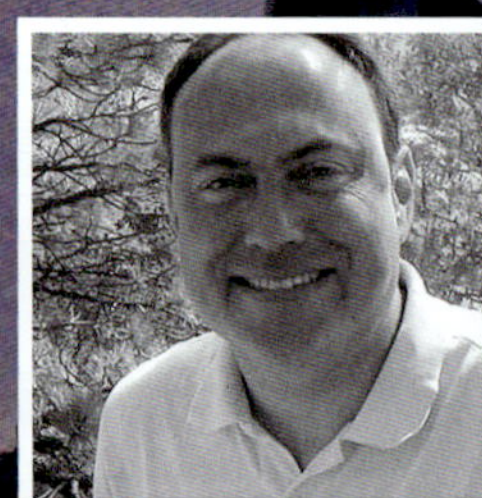

For 20 years, Alex Morris has been creating artwork and illustrations for the architectural market. He has produced and overseen the production of over 1200 images on more than 200 projects including landmark images of the Millennium Dome, Tate Modern, Chiswick Park, Gramercy Park North and 40 Bond St.

ALEX MORRIS

STEVEN STAHLBERG

Senior Figure Artist at Zenimax Online Studios, Stahlberg is internationally acknowledged as world class and the first artist to have a virtual character sponsored by a major modeling agency (1999). His game credits include *Army Men, Conquest, Free-lancer, Need for Speed, Eragon, Def Jam, Sims 3, Heavy Rain, Tabula Rasa, Reich, EVE Online* and *Elder Scrolls Online*. Steven has held nine sold-out workshops at CGSociety.org

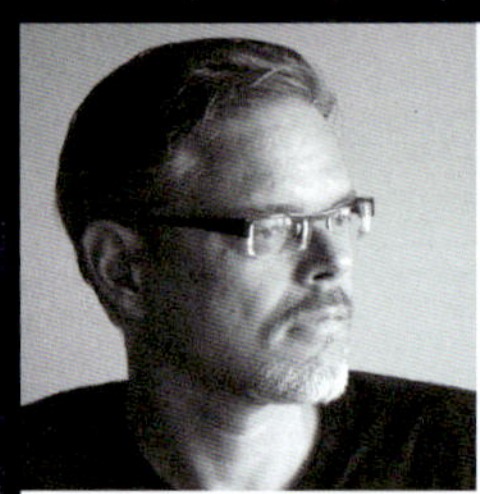

SYD MEAD

Syd Mead is the most celebrated 'visual futurist' and concept designer of our time. He was Grand Master of EXPOSÉ 6 in 2008. His most well-known works include production designs for *Blade Runner, Tron, Aliens* and *2010* – the pivotal sci-fi movies that have motivated so many amateur VFX artists to pursue professional careers in the field.

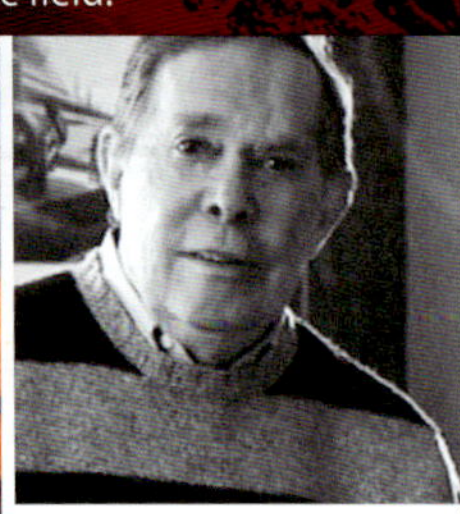

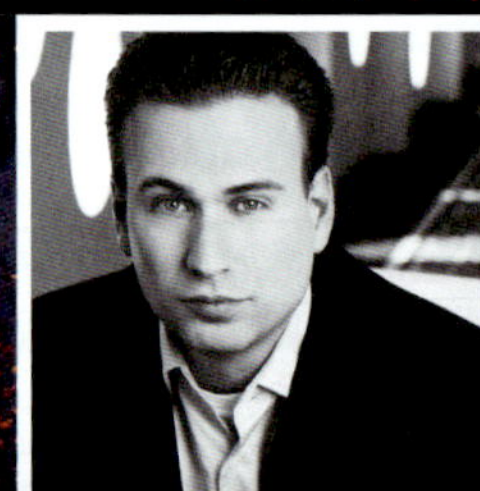

JEFF MOTTLE

Jeff Mottle is CEO and owner of leading online architectural site, CGarchitect. With 14 years in the architecture industry, Mottle co-founded the CGschool which caters to architectural visualization professionals, and writes editorial, performs market research/analysis and speaks internationally. In 2012 he was awarded the Joe Greco Community Award, the CAD Society's top honor.

MARK SNOSWELL

Dr Mark Snoswell is president of the CGSociety and founder of Ballistic Media. He has developed Absolute Character Tools and The Ultimate Human Model set, done film production work for Disney and Warner Brothers, and production work for National Geographic. He has also taught graphic design, 3ds Max and Painter.

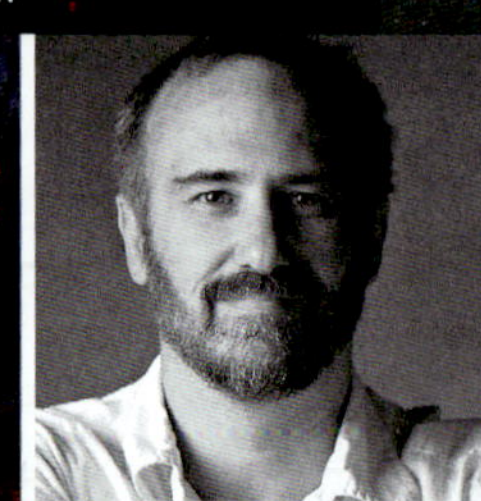

INTERNATIONAL JUDGES

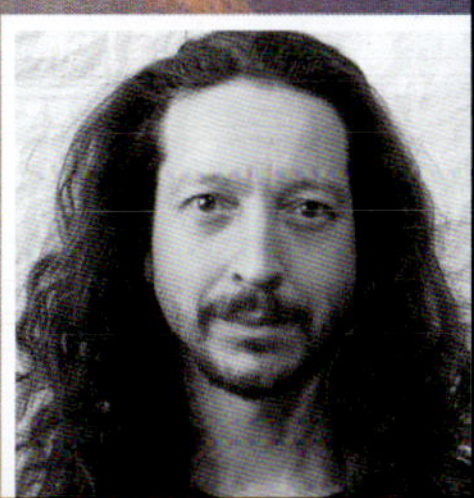

Taron Baysal freelanced his skills in Germany then moved to Los Angeles to work for various VFX houses such as StationXstudios and Computercafe, later known as CafeFX. He eventually joined the pmgWorldwide LLC to develop messiah:Studio. He moved to Croatia to design and create theme park venues and begin a new life of study and development.

TARON BAYSAL

DON SEEGMILLER

Don Seegmiller teaches visual design at Brigham Young University in Utah, and possesses a popular teaching method in advanced illustration, figure drawing and digital painting. He has work in galleries from Hawaii to England. Seegmiller worked as an art director at the Saffire Corporation. He offers regular CGWorkshops, speaks regularly at GDC, and is author of Ballistic's *d'artiste: Digital Painting 2* and *Painter* publications.

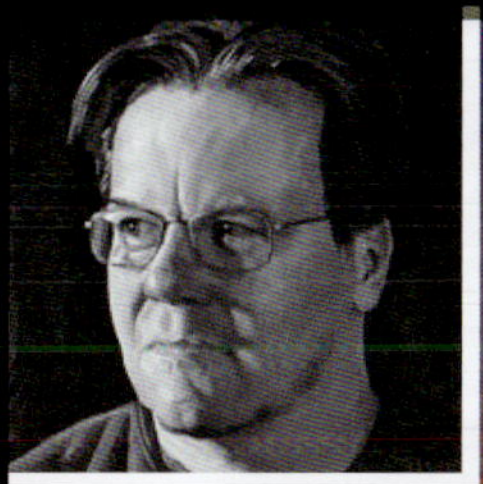

Leigh van der Byl has been a texture painter in the movie industry, and a freelance photographer for more than 10 years, working for numerous studios. She's currently based in London and her recent credits include *X-Men: First Class*, the final two chapters of the *Harry Potter* film series, and the space epic *Gravity* from Alfonso Cuaron.

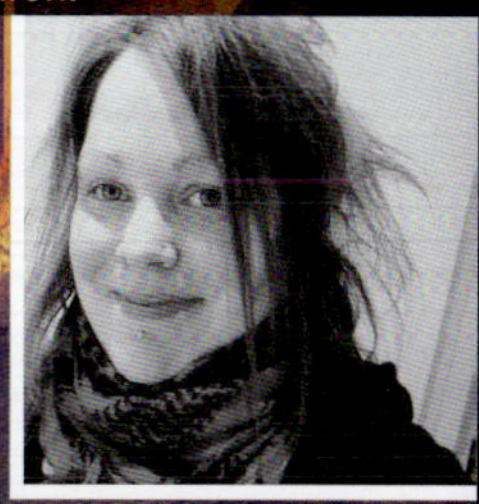

LEIGH VAN DER BYL

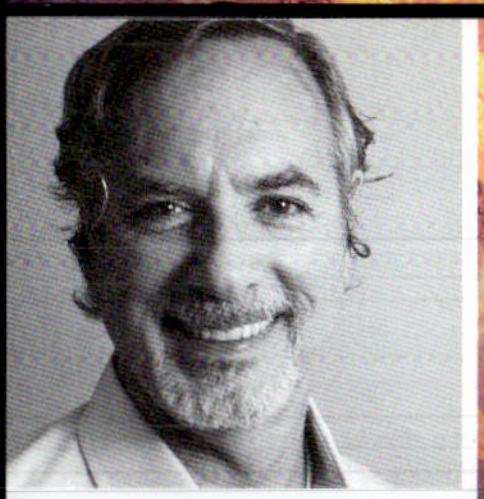

CHRISTOPHER SLOAN

Christopher Sloan is an award-winning art director and author who worked with *National Geographic Magazine* from 1992 to 2010 as art director and senior editor. He launched Science Visualization, Inc. in 2010 as a way of integrating visual approaches to science in multiple platforms, including film, exhibits and digital media.

PASCAL BLANCHÉ

After art school in Marseille, Pascal Blanché freelanced for *TILT Magazine*, Virtual Xperience, Xilam, Haiku Studio and Sony. As art director at Ubisoft Montréal, he worked on *Myst IV Revelation*, *Naruto Rise of a Ninja* and *Avatar: the game*. After two years of *Runescape* in the UK, he is now back at Ubisoft Montréal. He is also a well-rounded illustrator and worked for Wizards of the Coast, Autodesk, Funcom and Microsoft.

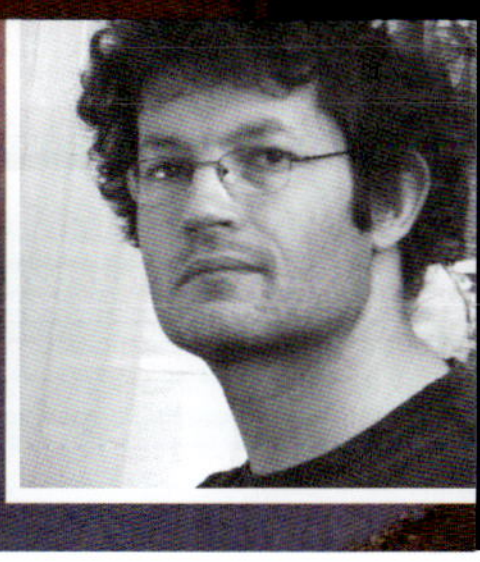

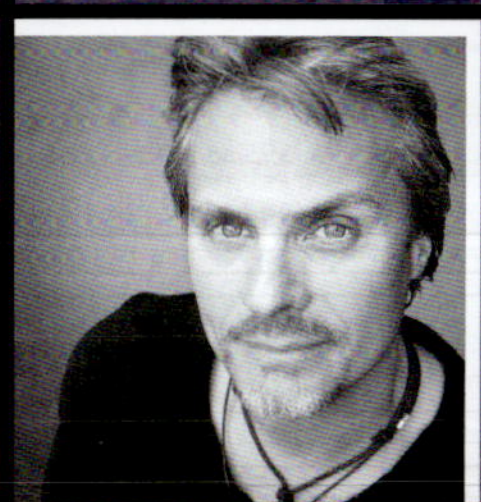

LORNE LANNING

Lorne Lanning's *Oddworld Inhabitants* has sold nearly six million copies, and garnered dozens of awards from the game industry, as well as the music, television and film industries, and illustration and design annuals. In 2010 Lorne co-founded Xmobb with Sherry McKenna, bringing a live social dimension to the online media landscape.

PAUL FRANKLIN

Paul Franklin set up Double Negative Visual Effects' 3D department and supervised the CG animation for a number of feature films the company worked on. As senior in-house VFX supervisor at DNeg, he's been front and center on many of the latest VFX triumphs such as *The Black Knight*, *Harry Potter: Half Blood Prince* and the VFX dream-laden, Oscar-winning *Inception*.

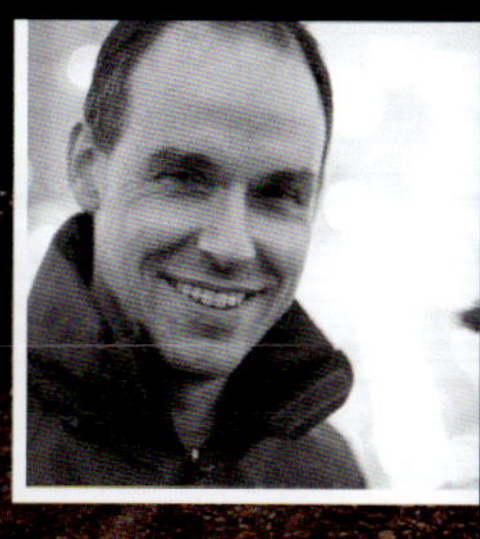

Background image: Shaddy Safadi, Planetside Lava

EXPOSÉ 11 GRAND MASTER ROGER DEAN

Roger Dean's father was in the army, so he grew up traveling all over the world. This gave him a unique overview of many different cultures and sparked in him an interest in the way design differs and changes in different countries. His family moved back to the UK from Hong Kong, and he left school at 16 and started at the Canterbury College of Art.

"I had this idea that I'd like to design the future. A lot of my paintings at school tended to lean into the future. That was the one motivating force in my being where I was."

As a younger man, Roger was also interested in natural history illustration. "I used to draw animals and birds ... but I was dragged out of a life drawing class by the principal at Canterbury, not for any reason but being young and impressionable. As I had maths and physics, I wasn't allowed to do art, and I was sent off to do industrial design."

At the time, the Canterbury College of Art was trying to get accredited to offer an industrial design course. This meant that Roger bypassed the foundation course and jumped straight into heavy duty industrial design.

"It was great that I was switched to design, but I didn't like the way it was being taught," he recalls. "I didn't like that everything was a 'box'. I used to challenge the tutors and ask 'Why are we put in boxes?' and I was given the old Bauhaus maxim in that 'Form follows function'. I'd be directed to Corbusier, the founding father of modern architecture."

Corbusier's idea was that the butcher, the baker and the banker should all live in identical boxes. Roger saw this as social engineering and was increasingly disillusioned with that aspect of design.

Although he completed his course, towards the end of it he had to make a choice between architecture and industrial design.

"One of my tutors said I shouldn't do either because I wouldn't like them and they wouldn't like me. He recommended strongly that I apply to the Royal College of Art and start a furniture design course, which I did."

Roger was using forms from nature as surface decoration and parts of 3D form in his creations. Organic forms were a huge inspiration for him. "I was designing a gyroscopic engine," he explains, "and I had these cubes on my sketchbook, and I sort of jokingly put pine trees on them, and they were bouncing around in the air, kind of detached from gravity. That was 'Flights' [see page 11], around 1966."

At the Royal College of Art, Roger conducted some unique research on the psychology of the built environment, or, as he refers to it, "the psychology of architecture". He studied what made people feel comfortable in buildings, and his research revealed that modern buildings presented problems for their inhabitants. It took a while longer for him to come up with some positive conclusions – a list of what to avoid and what to include in building construction.

Upon leaving university, Roger quickly exhibited a 'Sea Urchin' beanbag chair, a piece of furniture borne from his research. Almost as soon as Dean was out into the job market, he won a contract to design the interior of Ronnie Scott's jazz club in the Soho theatre district of London. The owner-saxophonist saw Roger's paintings he always carried with him, and asked if he would design an album cover for The Gun, a band he'd recently signed with his management company.

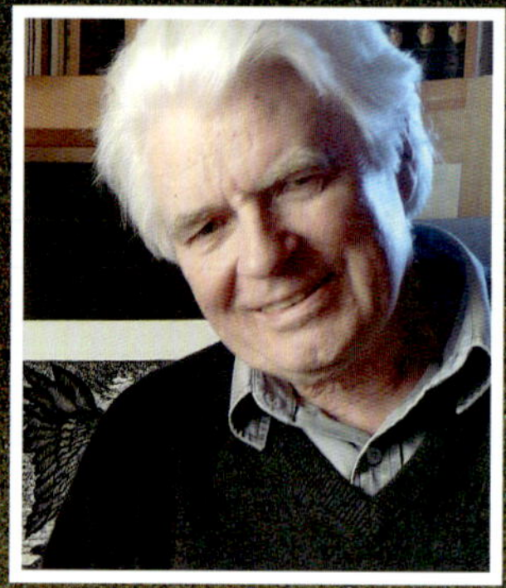

ROGER DEAN
Fantasy artist and designer

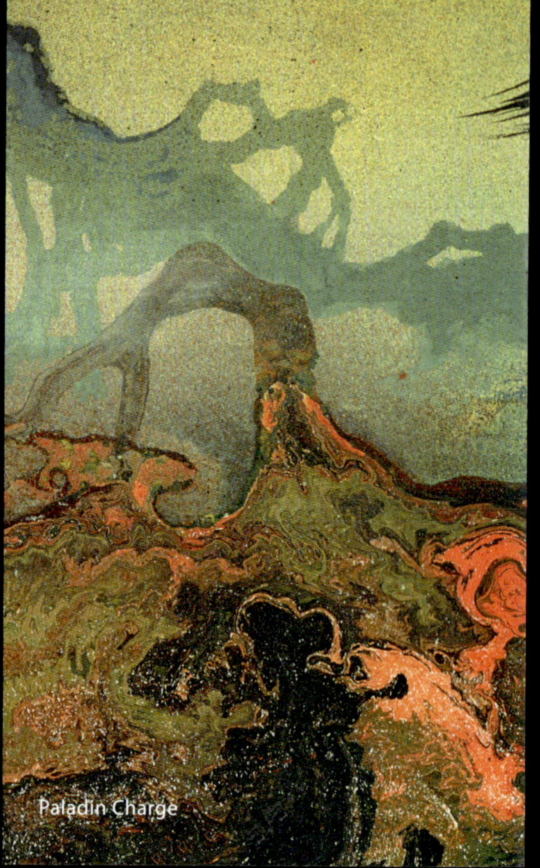

Paladin Charge

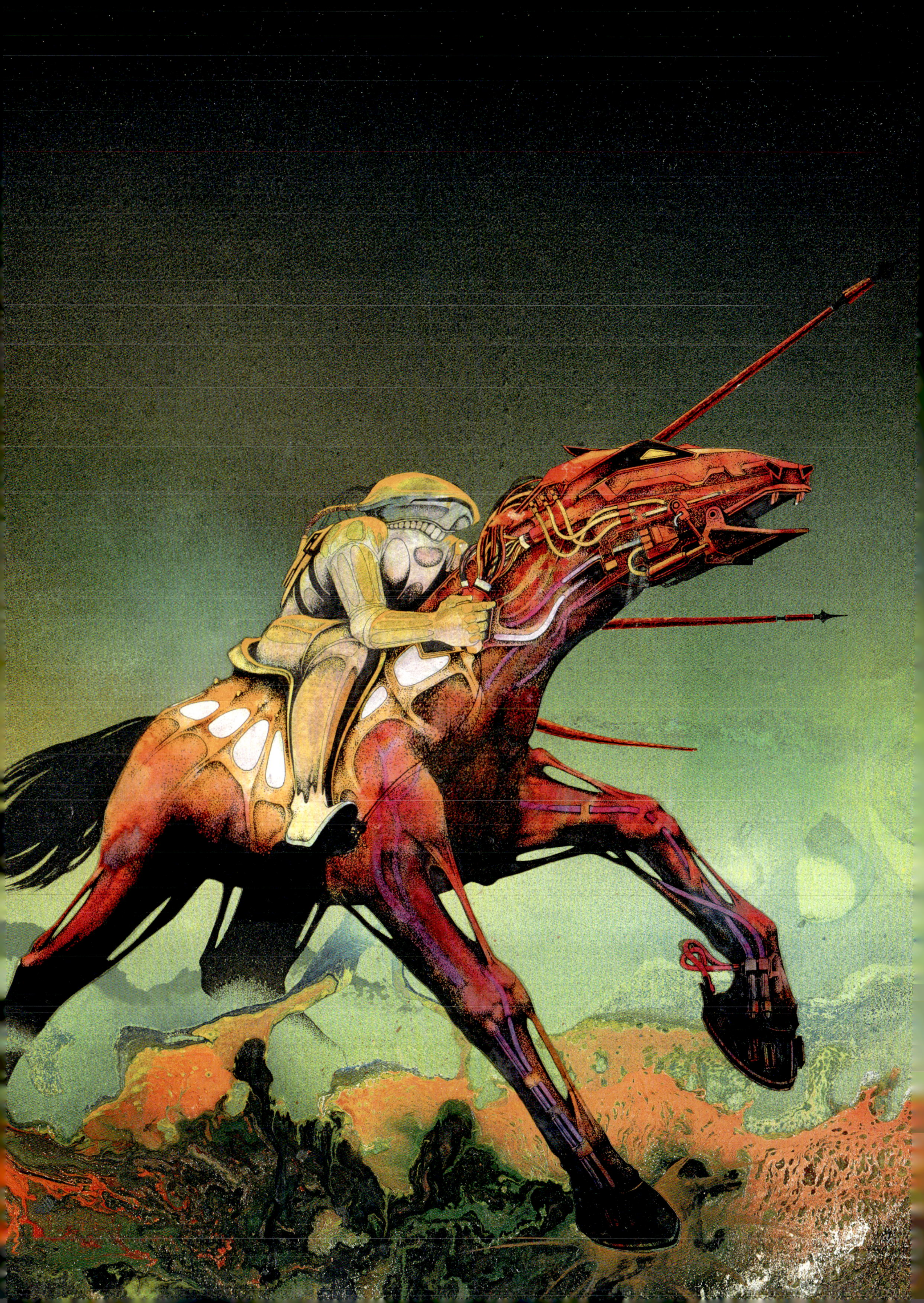

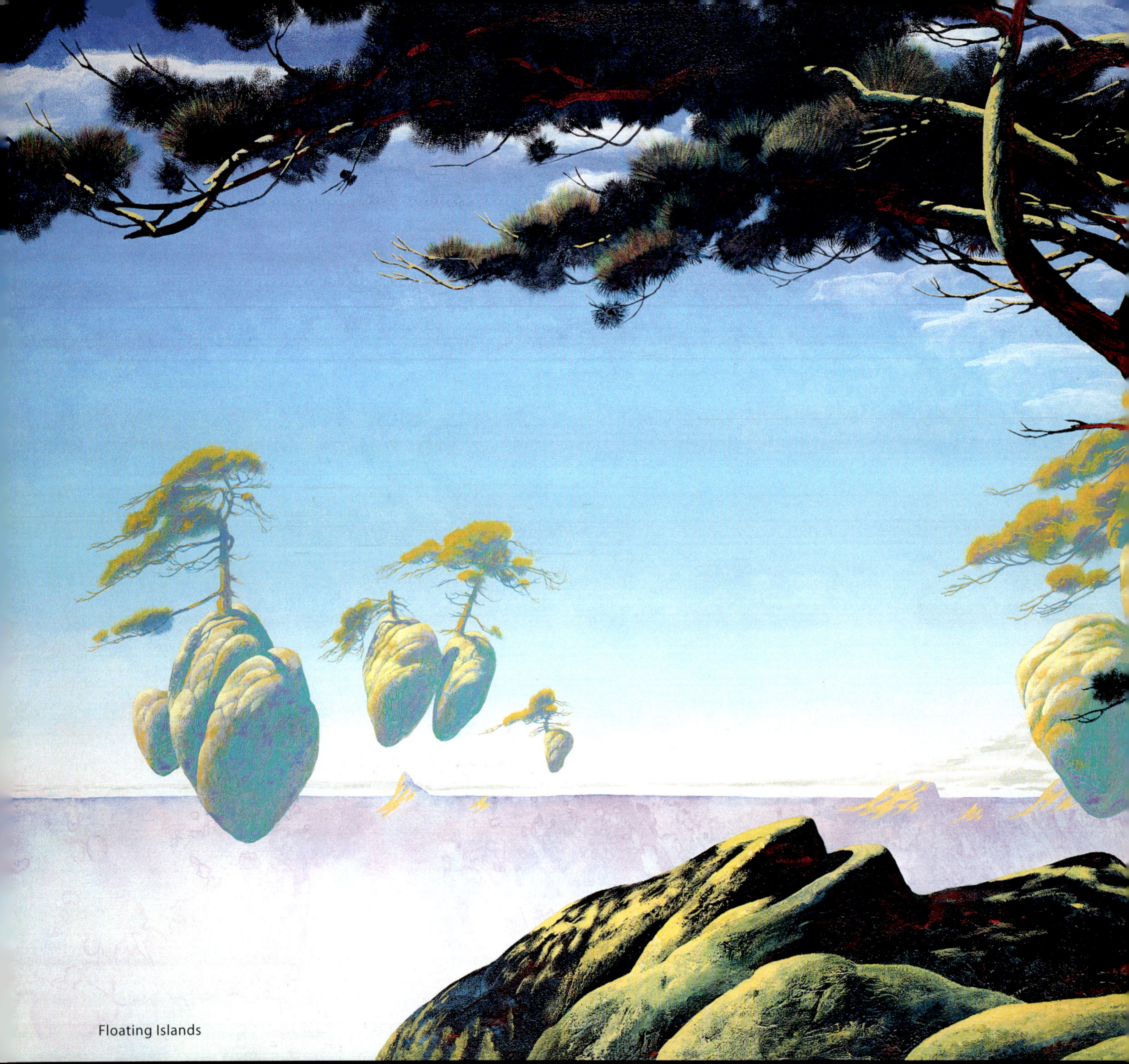

Floating Islands

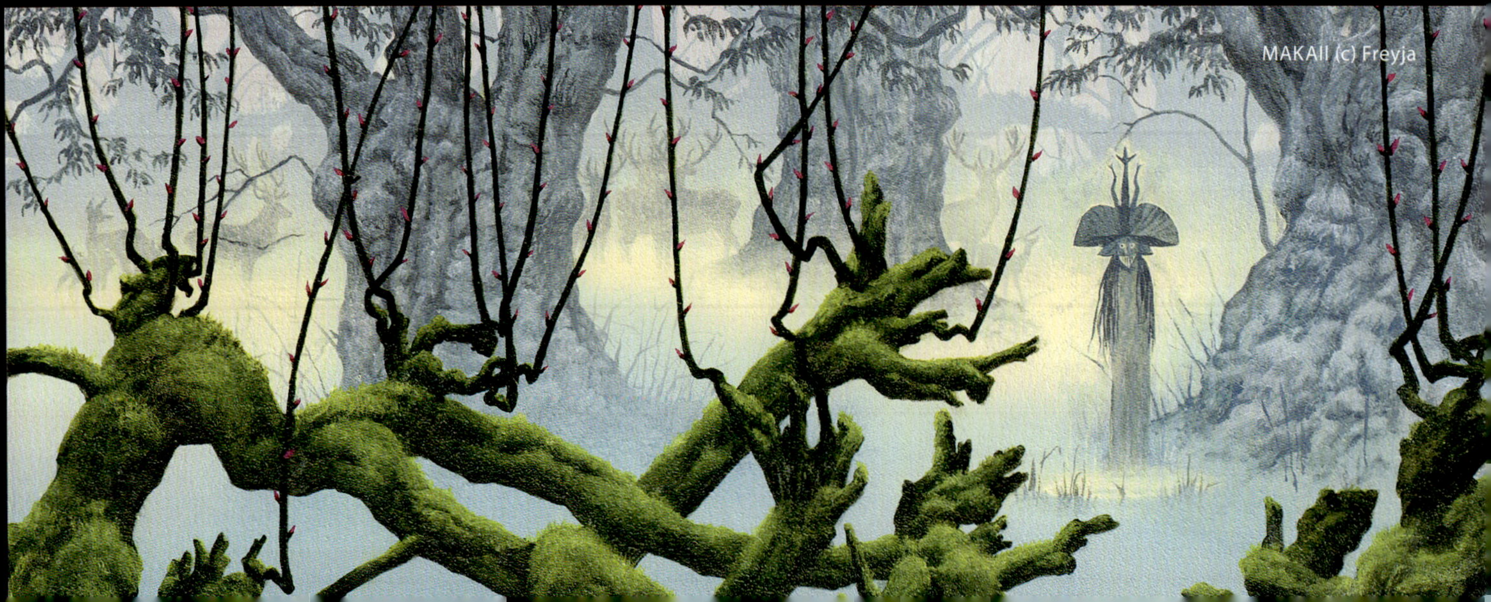

MAKAII (c) Freyja

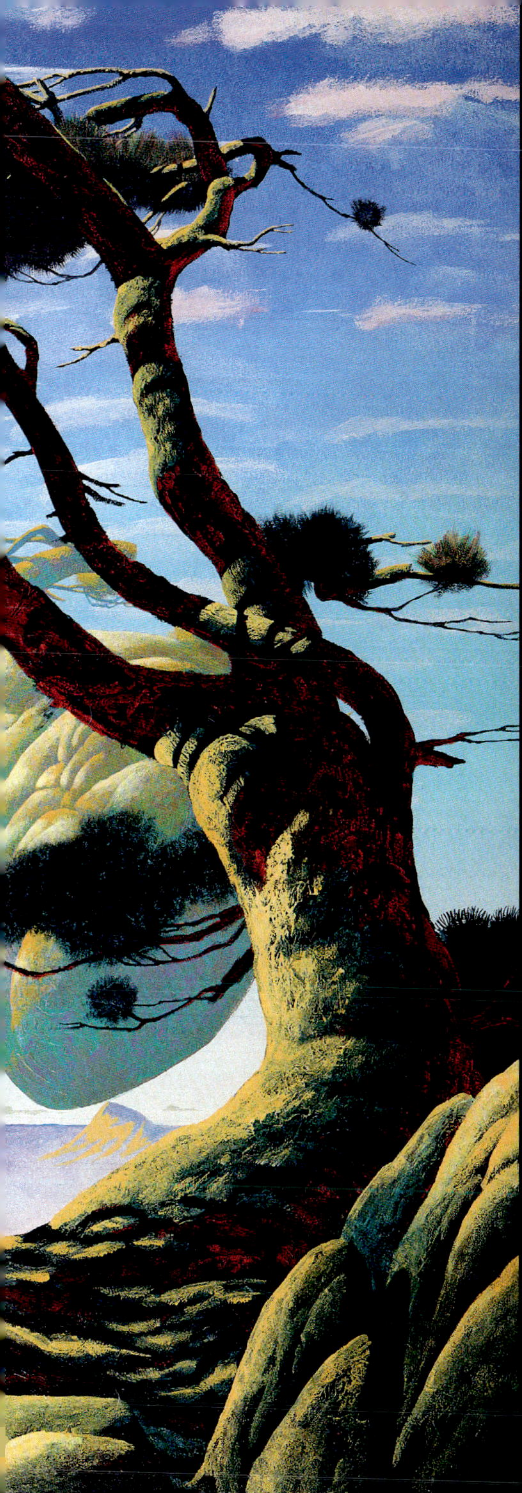

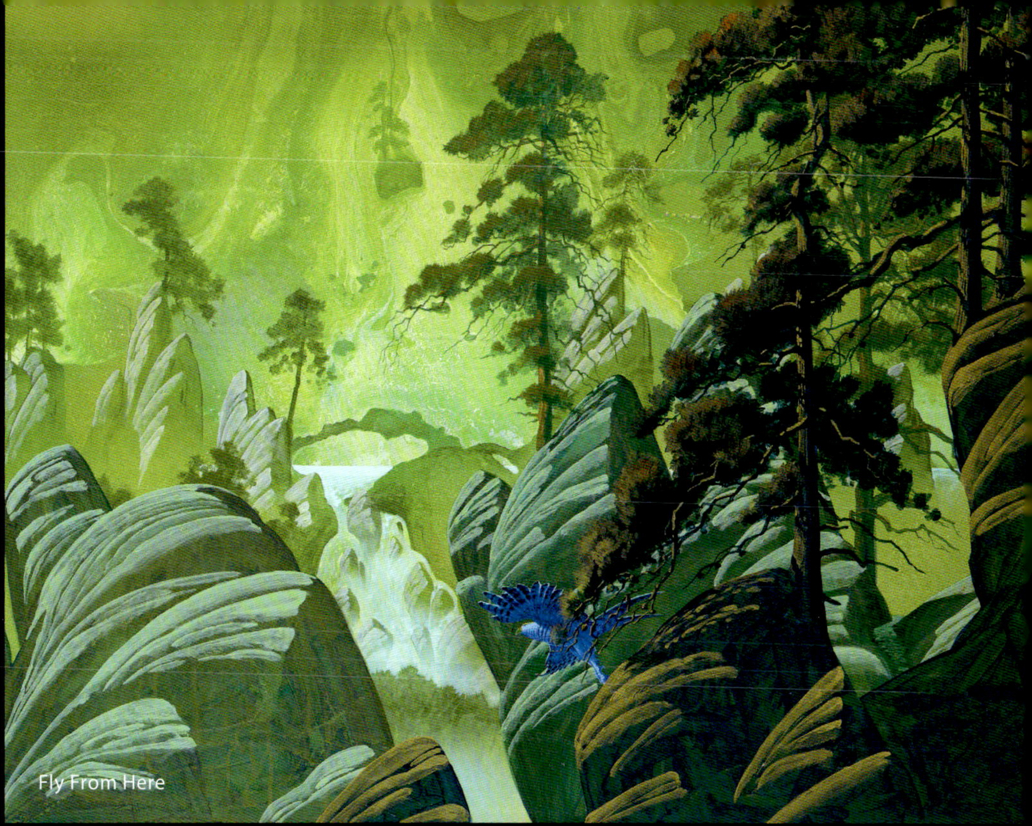

Fly From Here

This was Roger's chance to make some noise in the right crowd. "Doing the album covers, I could generate a very big audience and demonstrate an enthusiasm for my architecture through that," he explains.

Over the next few years, he featured a lot of his house and furniture designs, and, after his cover work for The Gun, he took on the album cover art world. "I did a cluster of jazz covers stemming from that first job, but they had a very fixed idea of what they wanted," Roger says. Even still, there were new clients lining up. Roger designed a cover for pop band Osibisa, a robotic horse image for a band called Paladin, and then some work for Uriah Heep. He also did work for the prolific bands Yes and Led Zeppelin.

There was an element of fantasy and science fiction in Roger's album work at the beginning, and he brought a degree of credibility to those genres with his designs. "If I put a machine into a painting, that machine had to look like it would work," he says. Also, the architectural side of his work was based on a certain practicality.

"Syd Mead once said he designs everything with the intention to be built, while I have designed buildings to be practical as well, and sometimes it just doesn't get built. I am much more interested in things that could be built and perhaps, should be built, than science fiction."

As his main focus at college was on mechanical devices and patents, Roger never studied illustration and had to learn as he went along. "I didn't have a clue about graphic design when I did my first cover," he admits.

When working for Marc Bolan of T-Rex fame, Roger couldn't get his typesetting done because he didn't know how to do it. "I went in with the letters done by hand just to show where the typesetting should be done, and their reaction was, 'Oh my god you've handwritten it, how cool!' From then on every single release he [Bolan] had me handwrite the label copy and lyrics."

In his training, Roger was taught to produce almost photographic-looking drawings with pencil and Chinese ink. The 'Ruleya' image, painted for Yes in 1974, was a pencil drawing and colored with dirty water. This was typical of the way he worked. His drawings were also very precise, another reflection of his training.

"It wasn't until 1979 that I switched to a much looser style of painting, for a couple of philosophical reasons. I switched from thinking my work was a window into a world, to being an object in its own right."

"I work in two ways. I have an idea and throw it down in a sketchbook. Sometimes fully formed," he says. He leaves it until one day he attempts to create it as a final painting, with the final looking pretty much the same as the original sketched thumbnail. "Sometimes, I experiment to see if the same scene in a different light might look better. I start with the canvas, and the initial sketch is incredibly loose and random," explains Roger. "But it feeds back on itself. I can be working on some detail while the background is constantly suggesting things. That suggestion process is interactive and the painting evolves from there. It starts with some idea, and evolves. That is the slowest process of all, but it comes up with the most satisfactory paintings of all, so I enjoy doing it. I hate doing it to a deadline because it doesn't work that way. But that's not the only way I work, nor is it my favorite way of working."

Later in his career, Roger made a foray into video game box covers and designed Psygnosis's famous owl logo. He sees a big difference between this work and his album cover art. "I'm looking to create a world on the package, the same way the music is looking to create a world," says Roger. He never played the computer games like

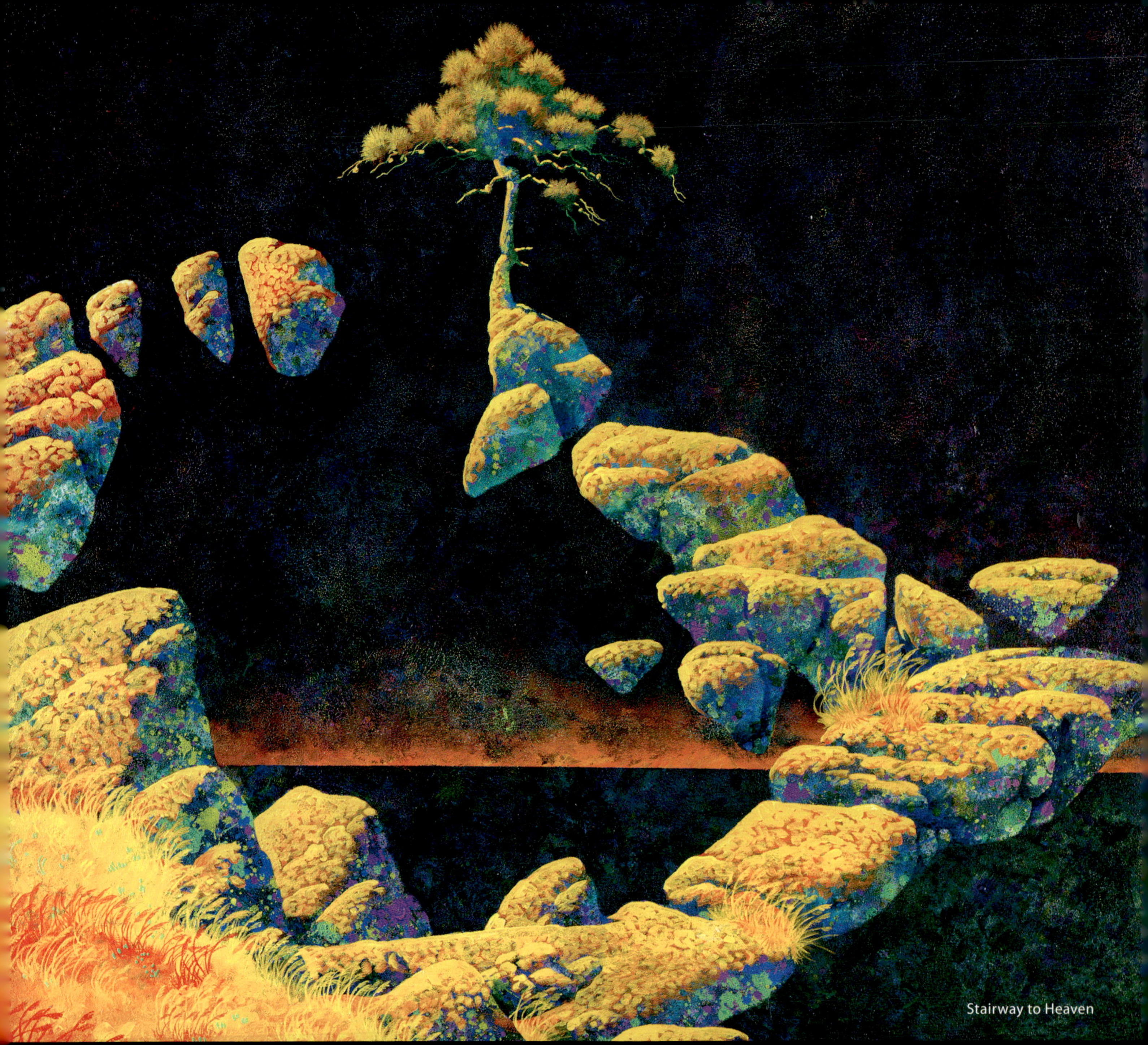

Stairway to Heaven

he'd play the band's music before painting the cover.

"But there can't be any challenge as to whether it's accurate or not ... Software development was so young at that stage, there wasn't a great deal to go on, and there wasn't any real relationship between what went on the box and what went in the box. The brief would be non-visual, essentially."

Roger also created covers for Brataccus, Air Supply, Barbarian, Chrono Quest, Ballistix, Lemmings, Shadow of the Beast, and many others. Lately he has moved away from the game and music industries.

Roger feels western culture suffered a major tragedy in the 1960s when the art world disengaged itself from craftsmanship. "That tragedy is serious because art doesn't exist without craftsmanship; for two reasons. Art is an expression of emotion and technique," he explains. "The Japanese say you train the body, and the body in turn trains the mind. The old cliché that you can't get a concert pianist without 10,000 hours of training, is absolutely true of art. If you dismiss the craftmanship, you're dismissing the training of the mind. Then if you're not training the hand to train the mind, you're missing the point. What makes art? You can have aesthetic skills and physical skills. It's when they are brought together."

"Artists have always used aids to generate art. Be that a brush or a set of compasses or an airbrush to achieve effects that are their signature," Roger says. "There's always been a certain aid to the artist, but nothing like what is available now since the explosion of digital creation."

Roger sees digital art as combining physical skill and aesthetic sensibility, and notes that it can be used to create "extraordinary images that would be almost impossible to do by hand".

He has used Photoshop and Illustrator for lettering, and for gradations and color selection, but most of his work has been hand-drawn from beginning to end. This work is more suitable to be shown in a gallery than on a screen.

Roger and his daughter Freyja share a studio in North London, and in 2008 worked on an exhibition together celebrating the 150th anniversary of Puccini's birth in Italy. "Her interests drift between science and art, like her father," he says.

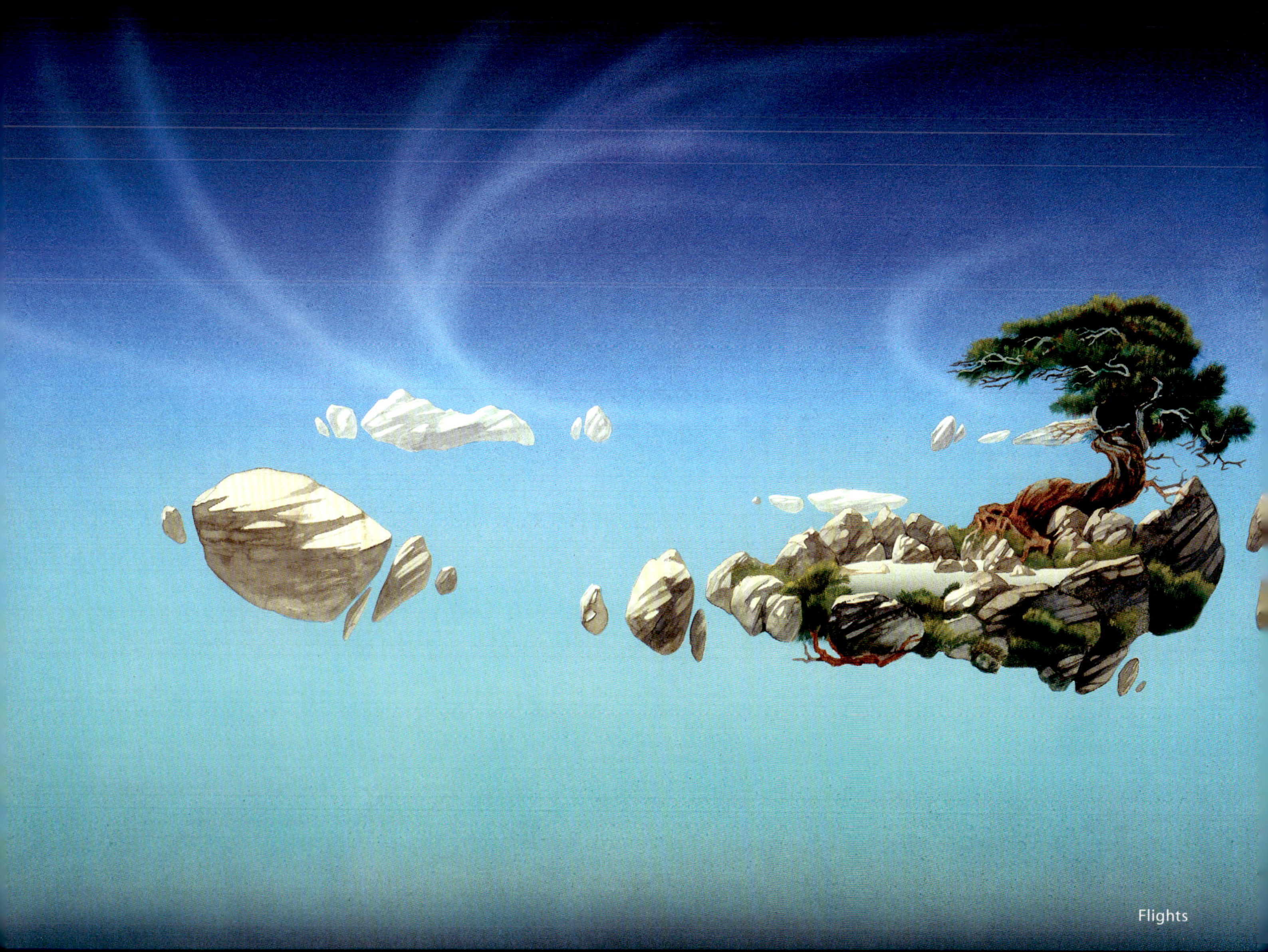
Flights

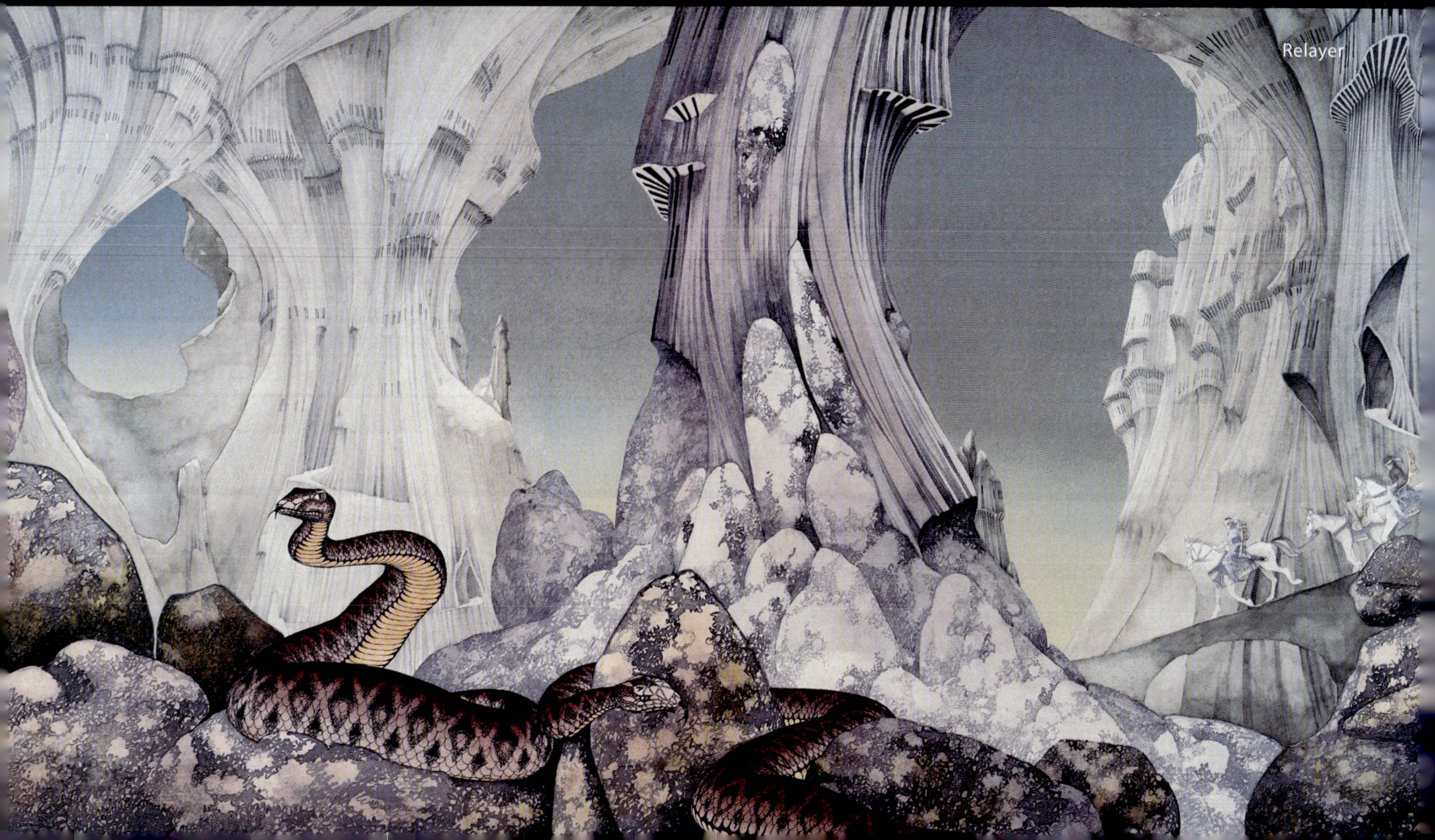
Relayer

We are proud to introduce the 22 Master Award winners of EXPOSÉ 11. The Master Award winners have been chosen by the EXPOSÉ 11 international judges for having produced the best work in their category of submission. Over the next few pages, you have the chance to see more of these Master Award winners as they share some of their influences, their work and their responses to winning this prestigious award.

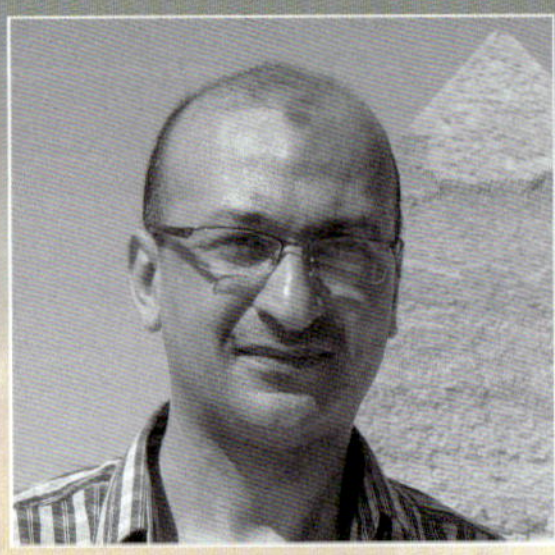

Portrait (Painted)
Mohamed Taaeb
Page 14, 21

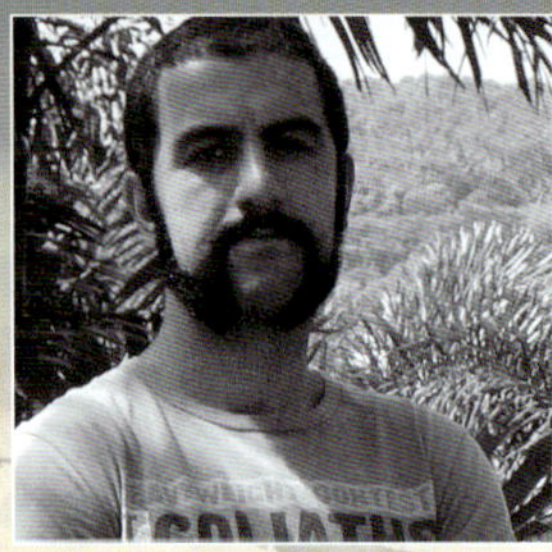

Portrait (Rendered)
Siamak Roshani
Page 14, 34

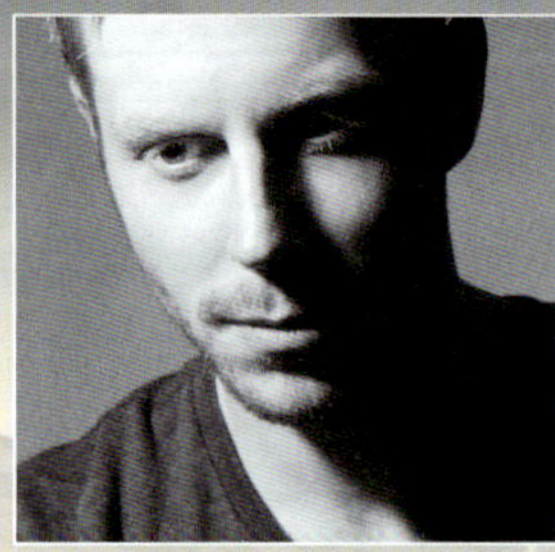

Portrait (Illustrated)
Stephen Molyneaux
Page 14, 49

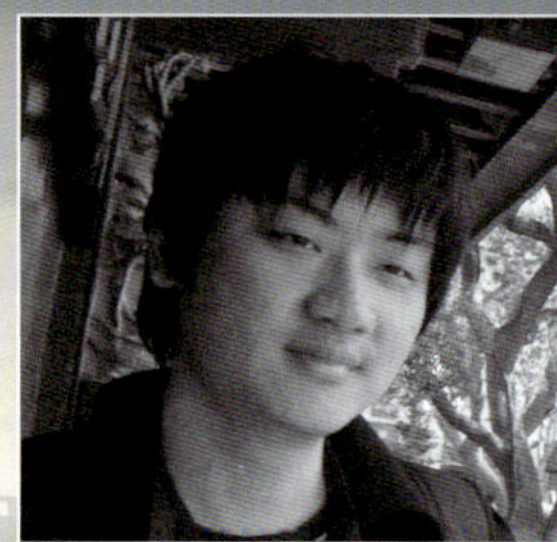

Warriors & Conflict
Guang Yang
Page 15, 63

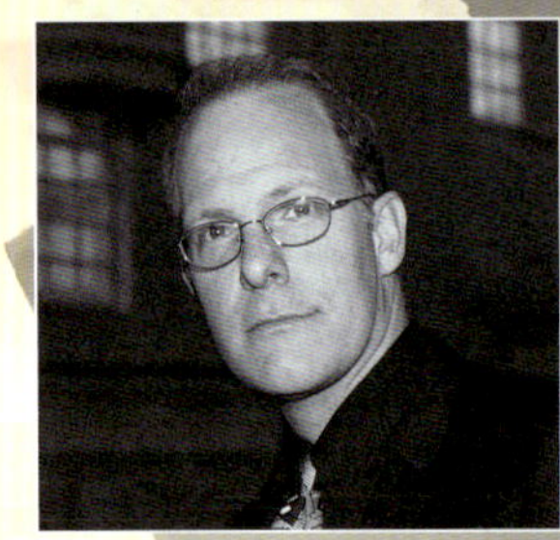

Science Fiction
Dave Seeley
Page 15, 74

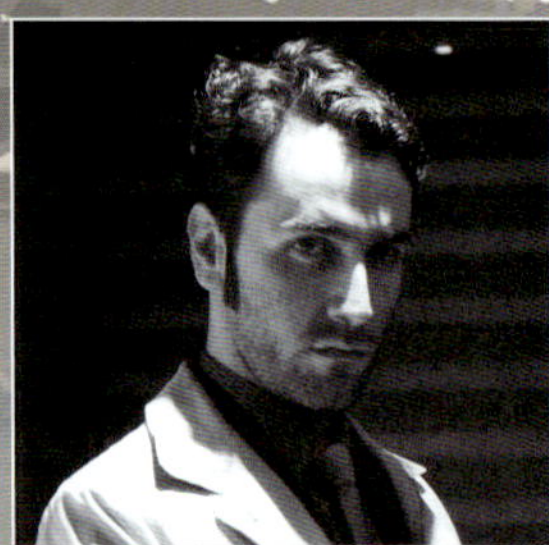

Fantasy
Kerem Beyit
Page 15, 90

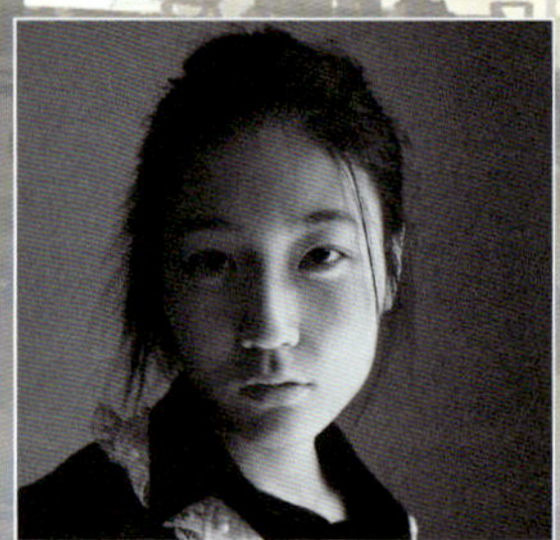

Character
Donglu Yu
Page 16, 105

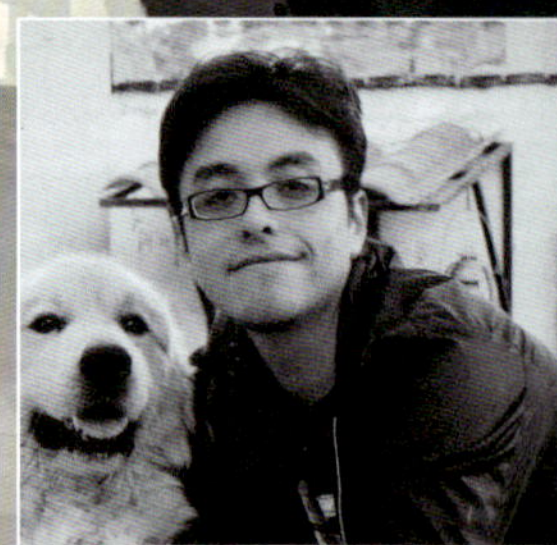

Fantasy Femmes
Carlos Ortega Elizalde
Page 16, 119

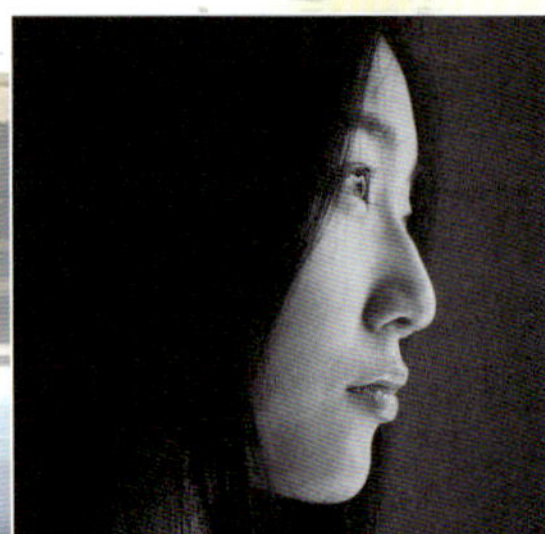

Concept Art
Donglu Yu
Page 16, 132

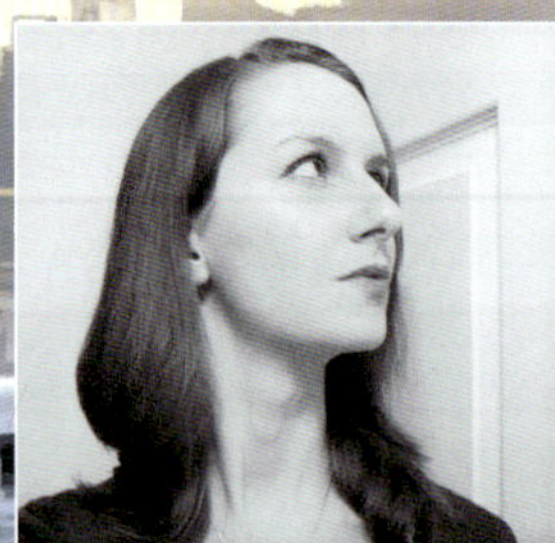

Comic / Manga
Wylie Elise Beckert
Page 16, 151

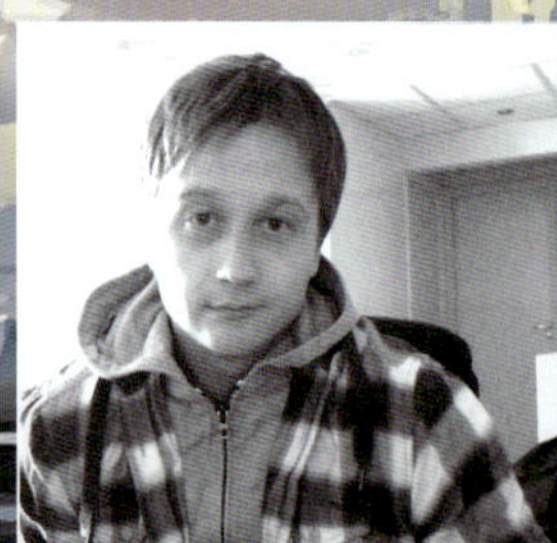

Matte Painting
Dmitry Zaviyalov
Page 17, 160

MASTER AWARD WINNERS

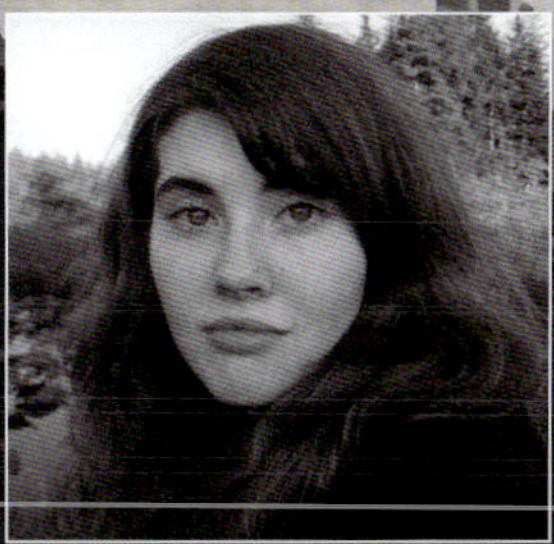

Environment
Sarah Webb
Page 17, 173

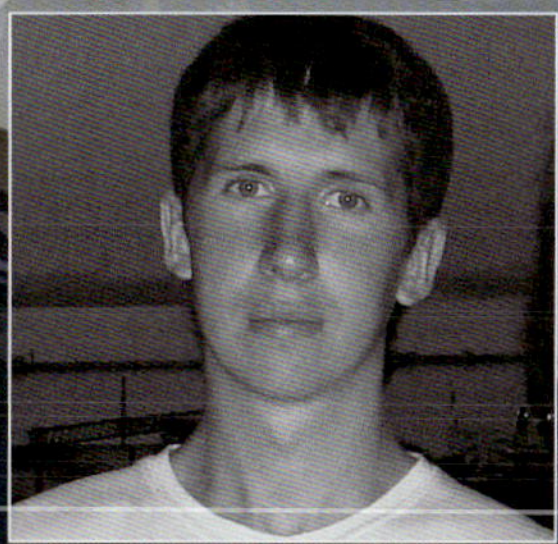

Architecture (Exterior)
Anton Cherenko
Page 17, 187

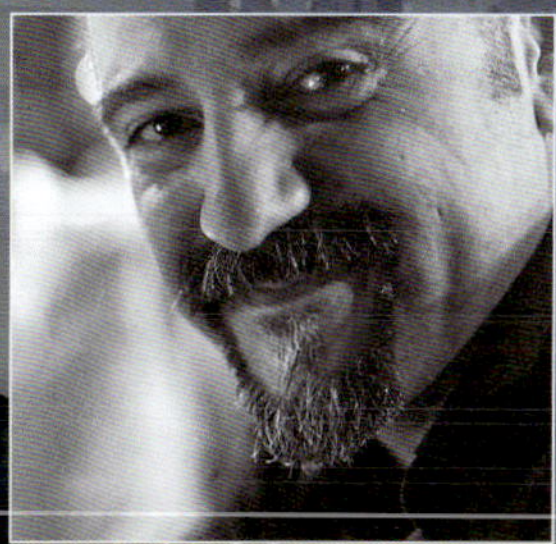

Architecture (Interior)
Andrea Bertaccini
Page 18, 197

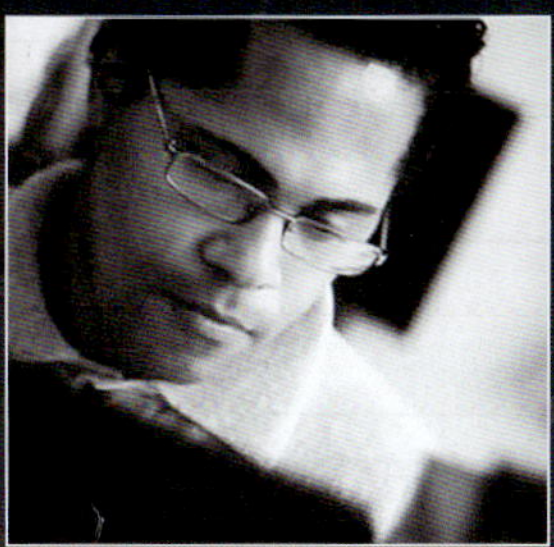

Robotic / Cyborg
Jacques Pena
Page 18, 205

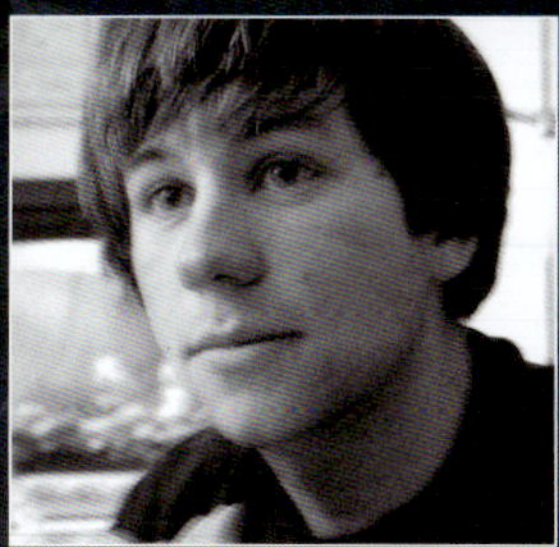

Game Art
Gabriel Verdon
Page 18, 213

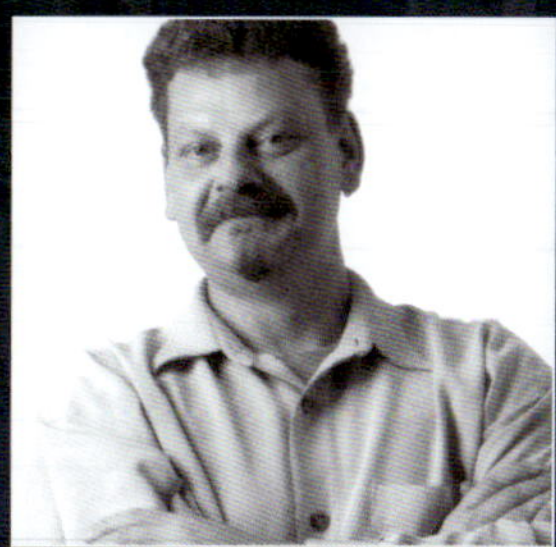

Abstract & Design
Ralf Stumpf
Page 19, 231

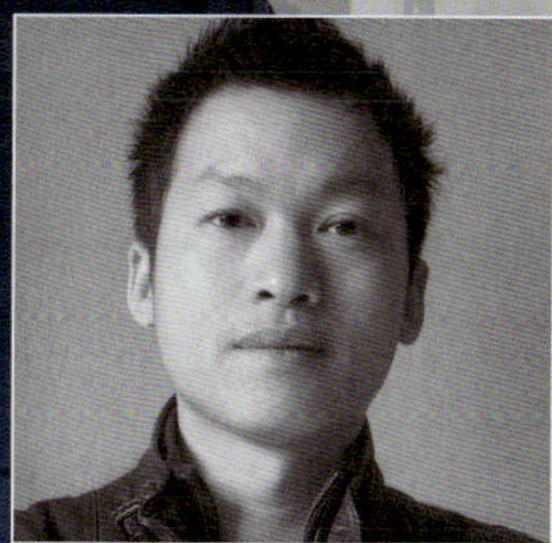

Whimsical
Xiao Yi
Page 19, 239

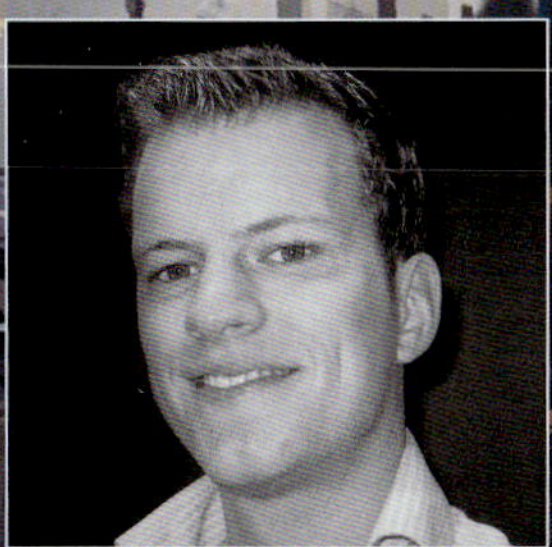

Transport
Jochem Aarts
Page 19, 247

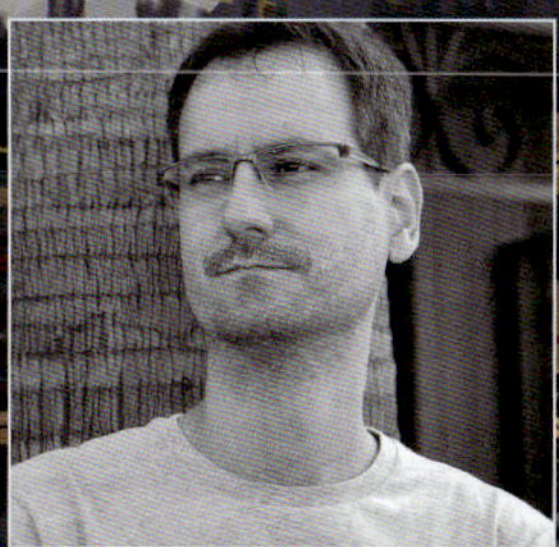

Steampunk
Toni Bratincevic
Page 20, 253

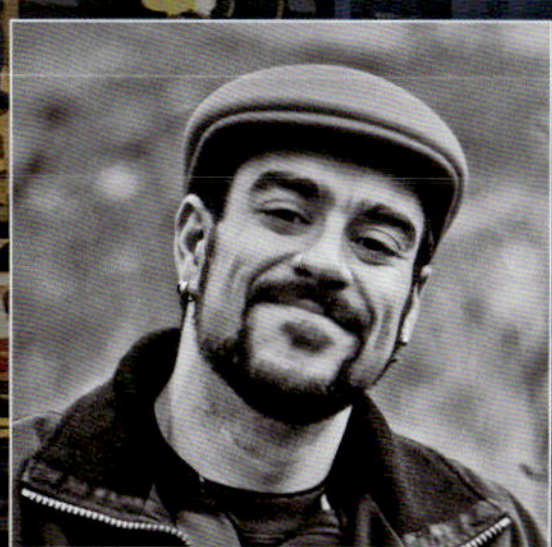

Surreal
Mario Sánchez Nevado
Page 20, 259

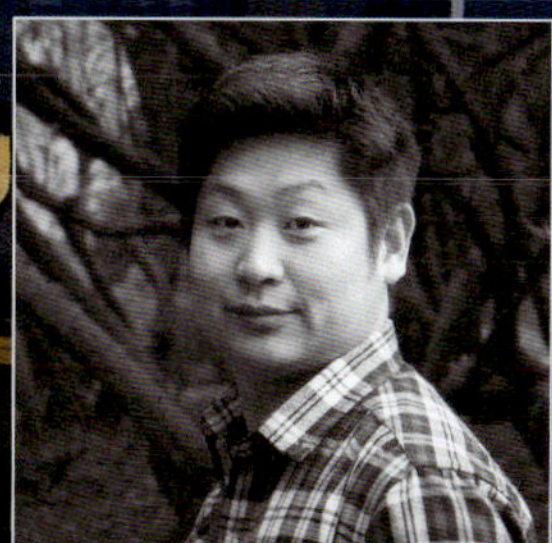

Storytelling
Hu Zheng
Page 20, 269

Background image: Jong-Won Park, Shipbuilding Town

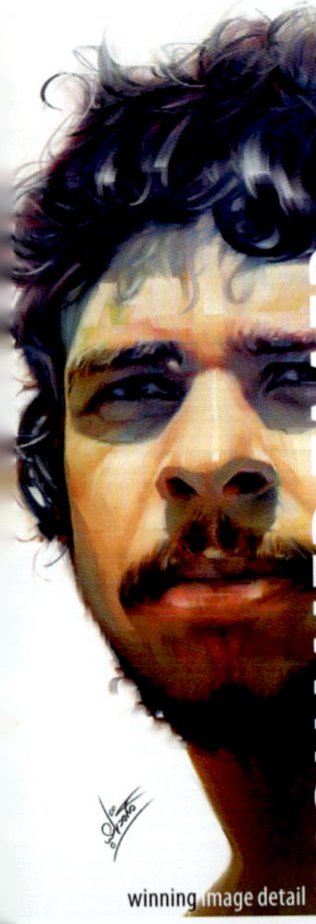

winning image detail

MOHAMED TAA'EB

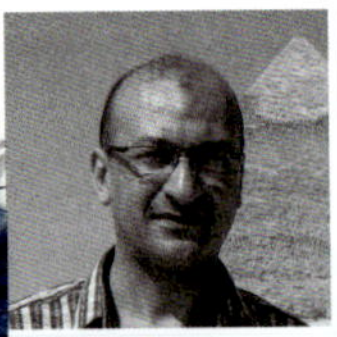

PORTRAIT (Painted)

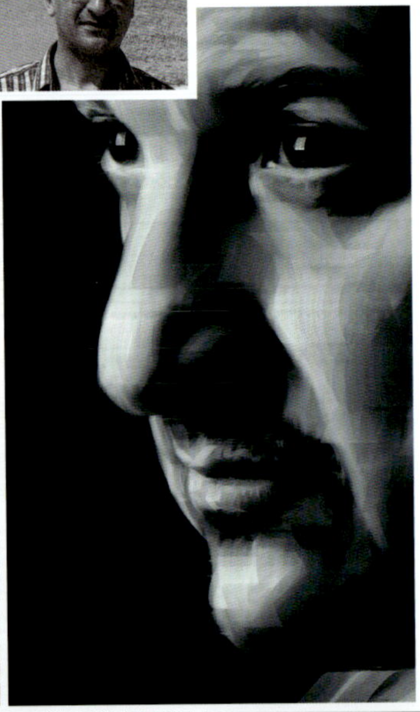

Mohamed Taa'eb is an Egyptian artist born in Cairo. His father, Abdel-Aziz Taa'eb, is a caricaturist. Mohammed completed his academic studies in graphics in the Faculty of Fine Arts at Helwan University in Cairo, obtaining his bachelor's degree in 1993. He later completed his Masters and PhD, and his research focused on science fiction and fantasy art.

After graduating, he joined a magazine where he created science fiction drawings, which until then the magazine had lacked. He used traditional techniques in his work, drawing pencil outlines on paper and using watercolors. In other work, the practical application of his art saw him design masks, toys and posters.

He worked as a freelancer for various magazines, publishing houses and advertising companies. In 1994 he decided to switch to digital art but had no guide, so he started a process of self-learning. He discovered the great potential of digital art software, culminating in him leaving behind his pencil and paper and switching to a graphics tablet.

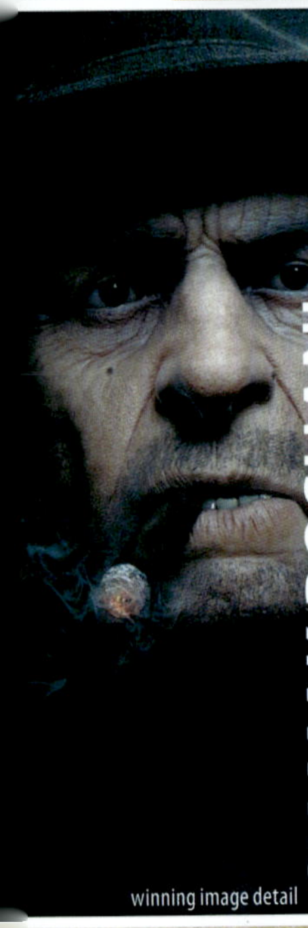

winning image detail

SIAMAK ROSHANI

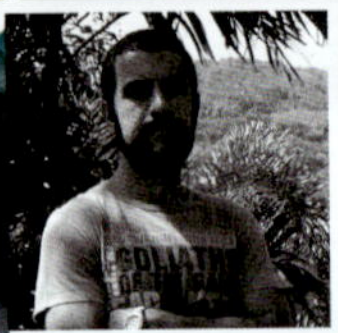

PORTRAIT (Rendered)

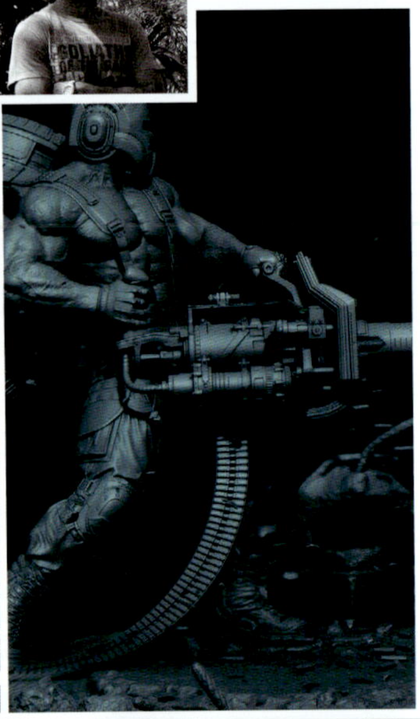

Siamak is an Iranian CG artist whose passion for video games led him to find out how the games he loved playing were created. He started learning CG while he was studying maths and physics. He now fosters a love of science and art.

In 2007 he got a job in Dubai as a modeler, working on character models and hard-surface models such as cars. He has also worked on environment modeling/texturing and as a character/texture artist. Currently he is employed as a freelance artist and also focuses on his ongoing personal projects, trying to give life to his ideas.

Siamak loves creating characters and enjoys the feeling that his characters are alive when he is finished. He has always been interested in how complex life evolved on earth; being a CG artist gives him the chance to create something digitally which doesn't exist in reality.

Siamak always enjoys what he does and says he has a long way to go before he is the best artist he can be – and there is no end to this path. Daily study is part of his everyday life, and he tries to be up to date in the industry. He is inspired by games, movies, nature, and other artists' work. In the future he hopes he will have the opportunity to travel and work in different countries.

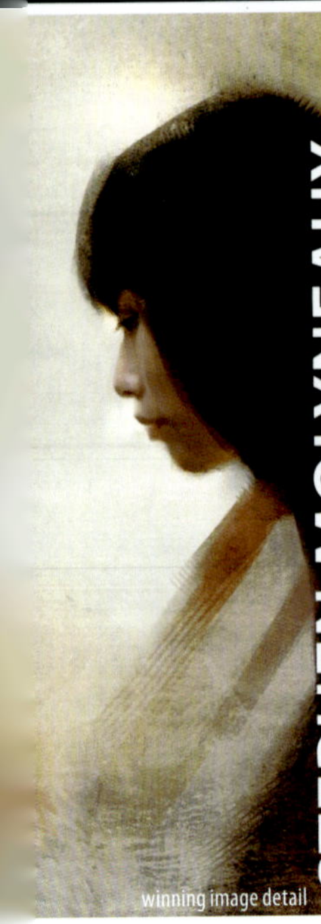

winning image detail

STEPHEN MOLYNEAUX

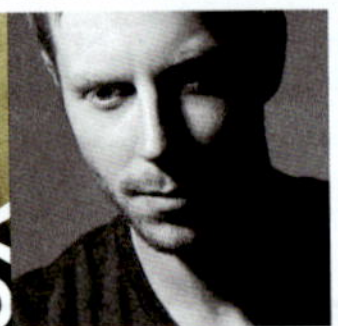

PORTRAIT (Illustrated)

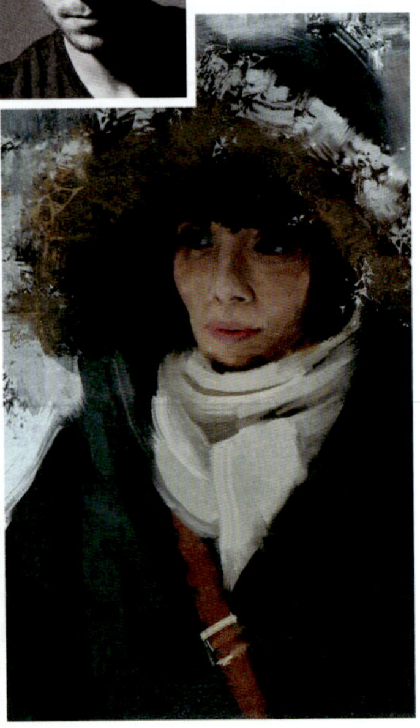

After graduating from Bradford University in 2004 with a degree in computer animation and special effects, Stephen Molyneux started his career as a digital artist in a small game company in the United Kingdom, working as a character artist on next-gen games.

He remembers being inspired by the work of epic games in Ballisitic's *d'artiste Character Modelling 2* book. His early work provided great experience and he made some close friendships with other enthusiastic young digital artists. He spent a lot of time building up his digital portfolio, attempting to create ultra-realistic renderings.

He moved from games into film VFX in 2008 and currently works for MPC London as a senior texture artist on feature films. He is proud to have worked on films such as *Prometheus*, *47ronin* and *Harry Potter and the Deathly Hallows*. He considers himself very lucky to have met some of the most talented artists in the industry – artists that inspire him to push himself further and explore new things.

As he has become a bit older and wiser he has developed a passion for fine art, and taught himself to work in traditional art mediums such as oil and charcoal. This has opened up new doors for his personal and professional digital artwork. His latest digital work has been heavily influenced by oil painting masters, old and new.

Over the next few years he hopes to keep developing his personal work and see where it takes him, and to move into the field of matte painting.

WARRIORS & CONFLICT

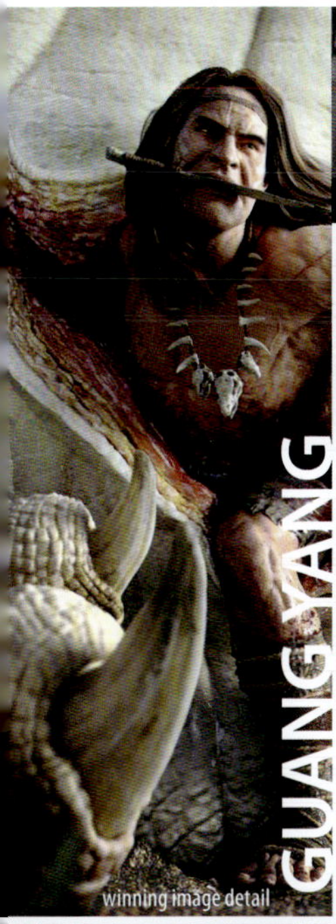

winning image detail

GUANG YANG

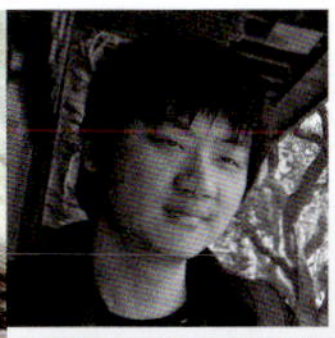

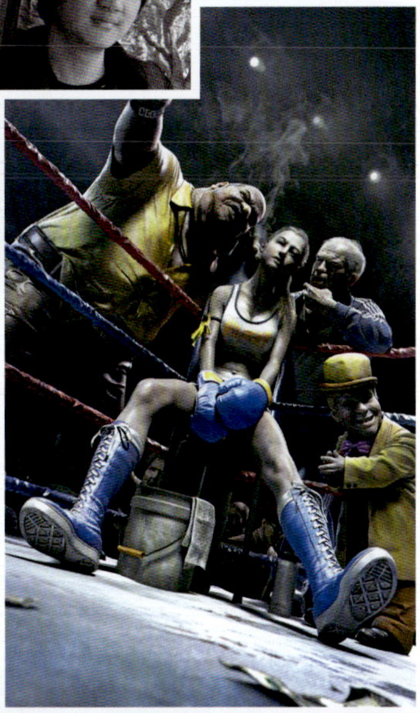

For Guang Yang, art is a kind of deep thinking, whether it be traditional or digital. Guang really started to get into digital art after graduation from university. His first contact with 3D software was with Zbrush, which made him love 3D design and production.

Guang has worked as a digital art teacher on various digital art projects, and currently works as a 3D art designer. He has done all sorts of work and is best at character art, which he sees as a very interesting process. He particularly likes creating biologically inspired characters – virtual organisms that have the soul of life.

For every art project he does, he tries his best to create an interesting work. He enjoys the process of production and design, and also experiencing the emotion embodied within a created artwork; each picture has a story, waiting to be explored.

He is hopeful for the future and hopes to do more quality work and meet more inspiring CG artists.

SCIENCE FICTION

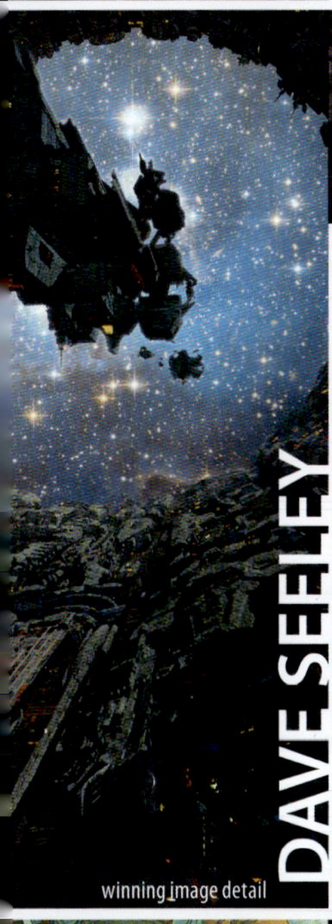

winning image detail

DAVE SEELEY

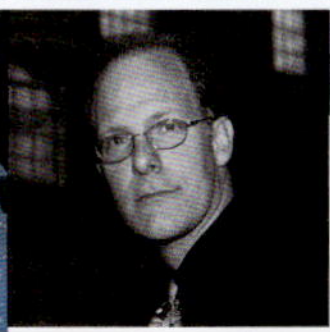

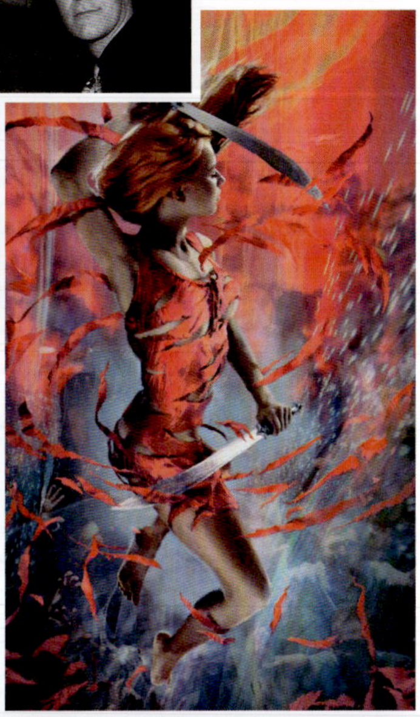

Dave Seeley's digital process involves kit-bashing photography and Frankensteining the bits together into new visions. Recently incorporating 3D image making. While many artists talk about the sheer love of their endeavor, he is a little more ambivalent about it.

"I don't love the act of making art, yet I'm compelled to do it. I love the discovery, and the results. I find making images a struggle, but when I find success, it's incredibly rewarding. That's what fuels my addiction to making art."

"I enjoy jumping in to a new picture, but after a short energetic sprint, it gets progressively messy as I arc outside my comfort zone. I most often find success there because that's where I find surprises (happy mistakes), and that can be exhilarating. That's where *all* the growth happens."

Dave has been drawing for as long as he can remember, and painting since high school. He decided to study architecture and fine art in college, and also began collecting comics and hunting down sci fi and fantasy art.

After 10 years working as an award-winning architect, Dave was seduced by the glamour of illustration and derailed his career for the "far more immediate gratification of image making".

Dave is far more influenced by contemporary science fiction film noir than by the legacy of science fiction illustration. He cites historical figures in fine art as influences, but says he is most influenced by respected fellow illustrators currently working in the genre.

FANTASY

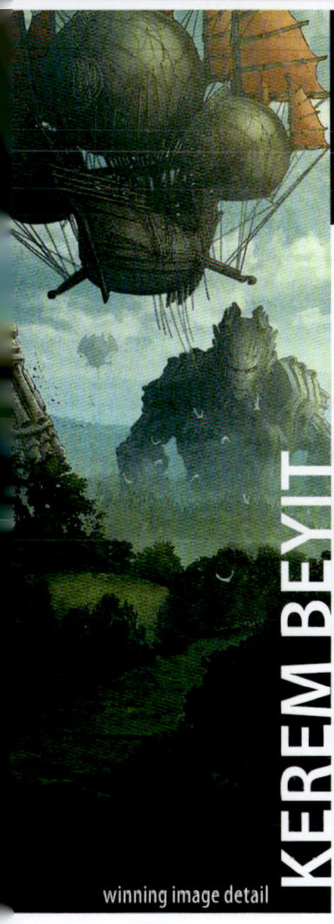

winning image detail

KEREM BEYIT

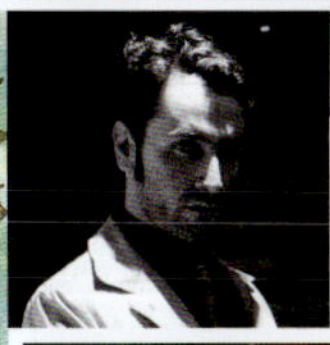

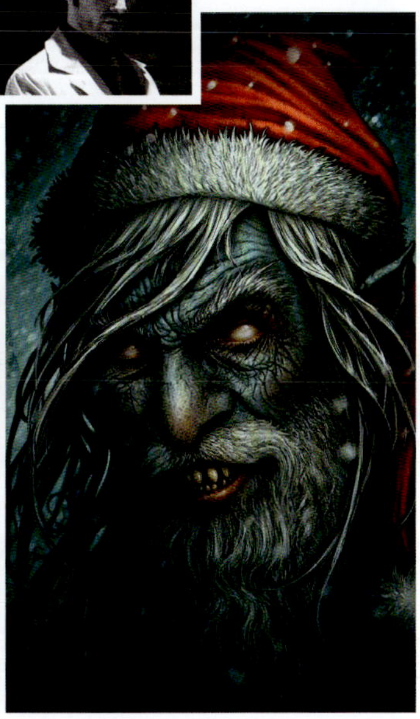

Drawing has been a passion for Kerem Beyit ever since he can remember, back into his childhood when he was also passionate about comic books. He remembers his father buying him the *Savage Sword of Conan* comic book, and he was blown away by its cover art.

Kerem went to college and studied graphic design and then worked as a graphic designer. But it didn't take long before he realised it wasn't right for him. He came across many impressive digital art pictures on the internet and decided to give digital art a try.

He started sharing his digital creations on the internet and began to receive commissions – his first step towards becoming a professional digital artist. He worked as a concept artist in the video game industry, but wanted to work as a freelance illustrator so he locked himself at home and worked on a new portfolio. Now he does freelance concept and card illustrations. In his free time he continues with his true passion – cover art.

Kerem is influenced with every visual input, and, more specifically, by the cover artists of *Conan*, the comic book he loved as a child. He loves learning new things and trying new shortcuts and techniques with every piece of art he produces. One of the best things about creating digital art, for Kerem, is CTRL-Z, which means he can go as far as he likes; there are no limits.

Kerem isn't sure what the next few years will bring, but he knows that he will continue to get better and better as a digital artist.

CHARACTER

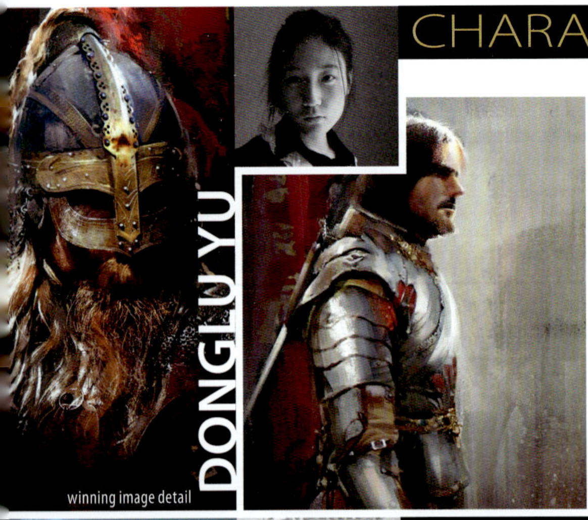

winning image detail

DONGLU YU

When Donglu was a little girl, her parents started sending her to art classes, in which she studied Chinese watercolour, calligraphy and oil painting. After emigrating to Canada with her parents at age 12, she continued to attend art classes during her college and university years.

Later, Donglu started to explore digital art tools and was amazed by the potential and flexibility they offered her. She now works for Ubisoft Entertainment and also enjoys freelance opportunities on such projects as iPhone/iPad games, card games, book illustrations and CG movie concepts.

Working on character art gives Donglu the chance to study anatomy, characters' emotions, and diverse cultures. Her work on portraiture allows her to more freely use brushstrokes and express colors.

Donglu spends most of her free time drawing, and also enjoys experiencing different people and cultures, and being in nature. In the future, she is looking forward to participating in more inspirational video games and film projects where she hopes to create a wide range of concept art and explore her artistic potential.

FANTASY FEMMES

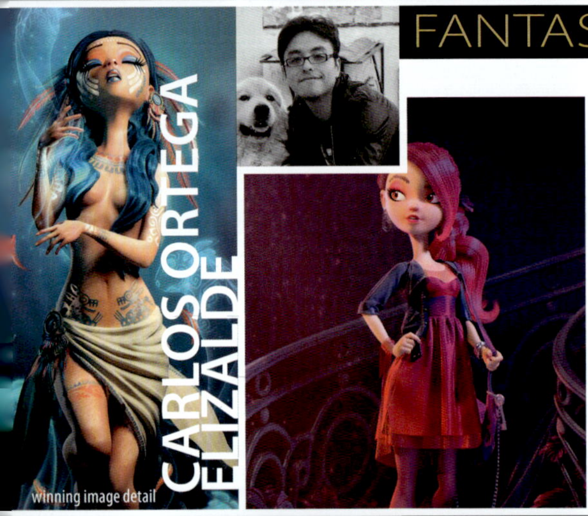

winning image detail

CARLOS ORTEGA ELIZALDE

Carlos Ortega Elizalde was enticed into the world of 3D through animated movies, VFX, video game cinematics, and the work of other digital artists. Accustomed to putting down most of his ideas on paper, 3D art presented him with a whole new world of possibilities – so he decided to use most of his free time learning to use 3D software.

Elizalde studied graphic design in Mexico and started his professional career as a multimedia designer for an advertising company. Later, he worked on motion graphics for documentaries and as a freelance character artist. He is currently studying animation, and he hopes to become a better animator in the next few years. He also works as a lead character artist on an animated feature film being made in Mexico.

Elizalde has been influenced and inspired by animation of all kinds, and also has great admiration for all traditional art, especially music and painting. He loves cartoons but is also very passionate about color, composition and atmosphere – and tries to merge all of these into his work. He believes it is important to continue to grow as an artist, to stay humble, and to keep himself motivated to learn.

CONCEPT ART

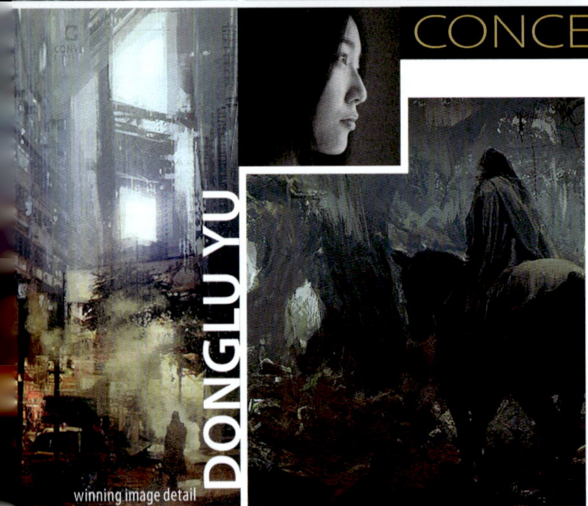

winning image detail

DONGLU YU

Donglu is a concept artist with over eight years of experience as a visual development artist. During her time at university studying film animation, Donglu explored different animation styles, including cell animation, stop motion and 3D animation.

After working as a texture artist and a 3D artist, she finally realized that concept art was what she most enjoyed. She is attracted to the position of concept artist because it requires lots of brainstorming, a fast sketching ability, and offers freedom to explore different visual materials.

Aside from her work as a freelance artist, recently Donglu has been making tutorials and video workshops to provide tips and insights to young artists.

Daily life observations, movies, novels and legends all provide Donglu with inspiration. Creating artworks has become an integral part of her life; art is her best friend, with whom she expresses her feelings and shares the fantasy world in her mind.

COMIC / MANGA

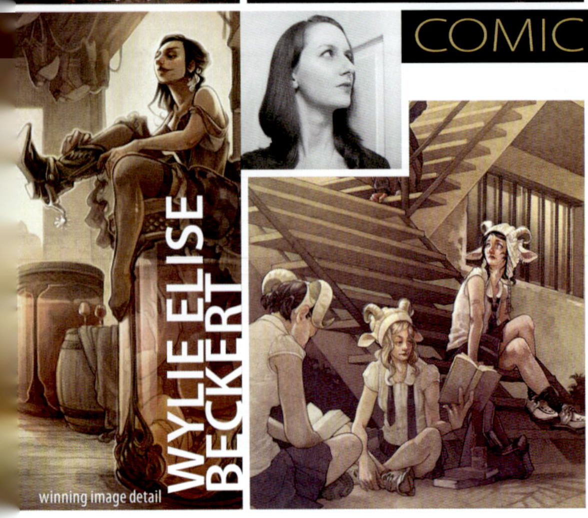

winning image detail

WYLIE ELISE BECKERT

Wylie Elise Beckert says she came from humble beginnings as a digital artist, and painted with a mouse for a long time before switching to a tablet just in time for the completion of her first professional portfolio.

As a child and budding artist, she was influenced by Old World fairytales and her work is defined by its darkness, whimsy and emphasis on characters and storytelling. She graduated with an art degree from the University of California and since then has increased her knowledge and experience with self-directed study.

For the last two years she has worked as a full-time illustrator, and looks forward to being able to look back and reflect upon the art she is creating now, of which she is so proud.

Wylie sees digital art as a playground and loves the freedom it provides her to explore different paths, and being able to produce a 16 x 20 painting on a rickety tray table on a crowded airplane.

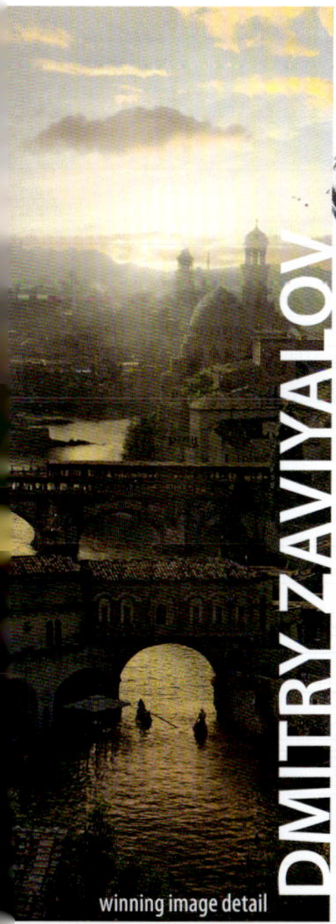

winning image detail

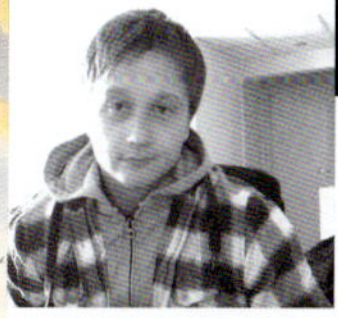

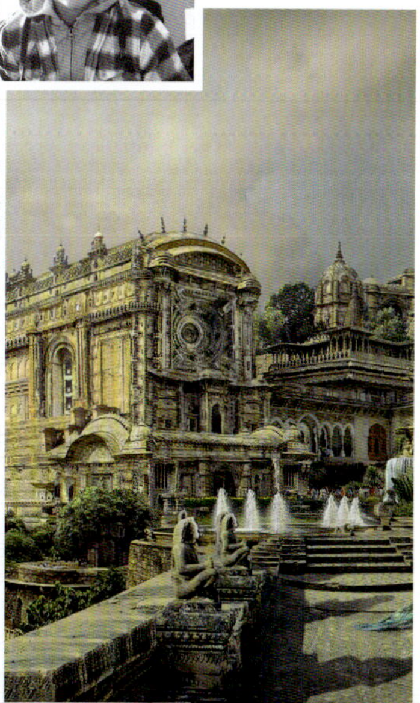

MATTE PAINTING

DMITRY ZAVIYALOV

Dmitry Zaviyalov's life as a digital artist began seven years ago when he came across a simple sketch on the website of well-known matte painting artist Yanick Dusseault. It wasn't fancy art, just a doodle; but there was something in it for Dmitry – something that got him dreaming that one day he could create such captivating environments in his art.

Dmitry finished art school, and also went to college where he gained a good understanding of traditional artistic mediums. He acquired most of his CG knowledge from searching the internet and completing manuals and tutorials. He has been working in the commercial graphics industry for a few years, on films and commercials, and had a stint in a studio in Brazil. He also continues to build up his freelance portfolio.

For Dmitry, art is not about making money. He believes art is amazing, and that digital art is the best construction kit you can get. His main artistic influence is the knowledge that he can create whatever he wants with his art – his own worlds, civilisations and universes; imaginable and unimaginable. He only wishes he had more time to create the art he loves.

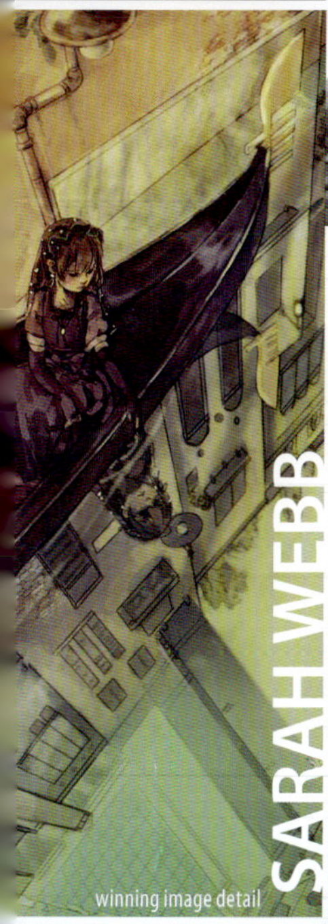

winning image detail

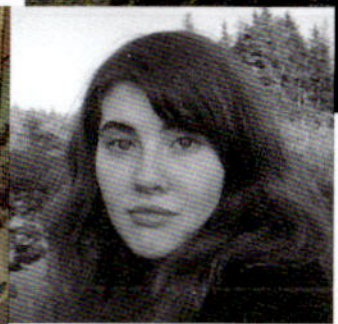

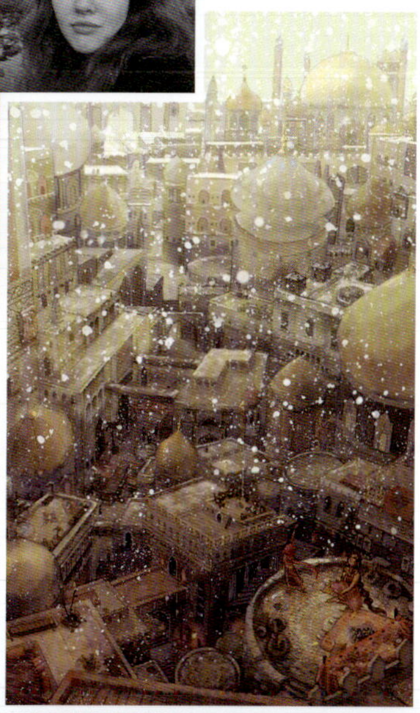

ENVIRONMENT

SARAH WEBB

Sarah Webb started painting digitally three years ago after her parents bought her a tablet for her birthday. She had learned about digital art online and wanted the same tools her favorite artists used.

While her early digital work was mostly motivated by her favorite artists and movies, recently she has been inspired by fantasy stories and photographs of the places she hasn't been able to visit yet.

Her favorite thing about painting digitally is being able to show people exactly what is inside her head, and having the flexibility to perfect a piece without worrying about ruining it with one mistake.

With her work she wants to bring the viewer (and herself) into amazing locales that can't be found anywhere else. She loves being able to show places that don't exist. For Sarah, painting the places she hasn't seen in real life is the second best thing to actually being there. She is very happy to be able to center her life and work around the thing she loves doing most.

So far she is self-taught, using the numerous resources online, but she looks forward to taking online art classes and starting college, working towards a BFA in illustration. She is excited for a future of working more in digital painting, finding new and interesting things to inspire her art, and continuing to improve her skills.

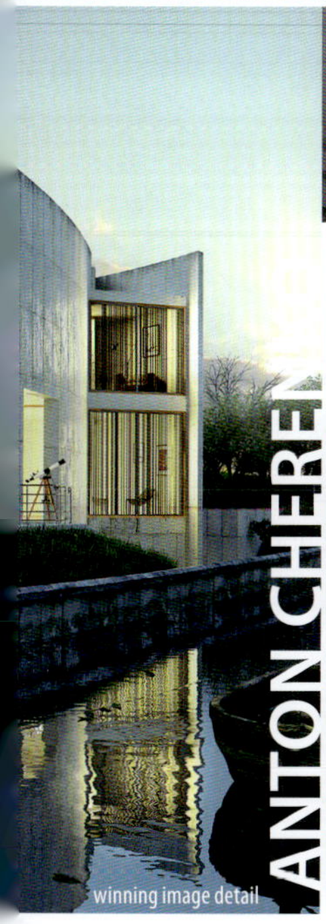

winning image detail

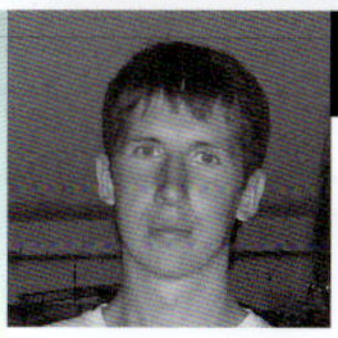

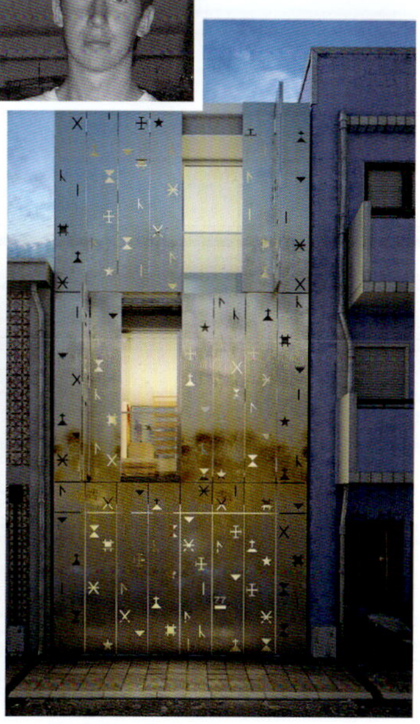

ARCHITECTURE (Exterior)

ANTON CHERENKO

Anton Cherenko has liked to draw ever since he was a child. He started to learn 3D when he was in high school after his brother brought home a book on 3D, and it soon became his hobby. At university, where he was studying to become an engineer, he started to take his hobby more seriously. He received his degree and started work in a design firm as an interior visualizer. Now he works for a game development company in Kiev.

Anton sees many aspects that make up his artistic style – from films he watches, journals and art books he reads, and being out in the world experiencing foreign cultures and the work of other artists.

He sees it as a great pleasure to be working in the fast-developing digital art field where he learns something new every day. The most rewarding part of being an artist for Anton is the ability to realize the creative ideas in his mind that are impossible to create in real life.

In the future he plans to participate in interesting and inspiring projects, to gain more experience, and to expand his knowledge base, especially in animation and motion design.

ARCHITECTURE (Interior)

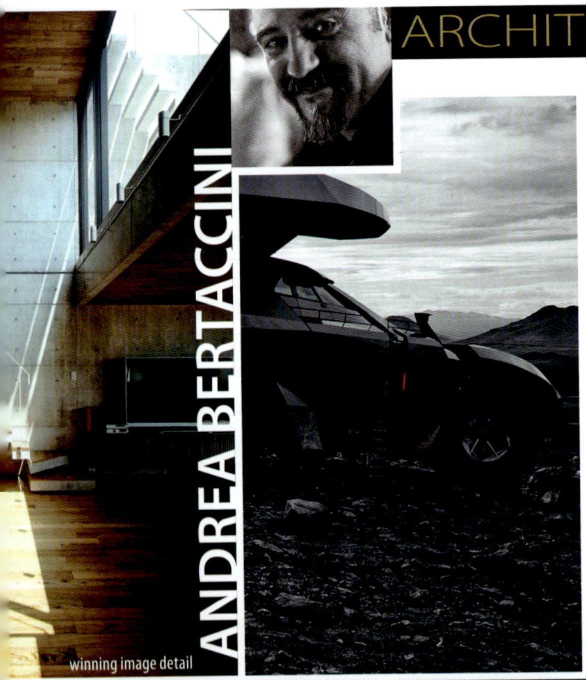

winning image detail

ANDREA BERTACCINI

Trained as an architect, Andrea Bertaccini entered the 3D world when one day he was given a computer. After a short time, Andrea became passionate and began to collaborate with an architectural studio (Studio Lucchi & Biserni). In 2000 he began TREDISTUDIO, a company that works in architectural visualization, concept design, advertising, animation – and anywhere they can use their creativity.

Reality and realism influence Andrea's artistic style. He loves recreating characters and real situations because he's immediately able to compare the quality of his work with the real world.

To Andrea, the best thing about creating digital art is being able to give life and emotion to something, an experience he is sure is similar for traditional painters or photographers. He is motivated by wanting to create a high-level project based on a good idea. Sometimes Andrea looks at an object and immediately has an idea; other times he concentrates for hours but is not able to come up with anything. He has high expectations and ambitions for his work and, sometimes, even after a work is complete, he looks at it and realizes there is something he could have added or changed.

Andrea sometimes laughs when he is called a 'digital artist', because it is just what he likes to do – it is his passion. When he gets home from work, he turns on the computer and keeps creating.

ROBOTIC / CYBORG

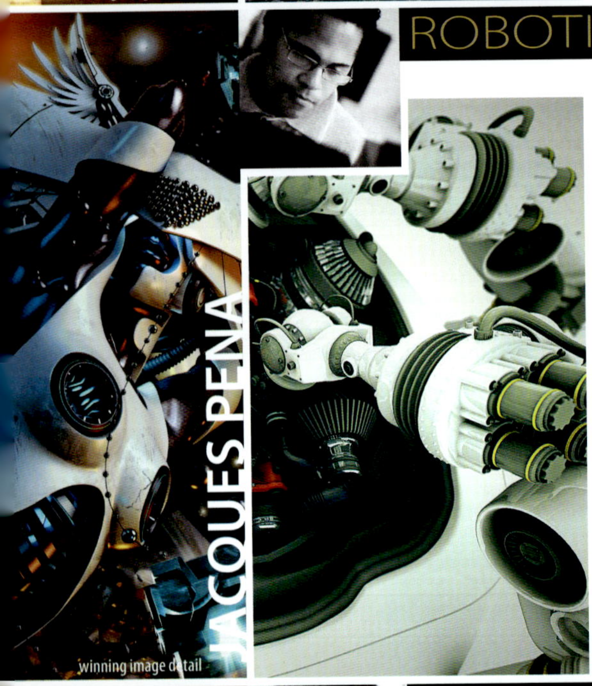

winning image detail

JACQUES PENA

Jacques Pena's foray into digital art began as an evolving transition from one art medium to another. Being a traditional young artist in the 1990s, the tools were there to support what he wanted to accomplish with his traditional skills. He mixed media, which opened new doors, but, as time went on, eventually everything became digital and a new world was born.

Jacques studied graphic design, architecture and illustration in Boston. Soon after graduation he began his professional career at Neoscape. In 2009 he embarked on a new venture into video games, working for Fire Hose Games, Sony Online Entertainment and Harmonix Music, while also contracting for Autodesk and PL Studios. Currently, he works at Fire Hose Games as senior artist, developing new and exciting stuff.

Growing up, Jacques was inspired by many influential artists. He fell in love with the mechanics and works of da Vinci, the illustrations of Gustave Doré, fantasy artist Luis Royo, Jean Giraud ('Moebius') and Syd Mead. They all challenged his imagination to create, engineer and form his own special style.

Through technology, Jacques sees the potential to create and express without limitations, to develop with an unending tool-set, and to create with new mediums.

Jacques loves the moment when he creates that one special image, and the satisfaction and accomplishment sinks in. For Jacques, it is this that makes being an artist rewarding and worth all the hard work.

GAME ART

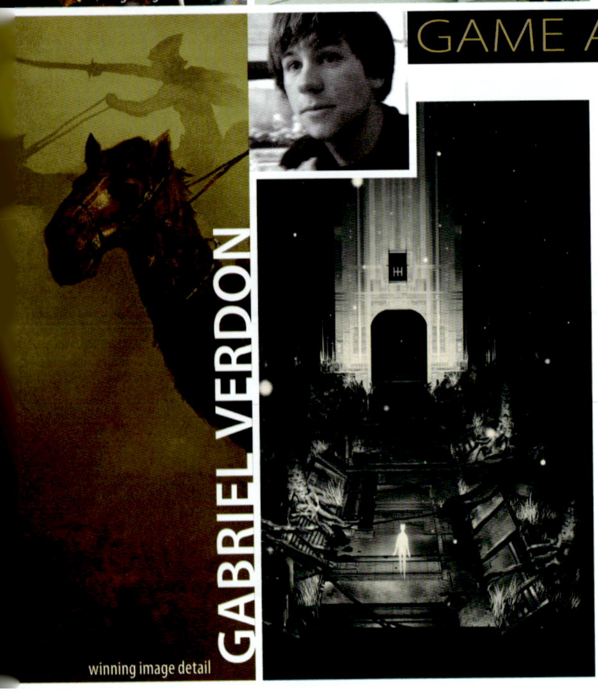

winning image detail

GABRIEL VERDON

Creating art is a compulsion for Gabriel Verdon. He enjoys the solitude and personal nature of painting most of all, and finds it is a way to meditate, reflect and test himself. Creating an interesting image tests his skill, motivation and patience, and its difficulty is what drives him to be better.

Gabriel started making digital art when he was in high school as a complement to his film and video game projects. He enjoyed his art making more than either and decided to pursue it as a career. He is entirely self-taught and has no formal education in any field related to art. All of his skill has come from practice and learning from resources found online and in books.

Gabriel currently works as a freelance illustrator and independent game developer. In the past, he has worked for game and software companies doing graphic design, web development, illustration and concept art.

In the next few years, Gabriel looks forward to developing and finishing more personal projects, and he hopes to build his own self-sustaining business where he can explore his own ideas.

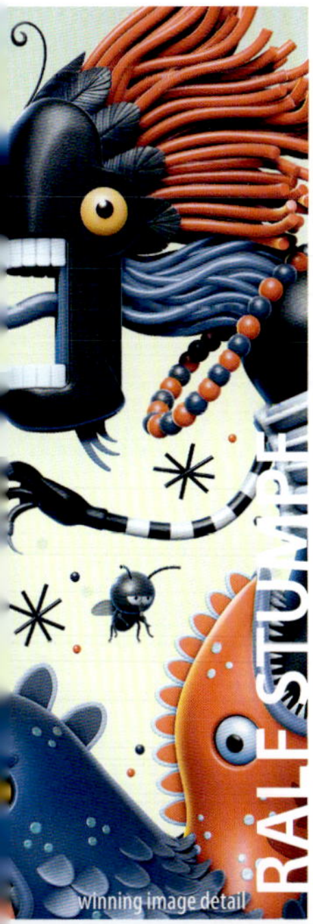

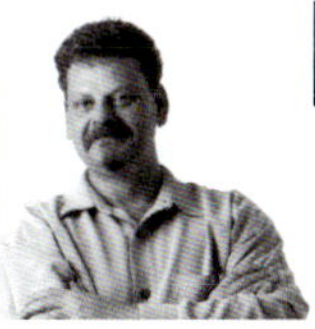

ABSTRACT & DESIGN

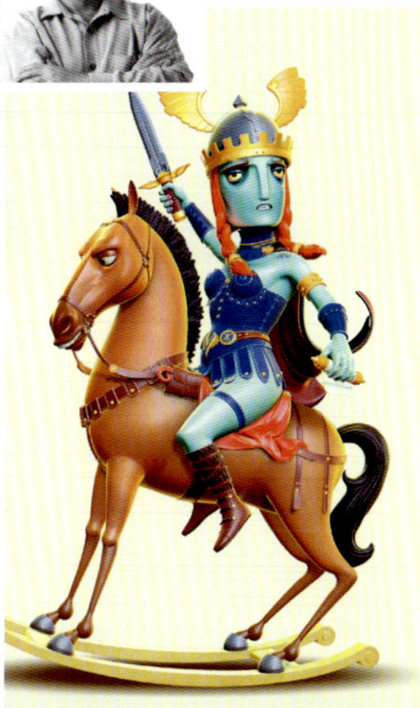

Ralf Stumpf studied communication design at the Folkwang School in Germany and since graduating has worked as a freelance artist on corporate designs, packaging, advertising, and many other kinds of illustrations. His real passion is for character design.

Ralf started working digitally on Macs in 1990, making logos, corporate designs and vector illustrations. He has been interested in 3D since he saw the first short movies from Pixar.

Over the years Ralf has worked as a freelancer on all kinds of characters while for his personal work he likes working on simplified cartoon-type characters. He is currently making his own series of characters, which continues to grow, and one day he hopes to transfer this digital work to produce some physical toys.

Ralf's design works are published in the *Graphis* design, letterhead and packaging series, and his character design and illustration works are shown in Ballistic Publishing's *Exposé*, *Exotique* and *d'artiste Character Modeling* series. He won an Animago Award, was in the top 10 in the Master and Servant Challenge, and won first prize in the Scared Silly Challenge.

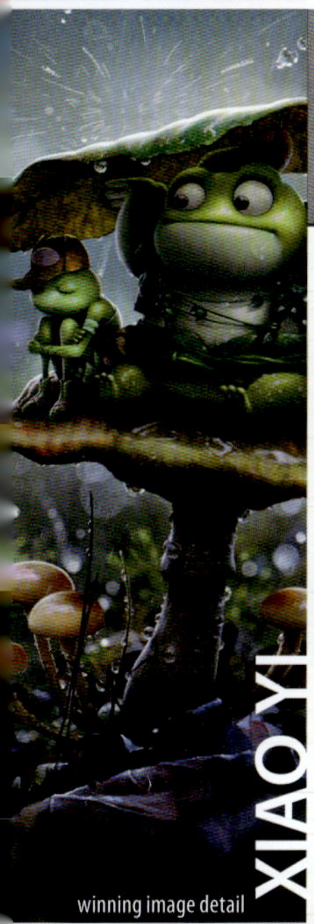

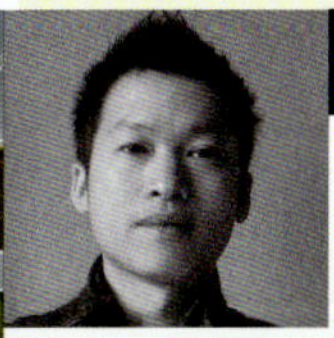

WHIMSICAL

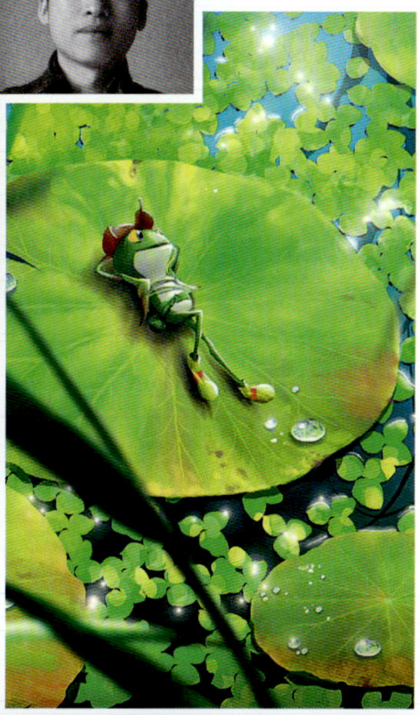

Xiao Yi was born and raised in NanNing, China. He has experience working as an editor for comic and youth magazines and a designer for games and commercials. In 2002 he moved into digital art when he was working as a storyboard and concept artist at the Institute of Digital Media Technology (Shenzhen).

He is inspired by photography, and in his creative work likes to make his characters and environments as realistic as possible, so the viewer can get a strong sense of the atmosphere in these artworks. He loves exploring the fantasy worlds he creates in his art.

Being an artist, Xiao appreciates being able to realize many of his bizarre and interesting ideas in images, and to share them with others.

Currently he works as a production designer and executive director in the Jilin Vixo Film Media, and *Kingdom of Frog* is their latest animated feature film. In the future Yi hopes to gain enough practical experience to be a director.

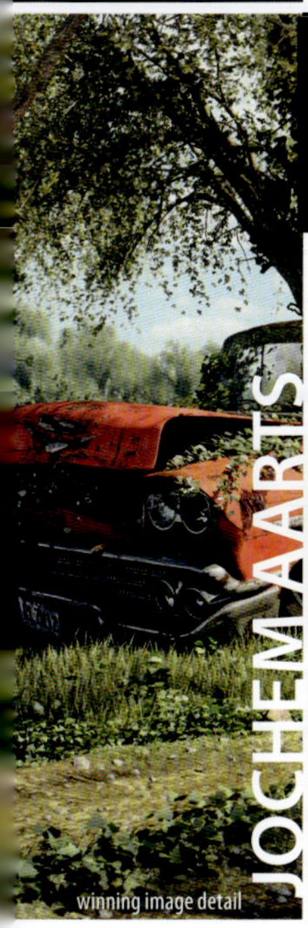

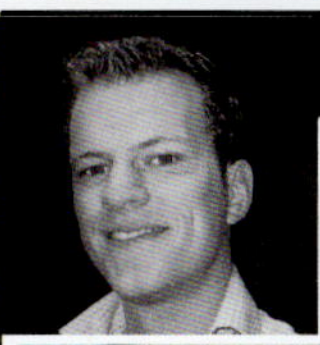

TRANSPORT

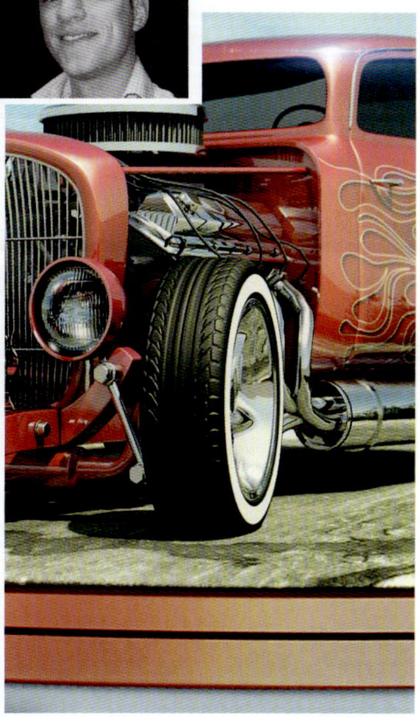

In the late 1990s Jochem Aarts completed his first Photoshop course. Before this, he had done some traditional drawing but digital art was completely new to him. Later, he studied multimedia design and was introduced to 3D software.

After receiving a bachelor's degree in 3D animation, Jochem wanted to learn more about the 3D aspect of art. This was at a time when there weren't many schools teaching 3D so he had to teach himself. At the same time he attended an art academy in The Netherlands where he learned more about (traditional) animation. However, his main focus was on the 3D side of animation.

Jochem worked as a 3D artist/Mocap operator in an Amsterdam-based production studio where he made pre-viz animations, animated commercials, TV series and feature films. Years later, he worked for a company as a 3D artist on the Nintendo games team. Over the last few years he has worked as a freelance CG artist, creating high-end 3D models, visuals and scenes for print media, commercials and feature films.

Jochem is not influenced by any particular style, but instead can be motivated by a variety of things he sees in books, on the internet, or just on the street.

For Jochem, the most rewarding aspect of his work is when people/clients really love his work. He sees this as the best motivation to make his next work even better.

STEAMPUNK

TONI BRATINCEVIC

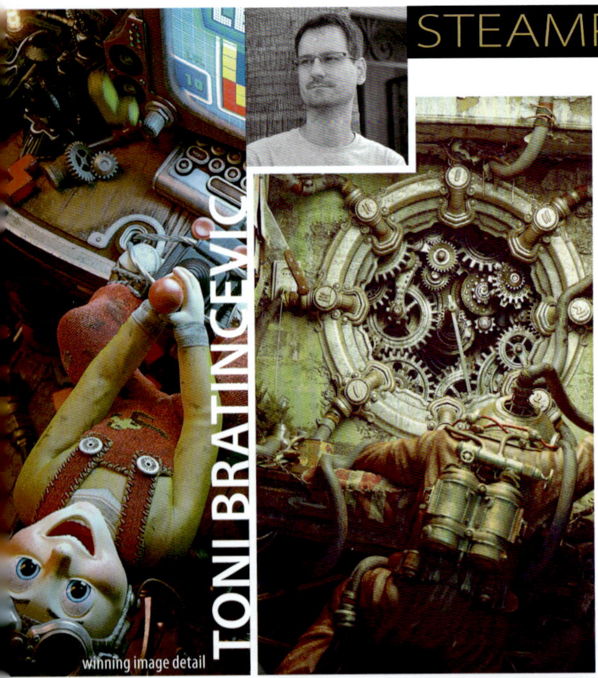

winning image detail

Toni's interest in 3D art started during the 1990s on an Amiga 500 computer after he saw images rendered in software called Real 3D. He remembers instantly falling in love with it, but it was not until he got his first PC that he started exploring 3D art, which later became his hobby.

He has a college degree in computer science and is a self-taught artist. After he graduated from college in 2002 he decided he wanted to work in the 3D industry and got his first job as a 3D generalist in a small Croatian VFX company.

All great art inspires Toni, whether it's digital art or the work of a French Renaissance painter. He usually goes for a realistic style in his art but it is also important for him to have a good story as a base for his work. This motivates him and keeps him focused on creation for a long time.

For Toni, one of the best aspects about doing digital art is the high efficiency of digital tools, and being able to distribute art to thousands of people with just a few clicks of the mouse. One of the main reasons he became a digital artist was because digital art enables him to explore new worlds with his art and to materialize his ideas and thoughts. He also loves the great community of people in 3D art, who are very passionate and willing to help each other.

Currently Toni works as a senior environment modeler for Blizzard Entertainment. In the future, he looks forward to improvements in realtime raytracing rendering and hopes that one day rendering will take minimal time compared to time spent creating scenes.

SURREAL

MARIO SANCHEZ NEVADO

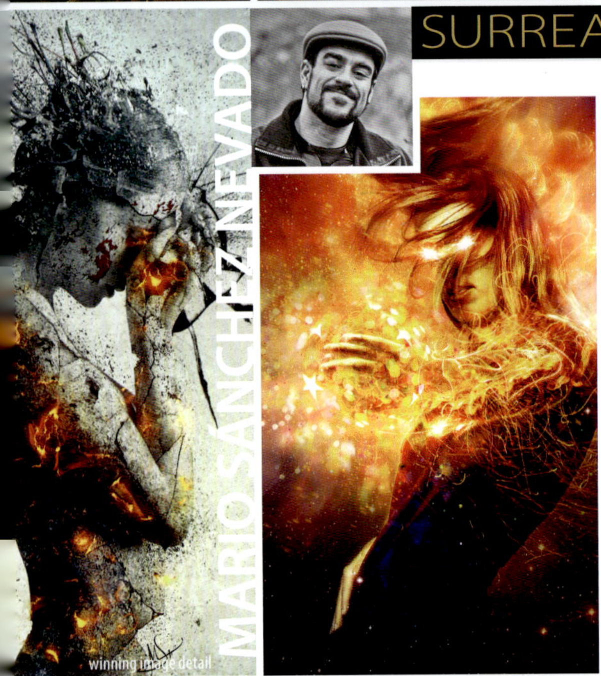

winning image detail

Mario Sanchez Nevado is a former traditional painter and web designer and has a passion for all things creative. After designing some wallpapers and banners for a website, he began experimenting with mixing photographs, which led to experimenting with vectors, 3D and digital painting.

Mario has an eye for mathematical composition, color psychology and visual narratives, and combines these skills with techniques in photograph manipulation and digital painting to create distinctive artworks.

For the last decade Mario has worked in illustration and design for bands and publishing houses. He now works as a freelance illustrator and is also the art director of the international art collective Hysterical Minds. He uses some of his free time to write Photoshop tutorials.

Although Mario admits he is an art lover and that illustrators and painters have had an influence on his artistic style, he sees his real inspiration coming from everyday life and nature.

Over the next few years, Mario would like to start his own artistic studio. Mario believes that the most rewarding aspect of being an artist is simple – to live doing what you love.

STORYTELLING

HU ZHENG

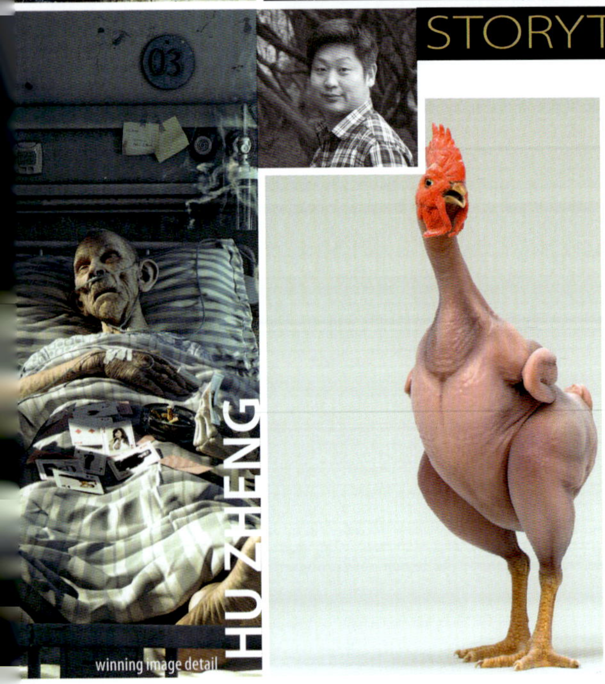

winning image detail

Hu Zheng graduated with a bachelor's degree from university, majoring in animation. Having always loved doodling, during university he began to learn about digital painting, using the CG 'pencil' to express his ideas. He has worked as a CG instructor and is currently working as a senior 3D designer at the Ultra Digital Animation Company in Shanghai.

During the stage of creating an artwork, Hu's emotions are 'uncertain' during the inevitably time-consuming process of creation. As he tries to create characters for his work, he walks in the shoes of his different characters, trying to make them real. His reward for his hard work is the indescribable joy he feels when he finishes a piece of art. Being able to create something greatly satisfies Hu, and he feels particularly fulfilled when his art resonates with other people.

Hu's career as a graphic artist has just begun, and he hopes to work overseas one day to gain international experience and hone his skills. He feels that as an artist he needs to be humble and continuously learn from others, and to follow the words of an old Chinese saying – 'live and learn'.

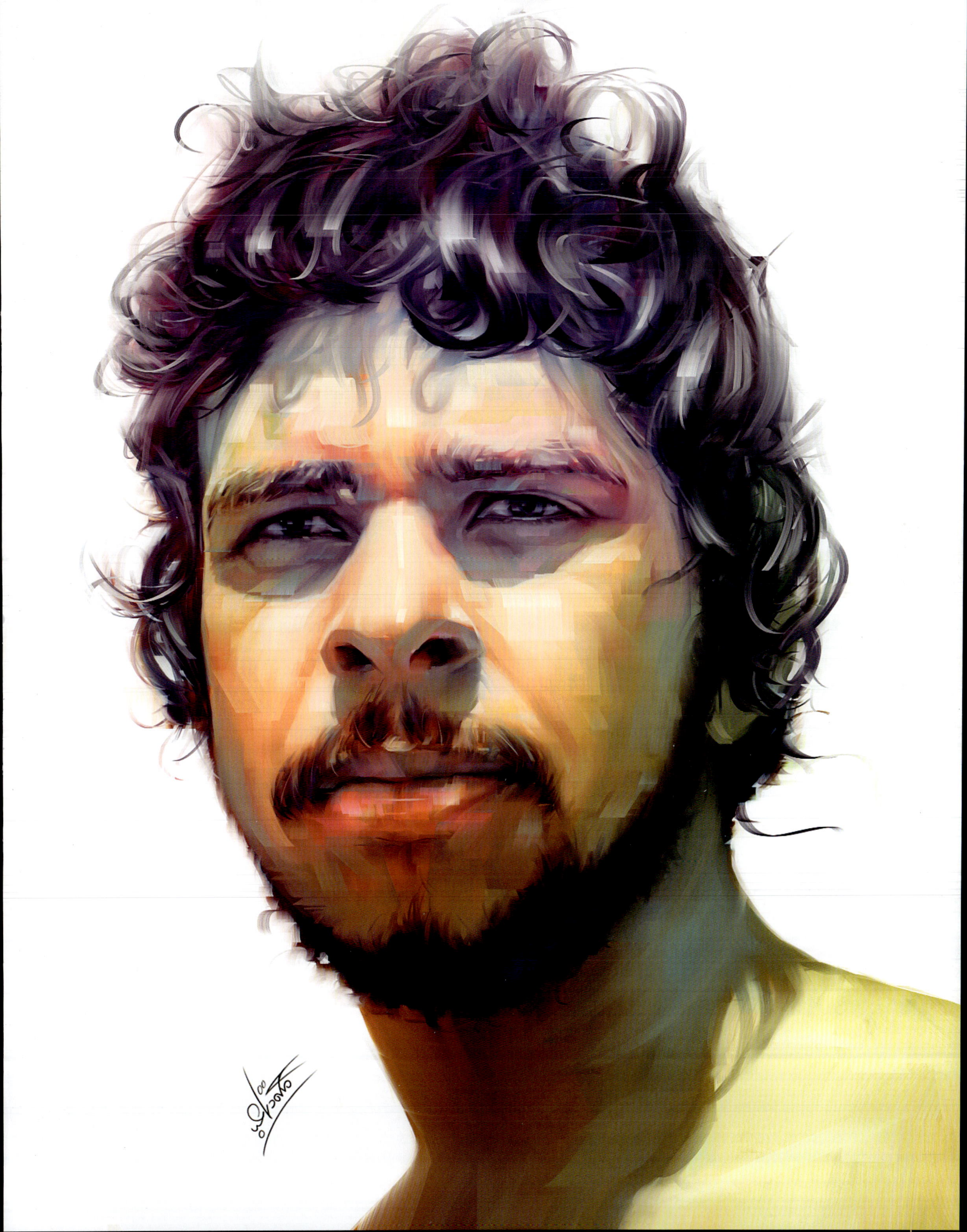

My Uncle
Painter
Mohamed Taaeb, Faculty of Fine Arts, EGYPT

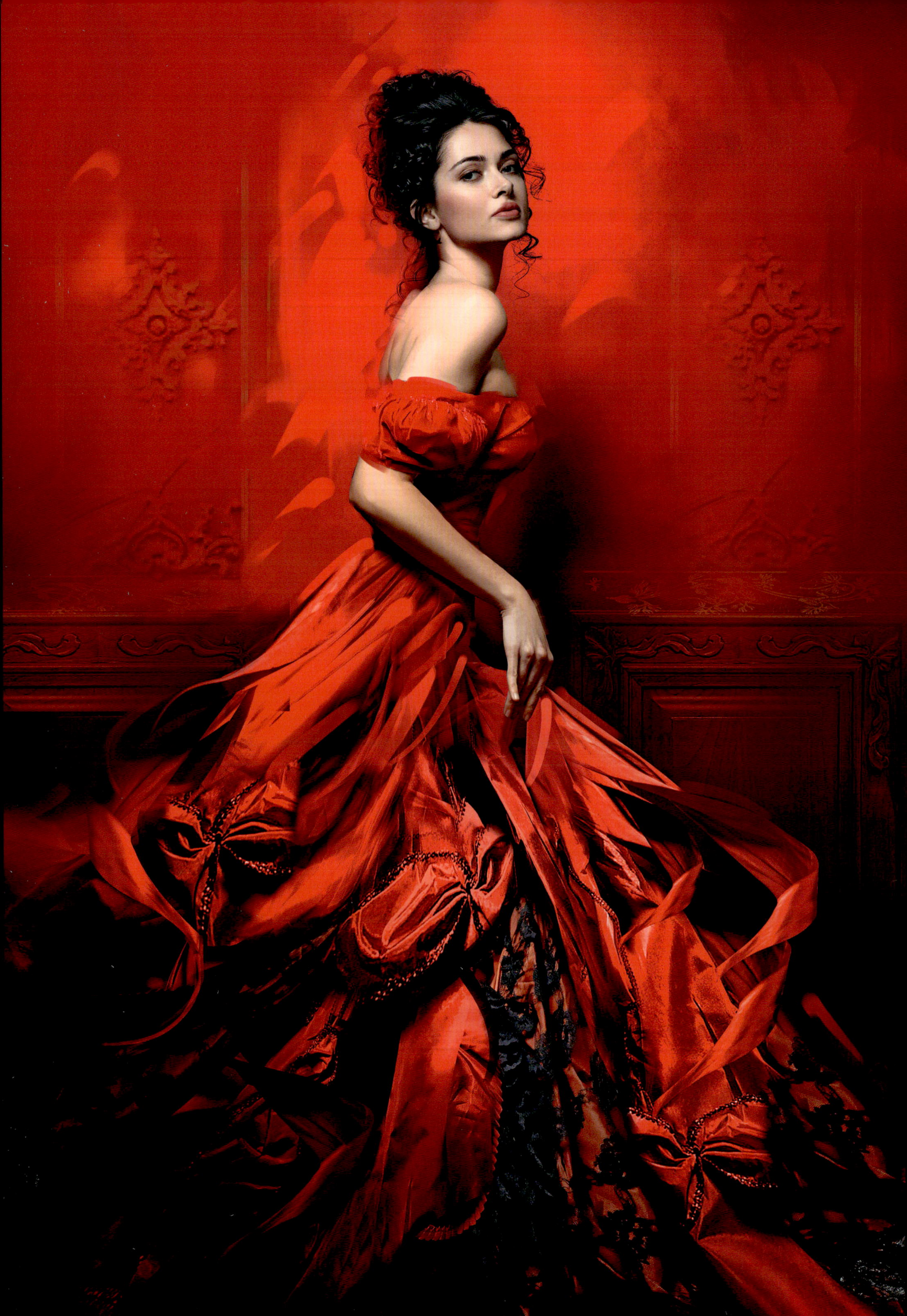

Excellence

Portrait (Painted)

Lady in Red
Photoshop
Jon Paul Ferrara, USA

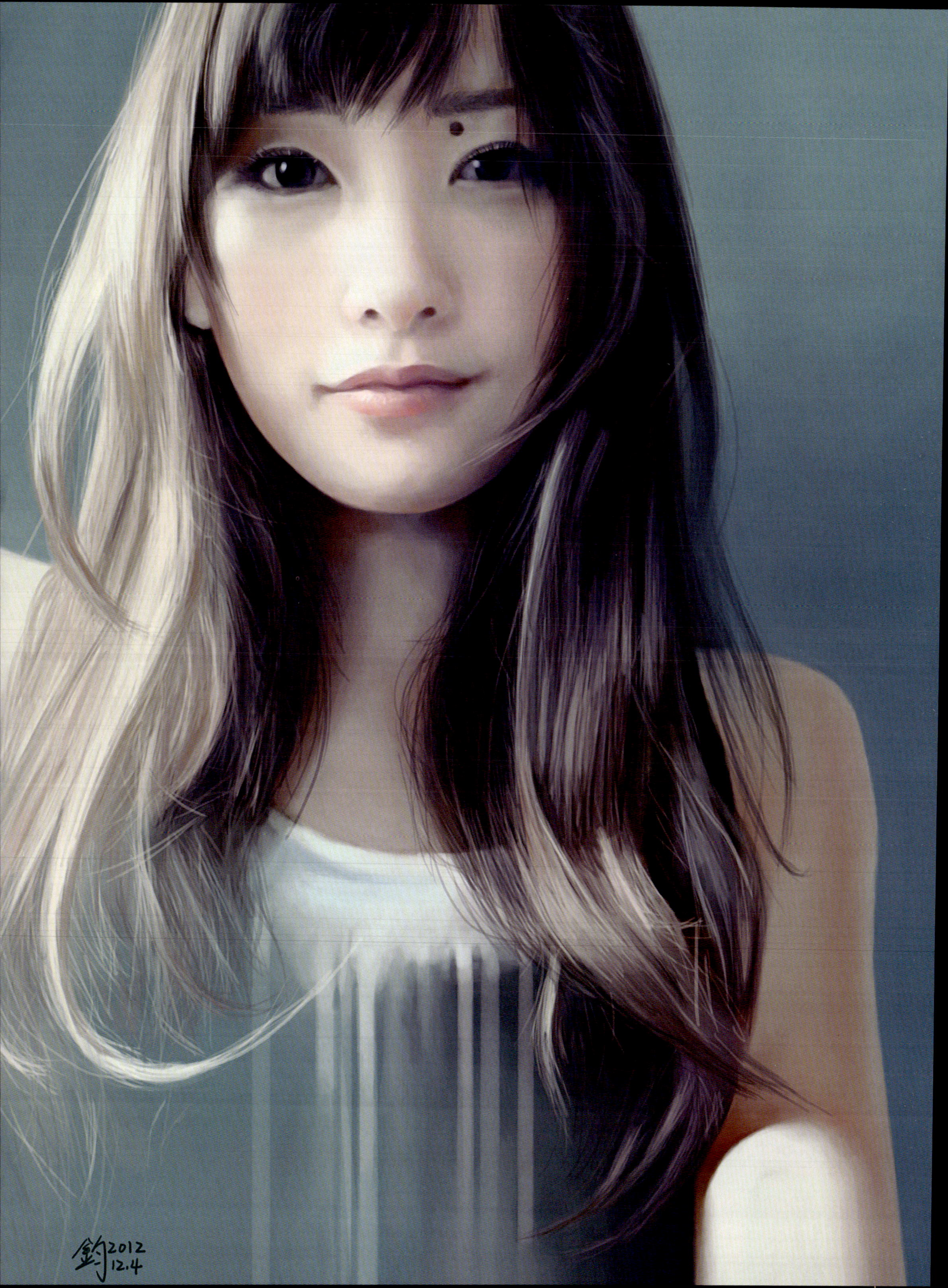

Sweet
Photoshop
Chang Chun Mao, TAIWAN

Excellence
Portrait (Painted)

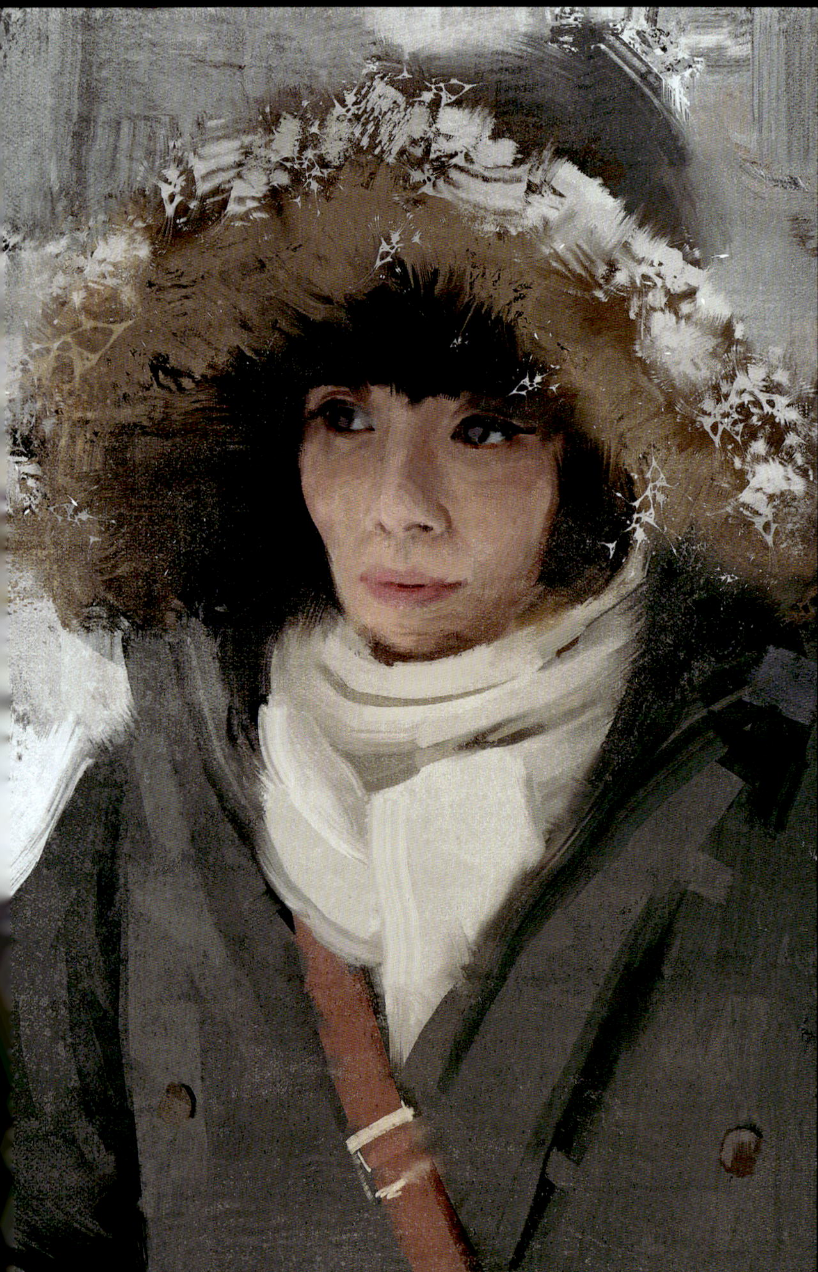

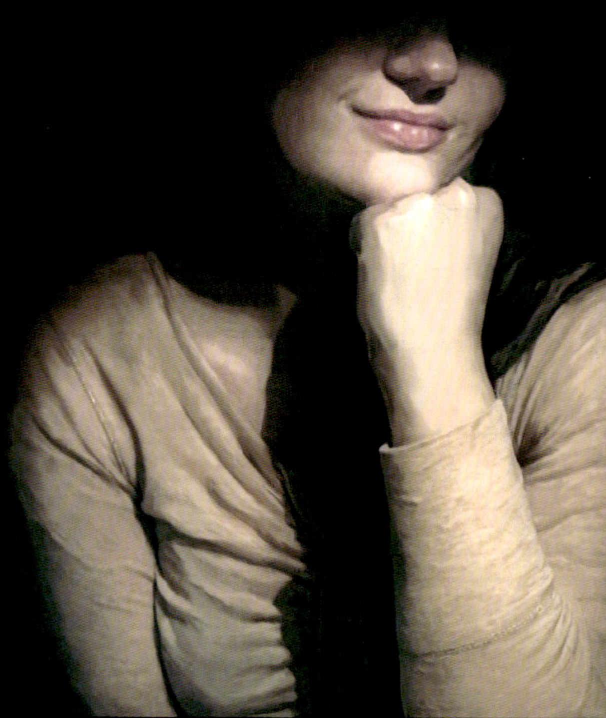

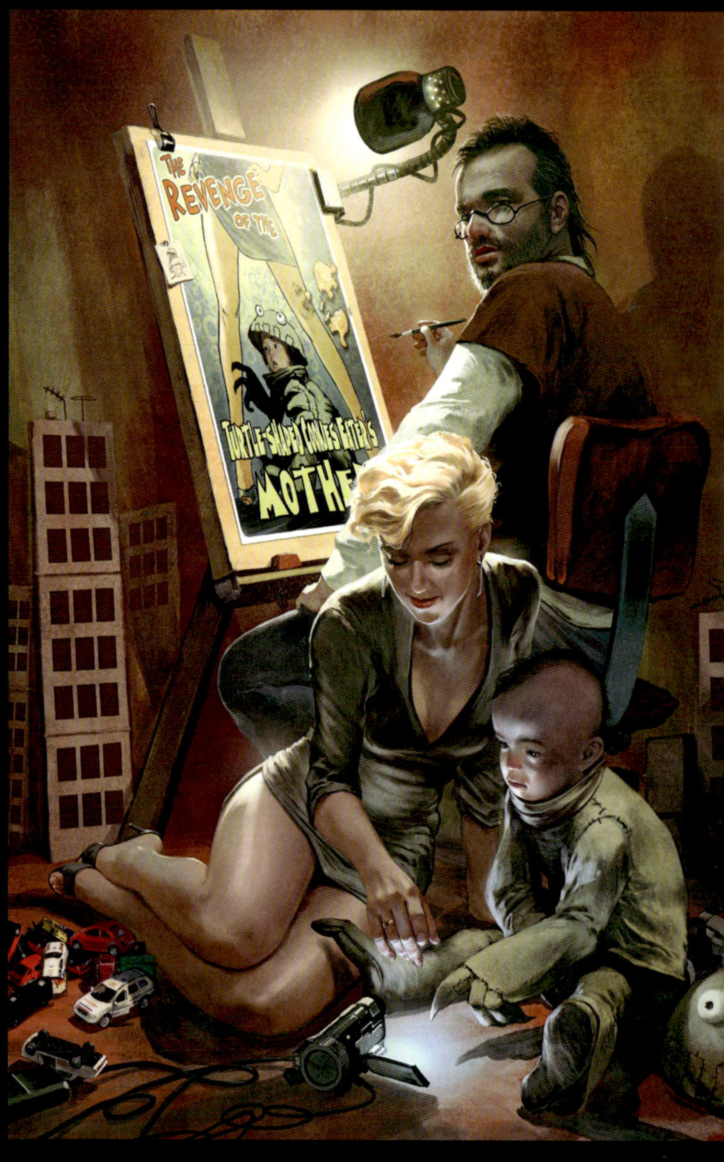

Winter
Photoshop
Stephen Molyneaux, GREAT BRITAIN
[above]

Shine
Photoshop
Rasmus Berggreen, DENMARK
[top right]

9 SQRM Production
Photoshop
Tomasz Jedruszek, POLAND
[right]

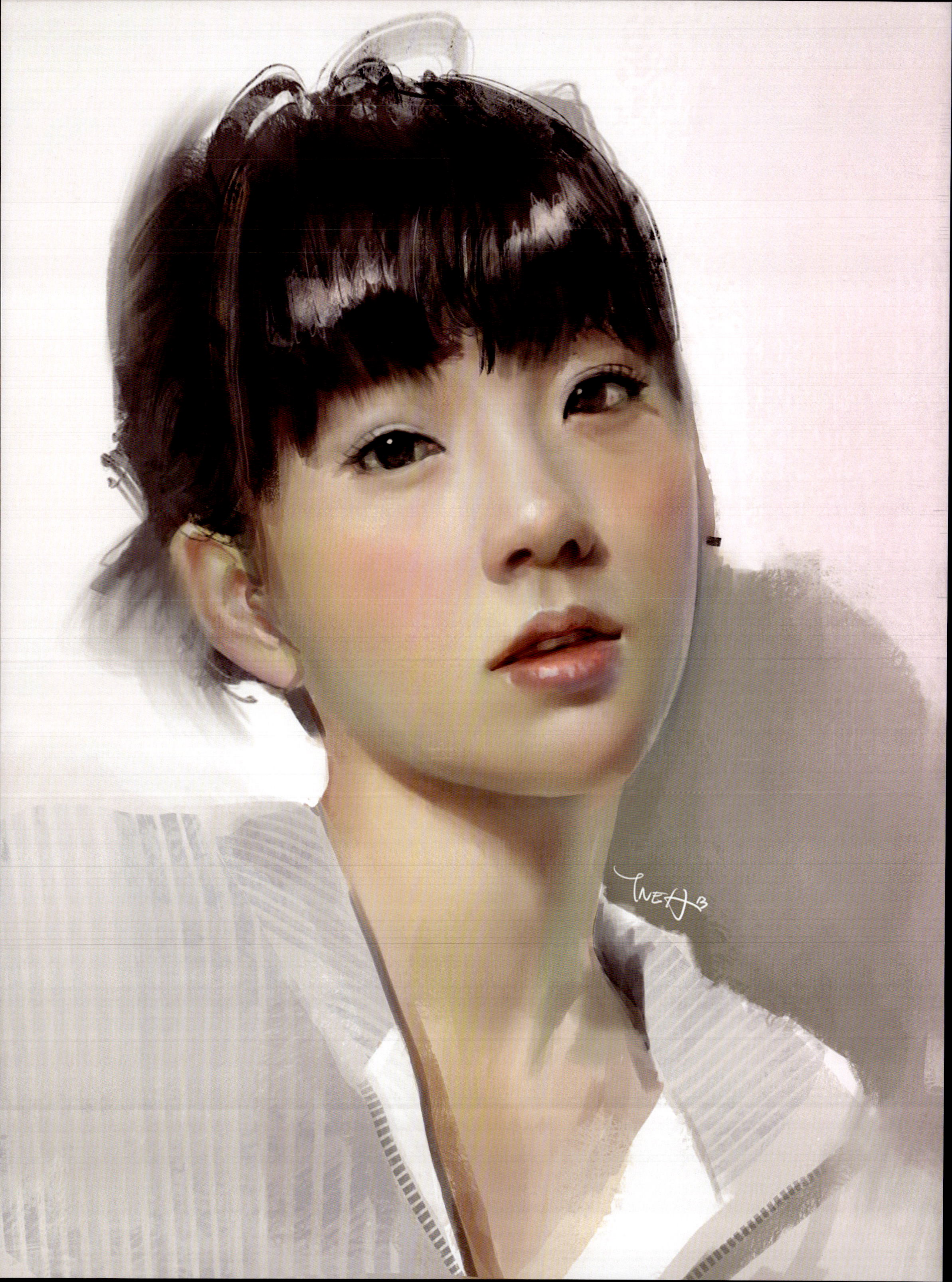

Tae Yeon
Photoshop

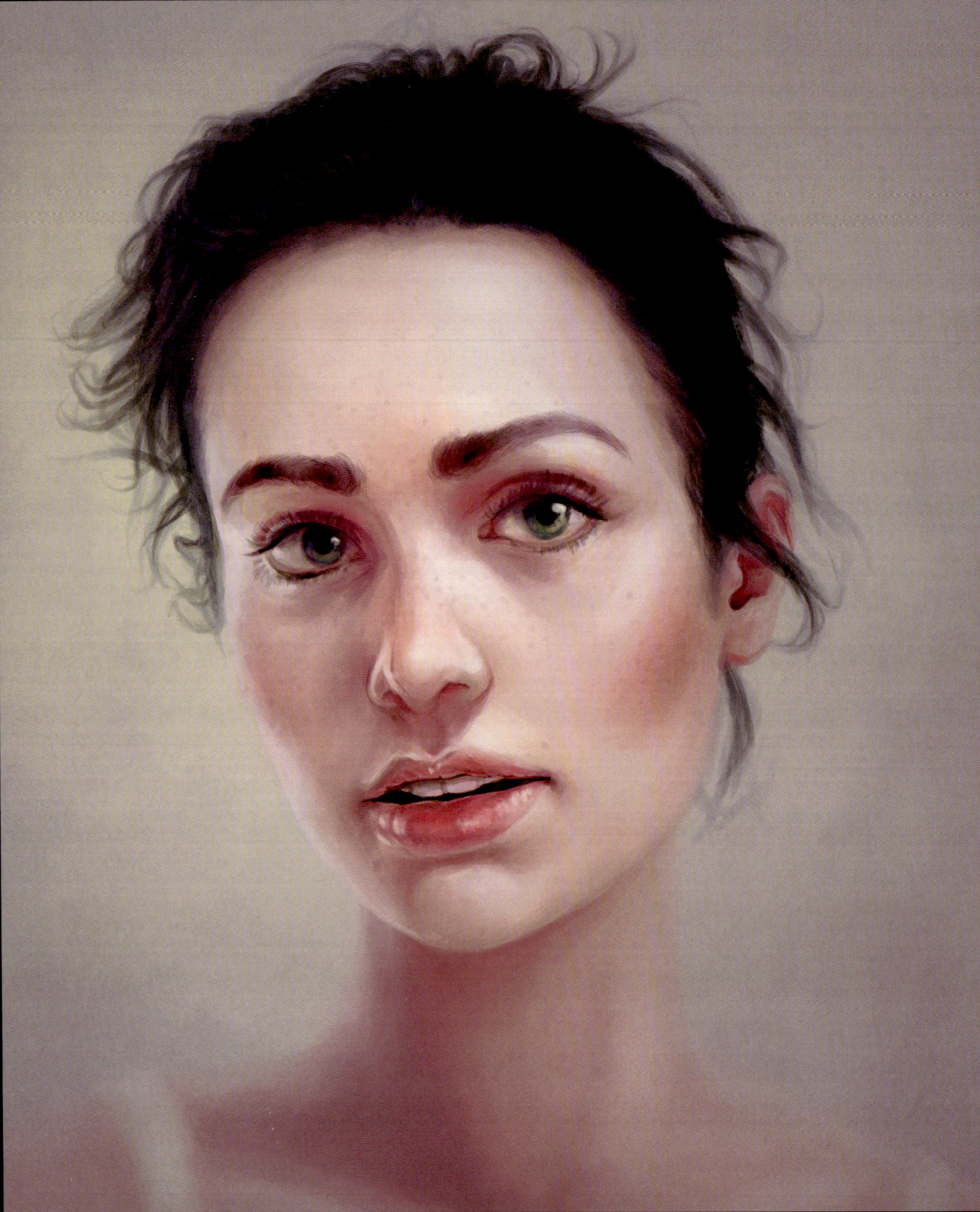

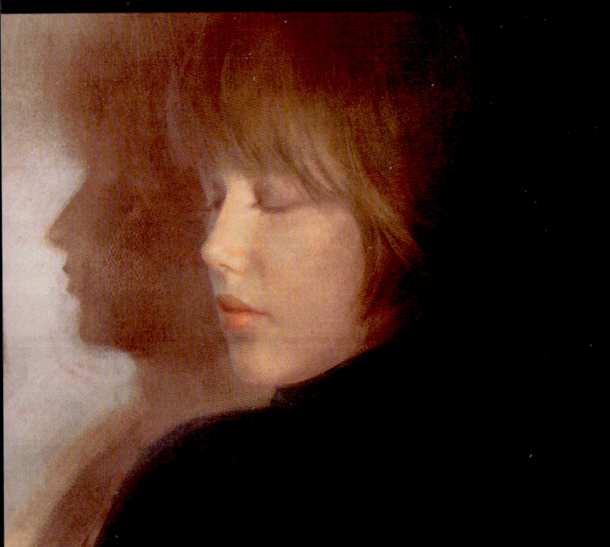

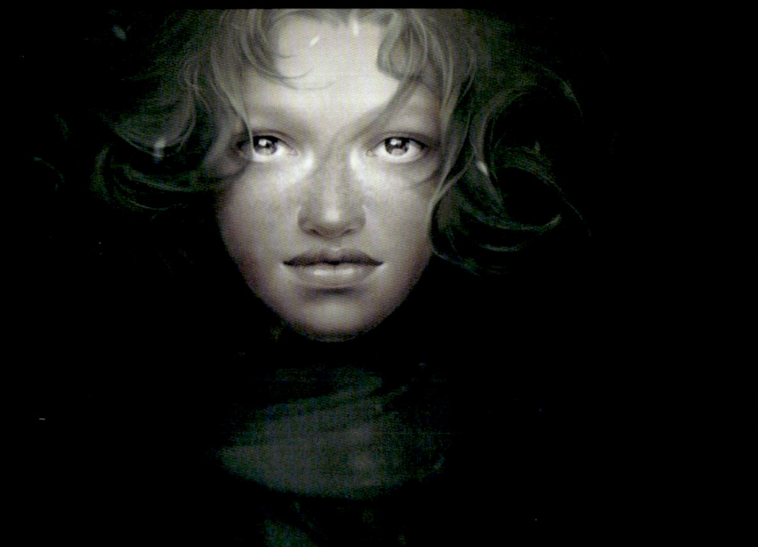

Sleep
Painter
Leng Jen Ting, MALAYSIA
[above]

Soft Portrait
Photoshop
Mominur Rahman, GREAT BRITAIN
[top]

Snowfall
Photoshop
Helen Rusovich, UKRAINE
[above]

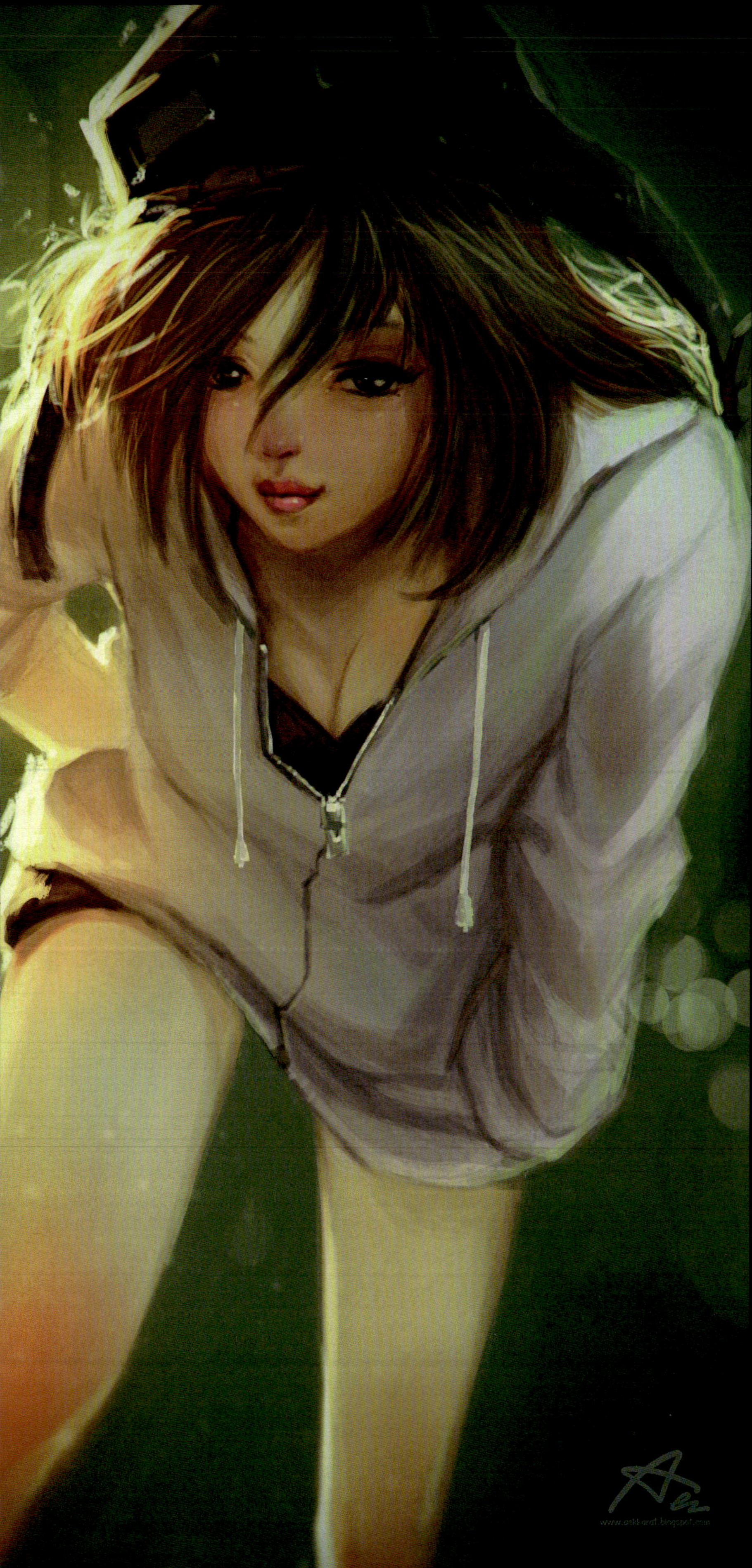

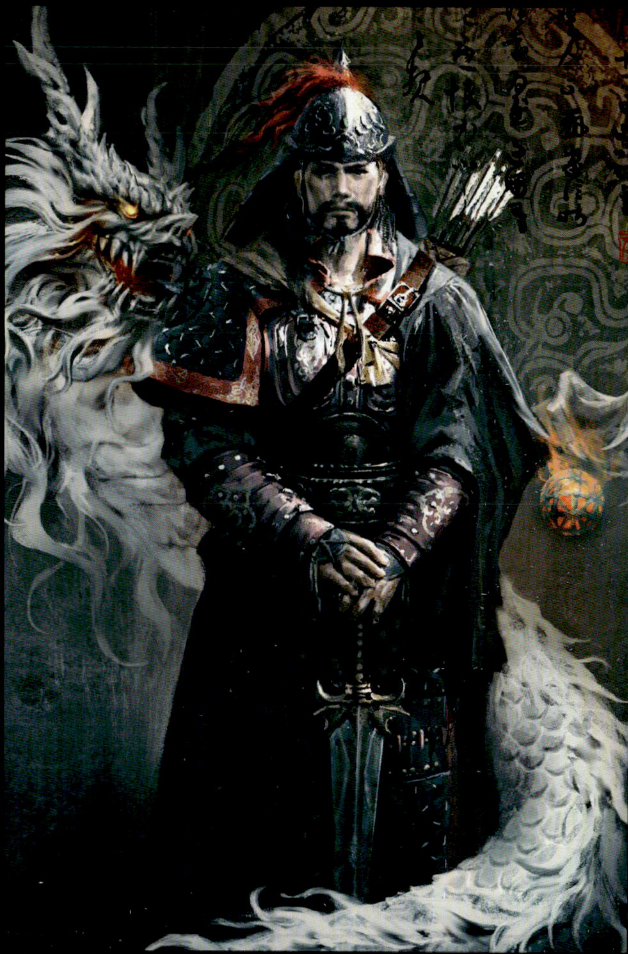

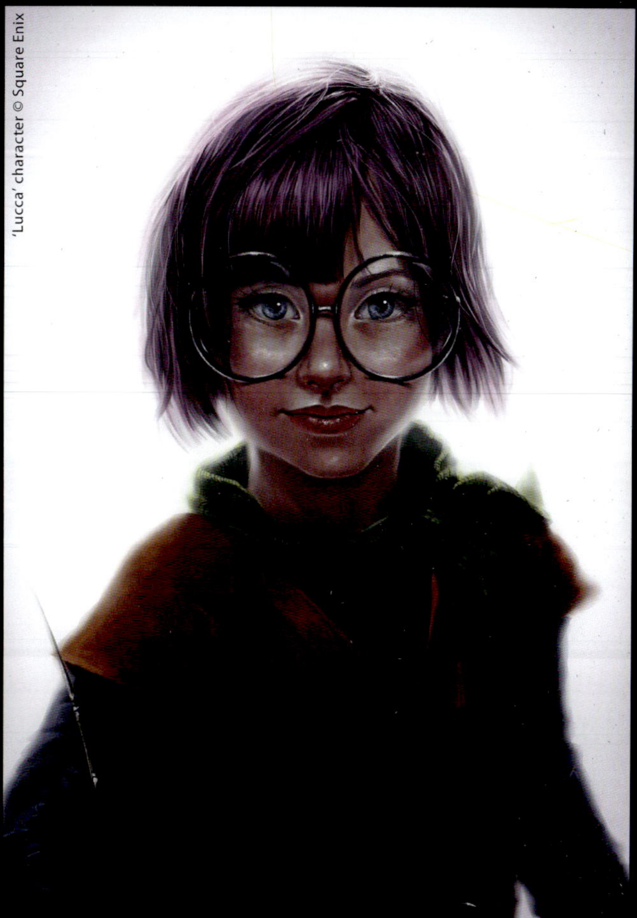

Air Corps
Photoshop
Aekkarat Sumuchaya, THAILAND
[above]

Genghis Khan
Photoshop
Wanglin Fang, CHINA
[top right]

Chrono Trigger: Lucca
Photoshop
2Minds Studio, BRAZIL
[above]

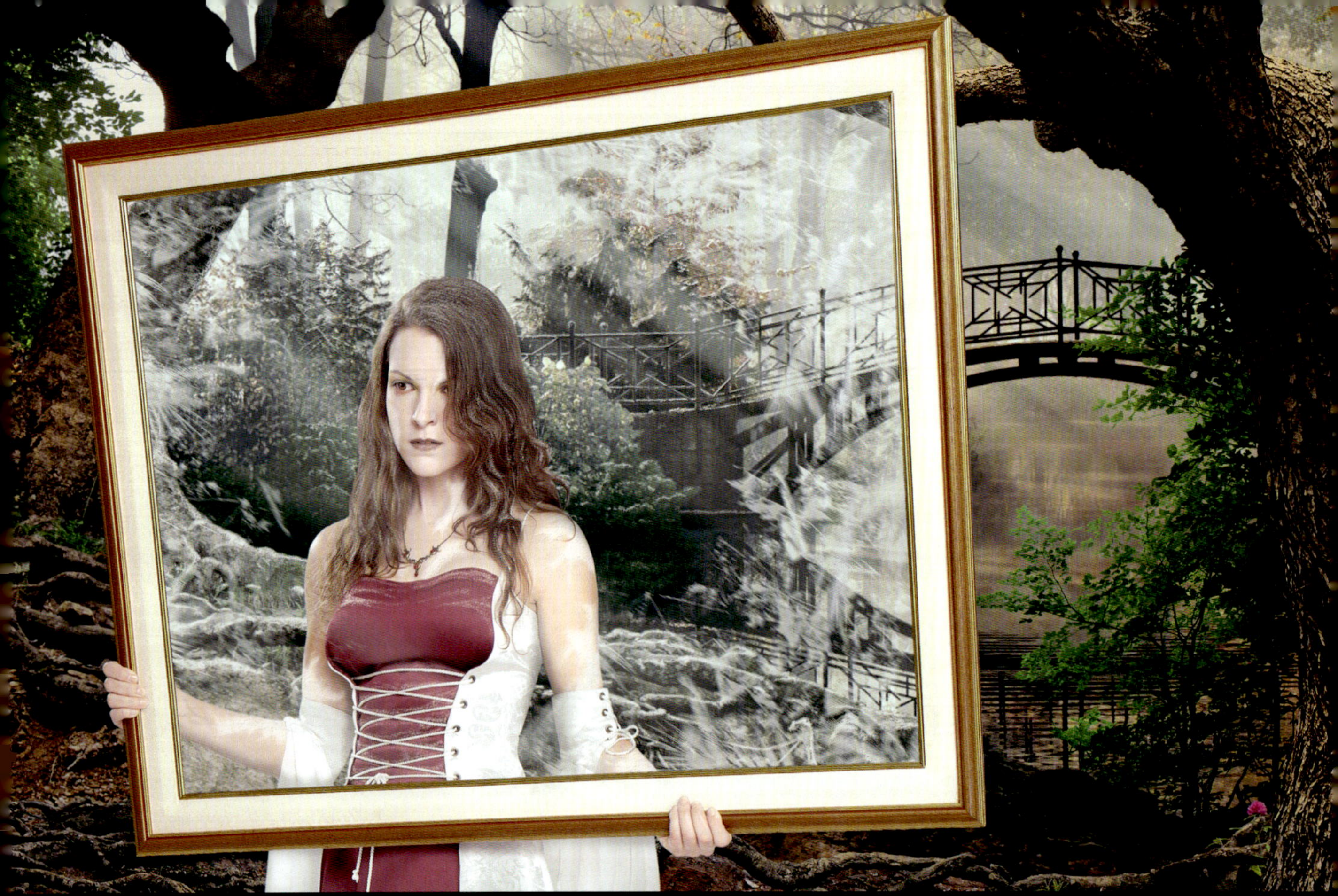

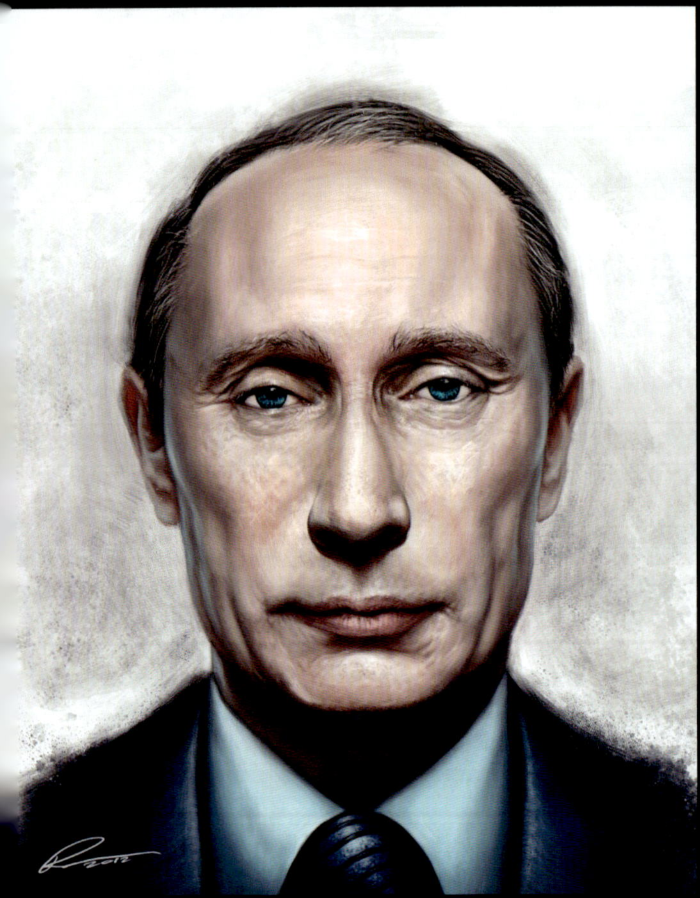

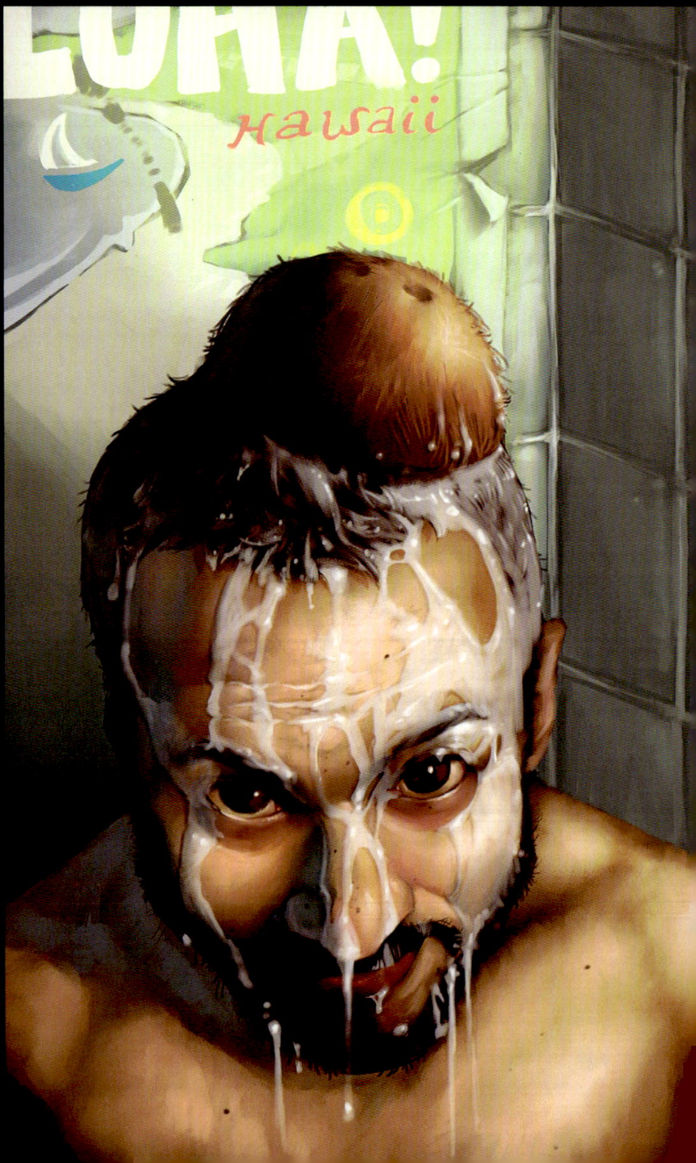

Soir d'hiver
Photoshop
Inspired by Emile Nelligan
Andre Faucher, CANADA
[top]

Vladimir Putin
Photoshop
Pavel Sokov, CANADA
[above]

Coconut
Painter
Stewart Craig, USA
[right]

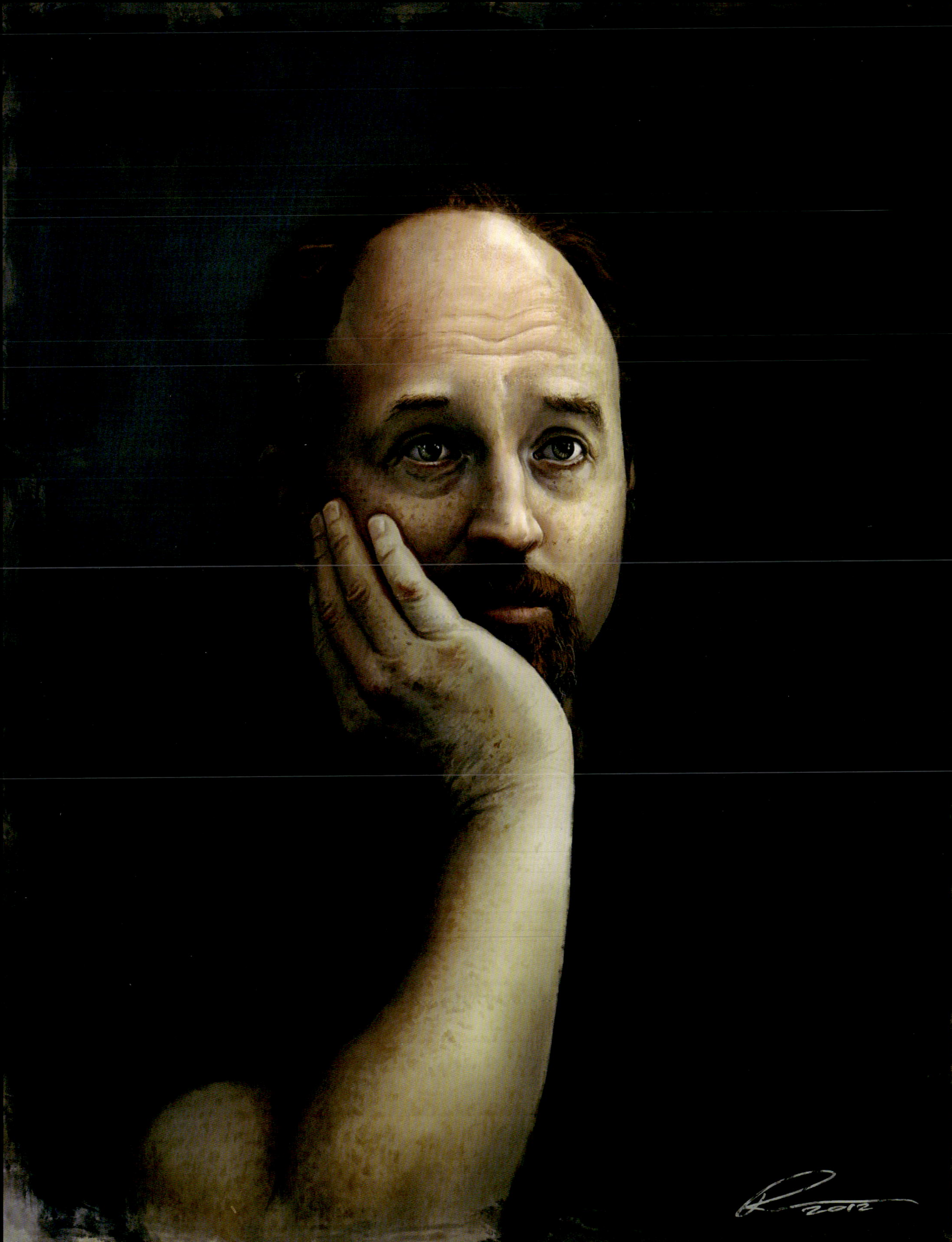

Louis CK
Photoshop
Pavel Sokov, CANADA

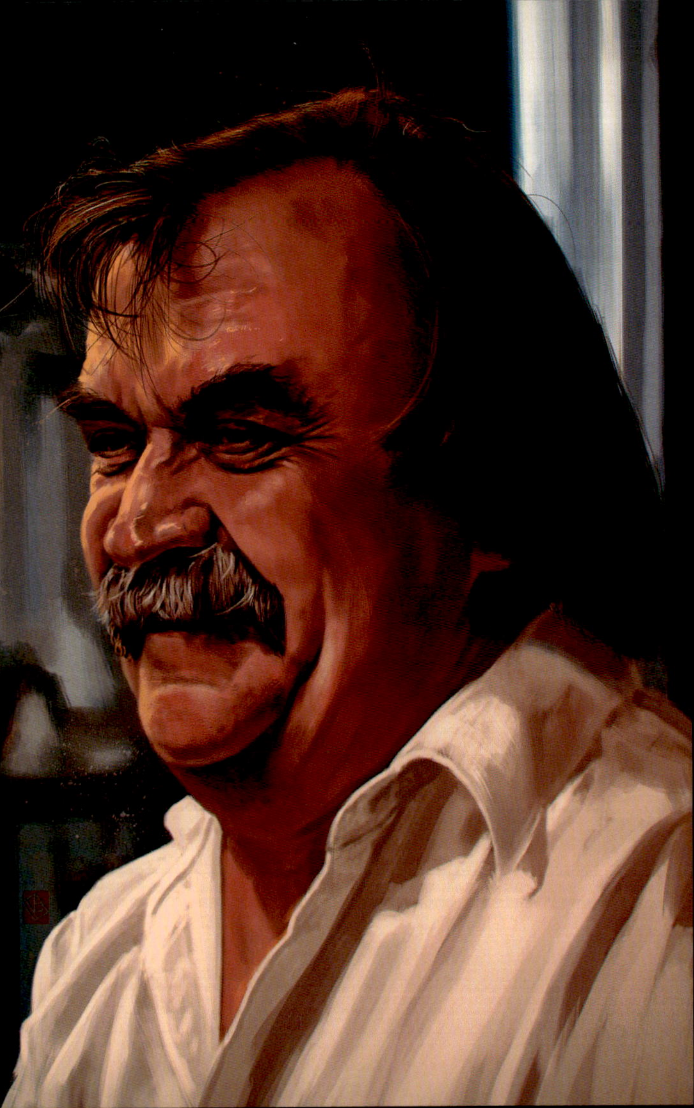

Meslay
Photoshop
Khasis Lieb, FRANCE

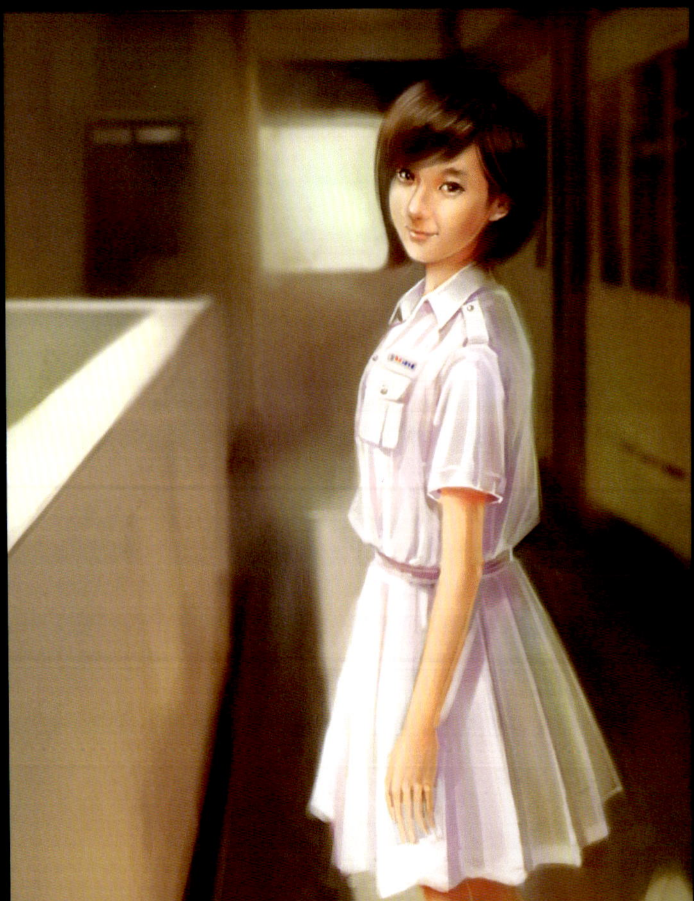

Recall: 1st Meet
Photoshop
Takashi Tan, MALAYSIA

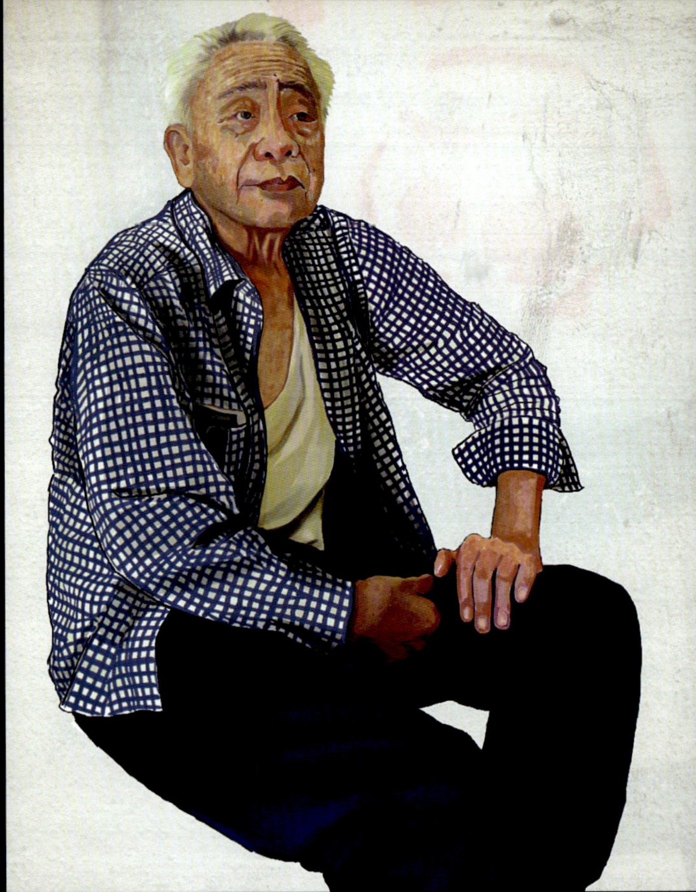

China Man
Photoshop
Lee Baskerville, GREAT BRITAIN

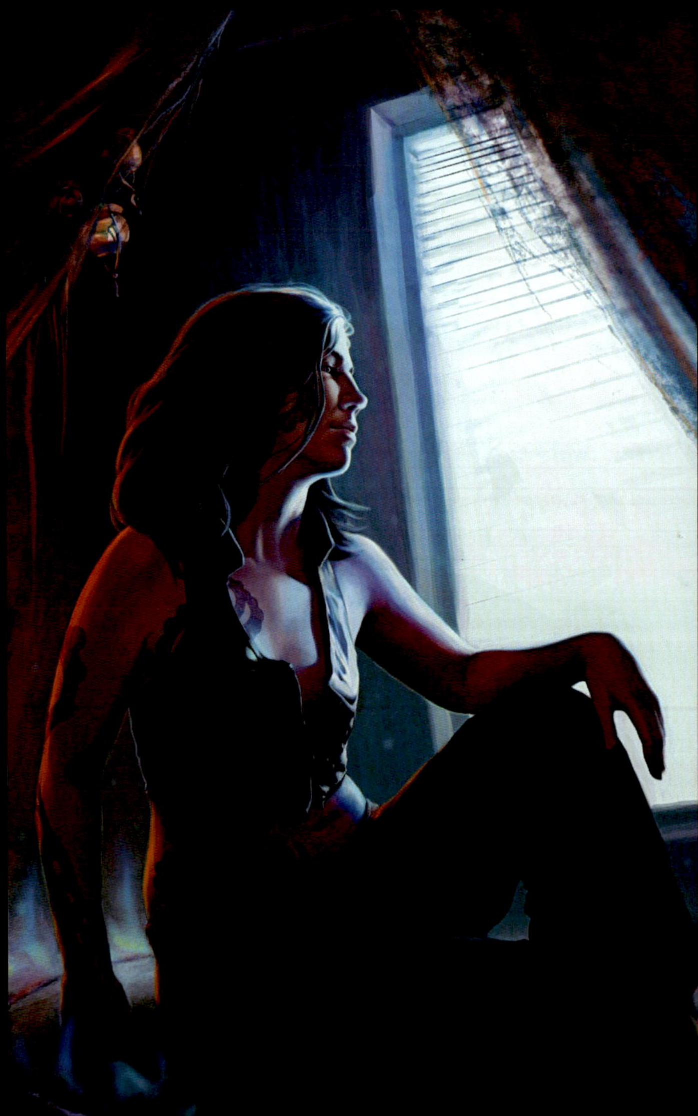

Safe Haven
Photoshop
Gabriella Eriksson, SWEDEN

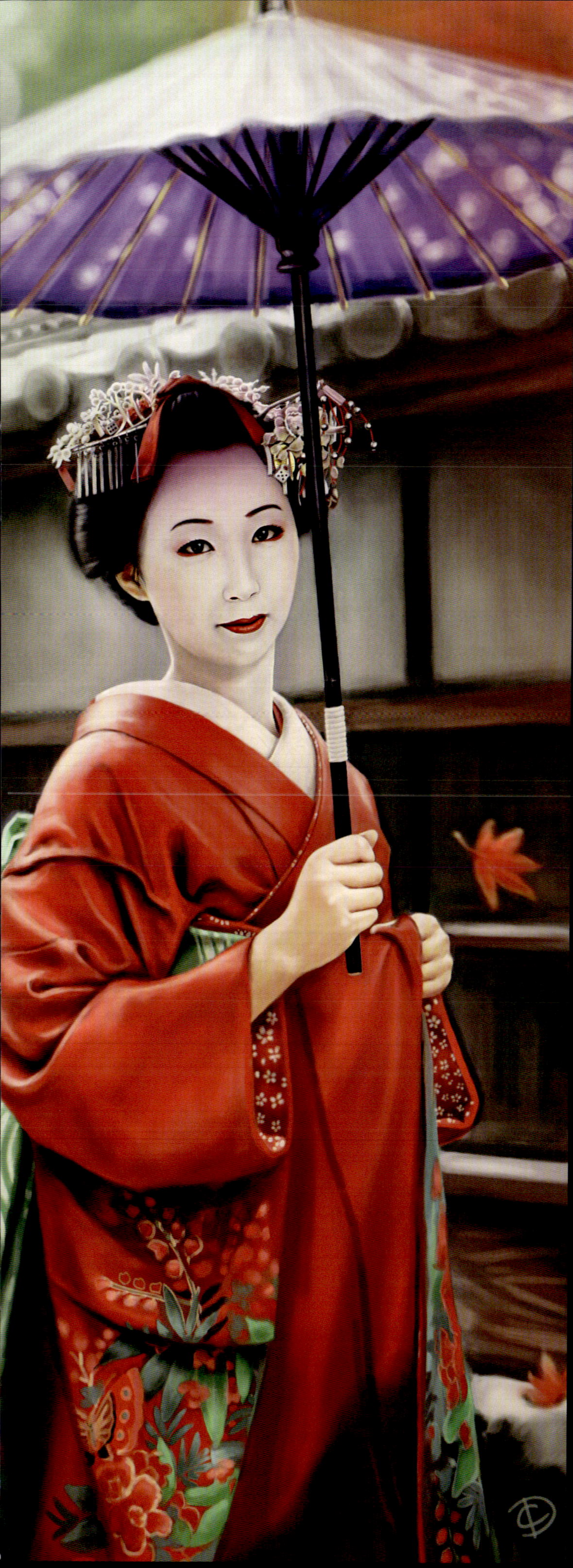

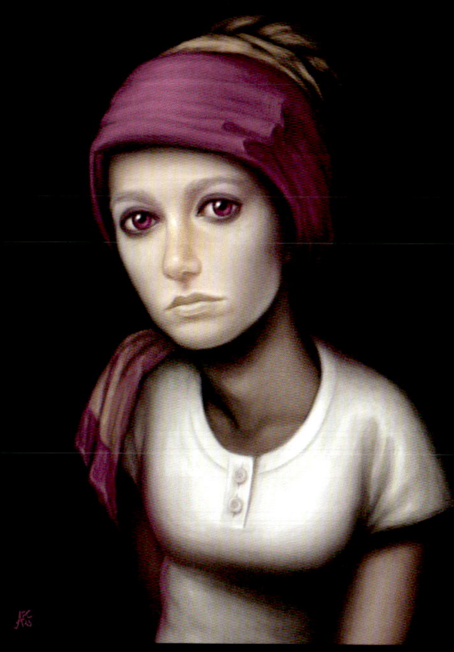

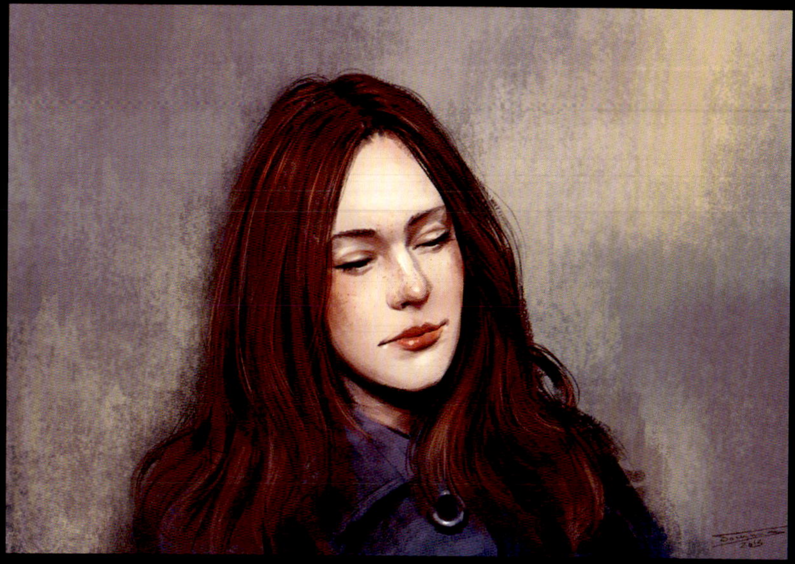

Maiko
Photoshop
Claudius Dreyer, GERMANY
[left]

White Disease
Photoshop
Alena Kubikova, CZECH REPUBLIC
[top]

Ioana
Photoshop
Alexandru Negoita, ROMANIA
[above]

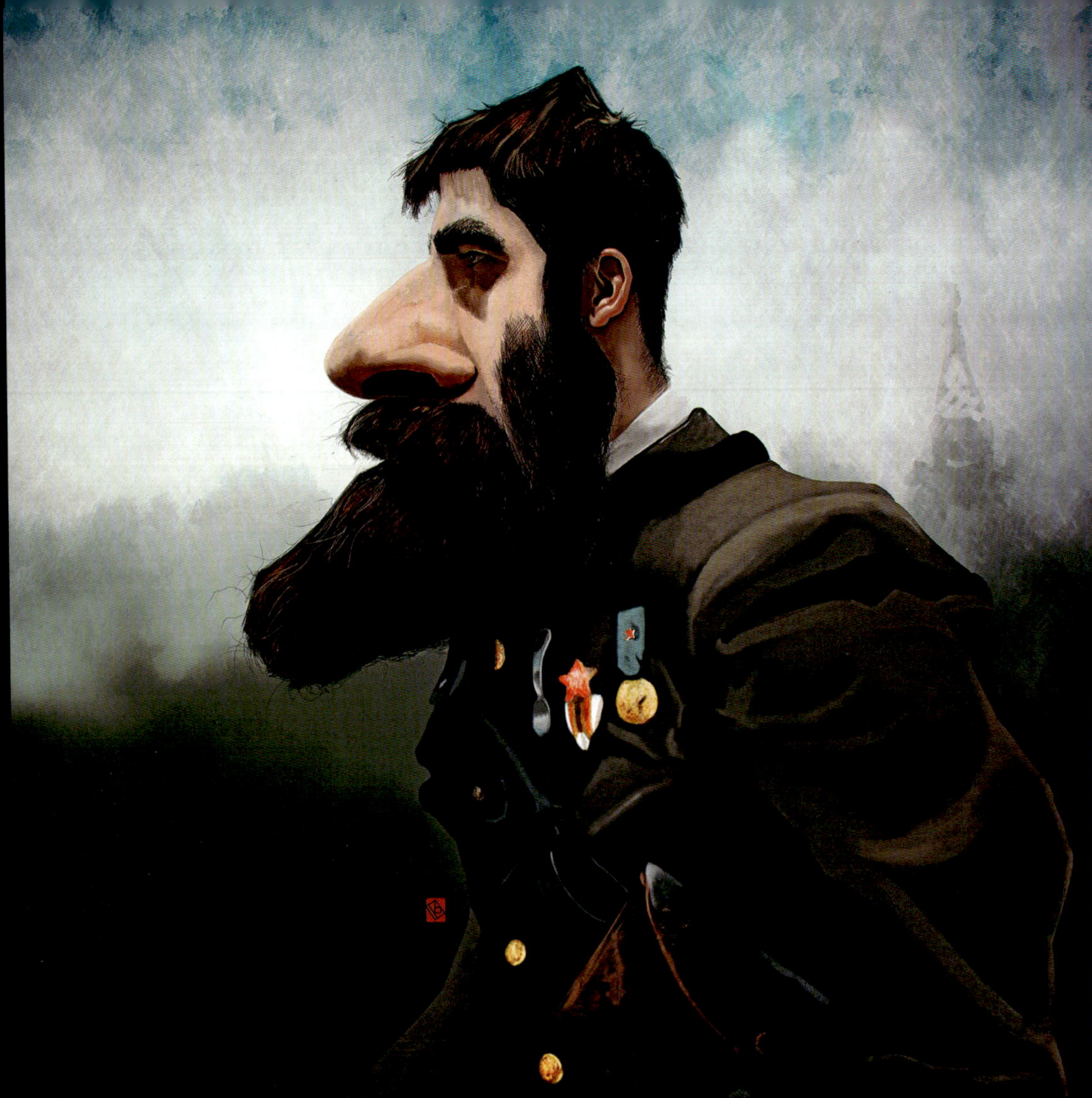

The Black Frog
Photoshop
Khasis Lieb, FRANCE
[left]

A Pilgrim
Photoshop
Mihir Joglekar, INDIA
[below left]

Natalia
Photoshop
Lane Brown, USA
[below]

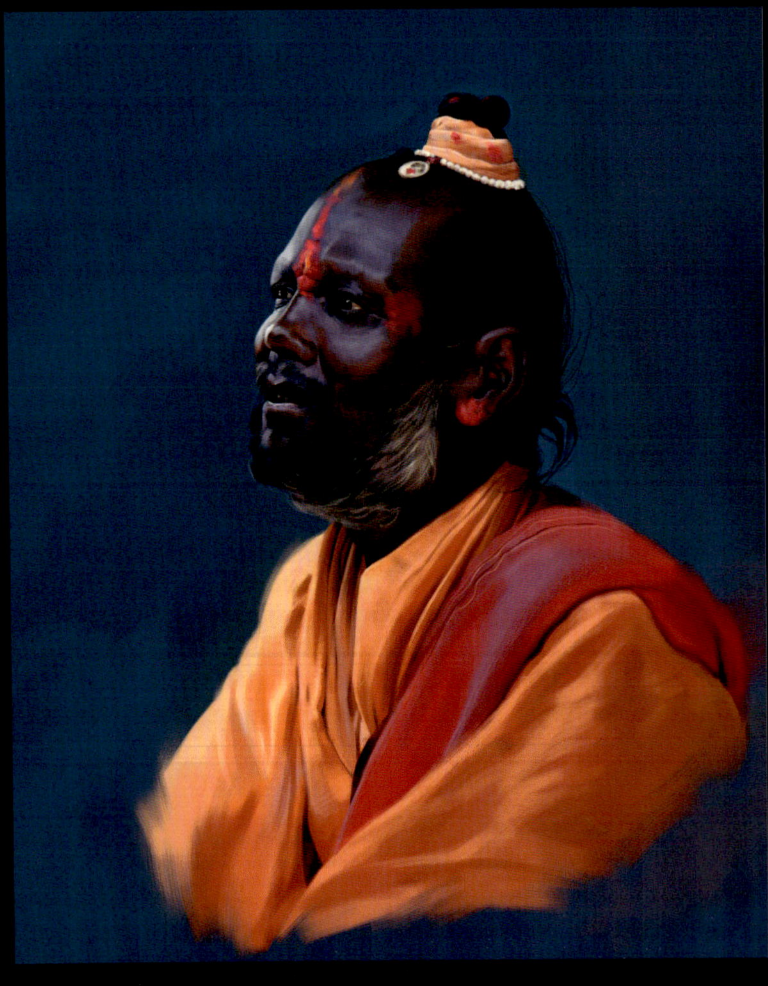

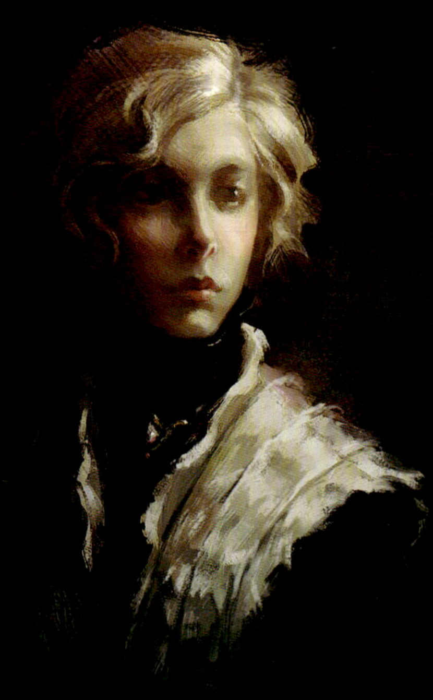

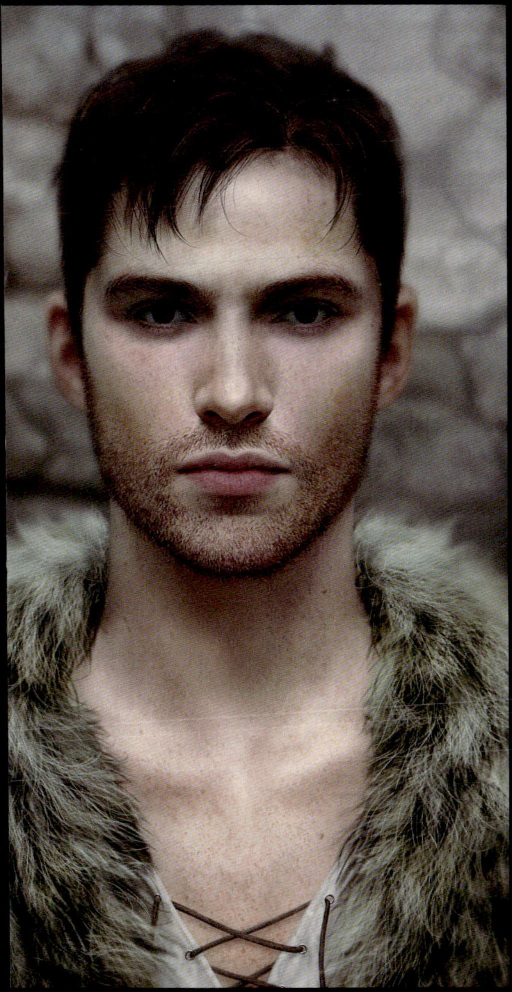

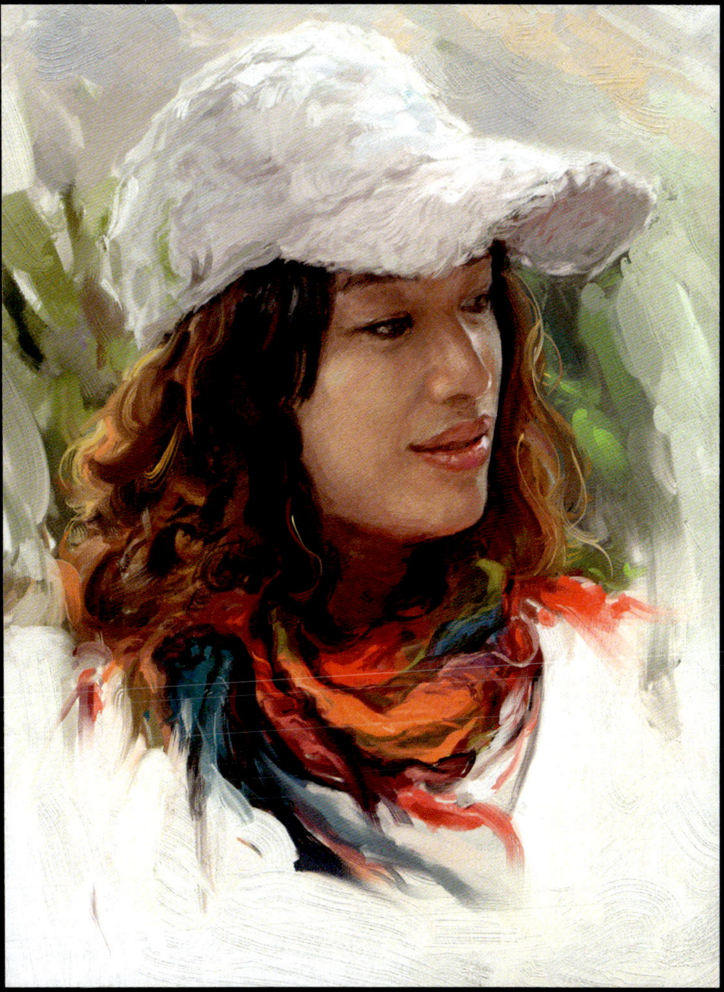

Without a Word
Photoshop
Sara Biddle, USA
[far left]

Ru Ru
ArtRage
Jinjie Bao, Tose Software,
CHINA
[left]

B&B
Photoshop
Gilberto 'Soren' Zaragoza
Metacube, MEXICO
[below]

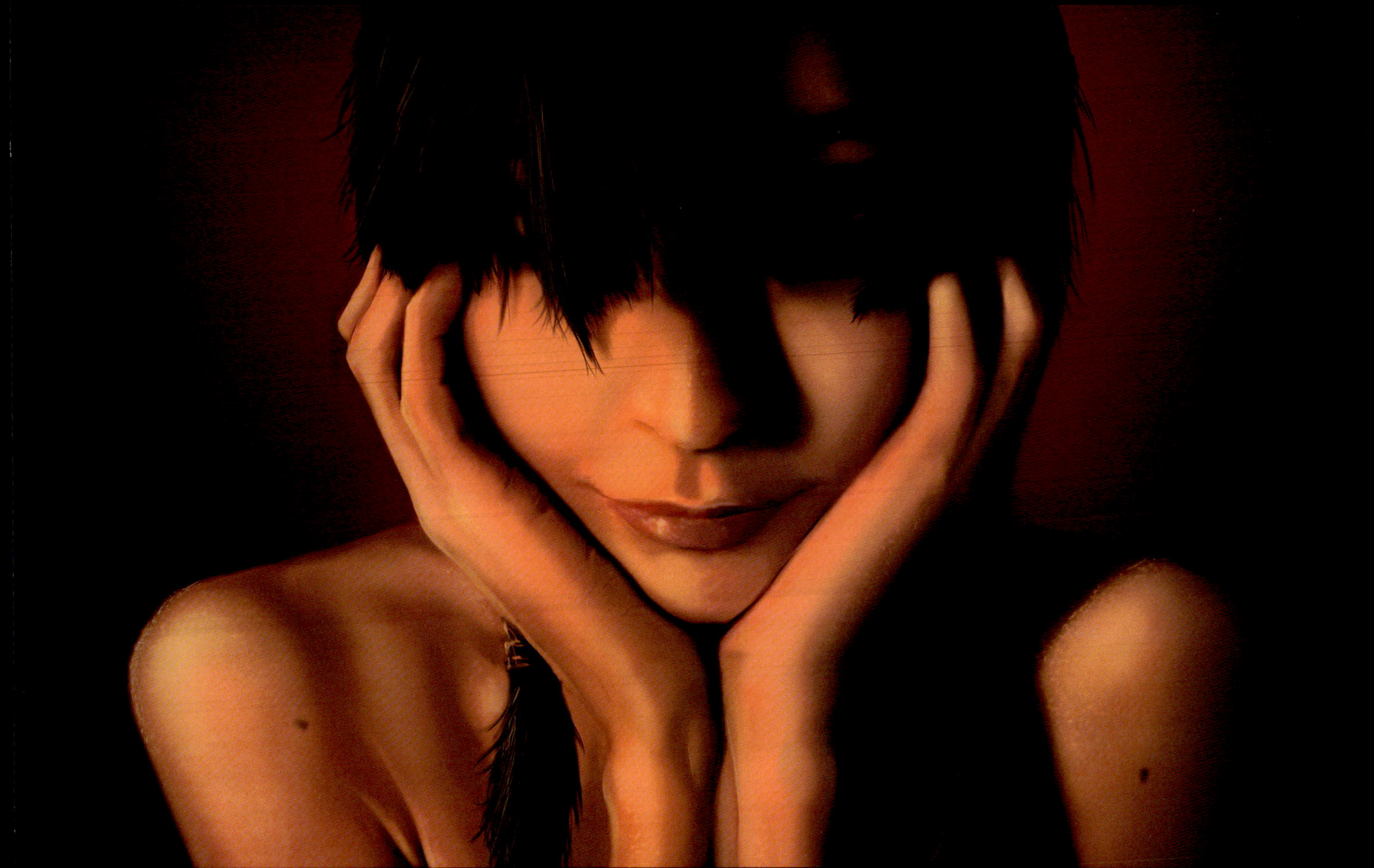

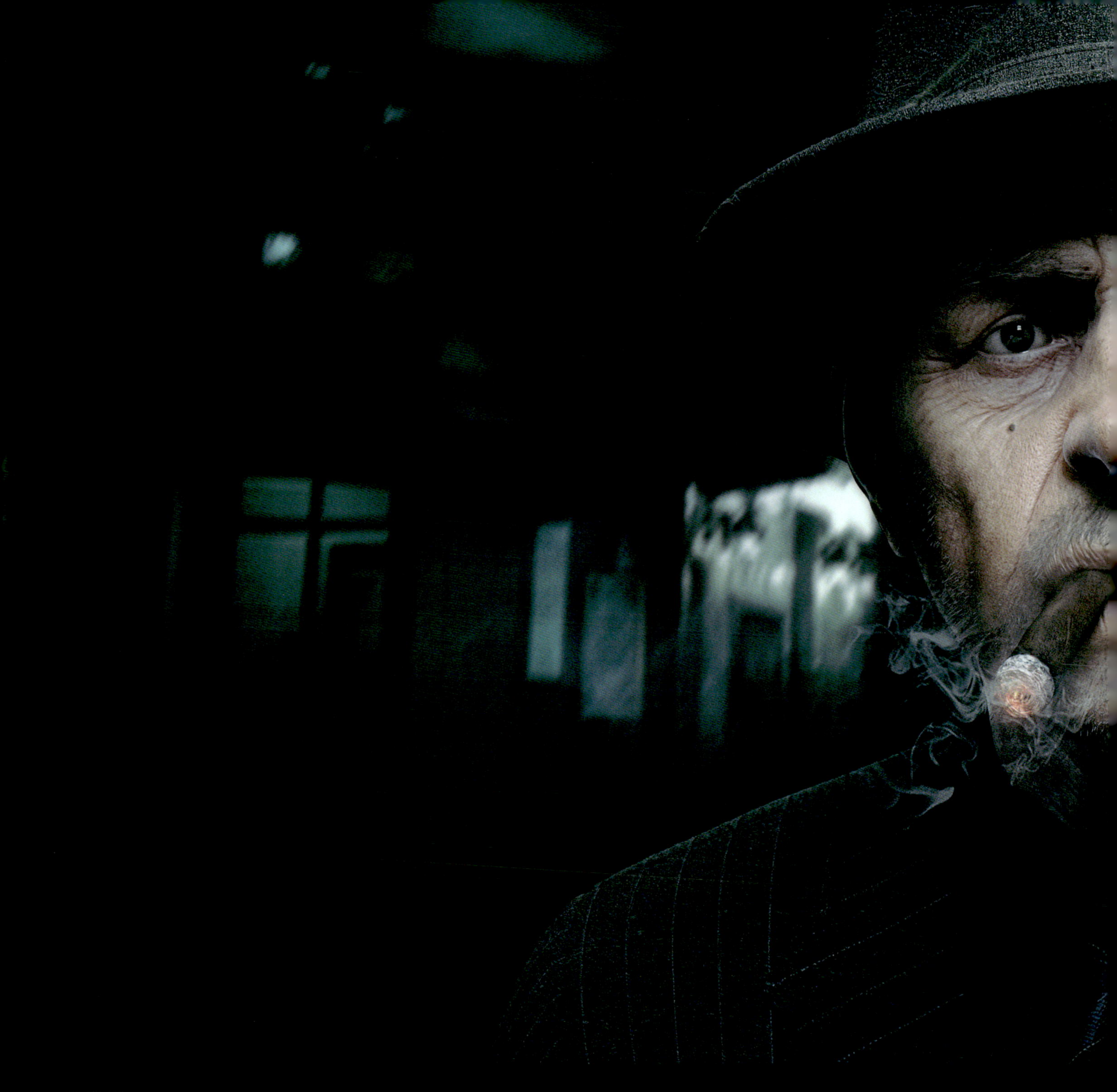

Mafia Man
ZBrush, Photoshop, Maya, mental ray
Siamak Roshani, UAE

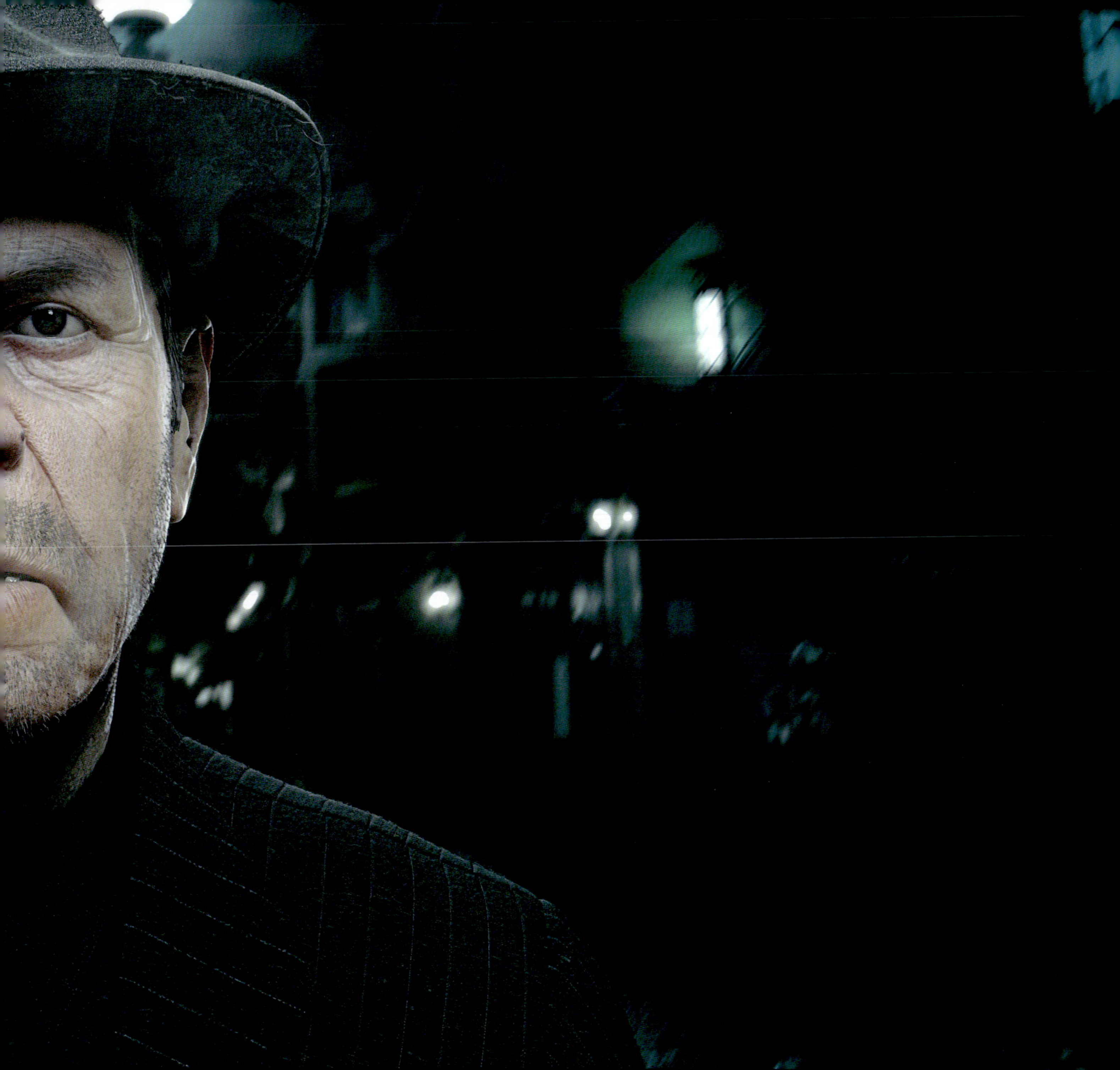

Master
Portrait (Rendered)

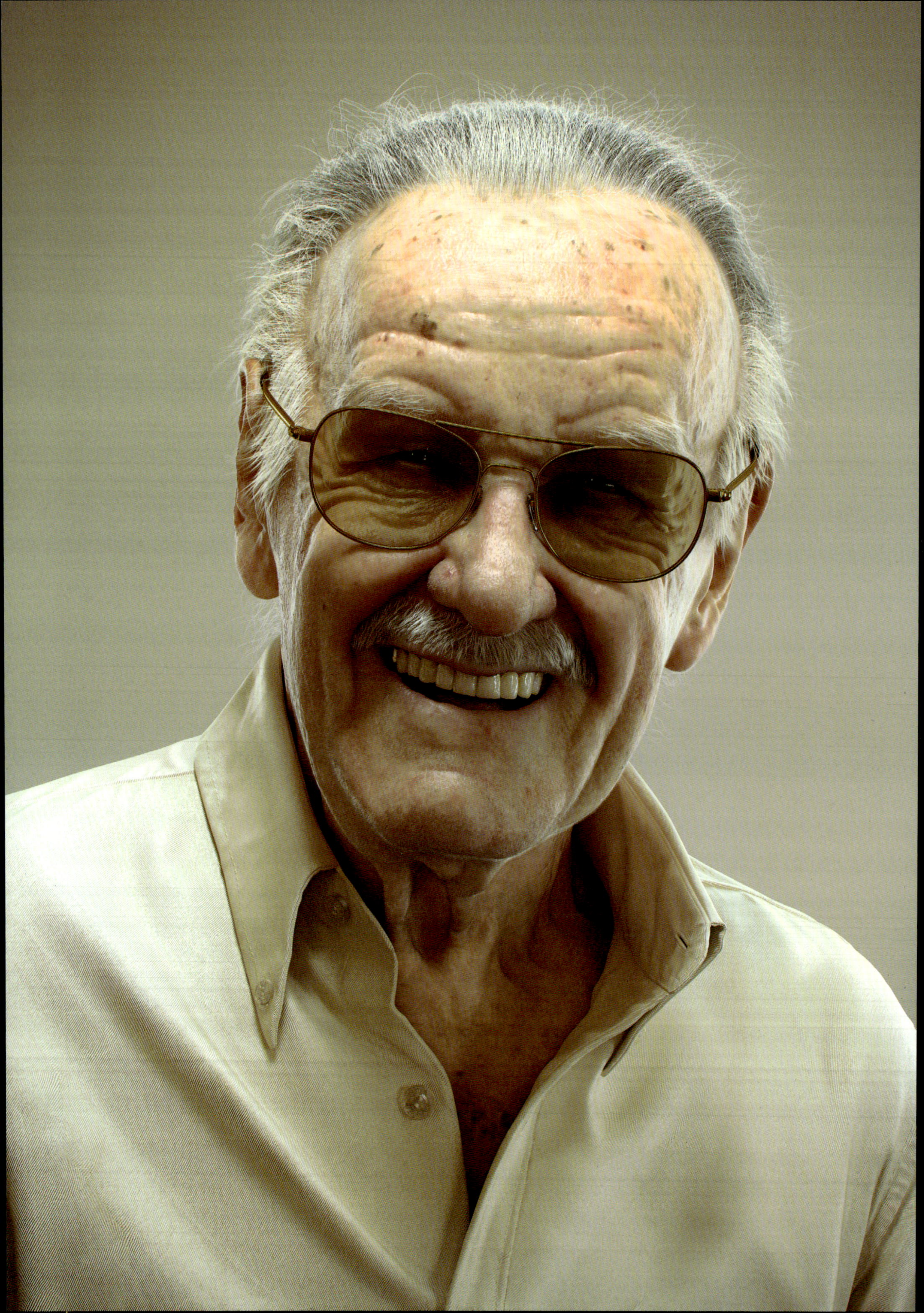

Excellence
Portrait (Rendered)

Stan 'The Man'
3ds Max, V-Ray, ZBrush, Photoshop
Andrew Lie, CHINA

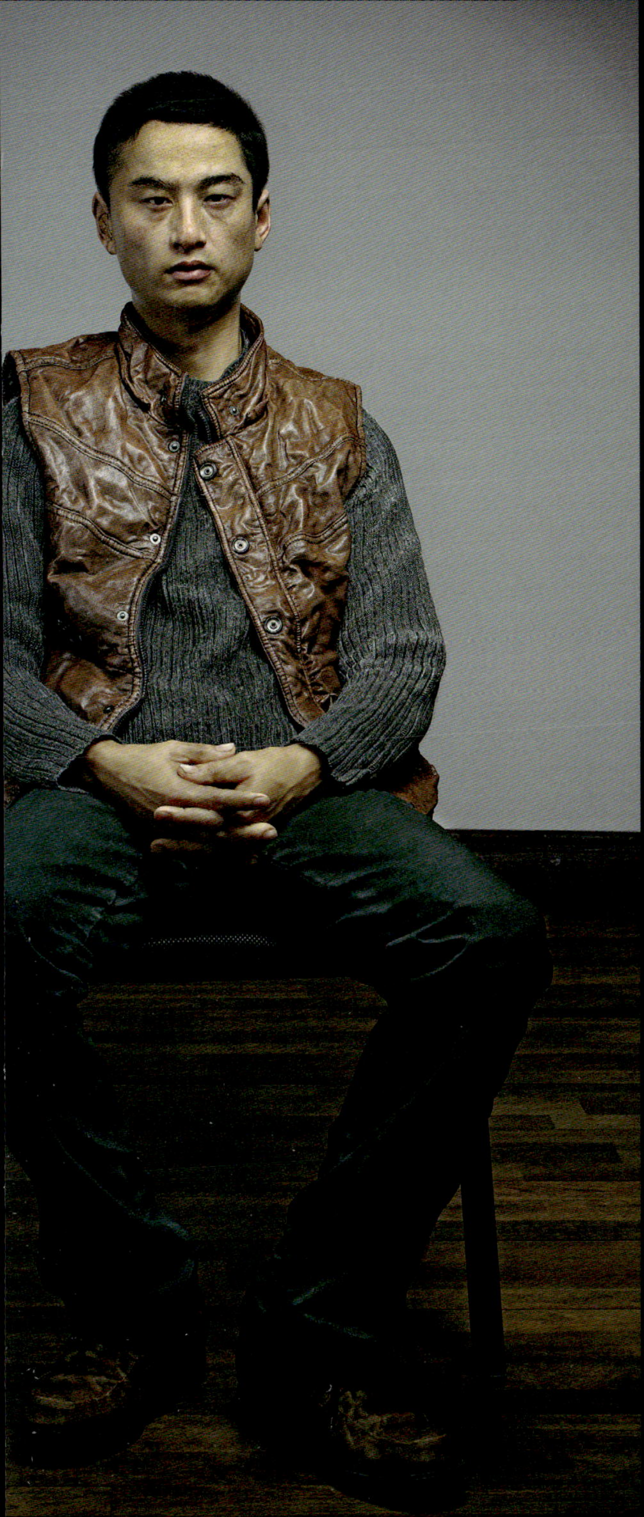

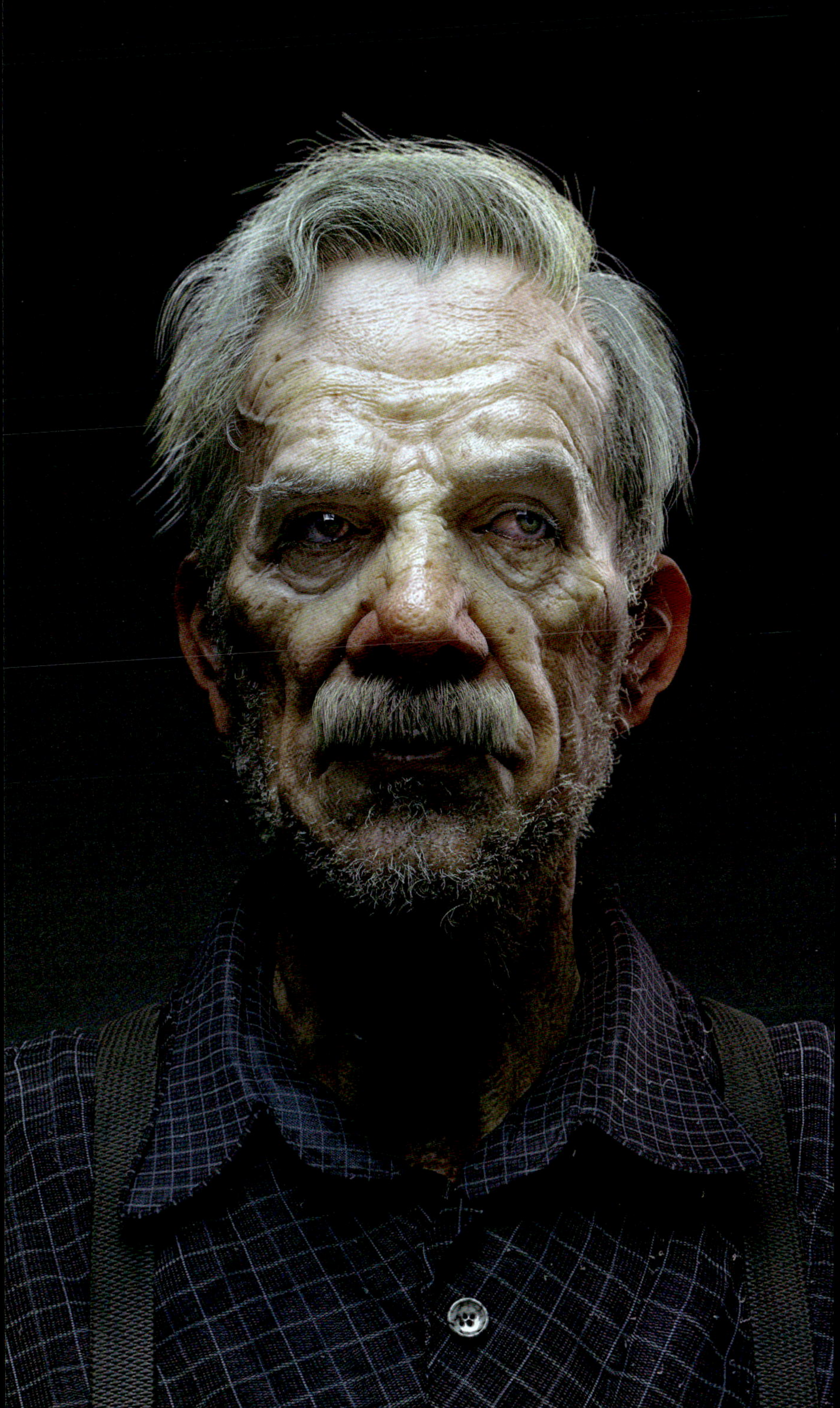

Excellence
Portrait (Rendered)

Excellence
Portrait (Rendered)

Meditation
3ds Max, ZBrush
Guang Yang, CHINA

An Elderly Curmudgeon
Maya, mental ray, ZBrush, Photoshop
Rokly Wang, AUSTRIA

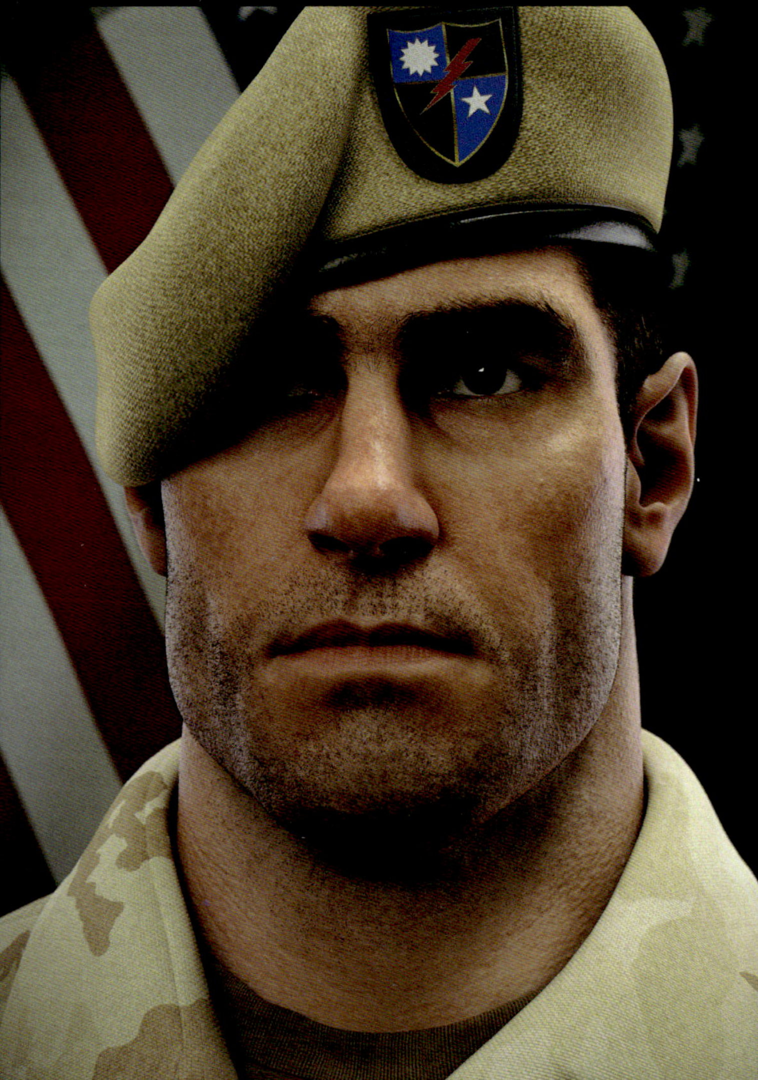

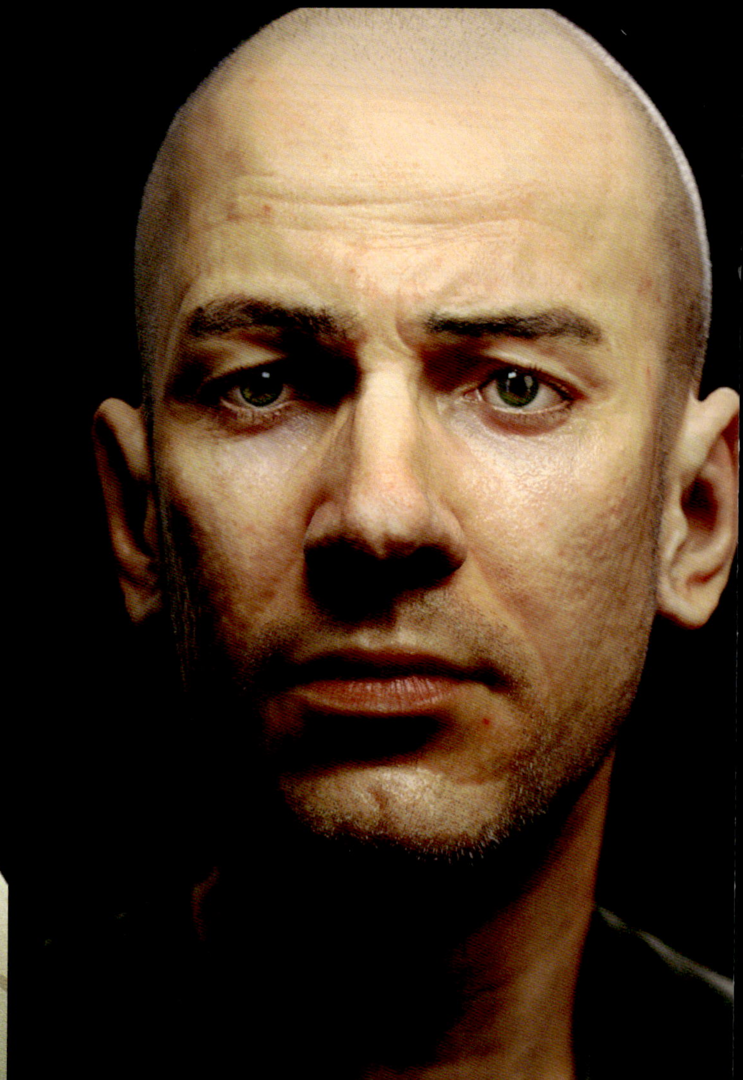

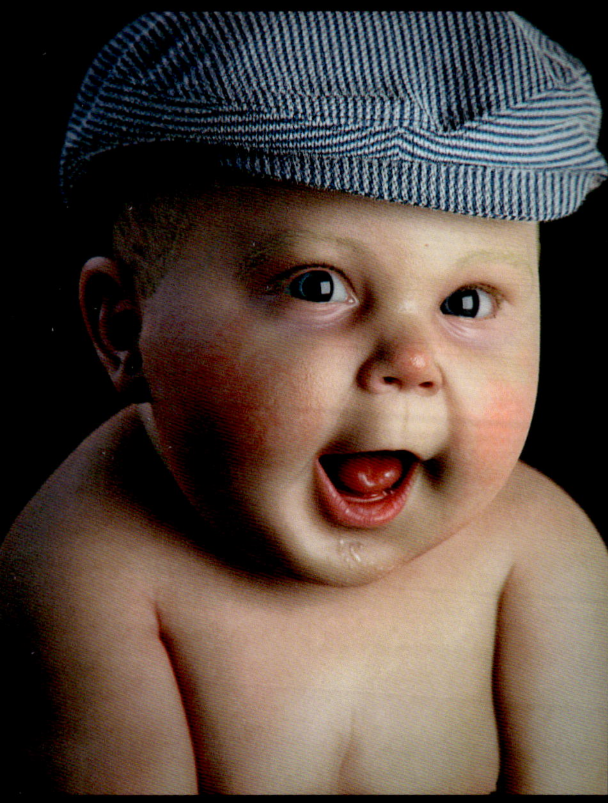

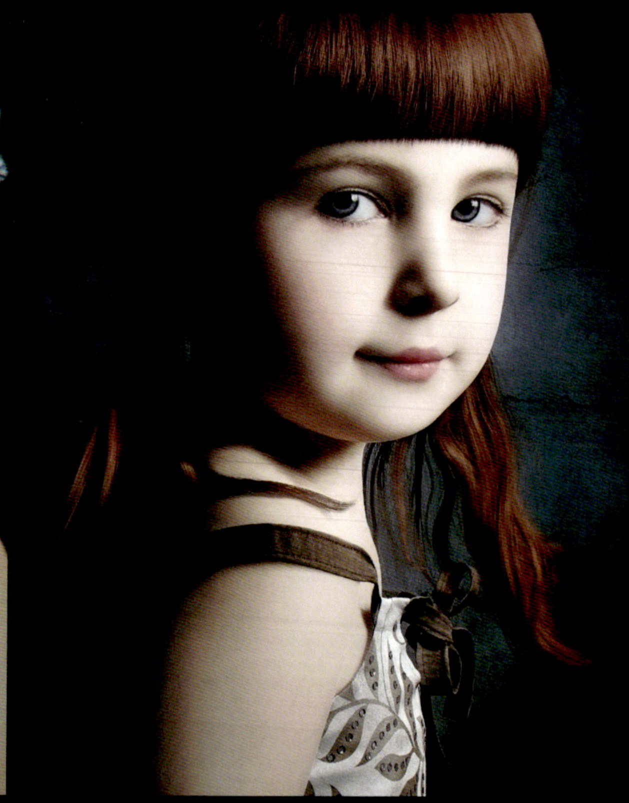

Ranger Portrait
Maya, ZBrush, Photoshop, Arnold
Render by Jeremy Celeste
Saimak Roshani, UAE

Fafal
Maya
Mohsen Fallah, TURKEY
[above]

Casual Man Portait
3ds Max, ZBrush, V-Ray
Mathieu Aerni, USA
[top]

Bonny
Maya, ZBrush, mental ray
Peyman Mokaram, IRAN
[above]

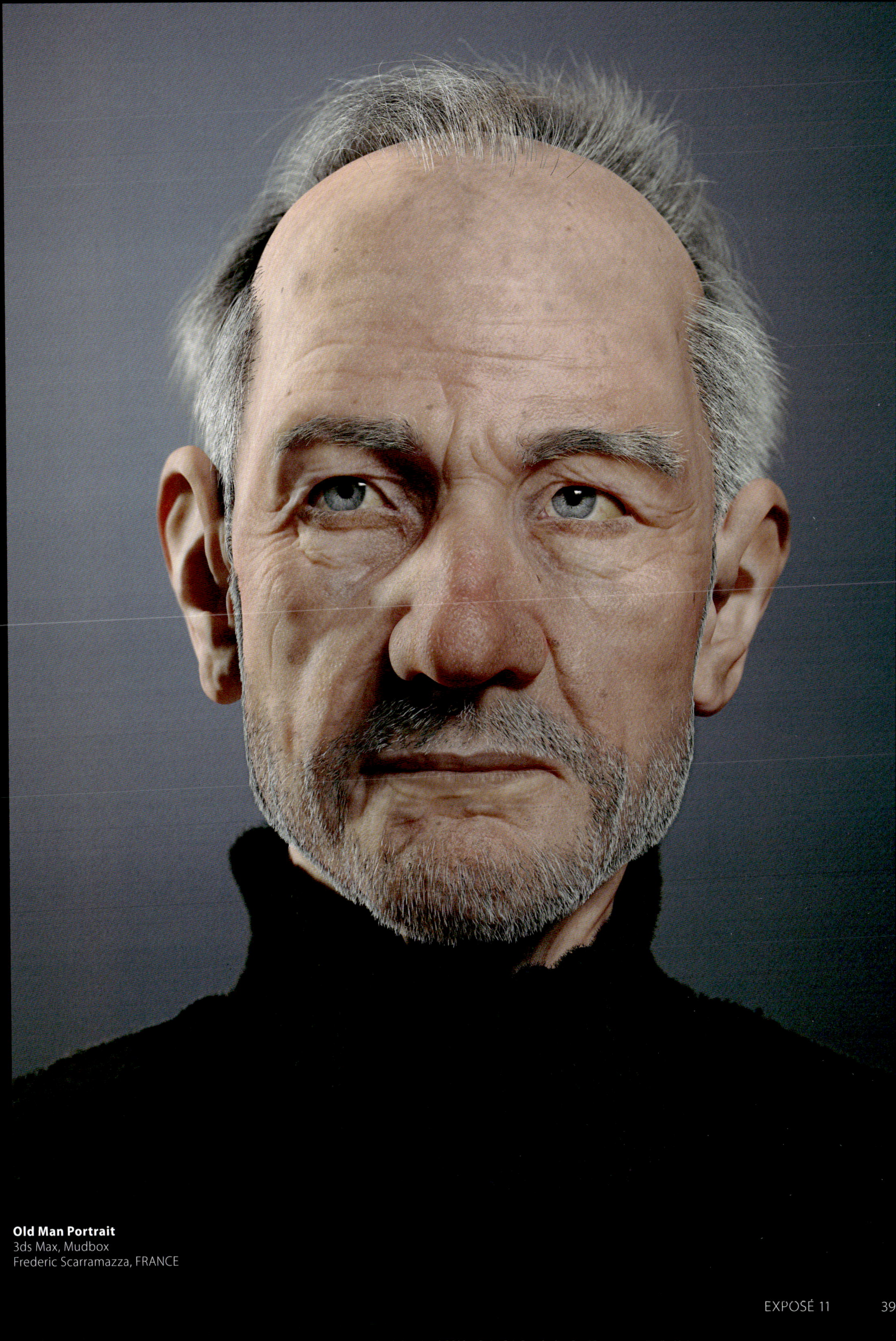

Old Man Portrait
3ds Max, Mudbox
Frederic Scarramazza, FRANCE

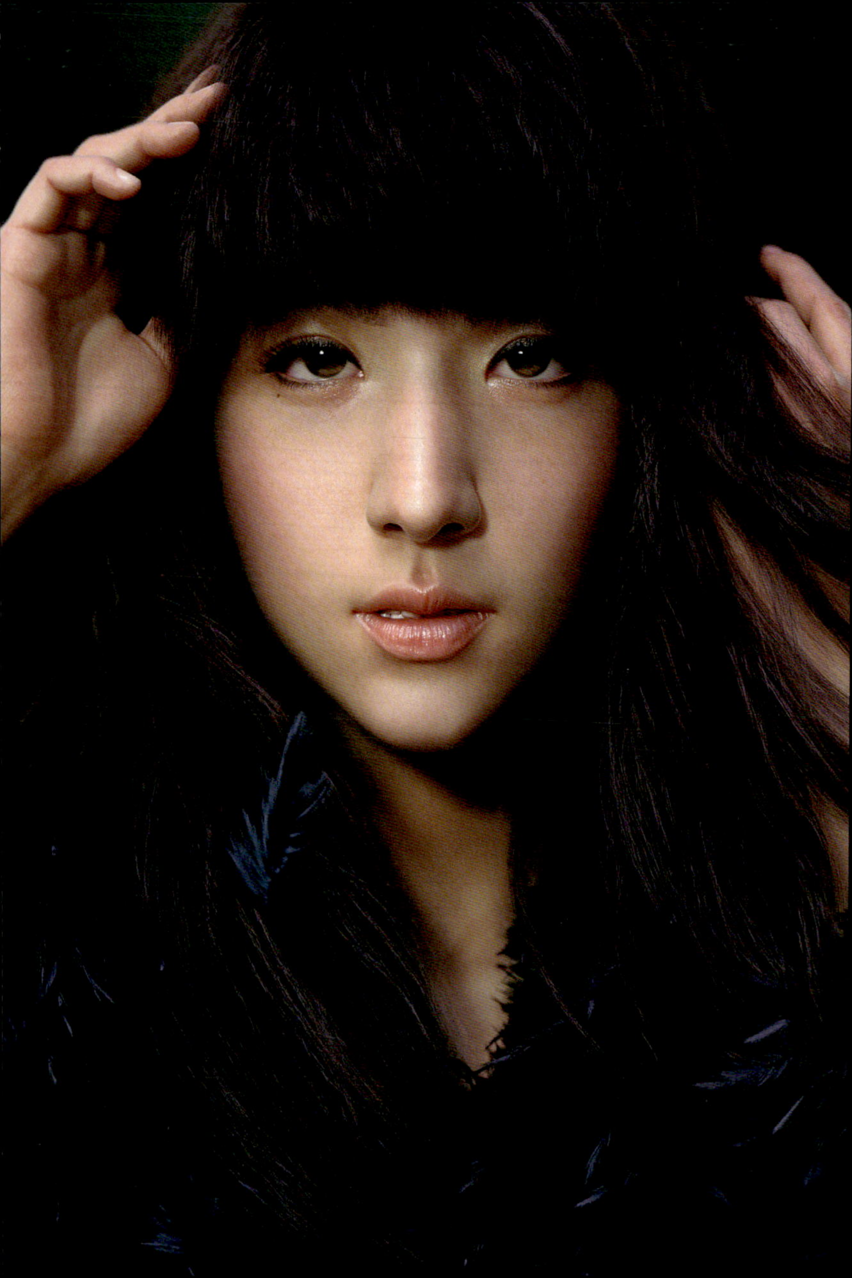

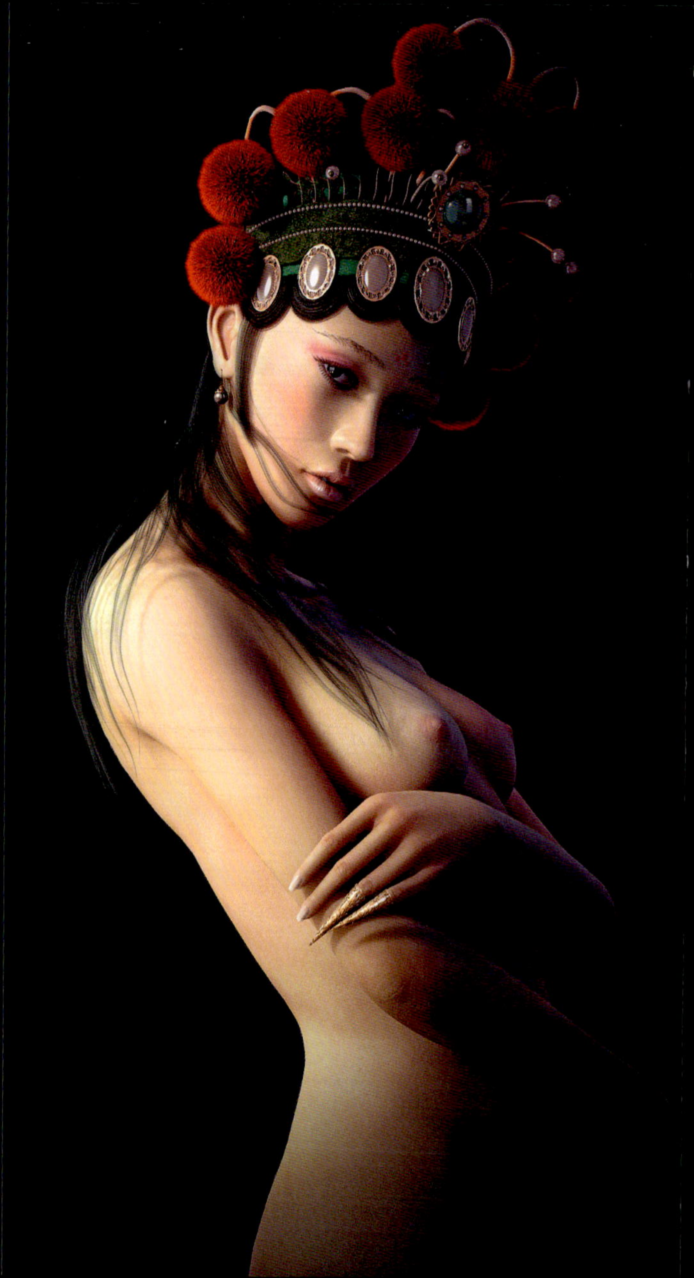

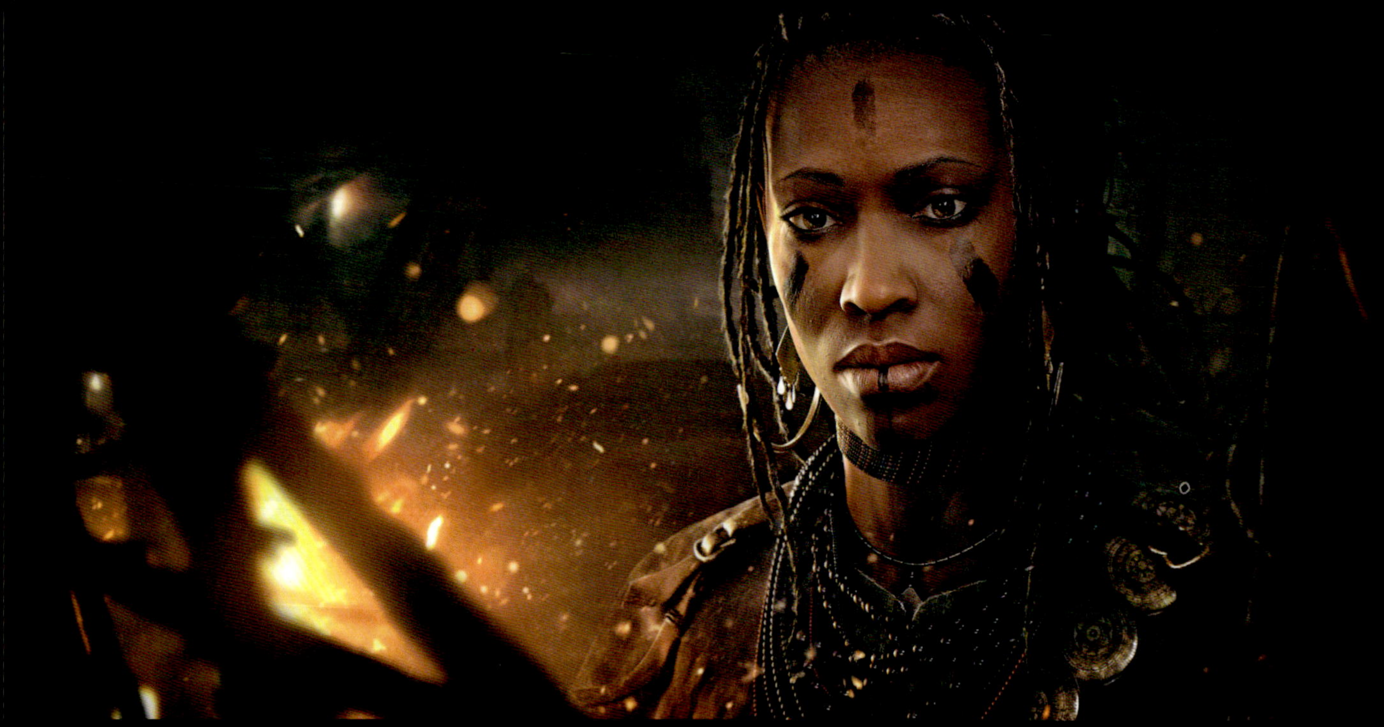

Renaissance
3ds Max, ZBrush, Photoshop, V-Ray
Anthony Guebels, CANADA
[above]

Then Flying the Youth
Maya, ZBrush, V-Ray, Photoshop
Leng ShangPeng, CHINA
[top left]

Opera Girl
Maya, mental ray, ZBrush, Photoshop
Zhangchendaxiao Zhang, CHINA
[top right]

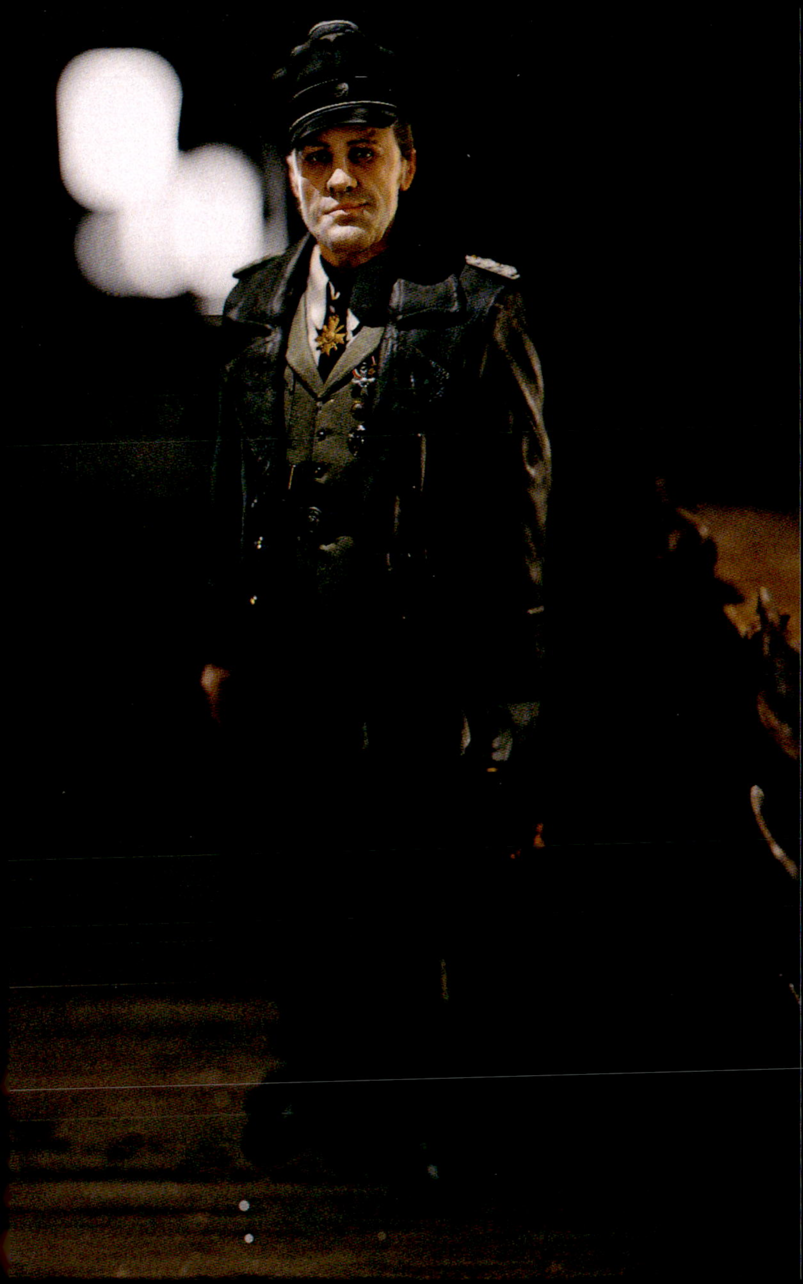

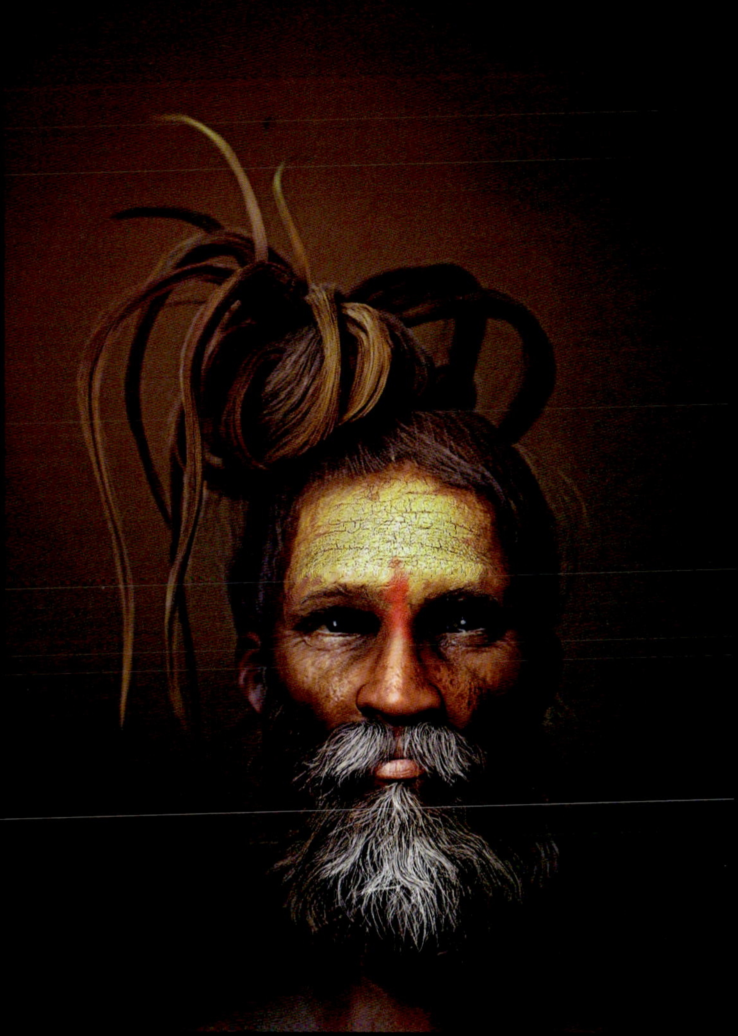

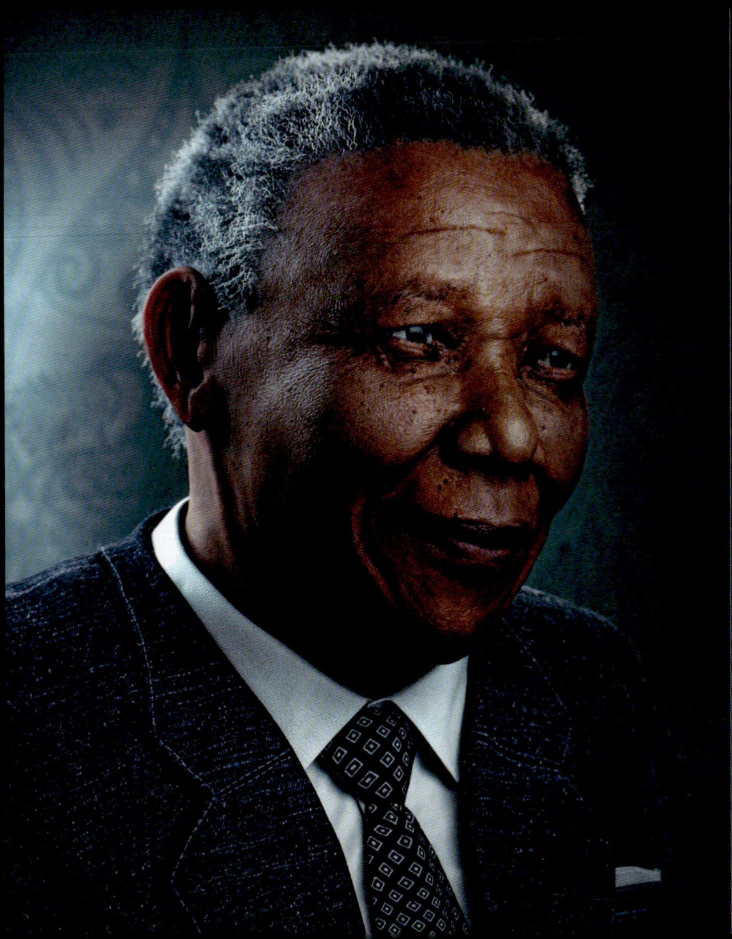

Col. Landa
Maya, ZBrush, mental ray
Lorenzo Serran, FRANCE
[above left]

Faces of the World
ZBrush, Photoshop
Pablo Munoz, AUSTRALIA
[above]

Nelson Mandela
ZBrush, Maya, mental ray, Photoshop
Mauro Baldissera, ITALY
[left]

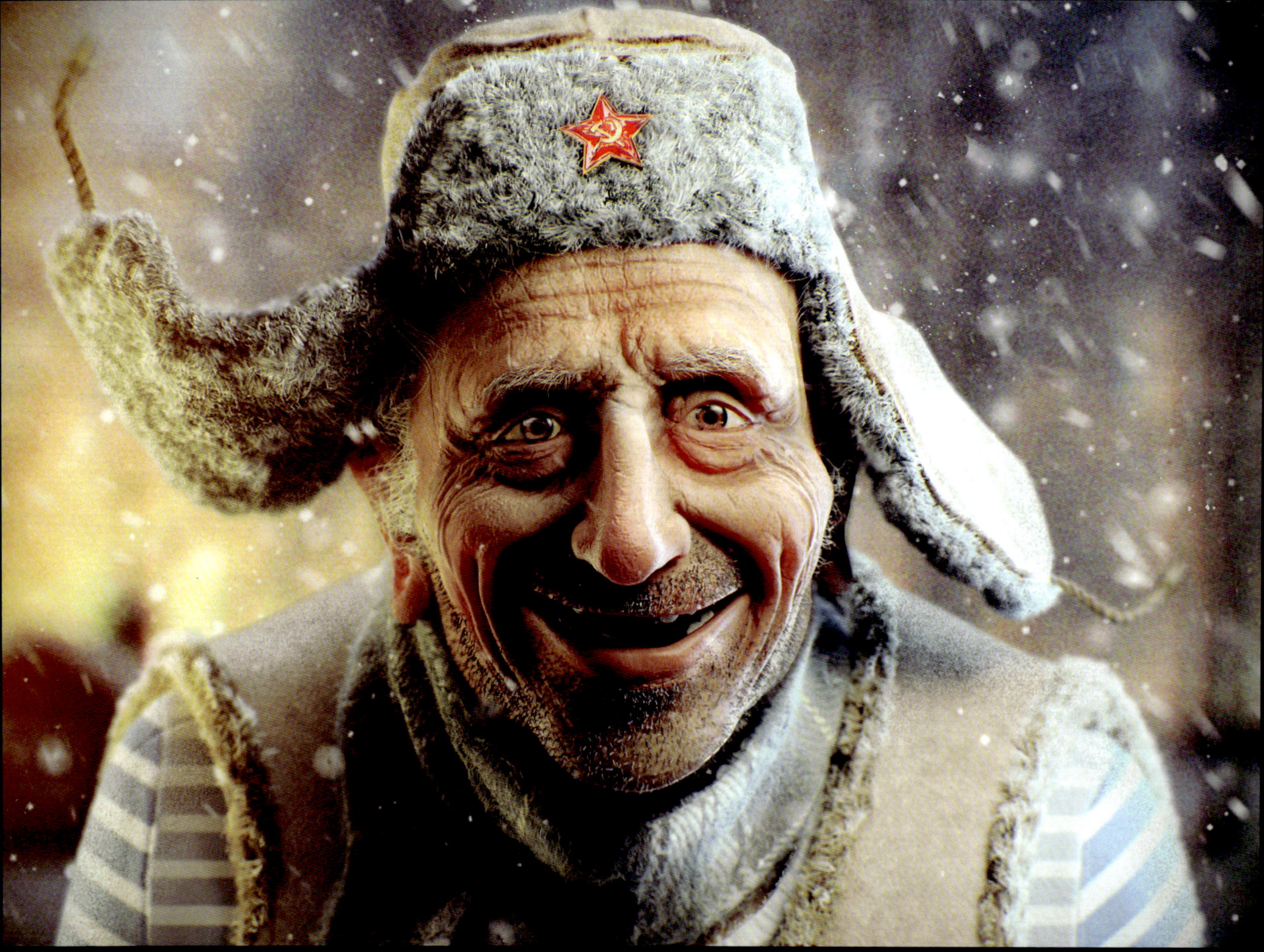

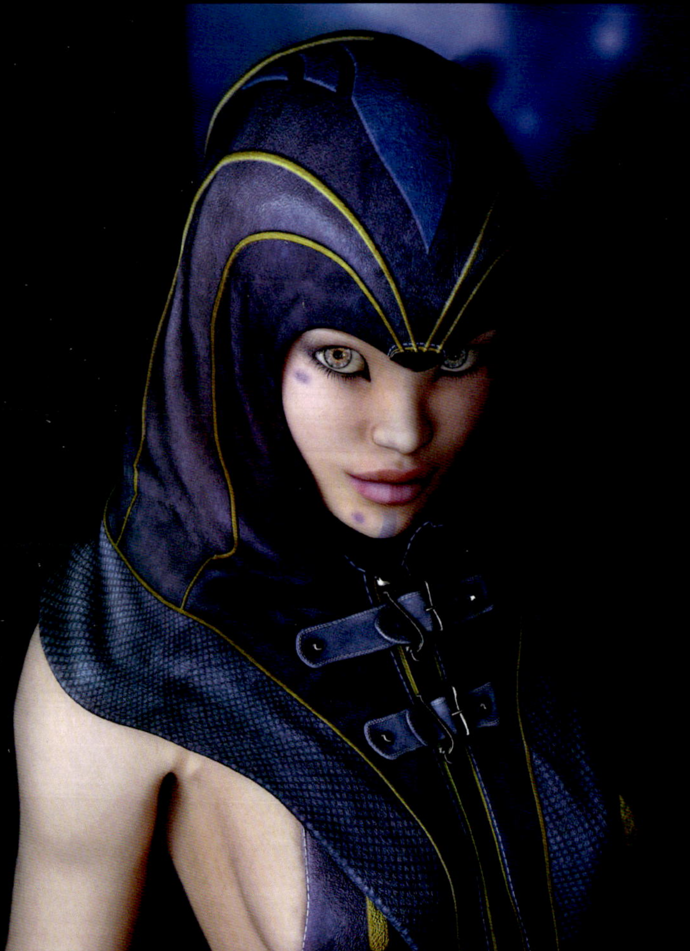

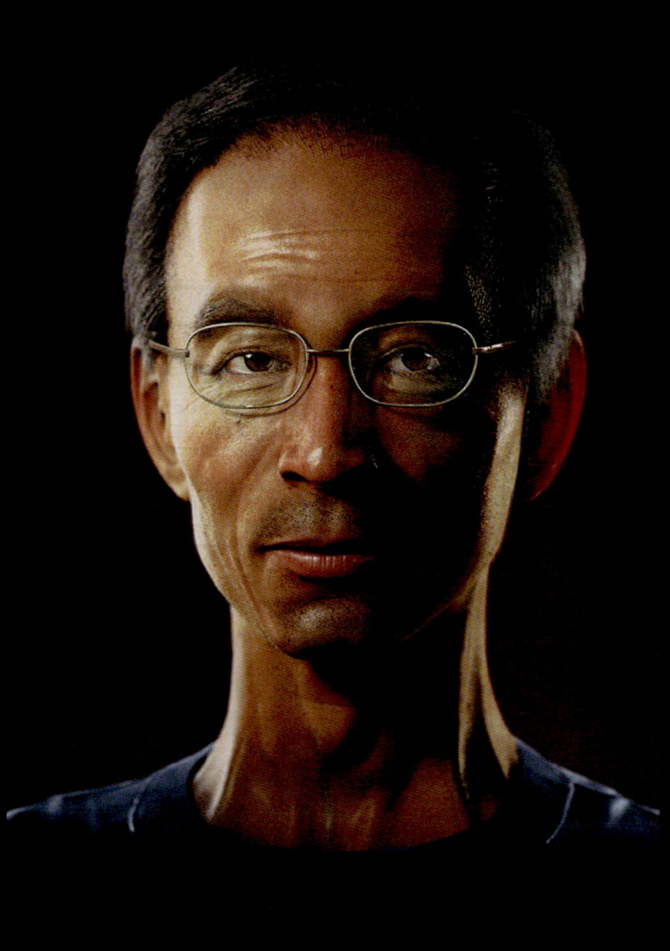

Last Year's Snow Falling...
3ds Max, V-Ray, Photoshop, ZBrush
Sergii Andreichenko, UKRAINE
[top]

Hooded
Maya, Photoshop, ZBrush
AlfASeeD, CANADA
[above]

Portrait
Softimage, Mudbox, Photoshop, mental ray
Yoshinobu Saito, Snowin, JAPAN
[above]

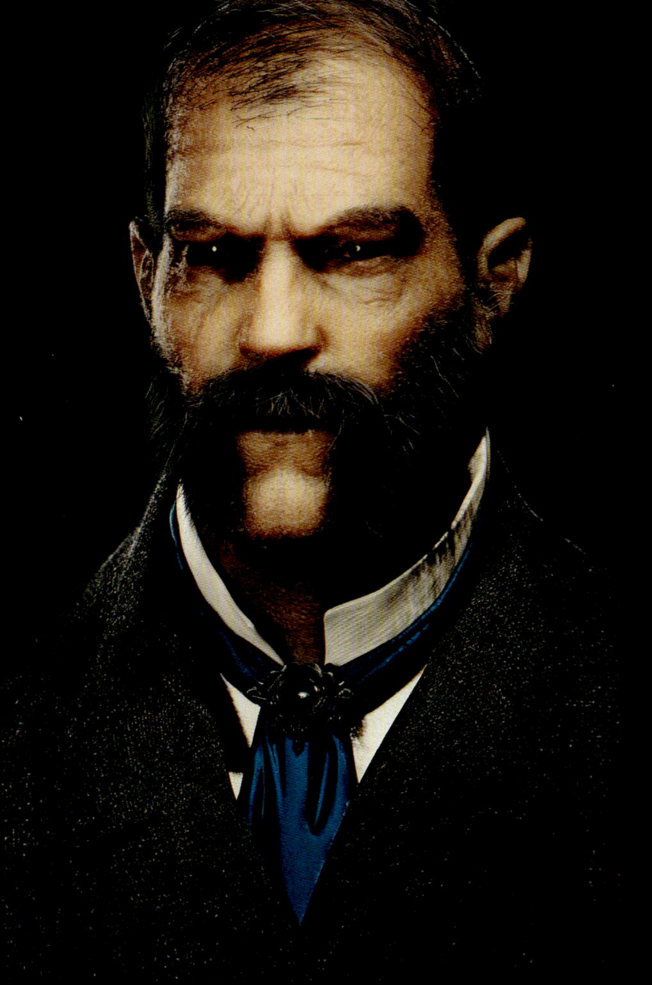

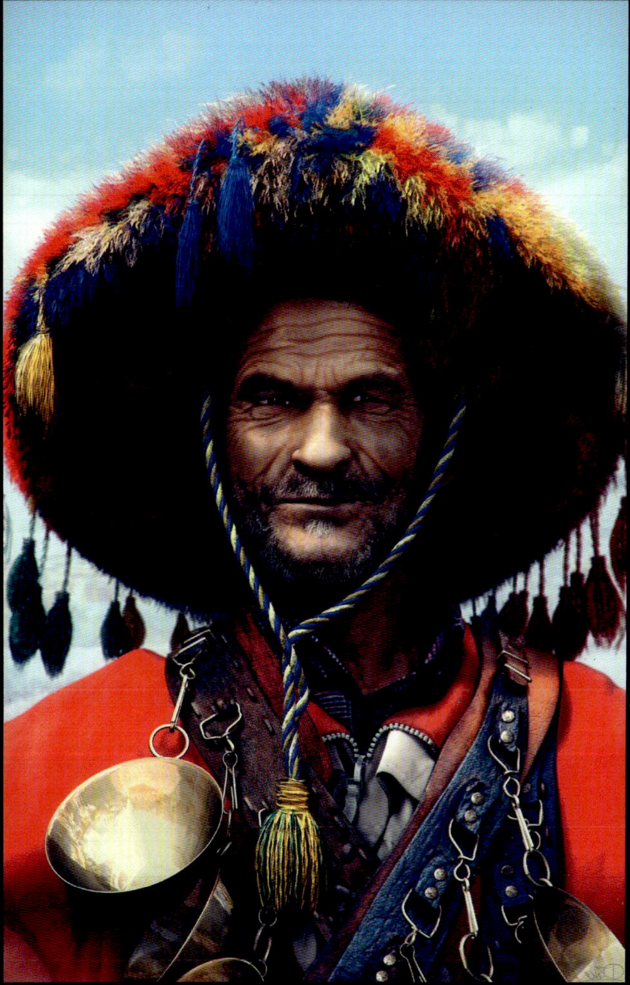

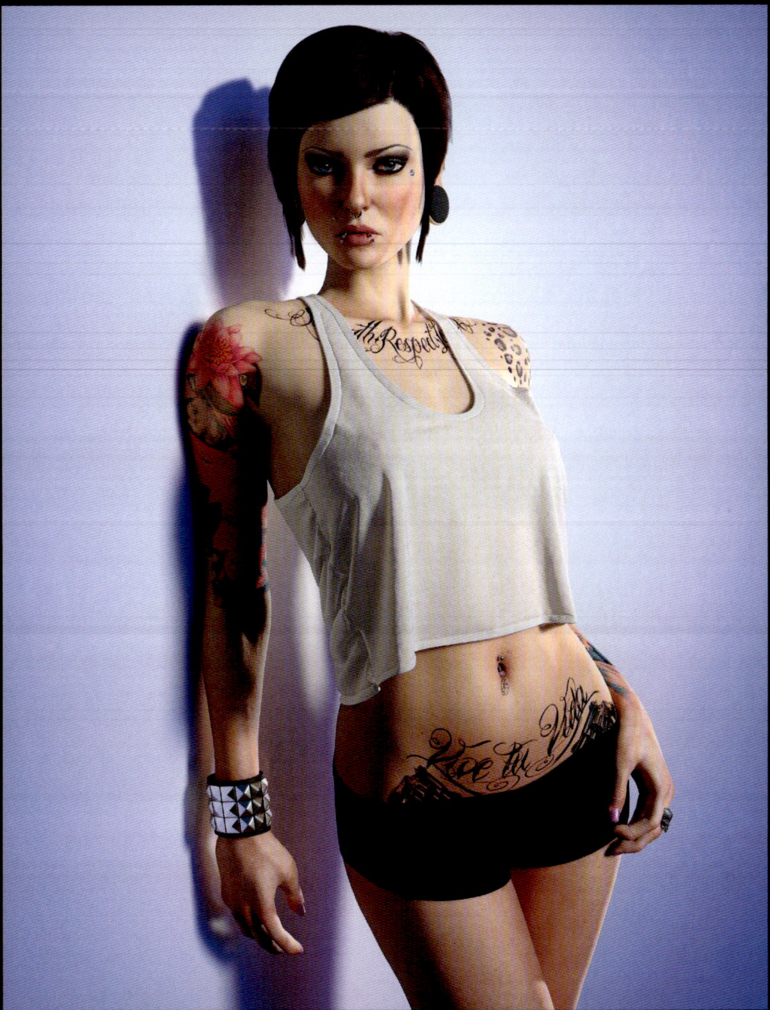

XVIII Century Portrait
Blender, GIMP
Andrzej Augustyniak, POLAND
[above left]

Carlos
LightWave 3D, Photoshop
Farkas Zsolt, HUNGARY
[above]

A Wolf in Sheep's Clothing
Maya, ZBrush, Mudbox, Photoshop
Kris Kelly, USA
[left]

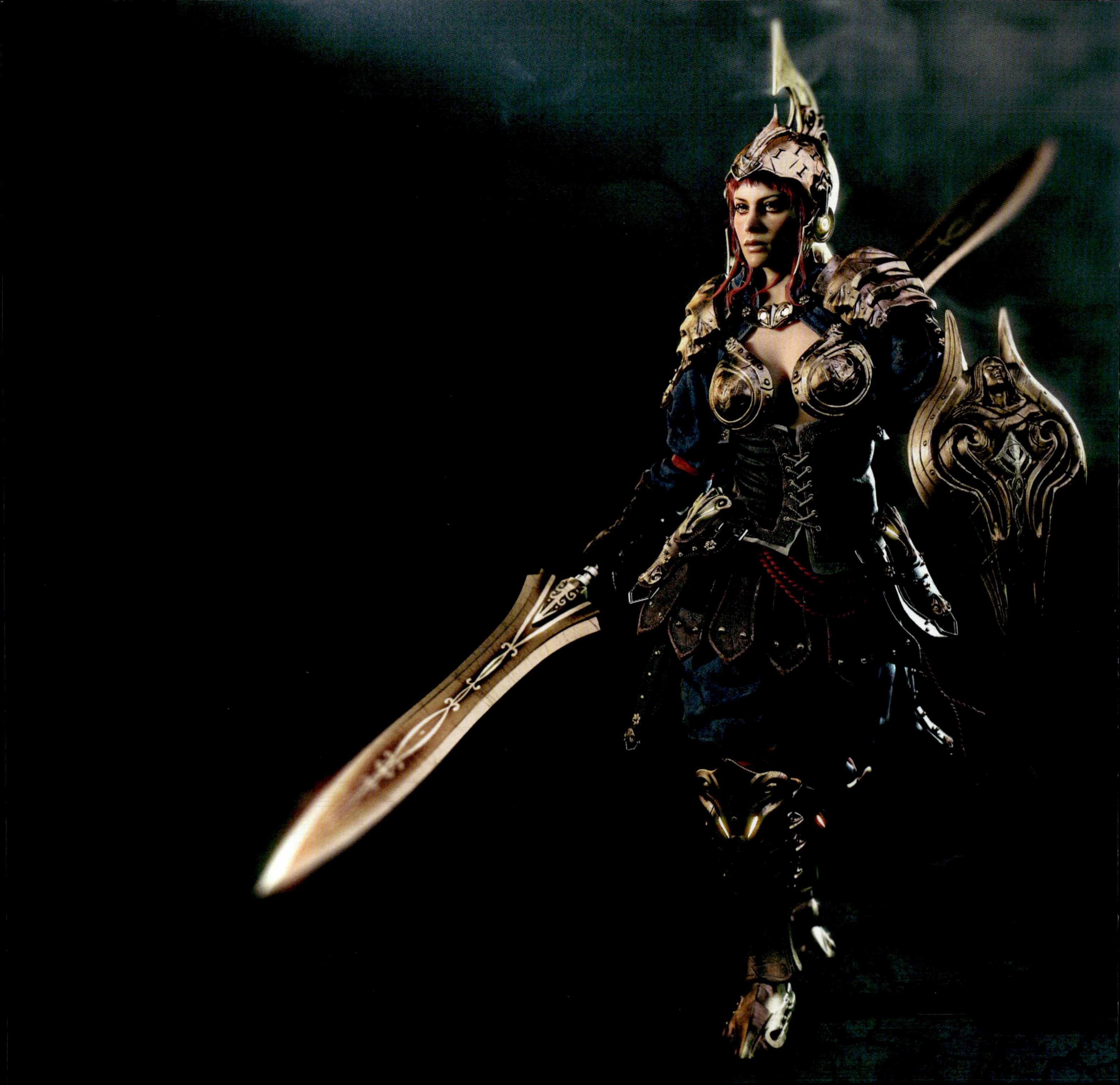

The Knight Girl
3ds Max, ZBrush
Inspired by Hahno Lee
Seid Tursic, BOSNIA AND HERZEGOVINA
[above]

Witch Doctor
Maya, MARI, V-Ray, Photoshop
Model: Jakob Kousholt
Lee Baskerville, GREAT BRITAIN
[far right]

Luciano
3ds Max, V-Ray, ZBrush
Inspired by Hans Holbein
Hasan Bajramovic, BOSNIA AND HERZEGOVINA
[right]

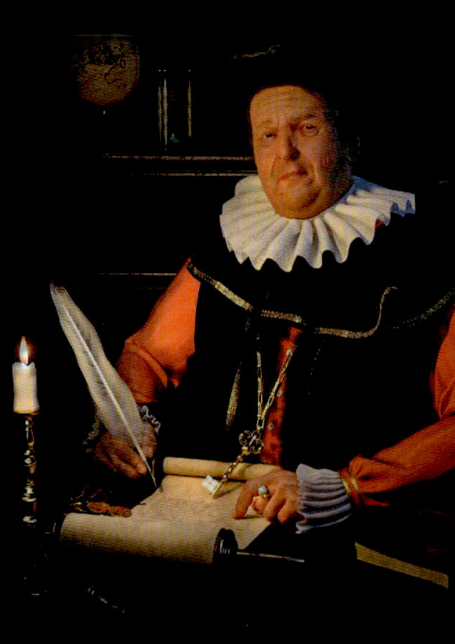

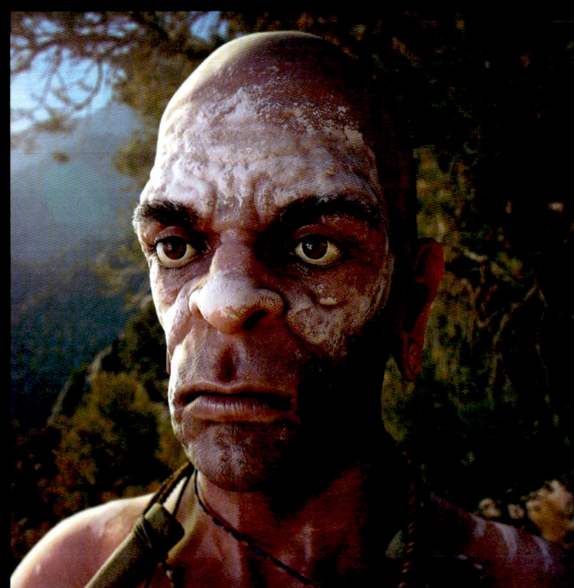

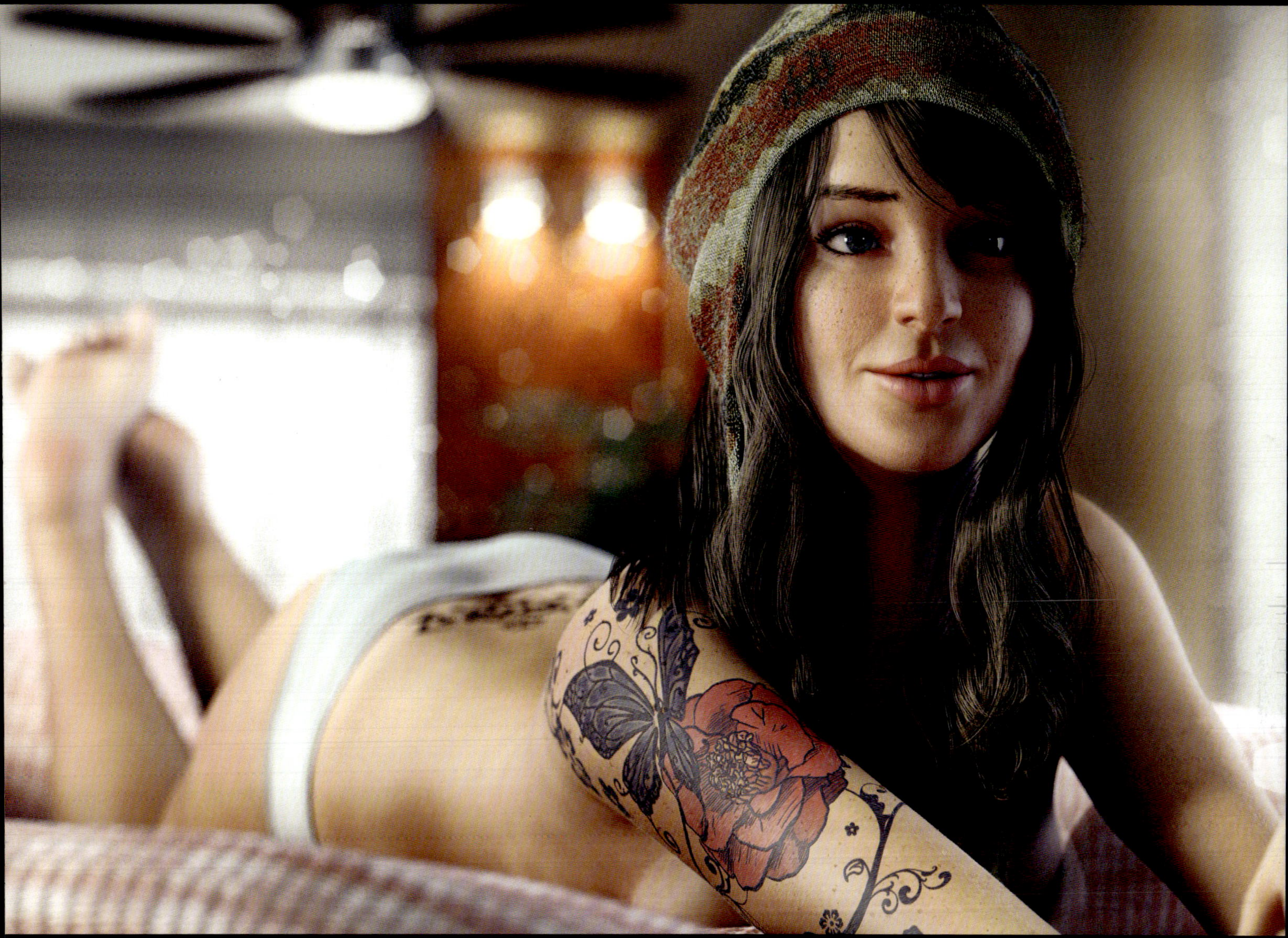

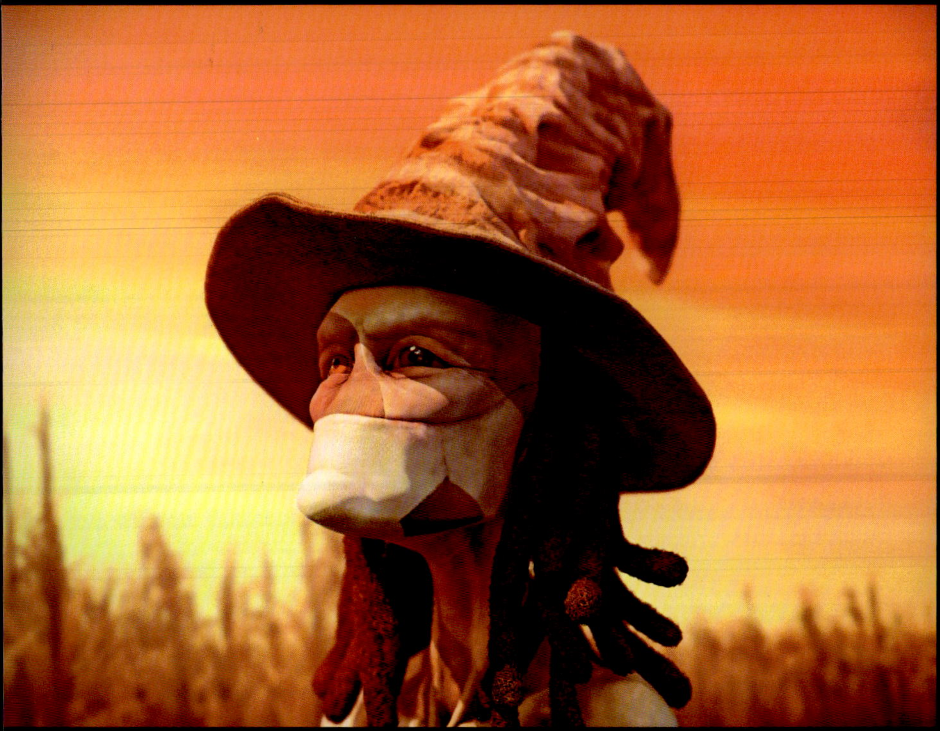

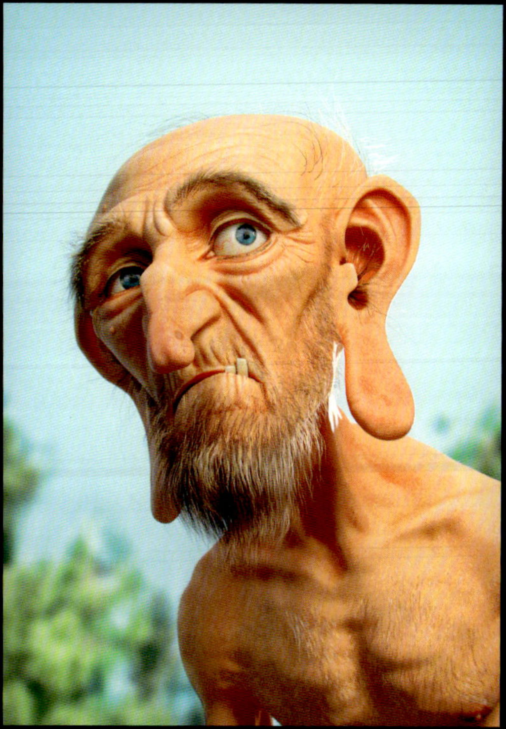

Morning Light
Maya, ZBrush
Gustavo Rios, BRAZIL
[top]

Richard
ZBrush, Photoshop
Pablo Munoz, AUSTRALIA
[above]

Hairy Old Guy
3ds Max, ZBrush, V-Ray
Jose Alves da Silva, PORTUGAL
[above]

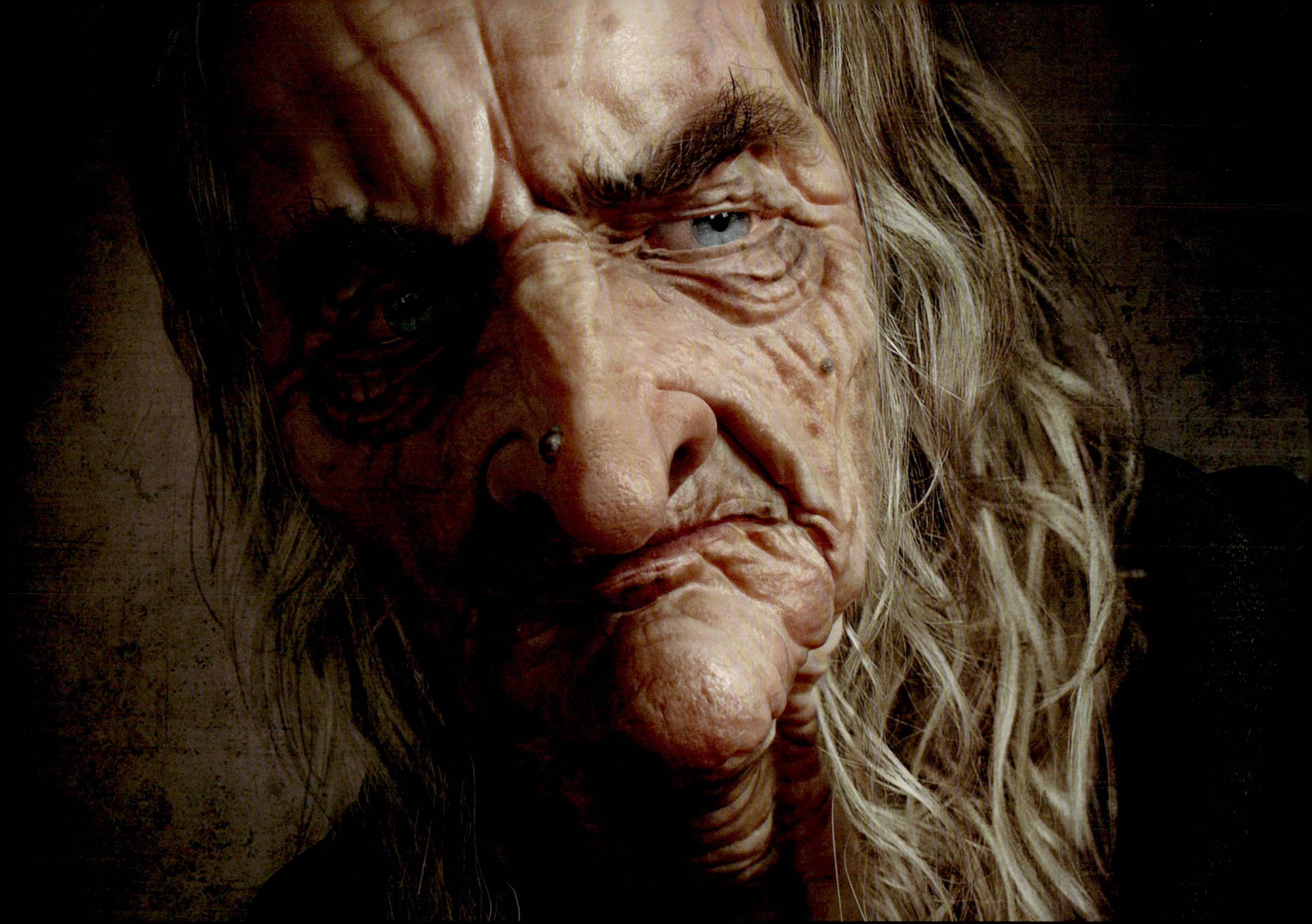

'Recycle' © Studio Munka/SFP

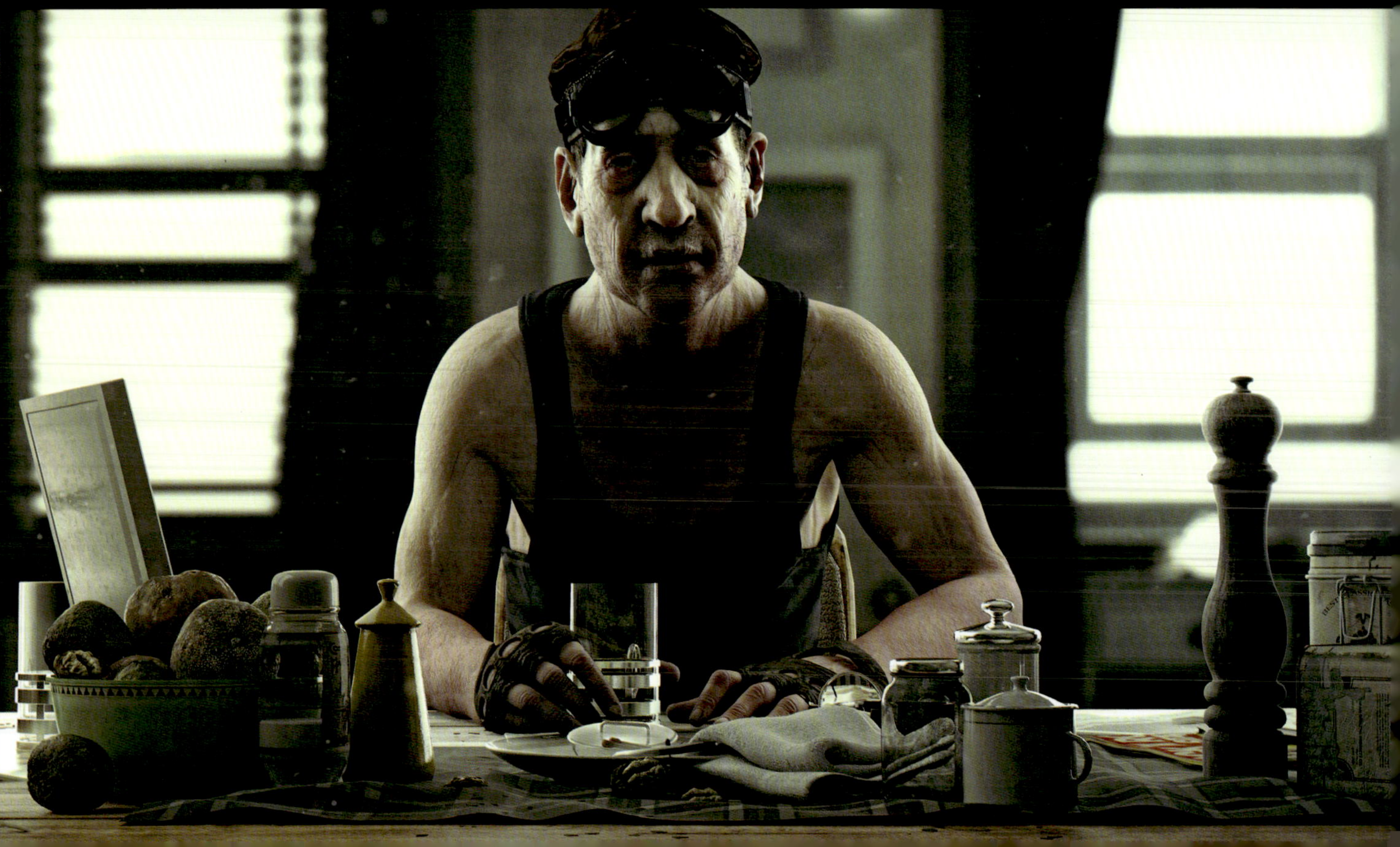

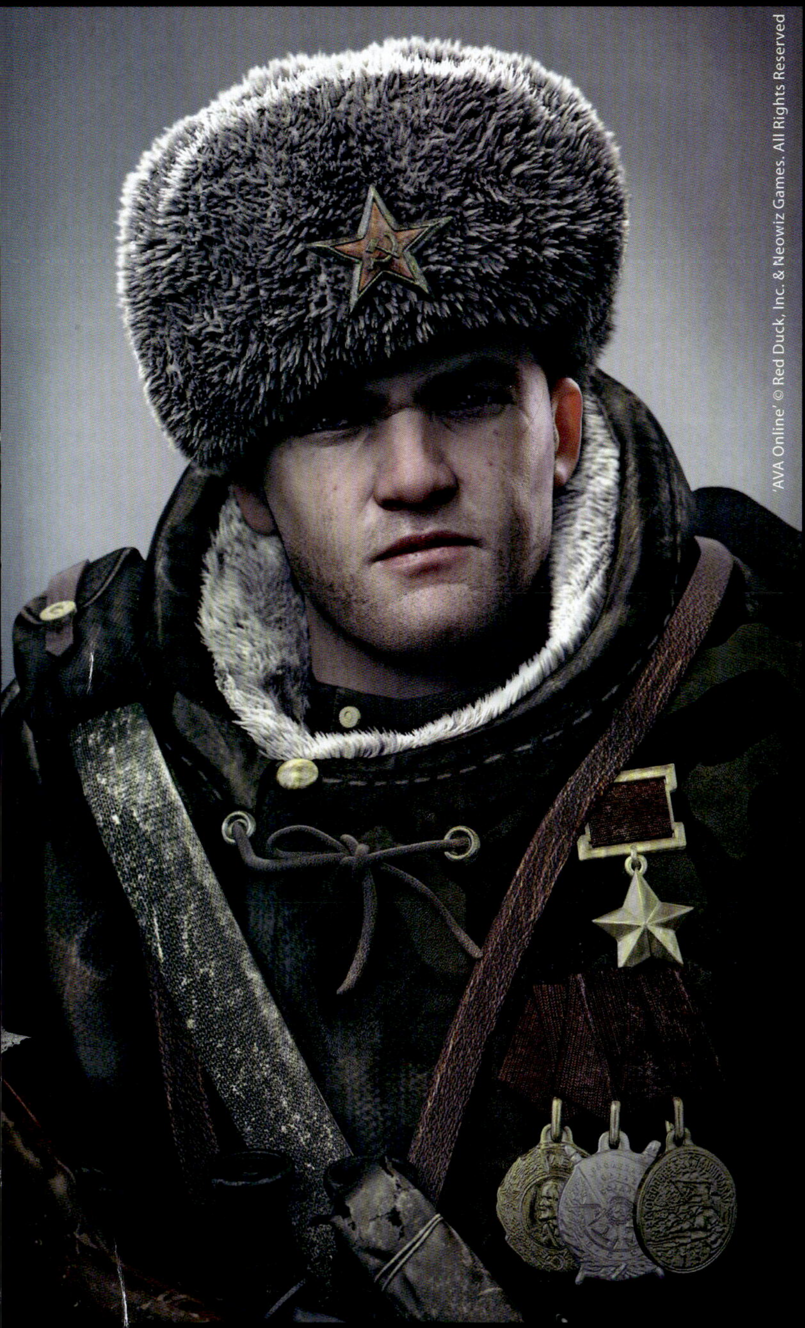

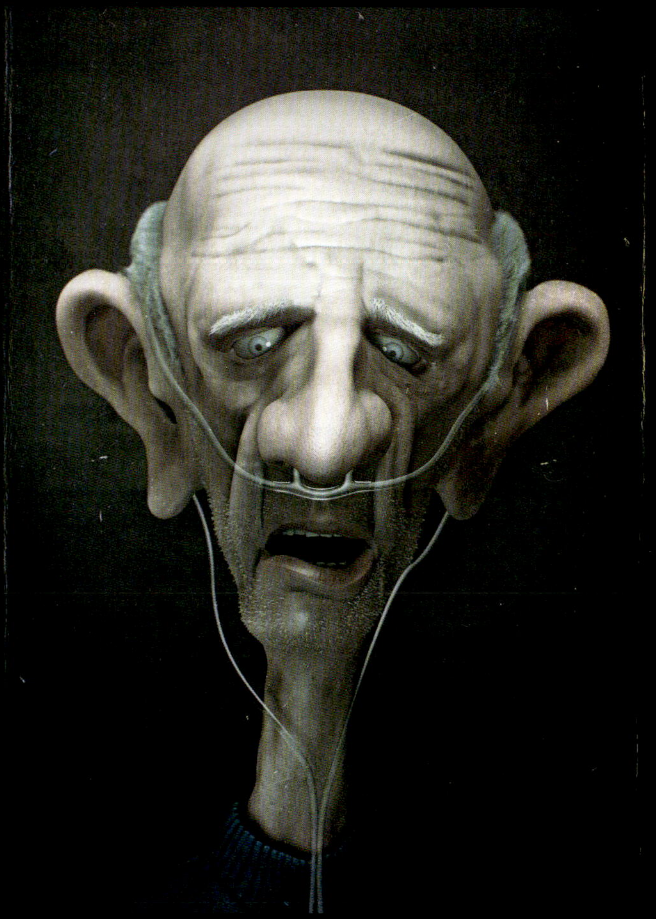

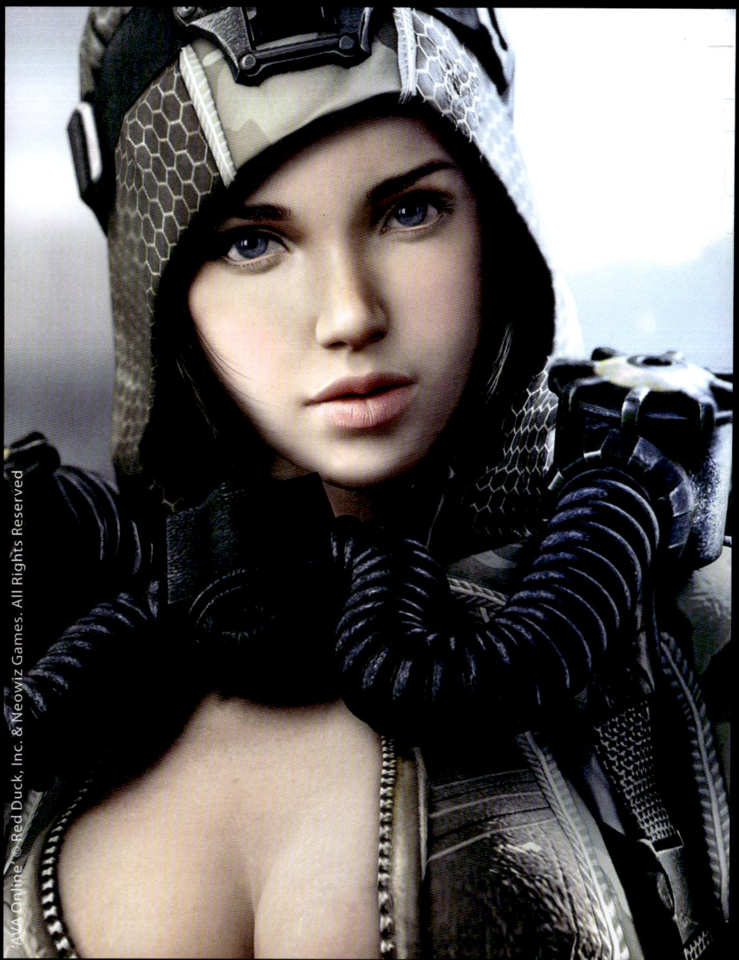

AVA Online: Sniper
3ds Max, ZBrush, Photoshop, mental ray
Client: Red Duck, Inc.
Young soo Choi, SOUTH KOREA
[above]

Old Man
ZBrush, CINEMA 4D, Photoshop
Jonathan Kemp, CANADA
[above right]

AVA Online: Ginny
3ds Max, ZBrush, Photoshop, mental ray
Client: Red Duck, Inc.
Jeongah Kwon, SOUTH KOREA
[right]

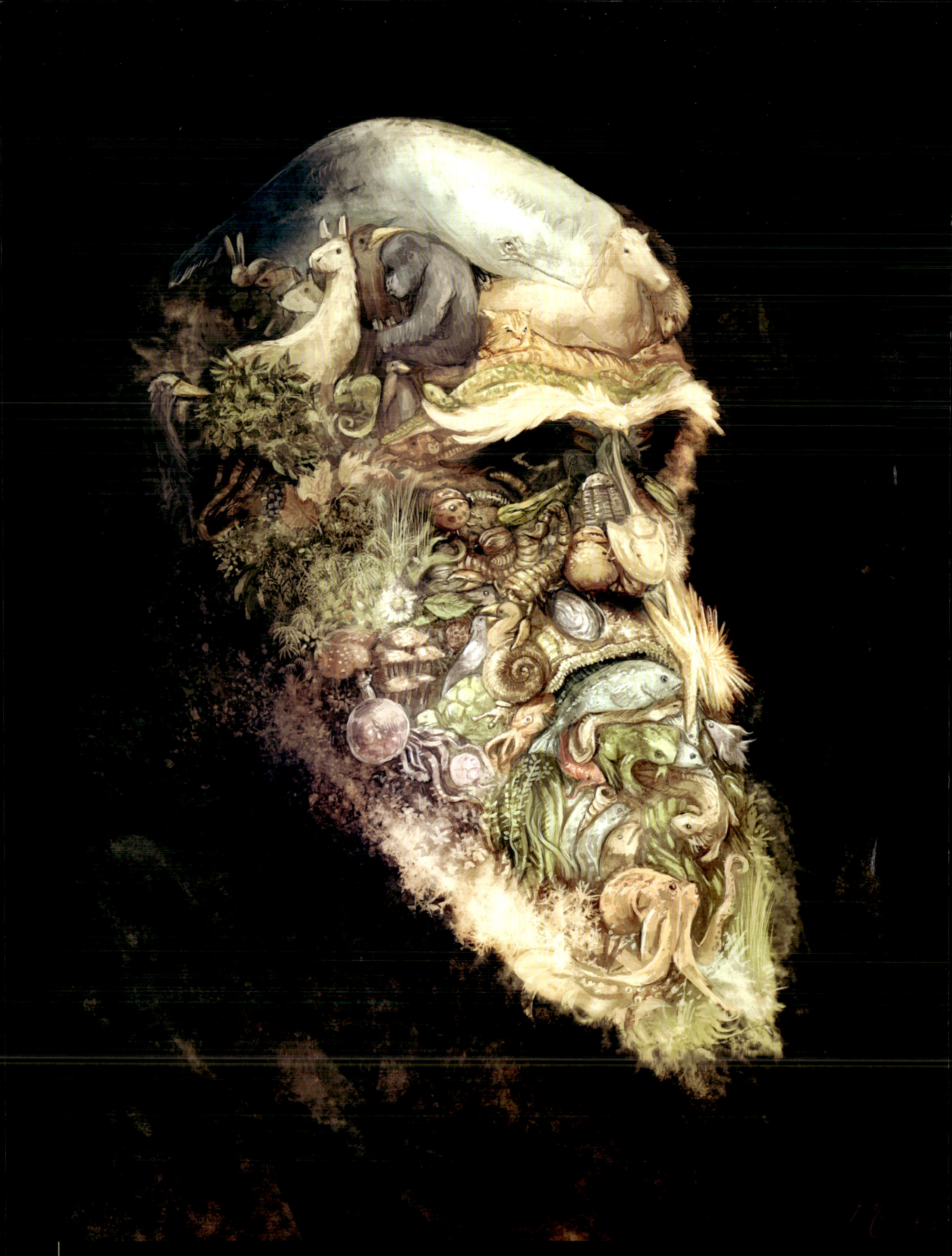

Excellence
Portrait (Illustrated)

Portrait of Charles Darwin
Krita
David Revoy, FRANCE

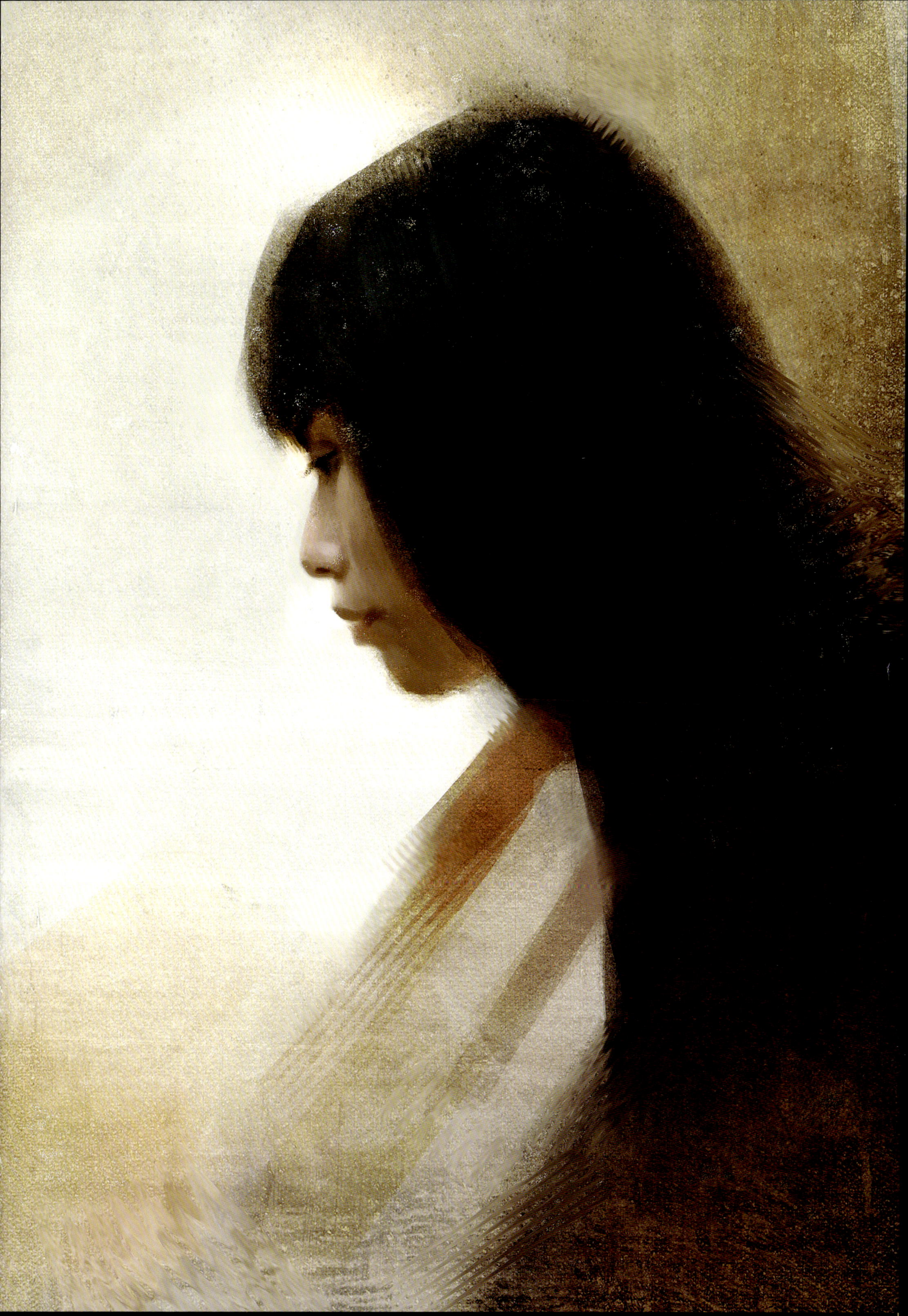

Love
Photoshop
Stephen Molyneaux, GREAT BRITAIN

Master
Portrait (Illustrated)

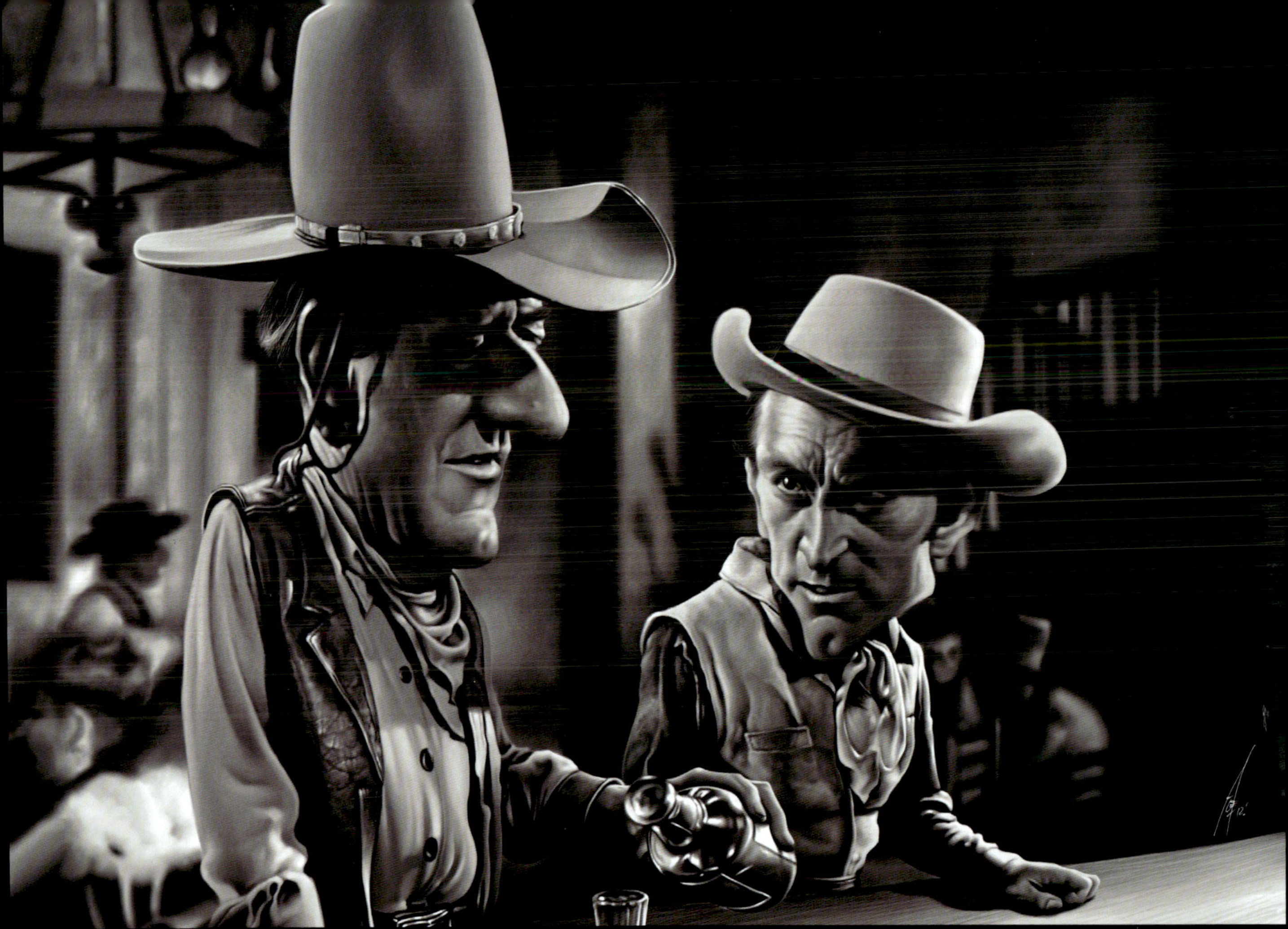

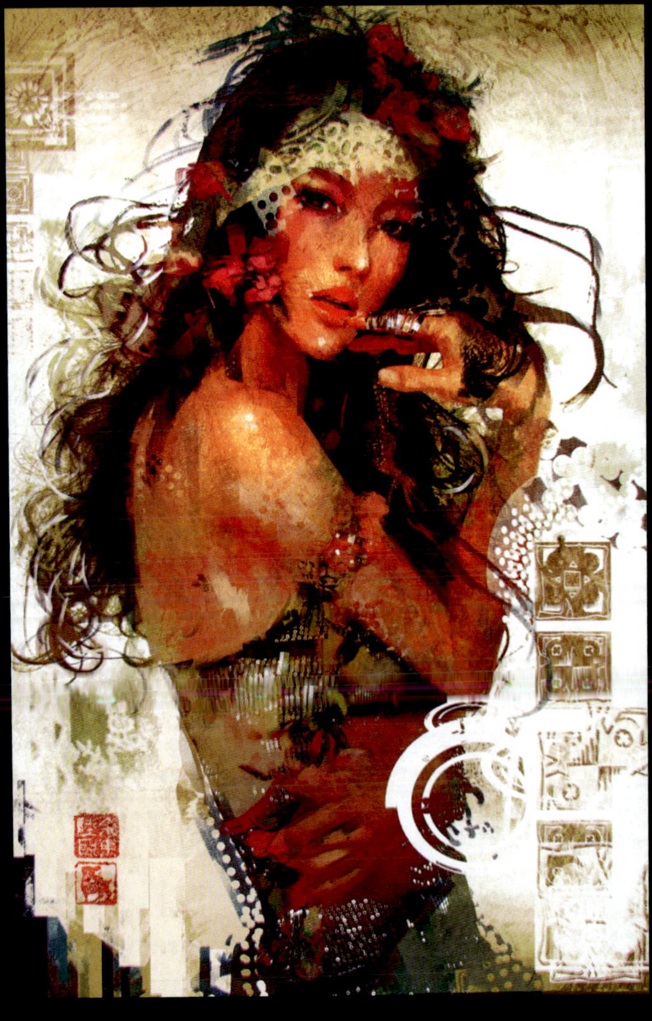

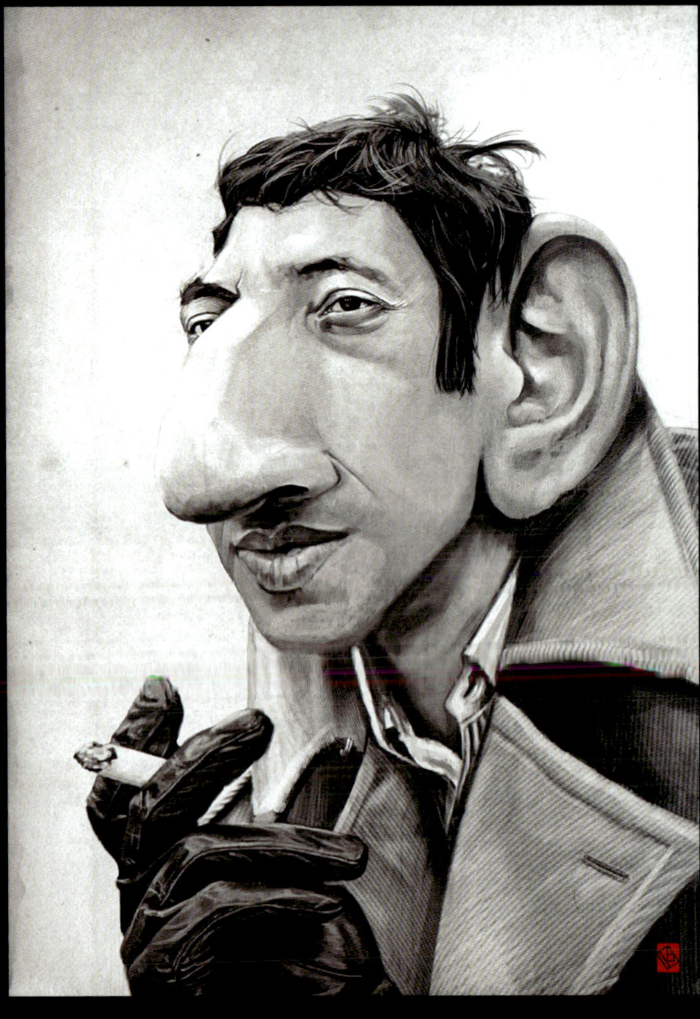

Wayne and Douglas
Photoshop
Alex Gallego, SPAIN
[top]

Springtime
Photoshop, ArtRage
Donglu Yu, CANADA
[above]

Gainsbourg Jeune
Photoshop
Khasis Lieb, FRANCE
[above]

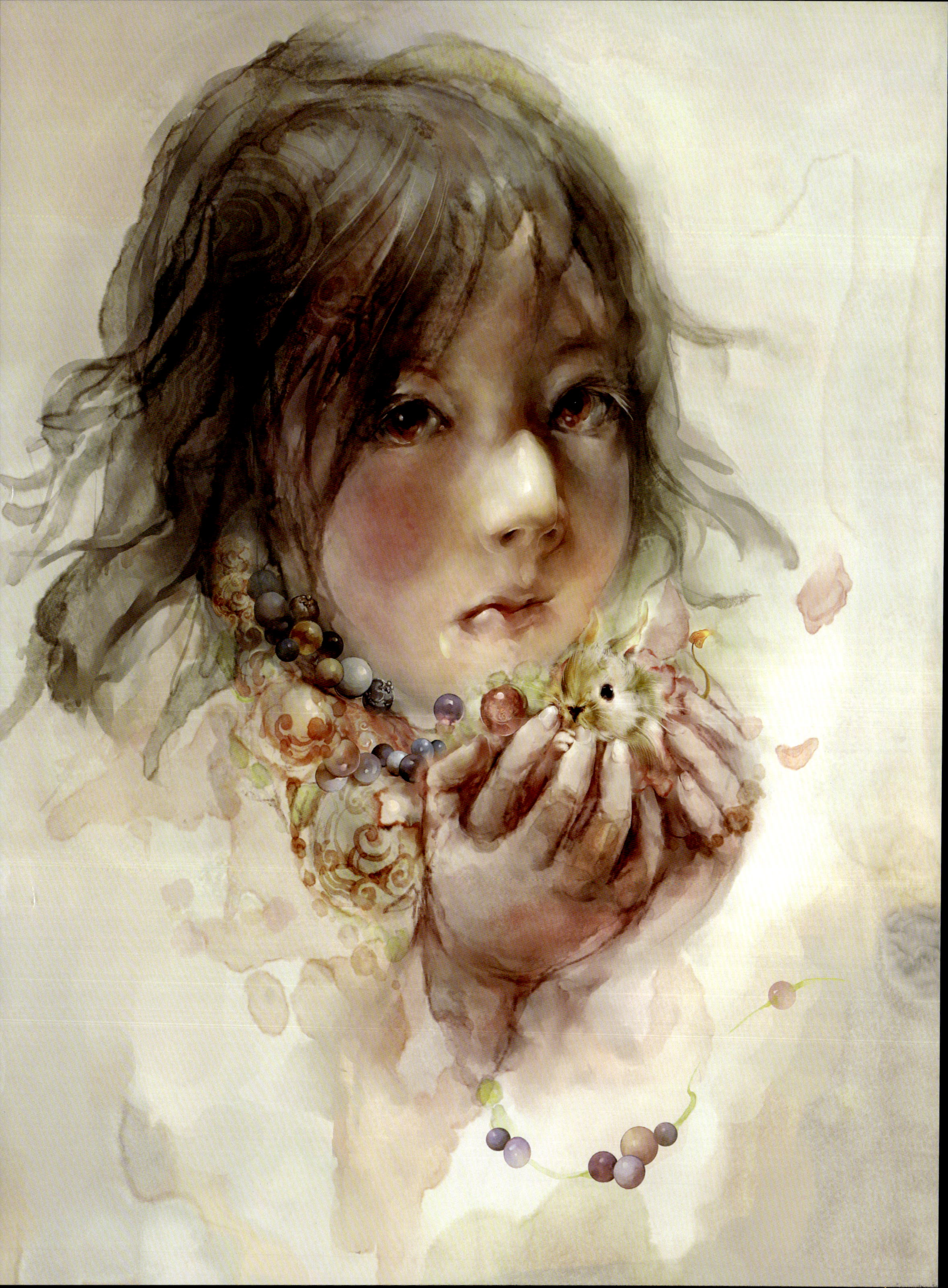

Hope
Painter, Photoshop
Te Hu, USA

Excellence
Portrait (Illustrated)

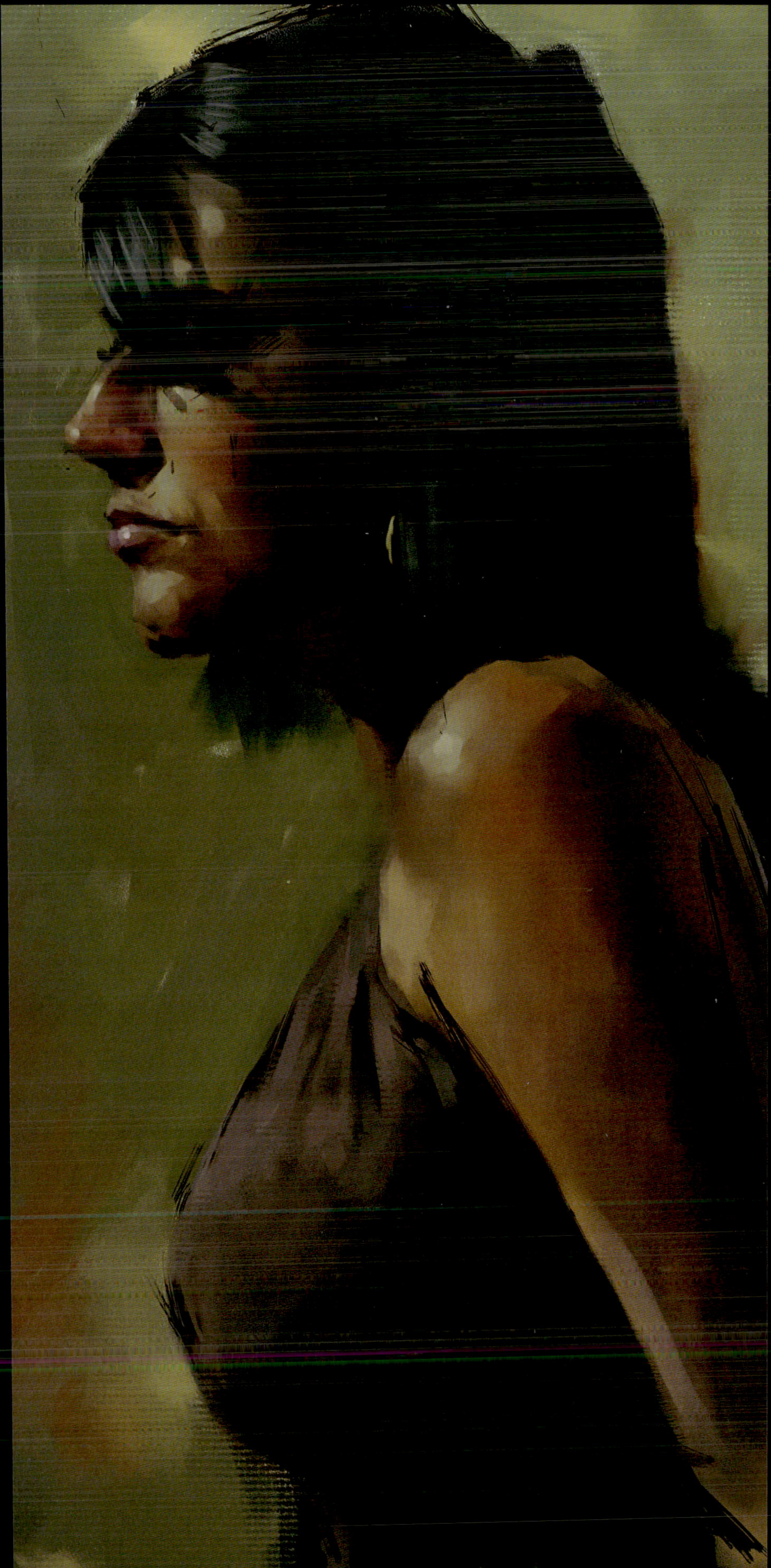

Tamra
Painter, Photoshop
Aaron Riley, USA

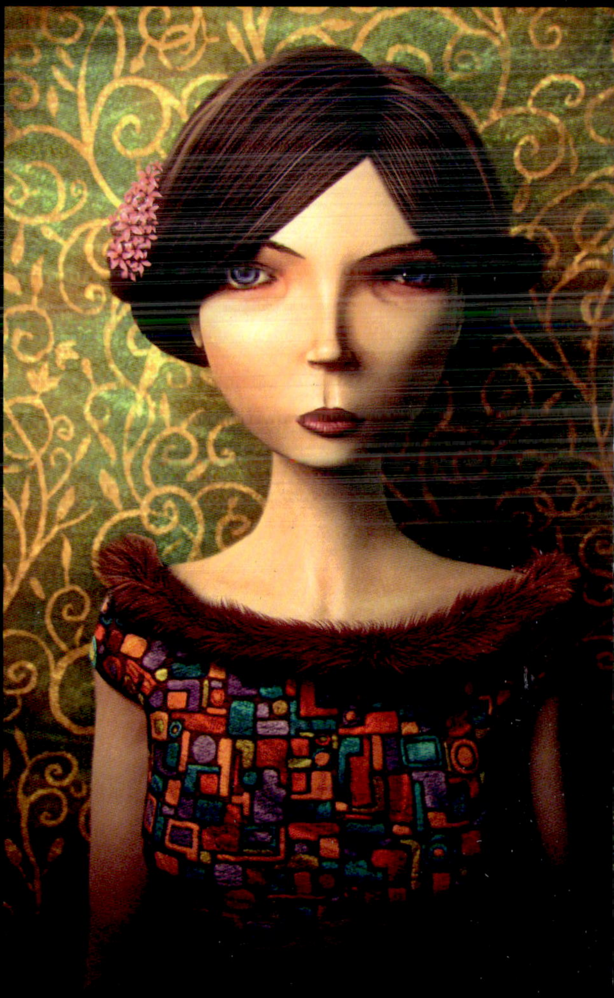

Fille Fleur
ZBrush, 3ds Max, After Effects
Inspired by Fabrice Backes
Pascal Ackermann, FRANCE

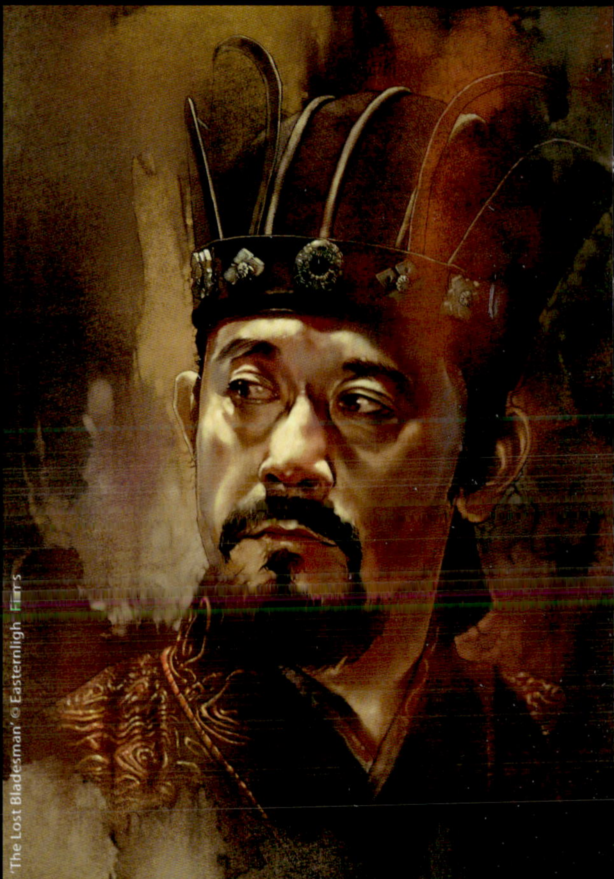

'The Lost Bladesman' © Easternlight Films

The Lost Bladesman: Cao Cao
Photoshop
Client: Easternlight Films

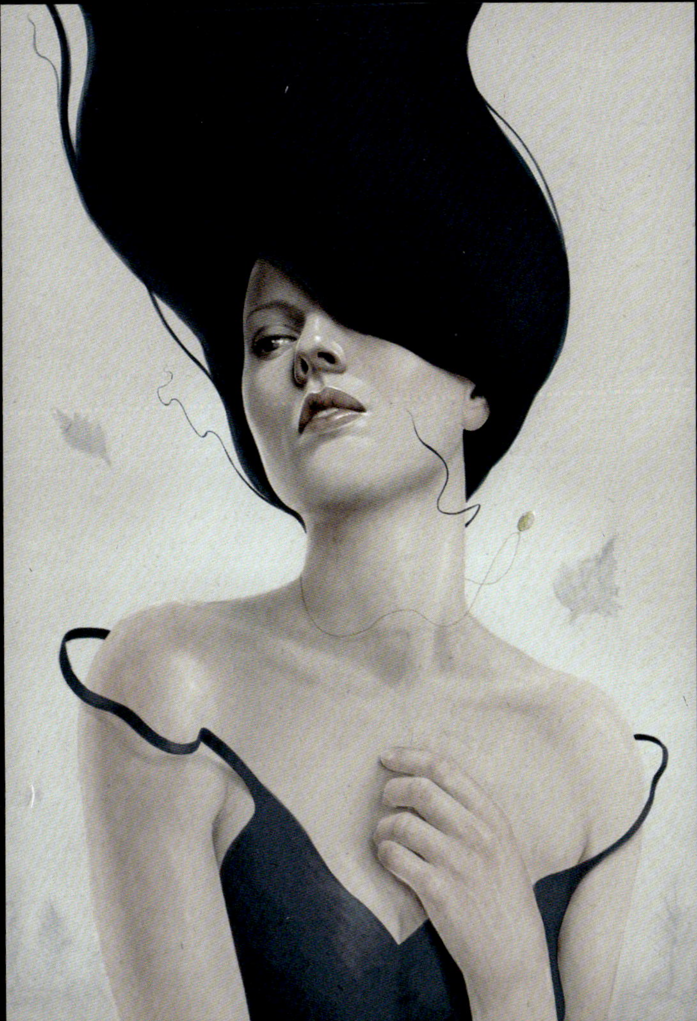

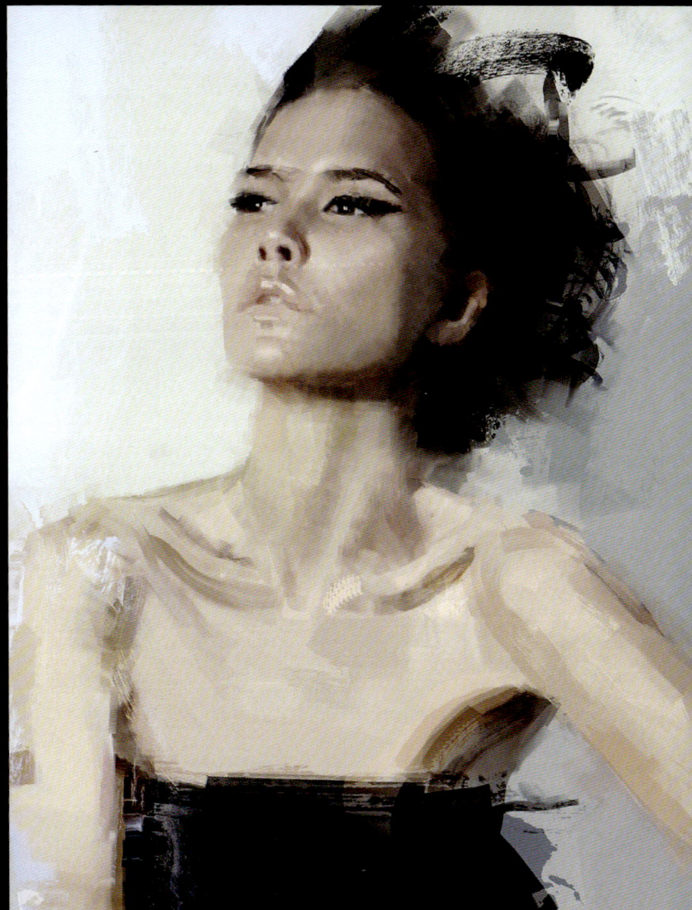

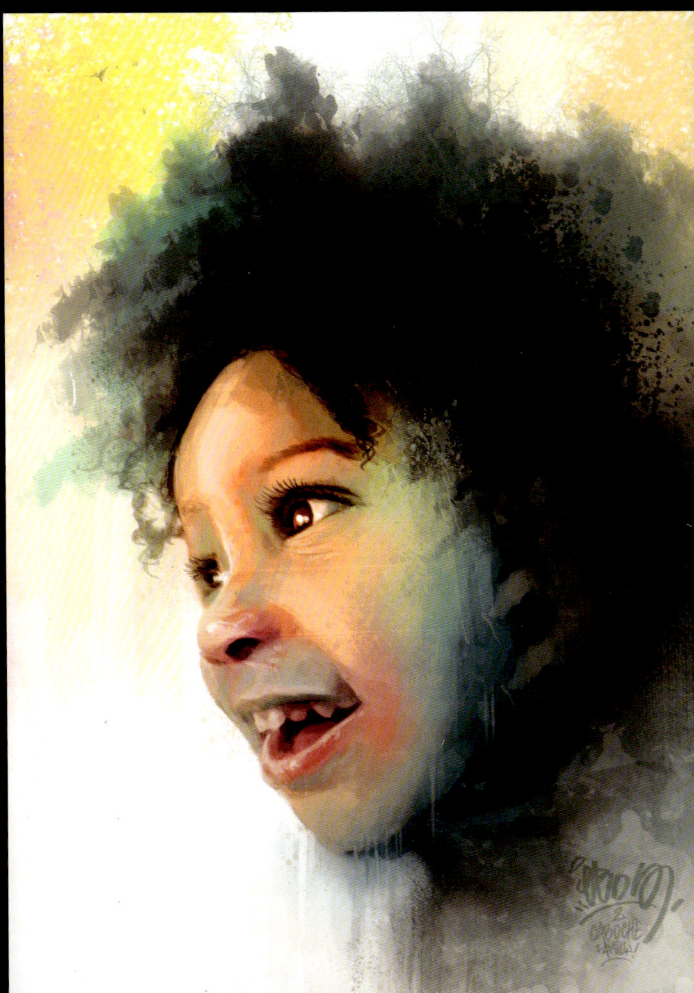

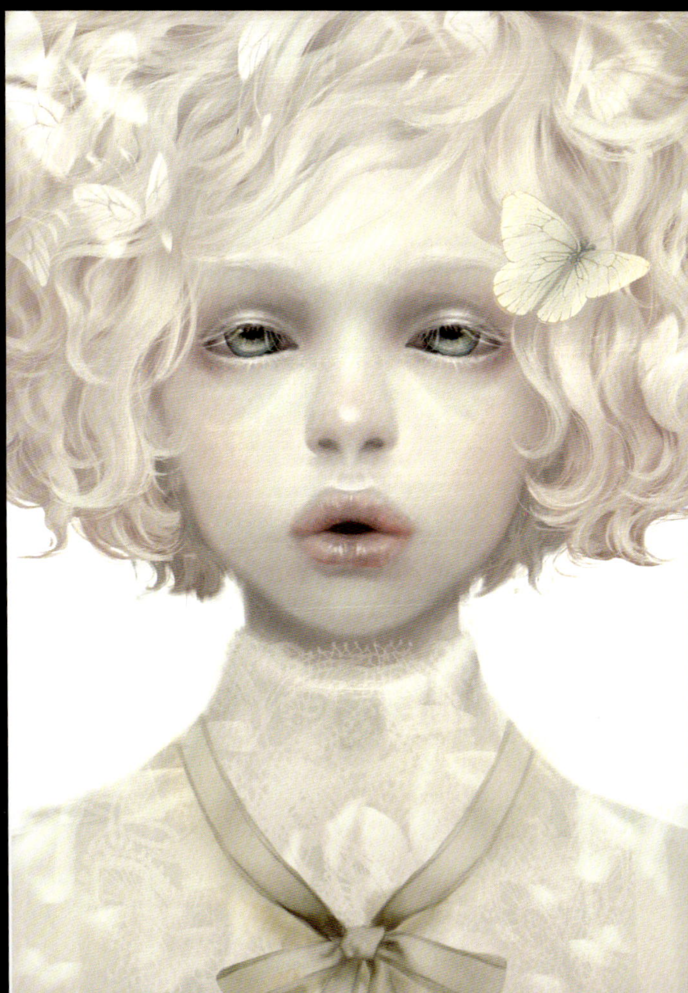

Ascension
Photoshop
Diego Fernandez, ARGENTINA
[top]

K6Dee
Photoshop
Renaud Taelemans, BELGIUM
[above]

Stacey
Photoshop
Stephen Molyneaux, GREAT BRITAIN
[top]

Among the White Butterflies
Photoshop
Nguy Thuyngan, VIETNAM
[above]

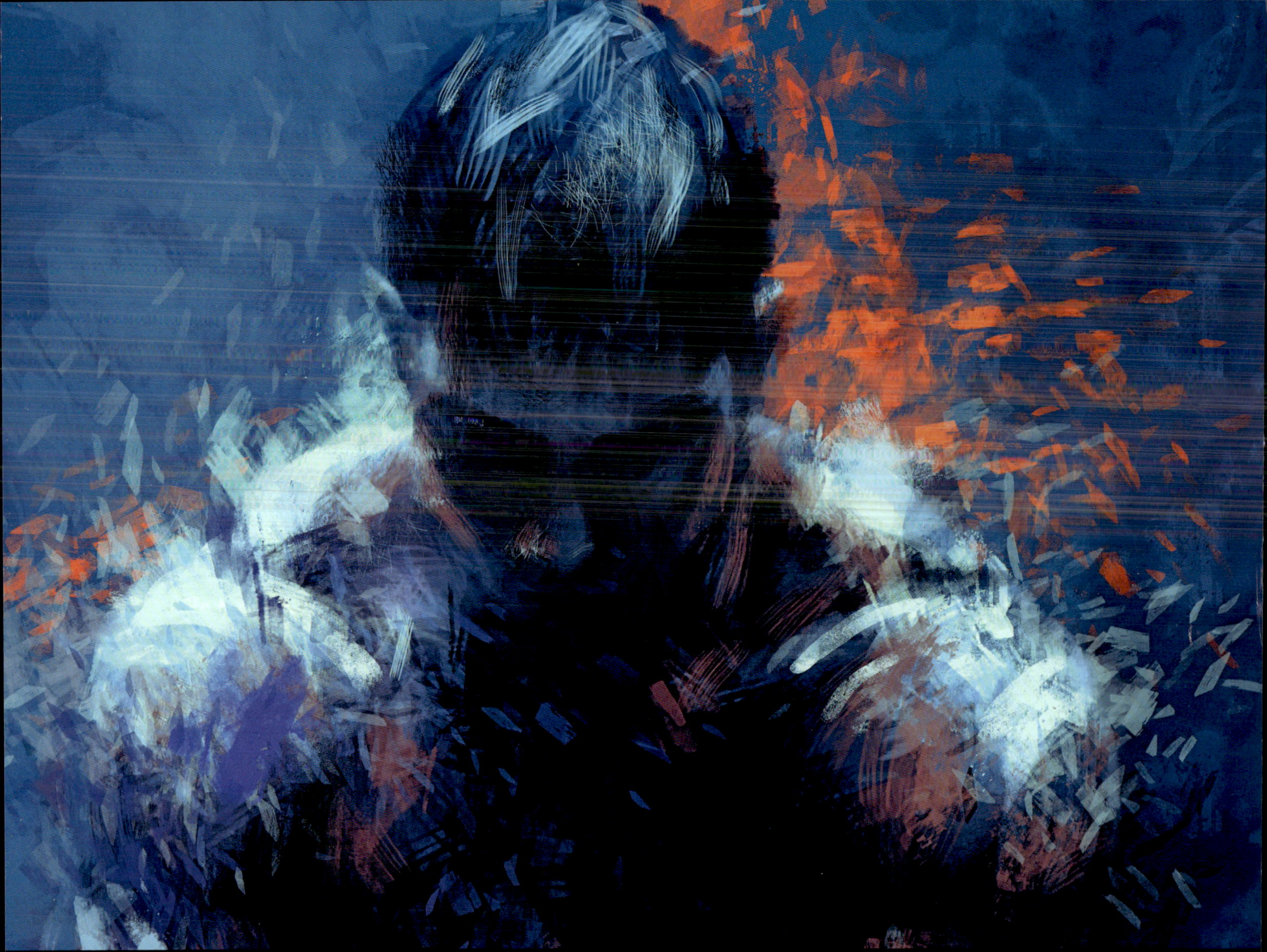

Warrior
Photoshop
Aleksandra Lech, POLAND
[top]

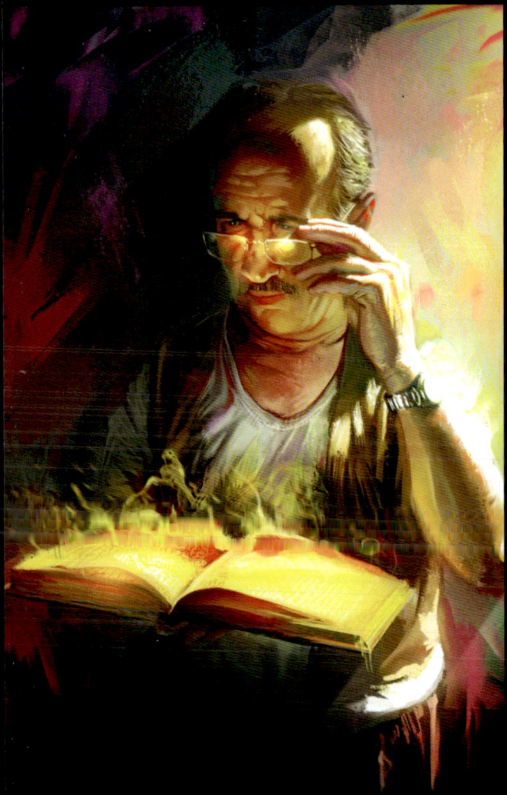

Passed Through Generations
Photoshop
Saeed Jalabi, IRAN
[above]

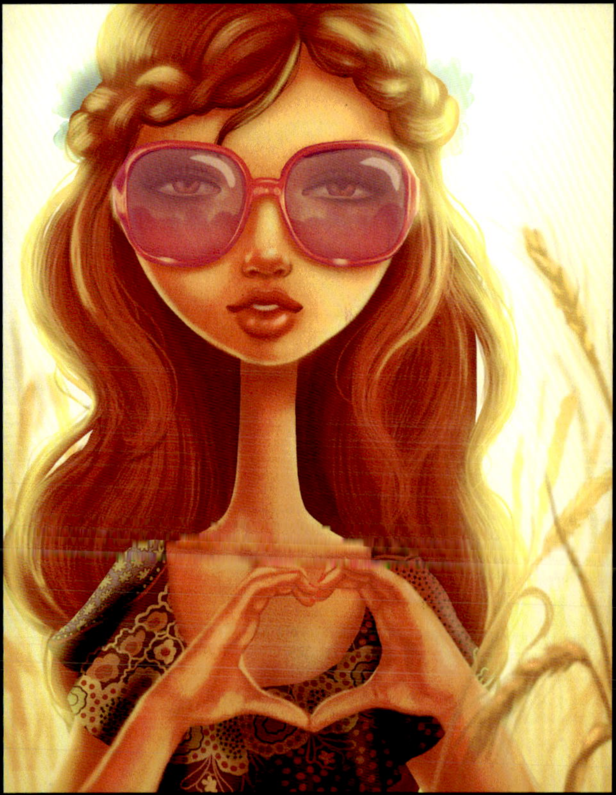

Sticky Sweet
Photoshop
Crystal Wall Lancaster, CANADA
[above]

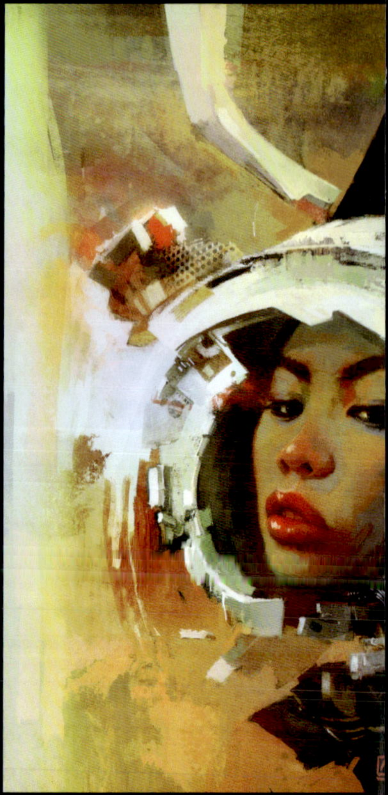

Binaural III
Photoshop
Loic Zimmermann, USA
[above]

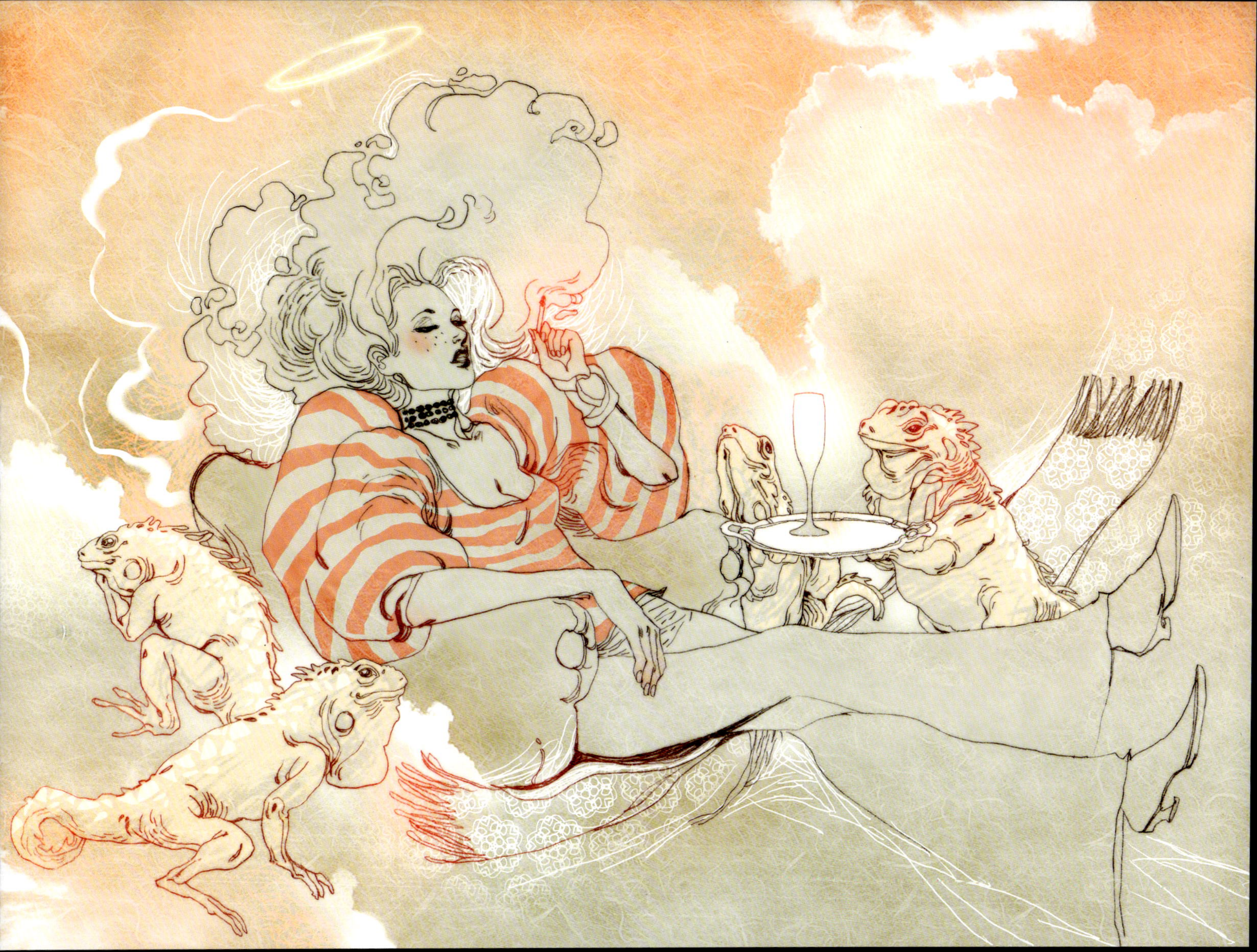

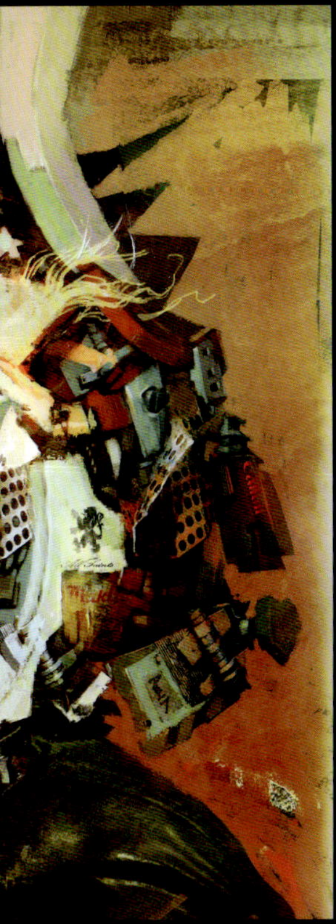

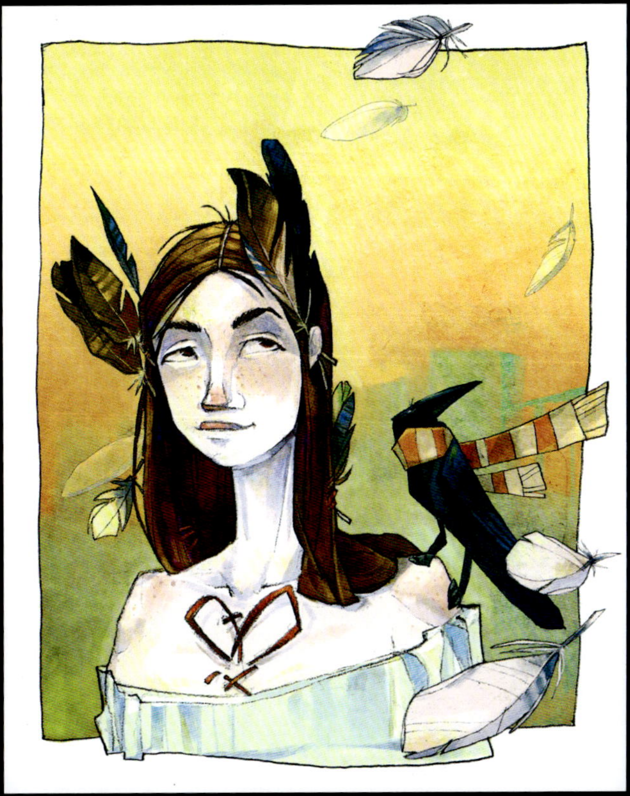

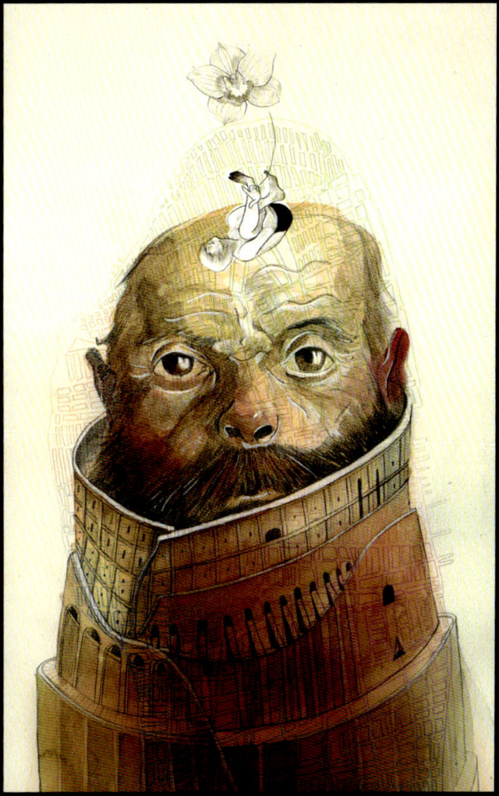

Omnipotence
Photoshop
Marguerite Sauvage, AUSTRALIA
[top]

Muse
Photoshop
Vadim Sverdlov, ISRAEL
[above]

The Tower of Babel
Photoshop
Inspired by The New York Trilogy
Richard Zela, MEXICO
[above]

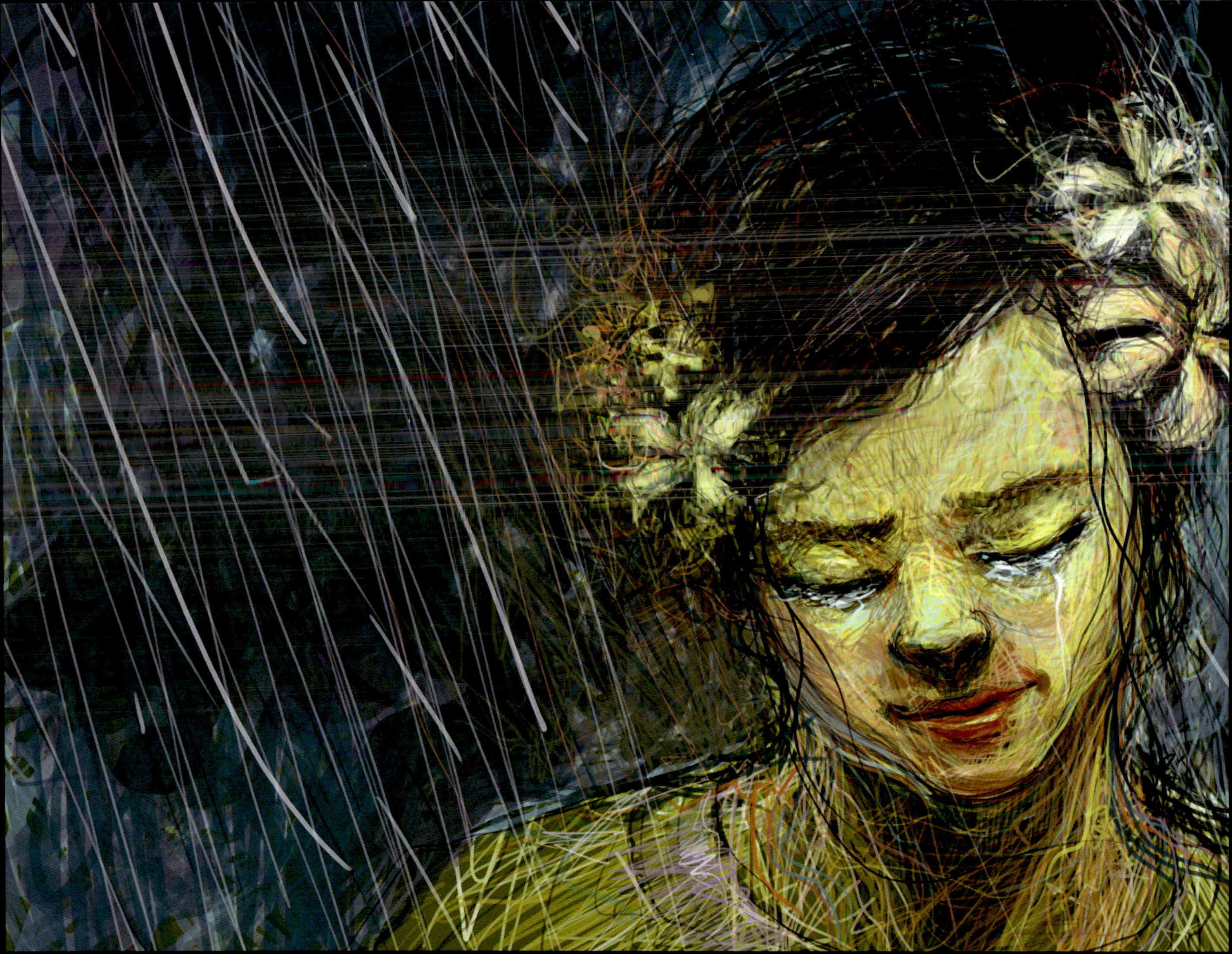

Shade of Rain: Cover
Photoshop
Client: Household Object Publishing
Sahaschai Pinmanee, THAILAND
[above]

The Warrior
Photoshop
Client: Taewon Entertainment
Takashi Tan, MALAYSIA
[right]

Cosmonaut
Photoshop
Richard Zela, MEXICO
[far right]

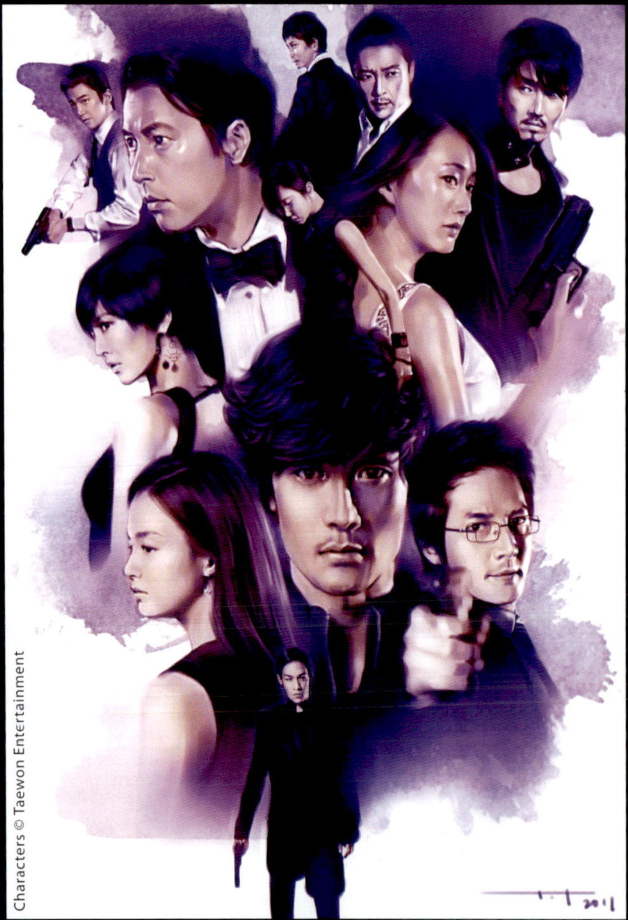

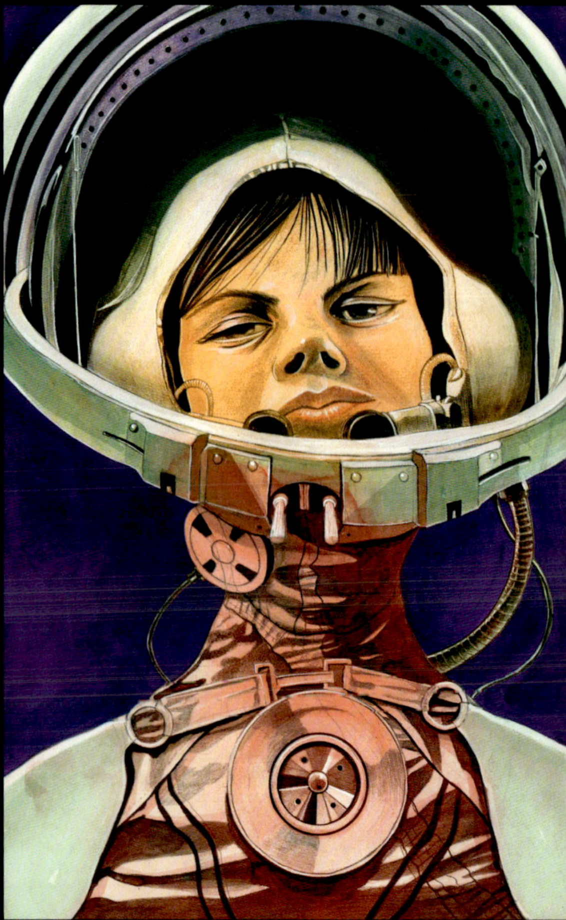

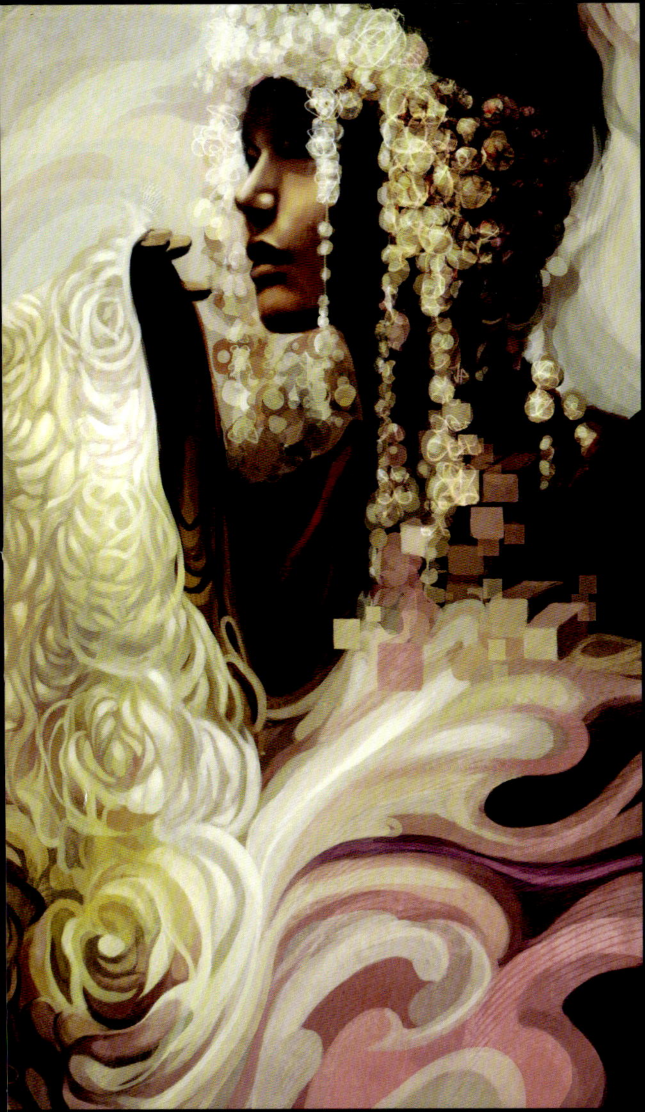

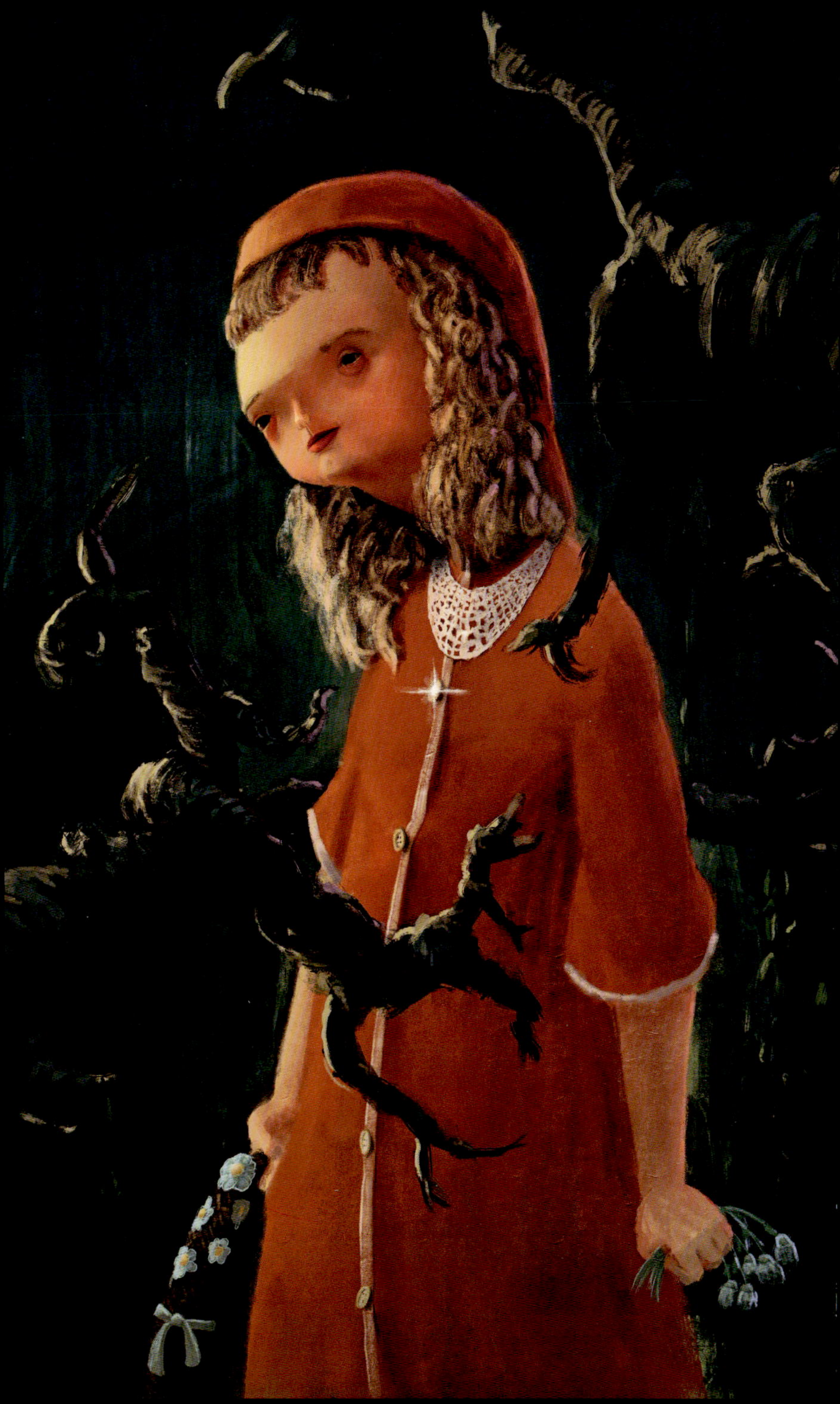

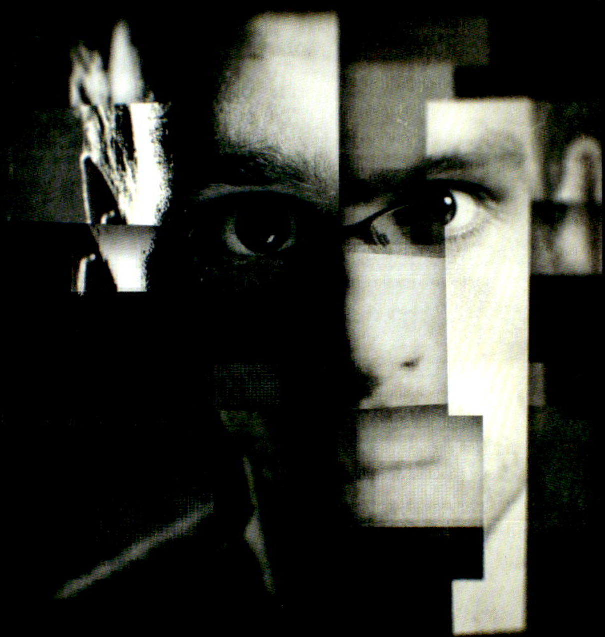

Potpourri
Photoshop
Kamille Areopagita, PHILIPPINES
[top left]

Little Red Riding Hood
Photoshop
Marco Piunti, ITALY
[above]

Guillaume
Photoshop
Jonathan Kemp, CANADA

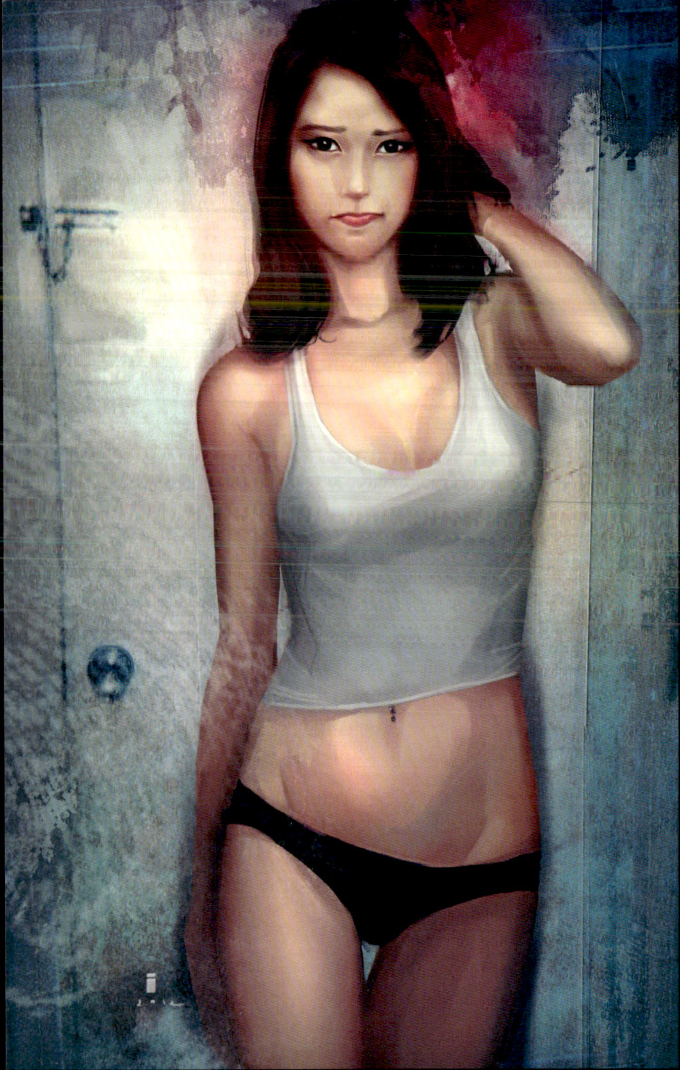

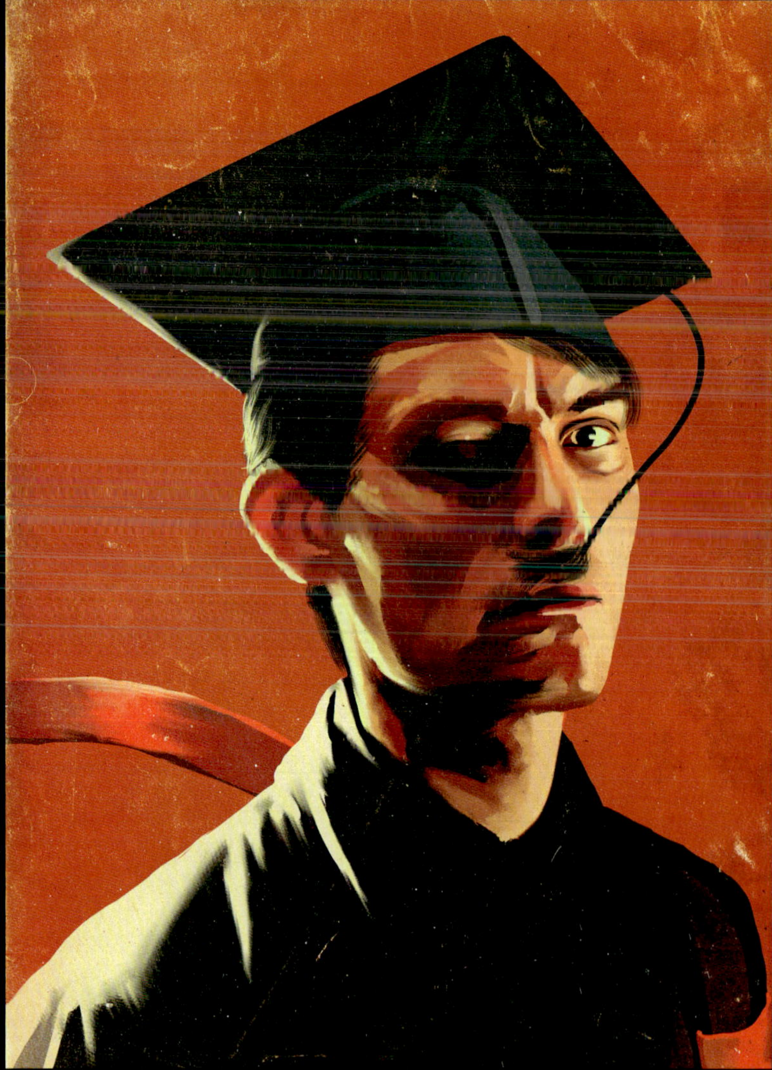

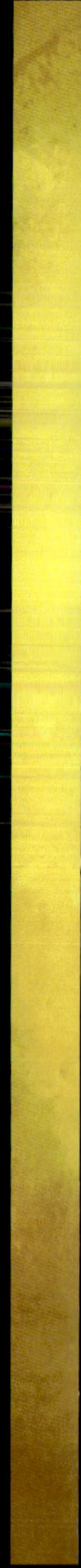

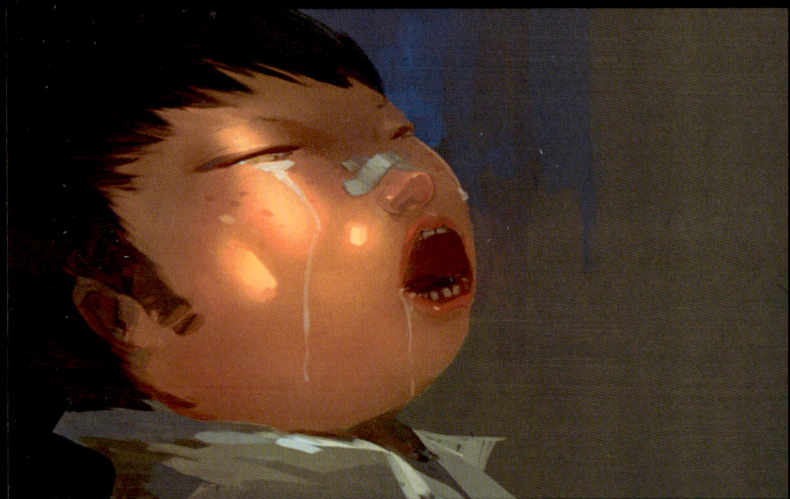

Korean ex GF
Photoshop
Ivan Tao, MALAYSIA
[top]

Cry
Photoshop
Yongming Yang, CHINA
[above]

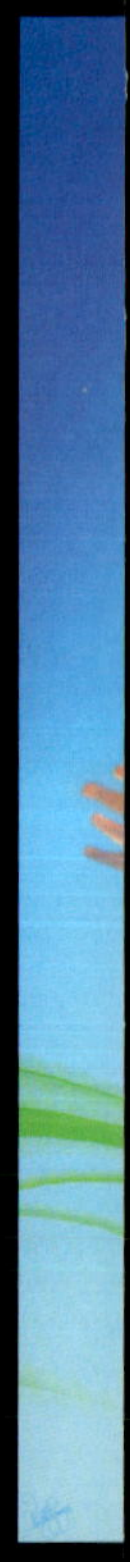

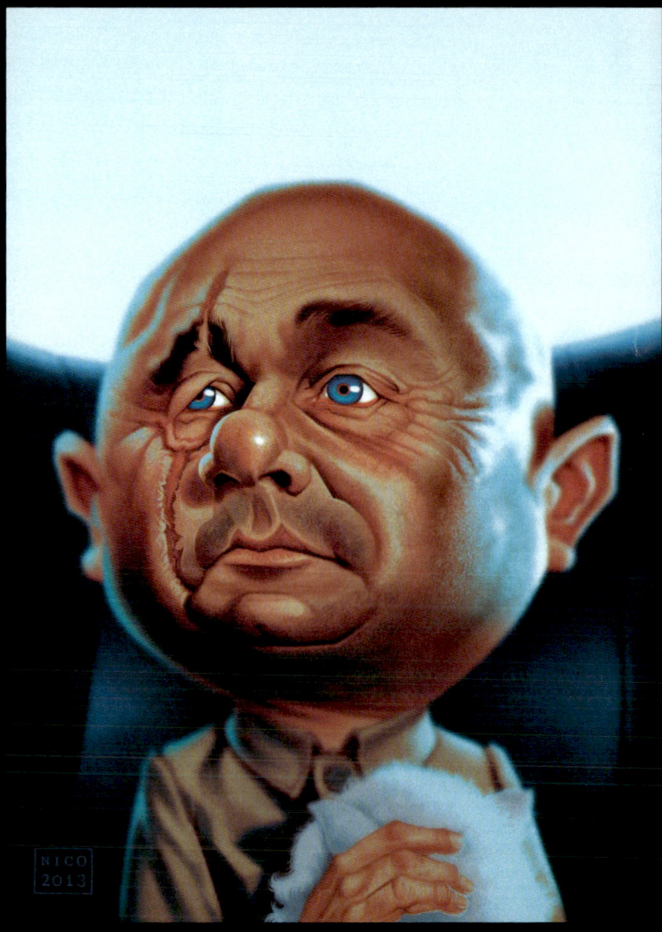

Nazi Student
Photoshop
Mart Klein, GERMANY
[top]

Blofeld
Photoshop
Nicolas Villeminot, FRANCE
[above]

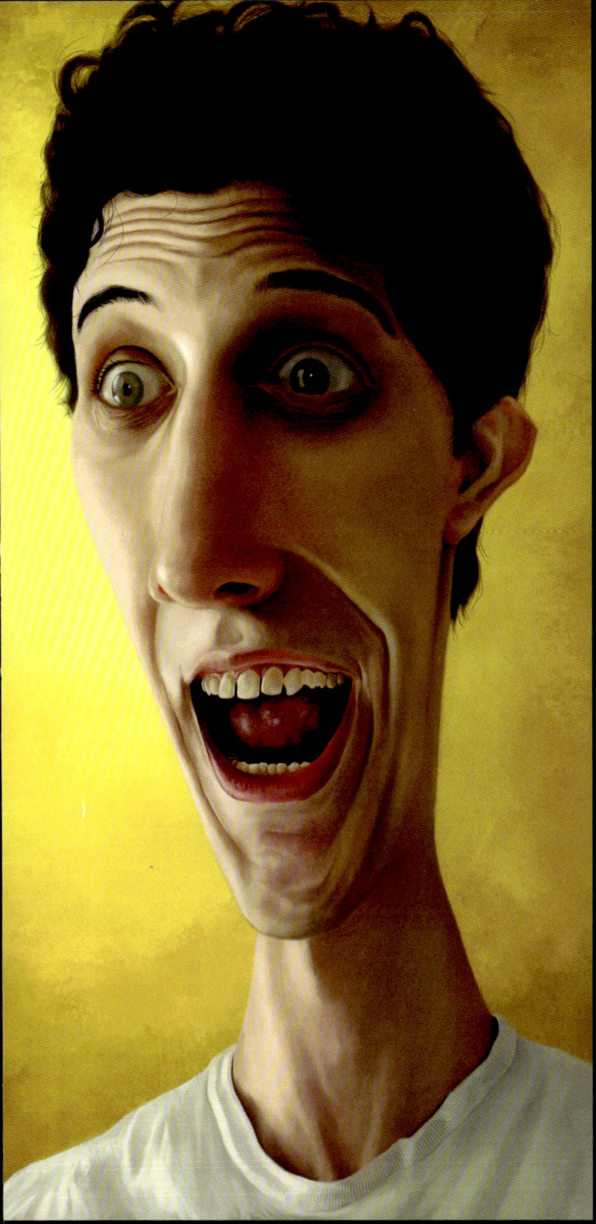

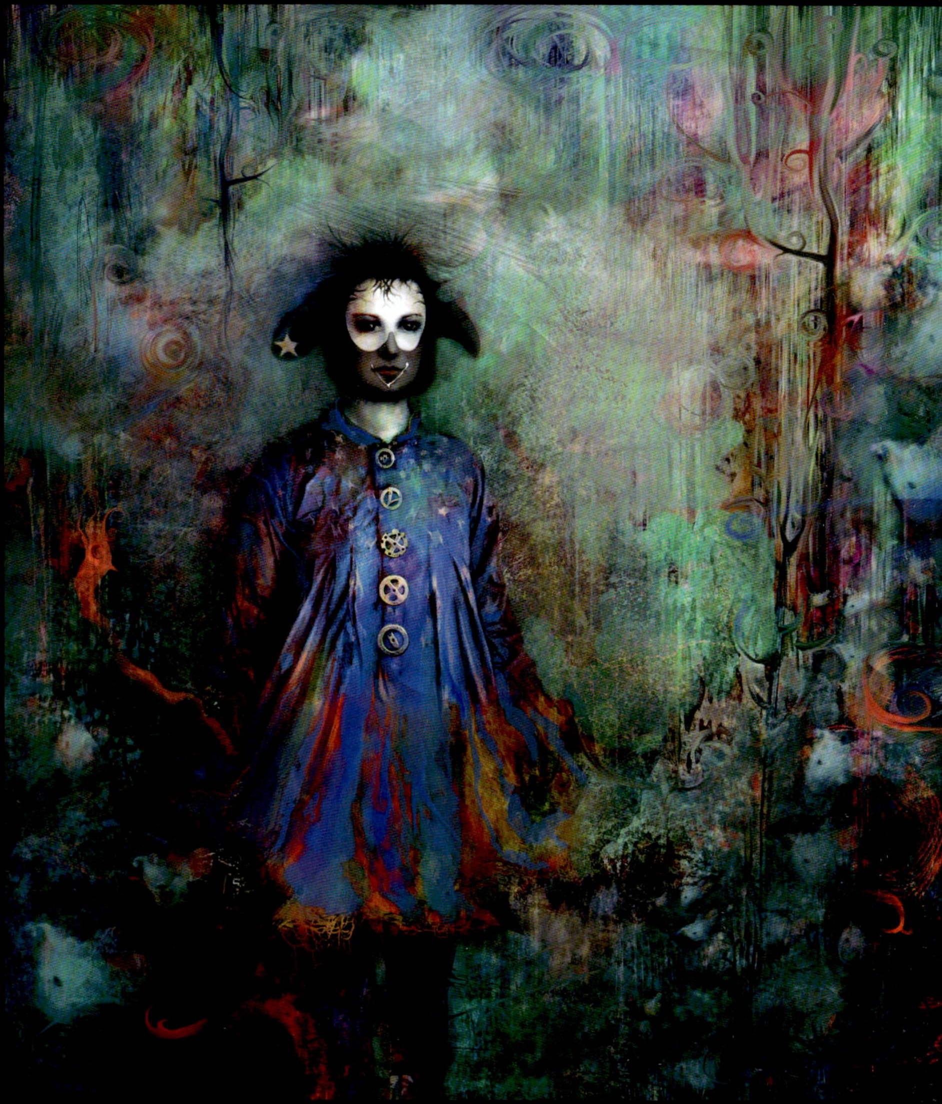

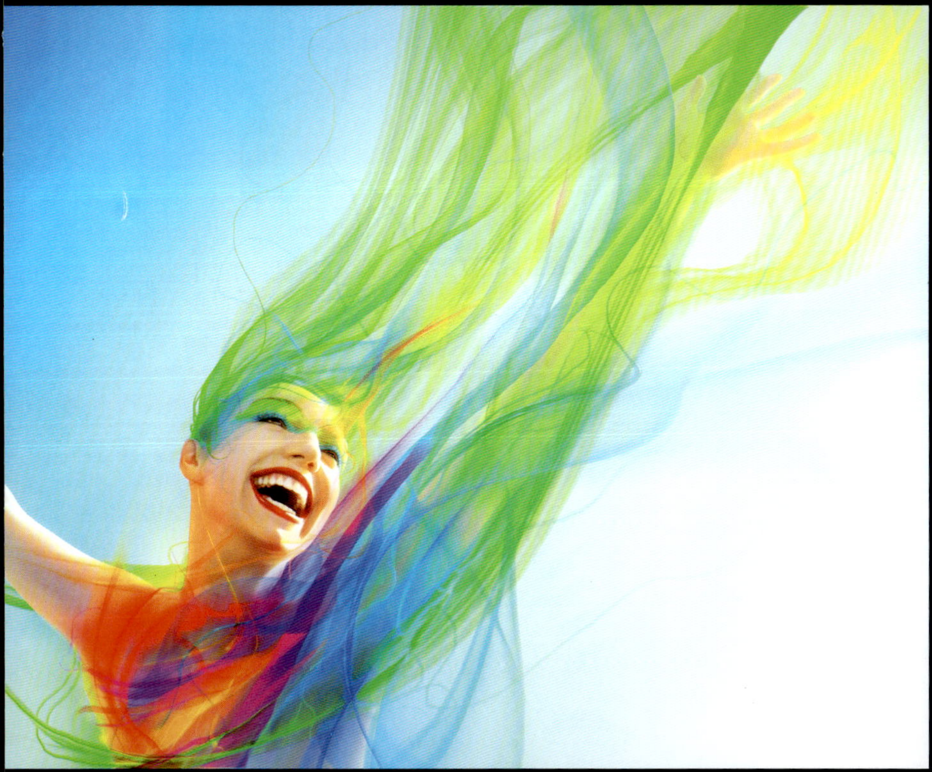

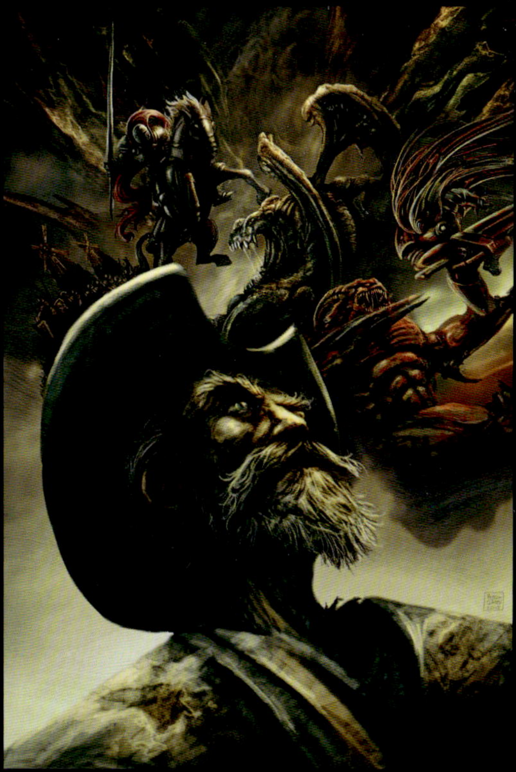

Iggy's Surprise
Photoshop
Igor Braulio, BRAZIL
[top]

Essence of Happiness
Photoshop
Neville dSouza, INDIA
[above]

Rita's Dream
Photoshop
Egle Zioma, LITHUANIA
[top]

Don Quijote
Photoshop
Patricio Clarey, SPAIN
[above]

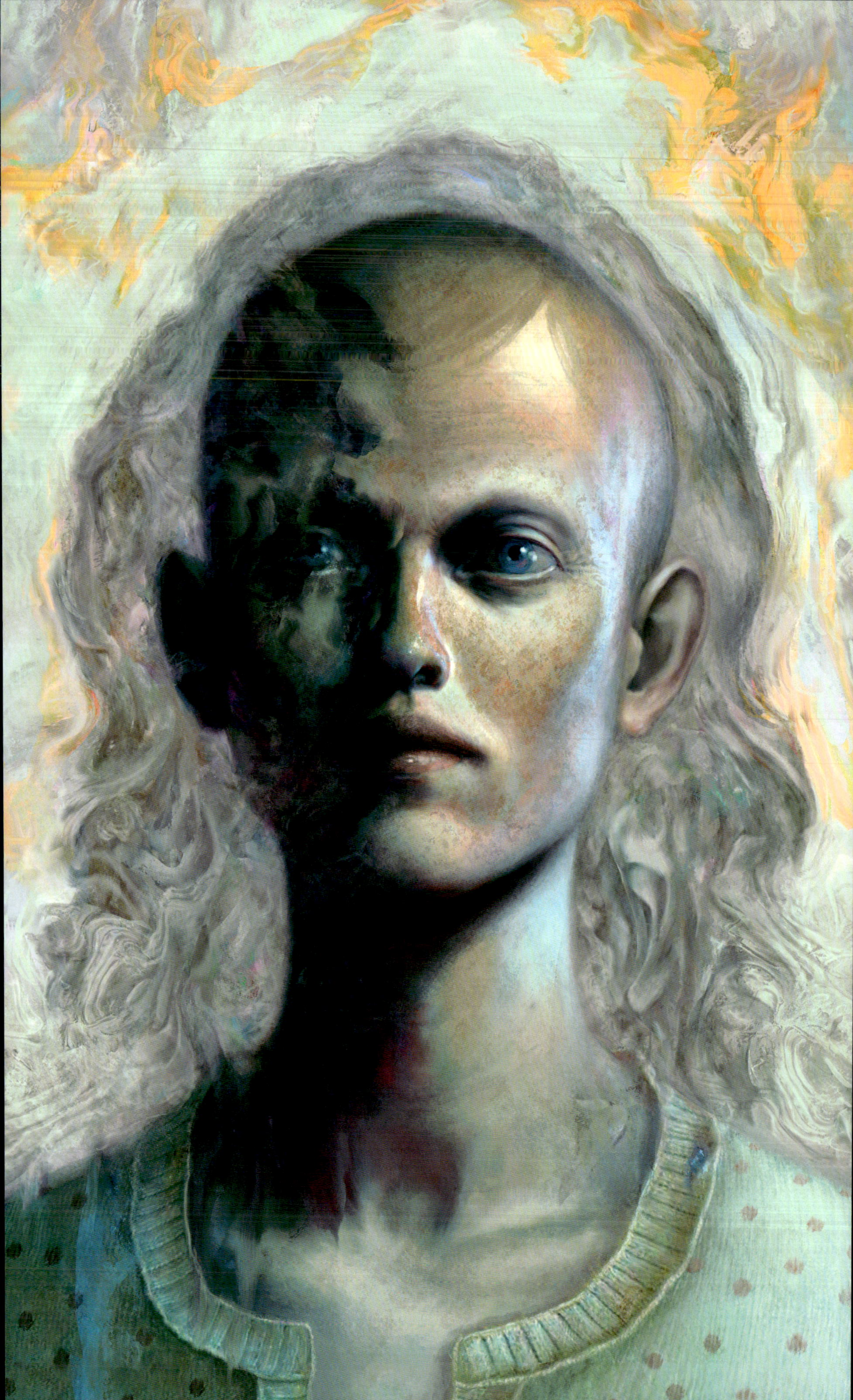

Ottoman
Photoshop
Michal Lisowski, POLAND

Holy Days
Photoshop
Aldo Katayanagi, USA

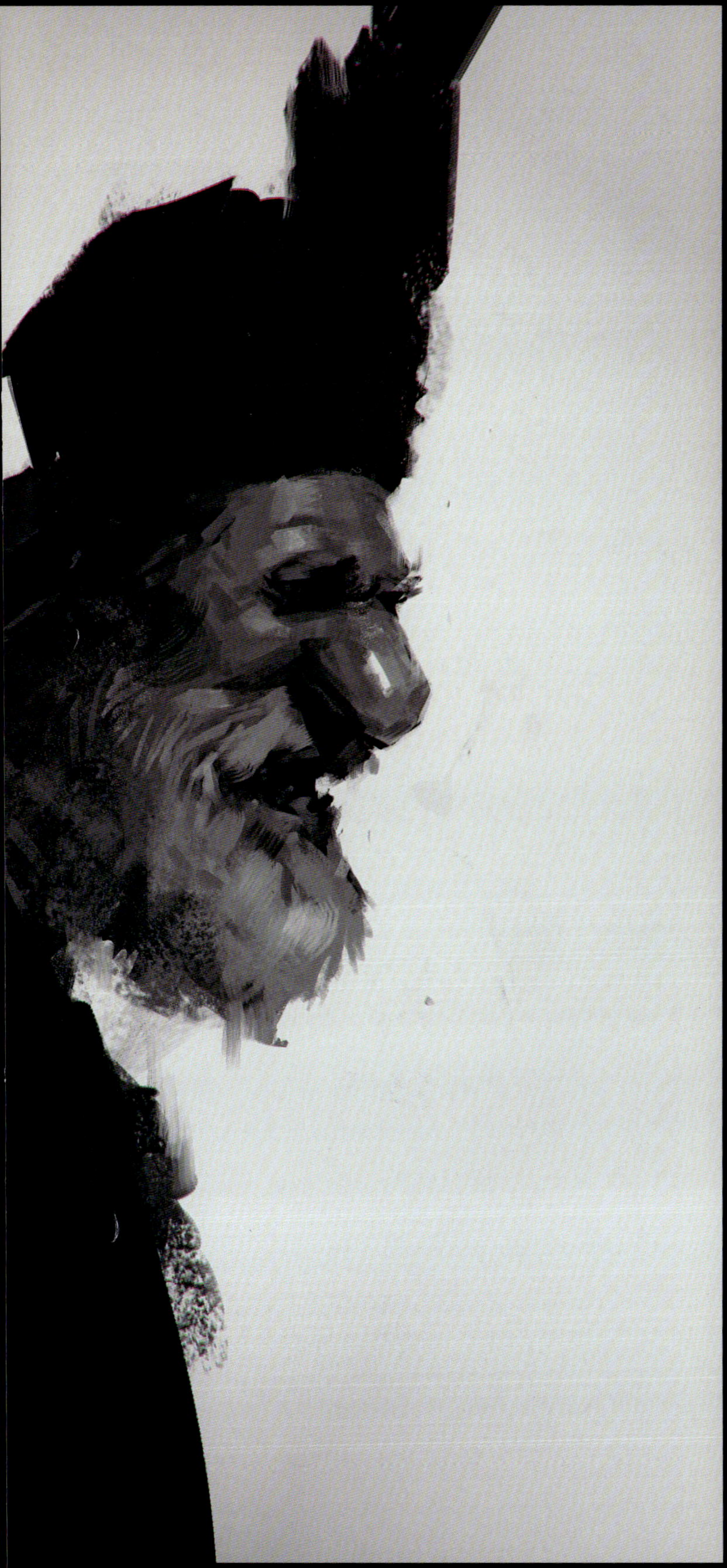

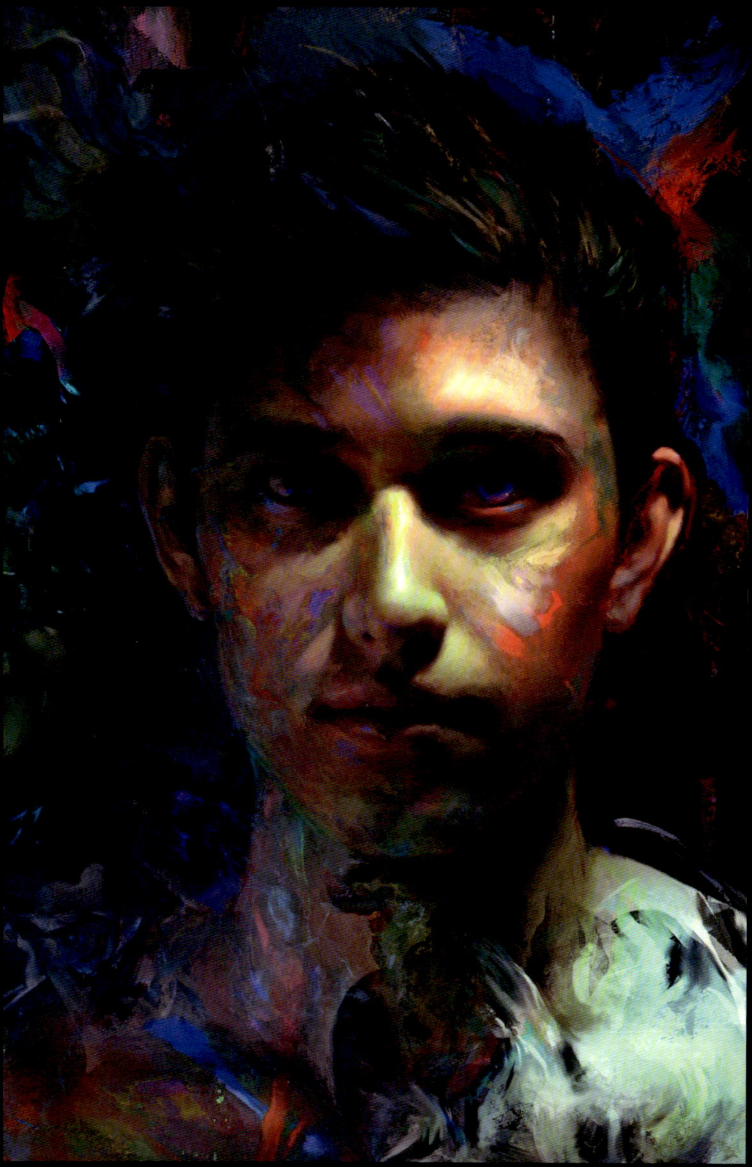

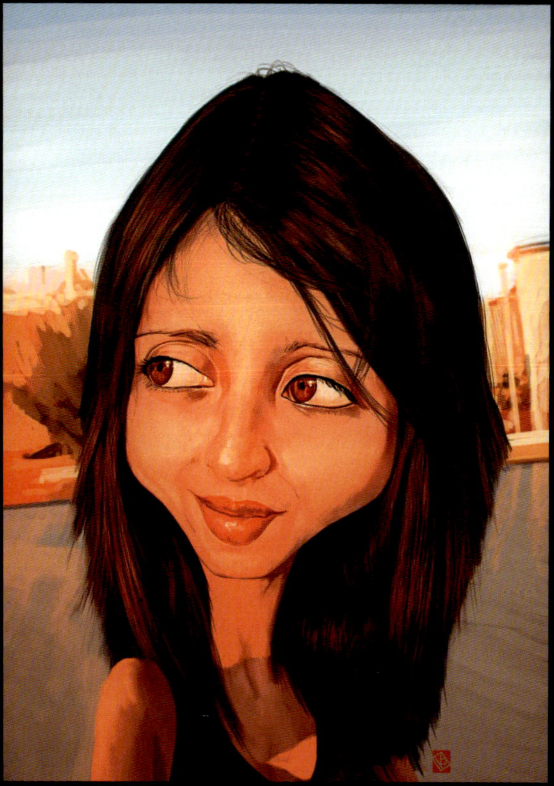

Portrait Experiment
Photoshop
Aldo Katayanagi, USA
[above right]

Atika
Photoshop
Khasis Lieb, FRANCE
[right]

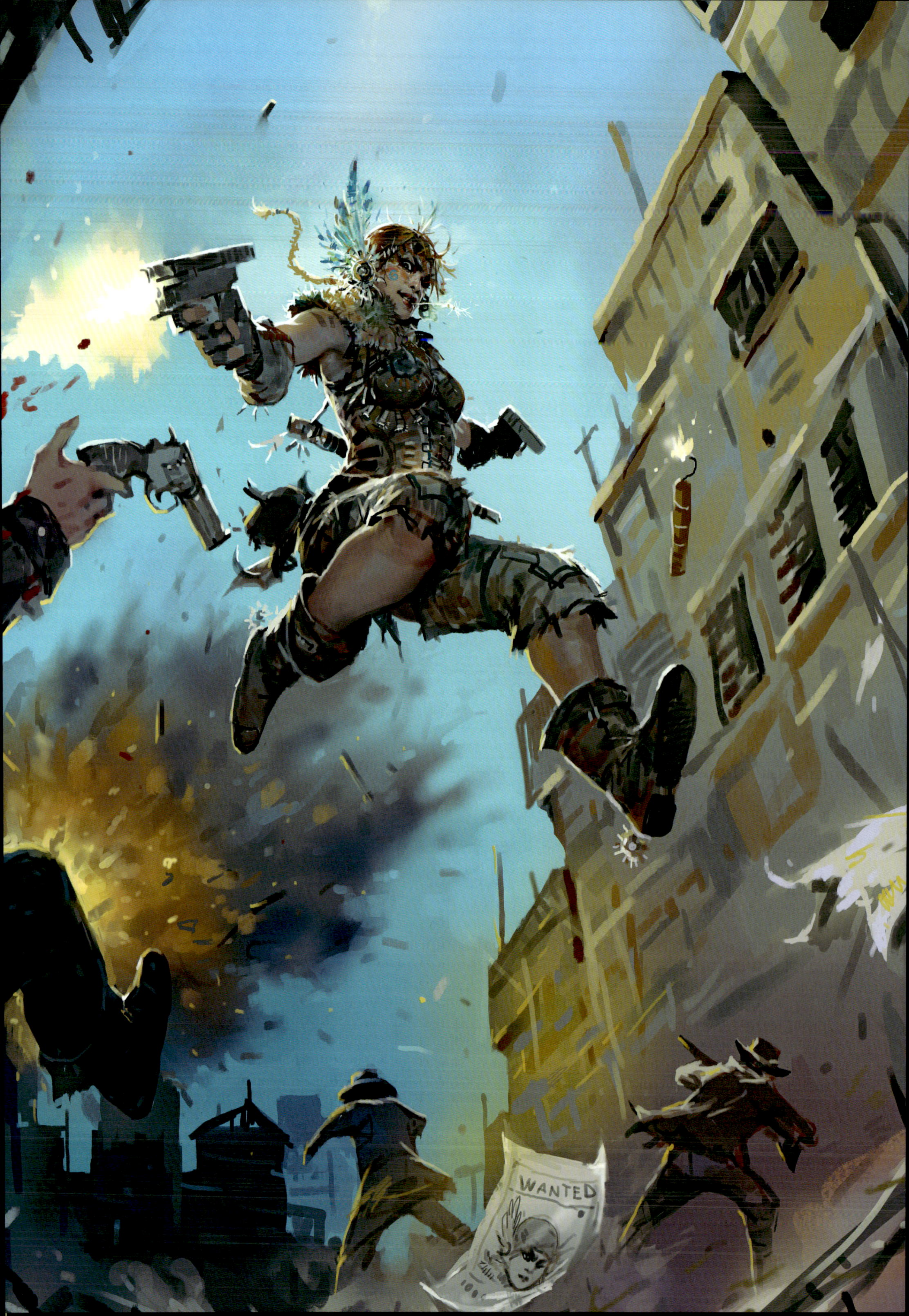

Ladyhawk
Photoshop
Kari Kallio, FINLAND

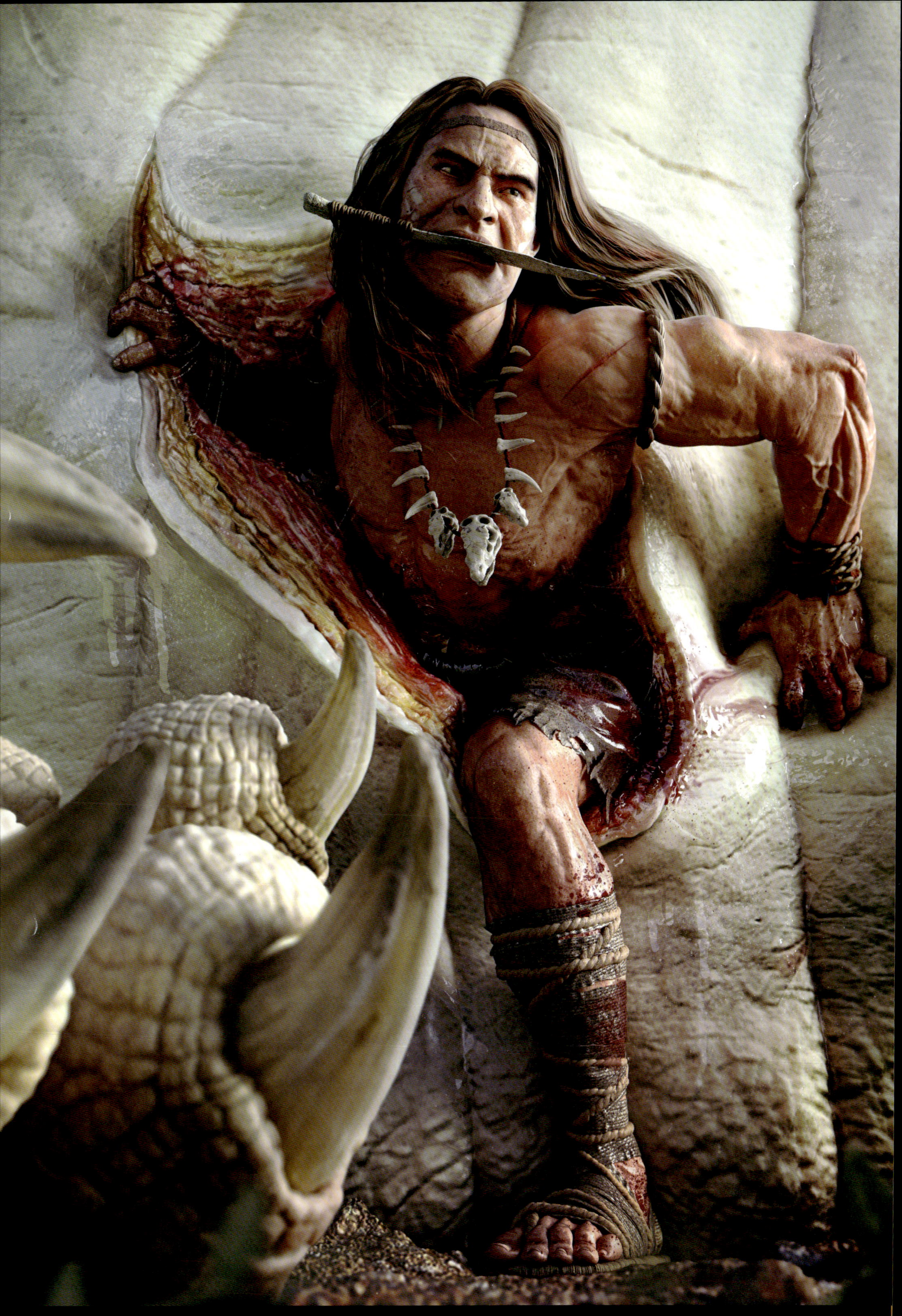

Slayer
3ds Max, ZBrush, V-Ray
Guang Yang, CHINA

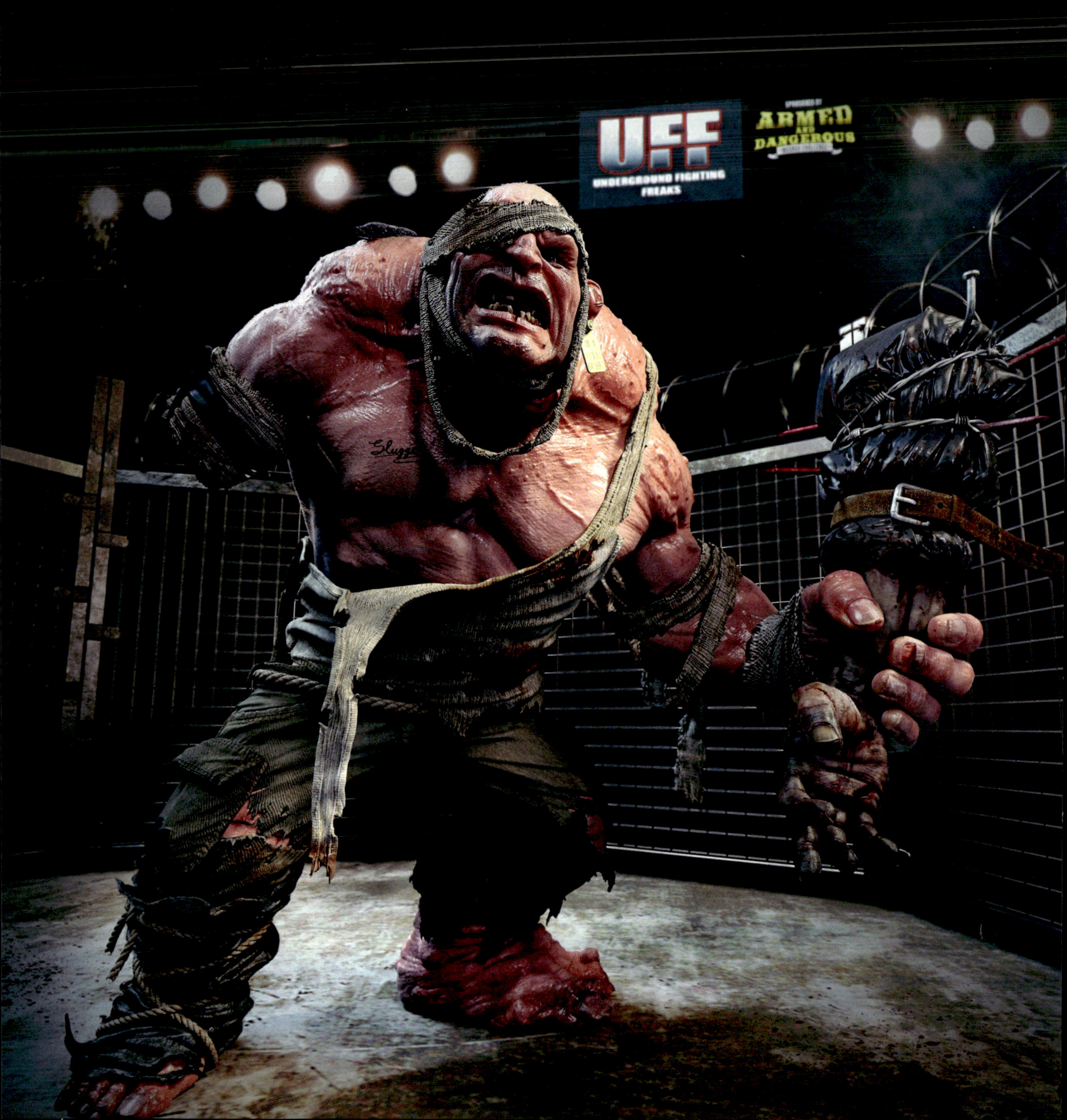

Excellence
Warriors & Conflict

The Slug
3ds Max, Mudbox, Photoshop, V-Ray
Benjamin Kym Davis, GREAT BRITAIN

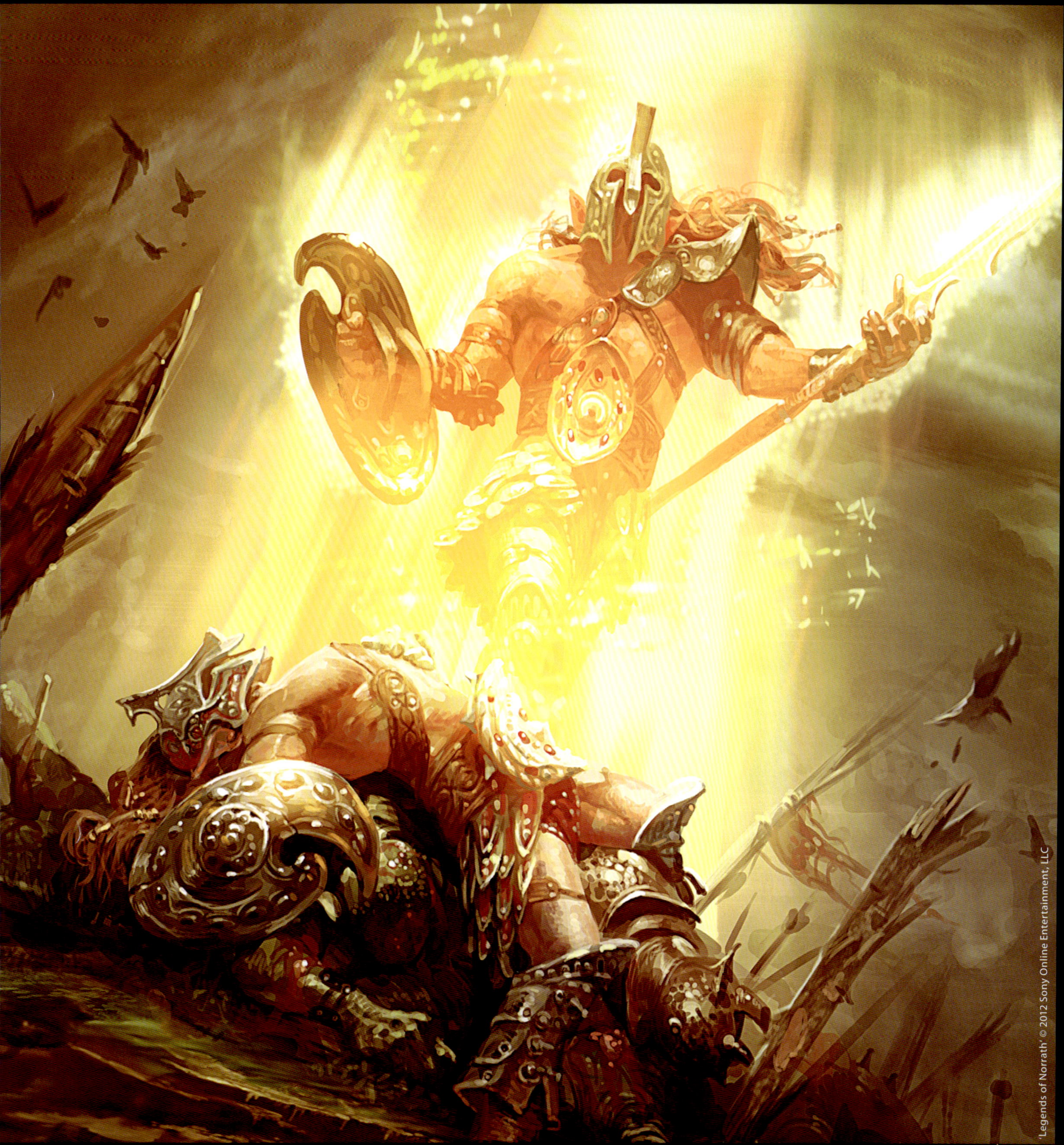

Legends of Norrath: Champion Reborn
Photoshop
Client: Sony Online Entertainment, LLC
Ryan Barger (Art Director: Mark Tuttle), USA

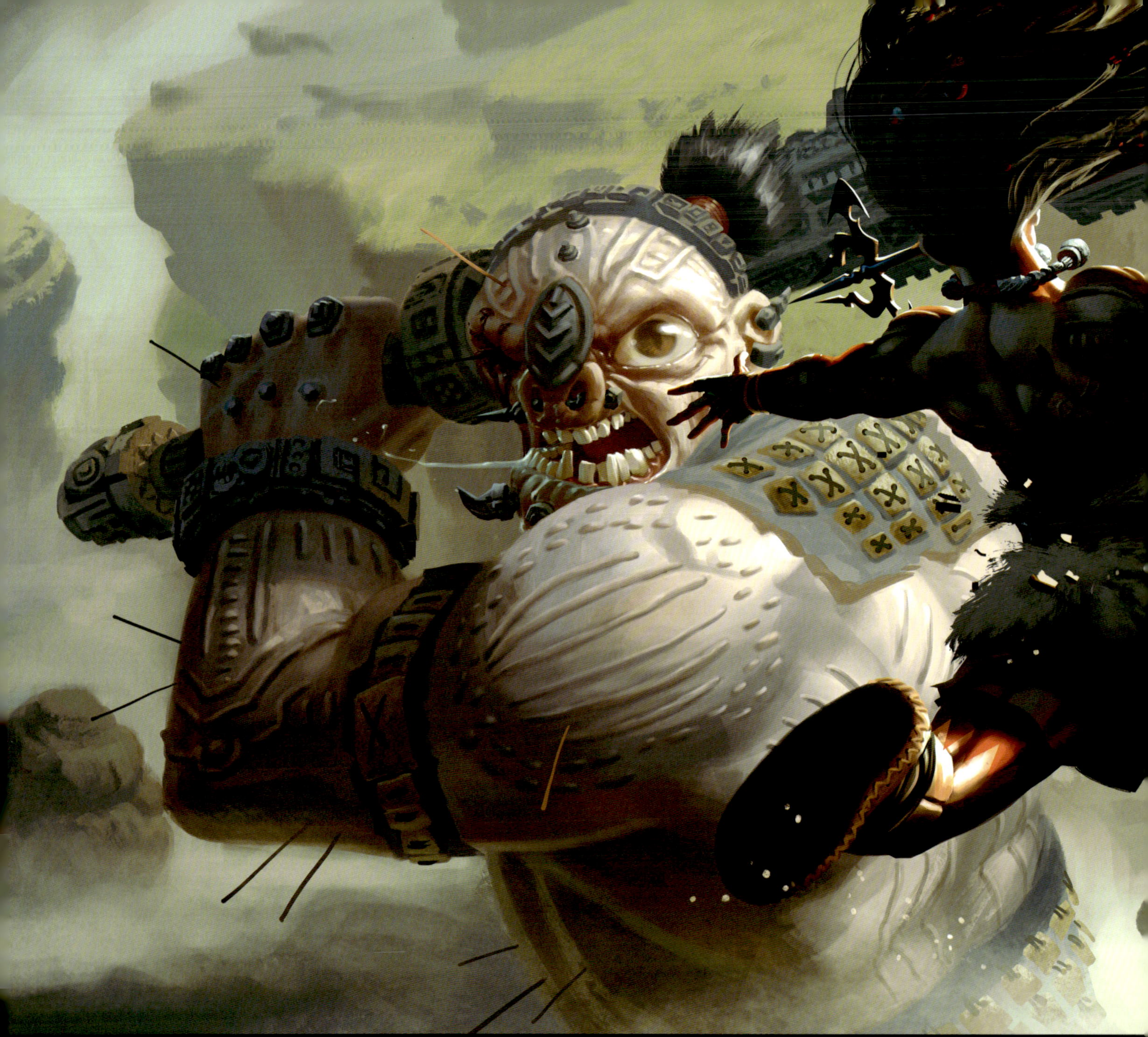

Giant Killer
Photoshop
Tony Weinstock, USA
[above]

Slayer
Photoshop
Frank Hong, CANADA
[right]

Legends of the Cryptids: Emperor
Photoshop
Client: Applibot, Inc.
Ivan Kashubo, RUSSIA
[center]

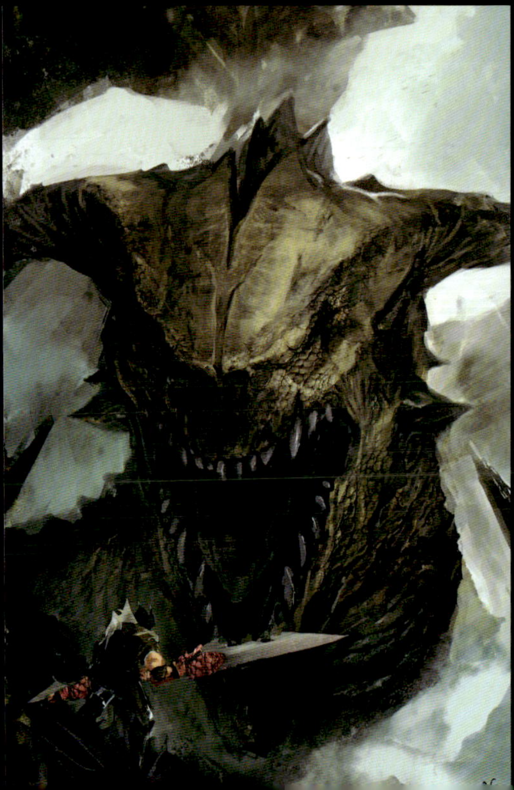

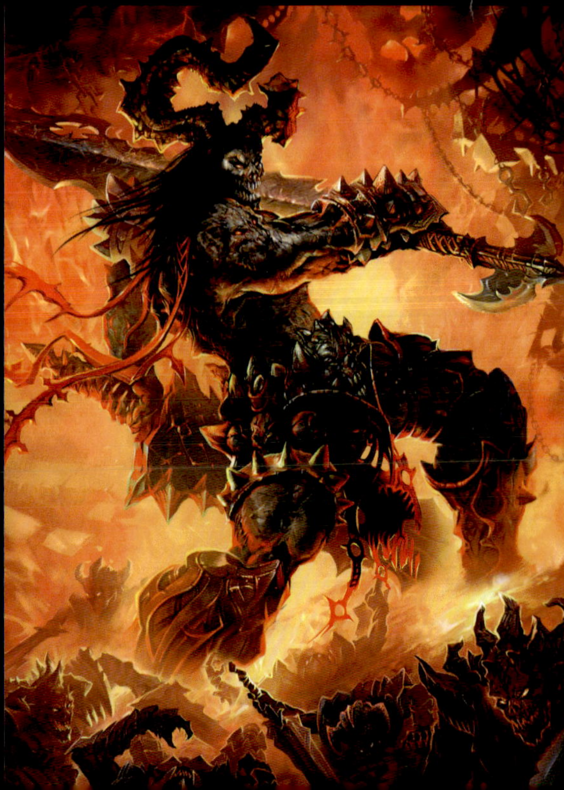

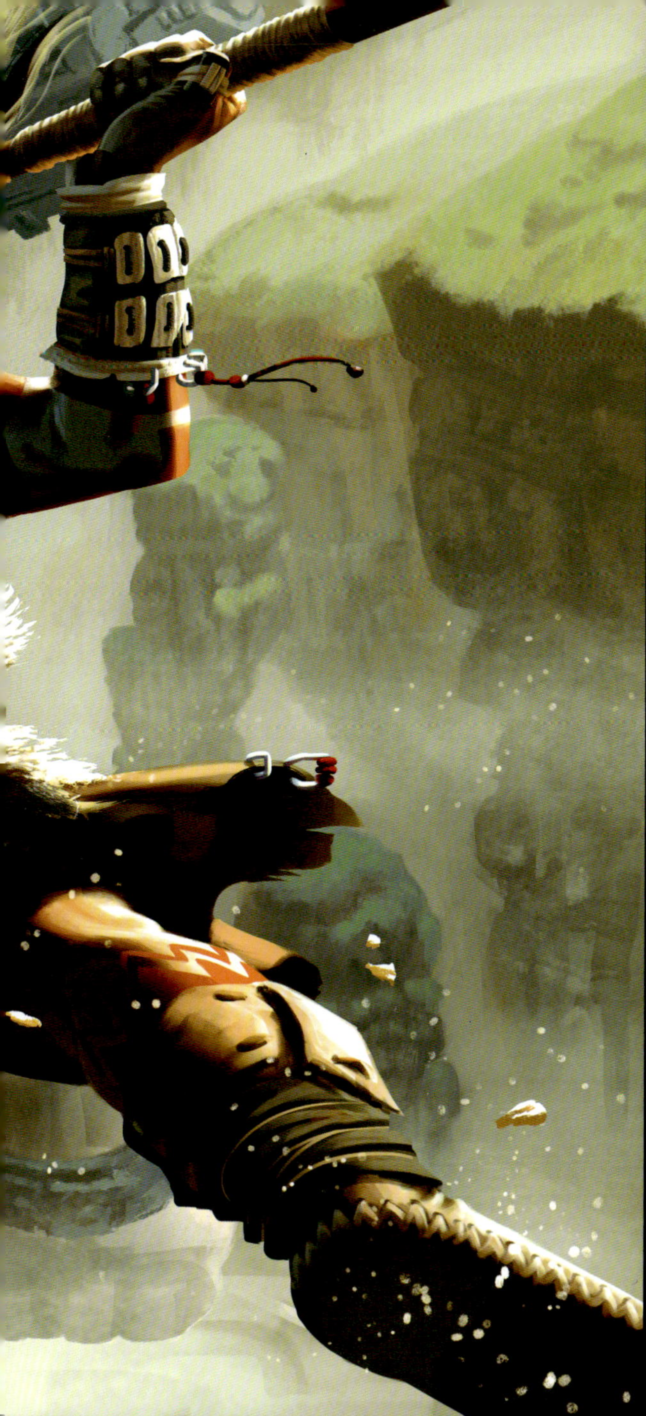

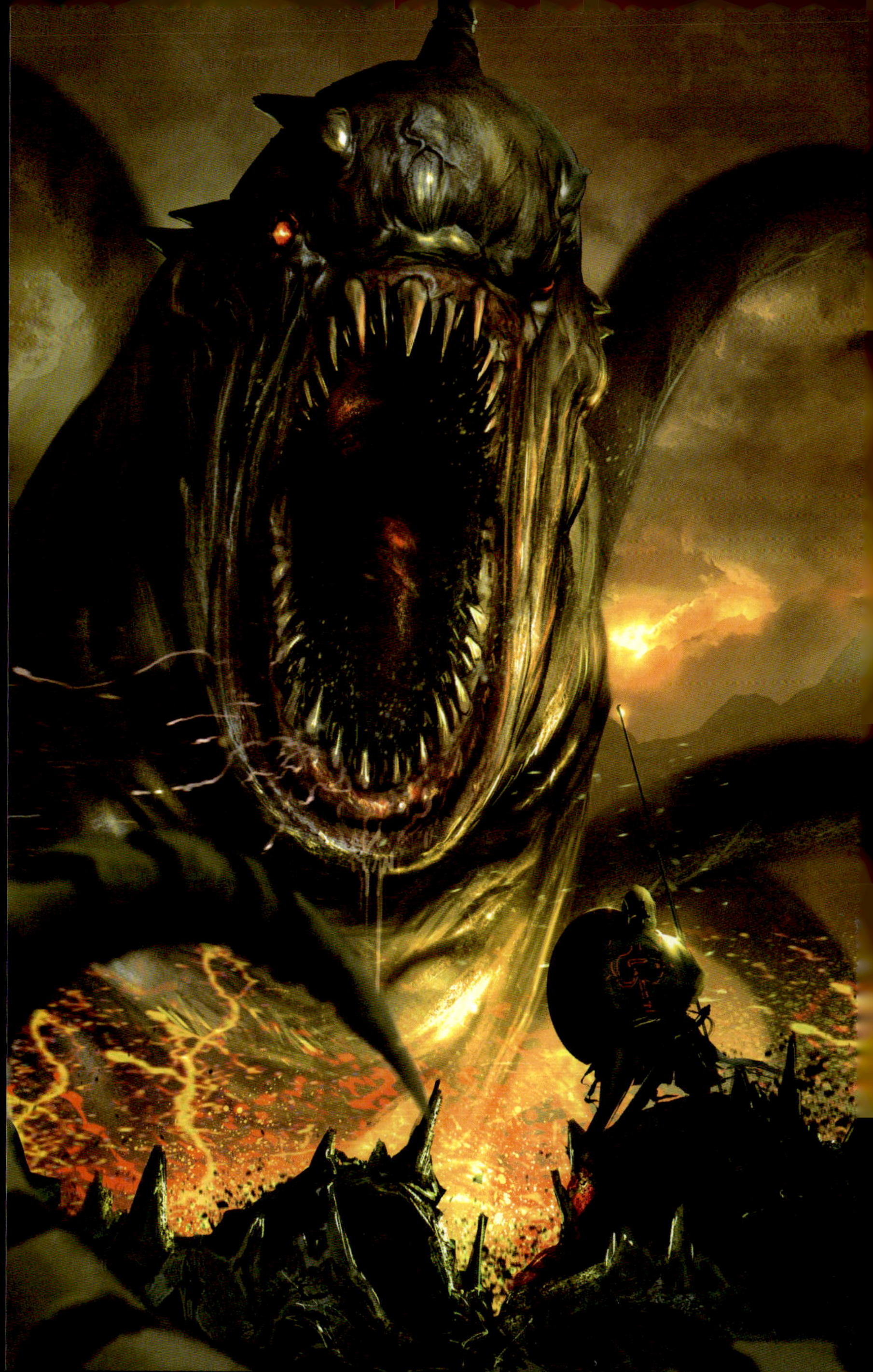

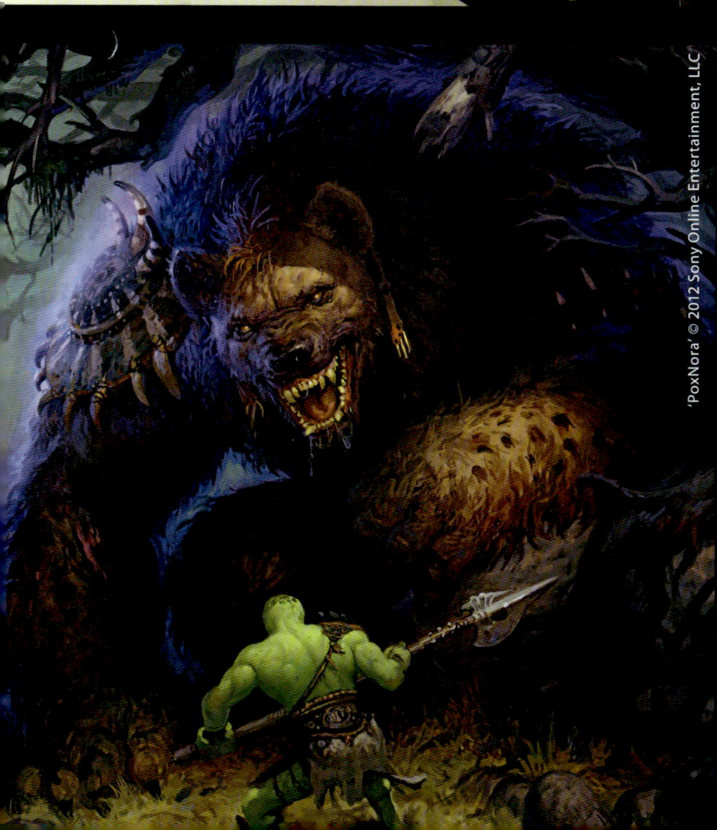

The Moglar
Photoshop
David Lecossu, FRANCE
[above]

PoxNora: Hyaenid Spiritspeaker
Photoshop
Client: Sony Online Entertainment, LLC
Jakub Kasper (Art Director: Anthony Lopes), POLAND
[left]

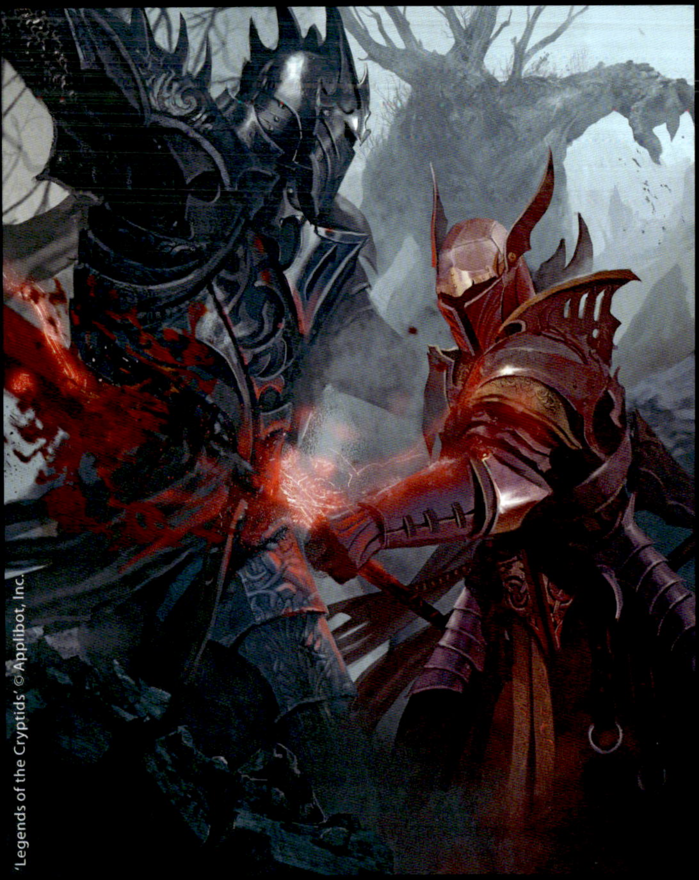

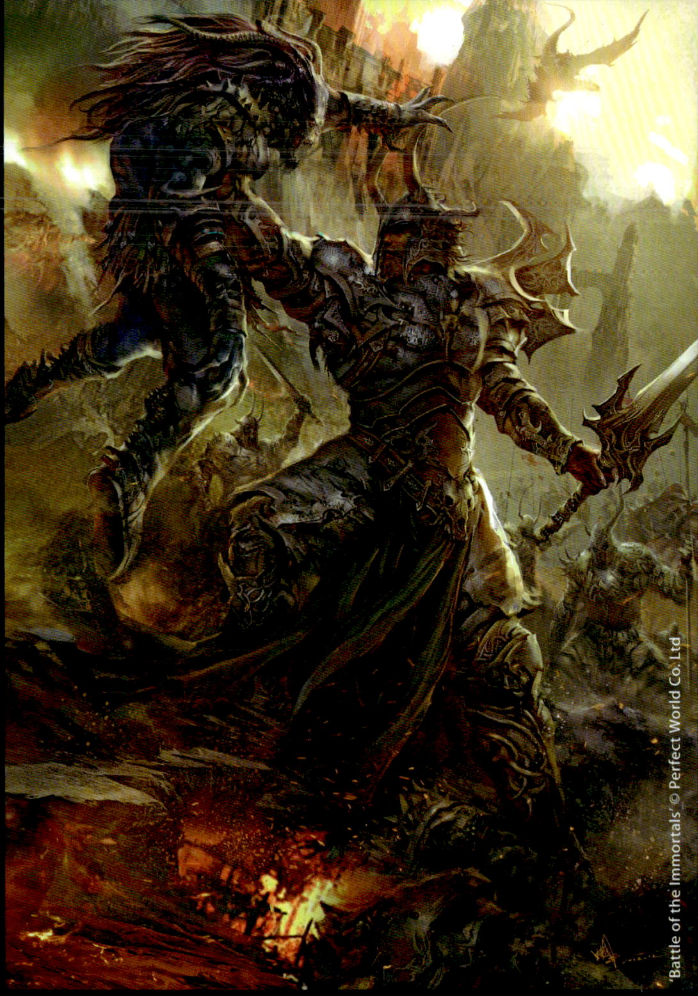

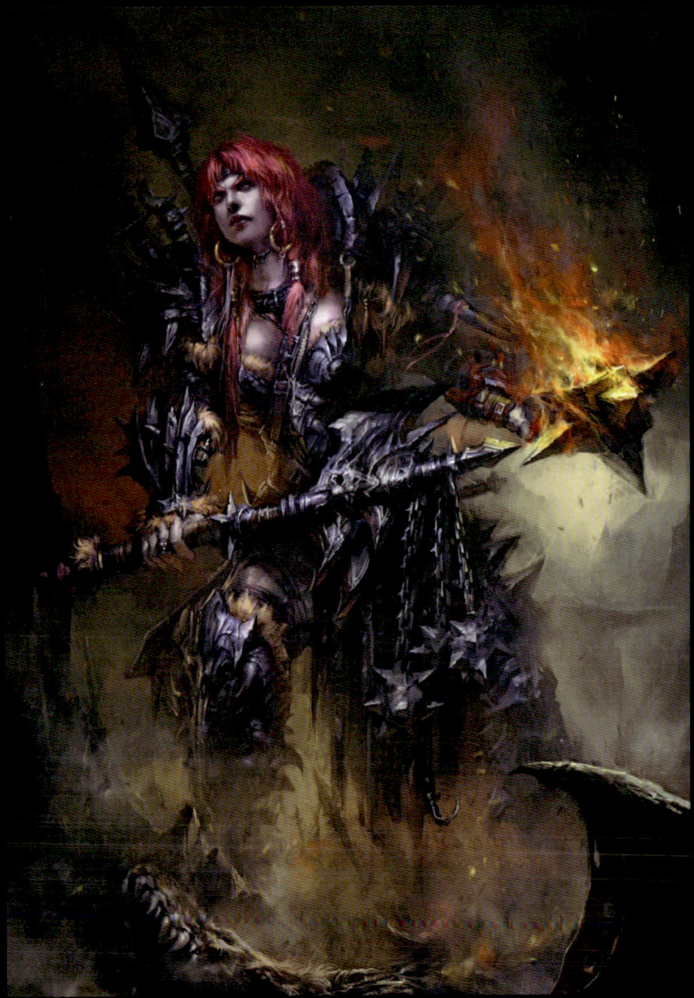

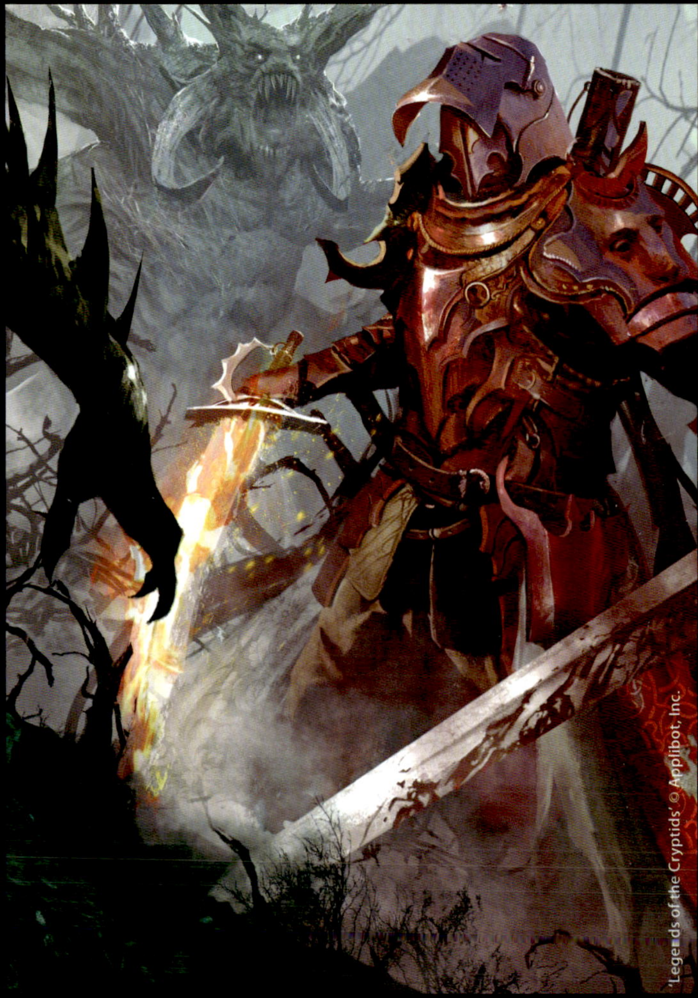

Legends of the Cryptids:
The Crimson Striker
Photoshop
Client: Applibot, Inc.
Diego de Almeida, BRAZIL
[top]

Fiir
Photoshop
Qiu jian Yuan, CHINA
[above]

Battle of the Immortals:
The Battle of Champions
Photoshop
Client: Perfect World Co. Ltd.
Feng Guo, CHINA
[top]

Legends of the Cryptids:
The Crimson Striker (Advanced)
Photoshop
Client: Applibot, Inc.
Diego de Almeida, BRAZIL
[above]

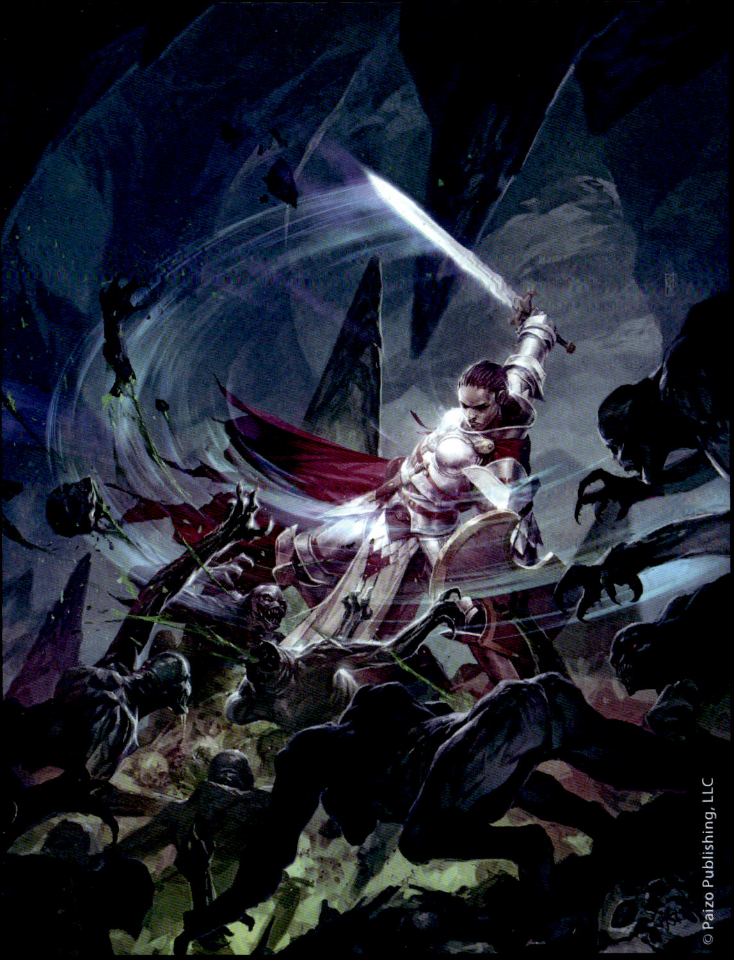

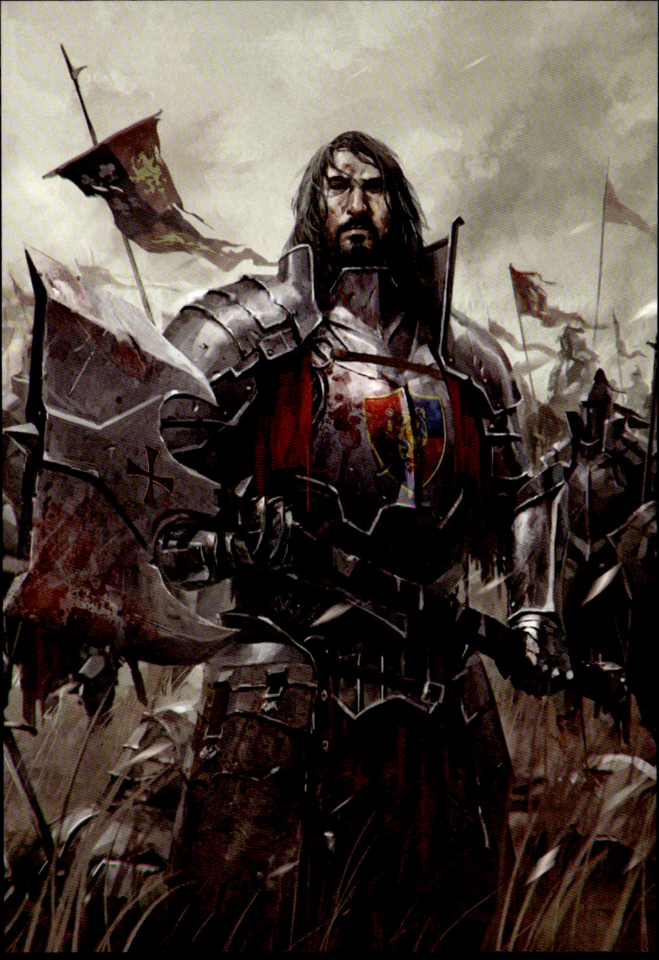

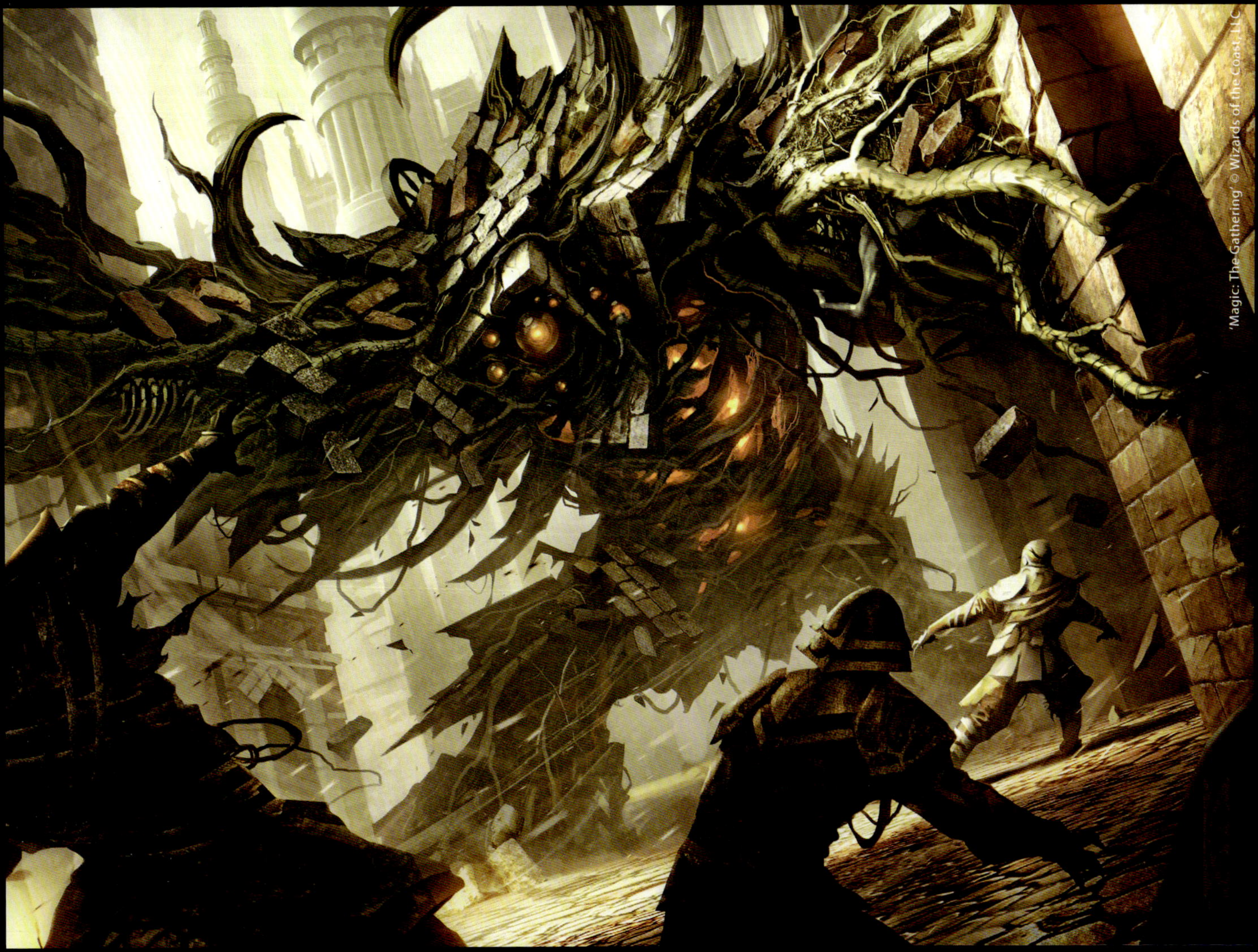

Champions of Purity
Photoshop
Client: Paizo Publishing, LLC
Michal Ivan, SLOVAKIA
[top]

Richard the Lionheart
Photoshop
Bagus Hutomo, IFS Jakarta, INDONESIA
[top right]

Magic: The Gathering (Rubblehulk)
Photoshop
Client: Wizards of the Coast, LLC
Raymond Swanland (Art Director: Jeremy Jarvis), USA
[above]

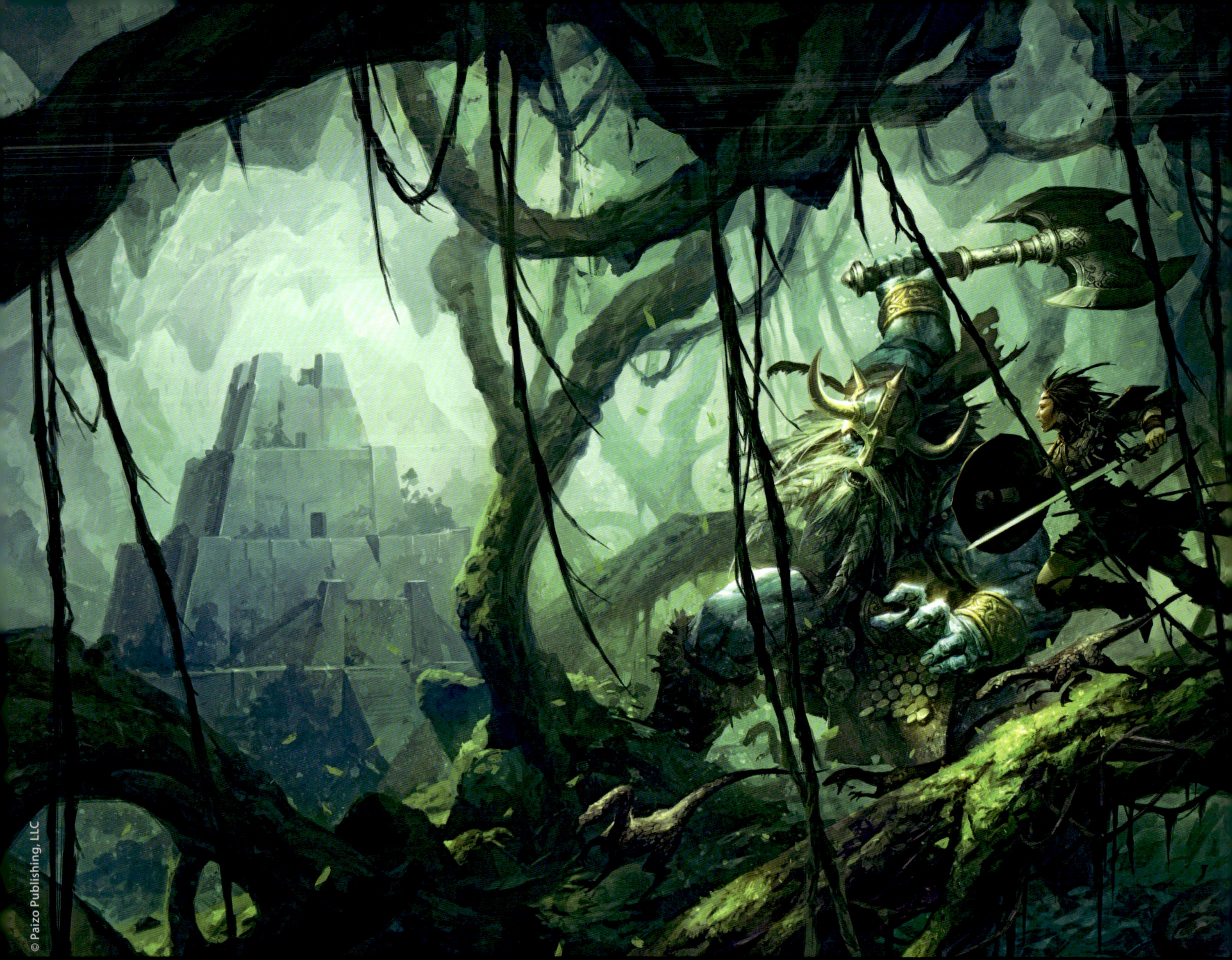

Called to Darkness
Photoshop
Client: Paizo Publishing, LLC
Michal Ivan, SLOVAKIA
[above]

Civil Wars Skeletons: Someone Should Tell Them...
Painter, Photoshop
Aaron Riley, USA
[right]

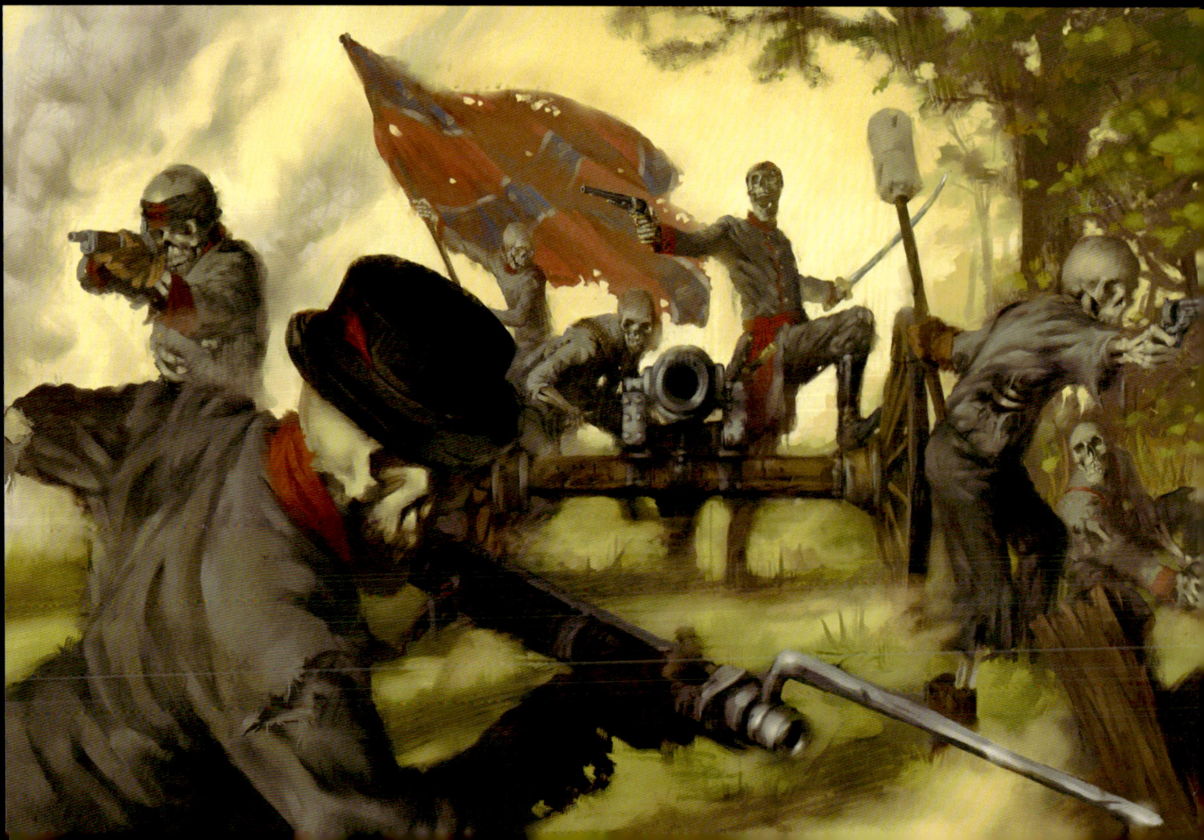

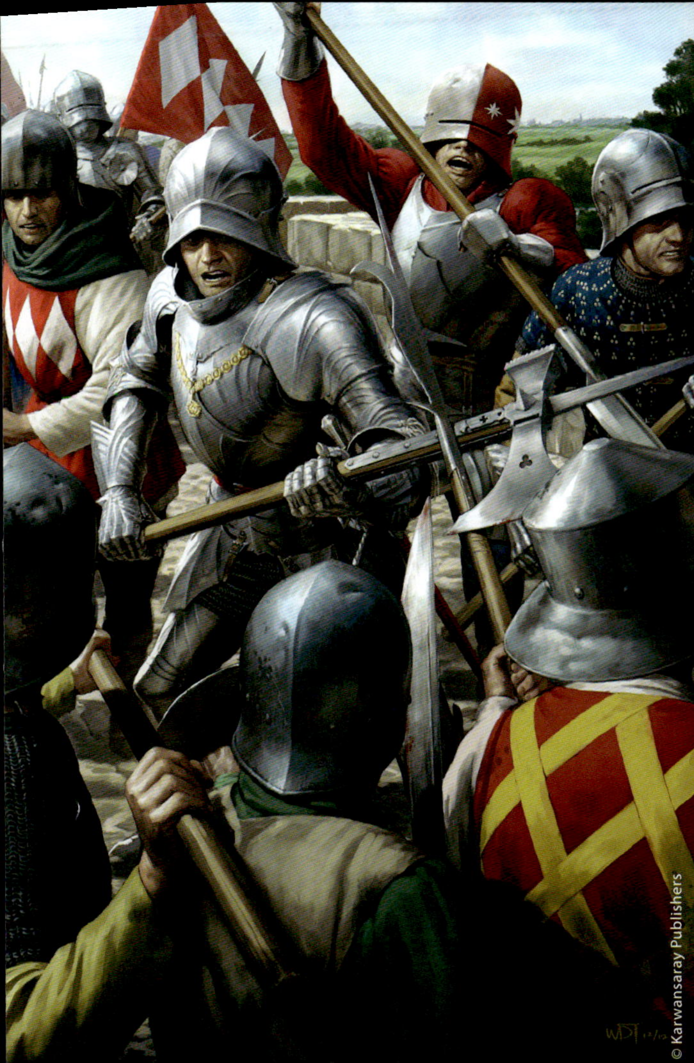

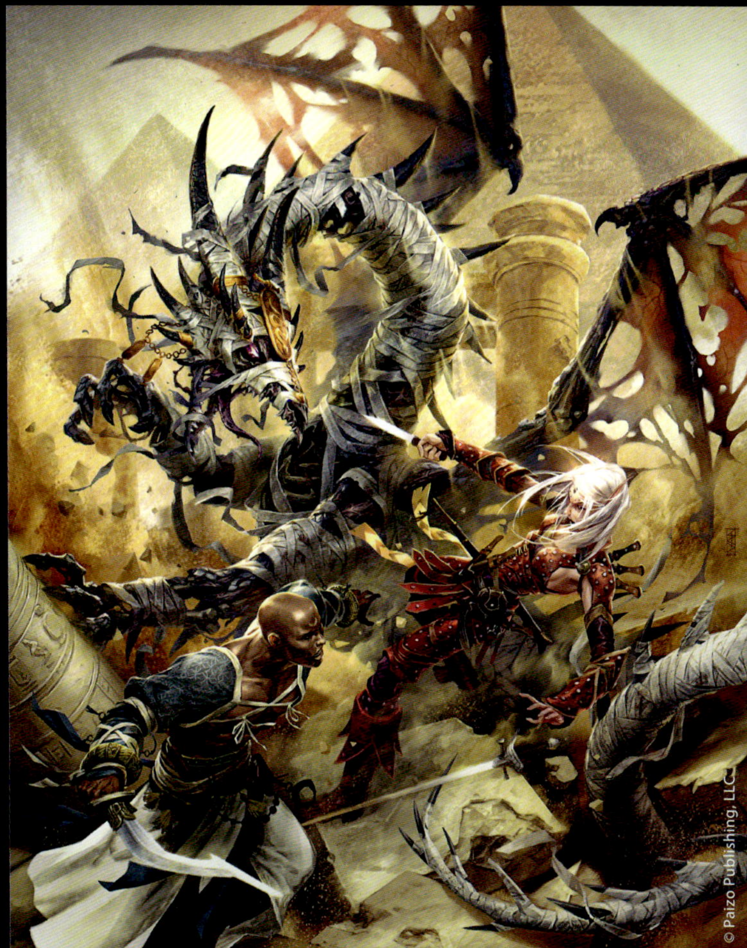

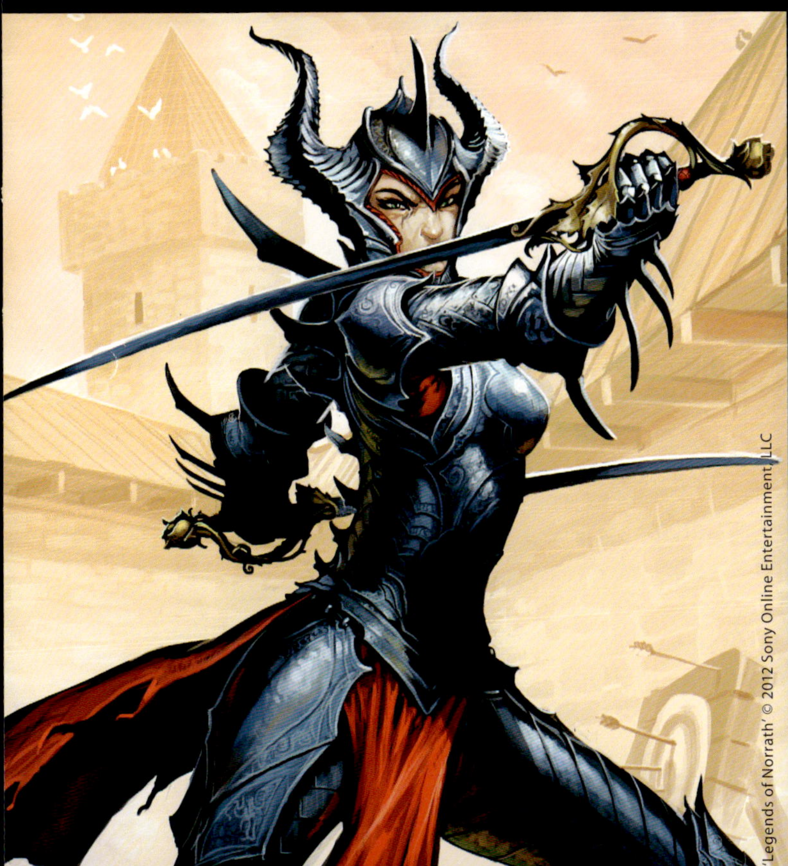

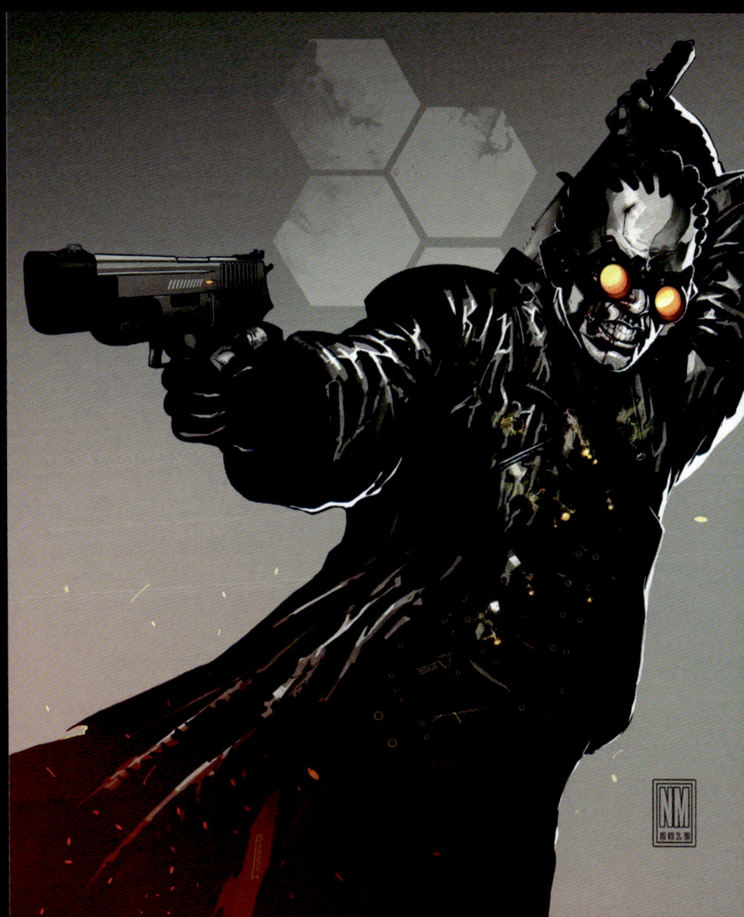

Battle Of Blackheath
Photoshop
Client: Medieval Warfare Magazine
Darren Tan, SINGAPORE
[top]

Legends of Norrath: Form of the Fighter
Photoshop
Client: Sony Online Entertainment, LLC
Ben Wootten (Art Director: Mark Tuttle), NEW ZEALAND
[above]

Lost Kingdoms
Photoshop
Client: Paizo Publishing, LLC
Michal Ivan, SLOVAKIA
[top]

End All
Photoshop
Neeraj Menon, INDIA
[above]

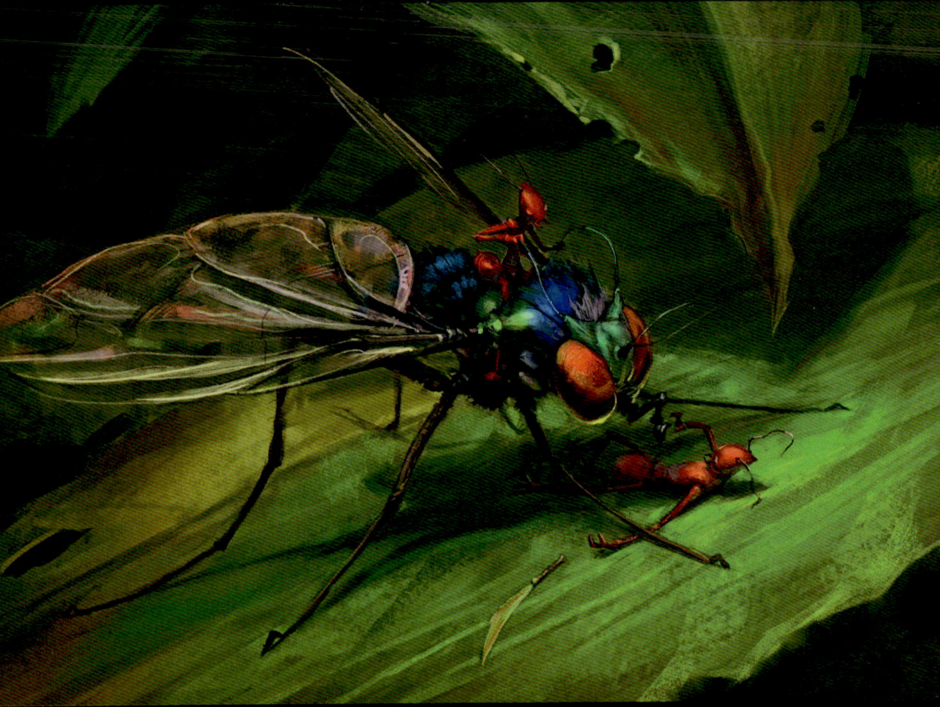

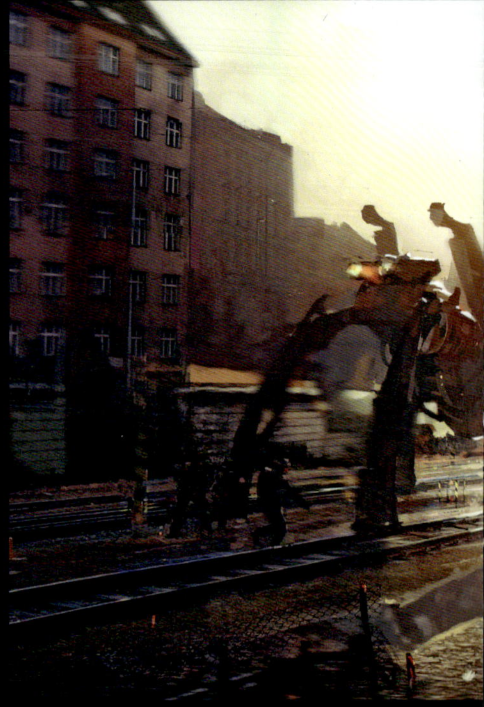

Antithesis
Photoshop
Lane Brown, USA
[above]

Enemy Mech Ahead!
Photoshop
Tomas Honz, CZECH REPUBLIC
[above center]

Trow's Pass
Photoshop
Alexandru Negoita, ROMANIA
[above far right]

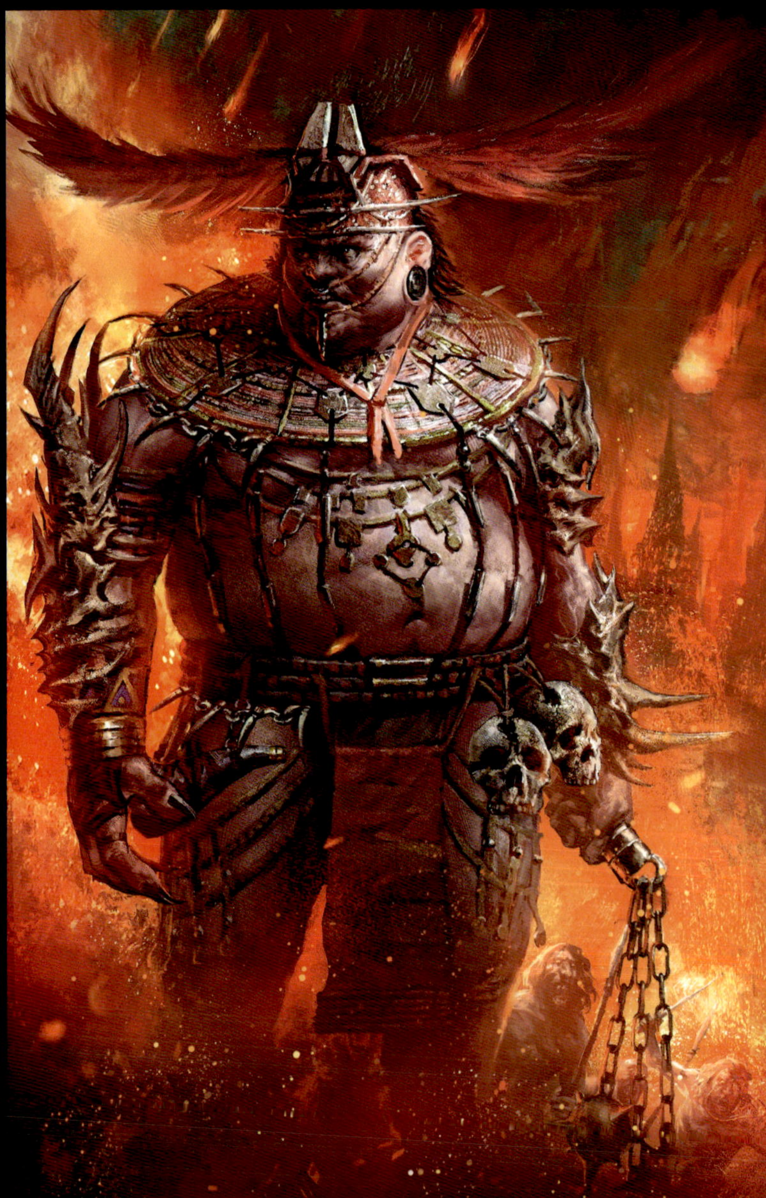

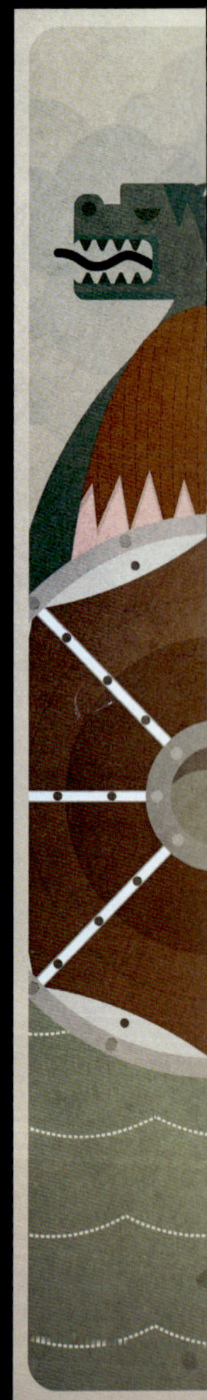

Disaster Strikes
Photoshop
Wanglin Fang, CHINA

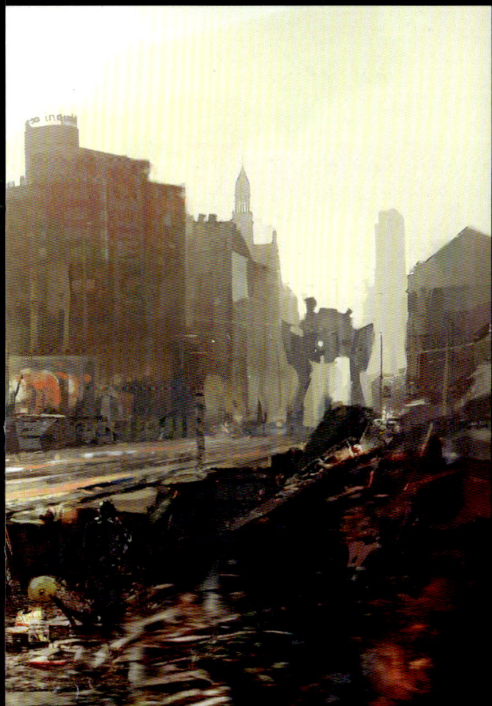

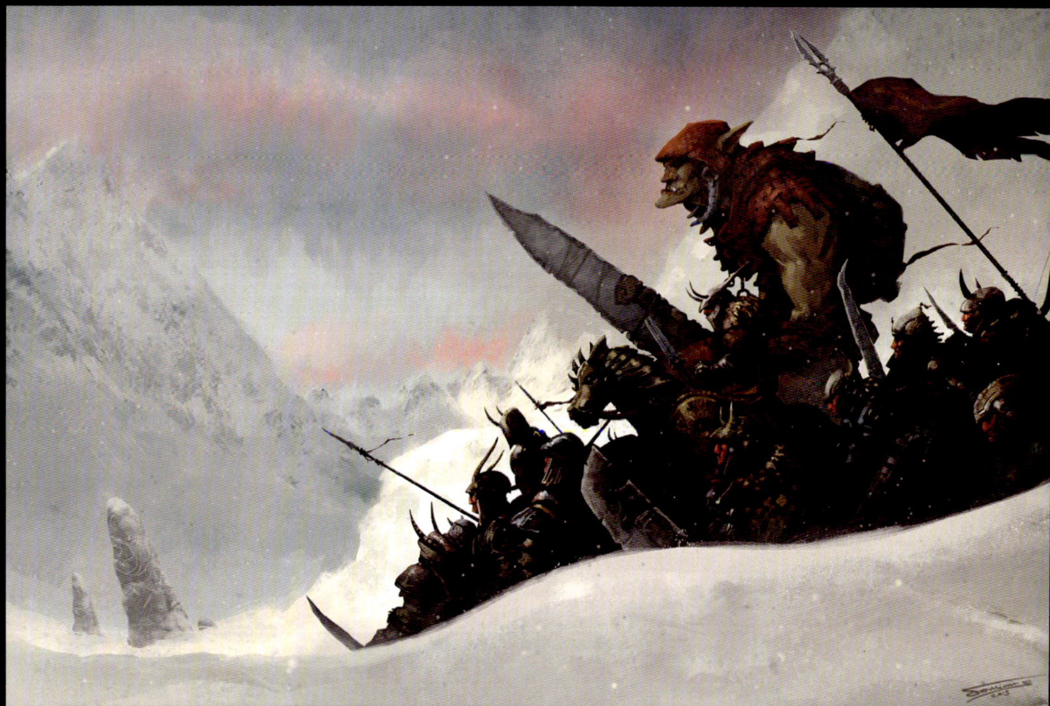

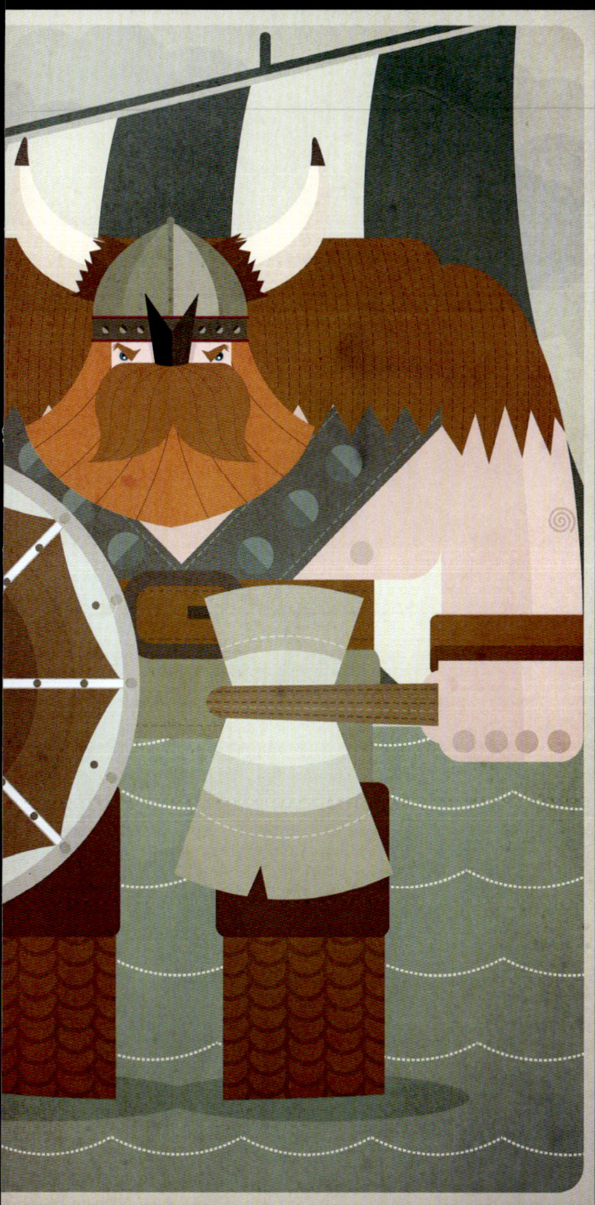

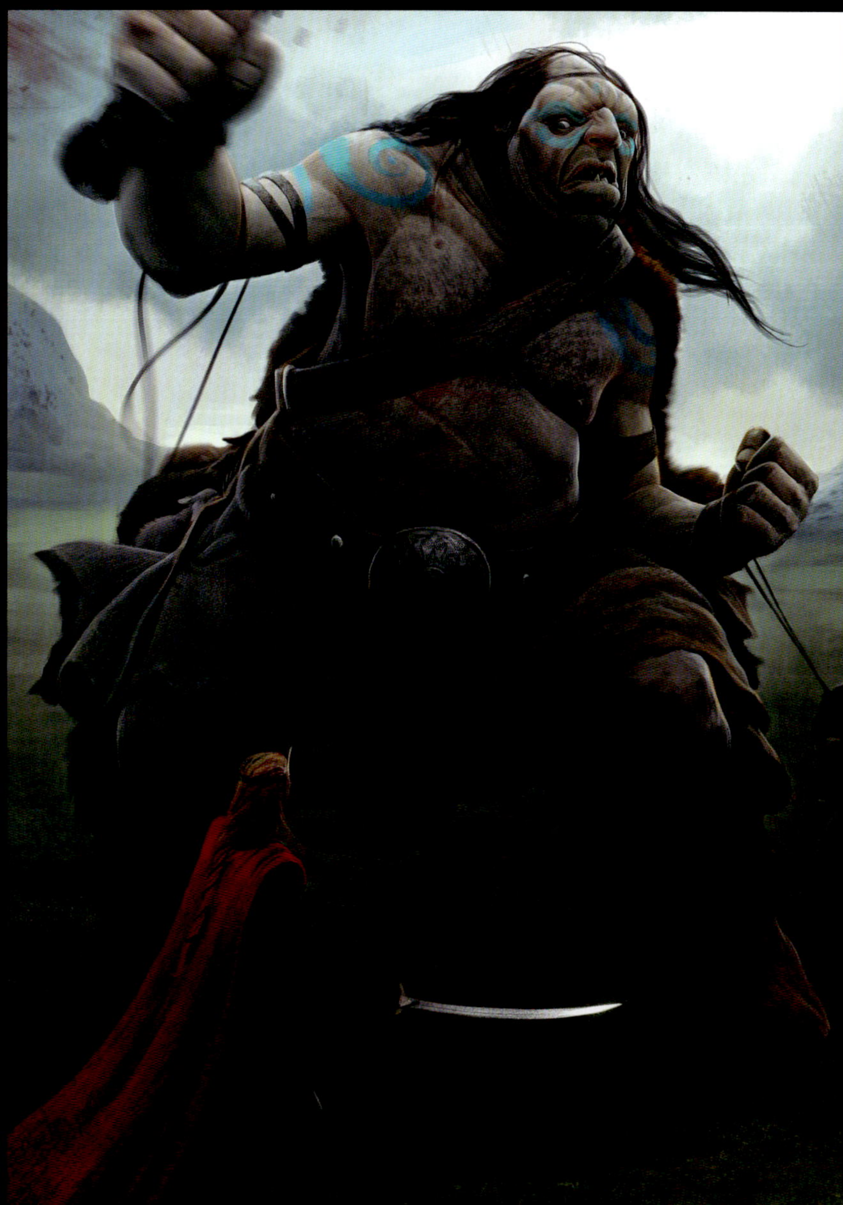

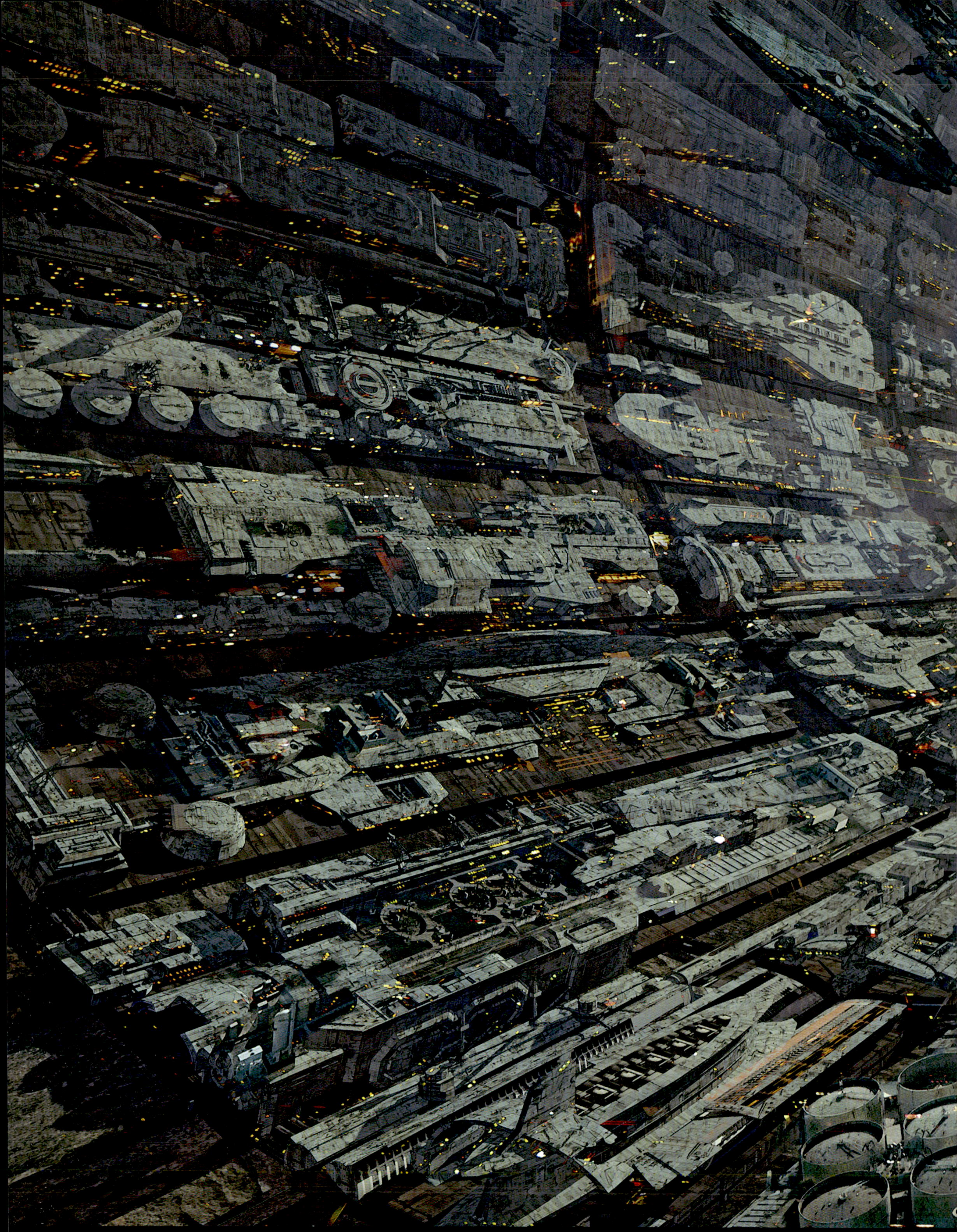

The Unincorporated Future
SketchUp, Photoshop
Client: TOR Books

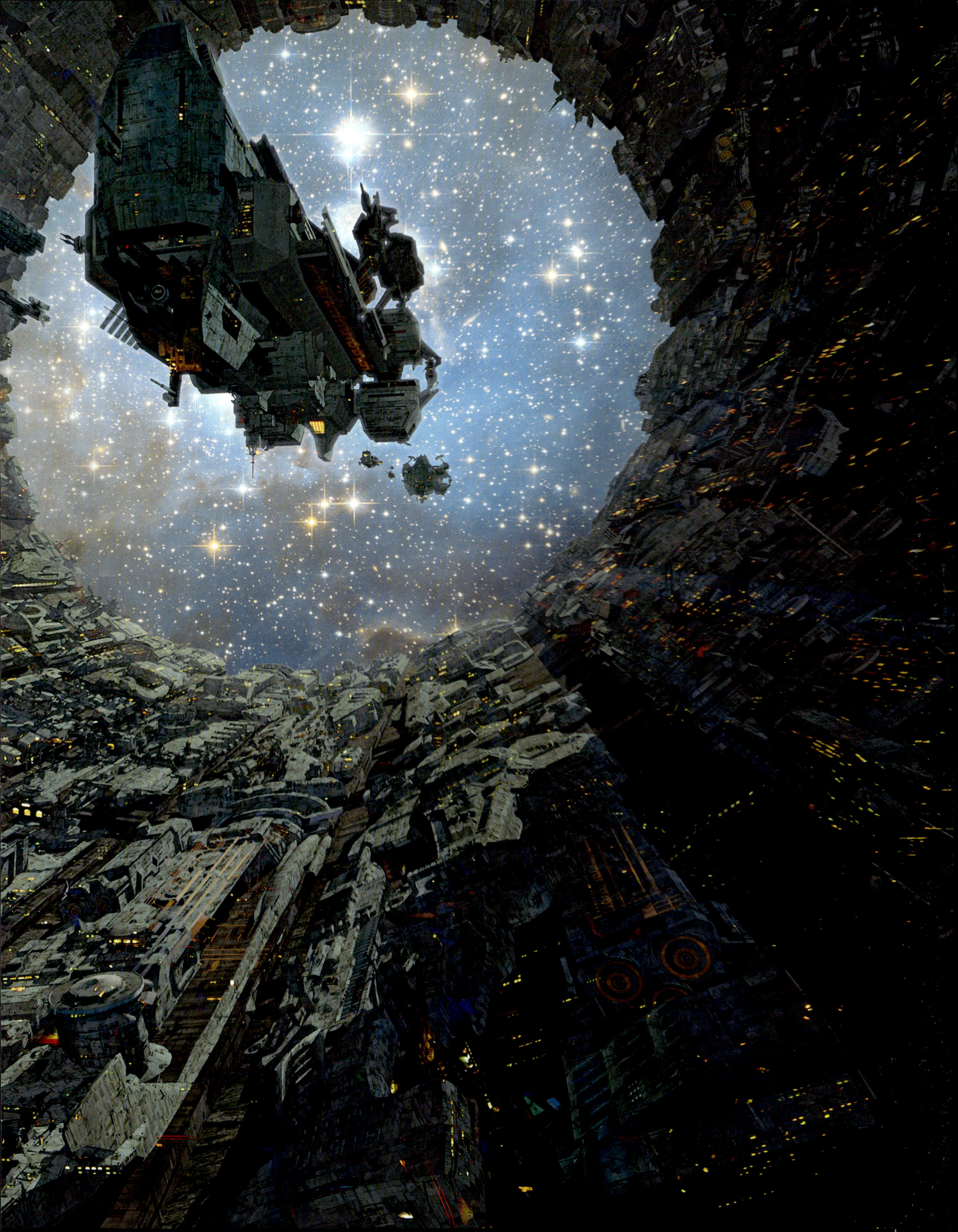

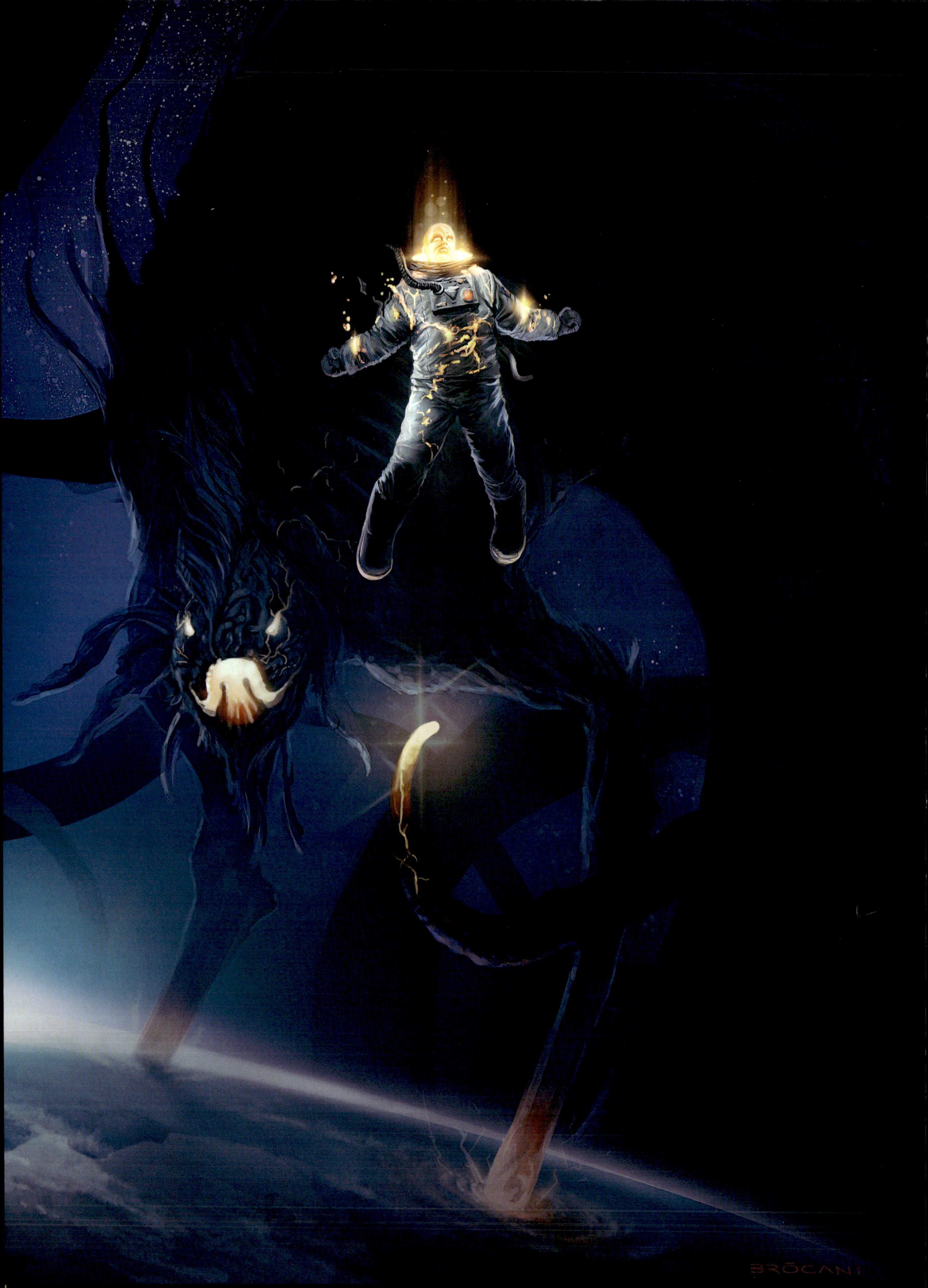

The Leviathan
Photoshop
Giuliano Brocani, Keller Adv, ITALY

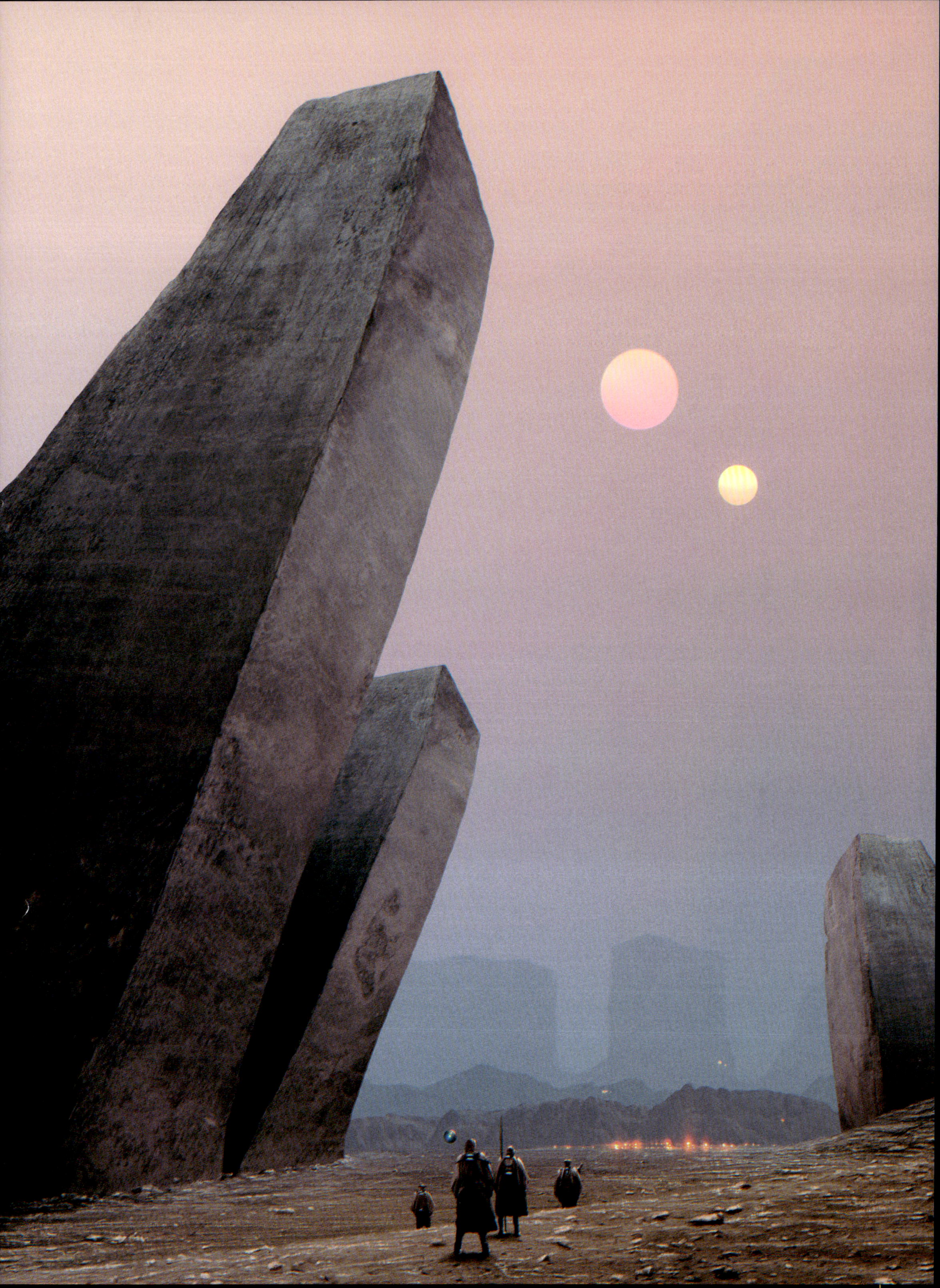

Eldion Passageway
Photoshop
Anthony Scime, USA

Excellence
Science Fiction

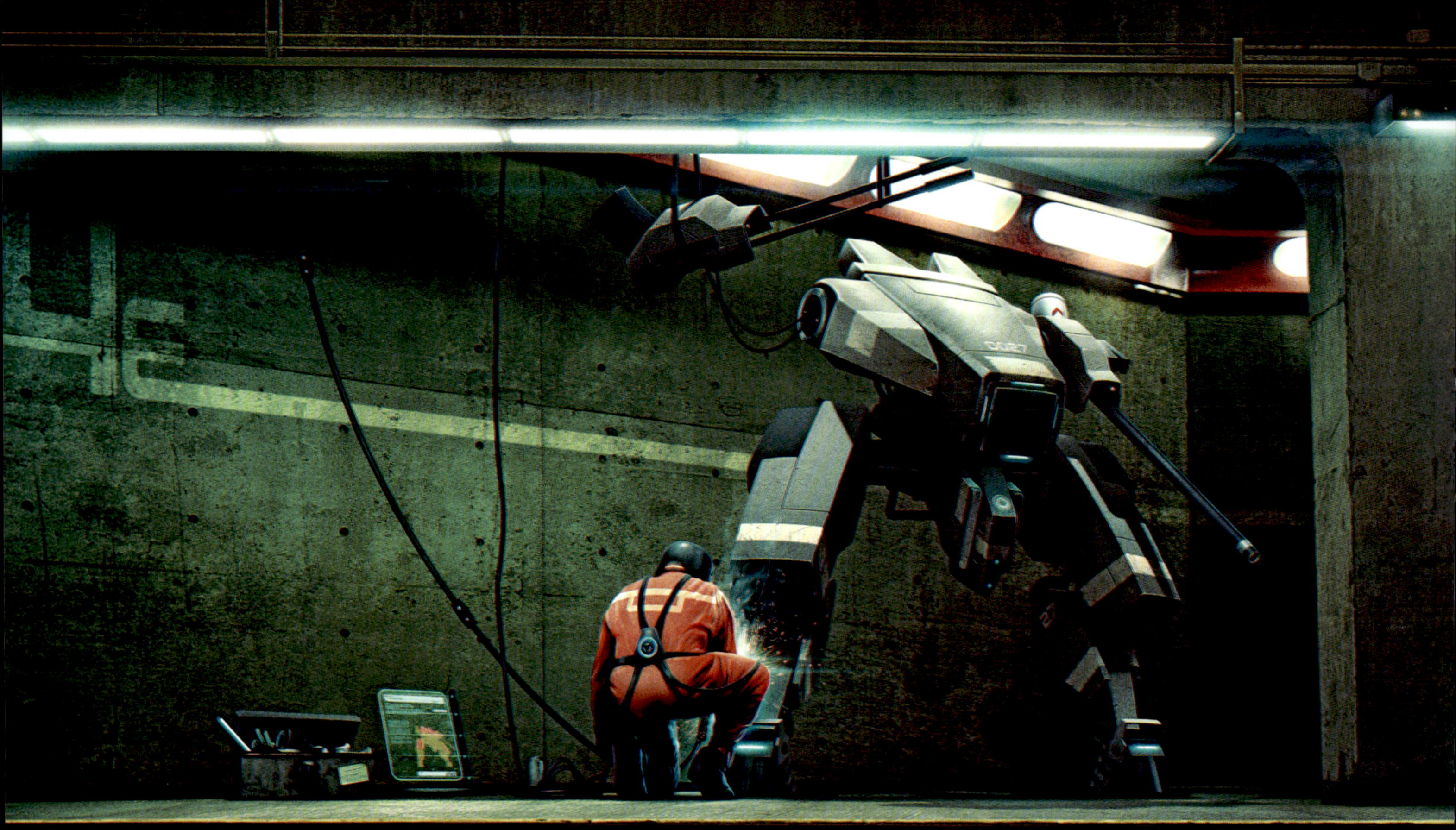

Bunker Level 4E
Photoshop
Anthony Scime, USA
[above]

The Burn Zone
Photoshop
Client: Penguin ROC
Dave Seeley
(Art Director: Patrick Kang), USA
[right]

Dead Space Girl
Photoshop
Sergio Diaz, ARGENTINA
[center]

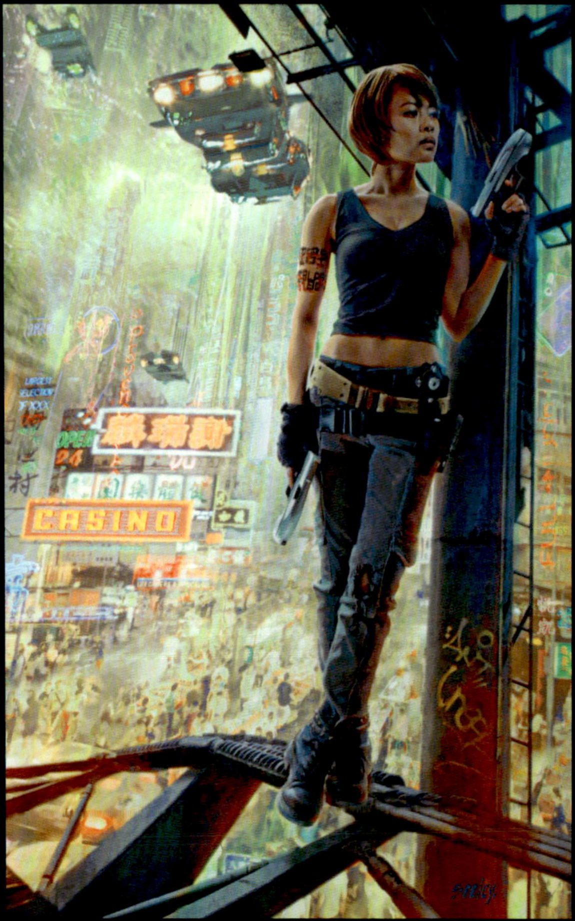

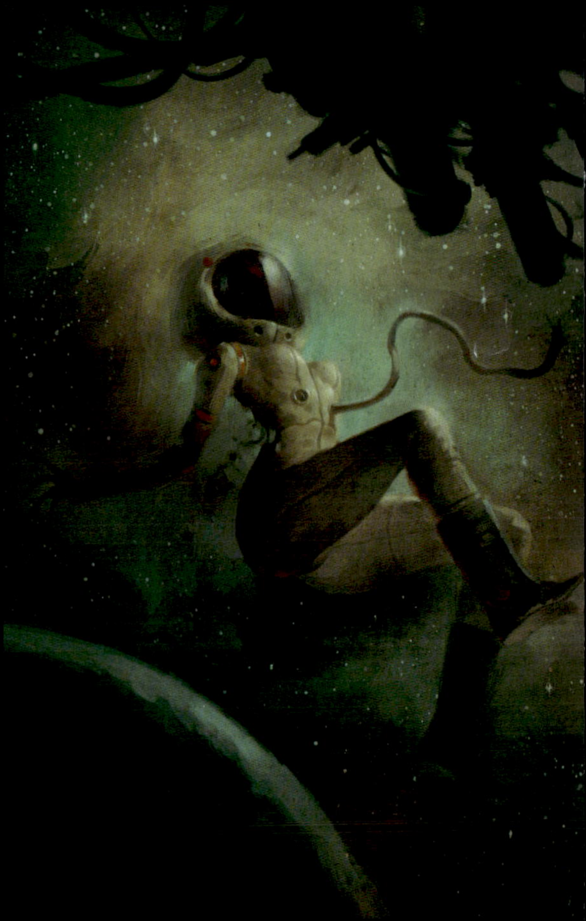

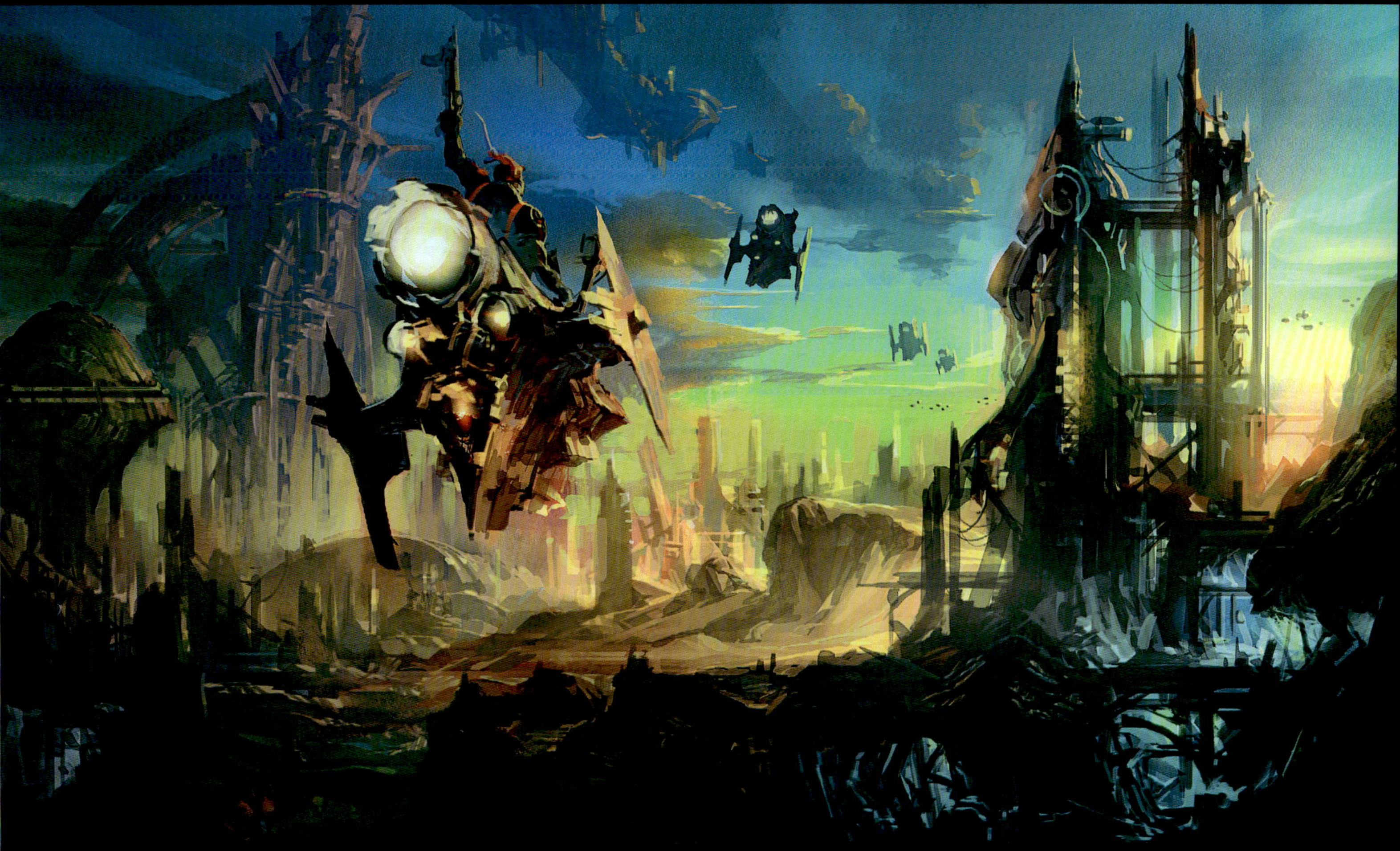

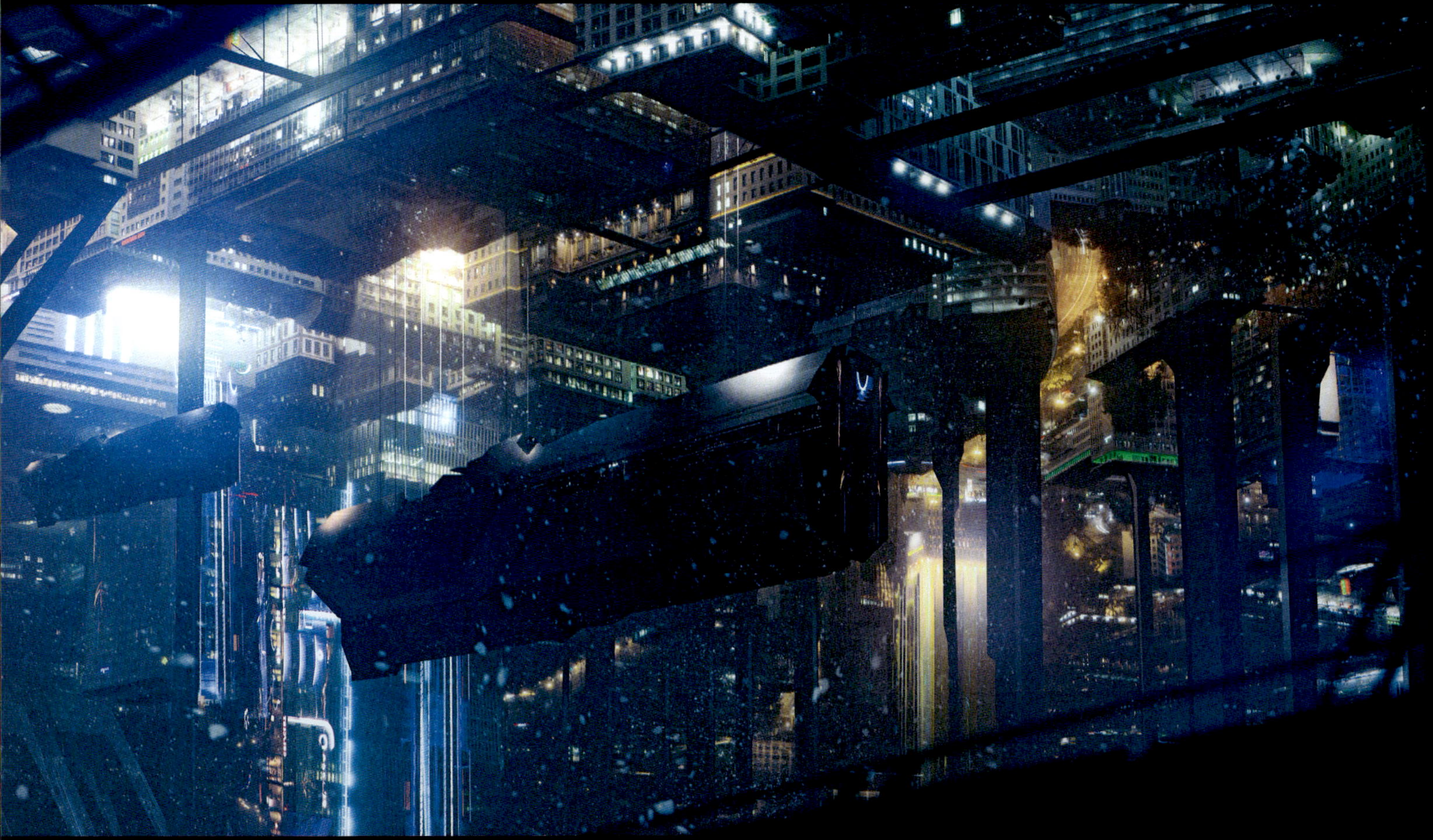

Sending Off
Photoshop, Painter
Kim Hyeong-seong, SOUTH KOREA
[top]

Another Winter
Photoshop
Bastien Grivet, FRANCE
[above]

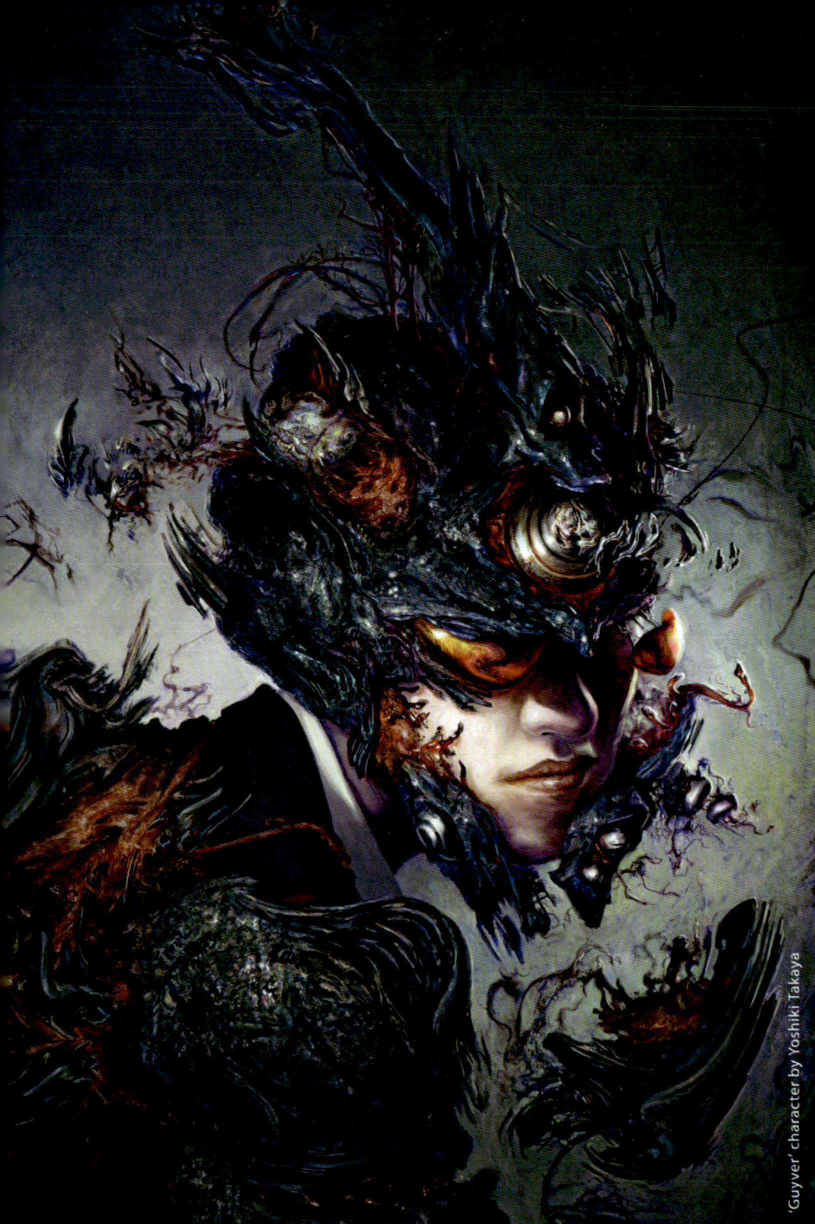

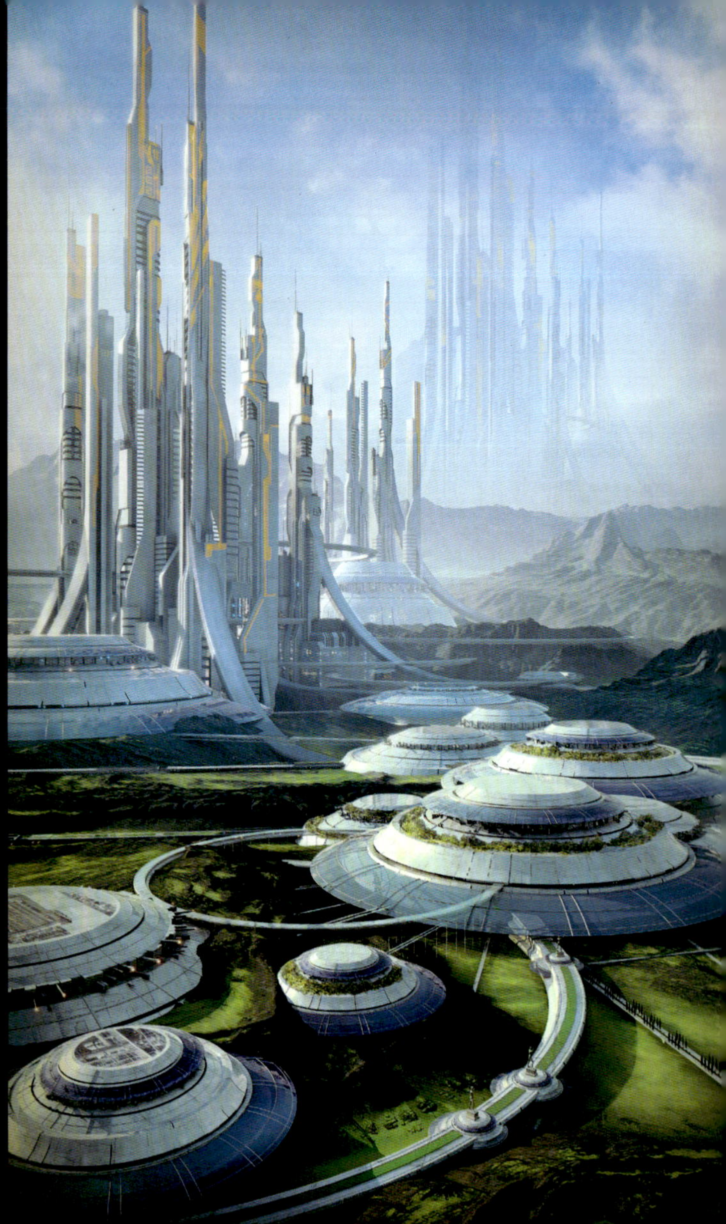

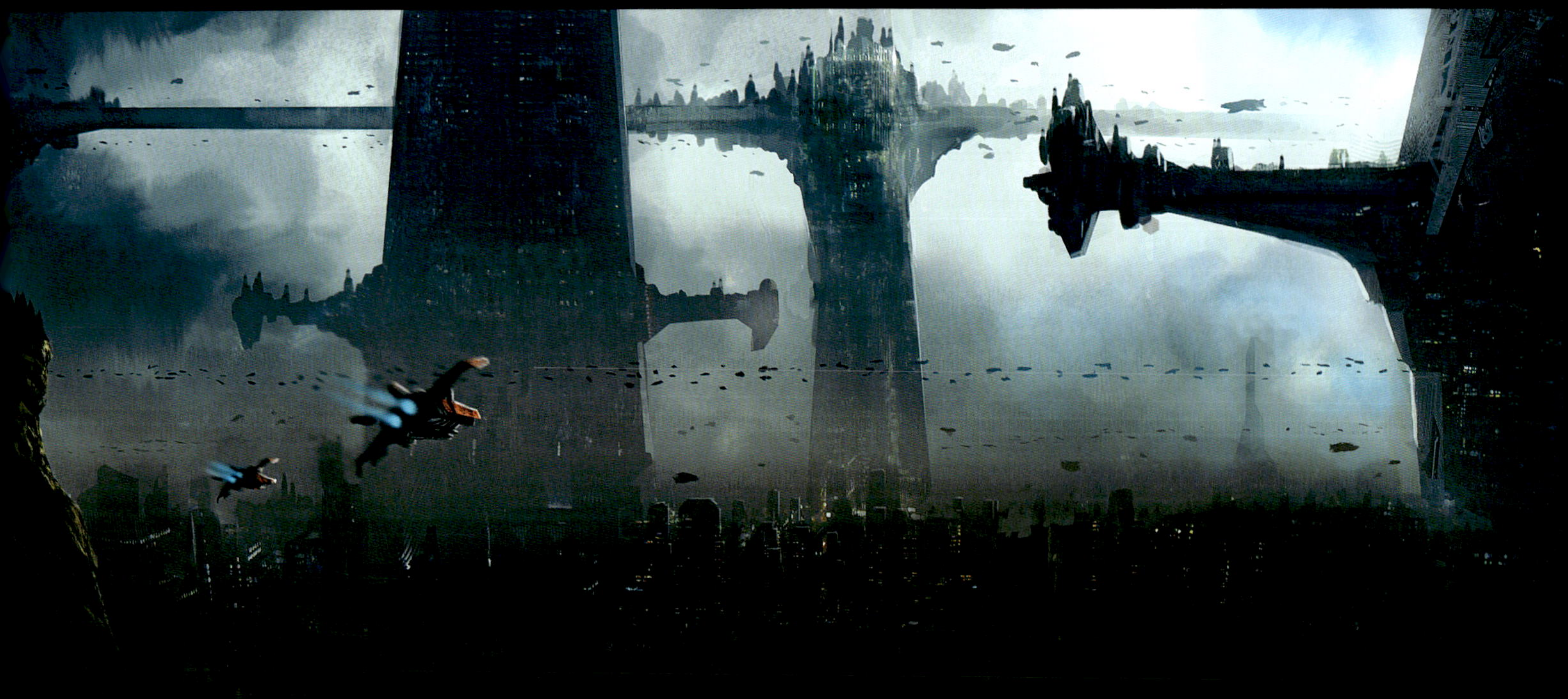

Guyver Portrait
Photoshop
Aldo Katayanagi, USA
[top left]

The 12th Colony
3ds Max, Photoshop
Stefan Morrell, NEW ZEALAND
[top right]

Giant City
Photoshop
Matthieu Rebuffat, FRANCE
[above]

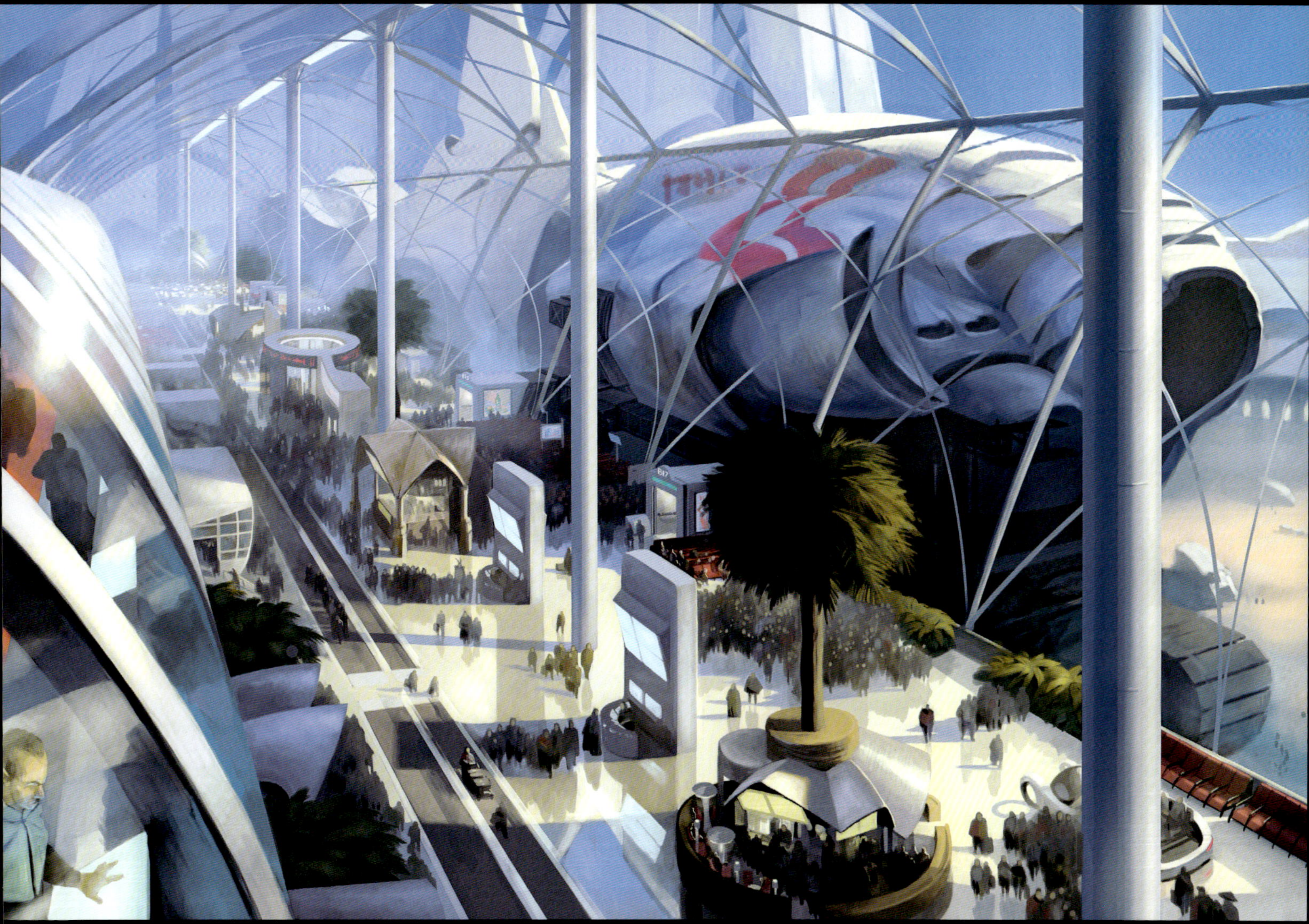

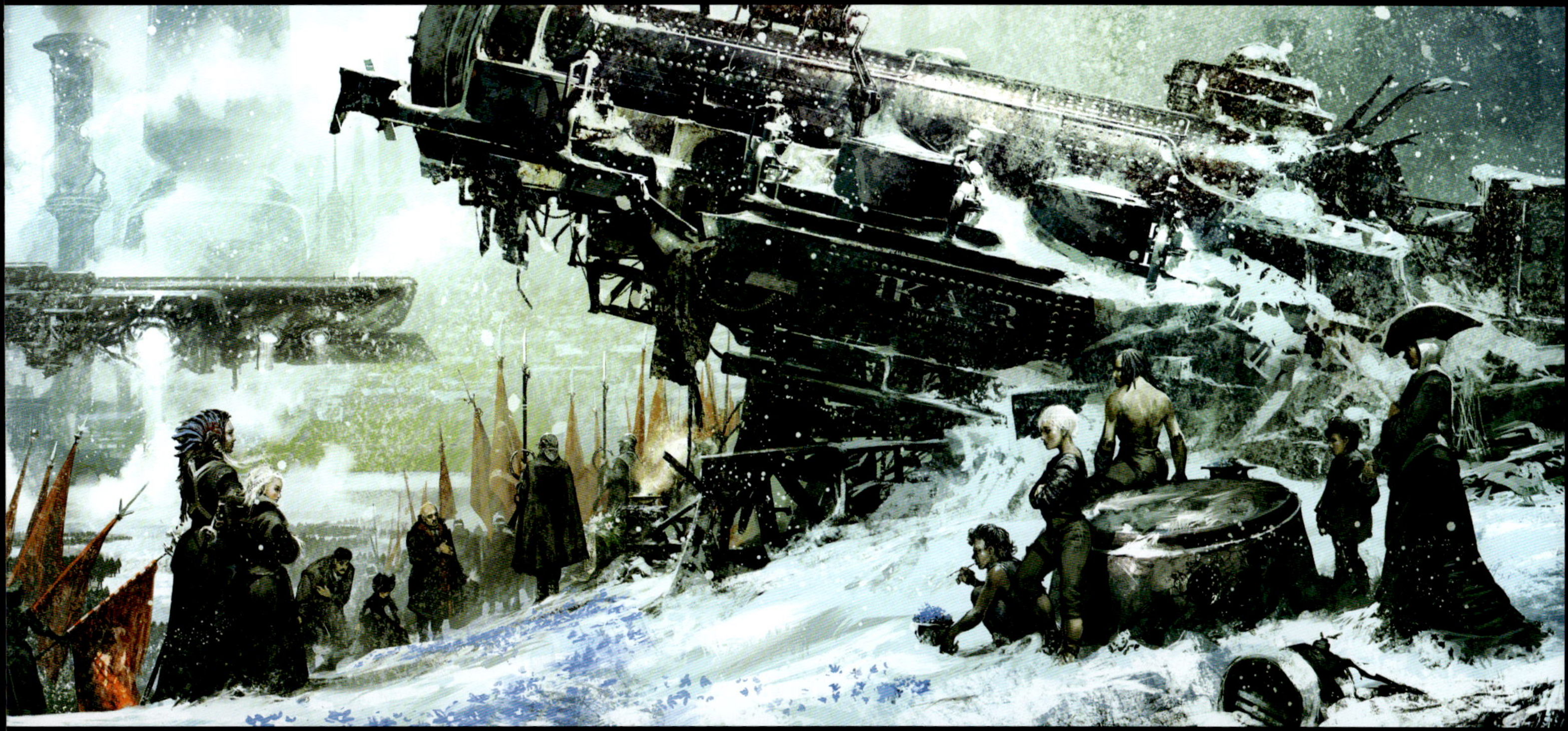

Spaceport
Photoshop
Sidharth Chaturvedi, USA

Icarus Day
Photoshop
Tomasz Jedruszek, POLAND

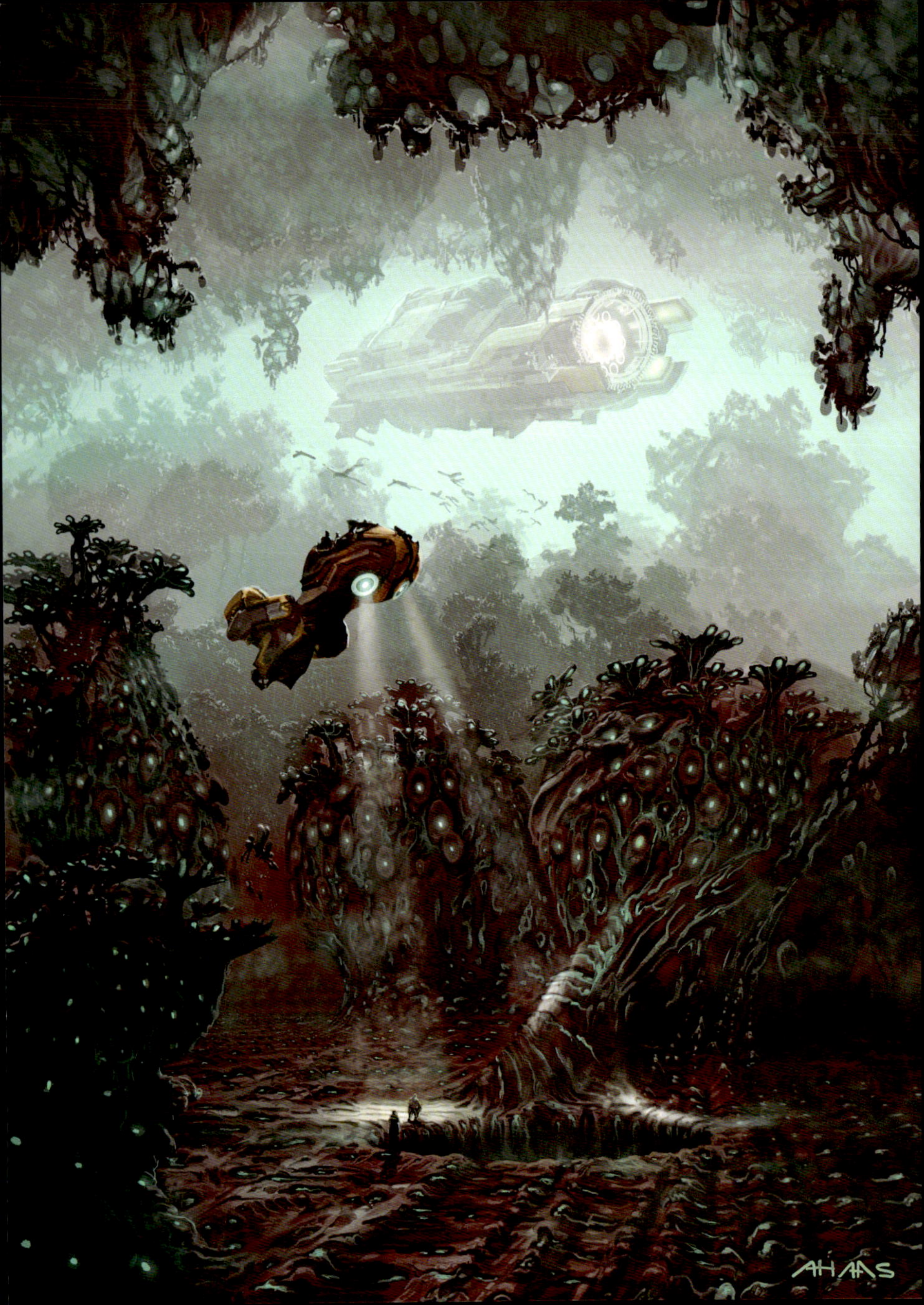

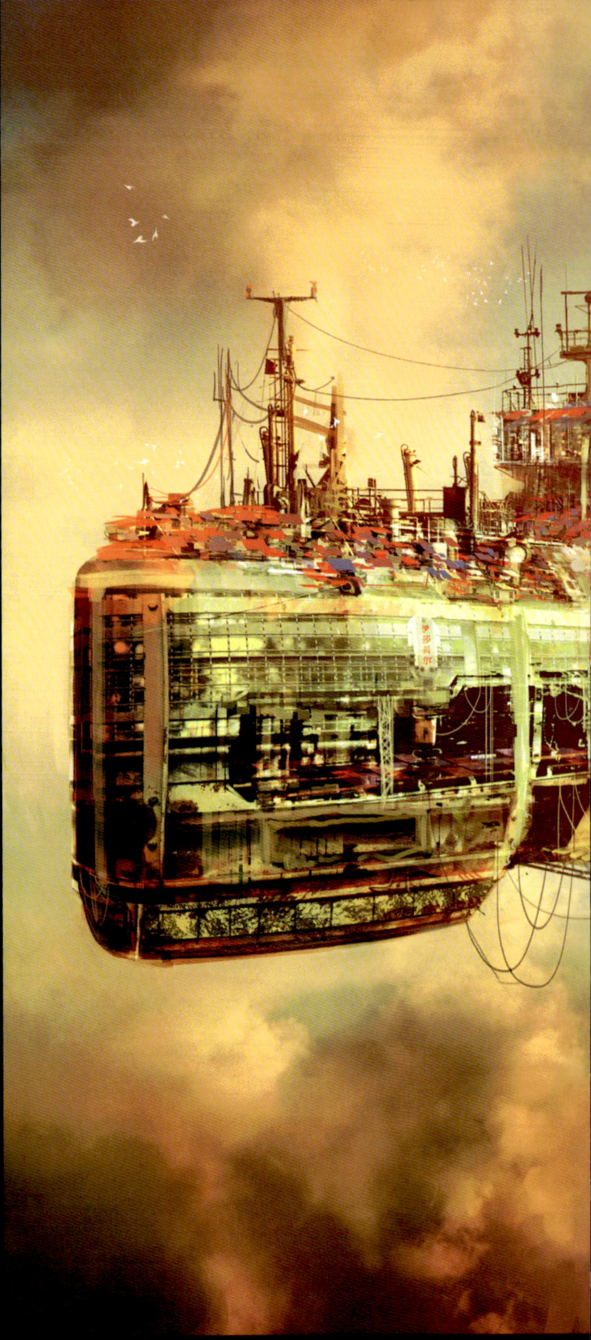

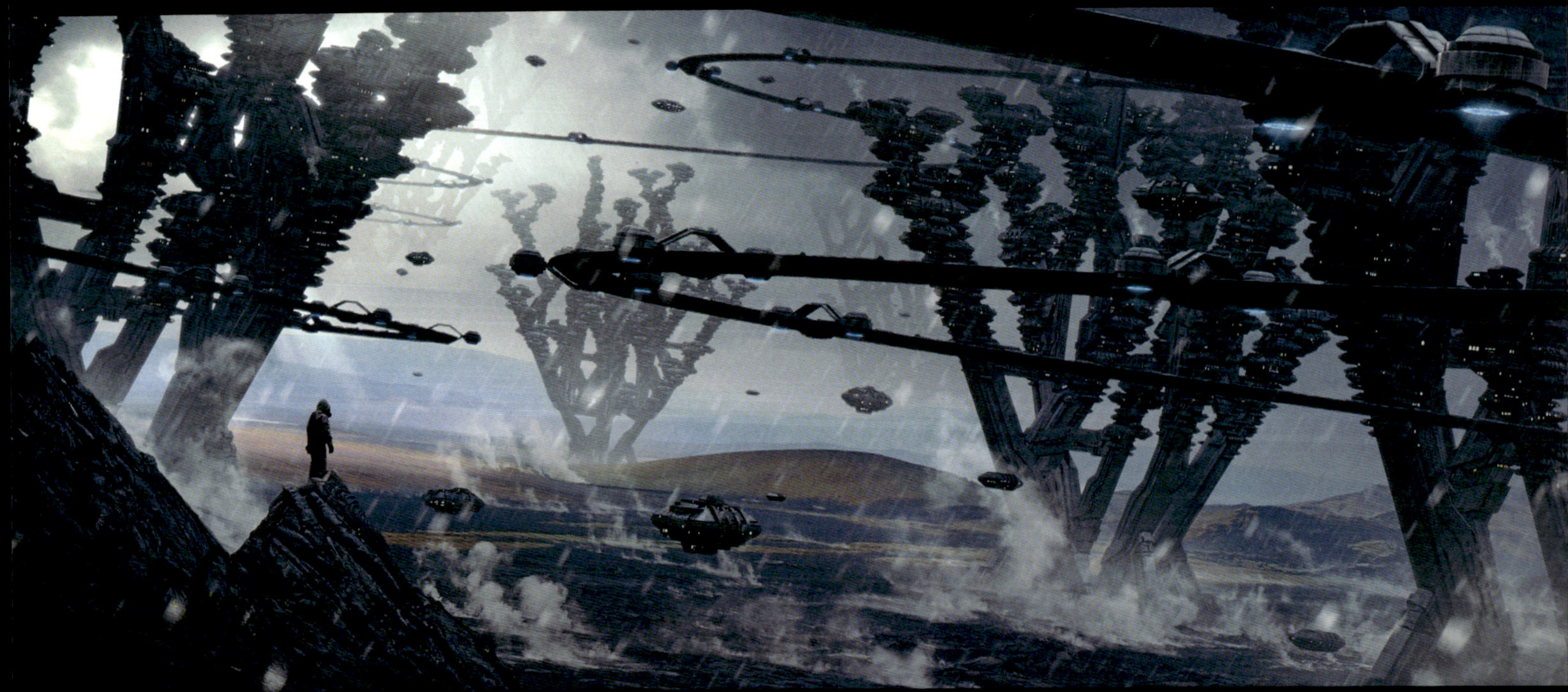

Cave
Photoshop
Arthur Haas, NETHERLANDS
[top left]

City Ship
Photoshop
Maciej Rebisz, POLAND
[top center]

Rest in Peace
Painter
Au yeung Chun Hay, CHINA
[top right]

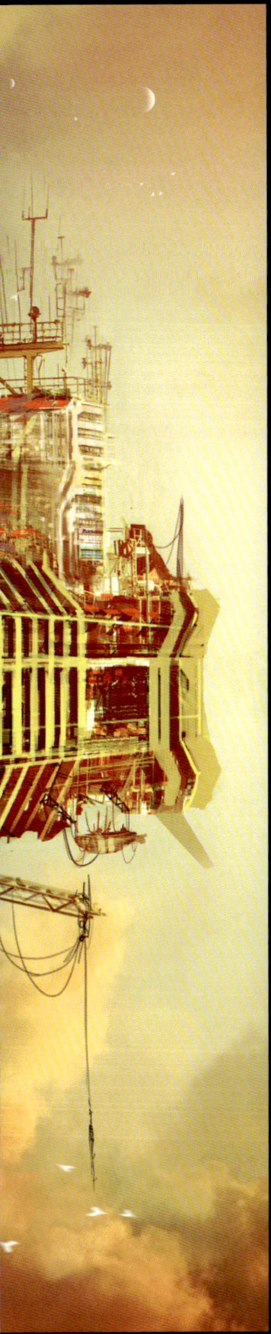

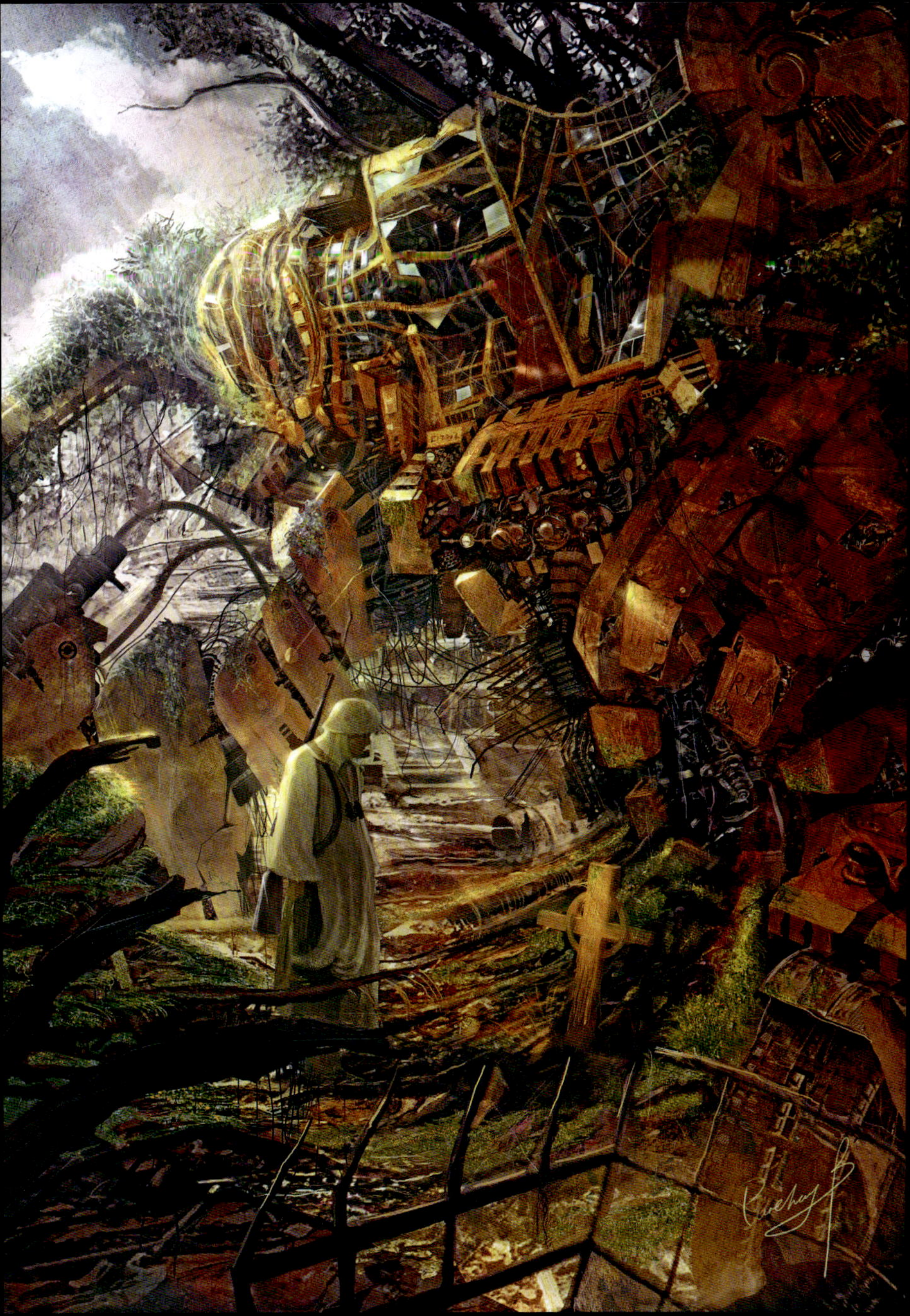

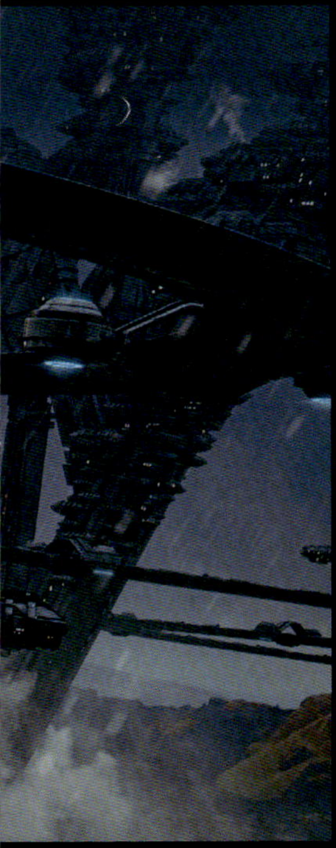

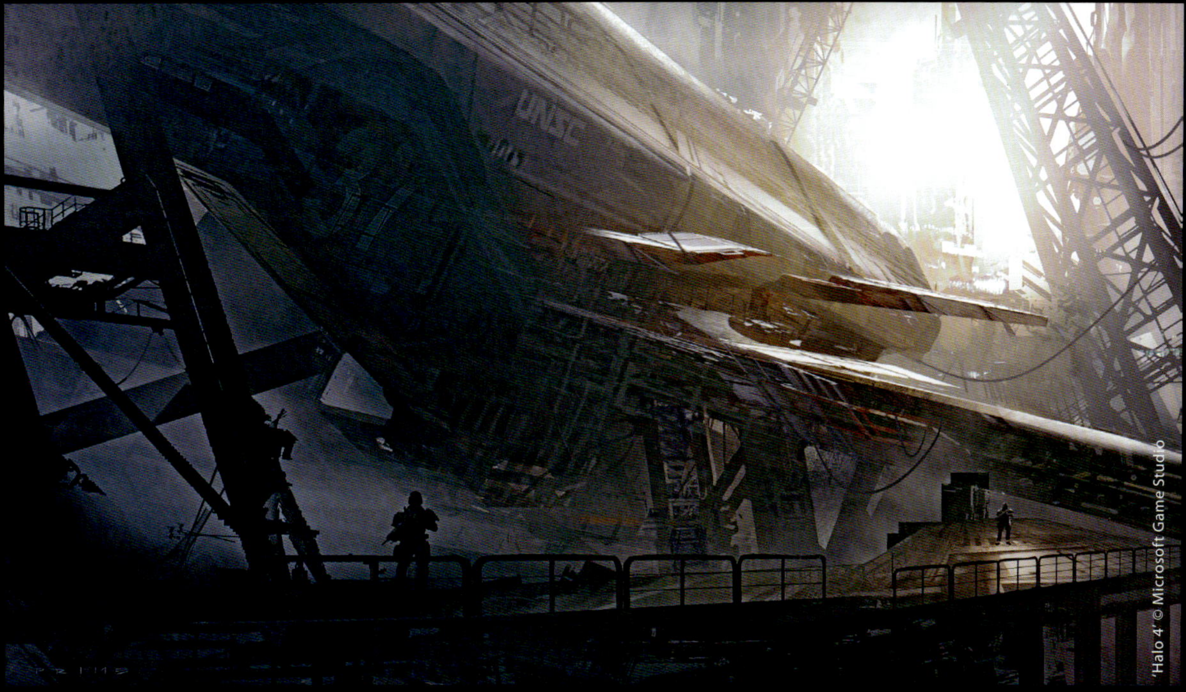

KX89
Photoshop, Maya, V-Ray
Francesco Corvino, ITALY
[above]

Halo 4: Landfall
Photoshop
Client: 343 Industries, Microsoft Game Studio
Michael Pedro, USA
[above]

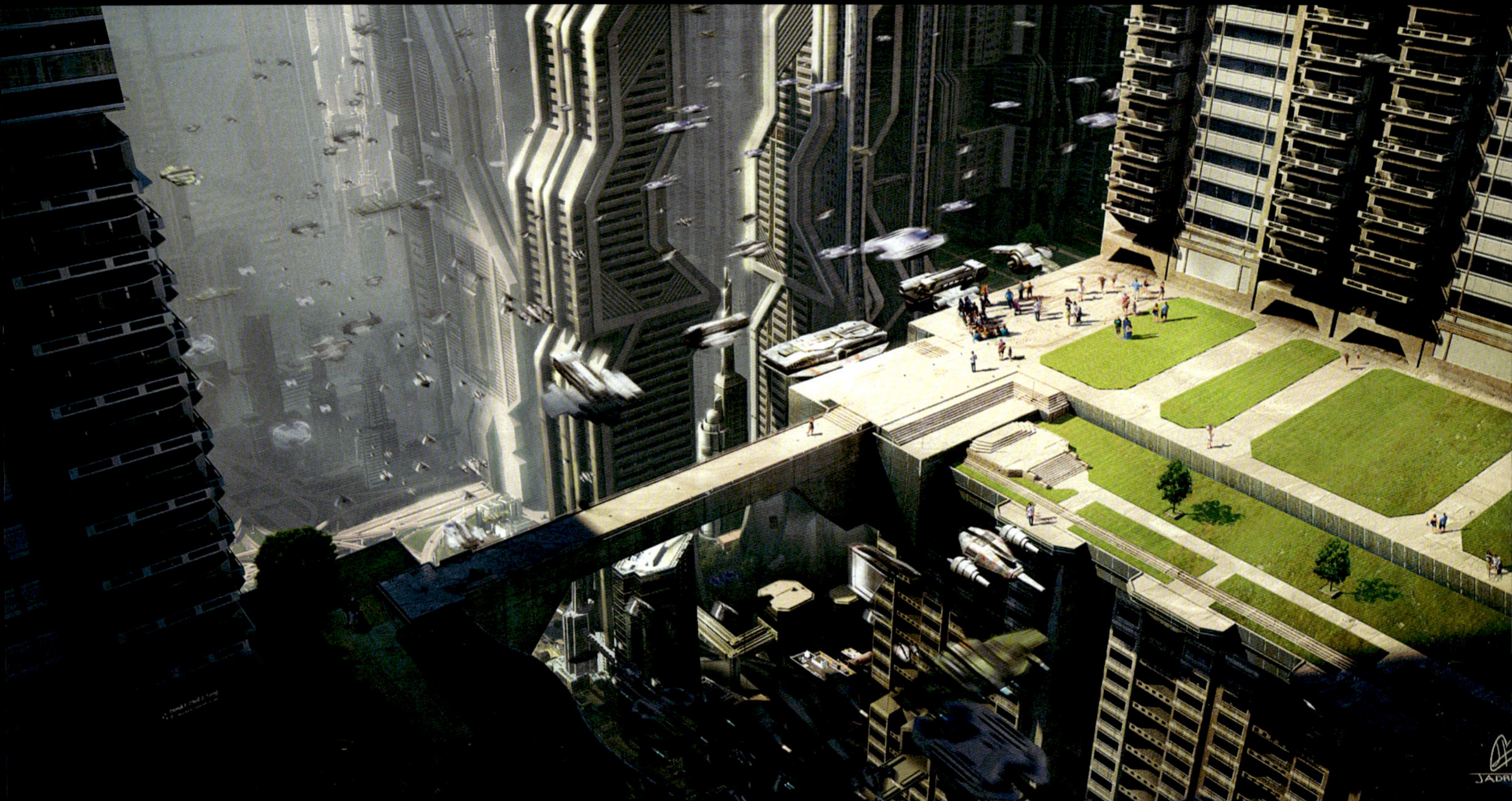

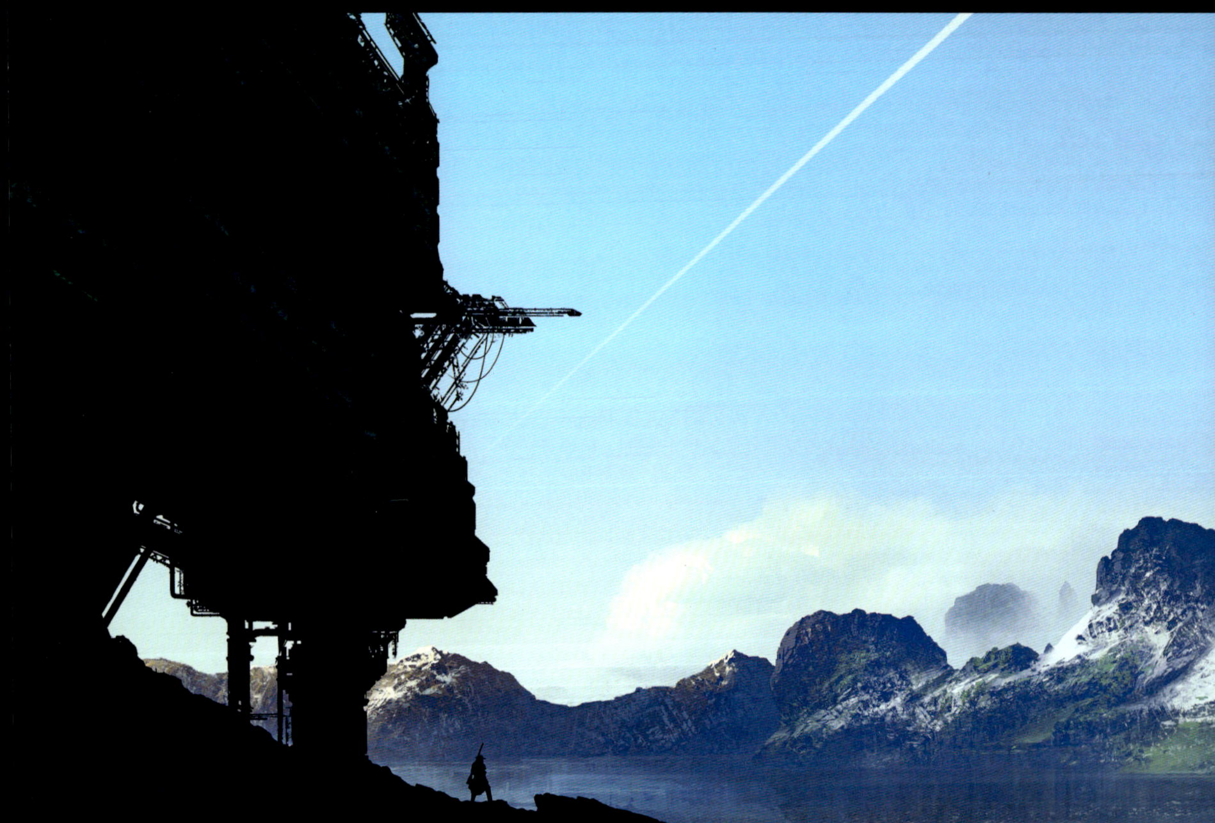

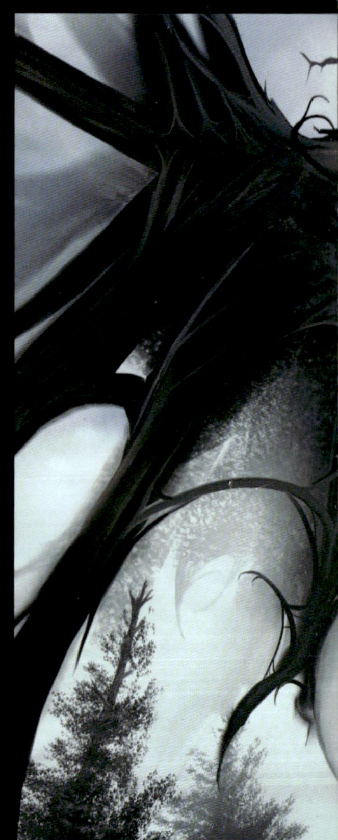

Downtown
Maya, Photoshop
Jadrien Cousens, USA
[top left]

Leaving the Fields of Steel
Vue Esprit, Photoshop
Christian 'Tigaer' Hecker, GERMANY
[top right]

Frontier
Photoshop
Hrvoje Beslic, CROATIA
[above]

Funeral Mantra
Photoshop
Ramses Melendez, MEXICO
[above]

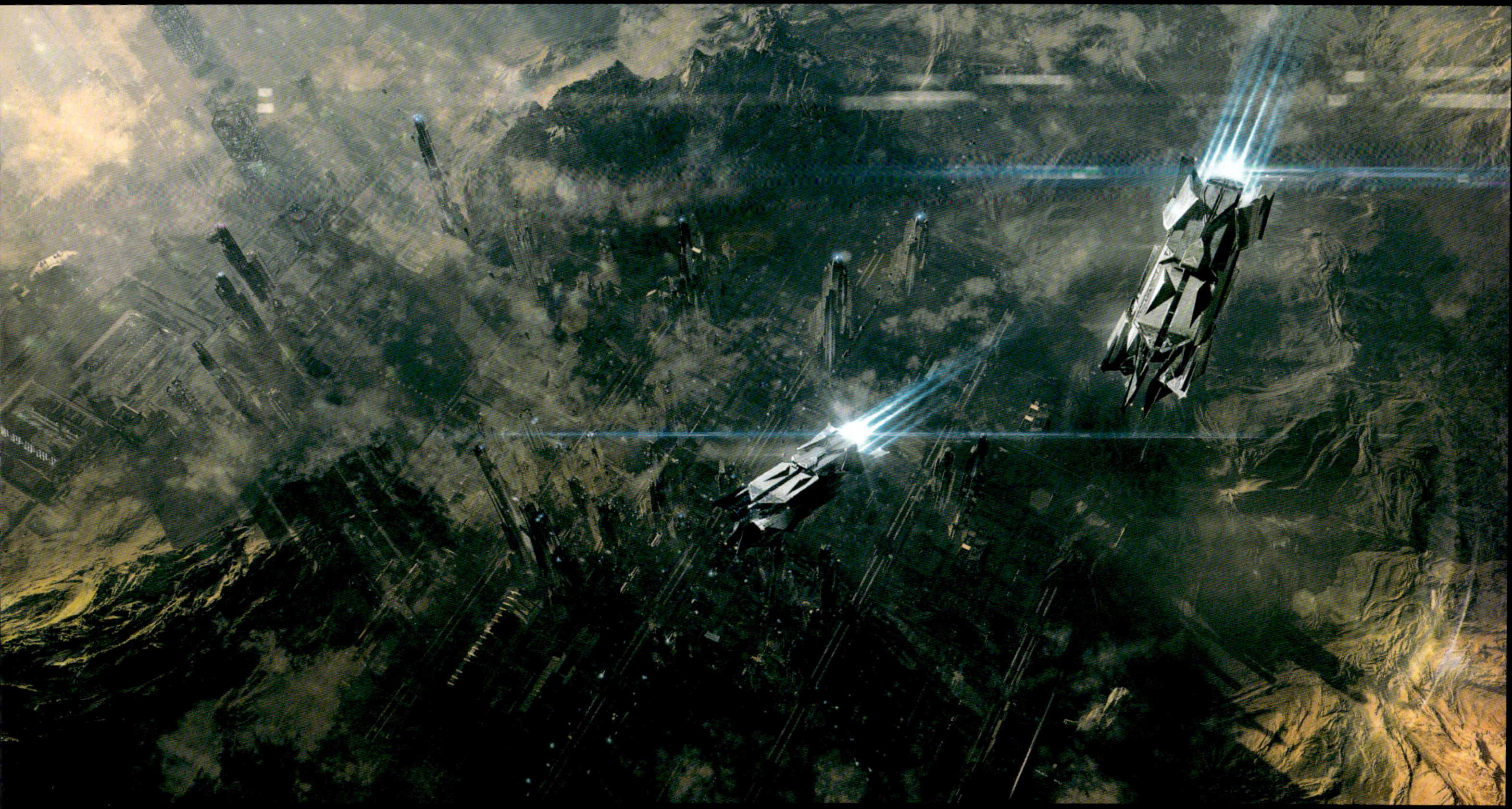

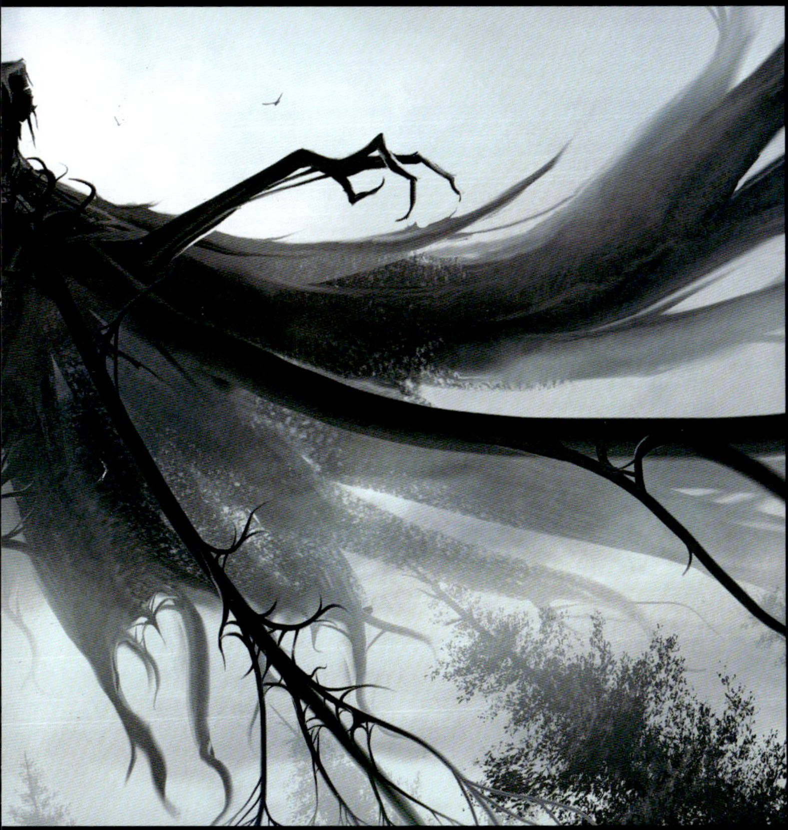

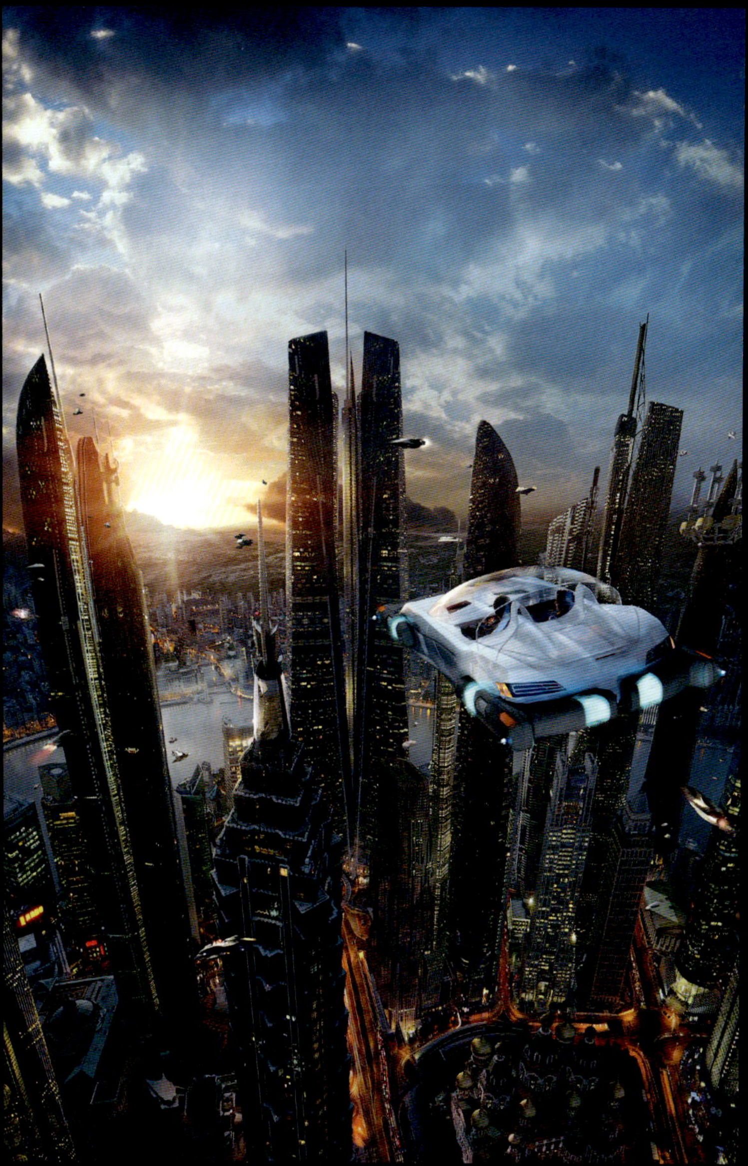

Captain Vorpatril's Alliance
Photoshop, SketchUp
Client: Baen Books
Dave Seeley (Art Director: Toni Weisskopf), USA
[right]

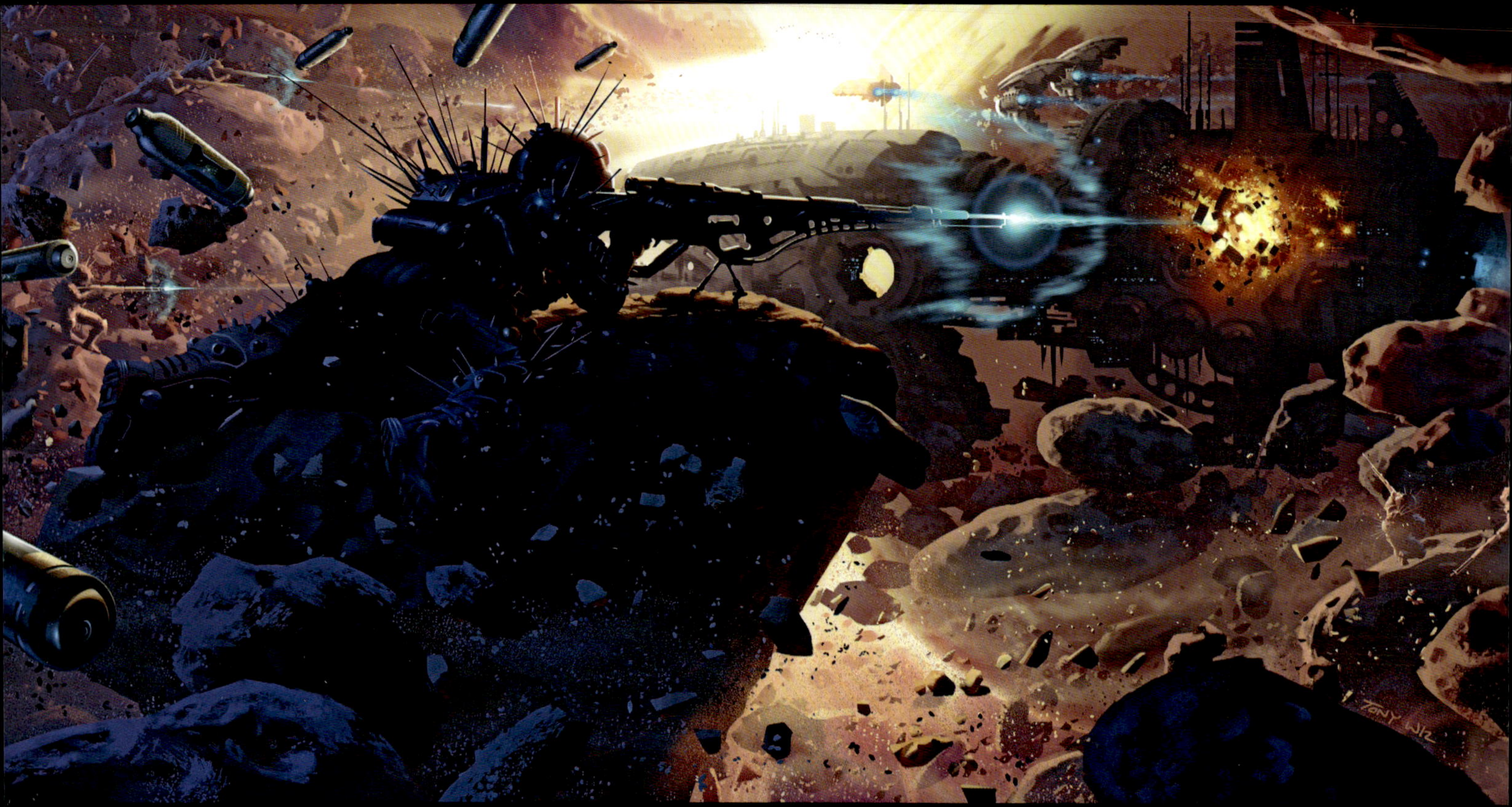

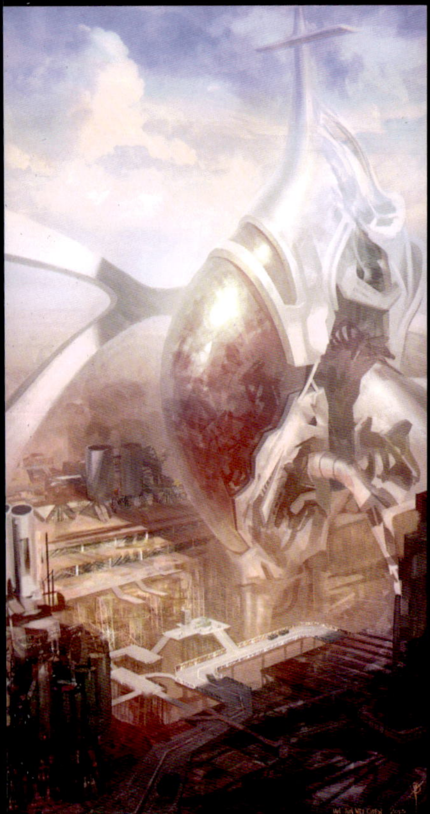

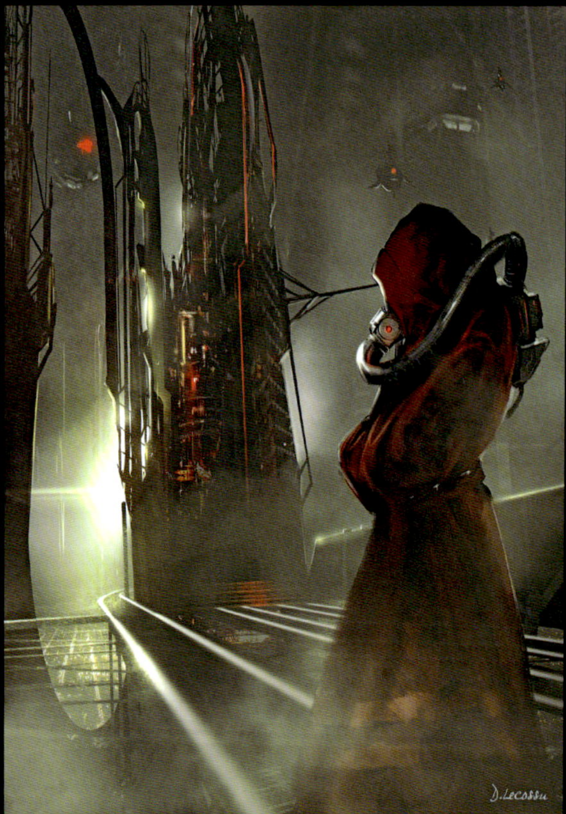

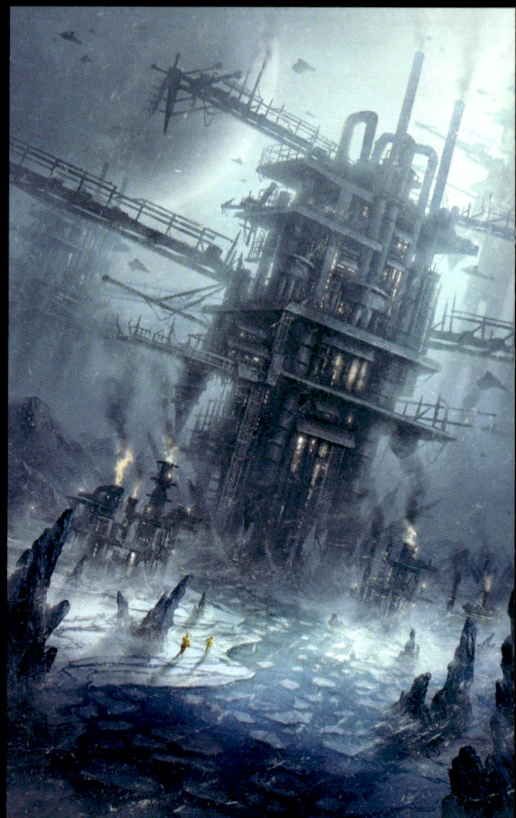

Cosmodrome
Photoshop
Ian Jun Wei Chiew, USA
[above]

Asteroid Sniper
Photoshop
Tony Weinstock, USA
[top]

POS 1
Photoshop
David Lecossu, FRANCE
[above]

Snowy Exploration
Photoshop
ZEZ Zhaoenze, CHINA
[above]

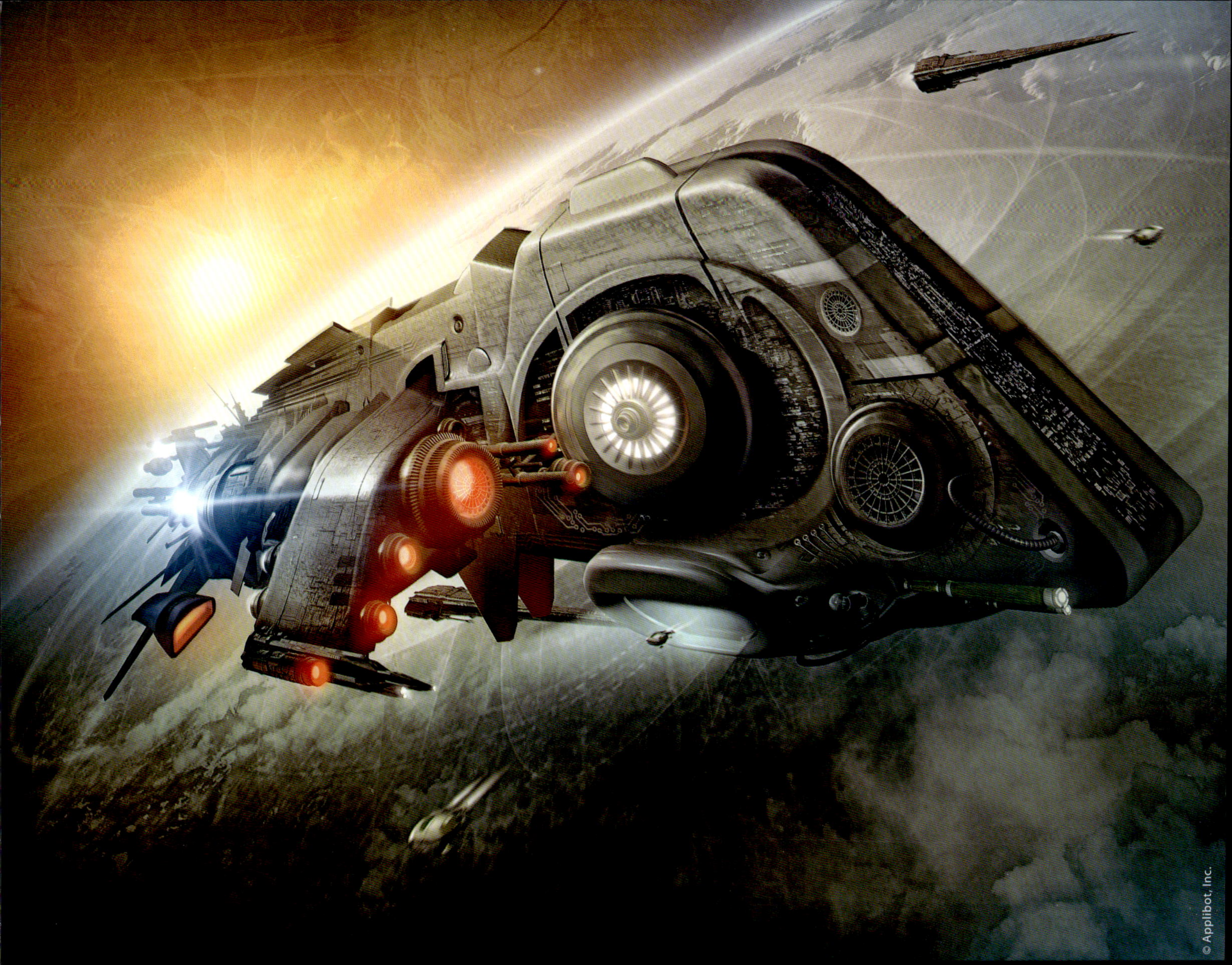

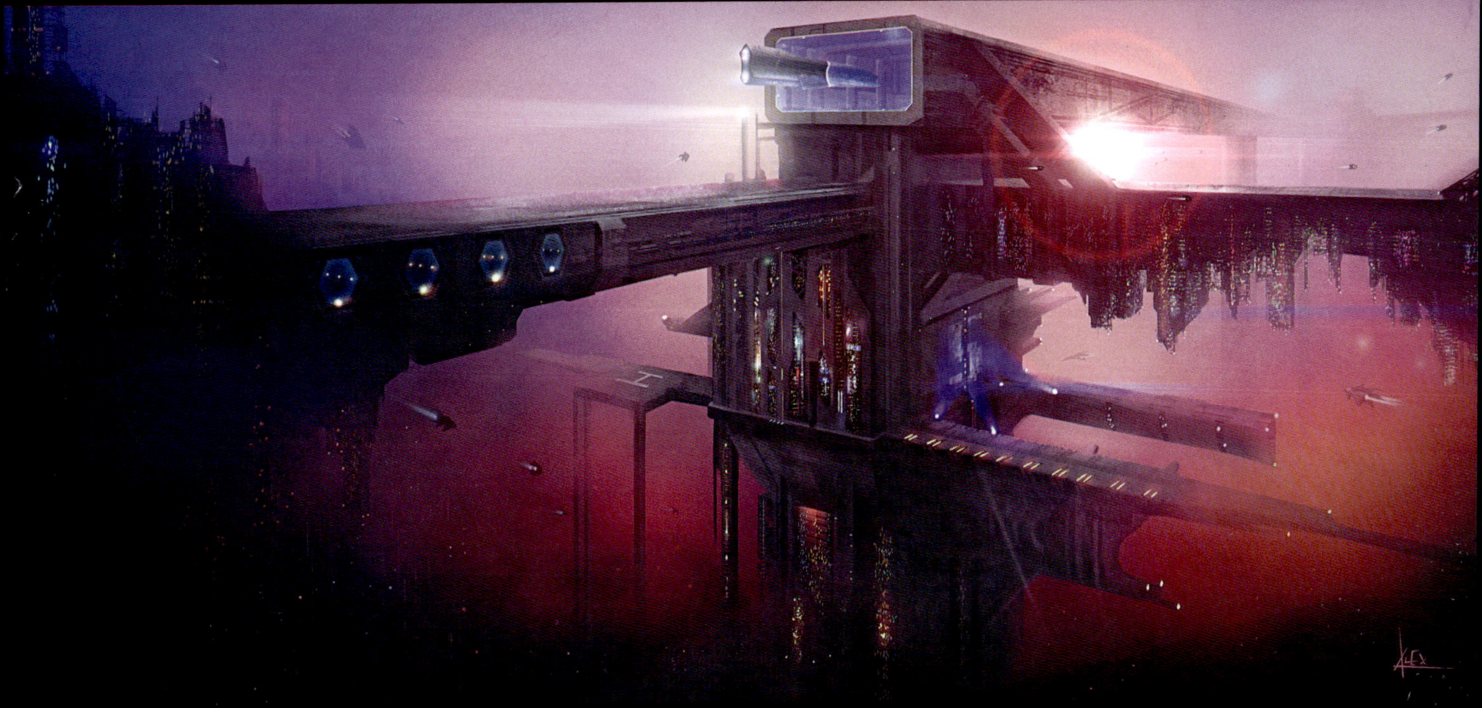

Starship

Sky Station

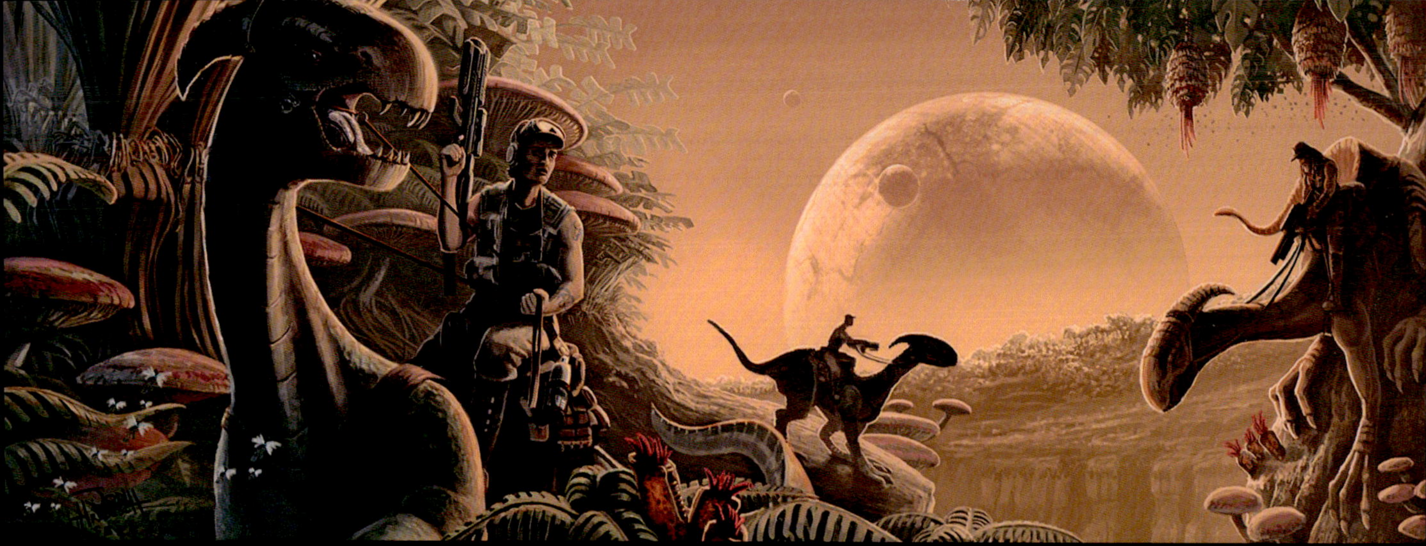

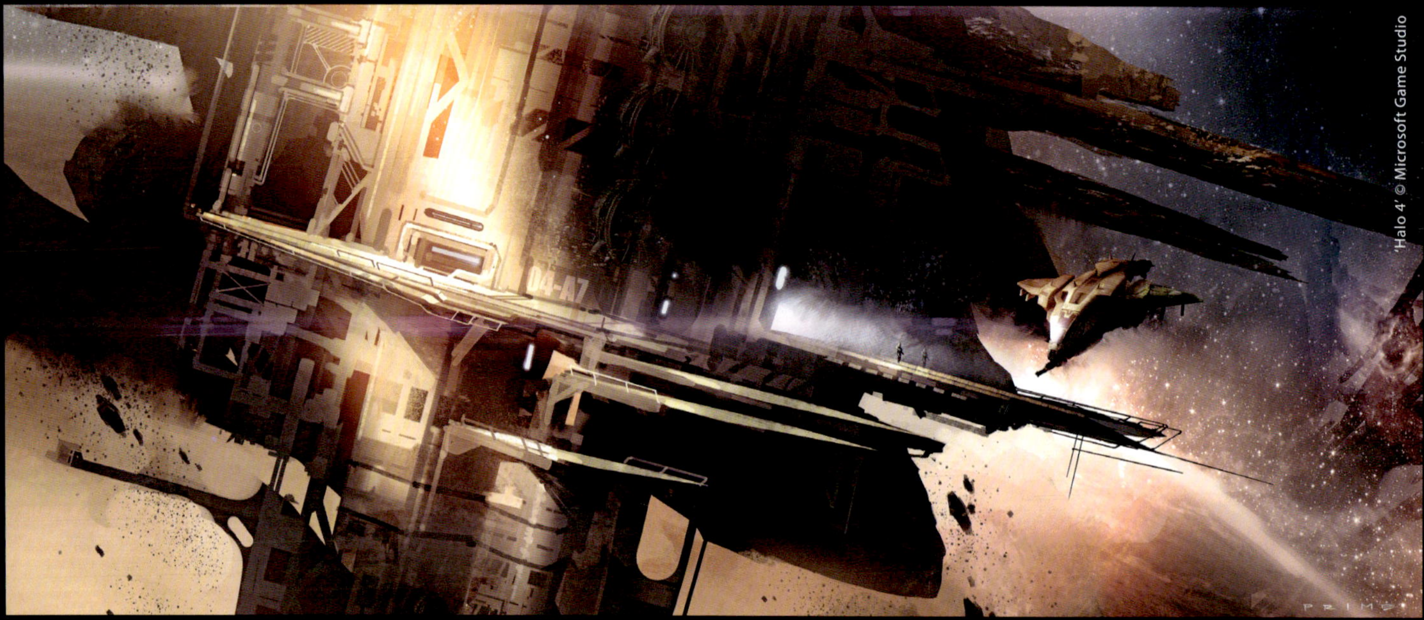

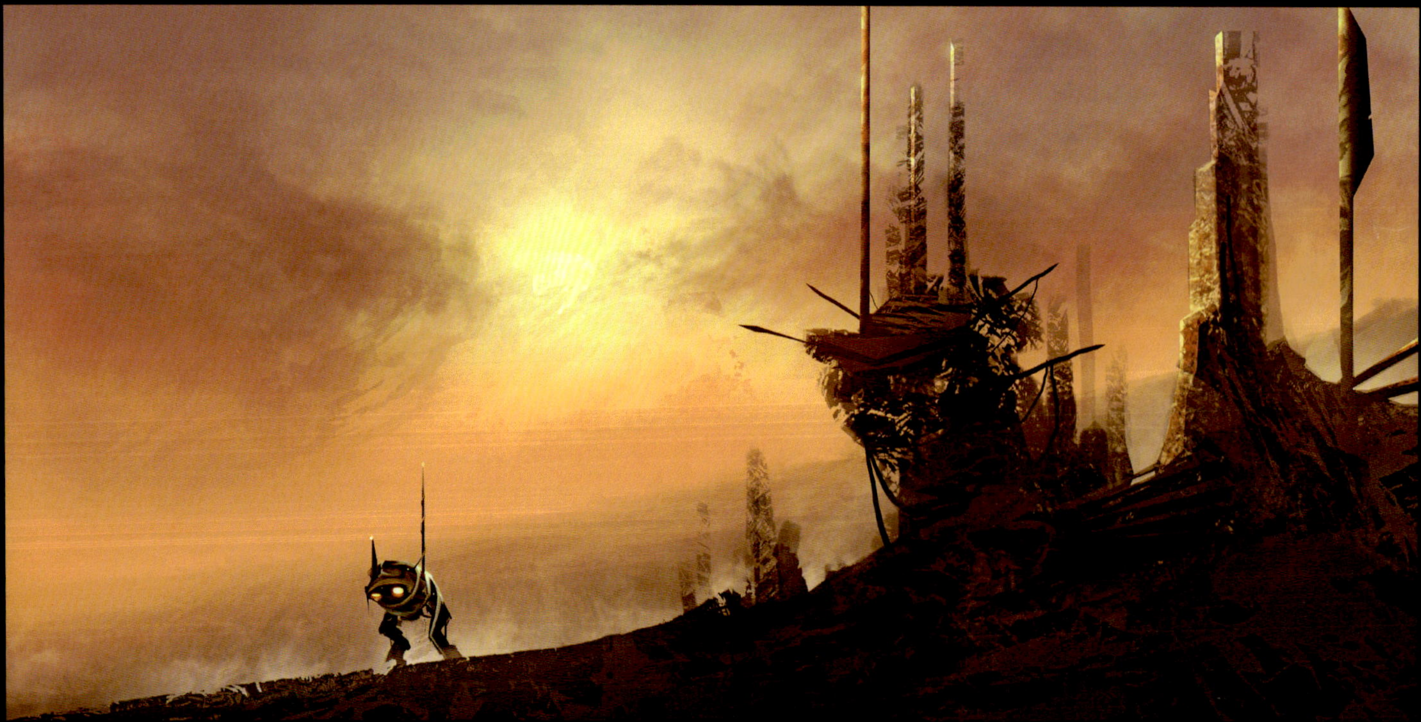

The Hunt
Photoshop
Jon Hrubesch, USA
[top]

Halo 4: Pylon 04
Photoshop
Client: 343 Industries, Microsoft Game Studio
Michael Pedro, USA

Robot 237
Photoshop
Ramses Melendez, MEXICO
[above]

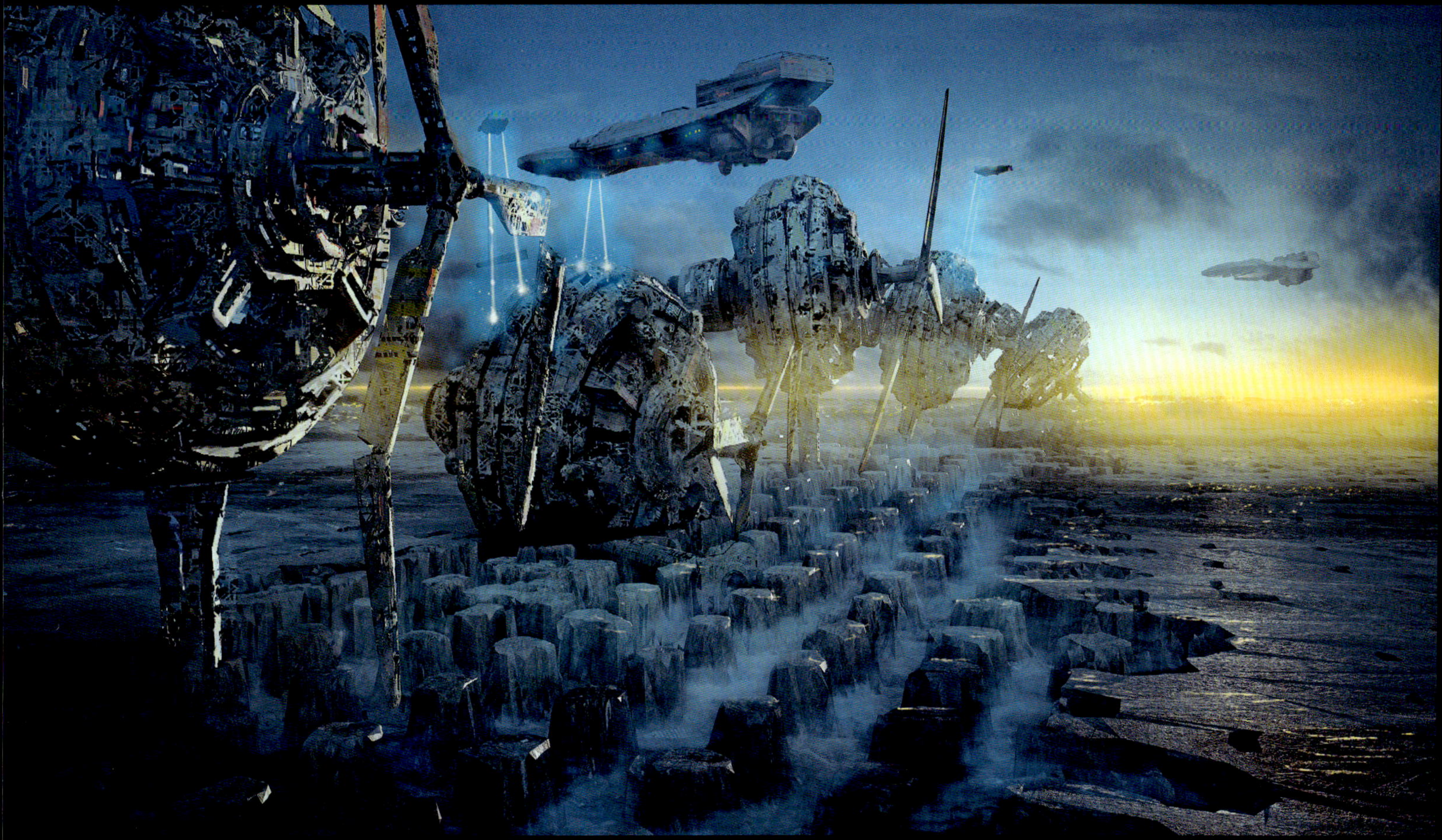

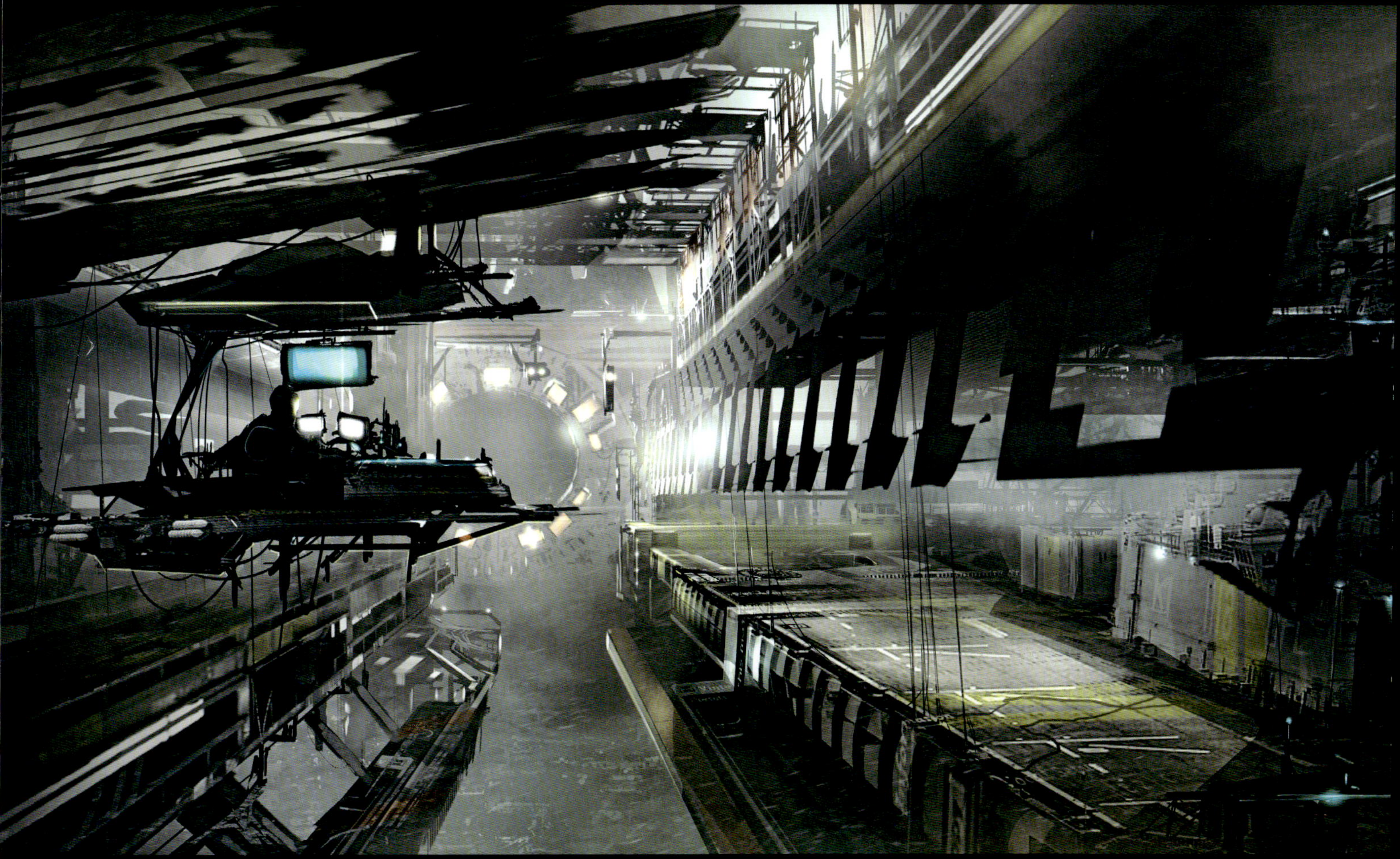

Salvage
LightWave 3D, Photoshop
Neil Maccormack, bearfootfilms,
SWITZERLAND

Simulator Control Room
Photoshop
David Lecossu, FRANCE
[above]

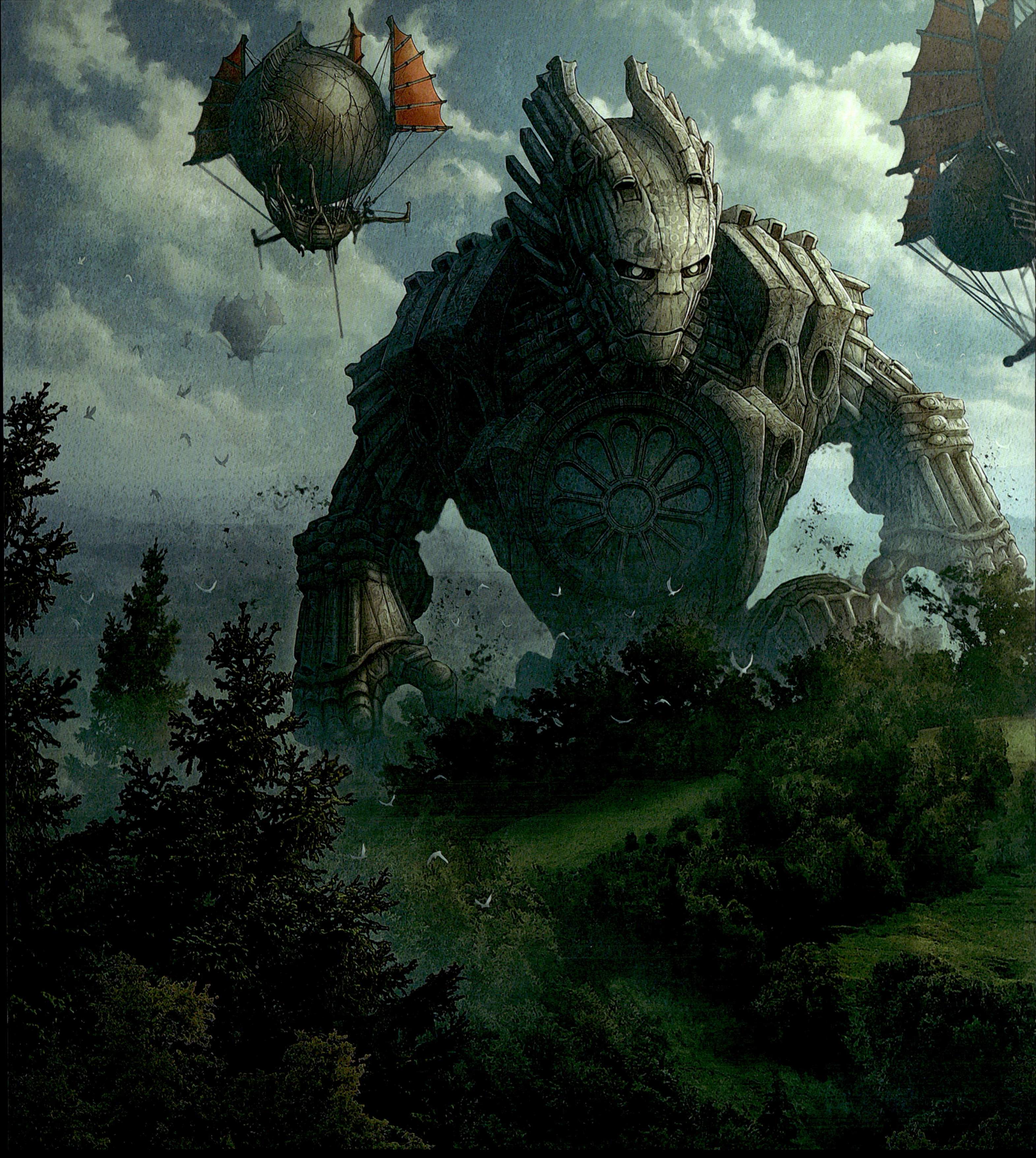

Invasion

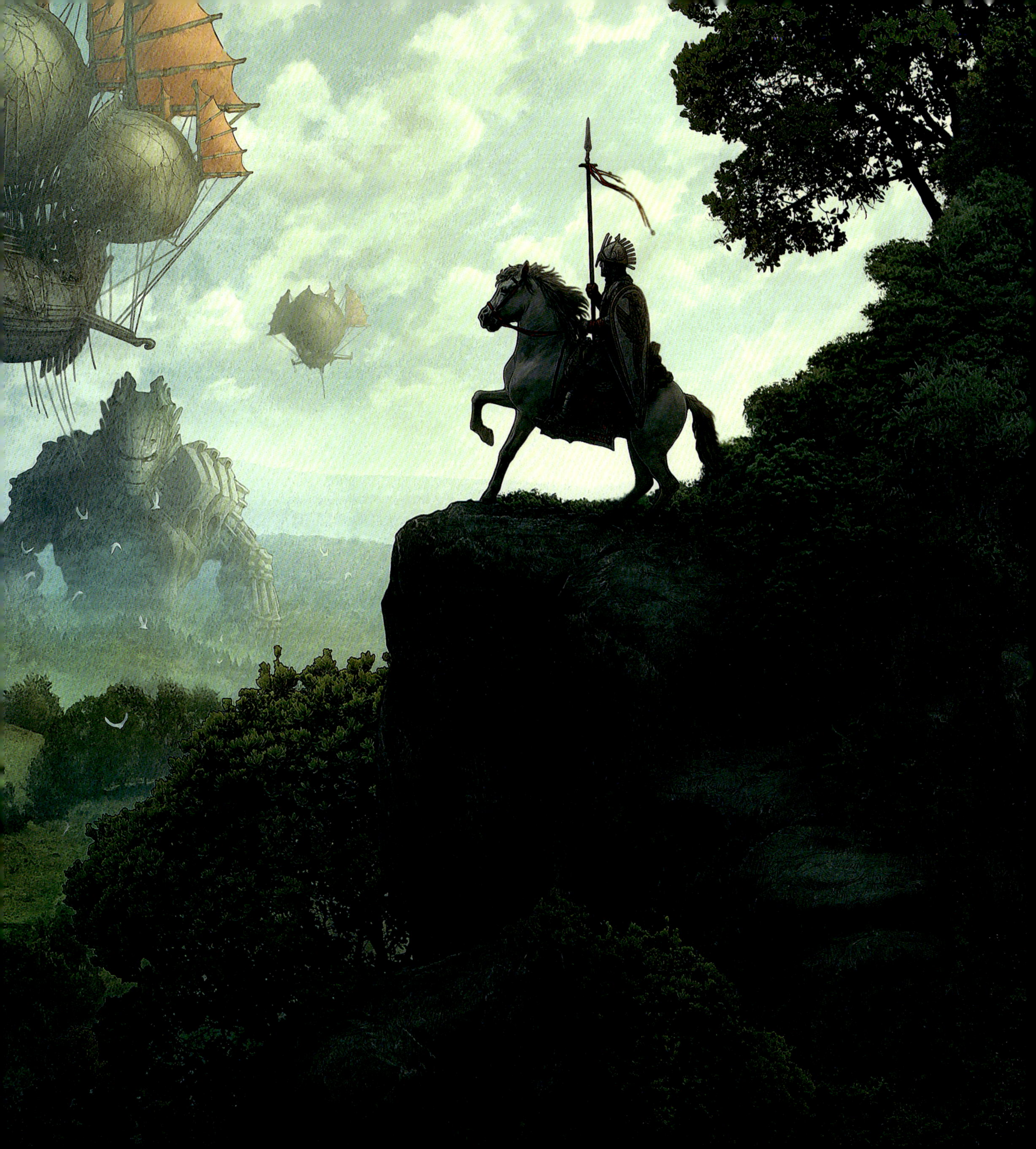

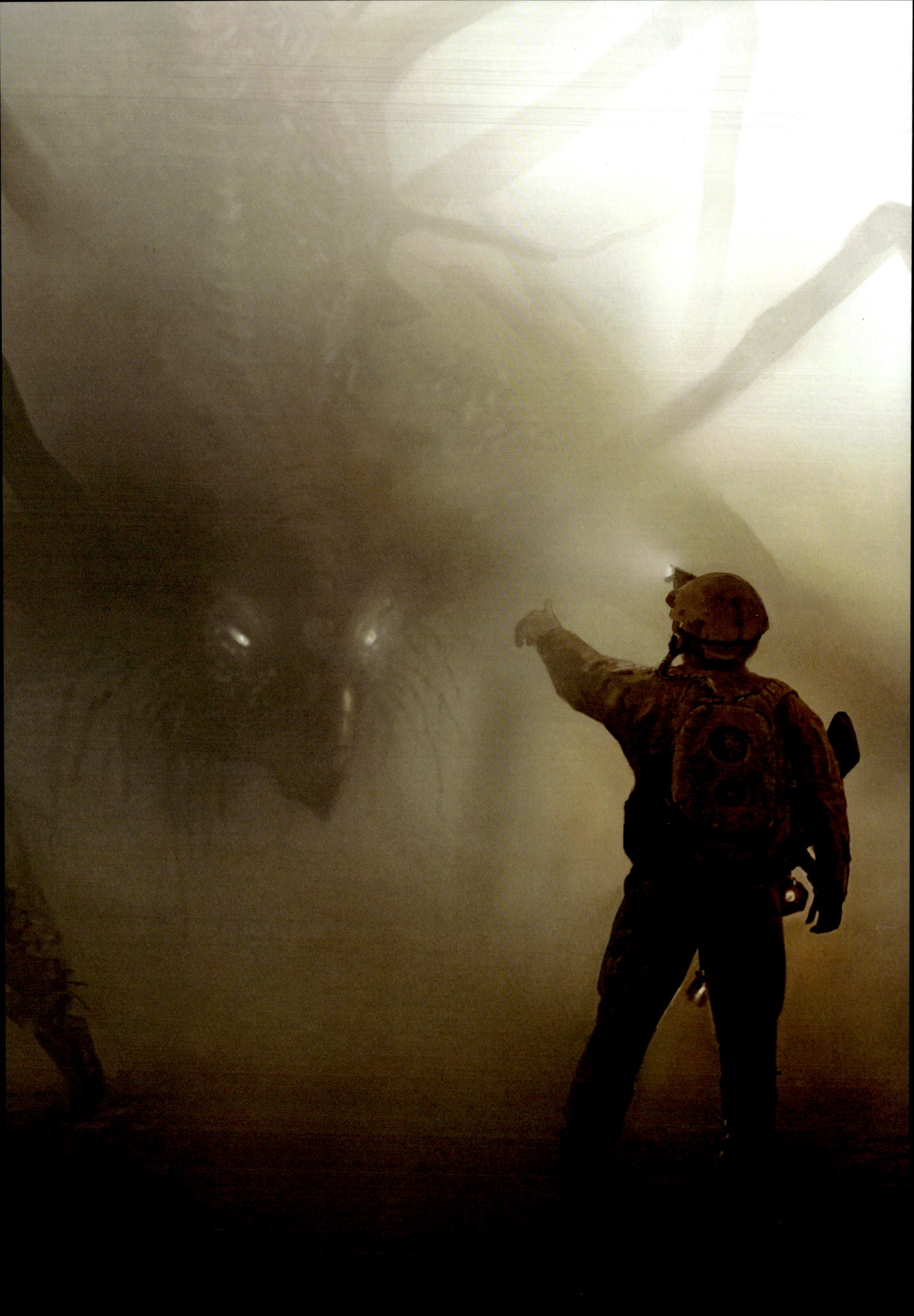

Excellence
Fantasy

Sandmonster
Photoshop
Rasmus Berggreen, DENMARK

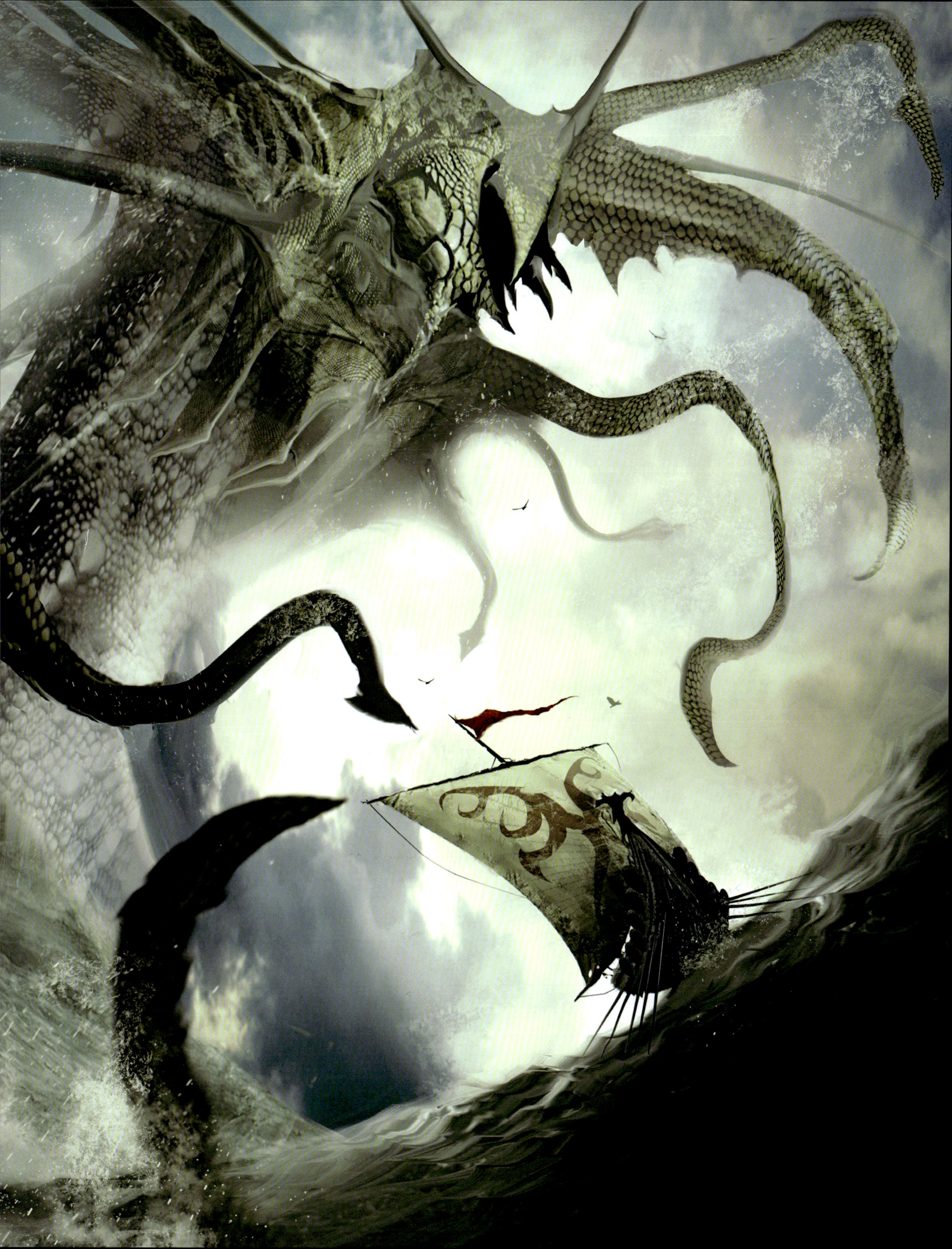

Kraken
Photoshop
Ramses Melendez, MEXICO

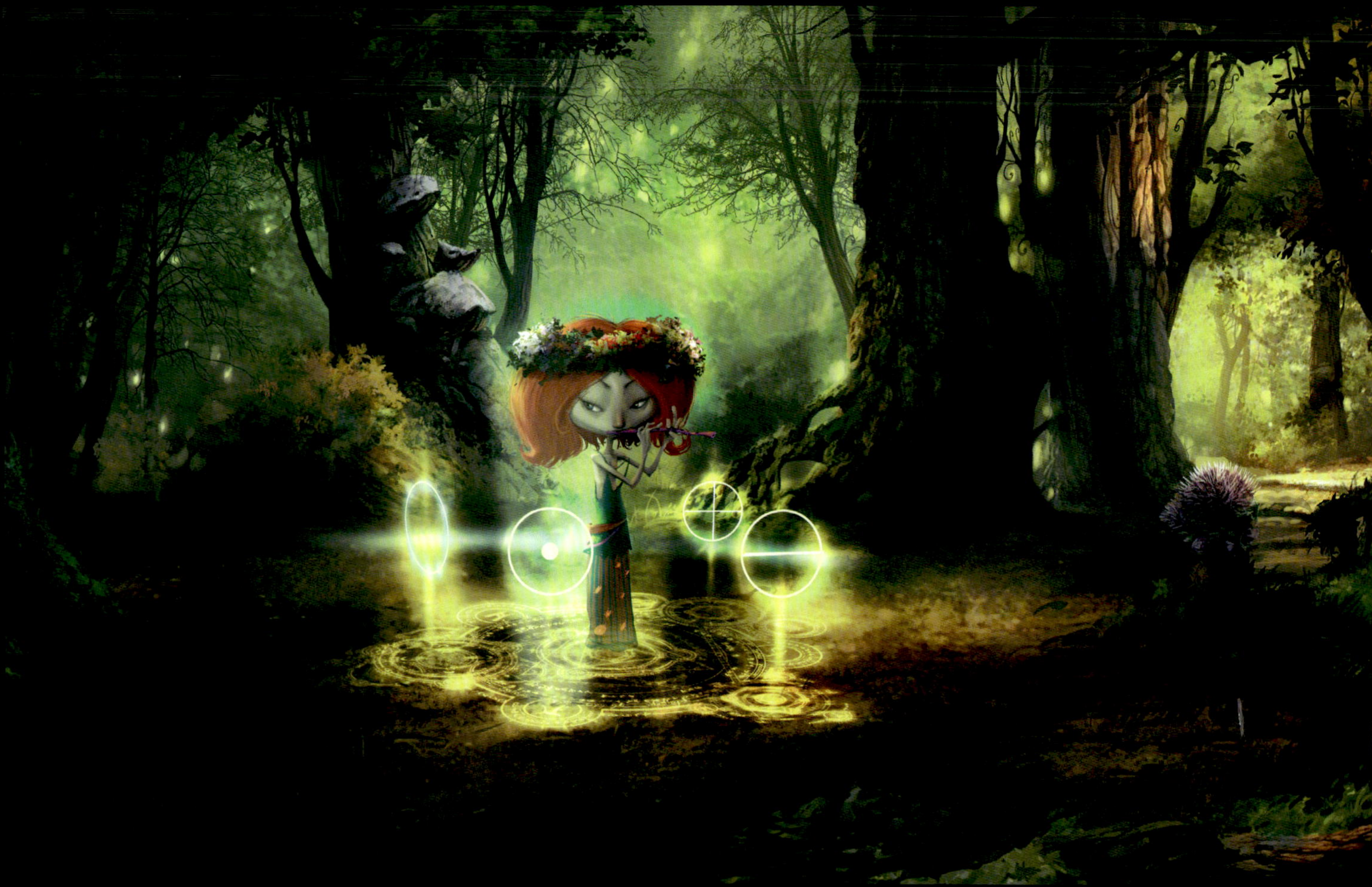

Enchanted Forest

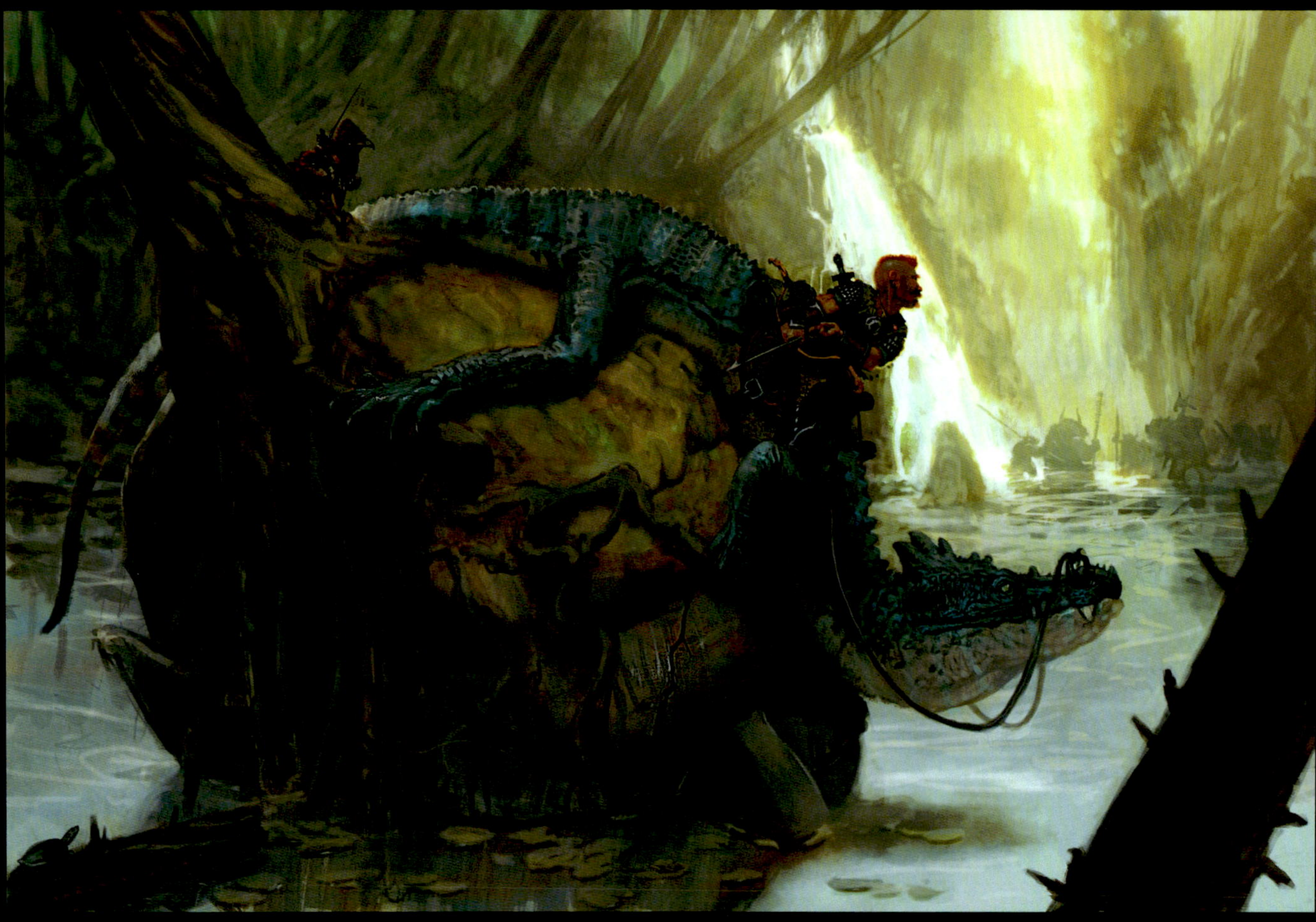

The Scouting Party

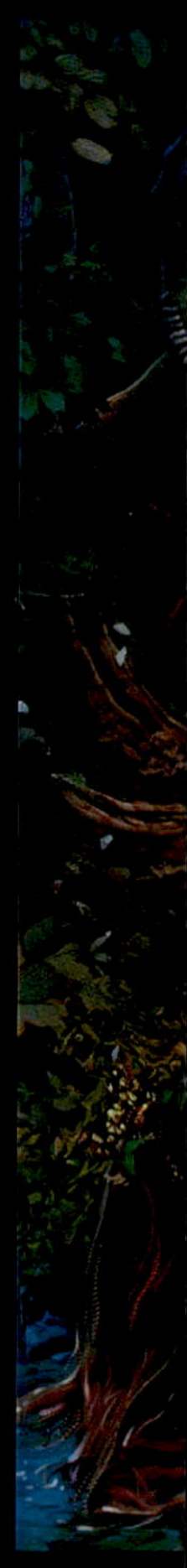

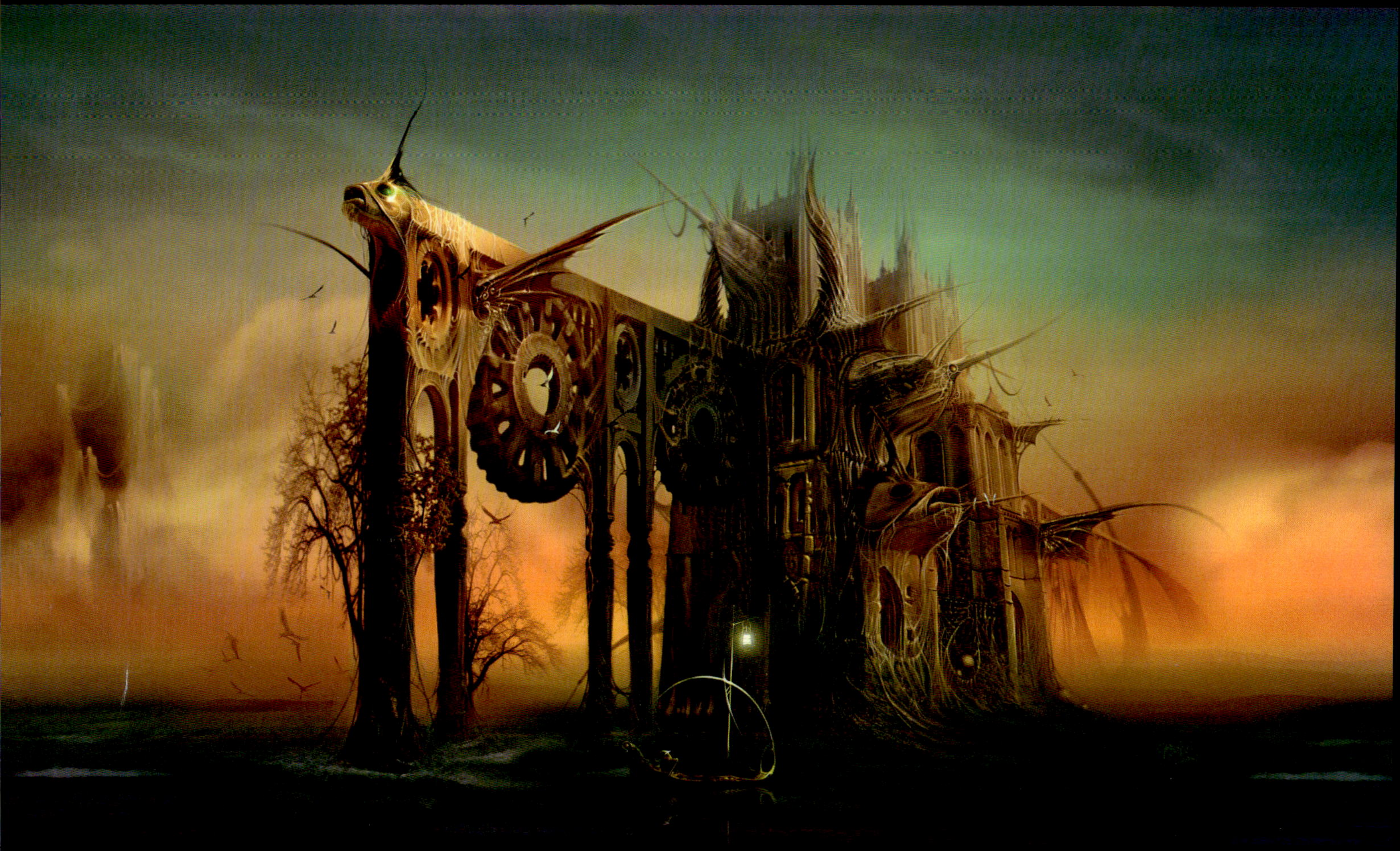

Sanctuary
PhotoPaint
Tomasz Maronski, POLAND
[above]

Traveller
Photoshop
Mike Dearden Clarke, GREAT BRITAIN
[left]

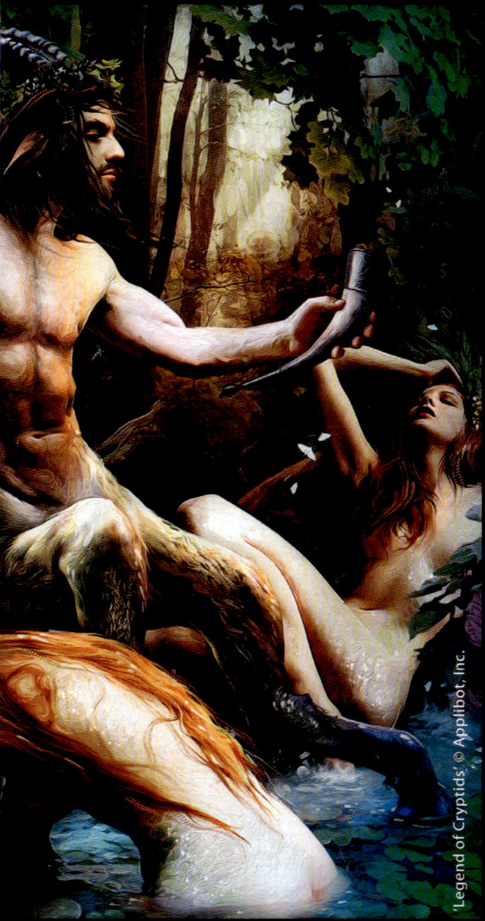

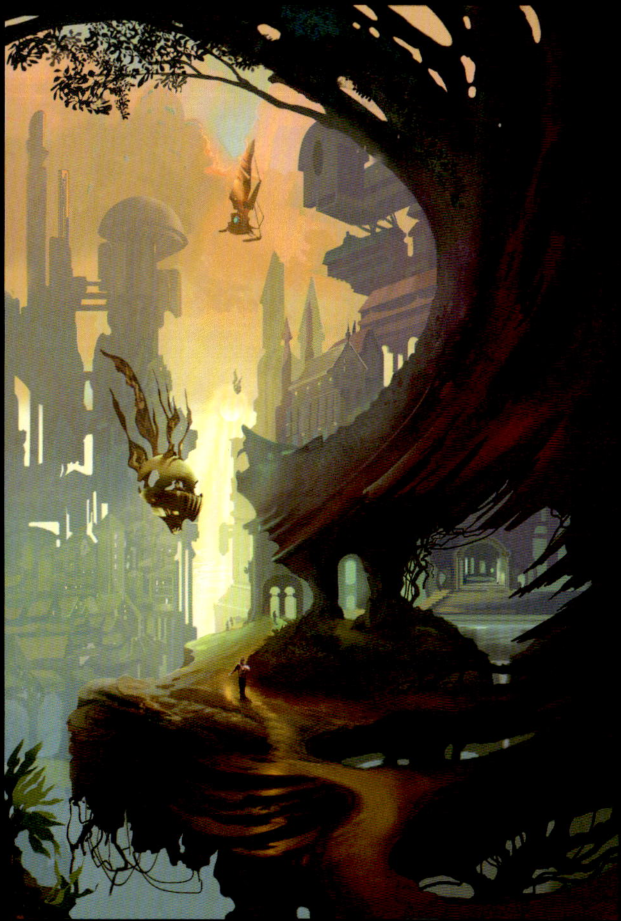

Legend of Cryptids: Satyr
Photoshop
Client: Applibot, Inc.
Bruno Wagner, FRANCE

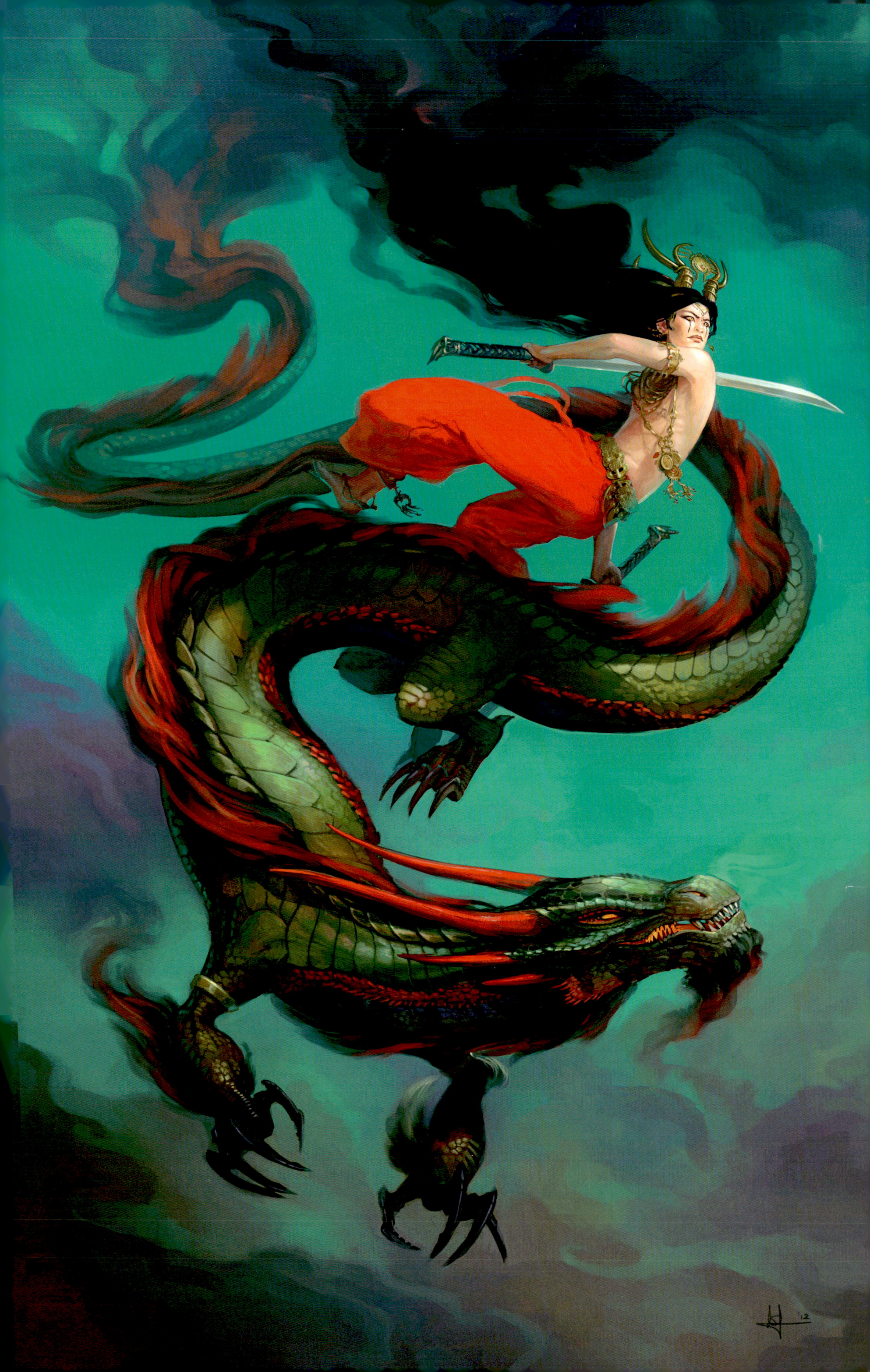

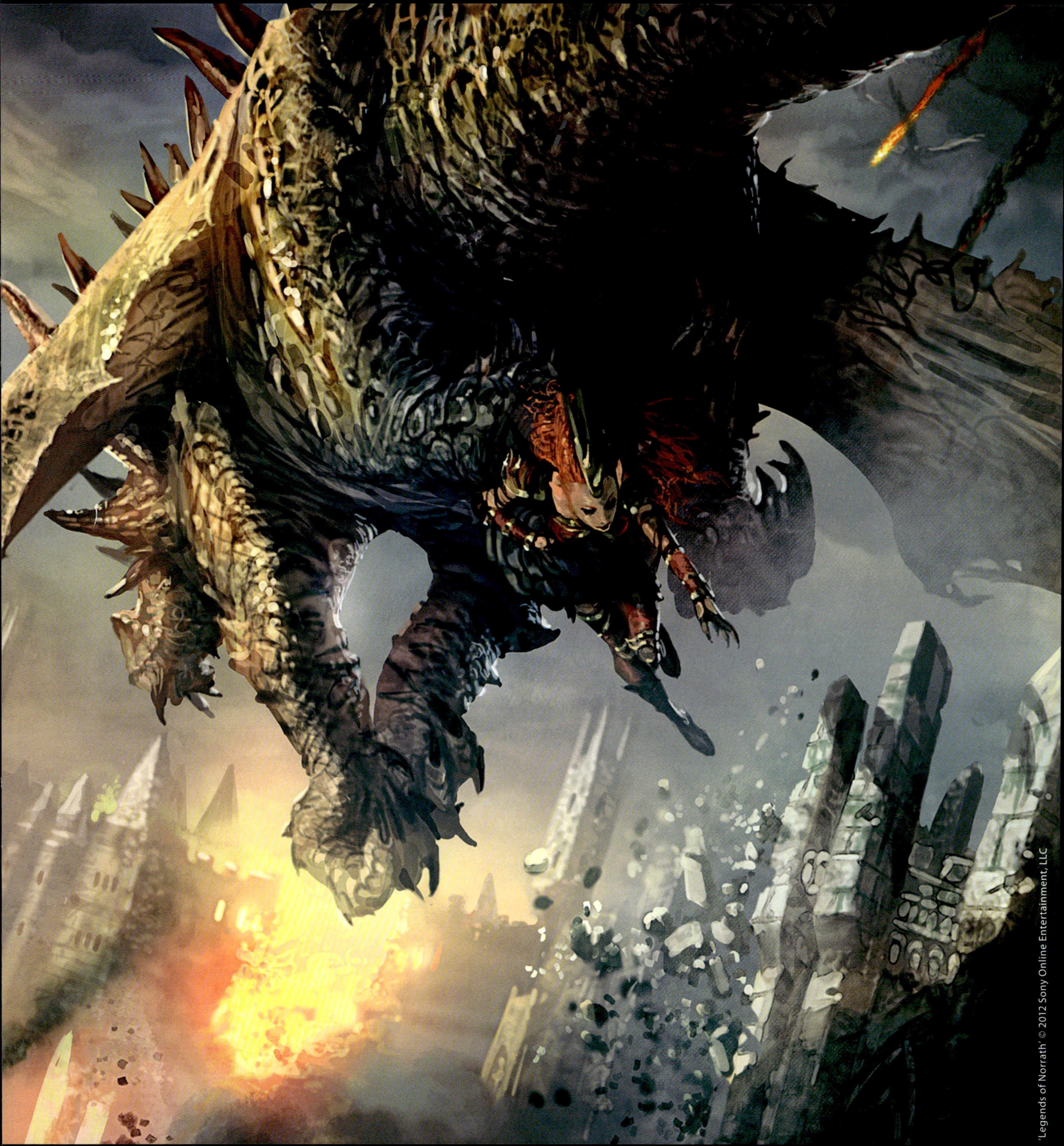

Legends of Norrath: Taken by the Anarchs
Photoshop
Client: Sony Online Entertainment, LLC
Ryan Barger (Art Director: Mark Tuttle), USA
[above]

Soul Spark
Photoshop
Sam Hogg, GREAT BRITAIN
[left]

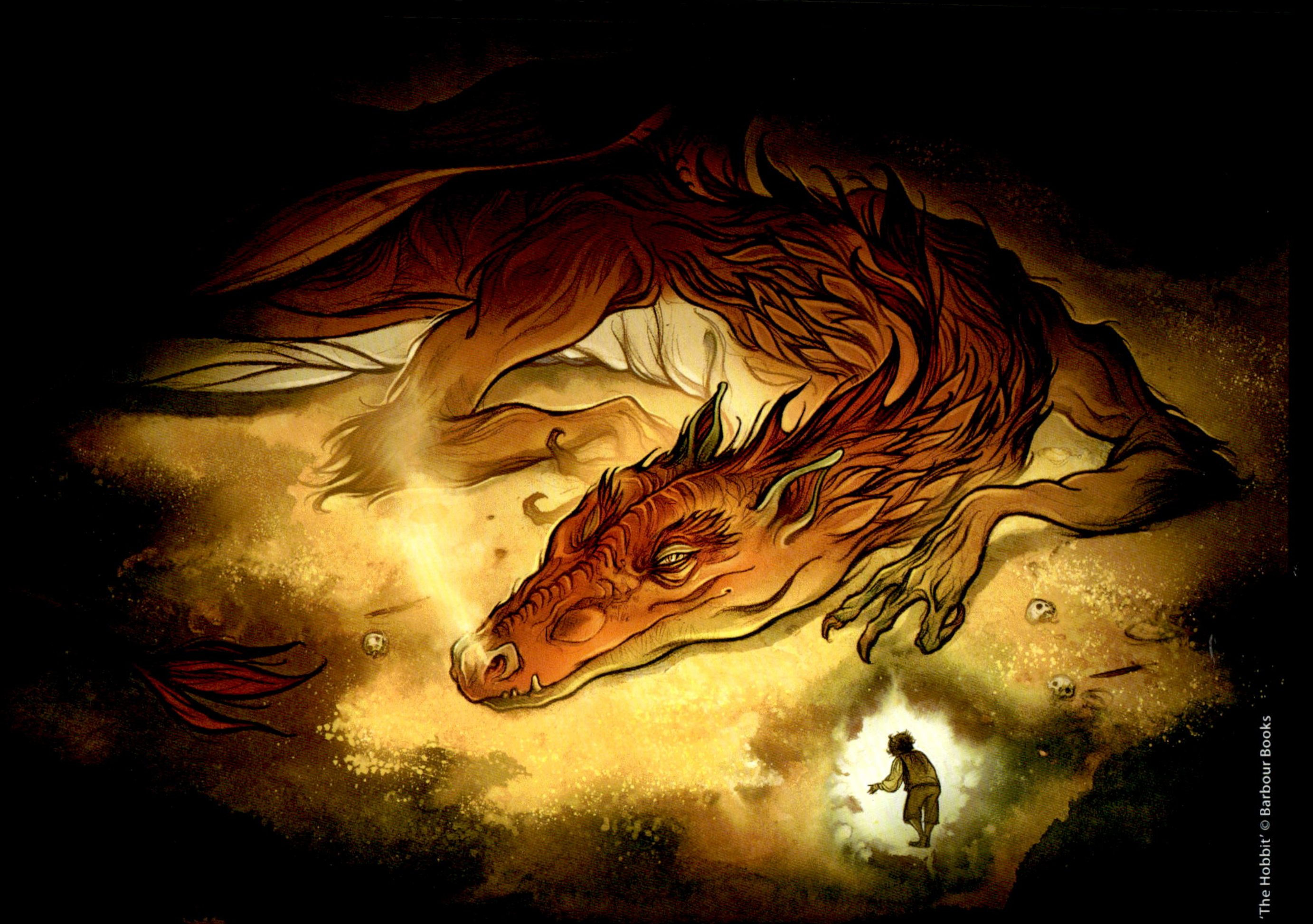

Smaug the Golden
Photoshop
Client: Barbour Books
Cory Godbey, USA
[above]

The Dragon Prince
Photoshop
Client: Consortium Books
Lane Brown, USA
[above center]

Into Dreamland
Photoshop
Bente Schlick, GERMANY
[above far right]

The Berserk Knight
Photoshop
Lius Lasahido, INDONESIA
[right]

Shells Desert
Photoshop
ZEZ Zhaoenze, CHINA
[far right]

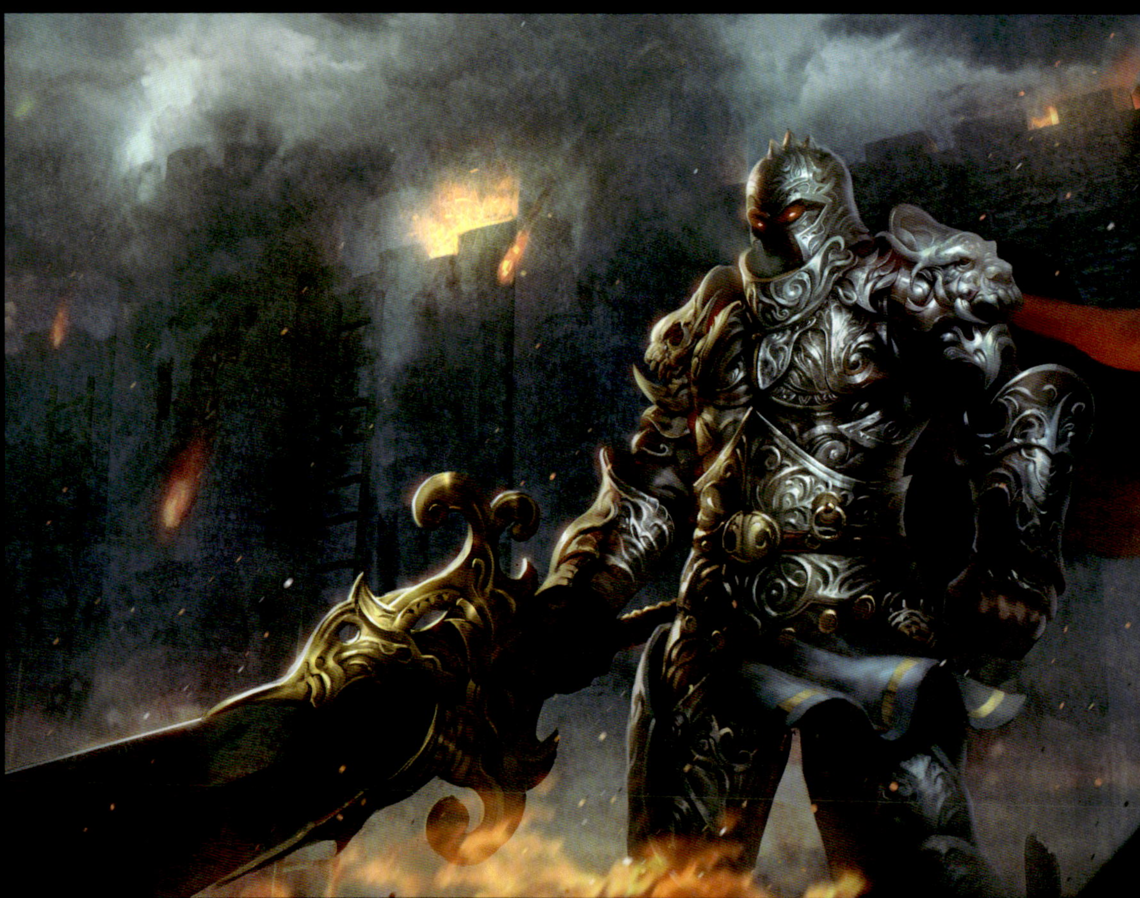

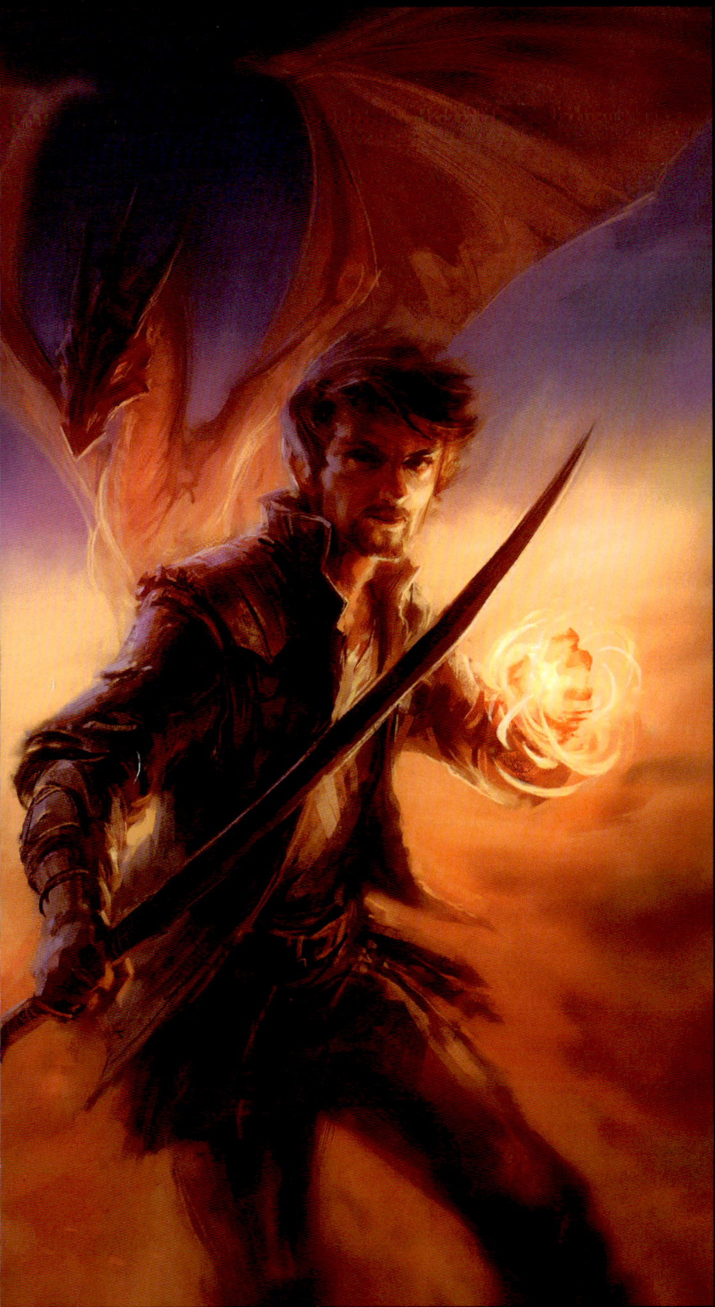

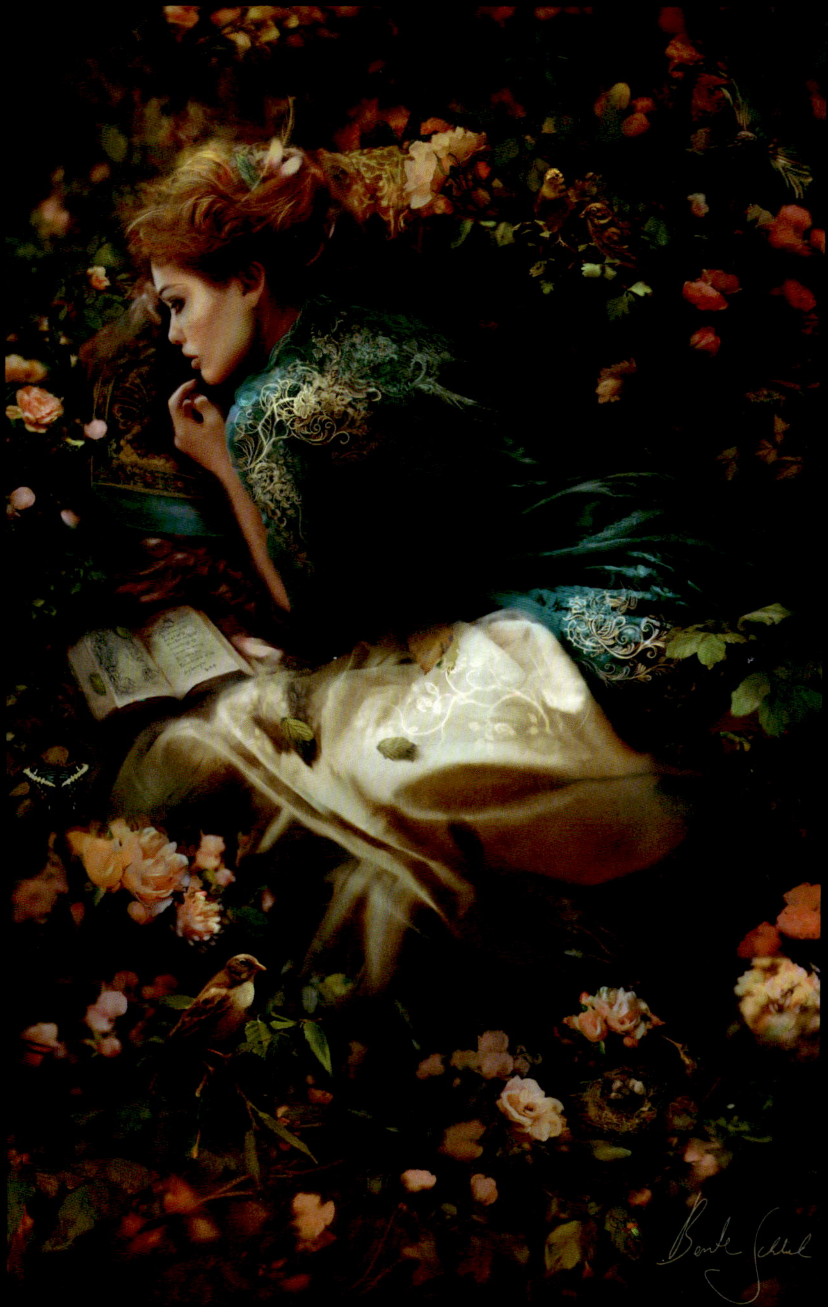

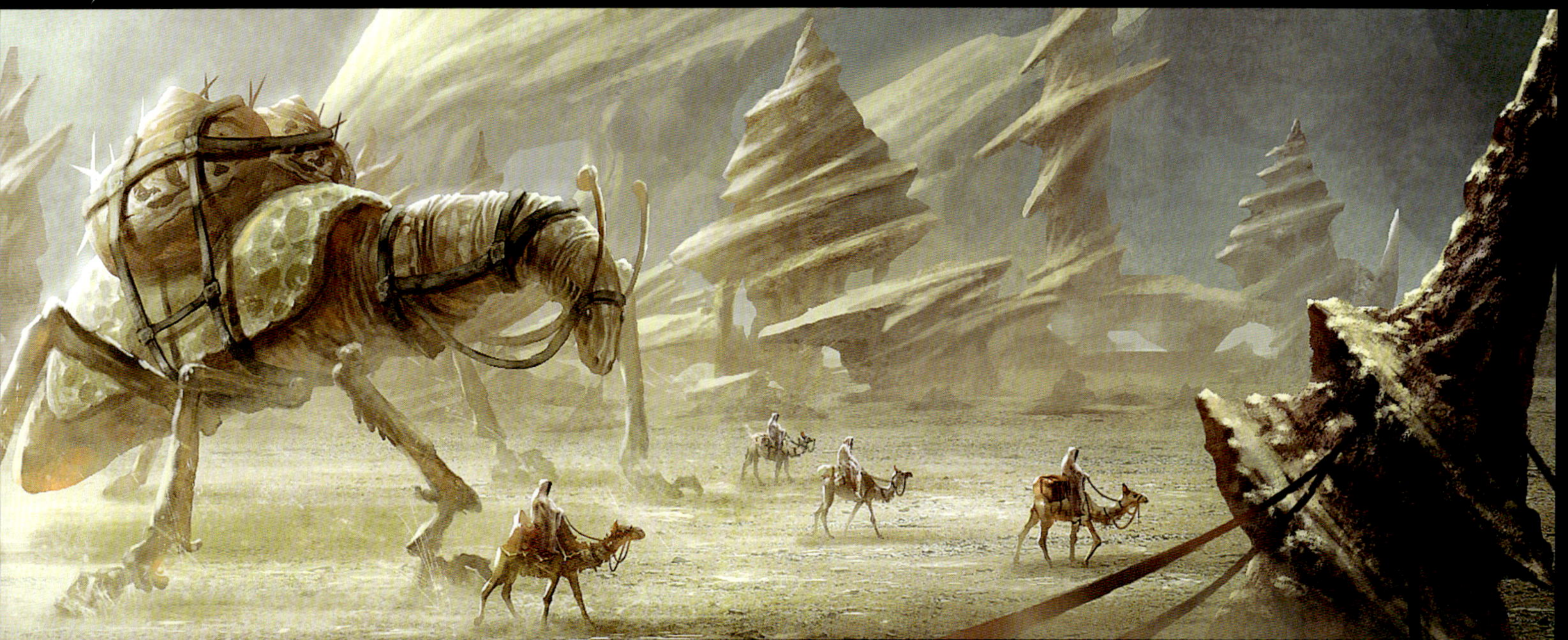

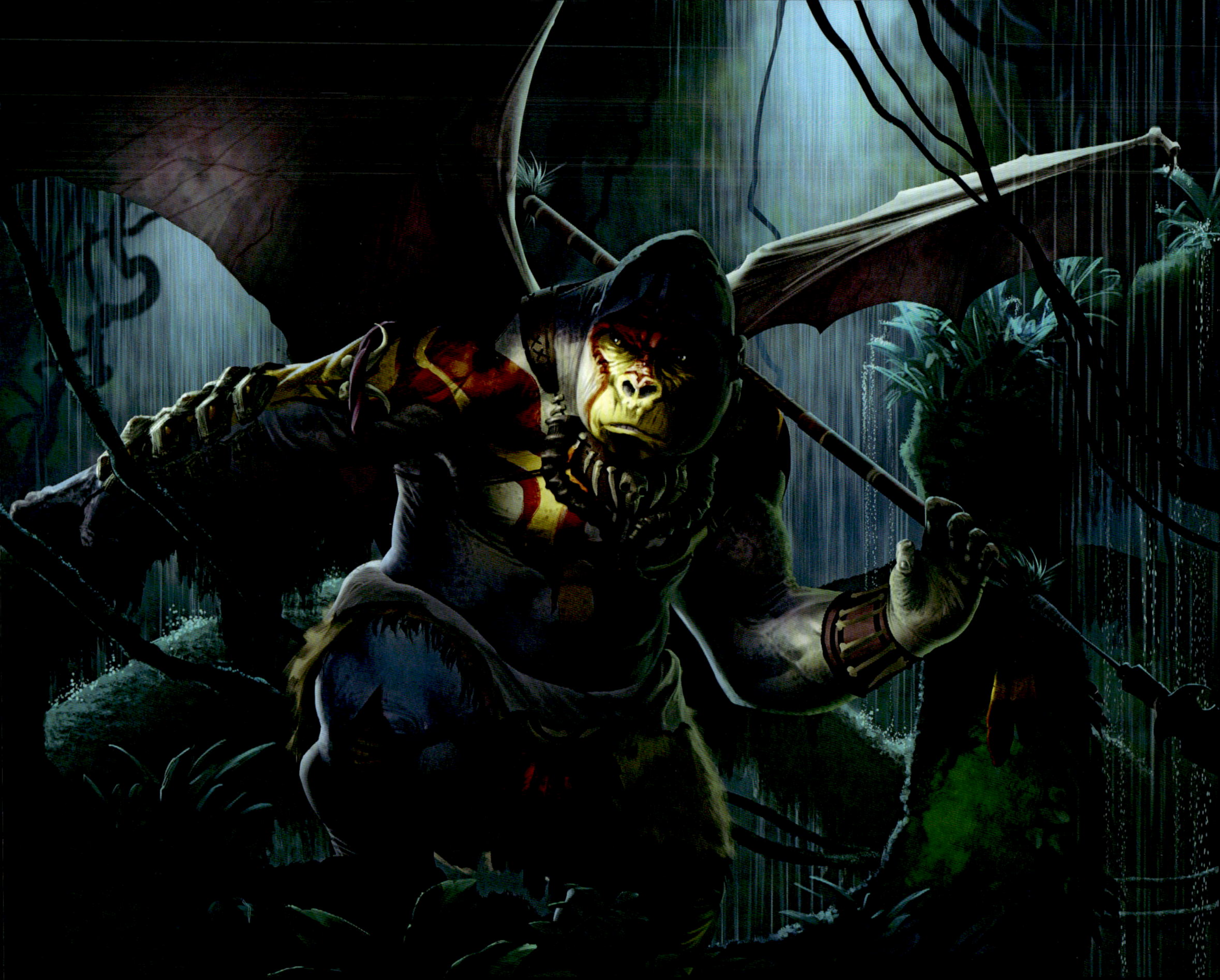

Winged Gorilla of the Emerald Forest
Photoshop
Tony Weinstock, USA
[above]

Vantage Point
Photoshop
Lane Brown, USA
[above center]

A Mermaid's Tale
Photoshop
Lawrence Mann, GREAT BRITAIN
[top far right]

Lavender Dragon
Photoshop
Galina Zhurkina, RUSSIA
[right]

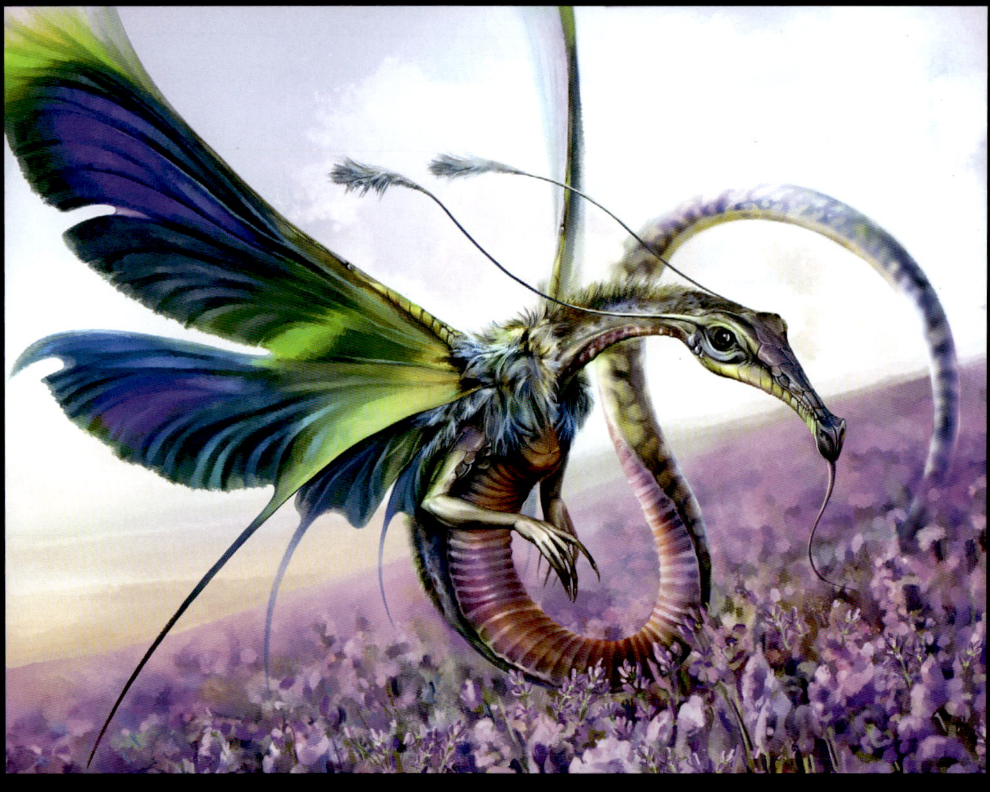

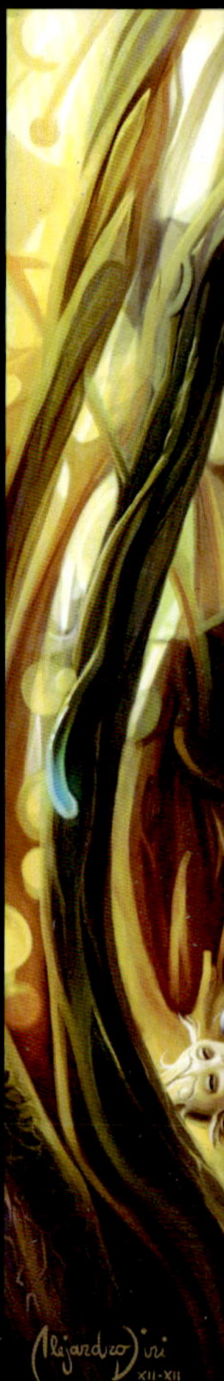

Blue Seeds
Photoshop
Alejandro Dini, CHINA
[right]

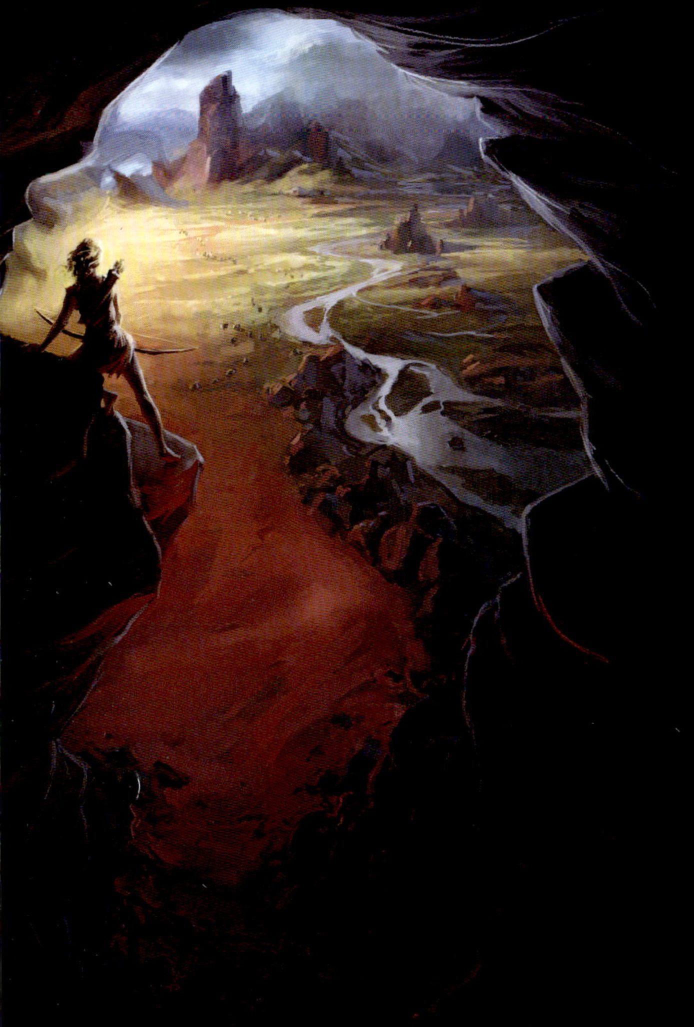

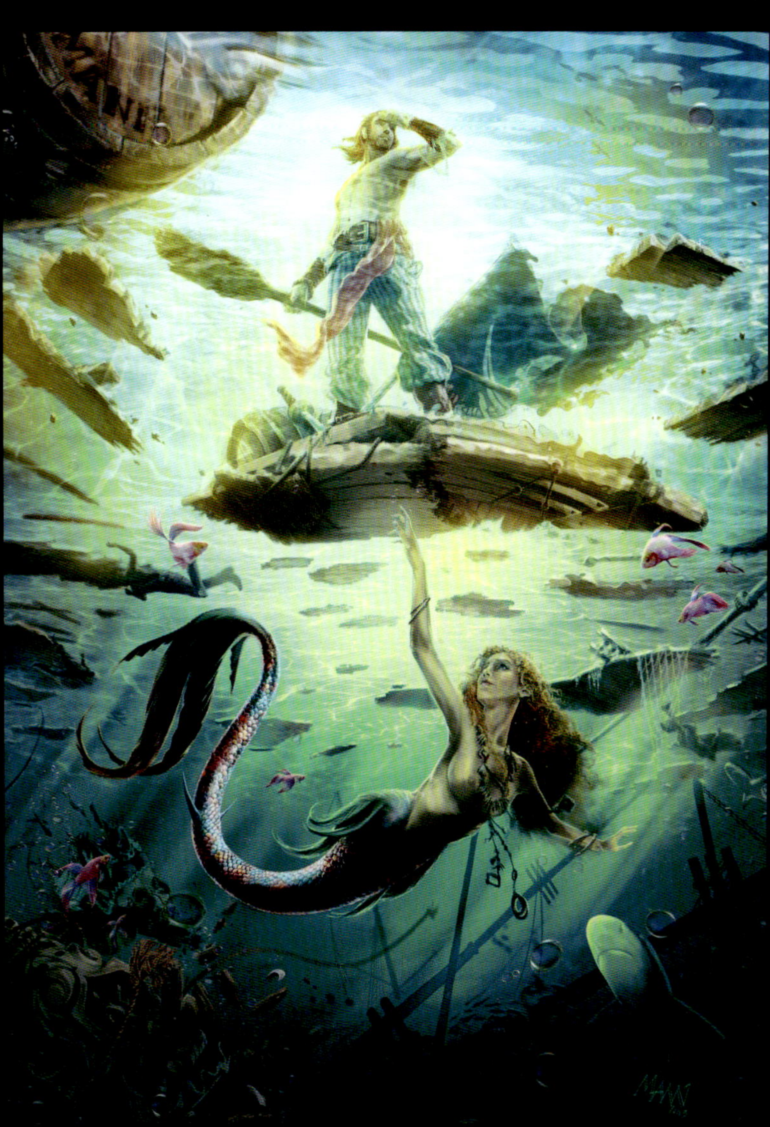

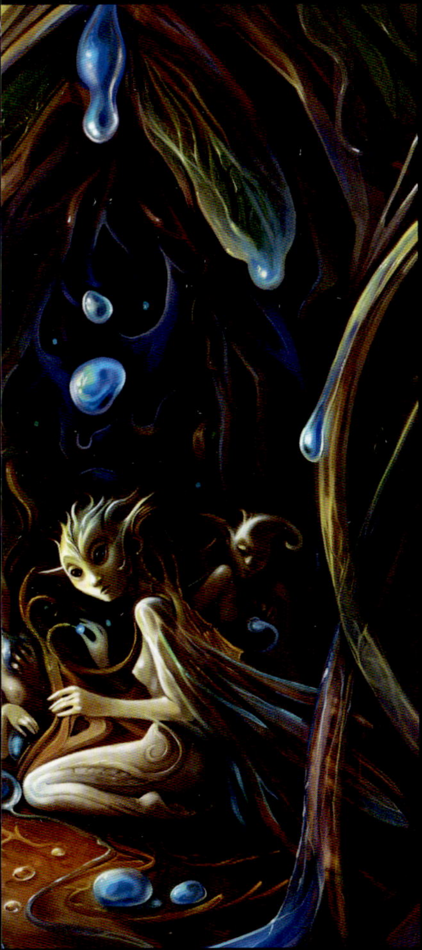

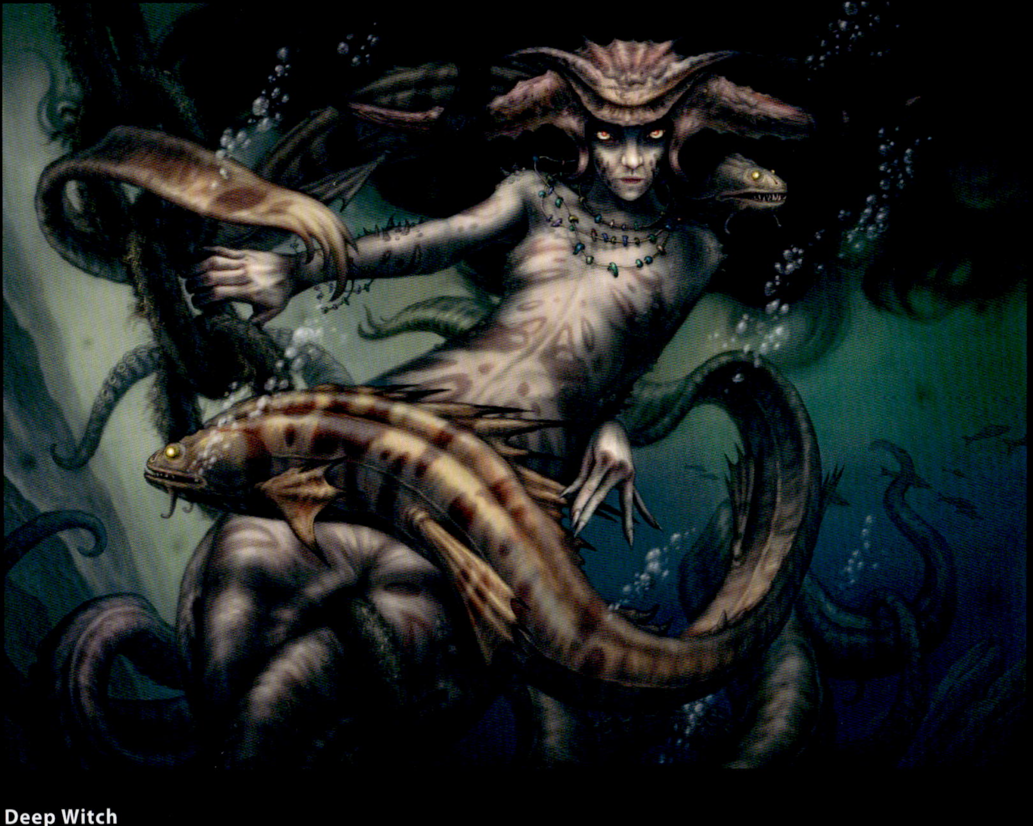

Deep Witch
Painter
Allen Douglas, USA
[above]

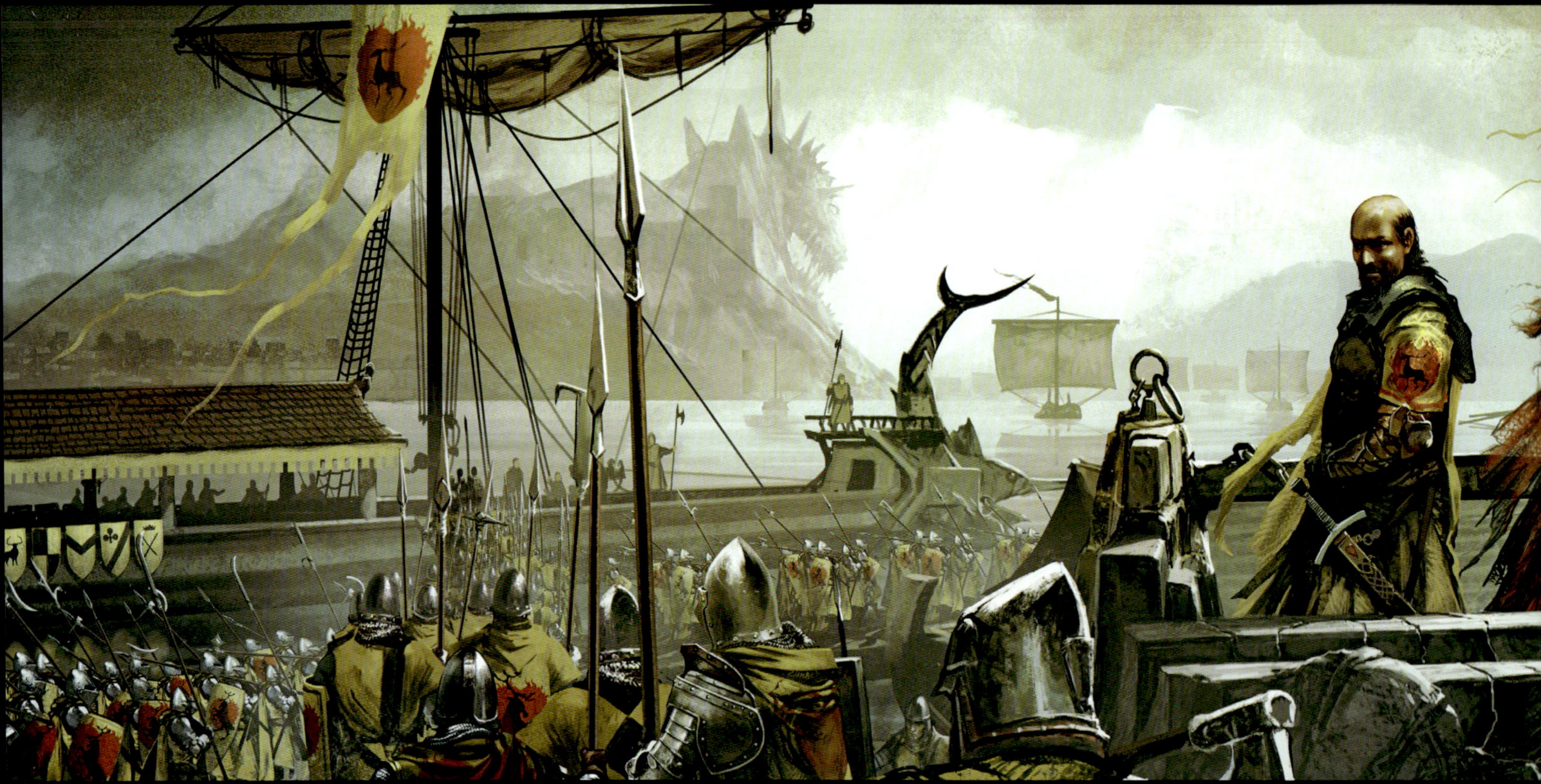

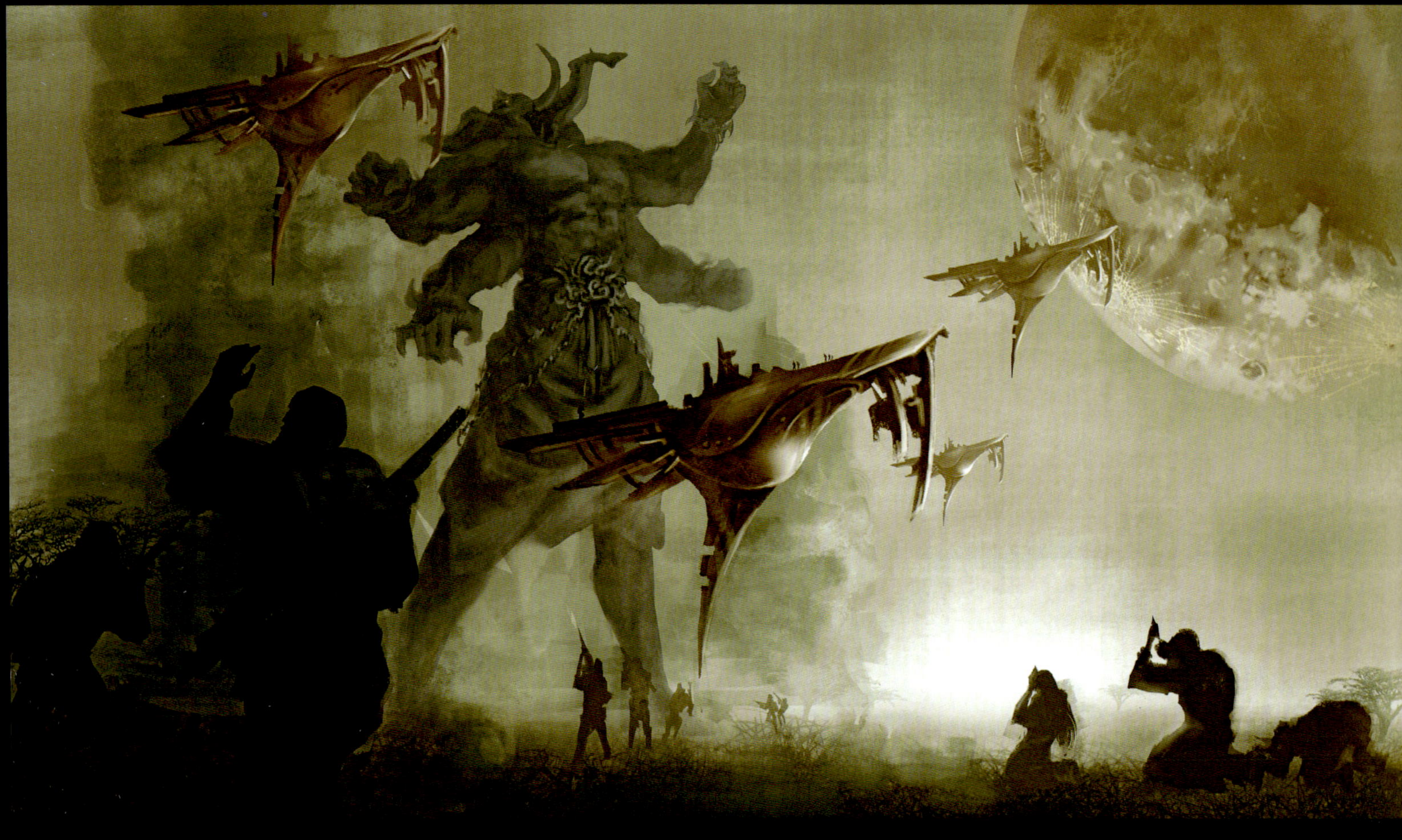

Battles of Westeros: House Baratheon Army Expansion
Photoshop
Client: Fantasy Flight Games
Tomasz Jedruszek, POLAND
[top]

Wrath of Ganesha
Photoshop
Apple Qingyang Zhang, Academy of Art University, USA
[above]

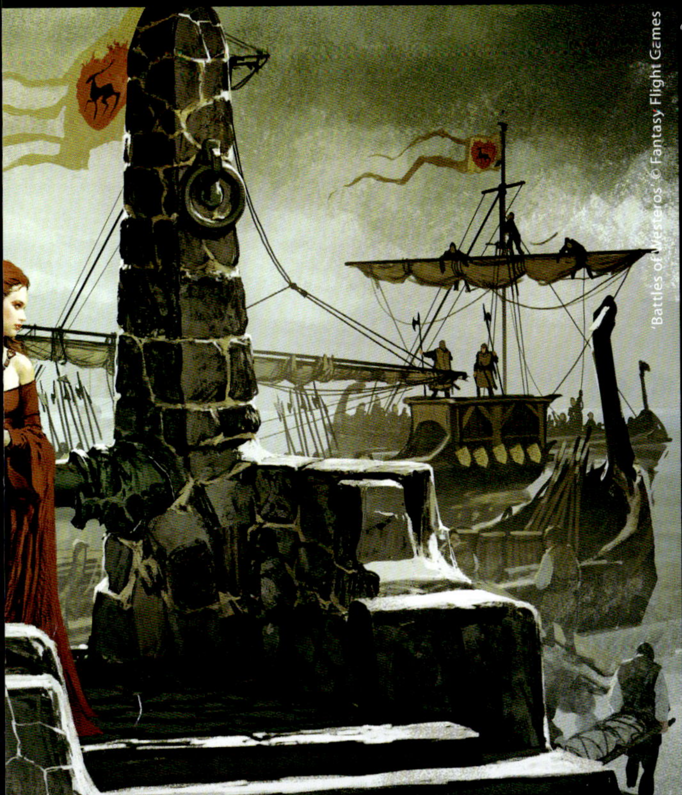

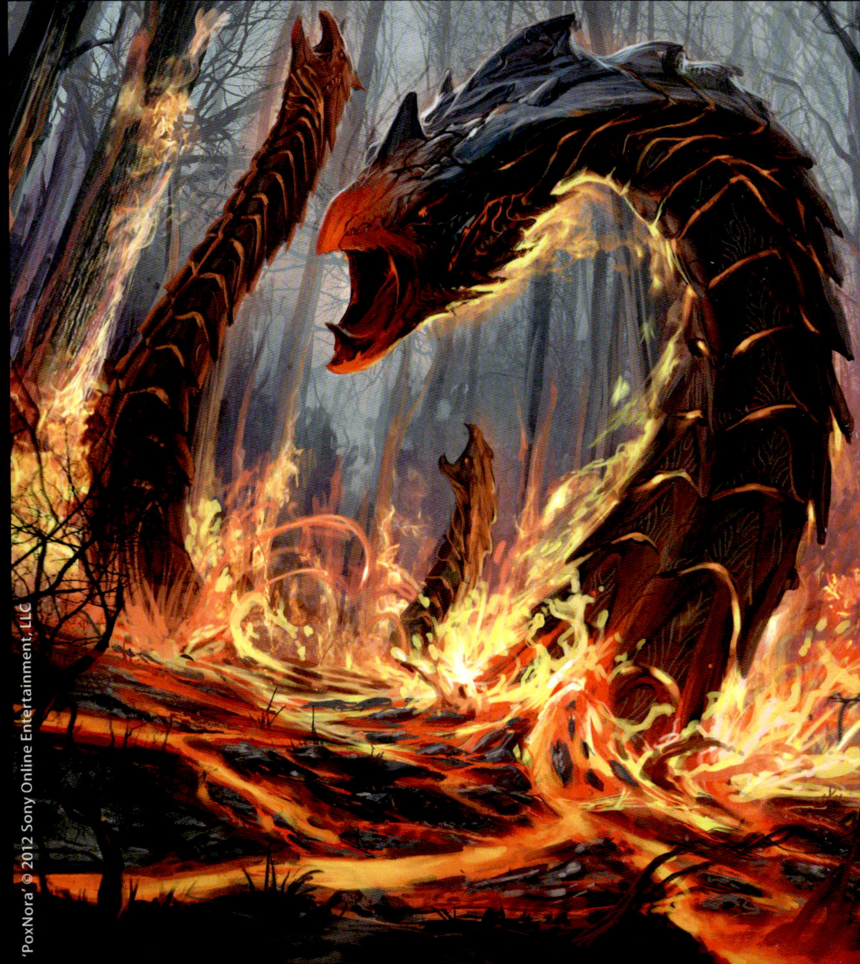

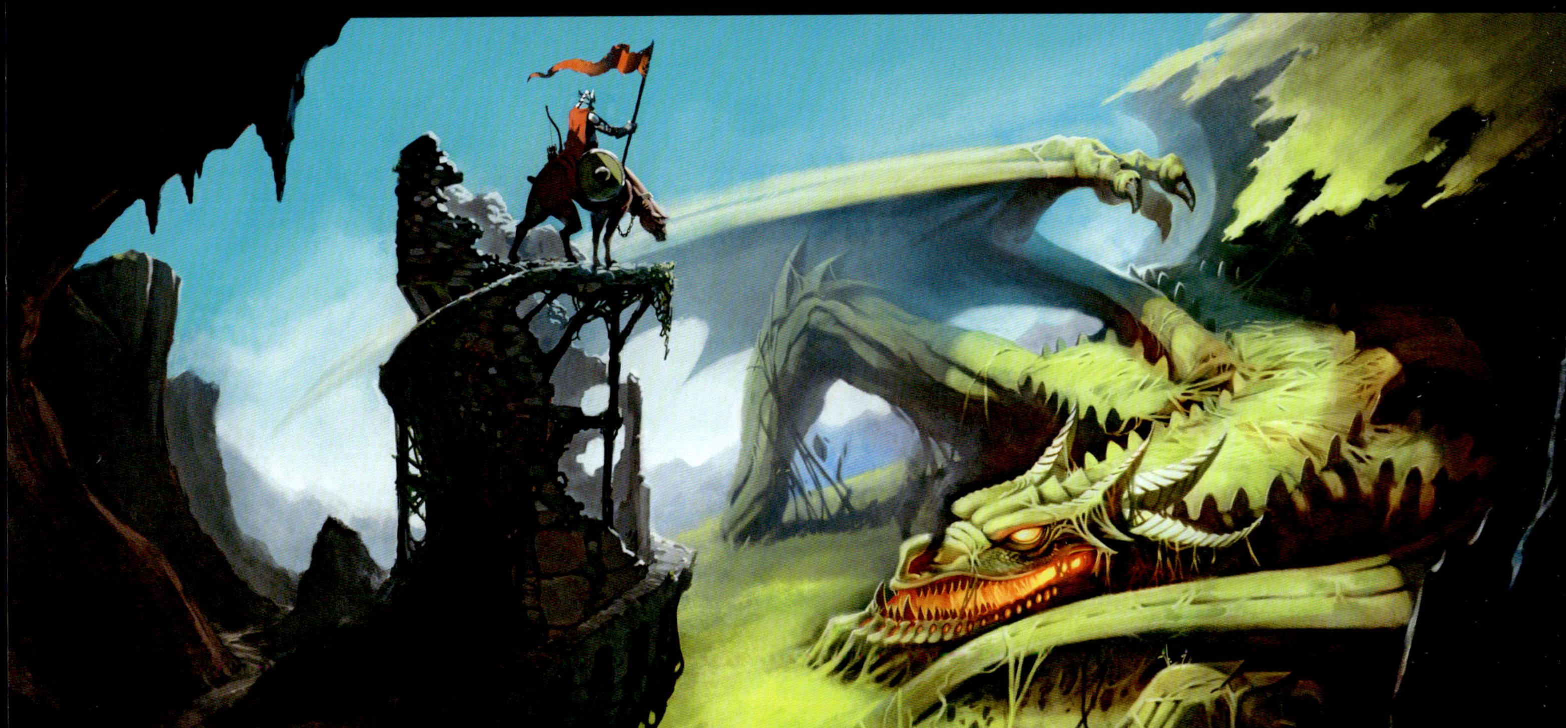

PoxNora: Heads of Osarius
Photoshop
Client: Sony Online Entertainment, LLC
Mateusz Ozminski (Art Director: Anthony Lopes), POLAND
[top right]

The Slumbering Tyrant
Photoshop
Victor Maury, USA
[above]

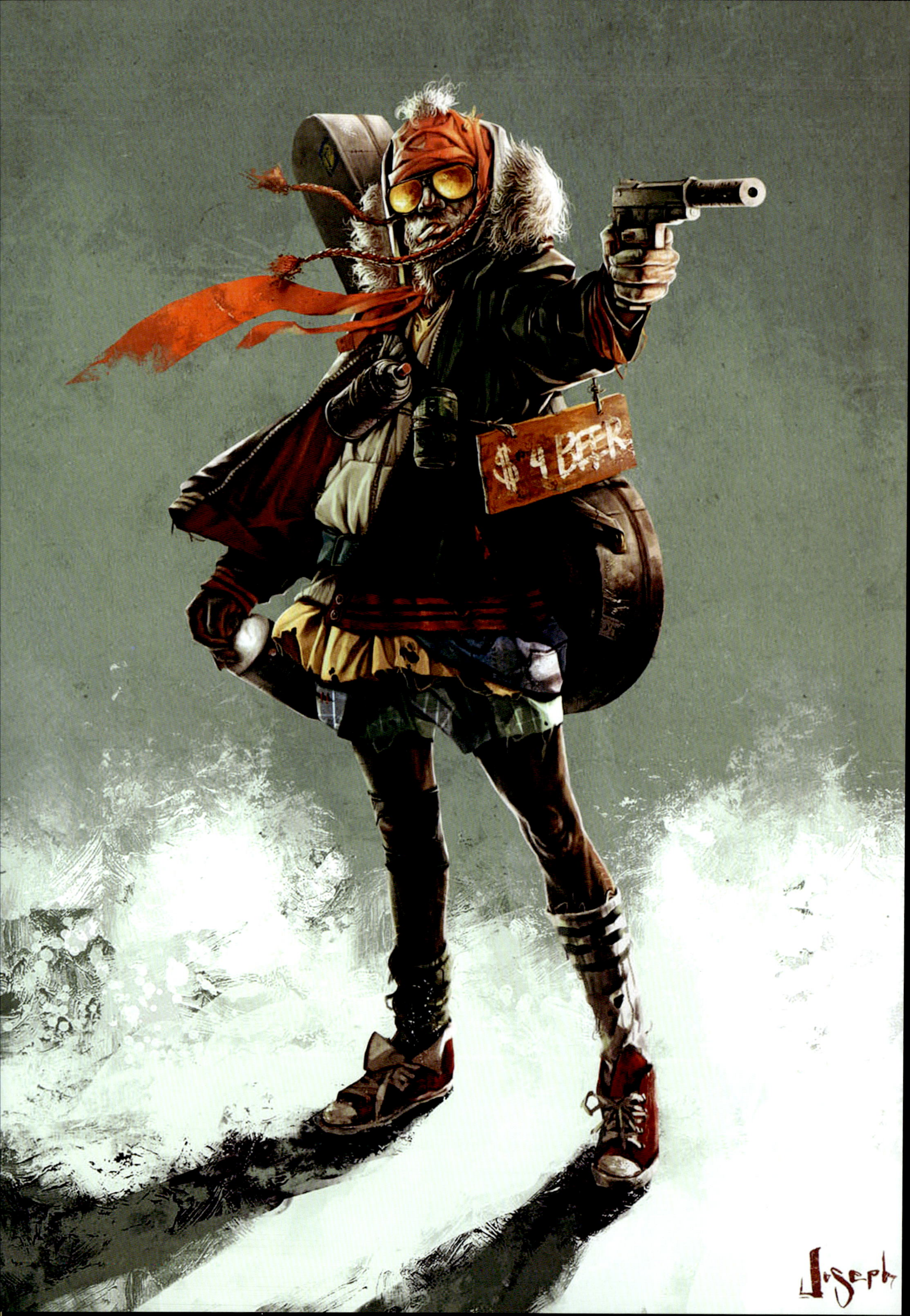

Excellence
Character

B.U.M.S. I
Photoshop
Joseph Descallar, USA

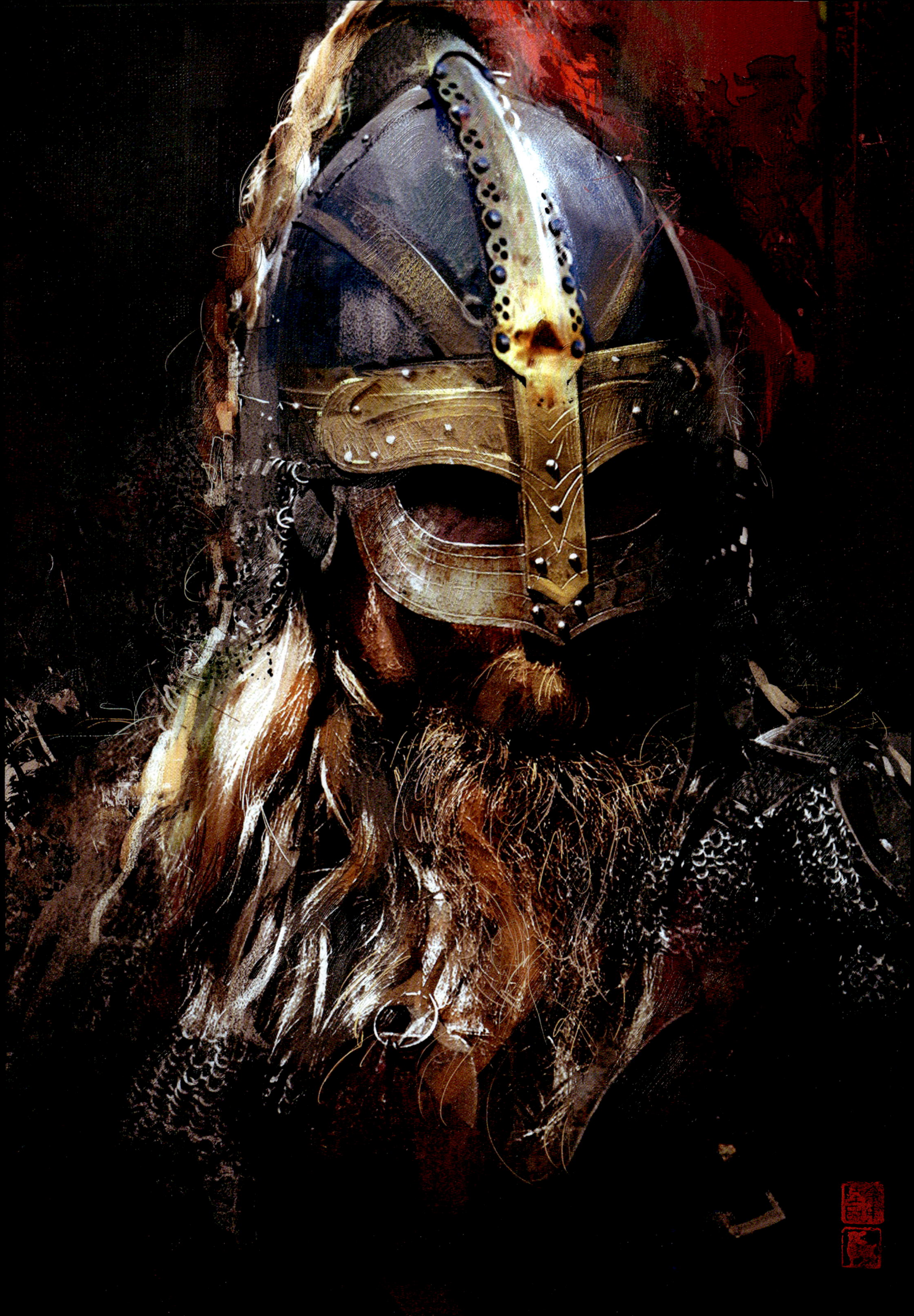

Medieval Lord
Photoshop, ArtRage
Donglu Yu, CANADA

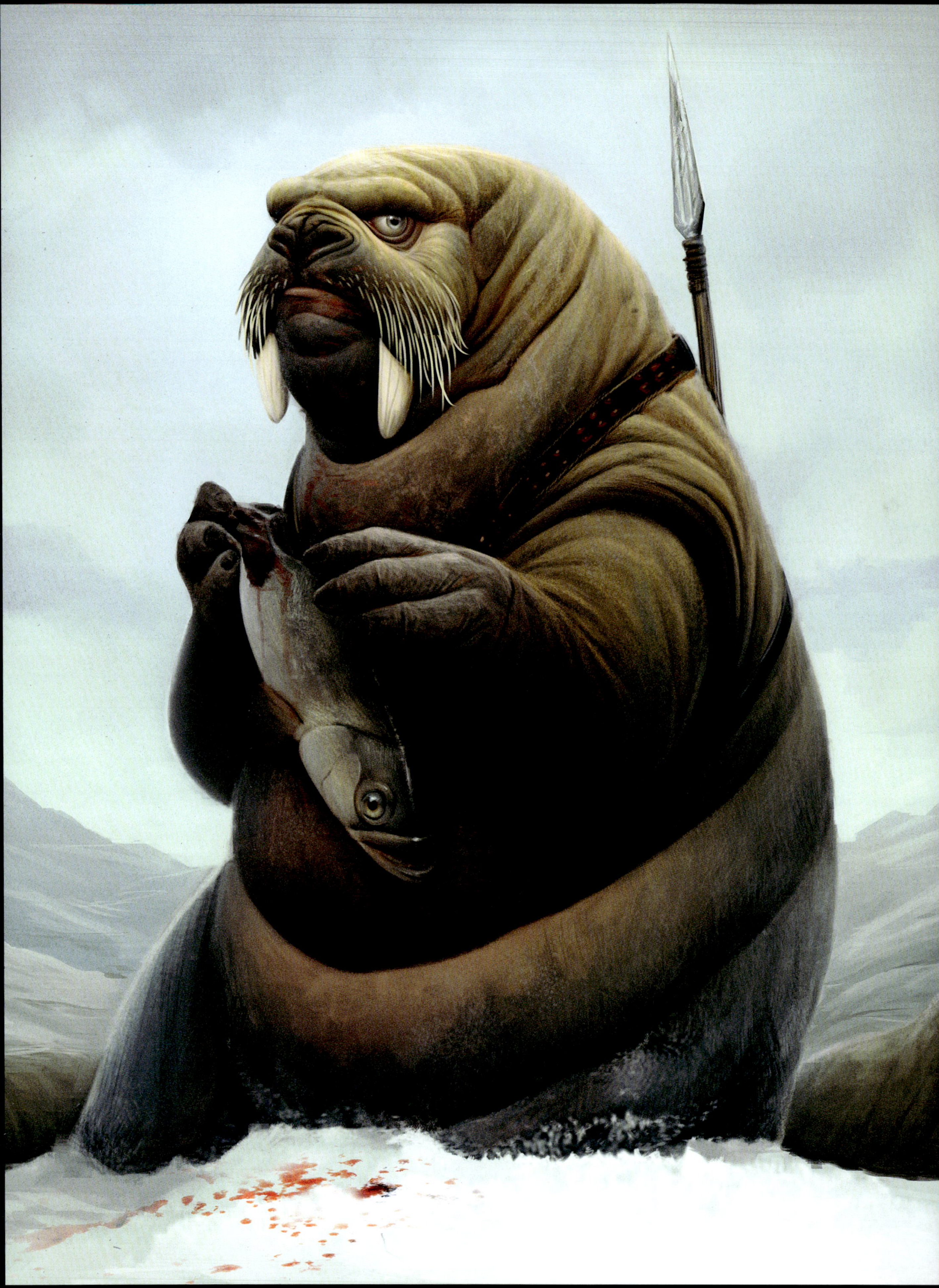

Walrus
Photoshop
Max Kostenko, RUSSIA

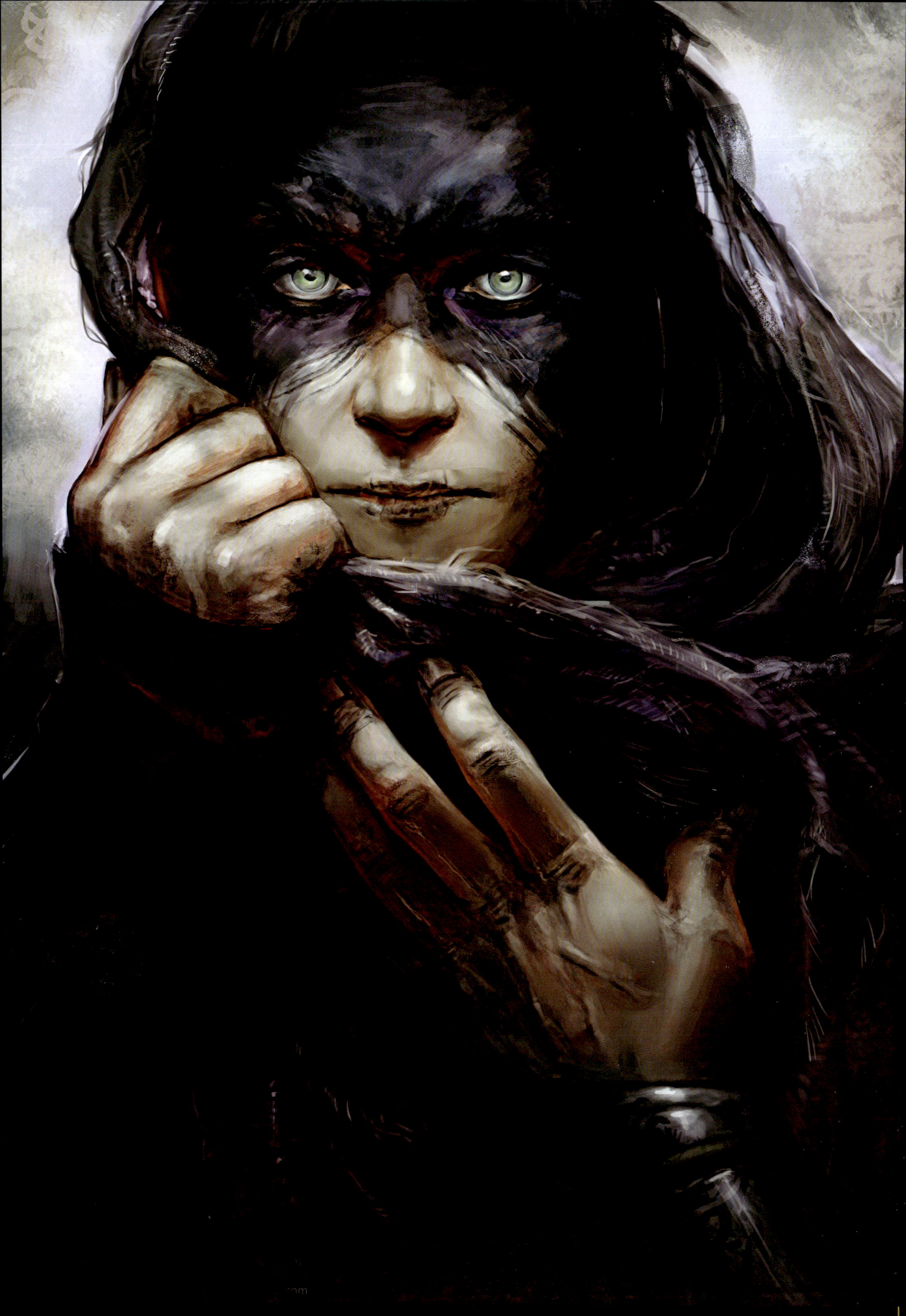

Seventh Devil
Photoshop
Monika Palosz, POLAND

Soul
Photoshop, Painter
Te Hu, USA
[right]

Tribal Leader
Photoshop
Client: Future Publishing
Mark Molnar, HUNGARY
[below]

Banner Freak: Rancid Rob
ZBrush, Photoshop
Andrew Baker, NEW ZEALAND
[below right]

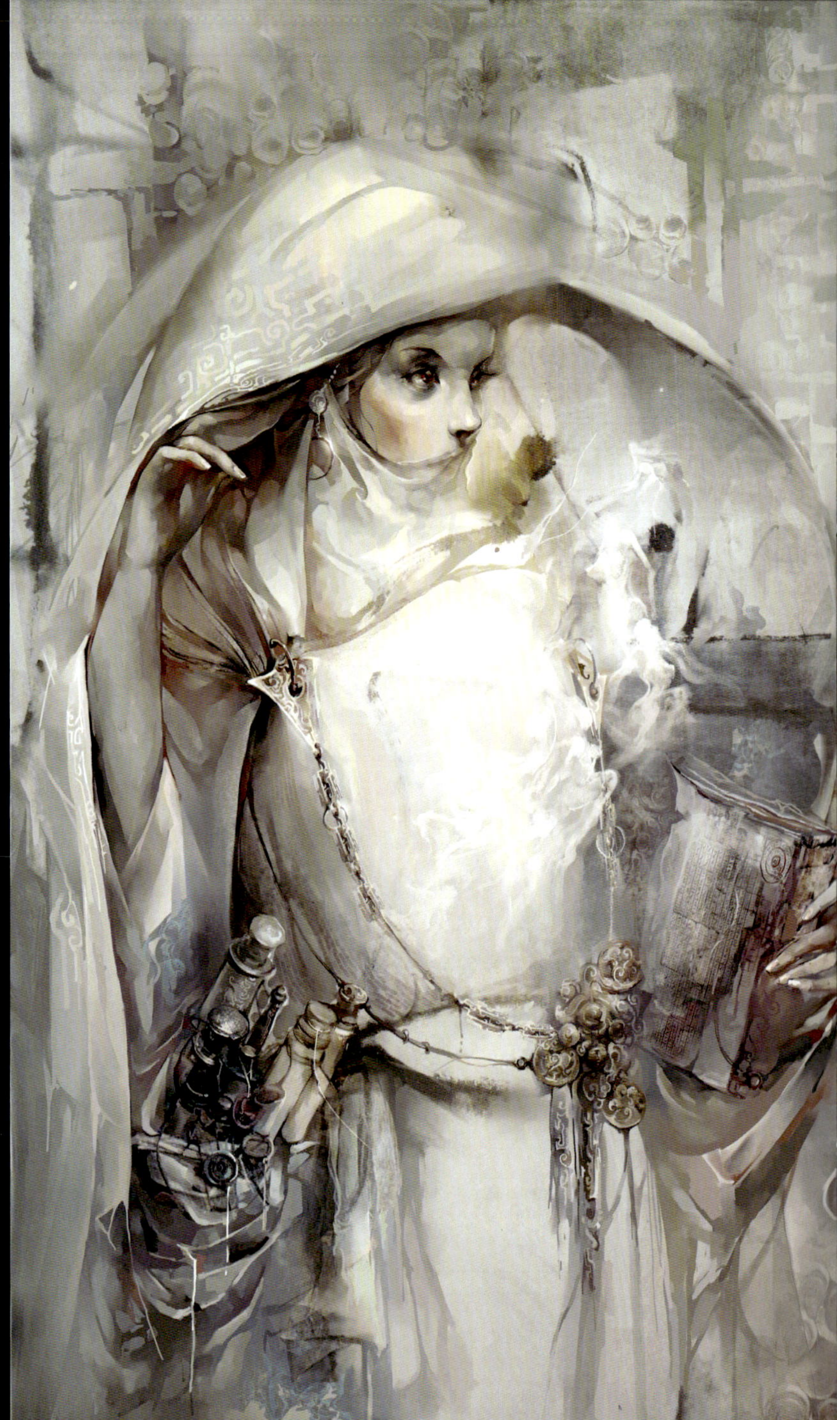

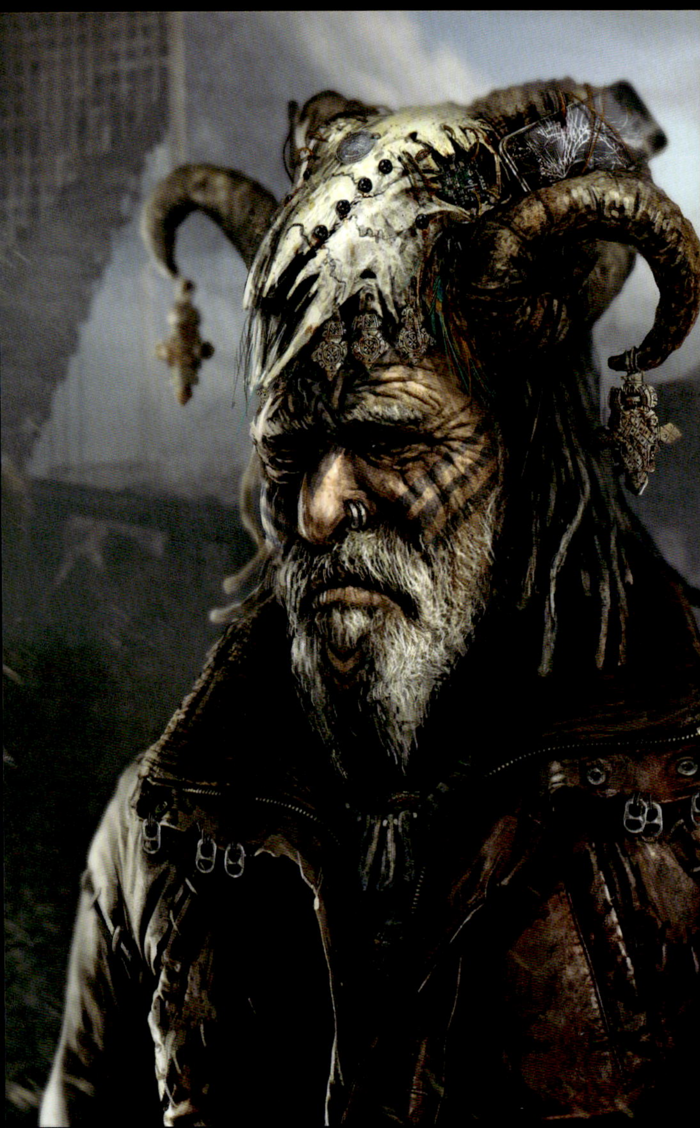

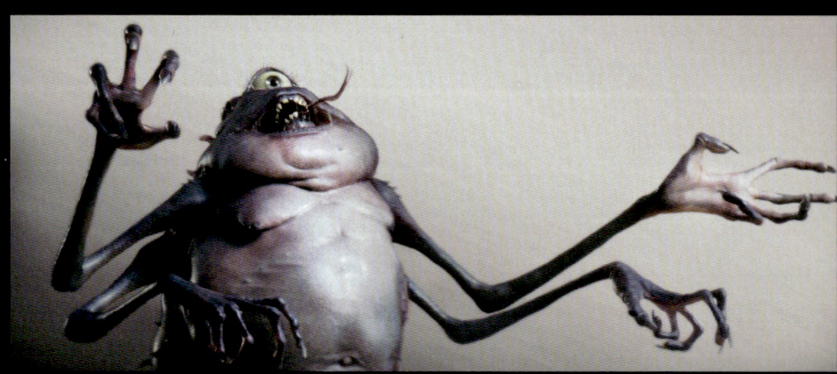

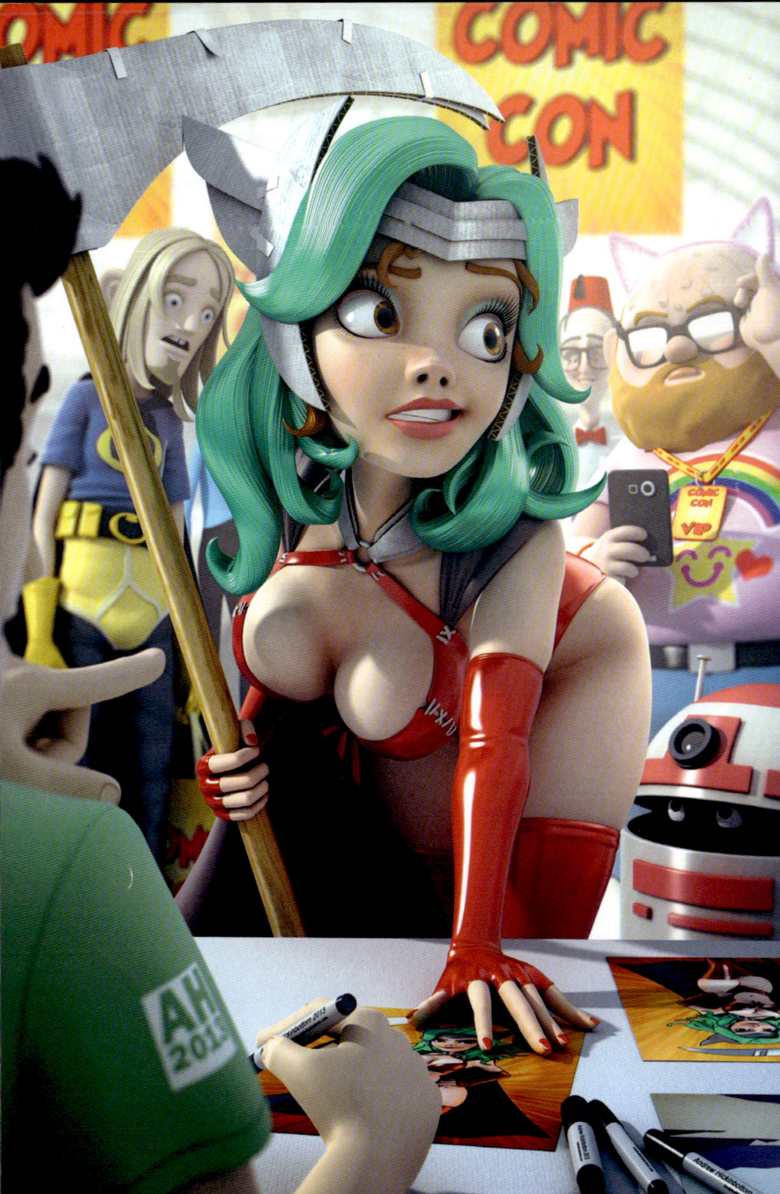

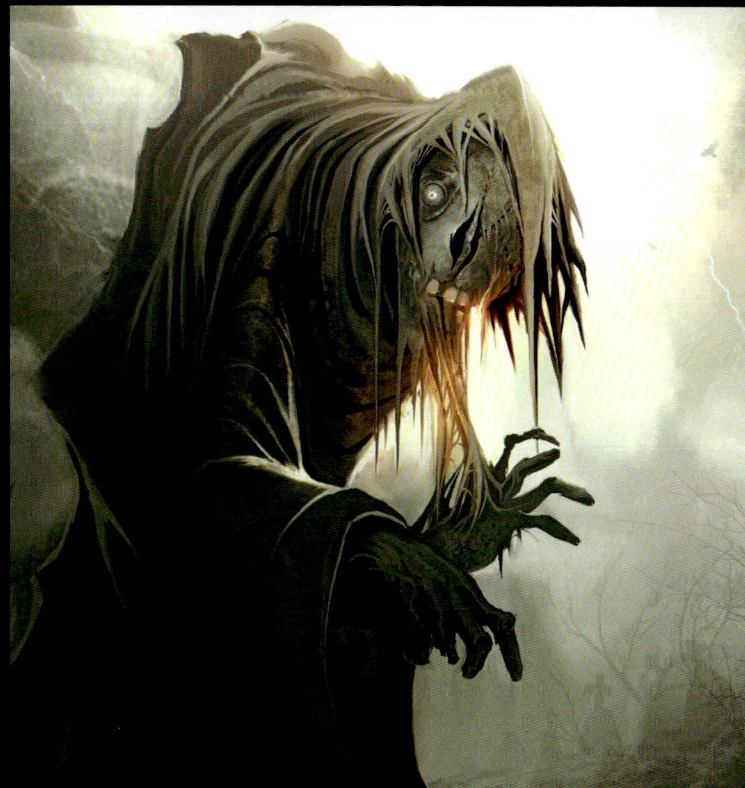

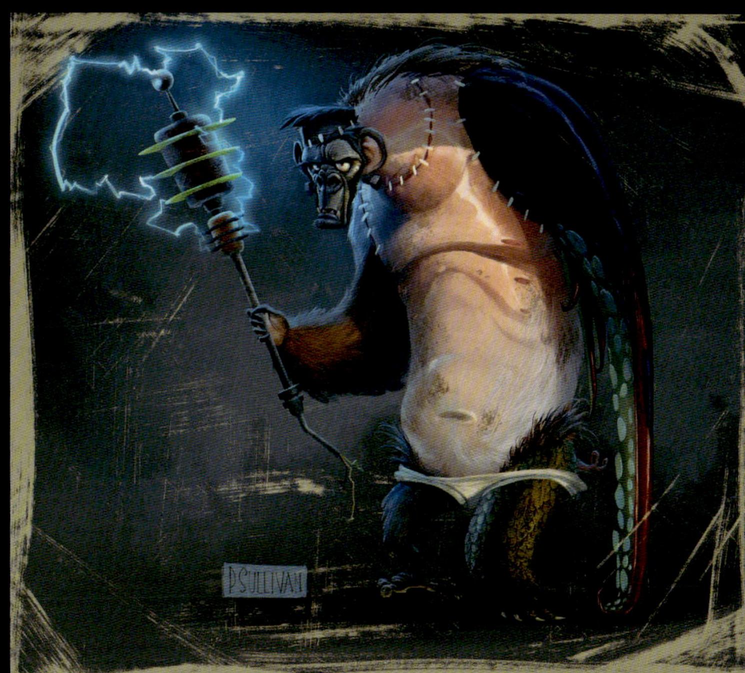

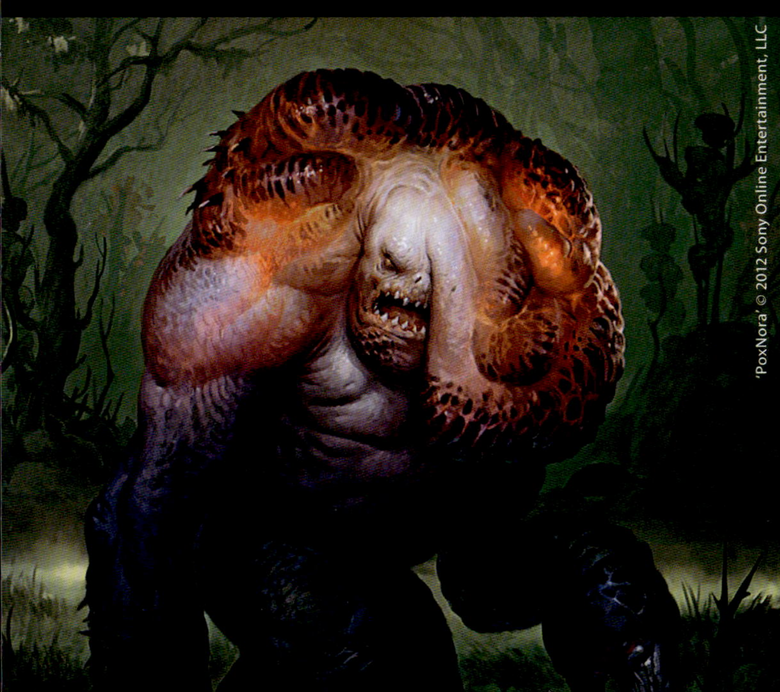

Comic Con Curves
3ds Max, V-Ray, Photoshop
Andrew Hickinbottom, GREAT BRITAIN
[above left]

Ghoul
Photoshop
Ramses Melendez, MEXICO
[top]

Frankenanimals

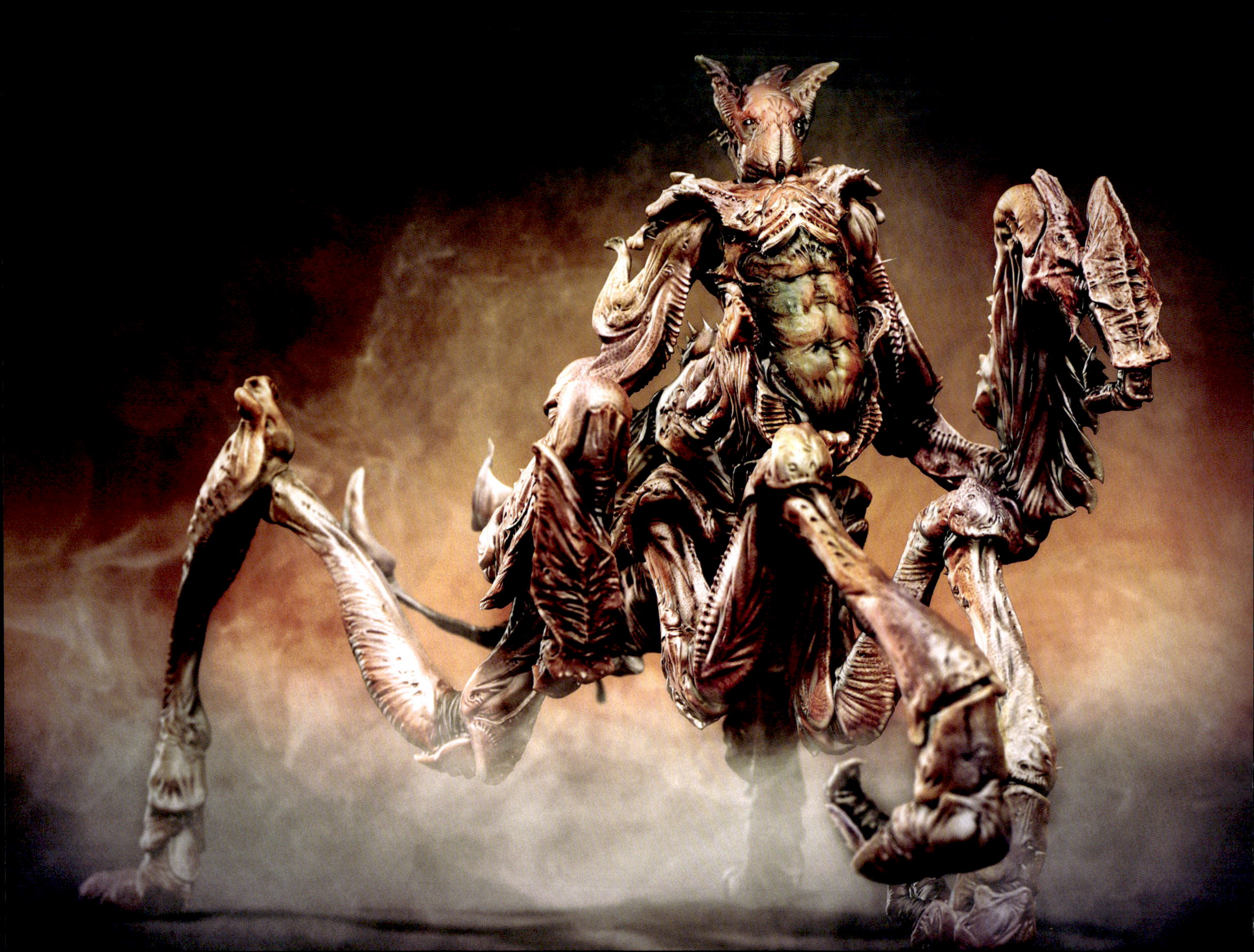

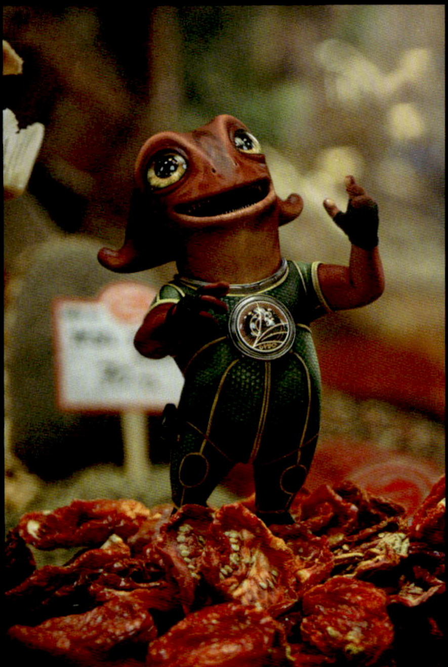

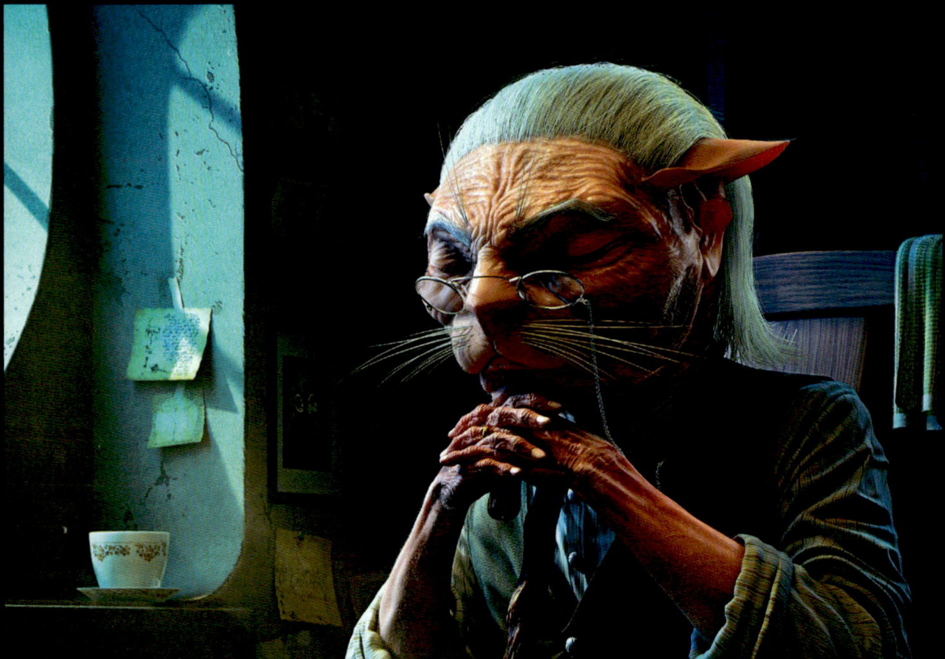

I Found It!
Maya, ZBrush, Photoshop, mental ray
Jean-Michel Bihorel, FRANCE
[above]

The Mantis
ZBrush, Photoshop
Tudor Fat, ROMANIA
[top]

Catman
Maya, mental ray, Photoshop, BodyPaint 3D
Xiaodong Li, HXSD, CHINA
[above]

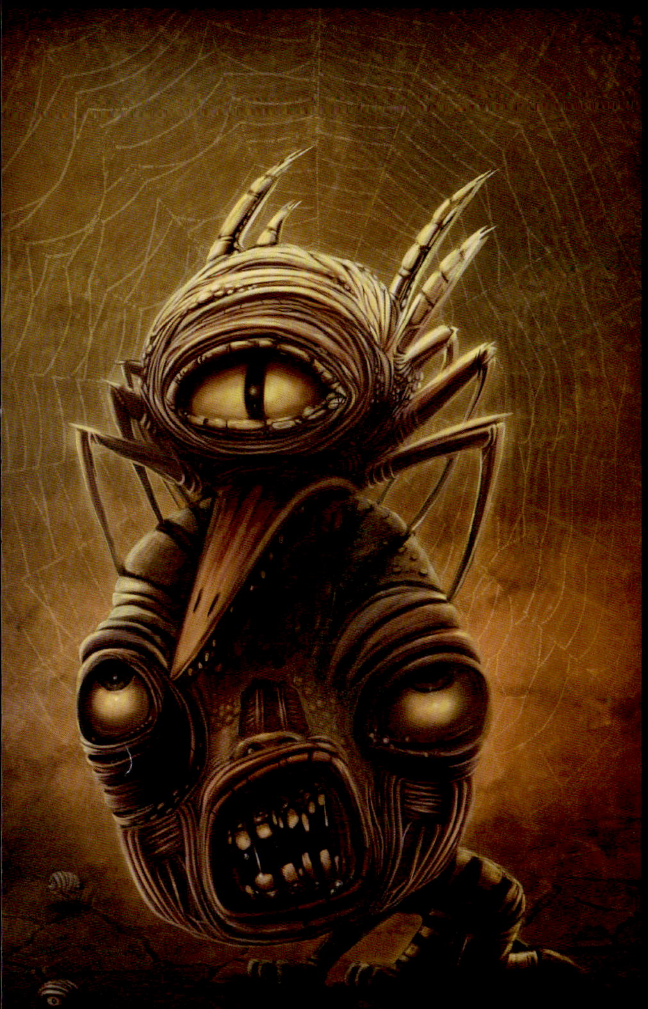

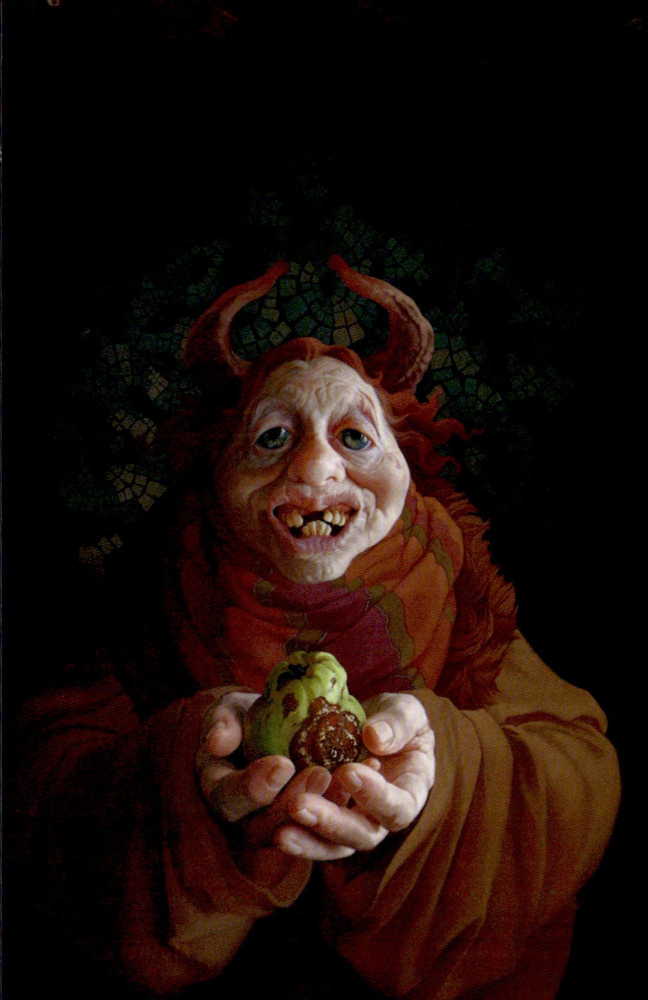

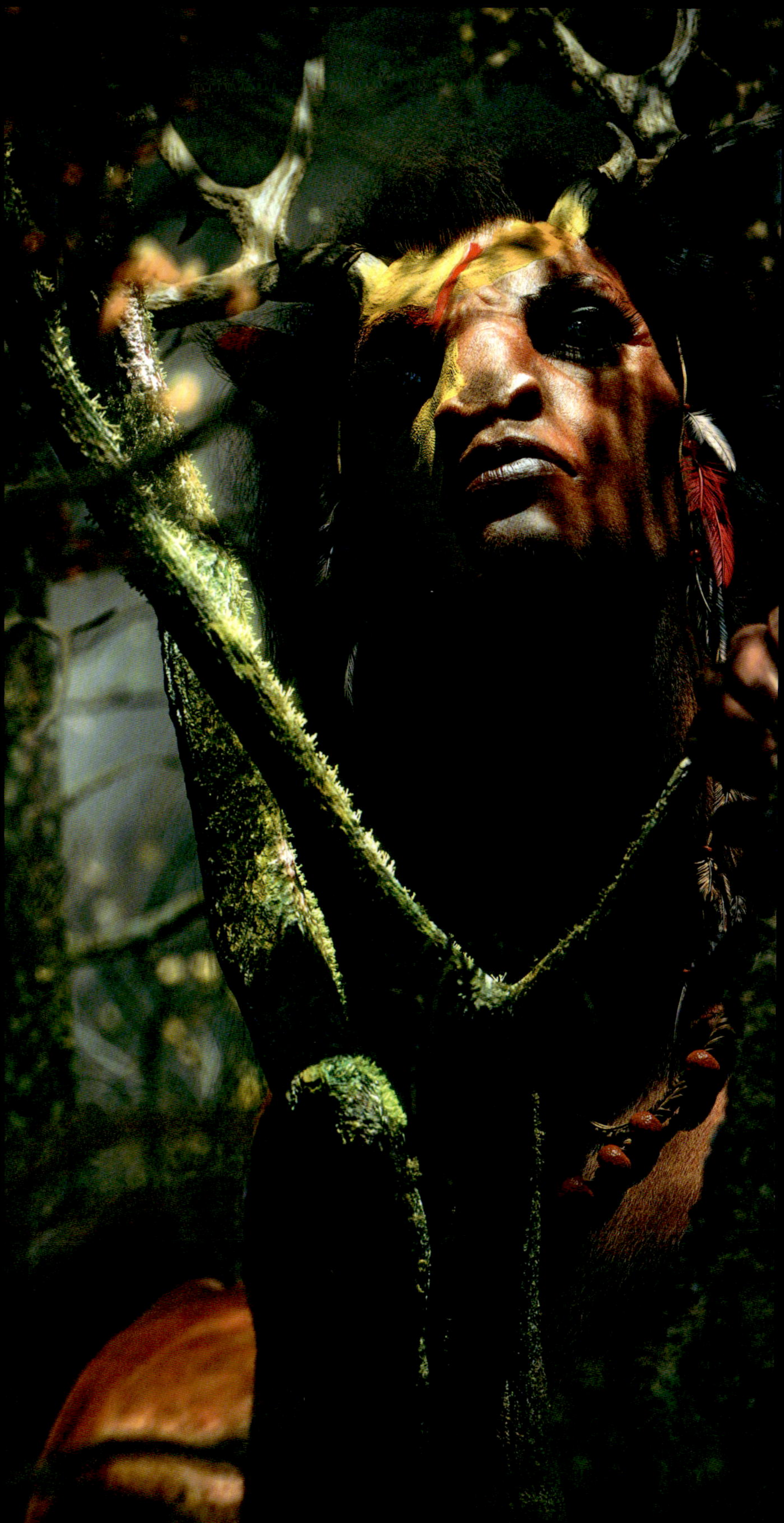

Nightmare
Photoshop
Liran Szeiman, SPAIN
[top left]

Offering
Photoshop
Romana Kendelic, CROATIA
[left]

Centaur
Maya, V-Ray, Mudbox, Photoshop
Igor Kudryavtsev, RUSSIA
[above]

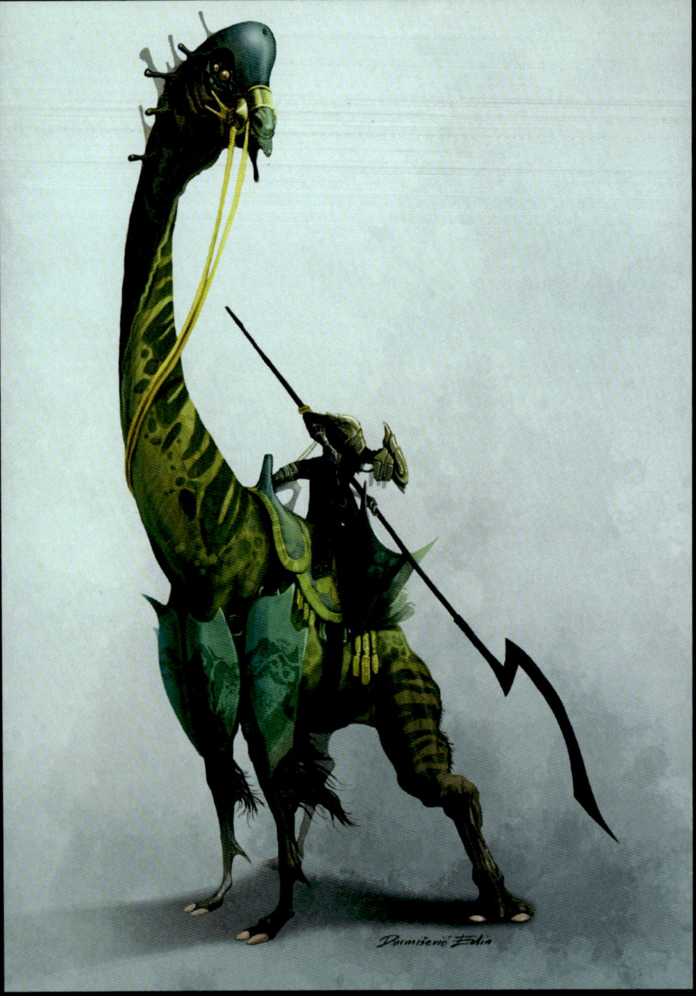

Heavy Cavalry
Photoshop
Edin Durmisevic,
BOSNIA AND HERZEGOVINA
[top]

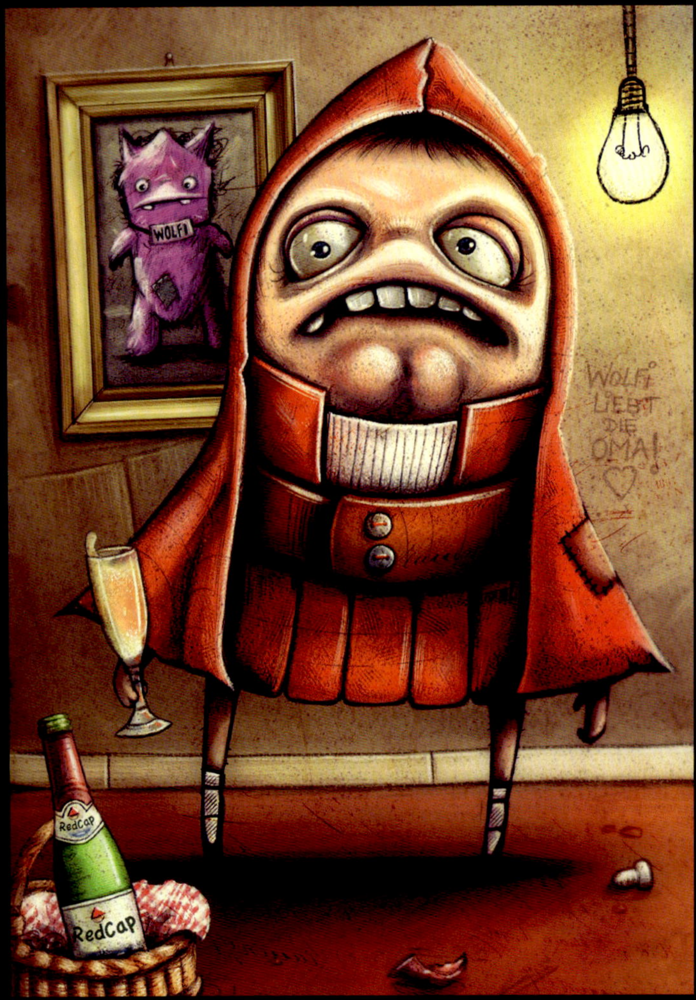

Red Riding Hood
Painter, Photoshop
Robin Kunzmann, LOPINE, GERMANY
[above]

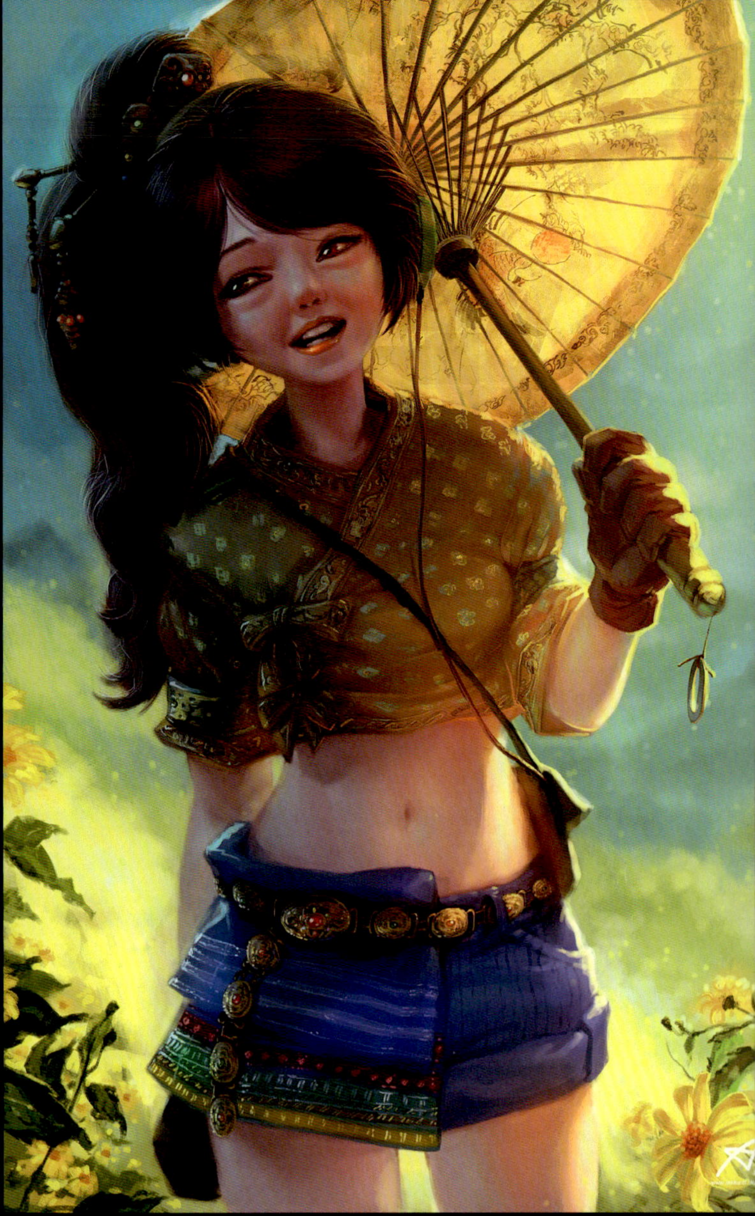

Boathong (Mexican Sunflower)
Photoshop
Aekkarat Sumuchaya, THAILAND
[top]

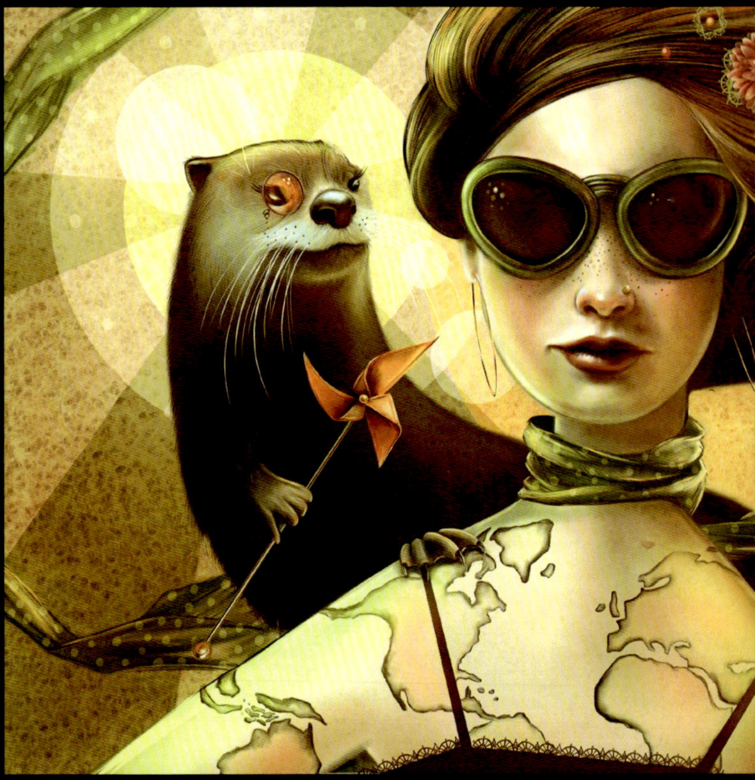

Mother Earth
Painter, Photoshop
Christina Hess, USA
[above]

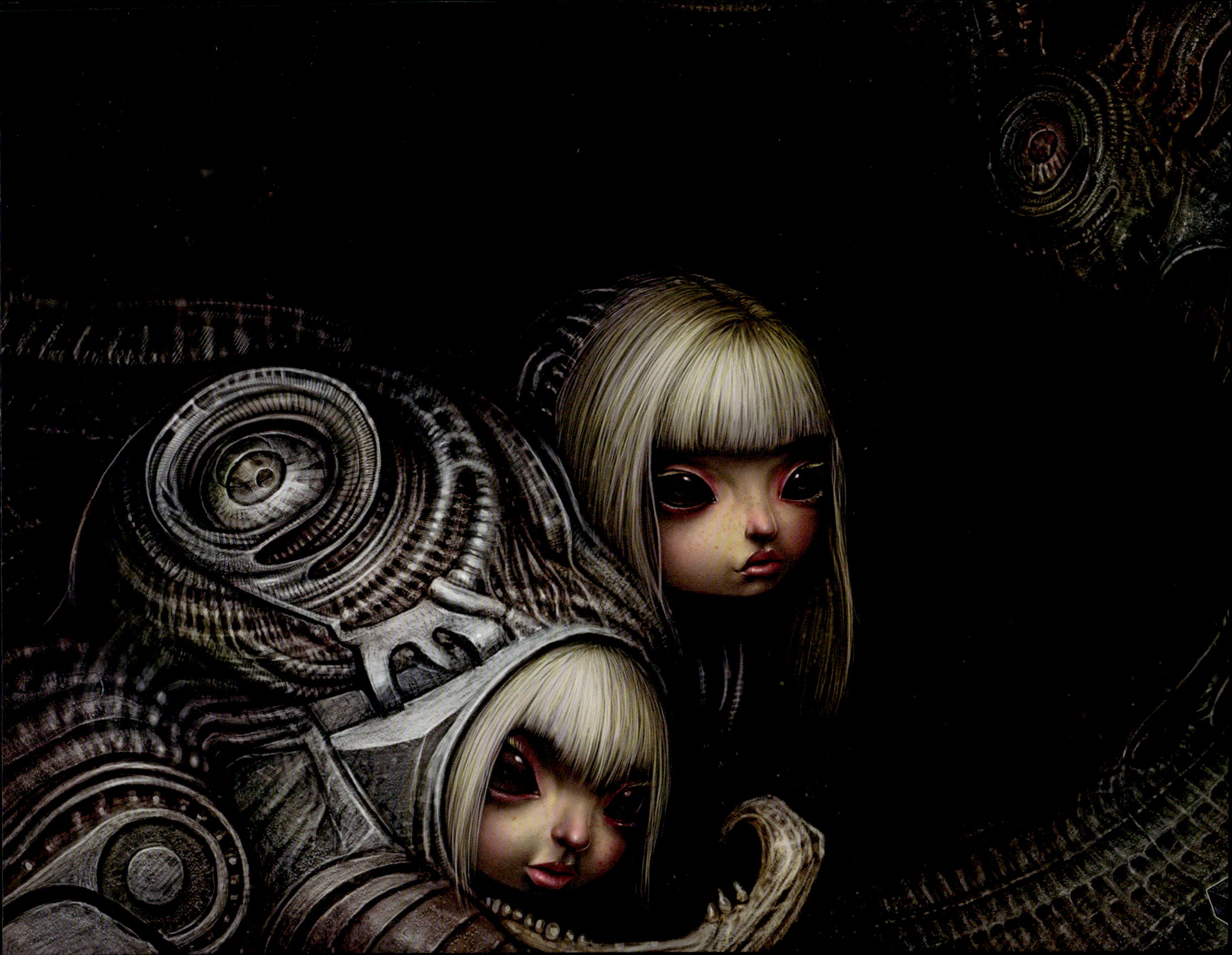

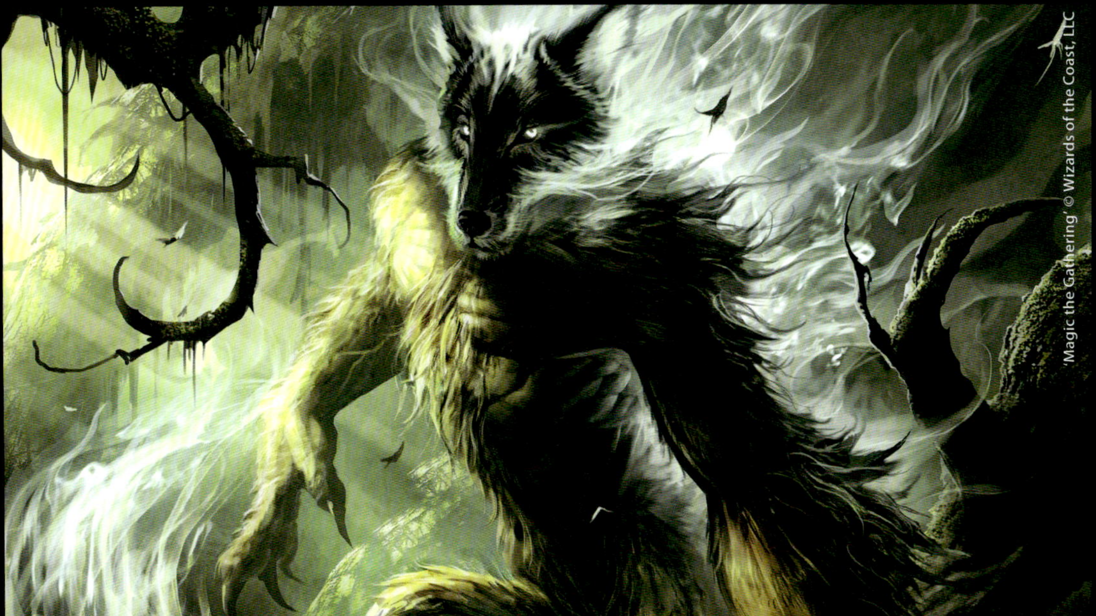

Dolls from the Hole
Photoshop
Liran Szeiman and Martin de Diego Sadaba,
Sugarflesh, SPAIN

Magic: the Gathering (Wolfir Silverheart)
Photoshop
Client: Wizards of the Coast, LLC
Raymond Swanland (Art Director: Jeremy Jarvis), USA

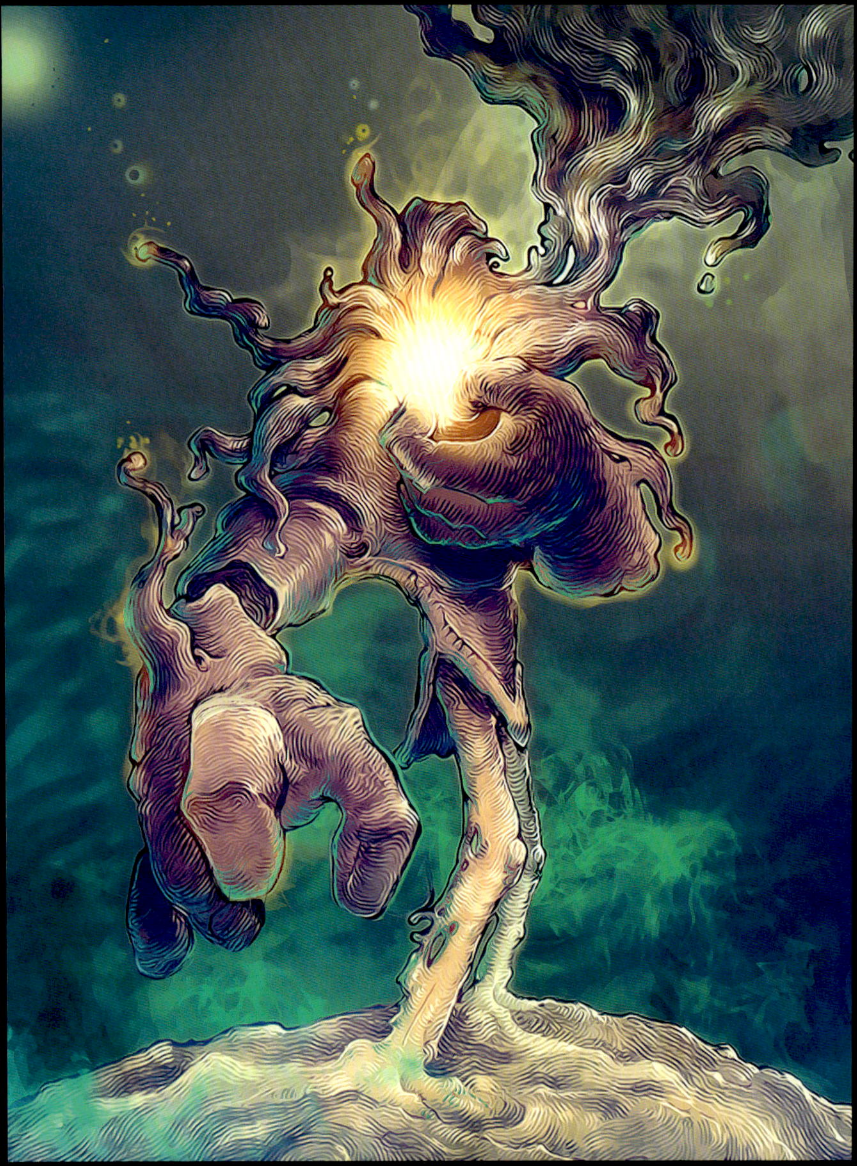

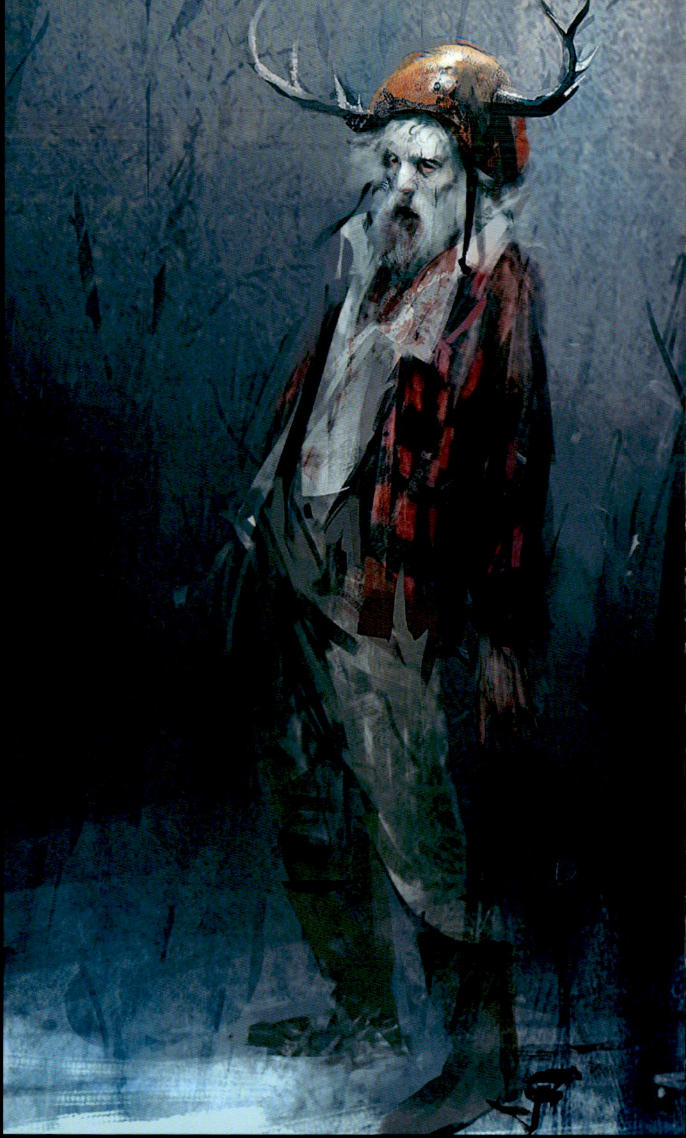

Starosta
Painter
Asdrubal Piedra Carvajal, COSTA RICA
[above]

Redneck
Photoshop
Morgan Yon, FRANCE
[above right]

Michita Warrior
Mudbox, Maya, Photoshop
Misael Barbosa Vazquez, MEXICO
[right]

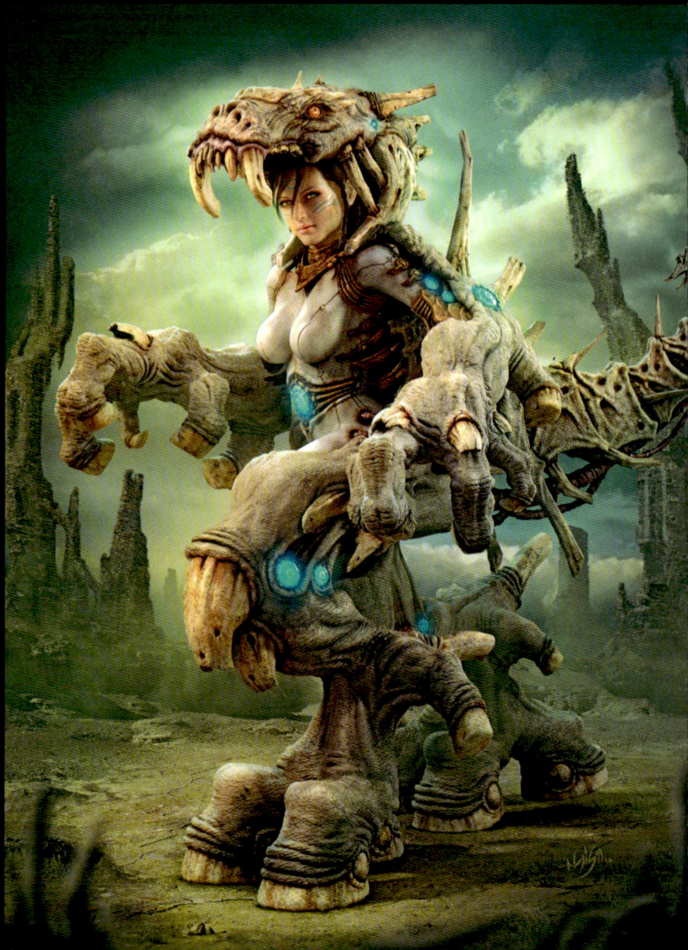

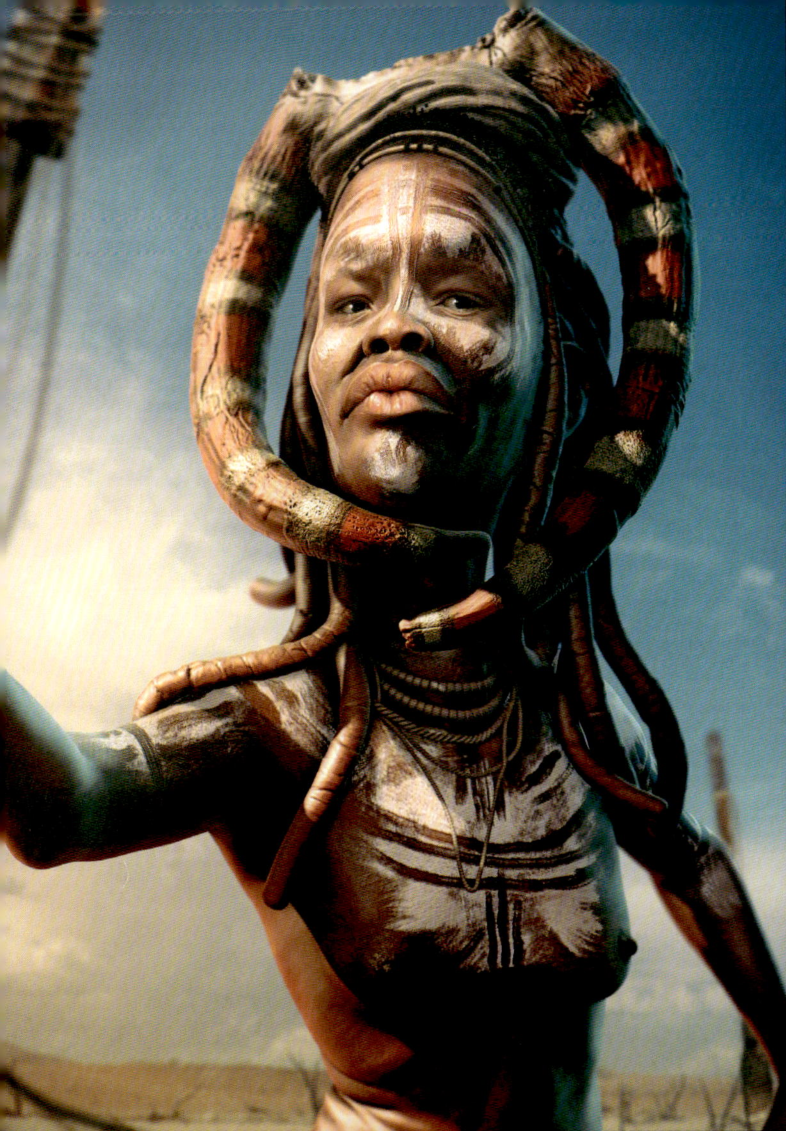

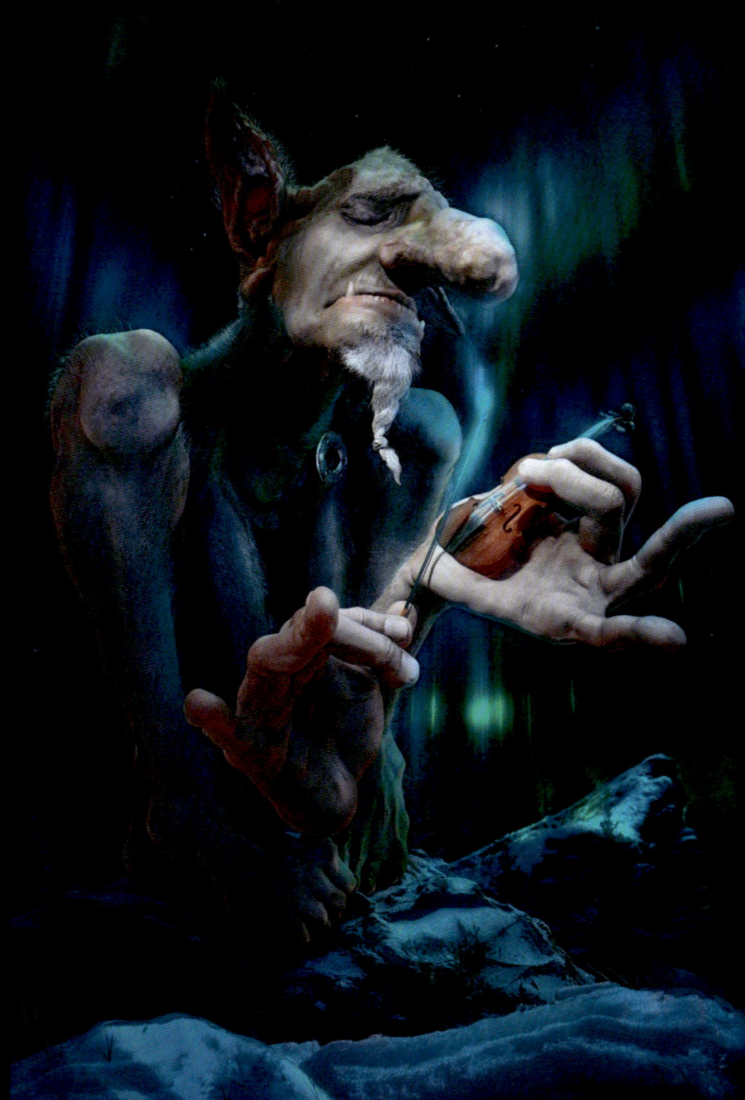

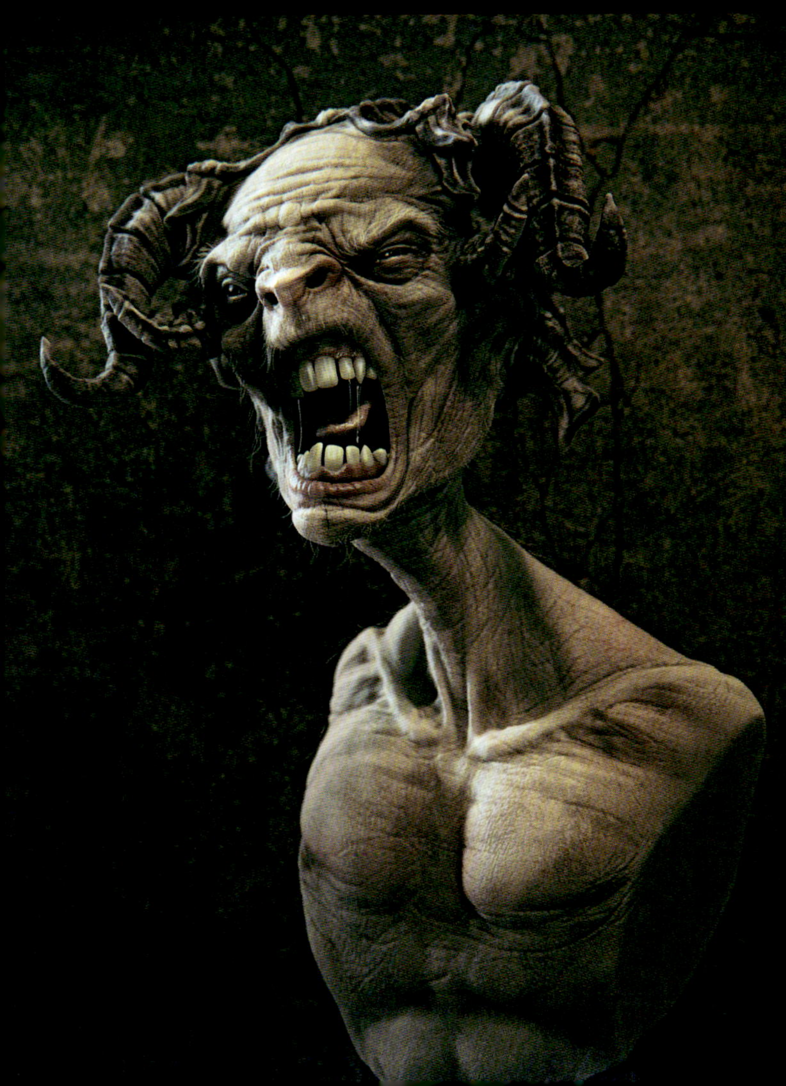

Unfathomable
ZBrush, Photoshop
Pablo Munoz, AUSTRALIA
[above left]

Nordlystroll
Maya, mental ray, Mudbox, Photoshop
Igor Kudryavtsev, RUSSIA
[above]

Angry faun
ZBrush
Daniel Bystedt, SWEDEN
[left]

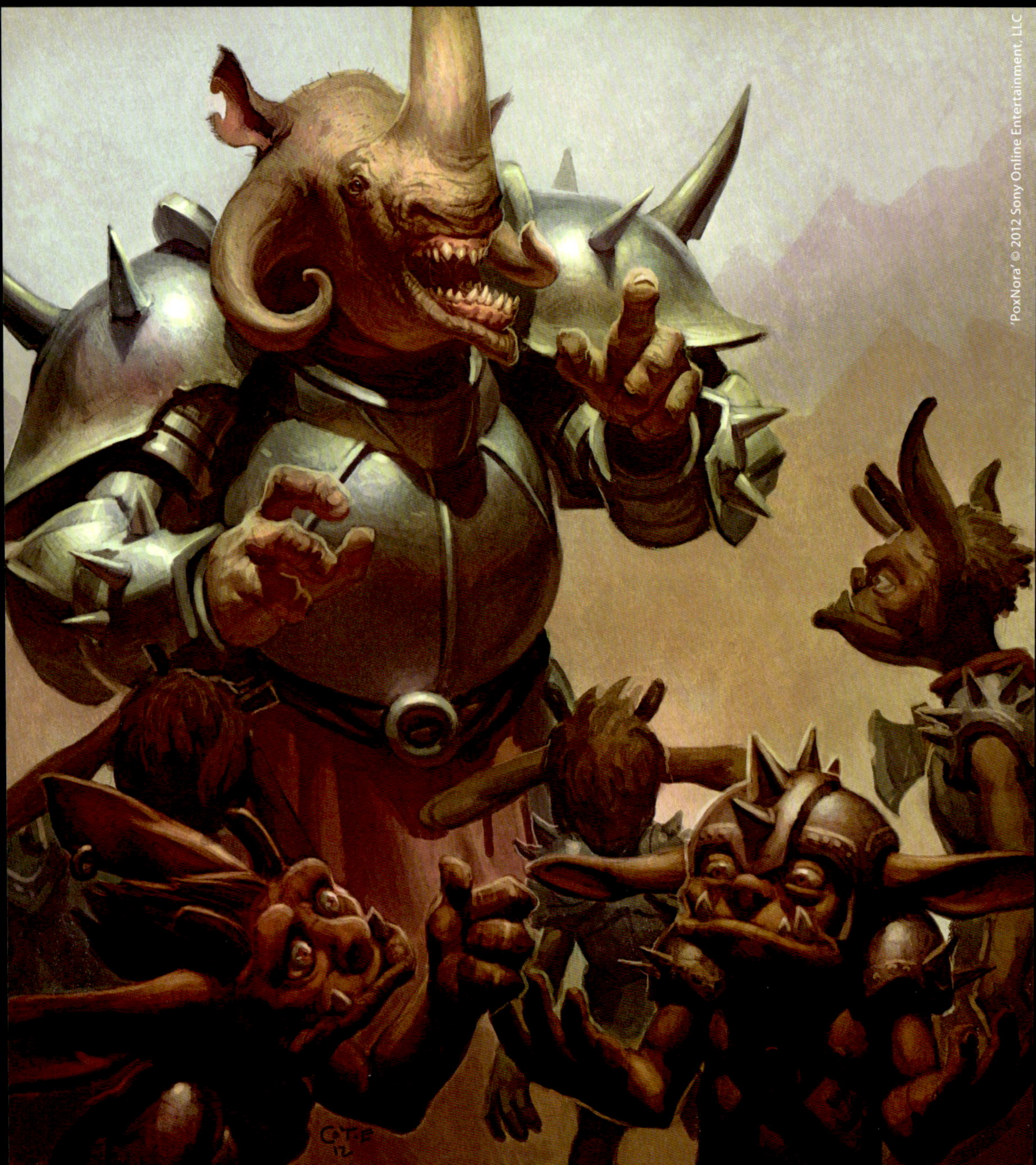

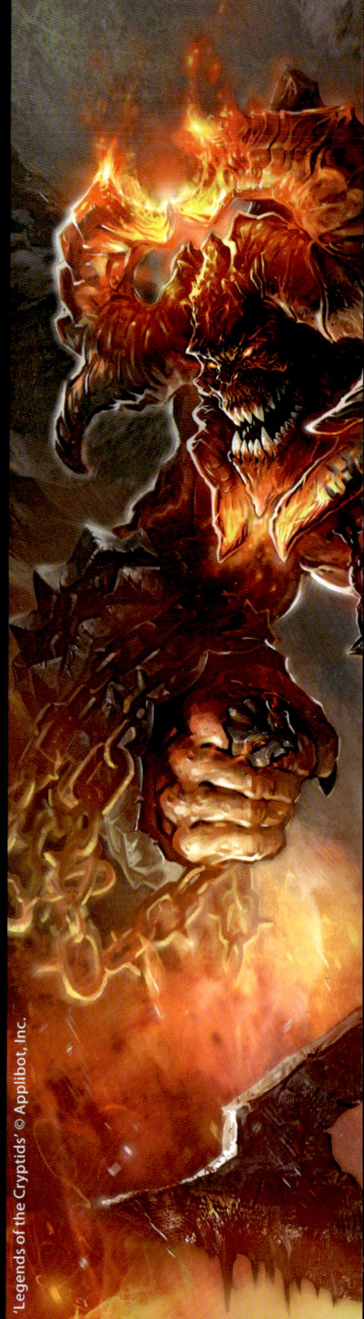

Legends of the Cryptids: Darkness Emperor
Photoshop
Client: Applibot, Inc.
Ivan Kashubo, RUSSIA
[above]

Frozen Hands
Photoshop
Renaud Taelemans, BELGIUM
[right]

PoxNora: Lethologica
Photoshop
Client: Sony Online Entertainment, LLC
Cory Trego-Erdner (Art Director: Anthony Lopes), USA
[above]

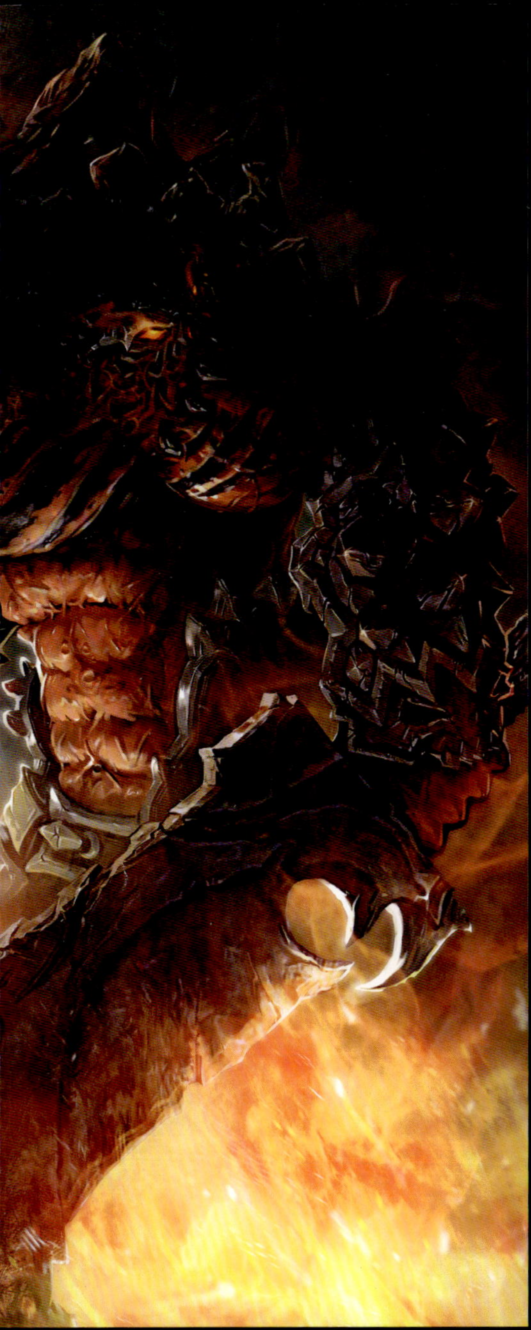

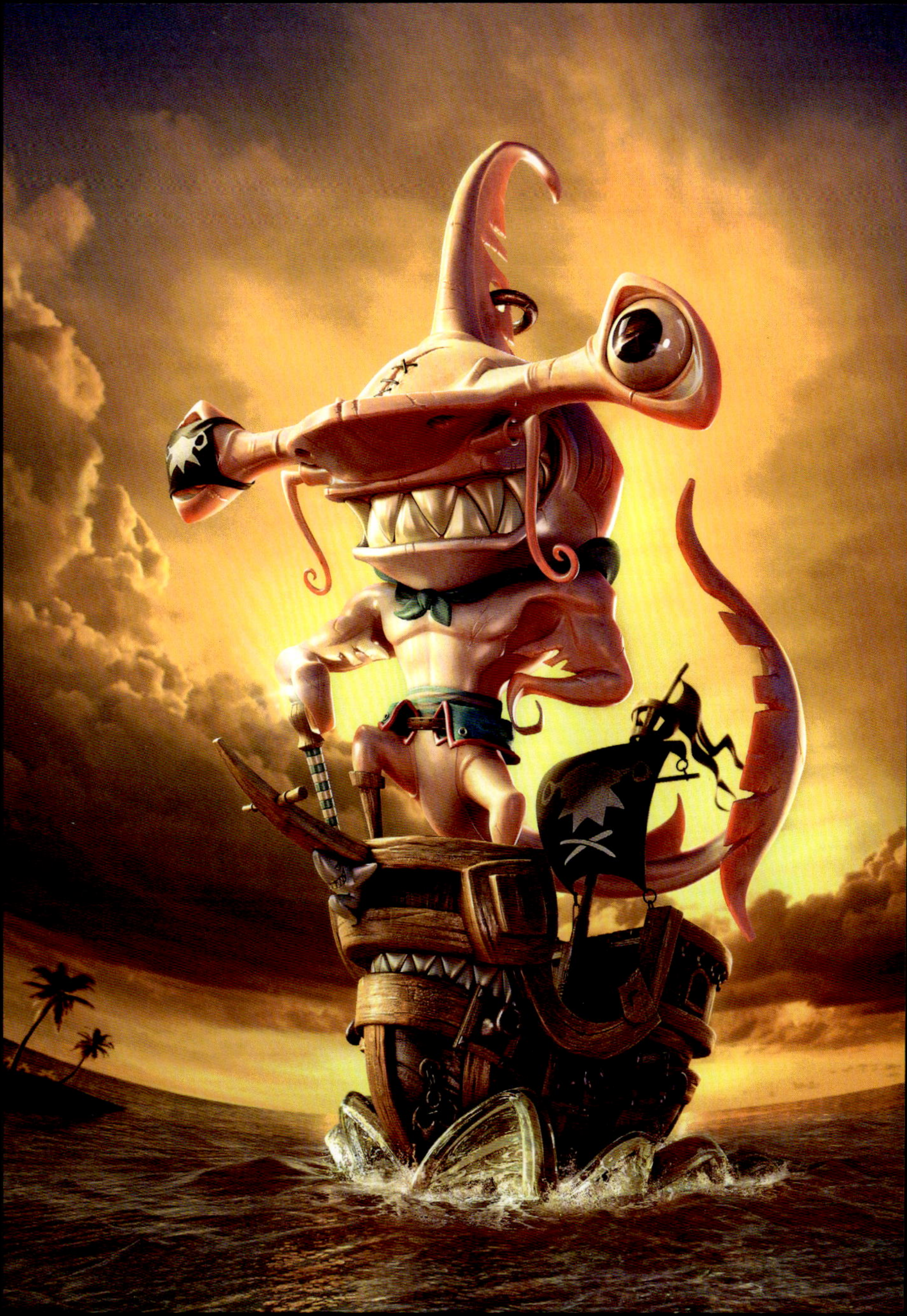

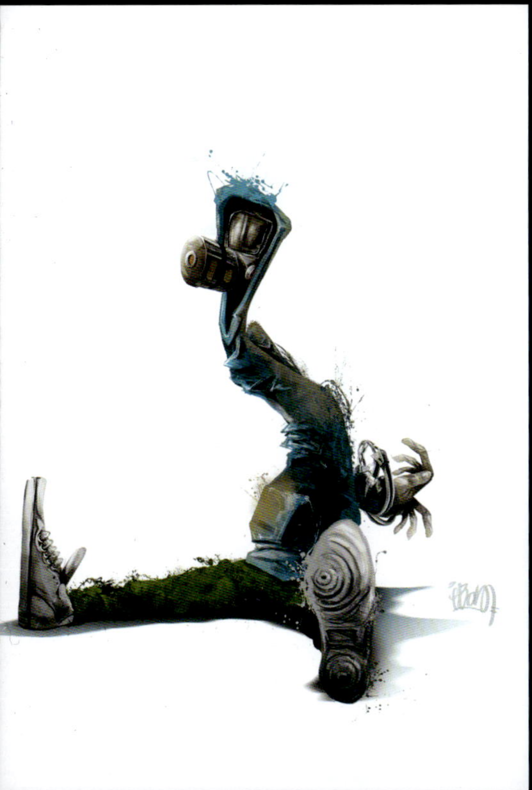

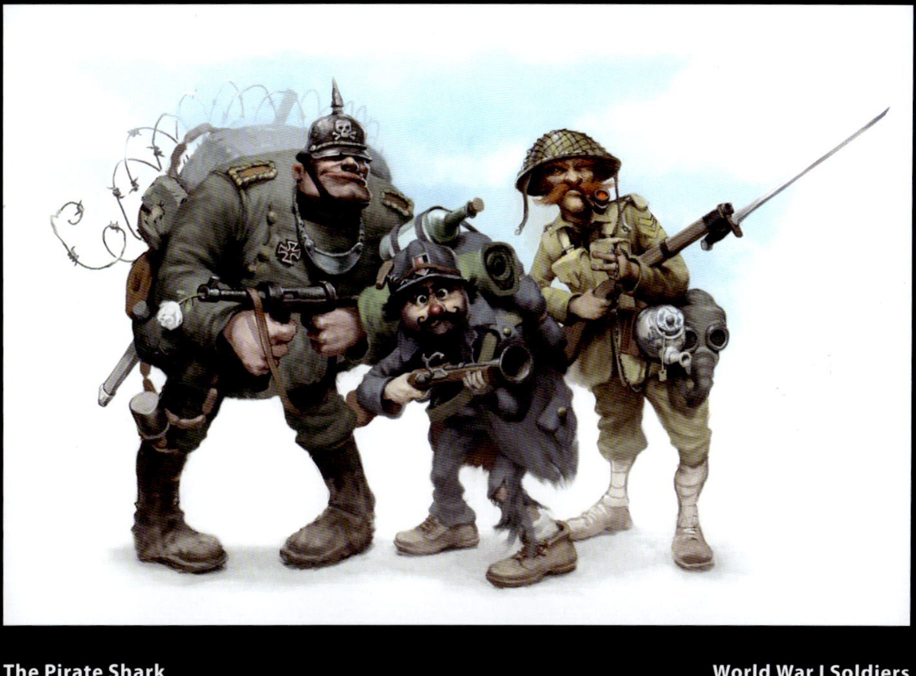

The Pirate Shark
3ds Max, Photoshop, ZBrush
Inspired by Xavier Houssin
Philip Herman, INDONESIA
[top right]

World War I Soldiers
Photoshop
Tor Jäger, SWEDEN
[above]

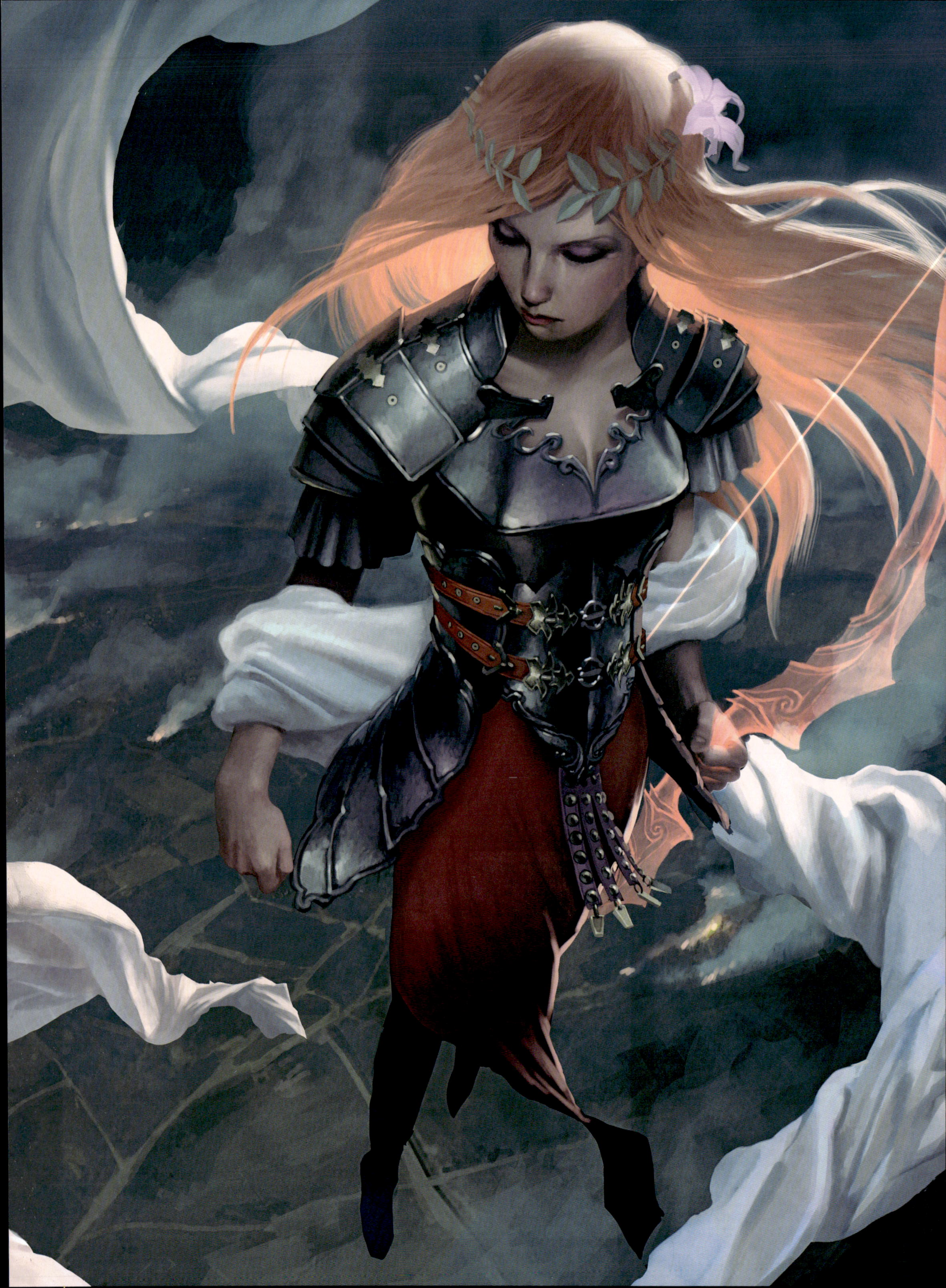

Legend of the Cryptids: Aurora
Photoshop
Client: Applibot, Inc.
Clint Cearley, USA

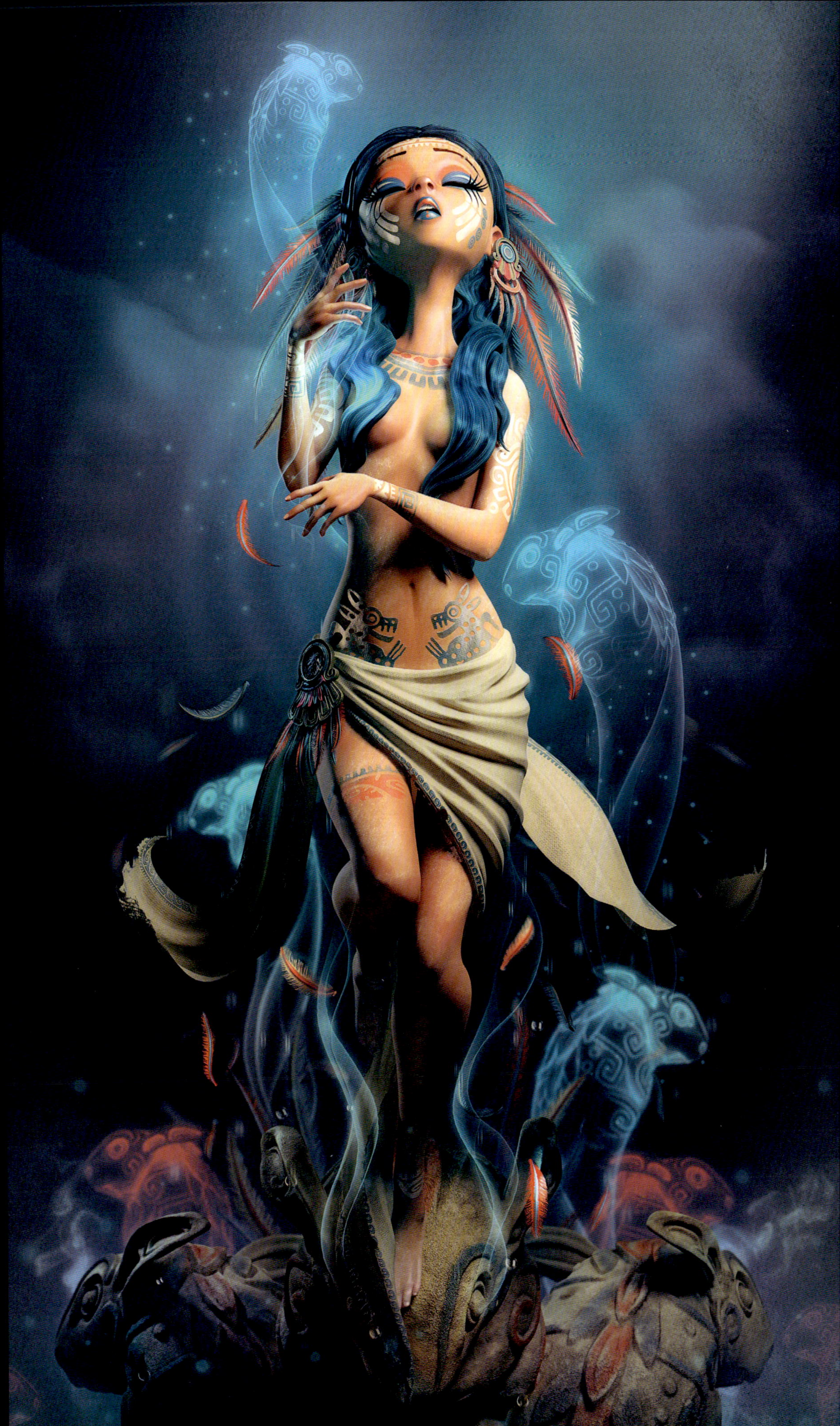

The Weeping Woman
Maya, Mudbox, mental ray, Photoshop
Carlos Ortega Elizalde, MEXICO

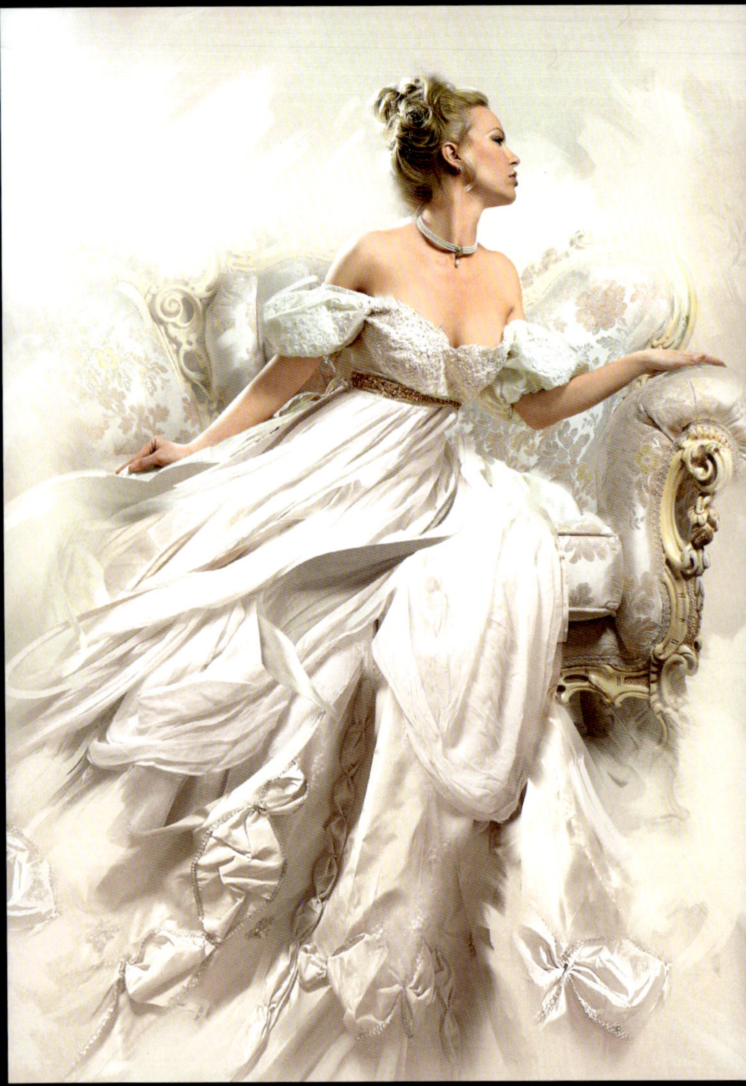

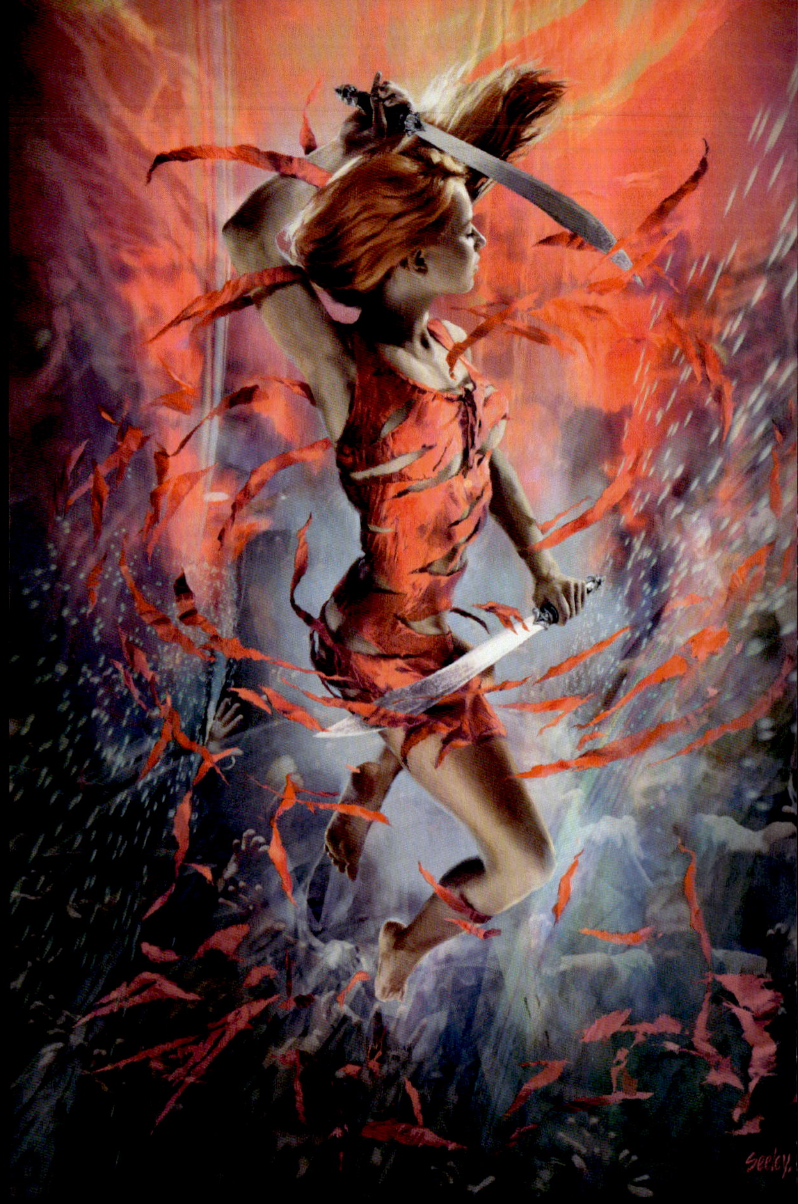
Seeley.

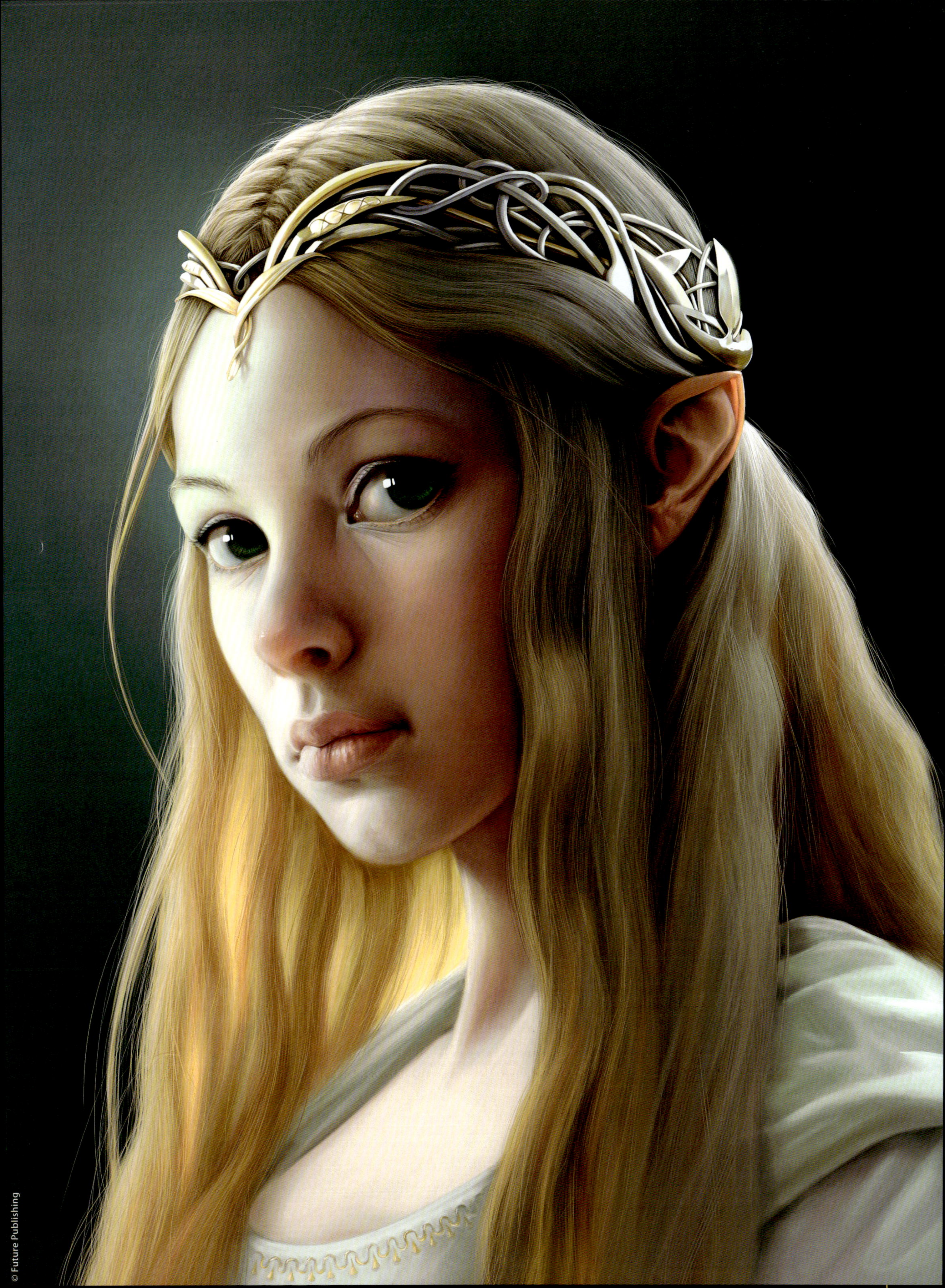

Elf Girl
Painter
Client: ImagineFX magazine
Corrado Vanelli, ITALY

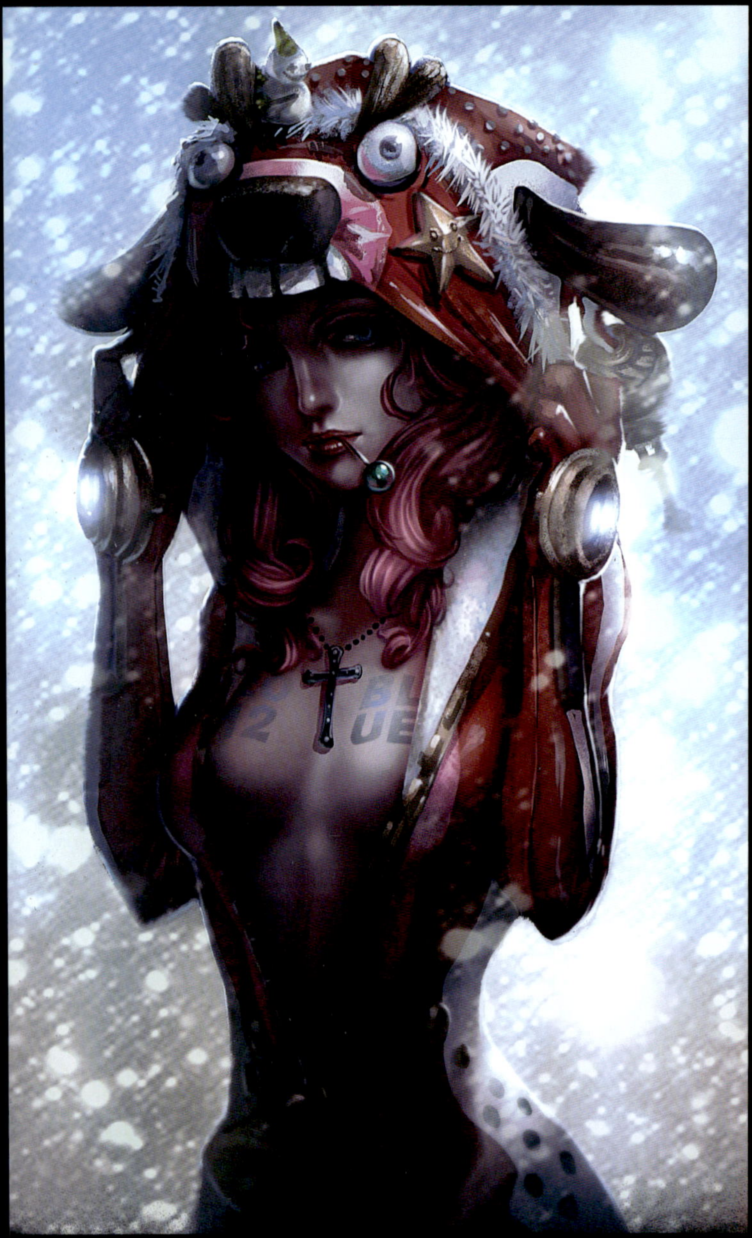

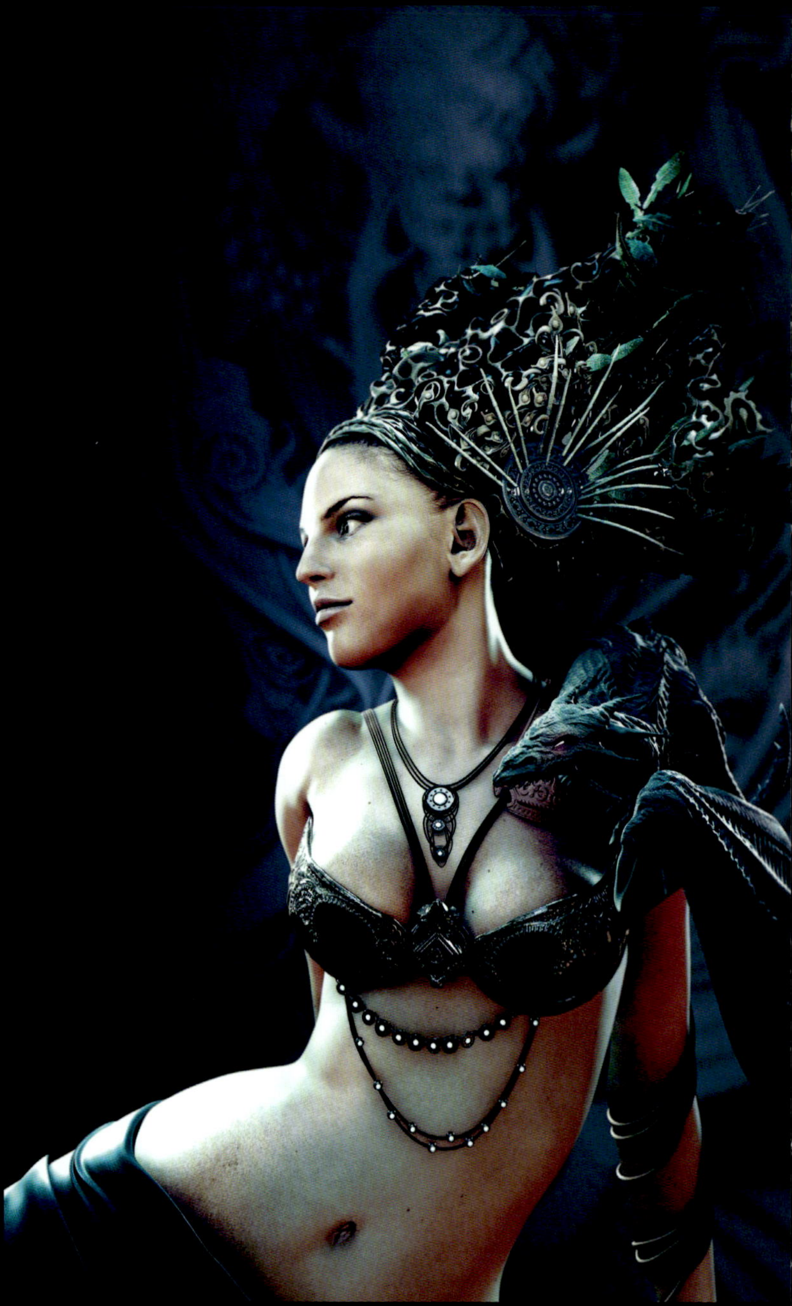

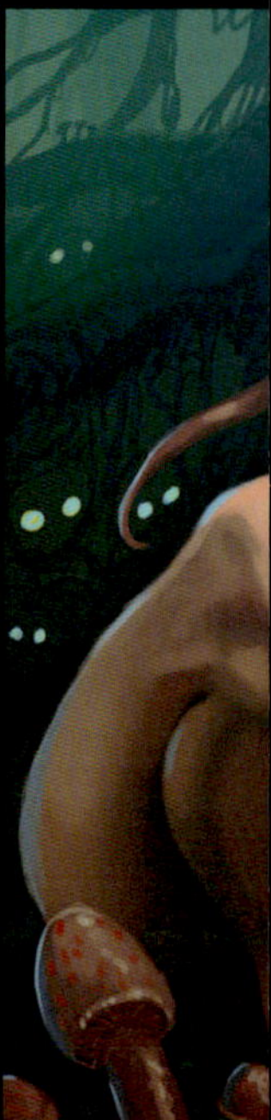

Christmas Girl
Photoshop
Kuo Feng Lan, TAIWAN
[above]

Mistress of Dragons
Maya, ZBrush
Daniele Scerra, ITALY
[above]

Rose
Photoshop
Chaichan Artwichai, THAILAND
[facing page top left]

Hunter
Photoshop
Bianca Draghici, SWEDEN
[facing page top right]

HellFire: Centaur Warrior
Photoshop
Client: DeNA Co., Ltd.
Michael Anthony Gonzales, PHILIPPINES
[facing page bottom right]

A Fine Form: I Got Me an Earworm
Photoshop, SketchBook Pro
Jhoneil Centeno, USA
[right]

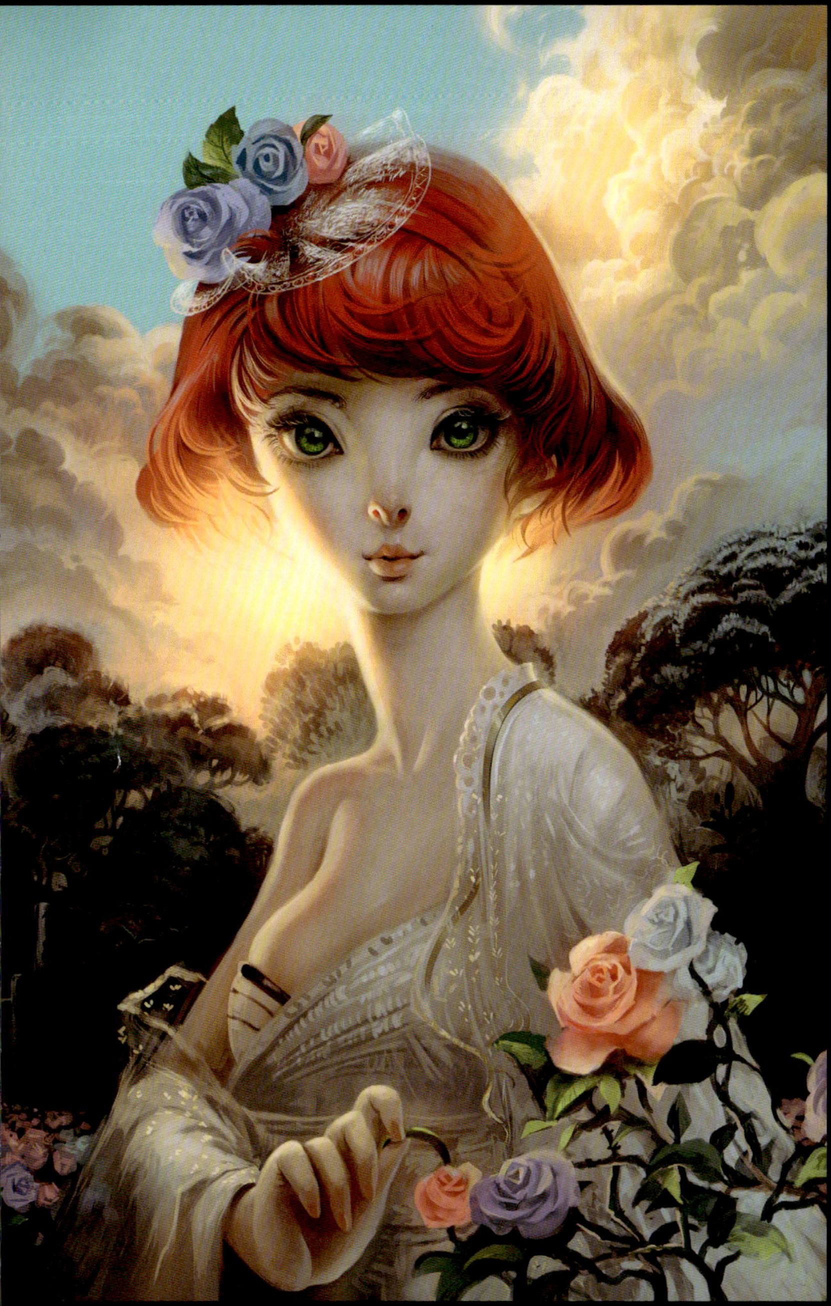

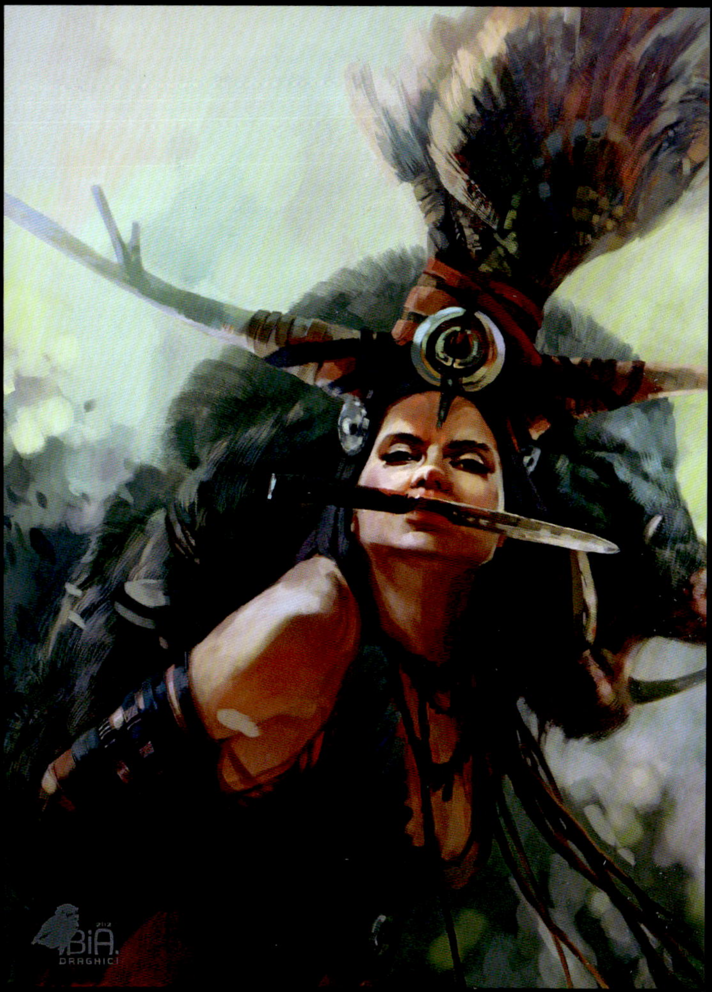

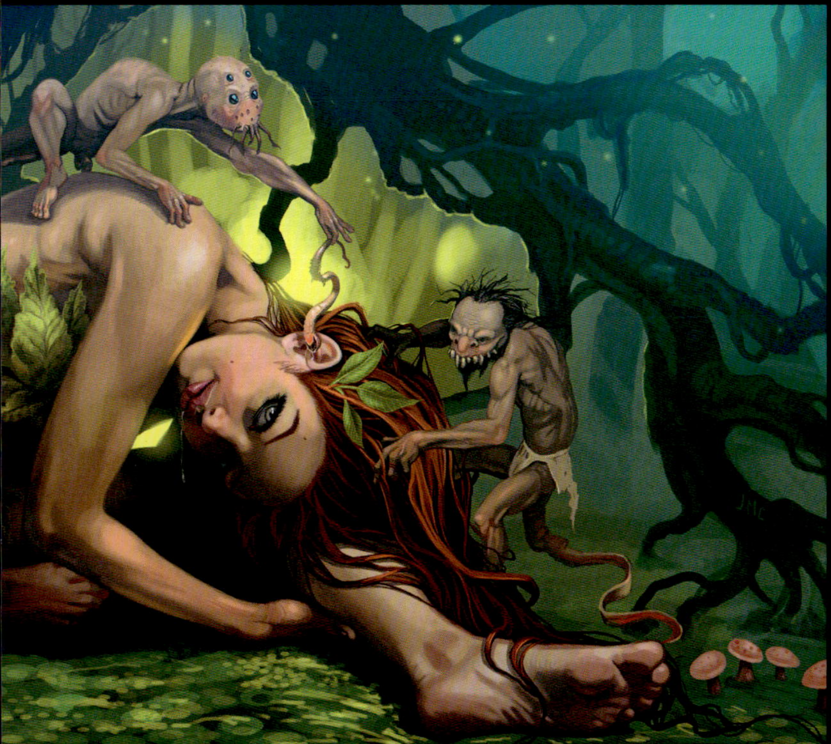

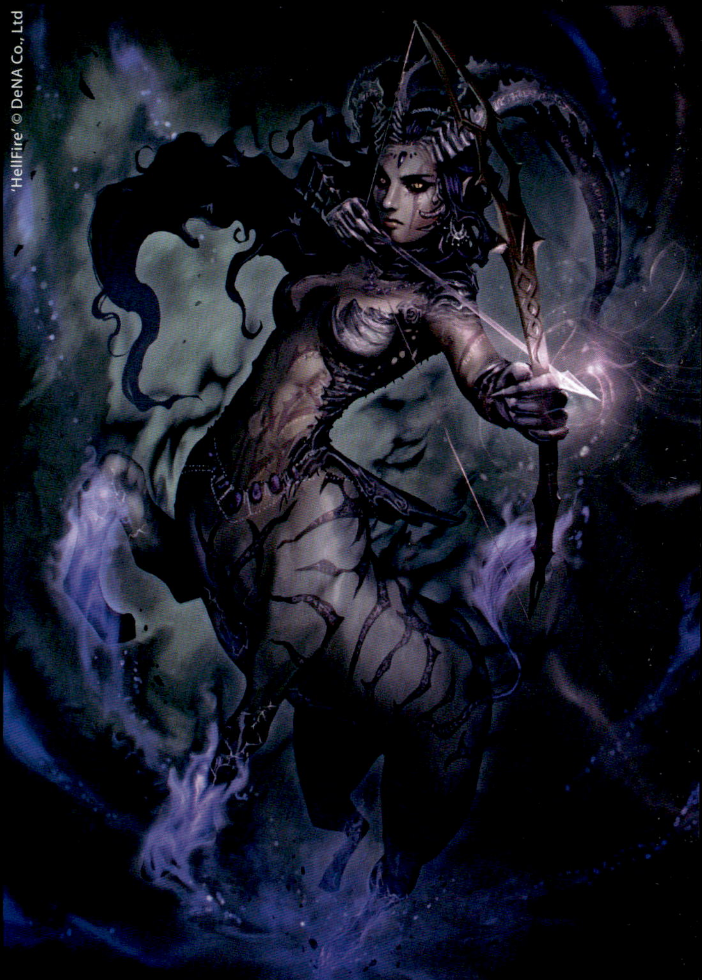

'HellFire' © DeNA Co., Ltd

Antissa
Photoshop
Desiree Delgado, SPAIN
[right]

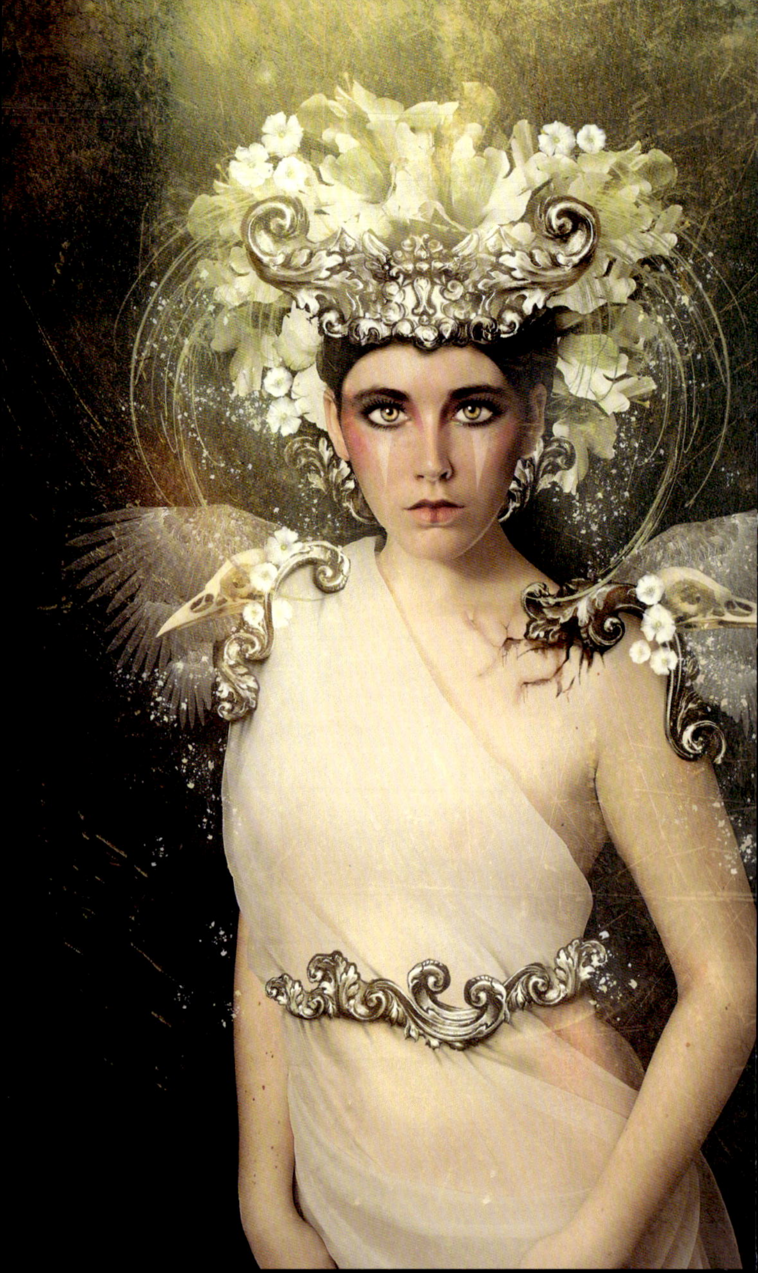

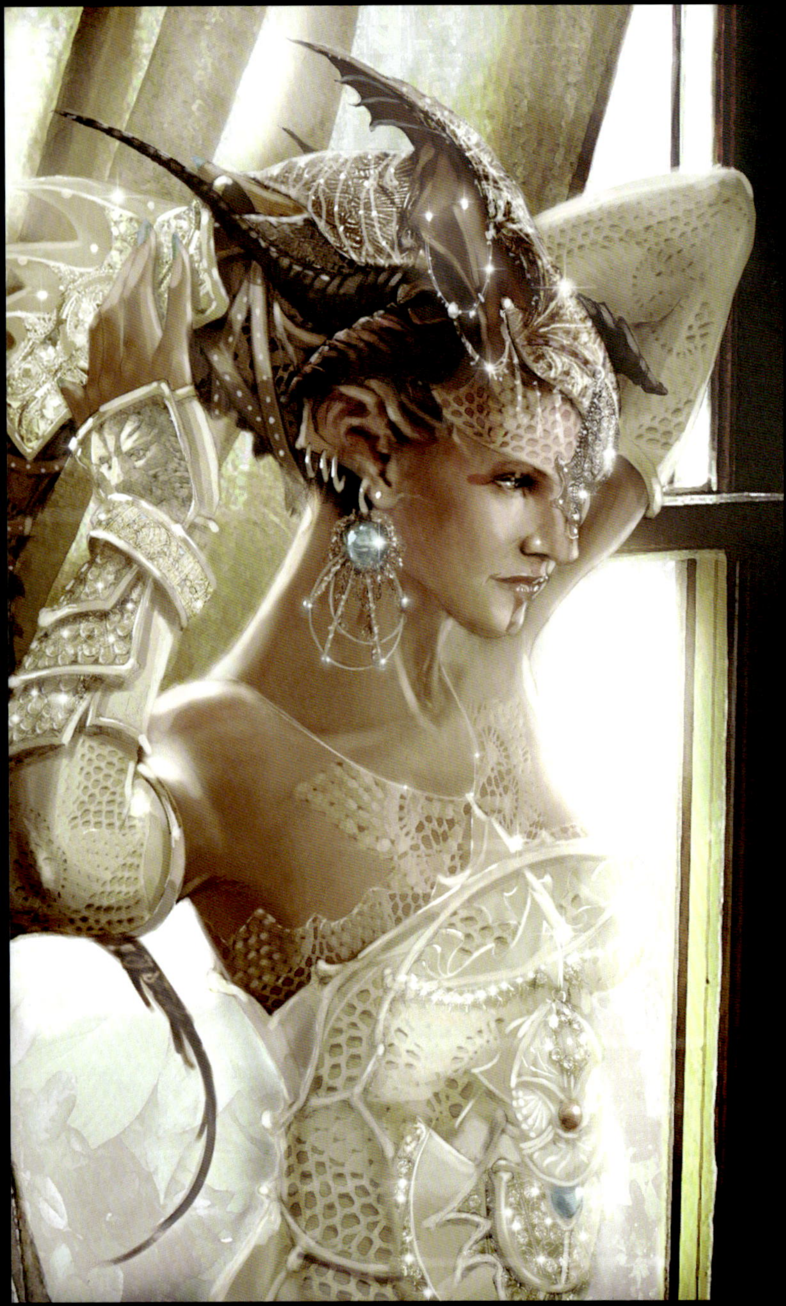

Solara
Photoshop
Lamin Martin, CANADA
[above]

Freya
Photoshop
Sue Marino, GREAT BRITAIN
[right]

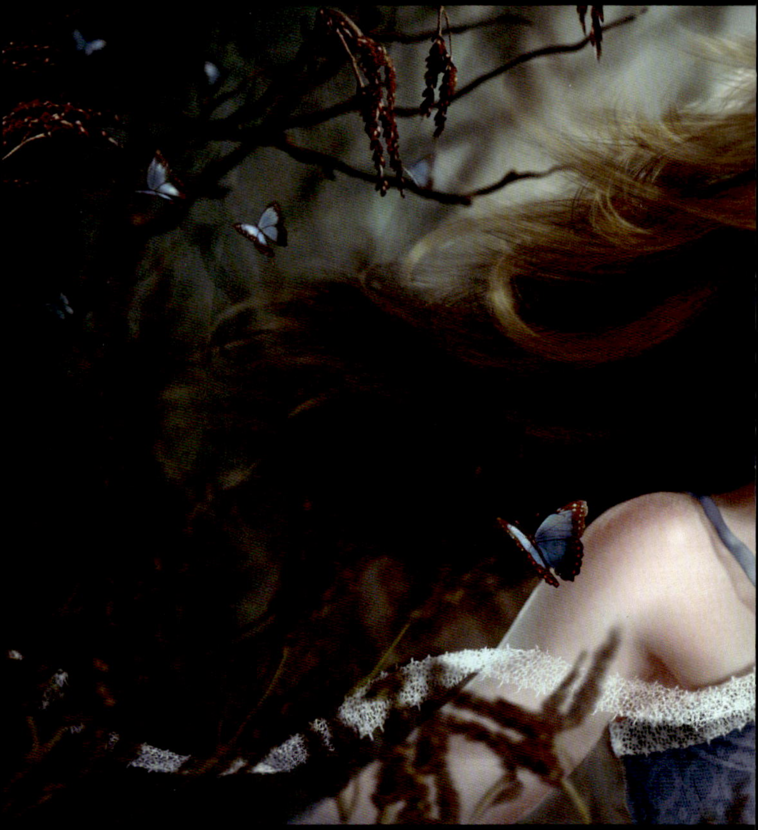

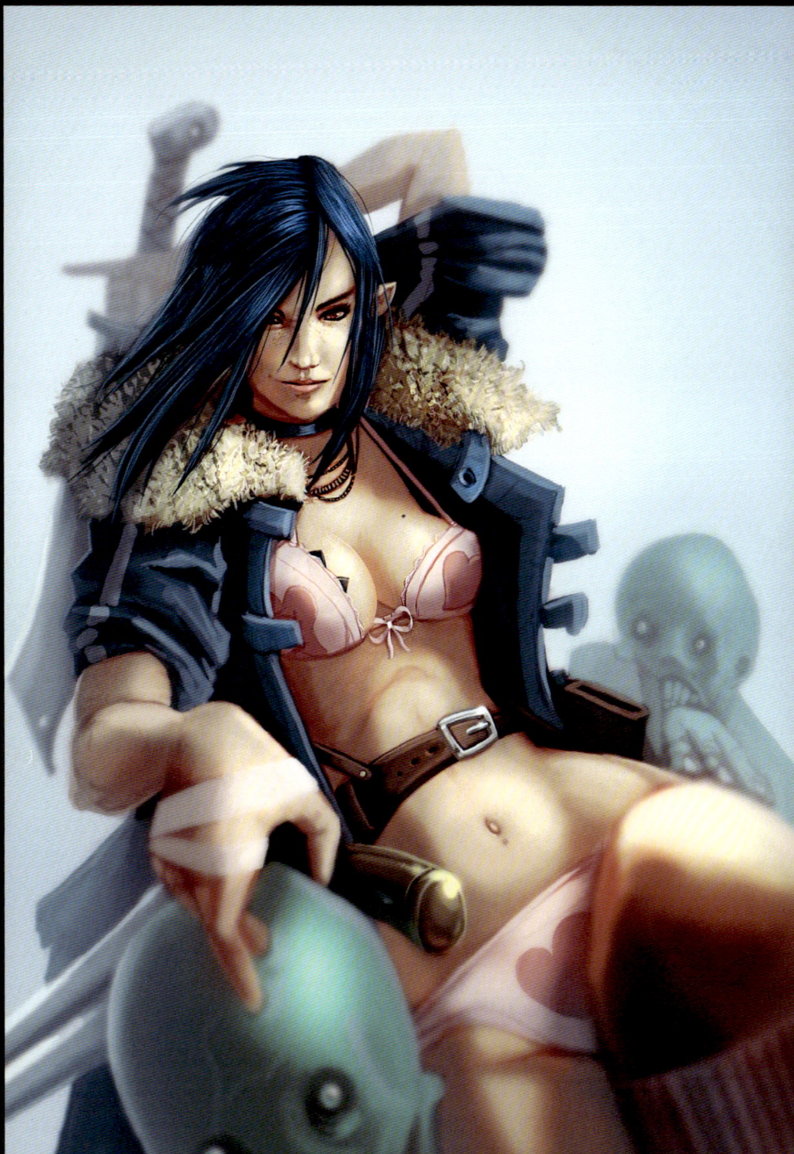

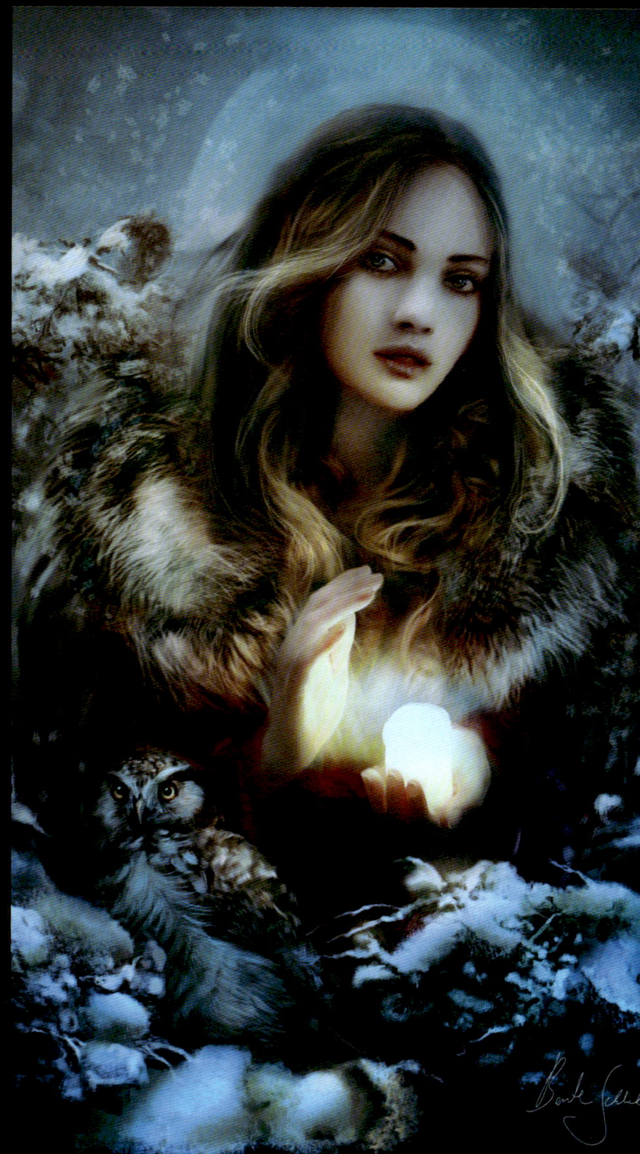

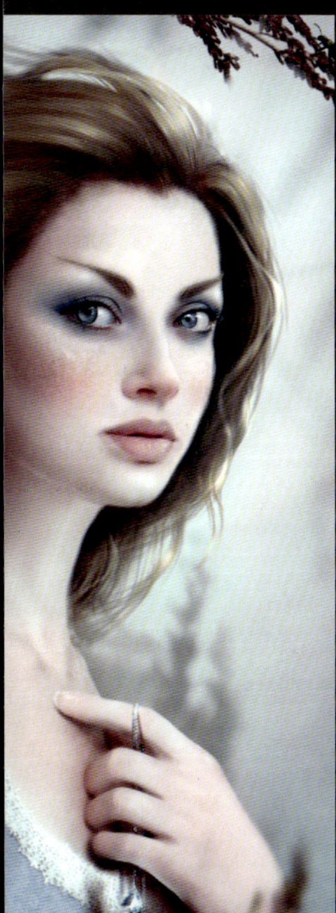

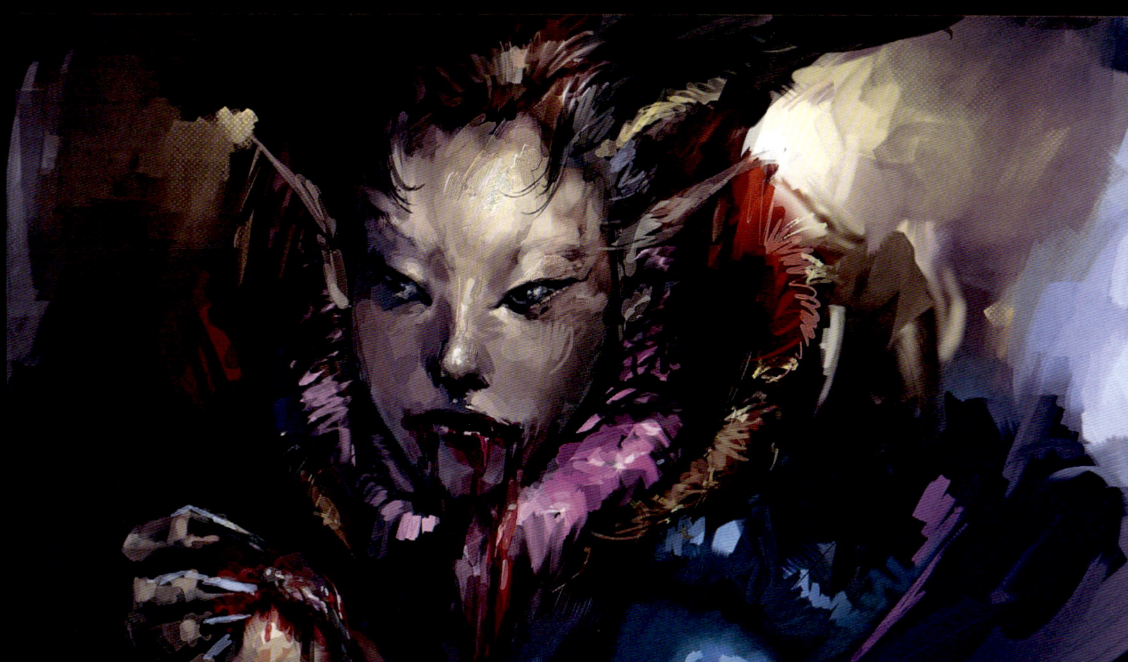

New Zombie Armor
Photoshop
Benjamin Schulz, GERMANY
[top left]

Winterheart
Photoshop
Bente Schlick, GERMANY
[top right]

Er
Photoshop
Qiu jian Yuan, CHINA
[above]

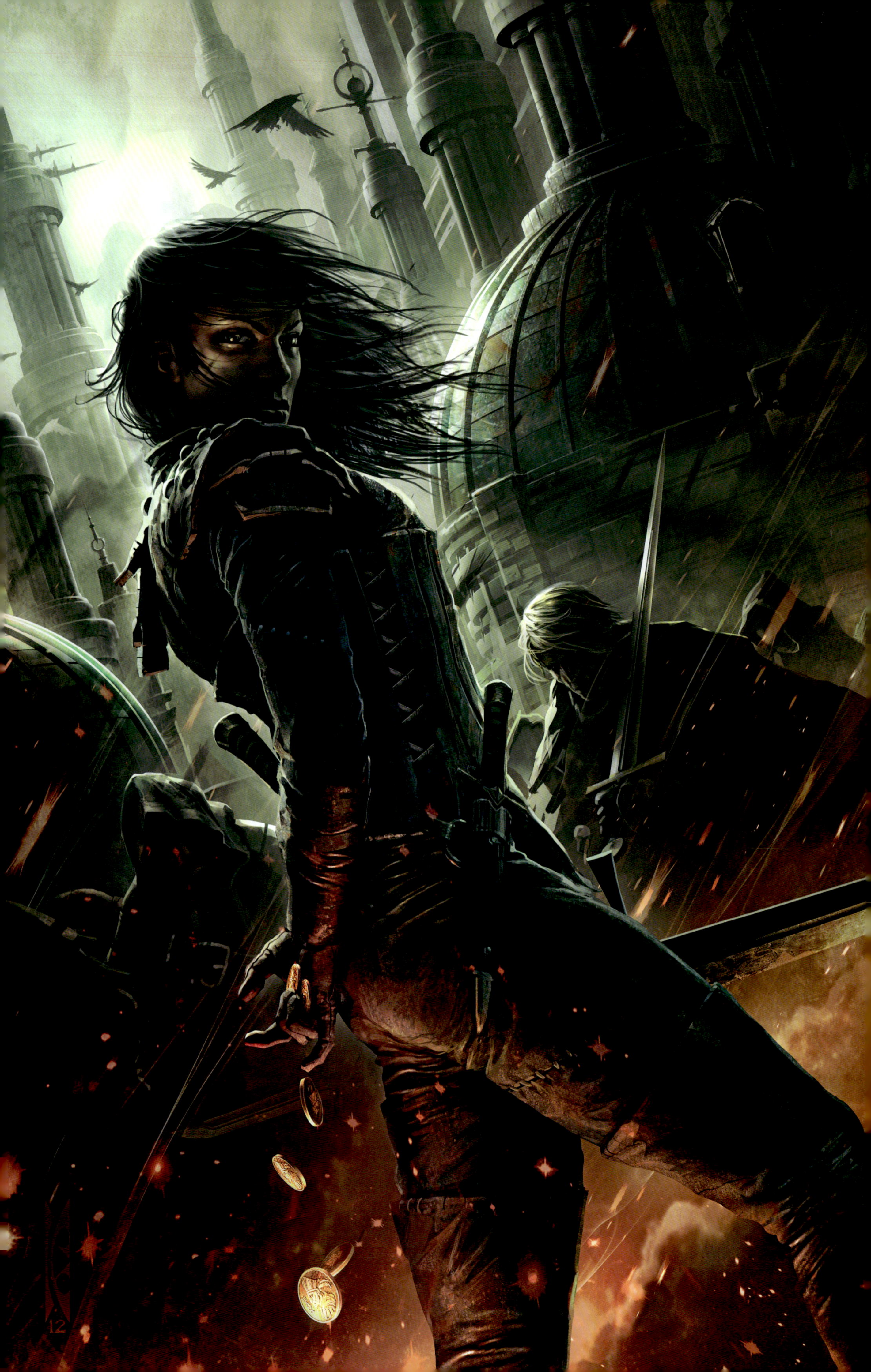

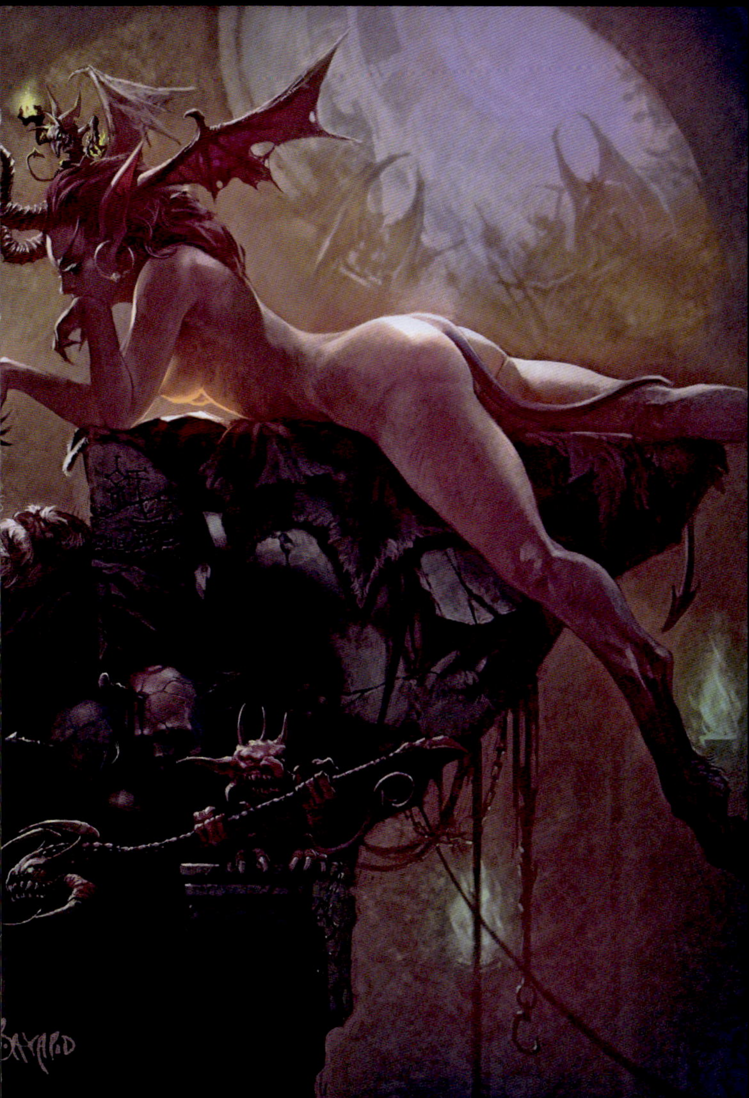

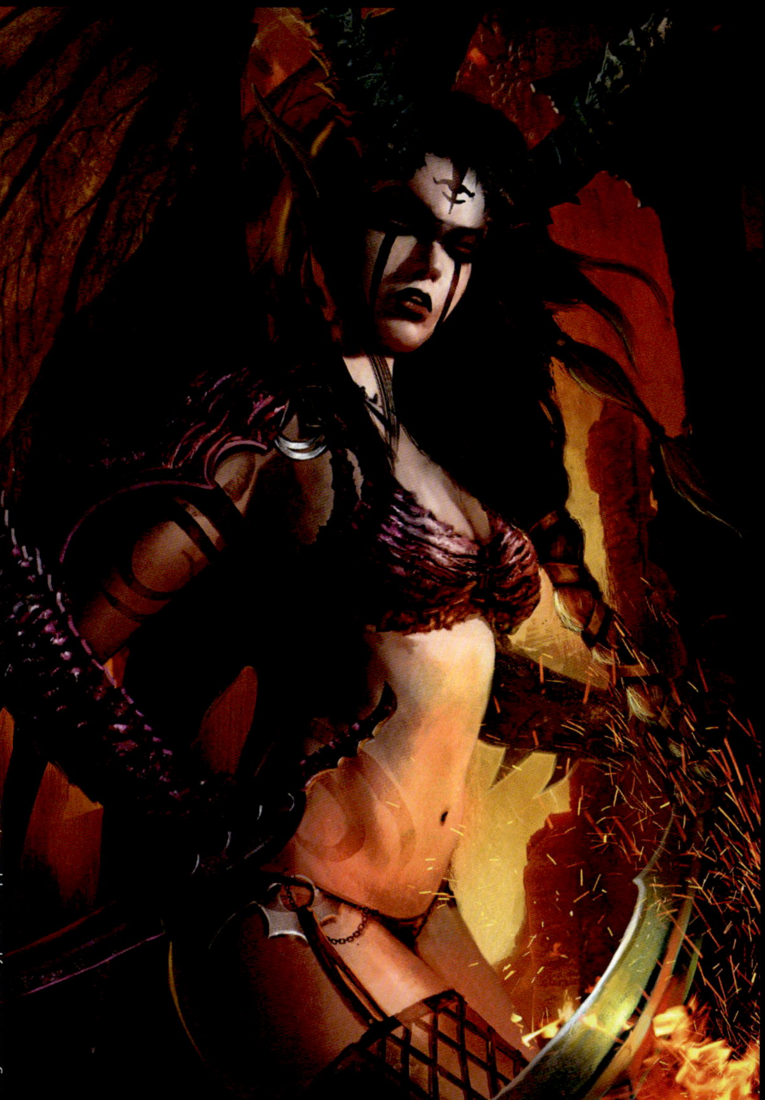

'Legends of the Cryptids' © Applibot, Inc.

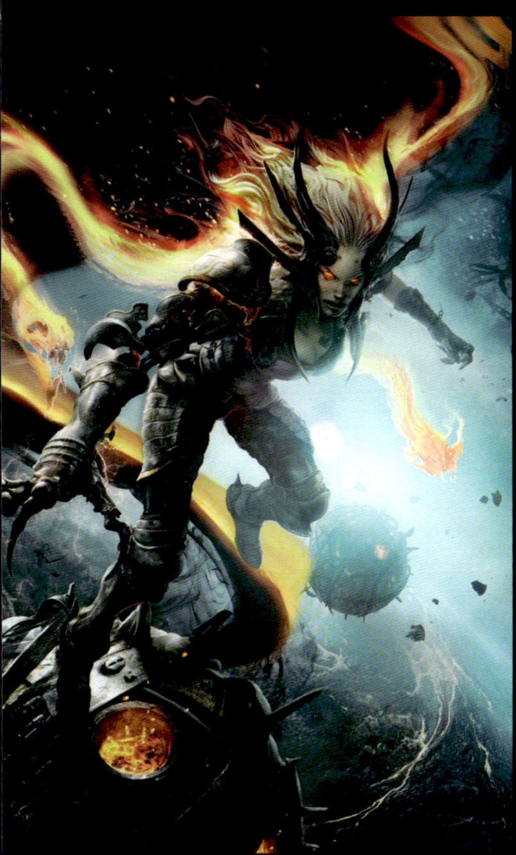

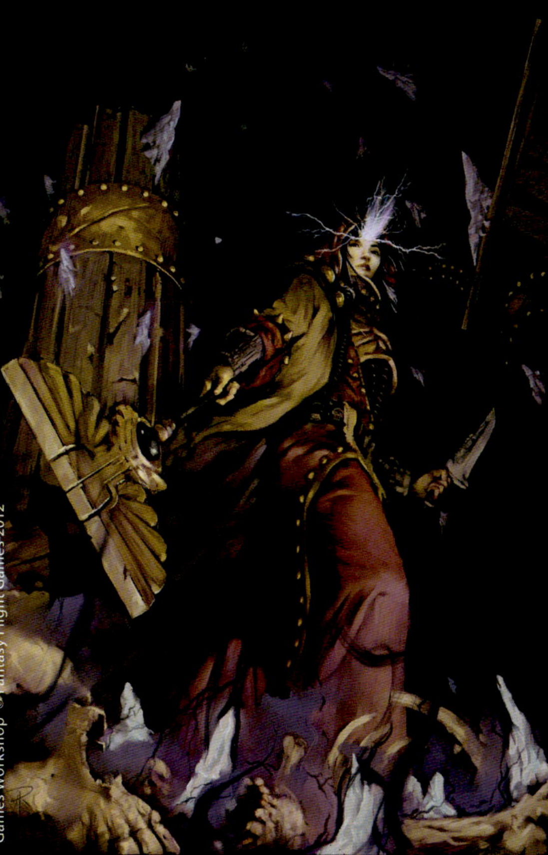

'Games Workshop' © Fantasy Flight Games 2012

Succubus
Photoshop
Bayard Wu, CHINA
[above left]

Legends of the Cryptids: Enlightened Fallen Angel
Photoshop
Client: Applibot, Inc.
Diego de Almeida, BRAZIL
[above right]

Worlds and Wonders: Azzar'Hi
Photoshop
Aleksi Briclot, FRANCE
[far left]

Games Workshop: Monster Slayer
Painter, Photoshop
Client: Fantasy Flight Games
Aaron Riley, USA
[left]

Best Served Cold
Photoshop
Client: Subterranean Press
Raymond Swanland, USA
[facing page]

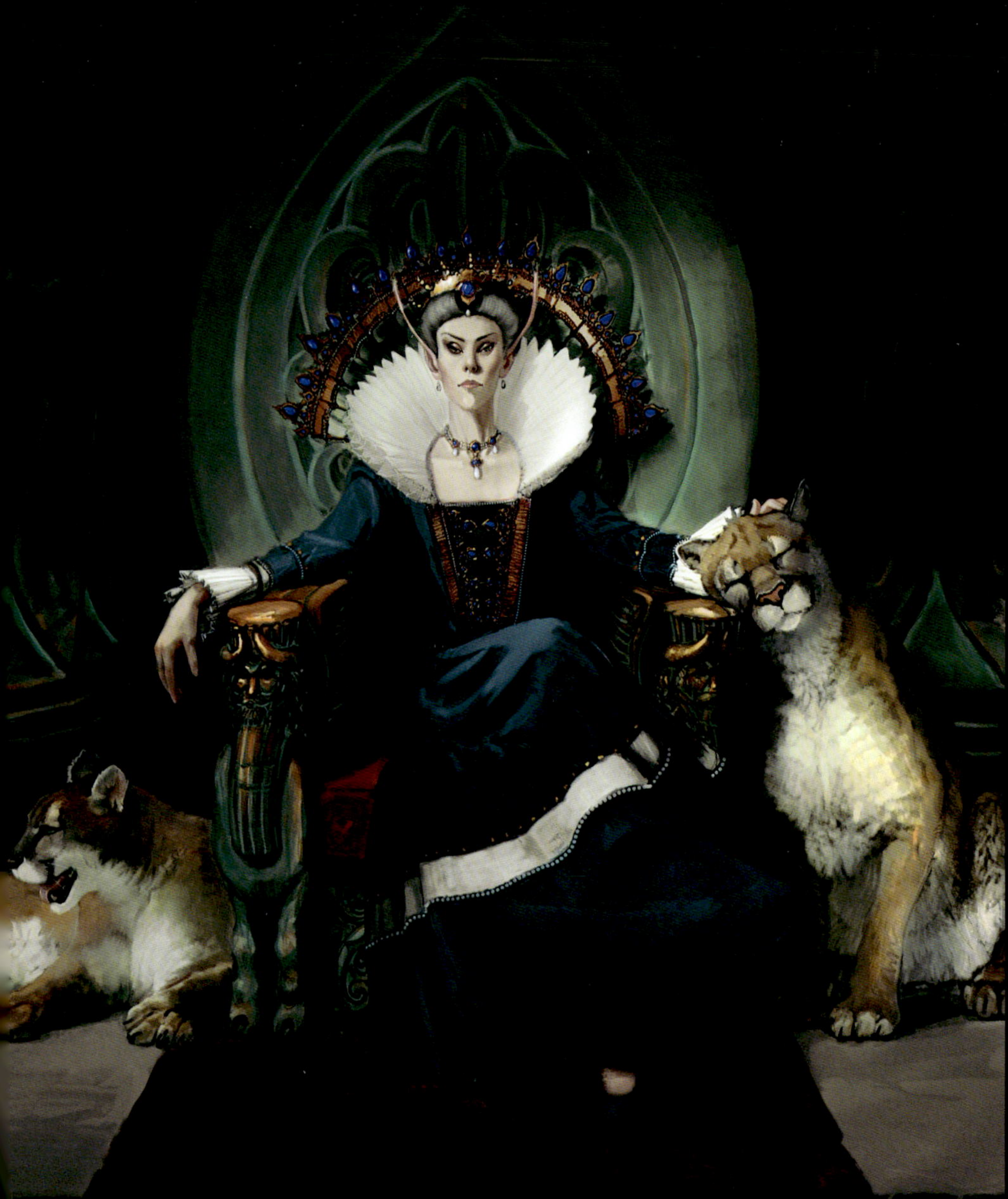

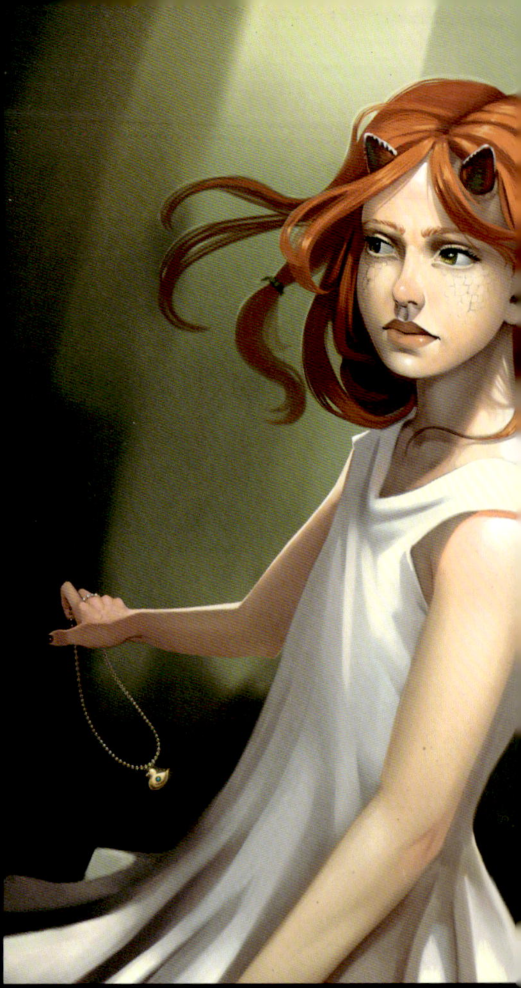

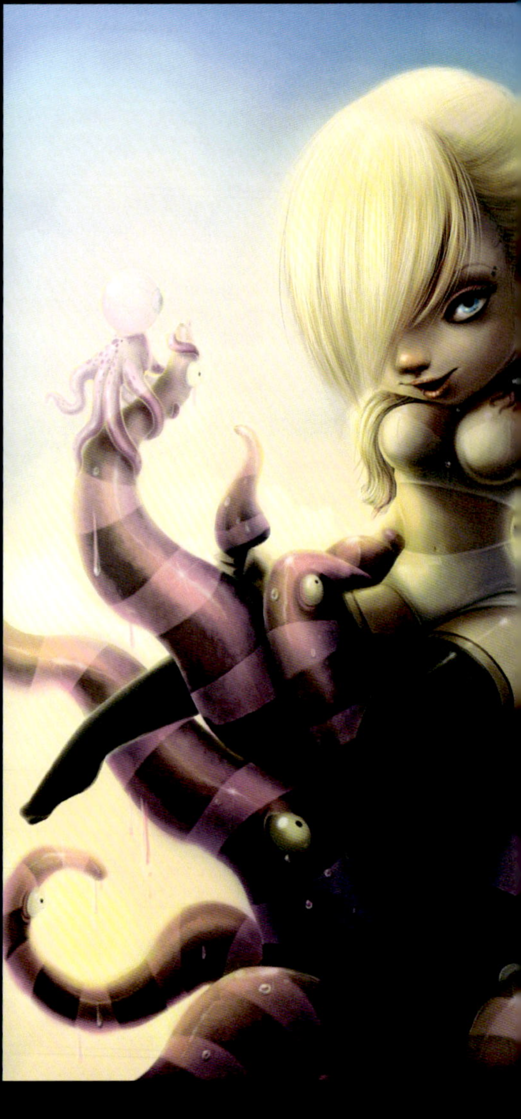

The Elf Queen
Photoshop
Aaron Miller, USA
[above]

Flame Child
Painter
Jacob Probelski, USA
[above right]

Desire
Photoshop
Liran Szeiman, SPAIN
[right]

Labyrinth of Jareth Masquerade
Painter
Client: Sypher Art Studios
Jacob Probelski, USA
[far right]

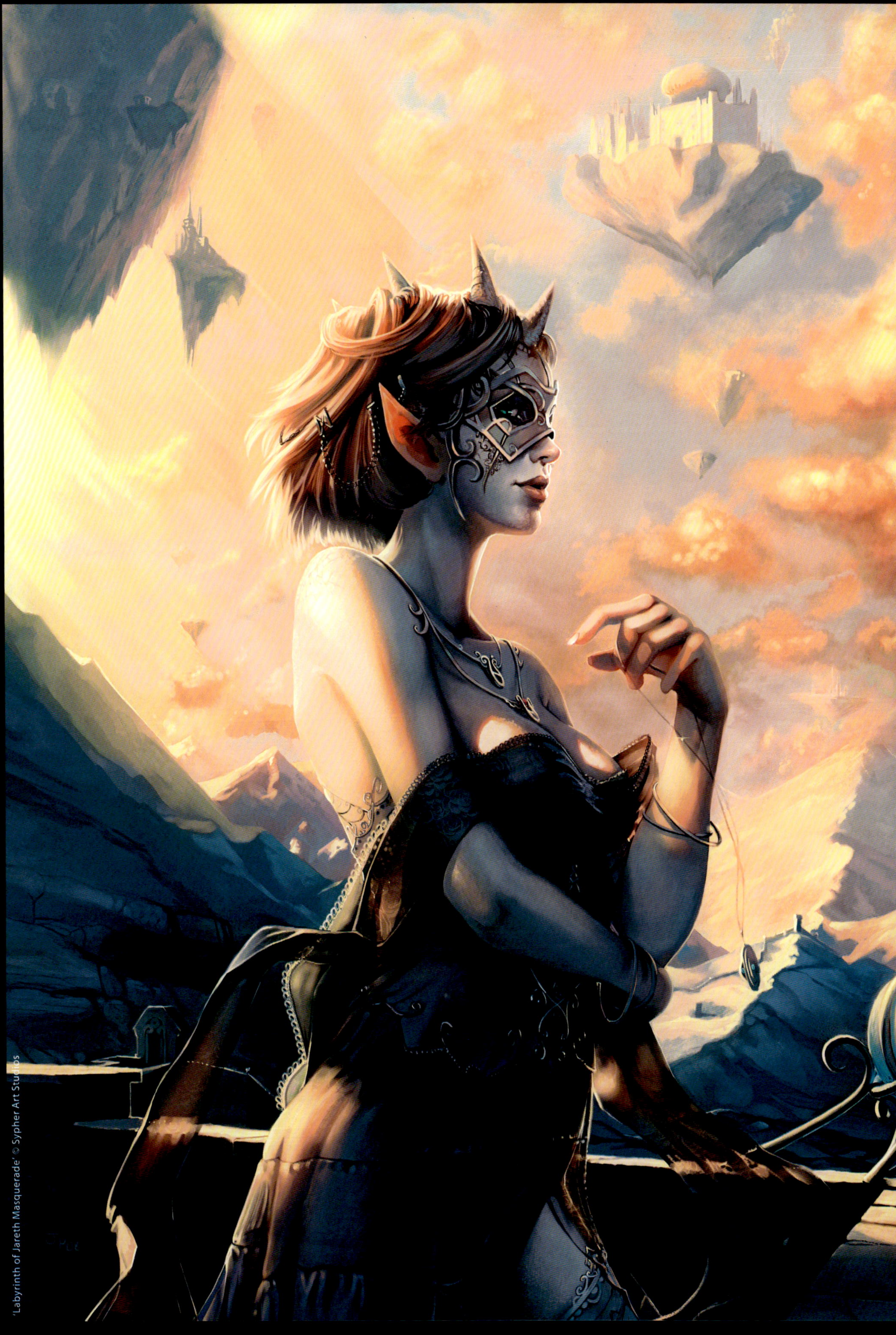

'Labyrinth of Jareth Masquerade' © Sypher Art Studios

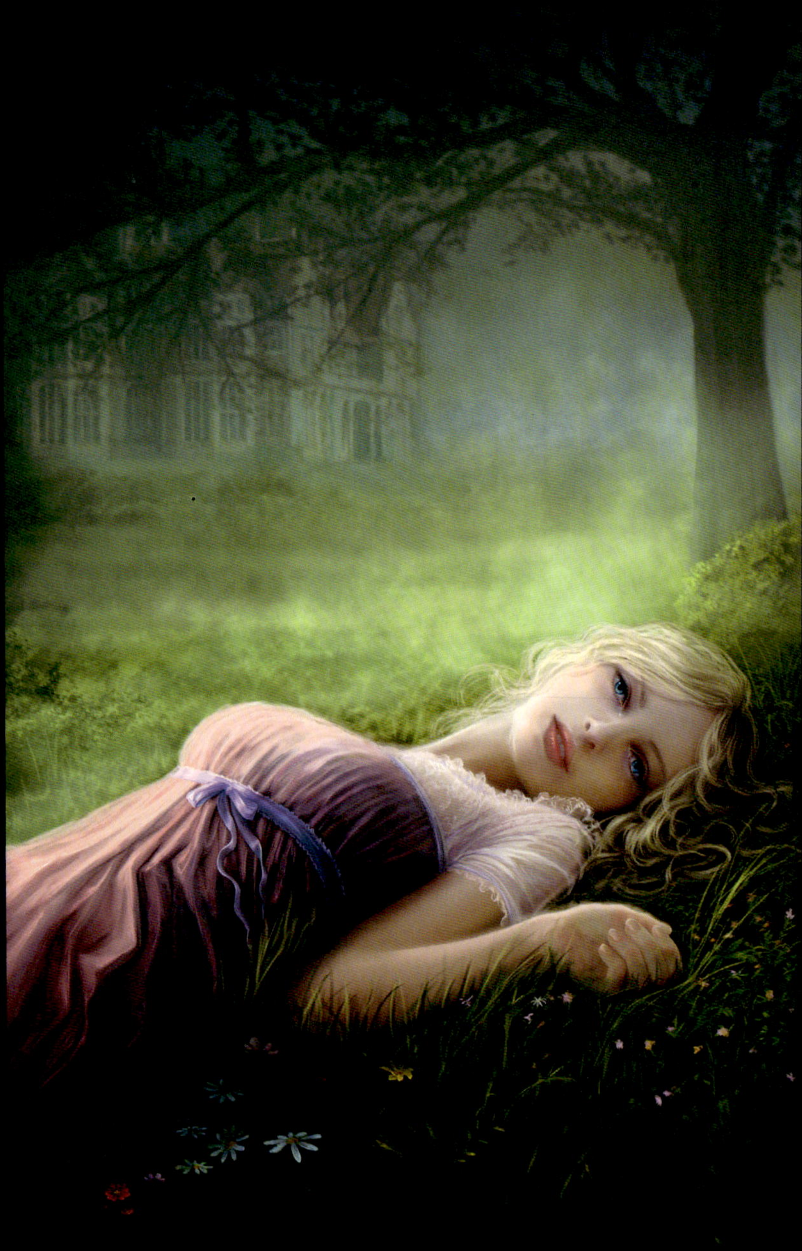

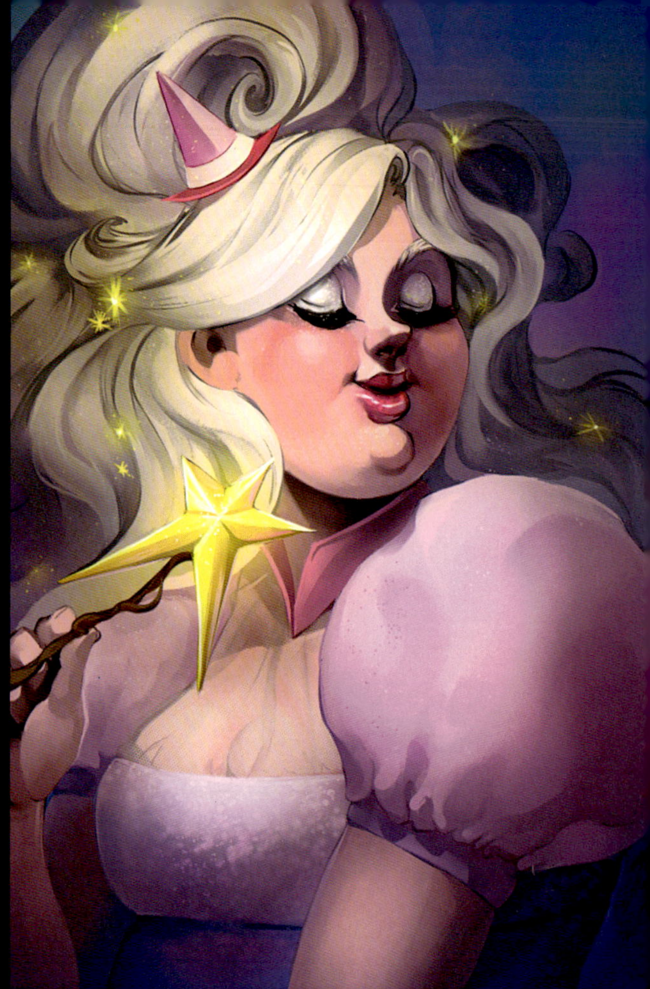

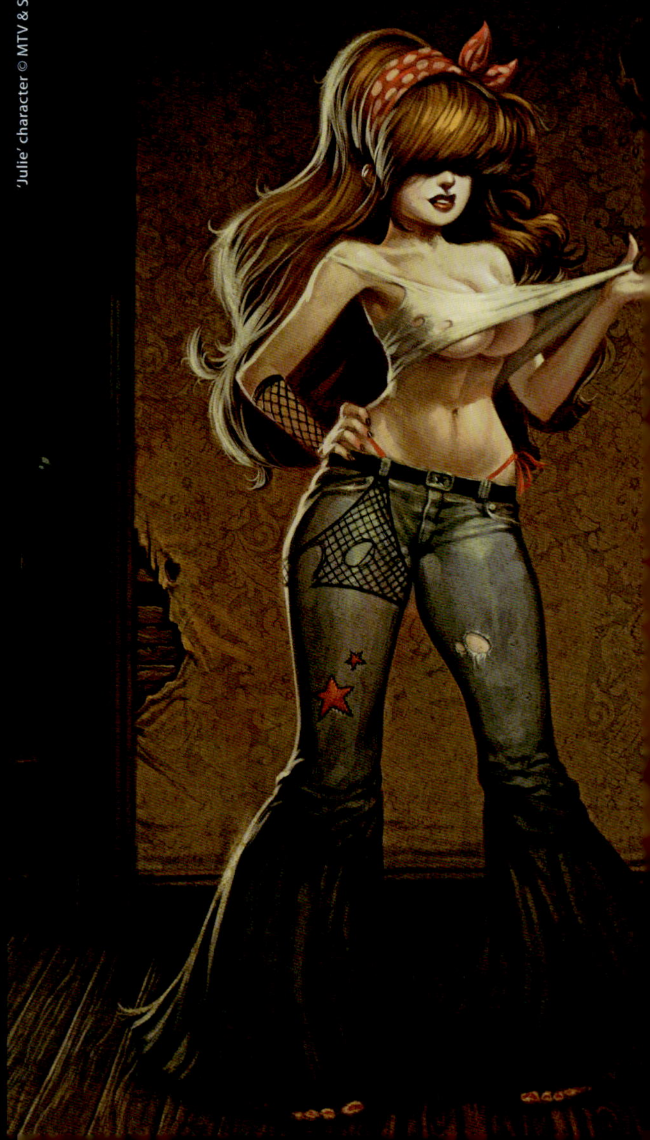

Naci Para Ti
Photoshop
Sonia Verdu, SPAIN
[above]

Glinda the Good
Painter, Photoshop
Keri Ruediger, USA
[above right]

The Maxx: Julie
Photoshop
Sergio Diaz, ARGENTINA
[right]

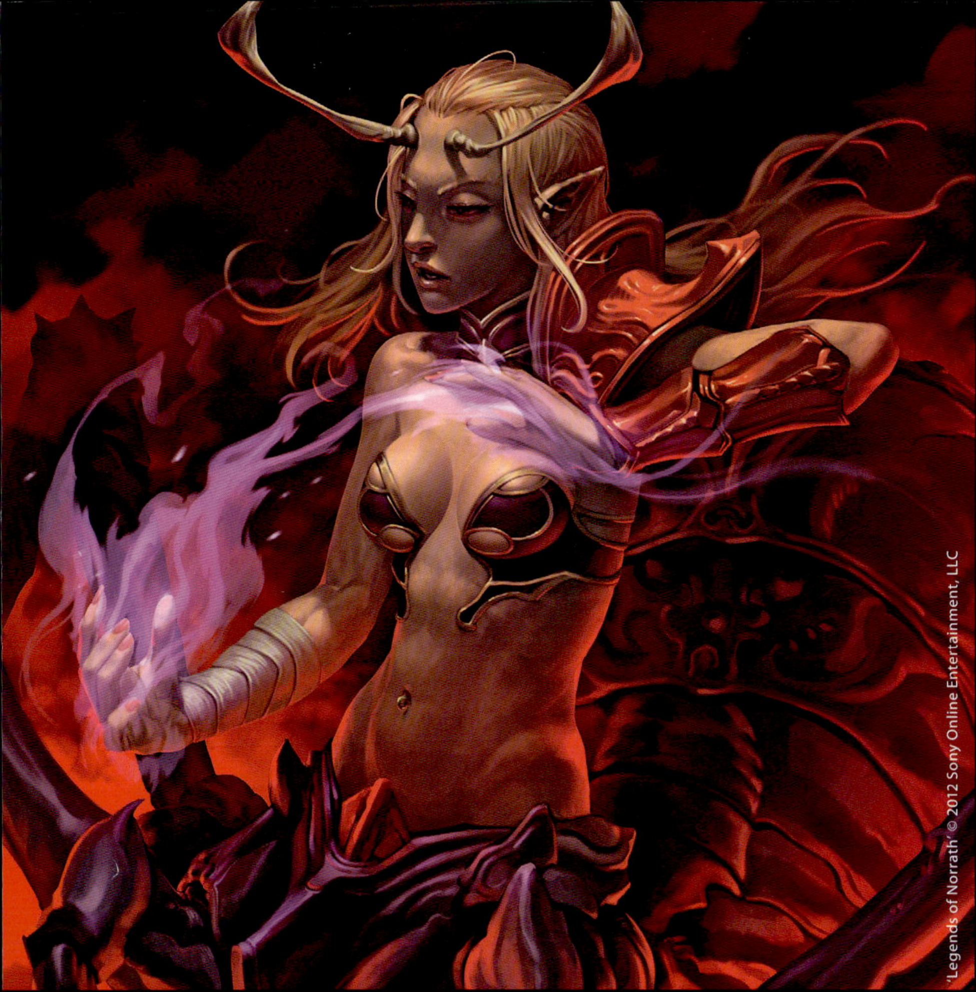

Legends of Norrath: Drachnid Enthraller
Photoshop
Client: Sony Online Entertainment, LLC
Derrick Chew (Art Director: Mark Tuttle), SINGAPORE
[left]

Fish
Photoshop
John Aslarona, USA
[below left]

Legend of the Cryptids: PoisonQueen
Photoshop
Client: Applibot, Inc.
Anna Mitura, POLAND
[below]

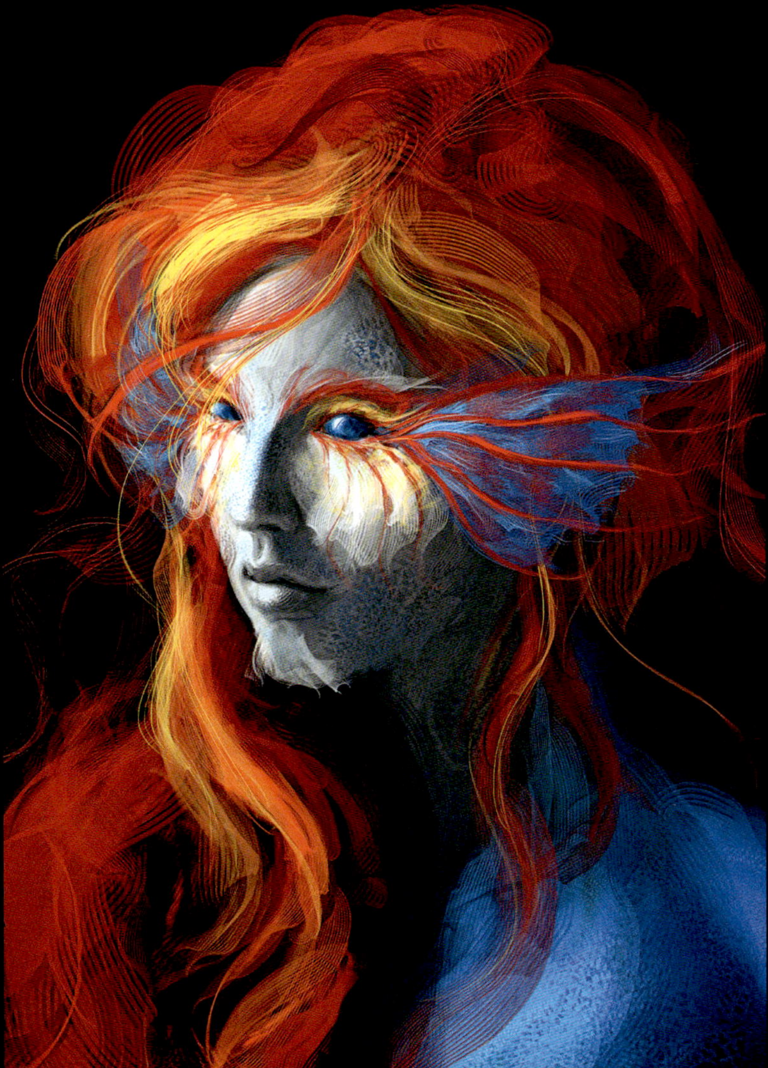

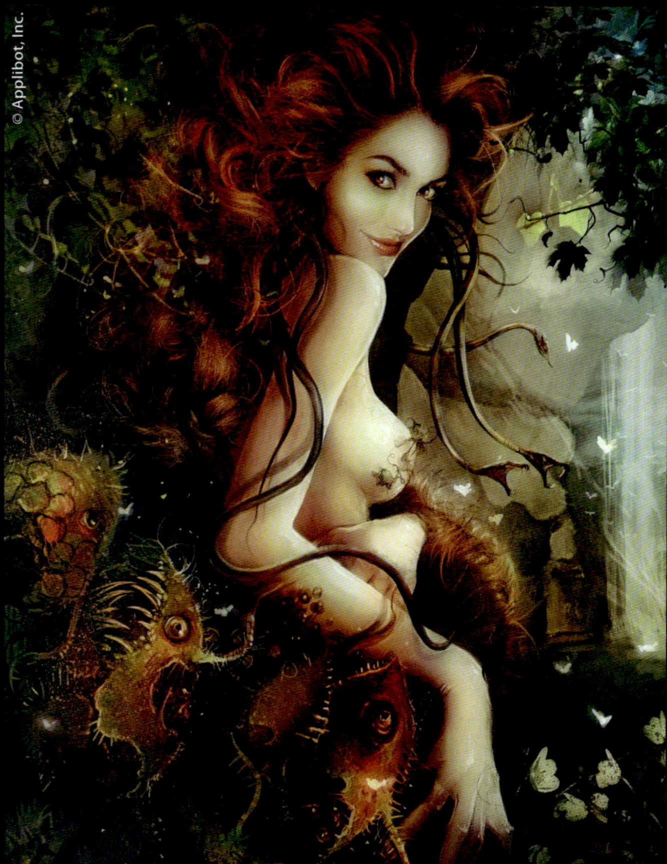

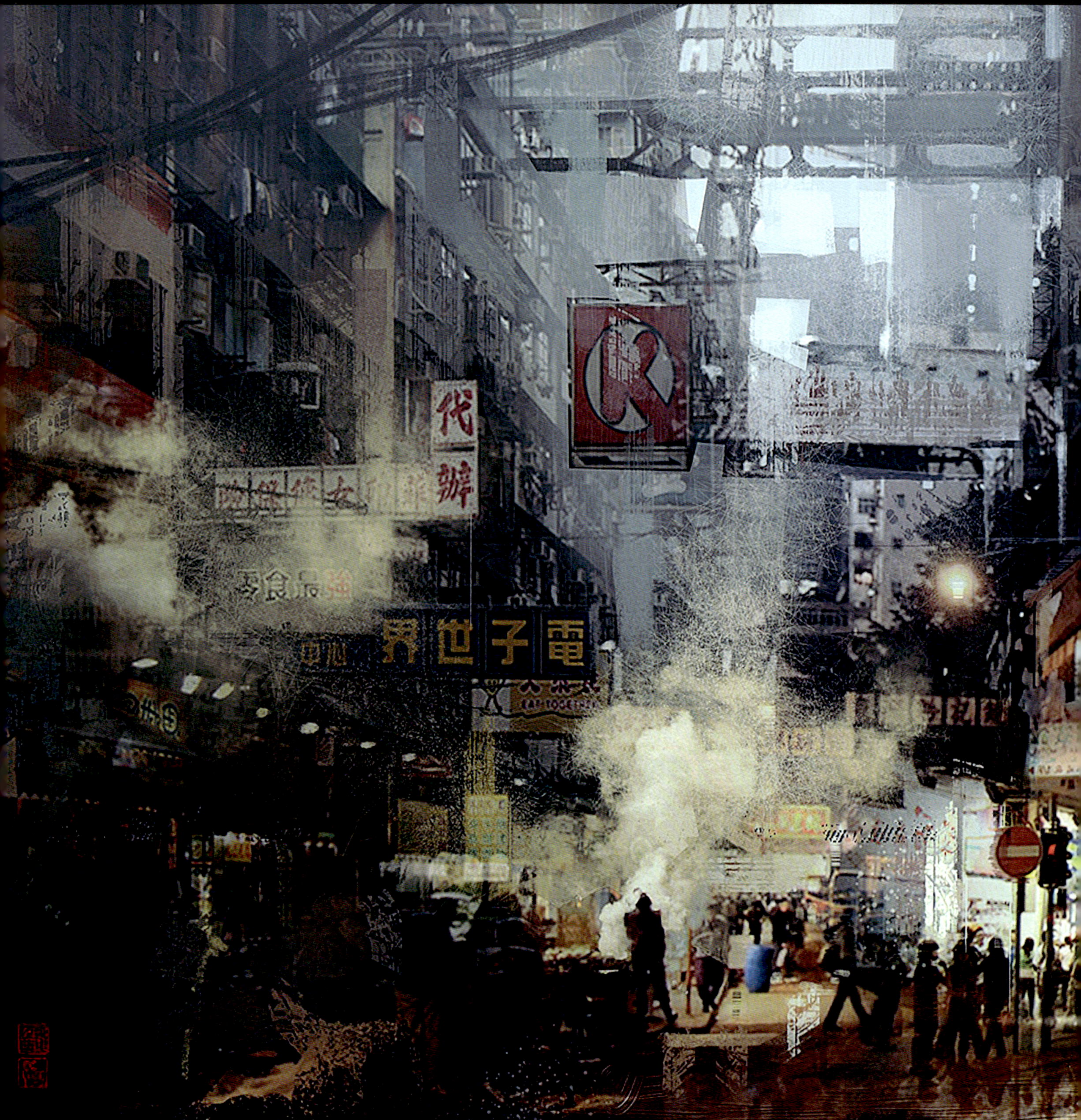

Chase Time
Photoshop
Donglu Yu, CANADA

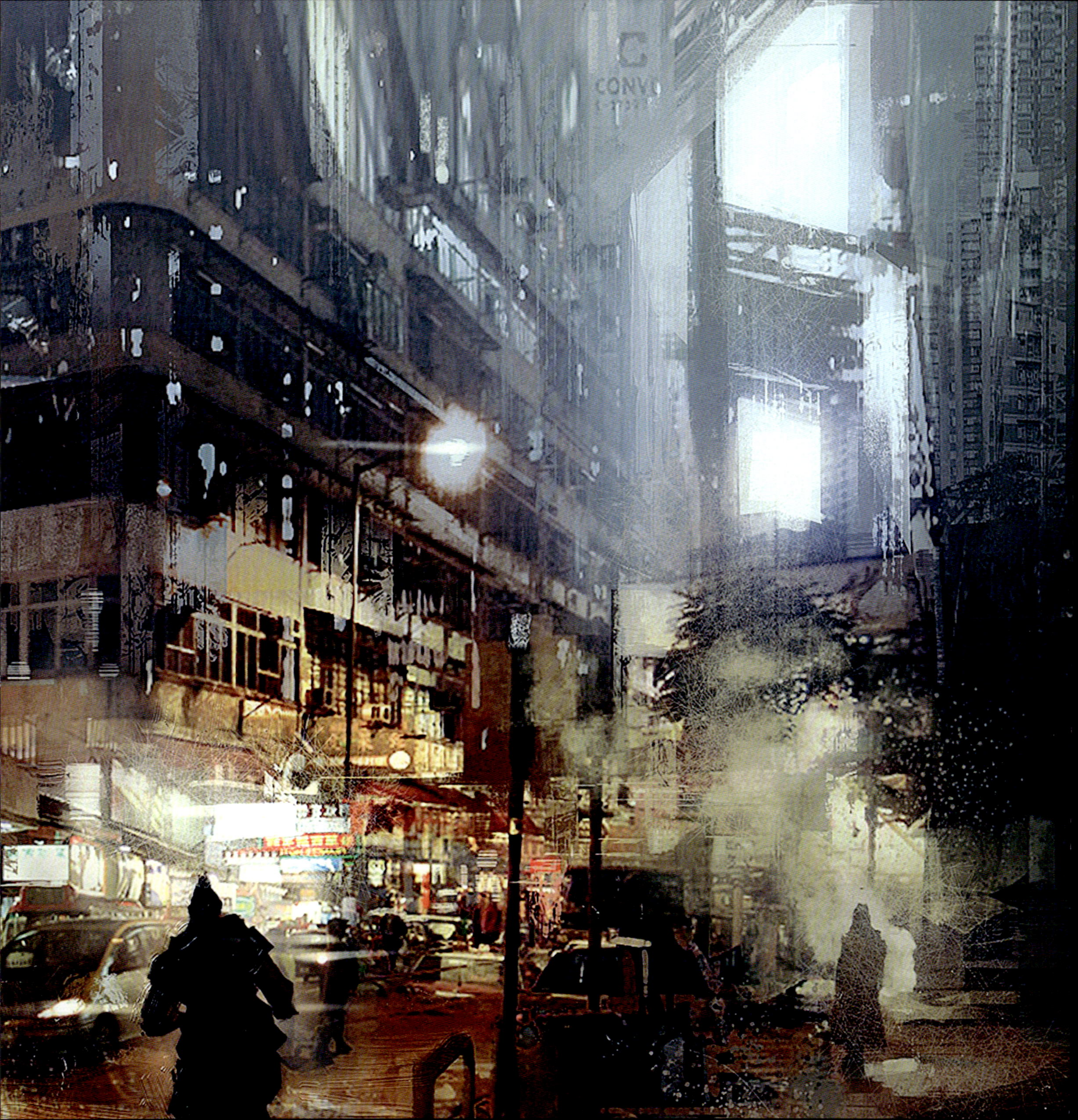

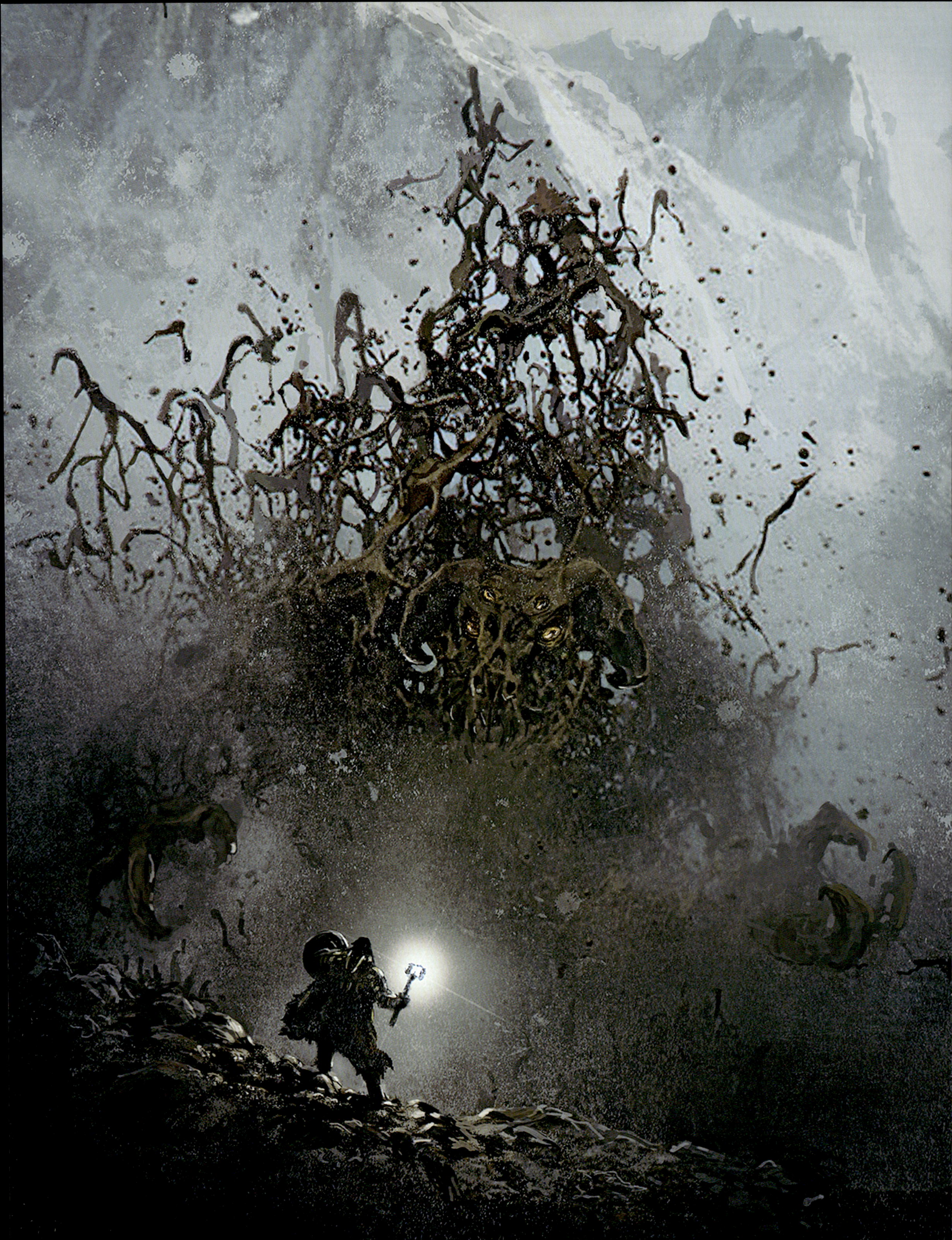

Excellence
Concept Art

Thor Fighting
Photoshop
Rasmus Berggreen, DENMARK

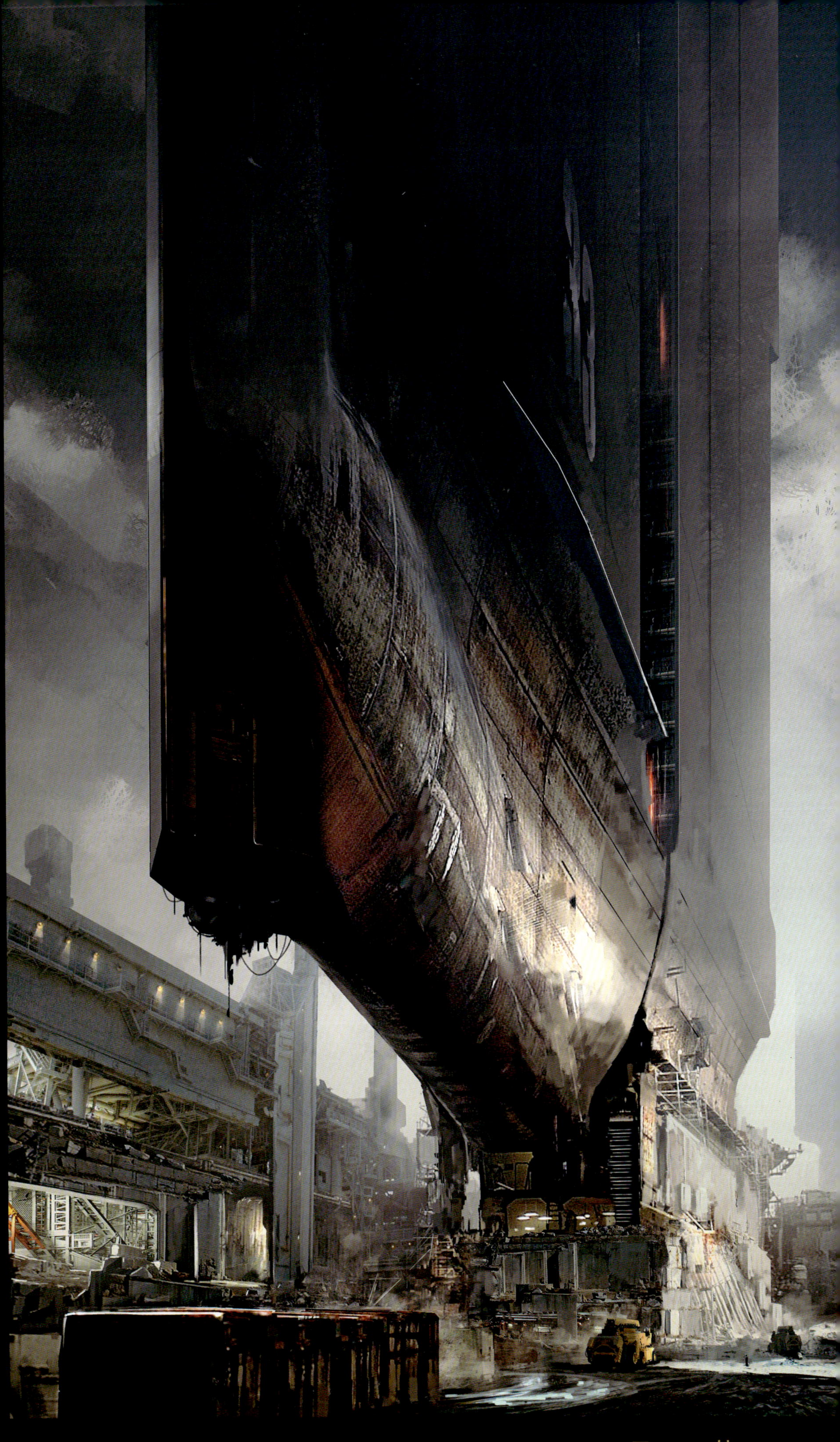

Fin
Photoshop
Jan Urschel, SINGAPORE

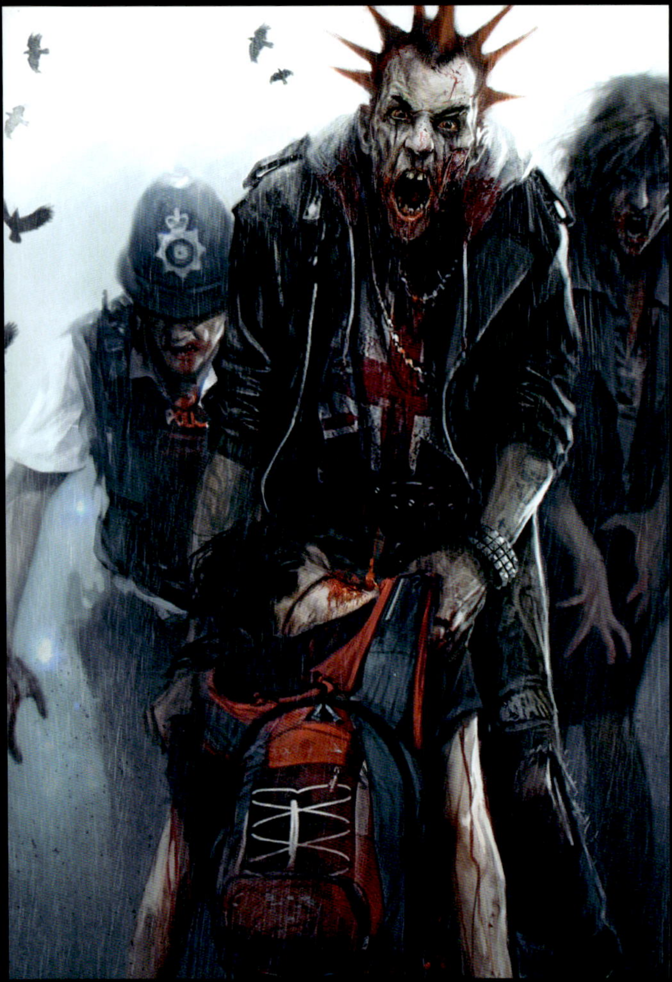

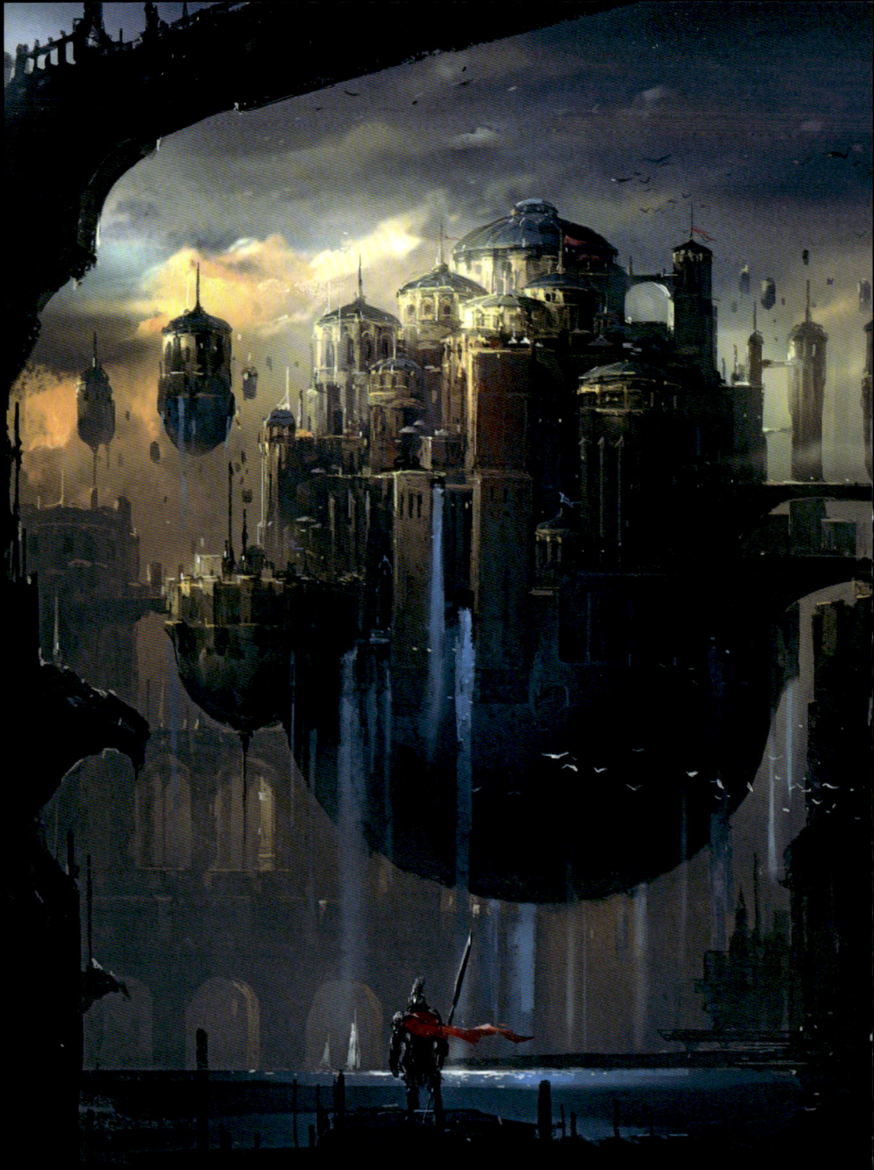

Hungry
Photoshop
Morgan Yon, FRANCE
[above]

City of Sunset
Photoshop
Jong-Won Park, SOUTH KOREA
[above right]

River Bank
Photoshop
Yun Ling, CANADA
[right]

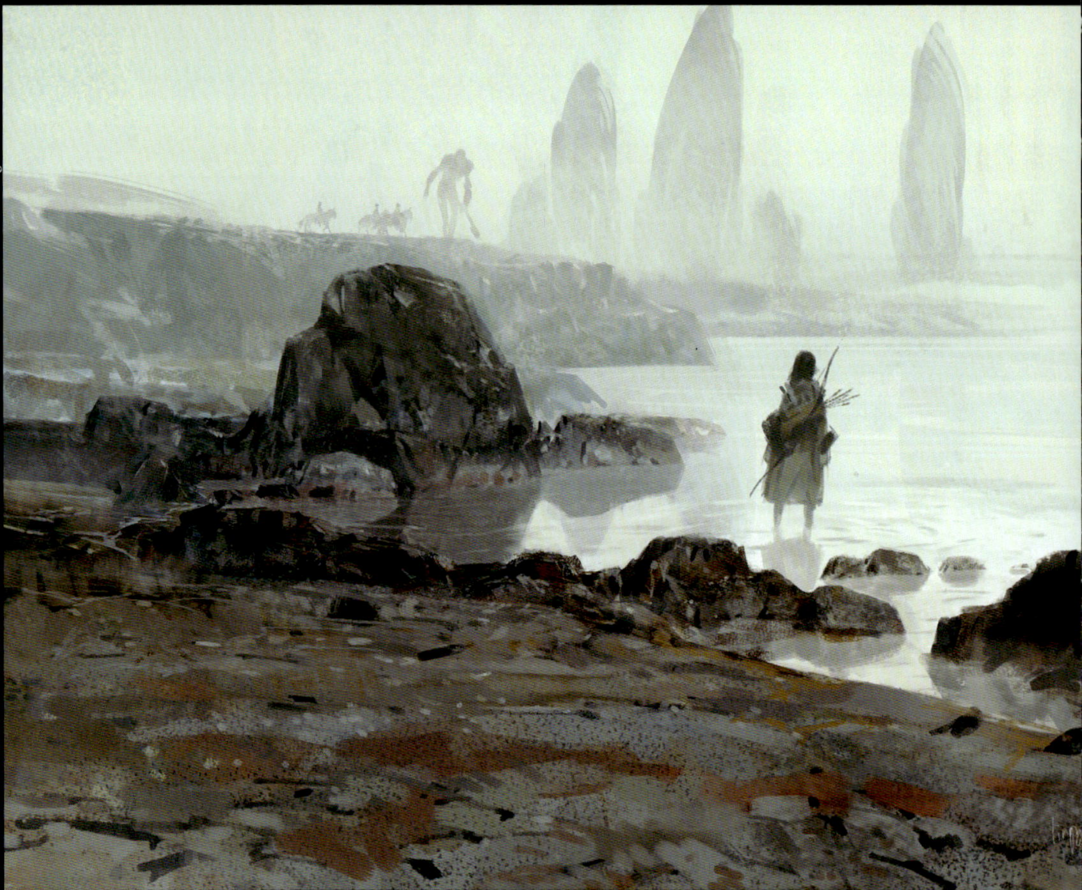

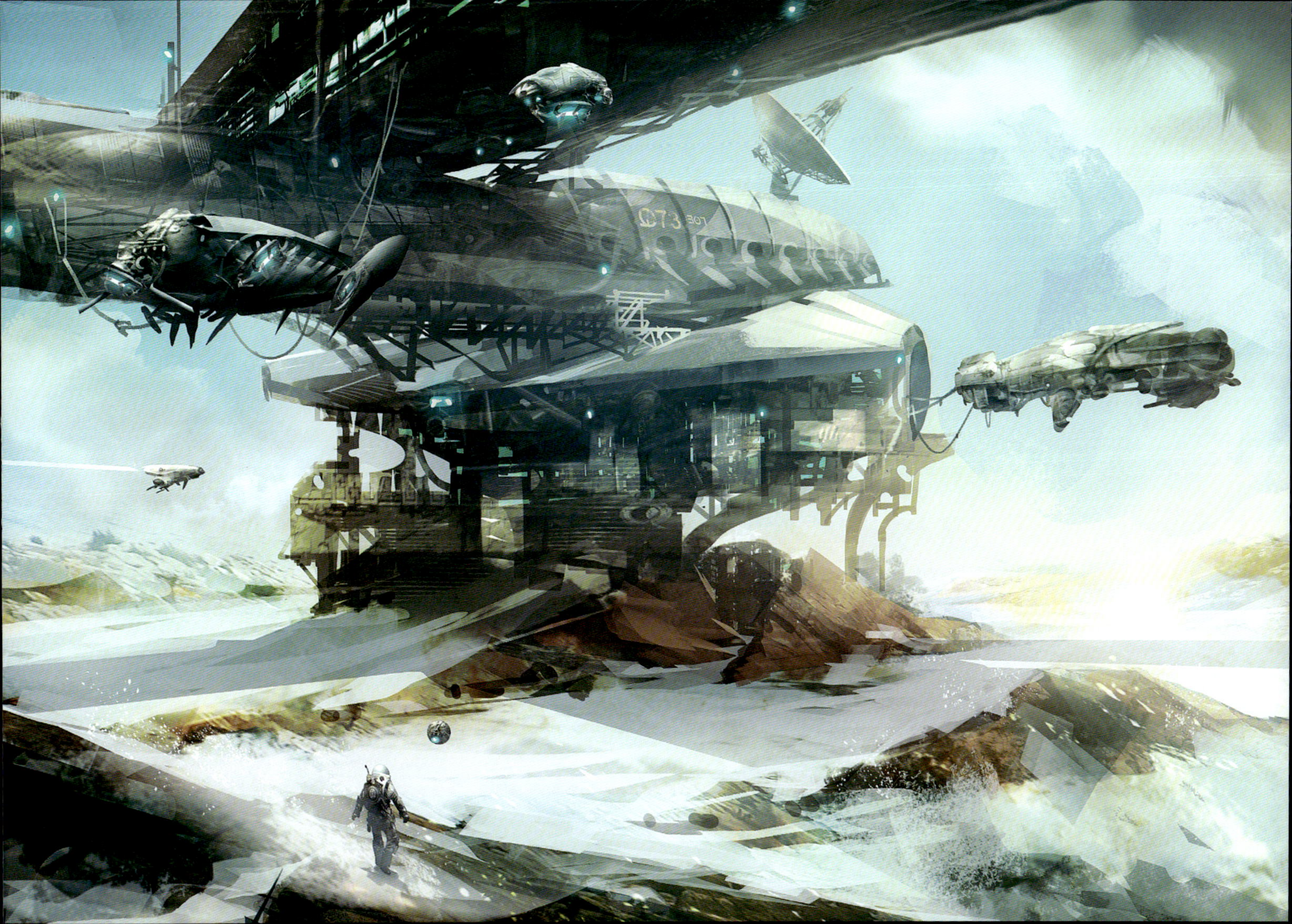

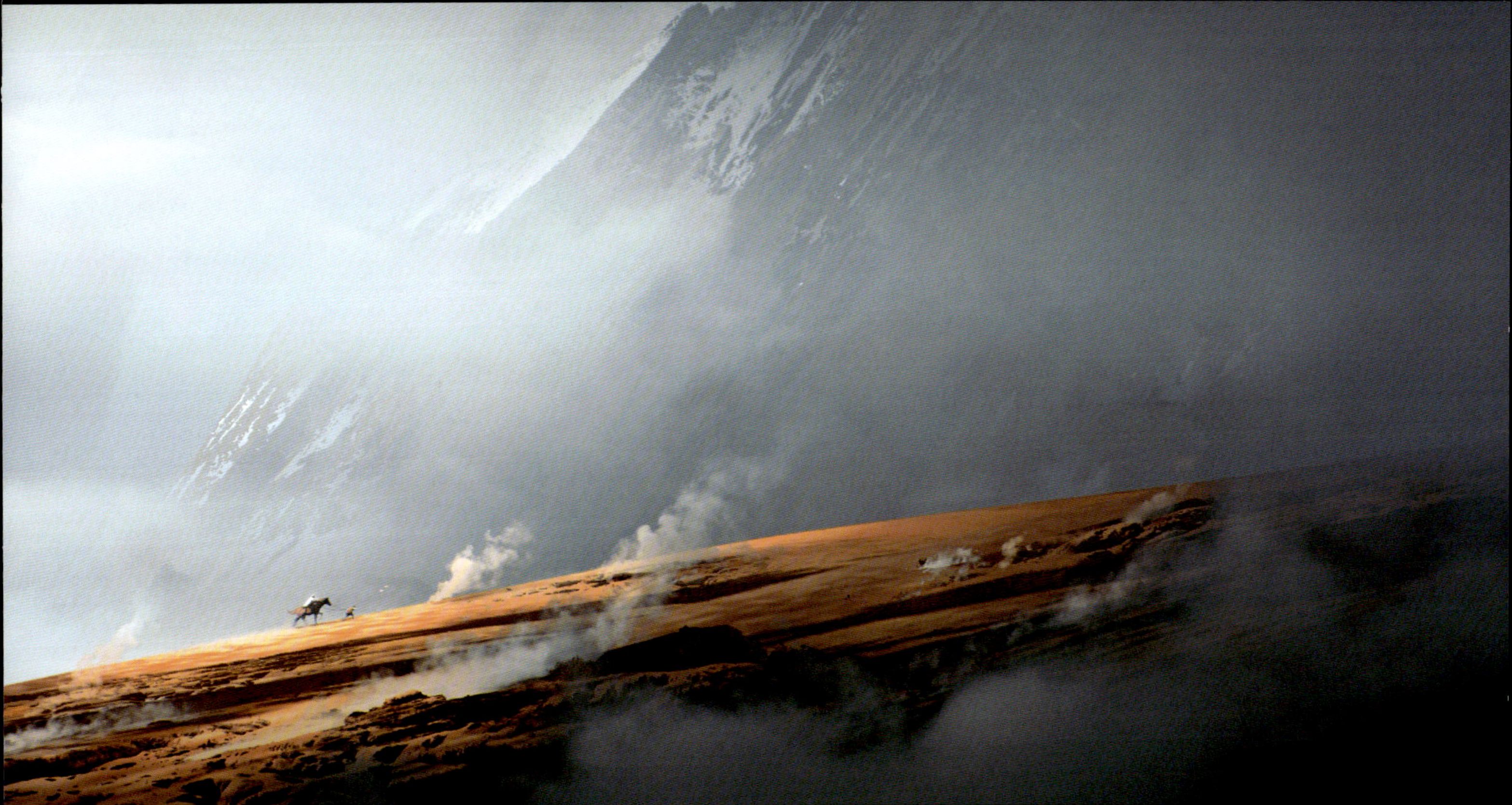

Base Q73
Photoshop
J Otto Szatmari, HUNGARY
[top]

The Ridge
Photoshop
Jama Jurabaev, TAJIKISTAN
[above]

Neo Air Force
Photoshop
Au yeung Chun Hay, CHINA
[right]

Fortress of Ogre
Photoshop
Jong-Won Park, SOUTH KOREA
[below right]

RED
Photoshop, Painter
Alexander Smolyakov, UKRAINE
[below]

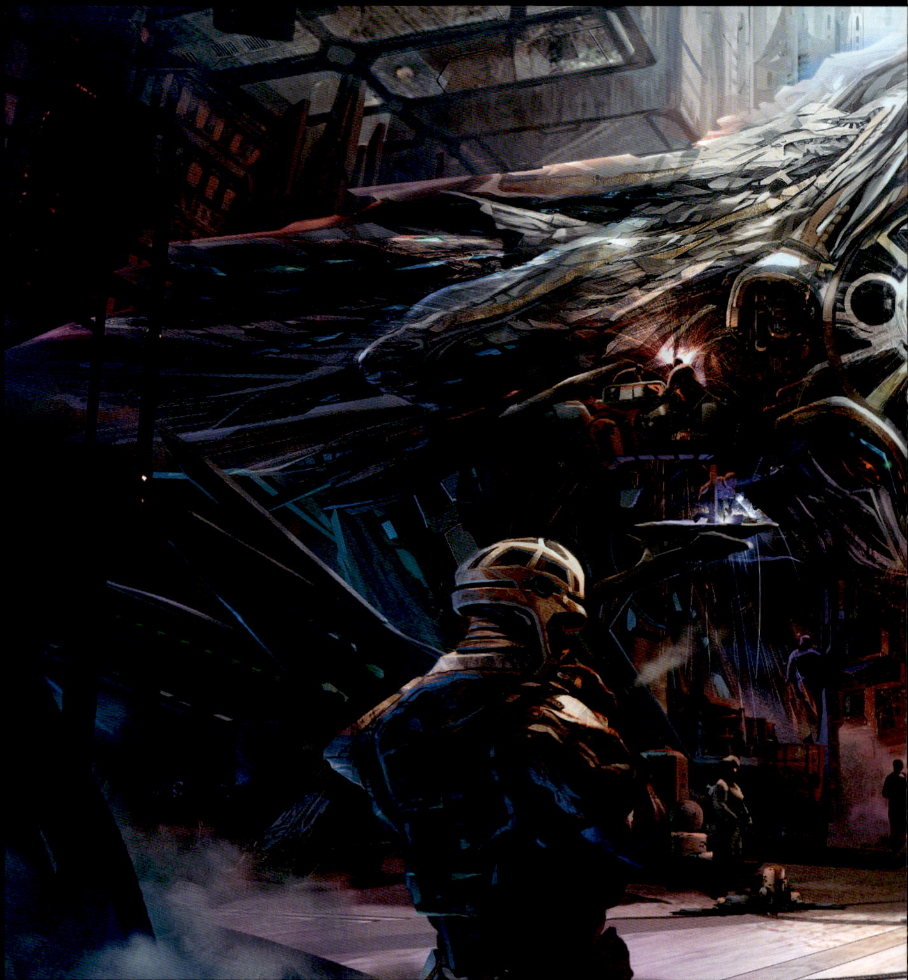

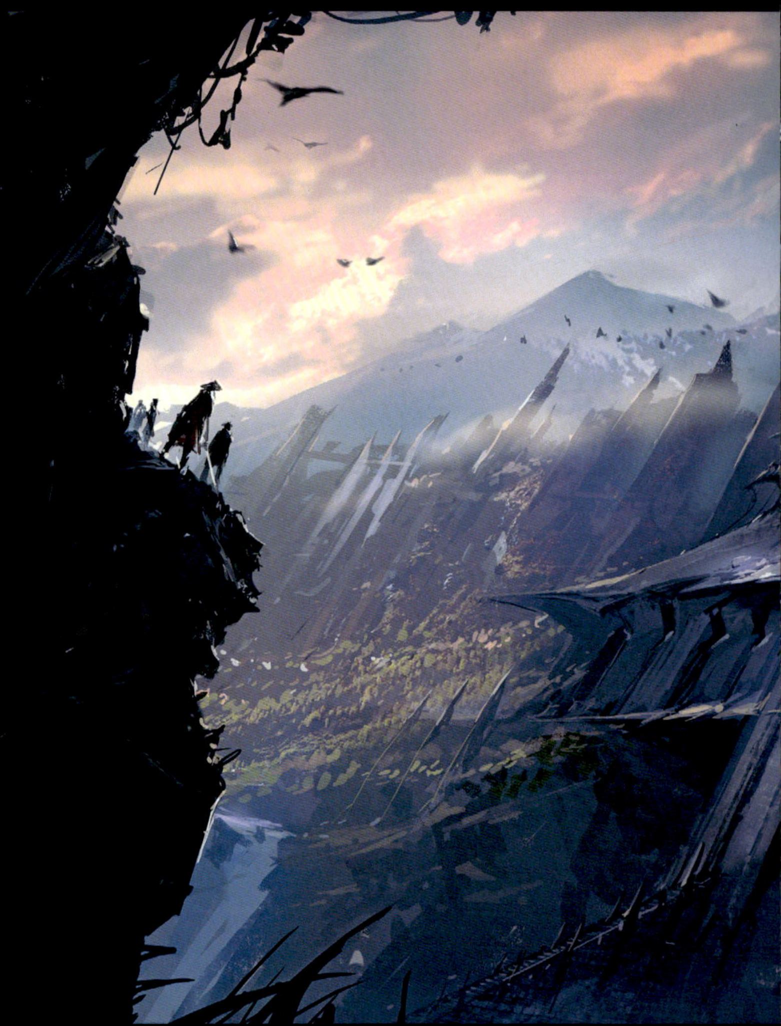

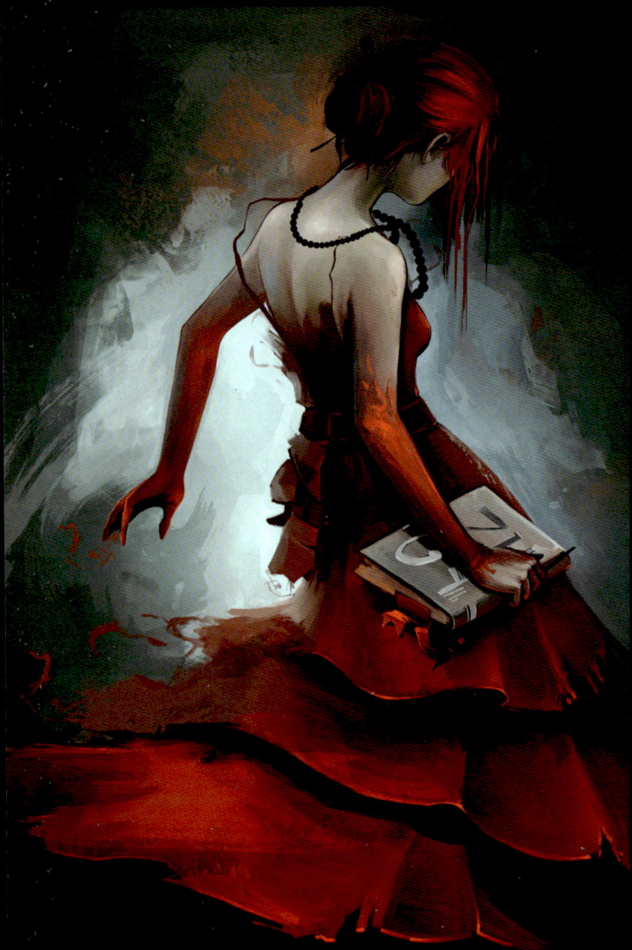

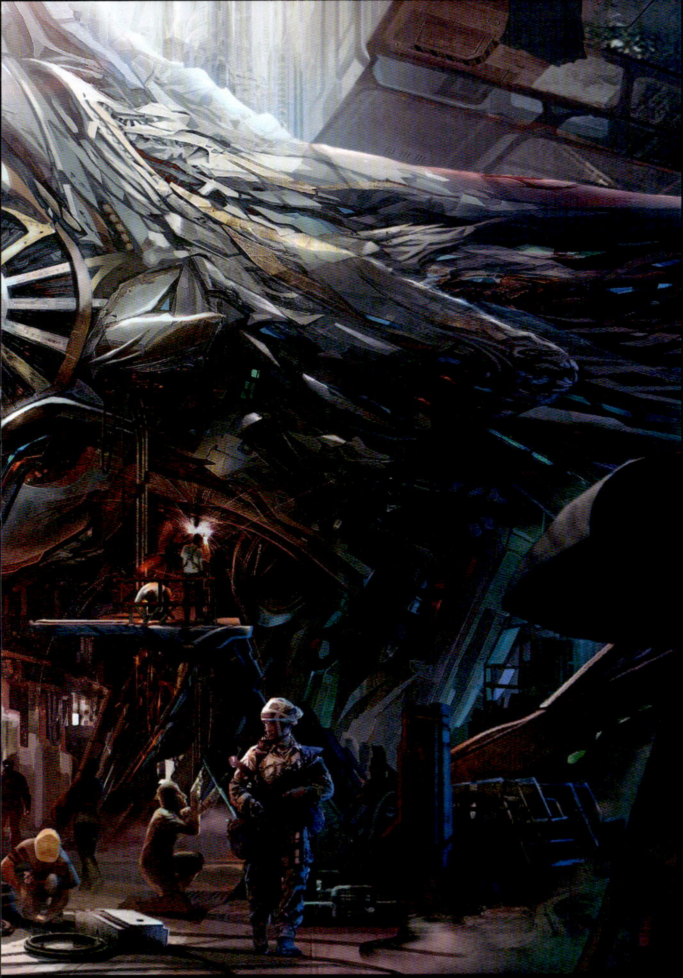

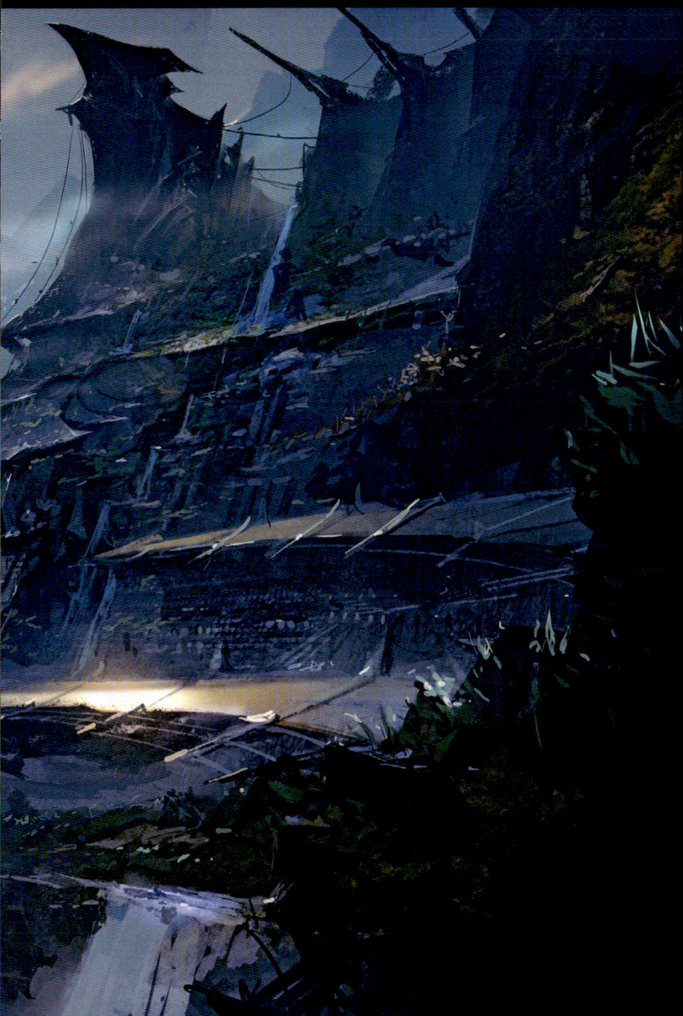

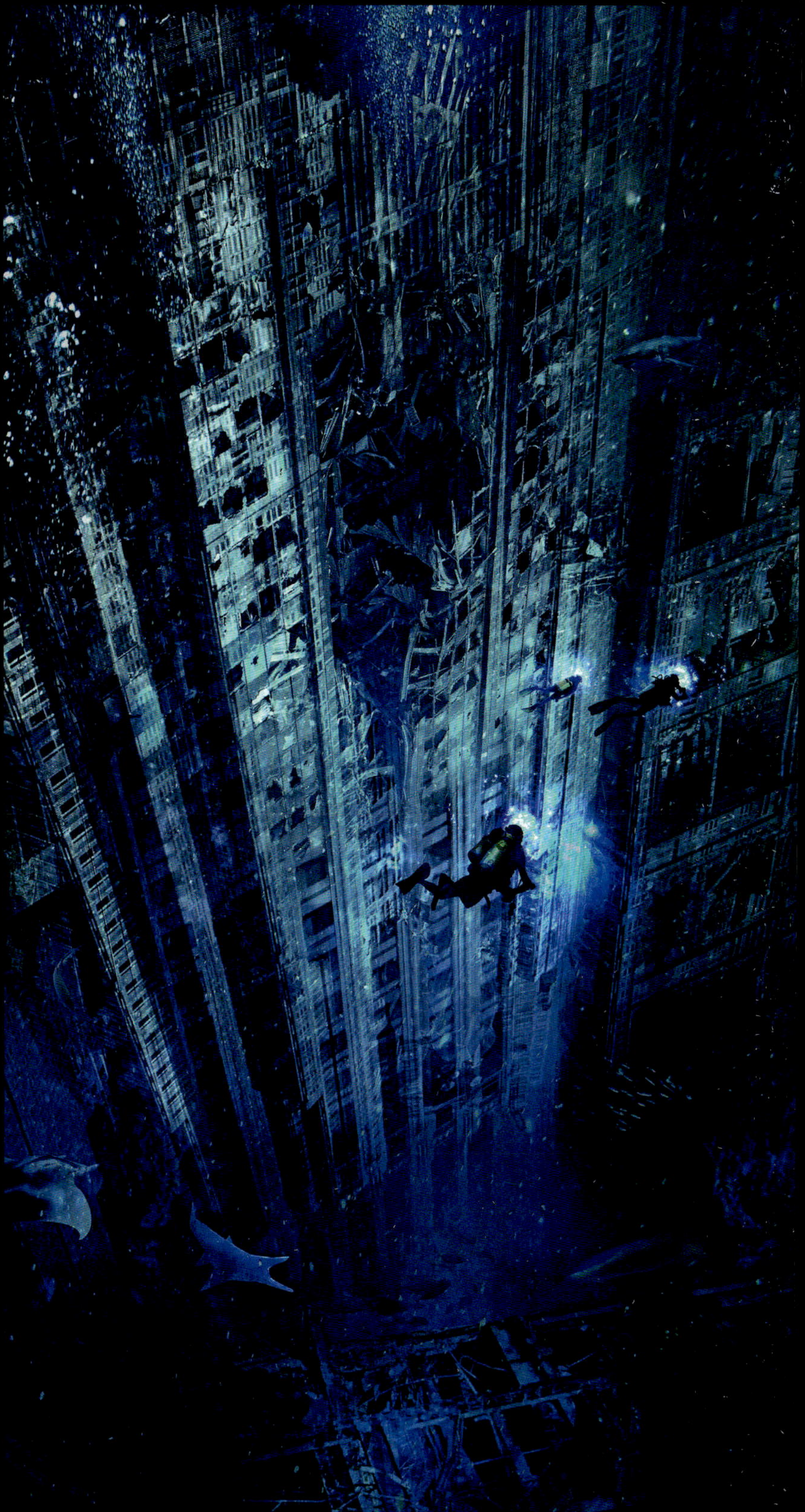

Underwater
Photoshop
Dong Kyun Ryu, USA
[above]

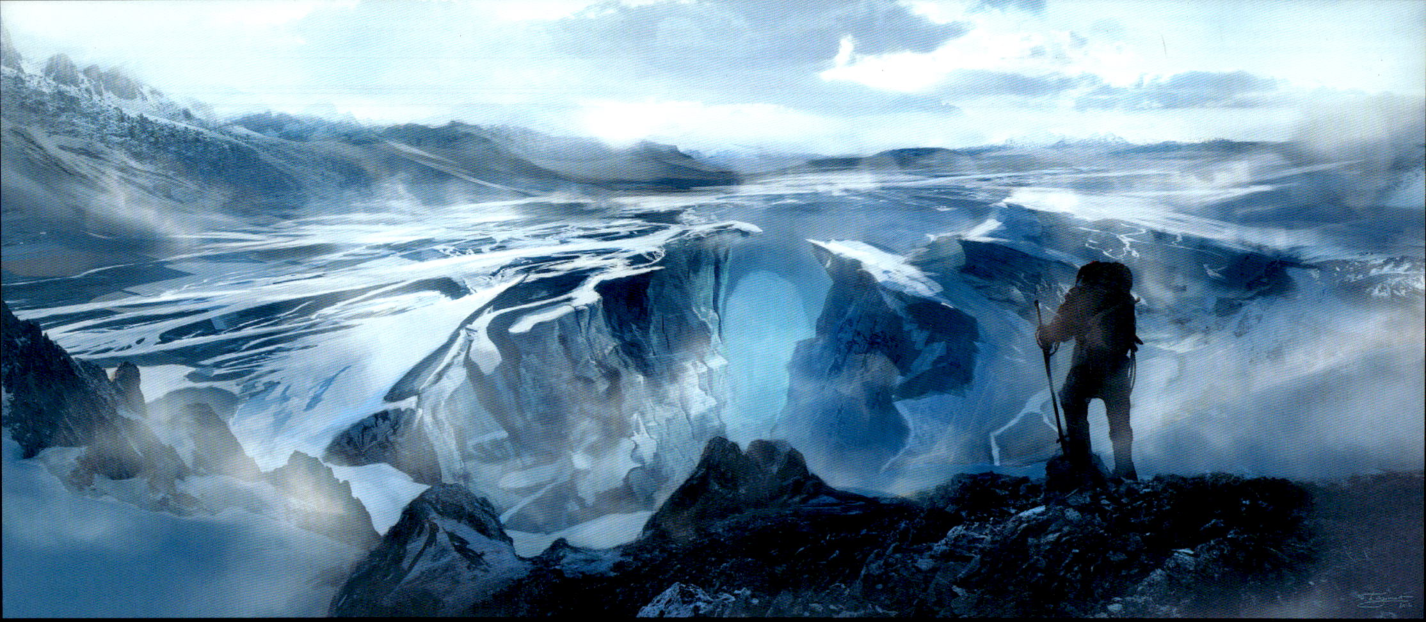

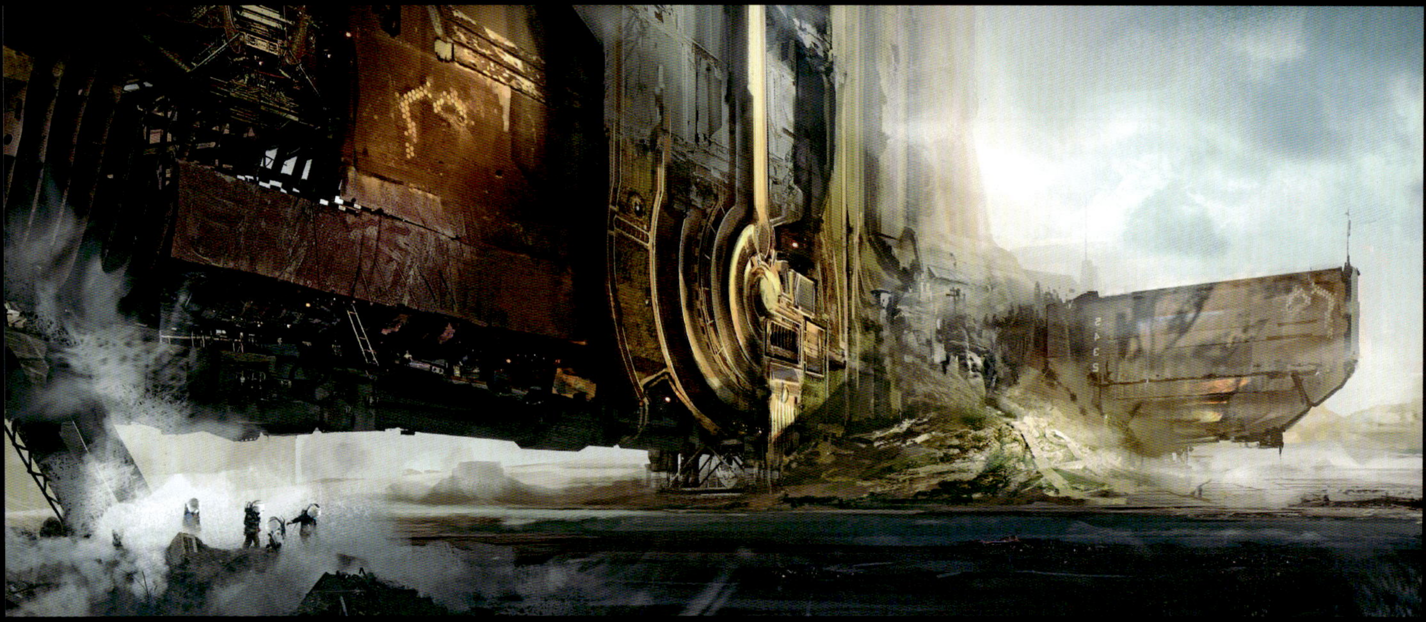

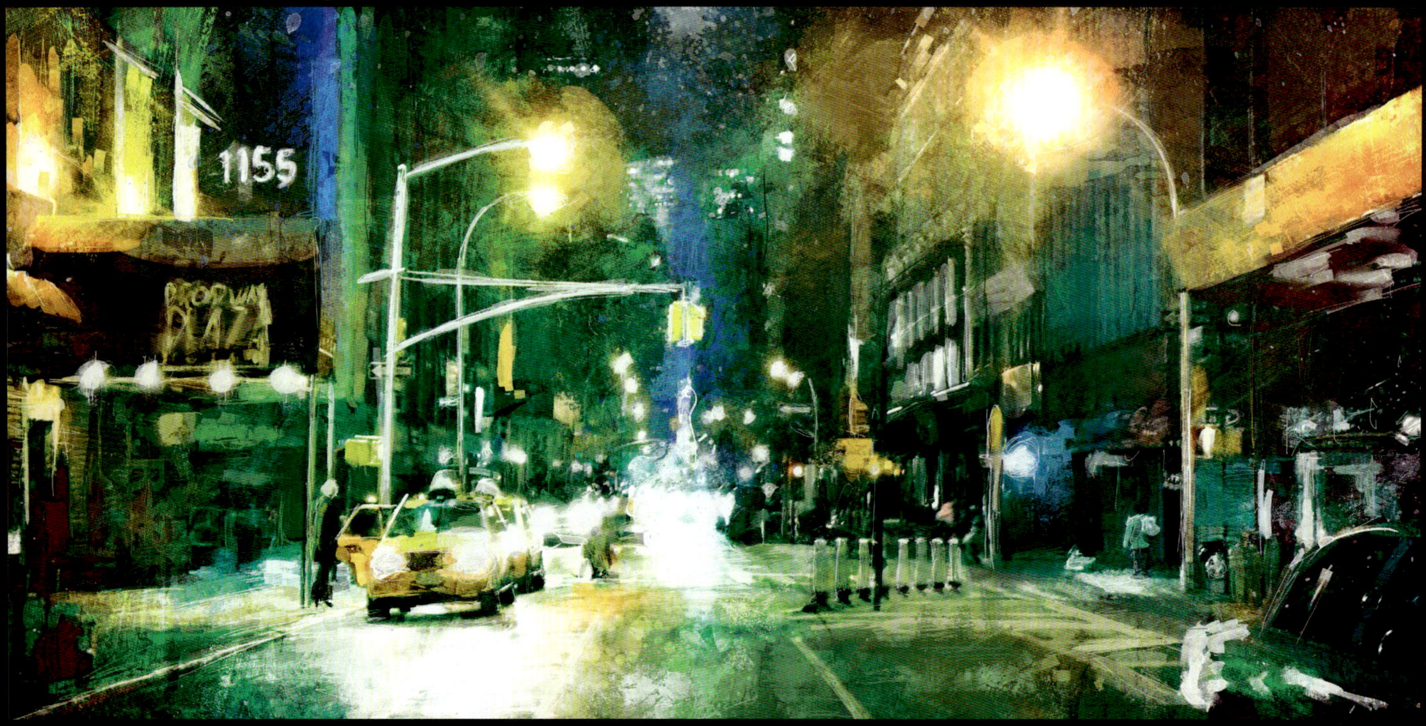

The Explorer
Photoshop
Florian de Gesincourt, FRANCE
[top]

Construction Site
Photoshop
Jan Urschel, SINGAPORE
[center]

NY lights
Photoshop, ArtRage
Guillem H Pongiluppi, SPAIN
[above]

Shipbuilding Town
Photoshop
Jong-Won Park, SOUTH KOREA
[facing page top]

Industrial Site
Photoshop
Daniel Dociu, USA
[facing page center]

Cloud Atlas: Submerged Slums of Neo Seoul
Photoshop
Client: Anarchos Productions
George Hull, USA
[facing page bottom]

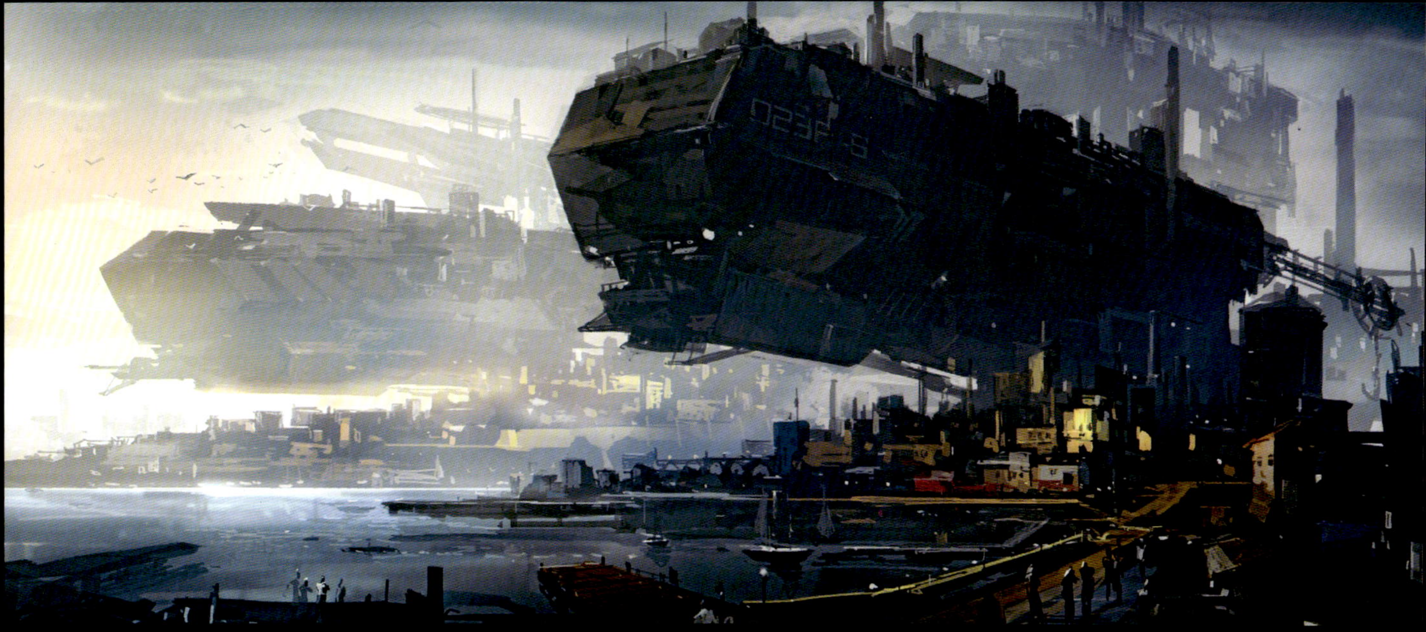

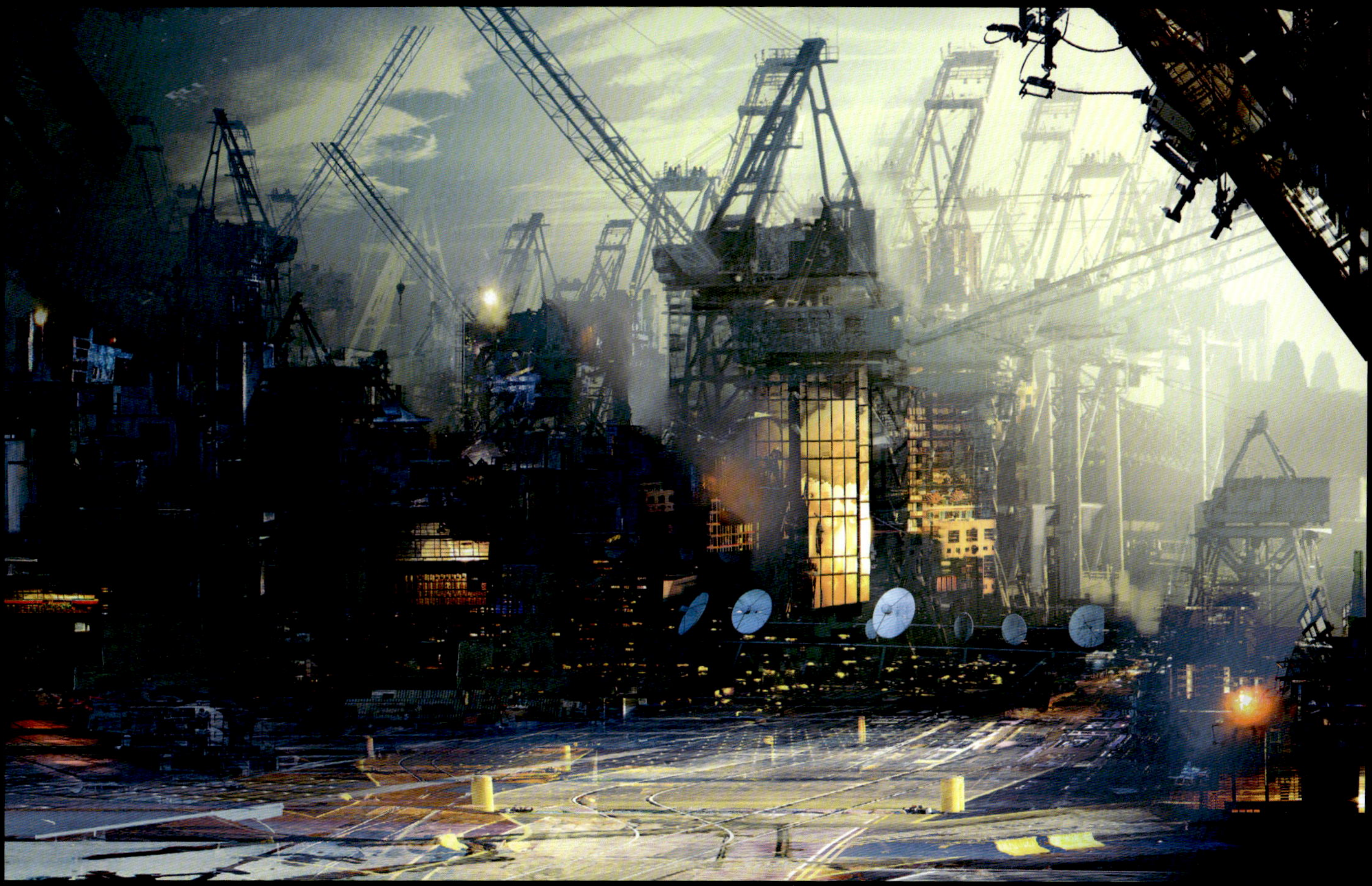

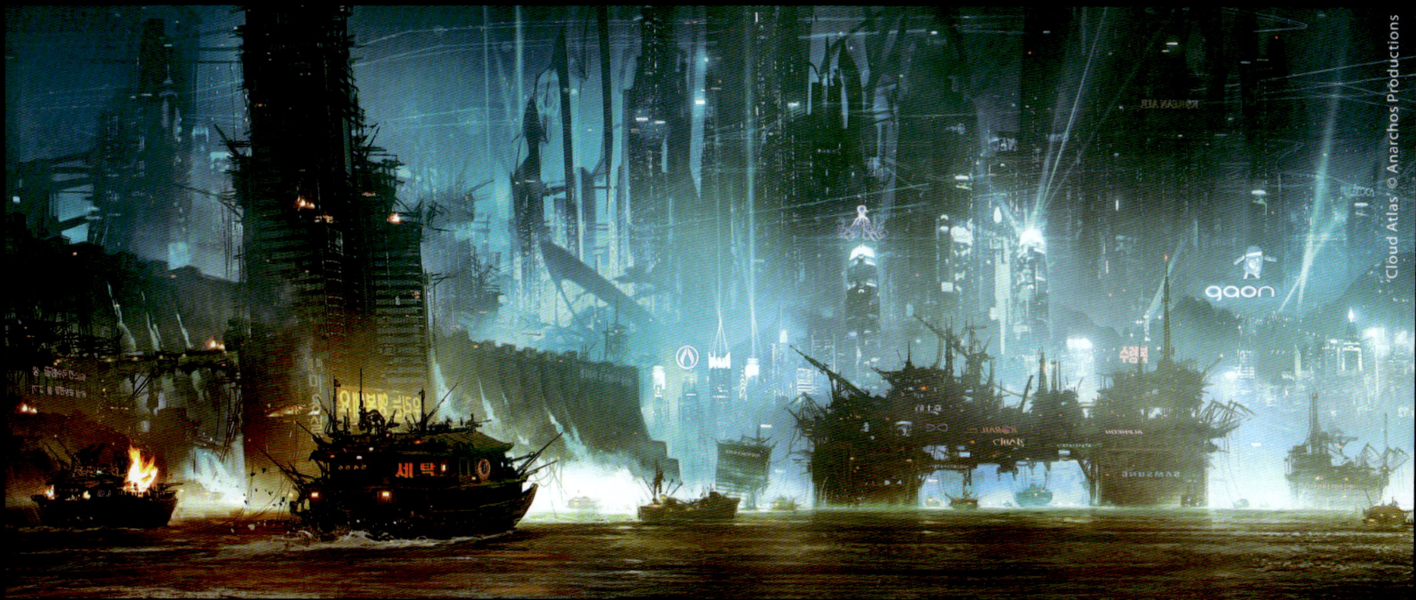
gaon
세탁

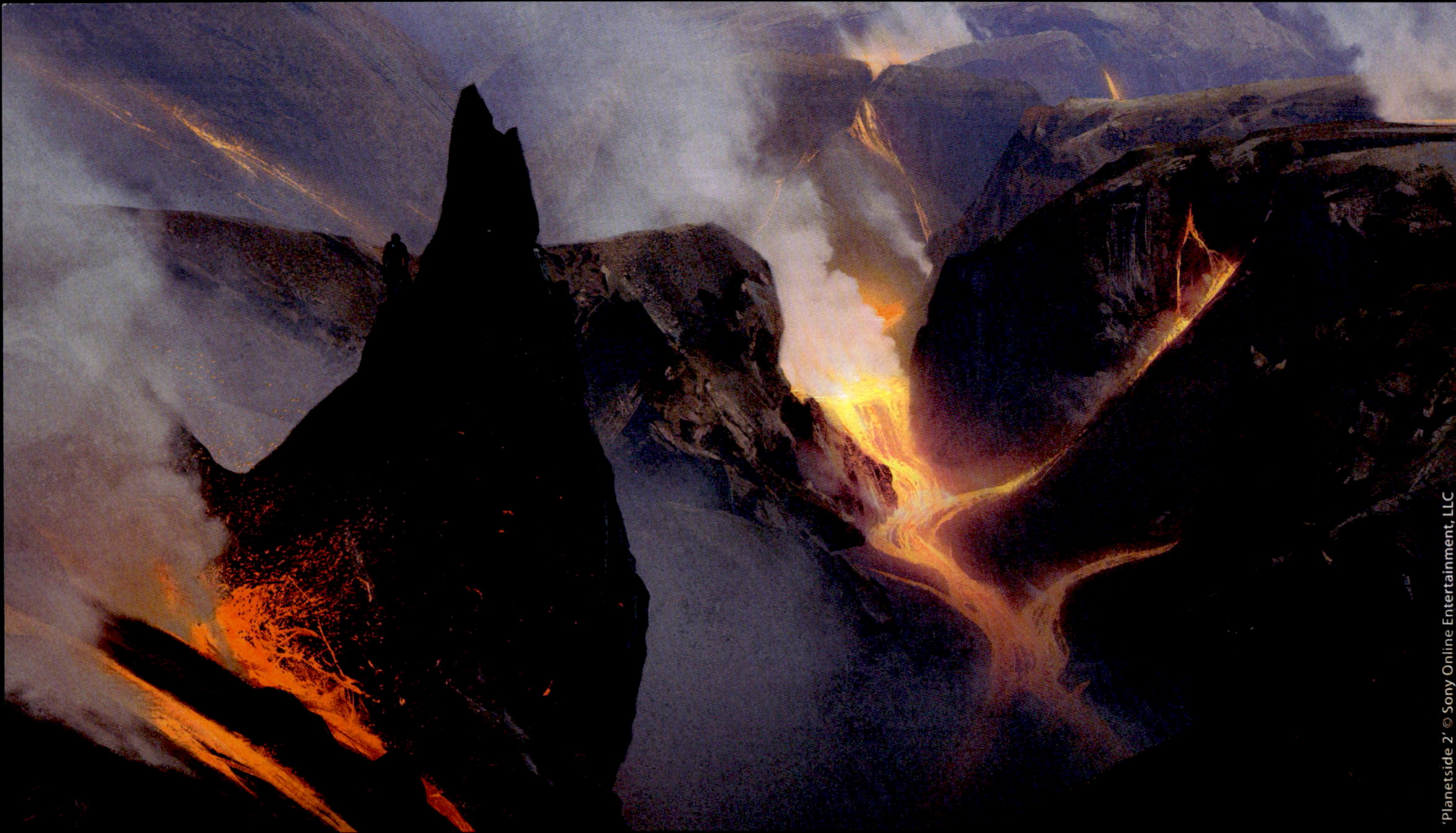

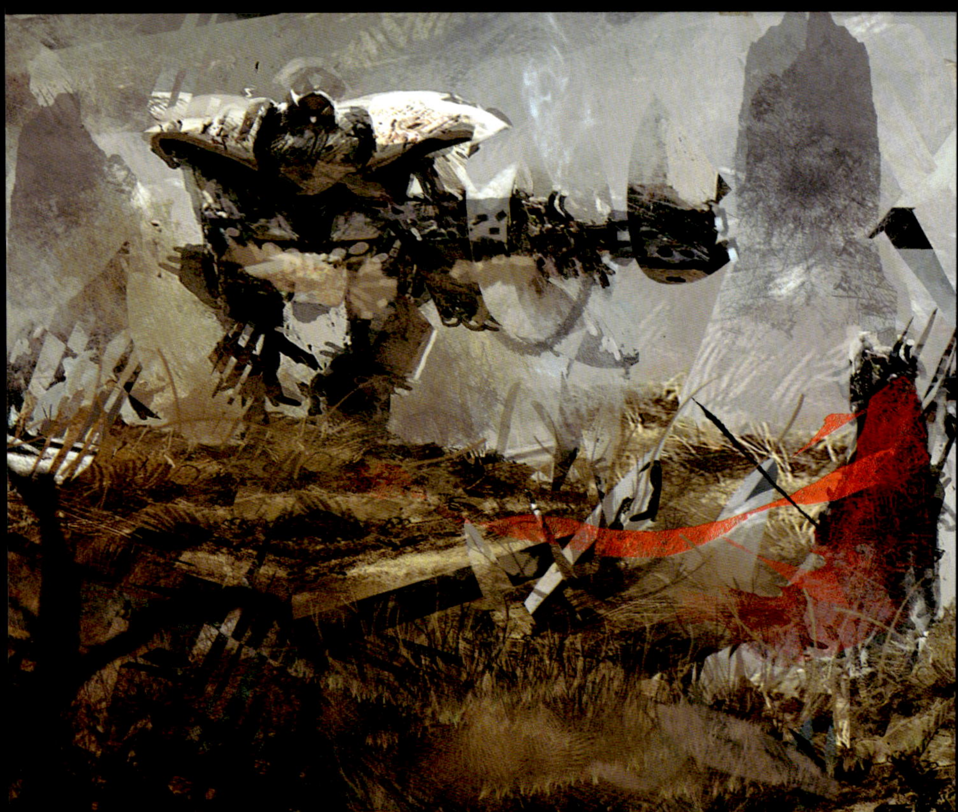

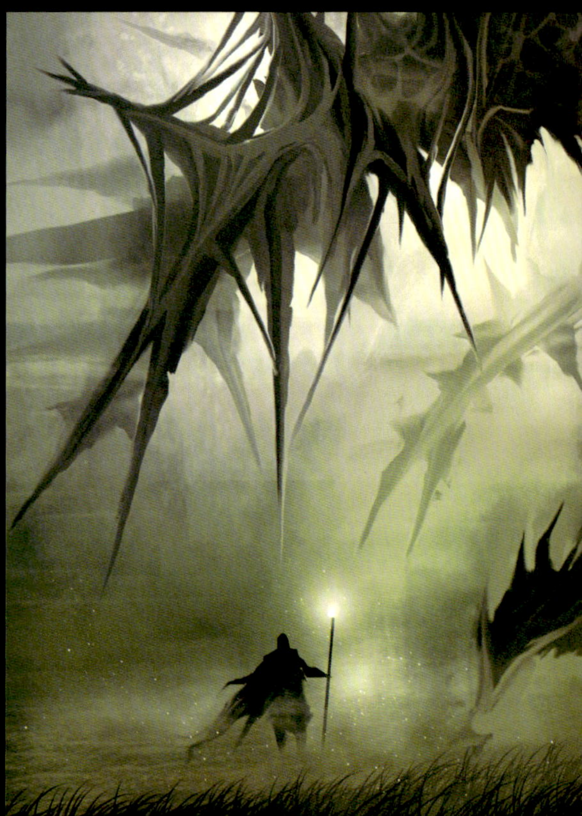

Planetside 2: Planetside Lava
Photoshop
Client: Sony Online Entertainment, LLC
Shaddy Safadi (Art Director: Tramell Isaac), USA

Strange Places
Photoshop
Ramses Melendez, MEXICO
[above]

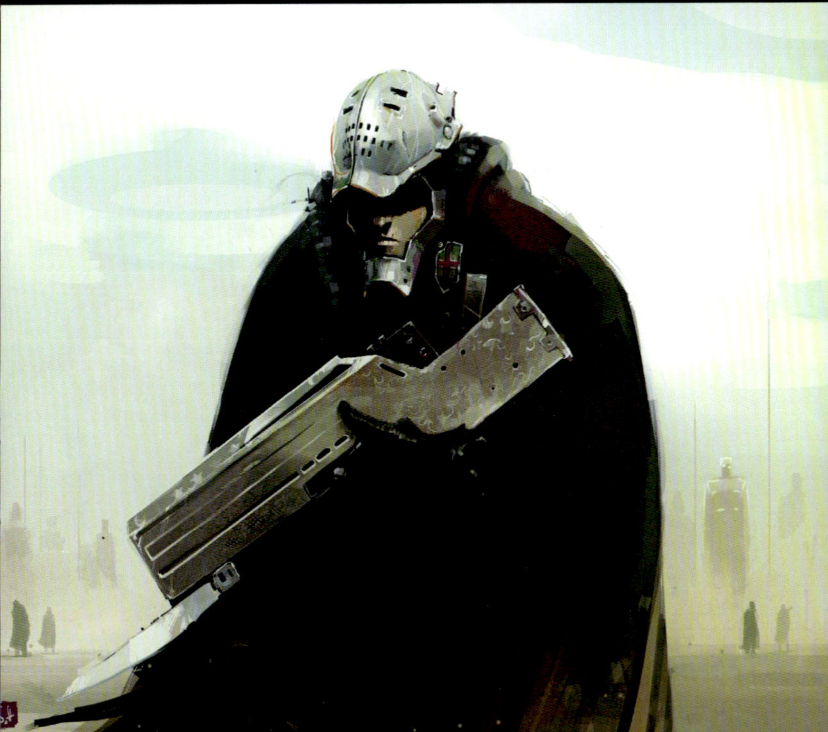

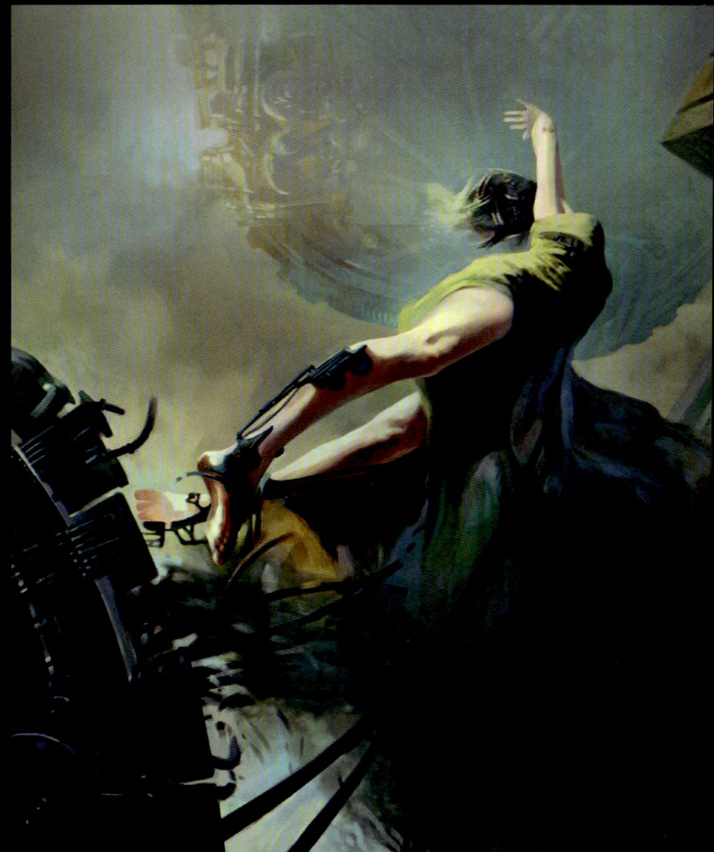

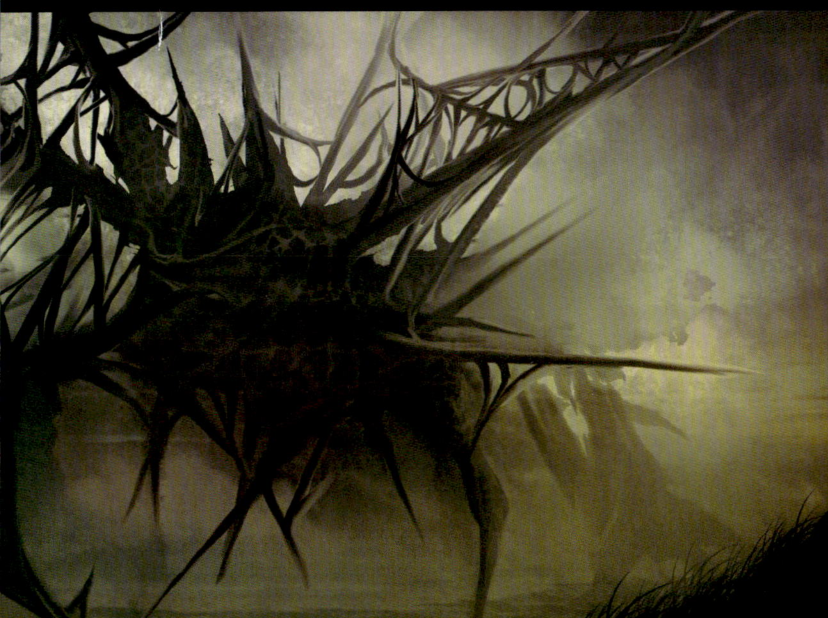

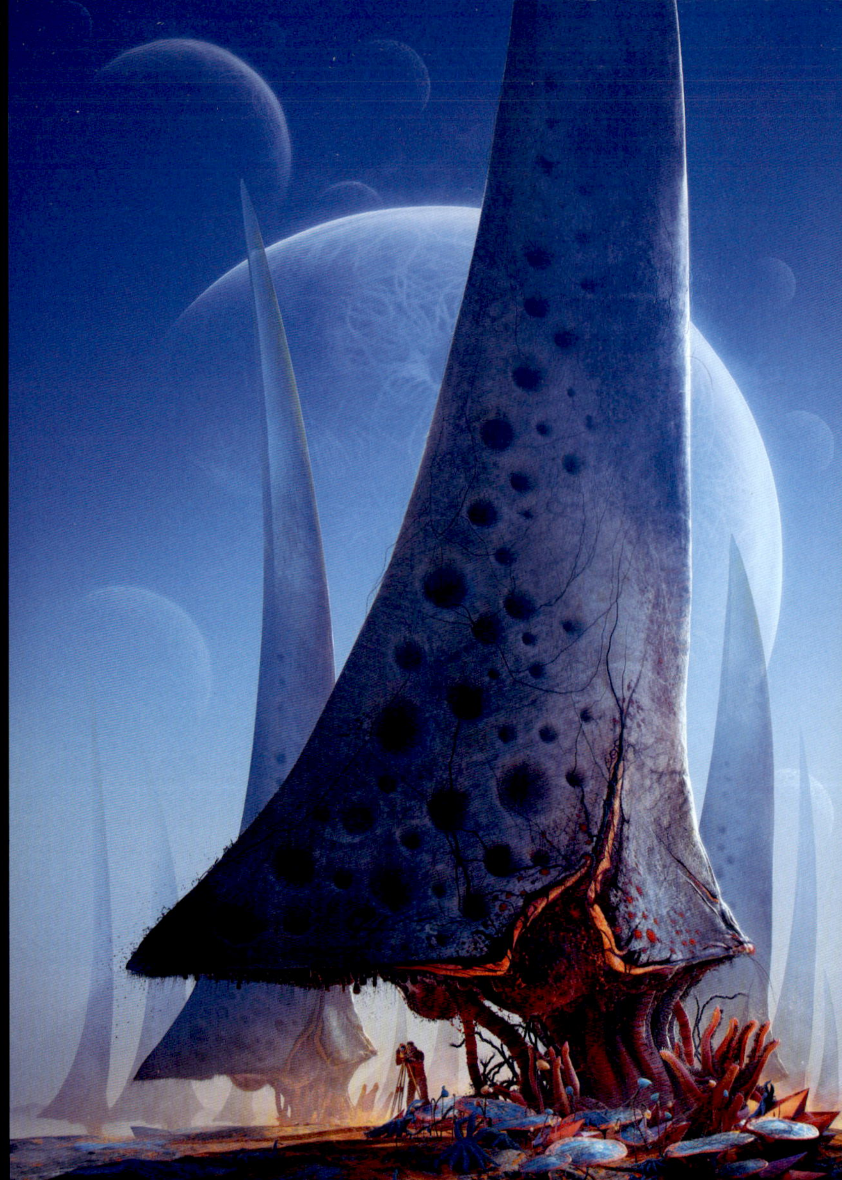

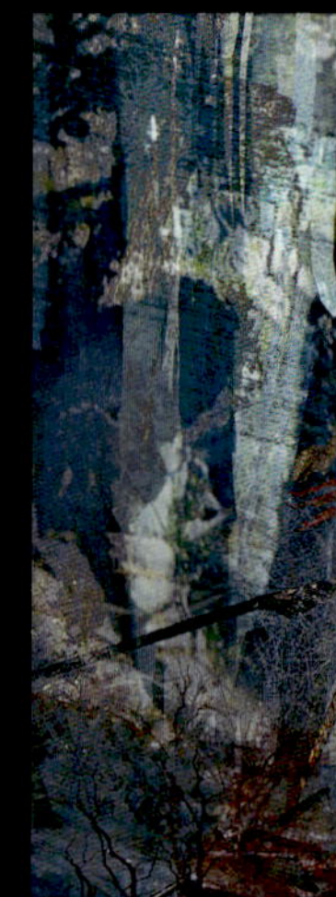

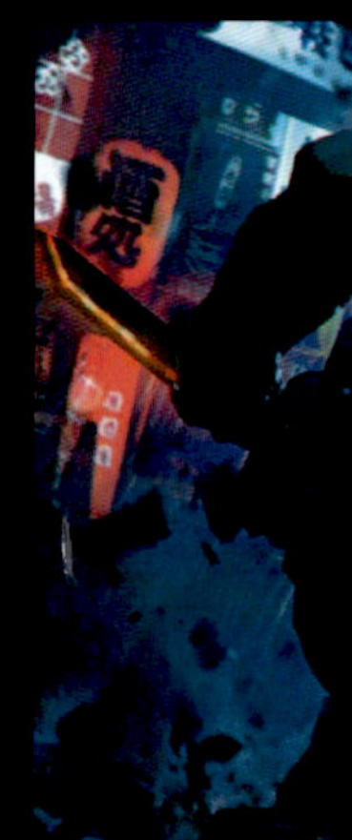

The Journey: Surveying BXT83-10
3ds Max, Photoshop, Wings3D, ZBrush
Andrzej Sykut, POLAND
[right]

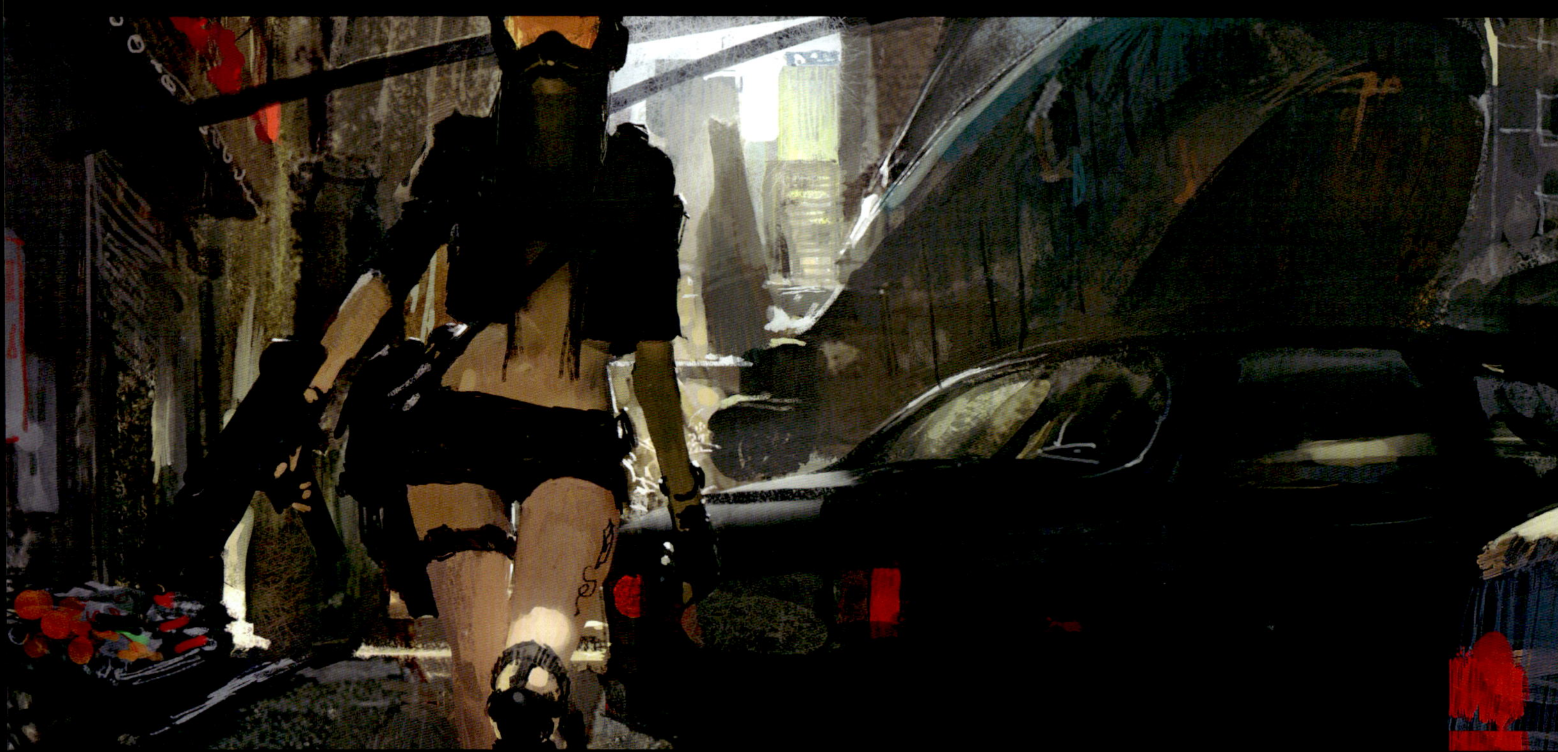

Gangstress
Photoshop

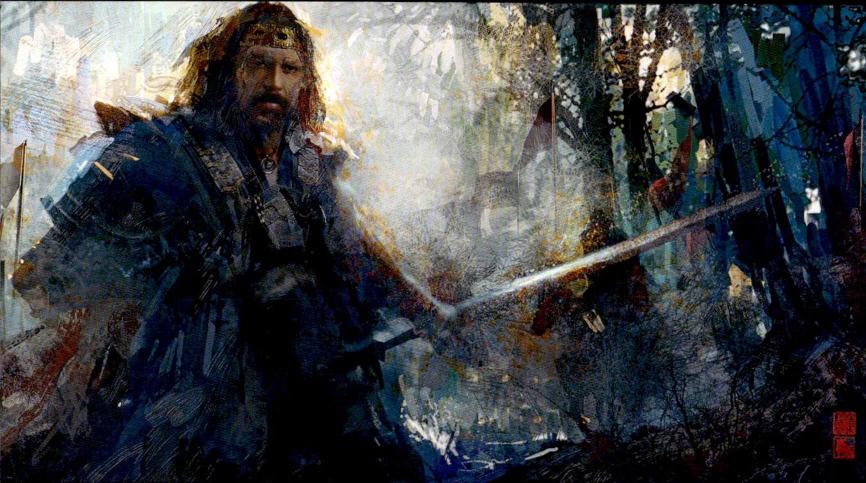

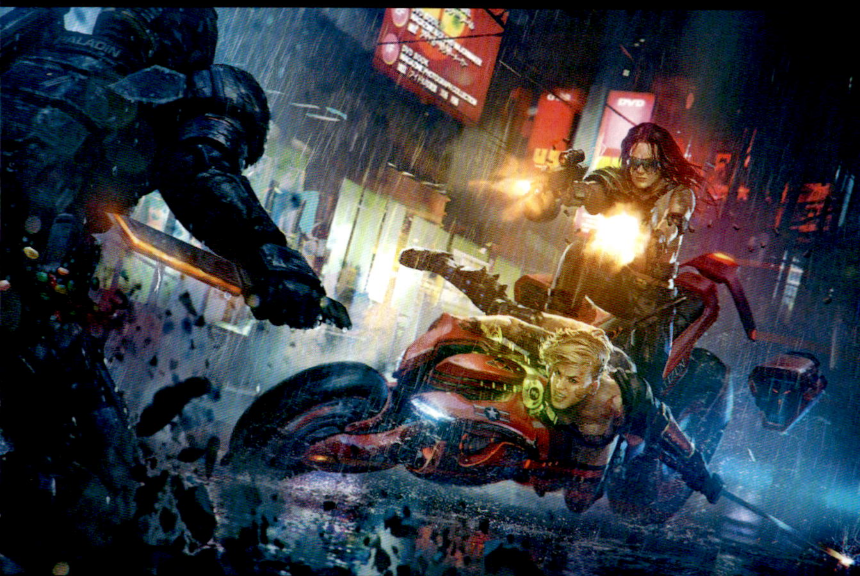

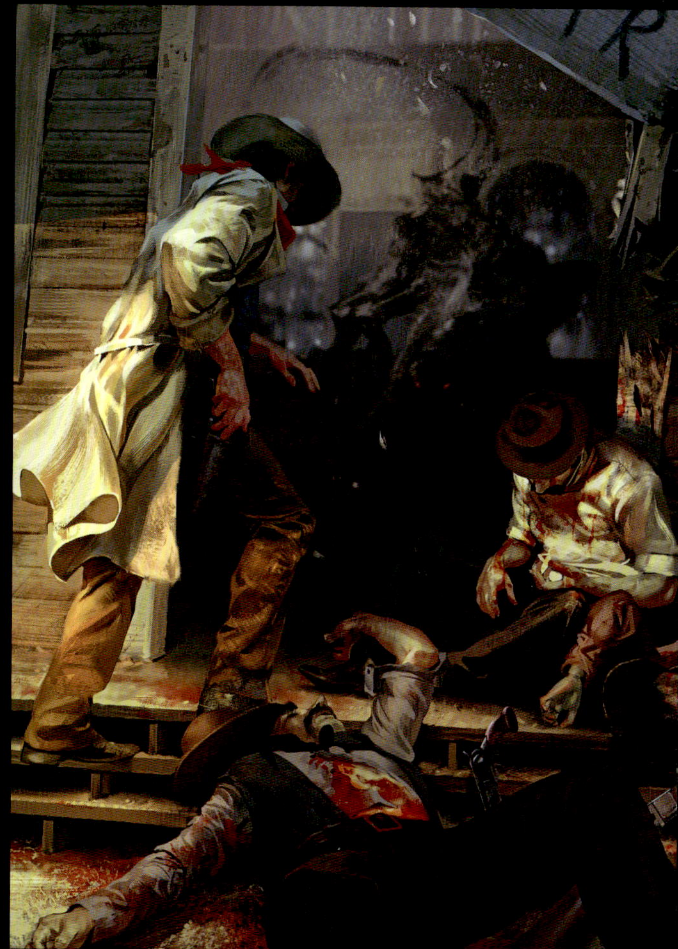

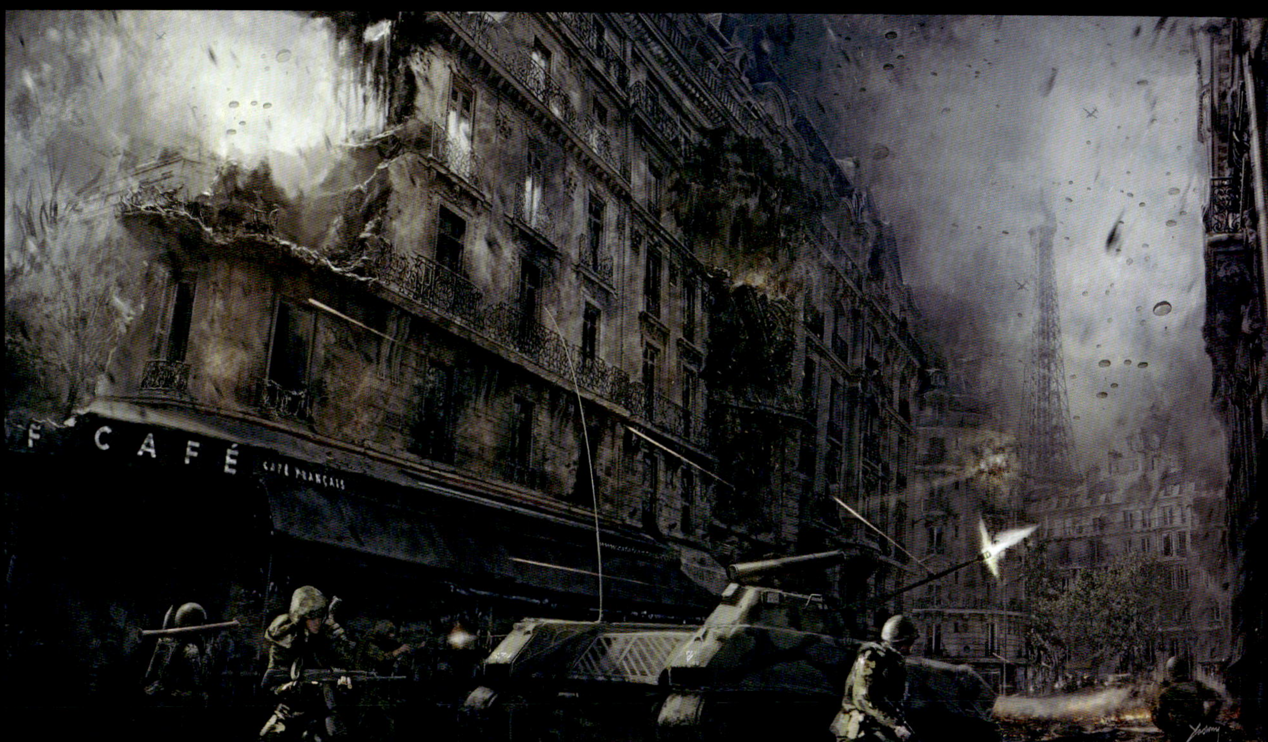

On the Horse
Photoshop
Donglu Yu, CANADA
[top]

Last Man Standing
Photoshop
Client: LMS: Killbook of a Bounty Hunter
Marek Okon, POLAND
[center]

Modern Warfare
Photoshop
Yaolong Liu, CHINA
[bottom]

The Hell Saloon
Photoshop
Andrei Pervukhin, RUSSIA
[top right]

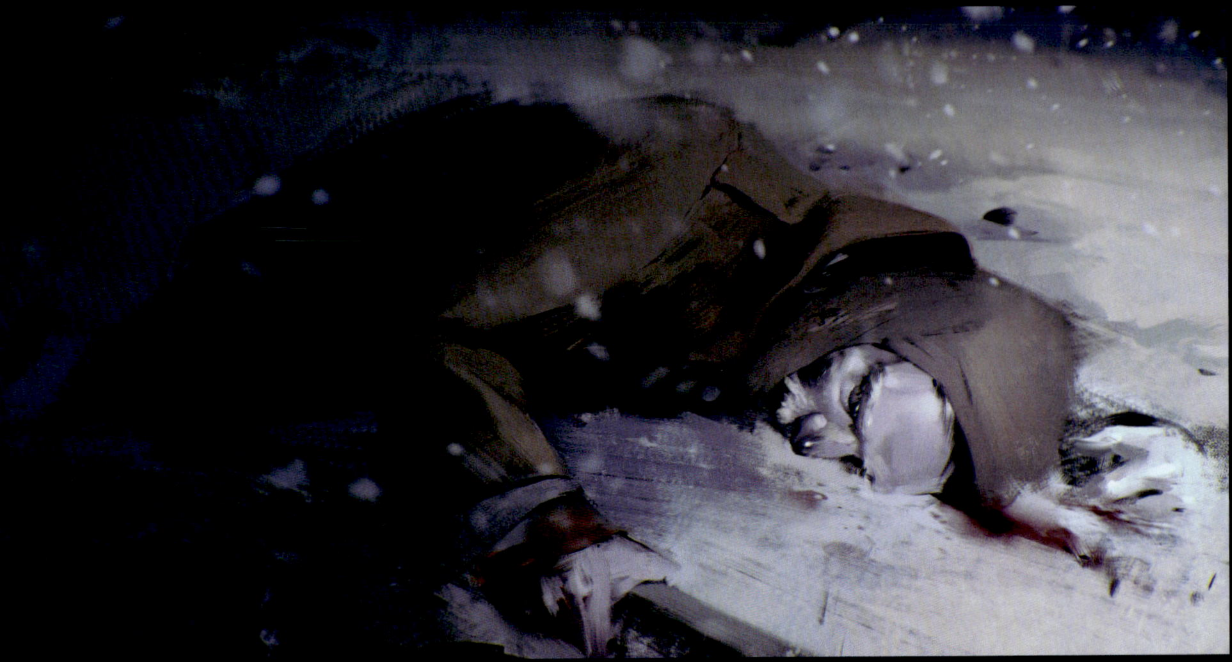

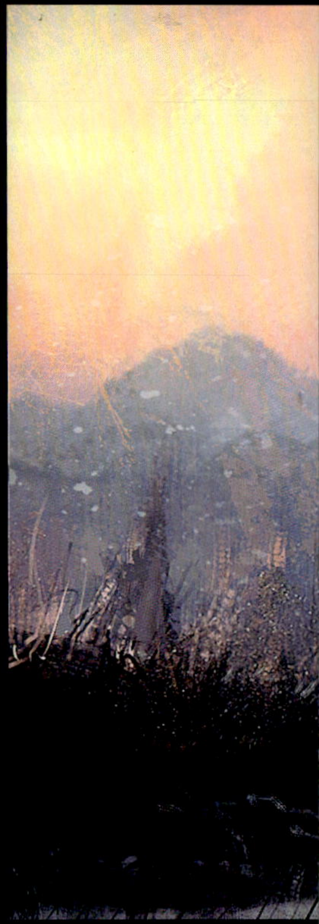

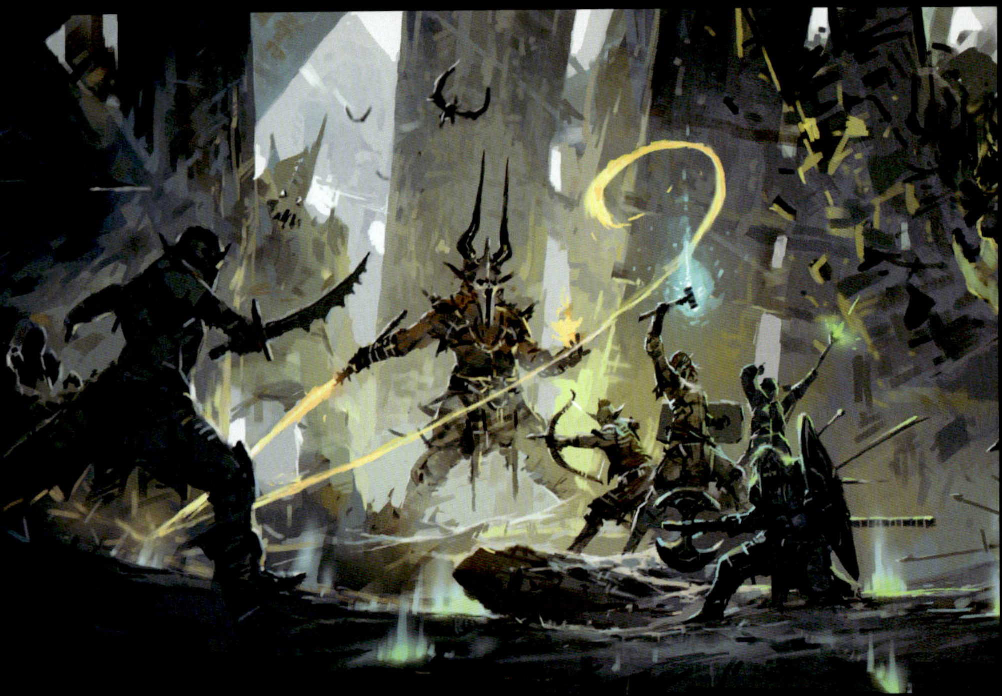

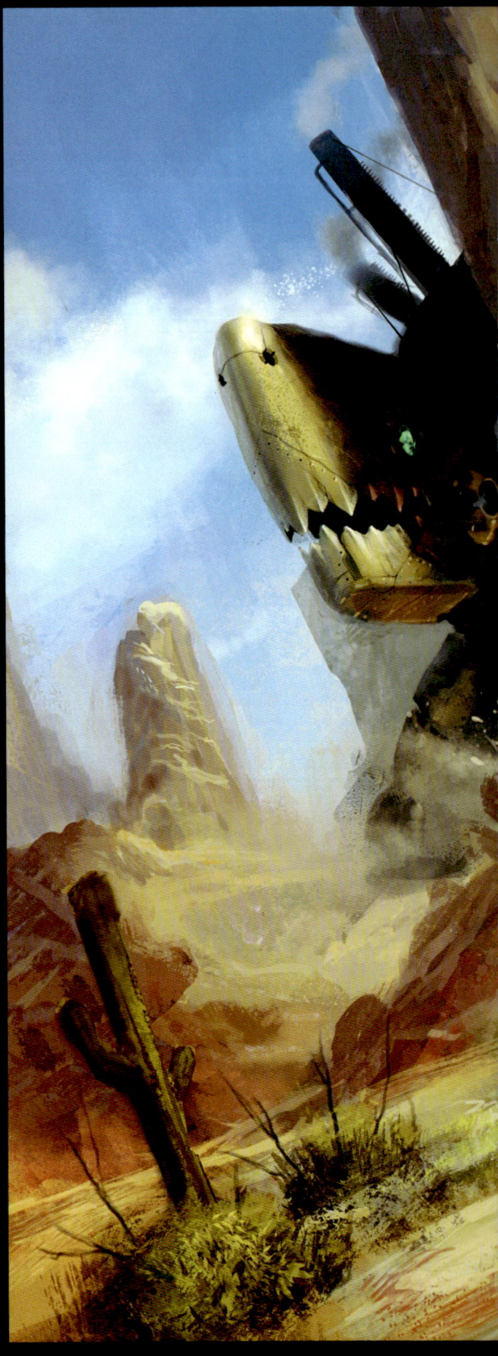

Dead Soldier
Photoshop
Jama Jurabaev, TAJIKISTAN
[top]

Against All Odds
Photoshop
Kari Kallio, FINLAND
[above]

Steambot Turtle
Photoshop
Logan Feliciano, USA
[right]

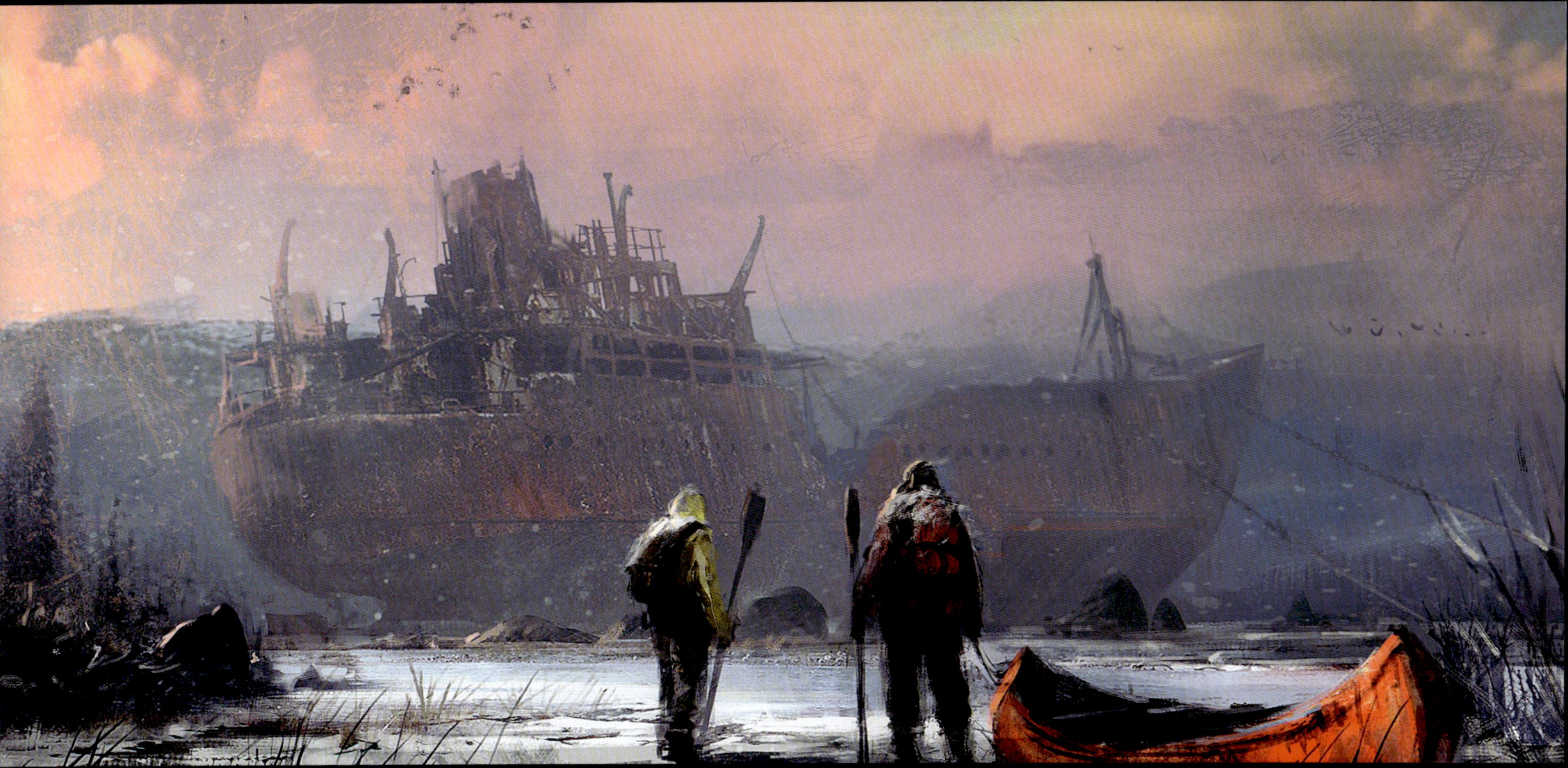

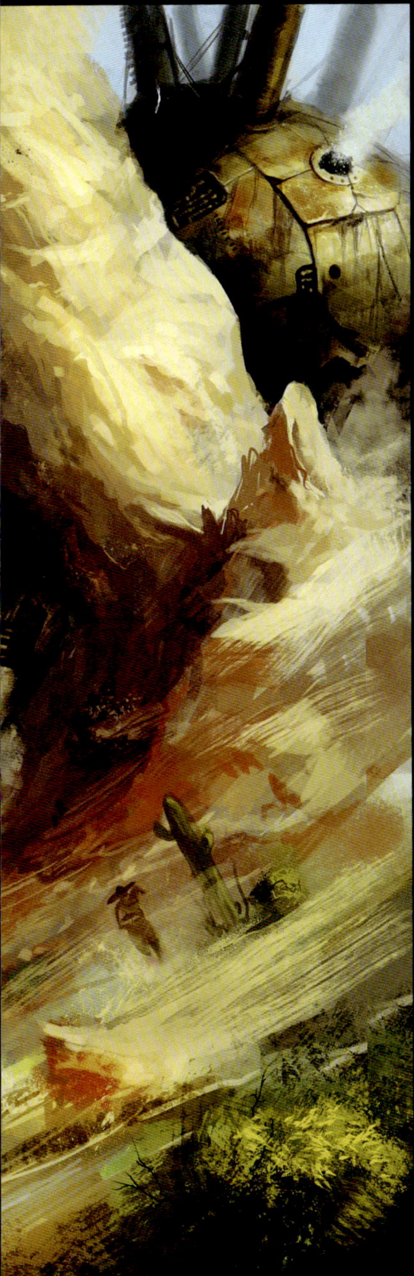

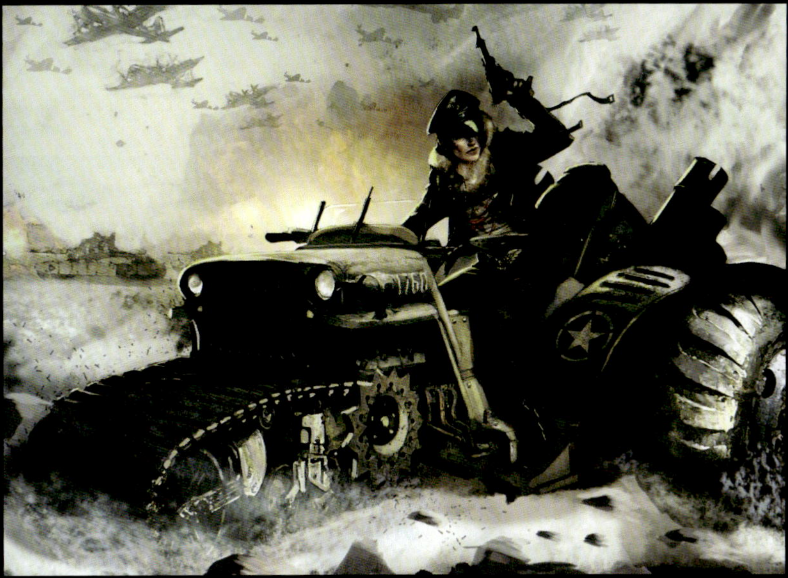

Wreck
Photoshop
Morgan Yon, FRANCE
[above]

Ursa Major
Photoshop
Lamin Martin, CANADA
[left]

A World Beyond
Photoshop
Andrew Katsuba, RUSSIA
[below left]

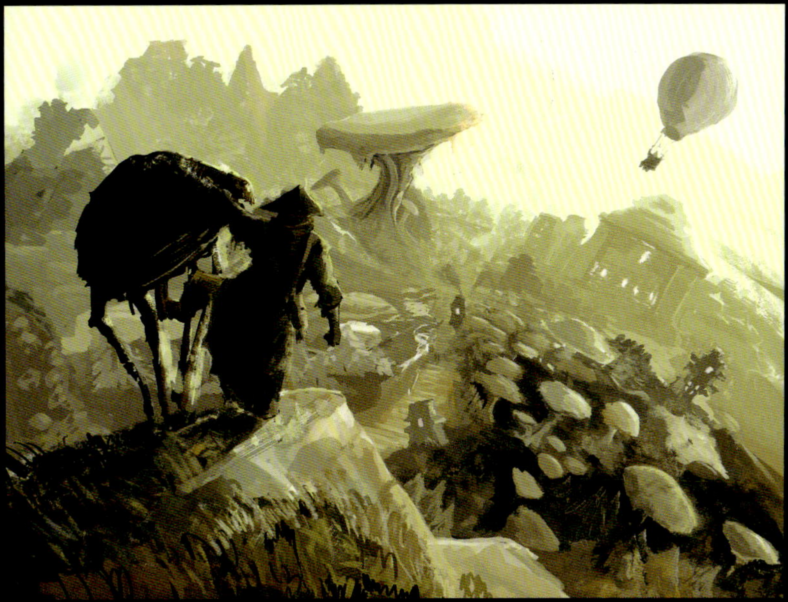

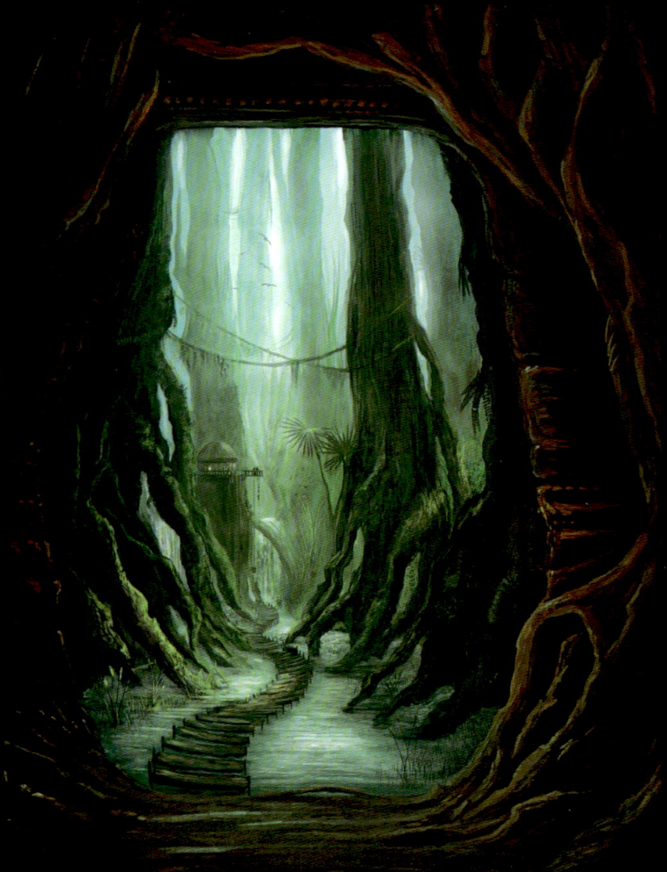

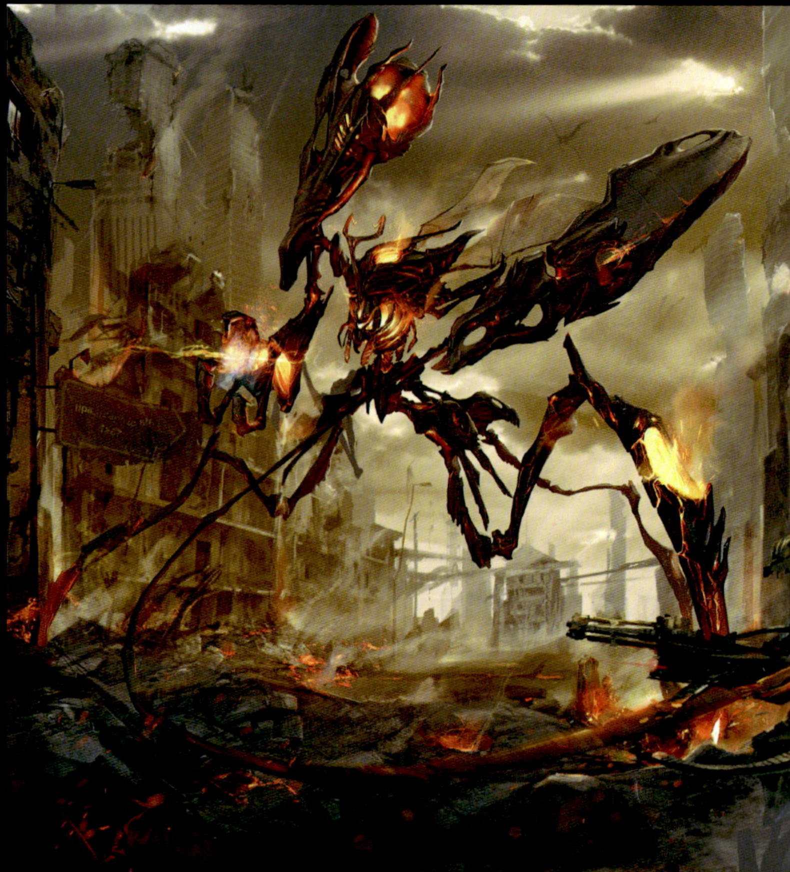

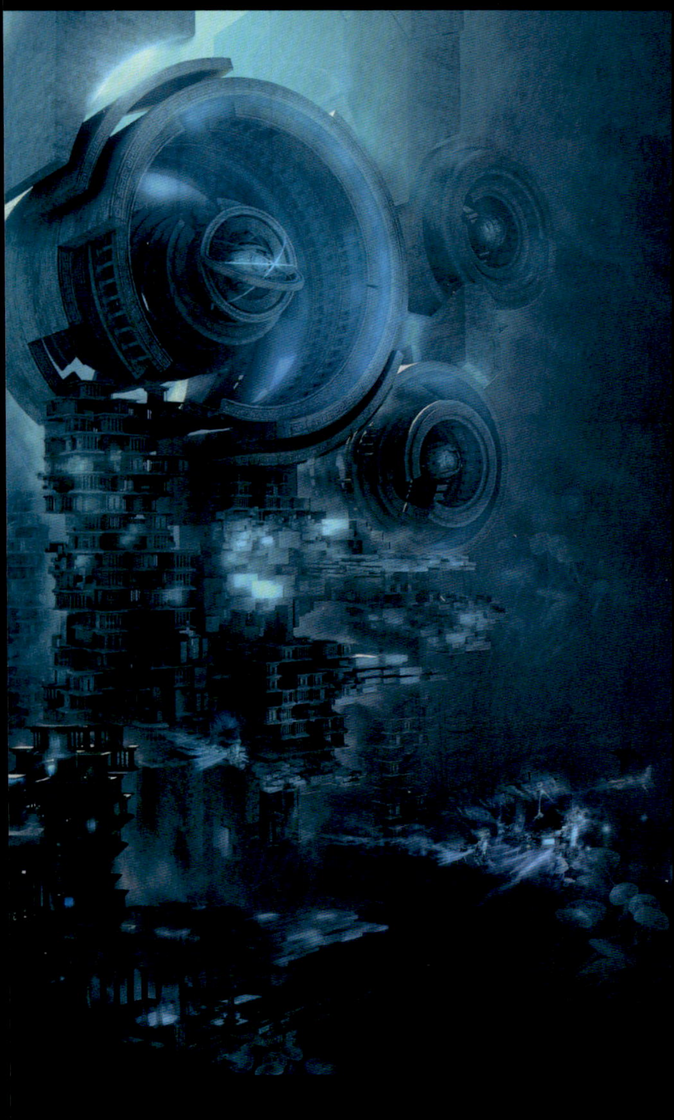

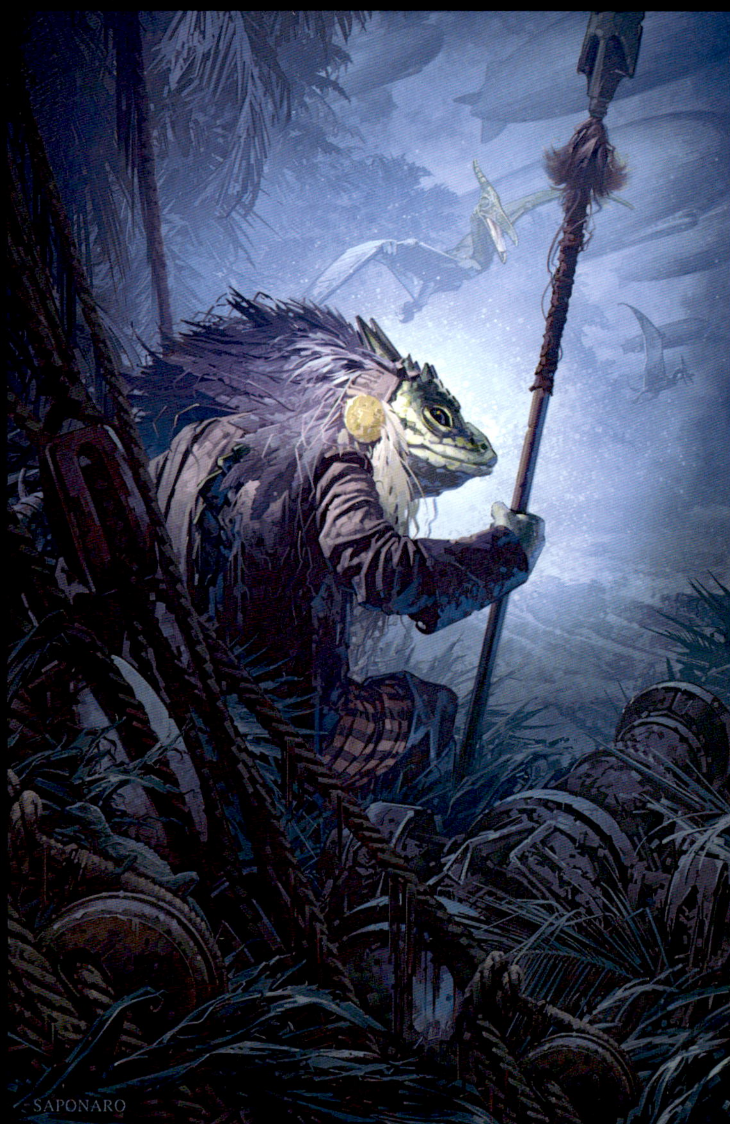
SAPONARO

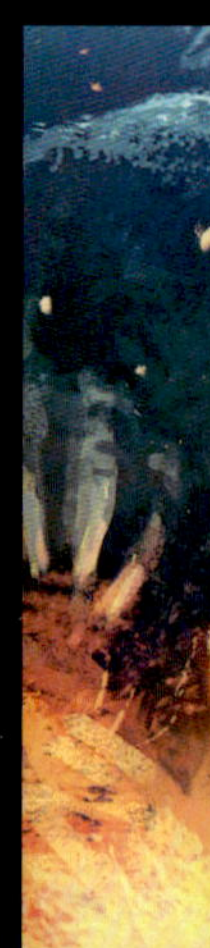

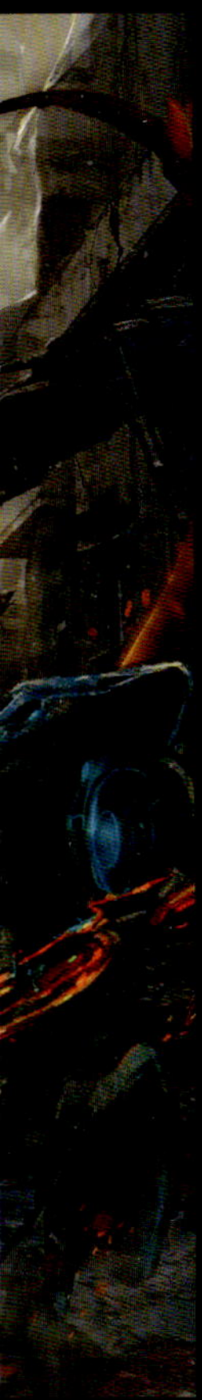

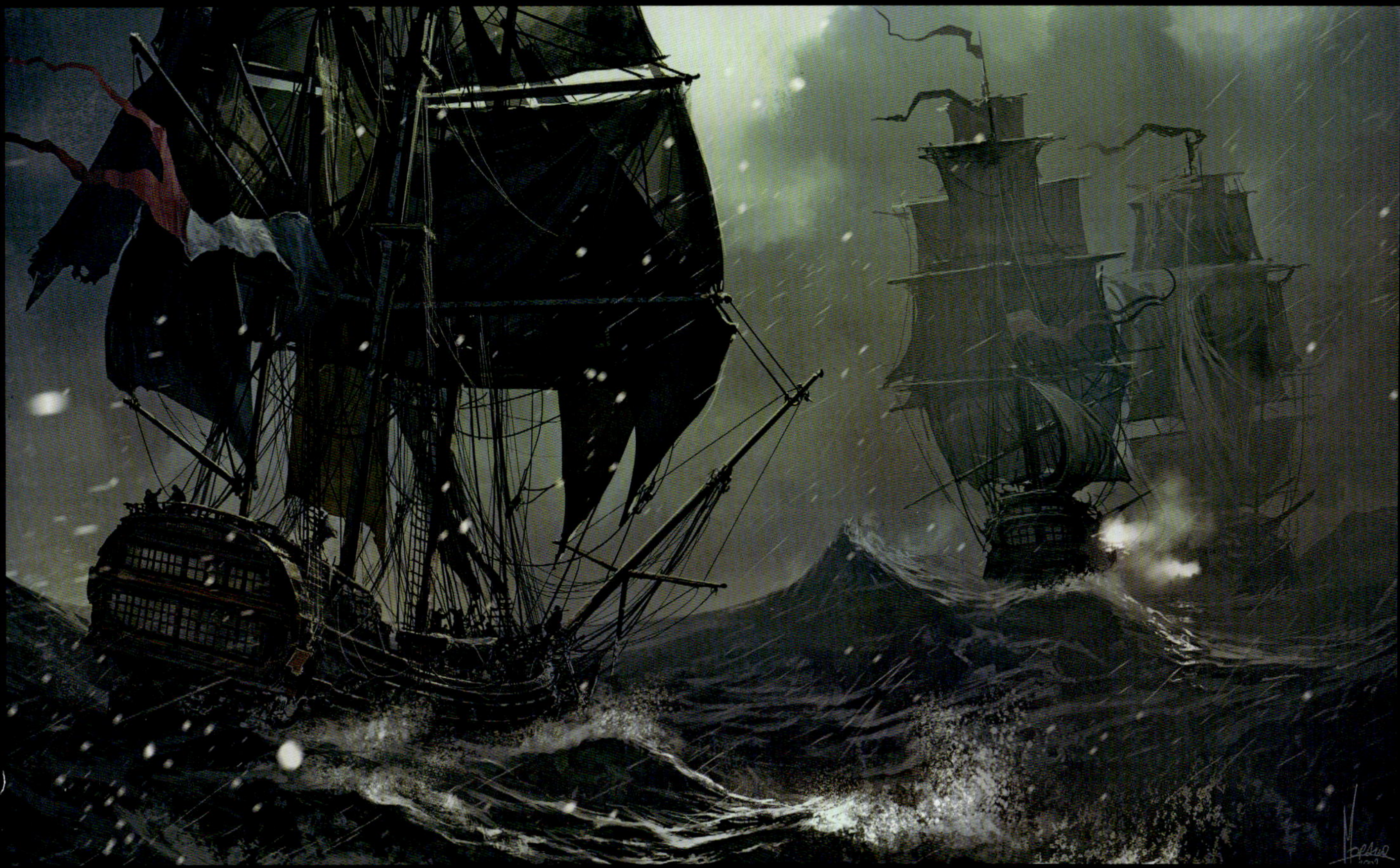

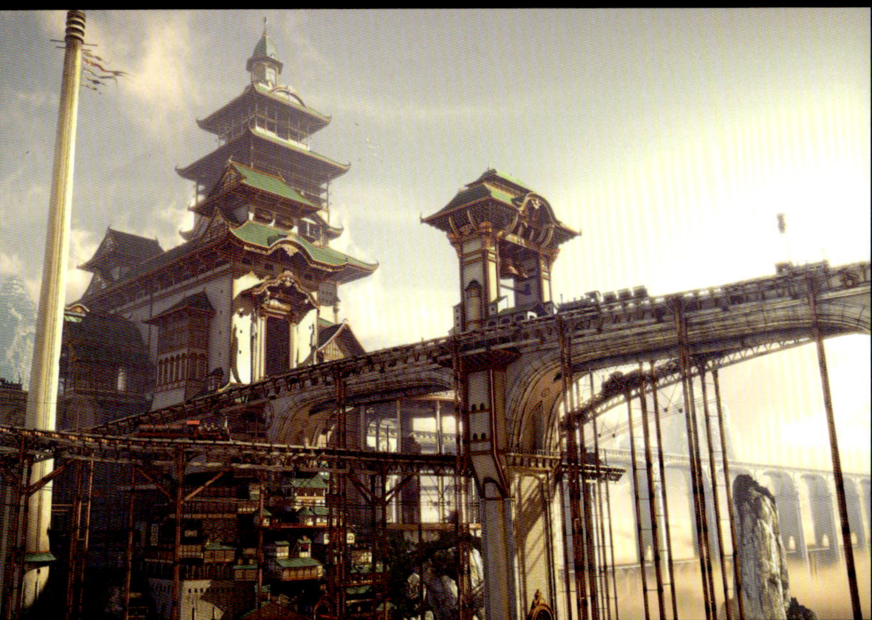

Winter Blockade
Photoshop
Tomasz Jedruszek, POLAND
[above]

The Train Station
Maya, Photoshop, Mudbox, mental ray
Jean-Michel Bihorel, FRANCE
[left]

The Golden Pitcher
Photoshop
Cristi Balanescu, ROMANIA
[below left]

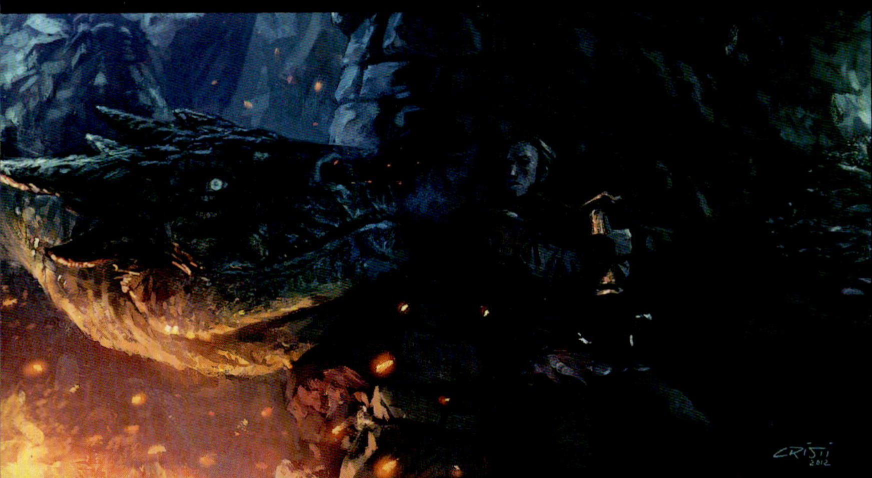

The Entrance to a Hidden Place
Photoshop
Christian Gerth, SWITZERLAND
[facing page top left]

Demon Lord
Photoshop
Vadim Sverdlov, ISRAEL
[facing page top right]

Atlantis
Maya, Photoshop
Te Hu, USA
[facing page bottom left]

Destroyermen: Rising Storm
Painter, Photoshop
Client: Science Fiction Book Club
Dominick Saponaro, USA
[facing page bottom right]

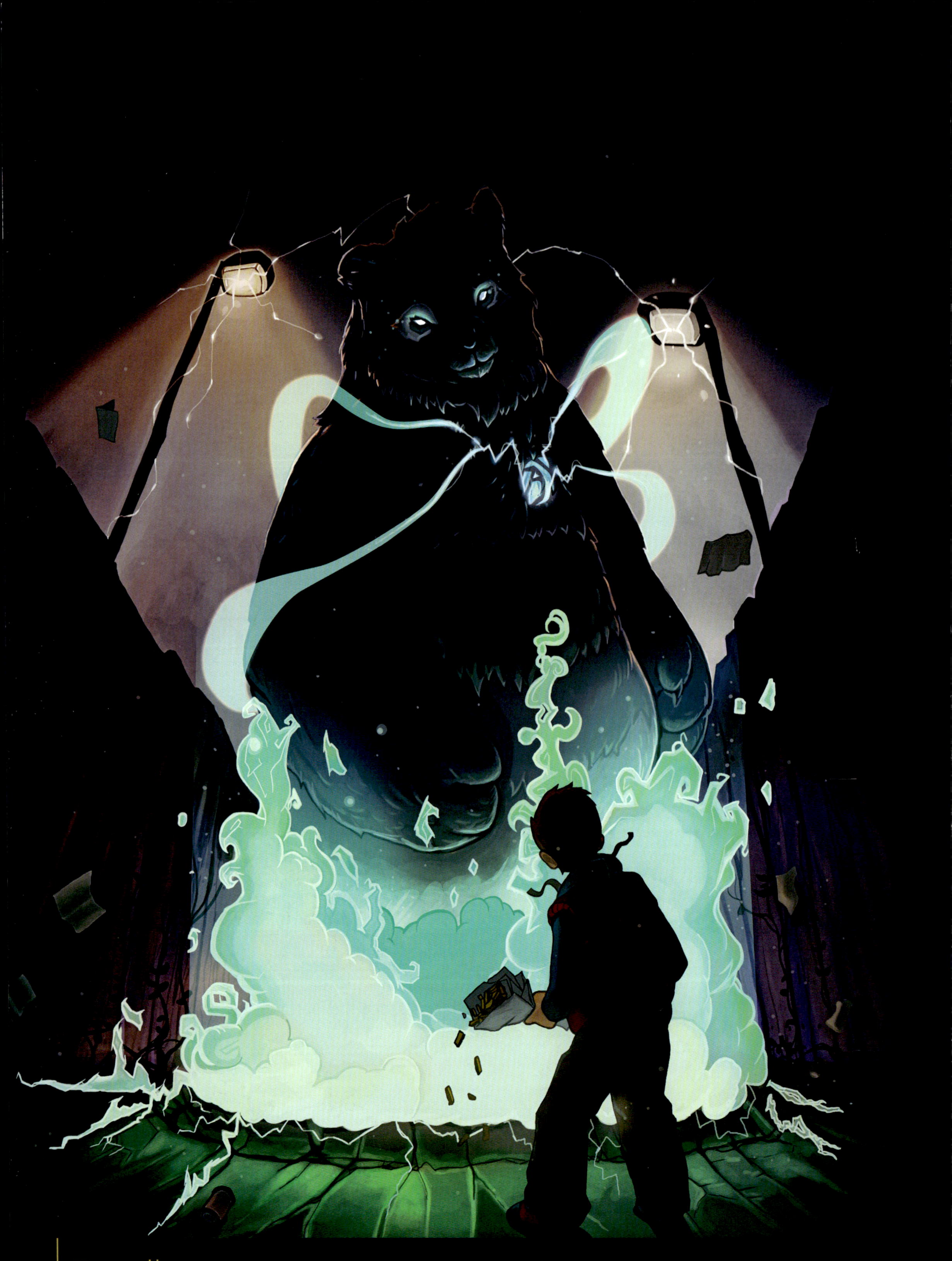

Excellence

Comic / Manga

You Called?
Photoshop
Guy Atherfold, GREAT BRITAIN

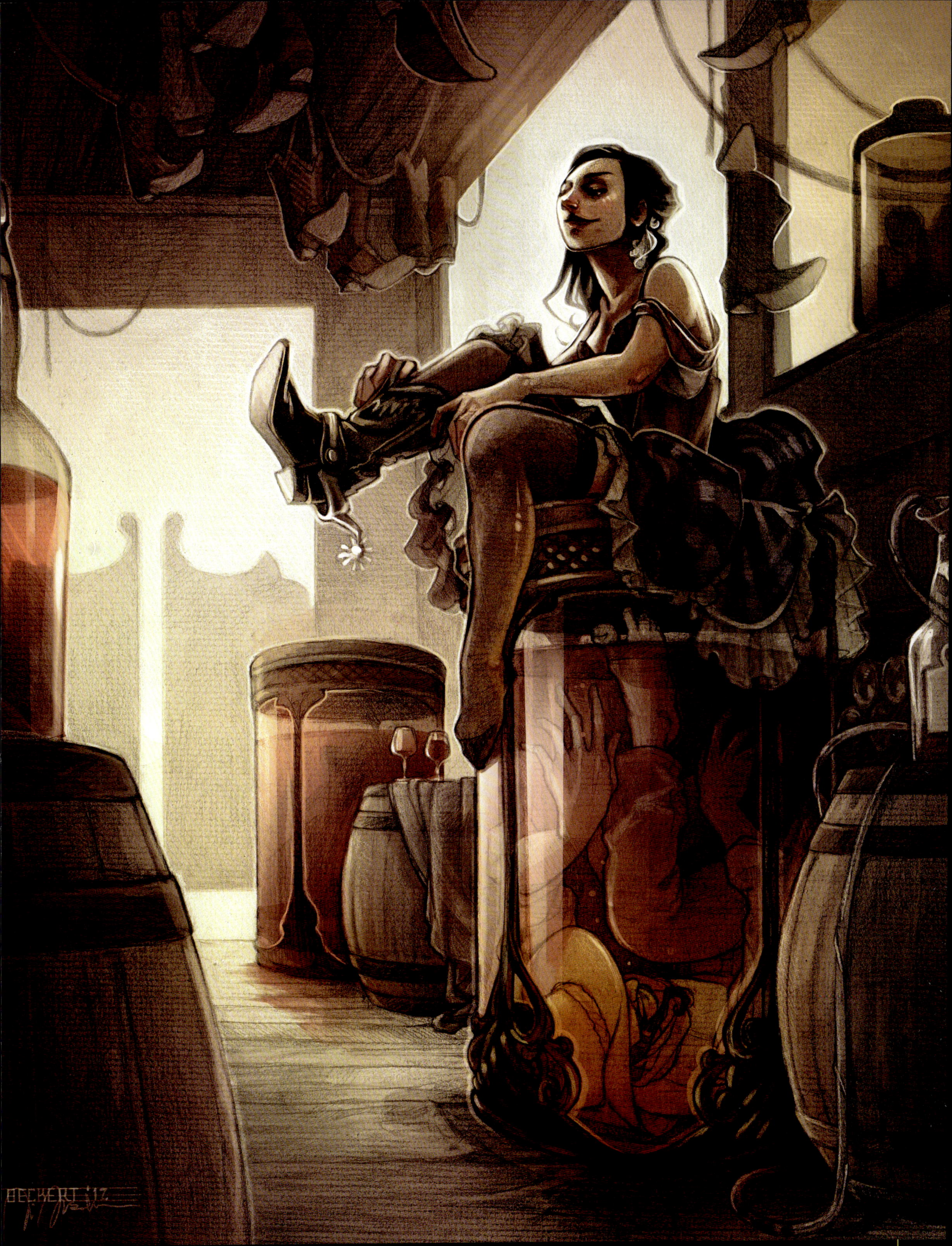

Summer Wine
Photoshop
Wylie Elise Beckert, USA

Master
Comic / Manga

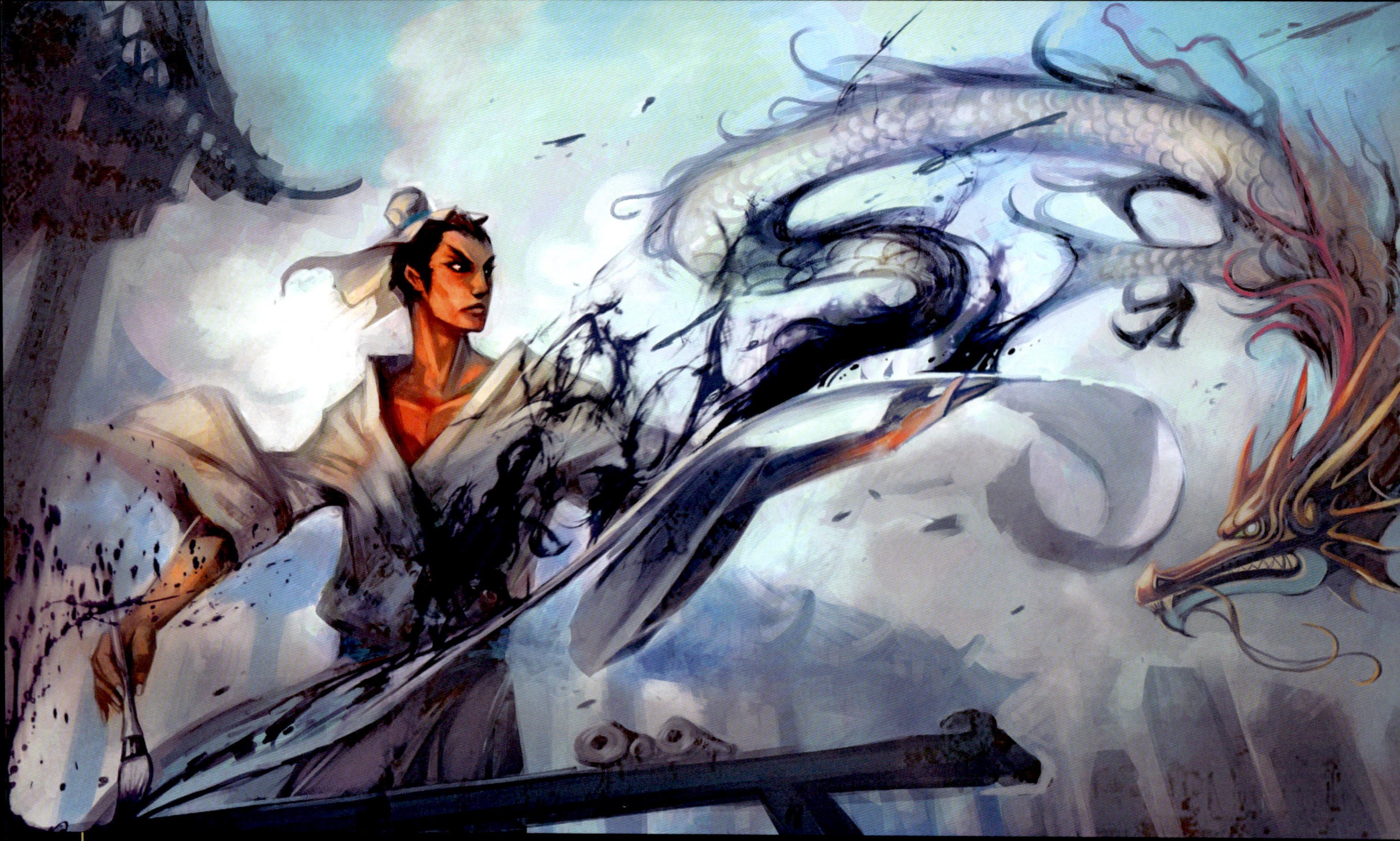

Excellence

Comic / Manga

Dragon Painting
Painter, Photoshop
Jian Guo, CHINA

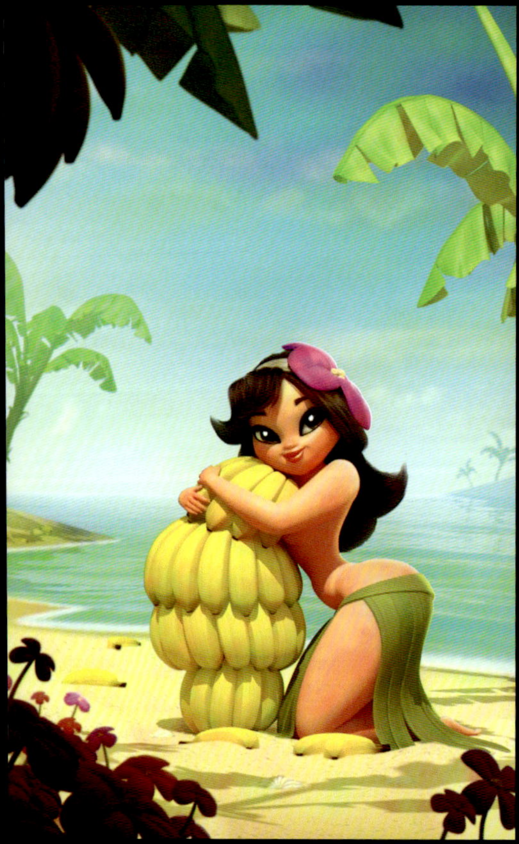

Banana Girl
3ds Max, V-Ray, ZBrush, LightWave 3D
Anders Ehrenborg and Bill Presing,
DigitalBananaStudio, NEW ZEALAND

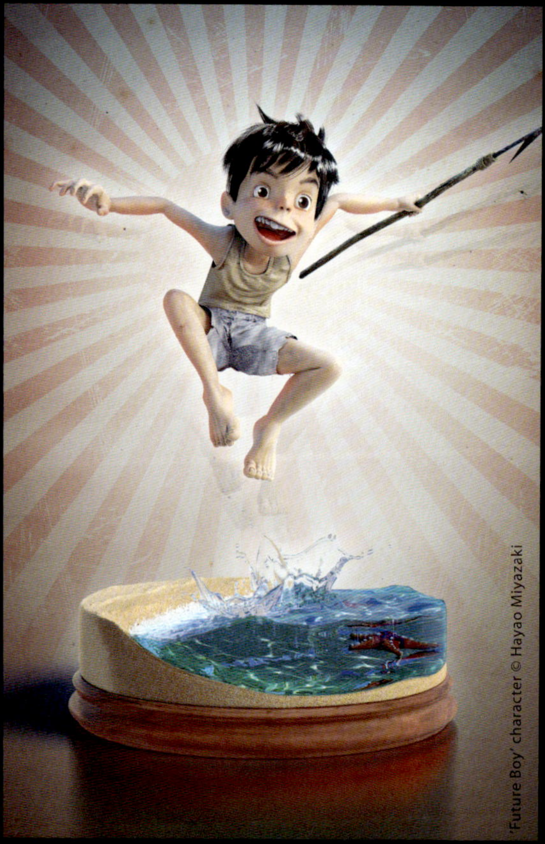

Conan Future Boy
LightWave 3D
Luis Lopes, PORTUGAL

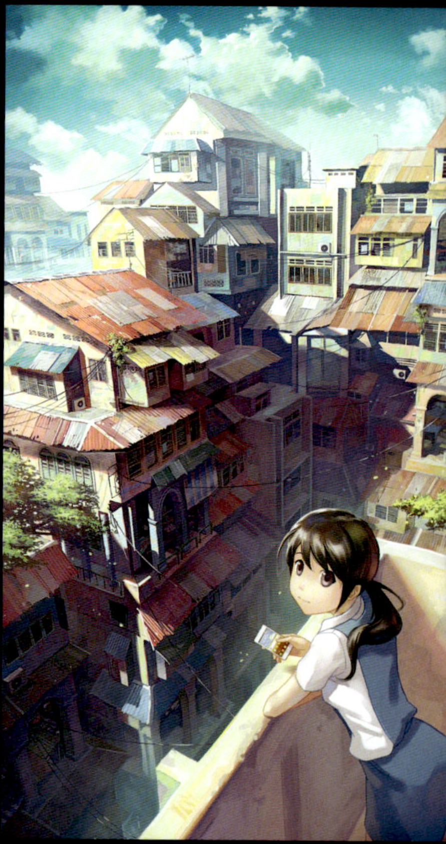

Balcony Girl
Photoshop, SketchUp
Fei Giap Chong, MALAYSIA

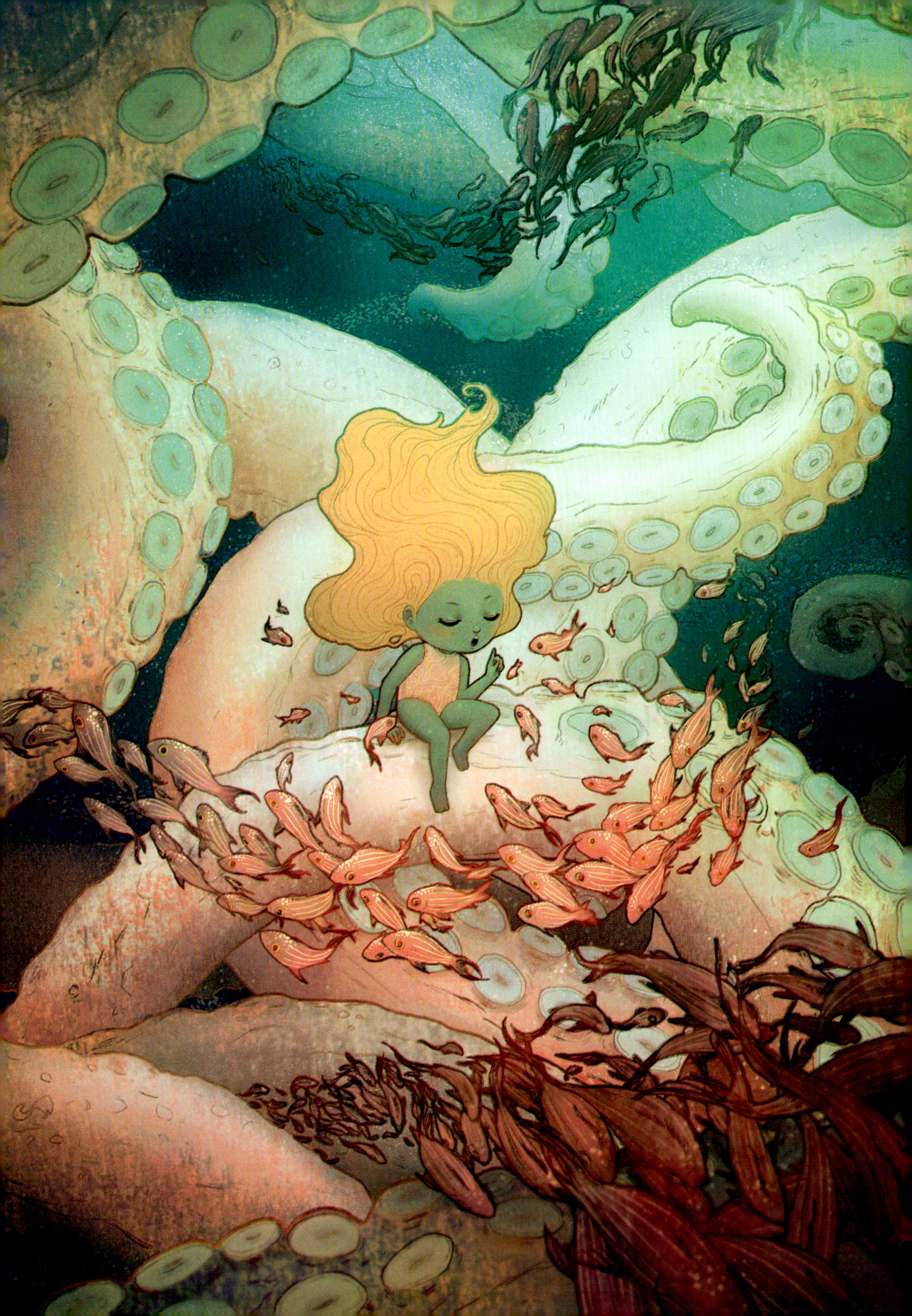

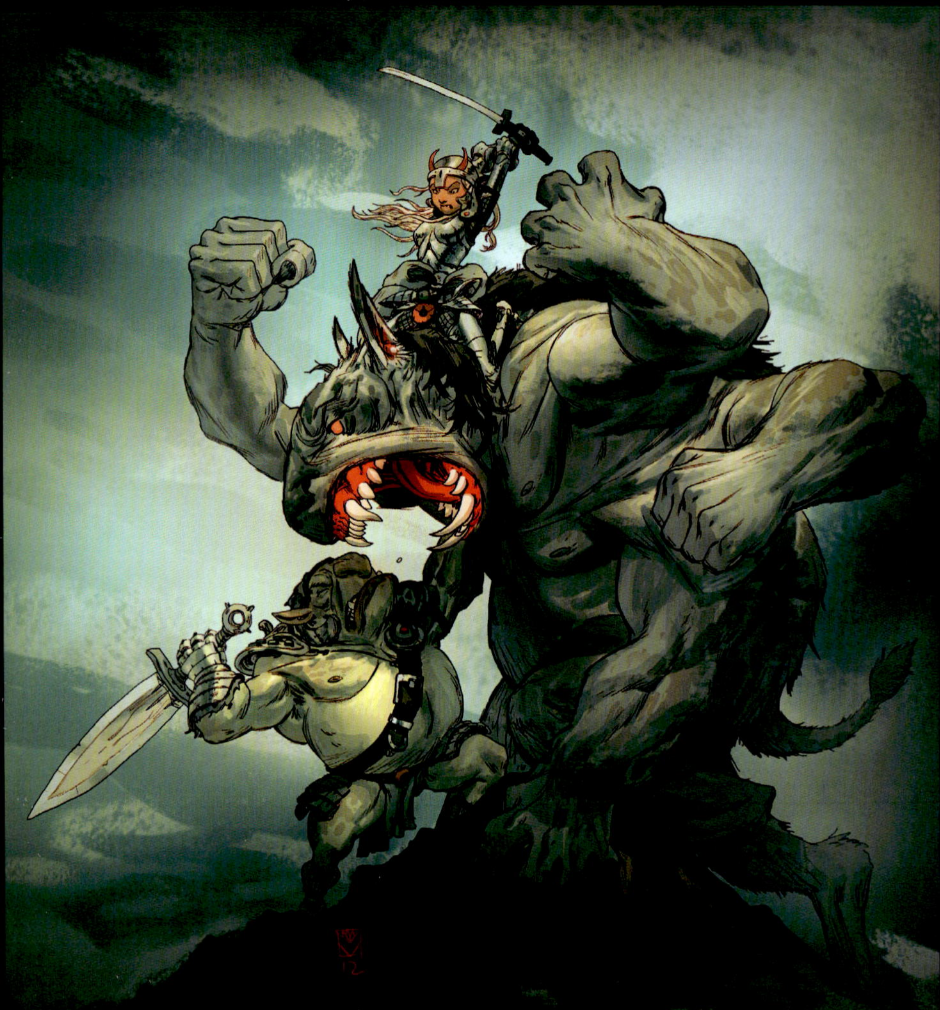

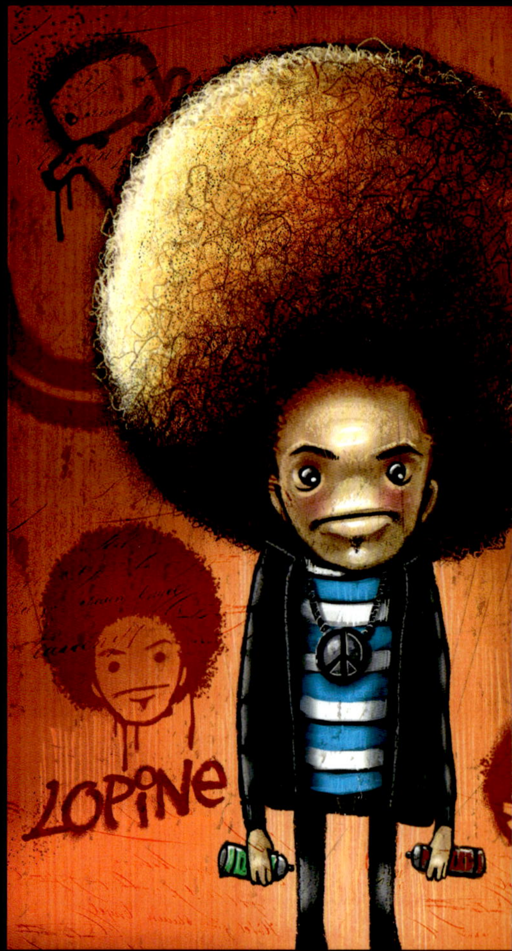

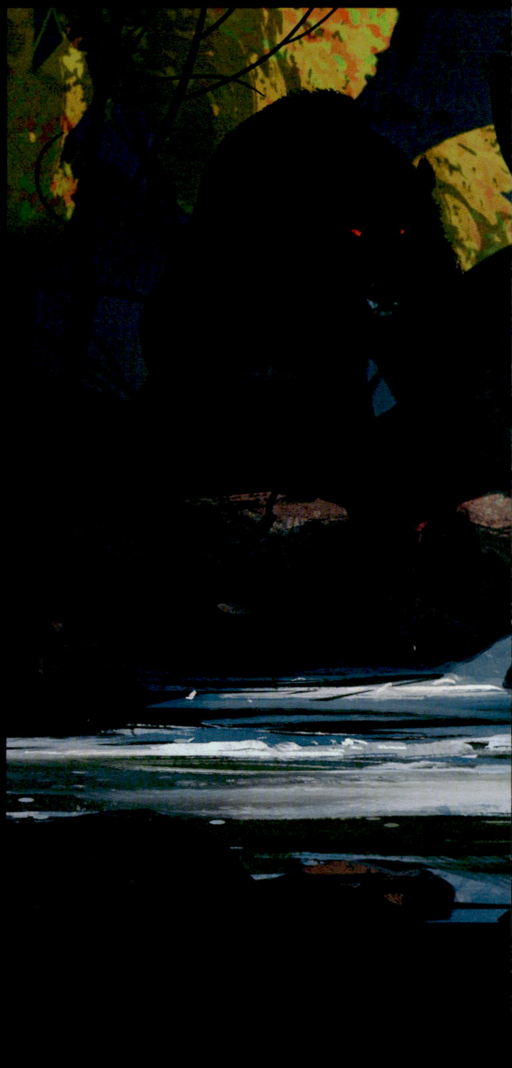

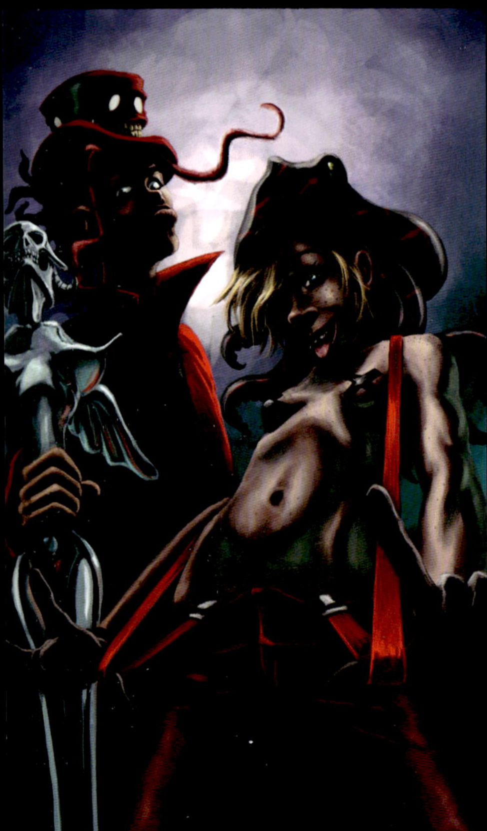

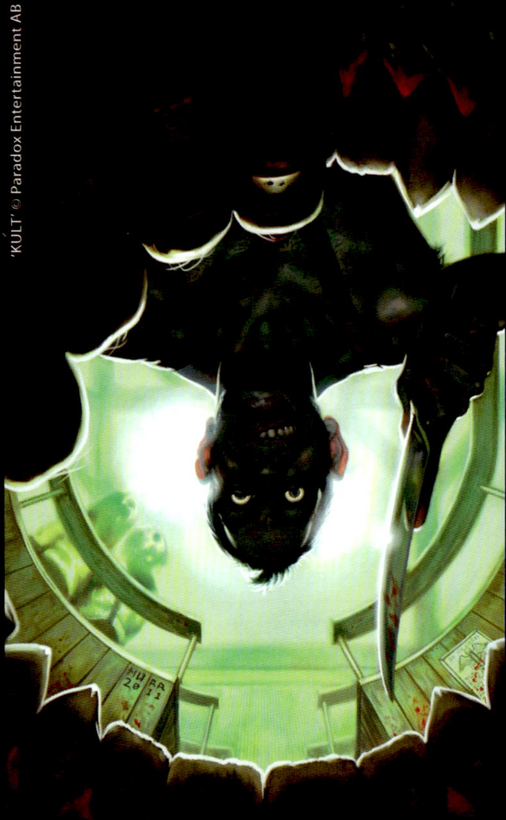

'KULT' © Paradox Entertainment AB

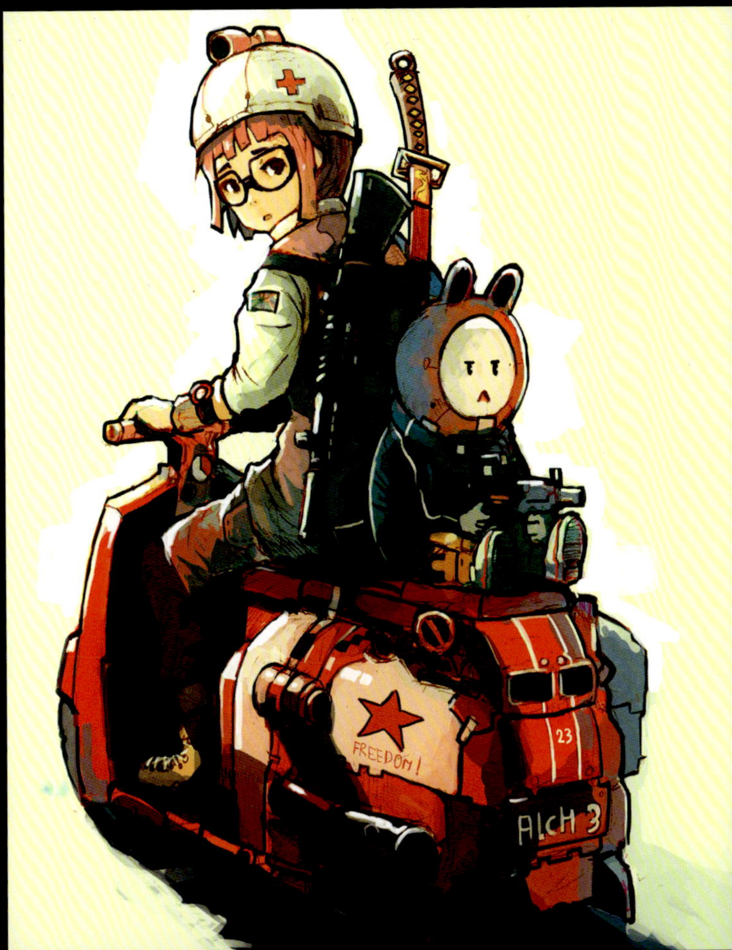

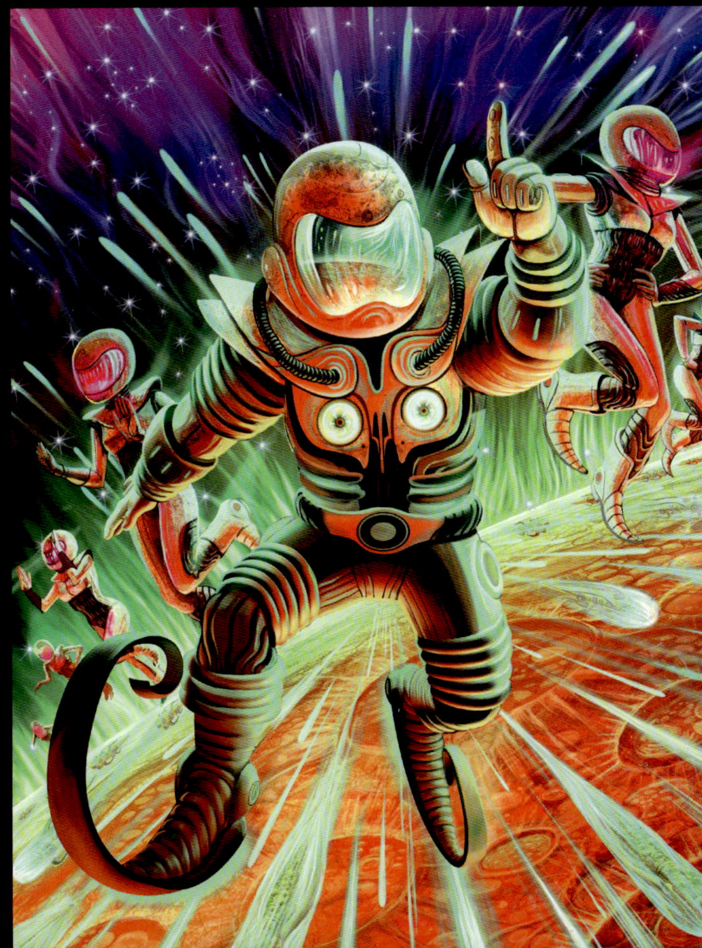

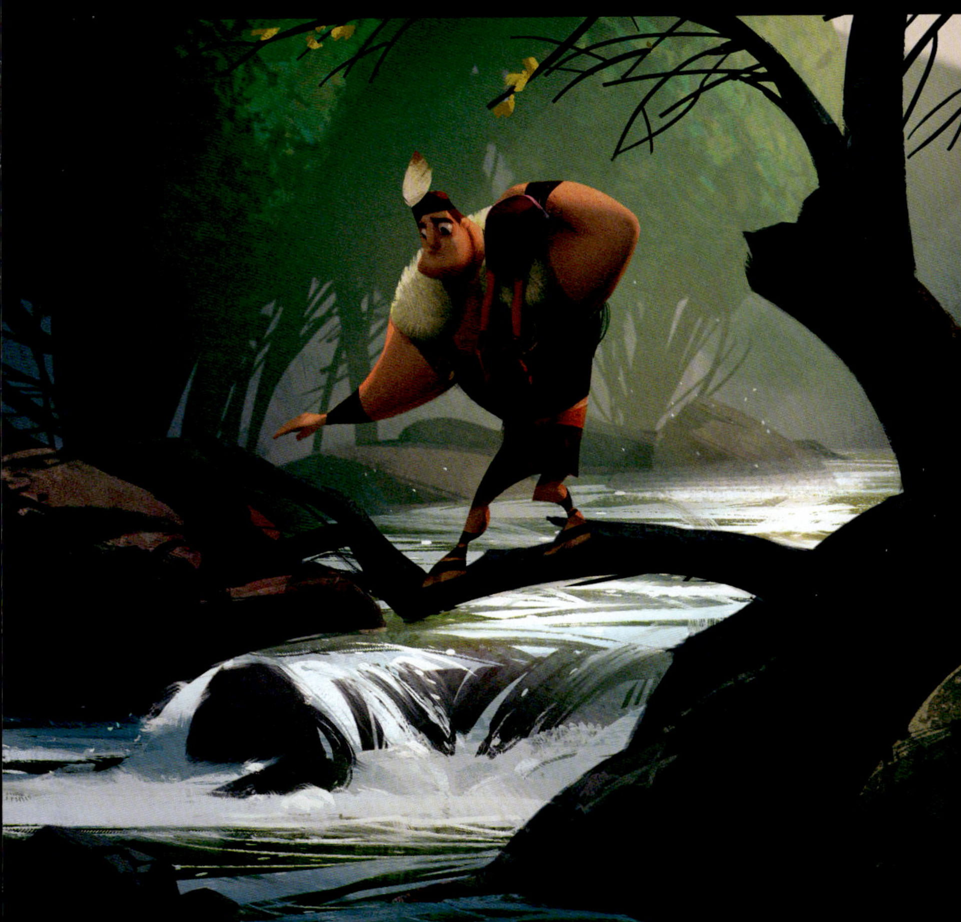

Big Fight
Photoshop
Tim Mcburnie, AUSTRALIA
[facing page top left]

Homey
Painter, Photoshop
Robin 'Lopine' Kunzmann, LOPINE, GERMANY
[facing page top right]

Motor Girl
Photoshop
Andrian Gilang, SINGAPORE
[above left]

Tribal Planet
Photoshop
Client: Picnic Magazine
Kamui Gomasio, MEXICO
[above right]

Rockstars of the Dreamtime
Photoshop
Andrew Blackman, BARBADOS
[facing page bottom left]

KULT #3
Painter, Photoshop
Client: Dark Horse Comics and Paradox Entertainment
Jake Murray, USA
[facing page bottom center]

Christo Crossing
Photoshop
Shaddy Safadi, USA
[left]

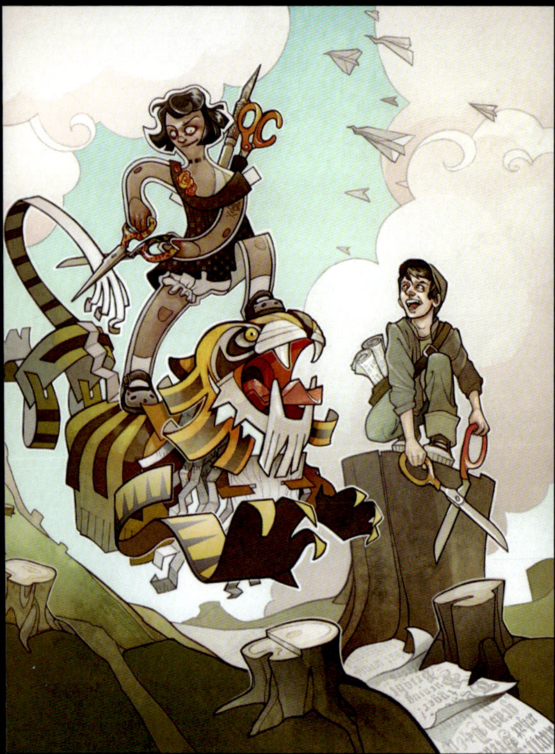

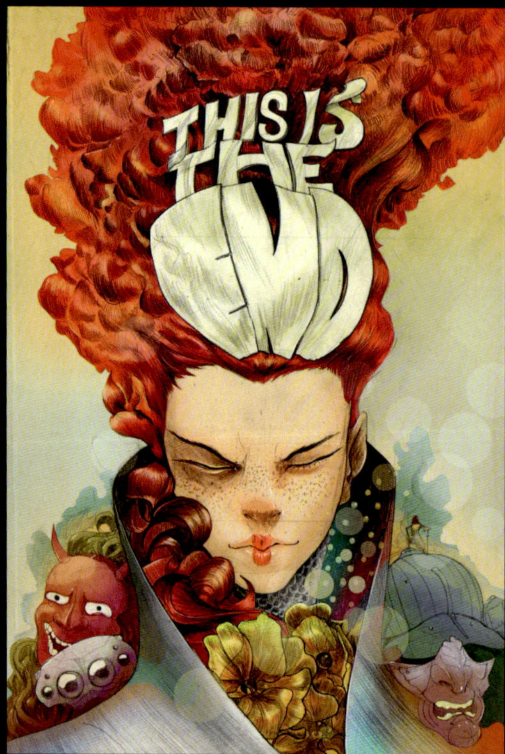
THIS IS

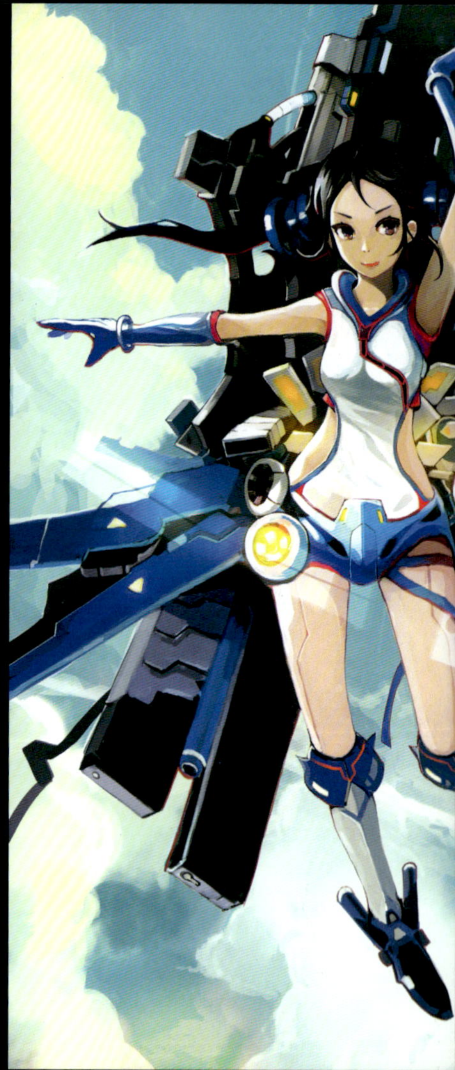

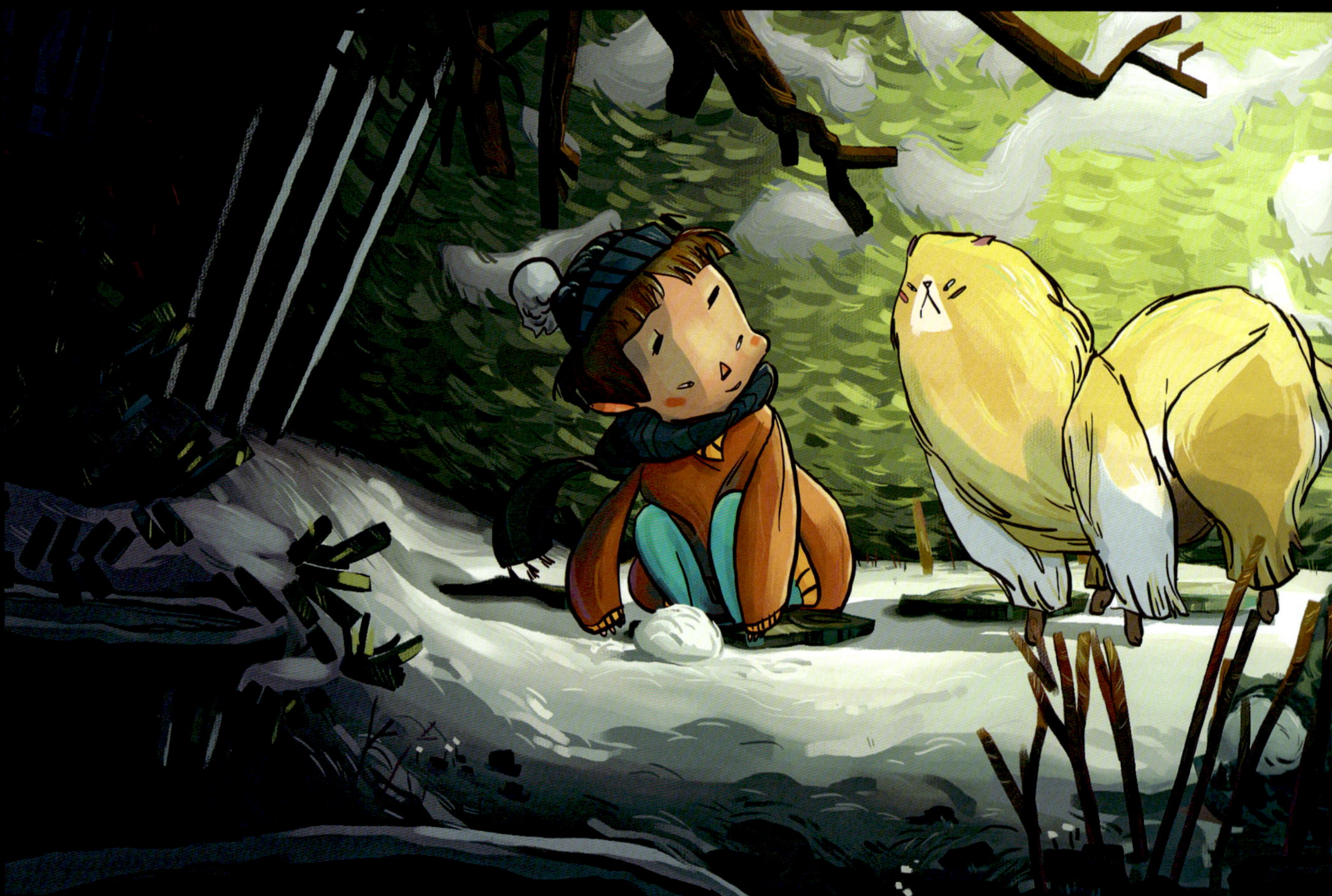

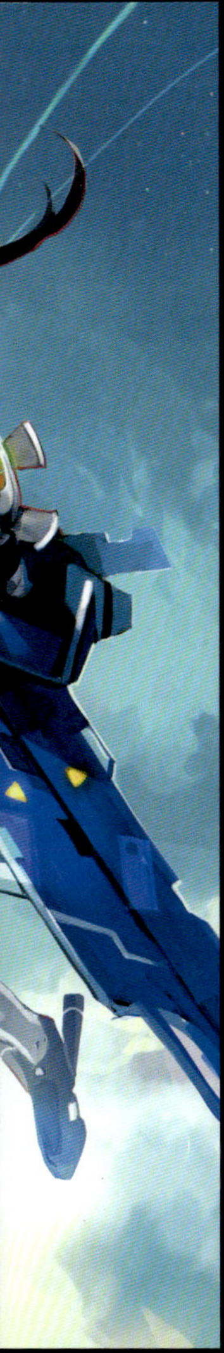

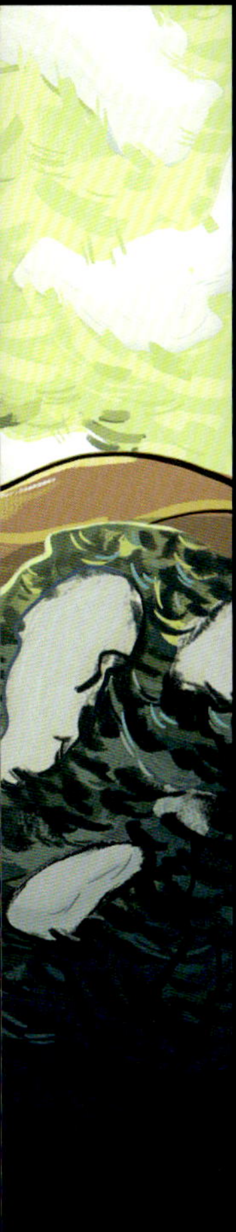

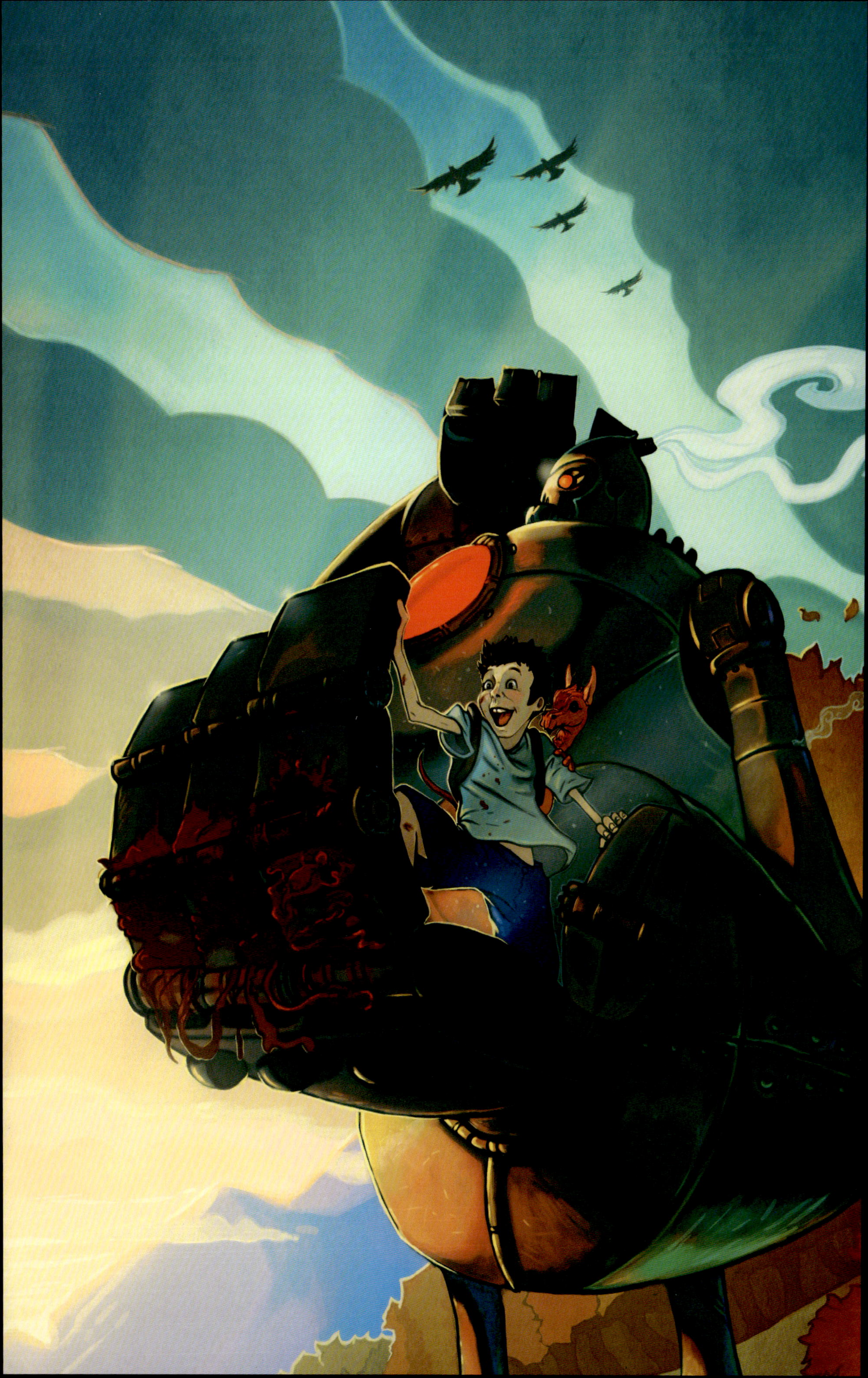

What a View
Photoshop
Guy Atherfold, GREAT BRITAIN
[above]

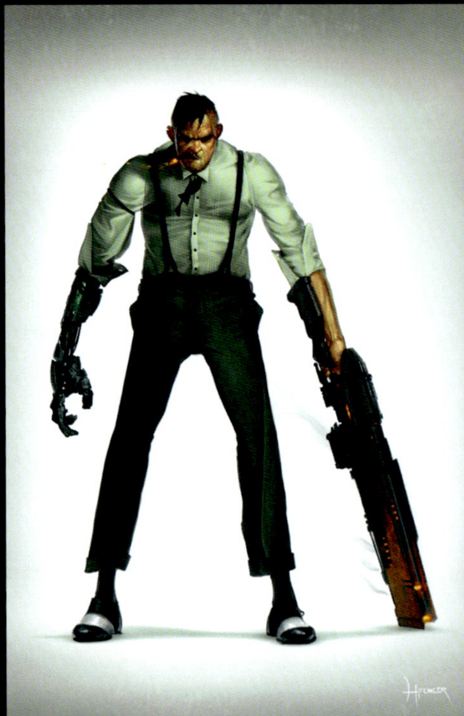

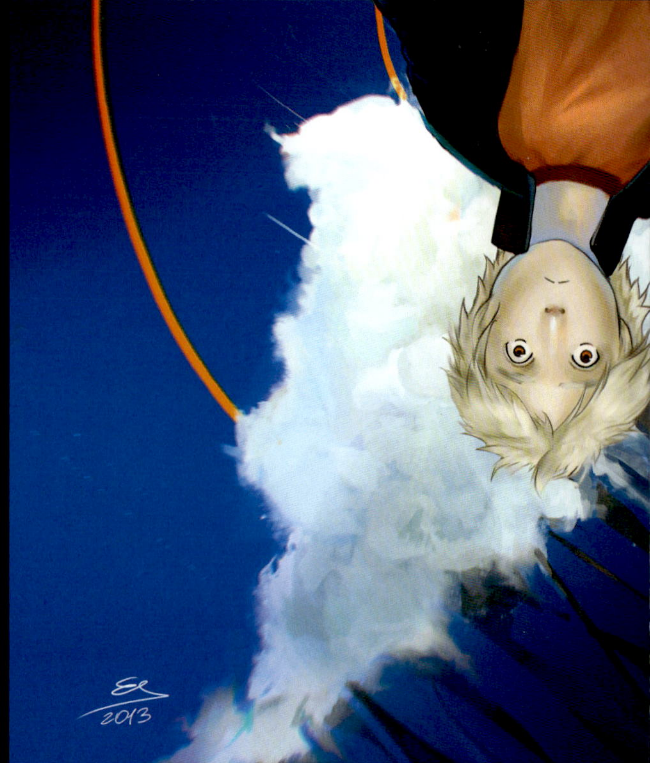

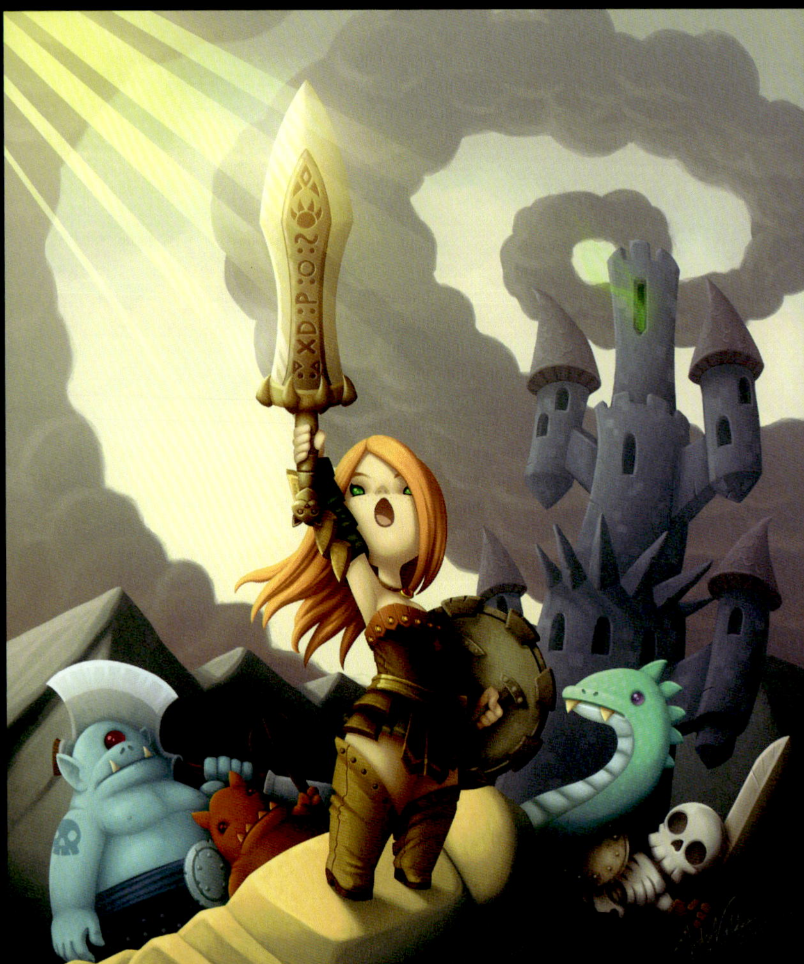

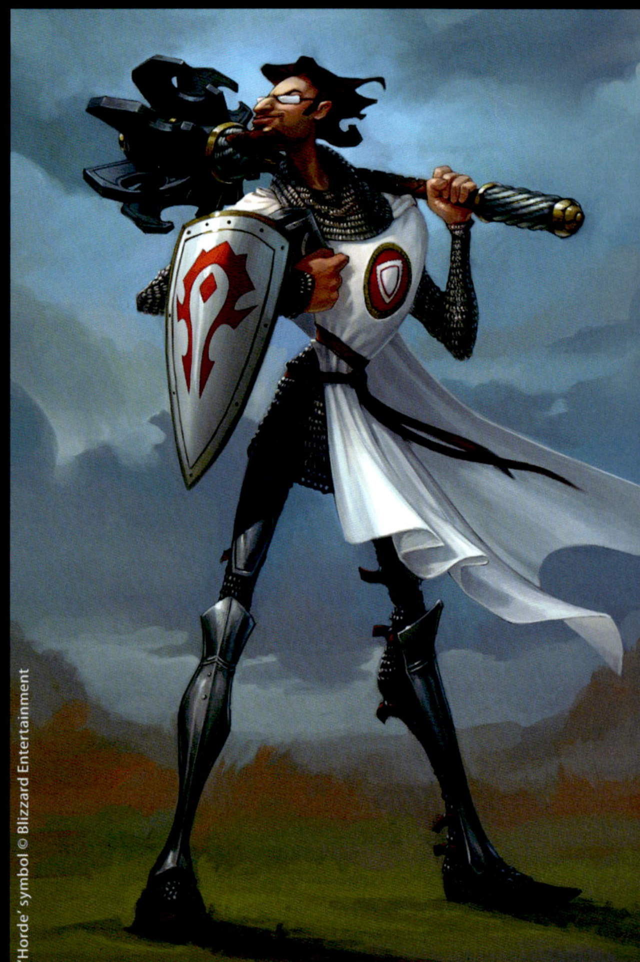

Big Eddie
Photoshop
Hardy Fowler, USA

Heroic Heroine
Photoshop
Jody Valdes, CANADA

The Tanklar
Photoshop
Sam Hogg, GREAT BRITAIN

Under Blue Skies
GIMP
Elwira Kolber, POLAND
[left]

Back in the Day
Maya, V-Ray, ZBrush
Alexandria Condon, USA
[below]

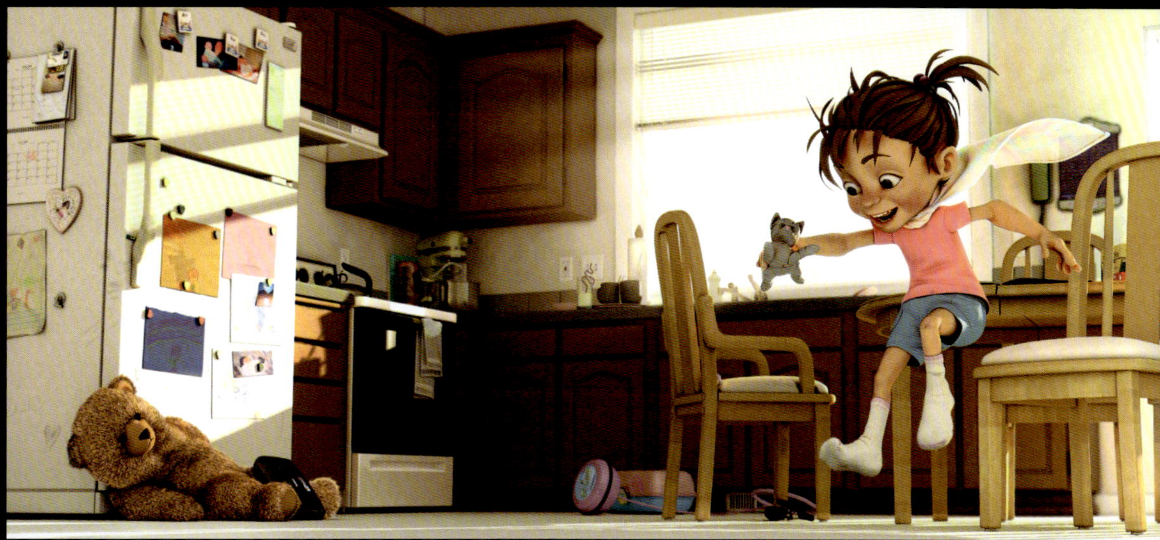

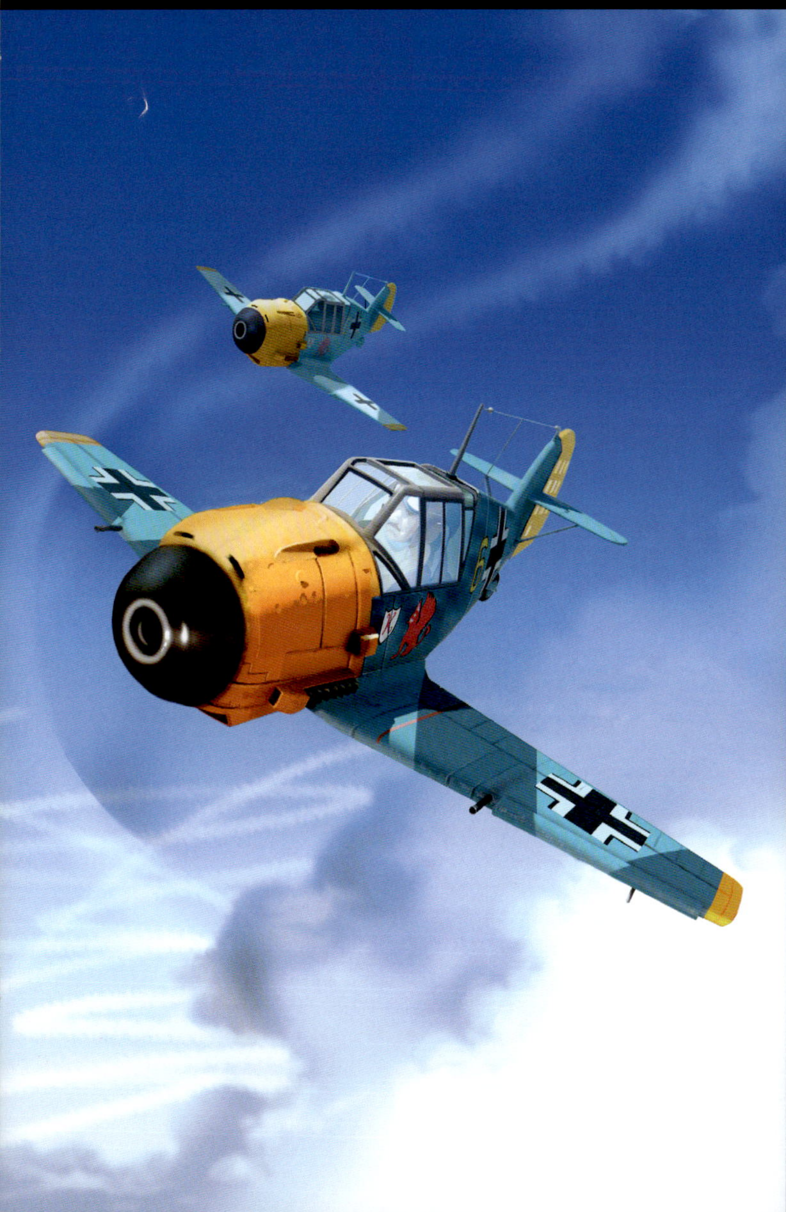

ME109 Caricature
Maya, Photoshop
Ken Fee, GREAT BRITAIN
[left]

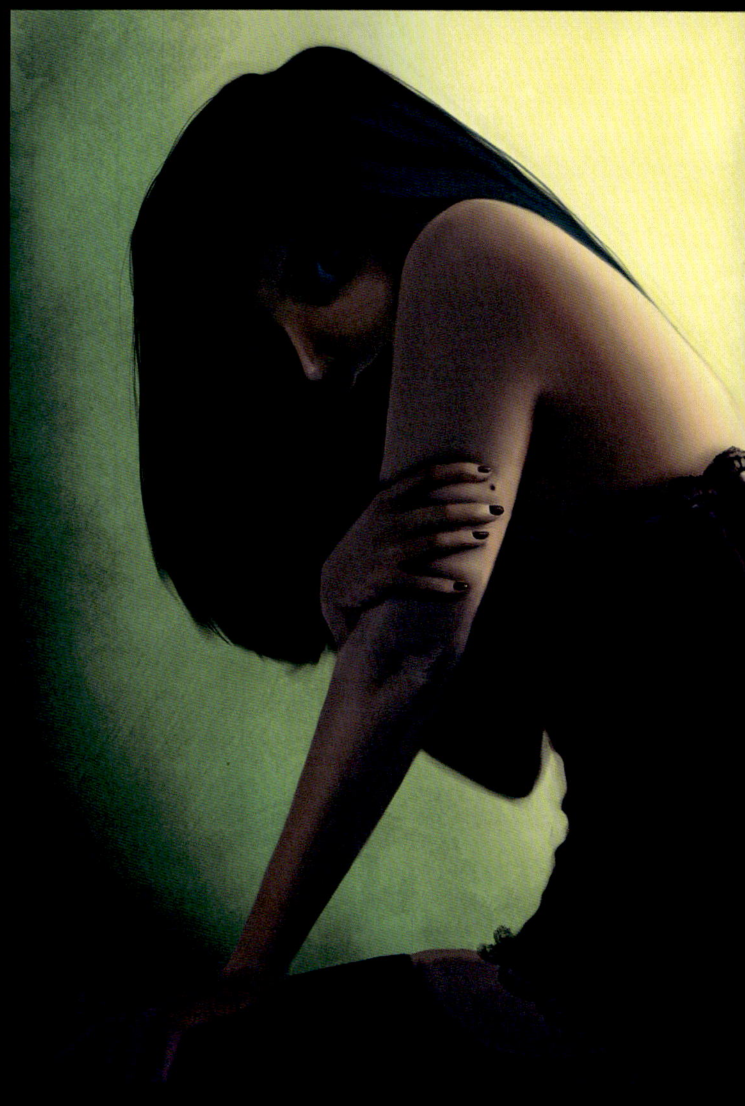

Beauty Spot
Photoshop
Renee Chio, MEXICO
[above]

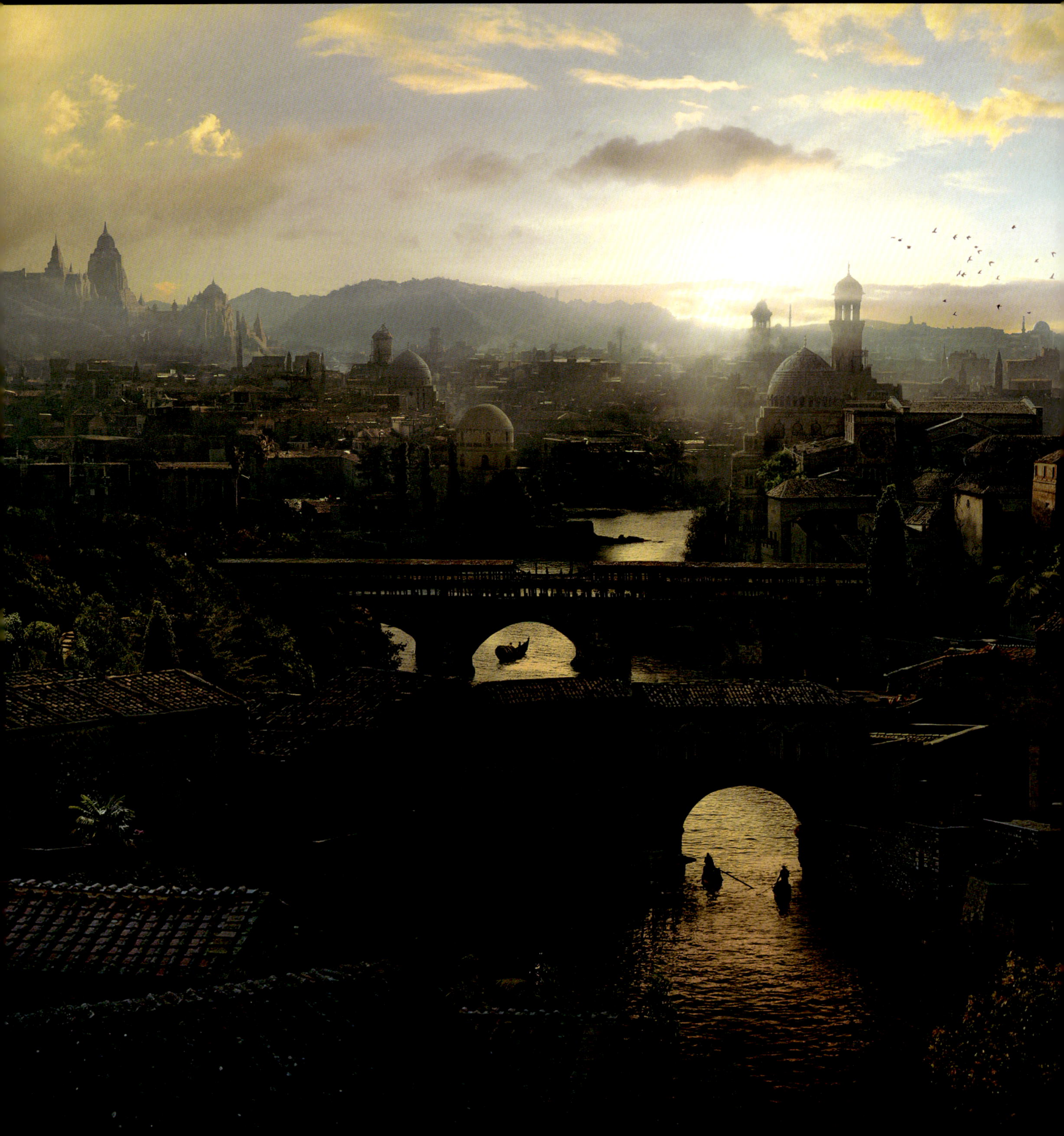

City of a Thousand Temples
Photoshop
Dmitry Zaviyalov, ESTONIA

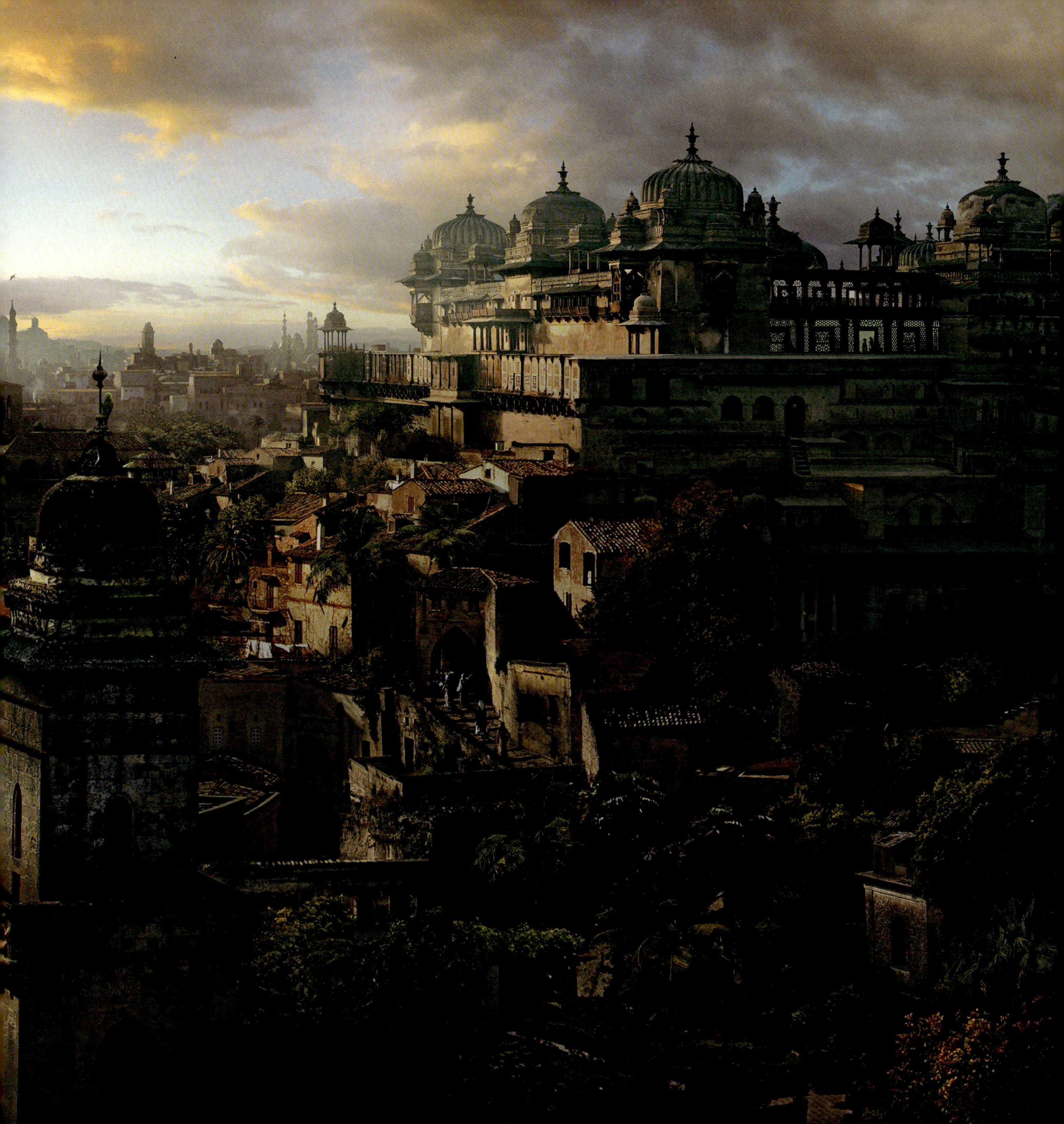

Master
Matte Painting

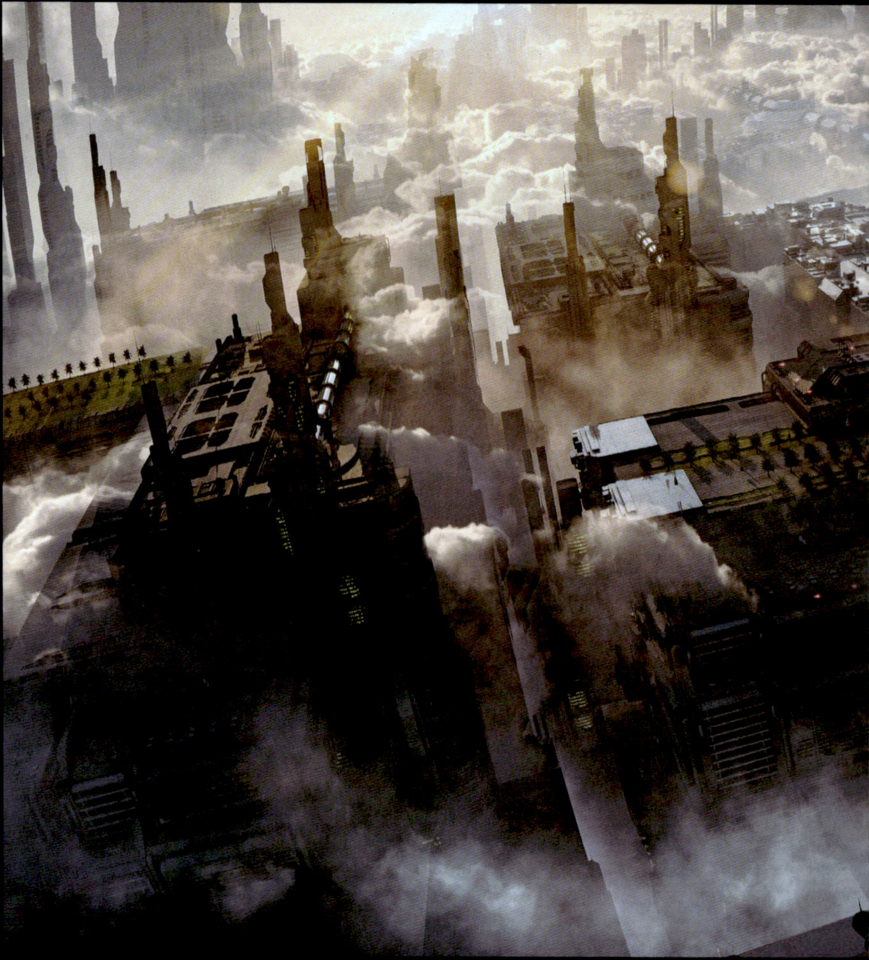

SuperCity
3ds Max, Photoshop, finalRender
Stefan Morrell, NEW ZEALAND
[right]

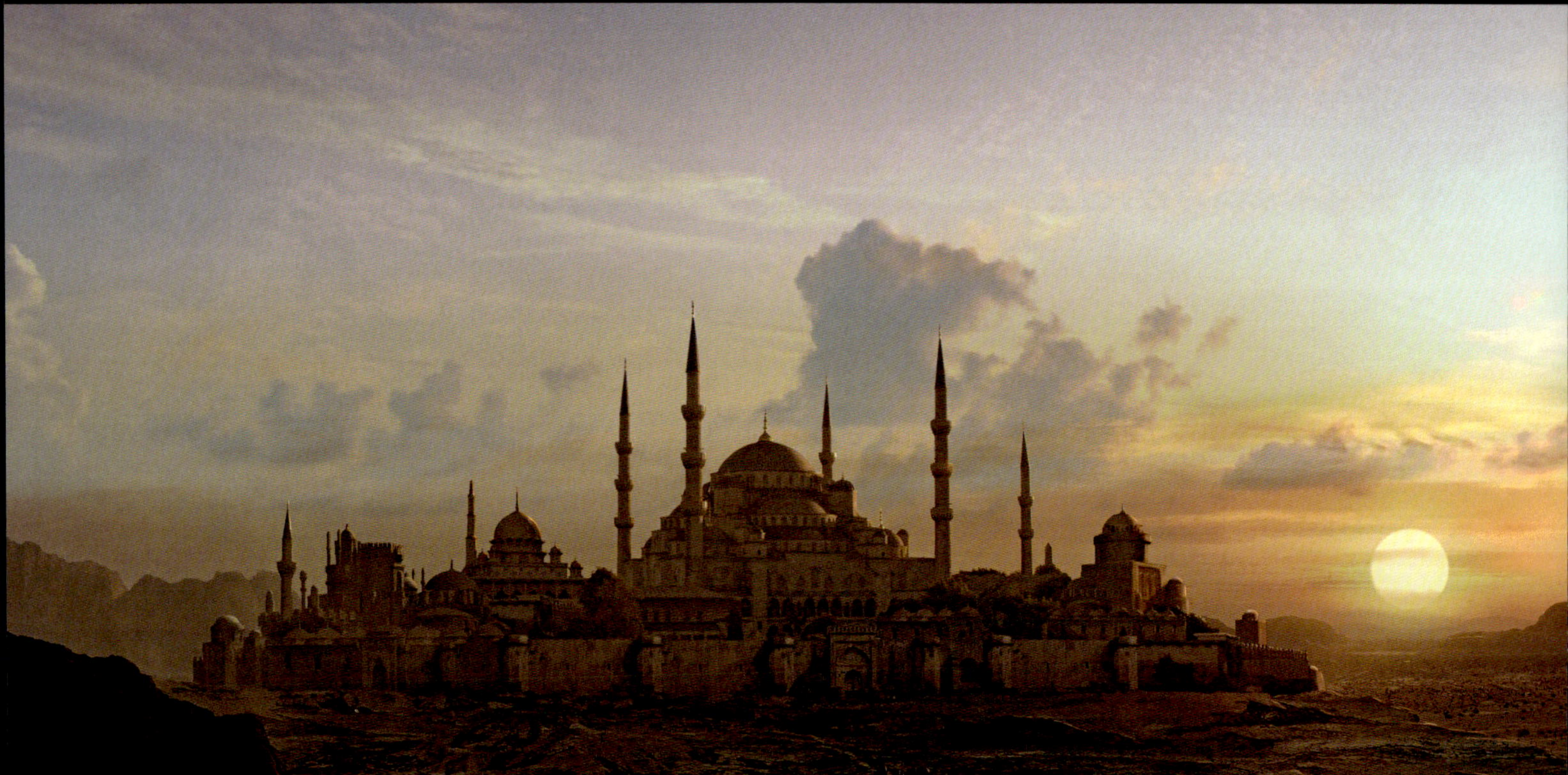

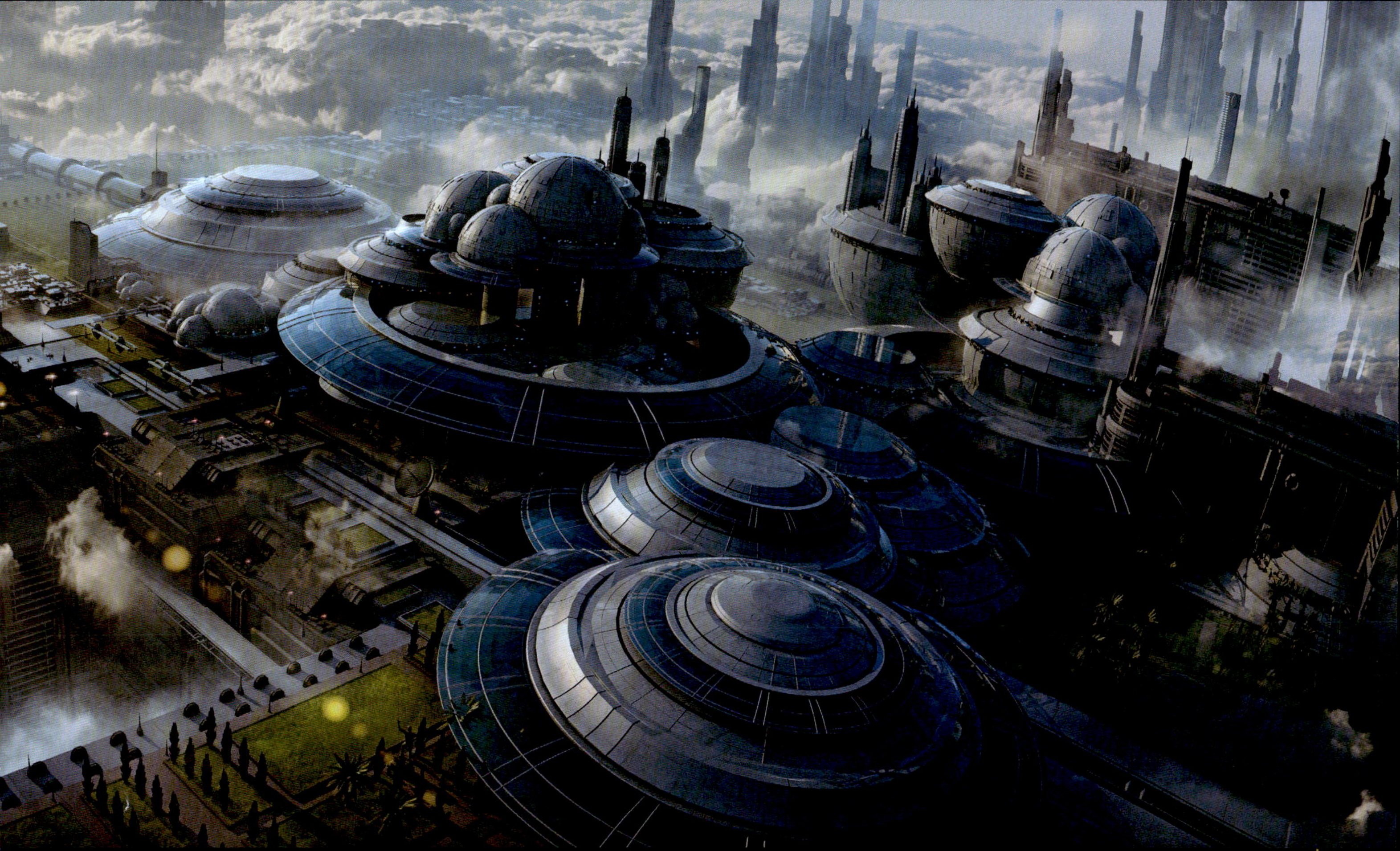

Excellence

Matte Painting

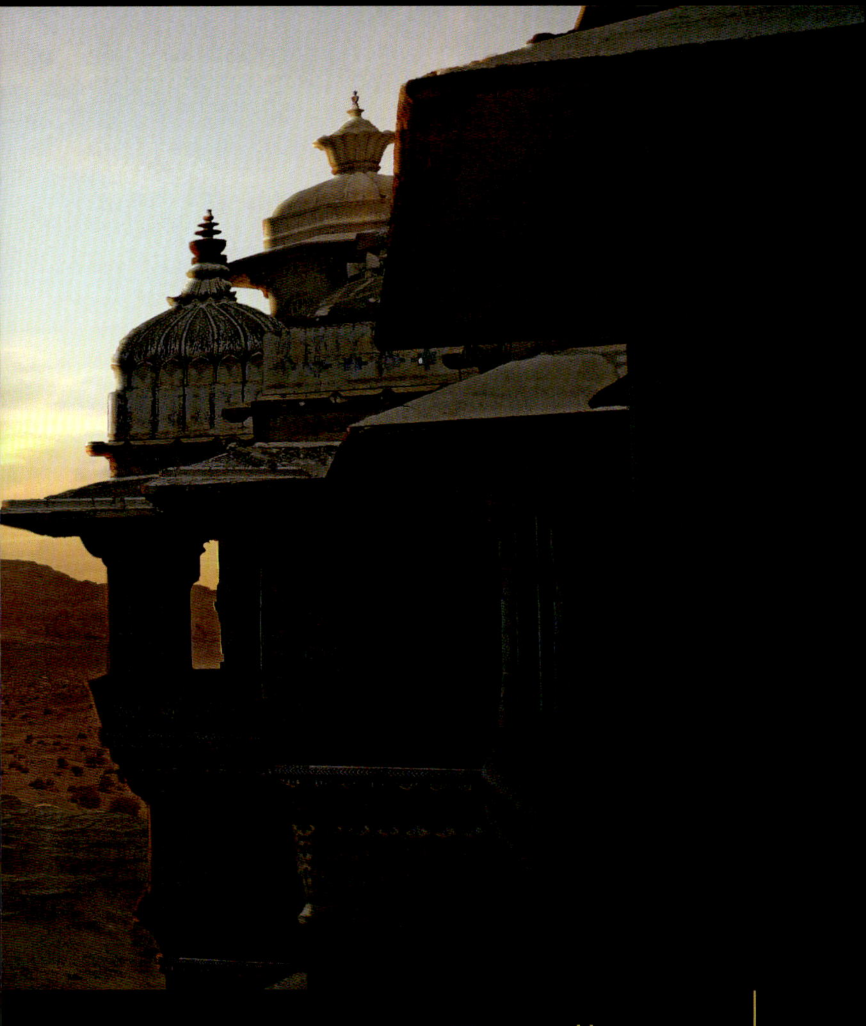

Desert Sunset
Photoshop
Pablo Palomeque, ARGENTINA
[left]

Excellence

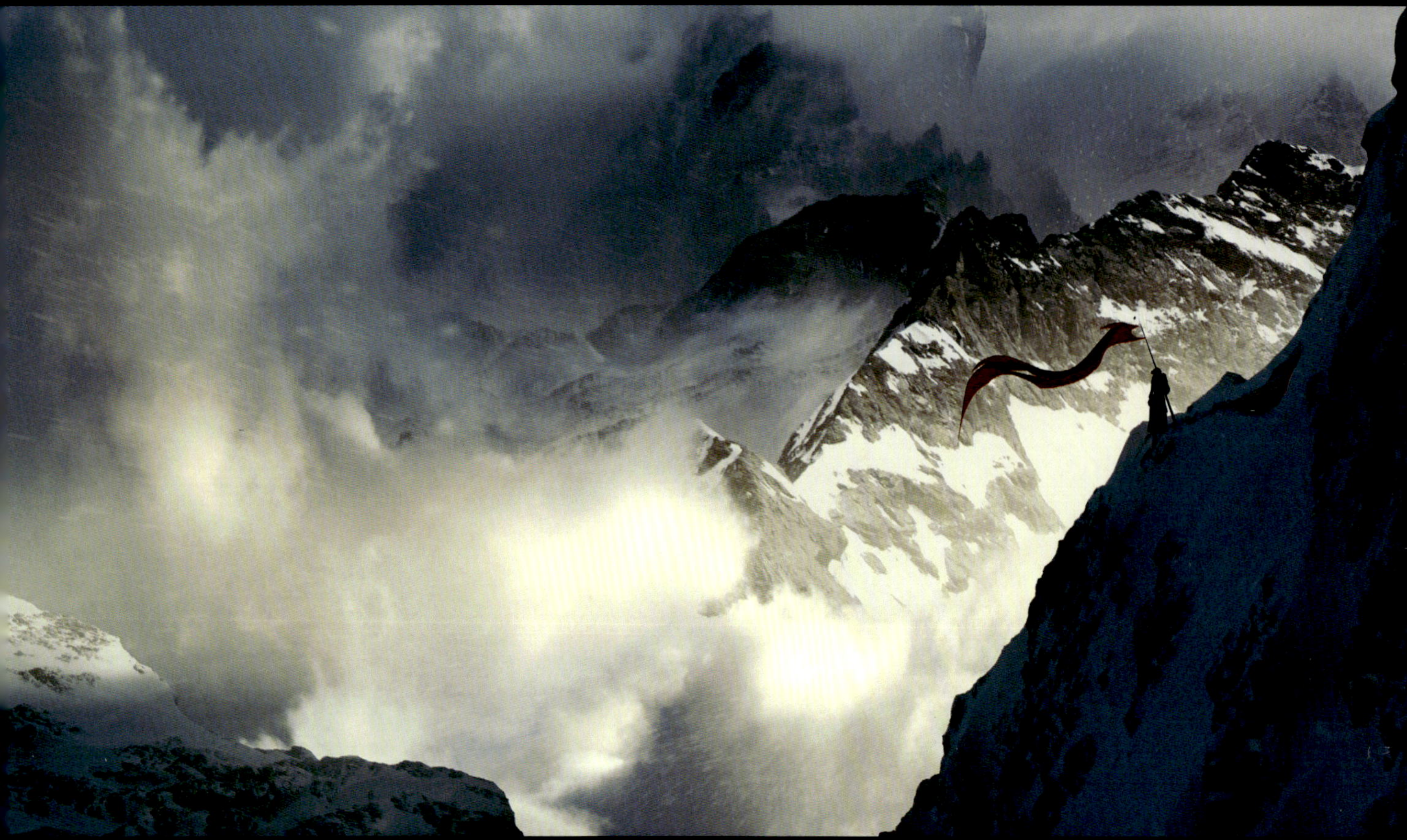

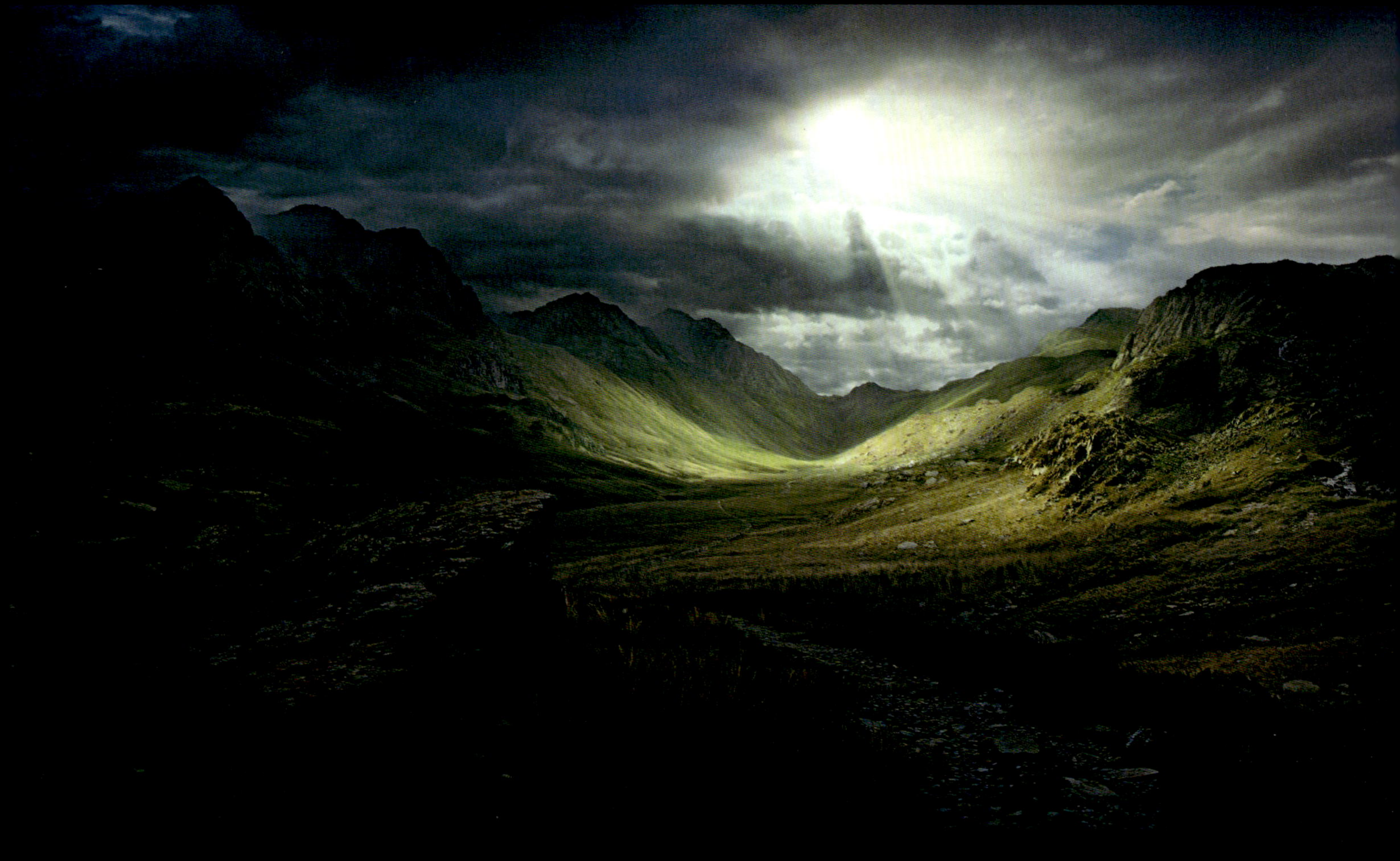

Flag Keeper
Photoshop
Jessica Rossier, FRANCE
[top]

The Messengers
Photoshop
Client: Wolfe Studios
Artur Zima, GREAT BRITAIN
[above]

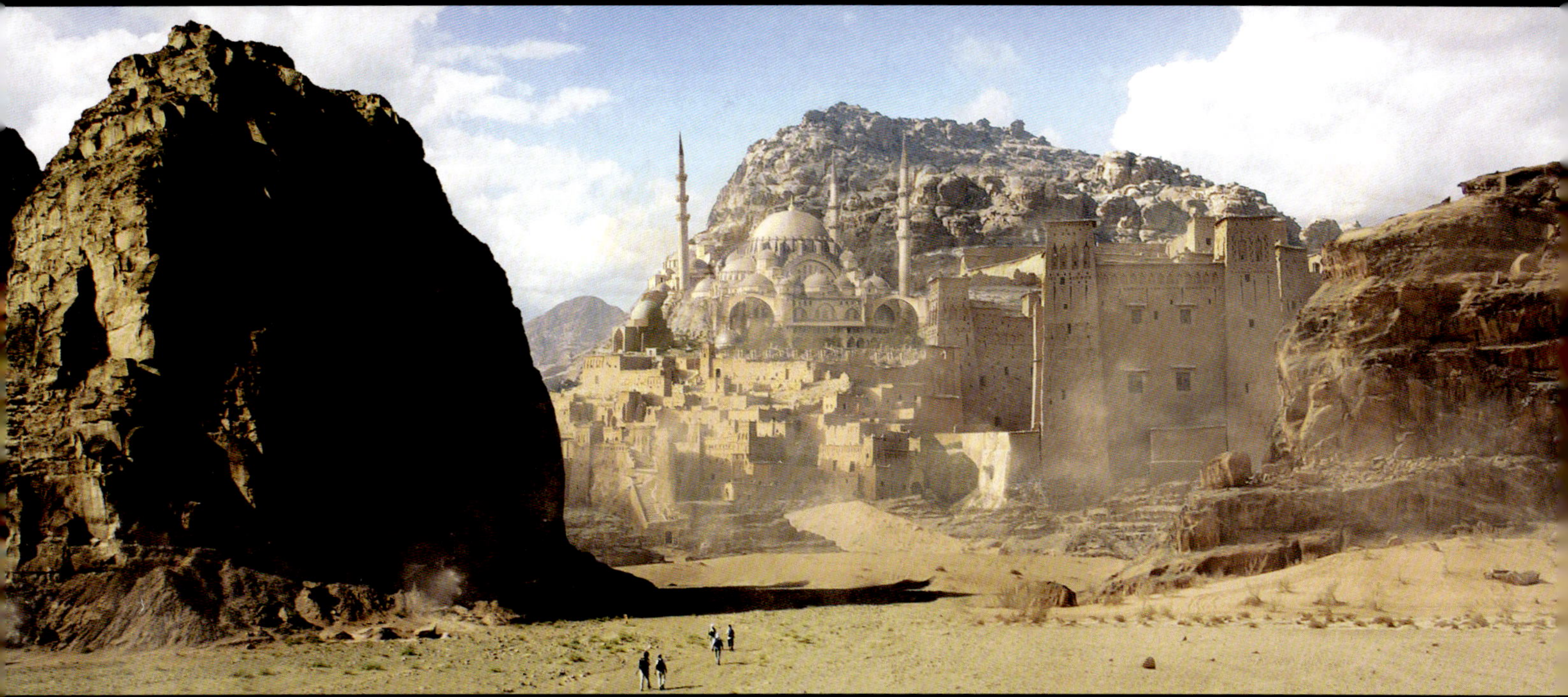

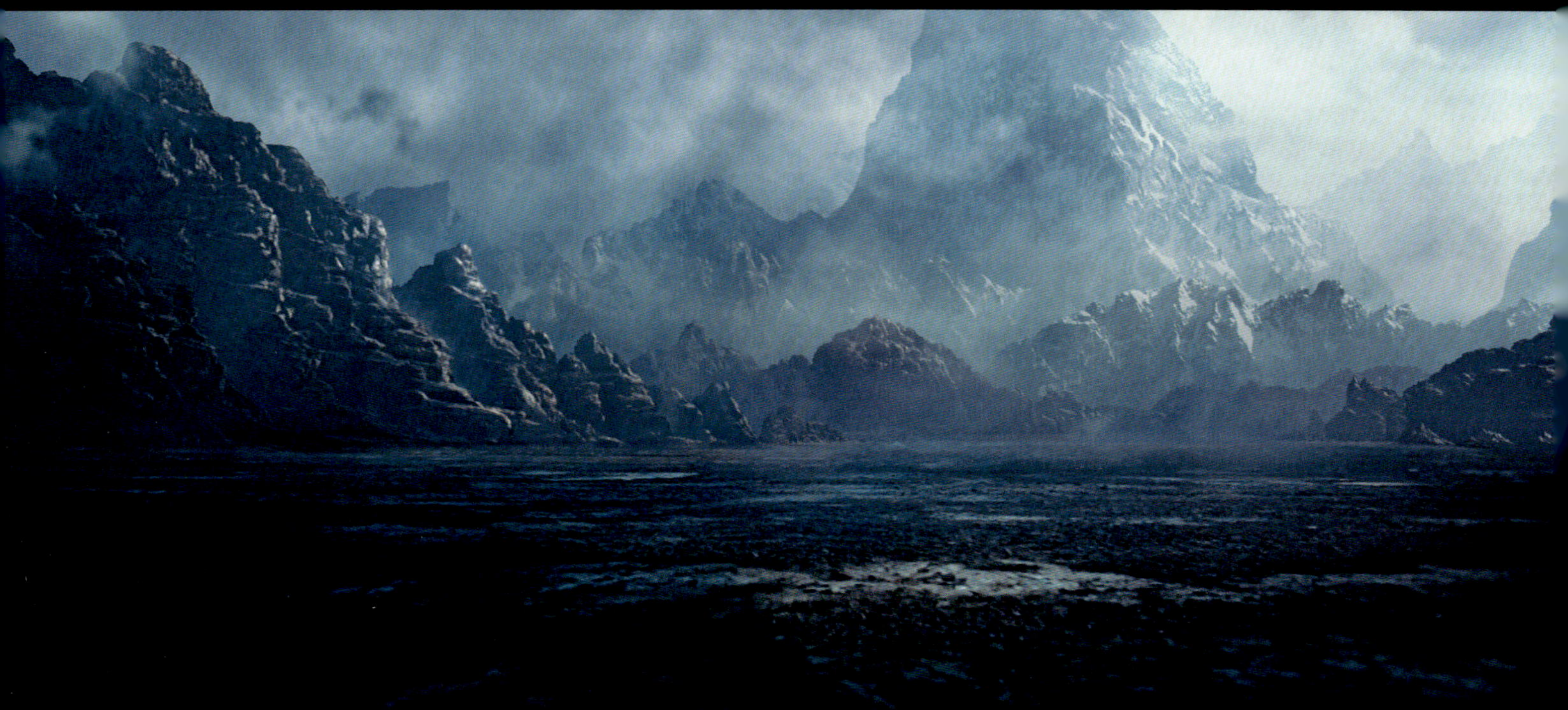

Desert Journey
Photoshop
Usama Jameel, INDIA
[top]

The Valley of a Huge Mountain
Photoshop
Igor Staritsin, RUSSIA
[above]

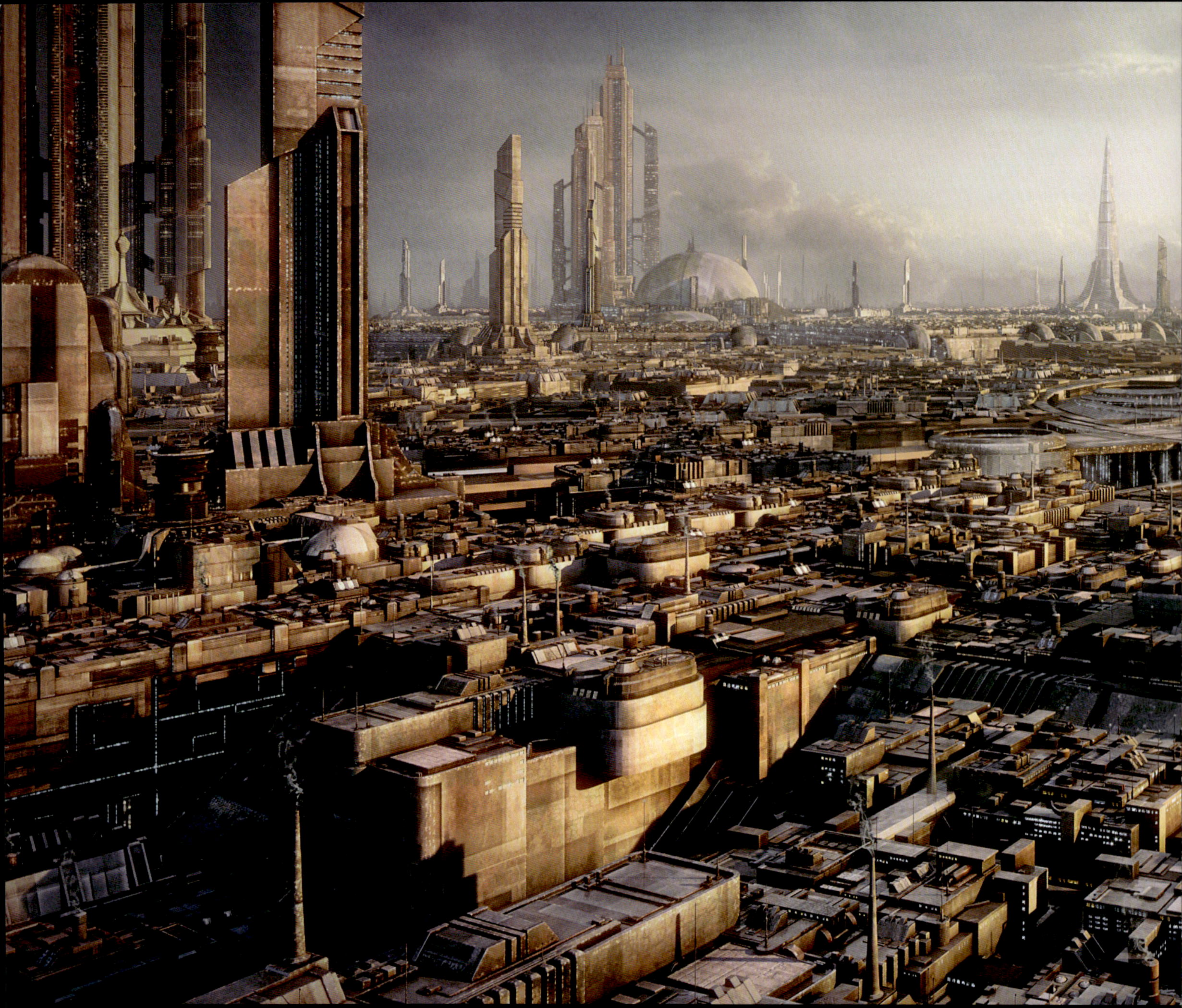

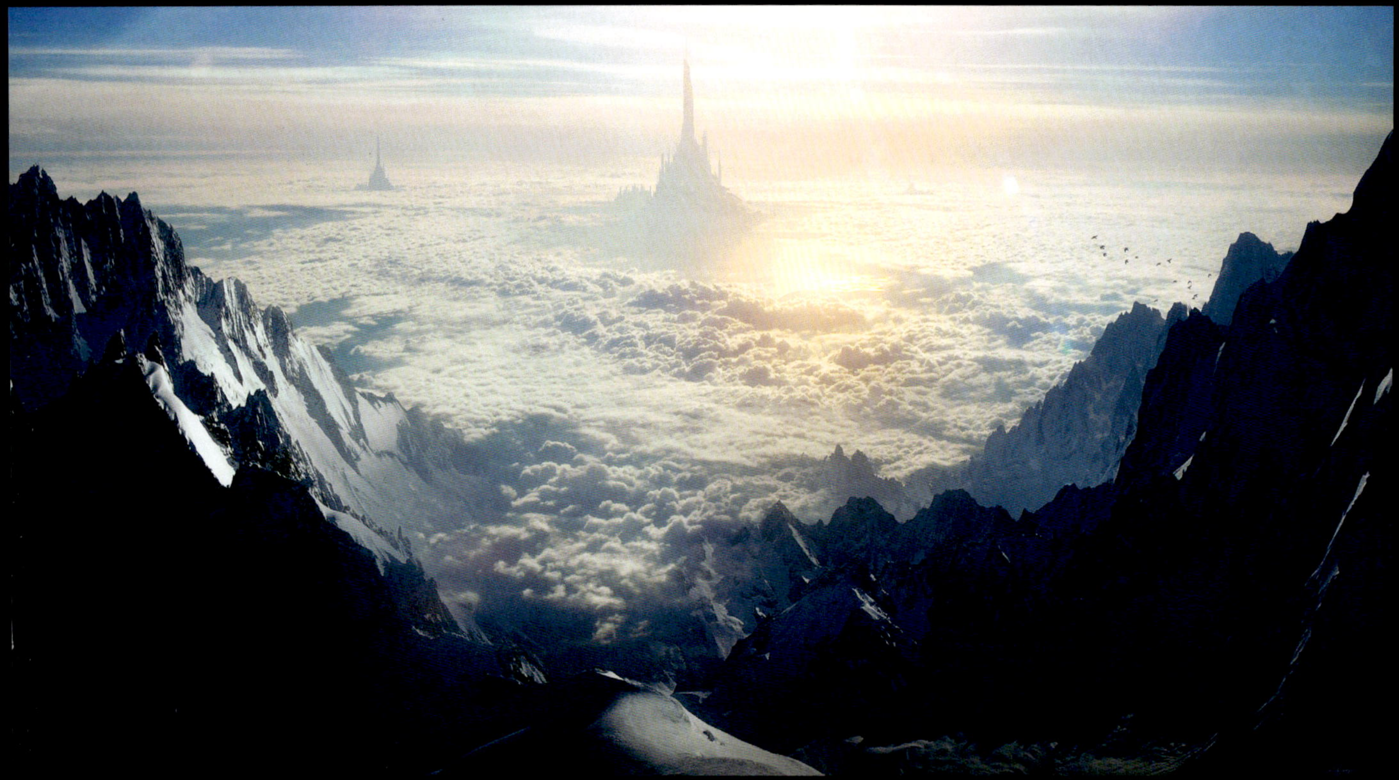

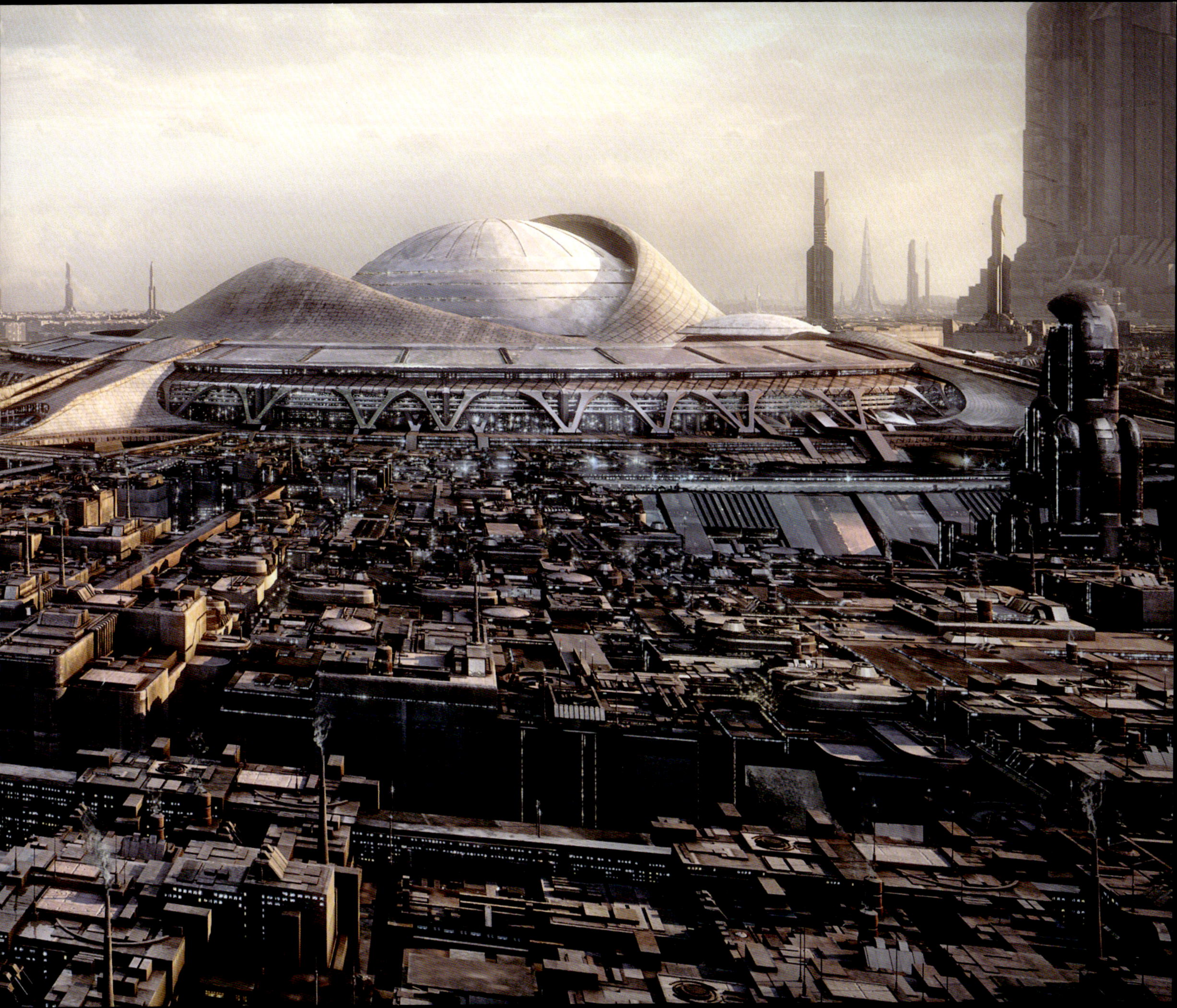

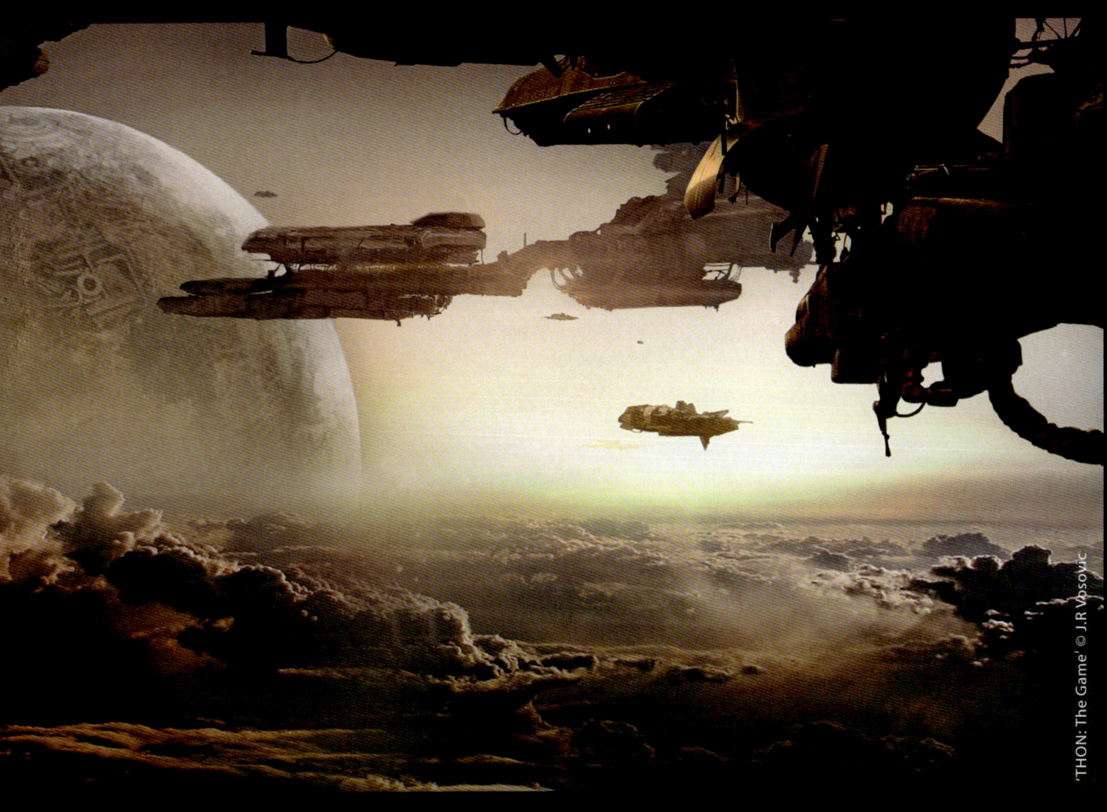

Brave New World
Maya, 3ds Max, Photoshop, V-Ray
Ashish Dani, CANADA
[above]

Over the Cold Mountain
Photoshop
Bastien Grivet, FRANCE
[facing page bottom left]

THON: View to a Space Station
Photoshop
Client: J.R Vosovic
Sourav Dhar, INDIA
[left]

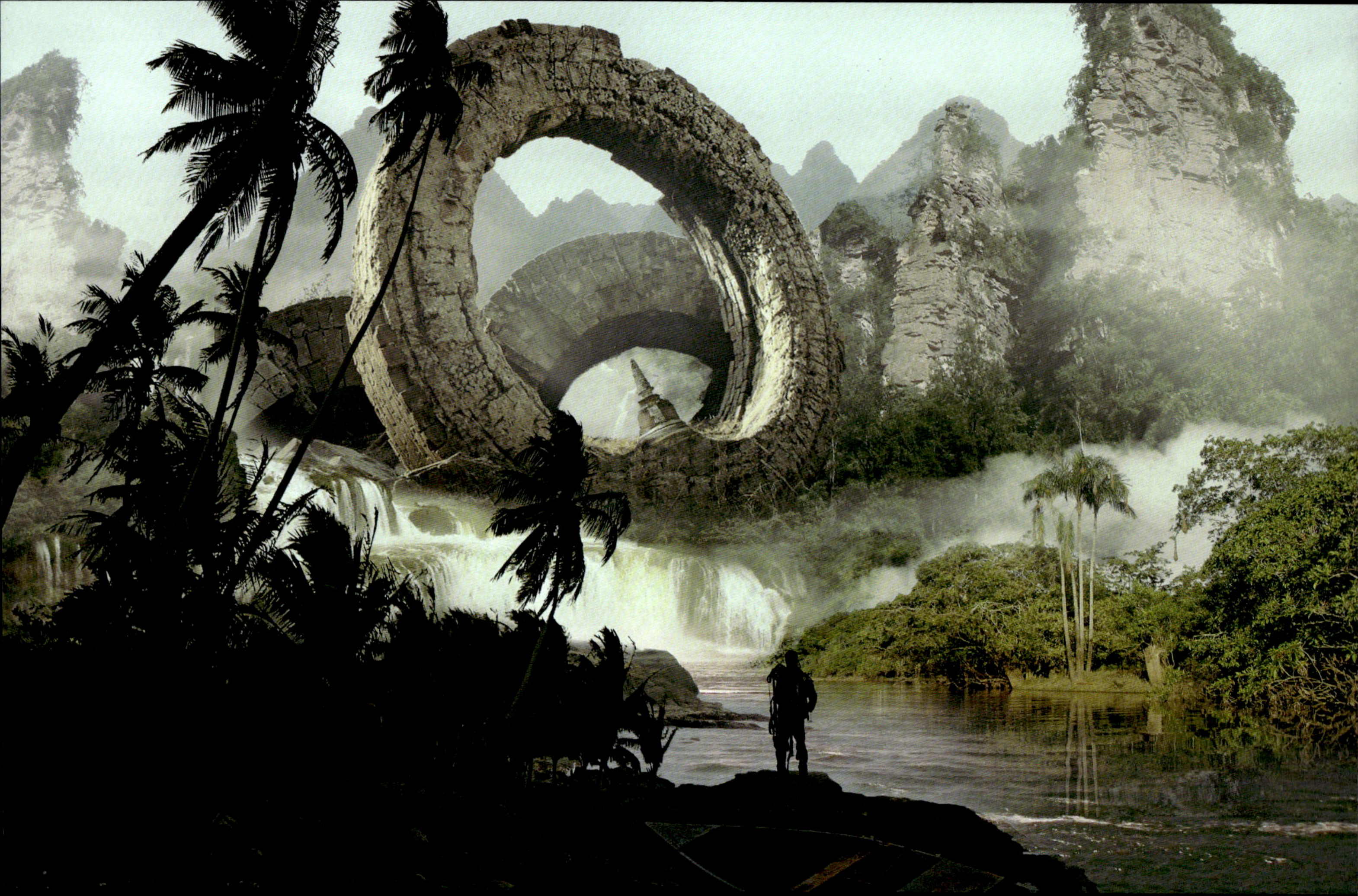

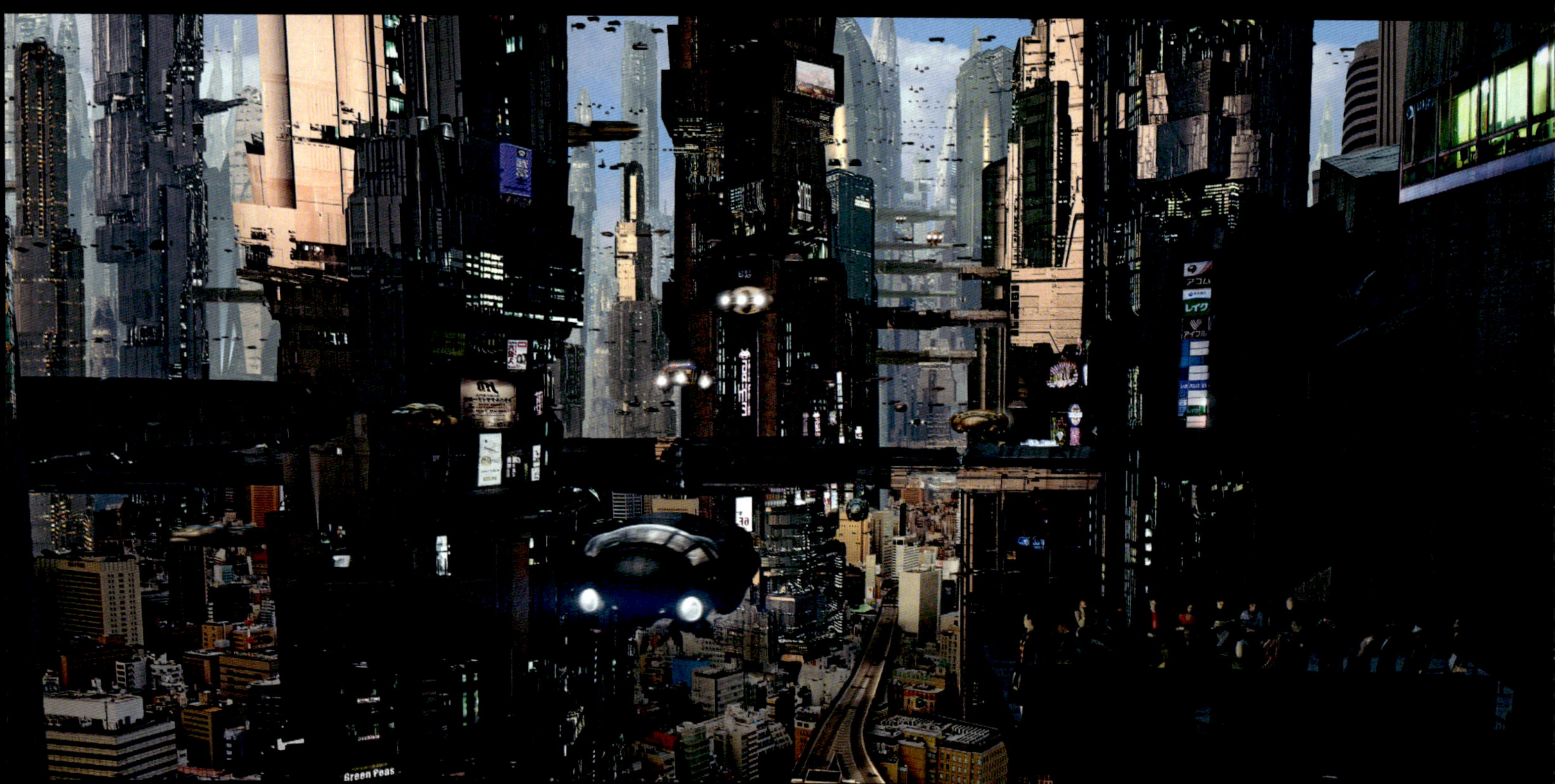

Rainforest
Photoshop
Guodong Zhao, CHINA
[top]

Matte City 2088
V-Ray, Photoshop
Scott Richard, USA
[above]

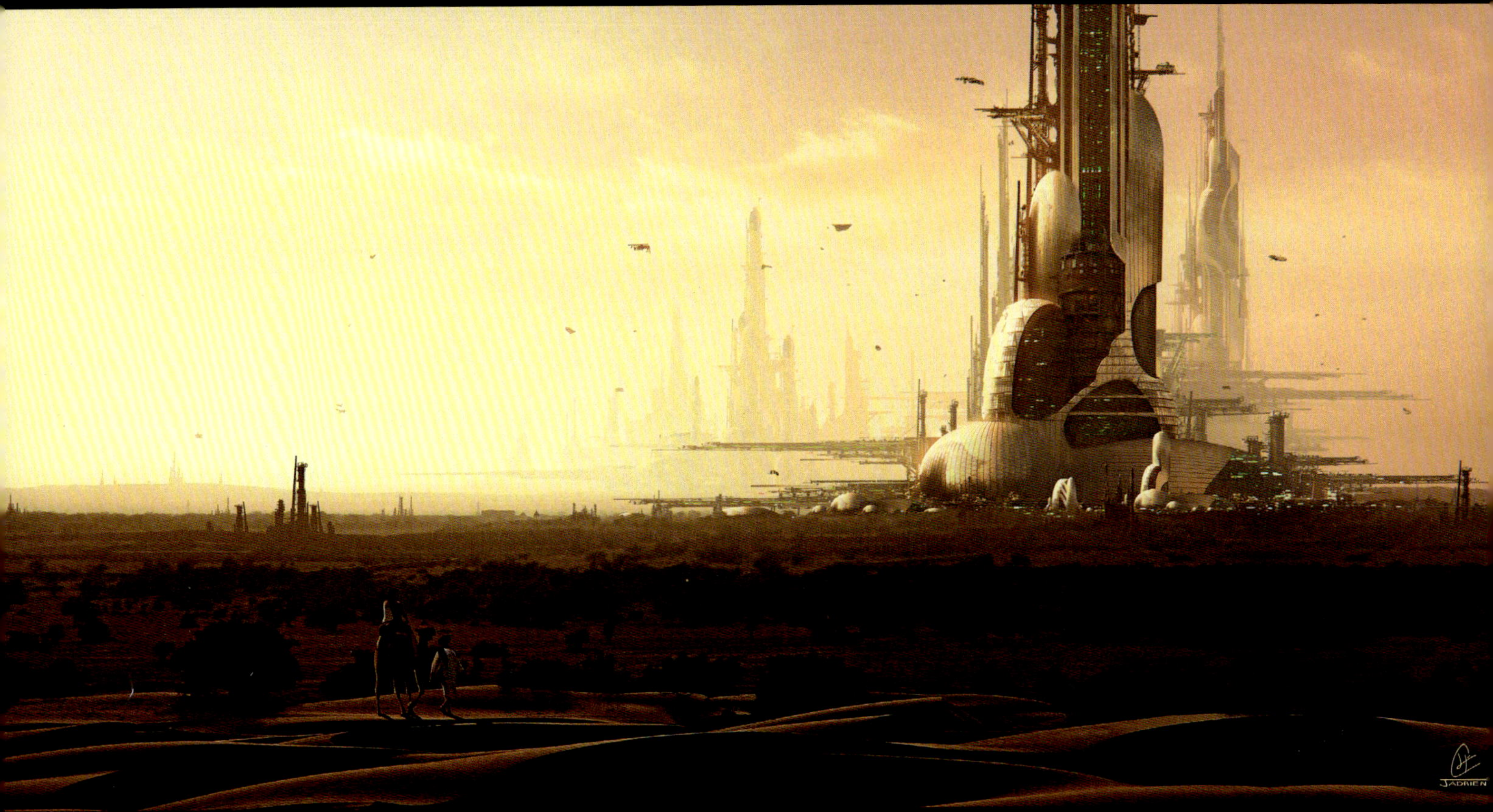

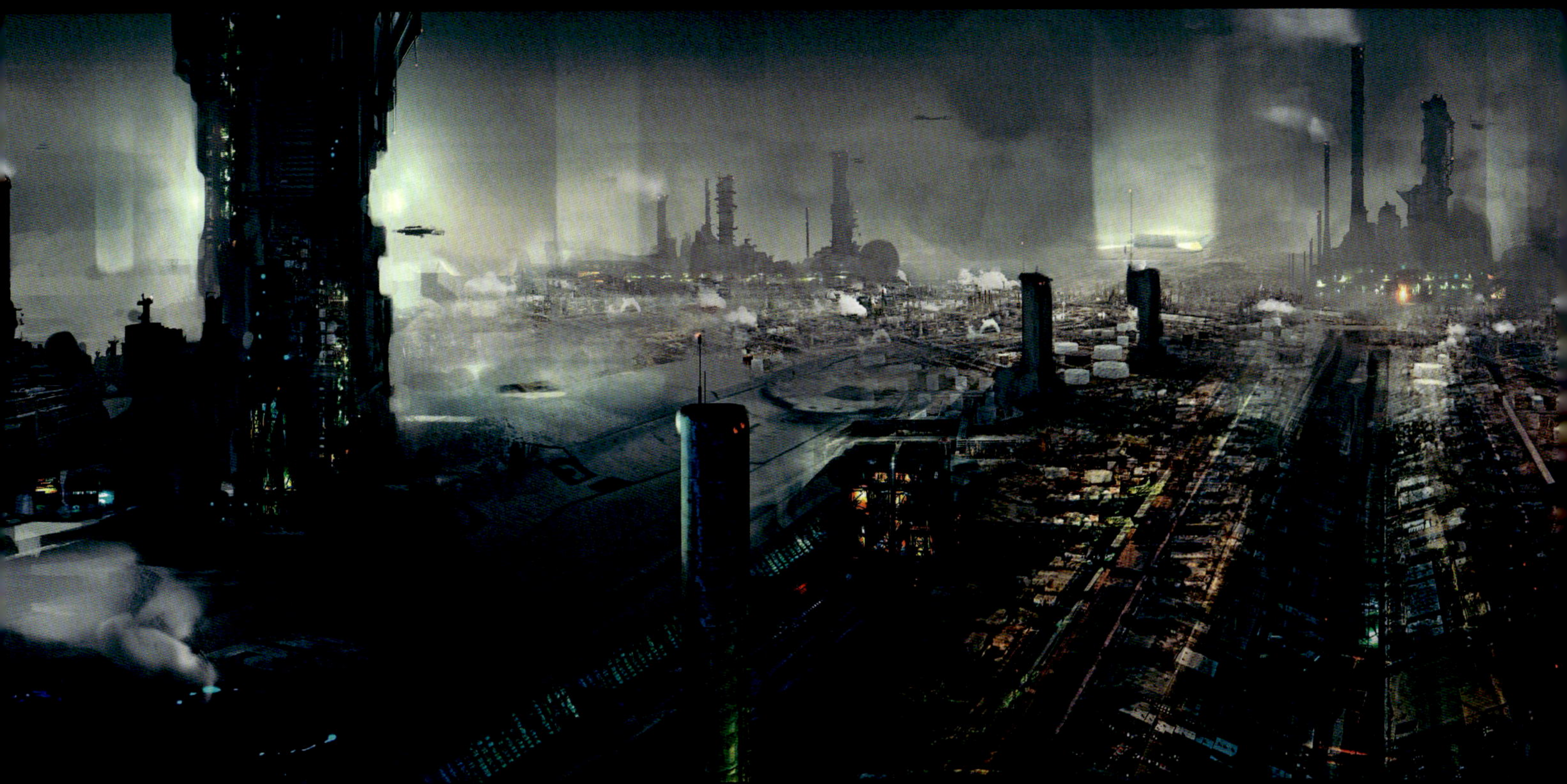

A Long Journey
Photoshop
Jadrien Cousens, USA
[top]

Industrialization
Photoshop
Jan Urschel, SINGAPORE
[above]

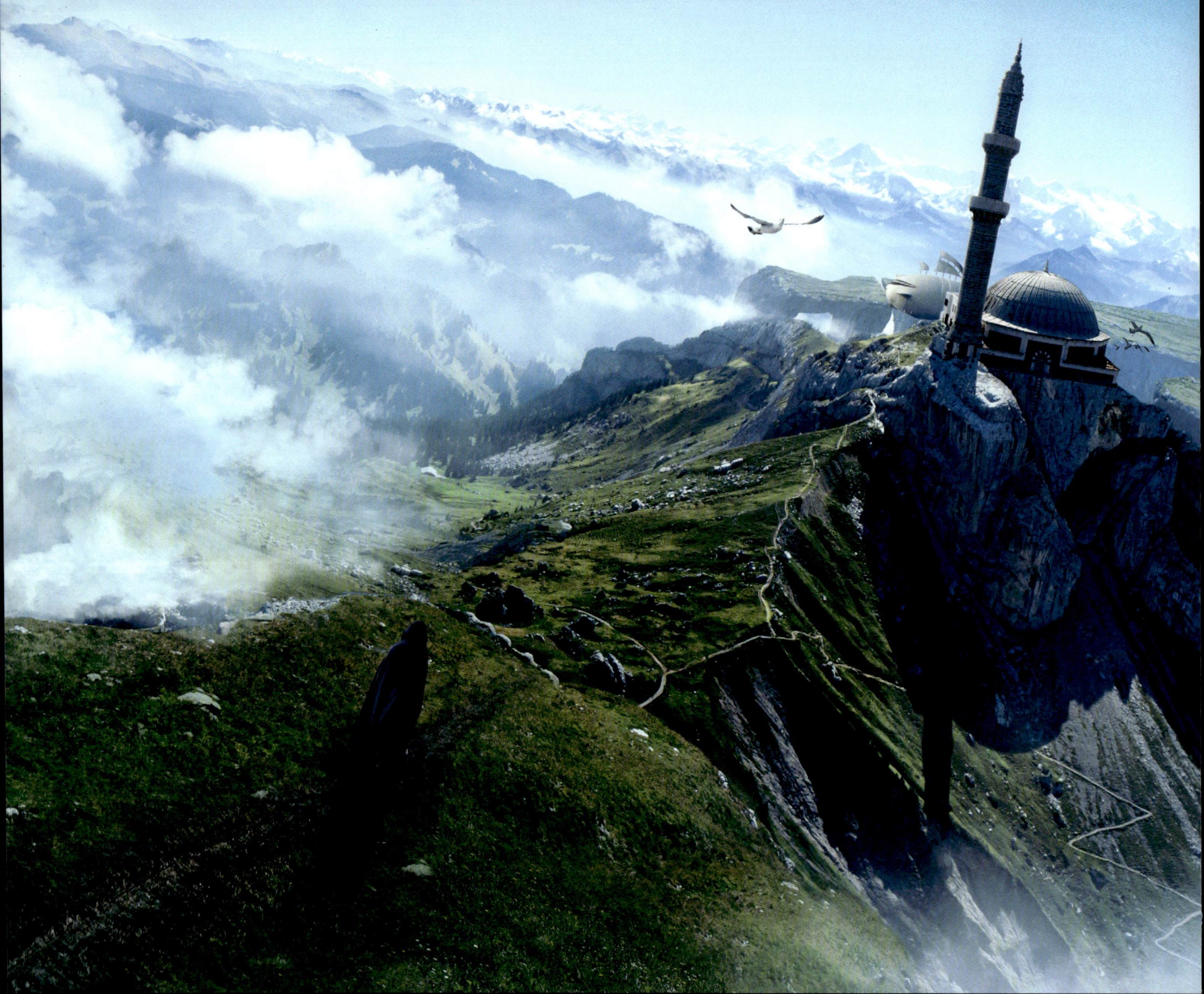

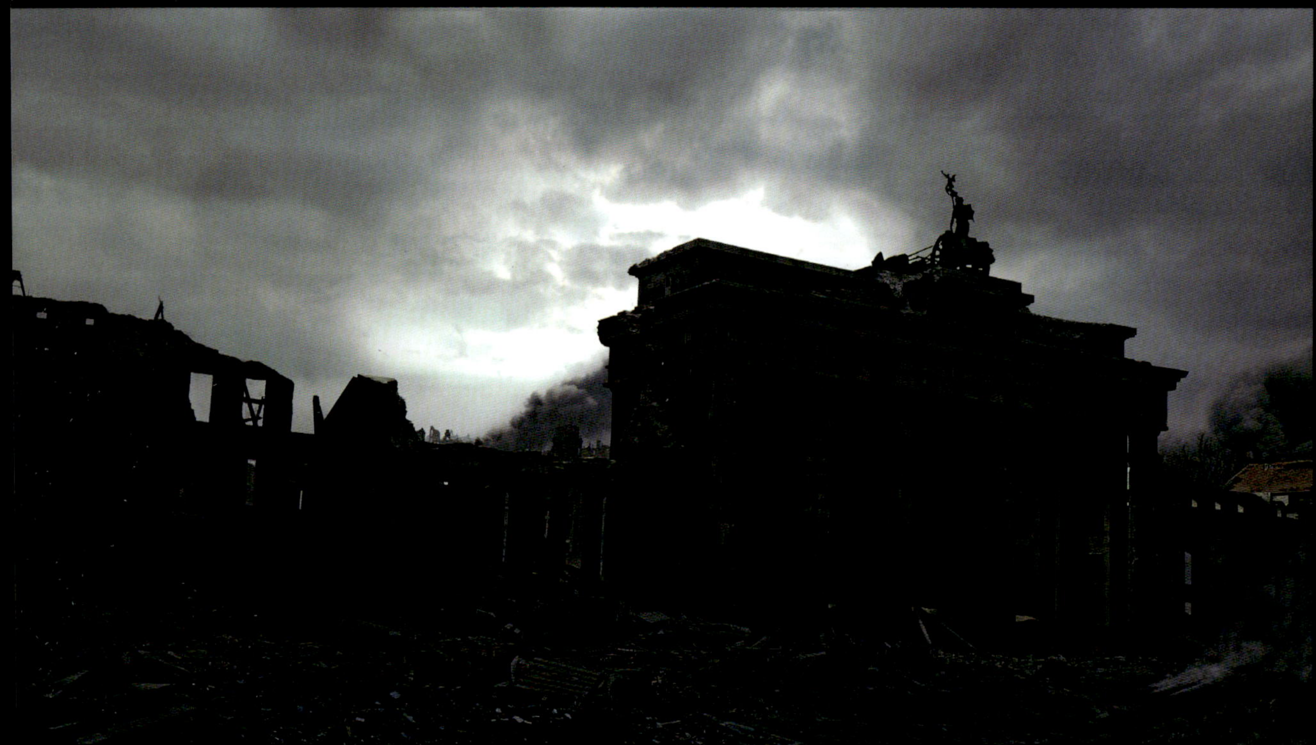

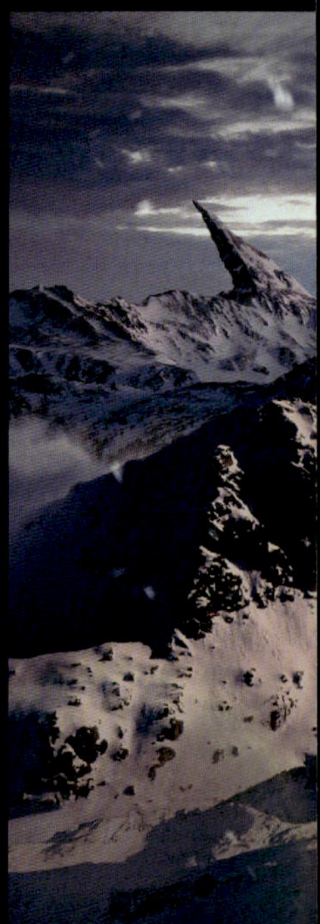

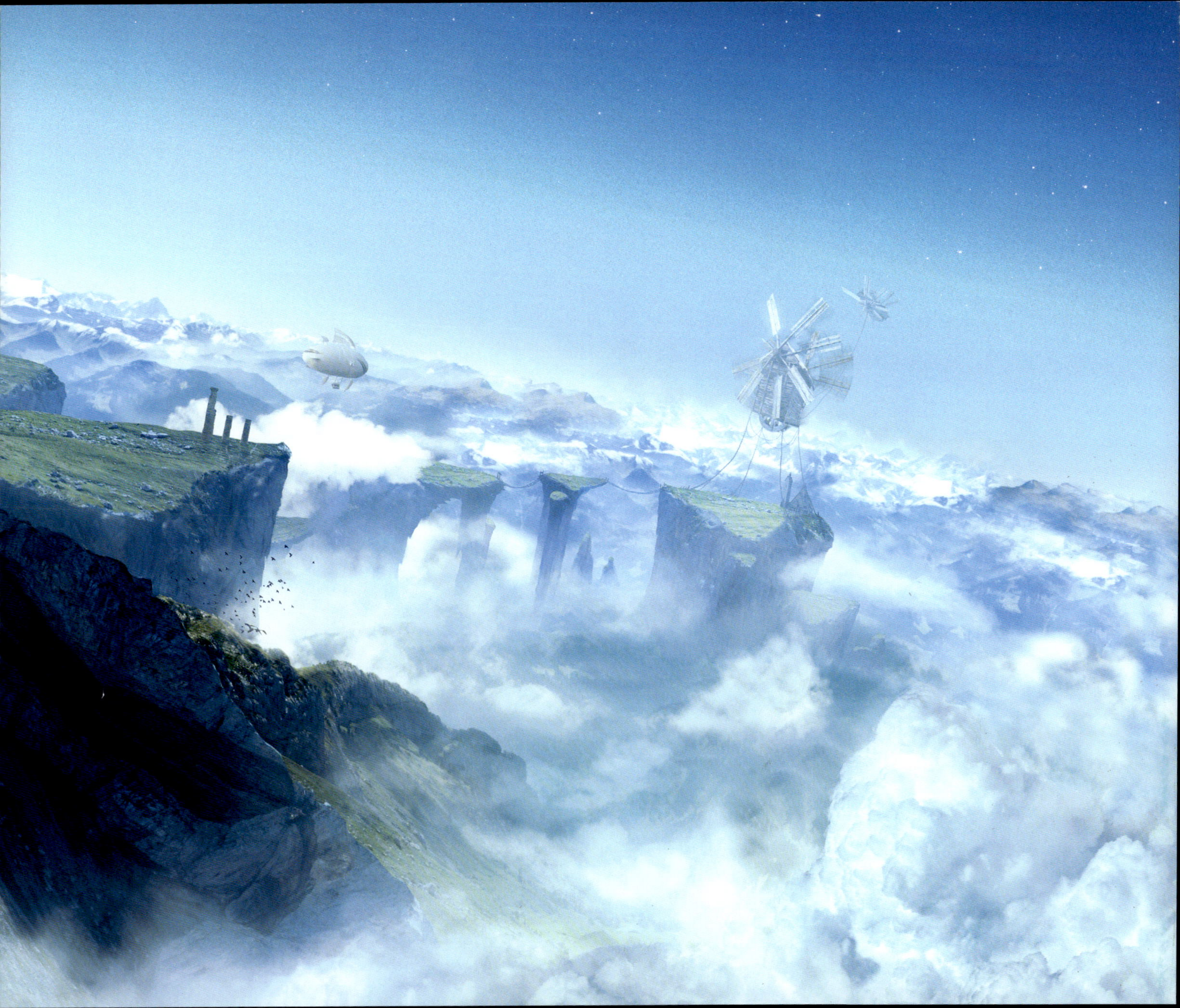

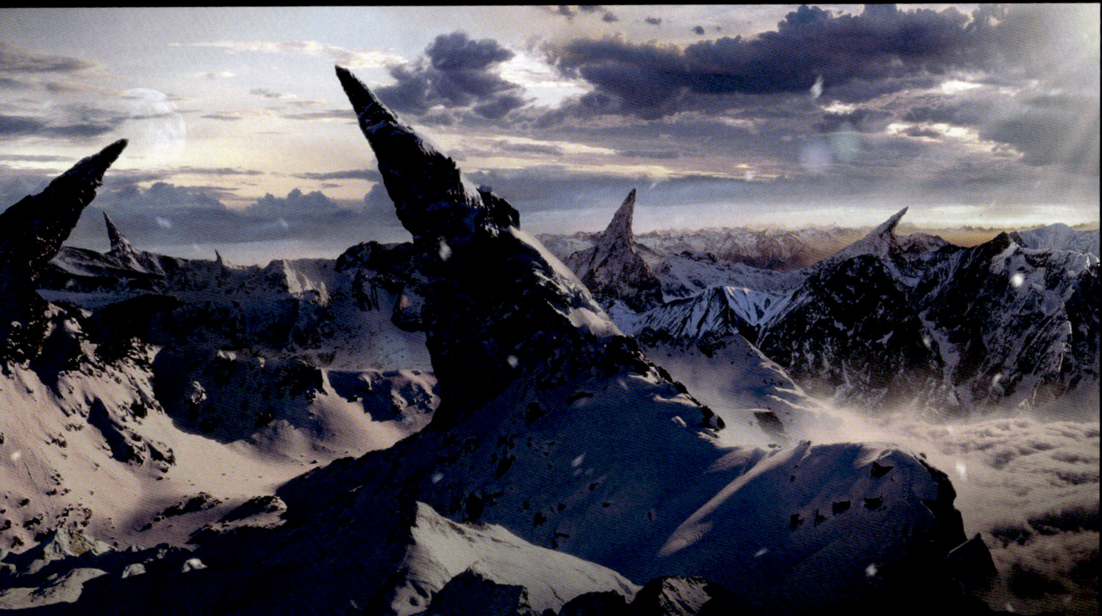

Journey to Shatter Island
Photoshop
Erik Schumacher, GERMANY
[above]

Brandenburger Gate WW2
3ds Max, V-Ray, Photoshop
Martin Hoehnle, GREAT BRITAIN
[facing page bottom left]

Kasternau
Photoshop
Francesco Corvino, ITALY
[left]

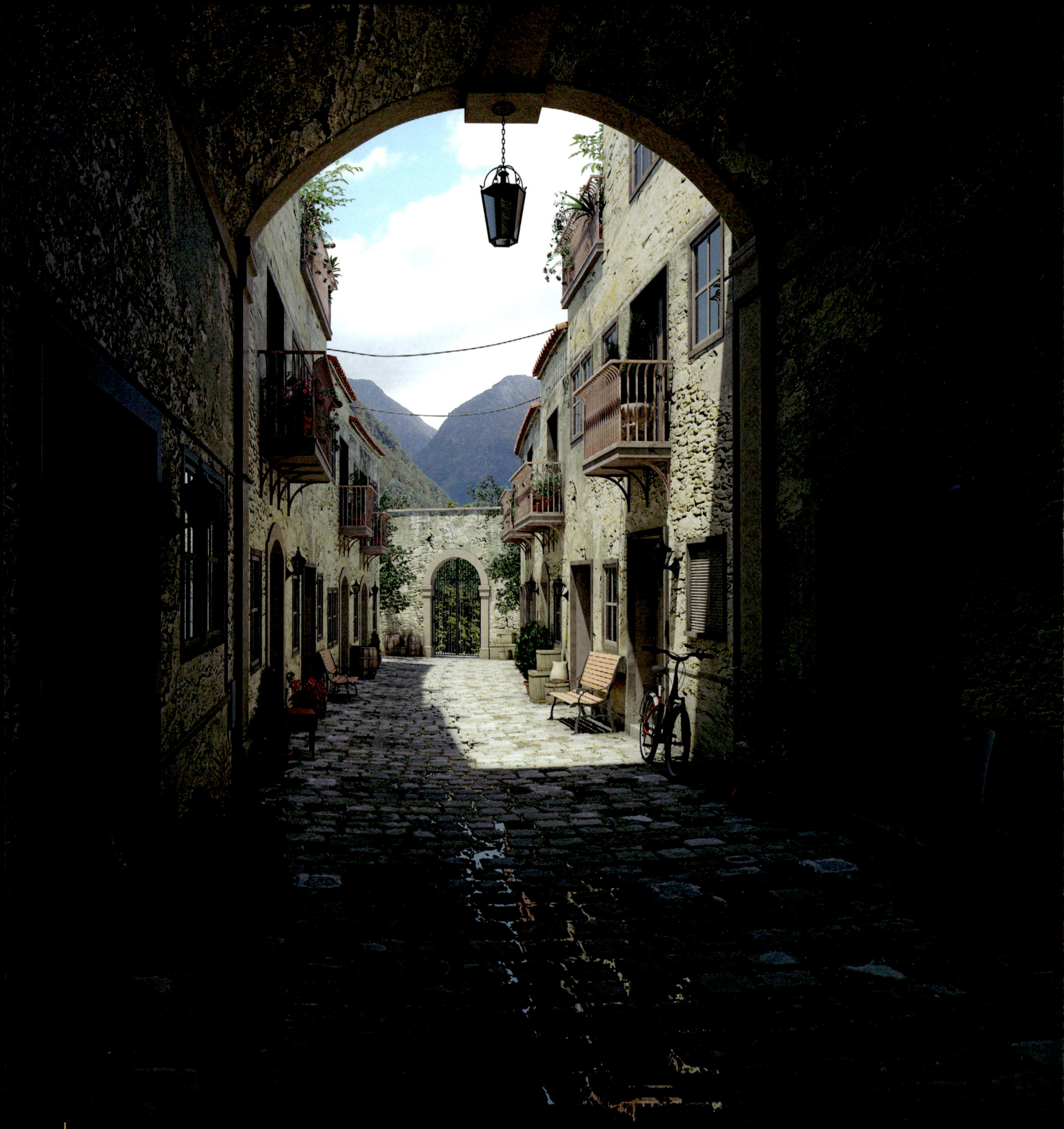

Old World Alley
3ds Max, mental ray, Photoshop
Rod DeWeese, USA

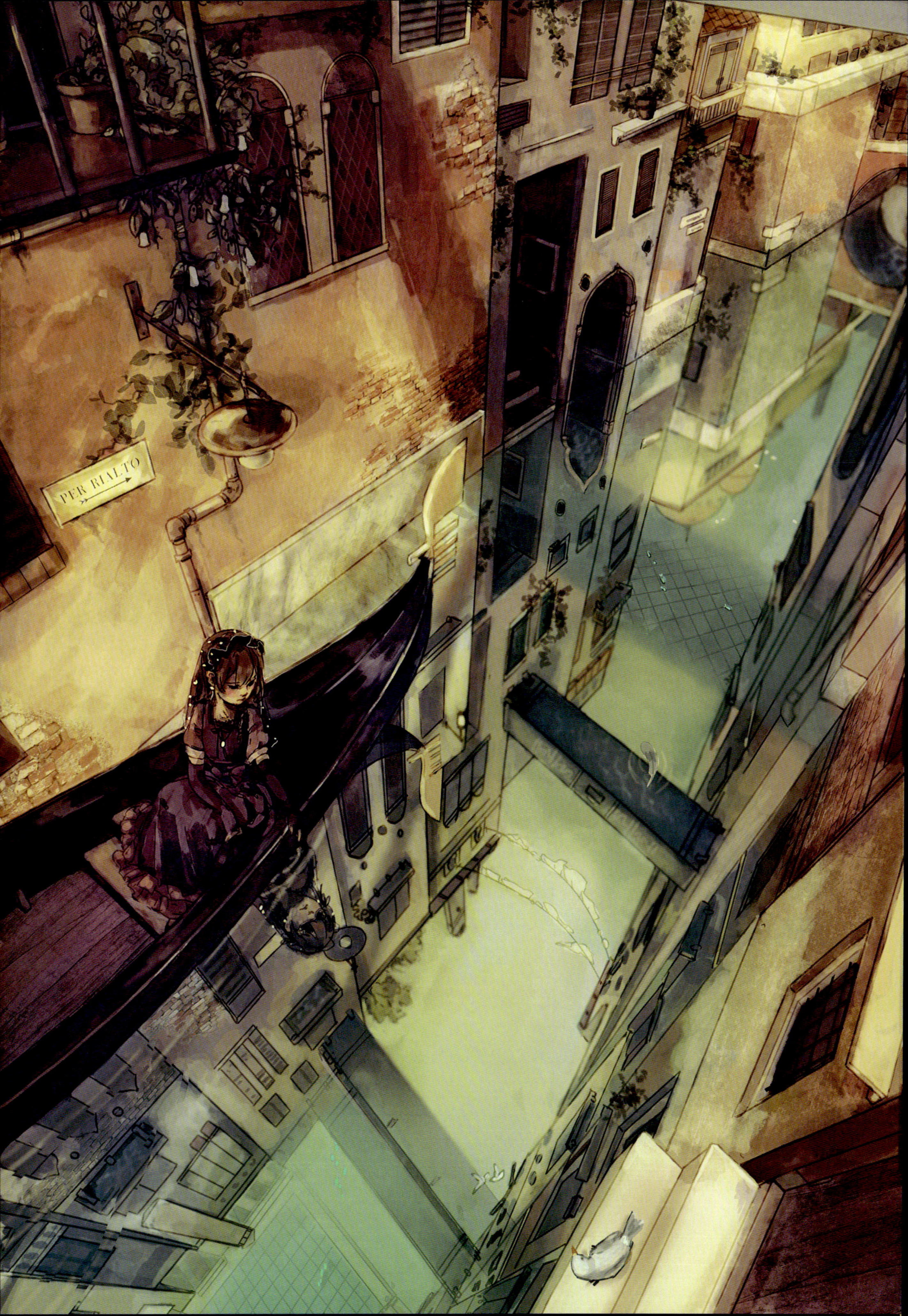

Gibigianna
Photoshop
Sarah Webb, USA

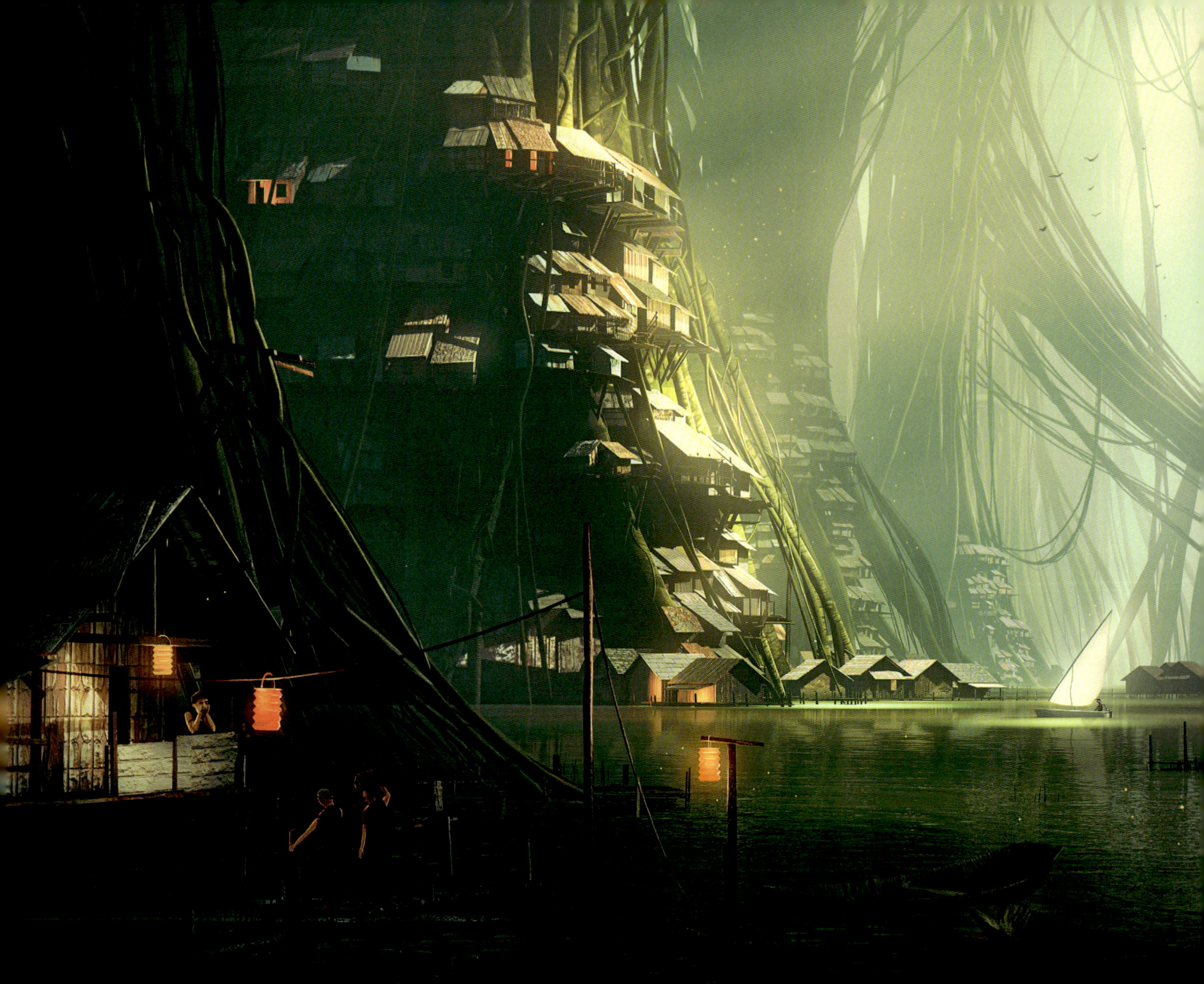

Excellence
Environment

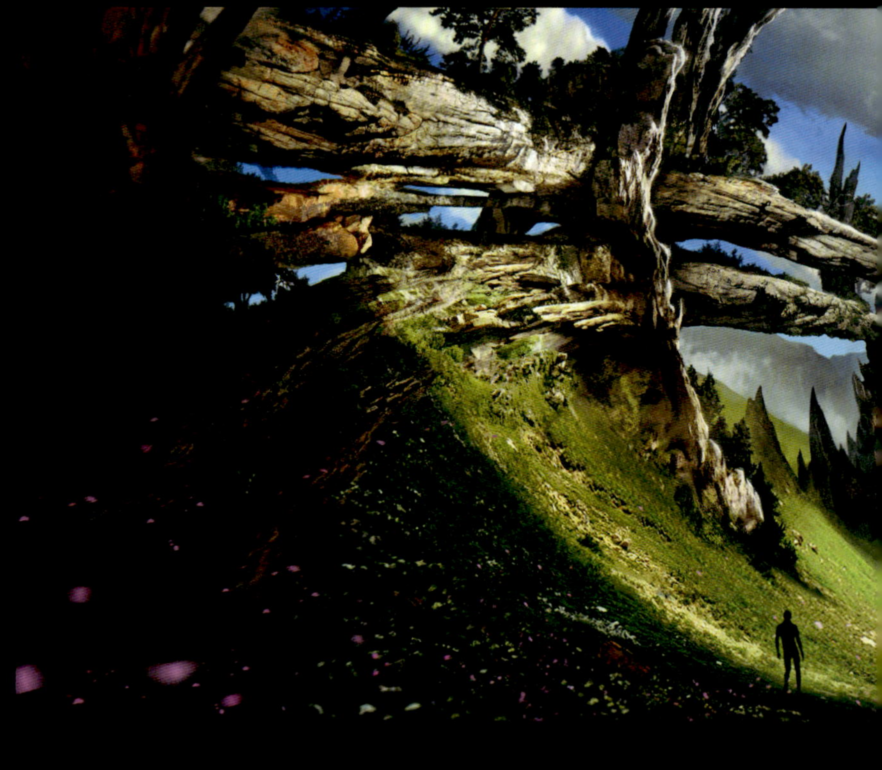

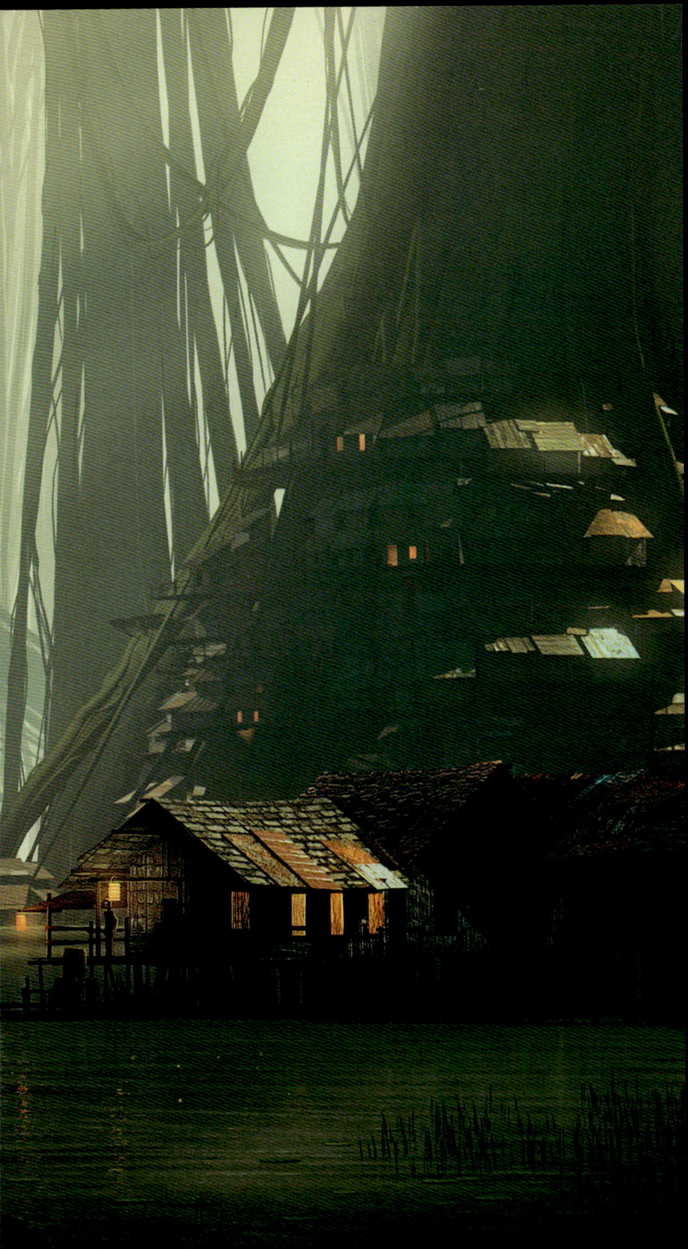

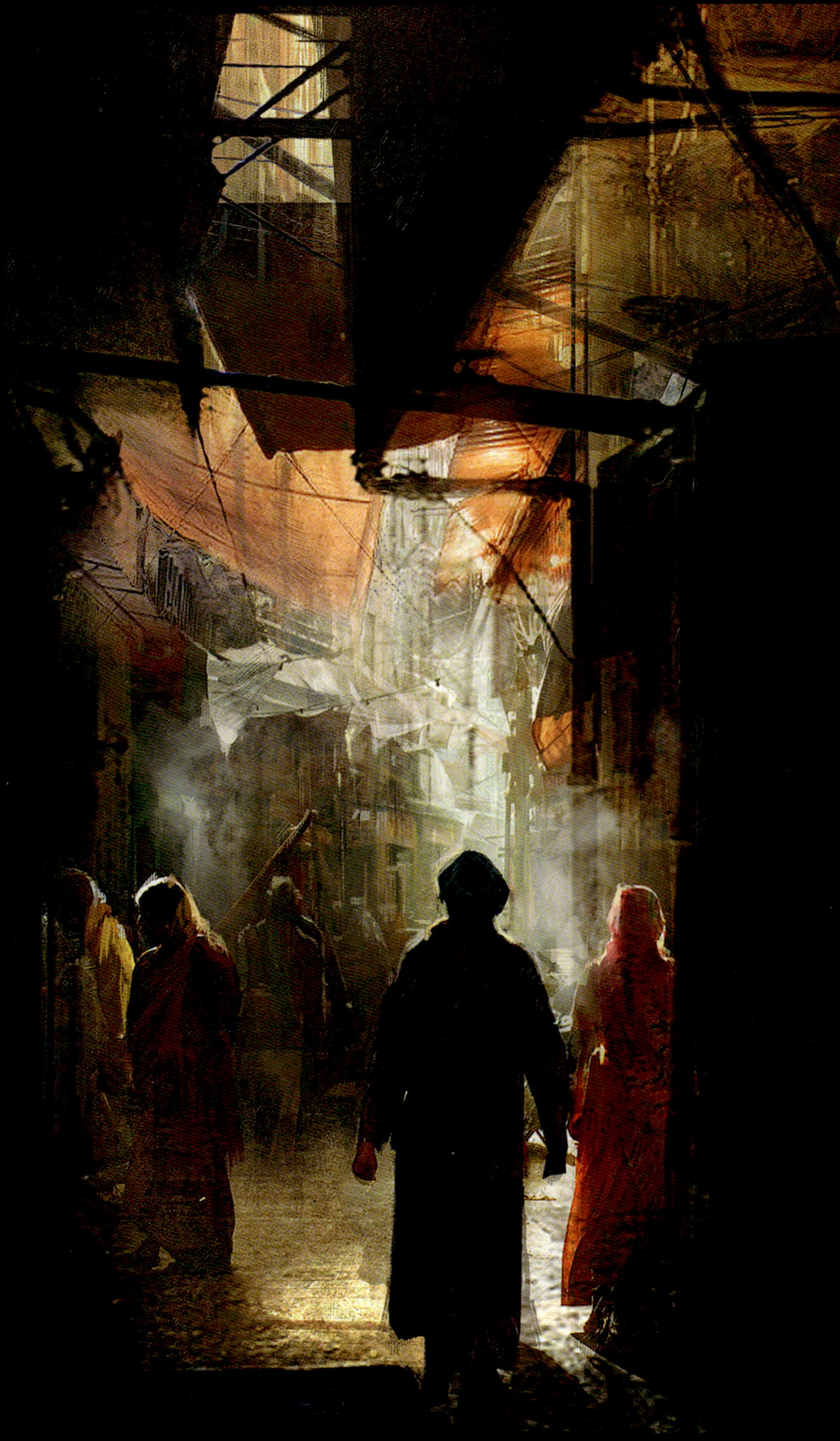

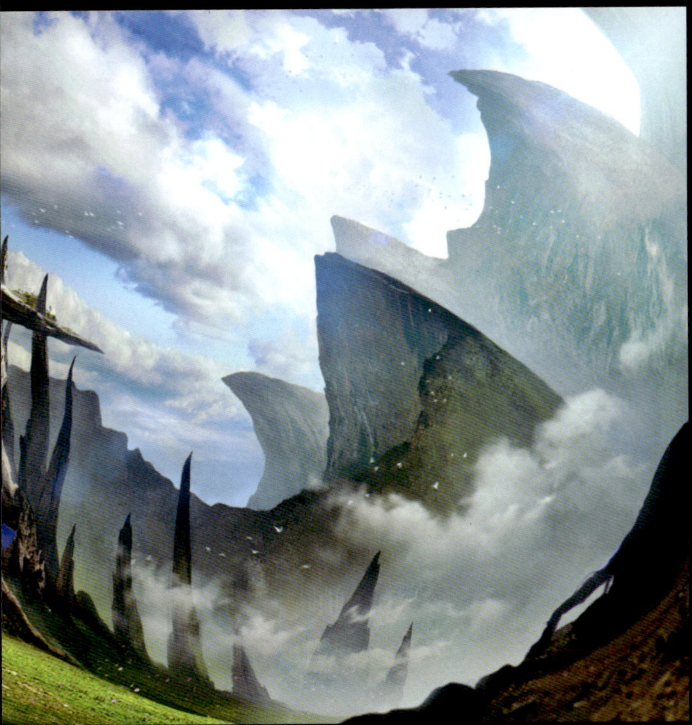

Home
Blender, Photoshop
Fabien Weibel, SWITZERLAND
[above left]

In the Alley
Photoshop
Donglu Yu, CANADA
[above]

Waiting for Spring
Photoshop
Lina Karp, RUSSIA
[left]

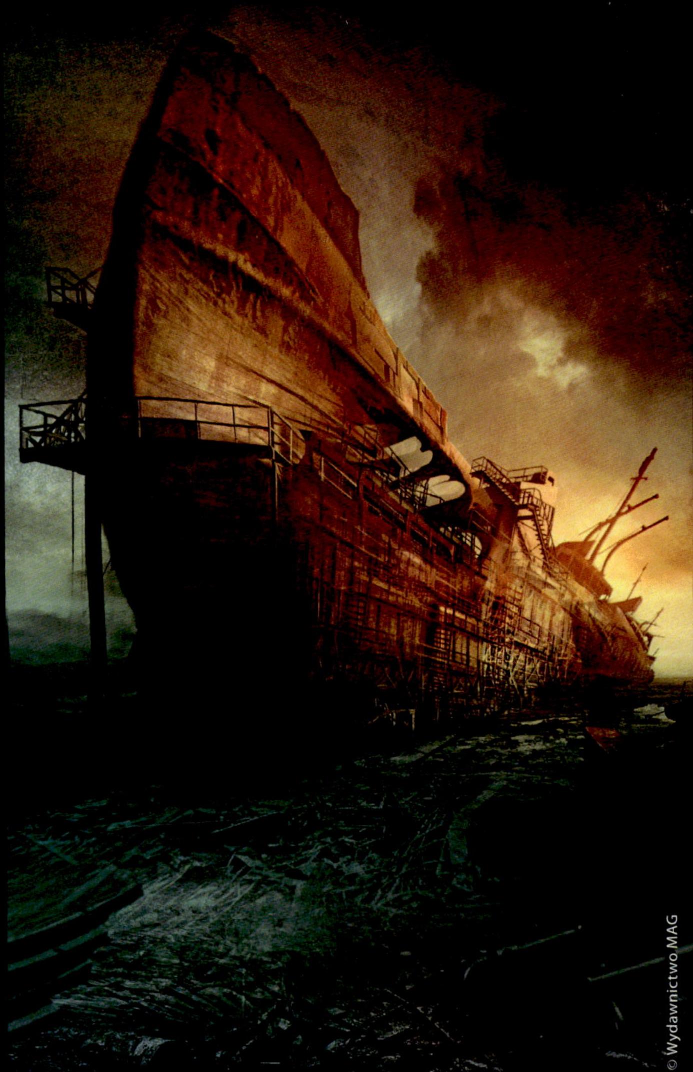

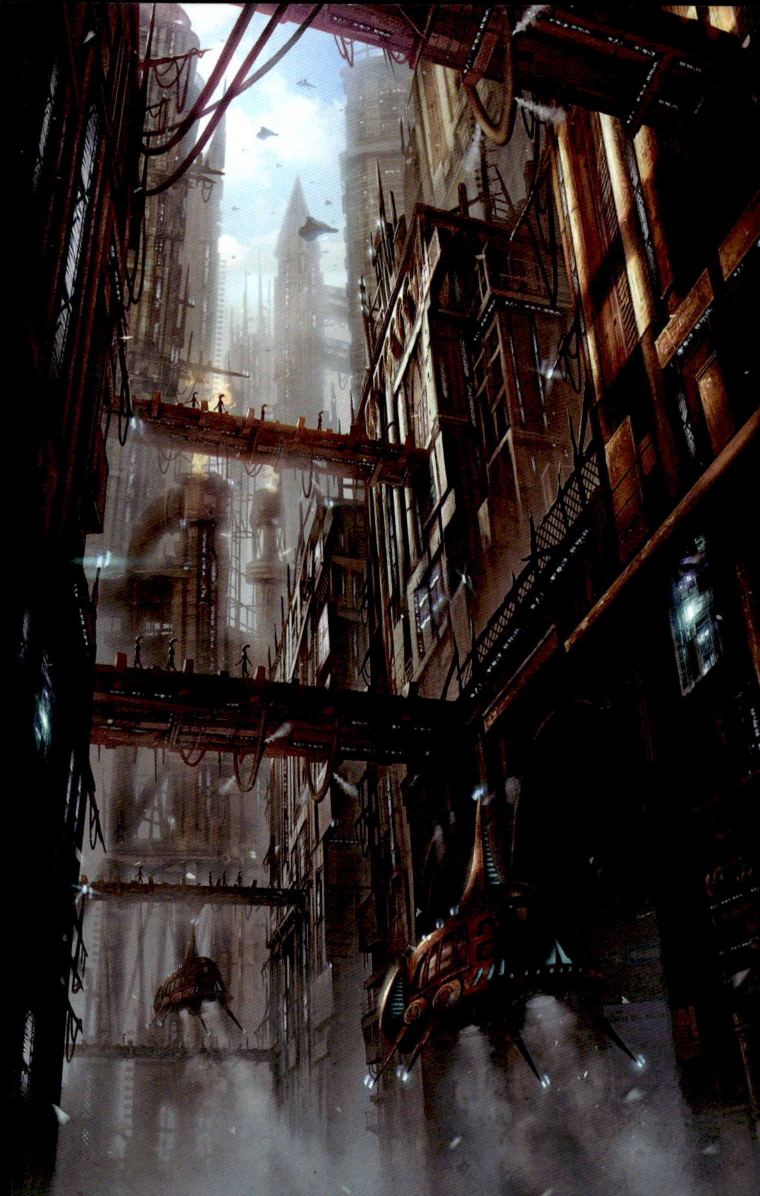

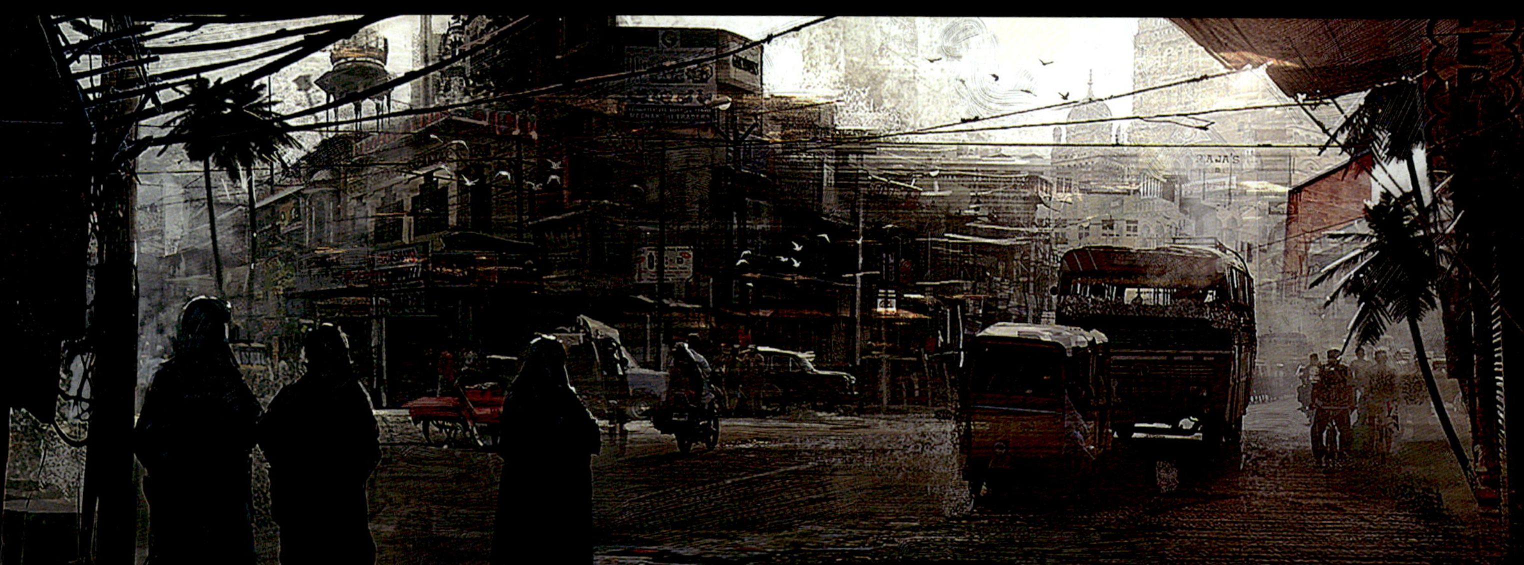

Wreck
PhotoPaint
Client: MAG Publishing
Tomasz Maronski, POLAND

City of Steam
Photoshop
ZEZ Zhaoenze, CHINA
[top right]

Street View
Photoshop
Donglu Yu, CANADA
[above]

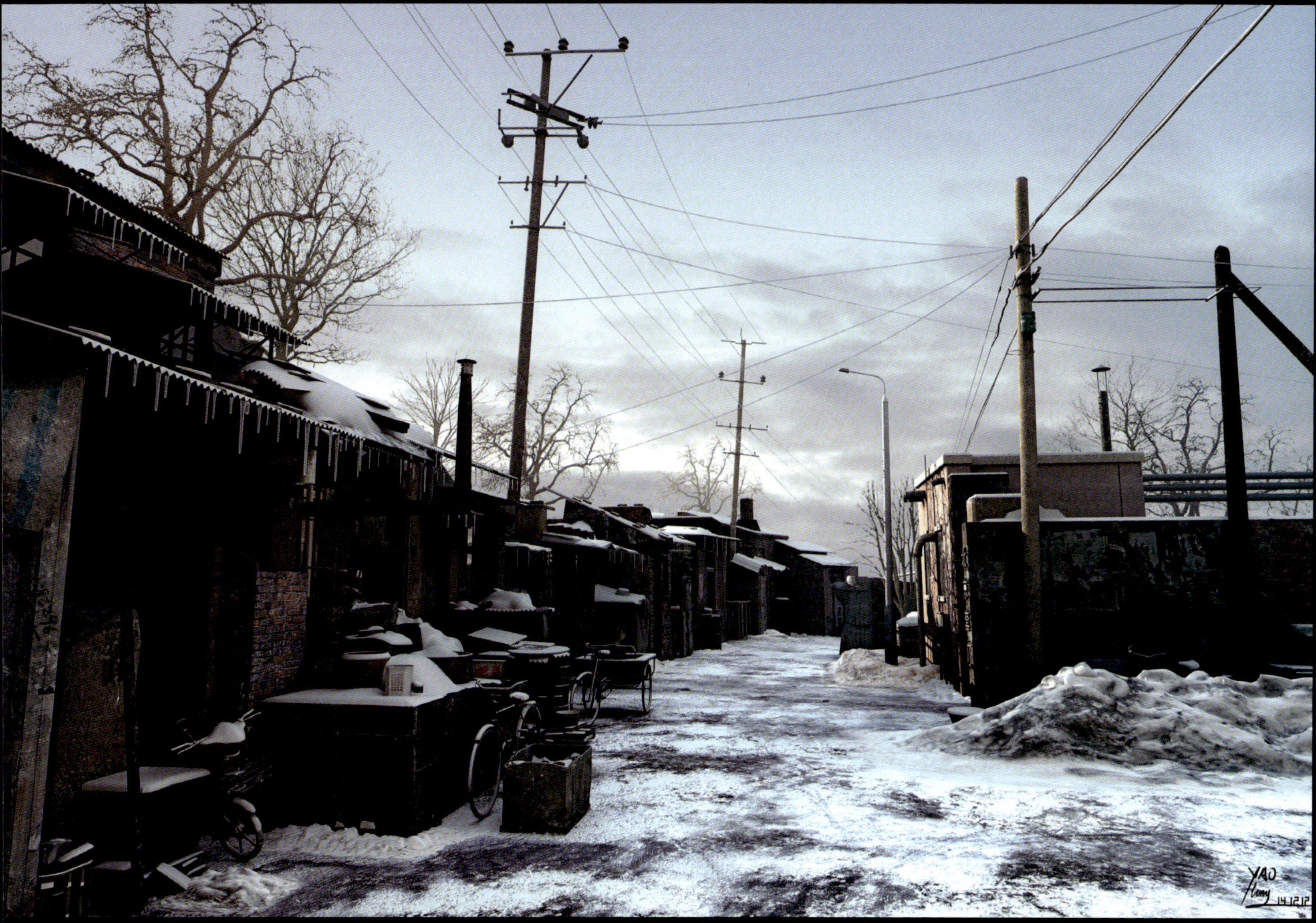

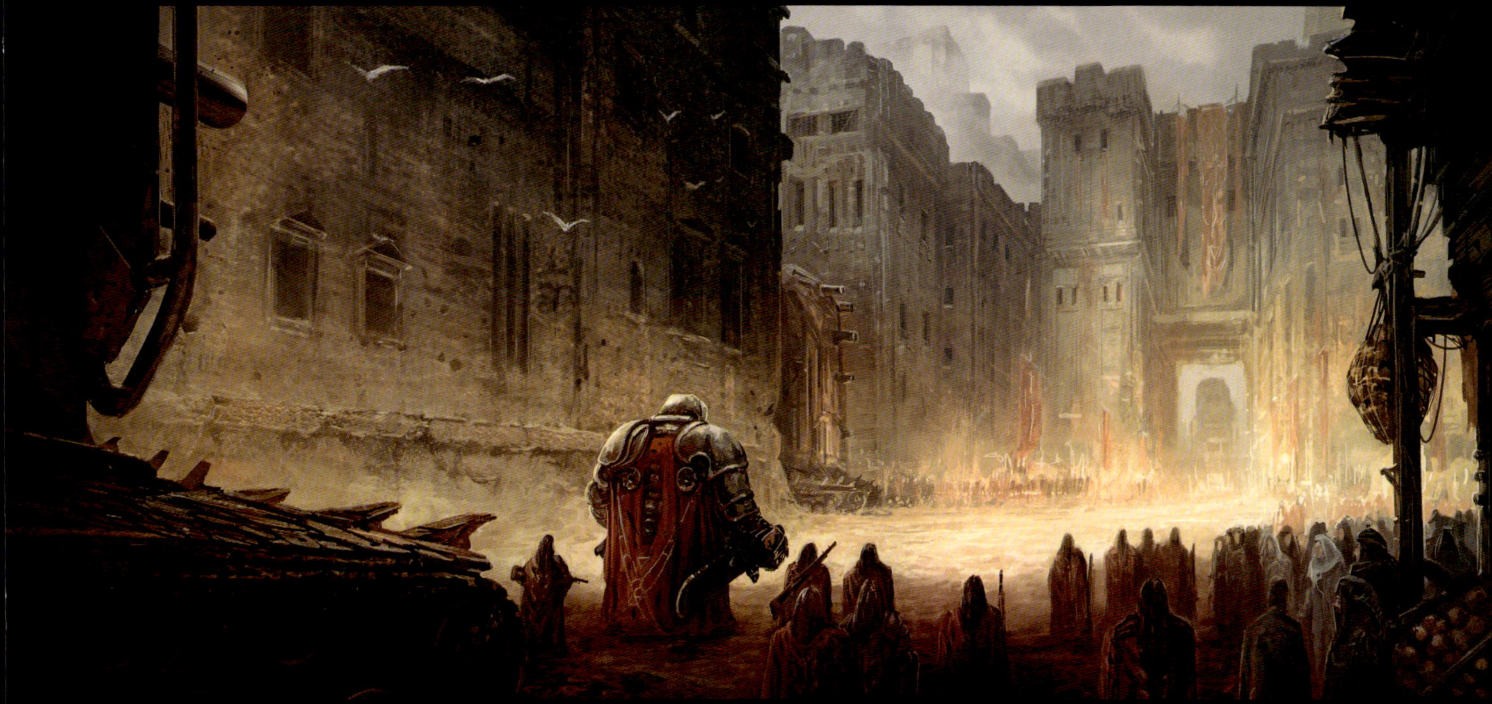

Winter Solstice
Maya, Mudbox, Photoshop

Marching Off
Photoshop

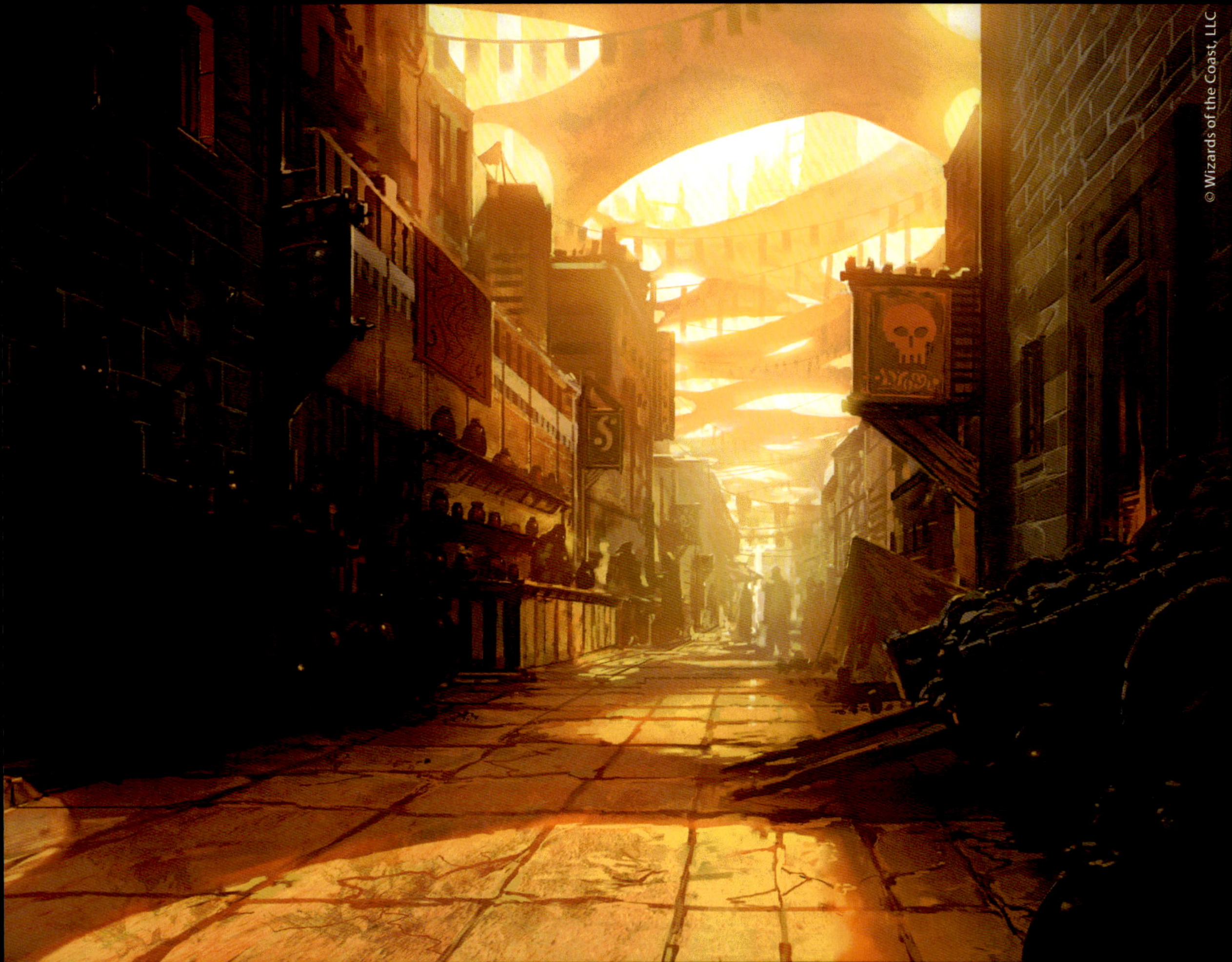

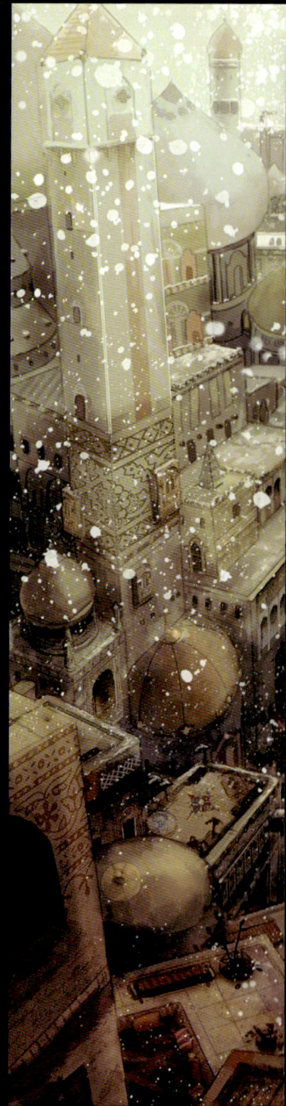

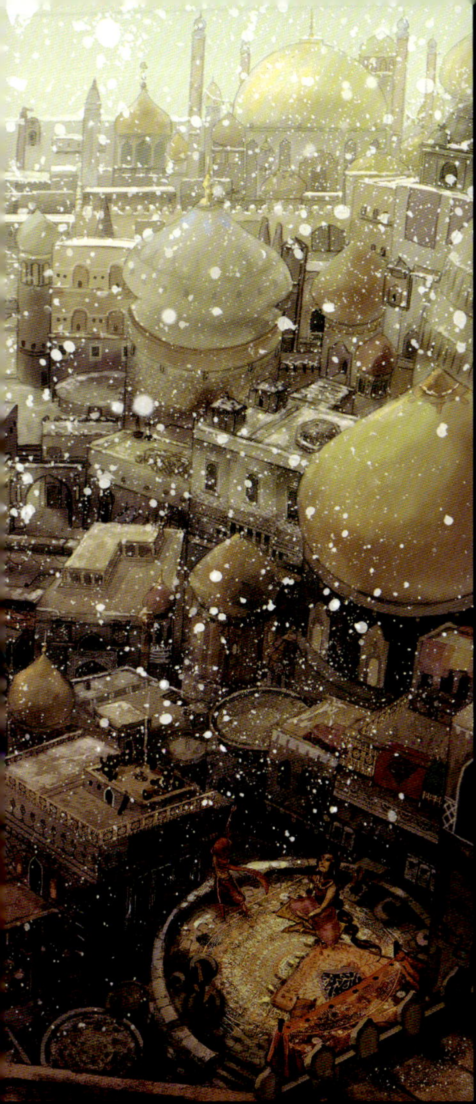

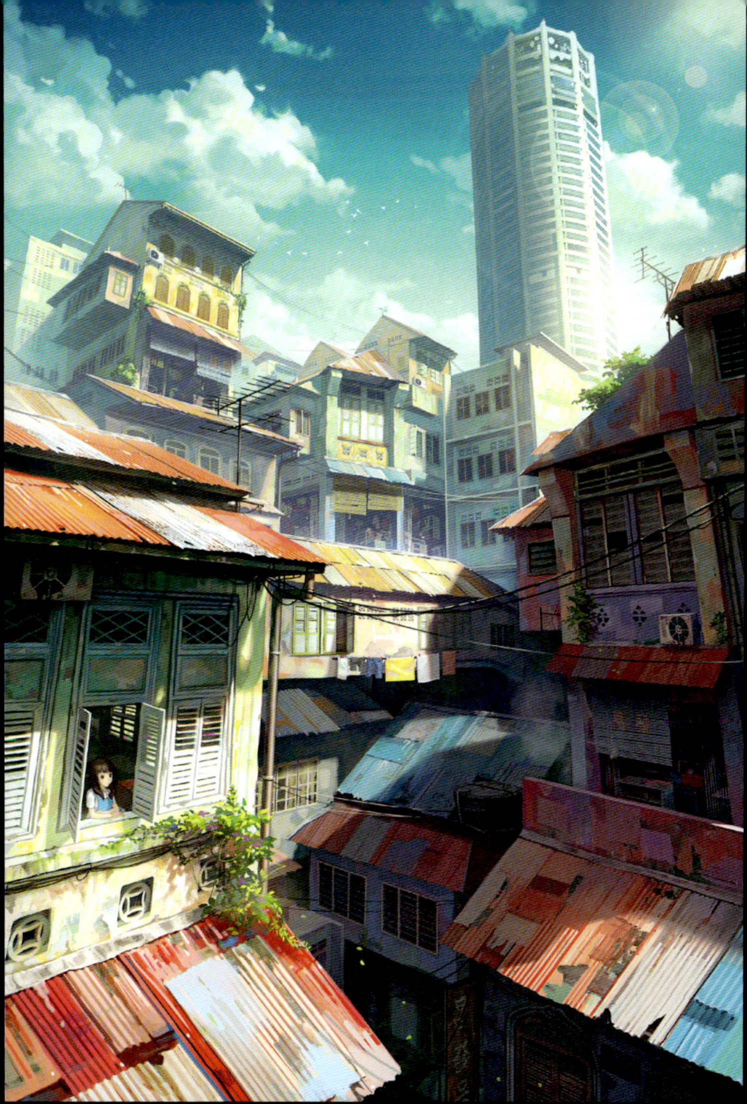

Tin Street Market
Photoshop
Client: Wizards of the Coast, LLC
Noah Bradley, USA
[facing page top left]

Snowfall
Photoshop
Sarah Webb, USA
[top center]

Fantasy Penang
Photoshop, SketchUp
Fei Giap Chong, MALAYSIA
[left]

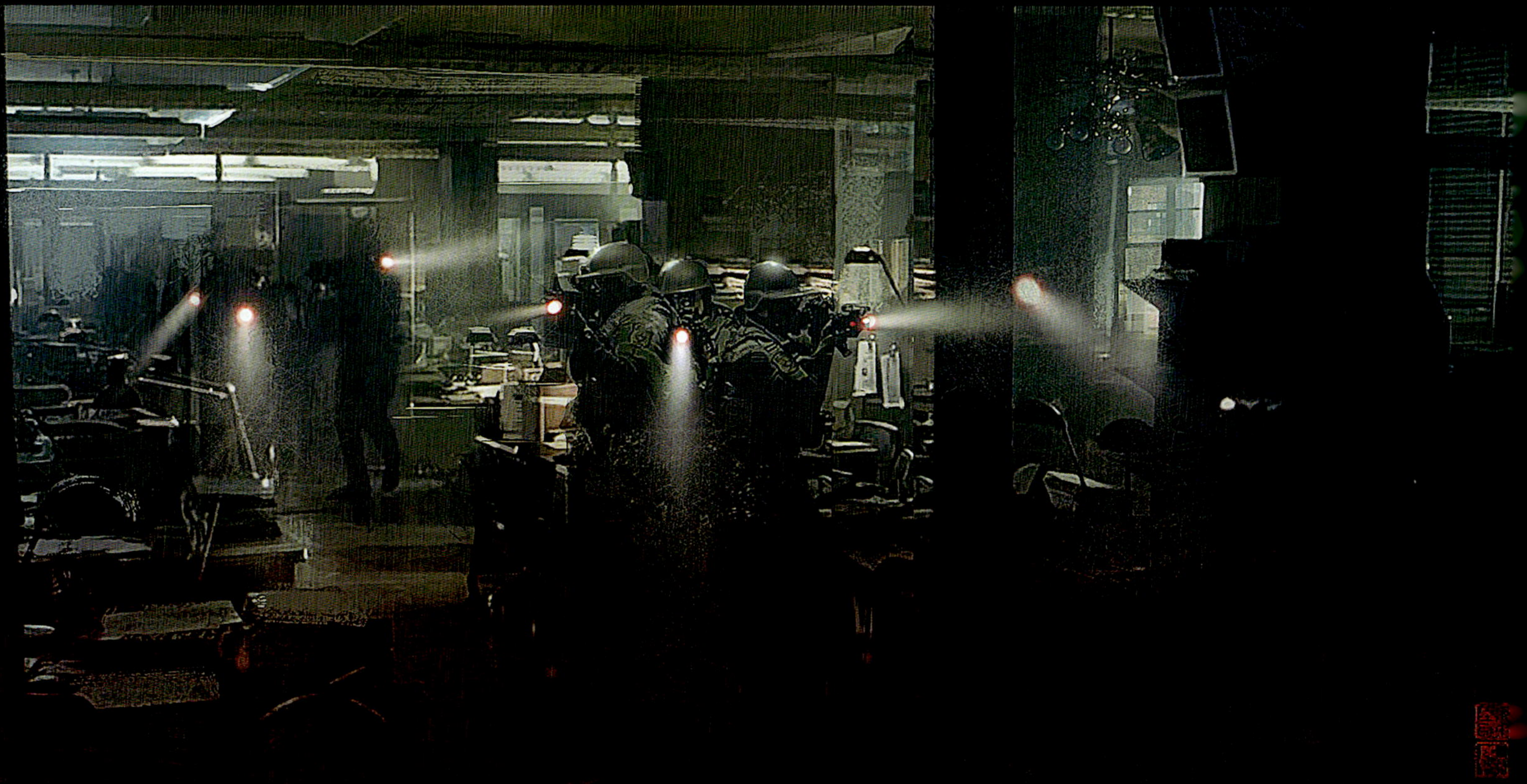

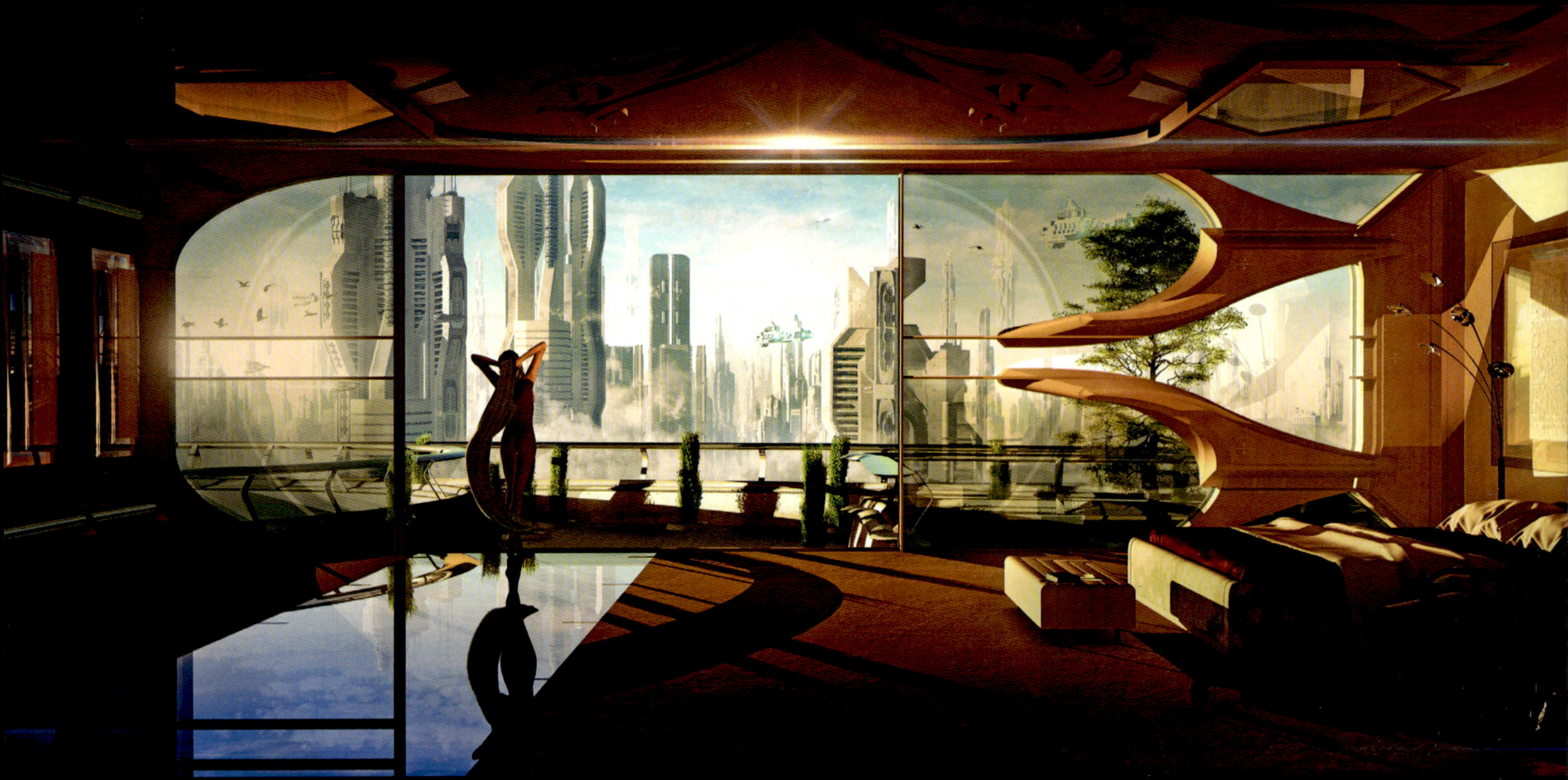

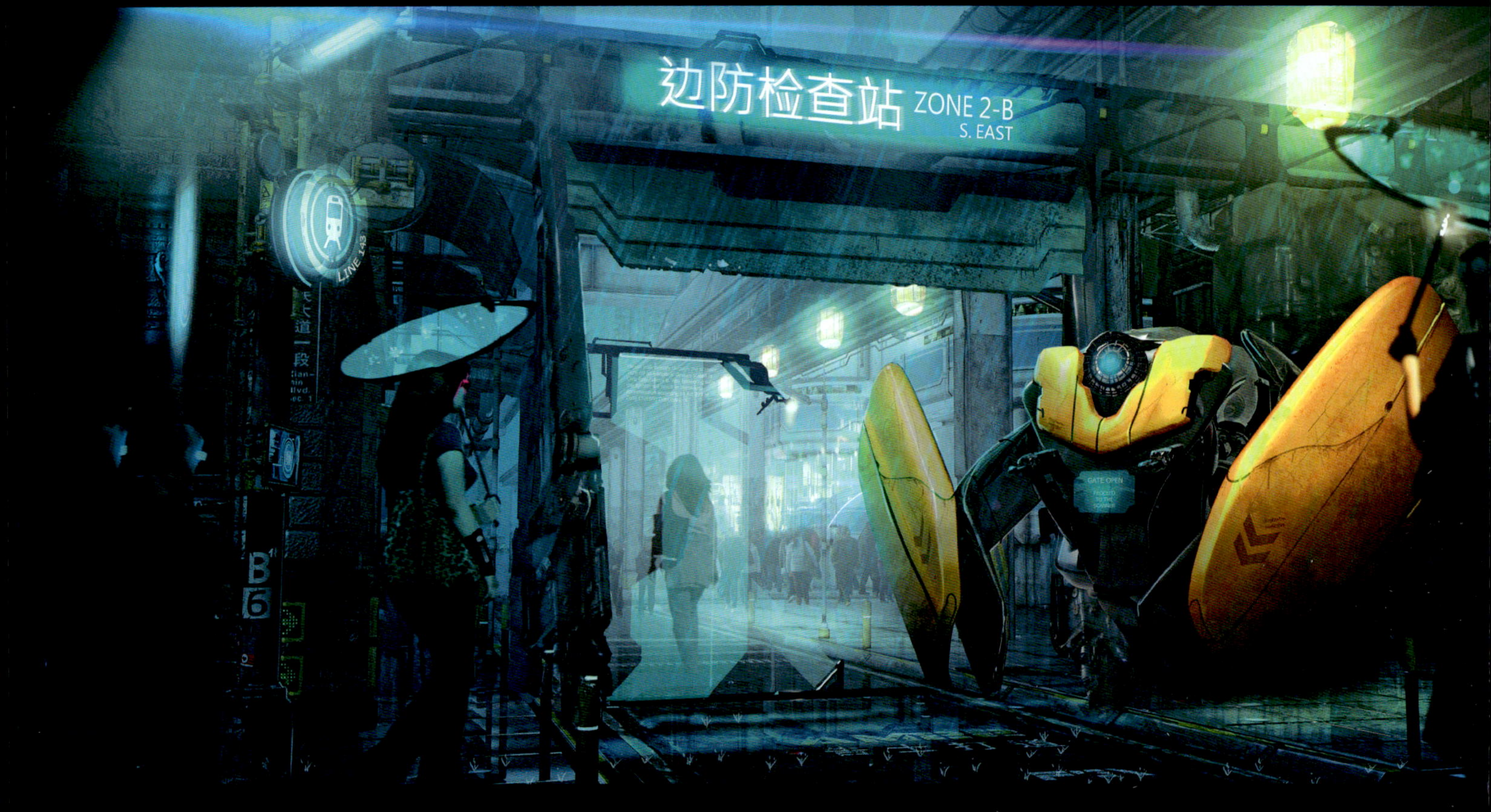

Room with a View
Vue Esprit, Photoshop
Christian 'Tigaer' Hecker, GERMANY
[top]

Checkpoint
Maya, Photoshop
Adam Kuczek, CHINA
[above]

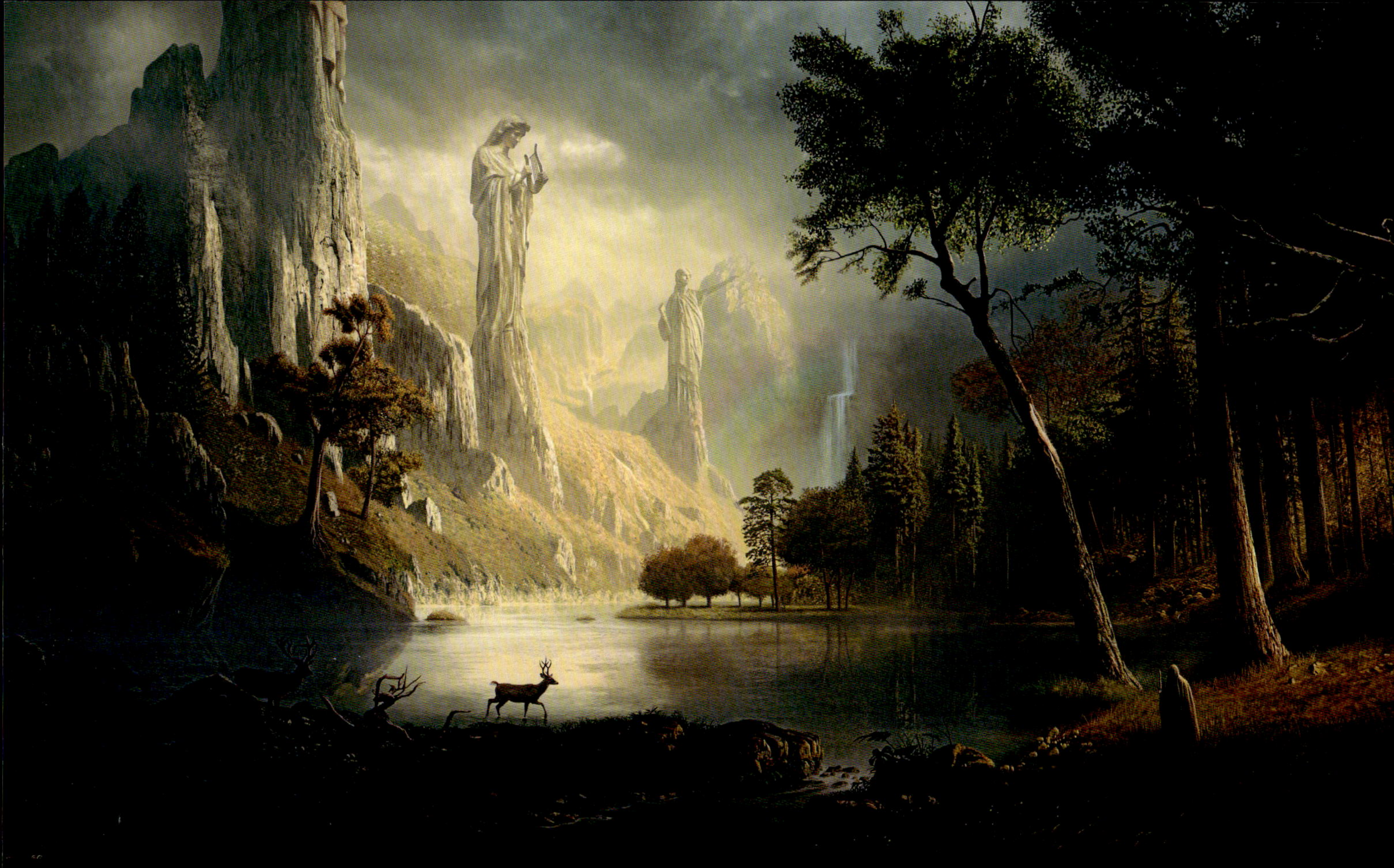

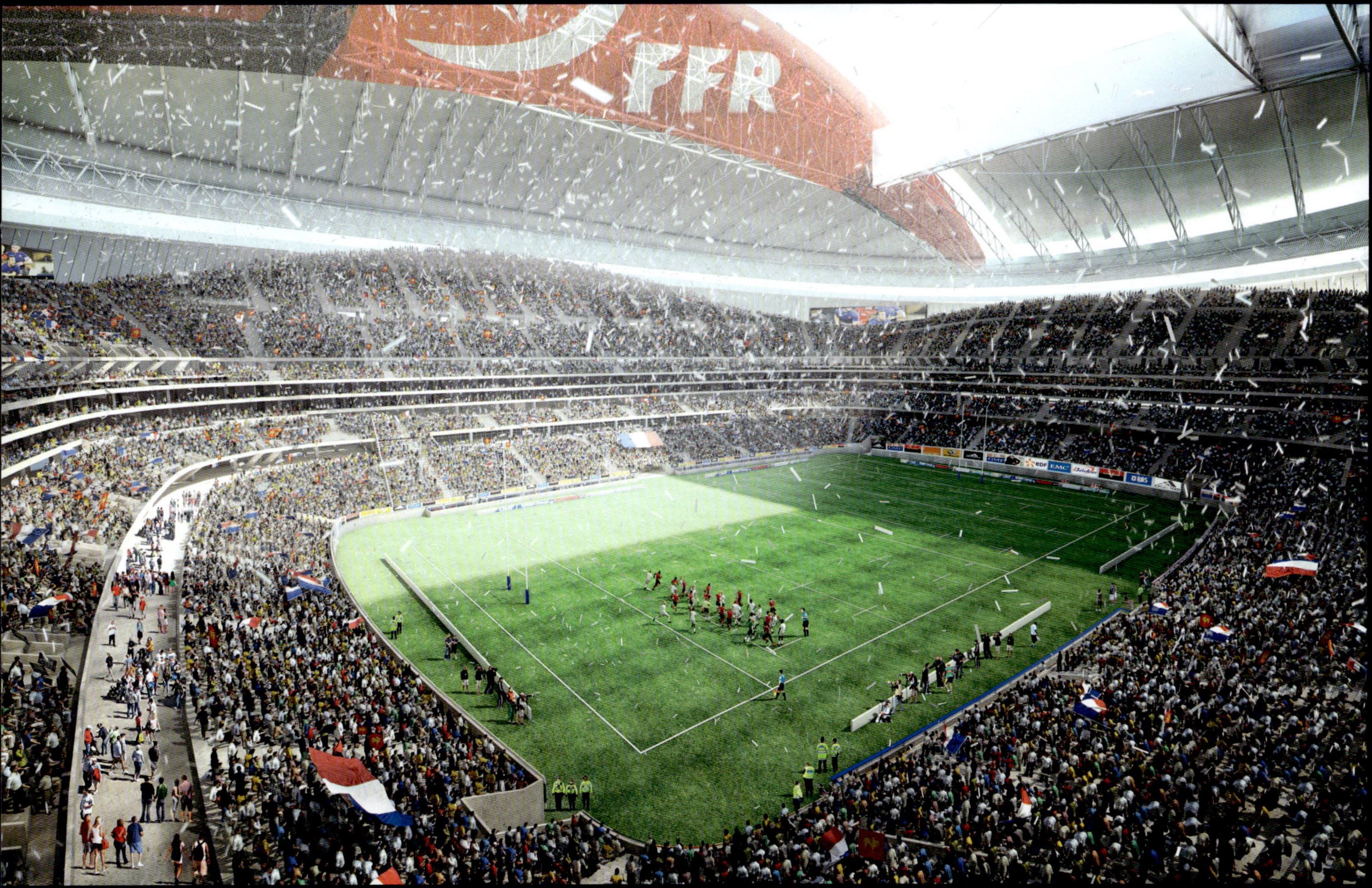

Solace
Photoshop
Inspired by Albert Bierstadt
Sarel Theron, SOUTH AFRICA

Stadium Bowl
3ds Max, mental ray, Photoshop
Judson Rogers and Nethra Ram Mohan, HKS Architects Inc., USA
[above]

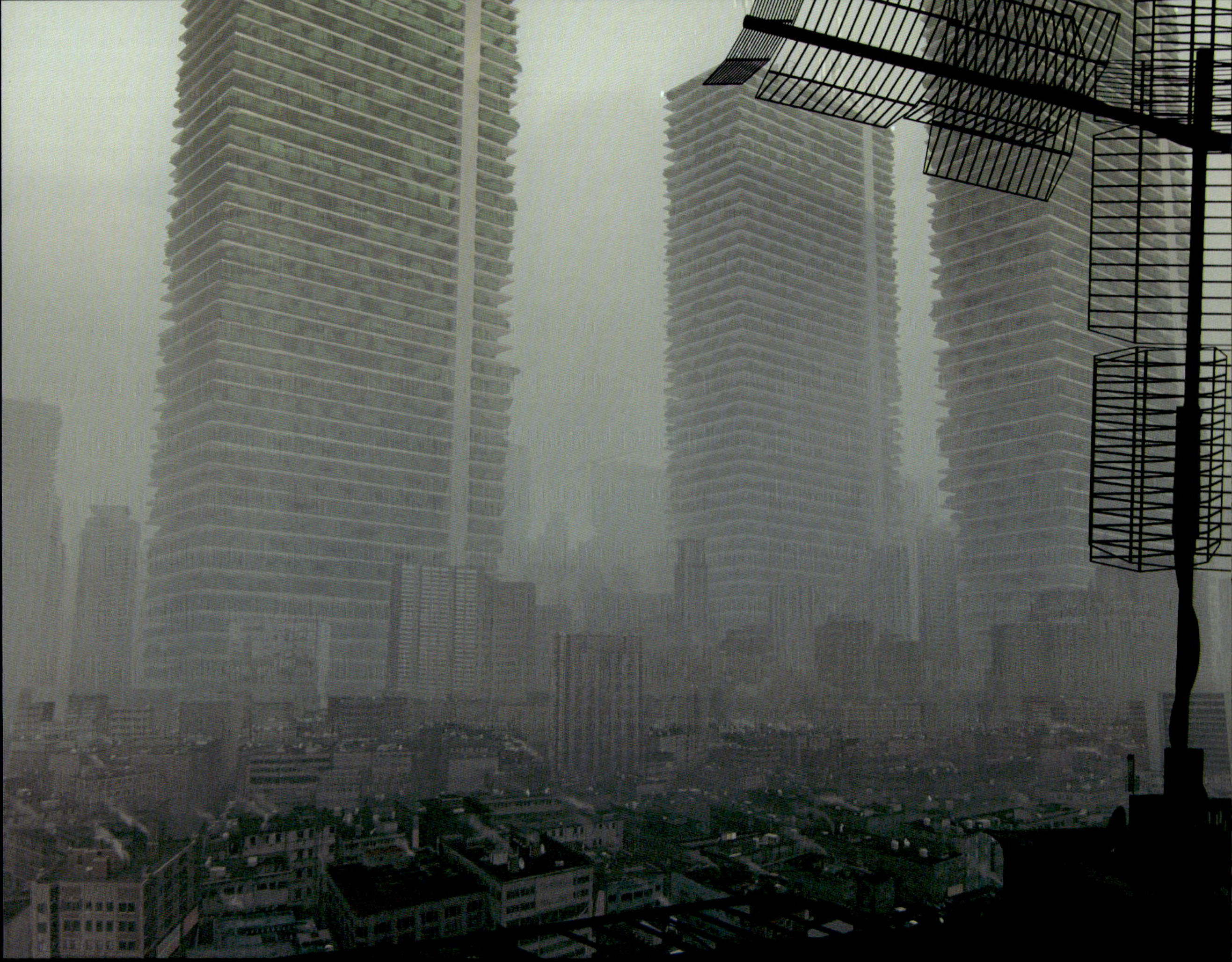

Smog
Photoshop,
3ds Max
Matus Garaj,
CZECH REPUBLIC
[right]

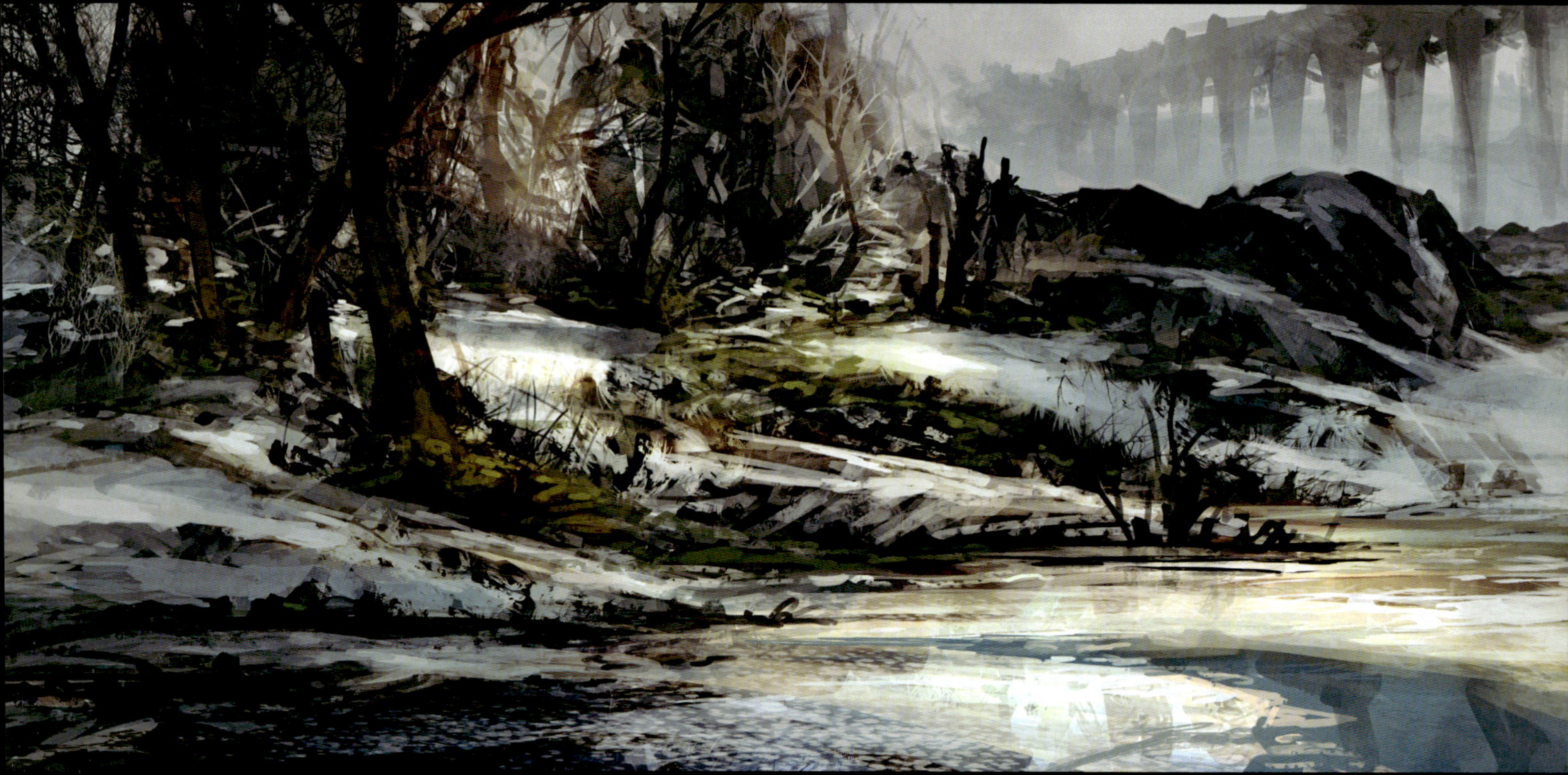

Icy Clearing
Photoshop
Lennart Verhoeff, NETHERLANDS
[above]

Clock Tower
Photoshop, 3ds Max
Howard Schechtman, USA
[facing page top right]

Agartha Discovered
Photoshop, Painter
Jeremy Vickery, USA
[facing page center]

The Race
3ds Max, V-Ray, ZBrush, LightWave 3D
Anders Ehrenborg, NEW ZEALAND
[facing page bottom]

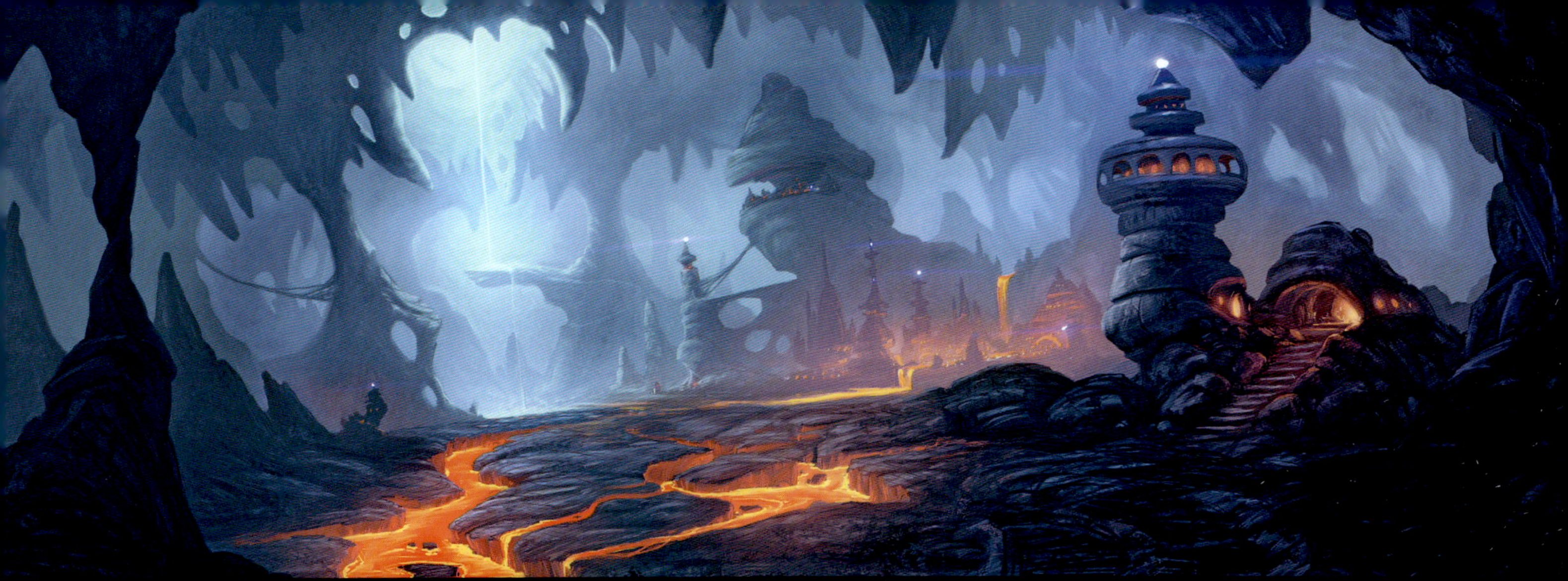

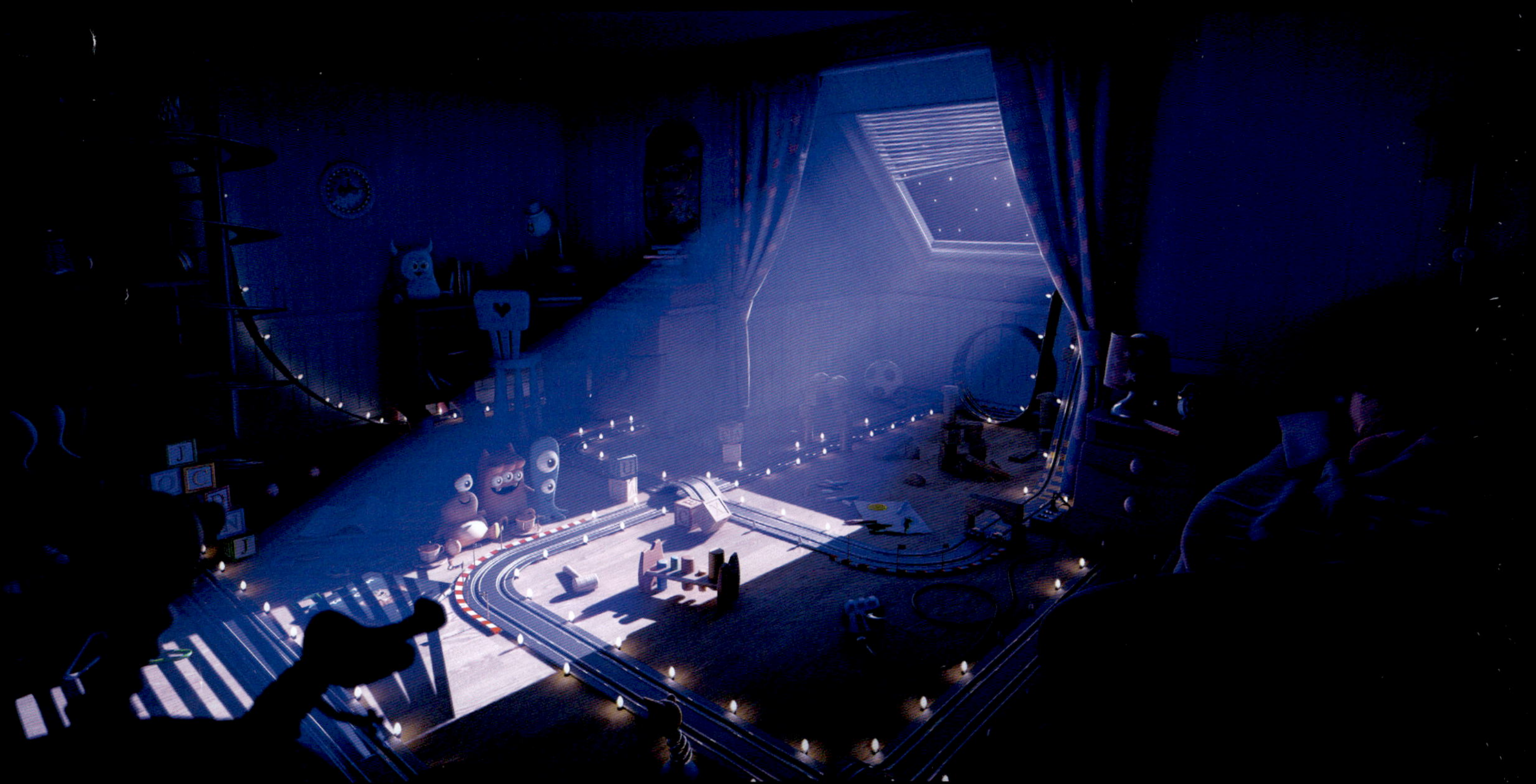

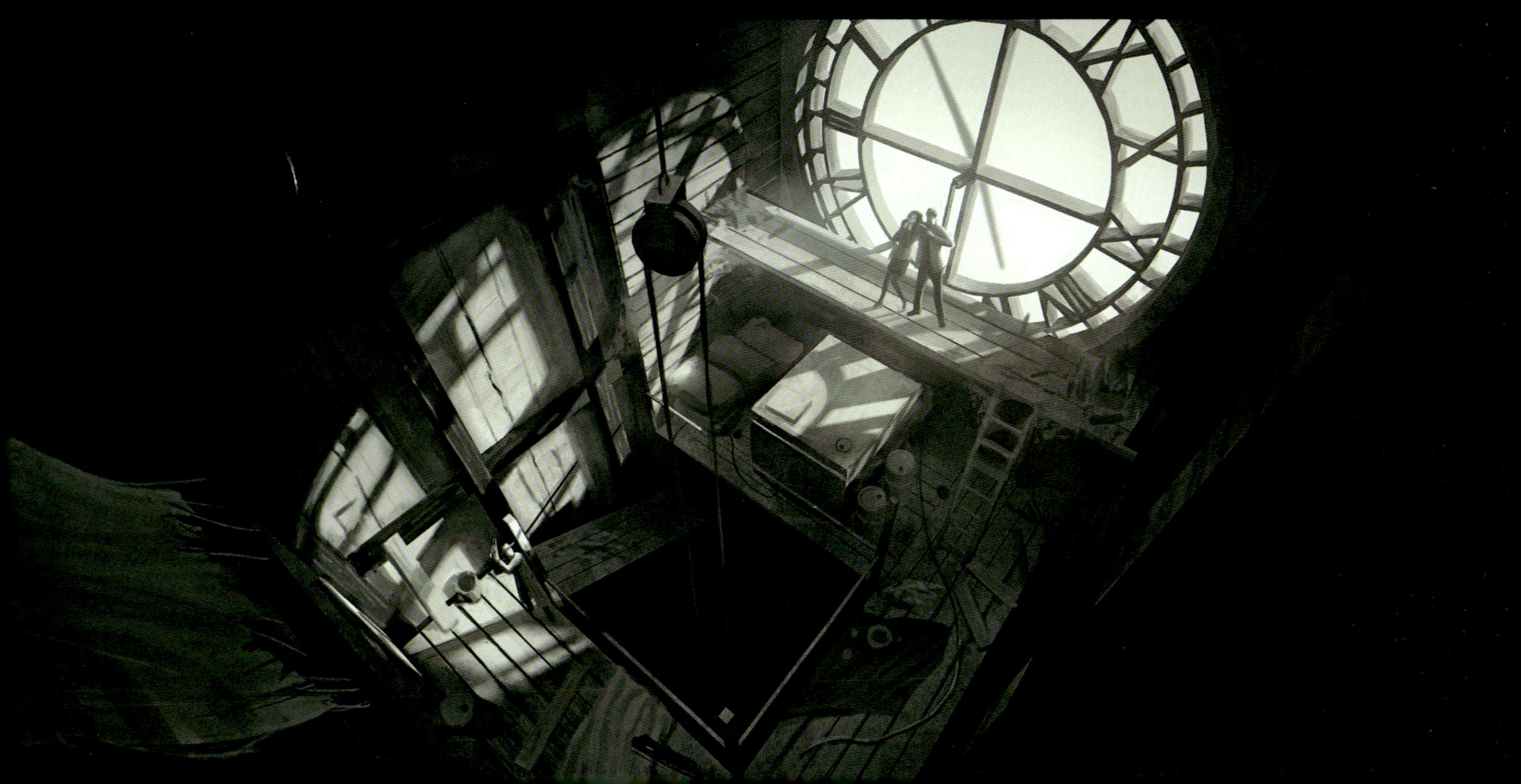

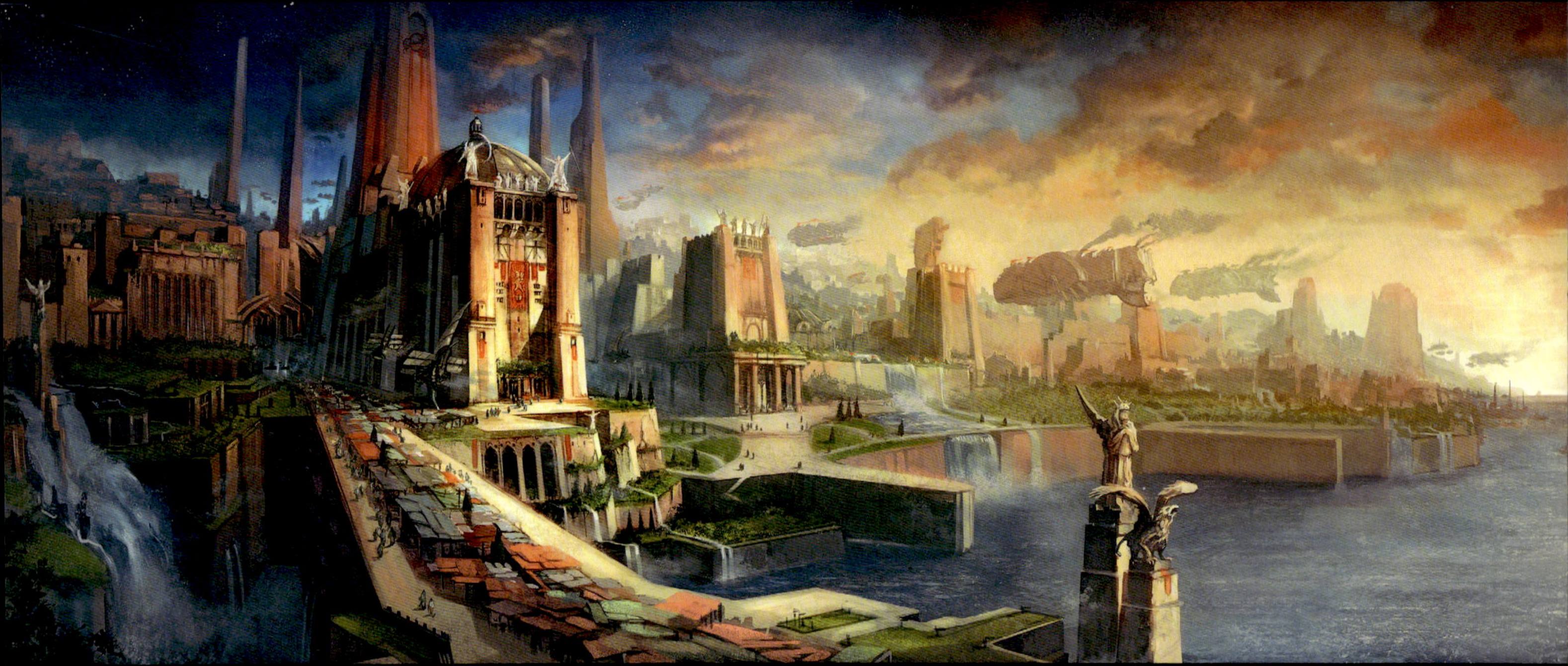

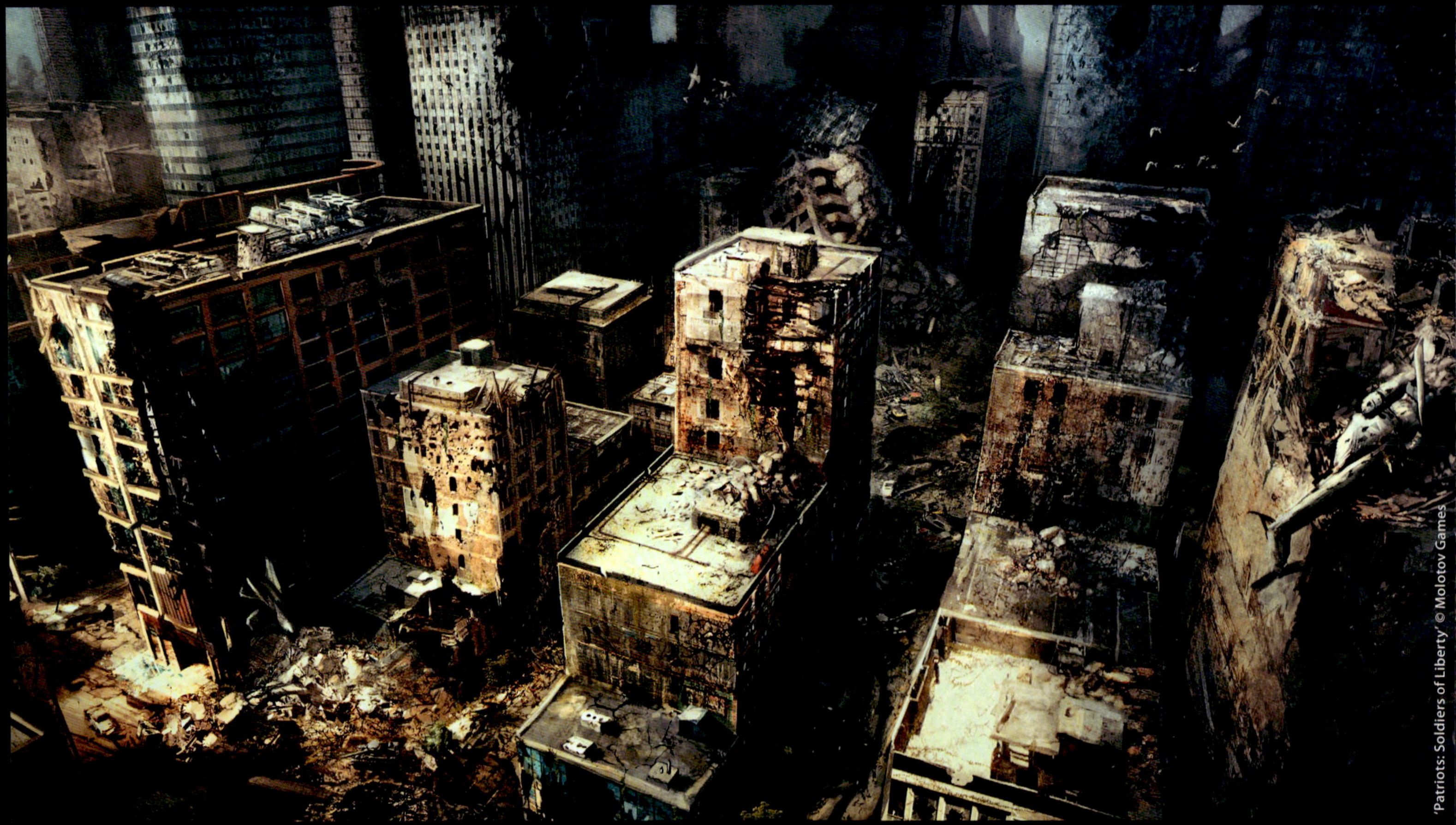

Bancur City
Photoshop
Flavio Bolla, SWITZERLAND
[top]

Patriots: Soldiers of Liberty (Chicago city)
Photoshop
Client: Molotov Games
Jesus De leon, MEXICO
[above]

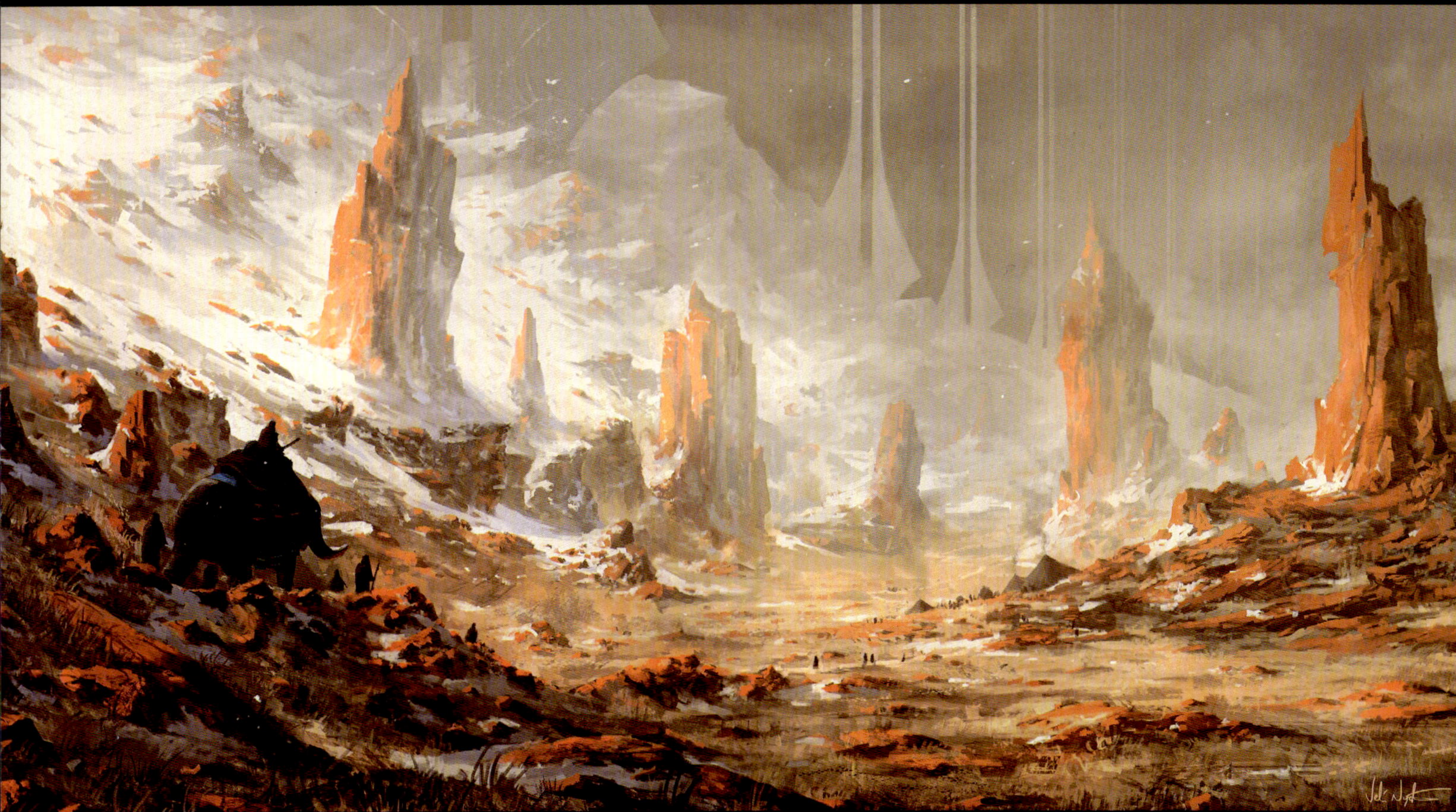

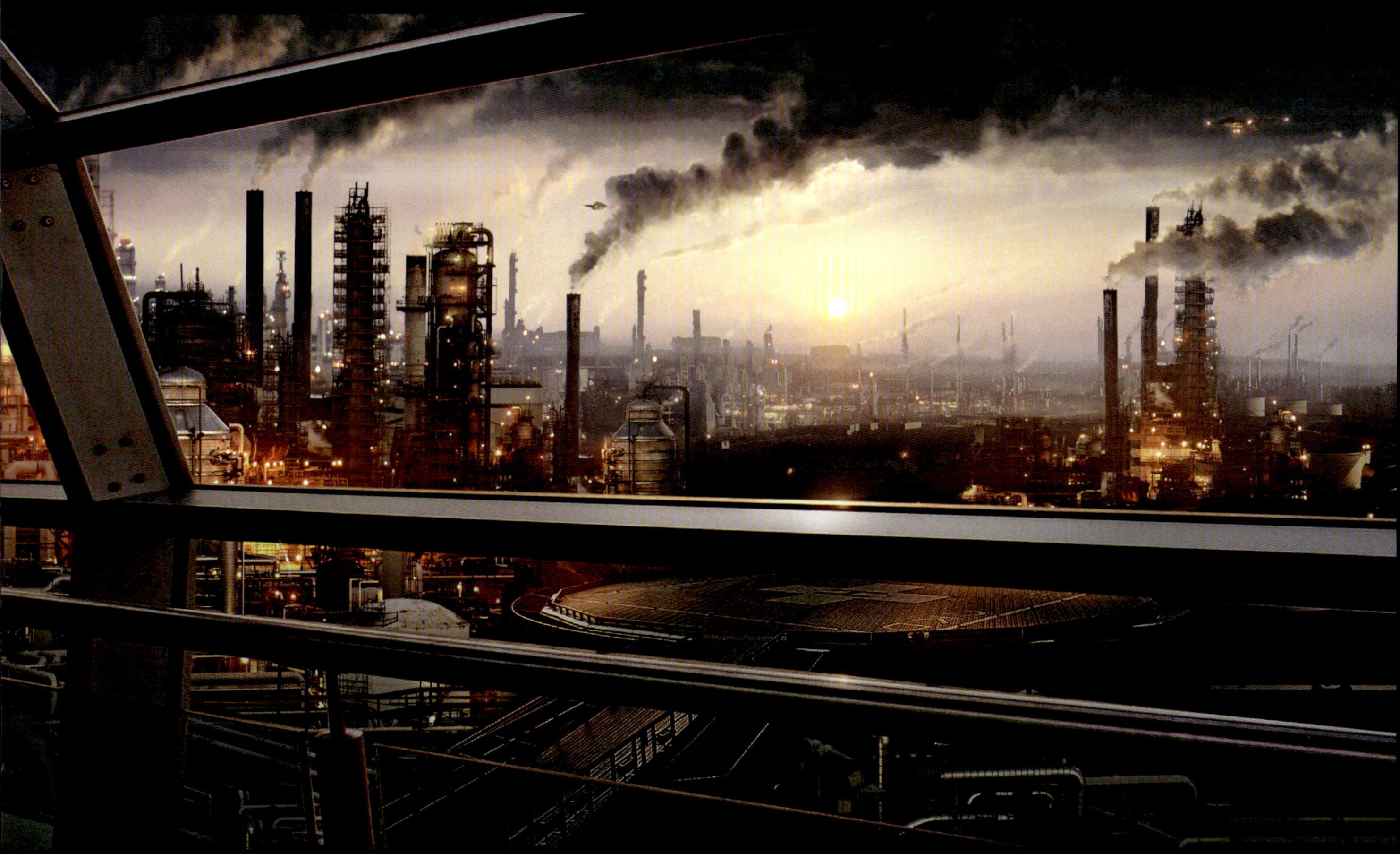

Journey
Photoshop
Veli Nyström, FINLAND
[top]

Landing Pad
Photoshop
Gordon Oscar, CANADA
[above]

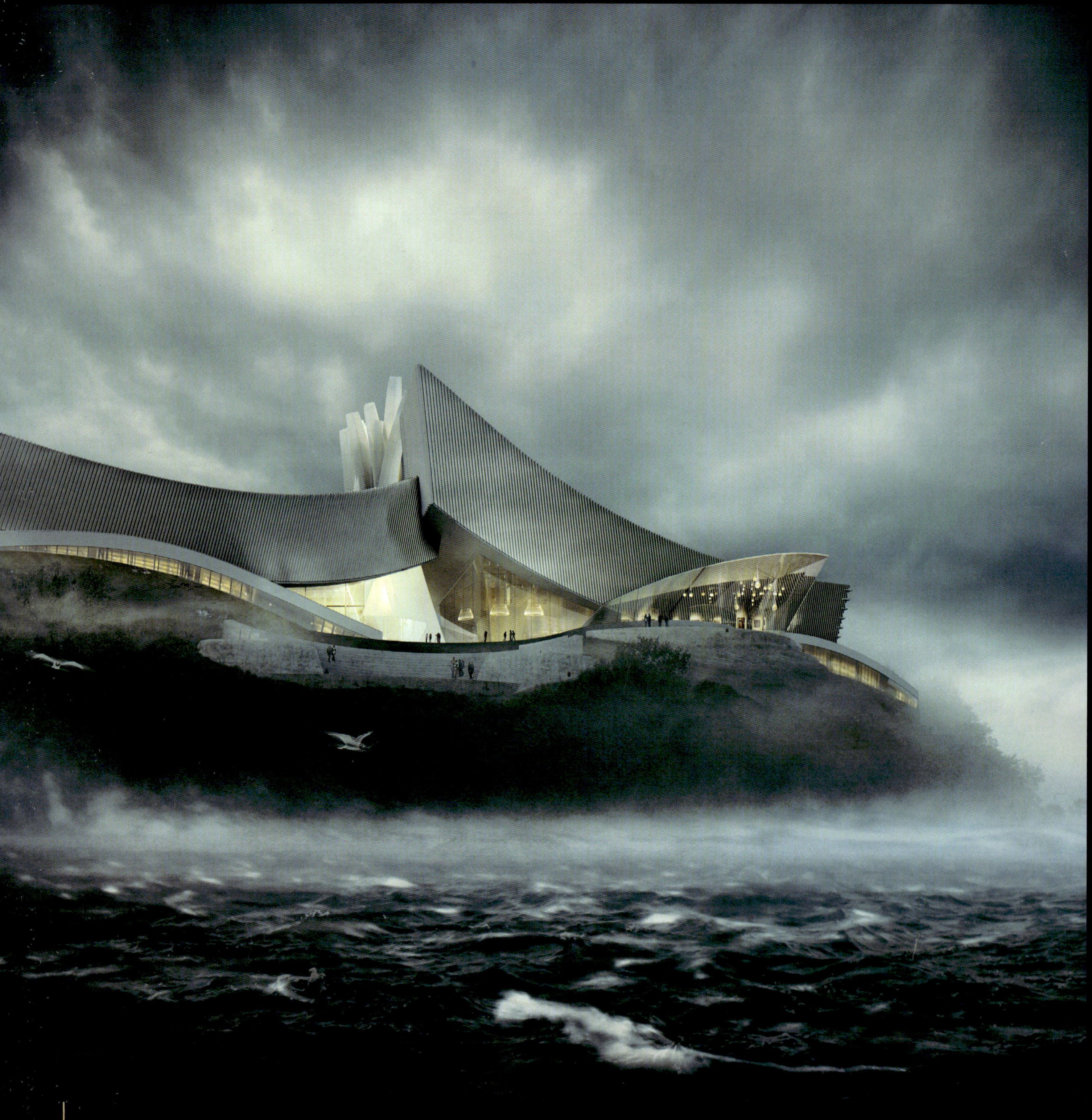

Excellence
Architecture (Exterior)

Crashing Waves
3ds Max, Photoshop, V-Ray
Client: Form4inc Studio
Tomek Miksa, POLAND

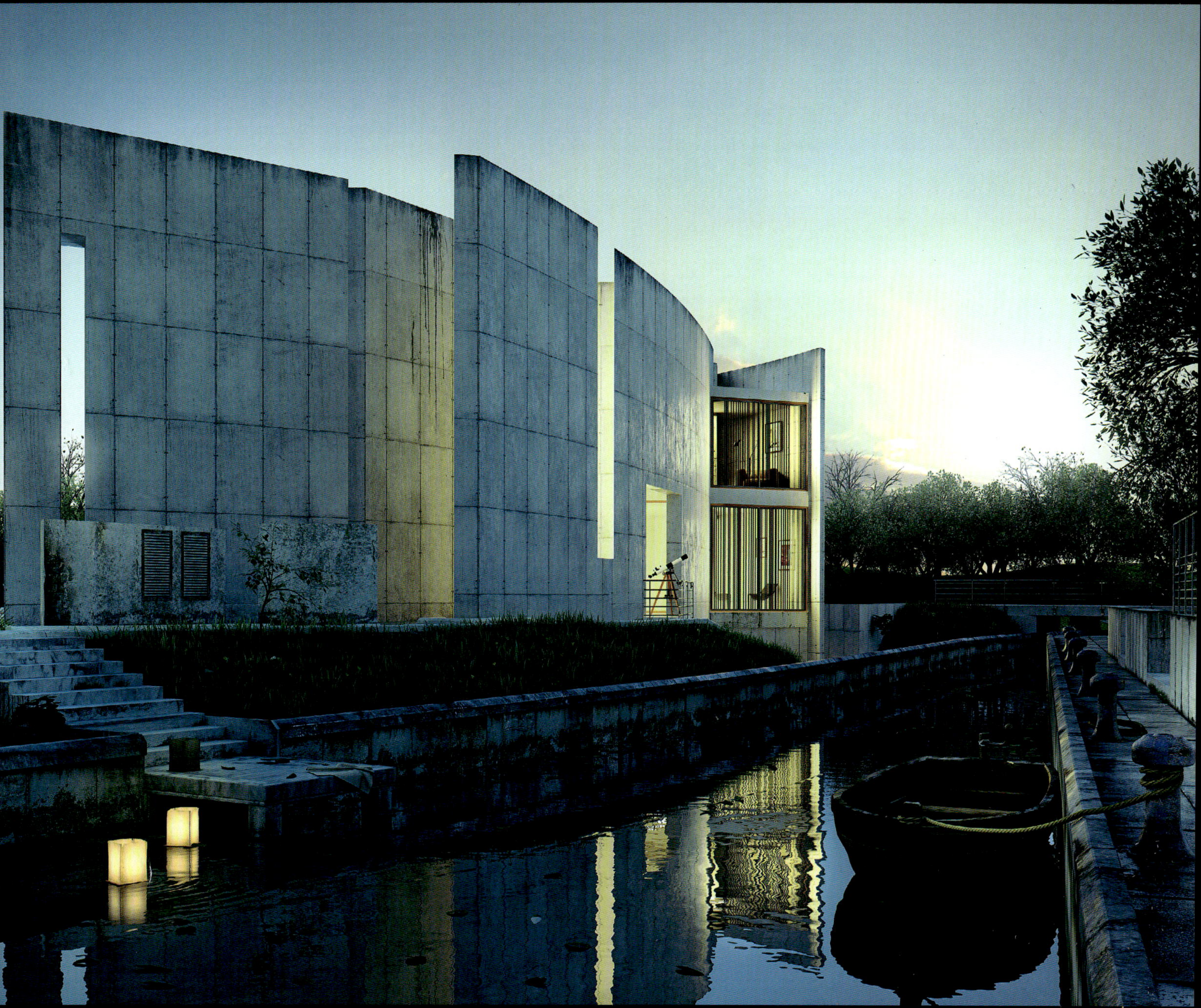

GH House
3ds Max, Photoshop, V-Ray
Anton Cherenko, UKRAINE

Master

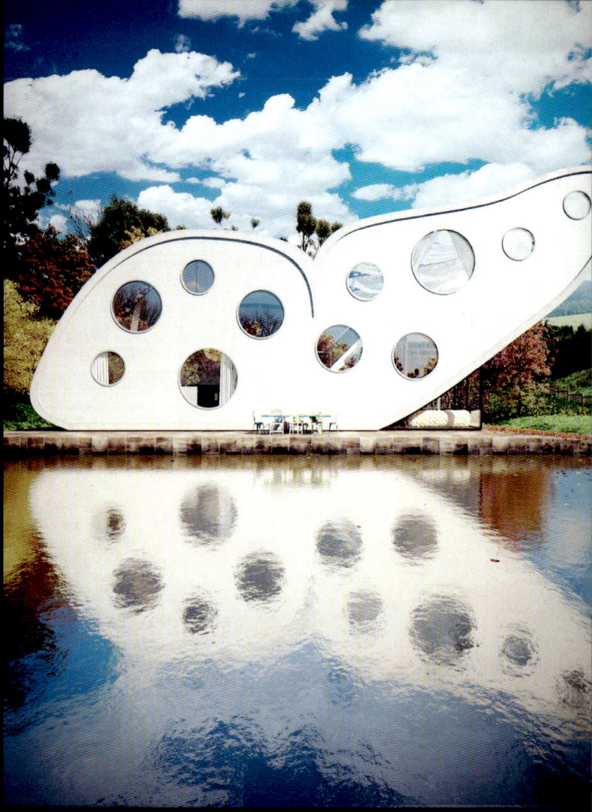

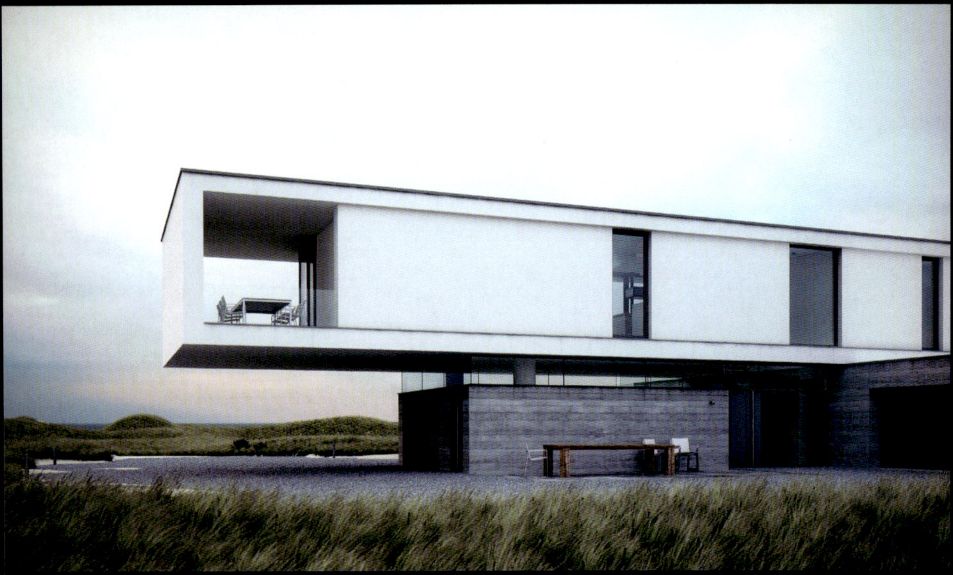

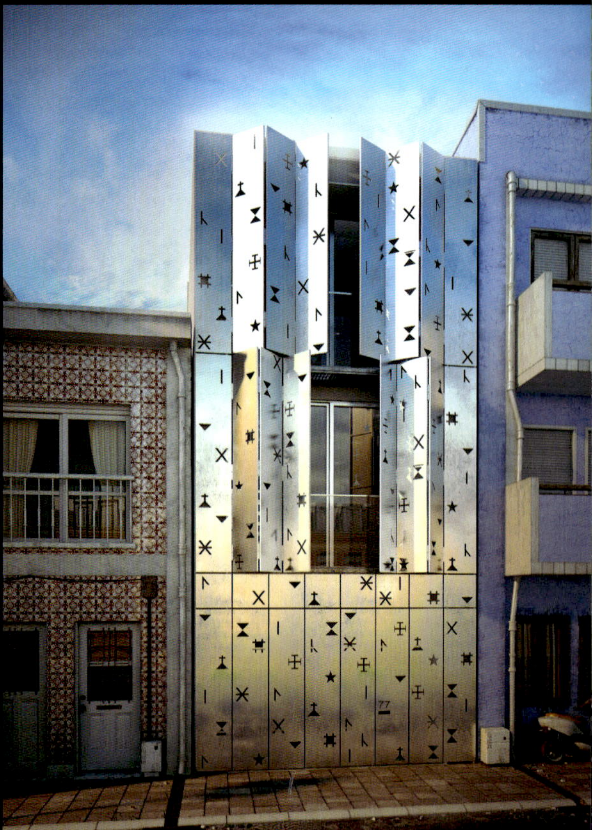

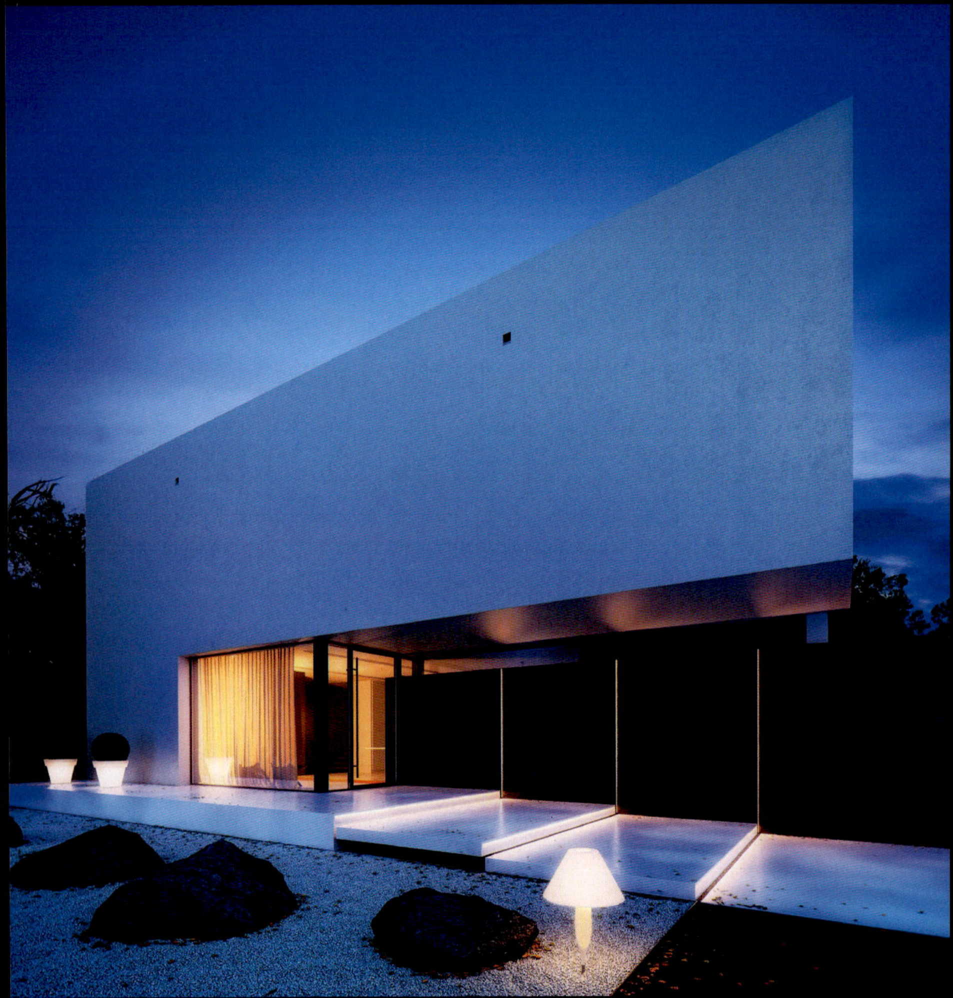

Butterfly: Front Lake
3ds Max, After Effects, V-Ray, Photoshop
Thiago Queiroz Lima, BRAZIL
[top]

House 77
3ds Max, Photoshop, After Effects, V-Ray
Anton Cherenko, UKRAINE
[above]

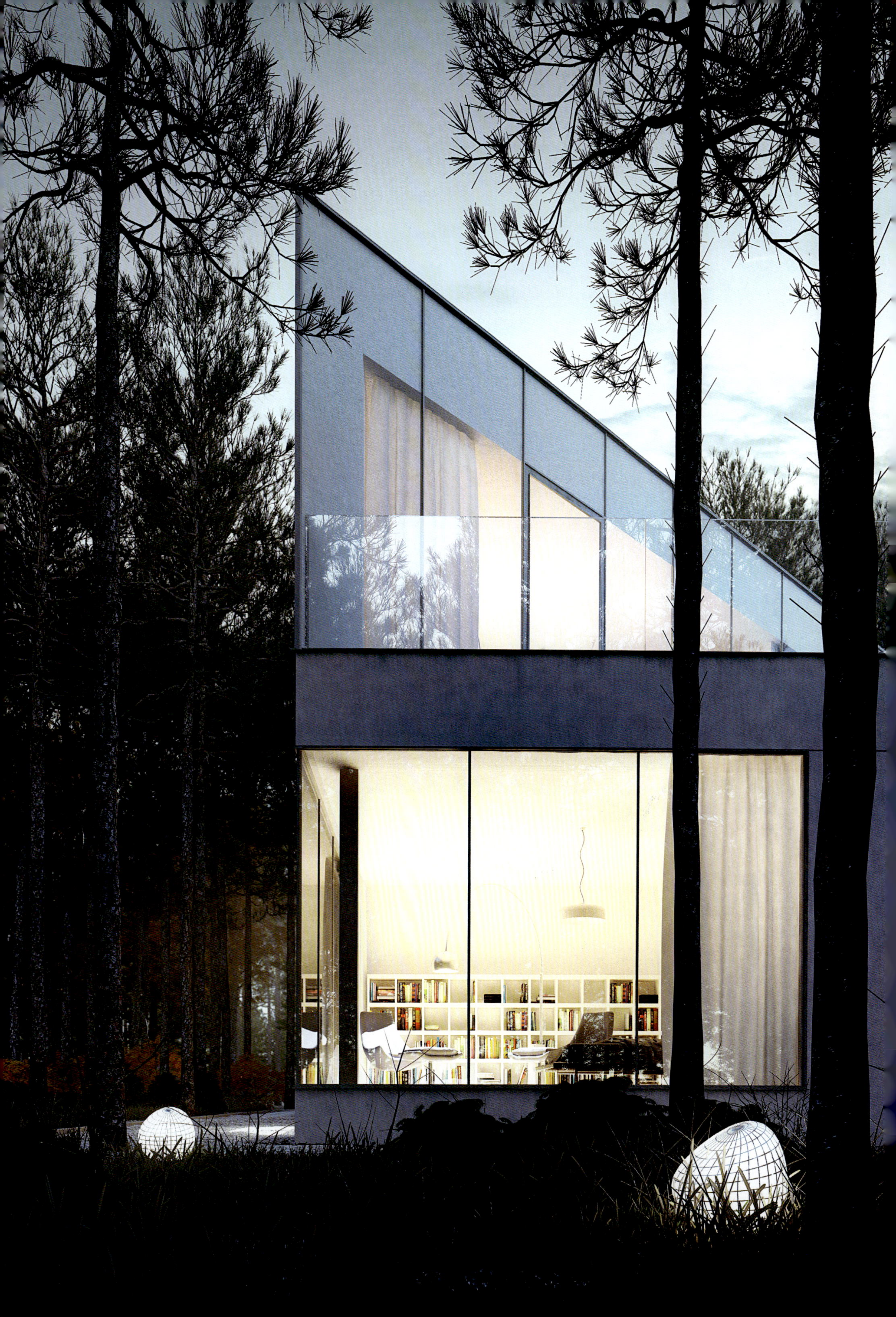

Forest House
ds Max, V-Ray, Photoshop
ndrzej Drawc, Architecture by: Kooperatywwa, Draw a Half-Circle, POLAND

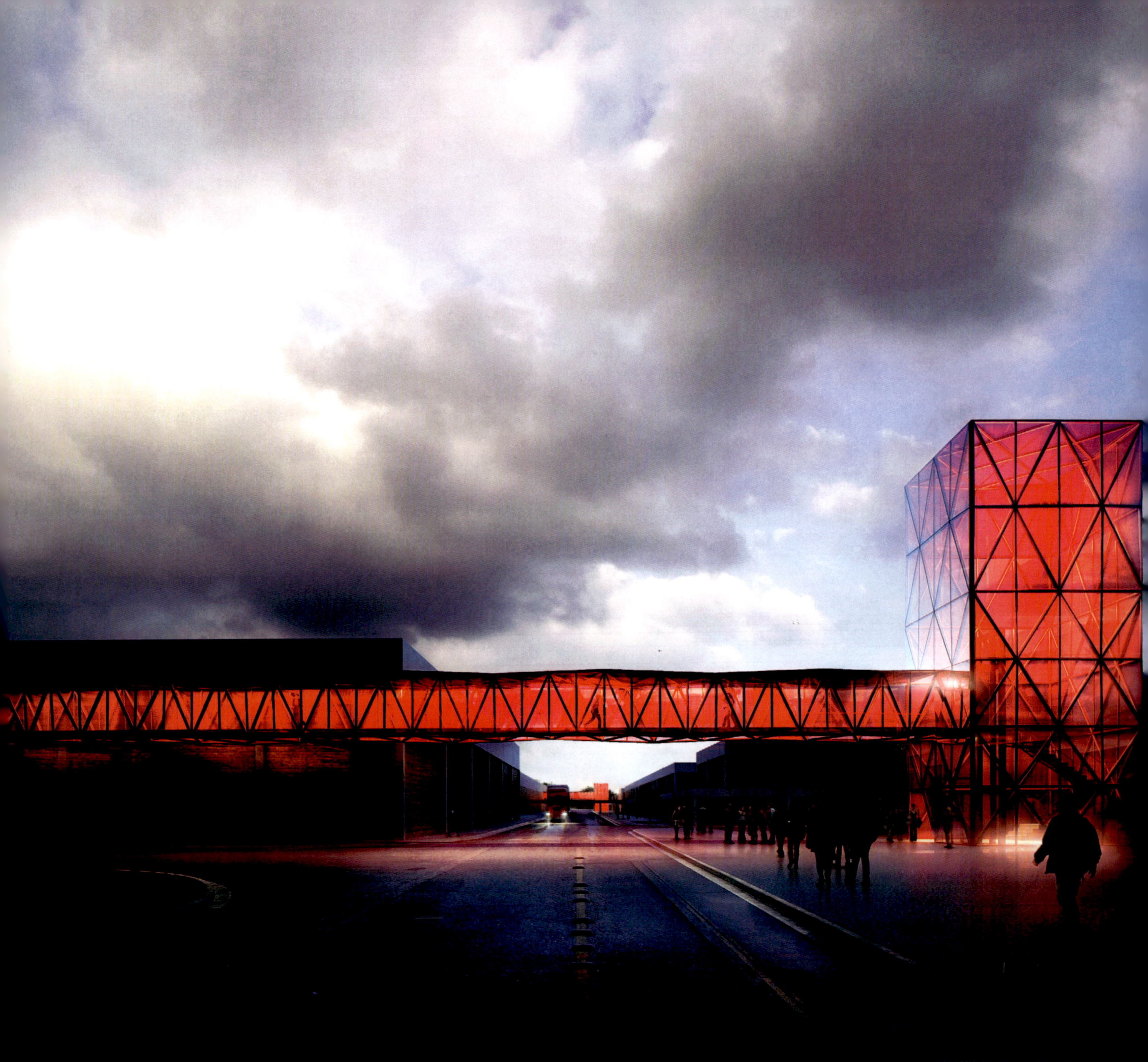

Nestlé Chocolate Museum
AutoCAD, 3ds Max,
V-Ray, Photoshop
Architect: Metro Arquitetos
Associados
Ricardo Canton, BRAZIL
[above]

Crown House
3ds Max, Photoshop, V-Ray
Michał Nowak, POLAND
[right]

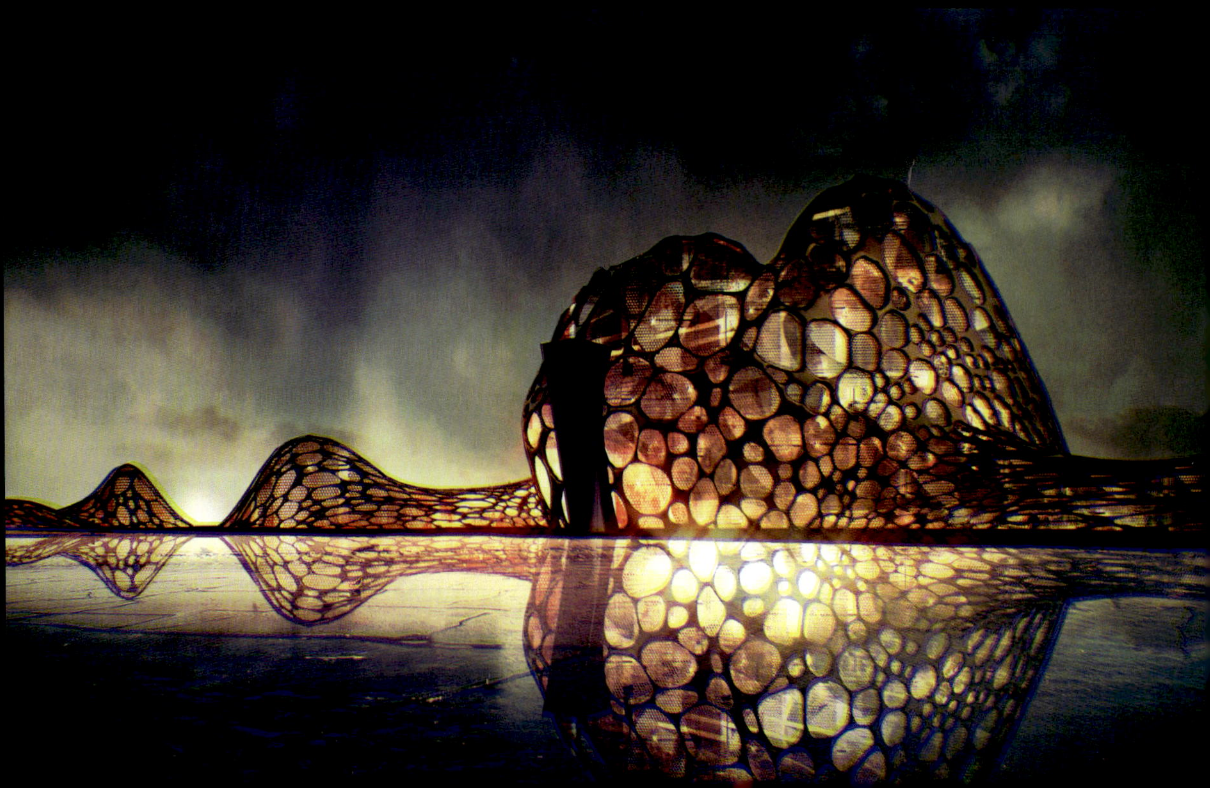

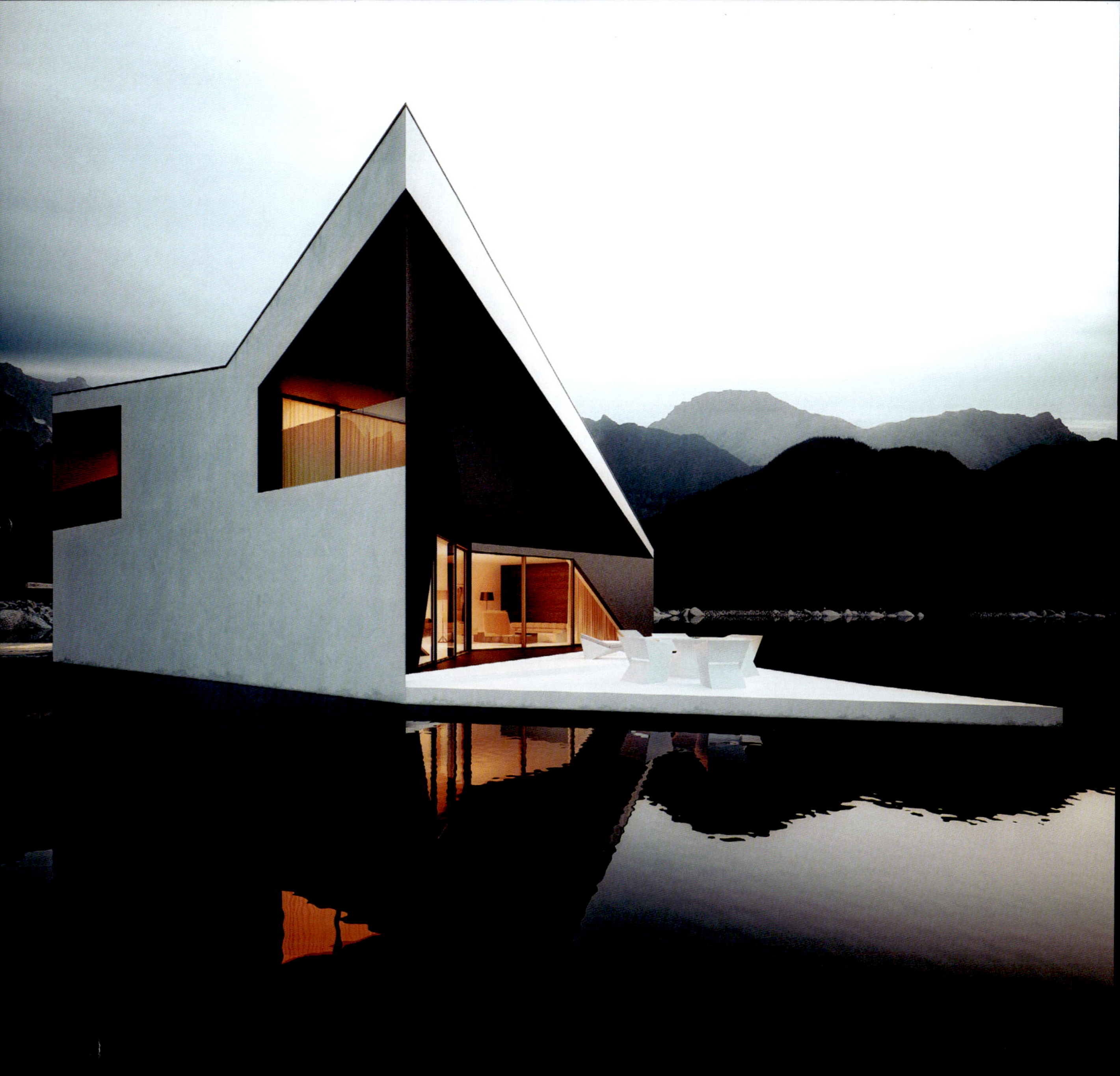

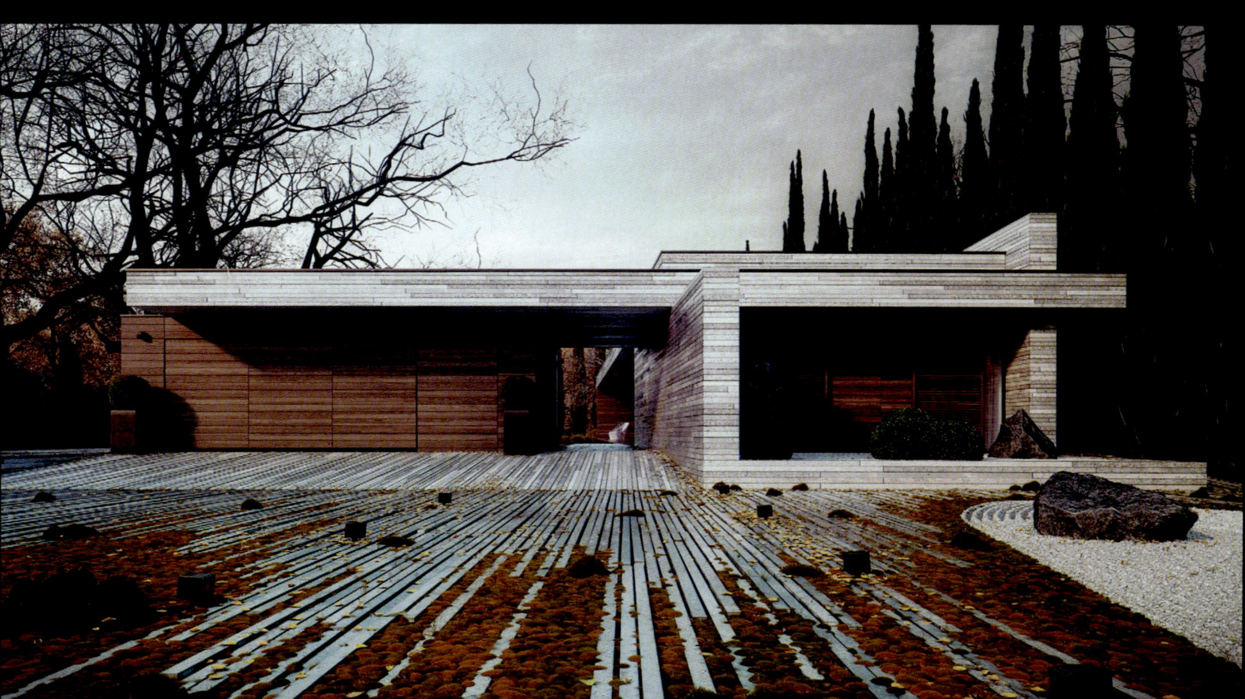

Art Halls
3ds Max, Photoshop, V-Ray
Sam A. Nassar, SYRIA
[top]

Horizontal House
3ds Max, Photoshop, V-Ray
Michał Nowak, POLAND
[above]

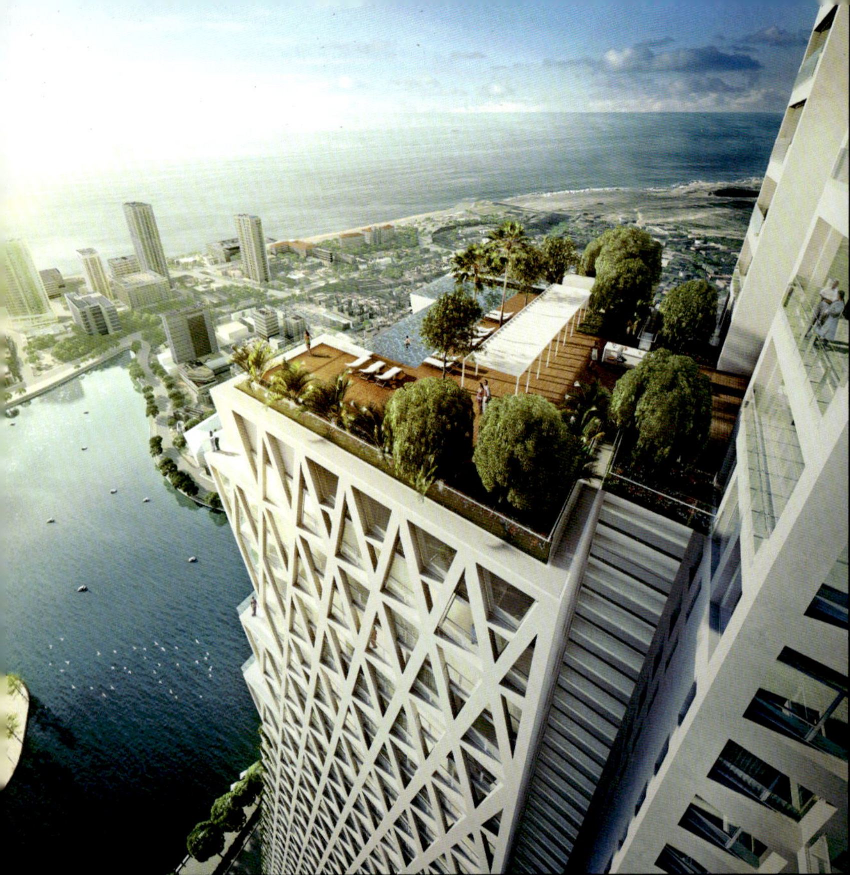

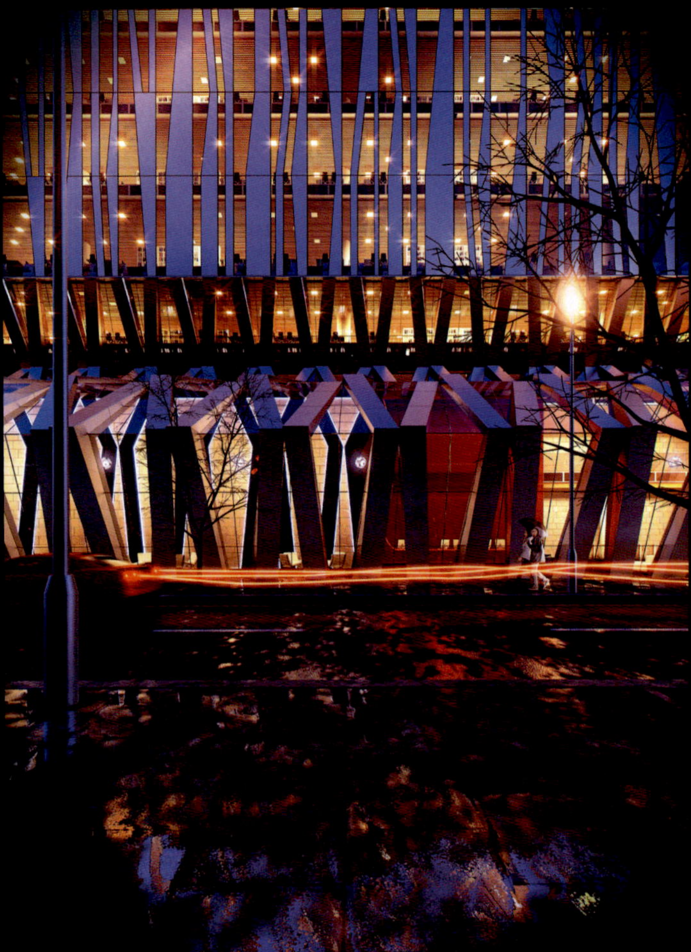

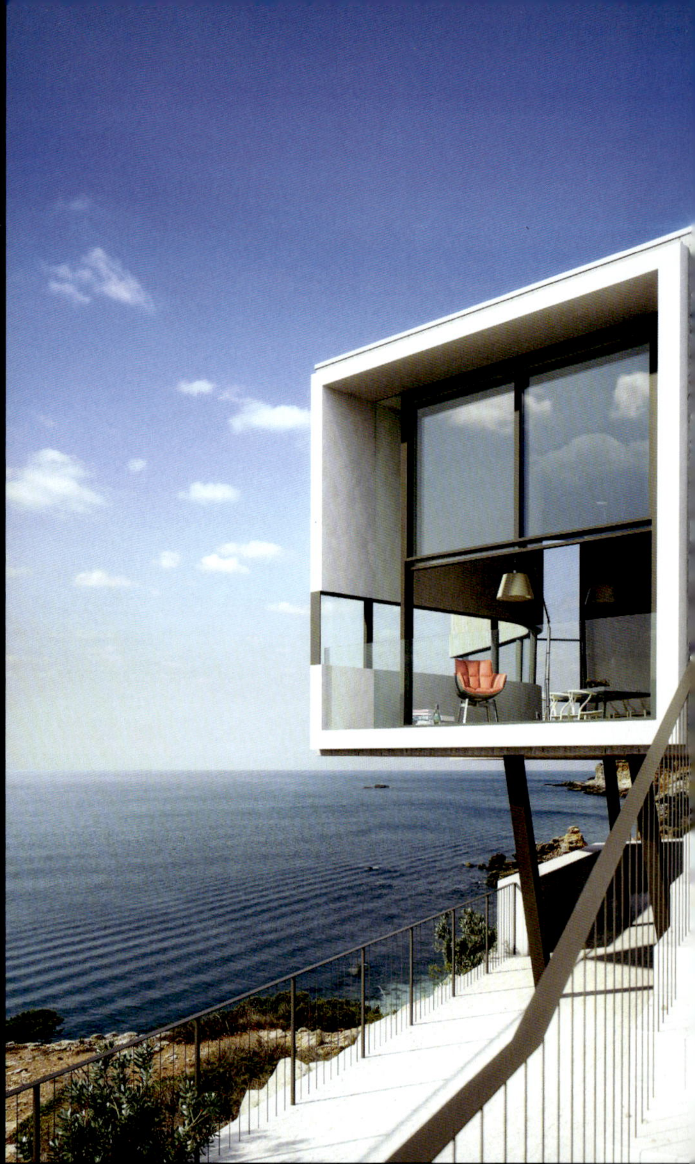

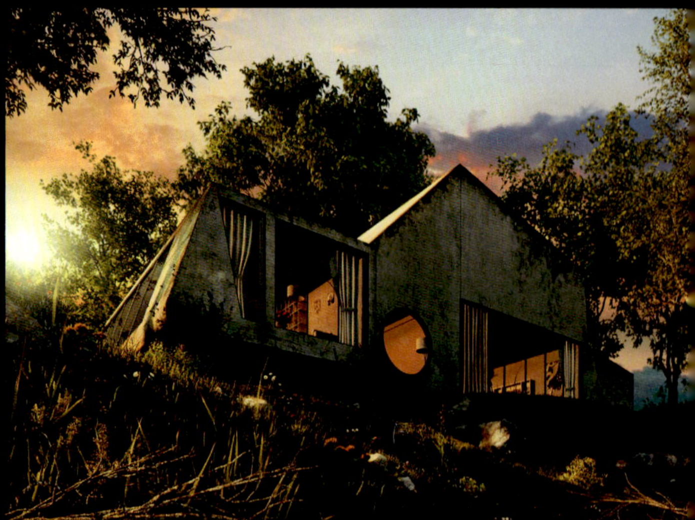

Holman House
3ds Max, V-Ray, Photoshop
Matthias Arndt,
lichtecht, GERMANY
[top]

Summer 69
3ds Max, Photoshop, V-Ray,
After Effects
Peter Ang, PHILIPPINES
[above]

Colombo
3ds Max, V-Ray, Photoshop
Client: Safdie Architects
Jerry Chen, USA
[top]

Public Library Competition Bid
3ds Max, V-Ray, Photoshop
Fernando Such, GC-VFX, GREAT BRITAIN
[above]

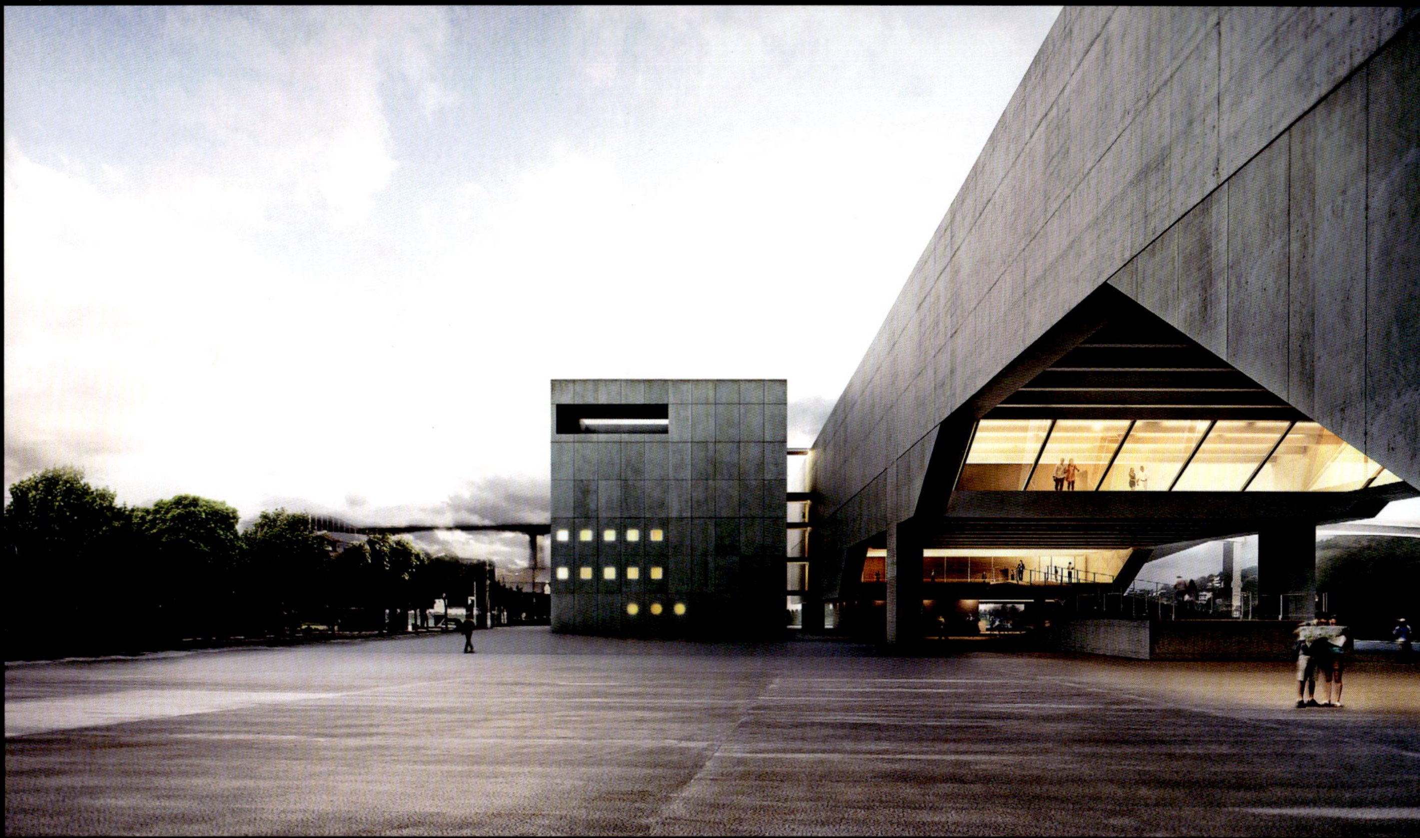

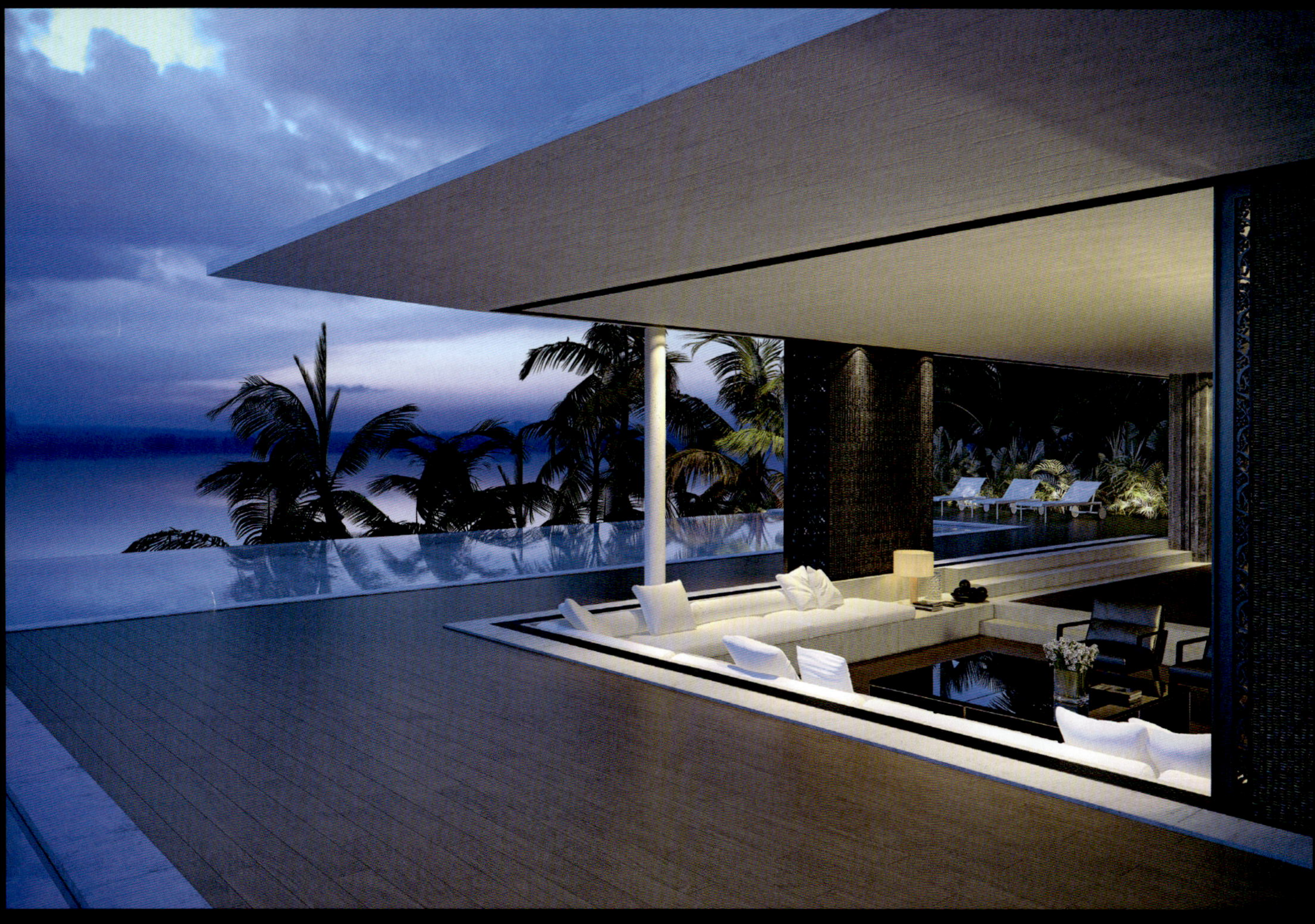

Cais das Artes (Quay of Arts)
AutoCAD, 3ds Max, V-Ray, Photoshop
Architect: Paulo Mendes da Rocha + METRO
Ricardo Canton, BRAZIL
[top]

Exotic: Living
3ds Max, V-Ray, Photoshop
Client: Domino
Miguel Miraldo and Alexandre Miraldo, PORTUGAL
[above]

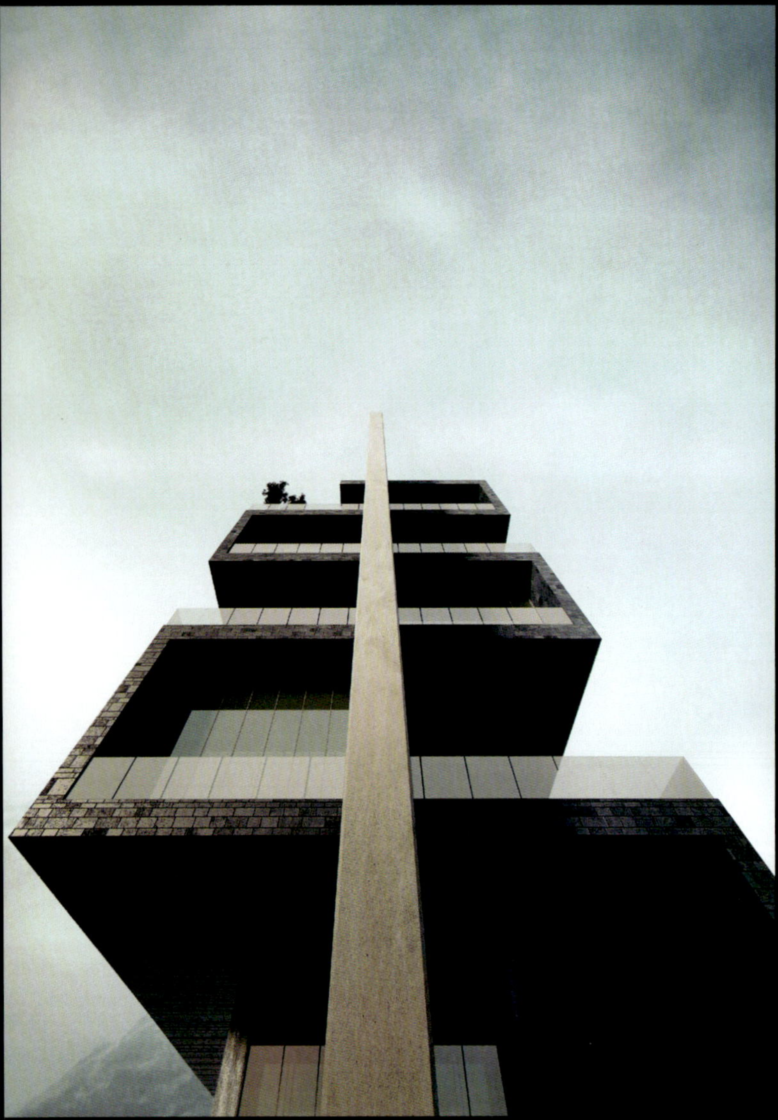

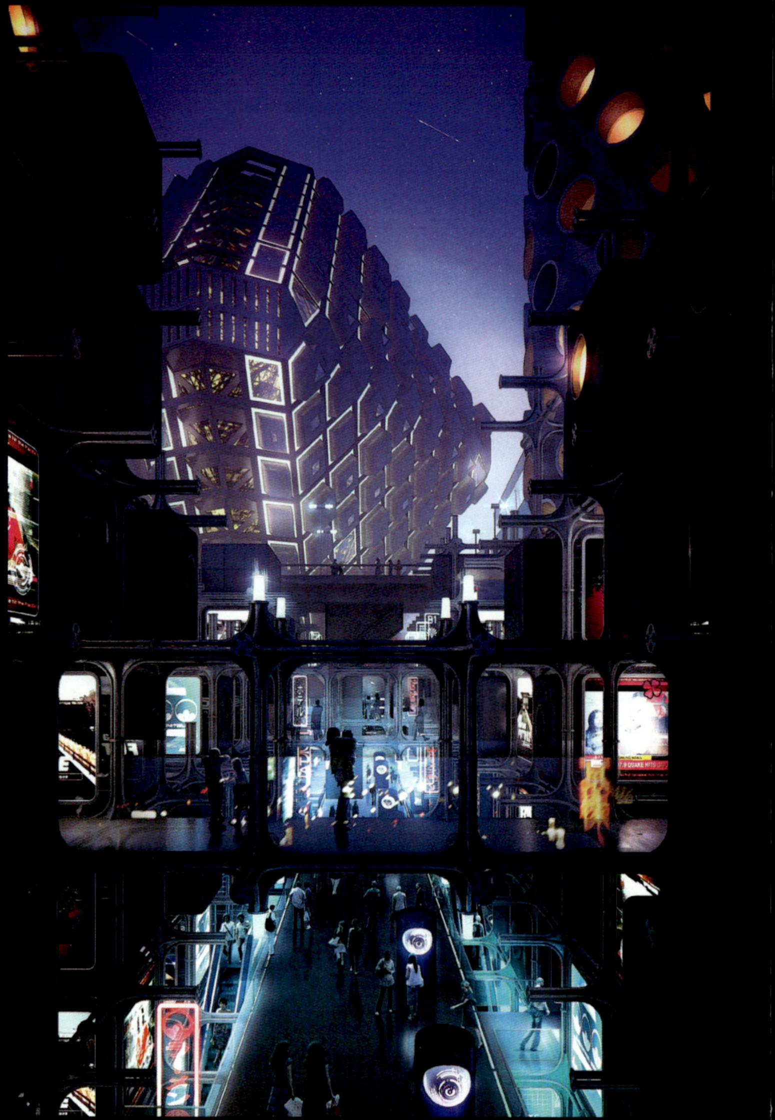

Z33
3ds Max, V-Ray, Photoshop
Sam A. Nassar, SYRIA
[above]

Tribute to Metabolism: Summer
3ds Max, V-Ray, Photoshop
Inspired by The Metabolists
Jean-Marc Emy, FRANCE
[above right]

Tampa Covenant Church (Sanctuary Entrance)
CINEMA 4D, V-Ray, Photoshop
Patrick Eischen,
Architect: Alfonso, LUXEMBOURG
[facing page top]

Wooden Cube House
3ds Max, Photoshop, V-Ray
Michał Nowak, POLAND
[facing page bottom]

Lugano | Apartment house
3ds Max, ArchiCAD, V-Ray, Photoshop
Bence Fischer, Brown-Blue.com, HUNGARY
[right]

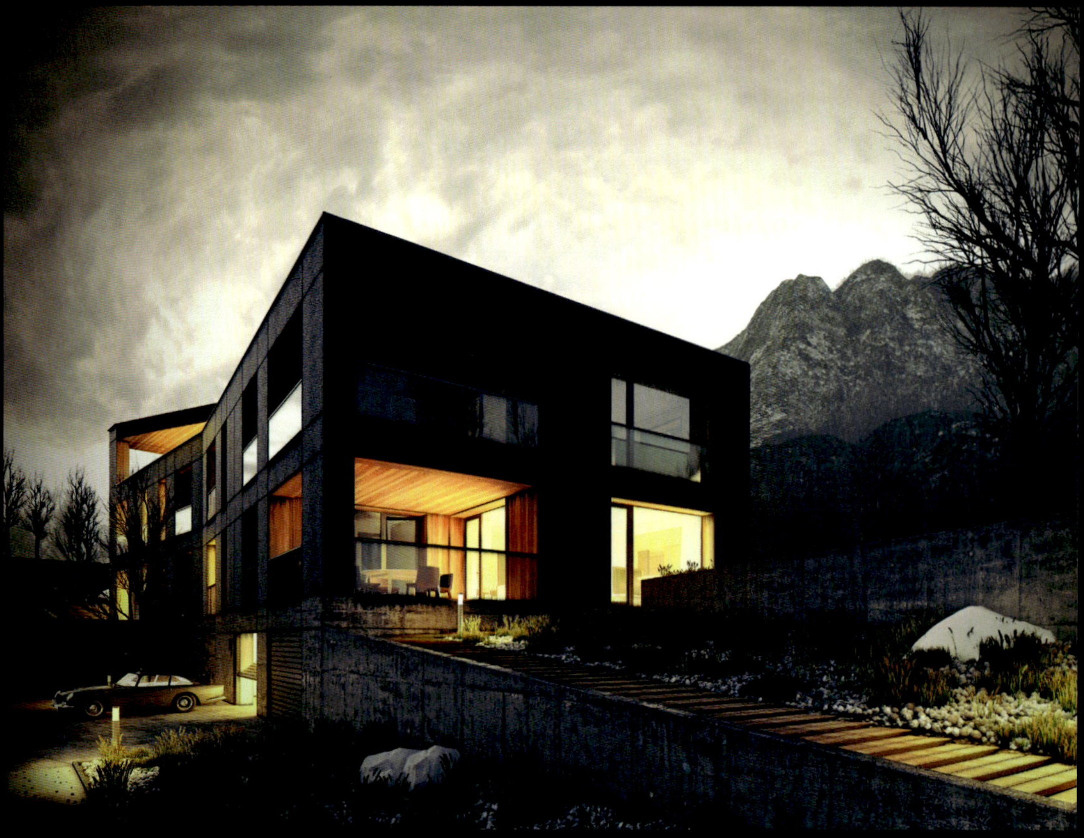

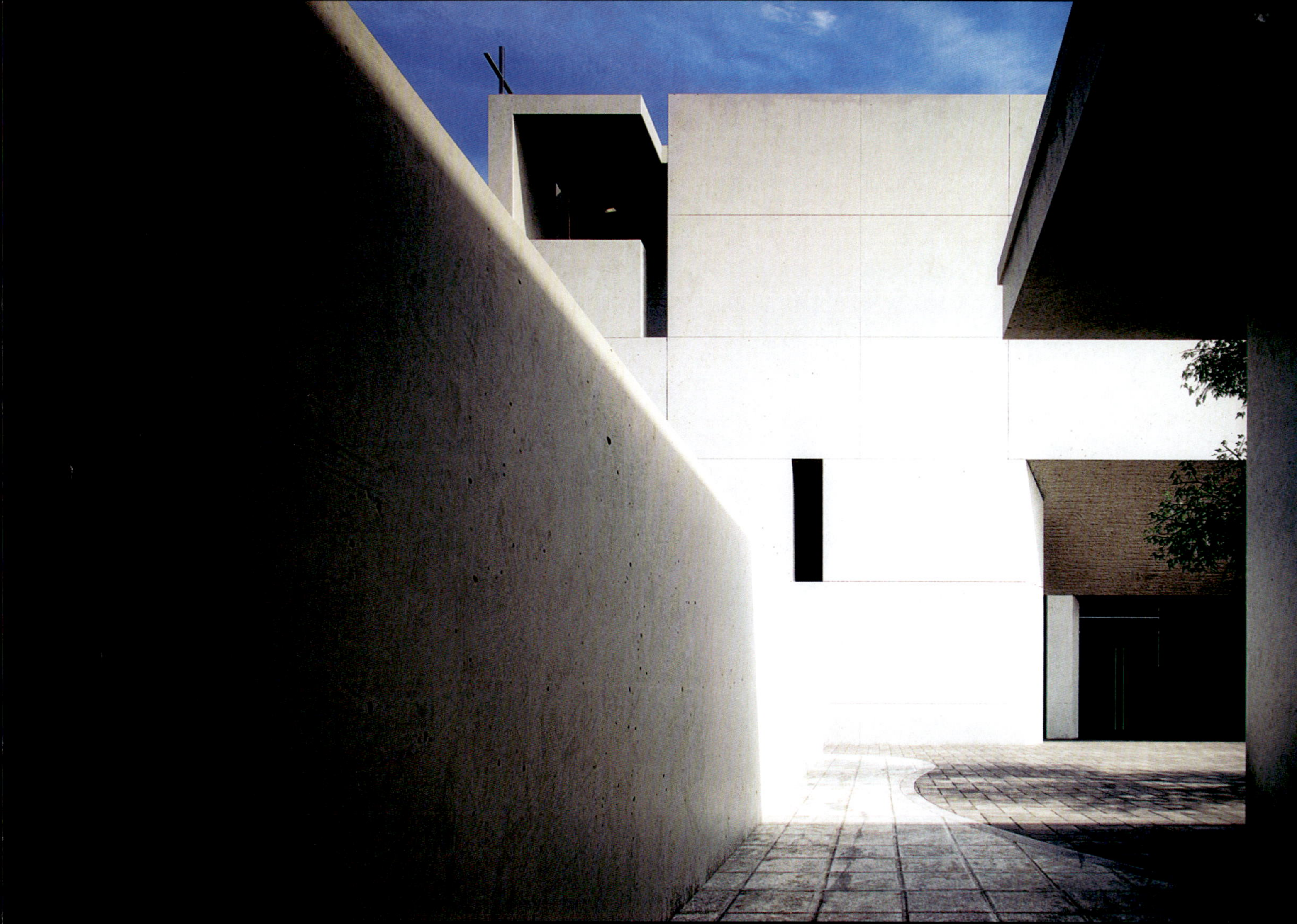

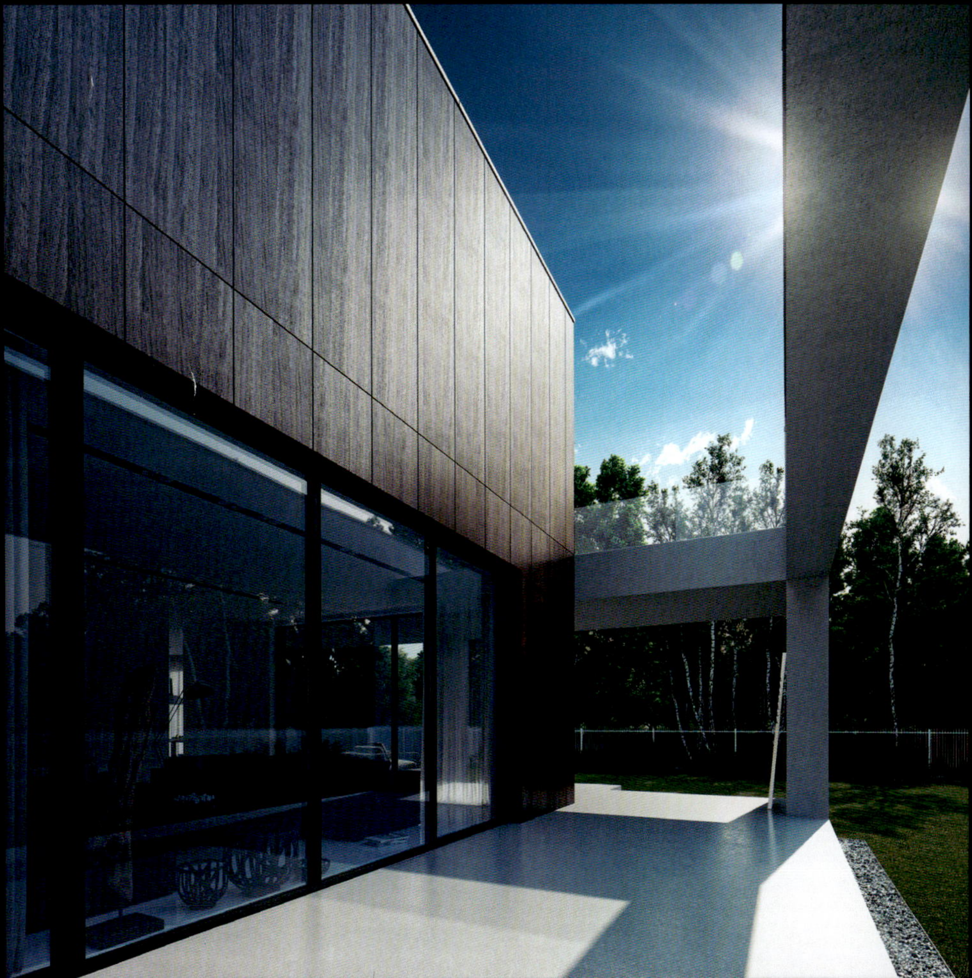

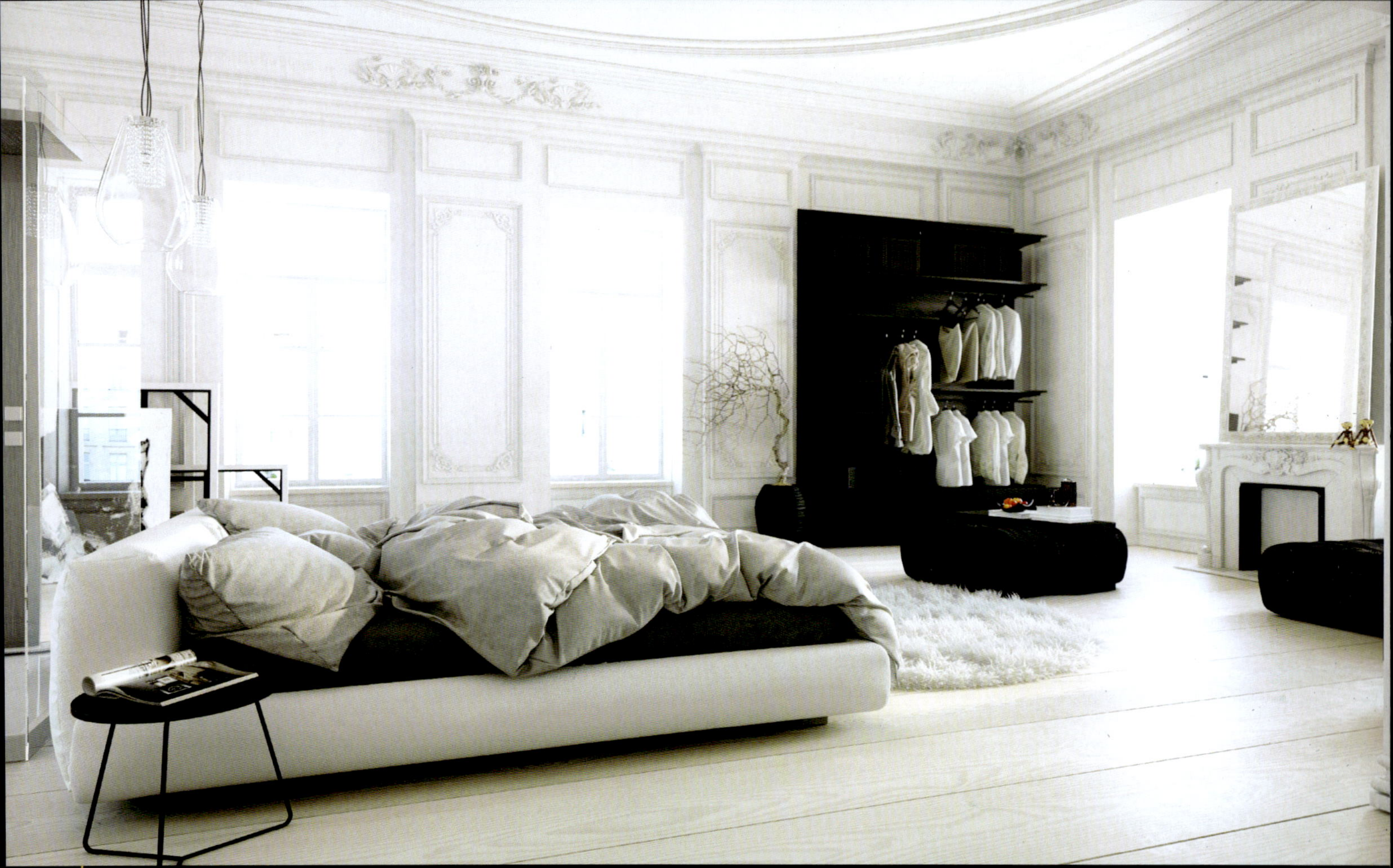

Excellence
Architecture (Interior)

White Bedroom
3ds Max, Marvelous Designer
Juraj Talcik and Veronika Demovicova, SLOVAKIA

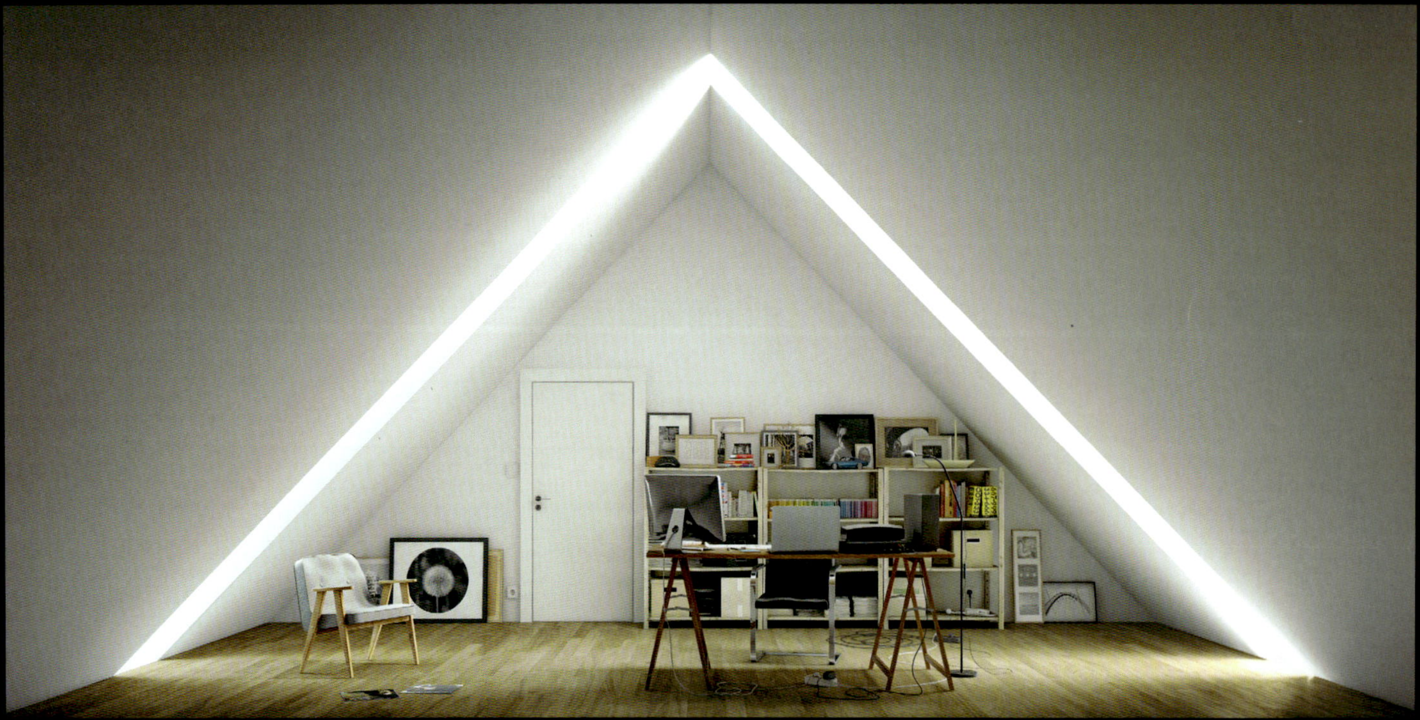

Attic Office
CINEMA 4D, V-Ray, Photoshop
Maciej Mackiewicz, POLAND

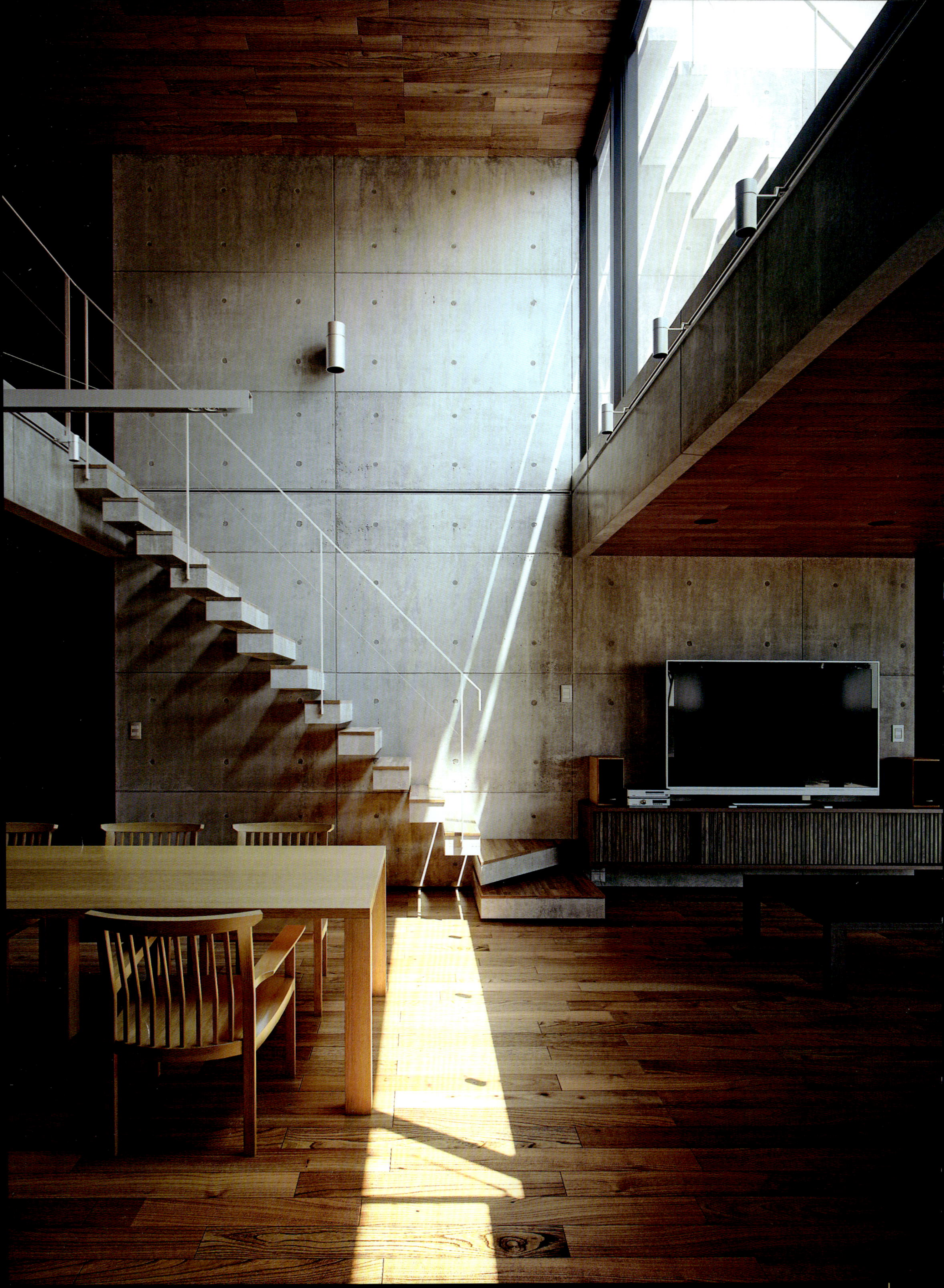

Foo House
3ds Max, V-Ray, Photoshop
Andrea Bertaccini, ITALY

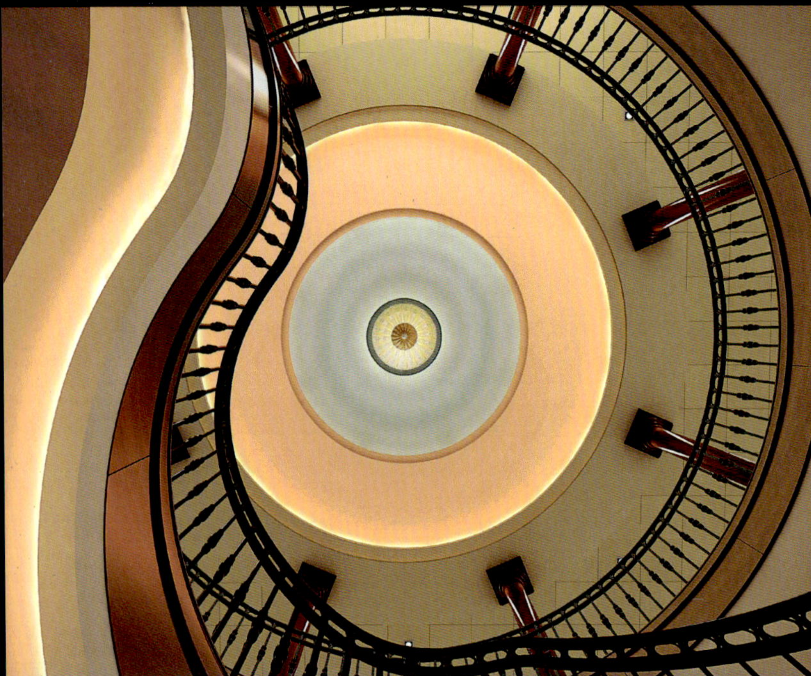

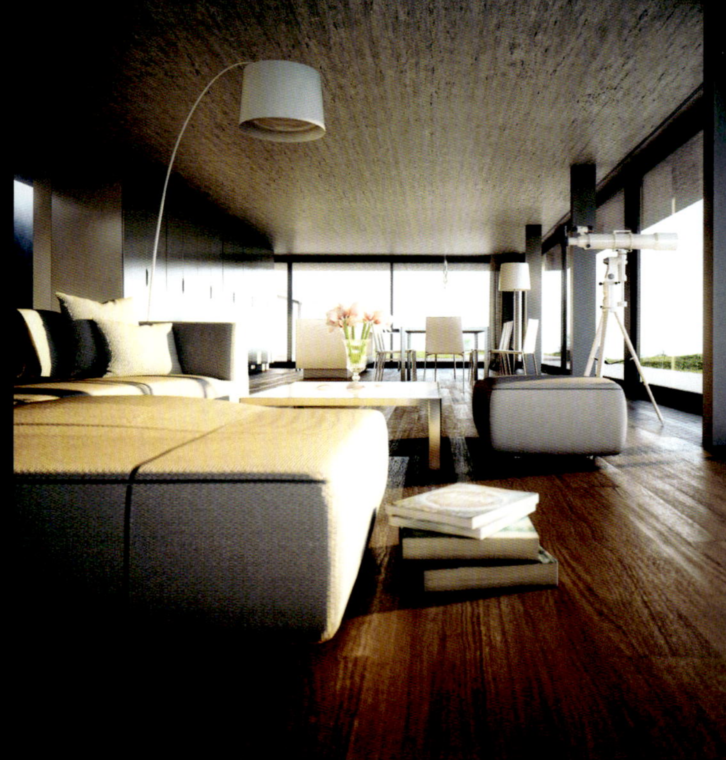

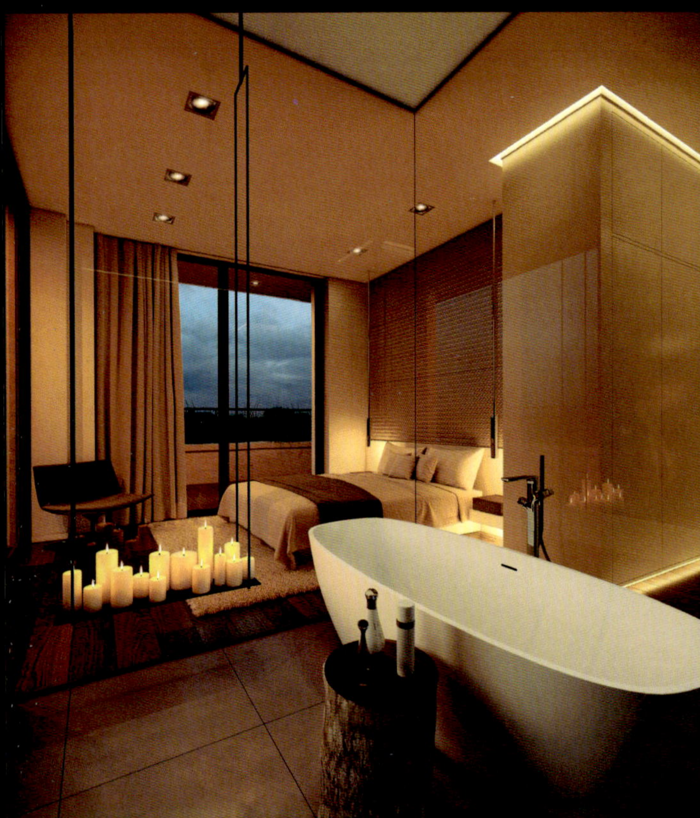

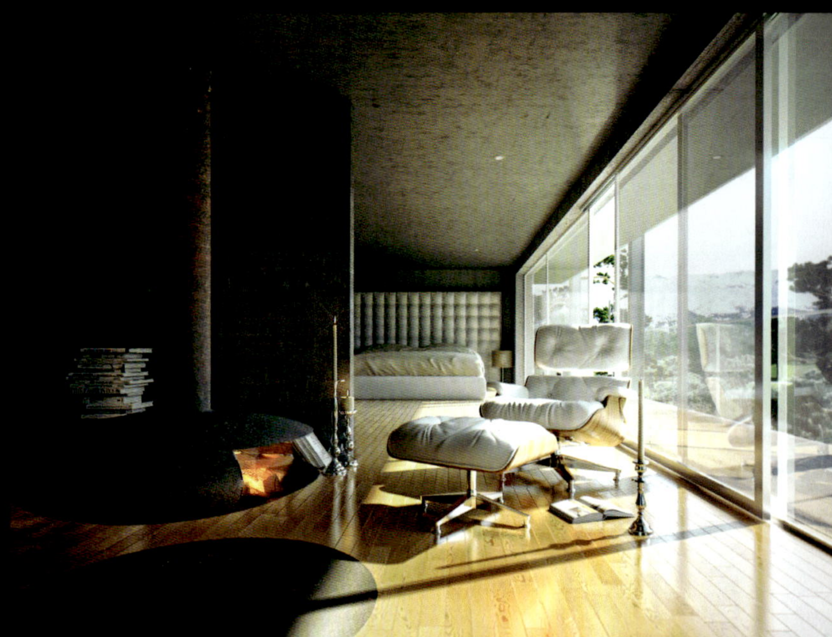

Labacaho House Reinterpreted
3ds Max, V-Ray, Photoshop
Matthias Arndt, lichtecht, GERMANY
[top]

Suishouen House
3ds Max, V-Ray, Photoshop
Stefanie Arndt, lichtecht, GERMANY
[above]

Look Up
3ds Max
Chen Qingfeng, Chen3D.com, CHINA
[top]

The Cond'Or: Deluxe Apartment Bathroom
3ds Max, V-Ray, Photoshop
Client: Quintessentially Benelux for Optima nv
Christophe Landrain, BELGIUM
[above]

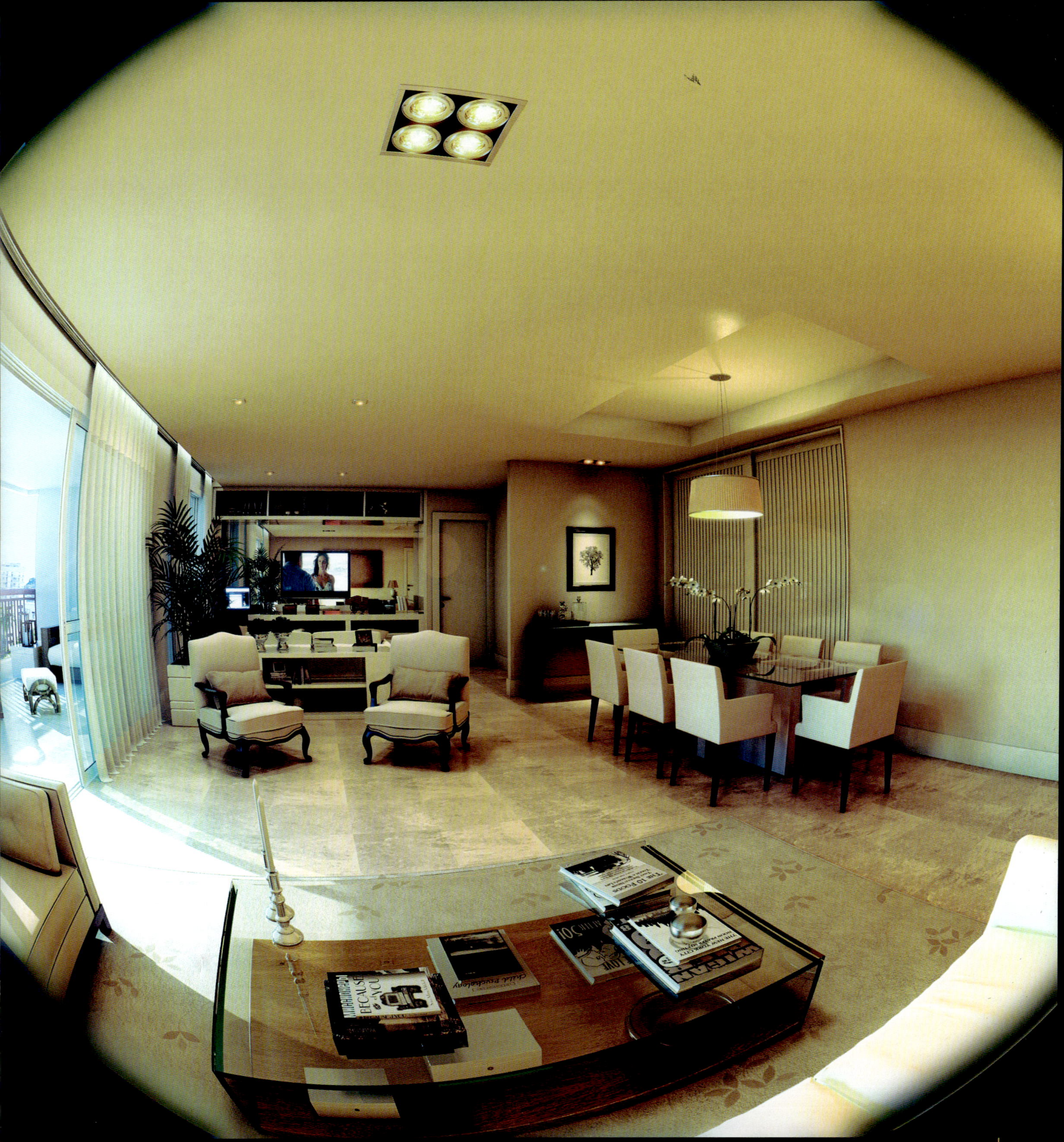

Fish Eye Living Room
3ds Max, V-Ray, Photoshop
Derek Guimares, BRAZIL

Excellence
Architecture (Interior)

The Cond'Or: Spa Pool
3ds Max, V-Ray, Photoshop
Client: Quintessentially Benelux for Optima nv -
Christophe Landrain, BELGIUM
[right]

BlackWhite Residence living Room
CINEMA 4D, V-Ray, Photoshop
Architect: David Jameson
Maciej Mackiewicz, POLAND
[facing page top]

Hunter's Bedroom
3ds Max, V-Ray, Photoshop
Micael (DIA) Dillner, Inspire Studios, SWEDEN
[below left]

Butterfly: Interior Flux Chair
3ds Max, After Effects, V-Ray, Photoshop
Thiago Queiroz Lima, BRAZIL
[below right]

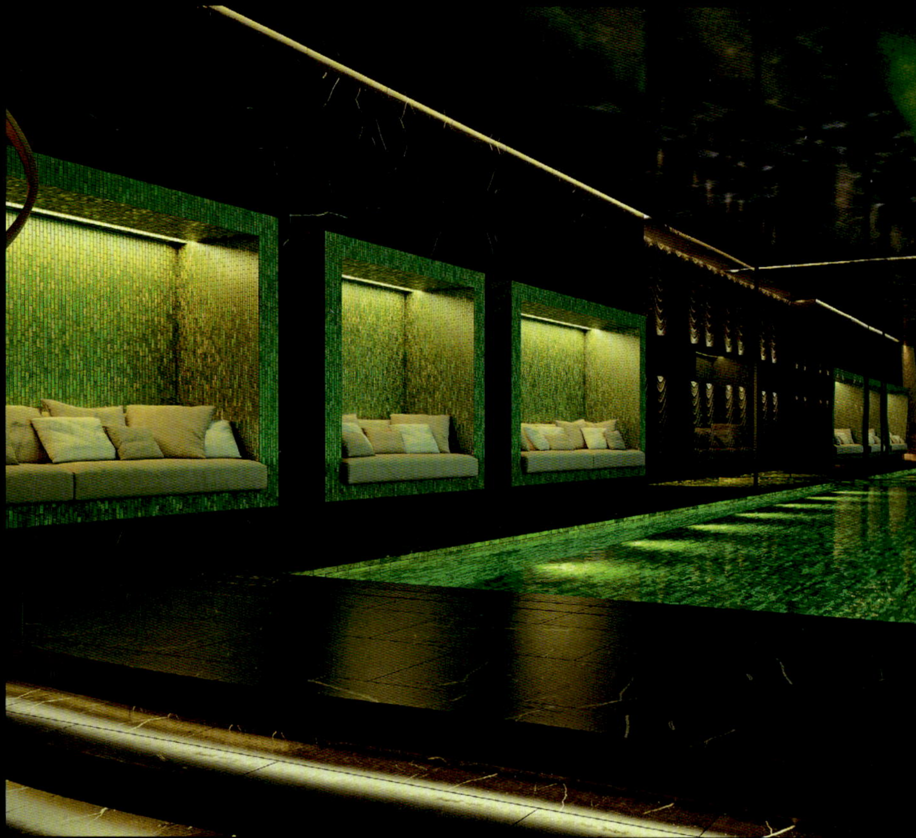

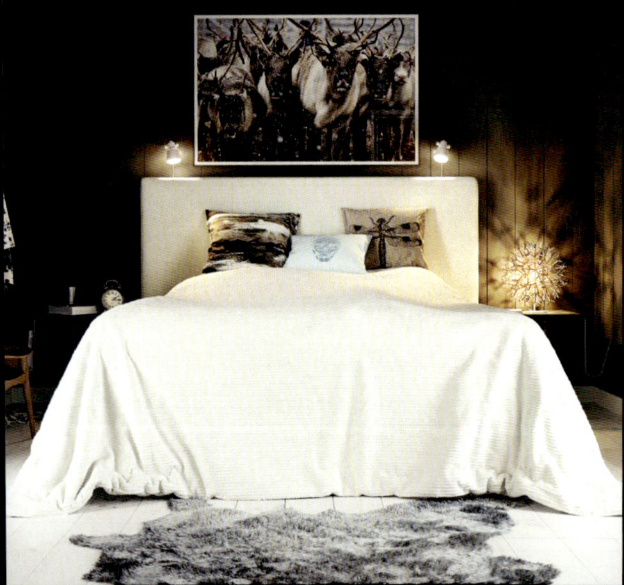

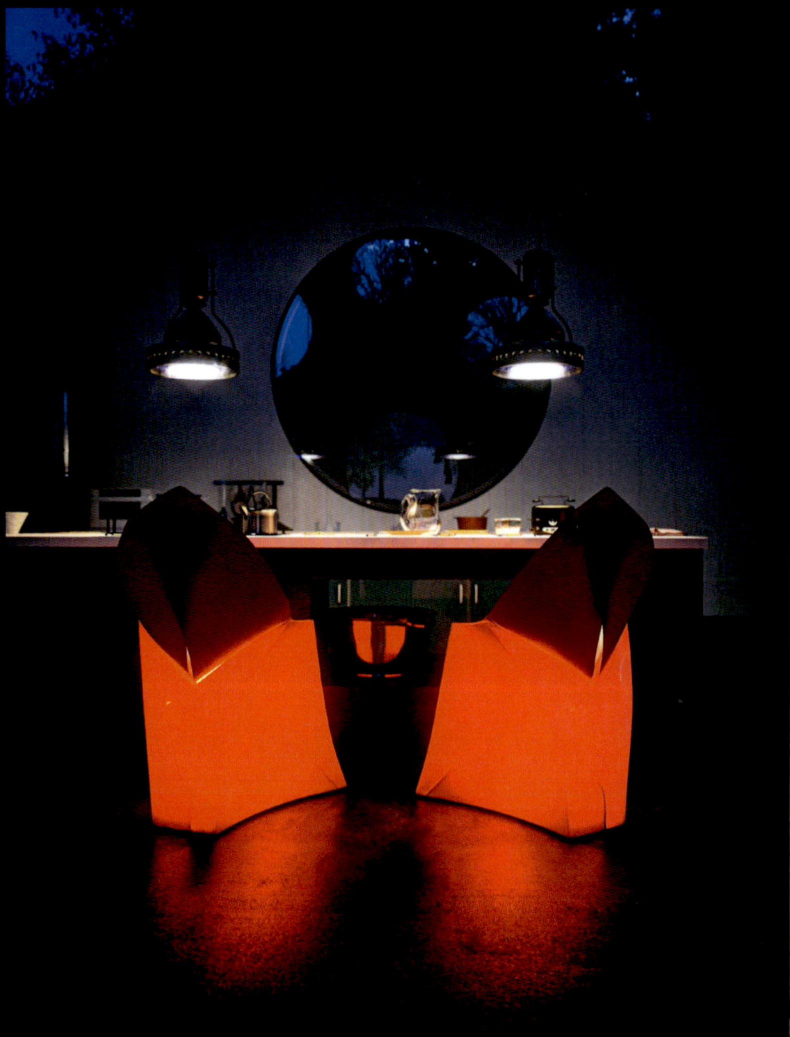

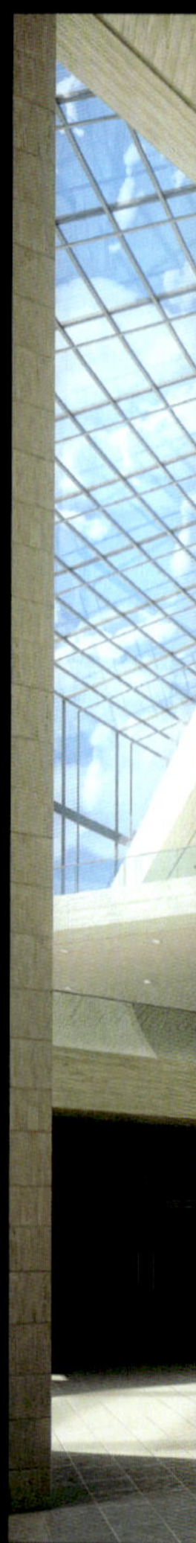

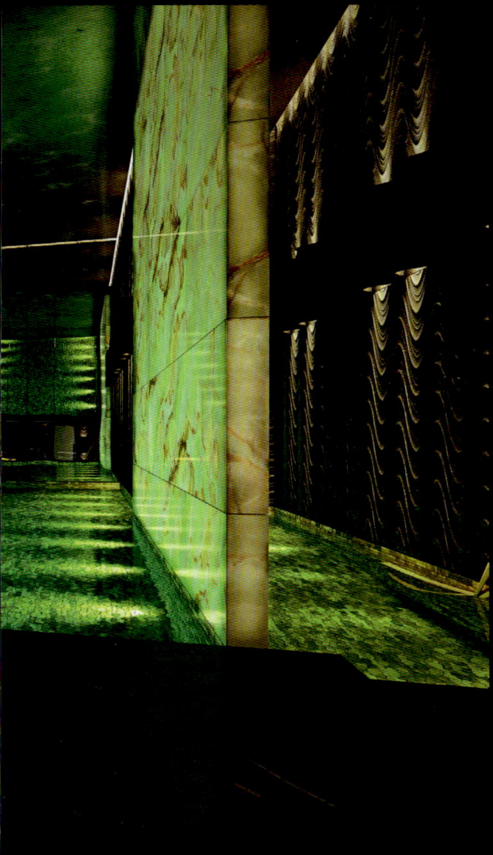

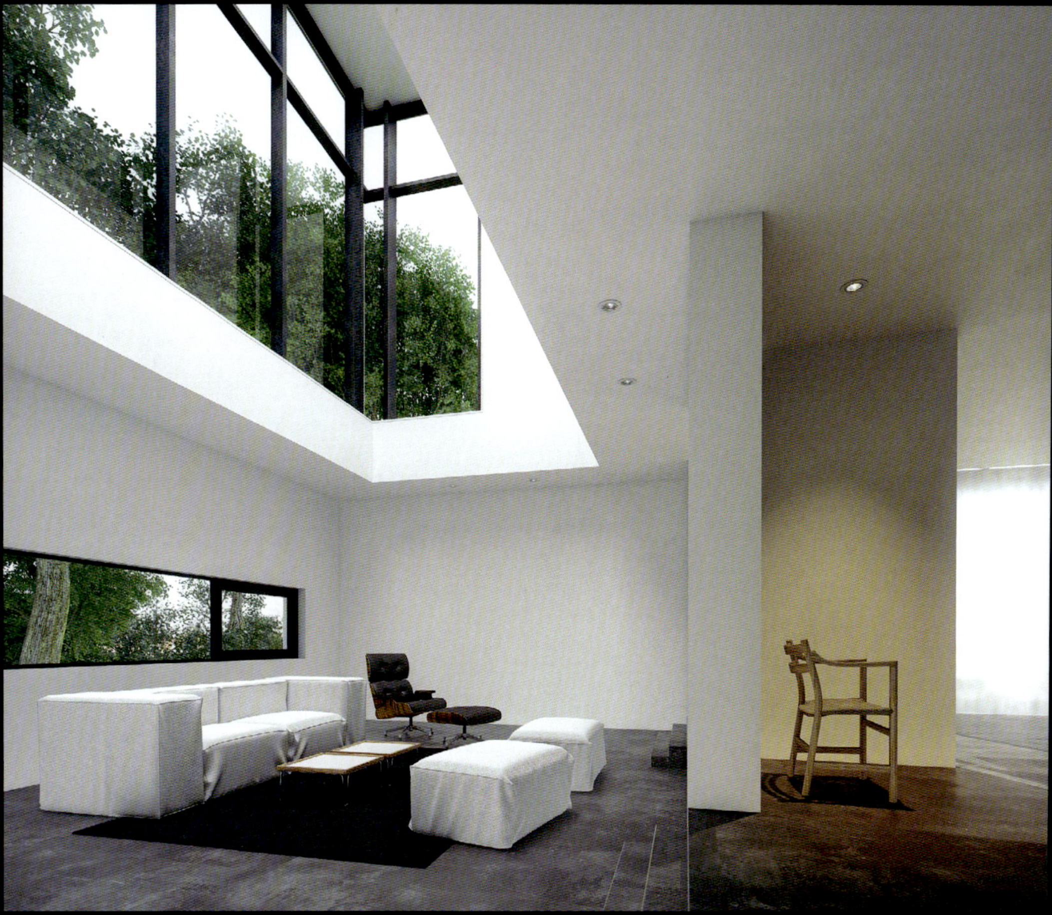

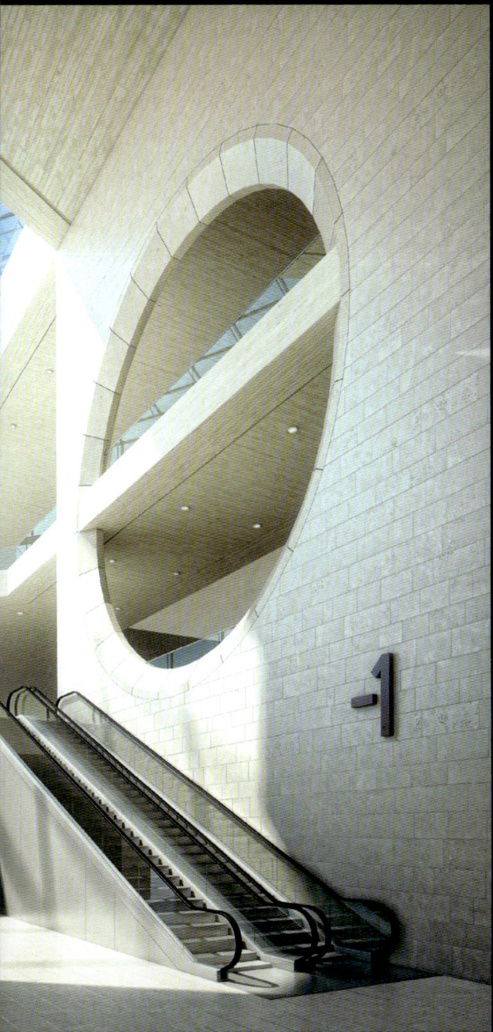

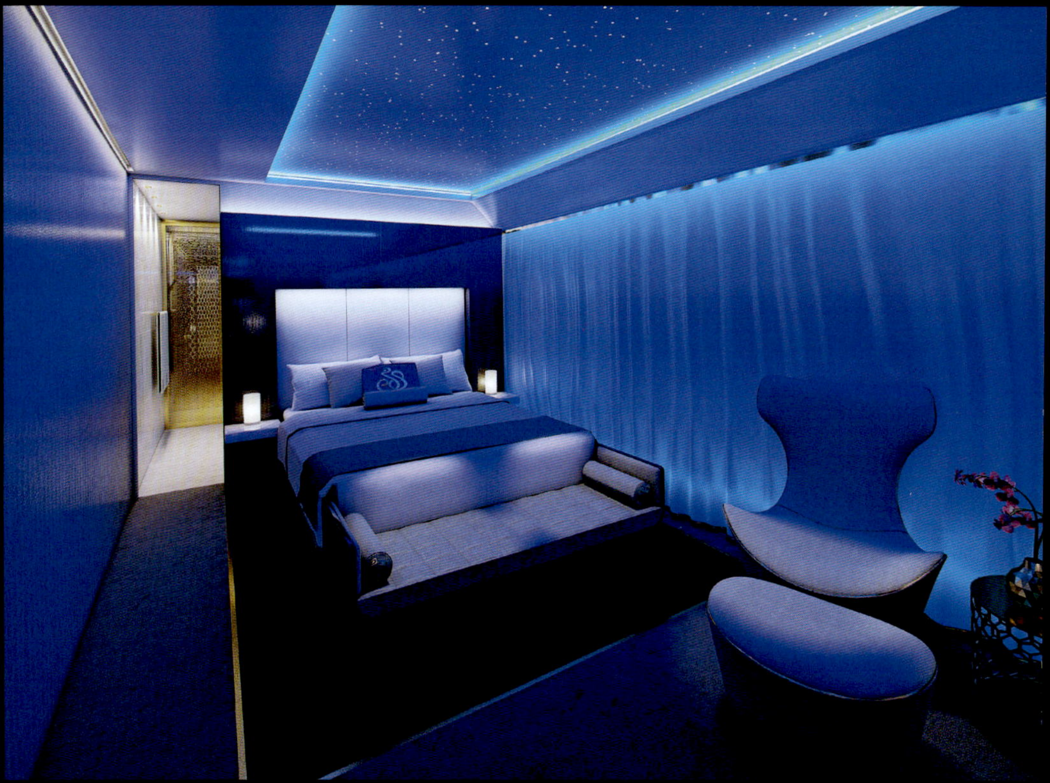

DHM Lobby
3ds Max, V-Ray
Daniel Yaqub, twentyfourpixel, GERMANY
[left]

Altitude 787 VIP Interior/Bedroom
3ds Max, V-Ray
Teague, USA
[above]

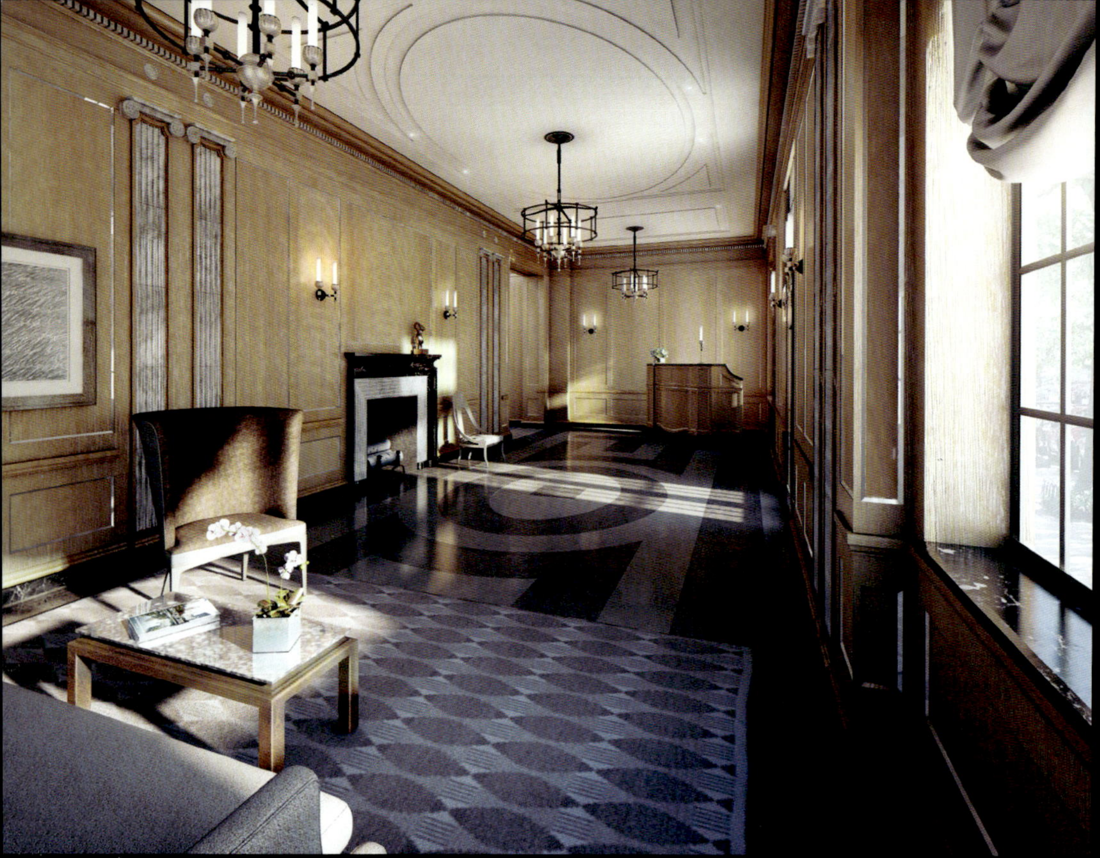

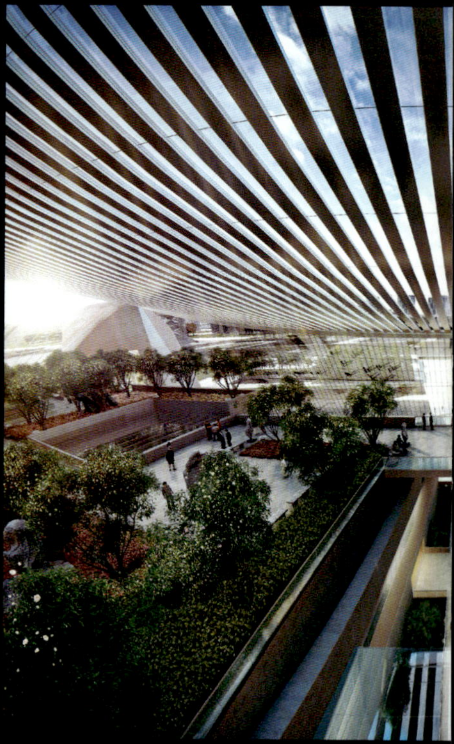

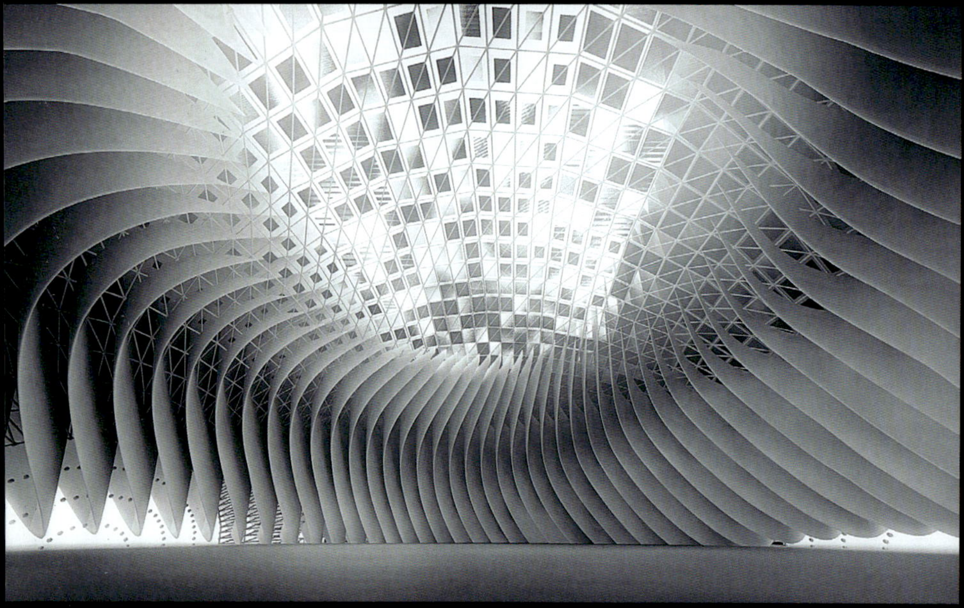

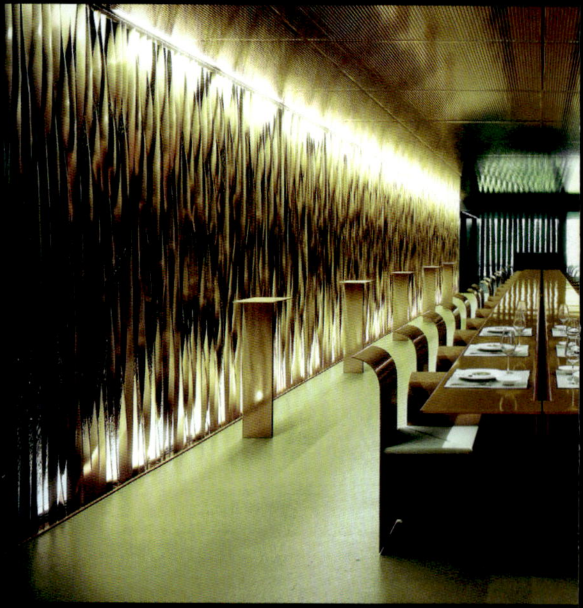

18 Gramercy Park South
3ds Max, V-Ray, Photoshop
Client: Zeckendorf Development

Corvette
CINEMA 4D, Photoshop
Levente Gyulai, HUNGARY

Restaurant Les Cols
3ds Max, V-Ray
Architect: RCR

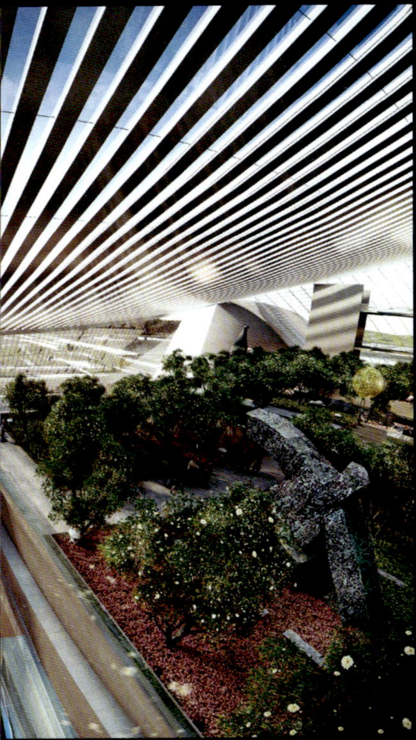

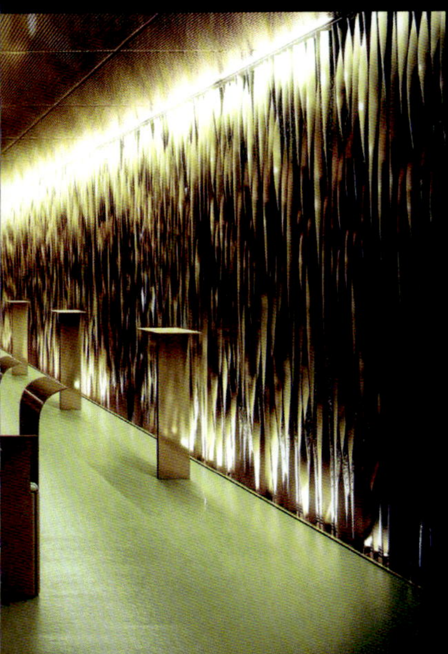

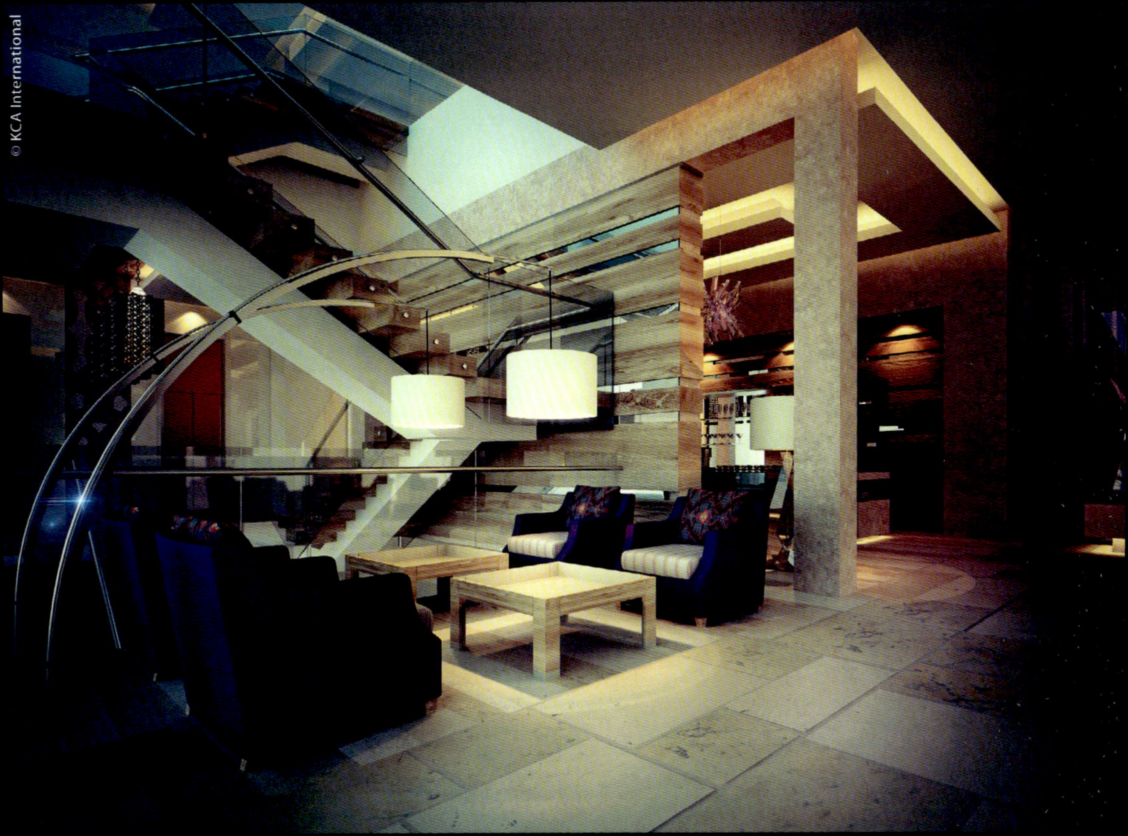

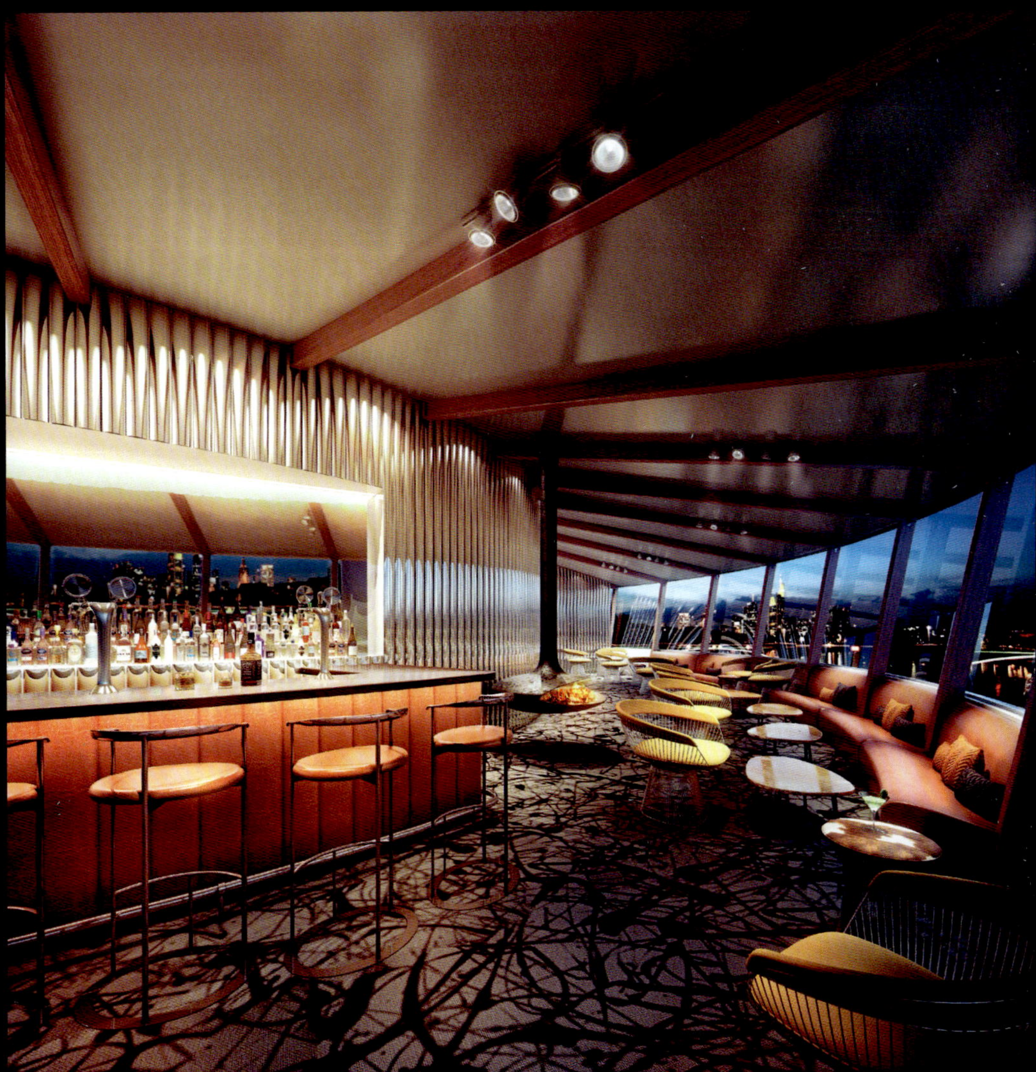

Museum
3ds Max, V-Ray, Photoshop
Jason Addy, Neoscape, USA
[top center]

Bar Zar
3ds Max, Photoshop, V-Ray
Client: Hilton Group
Rakan Jandali, UAE
[top right]

Pinnacle Bar
3ds Max, V-Ray, Photoshop
Hao La, USA
[right]

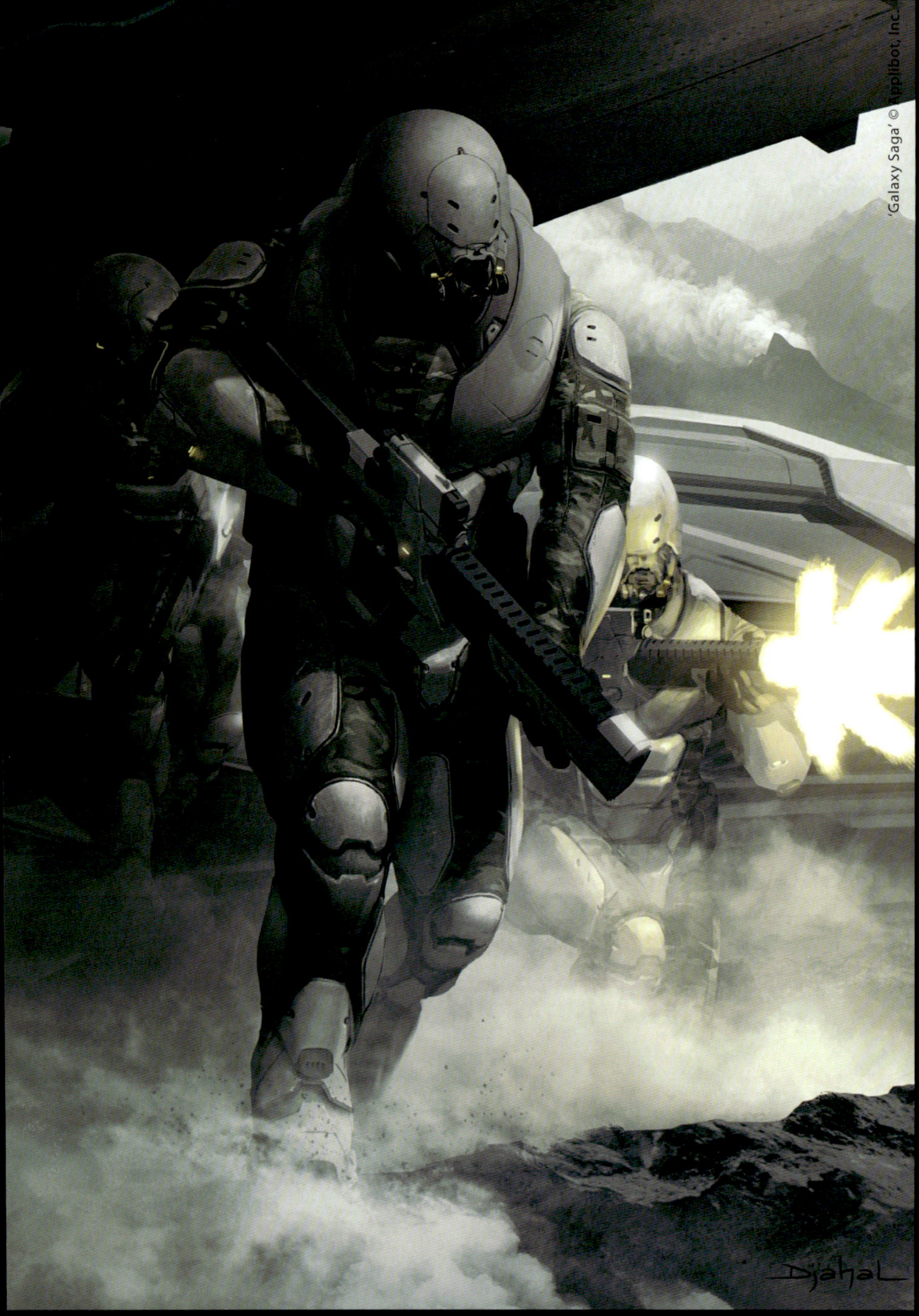

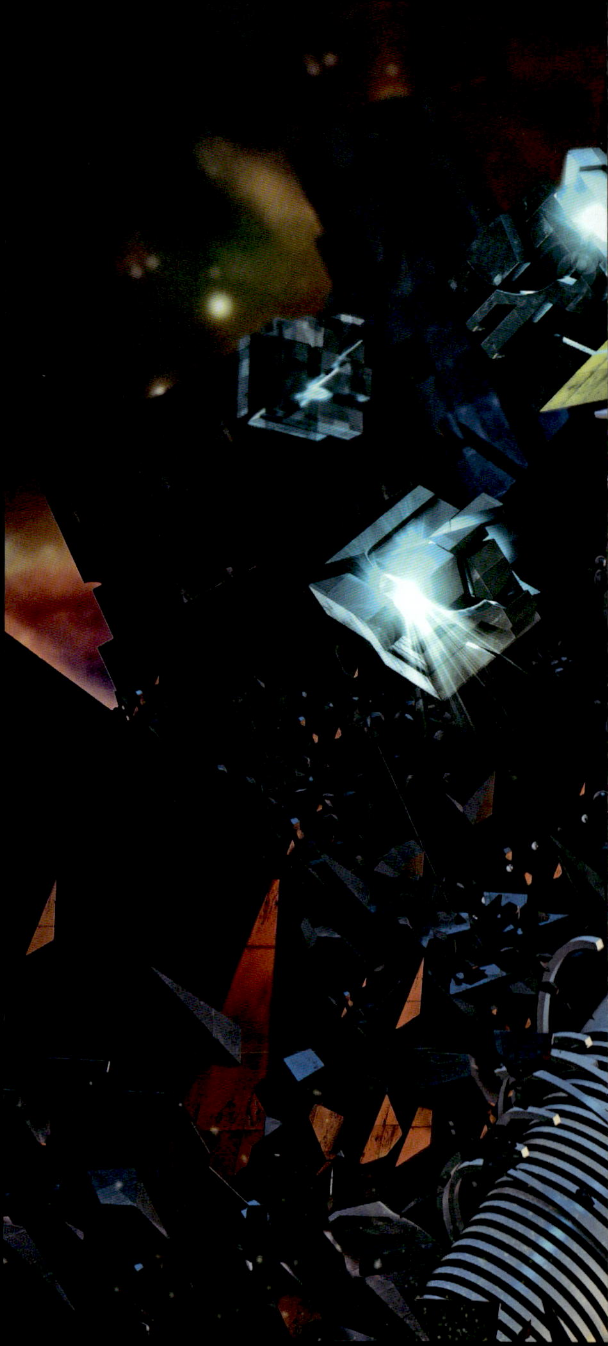

Galaxy Saga: Soldier of the Poison Planet
Photoshop
Client: Applibot, Inc.
Geoffroy Thoorens, FRANCE
[above]

Lobit
3ds Max, V-Ray, After Effects, Photoshop
Andrea Lazzarotti, ITALY
[right]

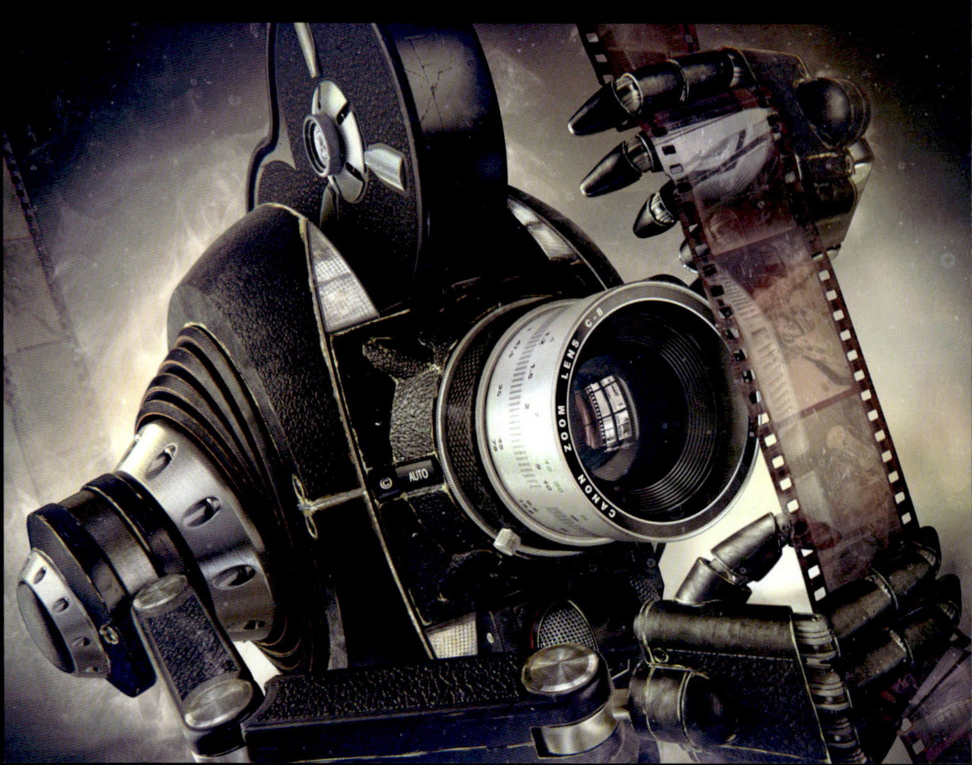

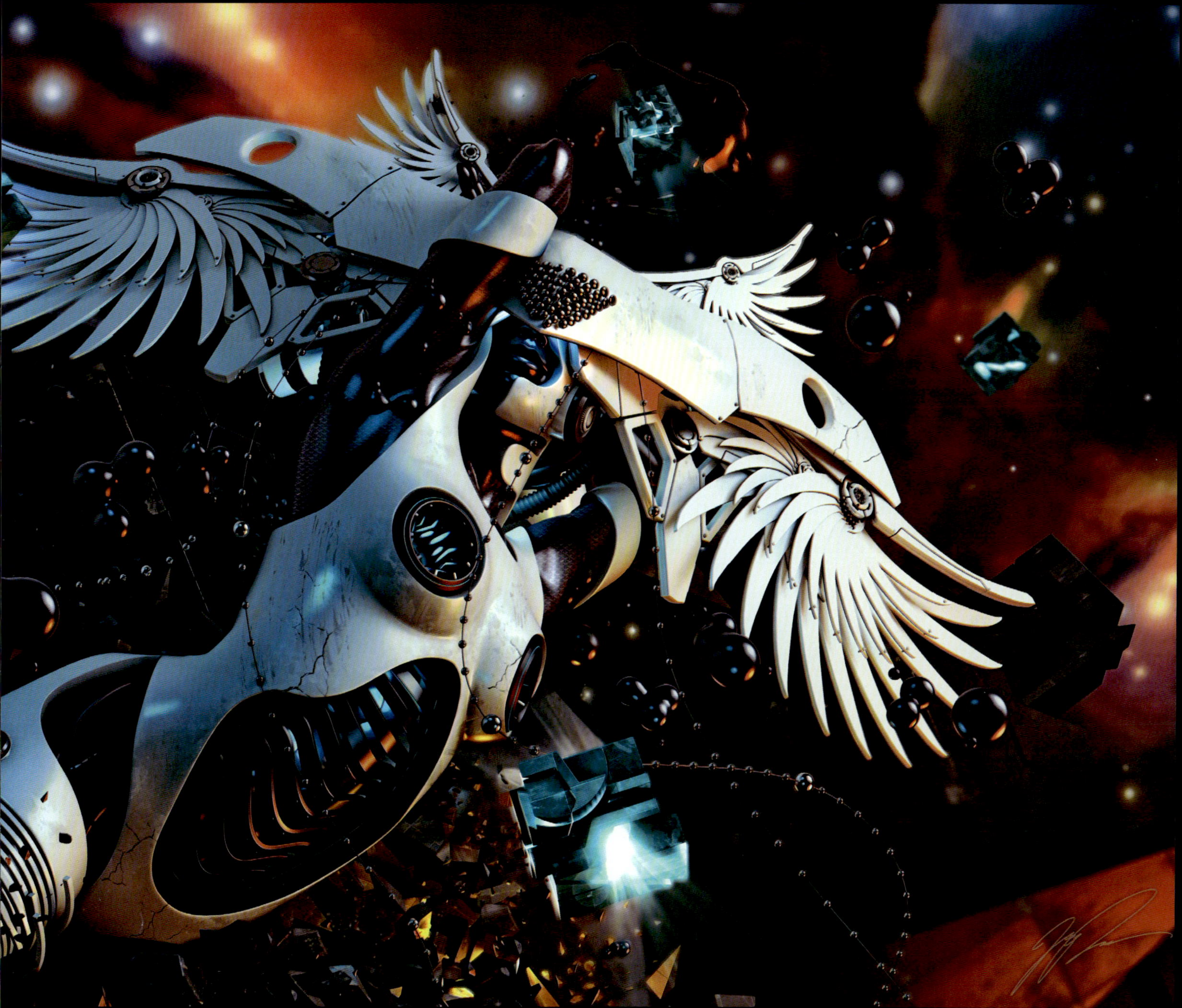

Rise
3ds Max, V-Ray, Photoshop
Jacques Pena, USA
[above]

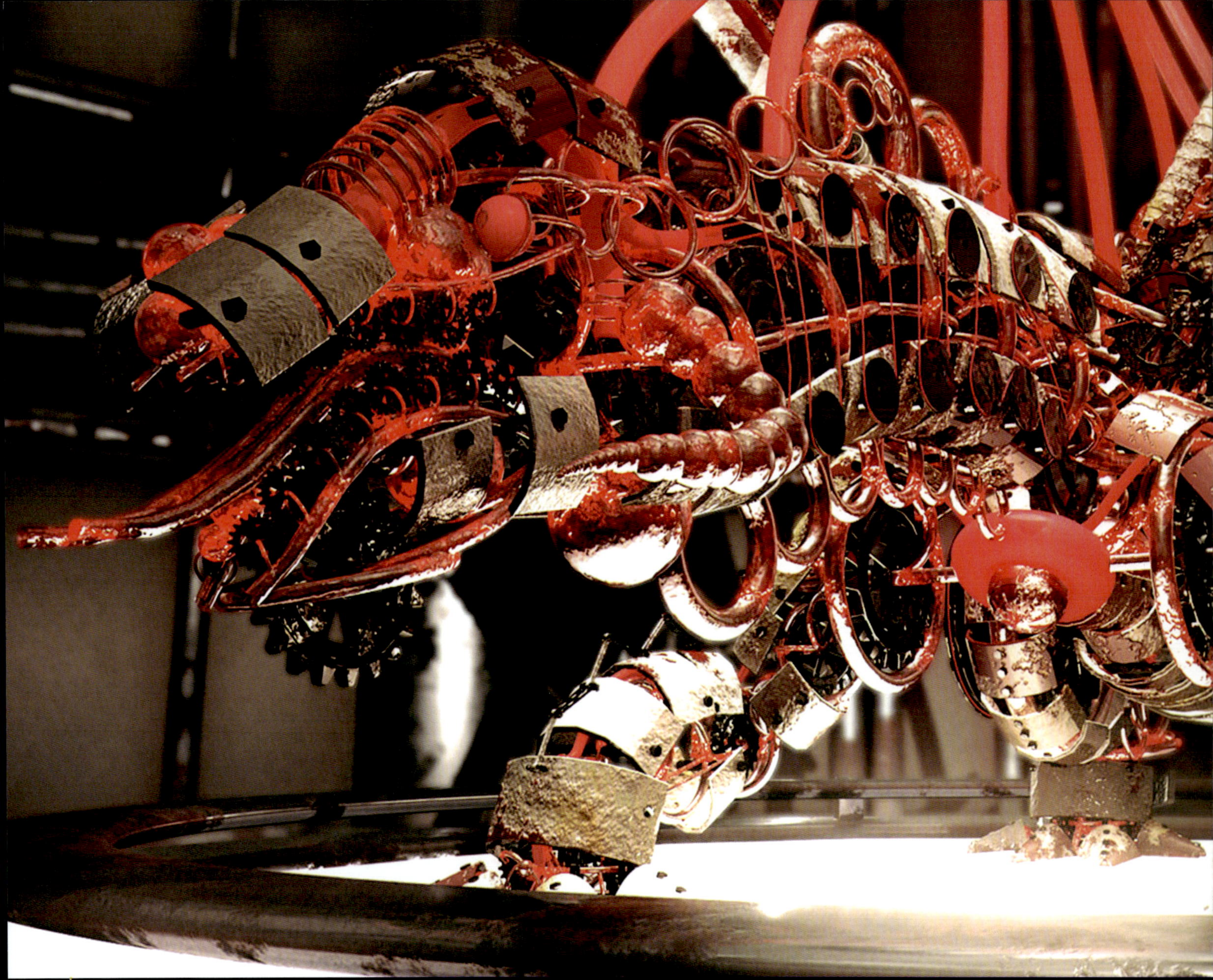

Excellence

Robotic / Cyborg

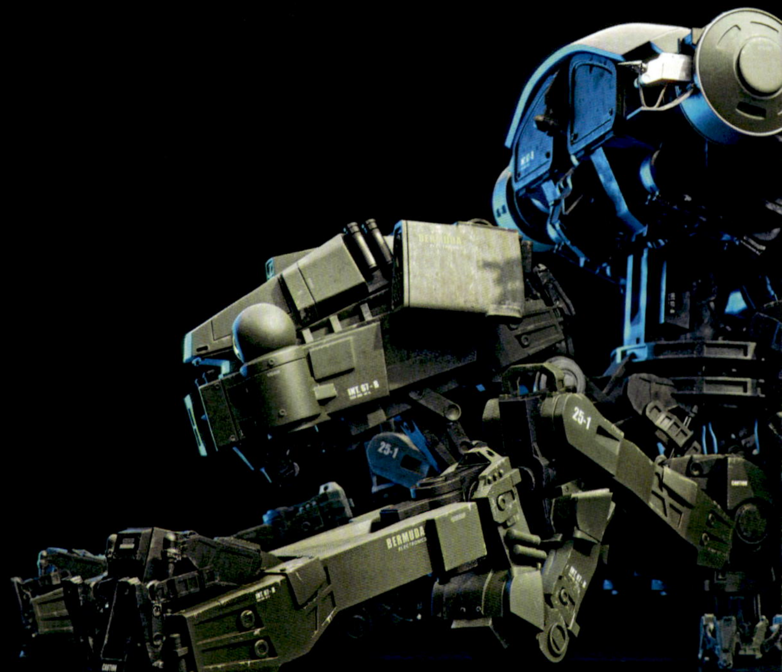

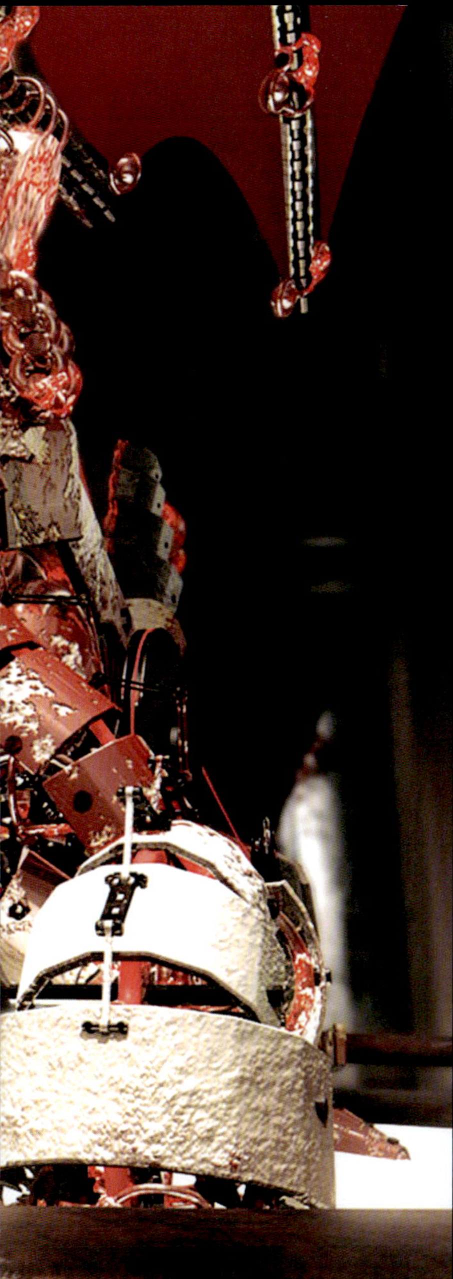

Mecha Fafnir Close Up
Maya, mental ray, Photoshop
William Helba, FRANCE
[left]

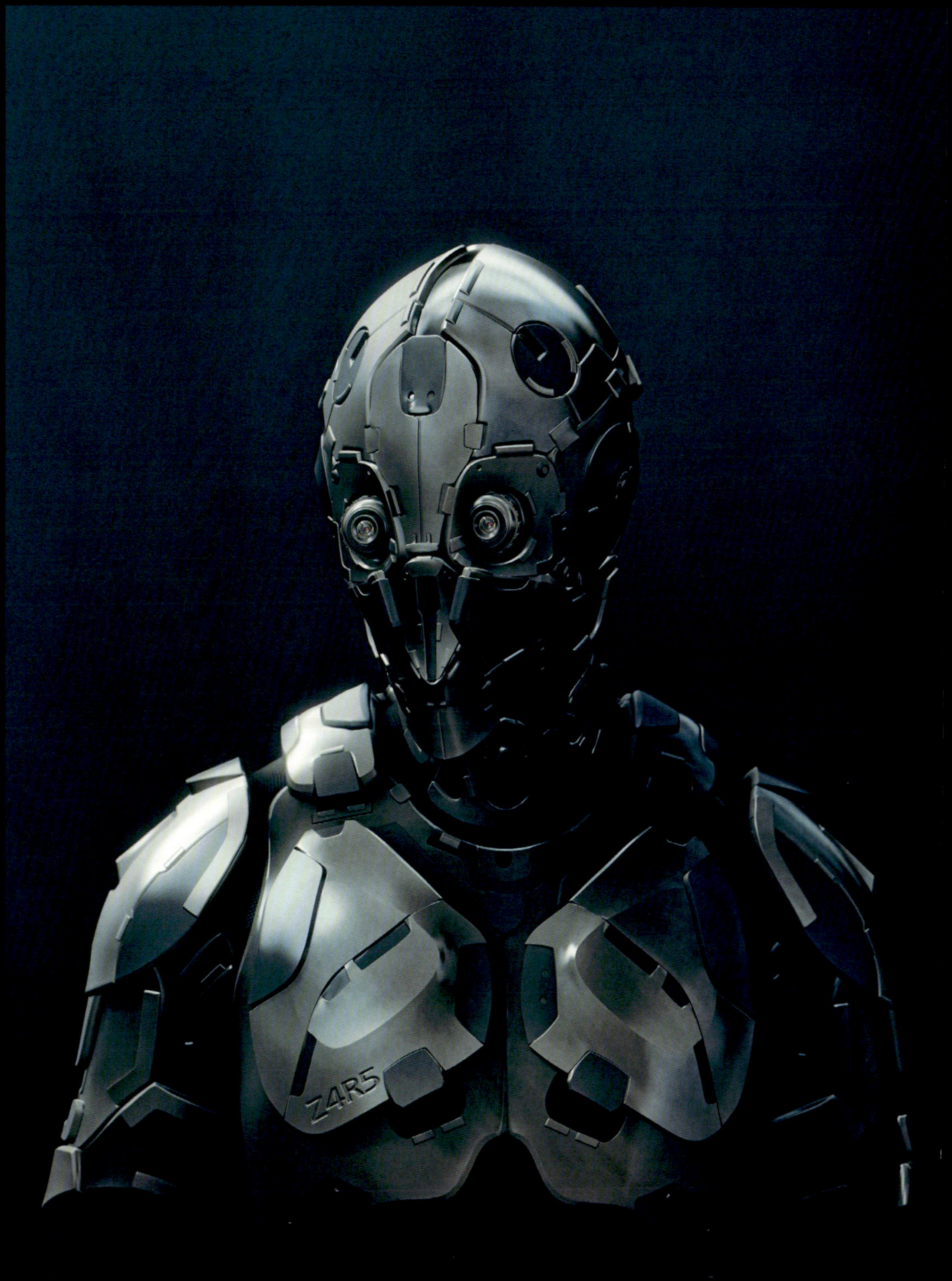

Robot
ZBrush
Daniel Bystedt, SWEDEN
[above]

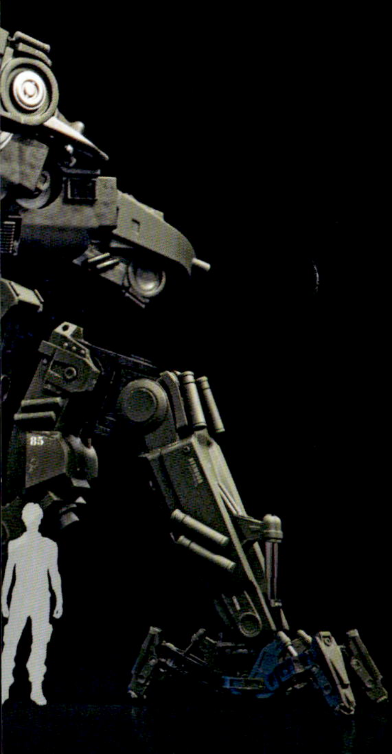

Int-67 Bergsteiger
3ds Max, V-Ray, Photoshop

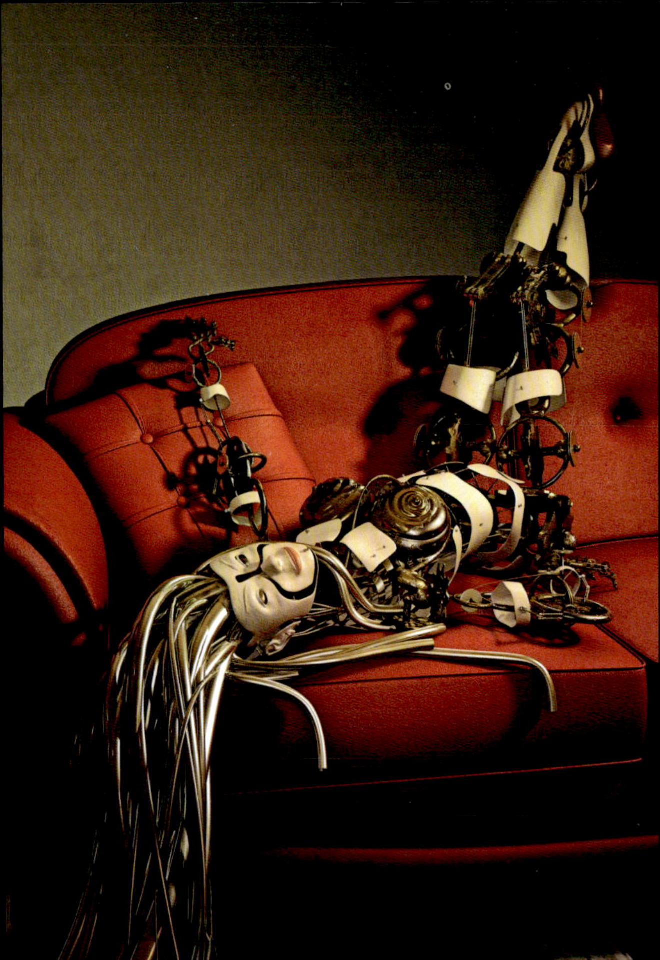

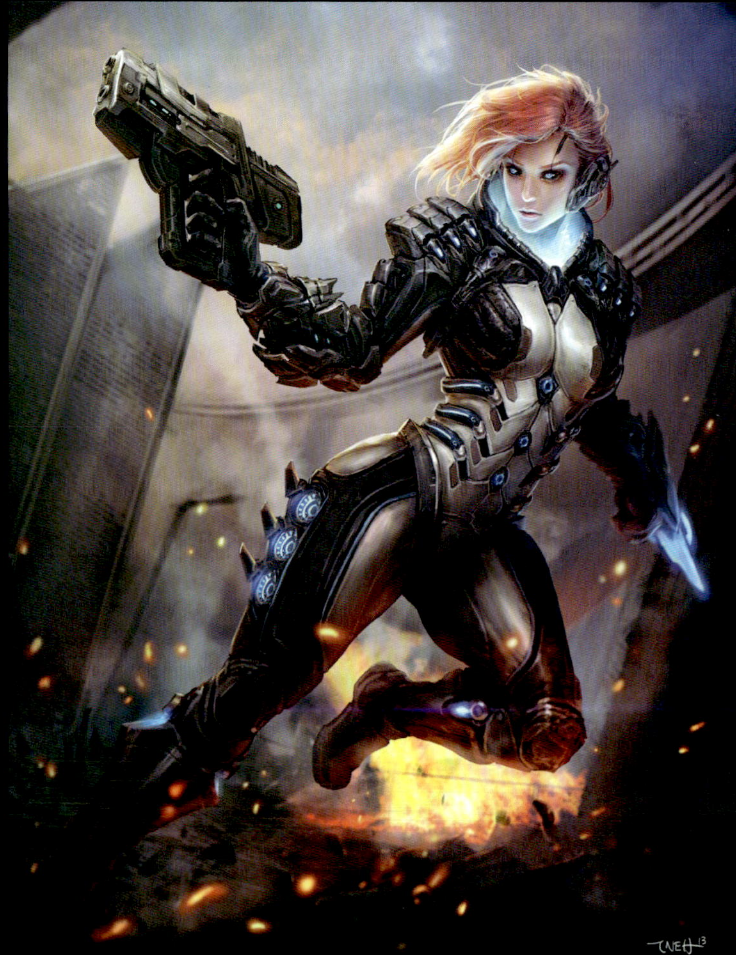

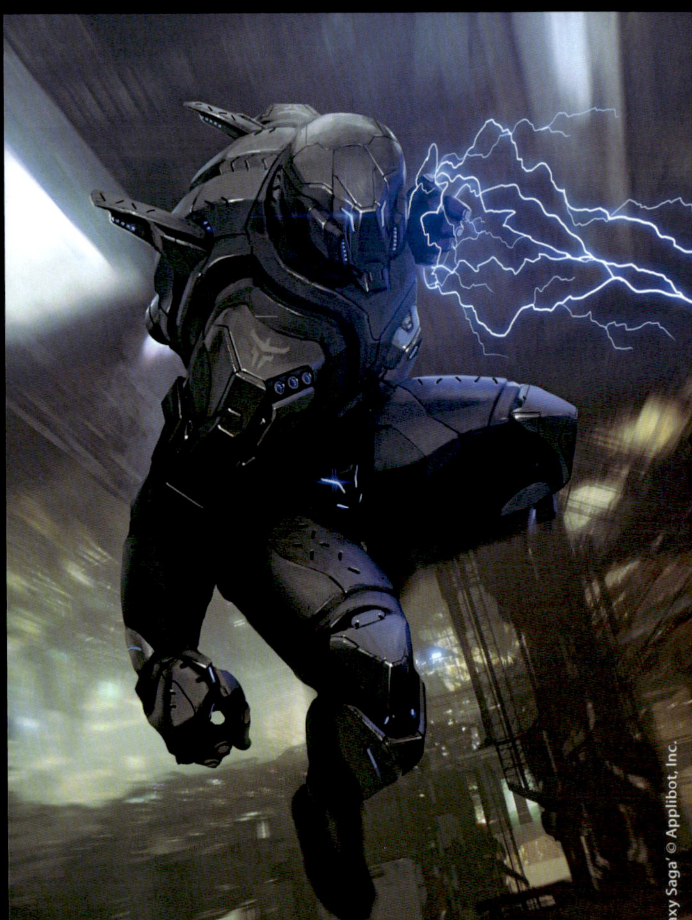

Galaxy Saga: Berserker of Destruction
Photoshop
Client: Applibot, Inc.
Geoffroy Thoorens, FRANCE
[above]

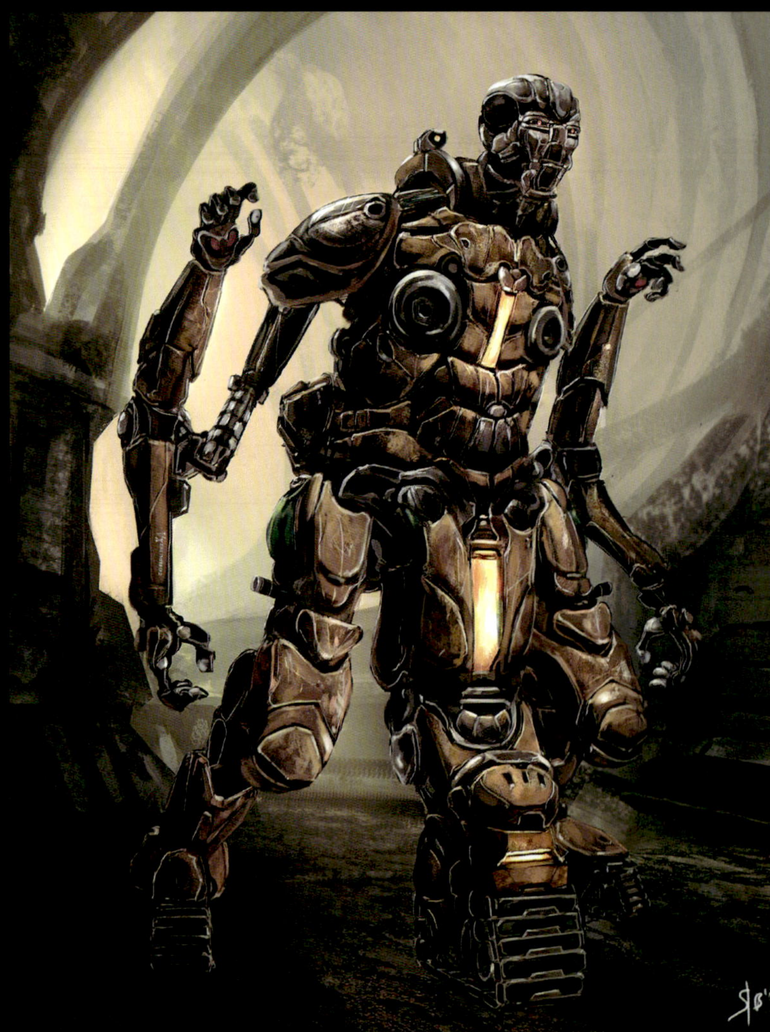

VX Unlimited 2
Photoshop
Rupy Bhogal, CANADA
[above]

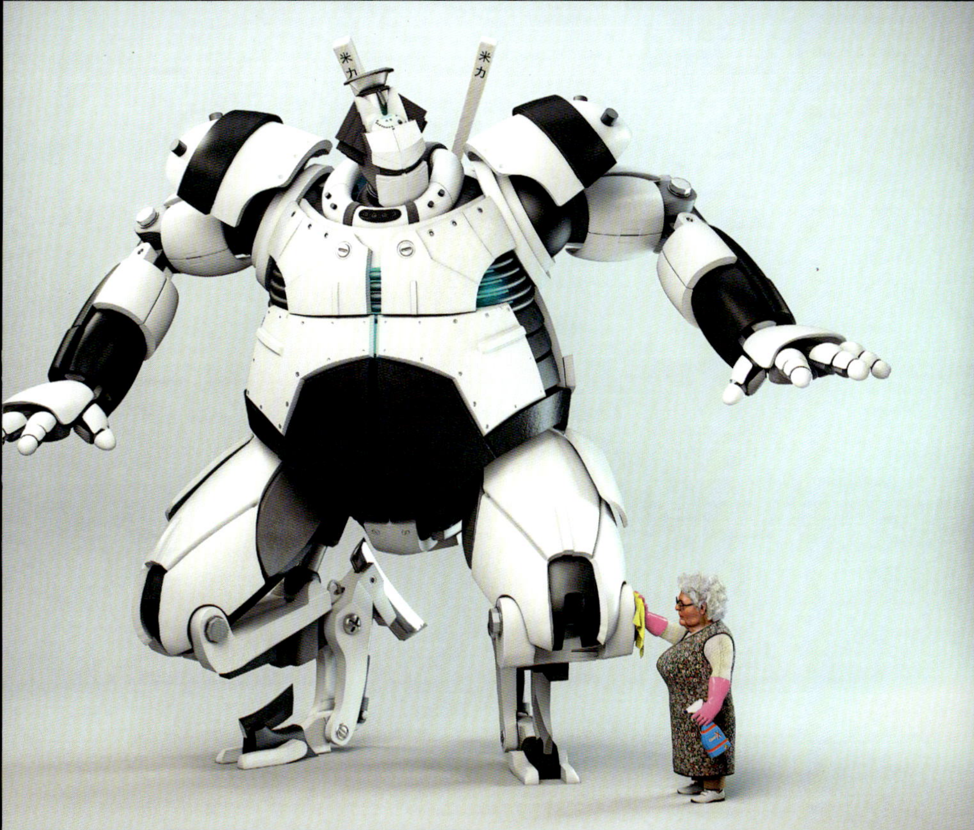

Gena Steampunk Pinup
Maya, mental ray, Mudbox, Photoshop
William Helba, FRANCE
[facing page top left]

War Cyborg
Photoshop
Tneh Sau Keong, MALAYSIA
[facing page top right]

Team 0: Bombi and Julia
ZBrush, 3ds Max, V-Ray, Photoshop
David AF, PORTUGAL
[left]

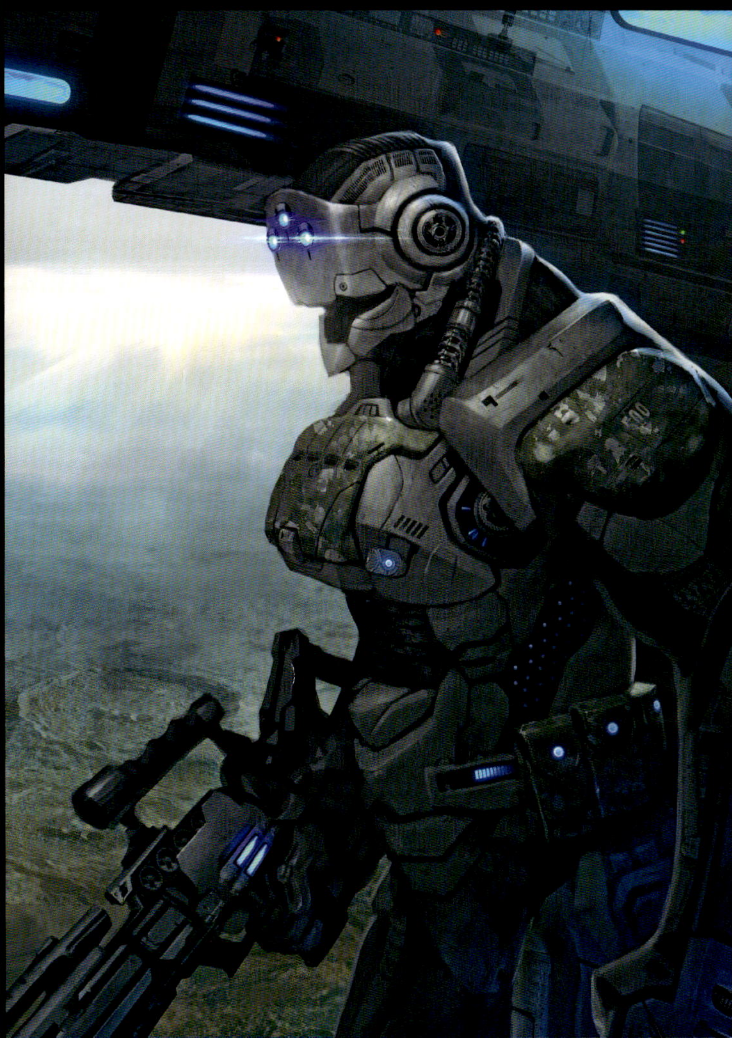

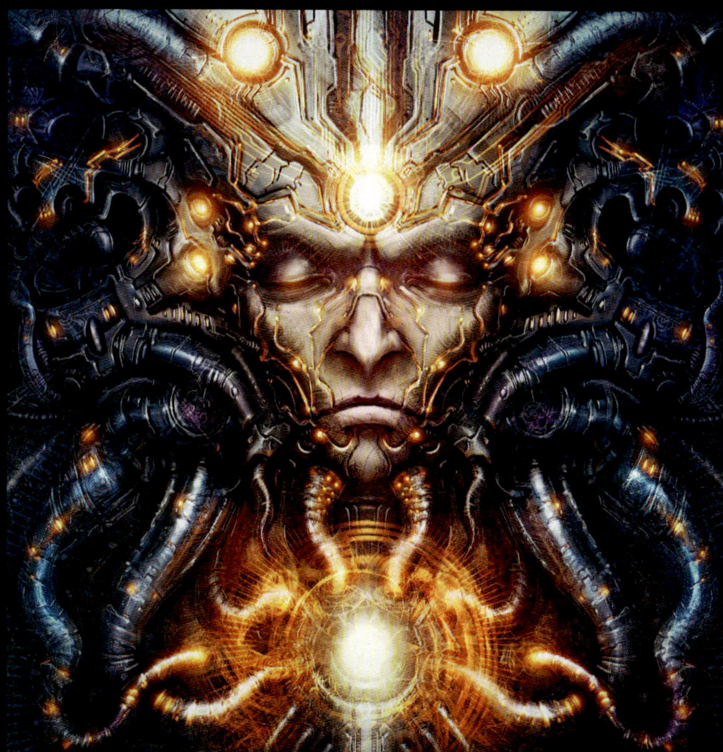

Galaxy Shaper
Painter, Photoshop
Mariusz Siergiejew, POLAND
[above]

Landing
Photoshop
Vinh Pham, VIETNAM
[left]

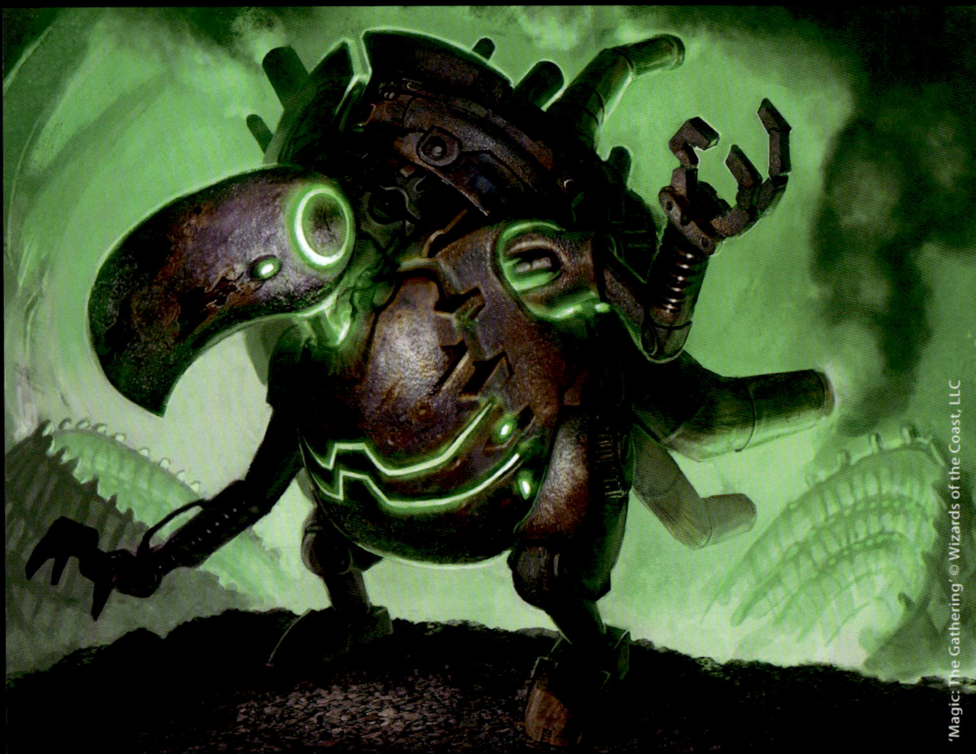

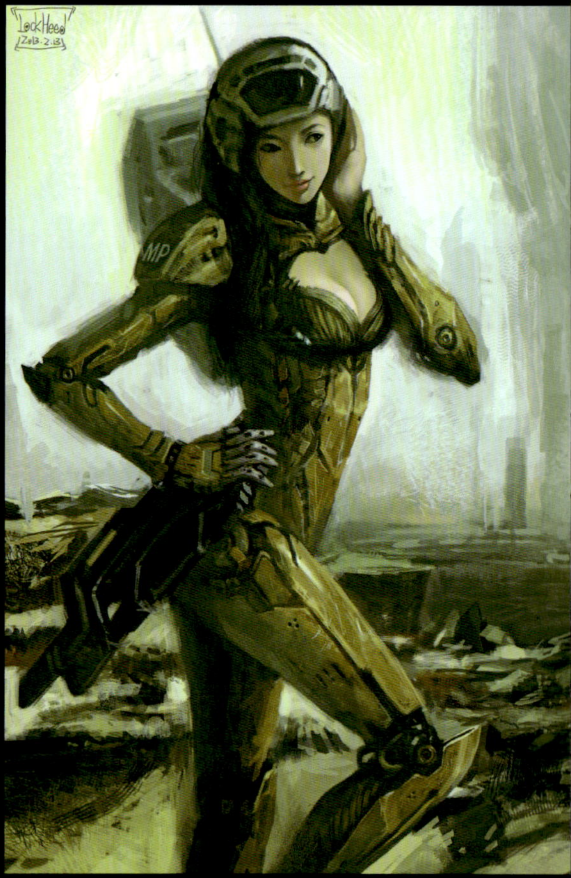

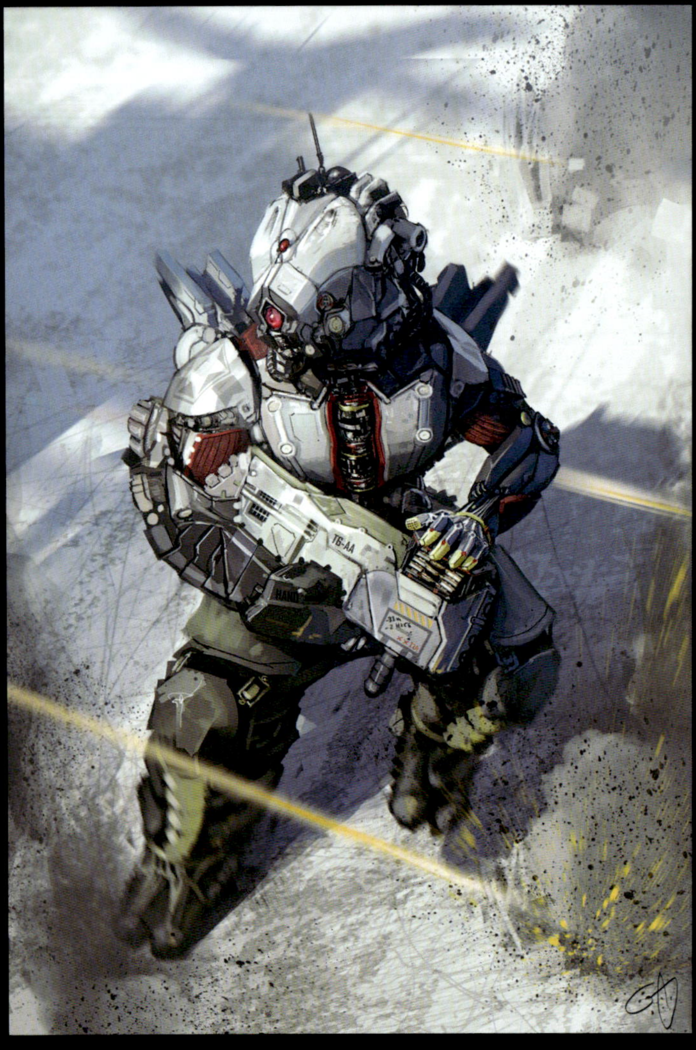

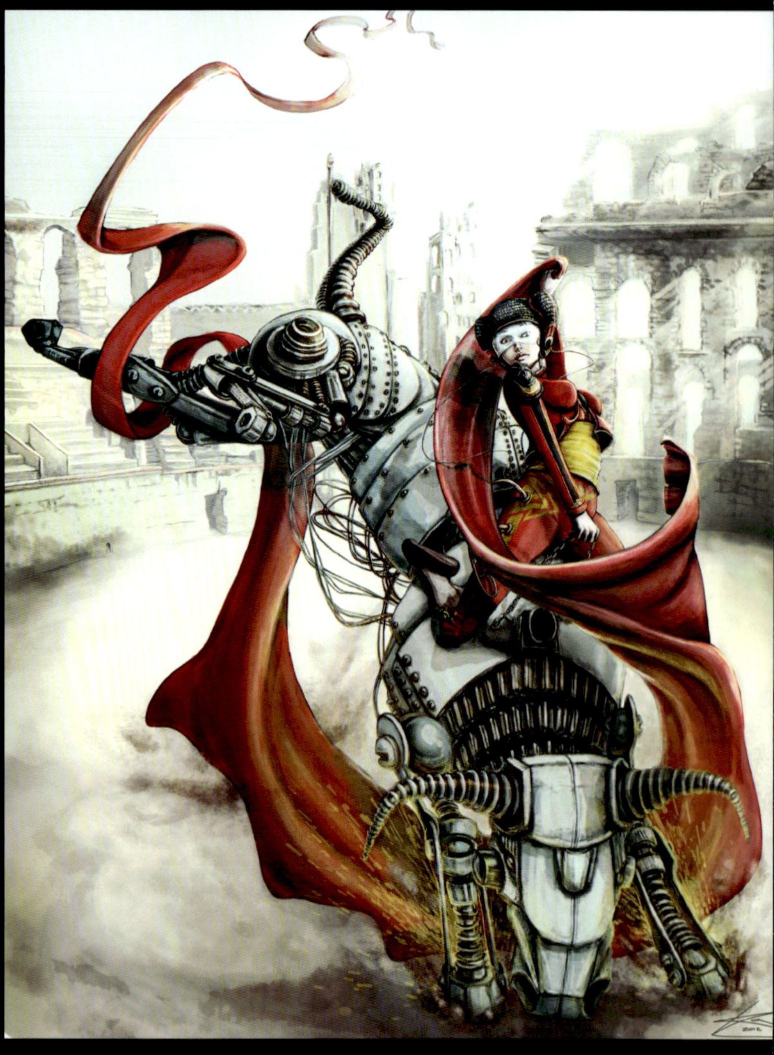

Anti-Air Unit
Photoshop, Illustrator
Garret AJ, USA

Pepper Matador
Photoshop
kEda Gomes, SOUTH AFRICA

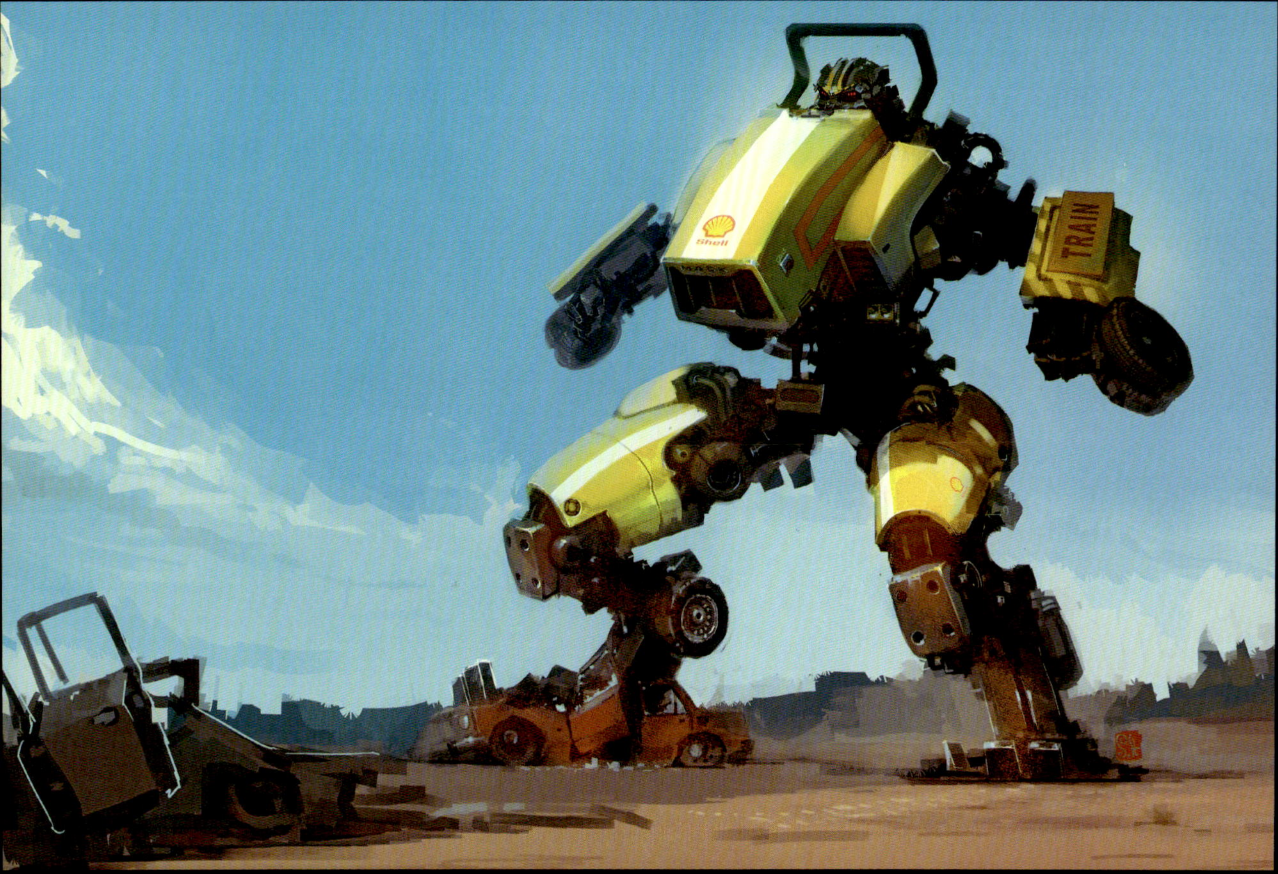

Magic: The Gathering (Poison Myr)
Photoshop, ArtRage
Client: Wizards of the Coast, LLC
Jason Felix (Art Director: Jeremy Jarvis), USA
[facing page top left]

Charm
Photoshop
Chang Chun Mao, TAIWAN
[facing page top right]

Mack
Photoshop
Eugene Lizin, RUSSIA
[left]

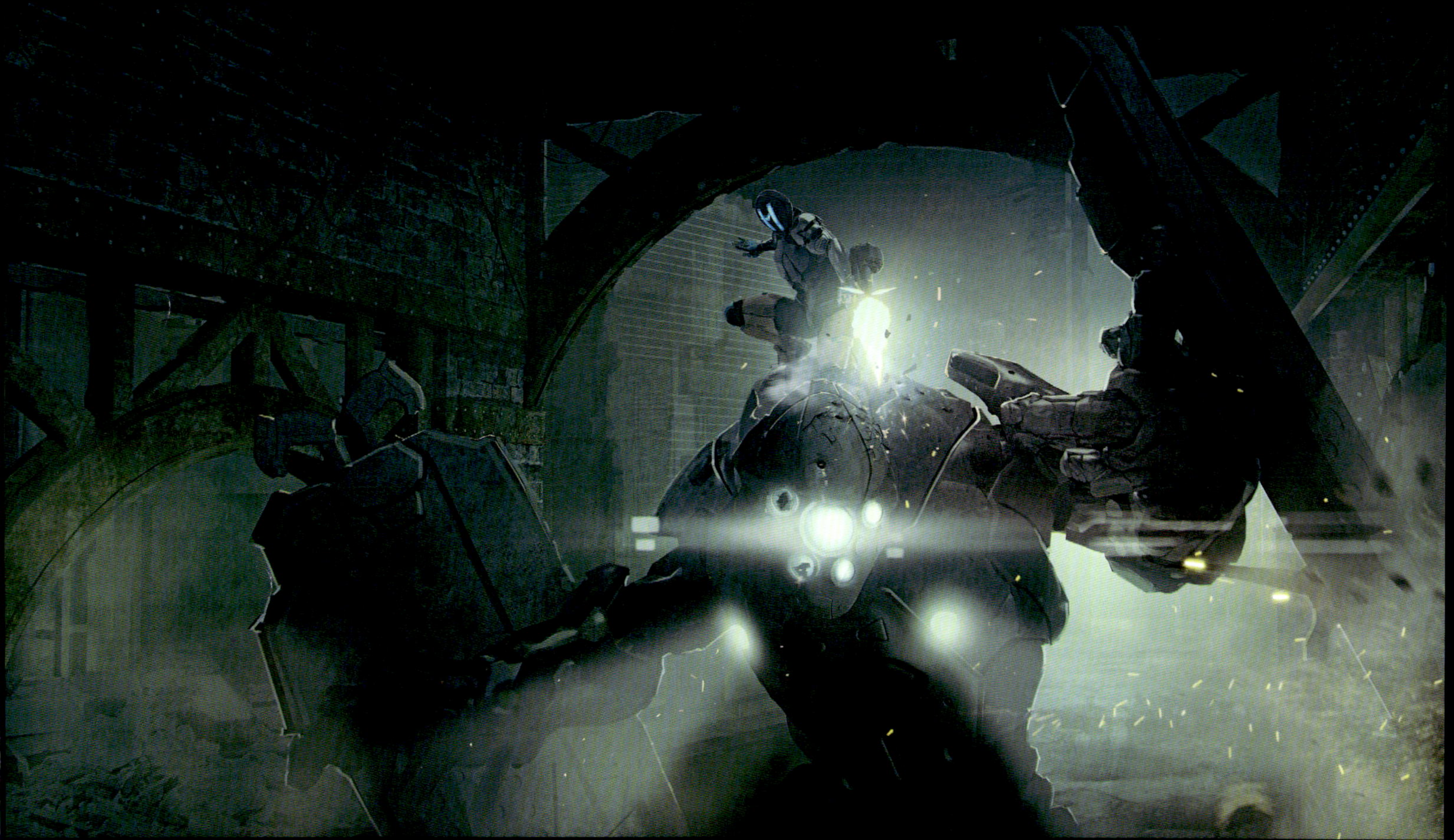

Firing at Reaper
Maya, Photoshop

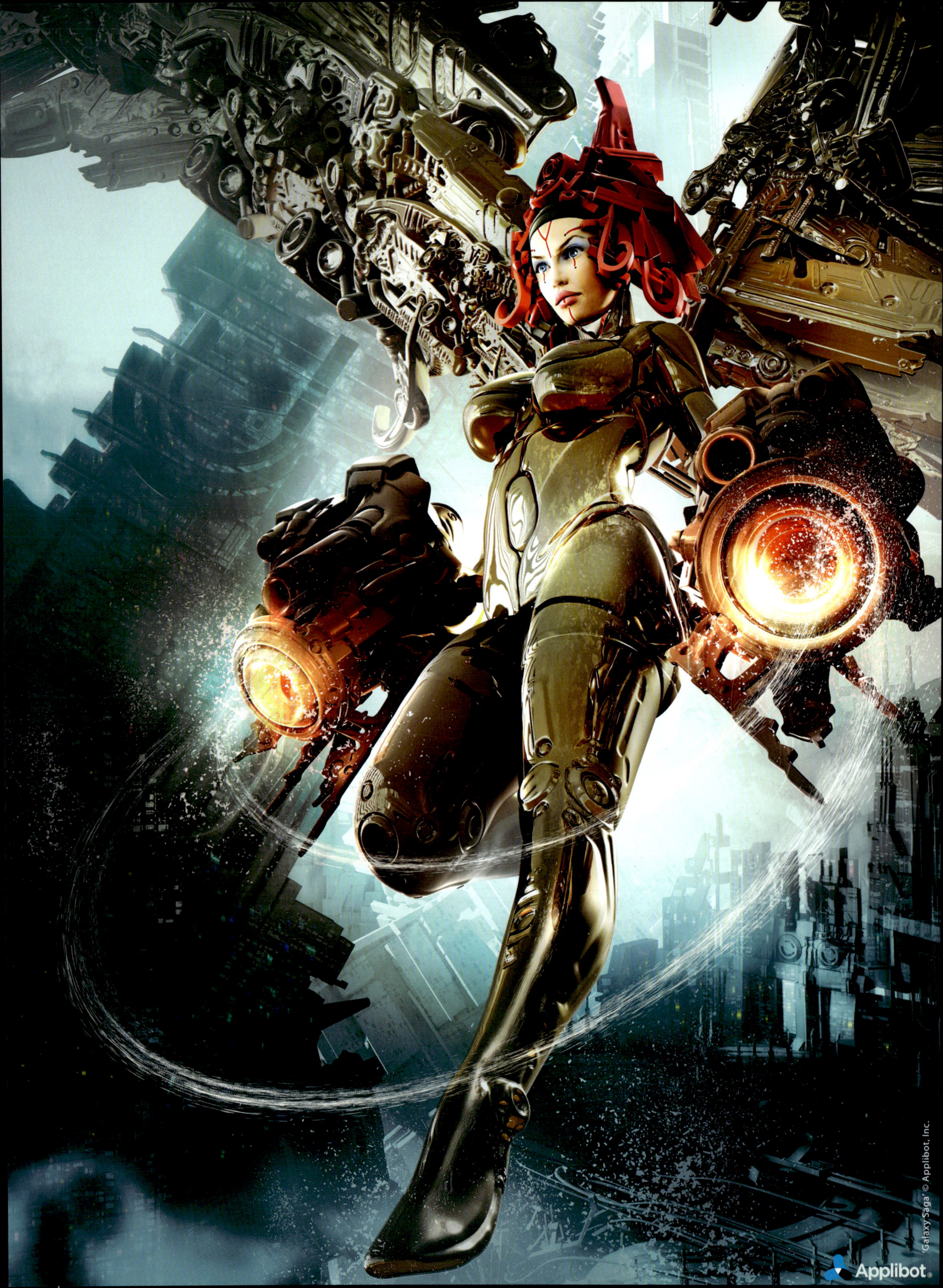

Excellence

Game Art

Galaxy Saga: Winged-Queen Perseus (Advanced Version)

Maya, ZBrush, Photoshop

Client: Applibot, Inc.

Daniele Scerra, ITALY

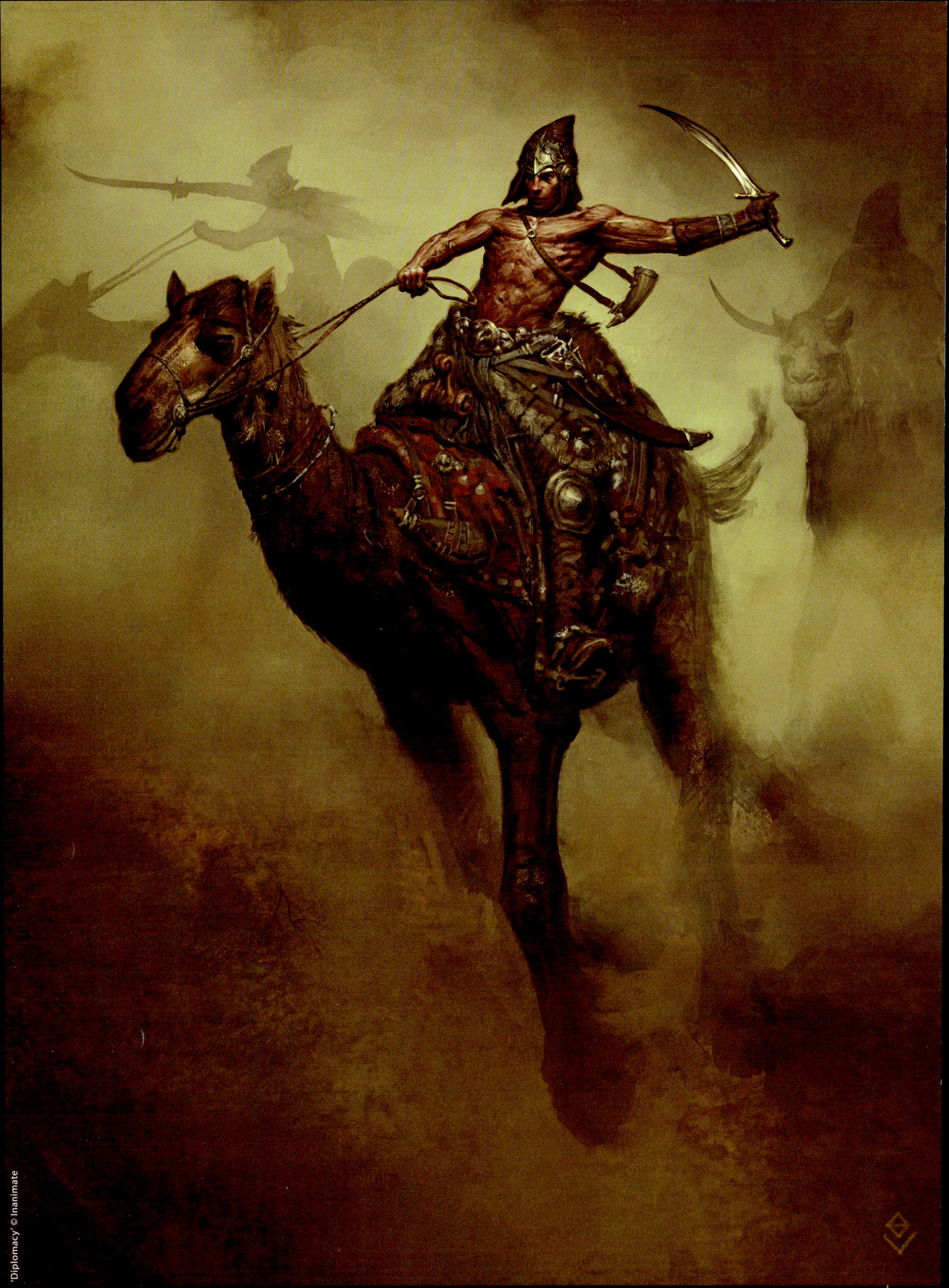

Diplomacy: Crusaders of Iram
Photoshop
Client: Inanimate
Gabriel Verdon, CANADA

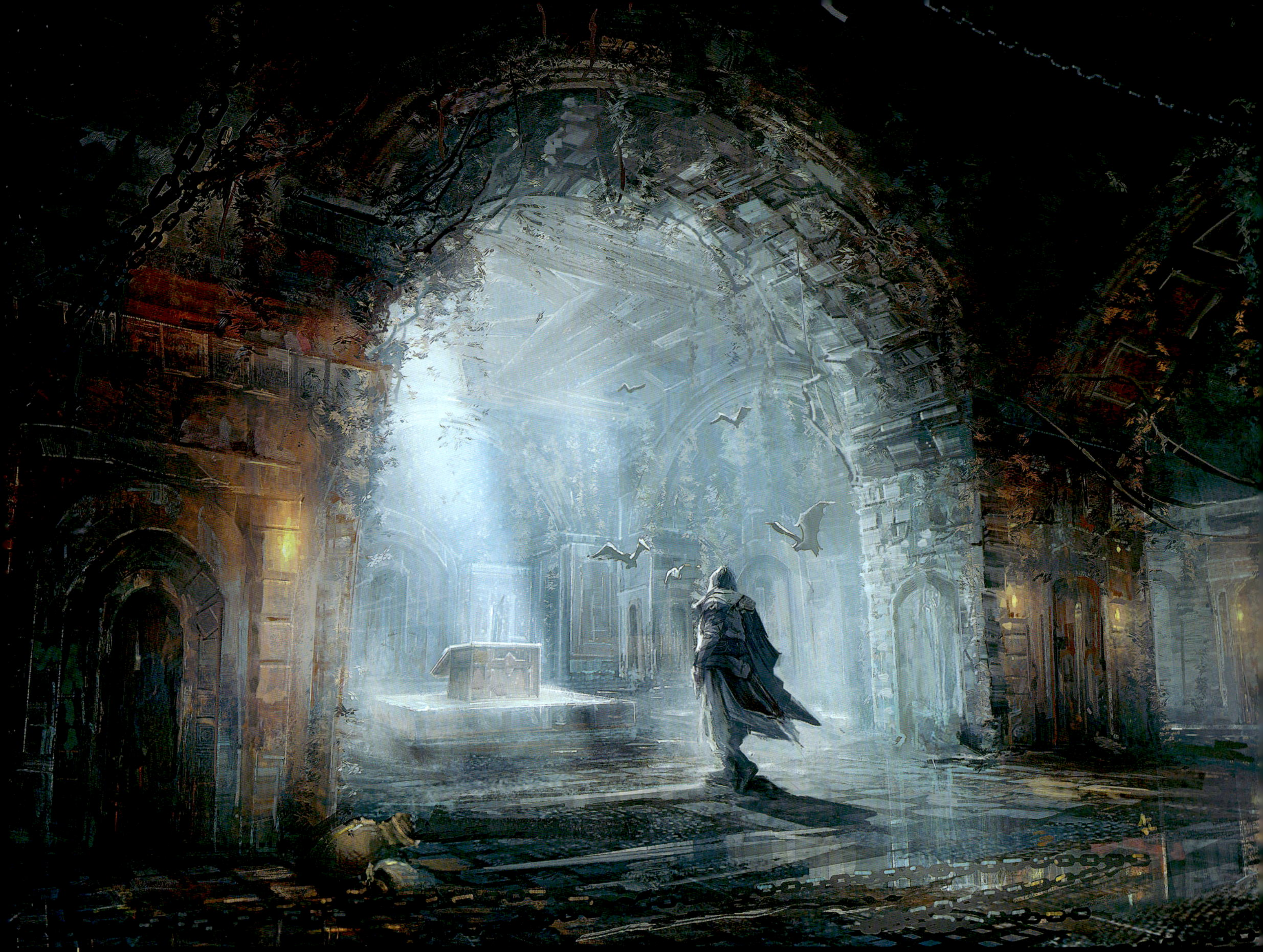

Excellence
Game Art

Assassin's Creed Brotherhood: Reward Room
Photoshop
Donglu Yu, CANADA
[above]

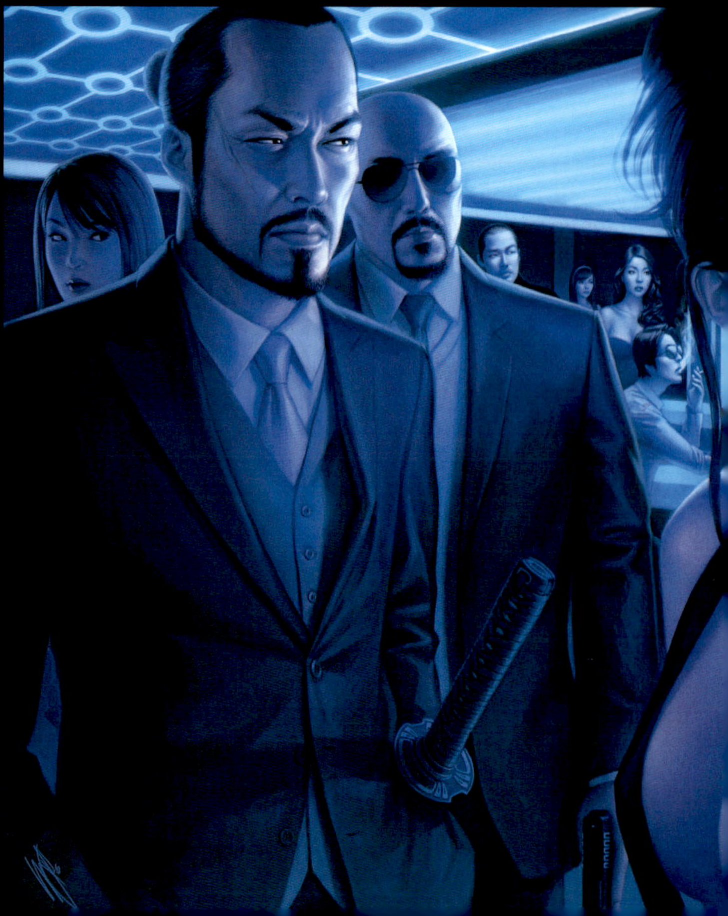

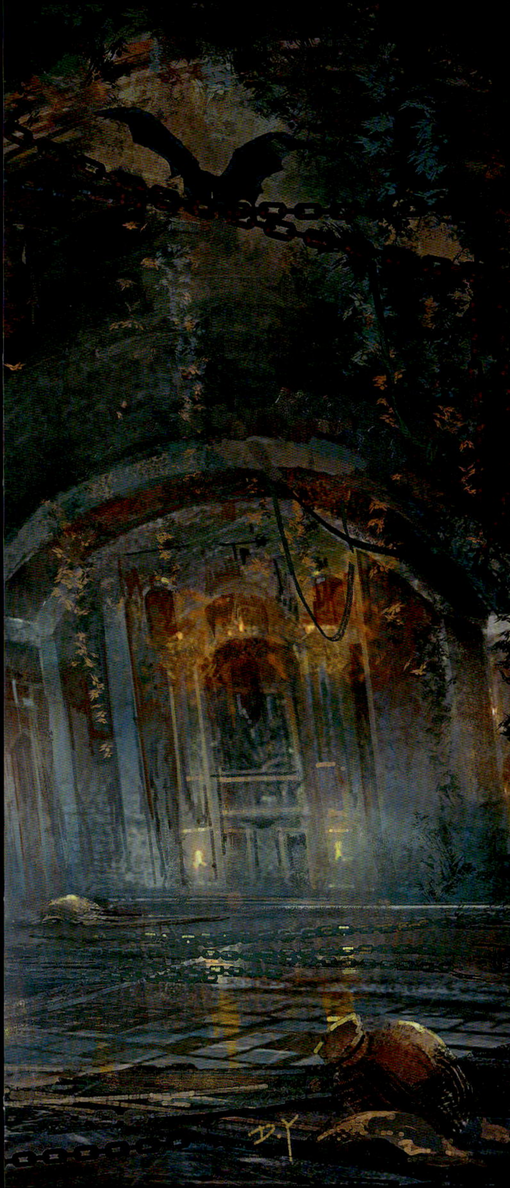

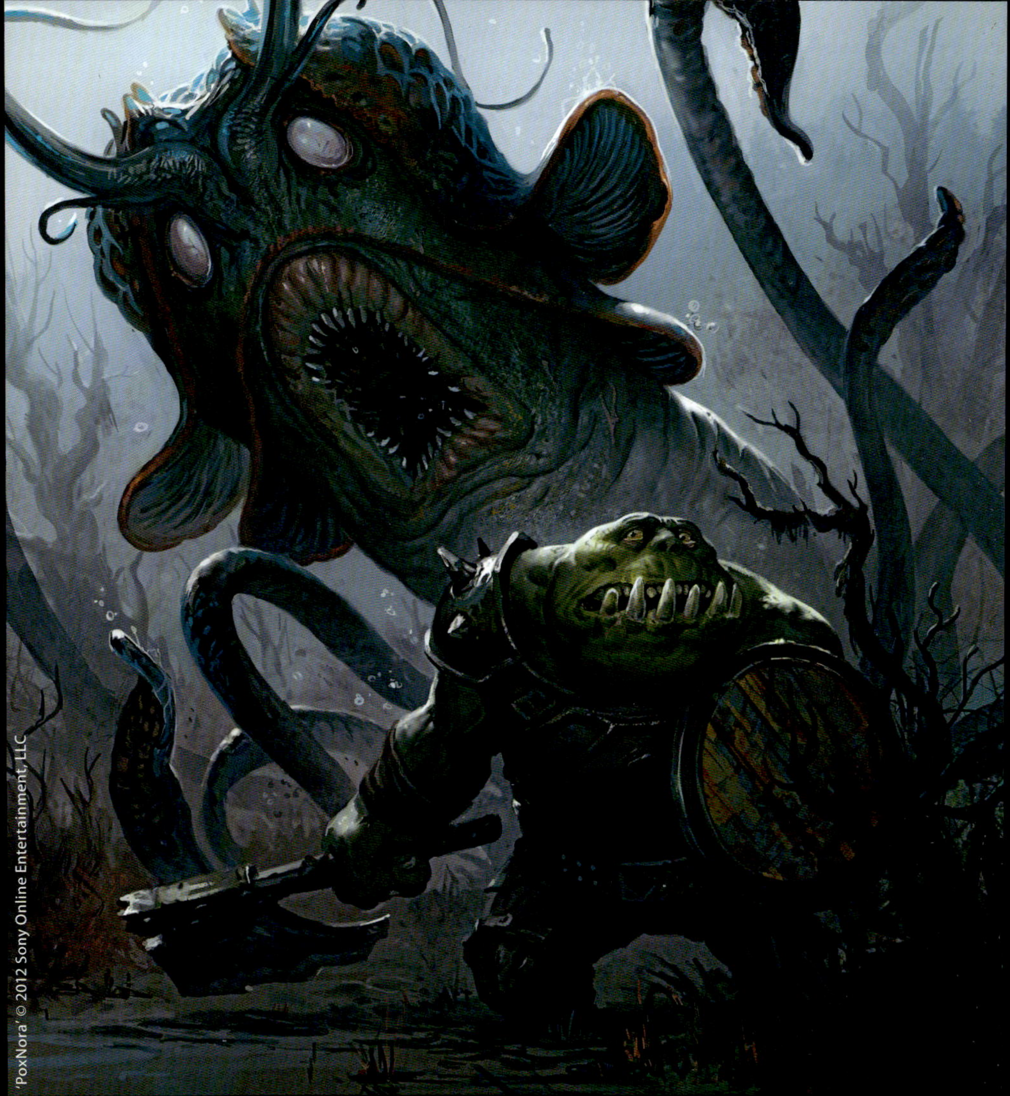

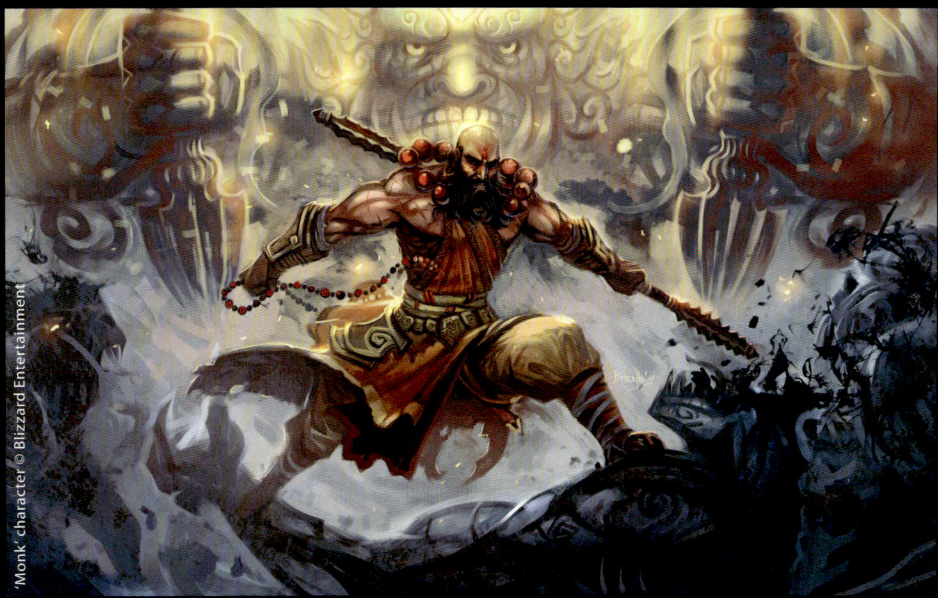

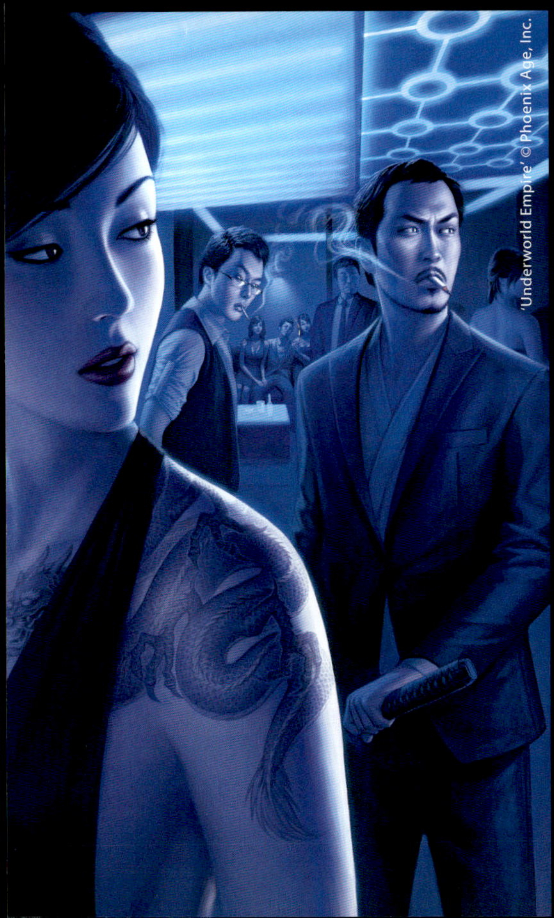

PoxNora: Extispicer
Photoshop
Client: Sony Online Entertainment, LLC
Jakub Kasper (Art Director: Anthony Lopes), POLAND
[top]

Monk
Painter
Jian Guo, CHINA
[above]

Underworld Empire: Sin
Photoshop
Client: Phoenix Age, Inc.
Warren Louw, SOUTH AFRICA
[left]

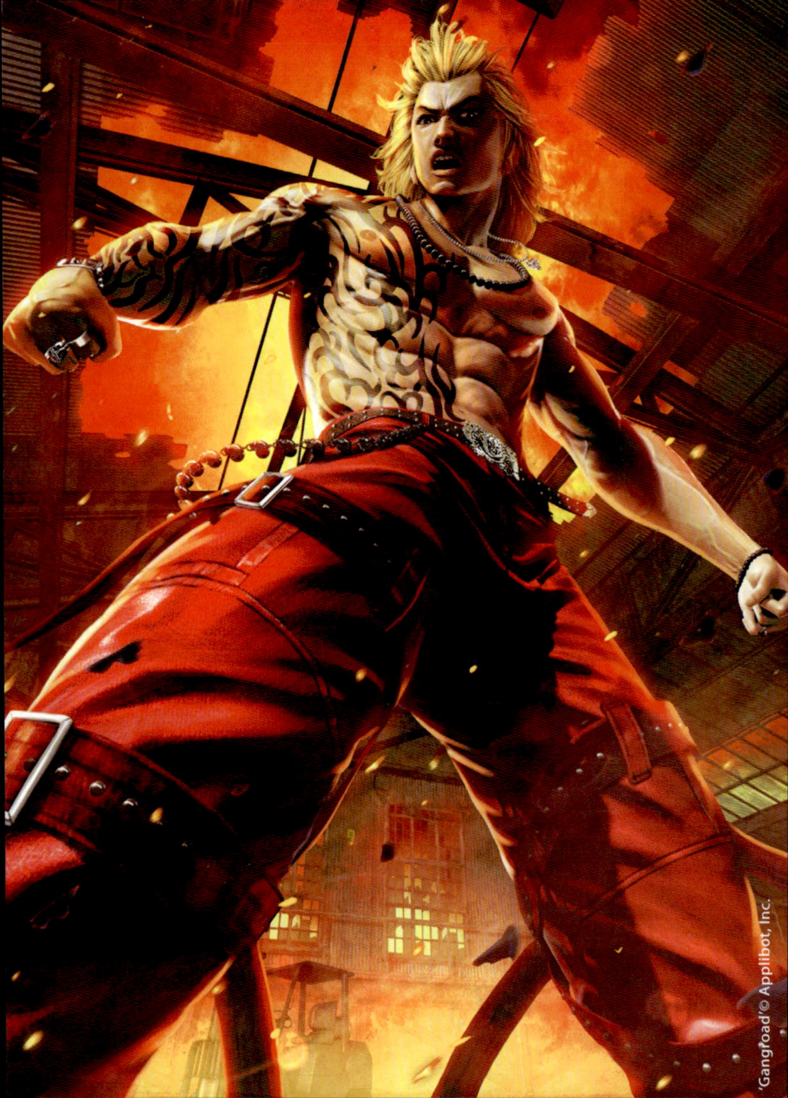

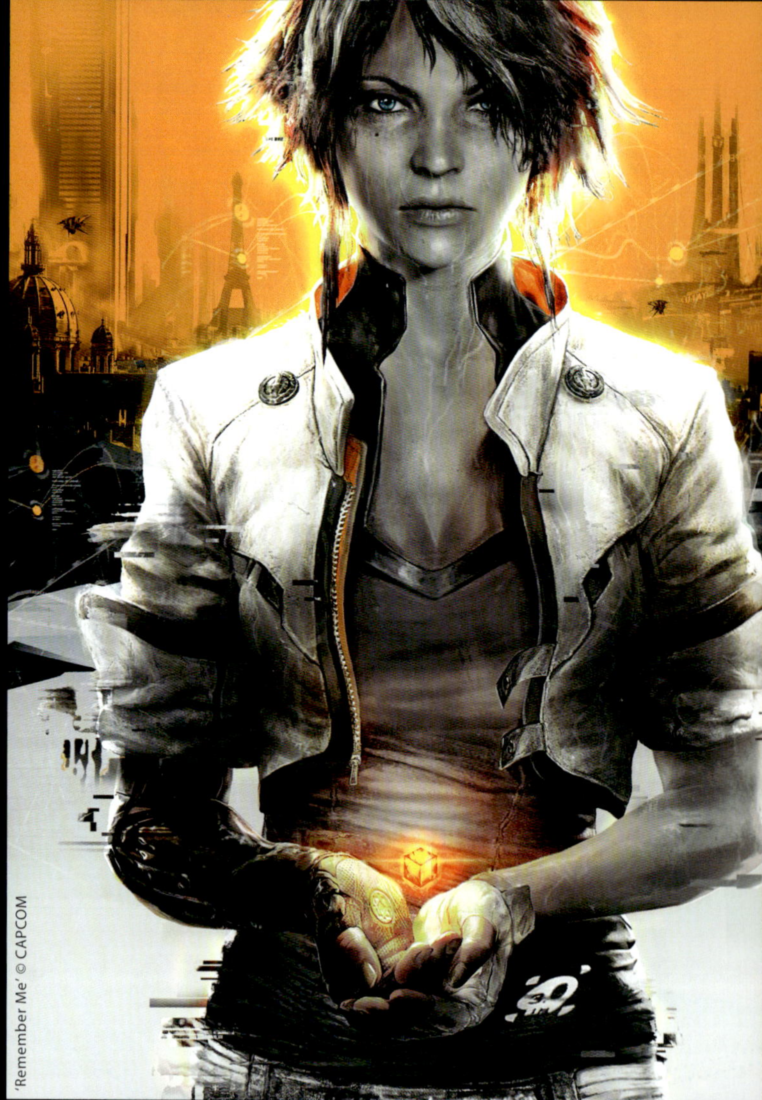

Gang Card Game Character Design
Photoshop, Softimage, Mudbox, Shade
Client: Applibot, Inc.
Yoshinobu Saito, JAPAN
[above left]

Remember Me: Nilin
Photoshop
Client: CAPCOM
Aleksi Briclot, FRANCE
[above right]

League of Legends: Zyra (Rise of the Thorns)
Photoshop
Katie De Sousa, Riot Games, USA
[right]

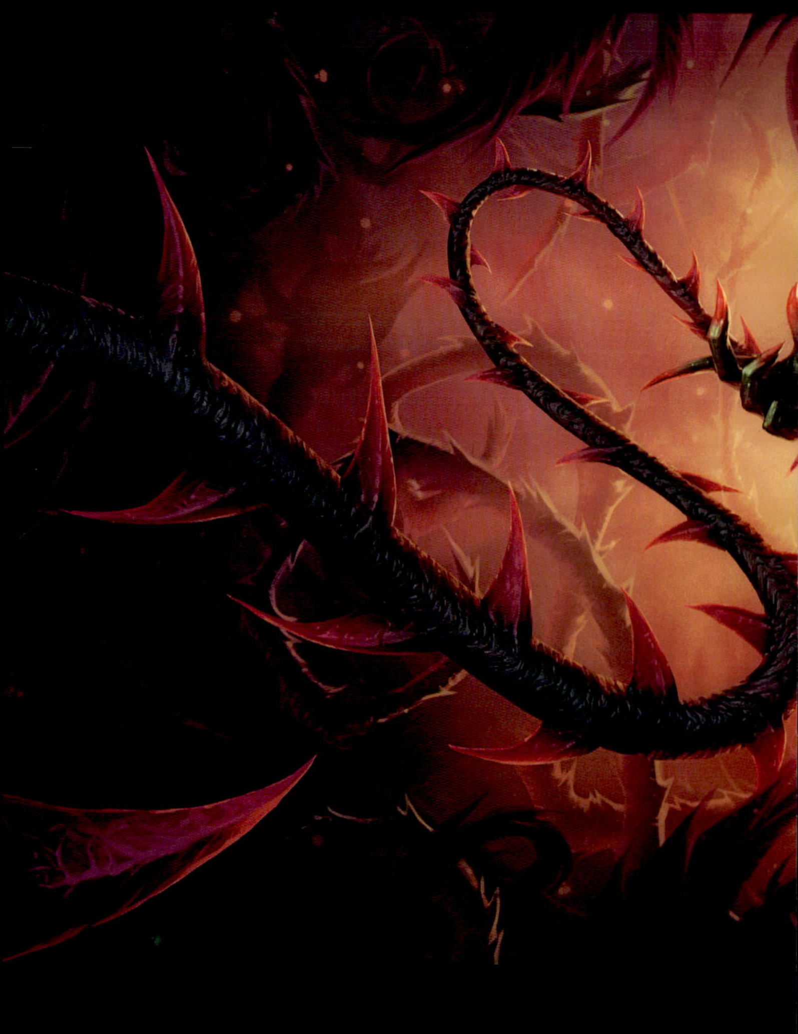

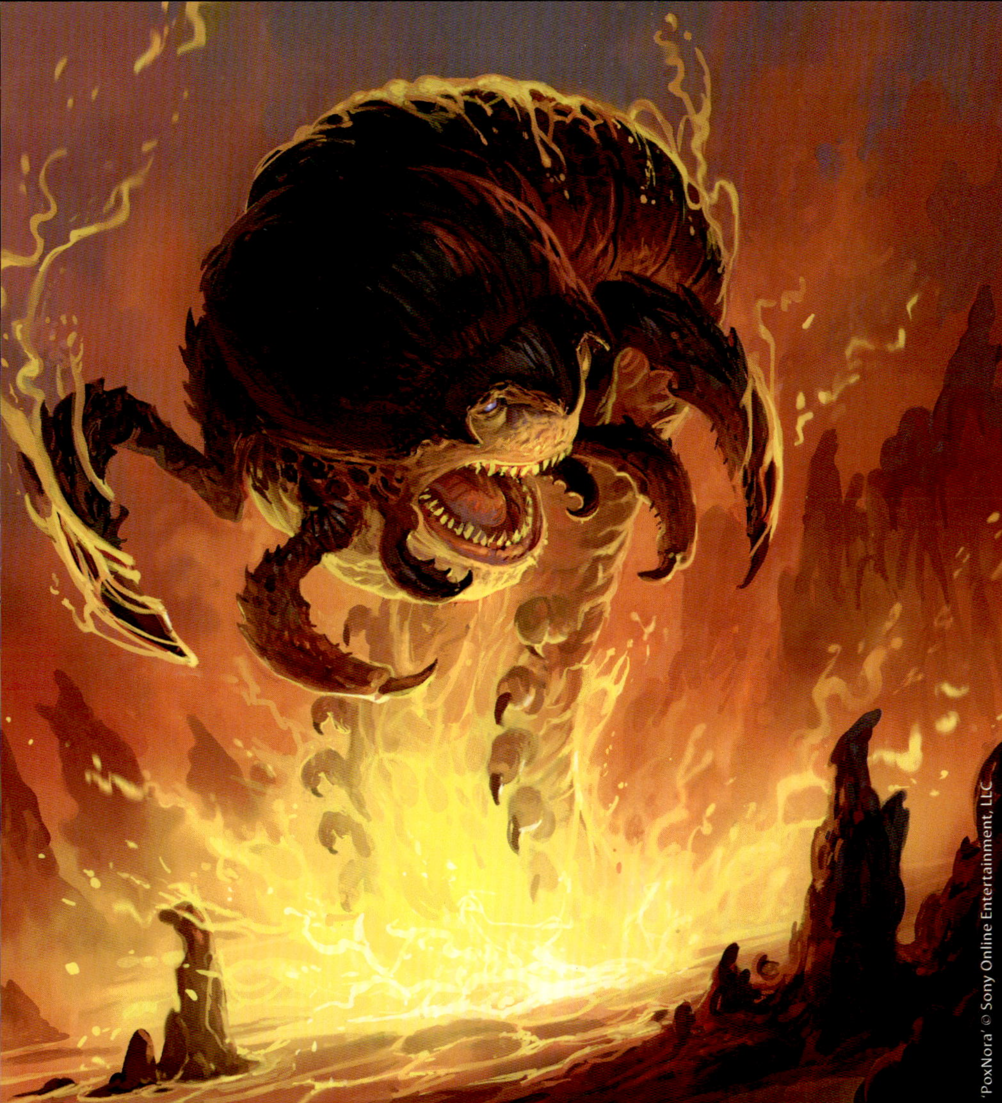

PoxNora: Cinderpede
Photoshop
Client: Sony Online Entertainment, LLC
Jakub Kasper (Art Director: Anthony Lopes), POLAND
[left]

Chains of Durandal: Dwarven King
Photoshop
Client: DeNA Co., Ltd.
Michael Anthony Gonzales, PHILIPPINES
[below]

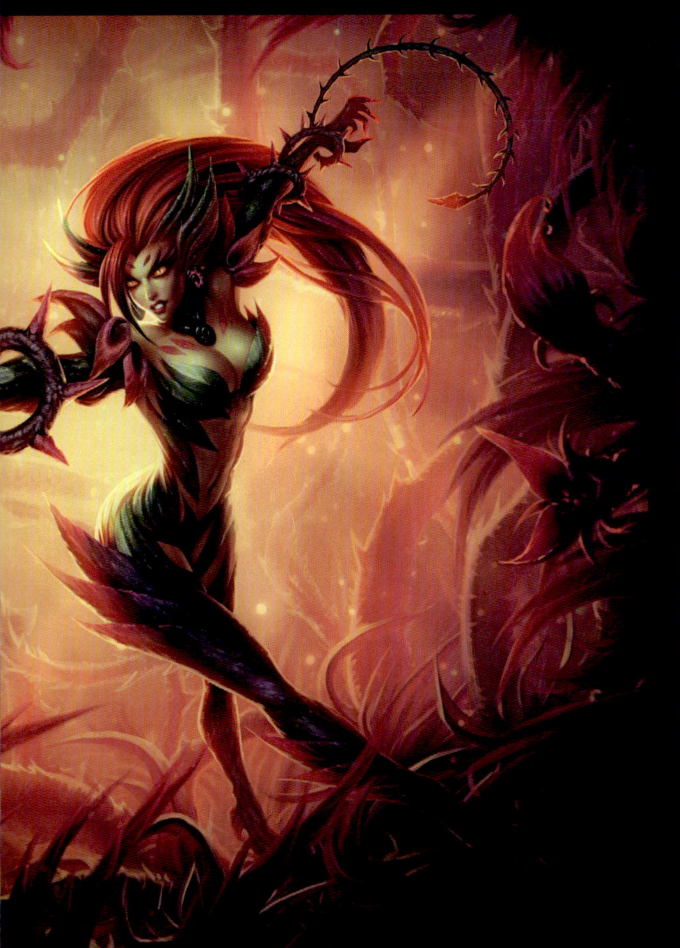

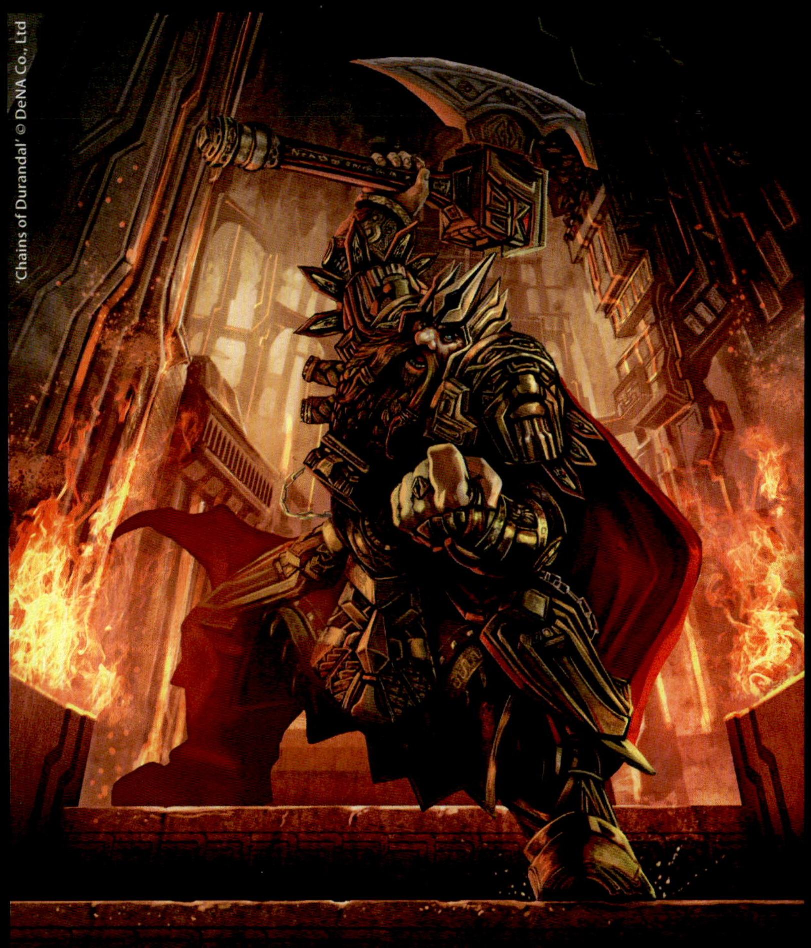

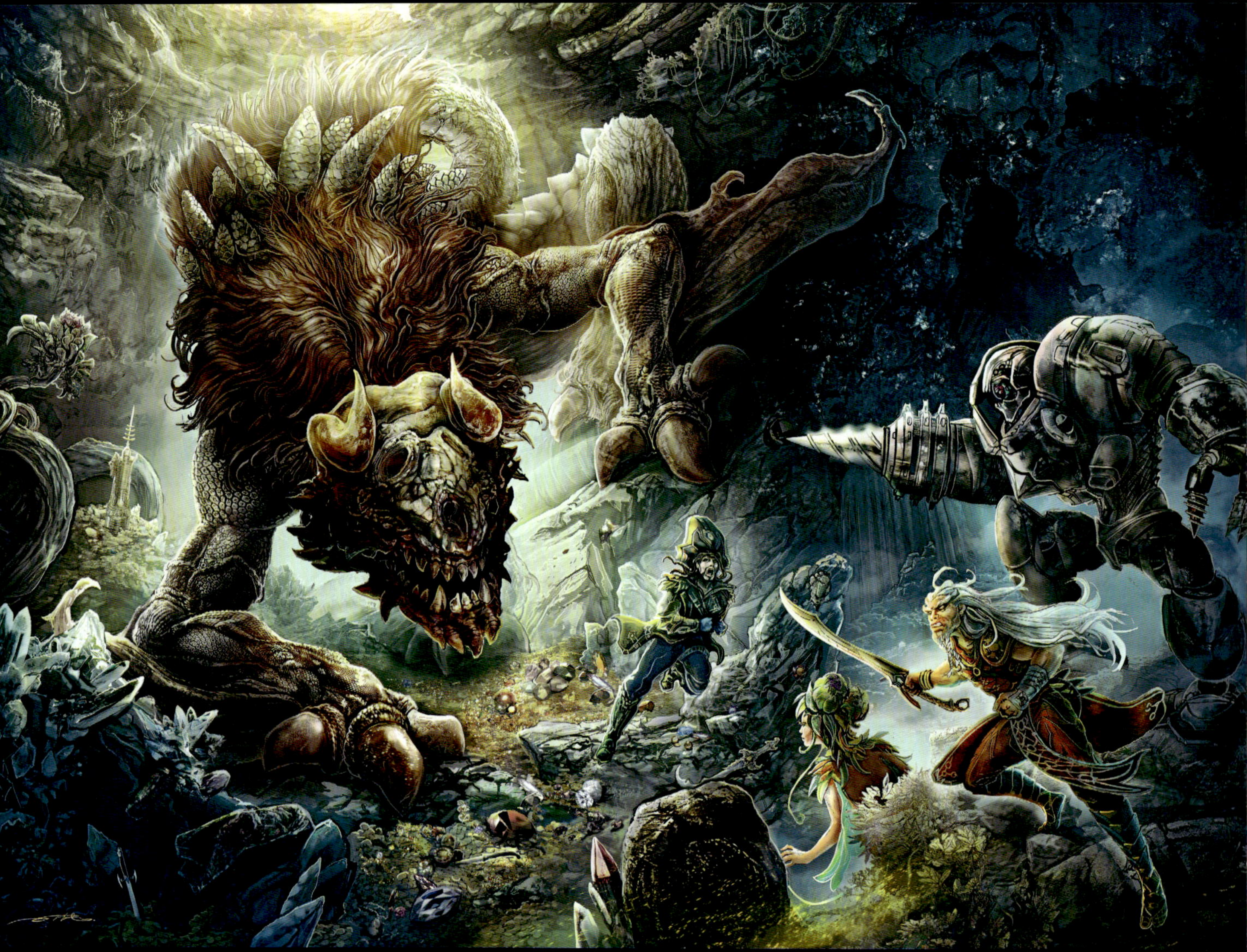

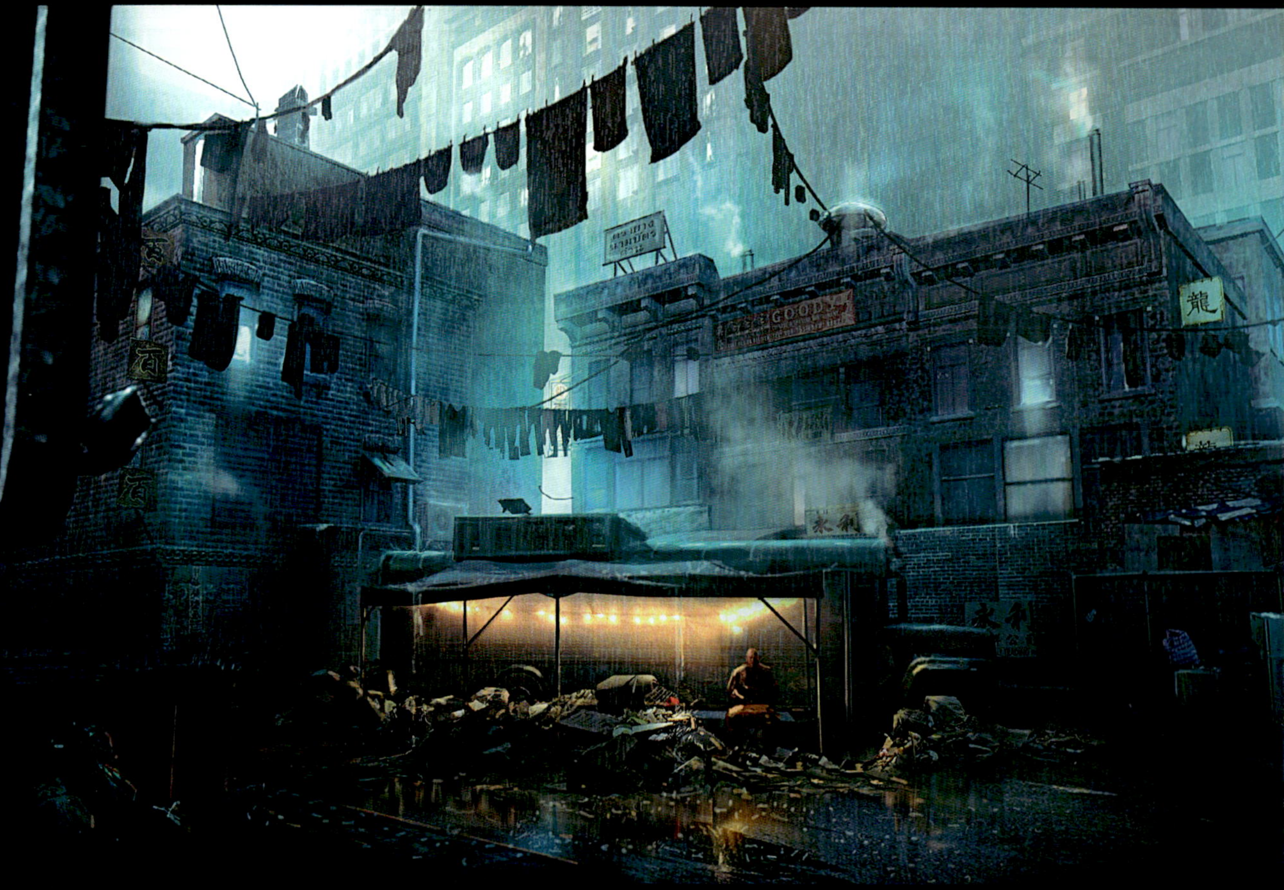

New Horizon: Lair of the Grimterror
Photoshop
Client: New Horizon Game Studios | Lypson Intelligent Systems
Ertaç Altinoz, TURKEY
[top]

Hitman Absolution: Birdies Nest
Photoshop
Client: Square Enix/IO Interactive
Rasmus Berggreen, DENMARK
[above]

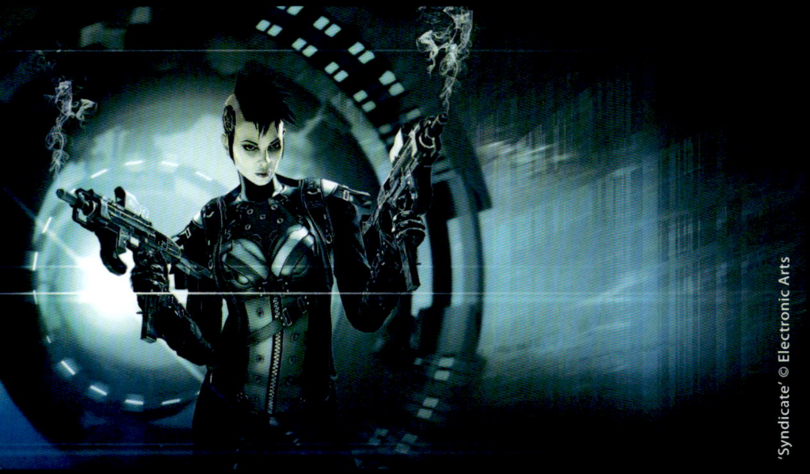

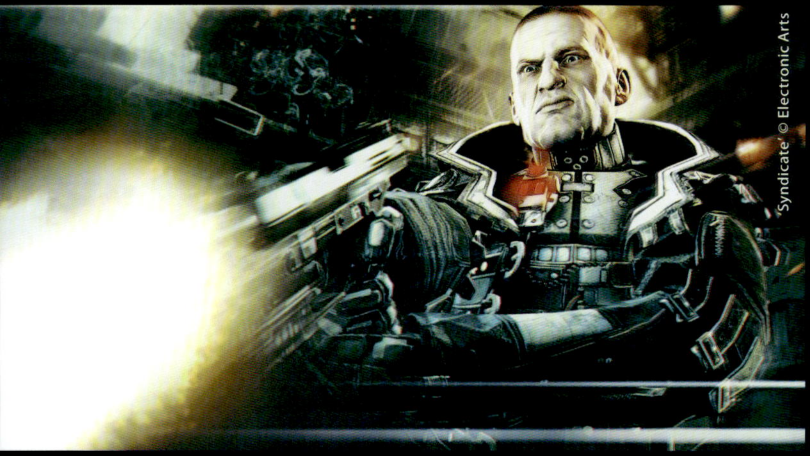

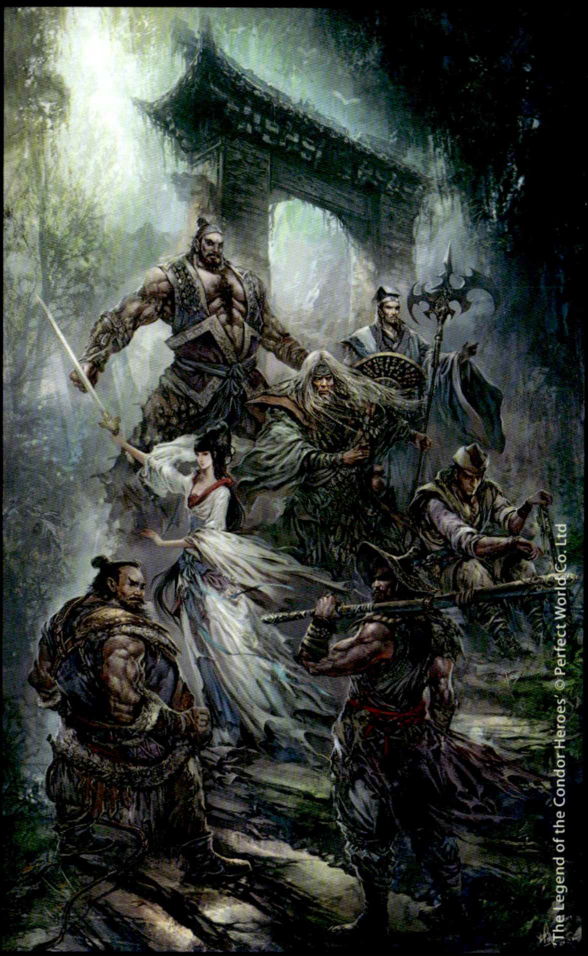

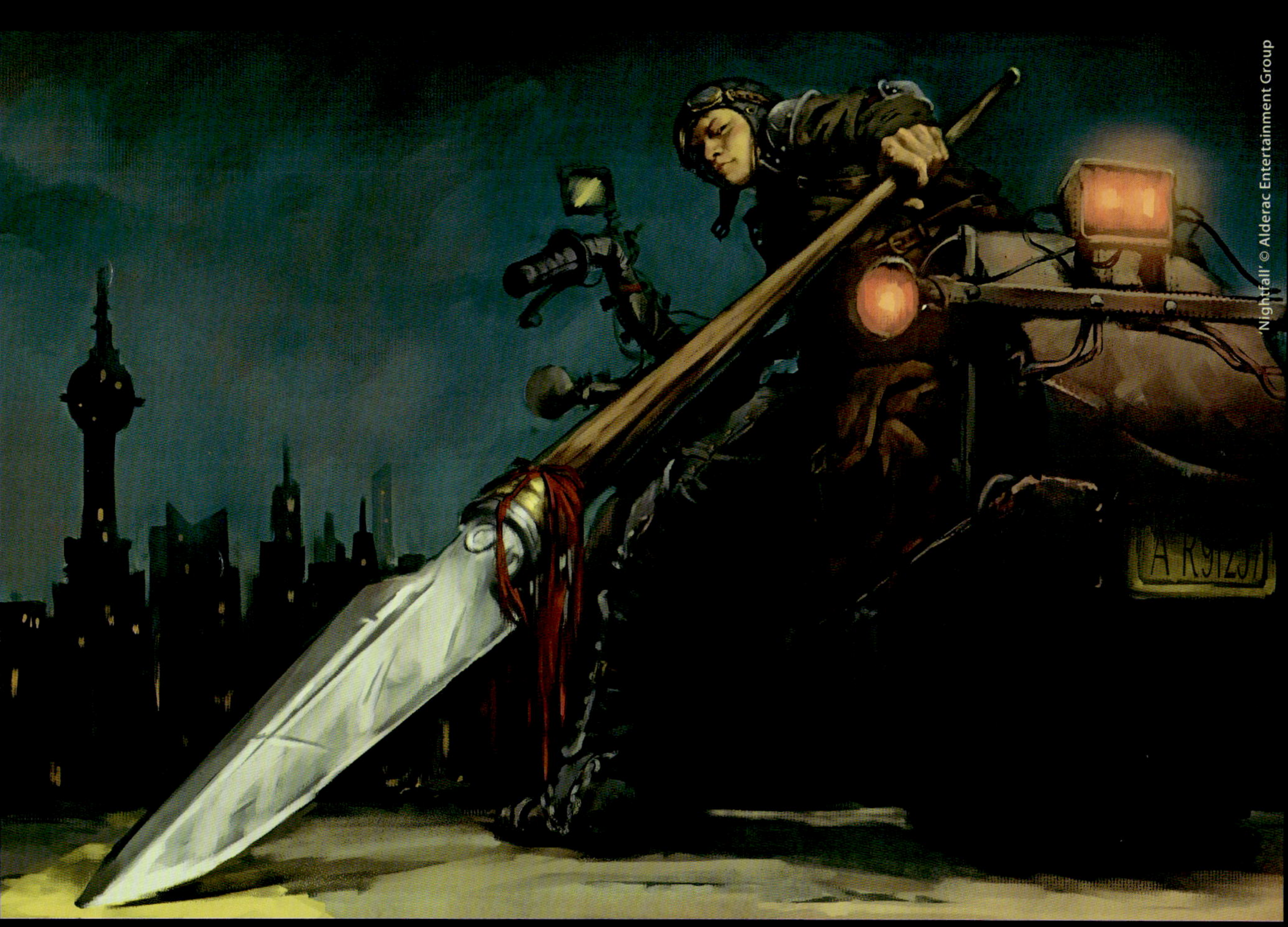

Syndicate: AKUMA
Maya, Photoshop
Client: Electronic Arts
Patrik Karlsson, SWEDEN
[top left]

Syndicate: Fall
Maya, Photoshop
Client: Electronic Arts
Patrik Karlsson, SWEDEN
[center left]

Nightfall: Did You See My Spear?
Painter, Photoshop
Client: Alderac Entertainment Group
Aaron Riley, USA
[above]

The Legend of the Condor Heroes: Seven Heroes
Photoshop
Client: Perfect World Co. Ltd.
Feng Guo, CHINA

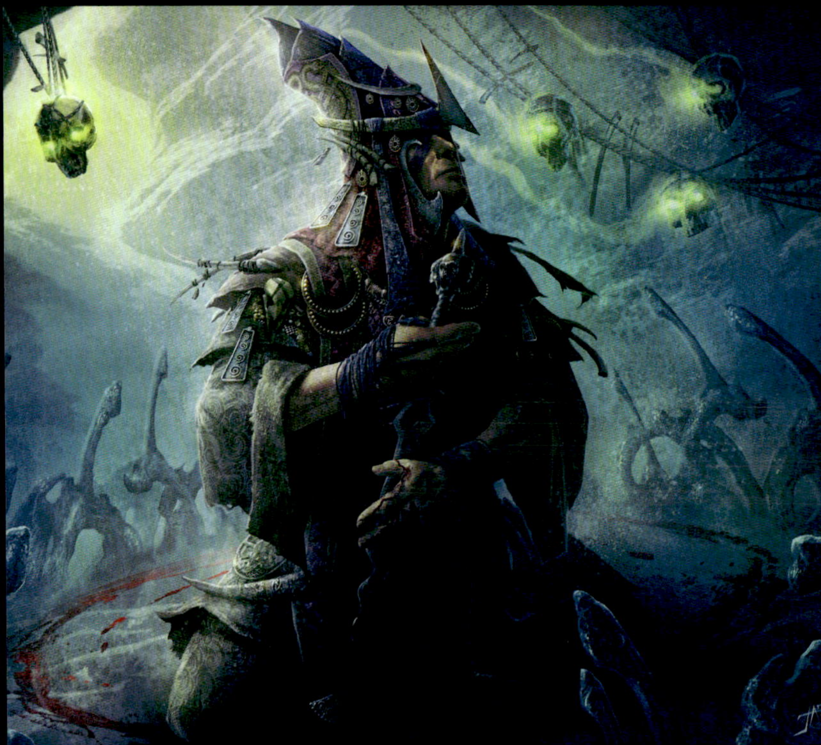

'Magic the Gathering' © Wizards of the Coast, LLC

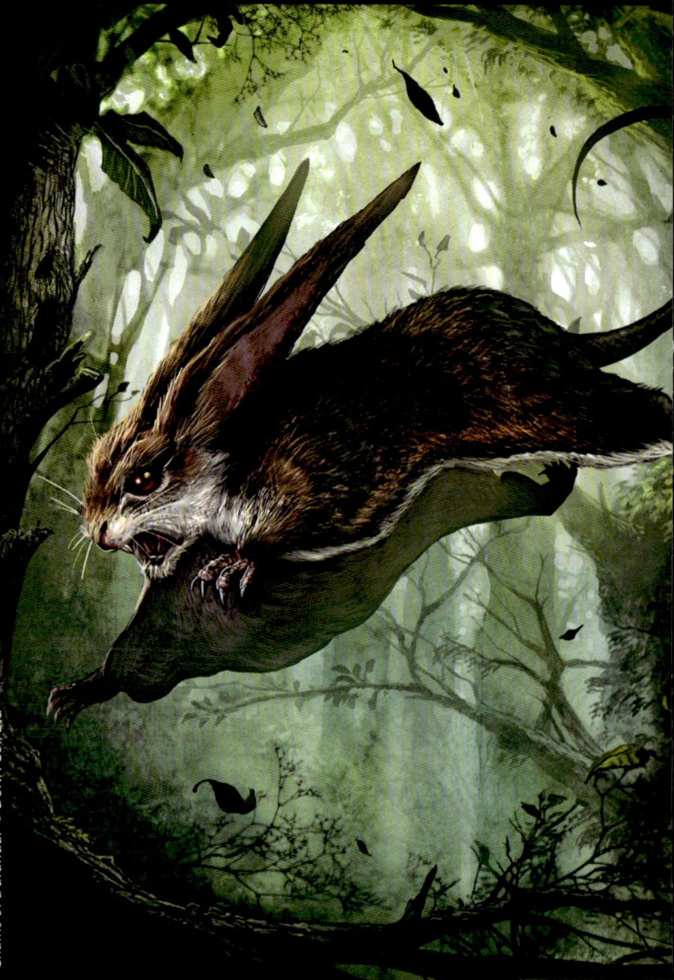

'Chains of Durandal' © DeNA Co., Ltd

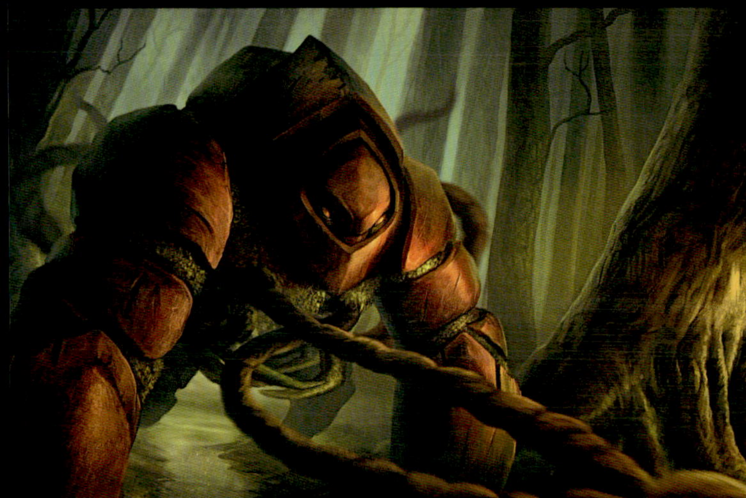

'Sins of a Dark Age' © Ironclad Games

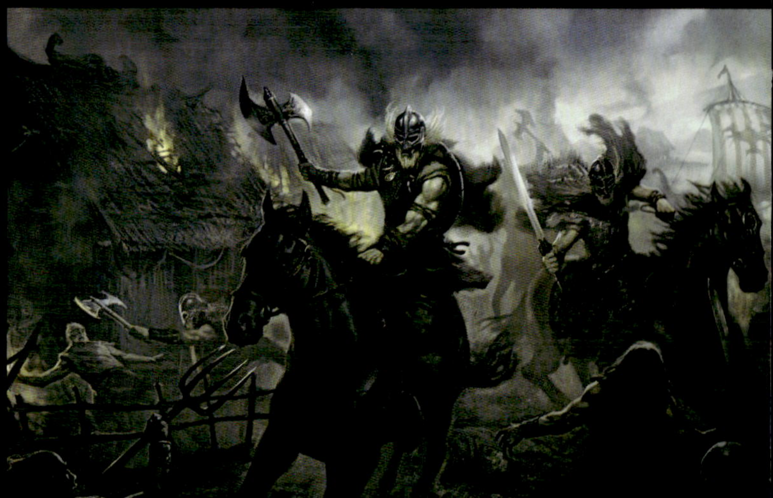

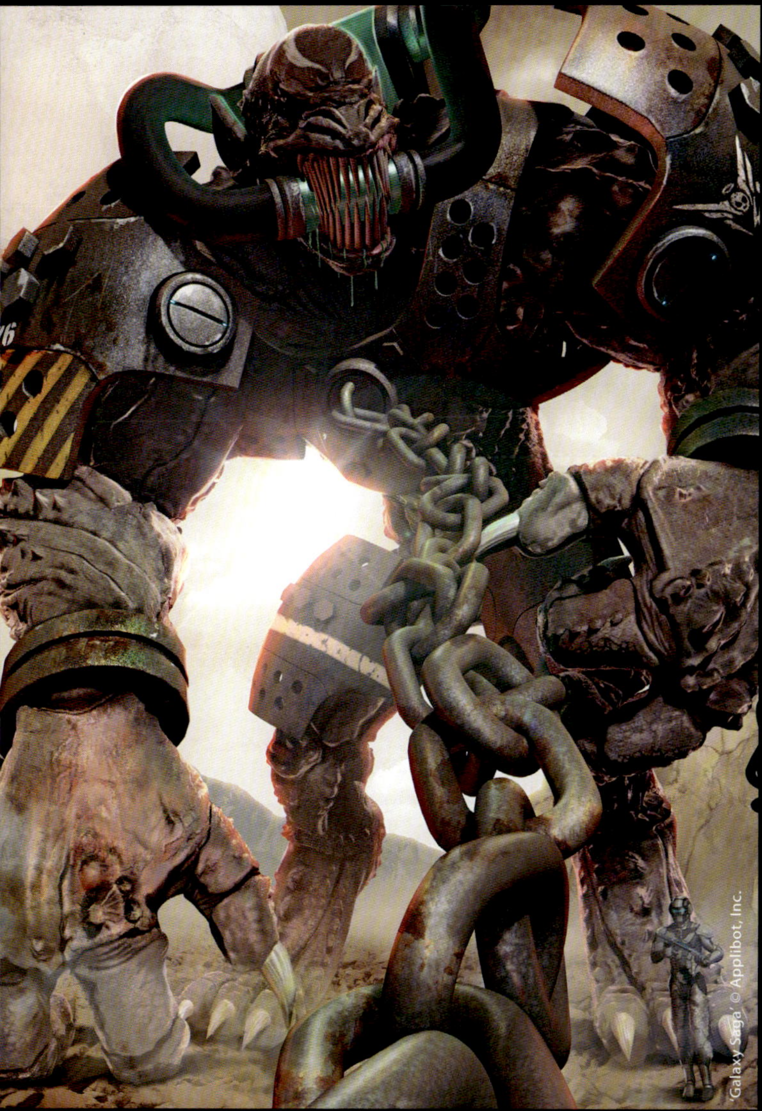

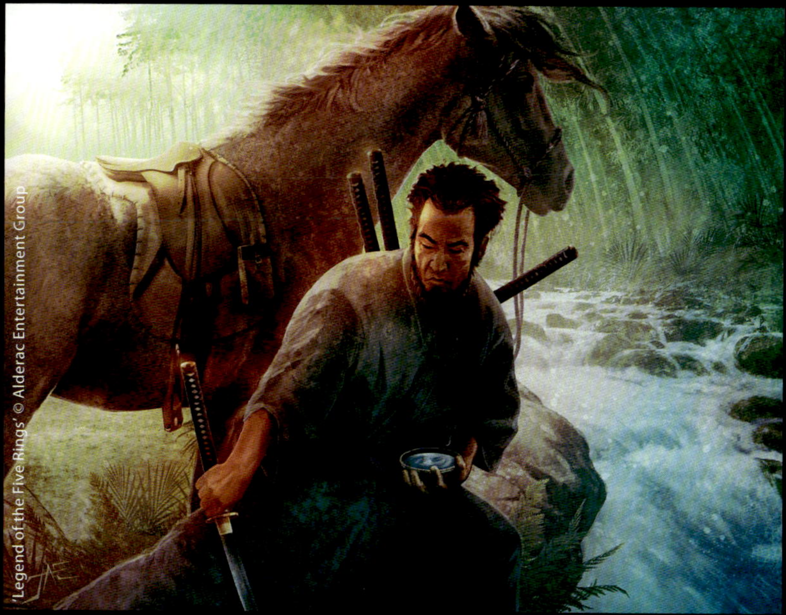

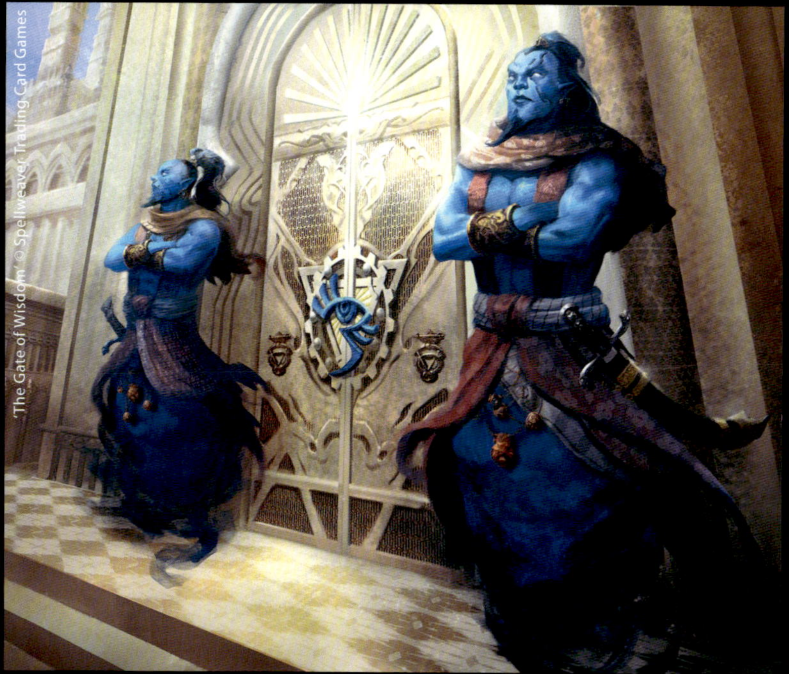

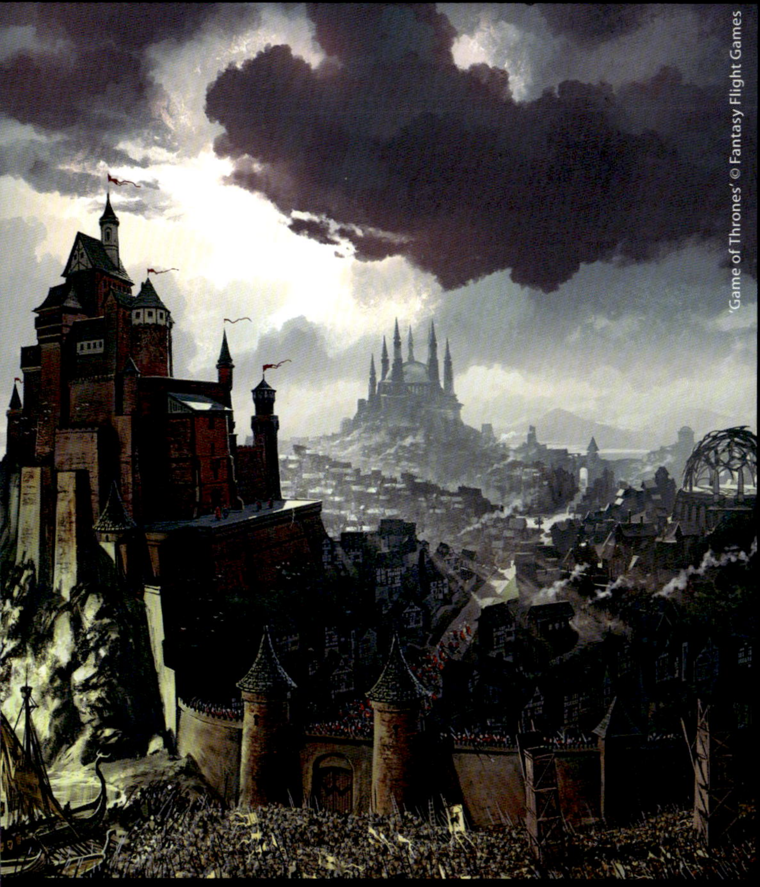

Bloody Venom
Photoshop, Softimage, Mudbox, Maya
Client: Applibot, Inc.
Yoshinobu Saito, JAPAN
[top left]

Legend of the Five Rings: Ronin
Photoshop
Client: Alderac Entertainment Group
Jason Engle, USA
[top right]

Game of Thrones: 2nd Ed. Box Cover
Photoshop
Client: Fantasy Flight Games
Tomasz Jedruszek, POLAND
[left]

The Gate of Wisdom
Photoshop
Client: Dream Reactor
Mihai Radu, ROMANIA
[above]

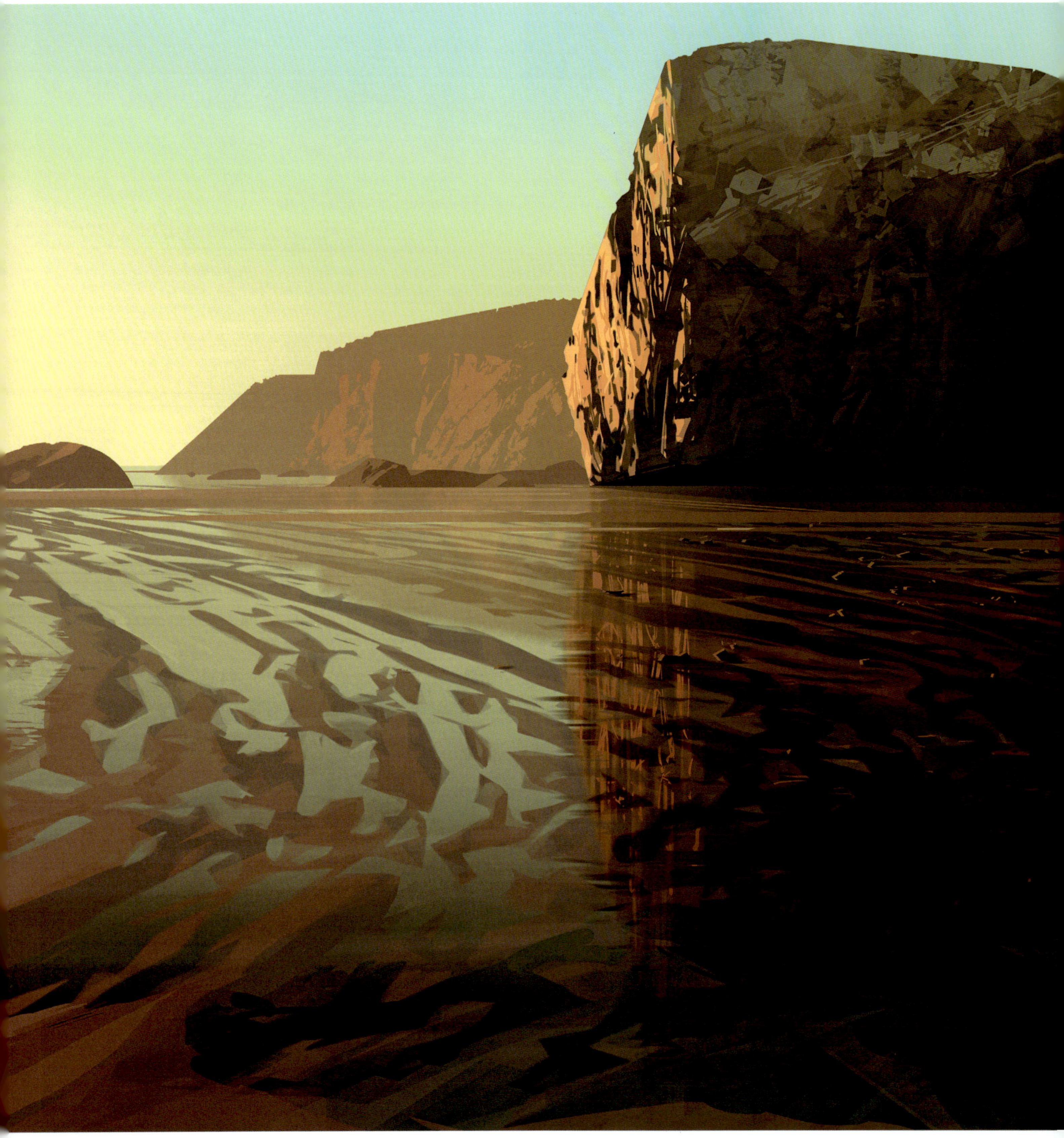

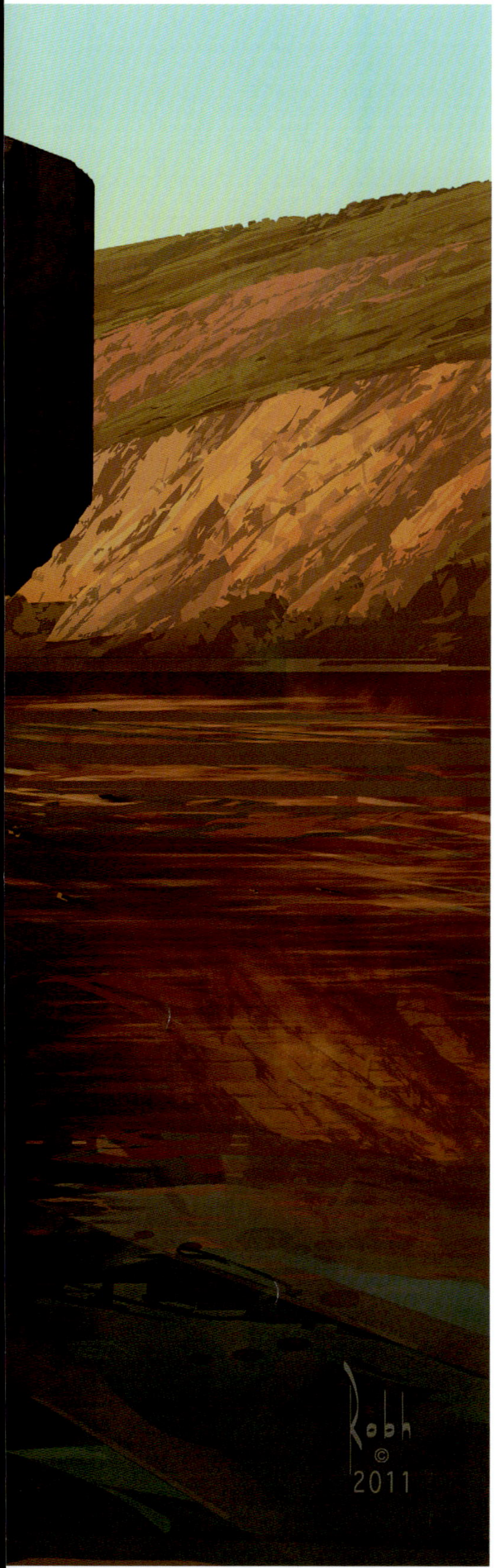

El Matador Beach
Photoshop
Robh Ruppel, USA

DIGITAL 'PLEIN AIR' PAINTING

ROBH RUPPEL (ART DIRECTOR OF *UNCHARTED 2* AT NAUGHTY DOG) IS A PIONEER IN DIGITAL 'PLEIN AIR' PAINTING. HE LIKES TO TAKE HIS IPAD AND GET OUTSIDE TO PAINT IN THE AMAZING CALIFORNIAN LIGHT. IT'S FRONTIER STUFF.

But truth is his digital paintings go way back – back to a group of French artists working in the late 1800s. The Impressionists were a small group of Parisian artists who began to challenge what was deemed 'acceptable' art. They produced works from the simple act of going outside to paint.

Painting en plein air – or 'in the open air' – emerged against a backdrop of political, social and industrial change, and flew in the face of the powerful Académie des Beaux-Arts (Academy of Fine Arts). Their works drew withering criticism from the Académie, but the artists responded with experimentation, ingenuity and invention.

Working outdoors required the artists to radically alter their approach to the physical act of painting. They were limited by the size of canvas they could carry, and they had to paint much more quickly to capture the angle, strength and color of shifting light. They changed the way they employed brushstrokes and the way they used colour – mixing directly on the canvas instead of the palette. They also capitalized on the new technology of oil paint in tubes, a 'portable paint' that gave the artists a wide range of colors in larger, more consistent quantities. According to Renoir, "Without tubes of paint, there would have been no impressionism".

The works they produced were like nothing that had been seen before – and the Académie rejected them by the hundreds. This meant little or no income, and, worse, obscurity for artists who were desperate to establish themselves. It wasn't until the end of the 1870s, when artists like Édouard Manet, Claude Monet and Pierre-Auguste Renoir began taking their canvases to the Salon des Refusés in Paris (literally, Exhibition of Rejects), that they began to find some acceptance.

The recent invention of the portable camera had one of the most profound influences on the Impressionist artists, changing the way they began to 'see' the world. It enabled them to study movement and gestures, and to capture a sense of real-life spontaneity rarely before seen on canvas. It inspired them to experiment with off-center focus, unusual perspectives and spontaneous compositions.

The Impressionists adapted existing tools and developed new technologies in order to more freely capture their impressions of the environment. This is the very essence of Robh Ruppel's work today.

Digital plein air painting is still in its infancy. Both digital and traditional artists experiment with new tools, innovating and ingeniously harnessing mobile digital technology to create artworks that capture their surrounding environments.

It's cutting-edge work born of a noble tradition.

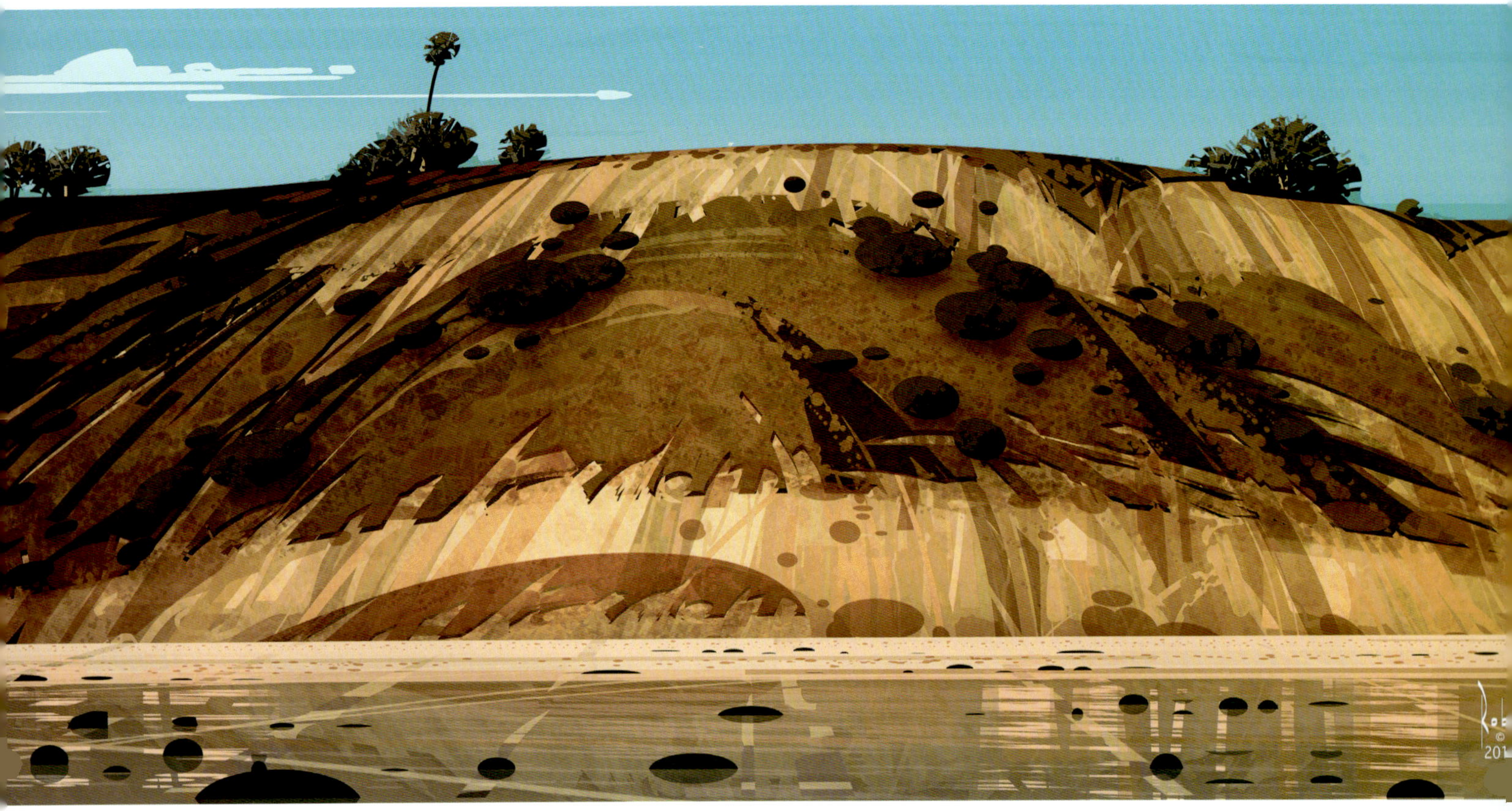

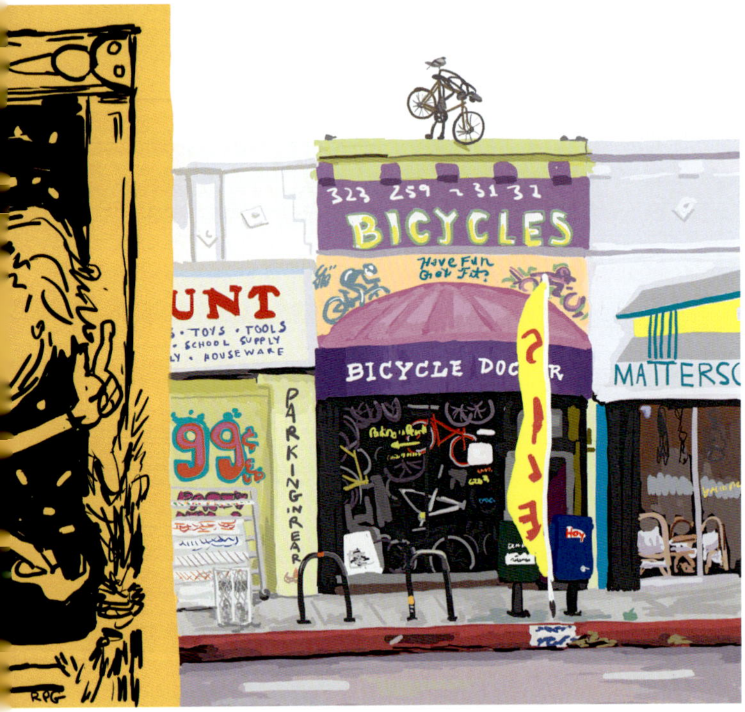

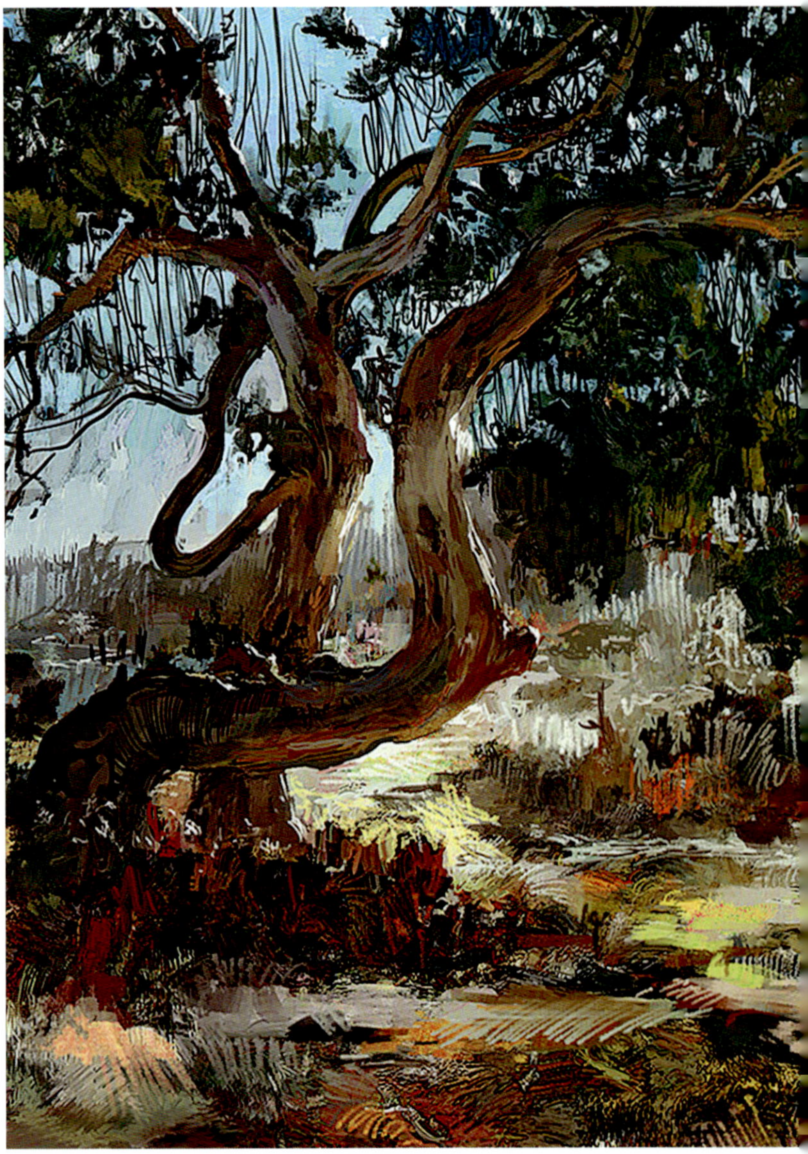

Coast
Photoshop
Robh Ruppel, USA
[top]

Bicycles on York
Painter
Ryan P Griffin, USA
[above]

Tree Study
Photoshop
Dan Ghiordanescu, GERMANY
[right]

Aigulle du Midi
Photoshop
Shaddy Safadi, USA
[facing page top]

[inset] Shaddy Safadi out on location

Colorado Blvd
Photoshop
Robh Ruppel, USA
[facing page bottom]

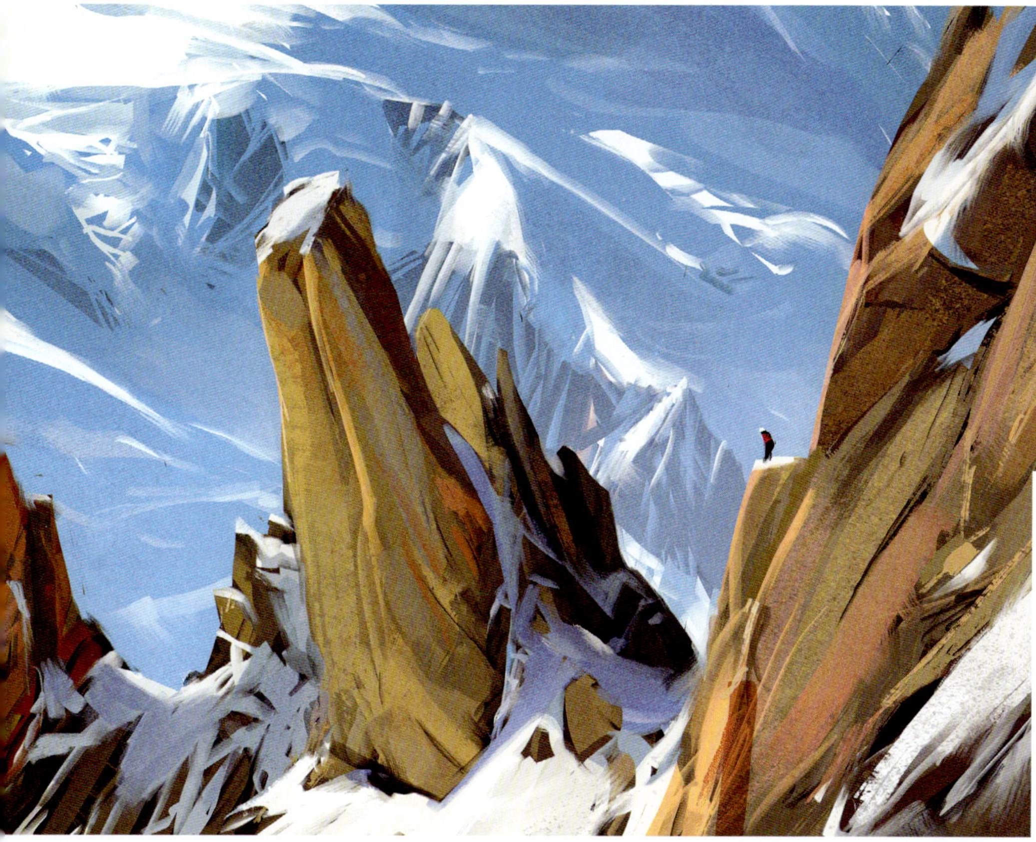

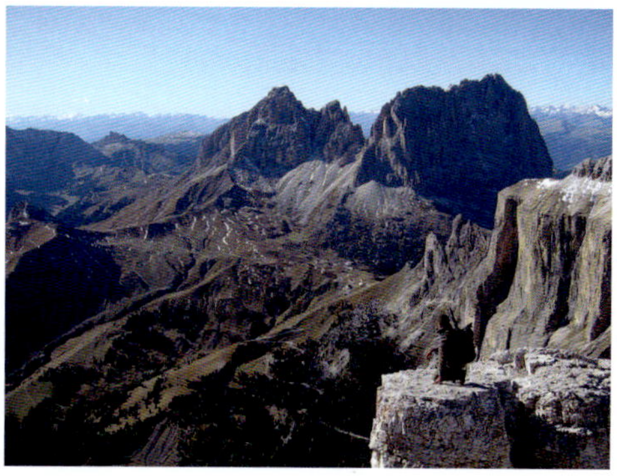

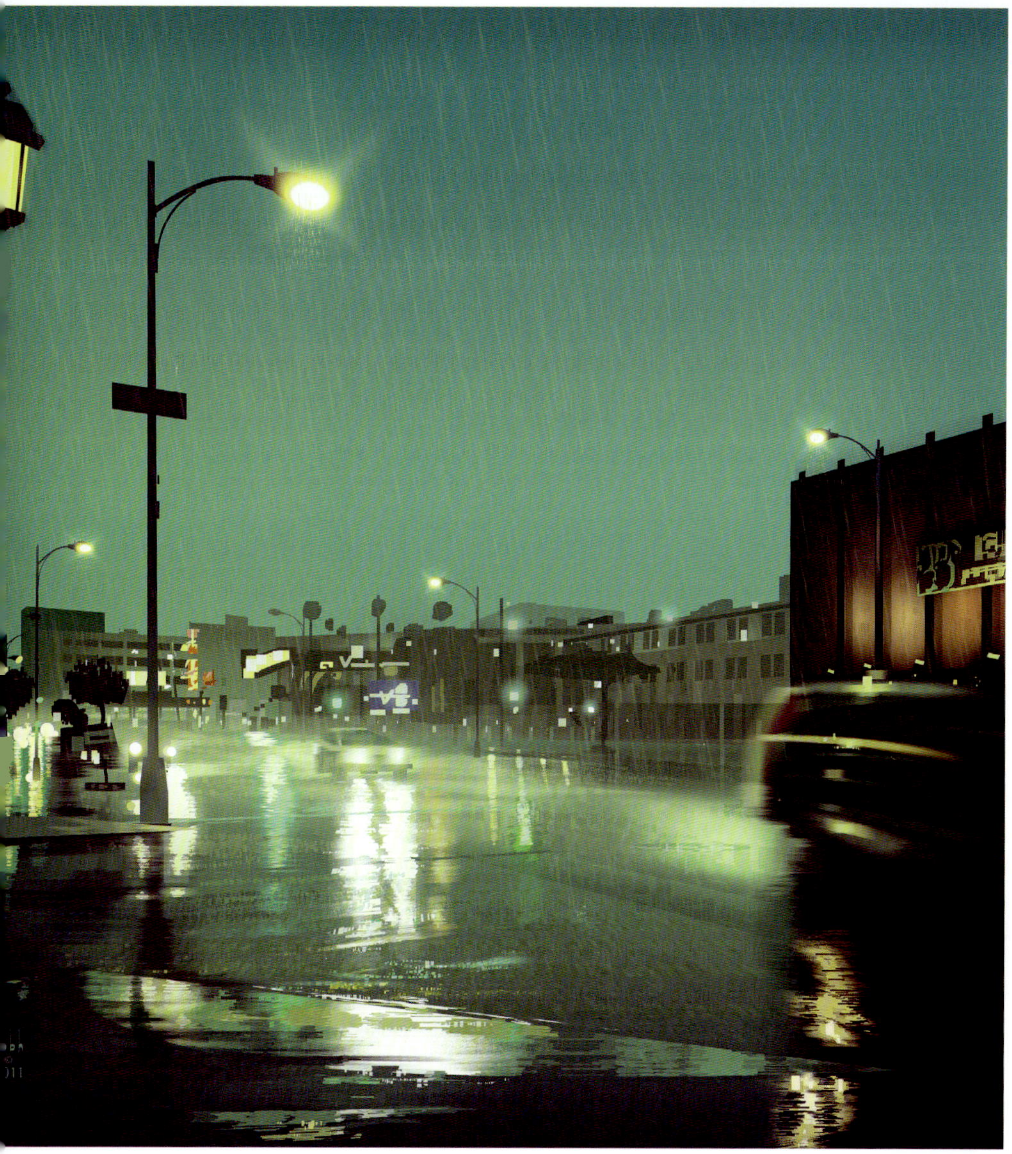

PAINTING FROM LIFE HAS HAS A FEW OBVIOUS BENEFITS, AND SOME SURPRISING ONES.

When painting from life, the artist can see color and light on its own terms, and which is not degraded by bad photography. The main revelation is that shadows aren't actually black, or even all that dark. Cameras tend to crunch the shadows to black or blow out the whites. When you start noticing how little actual black there is in real life, you can avoid the common pitfall of adding black to your images to create 'moodiness'.

When I hire concept artists, 'black' shadows are the first red flag that the artist has never really looked at natural light. Any artist who hasn't painted from life could simply walk outside and see how color and light works, then come back to their desk and apply it from memory. But so many don't – and it really affects the quality of their work.

The downside of course is that an artist can't go on location for every environment concept they do. The main benefit of life painting is to know how images sourced for reference are wrong. That is invaluable when you're collecting photo references for concept work, as images can be more carefully screened until they match what you inherently know is correct from your life painting experience.

Shaddy Safadi

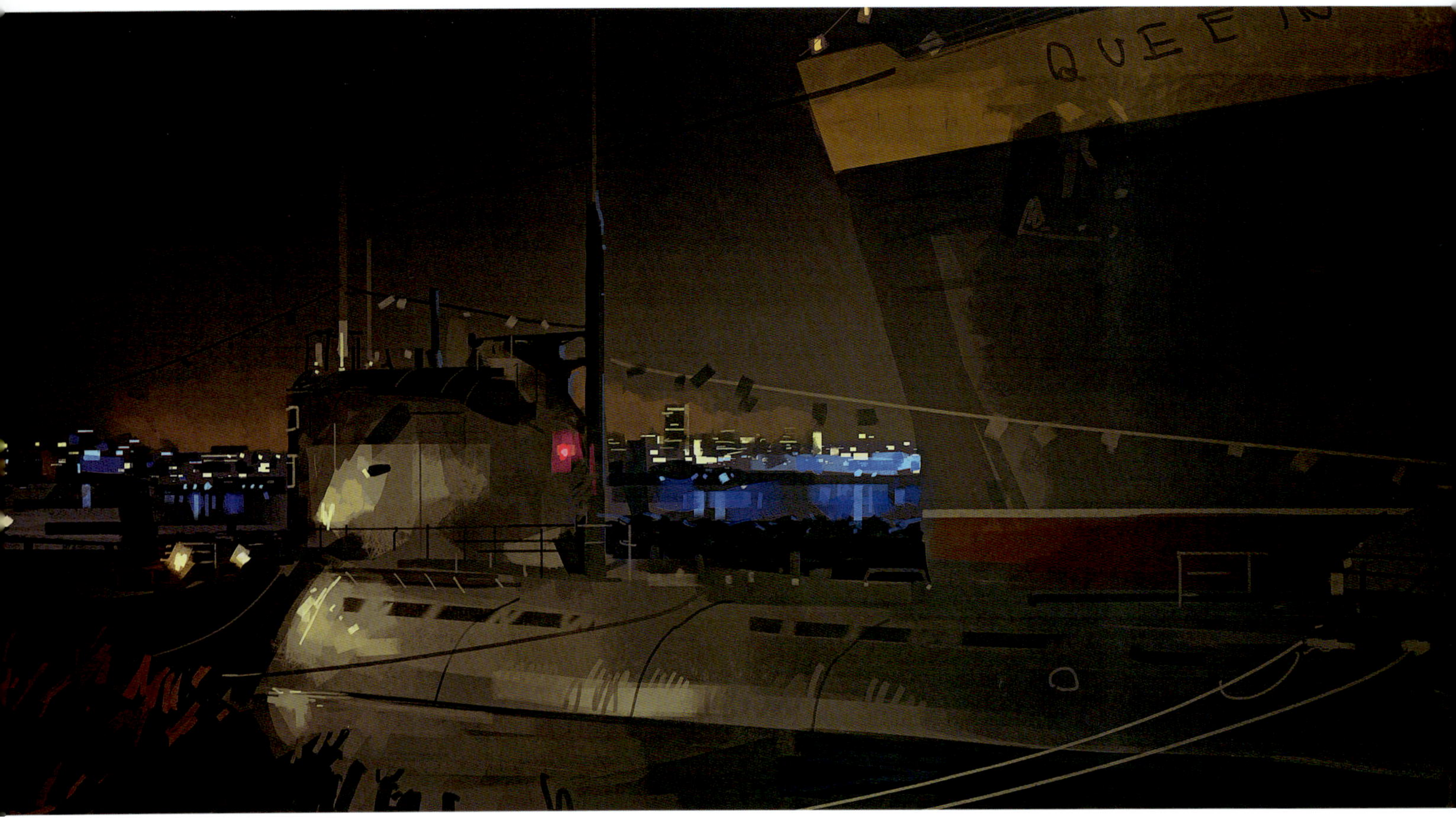

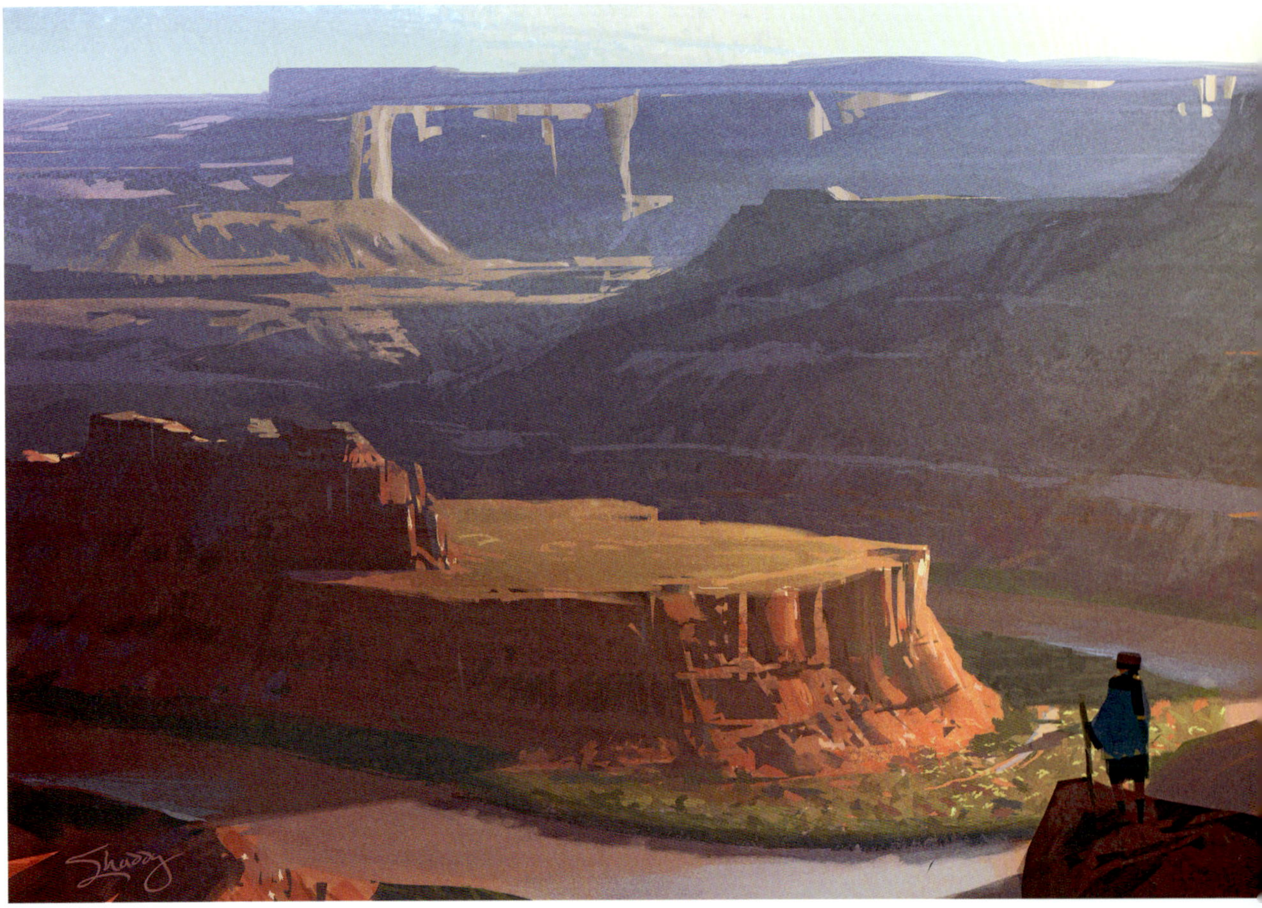

B-427, Long Beach
Photoshop
Patrick Faulwetter, USA
[top]

Dead Horse Point
Photoshop
Shaddy Safadi, USA
[above]

Elysian Valley at Dusk
Painter
Ryan P Griffin, USA
[facing page top]

Bucharest Street Winter
ArtRage, Photoshop
Dan Ghiordanescu, GERMANY
[facing page center]

El Matador Rock
Photoshop
Nick Gindraux, USA
[facing page bottom]

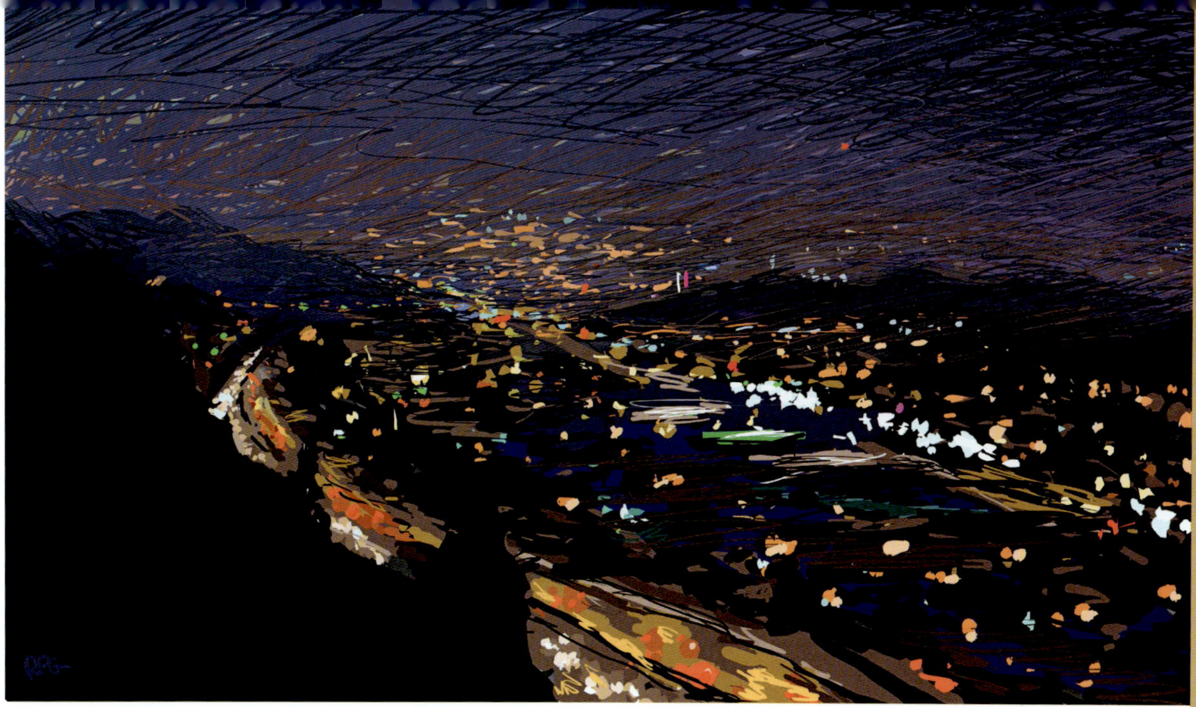

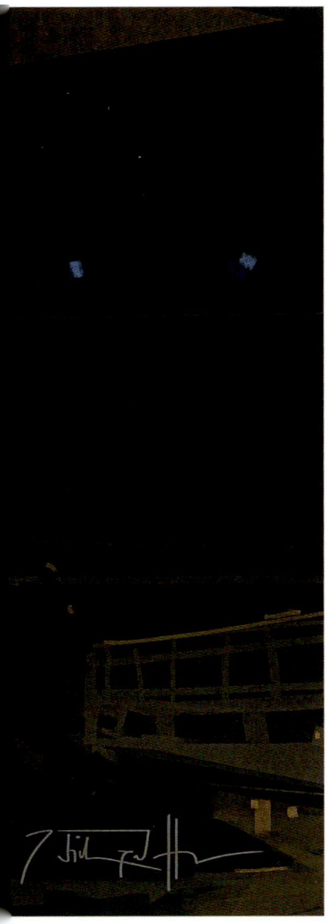

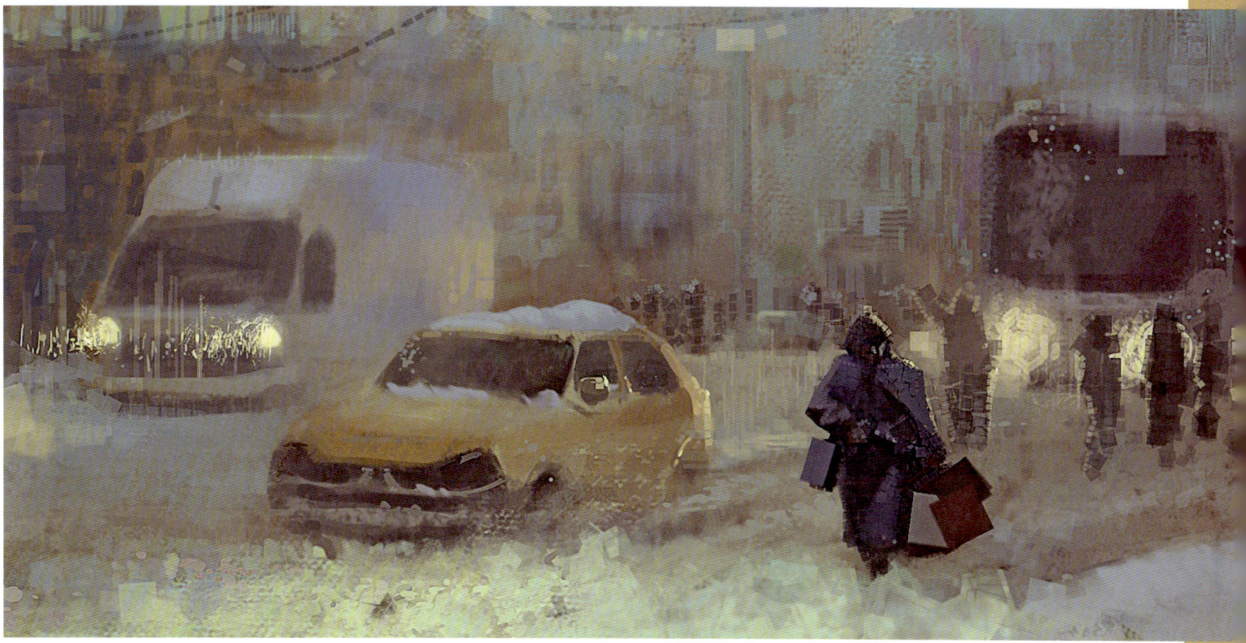

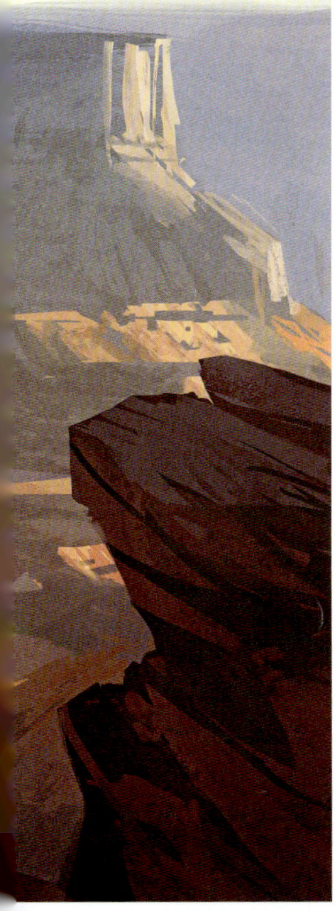

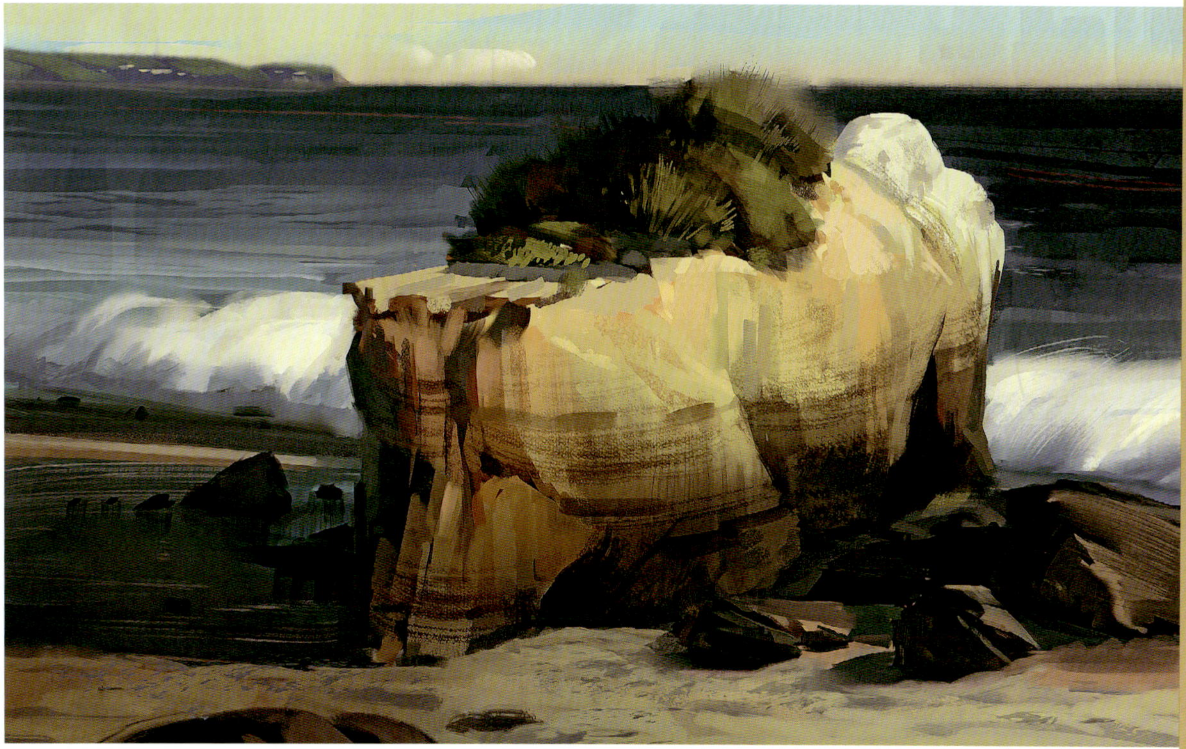

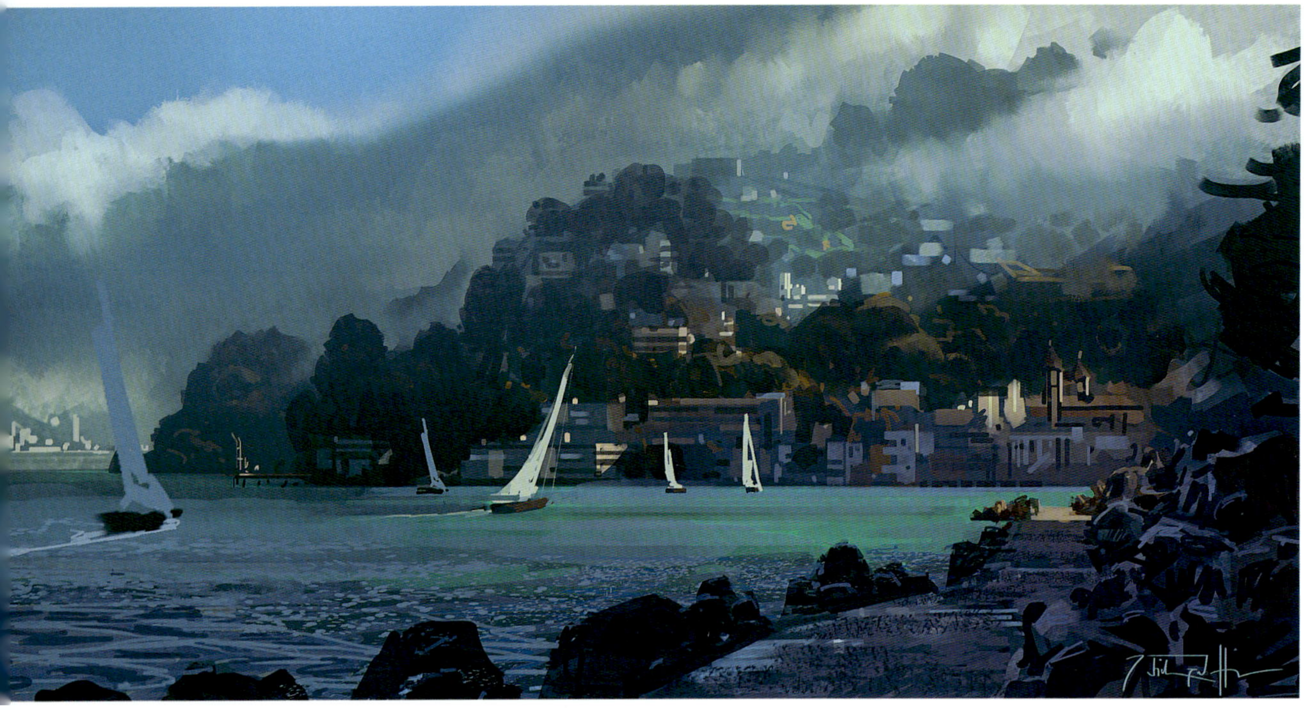

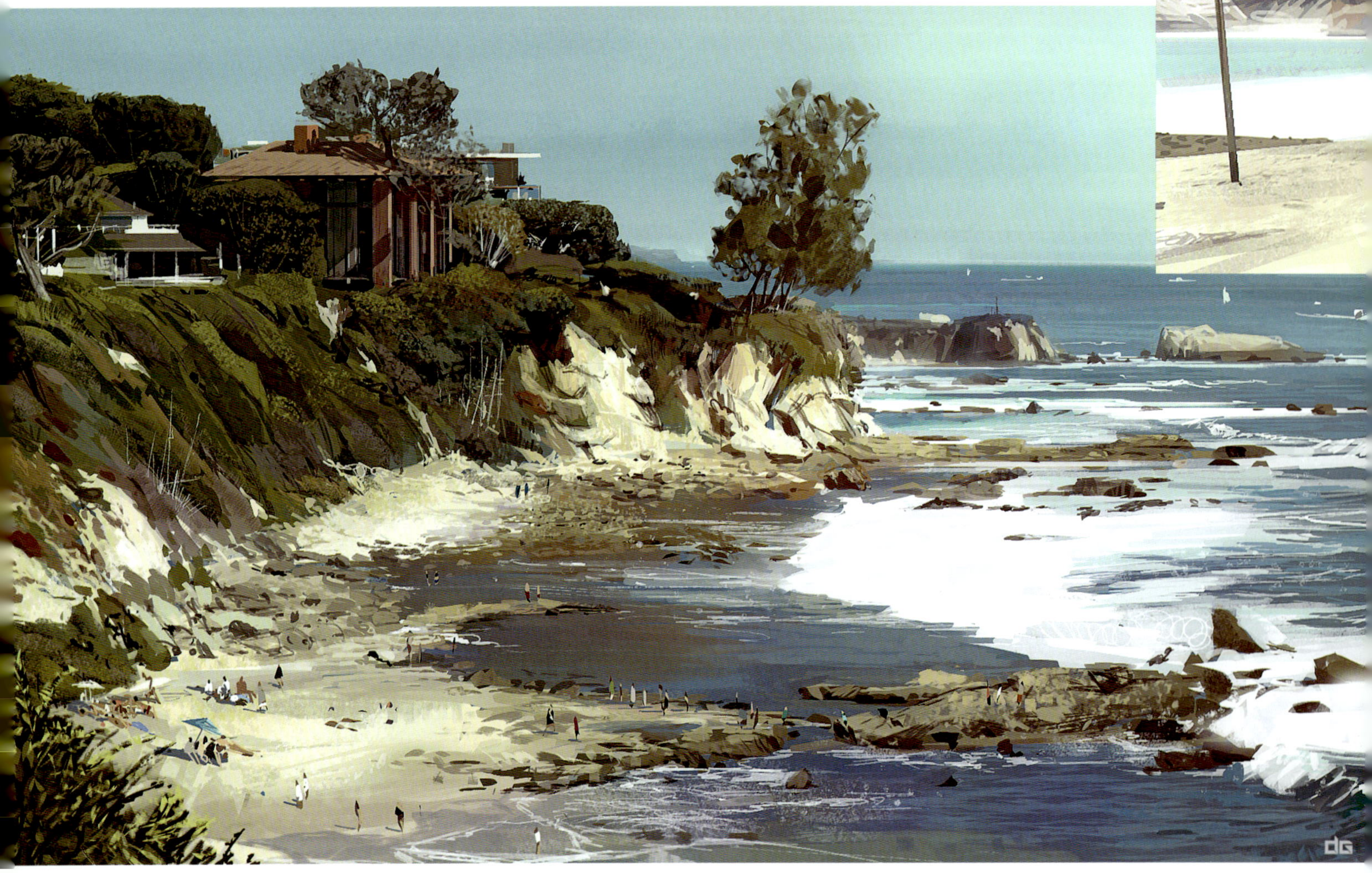

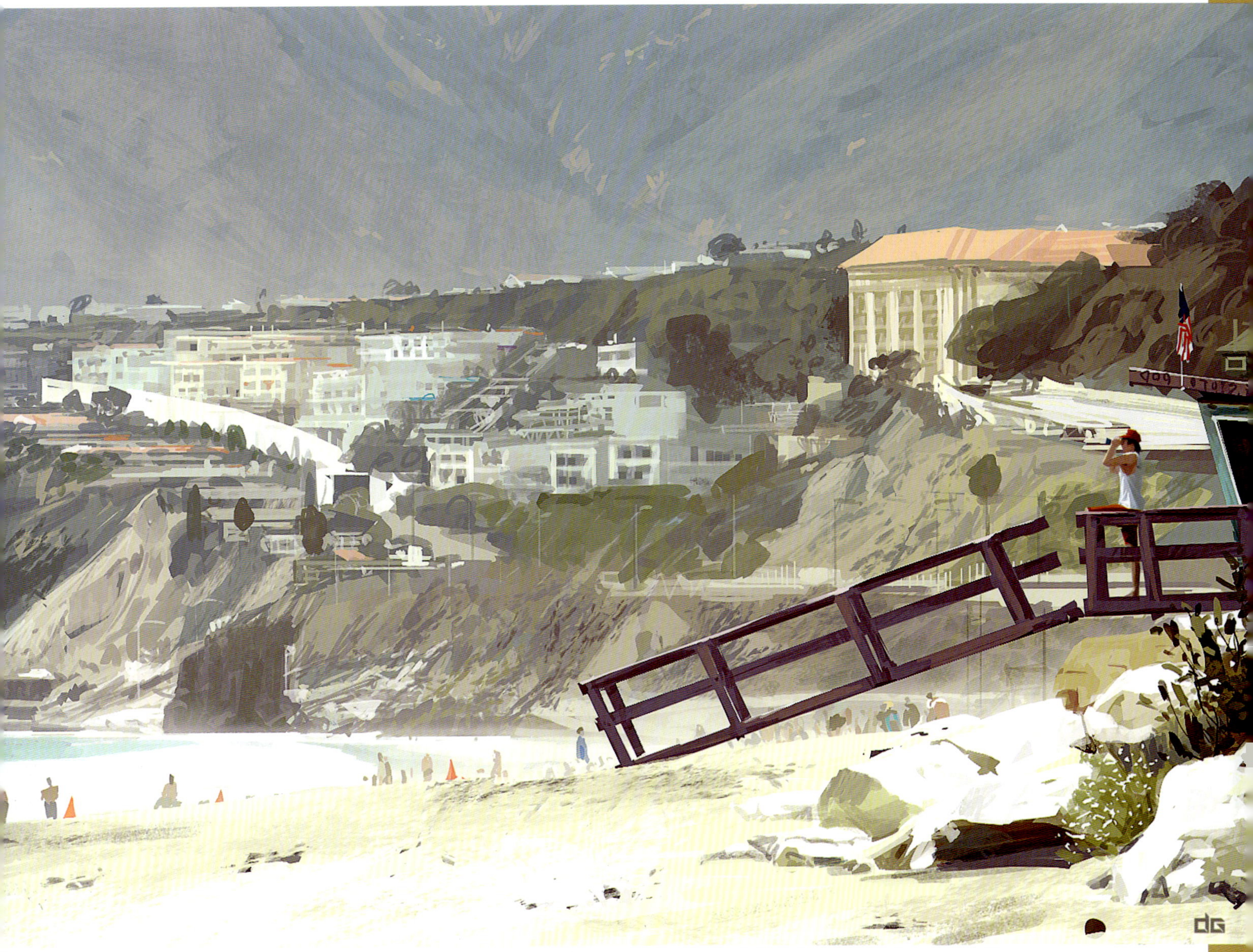

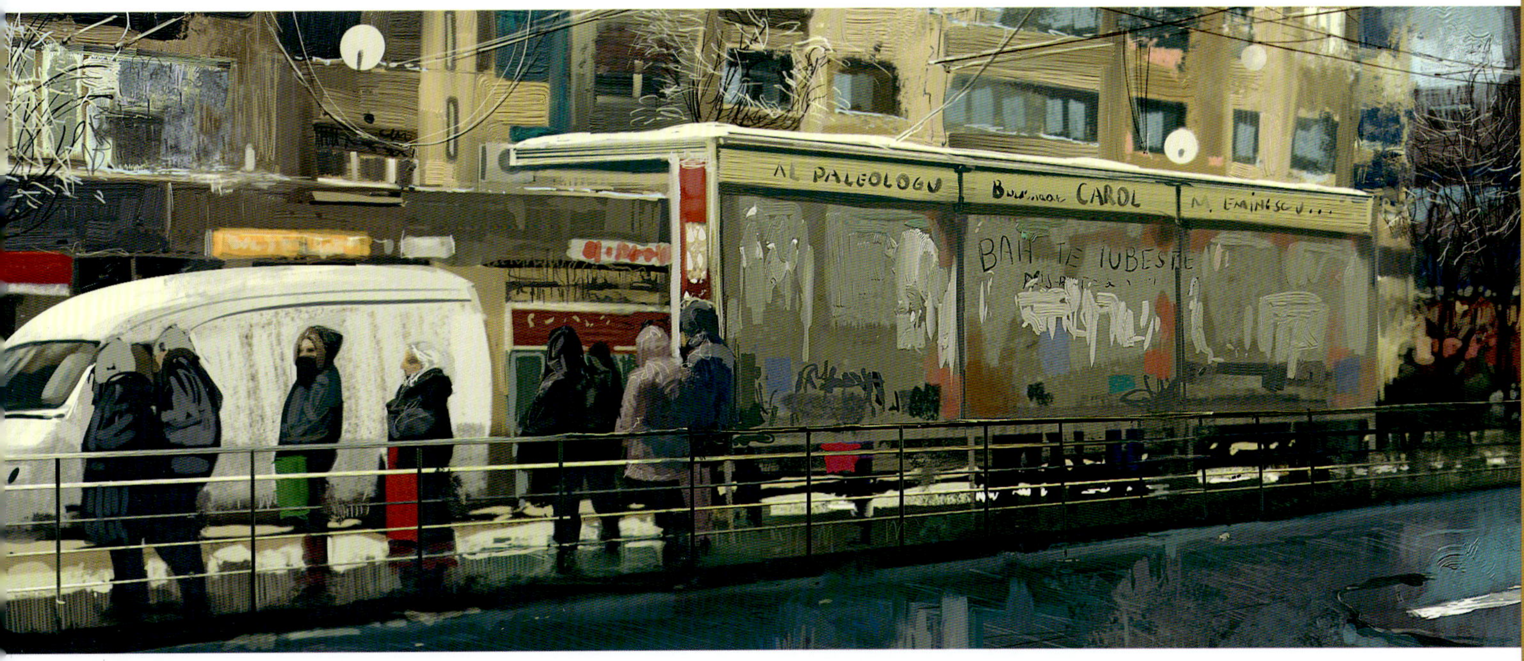

Marine Layer
Photoshop
Patrick Faulwetter, USA
[facing page top]

Carona del Mar
Photoshop
Danny Gardner, USA
[facing page bottom]

Malibu
Photoshop
Danny Gardner, USA
[top]

Tram Station Bucharest
ArtRage
Dan Ghiordanescu, GERMANY
[above]

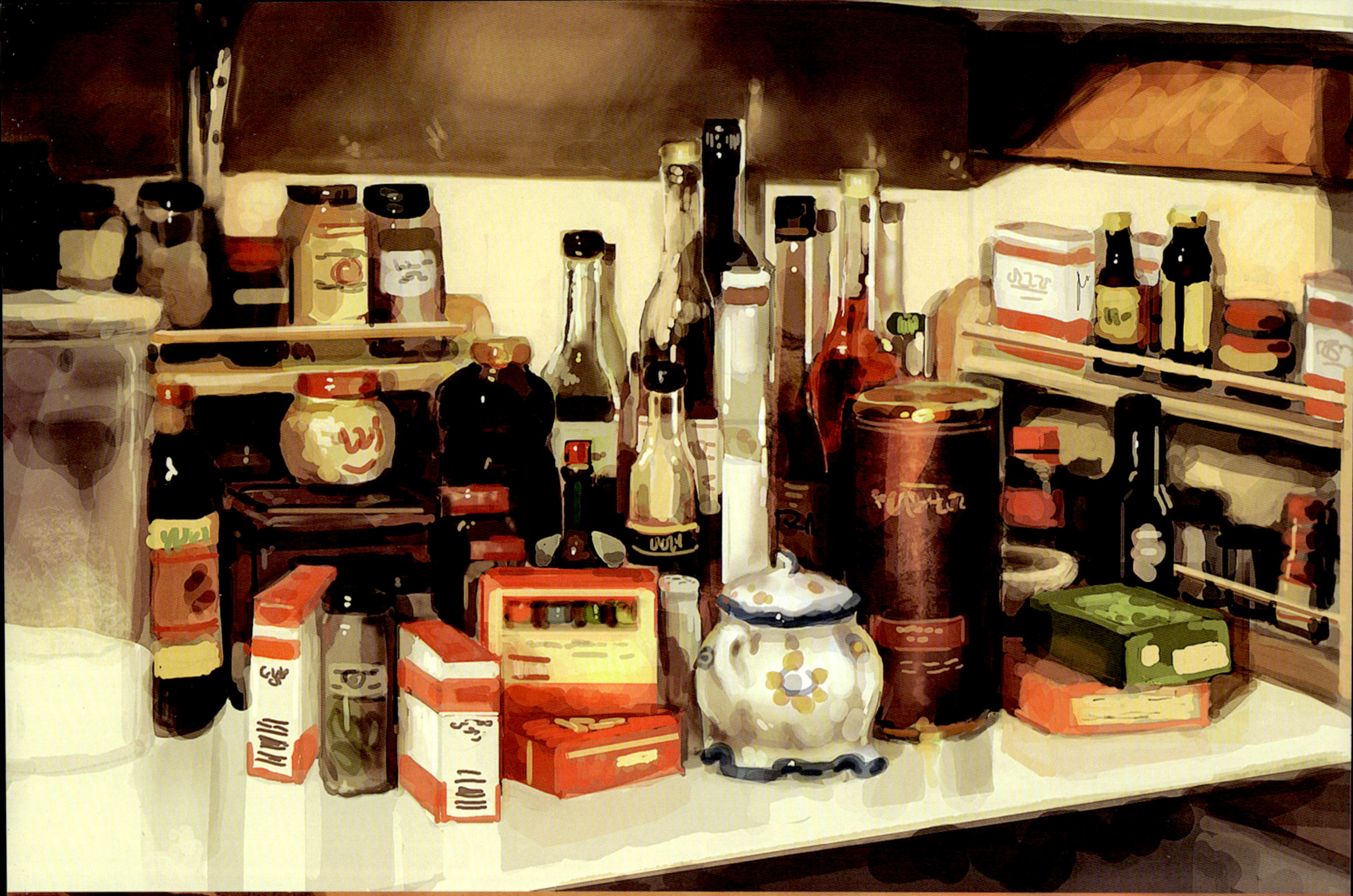

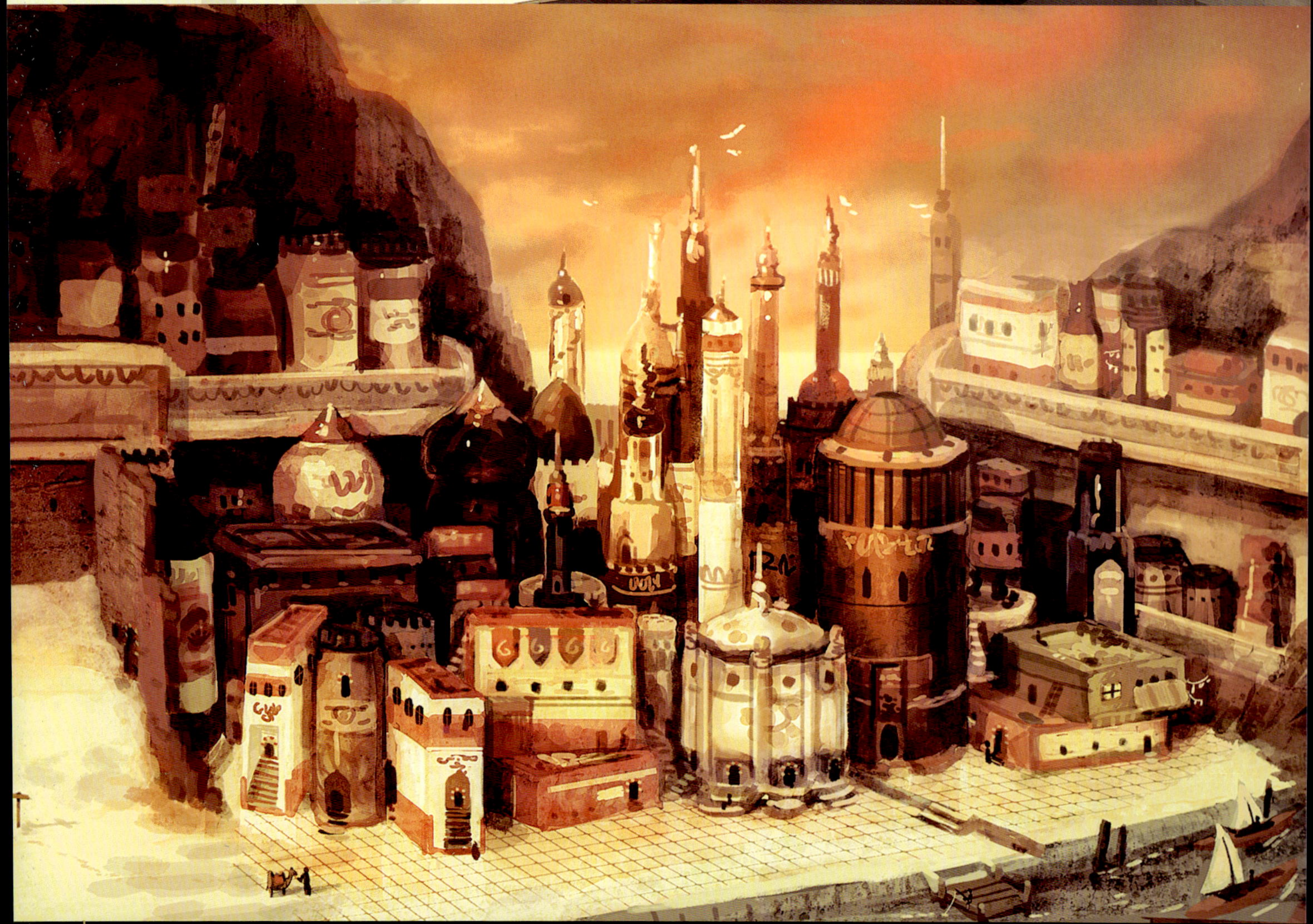

Cupboard City
Photoshop
Sarah Webb, USA

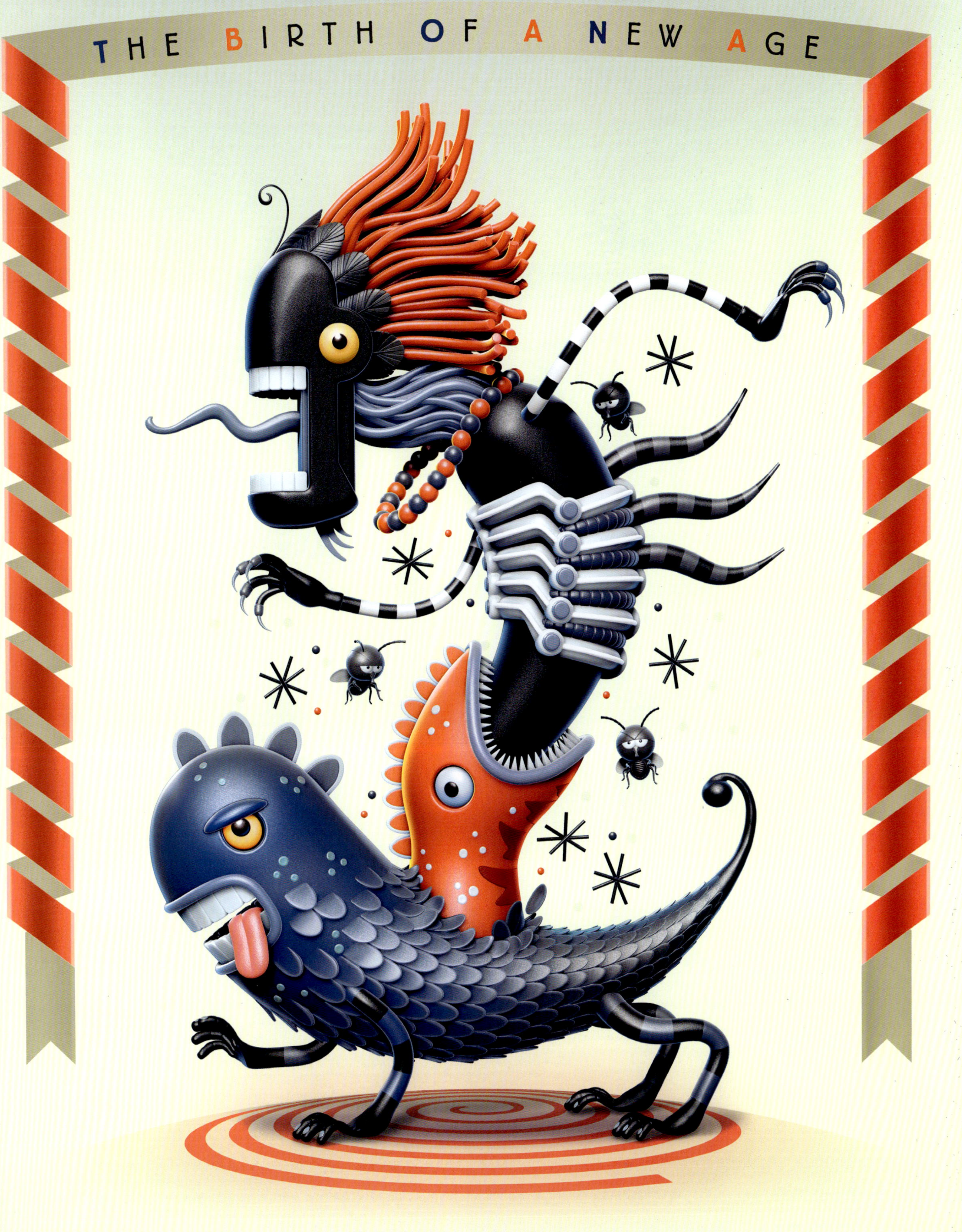

The Birth of a New Age
ZBrush
Ralf Stumpf, GERMANY

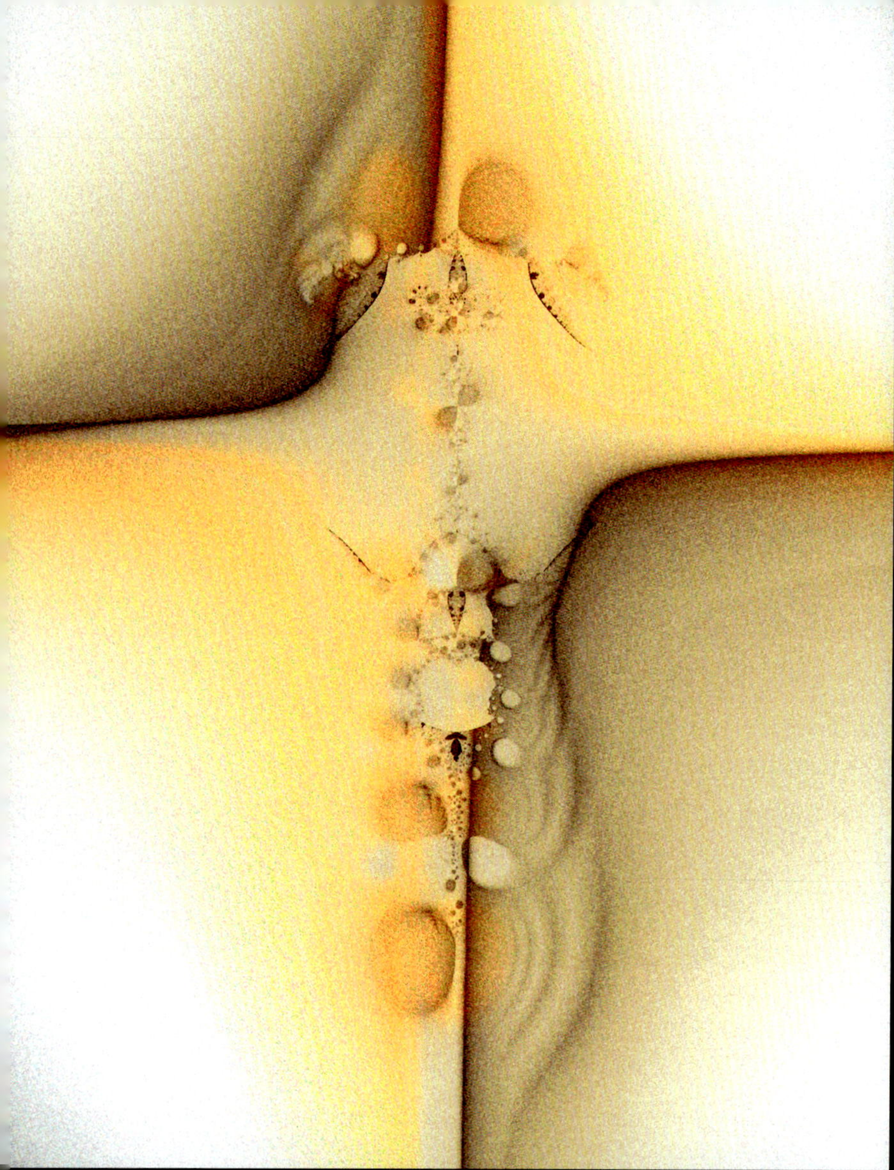

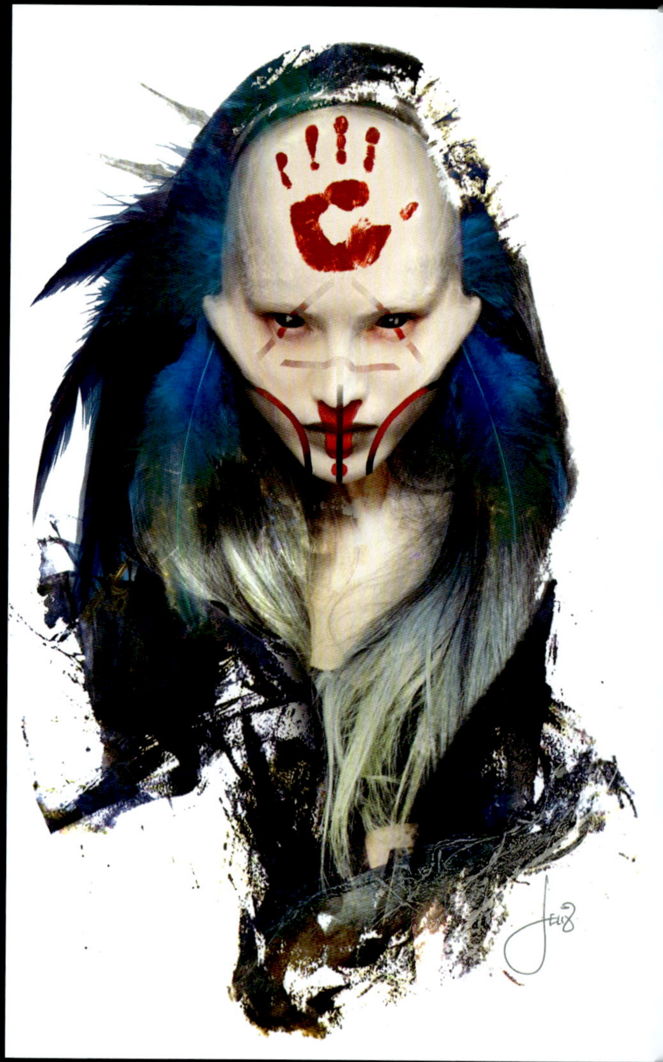

Sands of Time
Photoshop, Ultra Fractal
Osvaldo Buccafusca, USA
[above]

Queen Vampire
Photoshop, ArtRage
Jason Felix, USA
[above right]

Split Mind
Photoshop
Renaud Taelemans, BELGIUM
[right]

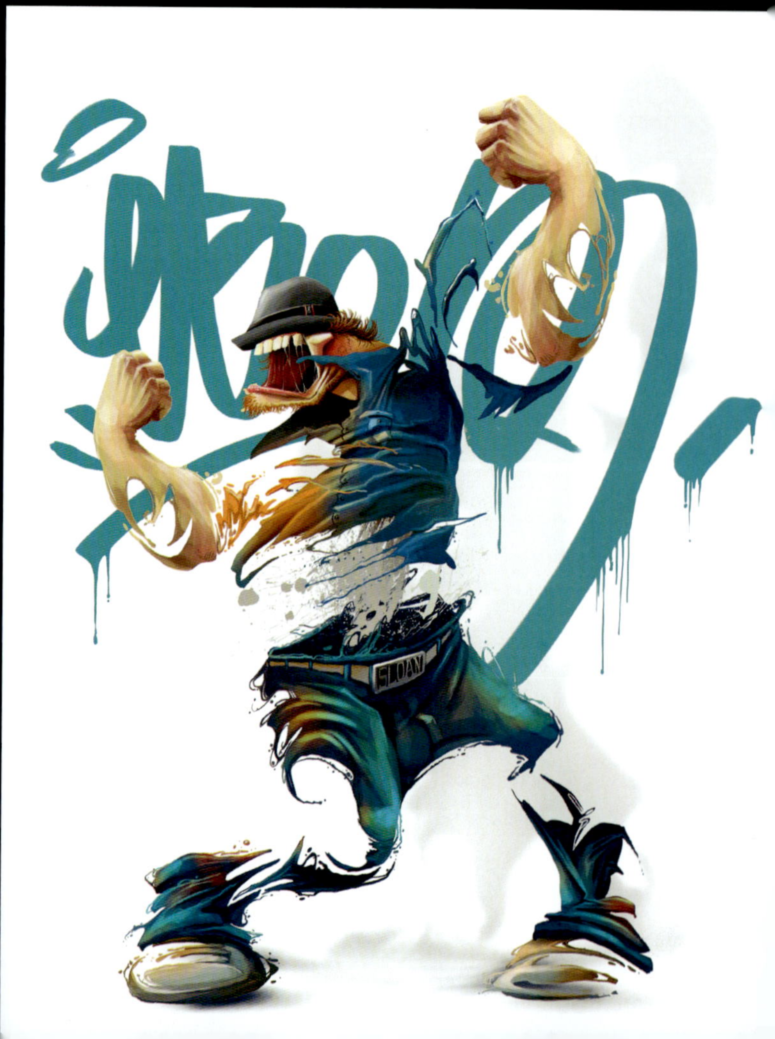

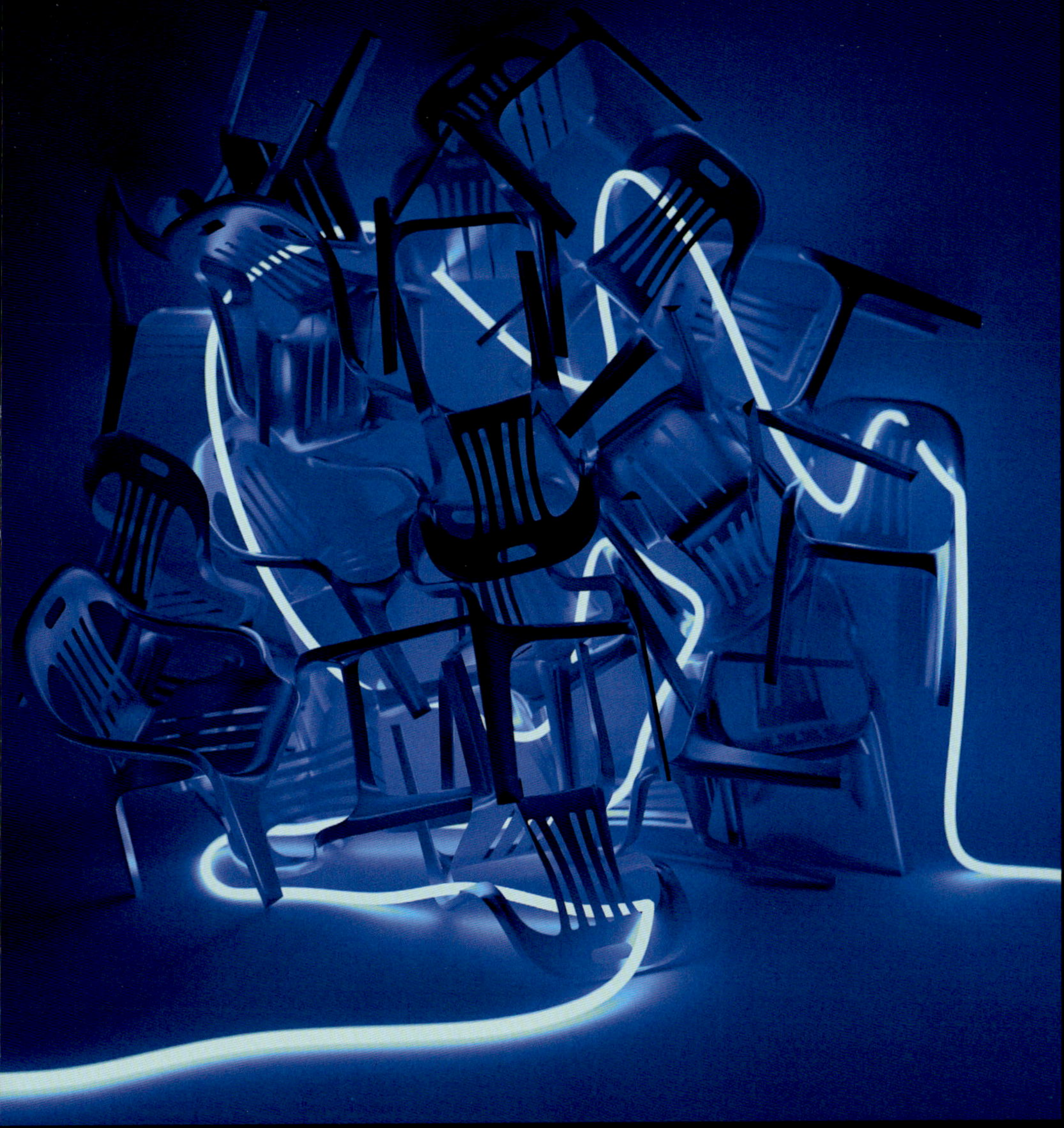

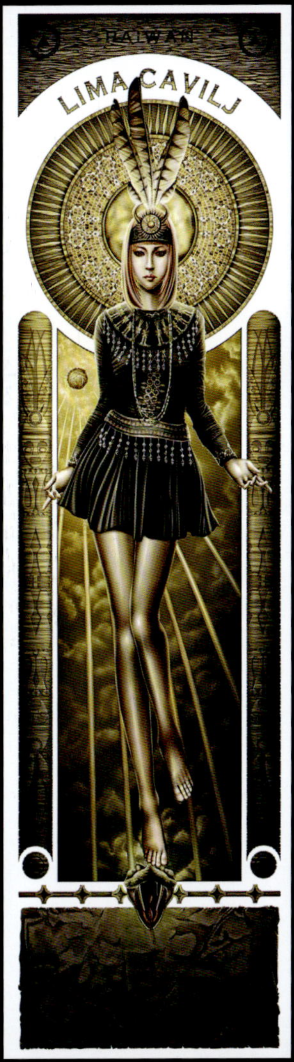

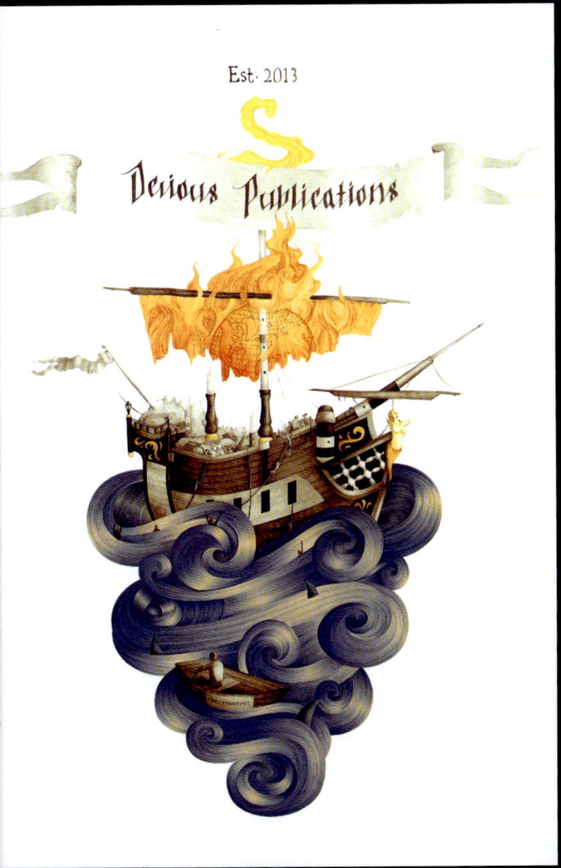

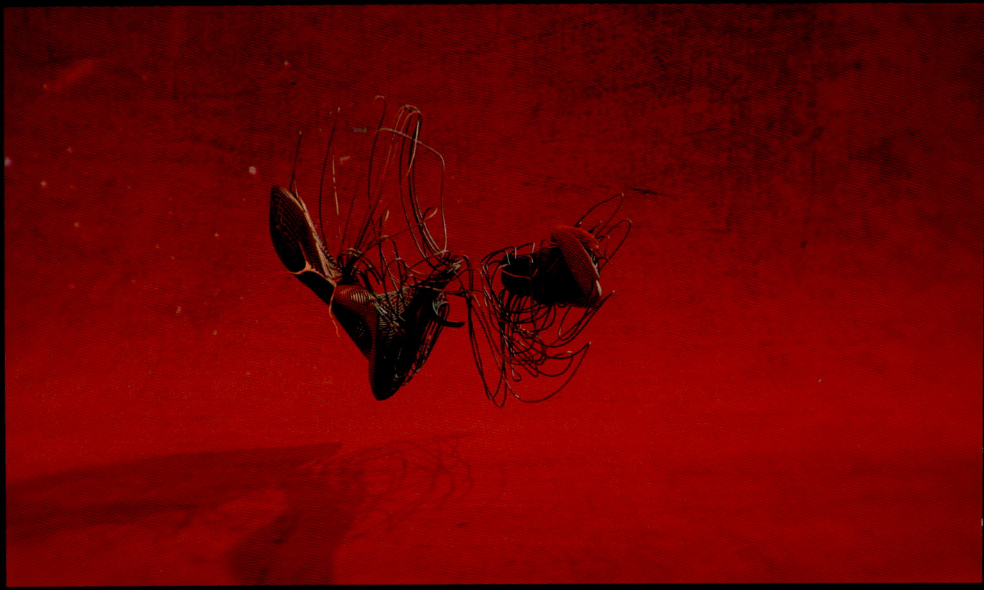

Mesh Light Chairs
Maya, Arnold
Lee Griggs, SPAIN
[top left]

Devious
Photoshop, Illustrator
Mitchell Nelson, GREAT BRITAIN
[left]

Paiwan
Painter, Photoshop
Chuan-Bin Chung OB, TAIWAN
[top right]

Anomaly v1
Softimage, After Effects
Emrah Gonulkirmaz, CANADA
[above]

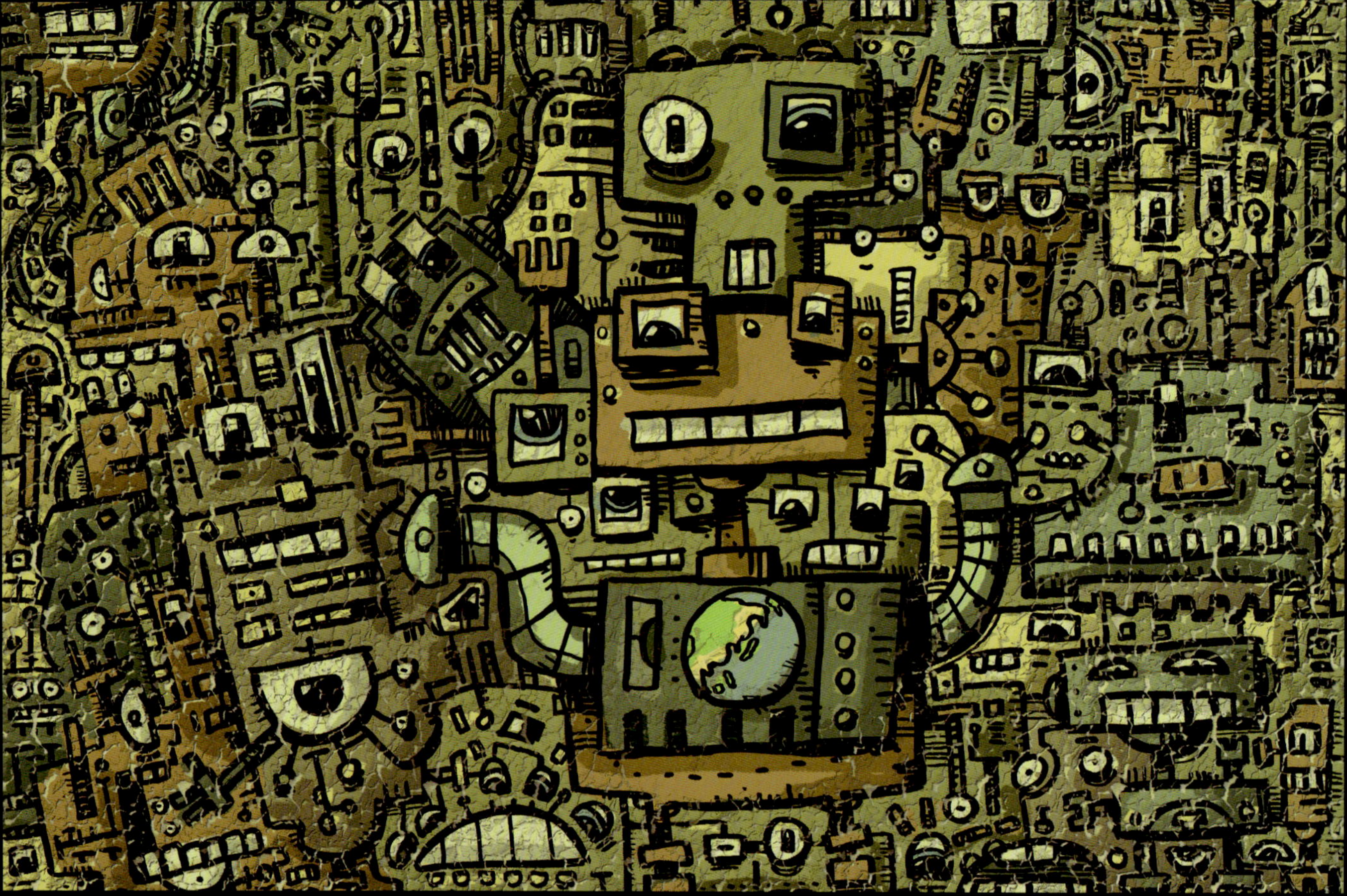

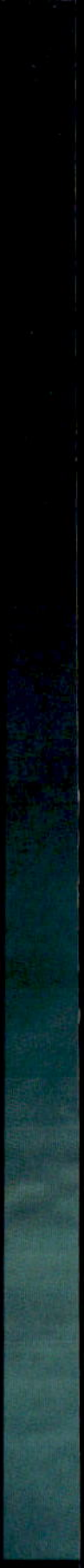

Mechenesis
Photoshop
Bryan Ballinger, USA
[above]

Anomaly v2
Softimage
Emrah Gonulkirmaz, CANADA
[facing page top]

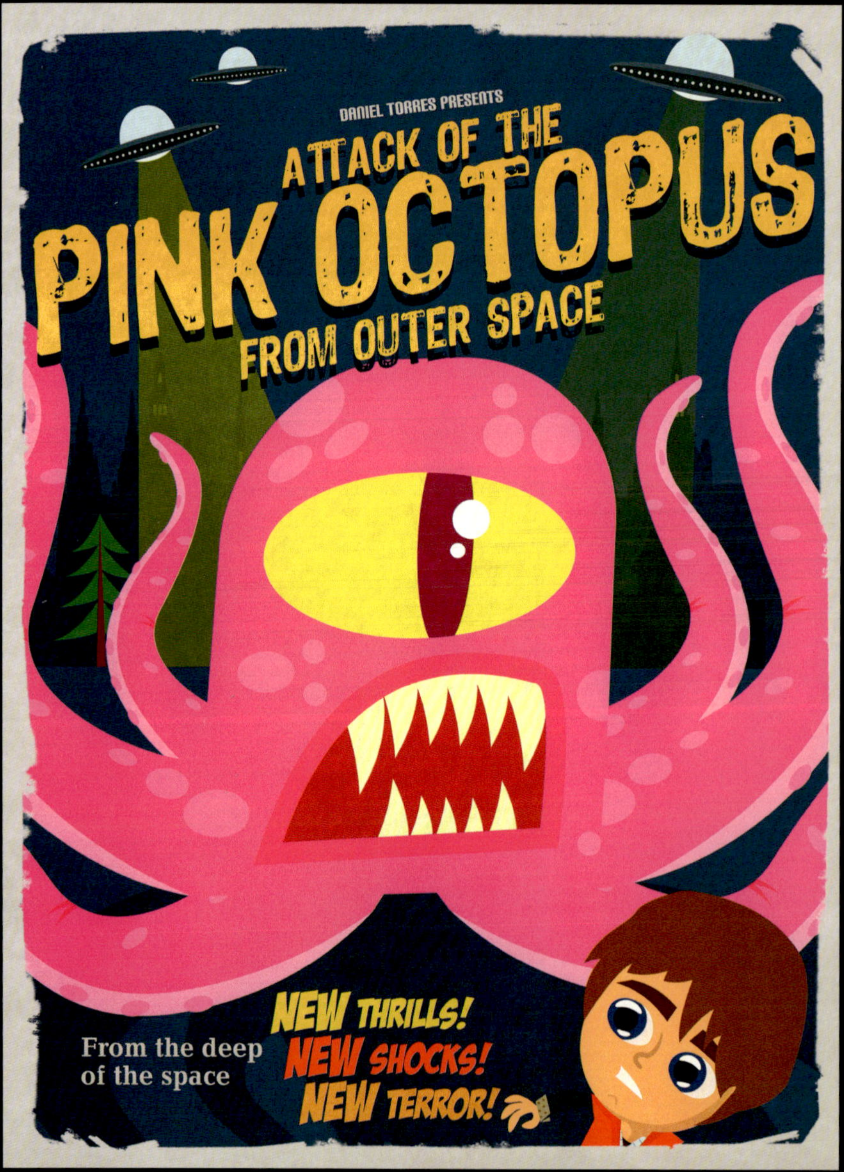

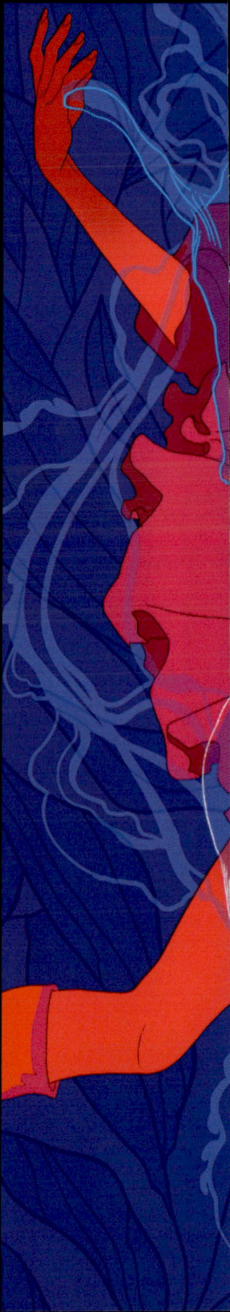

Pink Octopus
FreeHand, Photoshop
Daniel Torres, MEXICO
[right]

Cat Spirits
Photoshop
Marguerite Sauvage, AUSTRALIA
[center bottom]

IOKOSA
Photoshop
Client: Design Studio Press
Danny Gardner, USA
[facing page bottom right]

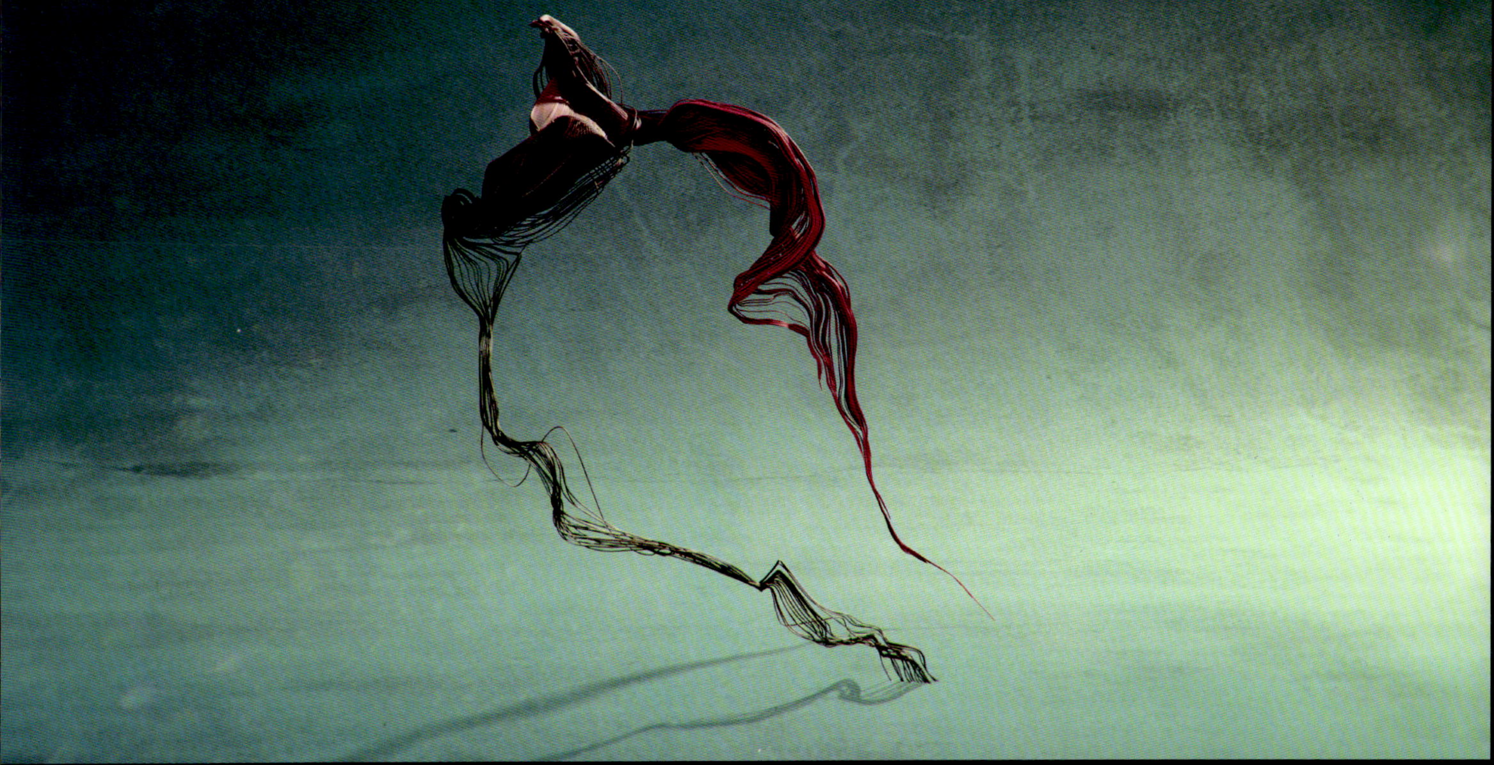

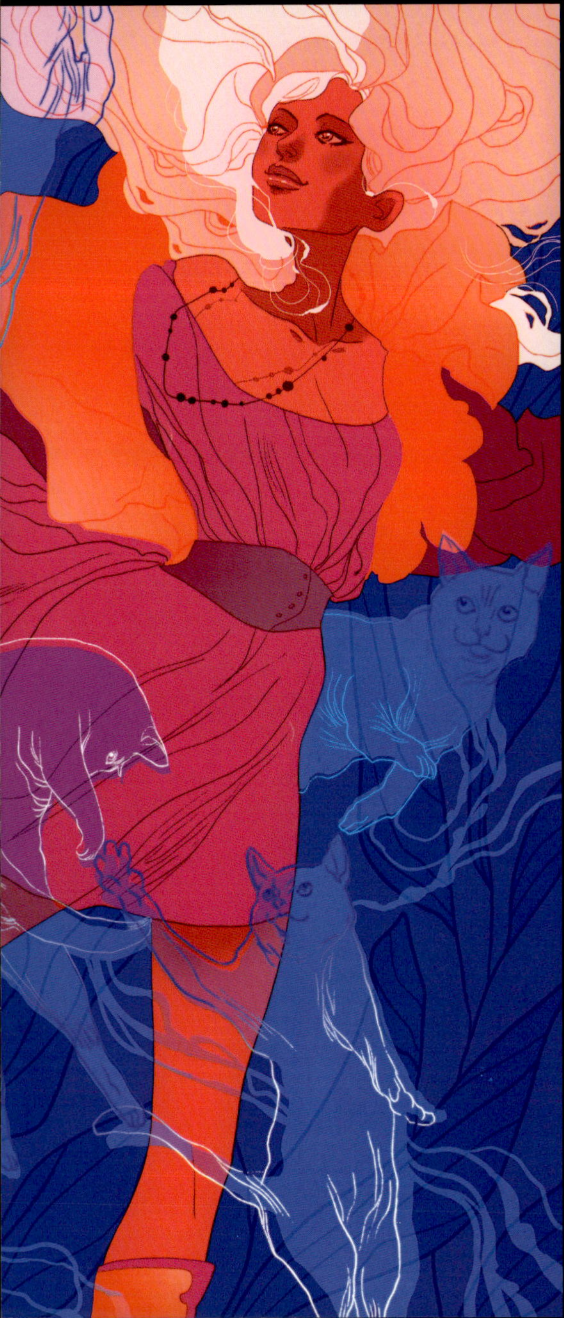

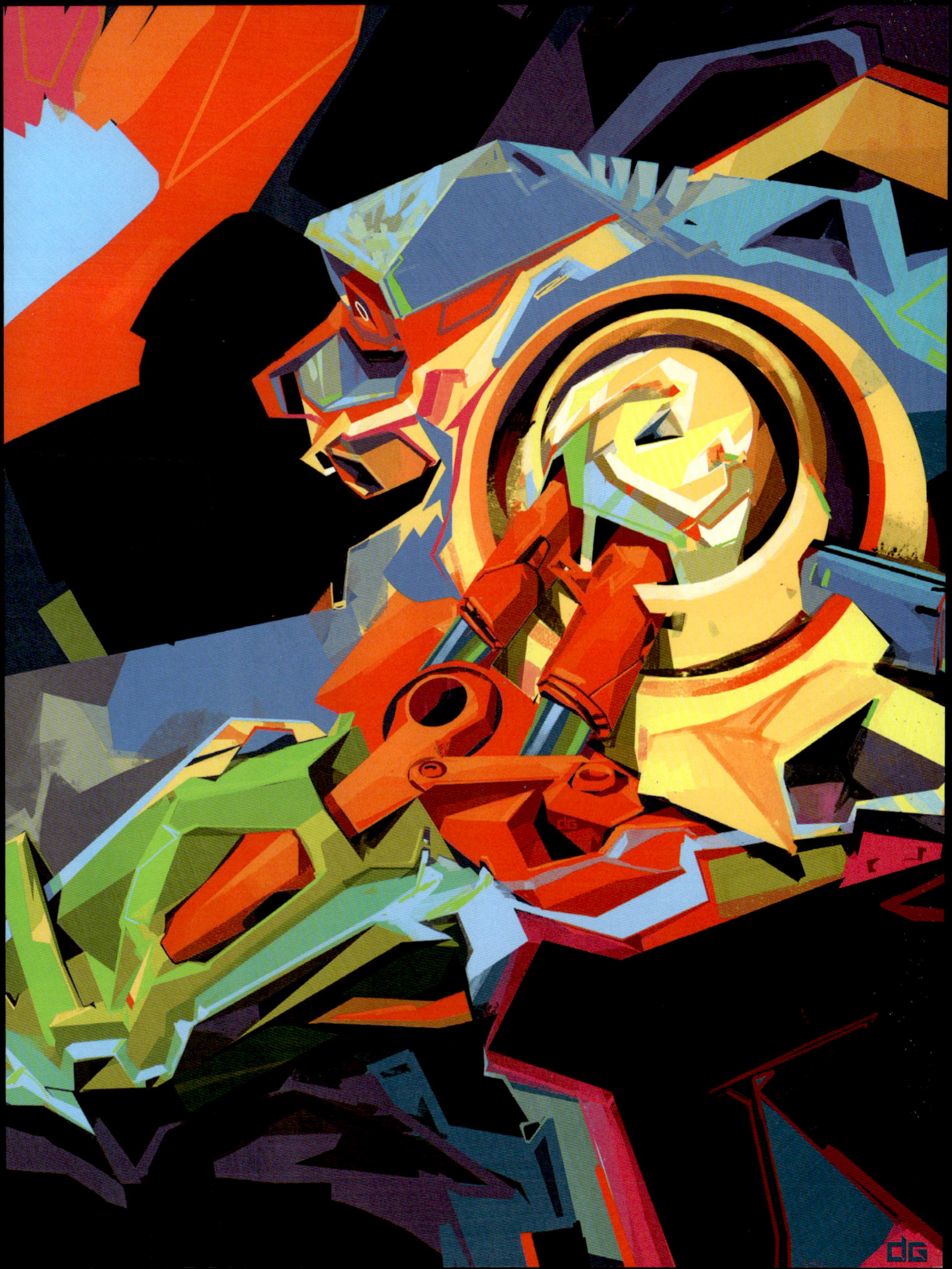

Unknown Disorder
V-Ray, 3ds Max, Photoshop
Client: Index Book
Fabien Meddour, FRANCE
[right]

Soc-Groaza-Exclusivitati
Photoshop
Sorin Bechira, ROMANIA
[below]

Paletero
Photoshop, Illustrator, Maya
Syndrome, USA
[bottom right]

Space Girl
Painter, Photoshop
Sergio Diaz, ARGENTINA
[bottom left]

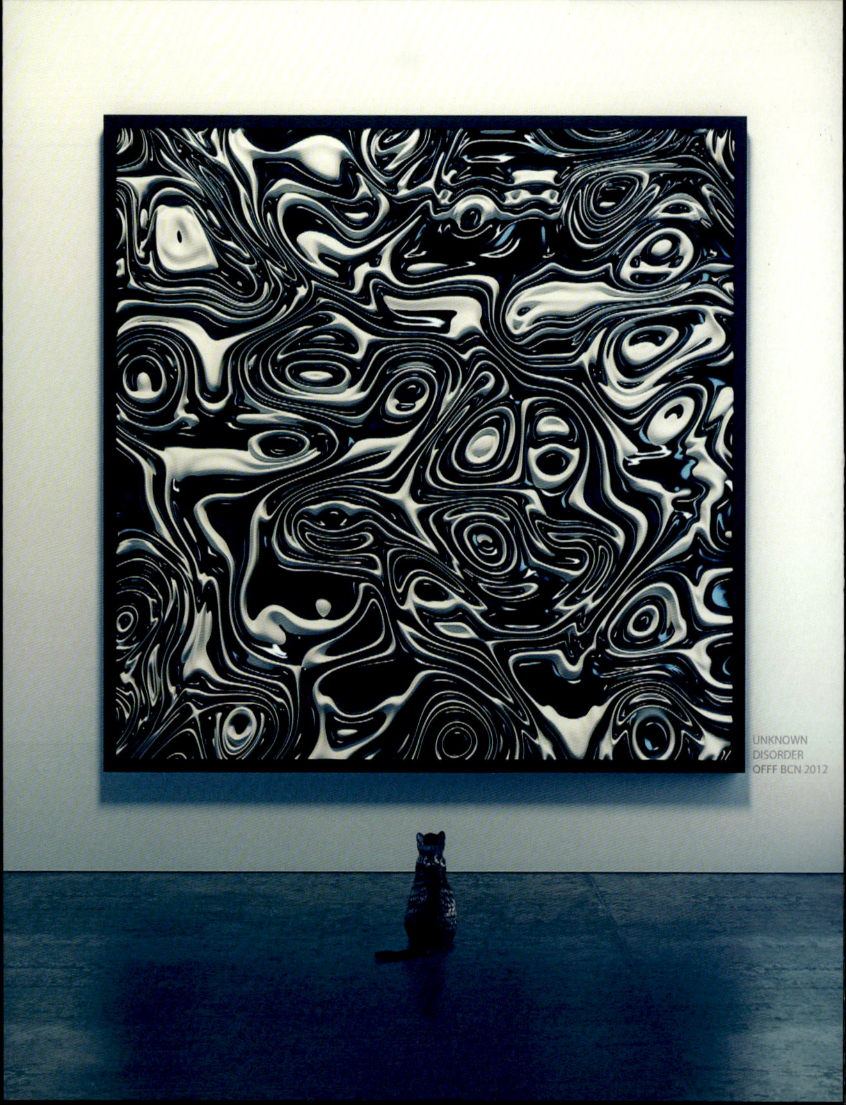

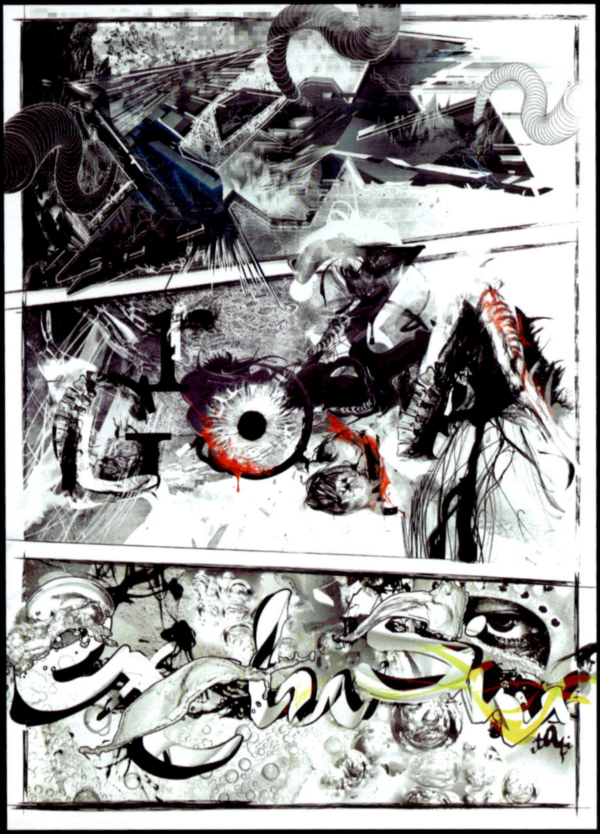

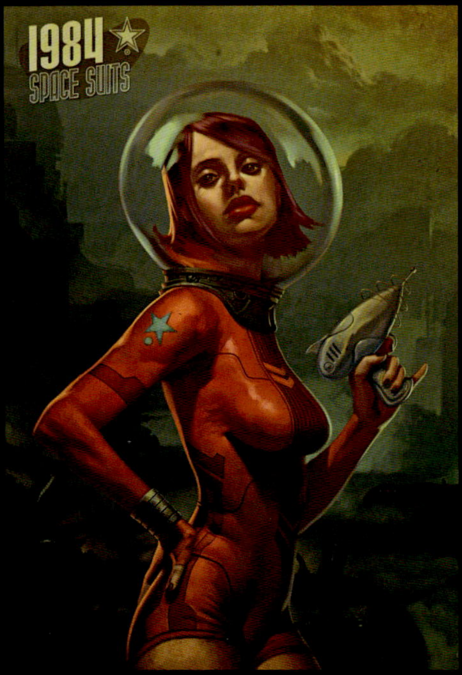

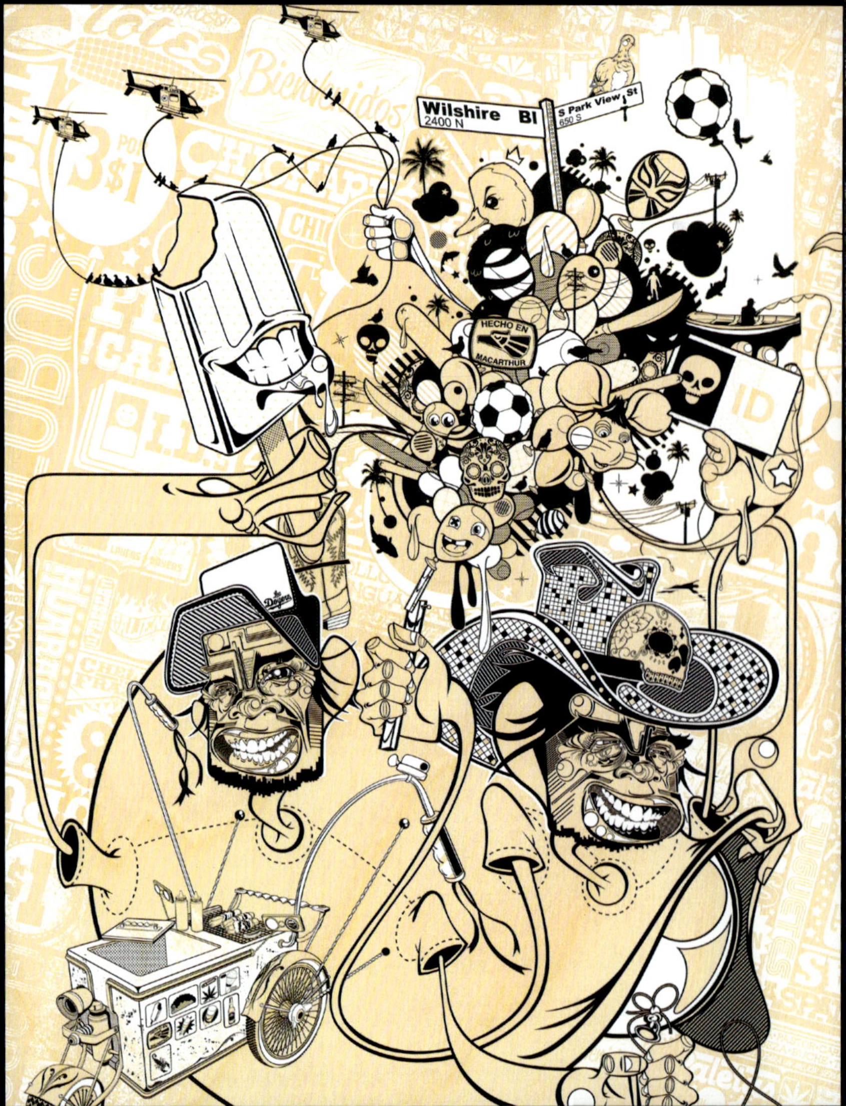

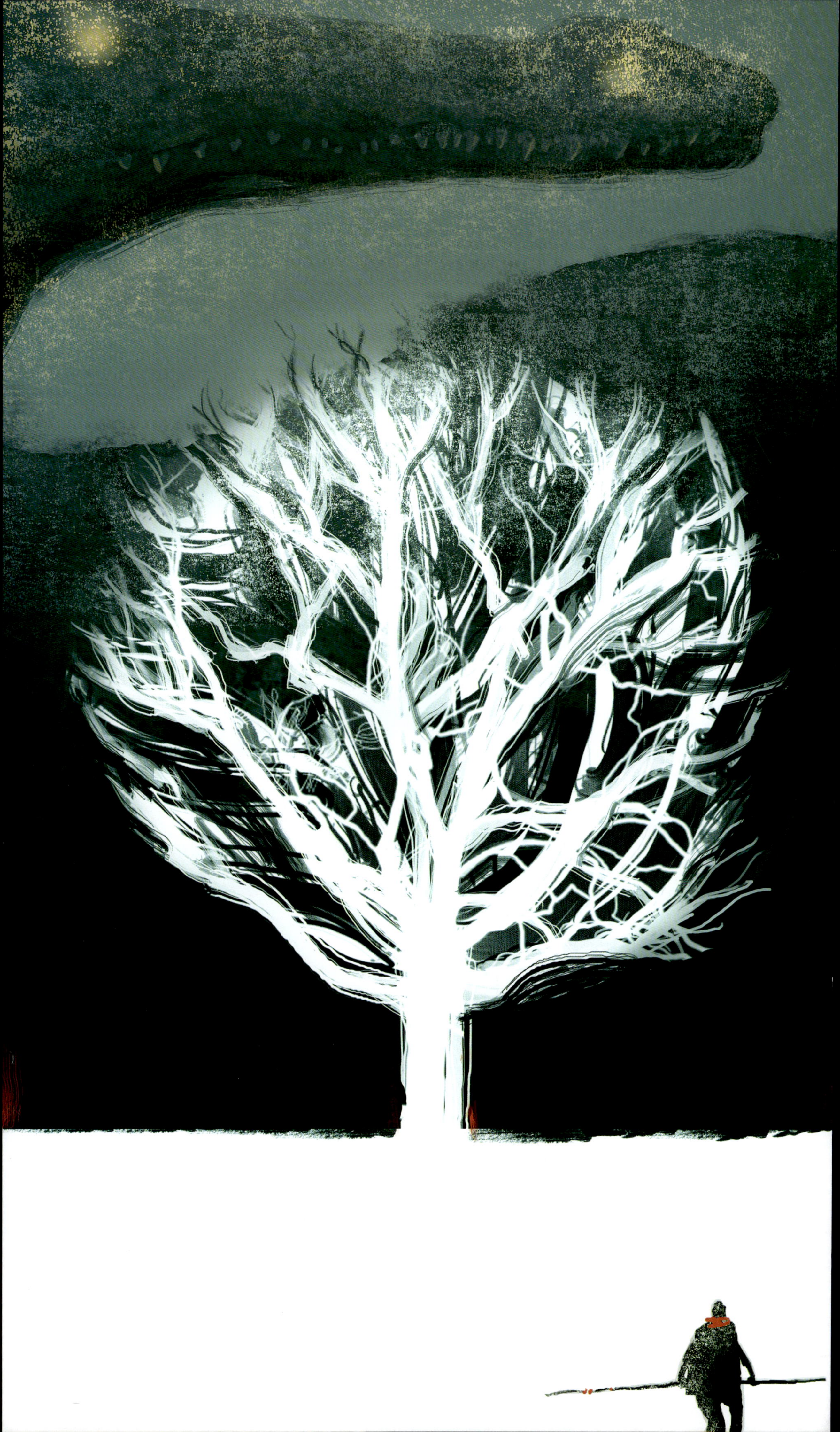

The Dragon Tree
Photoshop
Jeffrey Alan Love,
USA

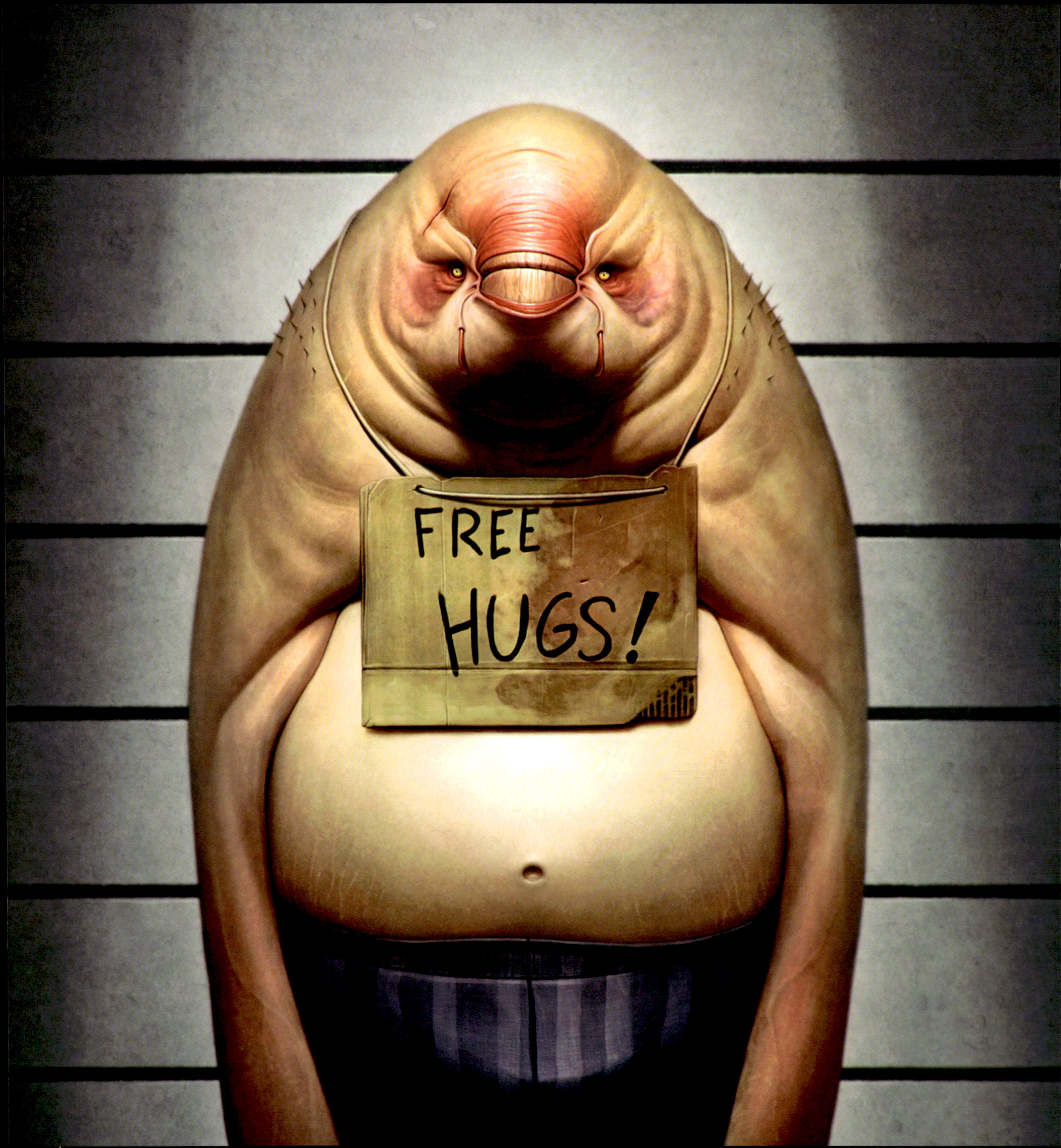

Free Hugs
Photoshop
Roberto Ribeiro Padula, BRAZIL

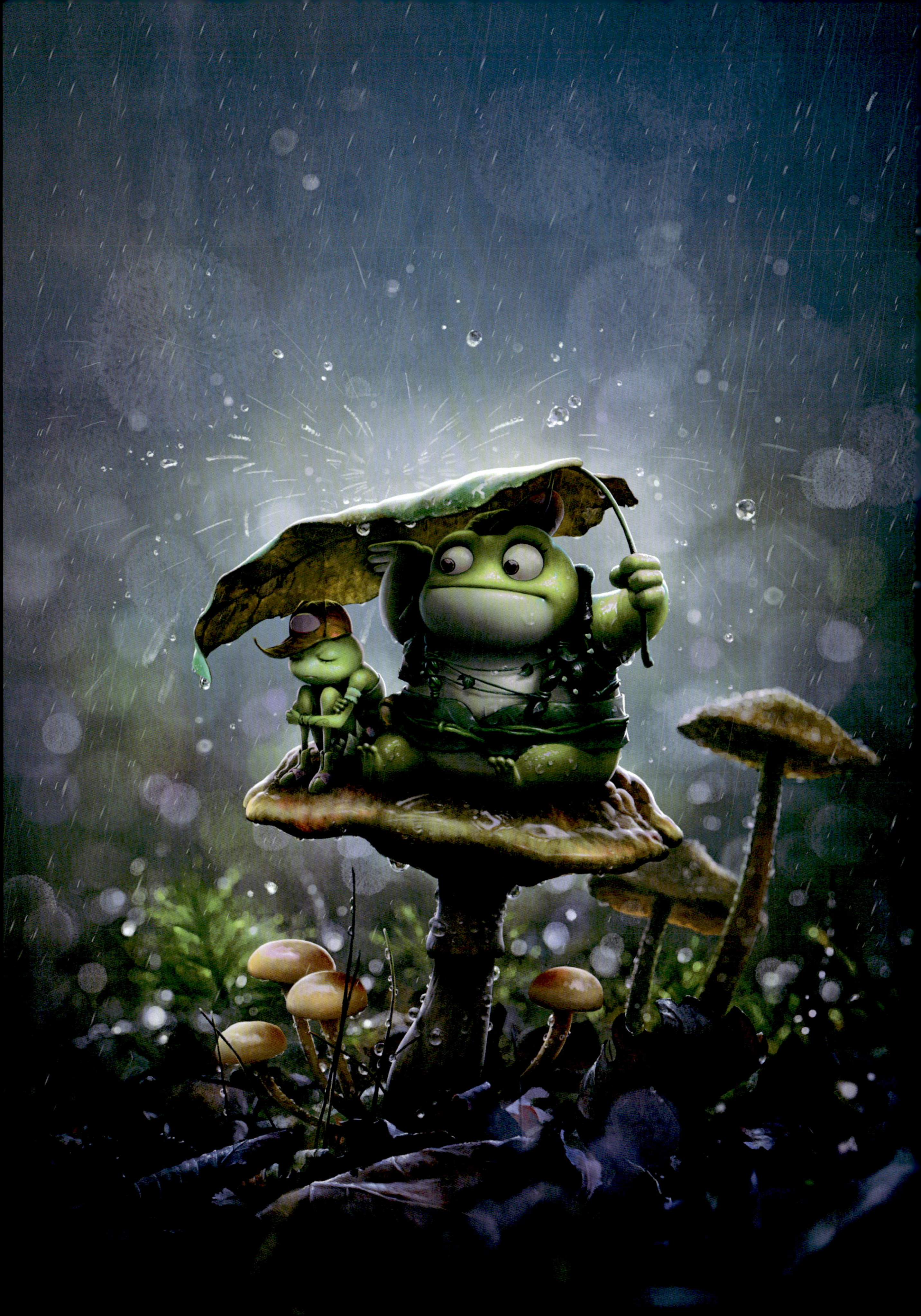

Raining
Photoshop
Xiao Yi, CHINA

Master
Whimsical

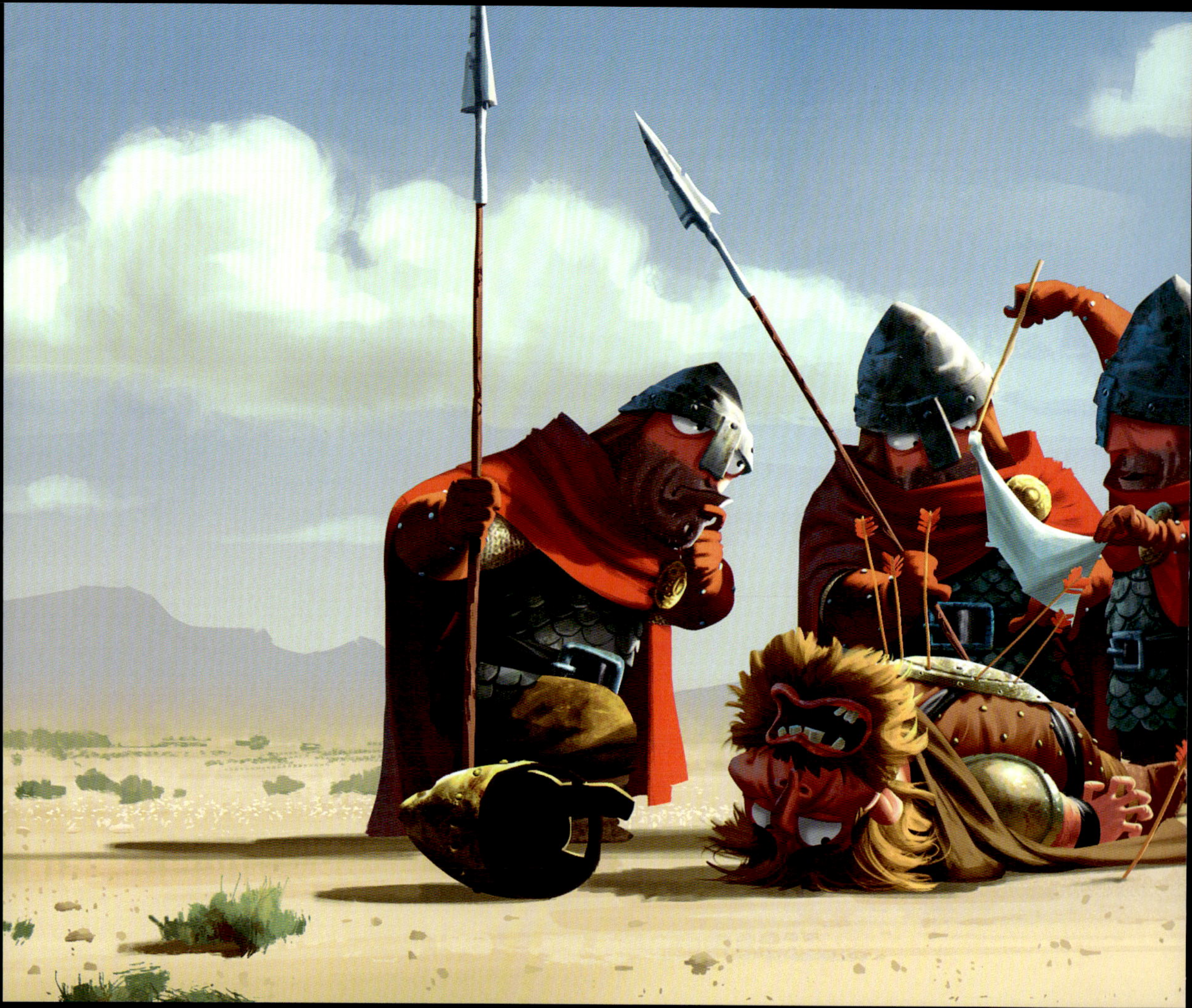

Lil' B!
3ds Max, V-Ray, ZBrush
Client: 3DArtist magazine
ose Alves da Silva, PORTUGAL
[below left]

Knight
Photoshop
Vinh Pham, VIETNAM
[below right]

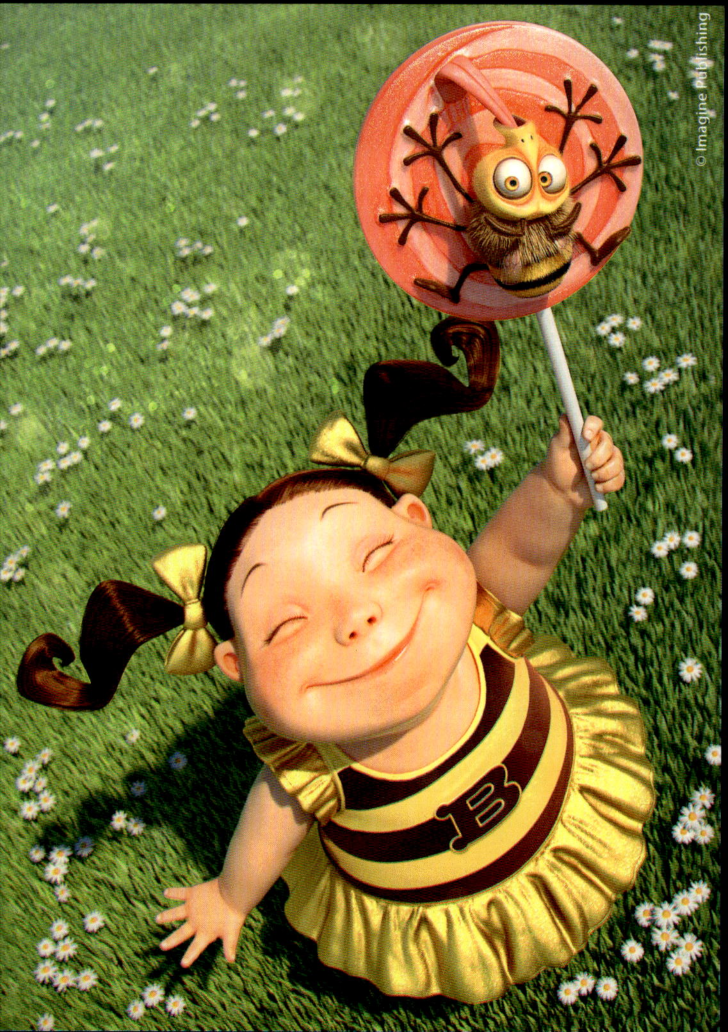

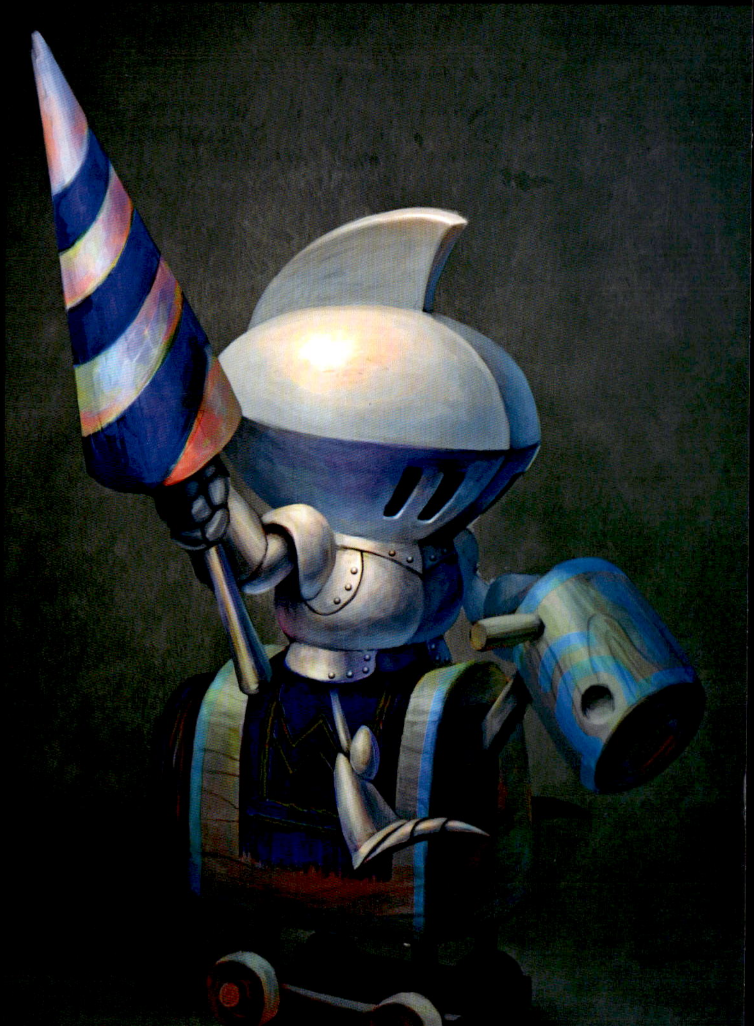

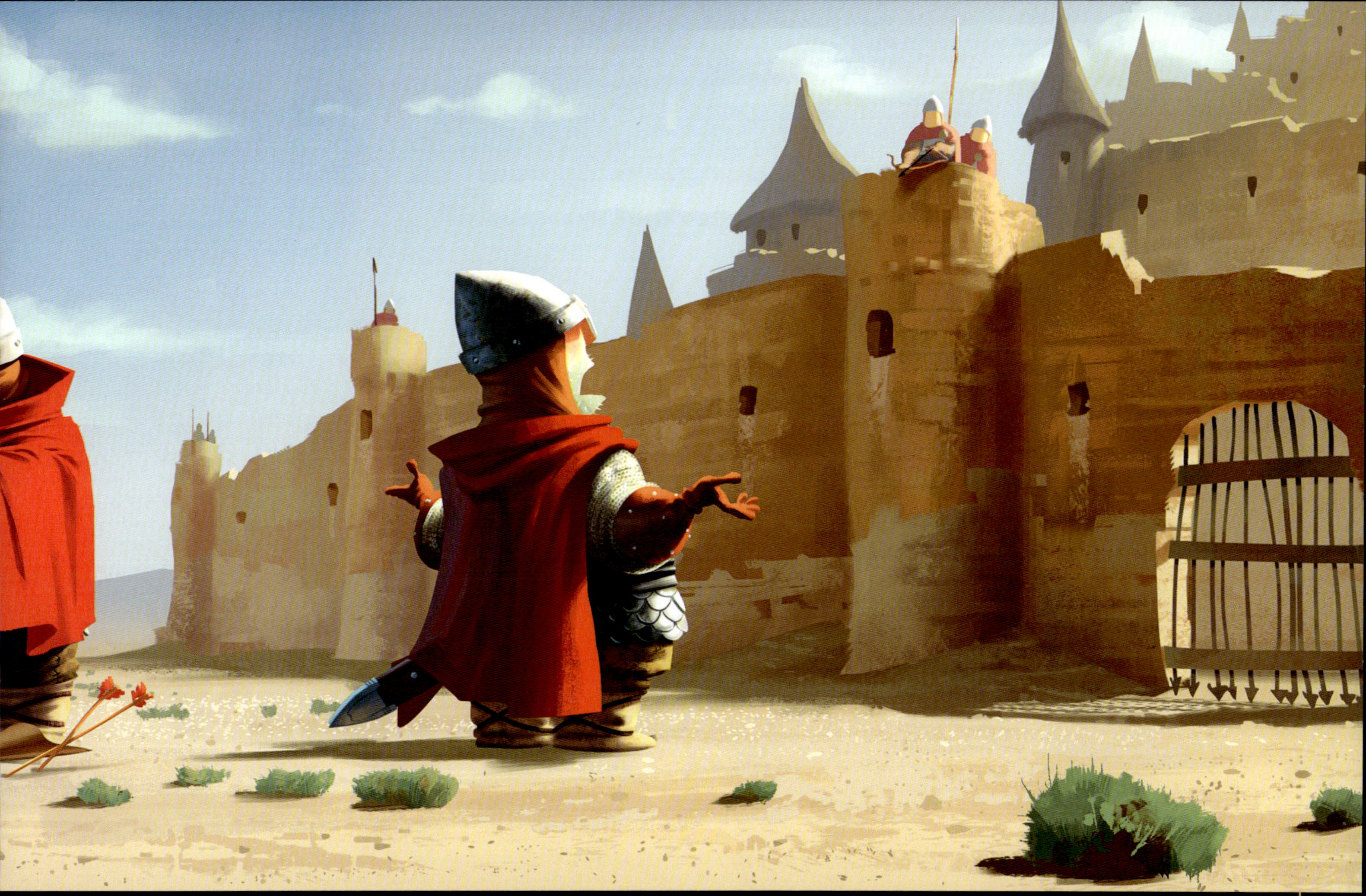

Don't Shoot the Messenger
Photoshop
Tony Weinstock, USA
[above]

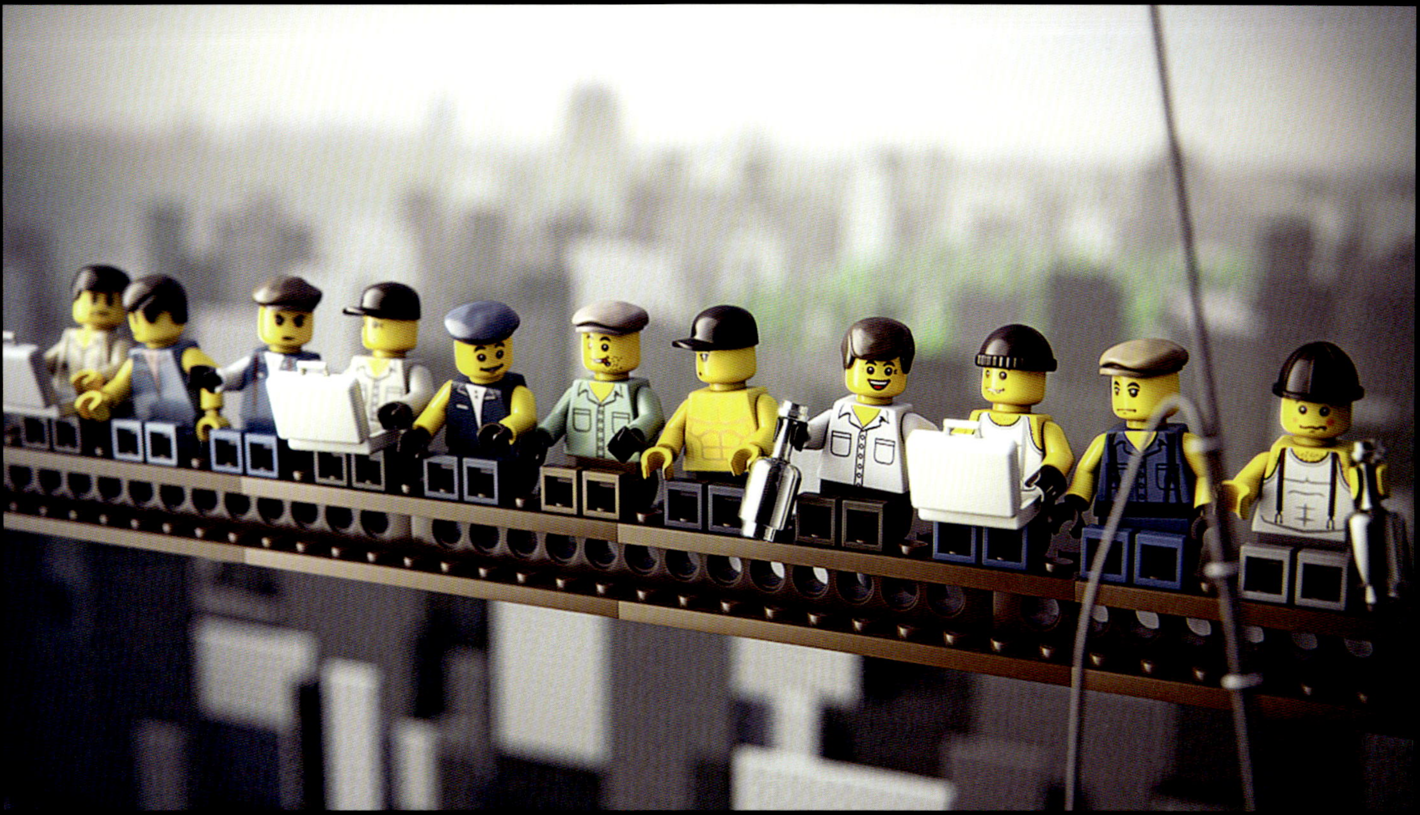

Lunch Atop a Skyscraper
CINEMA 4D, Photoshop
Inspired by Charles C. Ebbets
Patrick Eischen, LUXEMBOURG

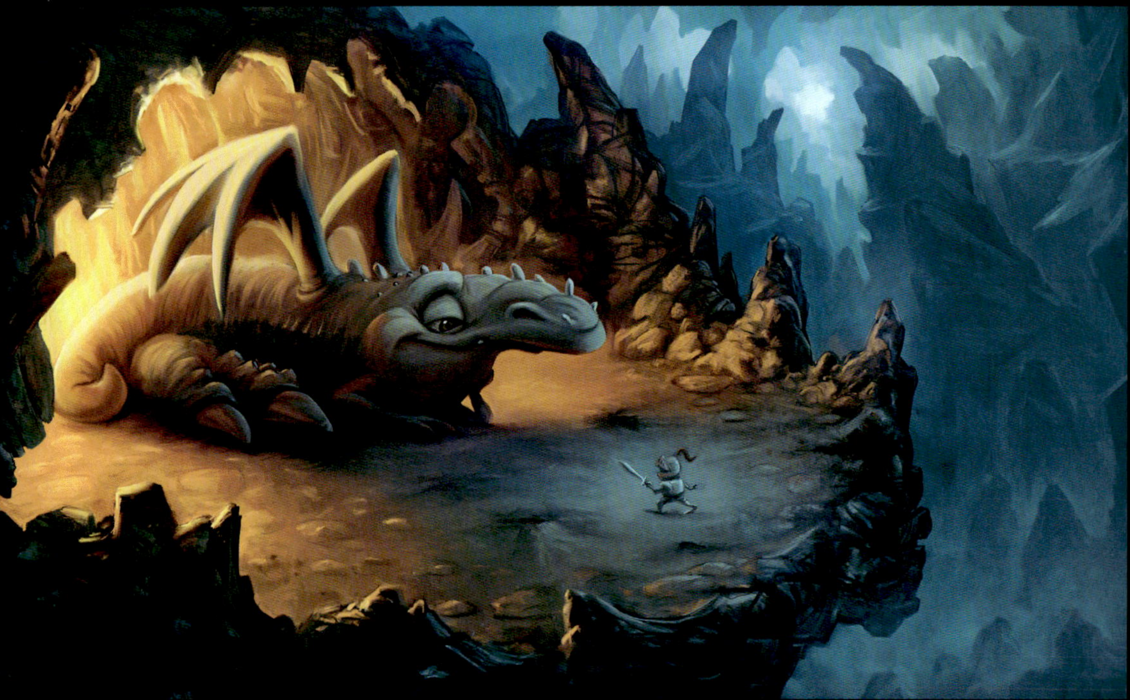

Don't Play With Your Food
Photoshop, Painter
Jeremy Vickery, USA
[right]

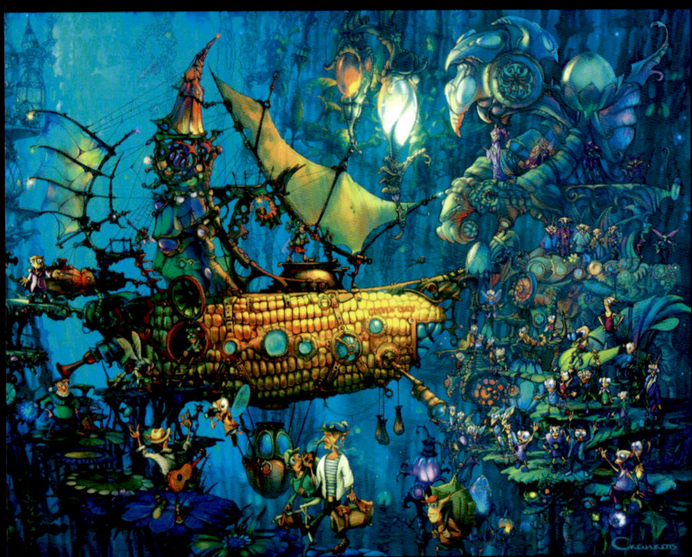

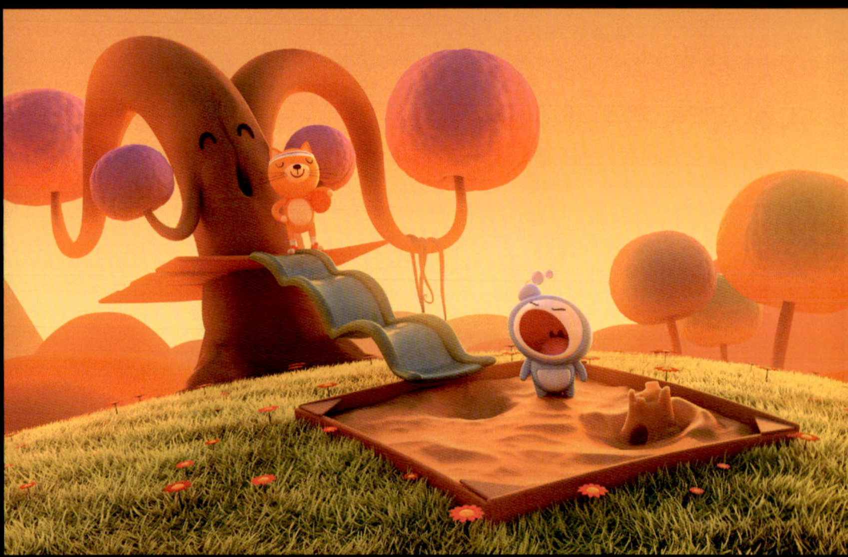

The Golden Corn
Photoshop
Sergey Skachkov, RUSSIA
[above]

Kimochis Playground
3ds Max, Maxwell Render, After Effects
Jonatan Catalan Navarrete, SPAIN
[above right]

Follow Me Yawn
Photoshop
Alben Tan, PHILIPPINES
[right]

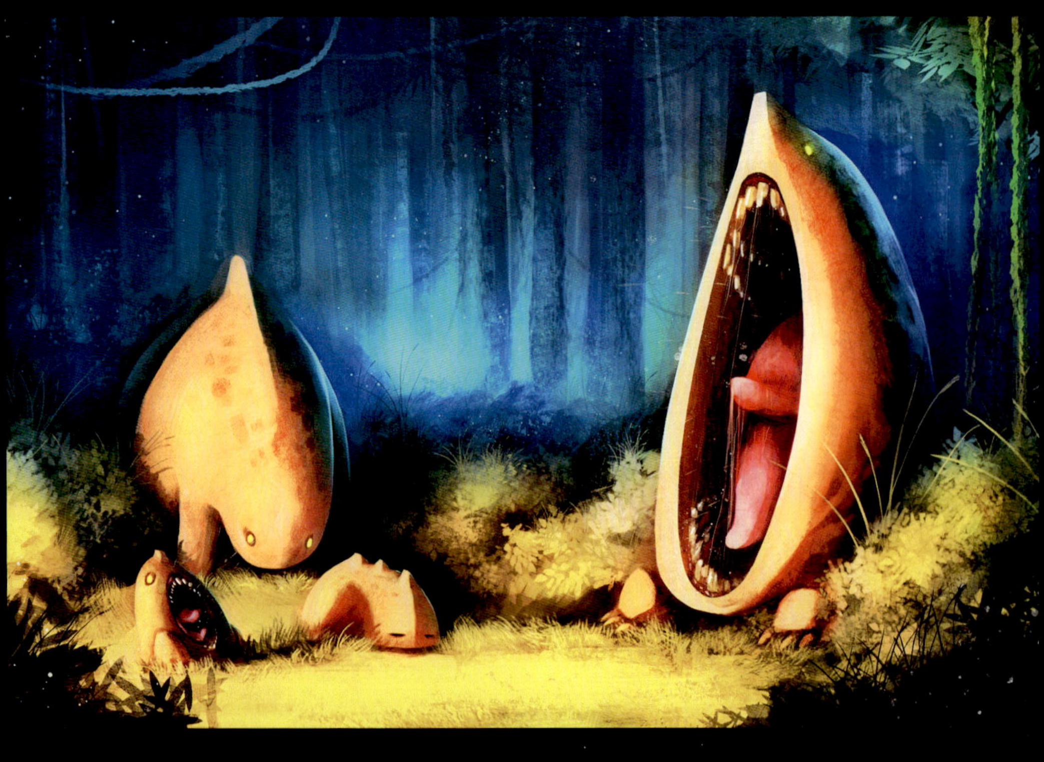

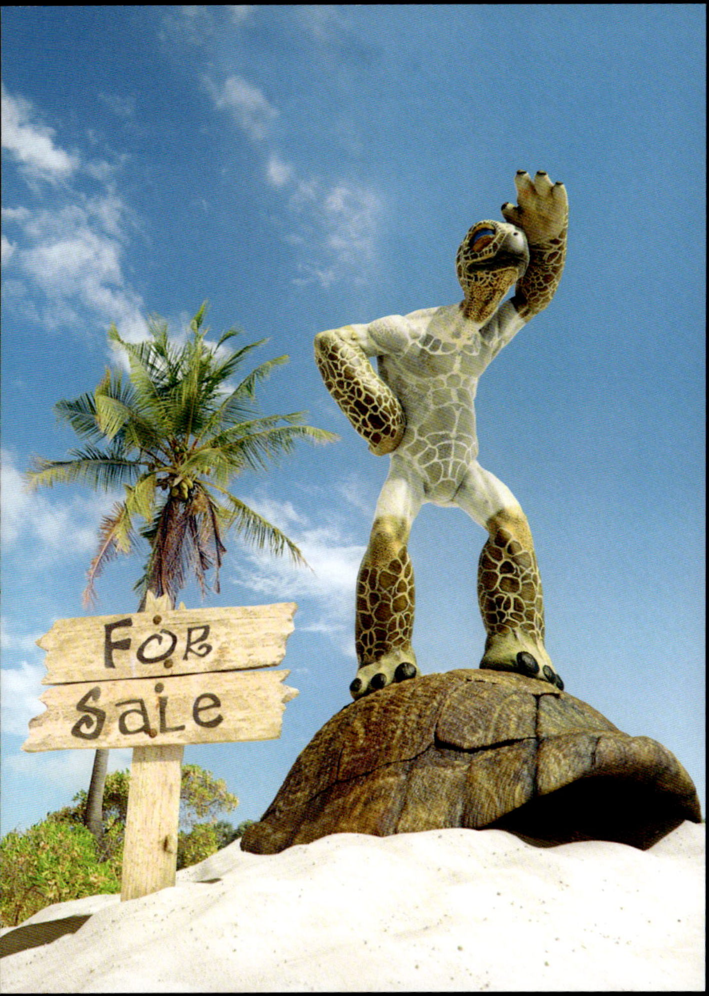

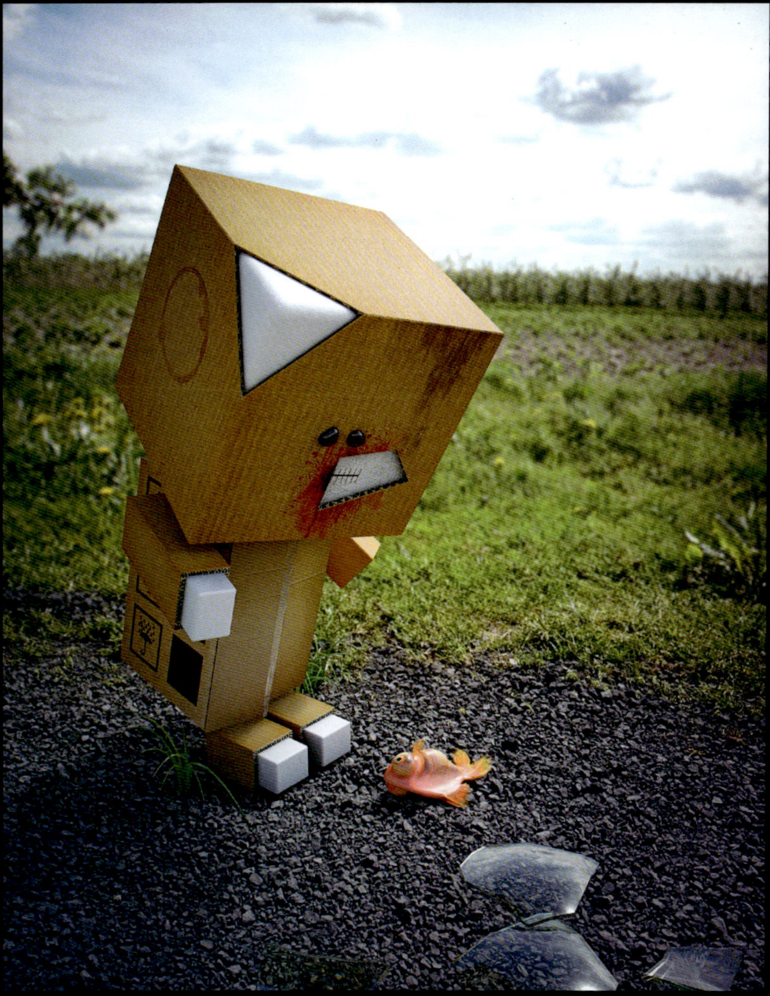

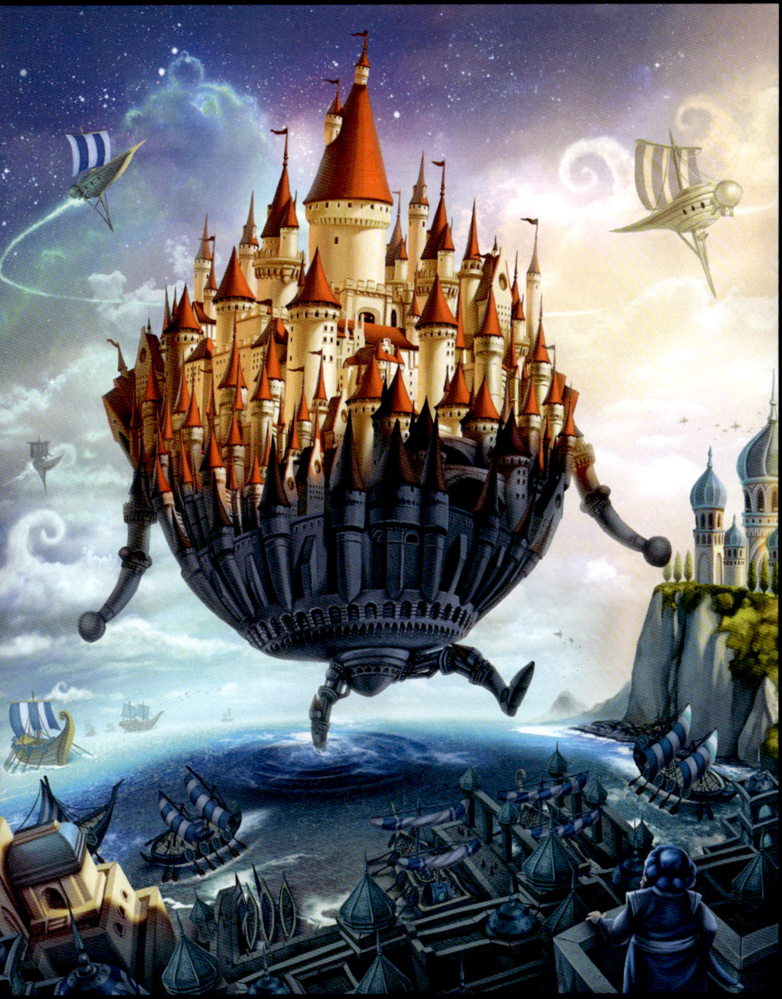

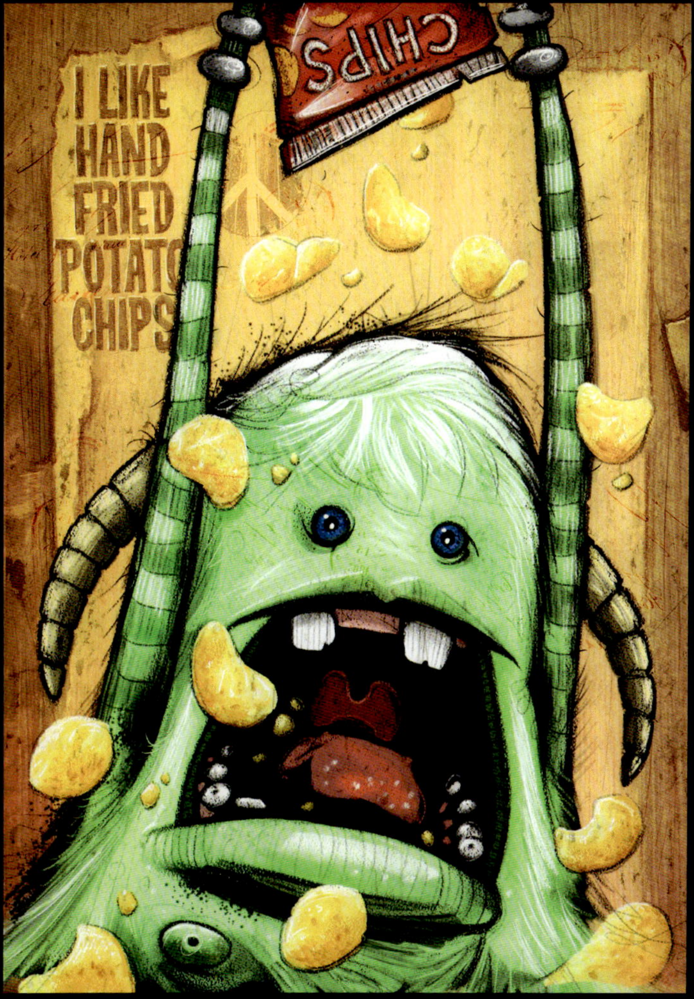

Turtle Freedom for Sale
3ds Max, ZBrush, V-Ray, Photoshop
David AF, PORTUGAL
[top]

Walking Ball of the North West Castle
Photoshop
Lee Chin Horng, MALAYSIA
[above]

Zombie Box Character
3ds Max, V-Ray, Photoshop
Vincent Jaramillo, USA
[top]

I Like Chips
Painter, Photoshop
Robin 'Lopine' Kunzmann, GERMANY
[above]

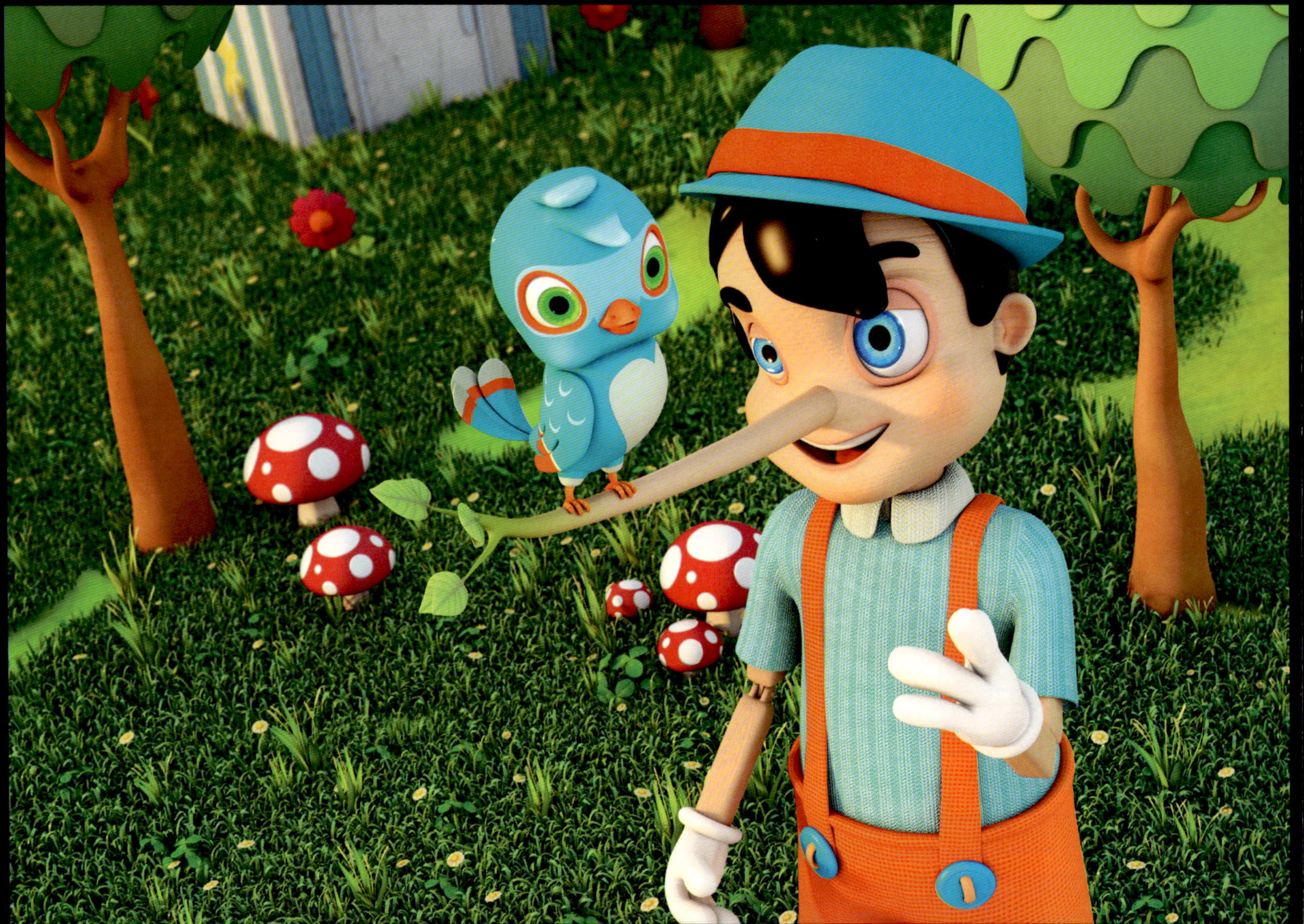

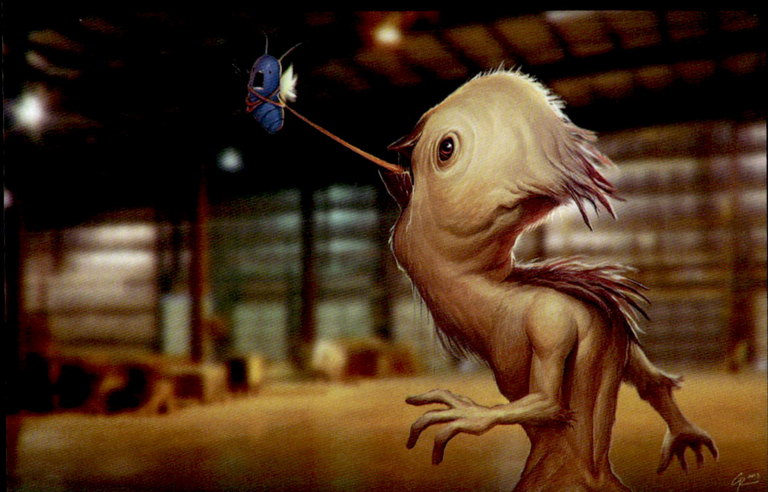

Pinocchio
modo, Photoshop
Teodoru Badiu, AUSTRIA
[top]

Slurp
Photoshop
Gibson Radsavanh, AUSTRALIA
[above]

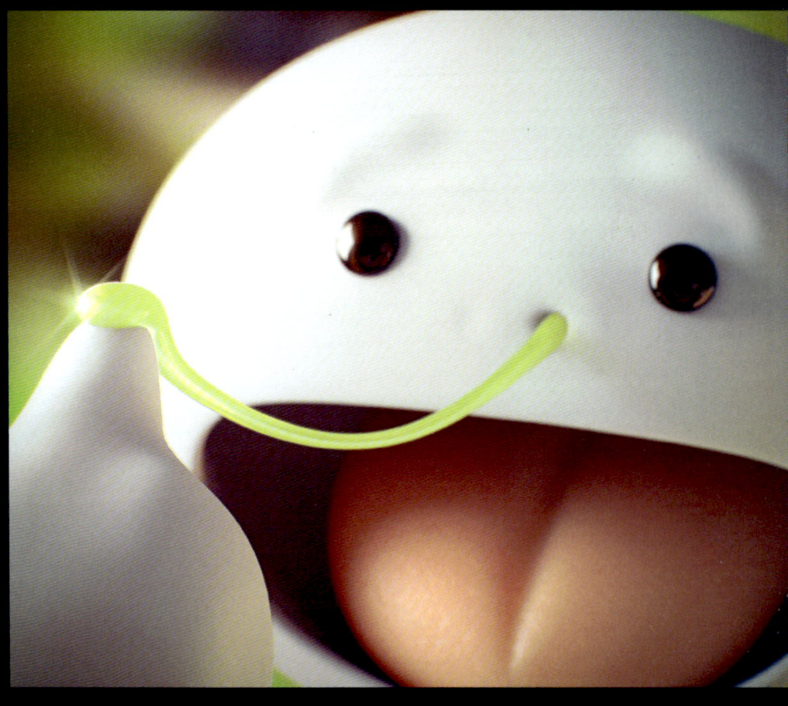

Stretch
3ds Max, V-Ray, Photoshop, Mudbox
Jose M. Andres Martin, USA
[above]

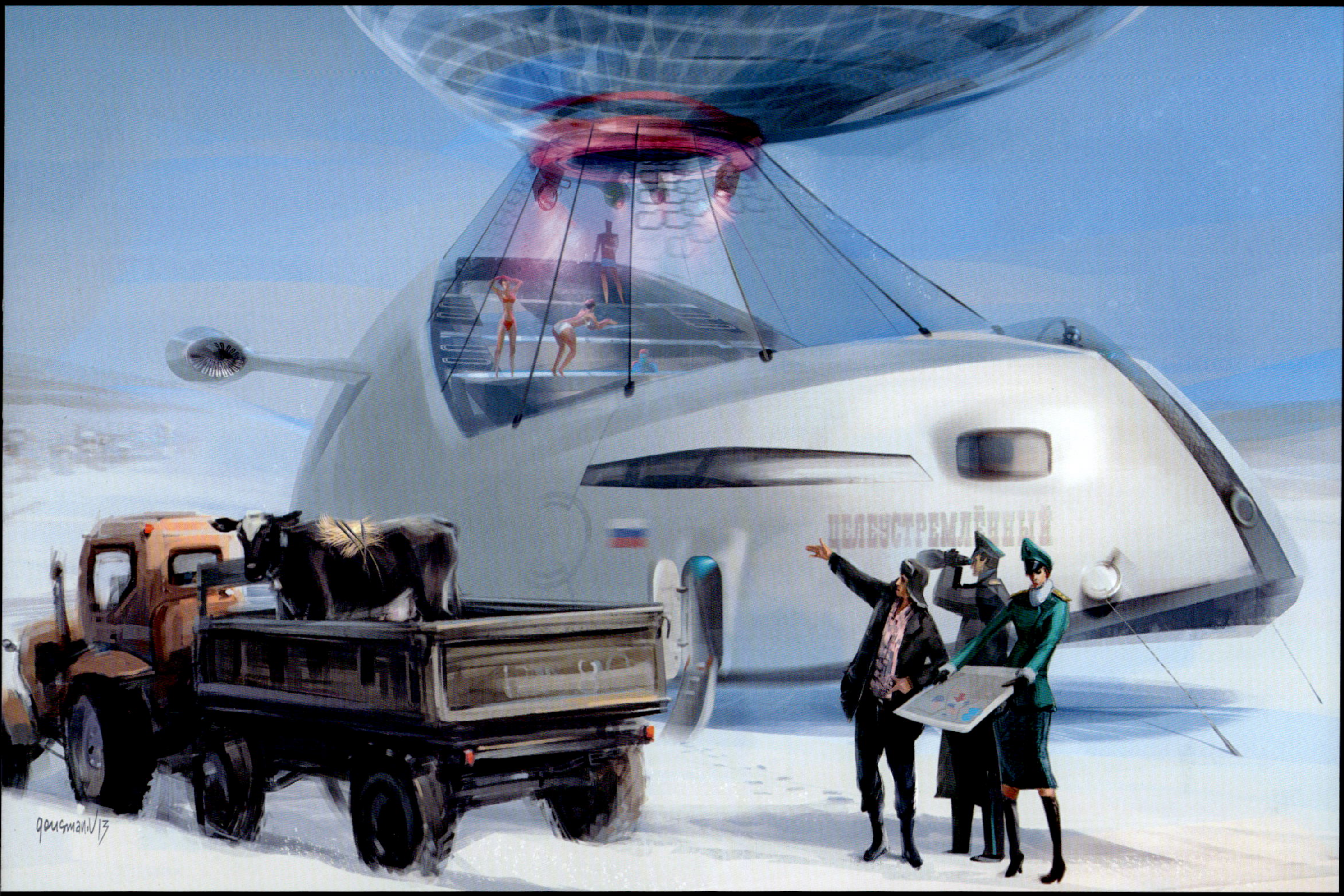

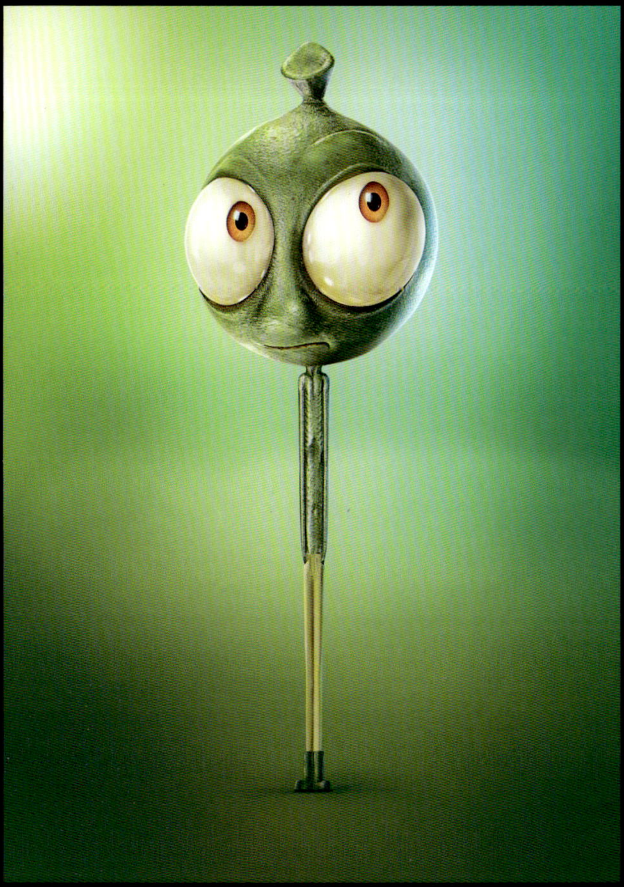

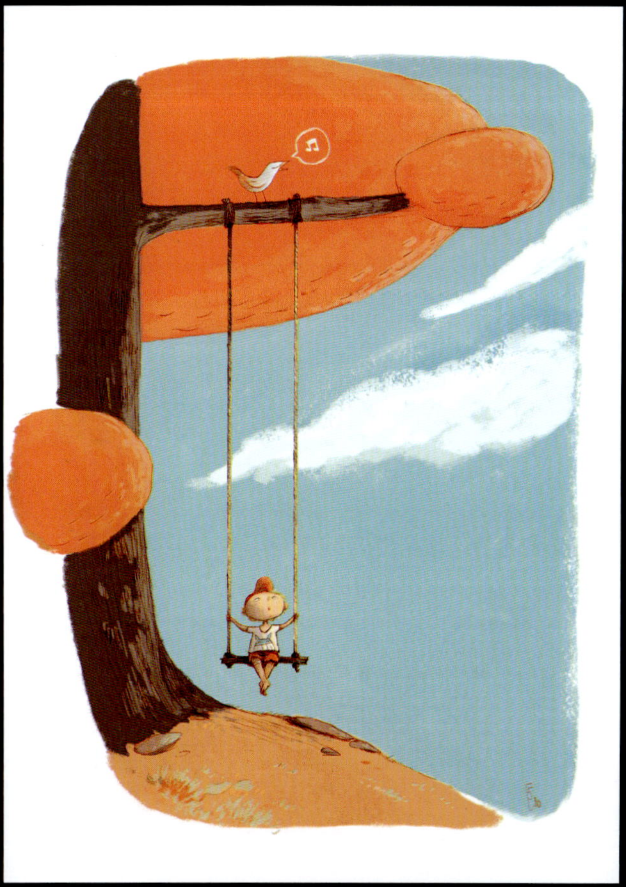

Alien Lollipop
3ds Max, Blender, Photoshop, ZBrush
Client: Vonpar Alimentos, Agency: Escala
Fescher Neoilustração, BRAZIL
[above]

Full Speed Ahead!
Photoshop
Vadim Gousmanov, RUSSIA
[top]

The Bird
Photoshop
Sabine Cazassus, FRANCE
[above]

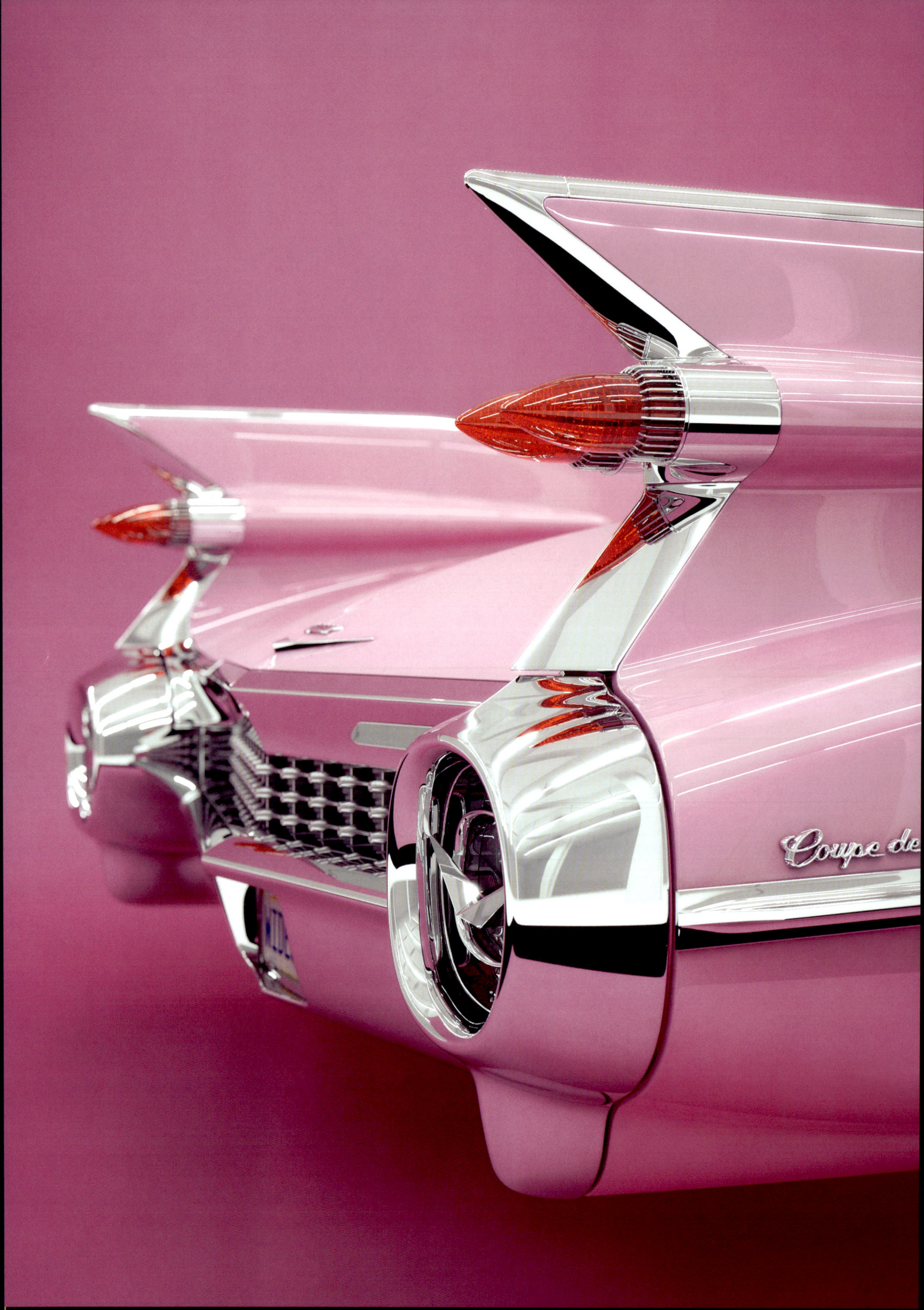

Excellence
Transport

Pink on Pink
3ds Max, V-Ray, Rhino
Tom Winberg, NORWAY

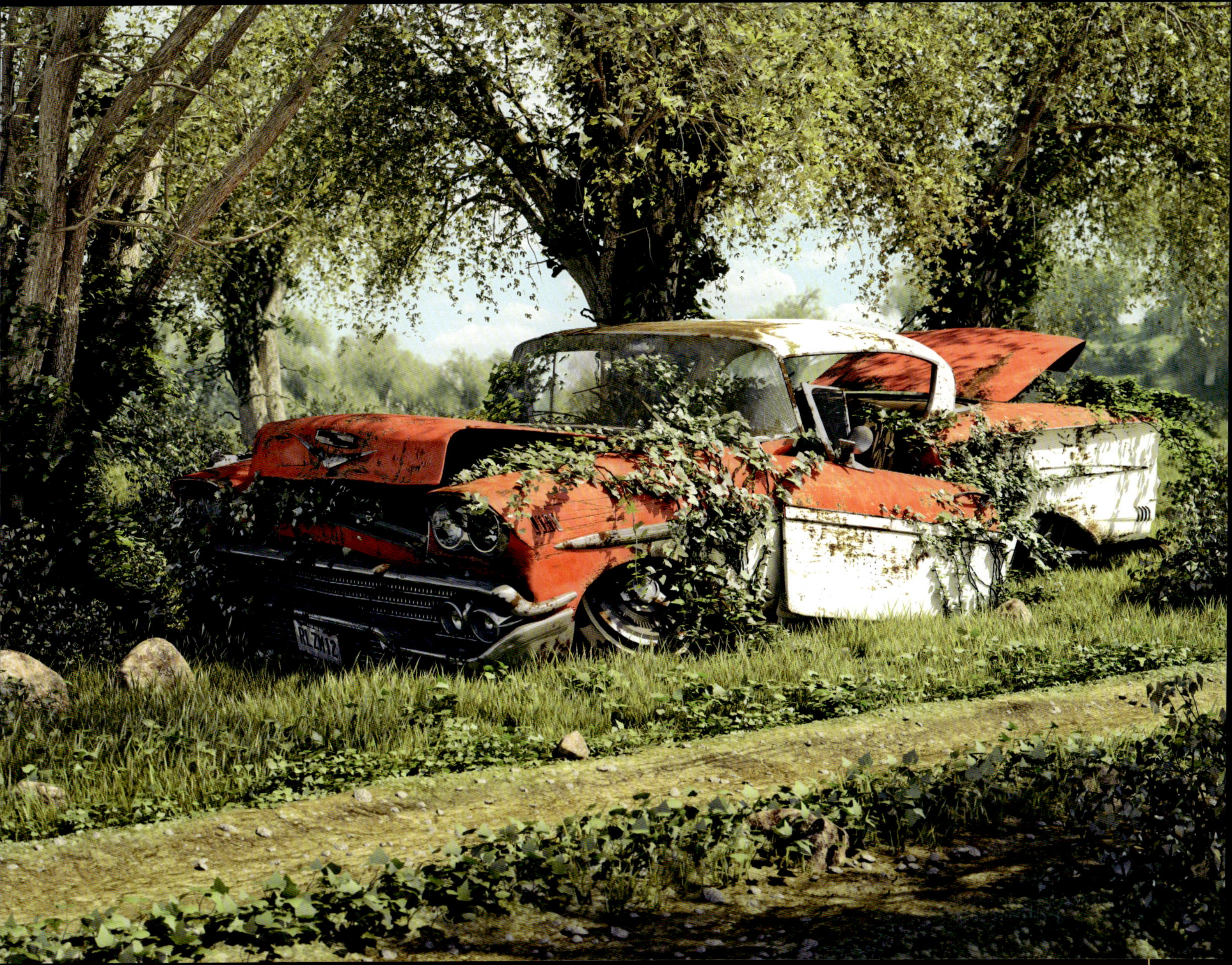

Abandoned Bel Air
Maya, Mudbox, Photoshop
Jochem Aarts, NETHERLANDS

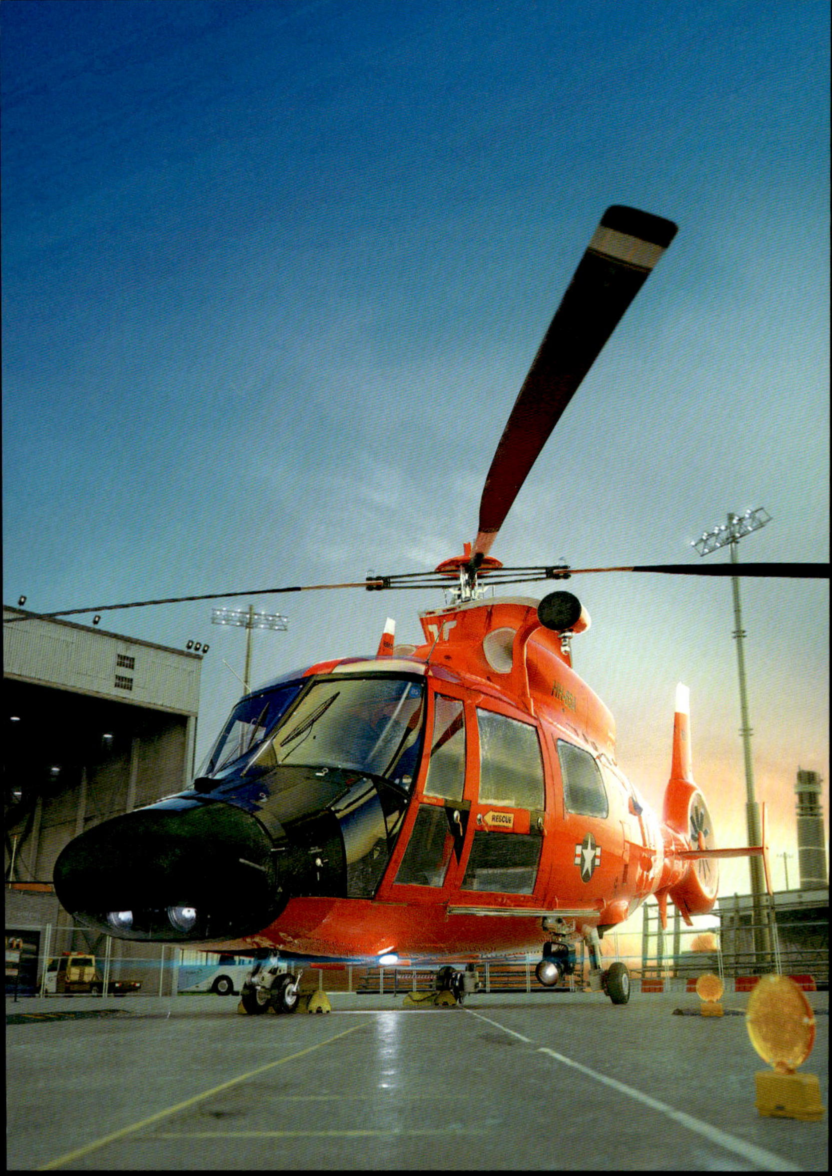

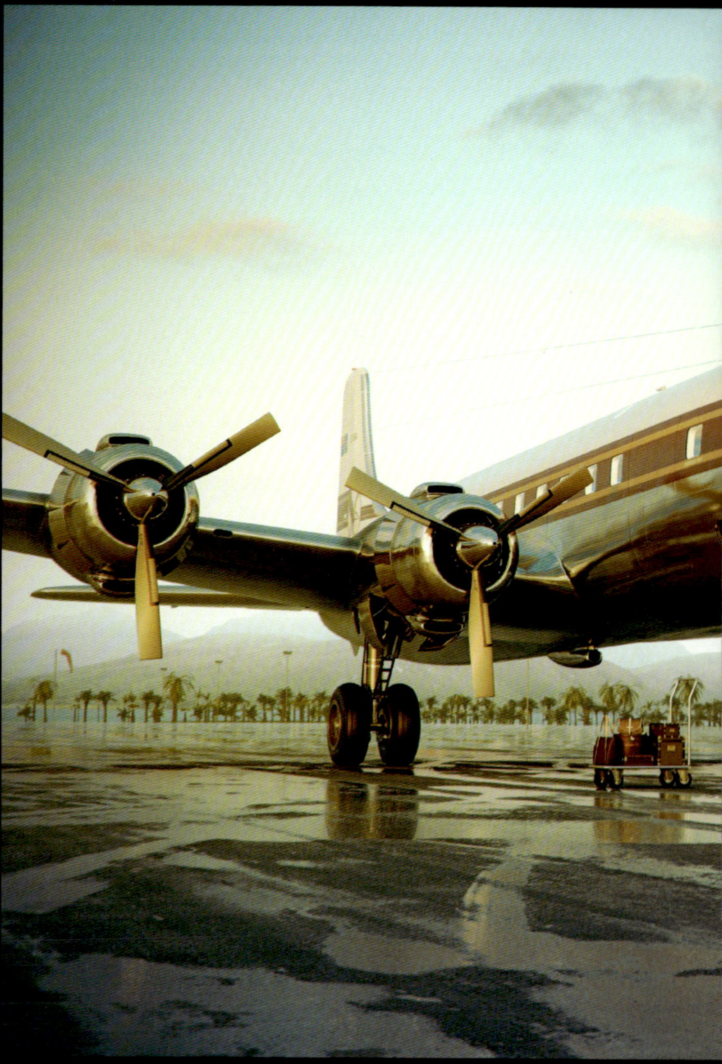

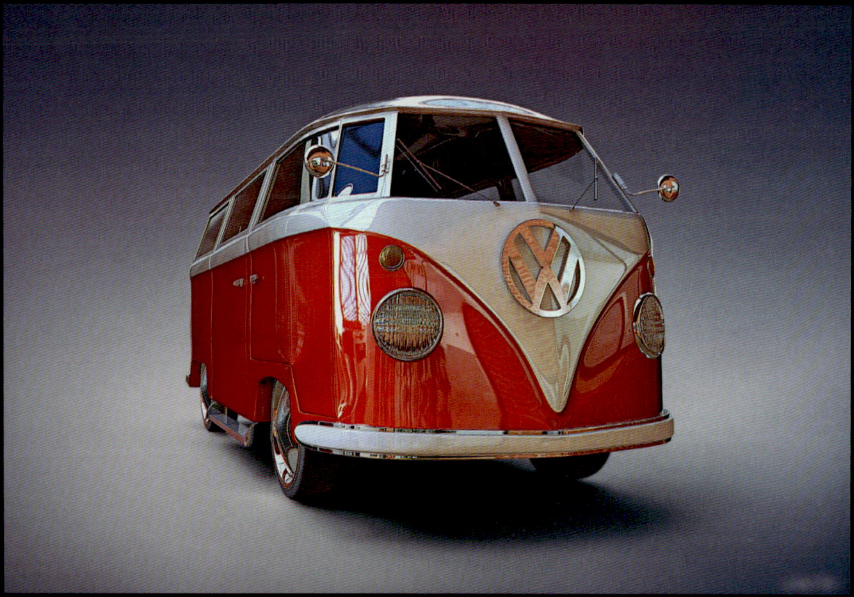

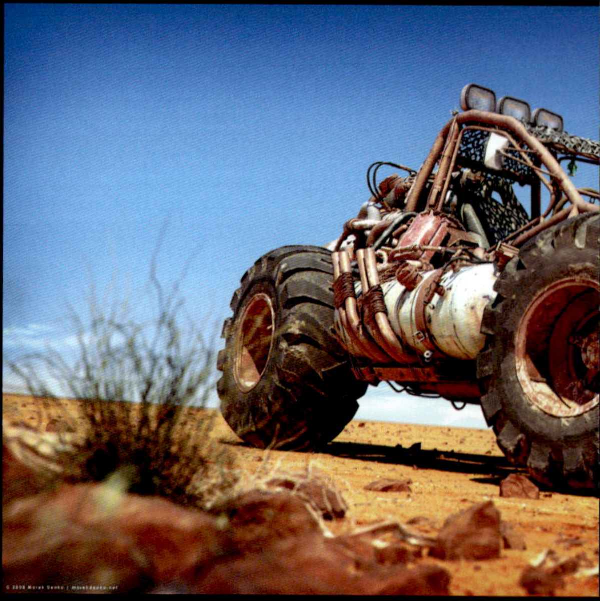

Eurocopter HH-65 Dolphin
3ds Max
Luis Miguel Duran Ramon, SPAIN
[top]

Red VW Camper
3ds Max, mental ray, Photoshop
Jake Denham, GREAT BRITAIN
[above]

Cloudmaster DC-6: An Early Start
3ds Max, V-Ray, Photoshop
Client: Cloudmaster Limited
Richard Booth, GREAT BRITAIN
[top]

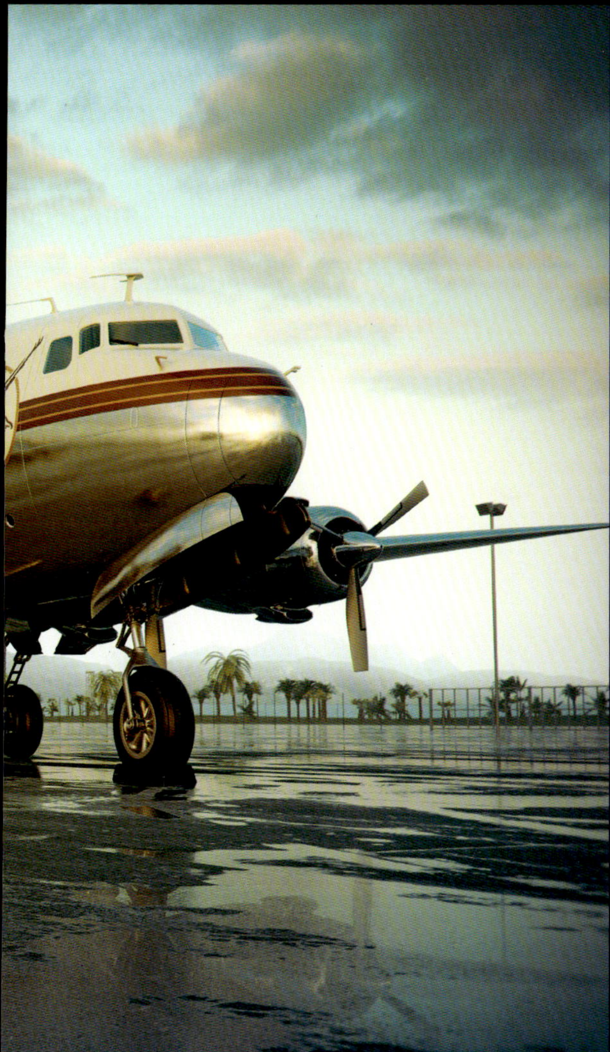

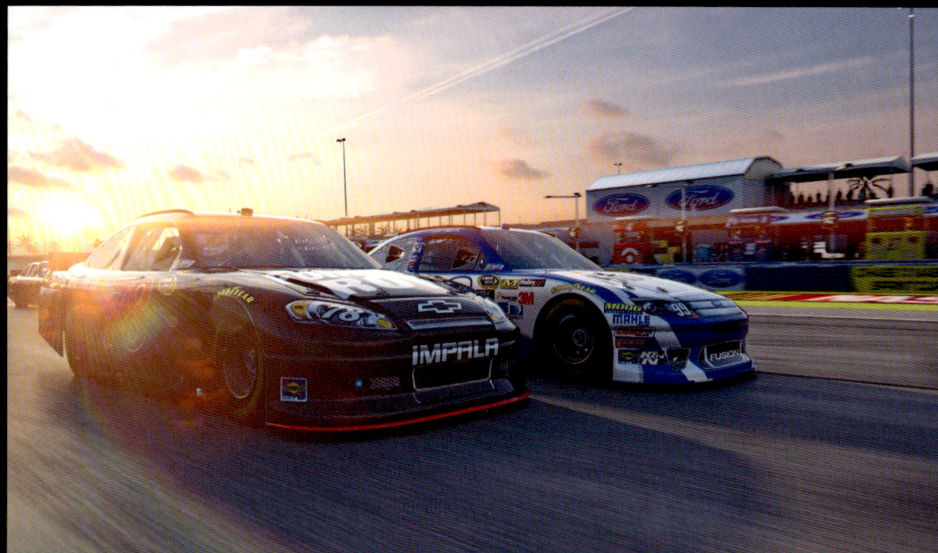

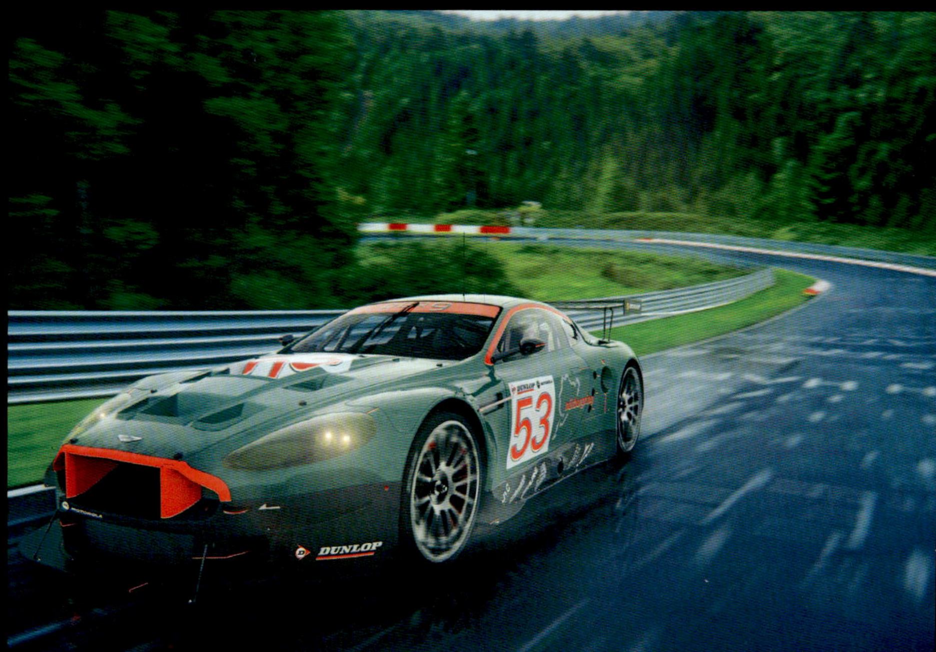

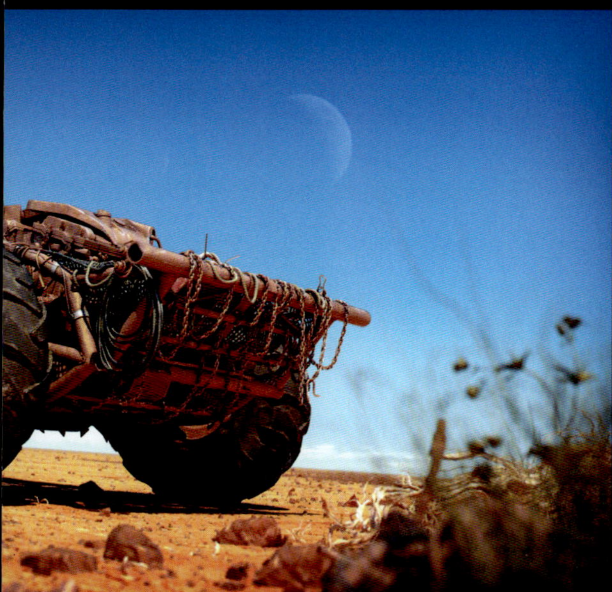

Sunset Race
3ds Max
Gareth Thatcher, Mi, GREAT BRITAIN
[top]

DBR 9
3ds Max, Photoshop, After Effects
Yegor Kalynychenko, PORTUGAL
[above]

Desert Rose
3ds Max, V-Ray
Marek Denko, SLOVAKIA

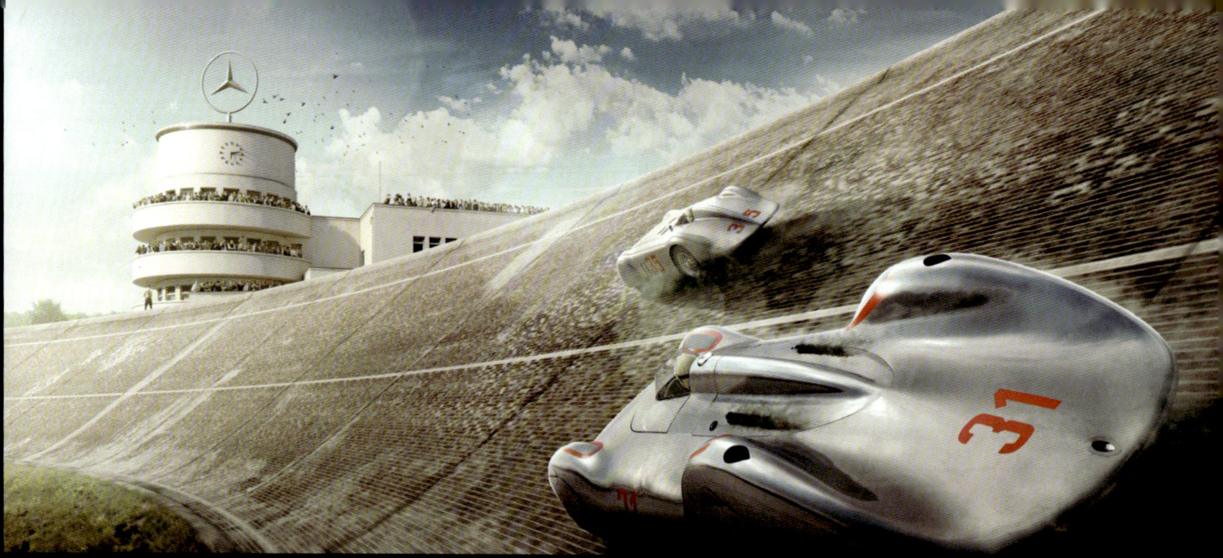

Silver Arrows
3ds Max, Photoshop,
V-Ray, ZBrush
Playground,
CZECH REPUBLIC
[right]

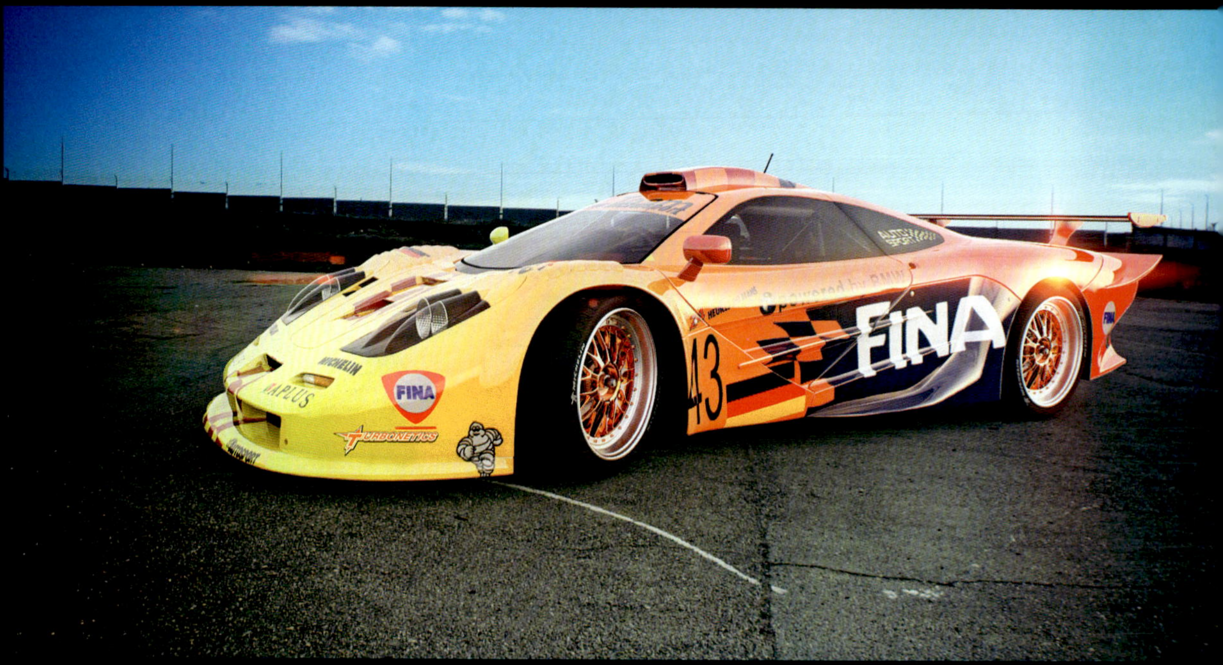

McLaren F1
3ds Max, Photoshop,
After Effects
Yegor Kalynychenko,
PORTUGAL
[right]

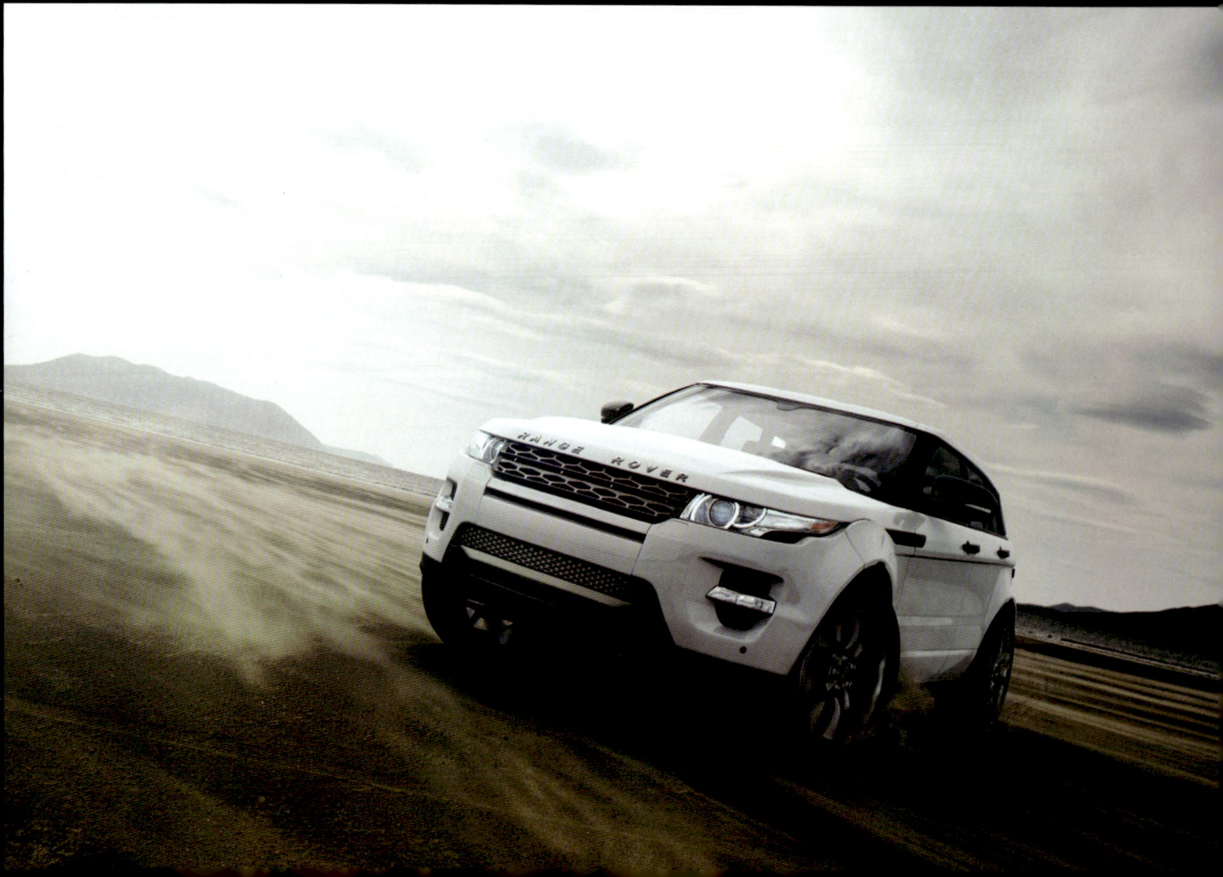

Range Rover Evoque
modo, Photoshop
Pascal Dalstein, GERMANY
[right]

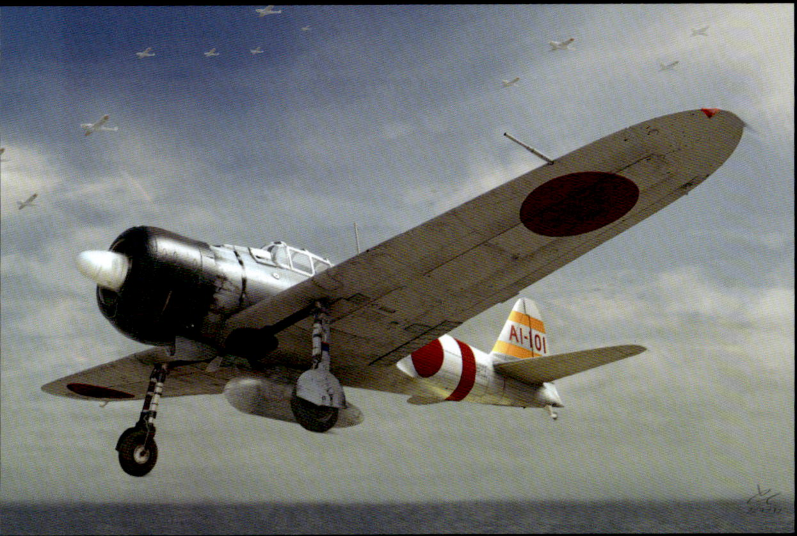

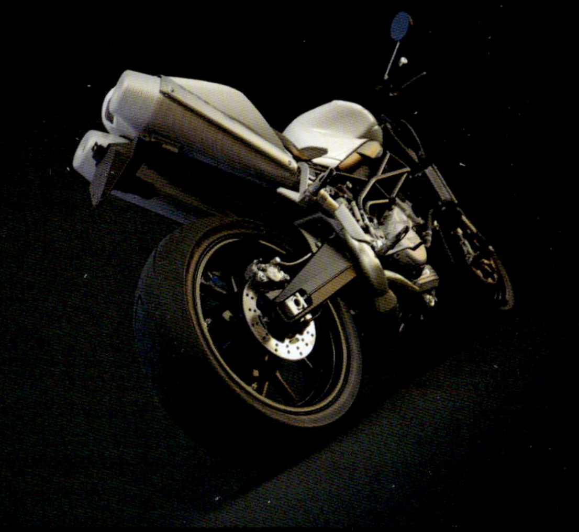

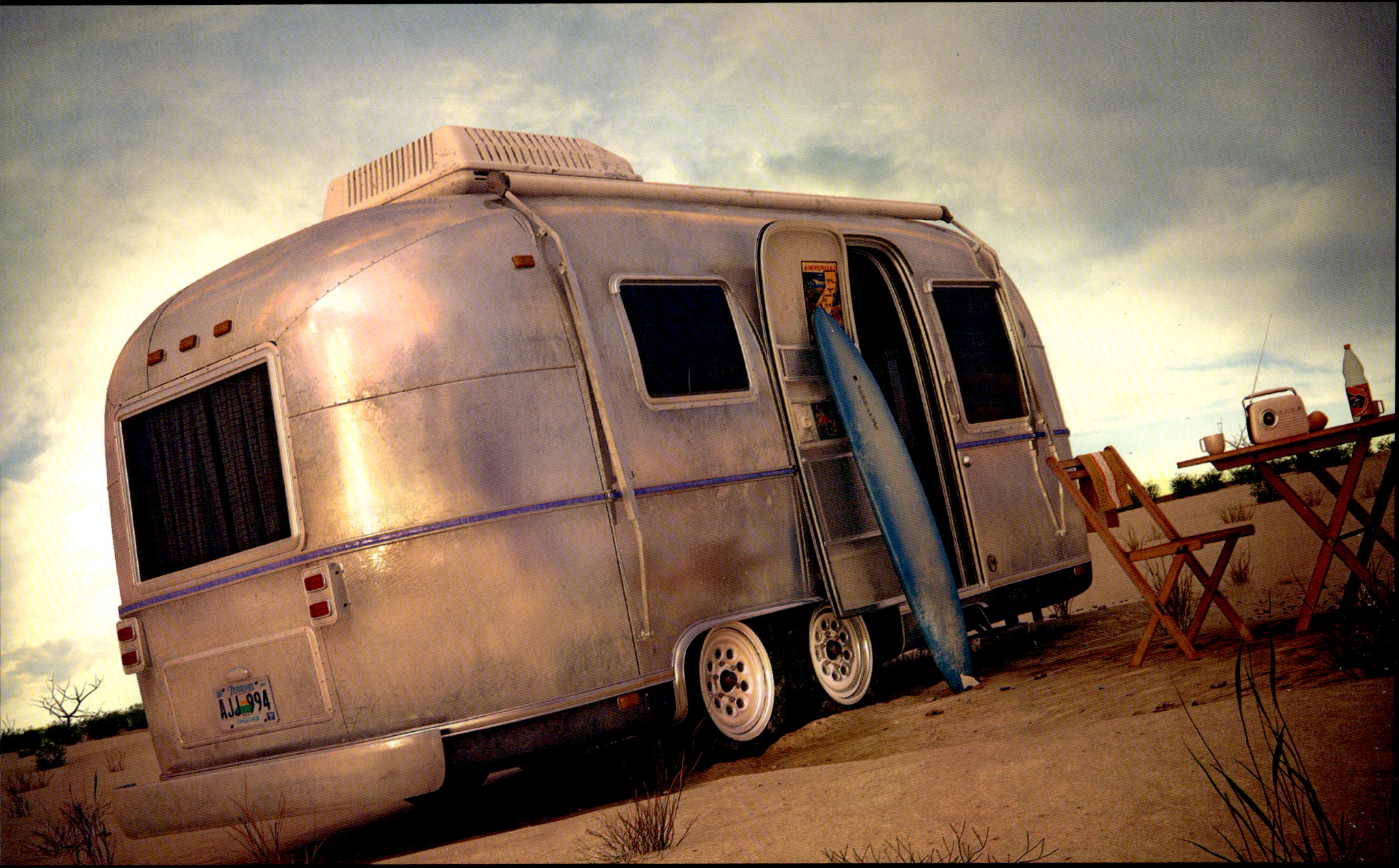

Tian Gou
Maya, Photoshop
Yaolong Liu, CHINA
[above center]

On Wheels
3ds Max, After Effects, V-Ray
Anton Cherenko, UKRAINE
[above]

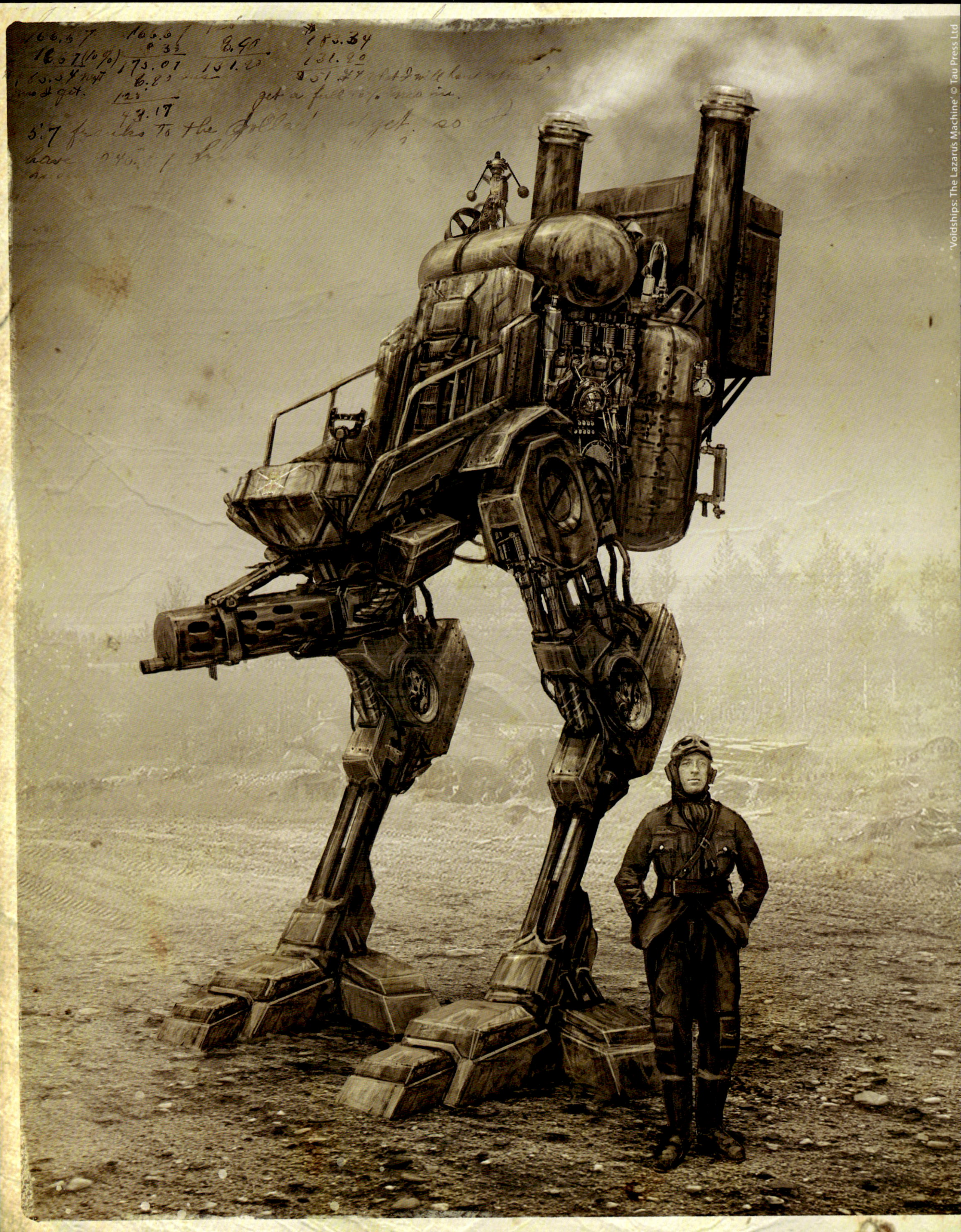

Voidships: The Lazarus Machine (Steampunk Walker)
Photoshop
Client: Tau Press Ltd
Mark Molnar, HUNGARY

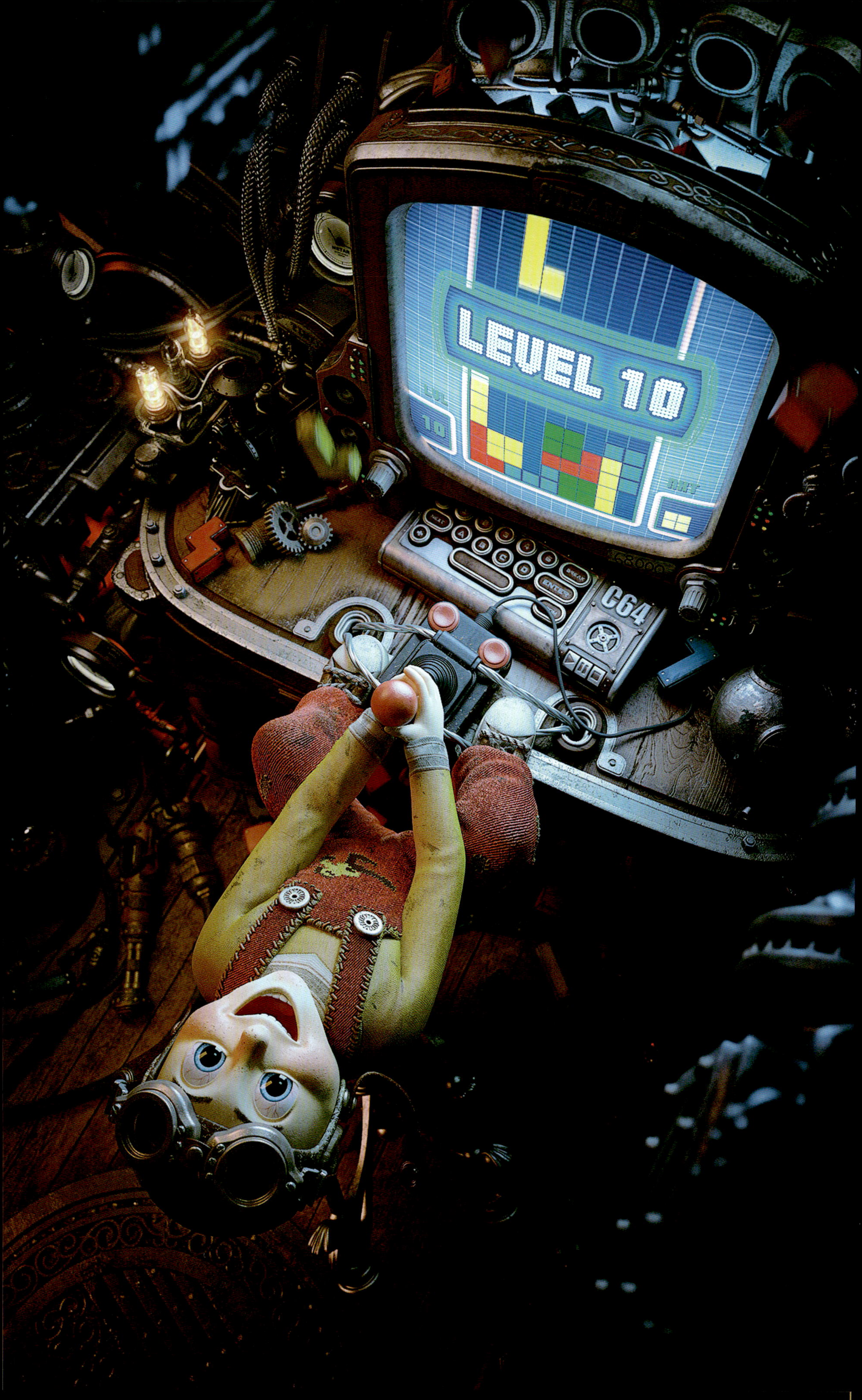

Level 10
3ds Max, V-Ray, ZBrush, Photoshop
Toni Bratincevic, CROATIA

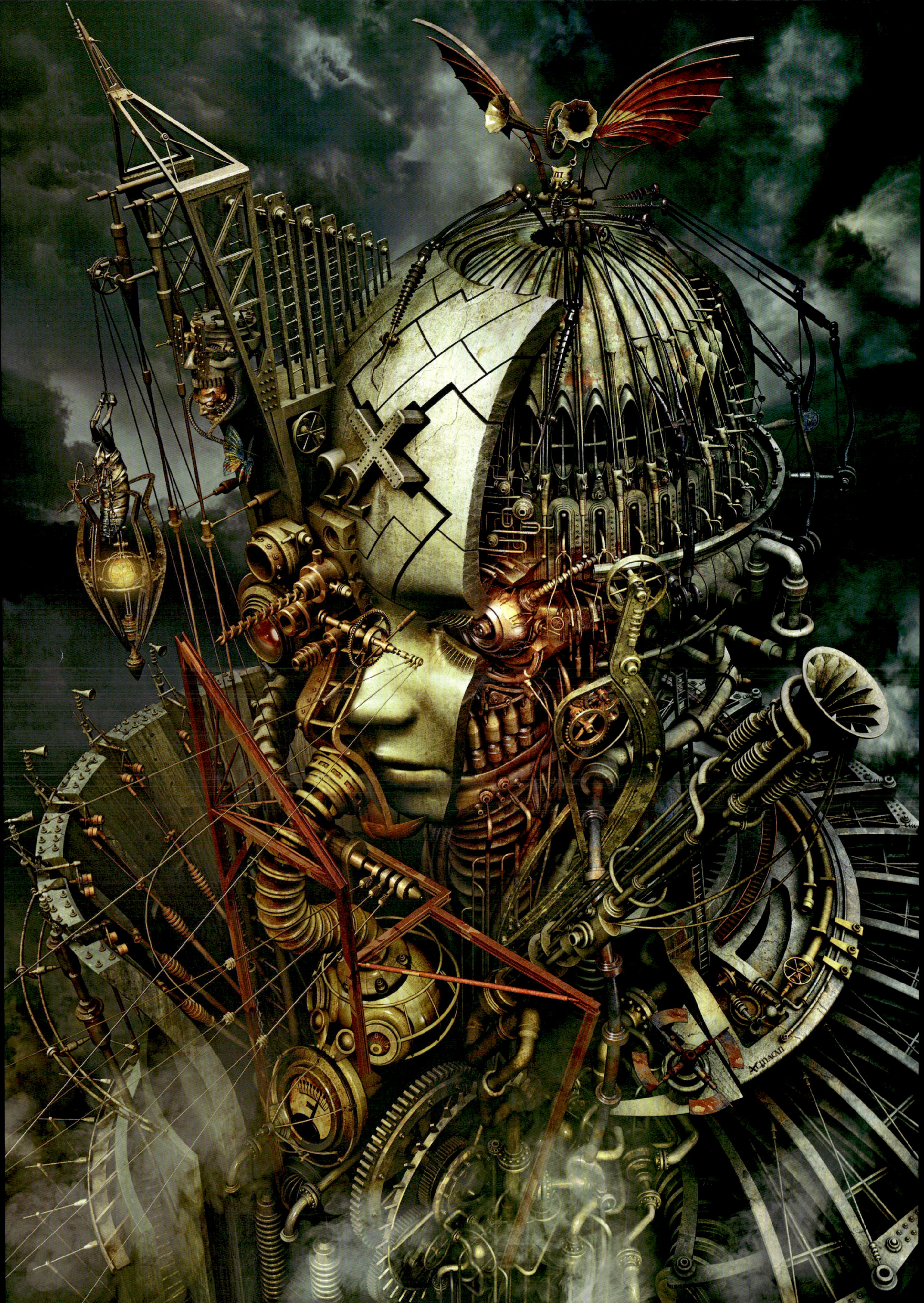

ZYGOSIS: Anatomical Architecture
Shade, ZBrush, Photoshop
Kazuhiko Nakamura, JAPAN

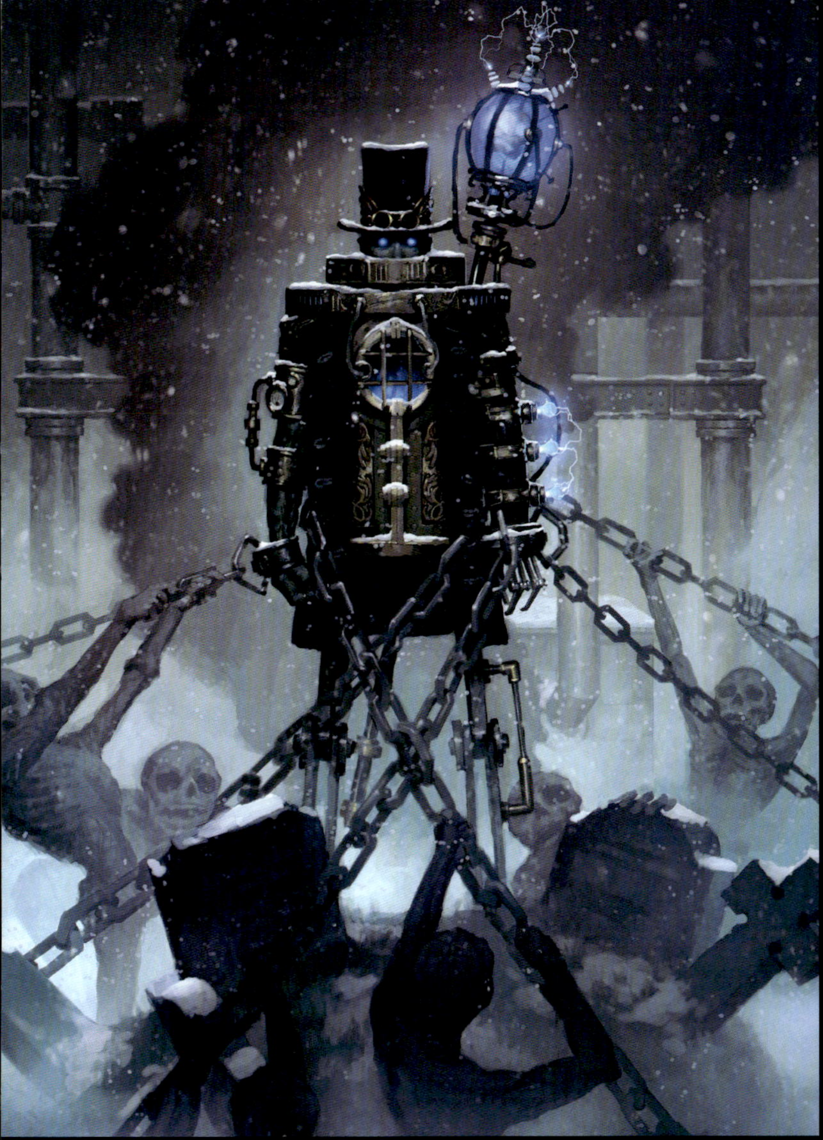

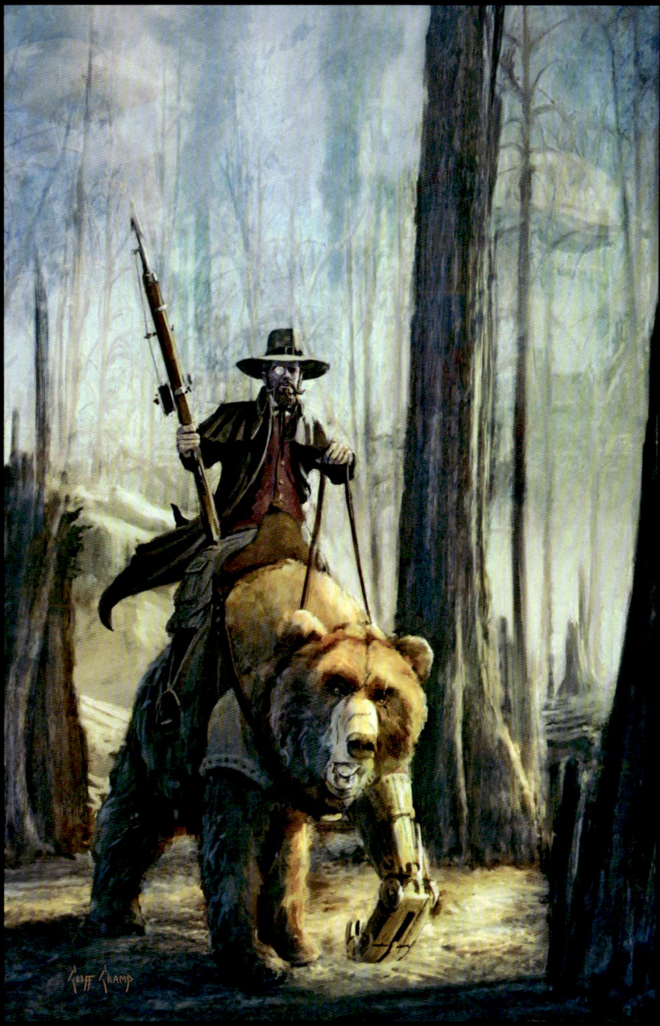

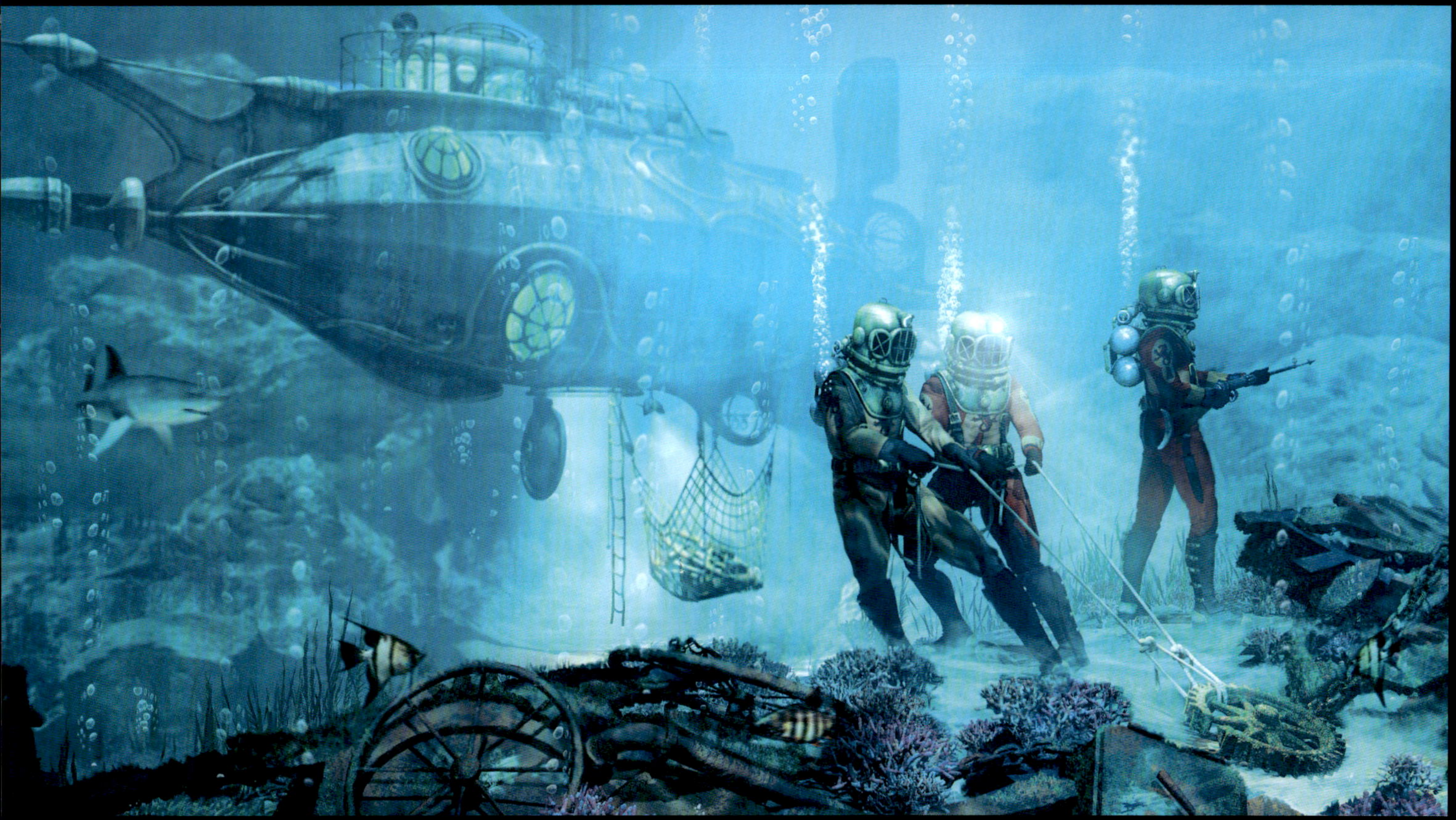

Necrolurgy
Photoshop
Clint Cearley, USA
[top left]

A Hunting We Will Go
Painter, Photoshop
Cliff Cramp, USA
[top right]

Scavengers
Maya, ZBrush, Vue Esprit, Photoshop
Peter Pohle, USA
[above]

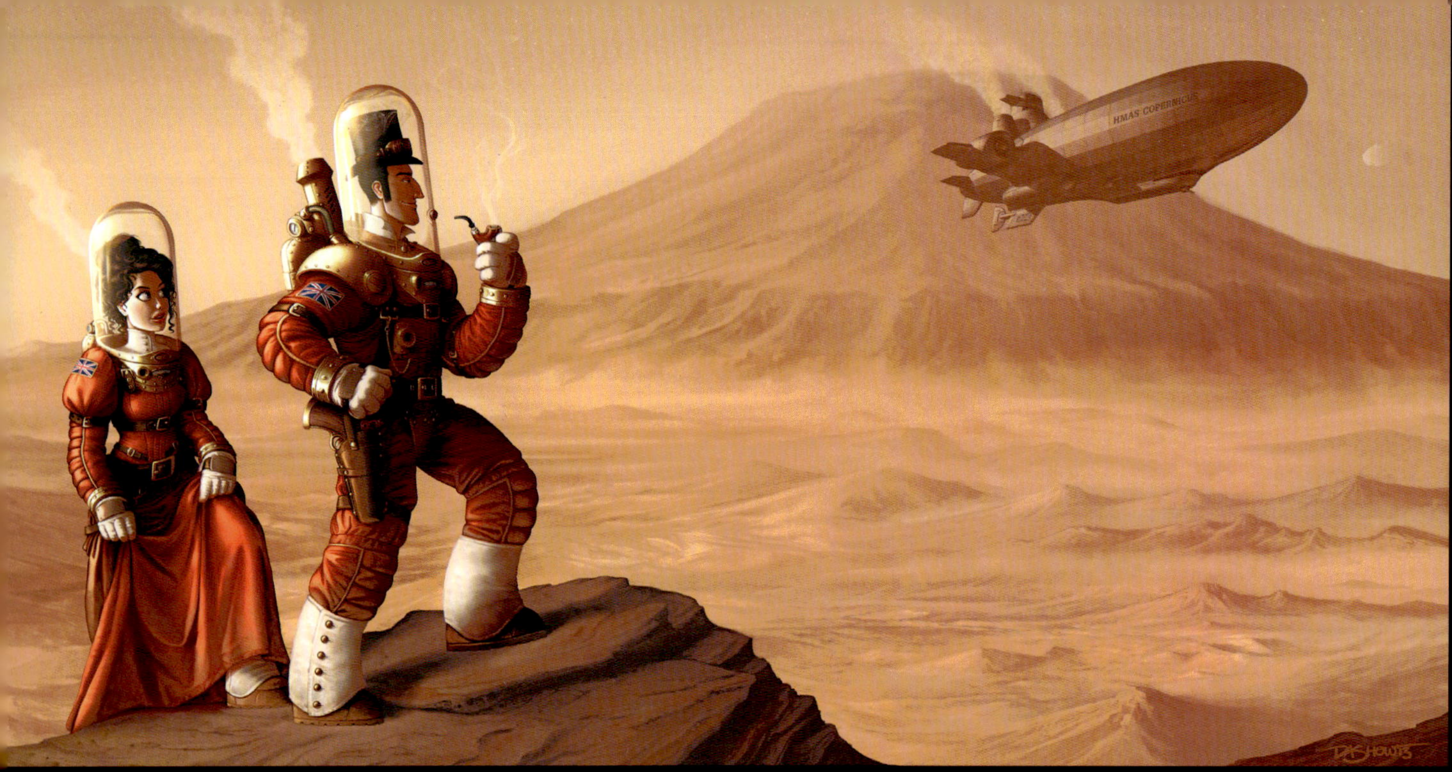

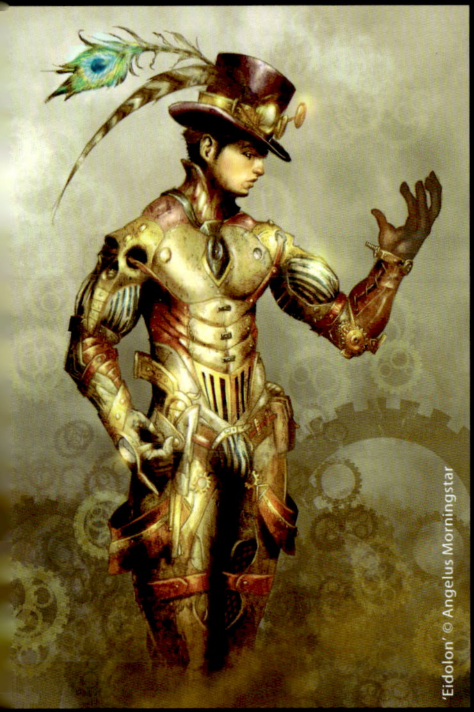

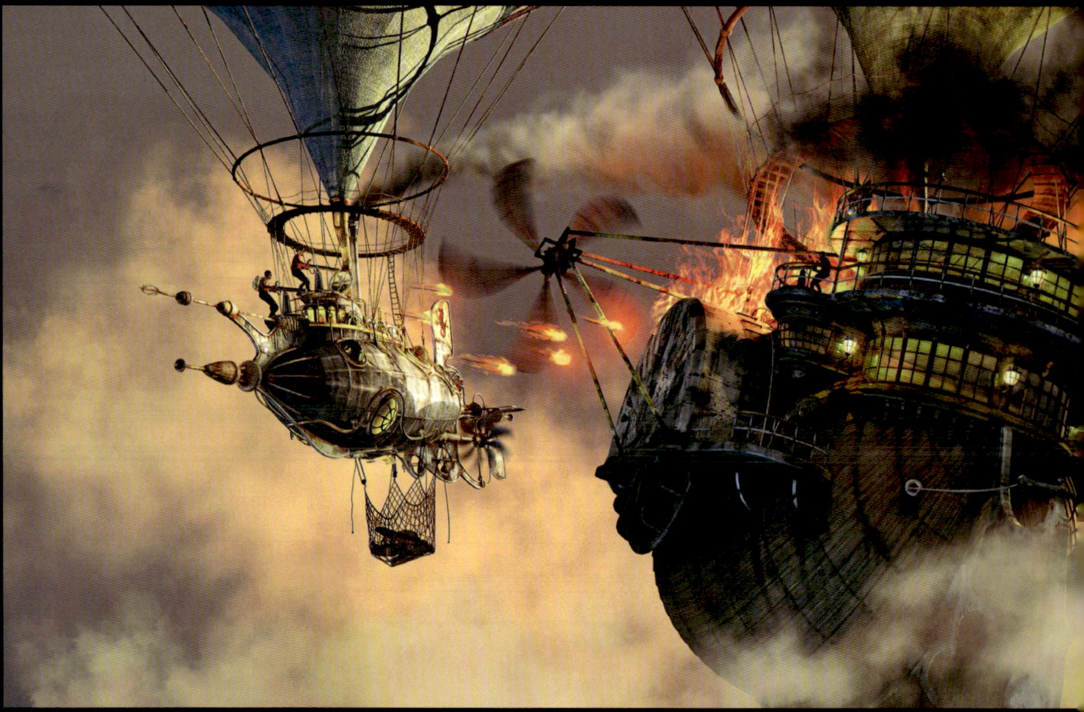

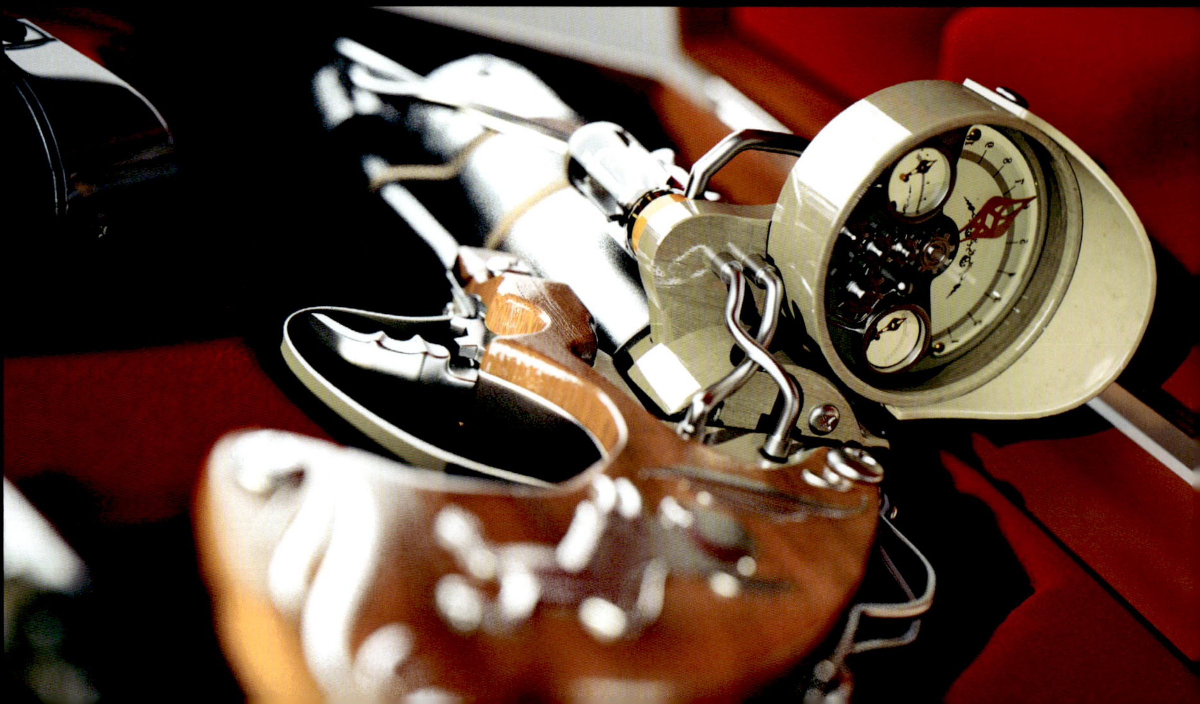

Olympus Mons
Photoshop, 3ds Max
Client: Nova Albion
Steampunk Exhibition
Michael Dashow, USA
[top]

Cyborg
Photoshop
Client: Angelus Morningstar
Roberto Quintero, VENEZUELA
[above left]

Steampunk Pirates
Maya, ZBrush, Vue Esprit,
Photoshop
Peter Pohle, USA
[above right]

Steampunk Raygun
3ds Max, Photoshop, V-Ray
Etienne Fraisse, FRANCE
[right]

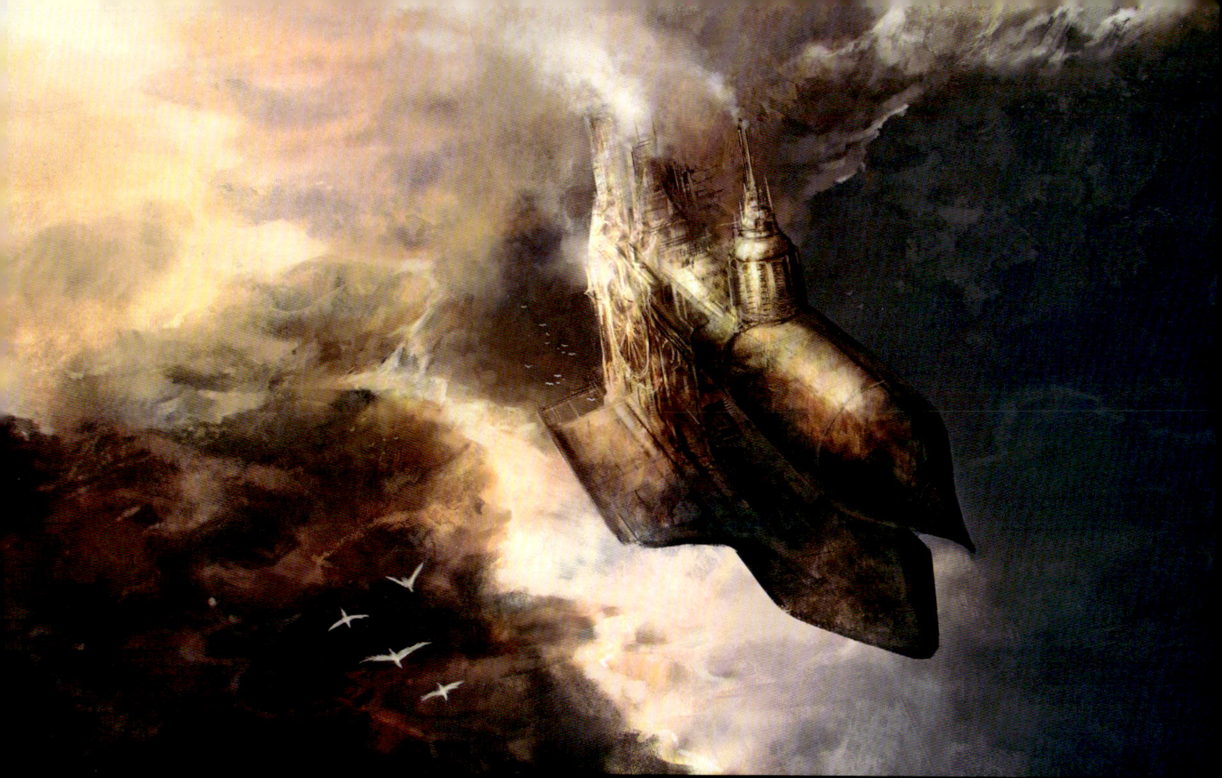

Ventura
Photoshop
Juan Carlos Barquet, MEXICO
[left]

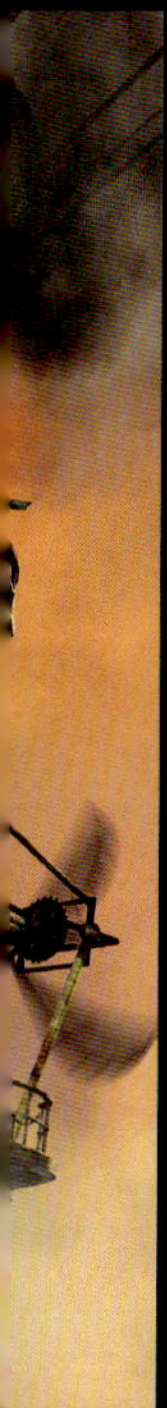

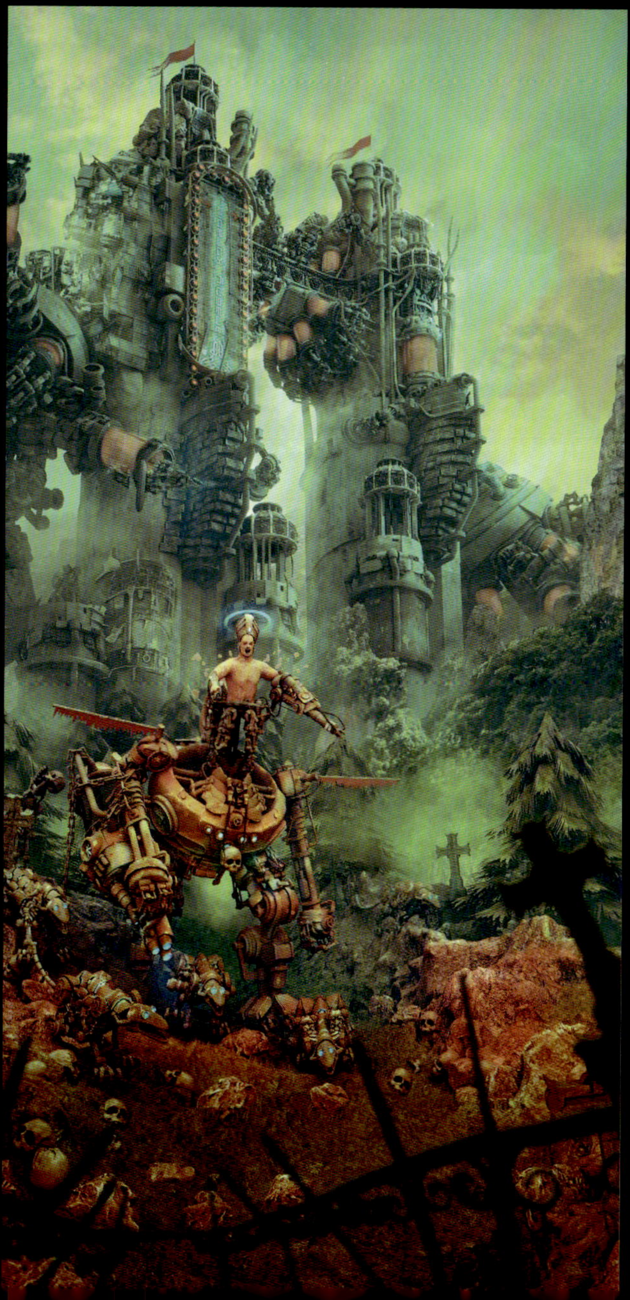

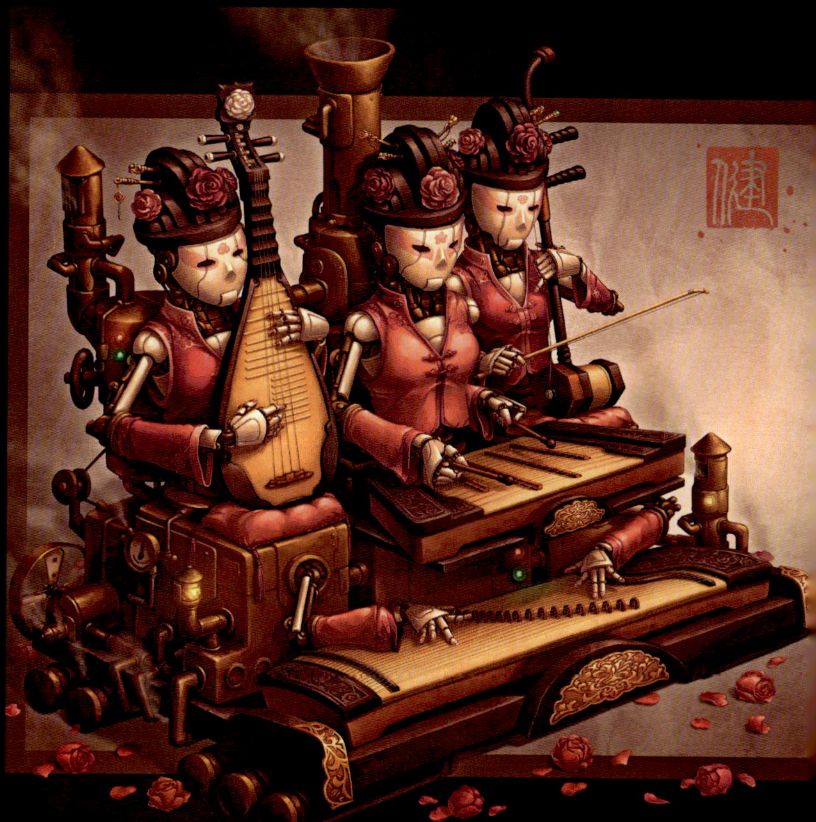

Court Band
Painter, Photoshop
James Ng, HONG KONG
[above]

Steel Creed
3ds Max, ZBrush, V-Ray, Photoshop
Arseniy Korablev, RUSSIA
[left]

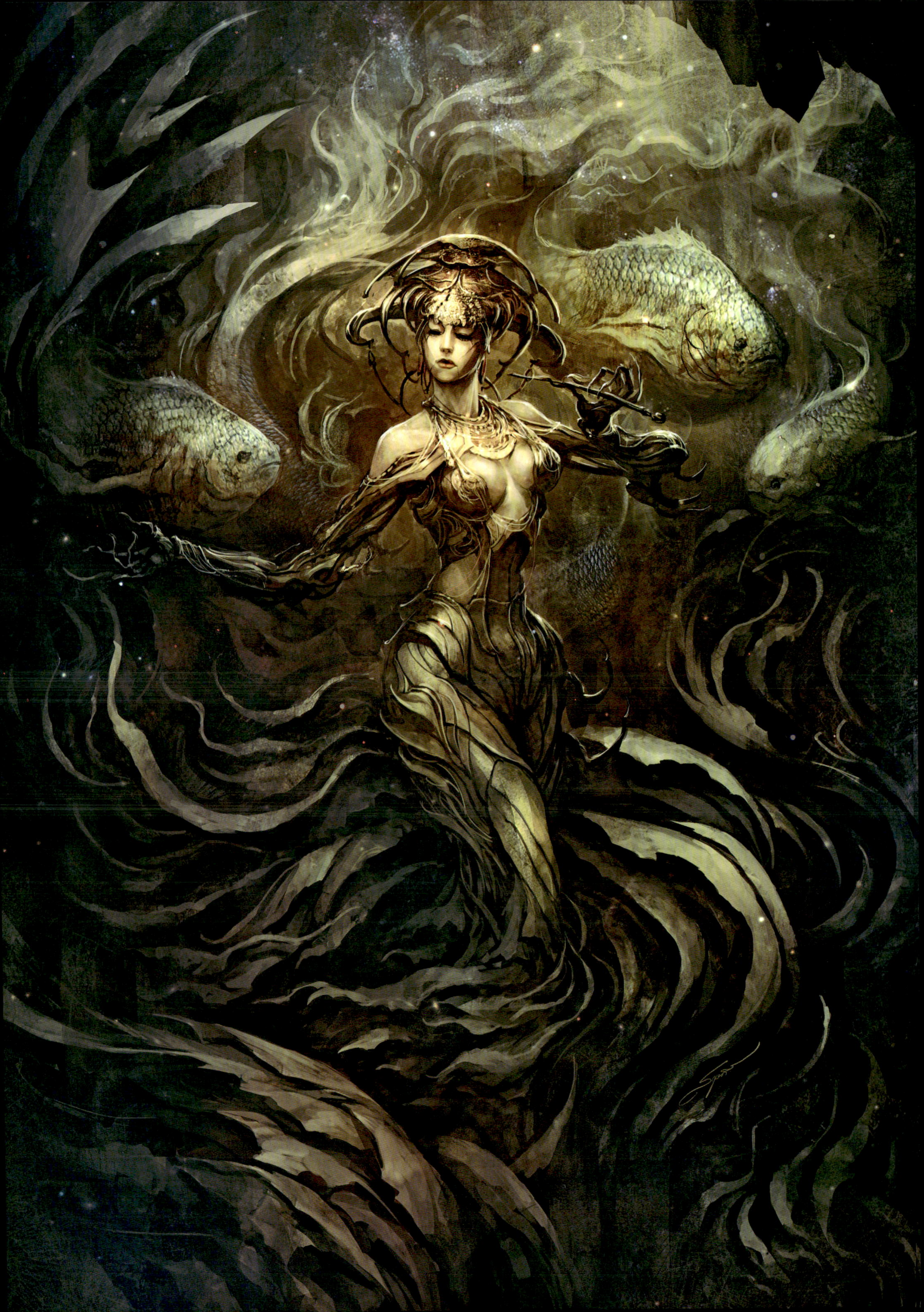

Excellence
Surreal

The Flower of the River
Photoshop
Saryth Chareonpanichkul, THAILAND

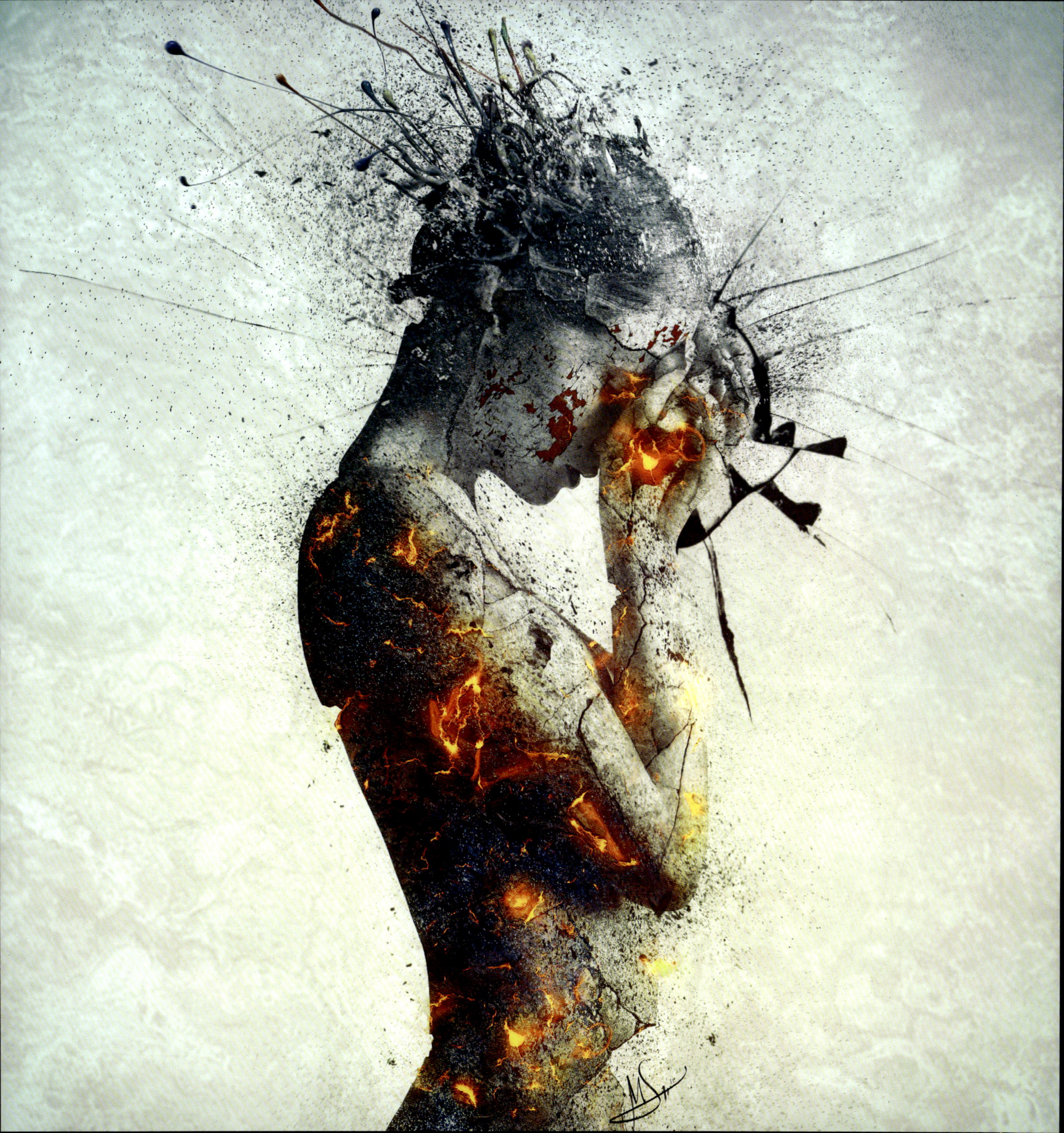

Deliberation
Photoshop
Mario Sánchez Nevado, SPAIN

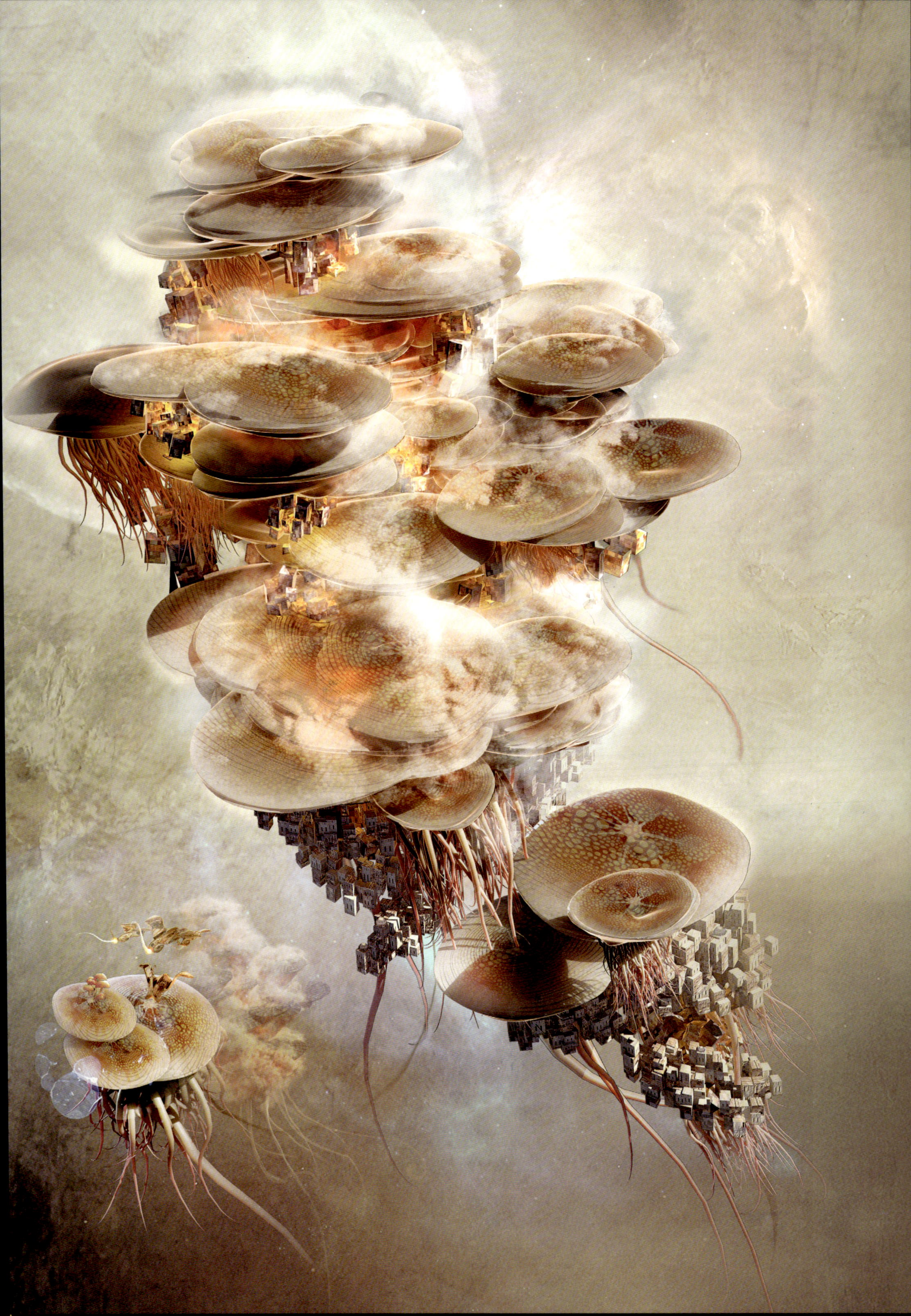

Excellence
Surreal

Flow
Maya, Photoshop
Te Hu, USA

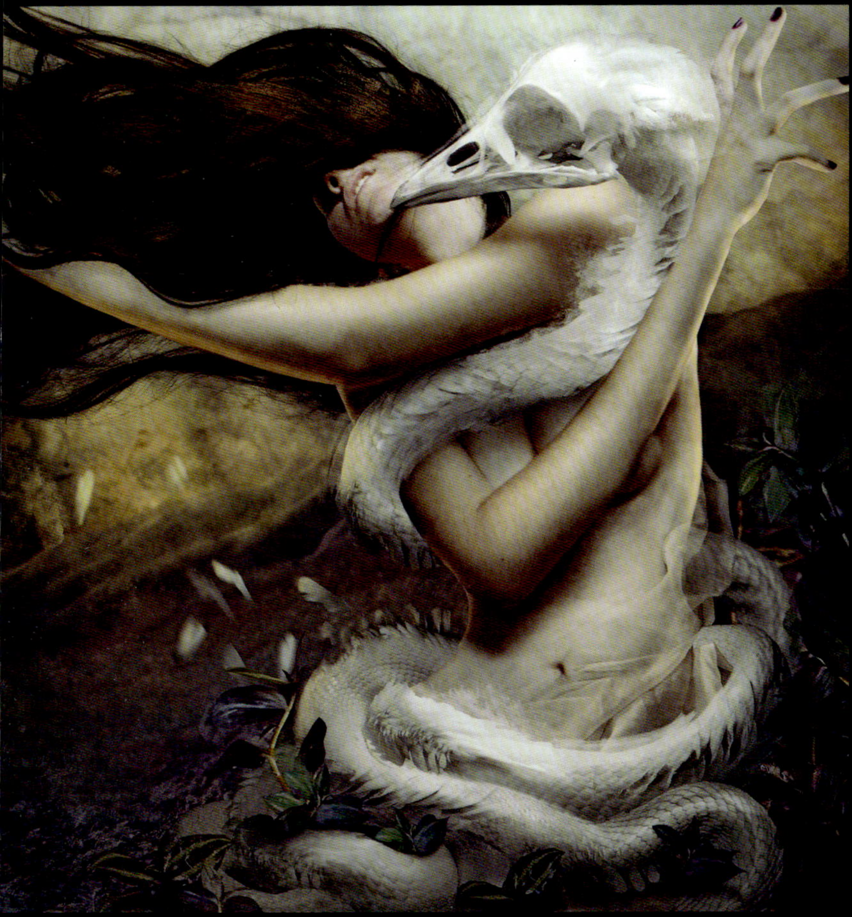

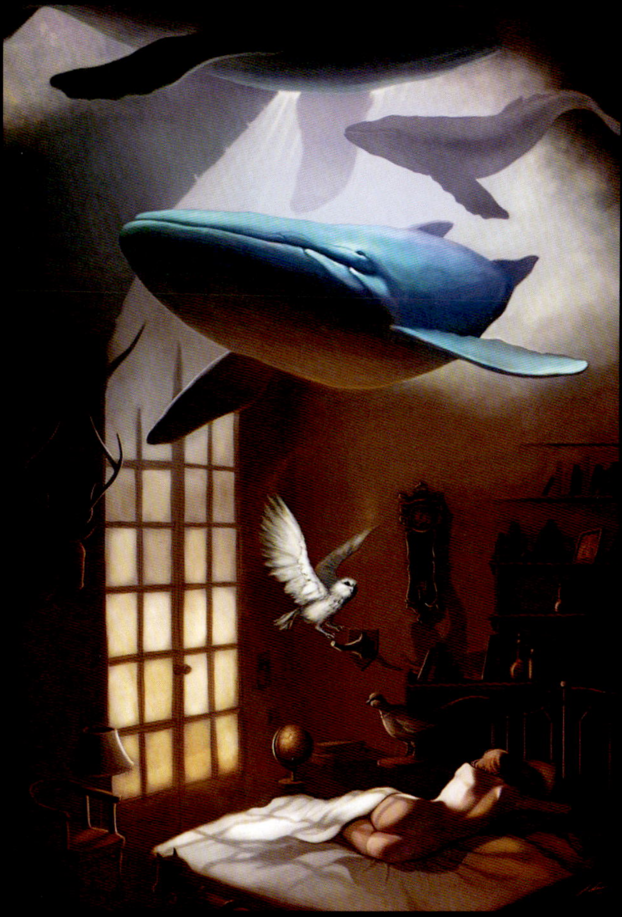

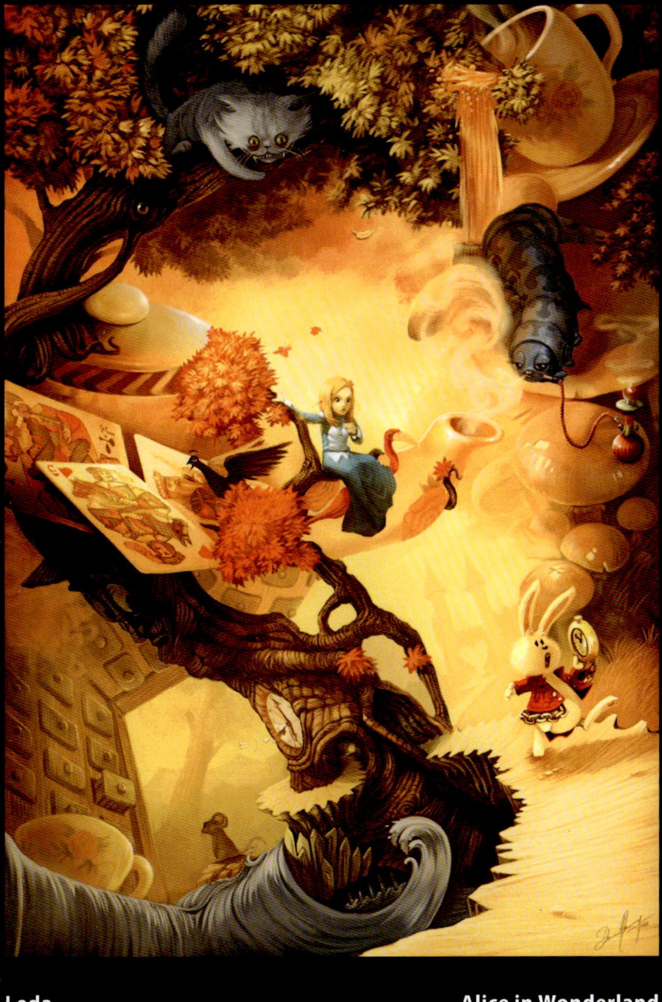

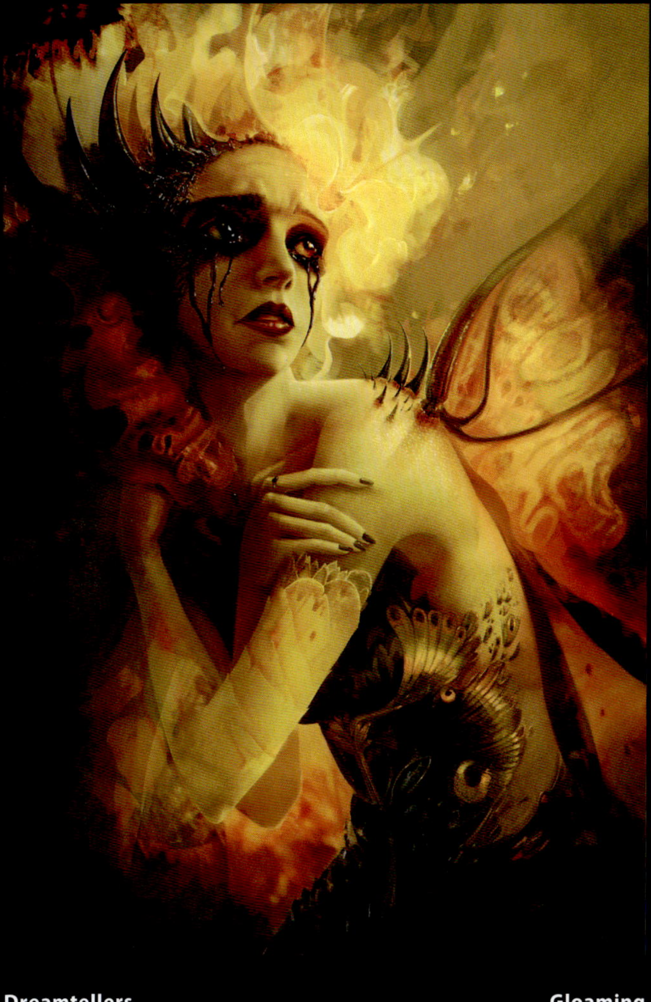

Leda
Photoshop
Marcela Bolivar, COLOMBIA
[top]

Alice in Wonderland
MyPaint, GIMP
David Revoy, FRANCE
[above]

Dreamtellers
Photoshop
Gabriella Eriksson, SWEDEN
[top]

Gloaming
Photoshop
Nicholas Miles, GREAT BRITAIN
[above]

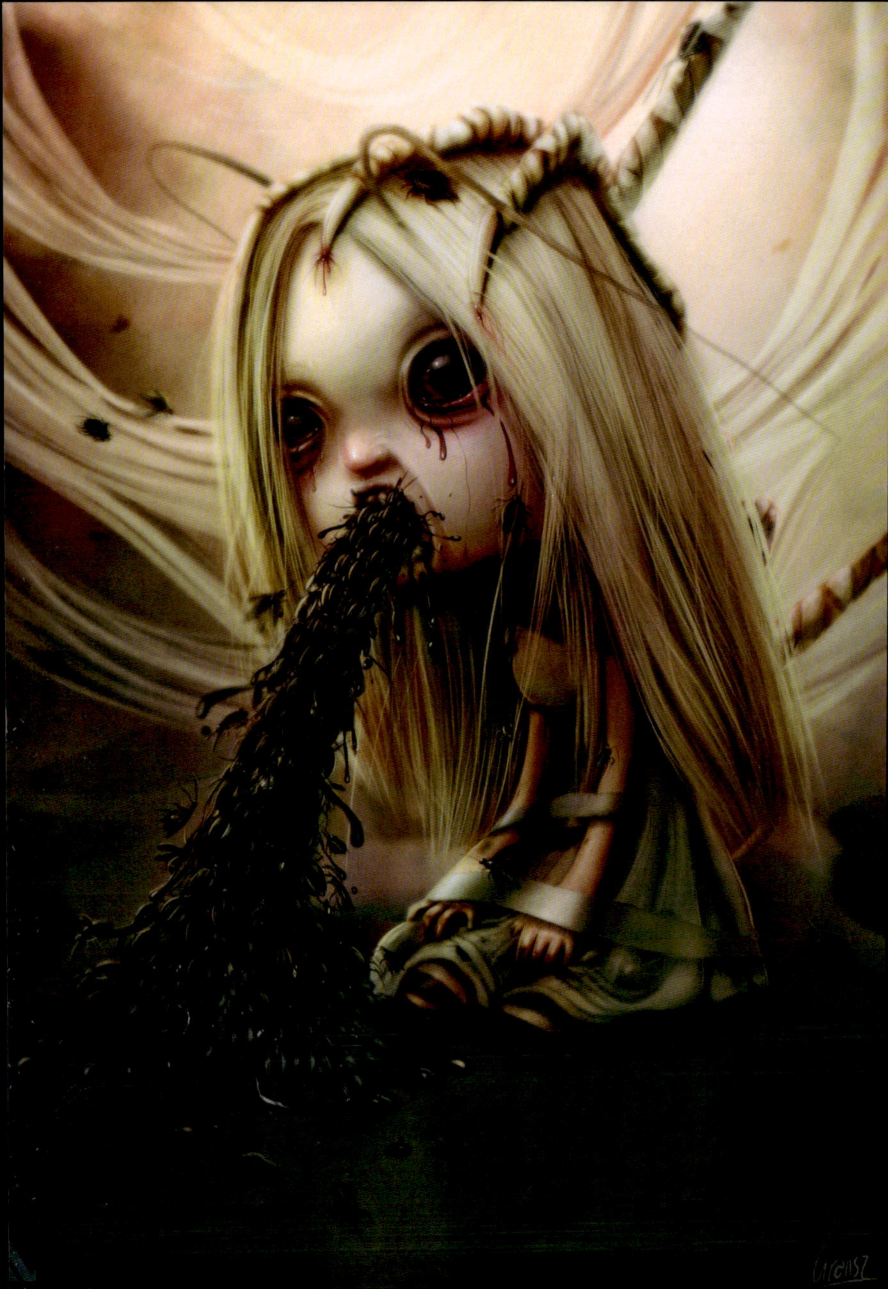

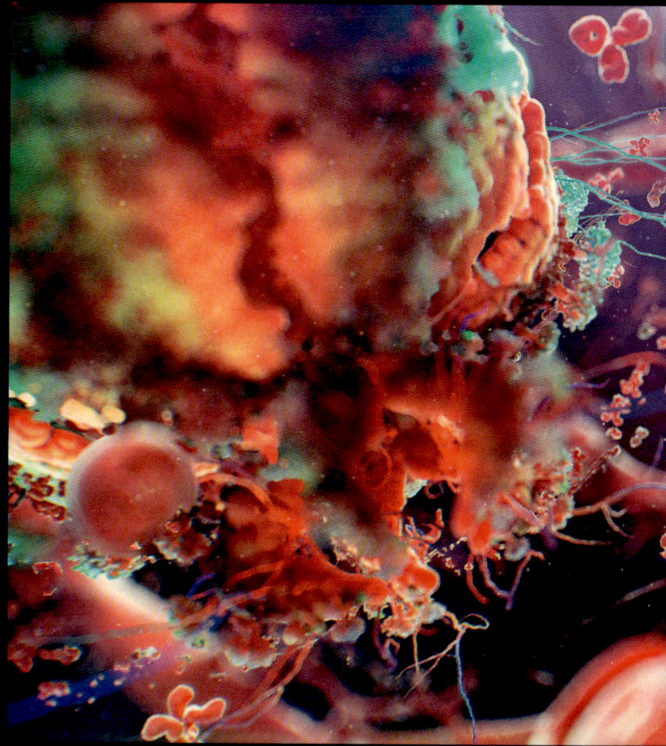

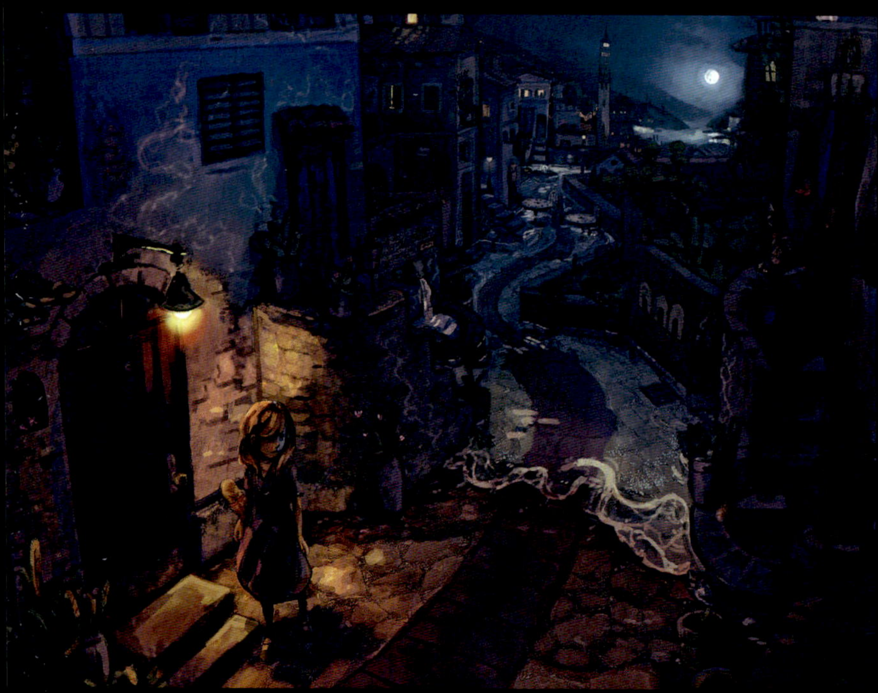

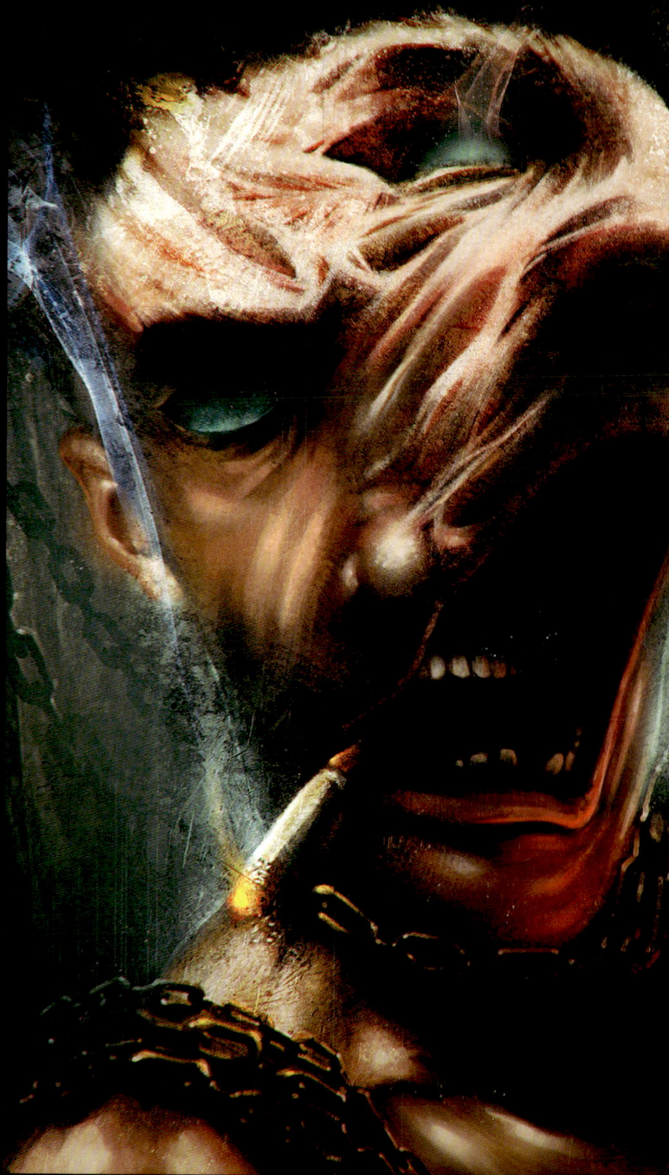

Ordeal
Photoshop

Acqua Alta
Photoshop

Struggle
Photoshop

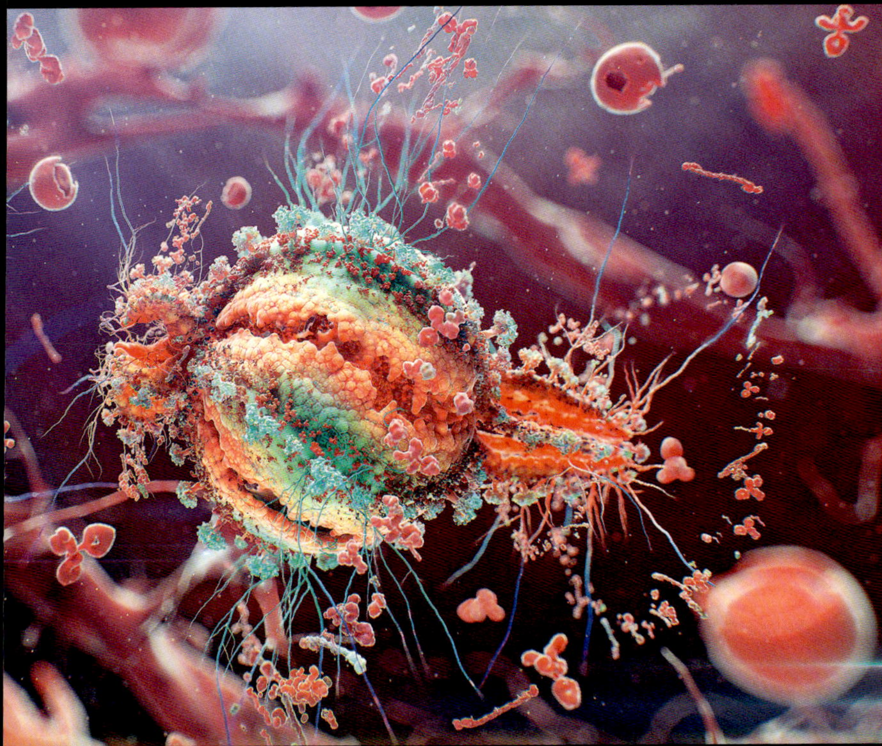

Human Immunodeficiency Virus
3ds Max, After Effects, ZBrush, V-Ray
Alexey Kashpersky, UKRAINE
[left]

Requiem For a Dream
Photoshop
Murat Turan, TURKEY
[below]

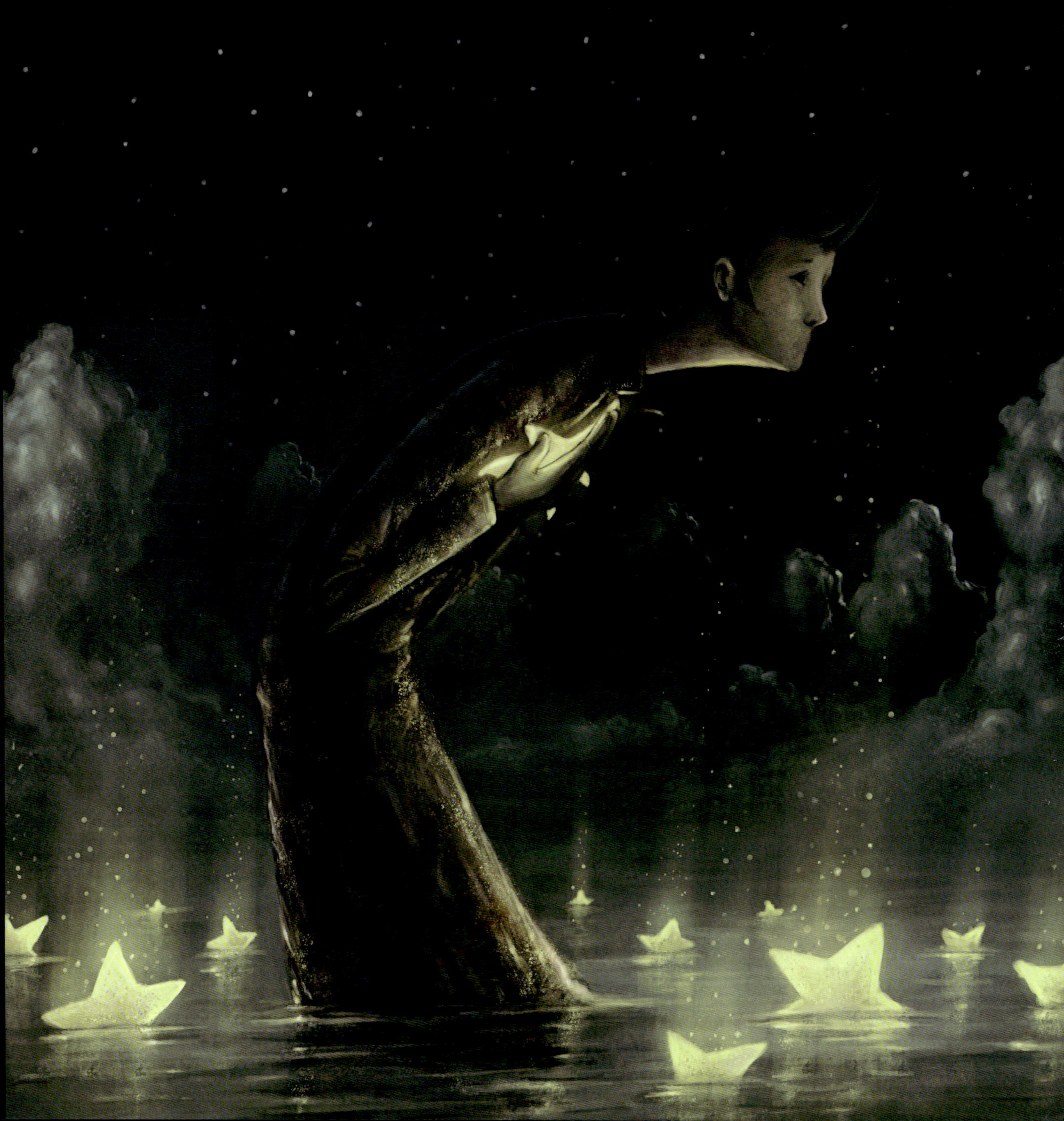

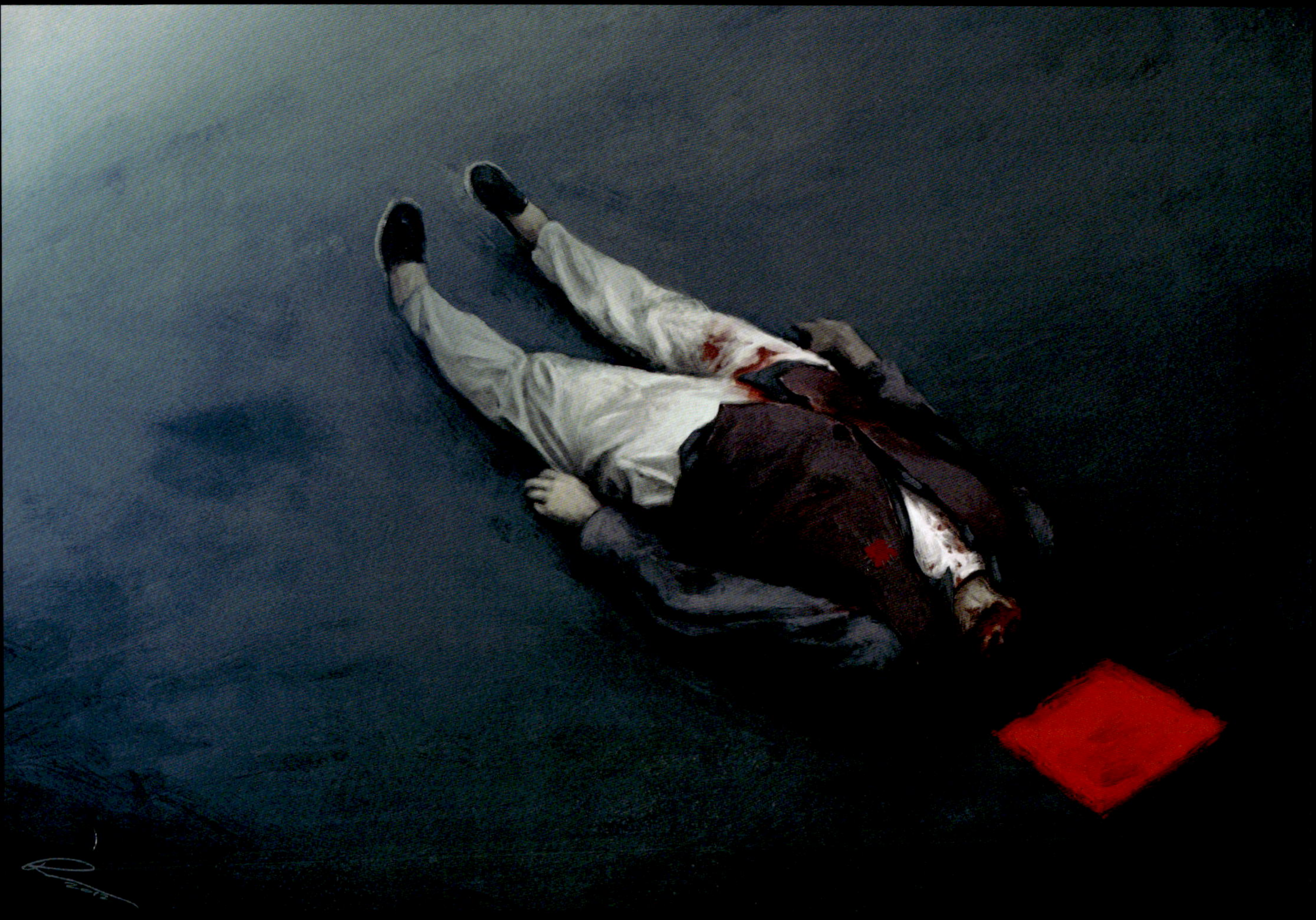

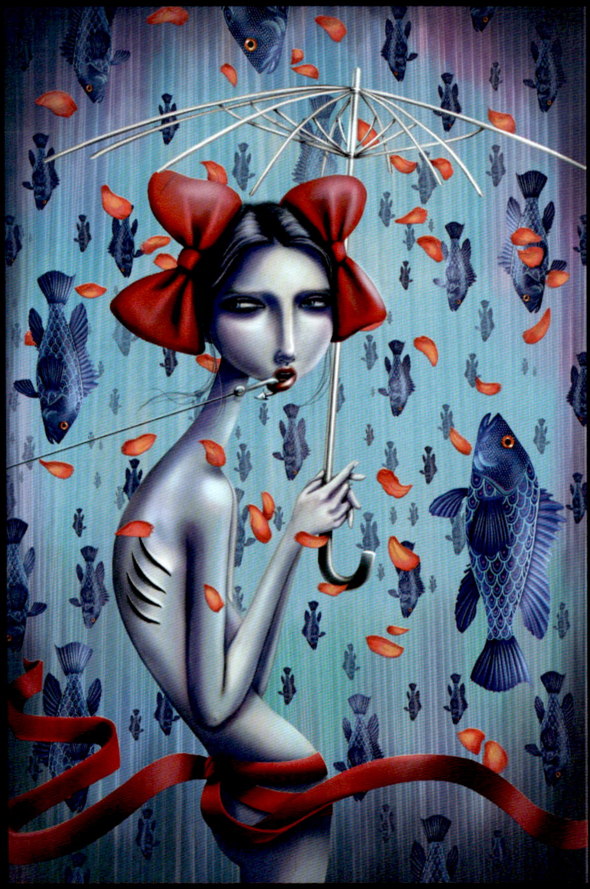

Caught

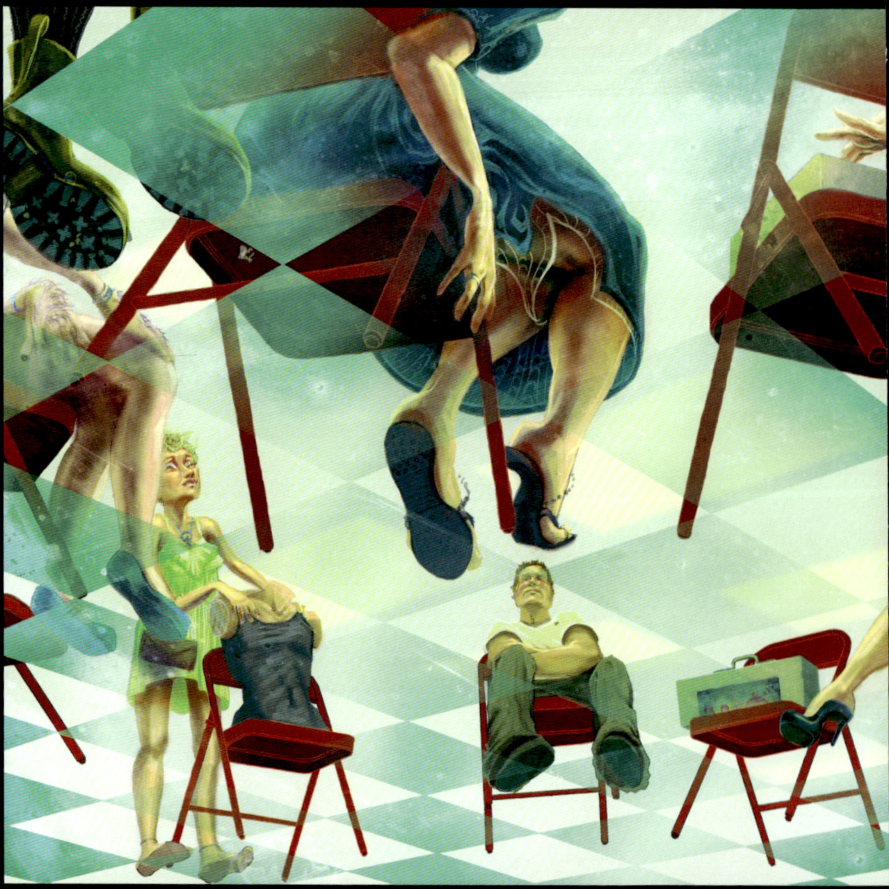

Her Husband's Hands: Support Group

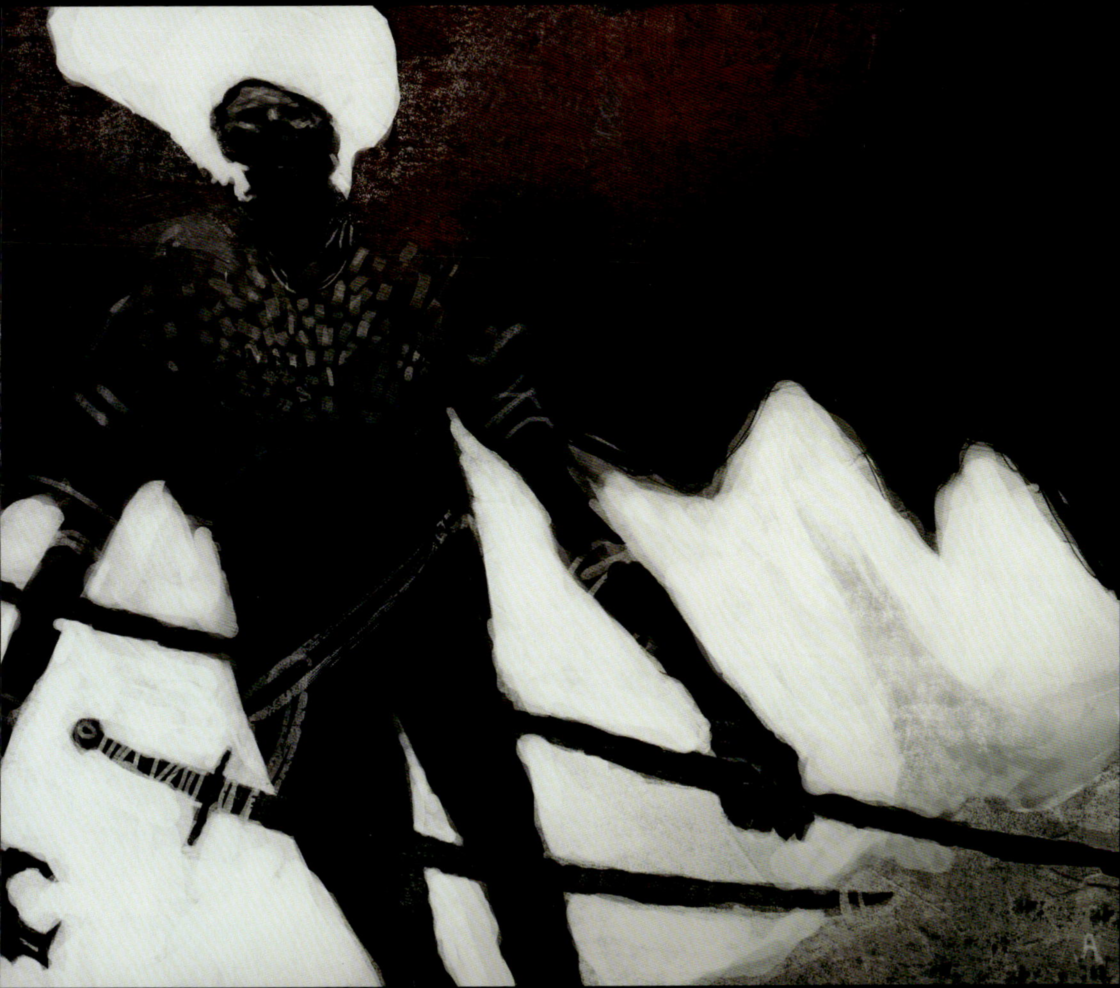

It's a Matter of Class
Photoshop
Pavel Sokov, CANADA
[facing page top]

With Spear and Sword
Photoshop
Jeffrey Alan Love, USA
[left]

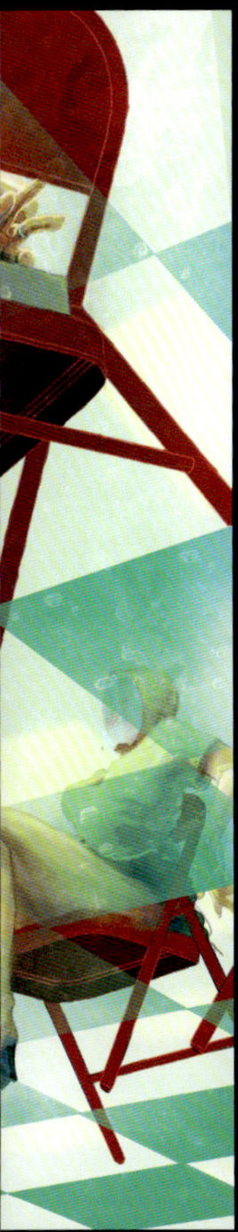

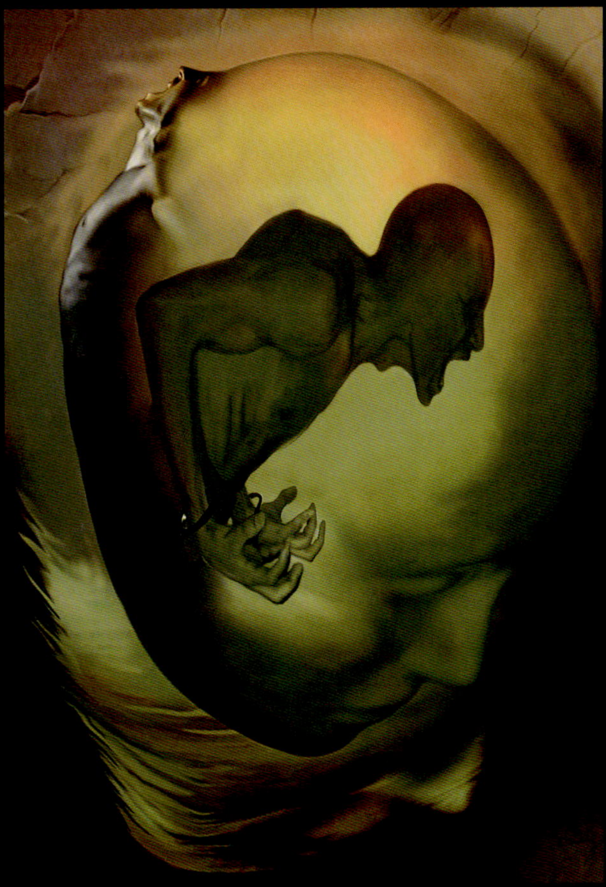

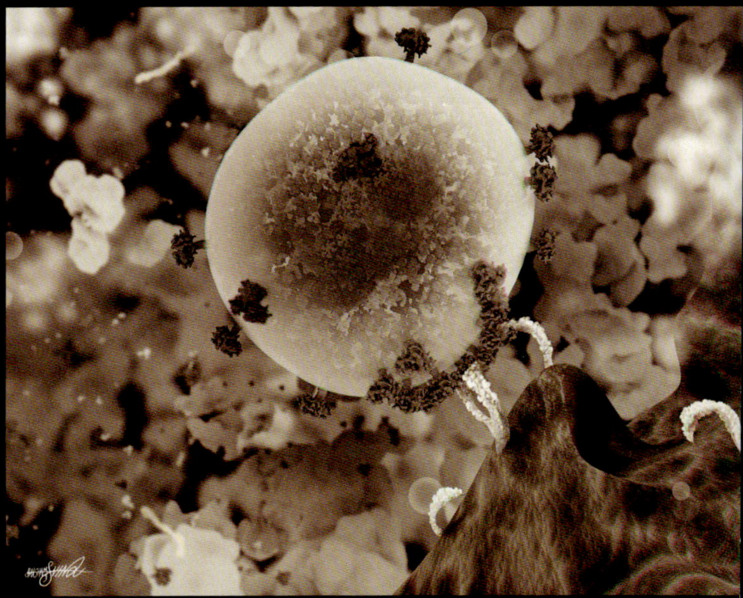

HIV Virus in Plasma
Blender, Photoshop
Alhaitham Jassar, USA
[above]

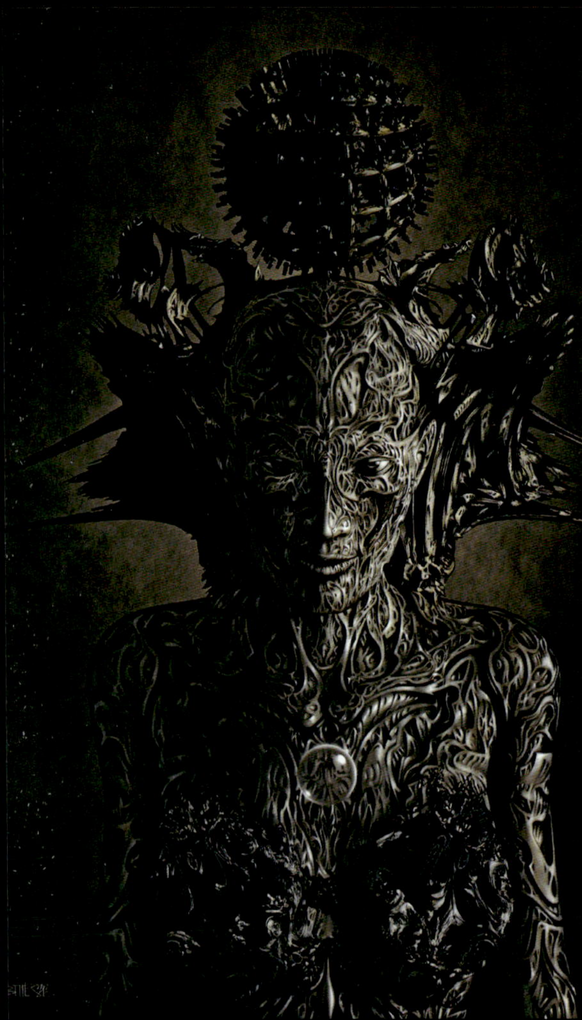

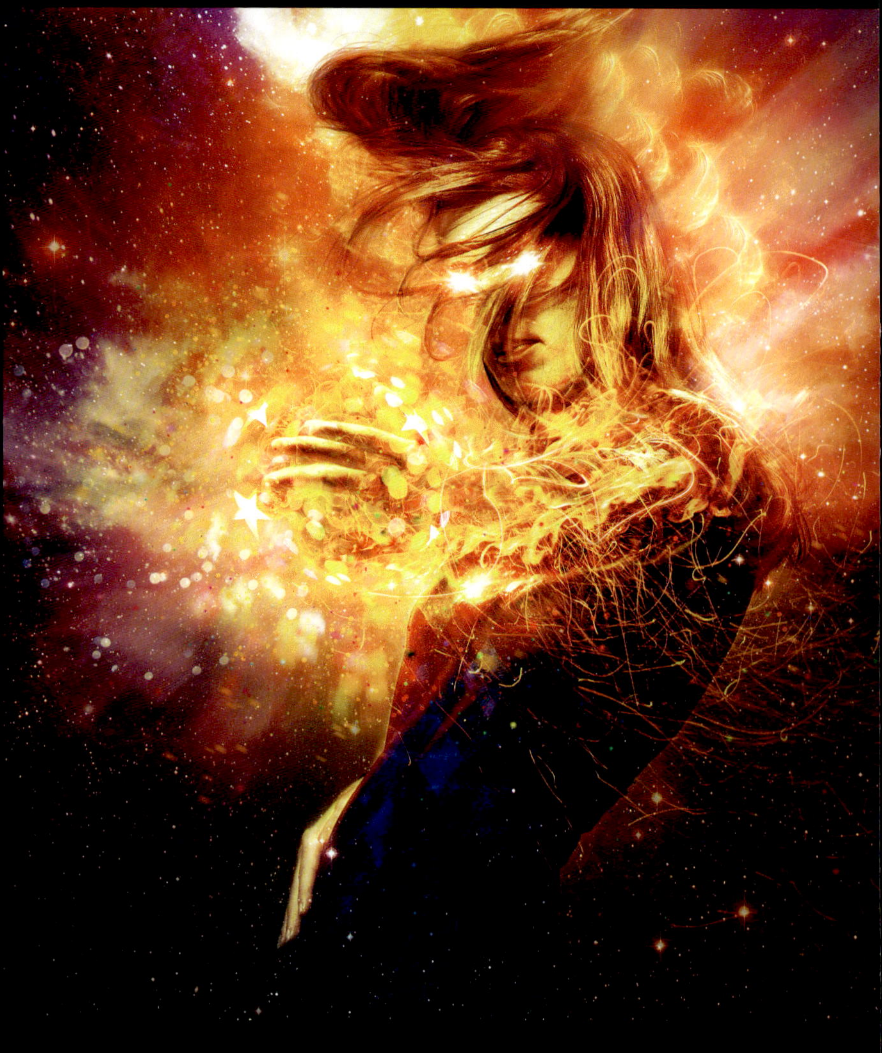

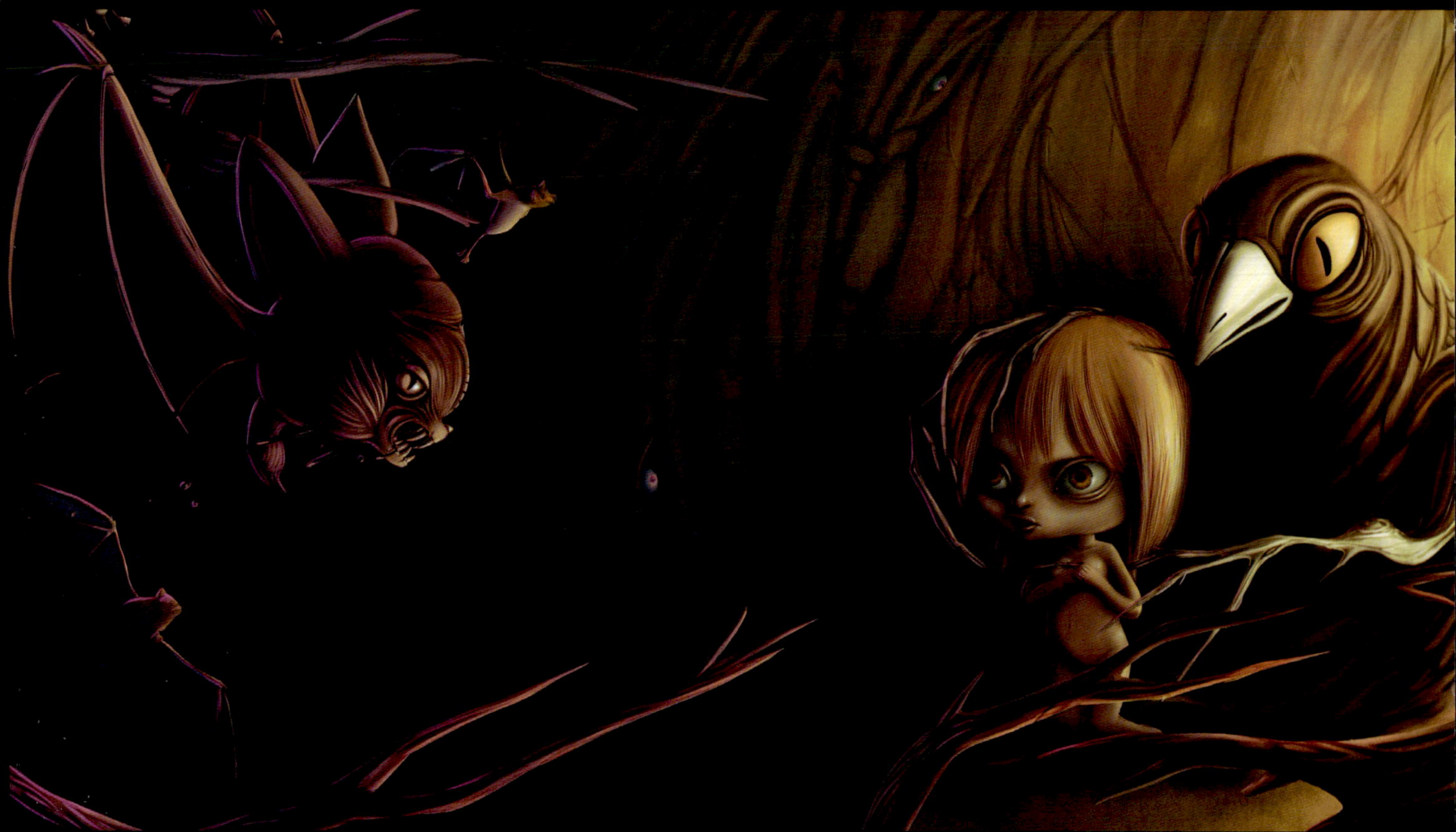

Sphaera Tenebris
GIMP, Mandelbulb3D, MyPaint
Bernard Bittler, FRANCE
[top left]

Spell On You
Photoshop
Mario Sánchez Nevado, SPAIN
[top right]

Lurking Back
Photoshop
Liran Szeiman, SPAIN
[above]

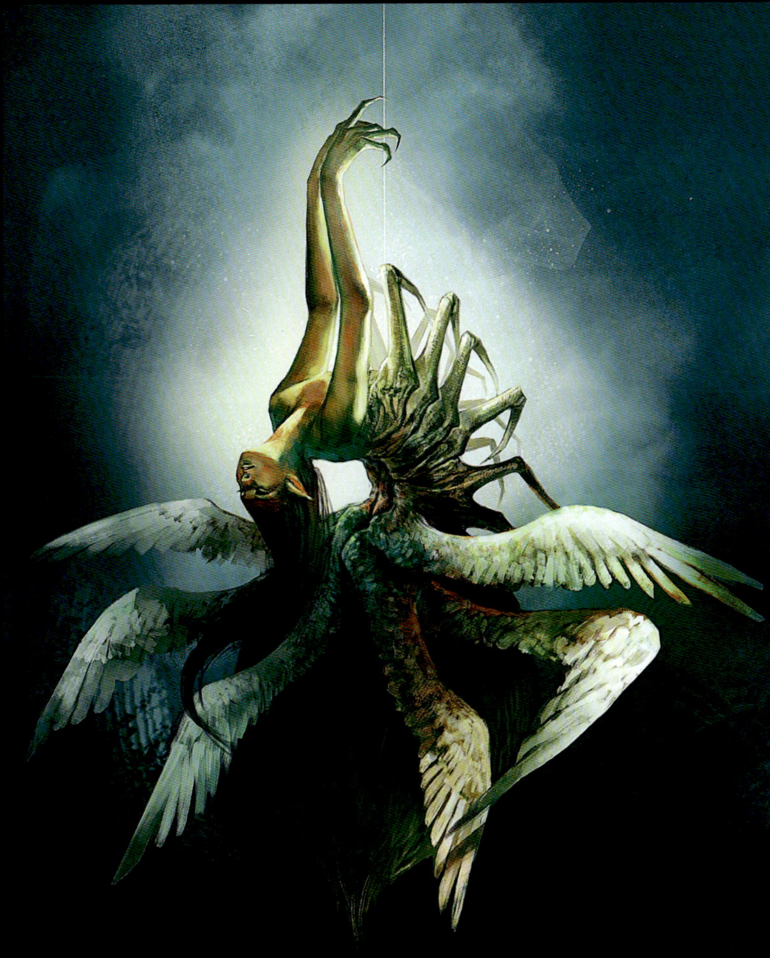

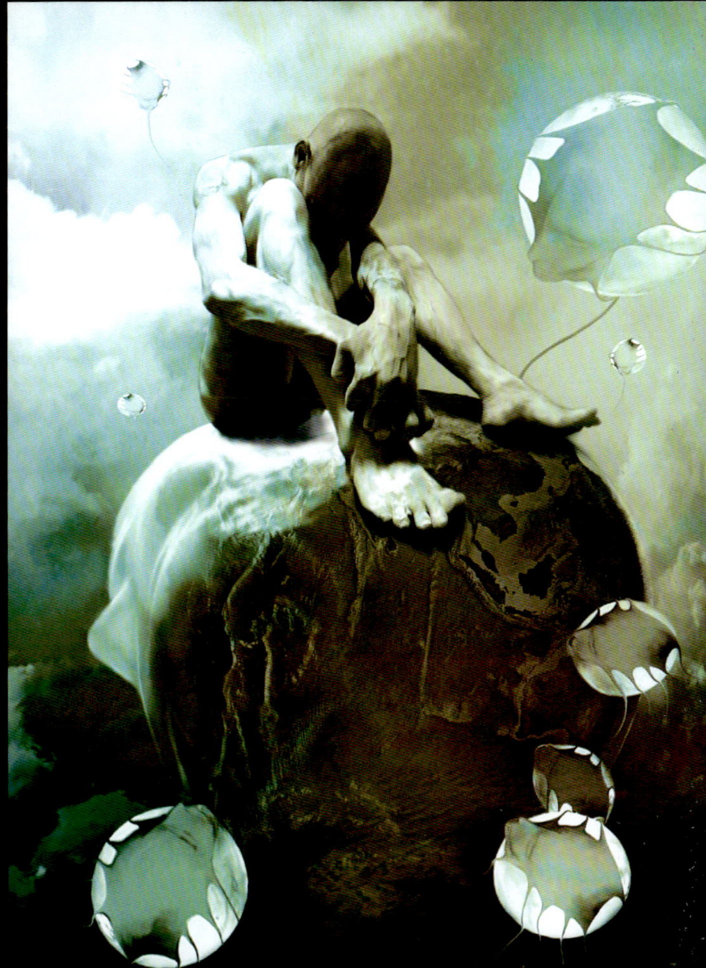

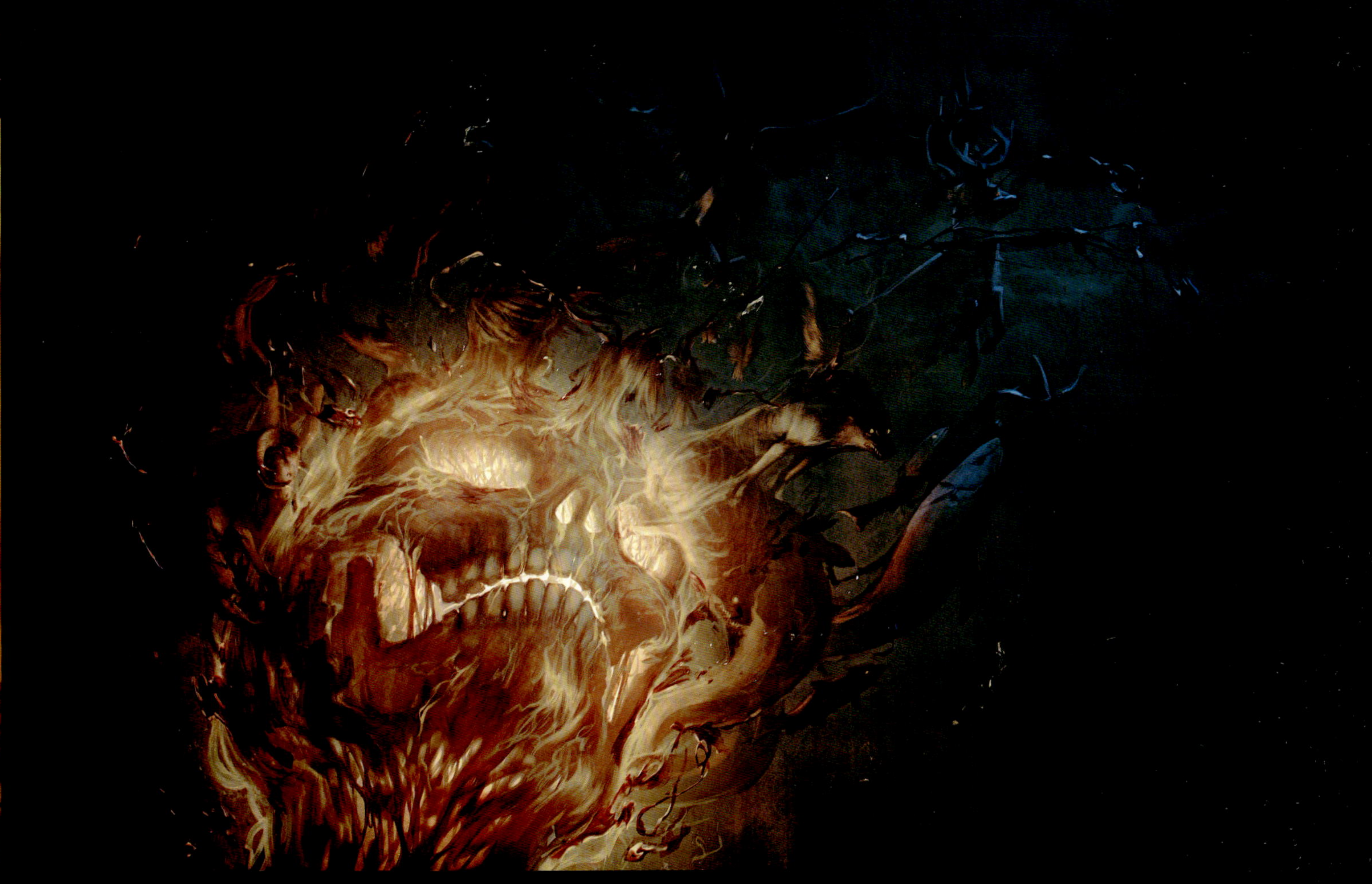

Her Will (The Other Side)
Photoshop
Reiko Murakami, USA
[top left]

I Can't Go
Painter, Photoshop
Bogdan Szot, POLAND
[top right]

Litany for Singularity
Photoshop
Justin Cherry, USA
[above]

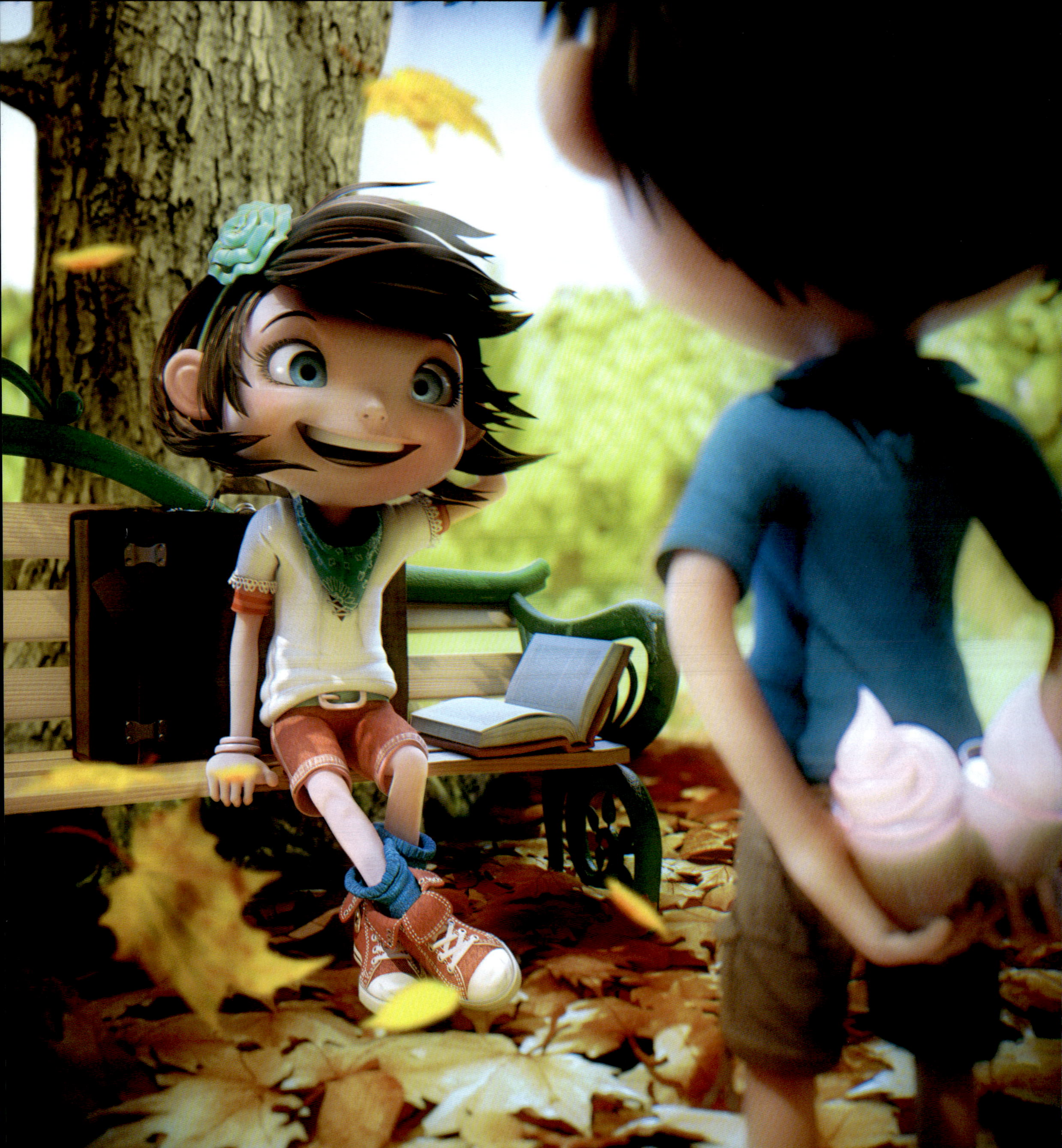

Excellence

Storytelling

Frozen Frame
3ds Max, V-Ray, Photoshop
Guillermo Soria, Salvador Ramirez
and Omar Sealtiel, MEXICO

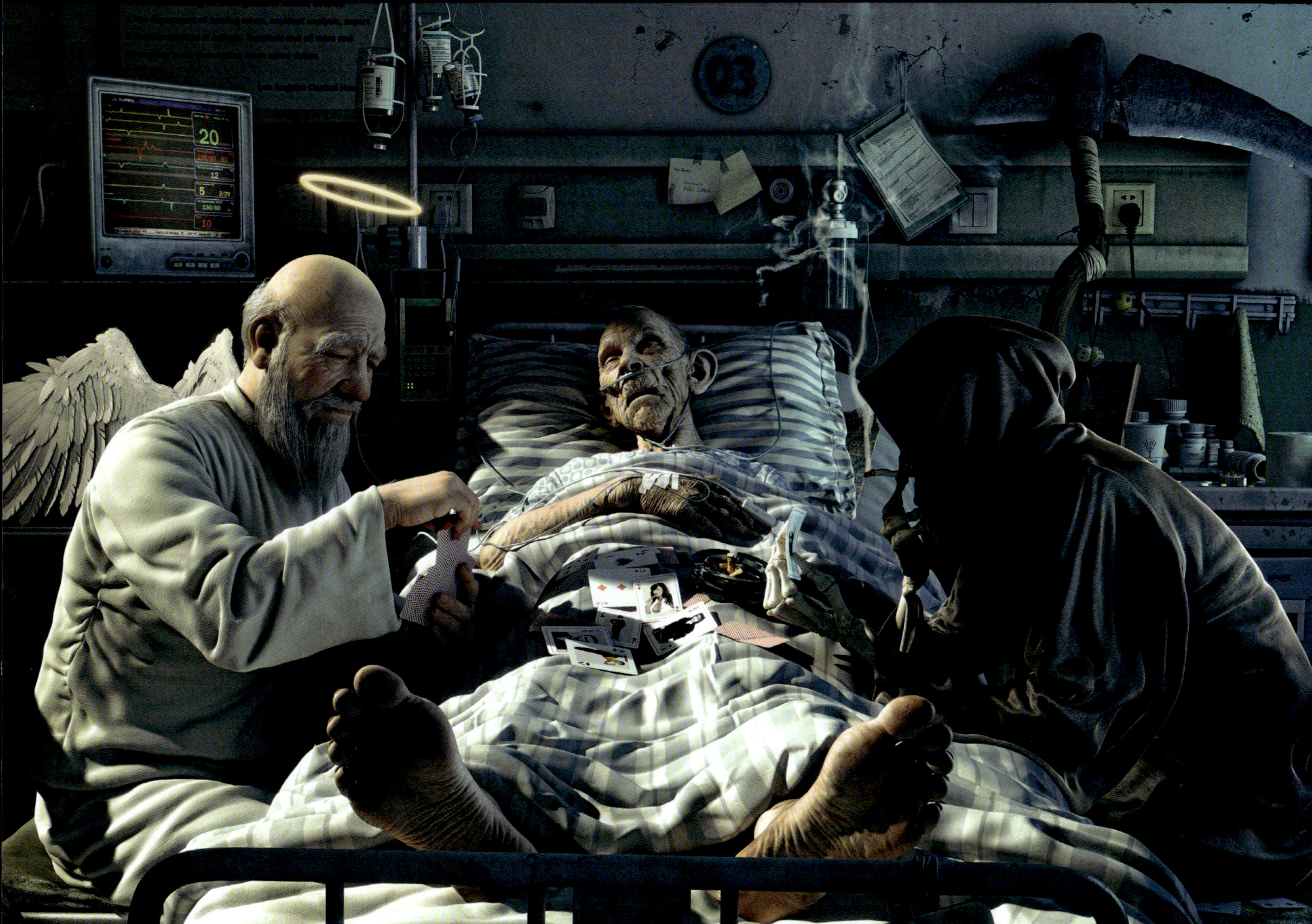

Game of Life
3ds Max, V-Ray, ZBrush, Mudbox
Hu Zheng, CHINA

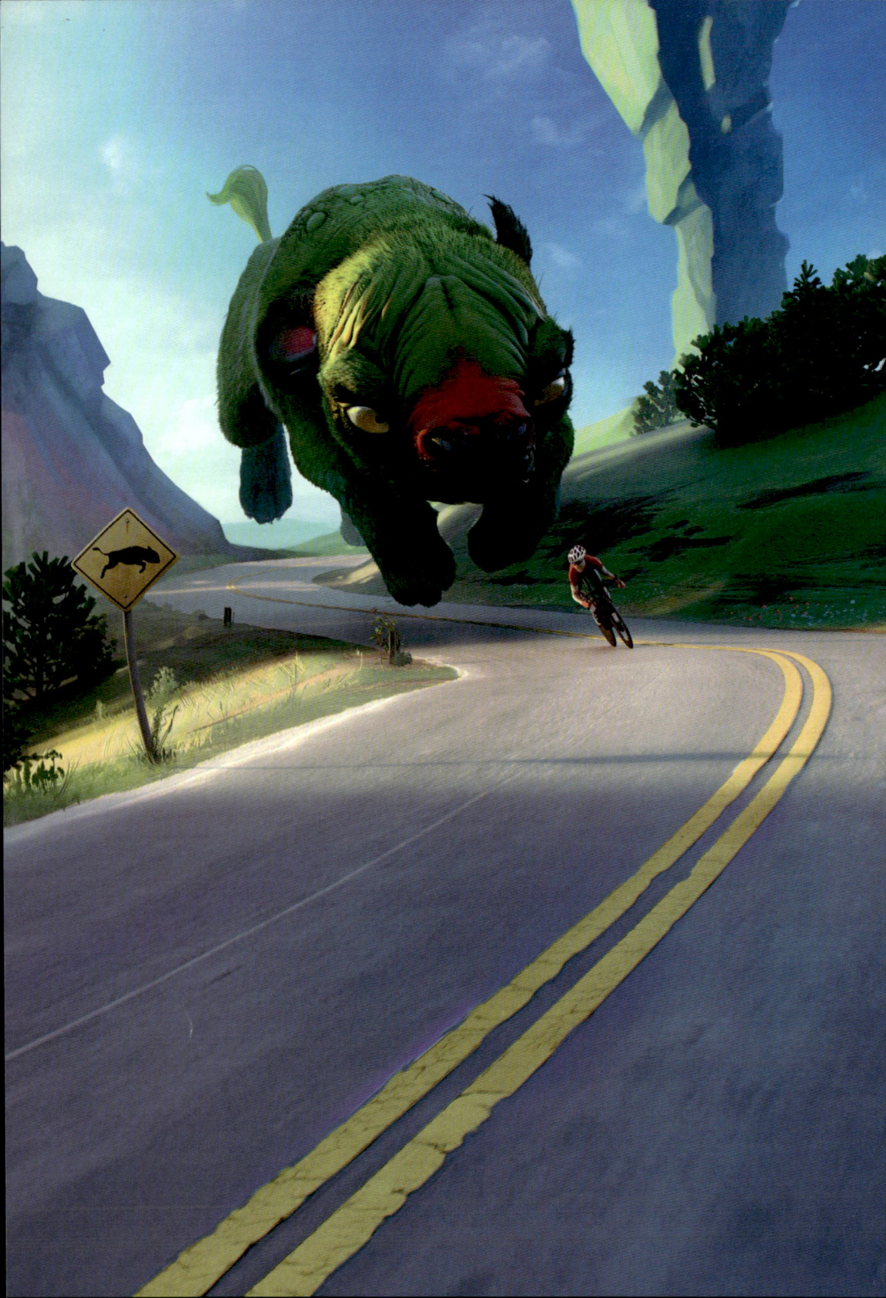

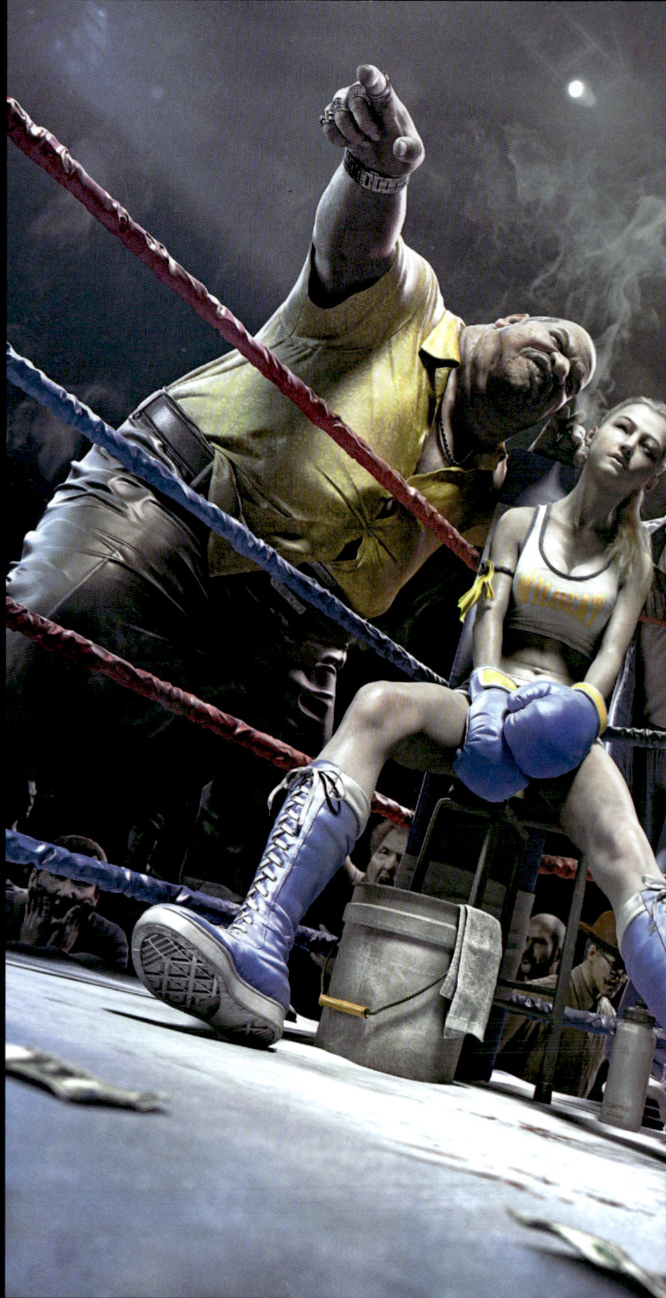

Chase
3ds Max, Photoshop, ZBrush
Nikita Veprikov, UKRAINE
[above]

Fight in the Dark
ZBrush, 3ds Max, mental ray
Guang Yang, CHINA
[above right]

My Equal
Photoshop
Rasmus Berggreen, DENMARK
[right]

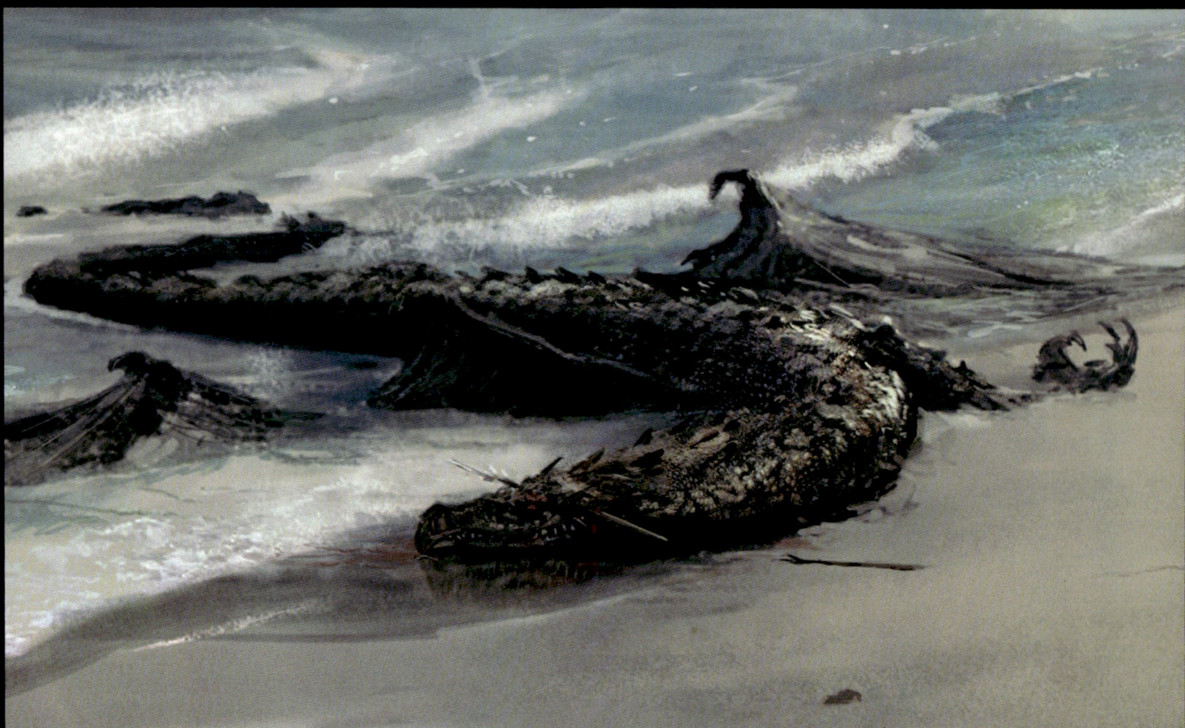

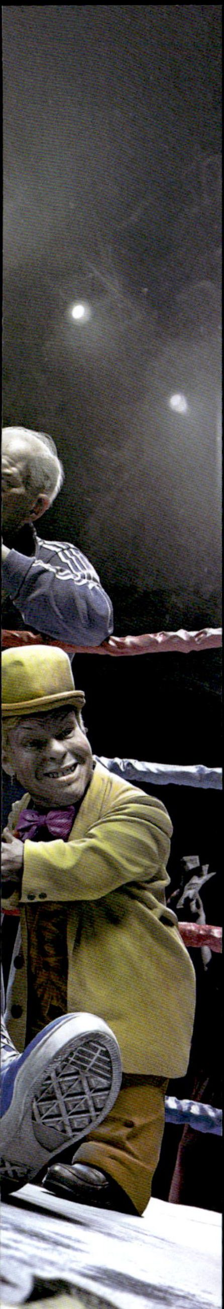

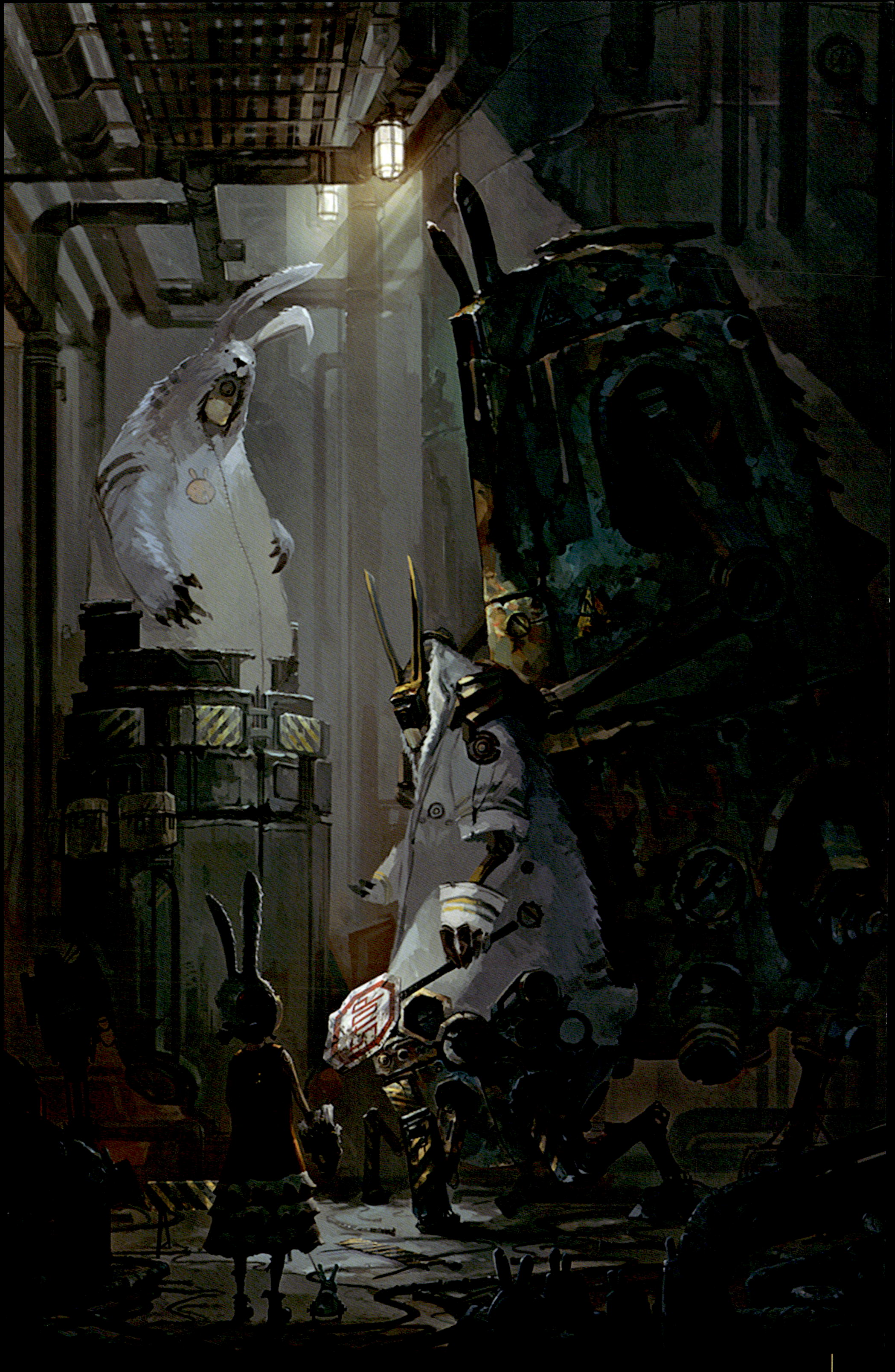

Rabbits
Photoshop
Yongming Yang, CHINA

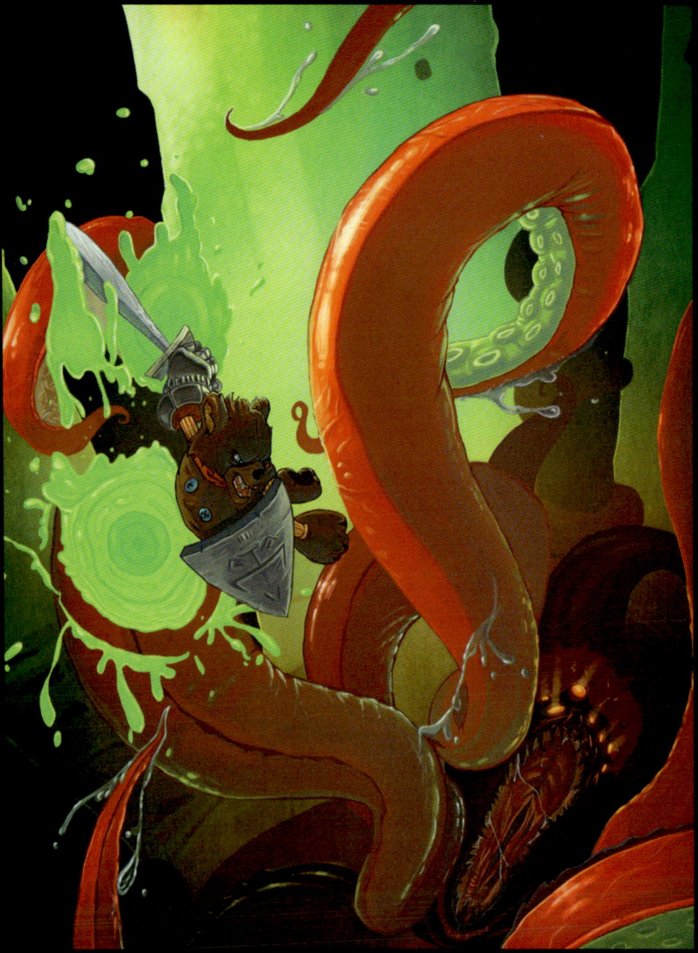

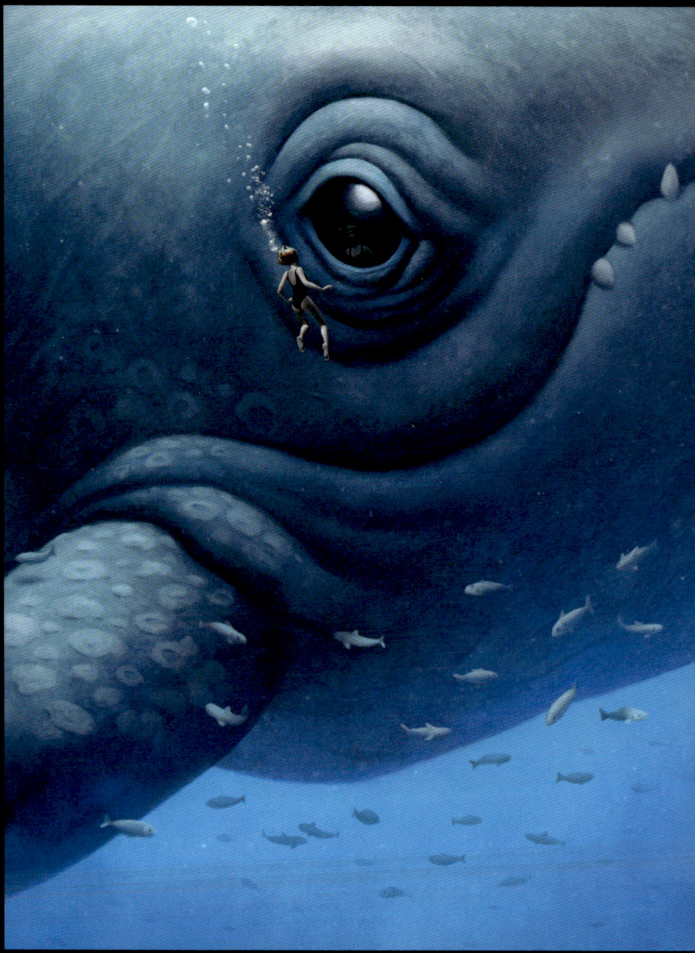

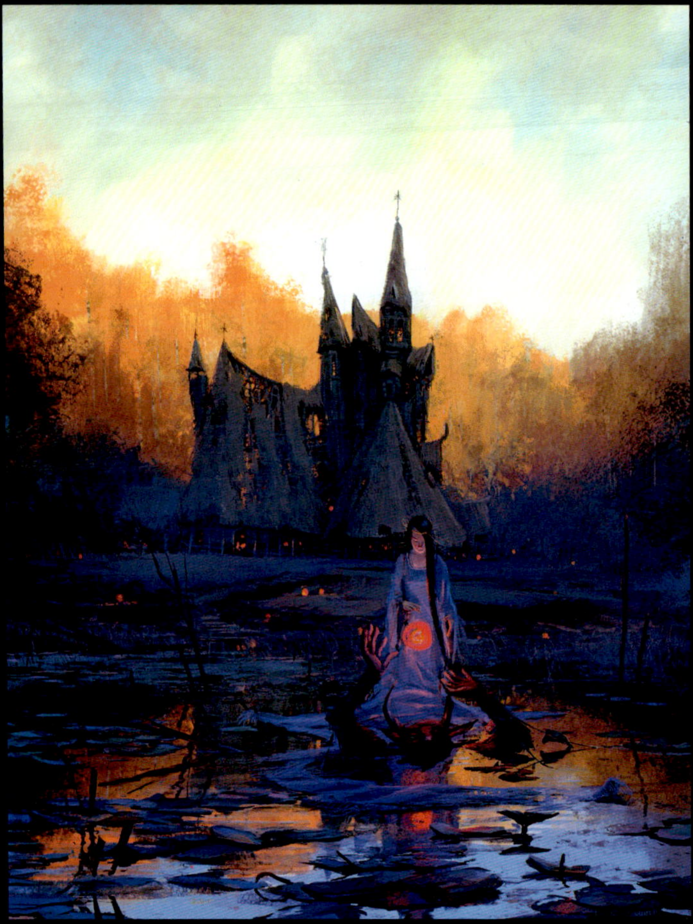

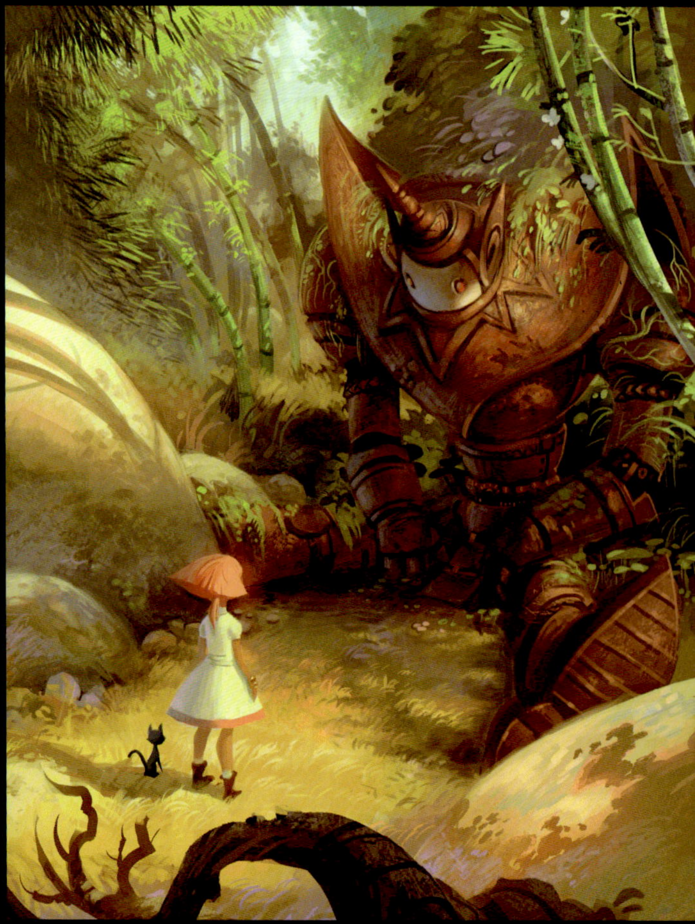

The Rescue
Photoshop
Guy Atherfold, GREAT BRITAIN
[top]

Fragile Love
Photoshop
Vilius Petrauskas, LITHUANIA
[above]

Beneath
Photoshop
Client: Tähtivaeltaja magazine
Ture Ekroos, FINLAND

An Old Puppet
Photoshop
Chaichan Artwichai, THAILAND
[above]

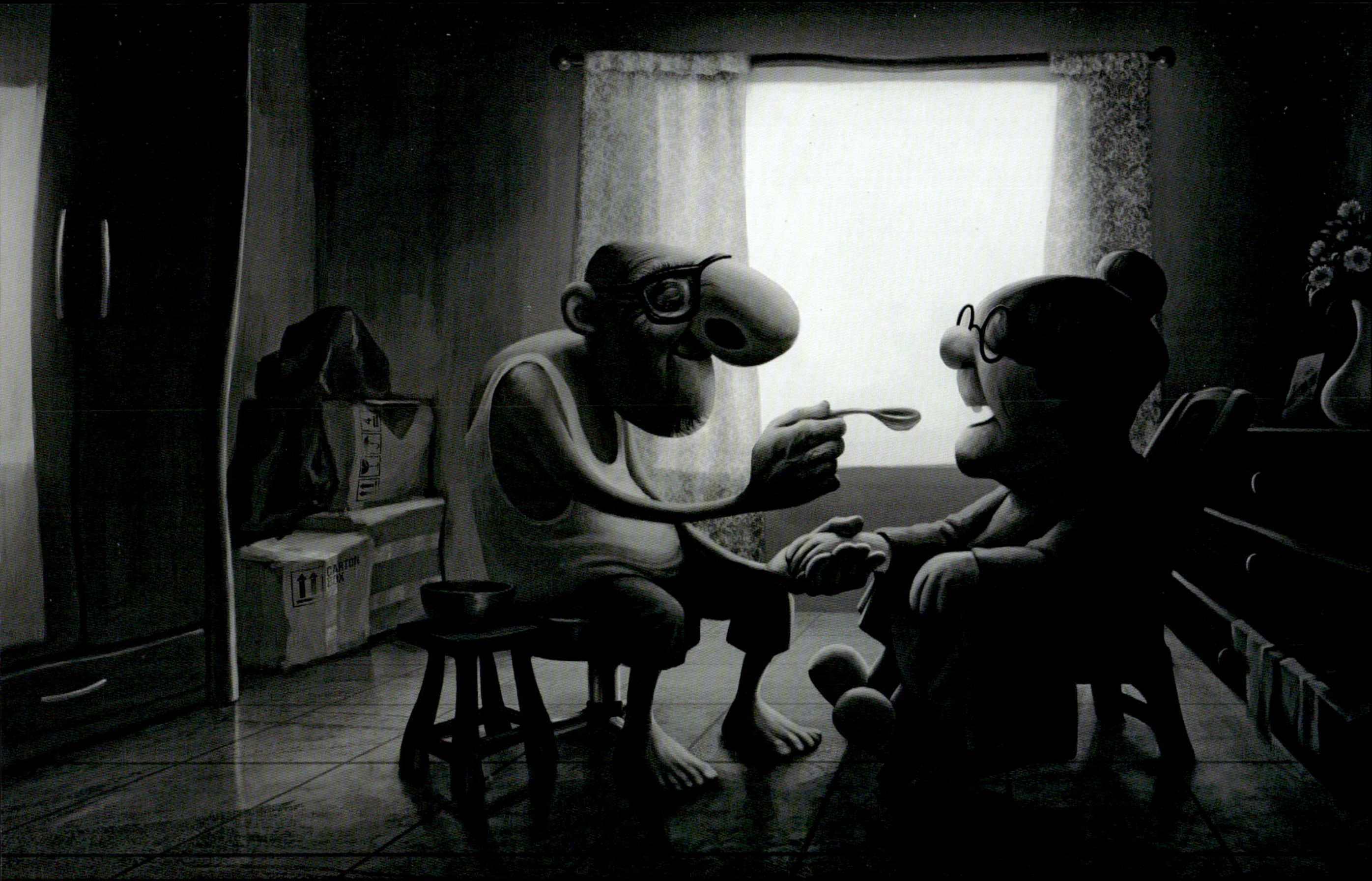

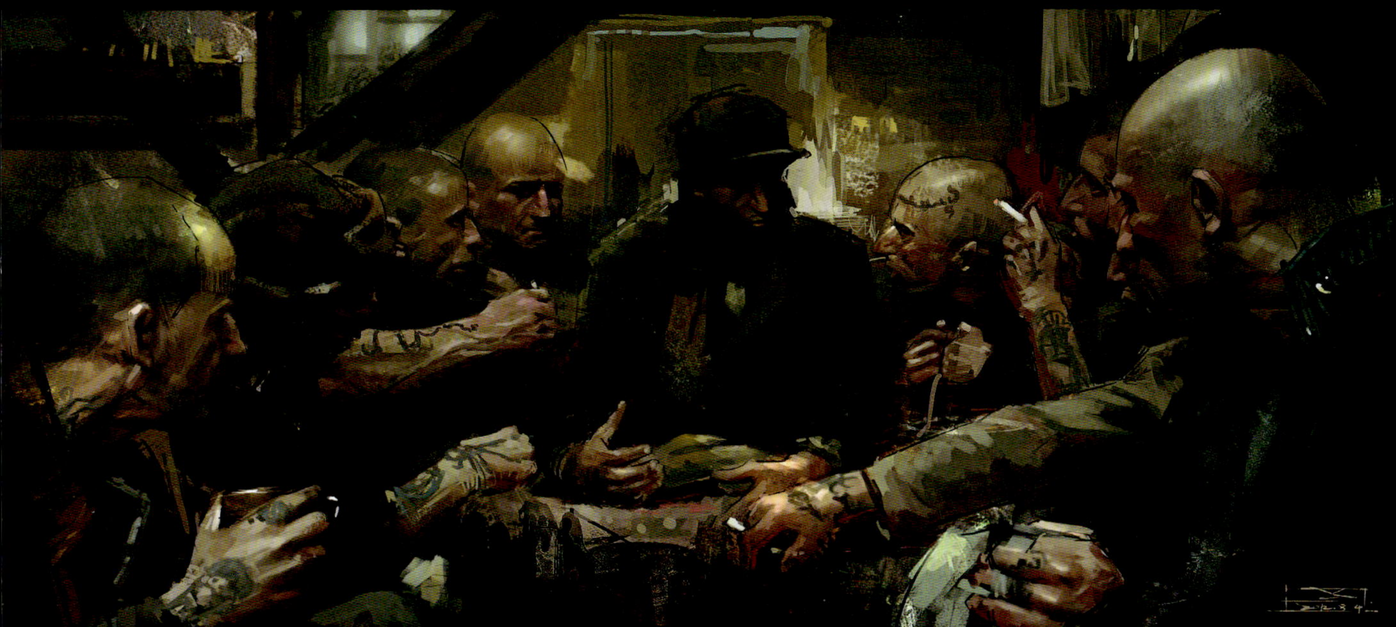

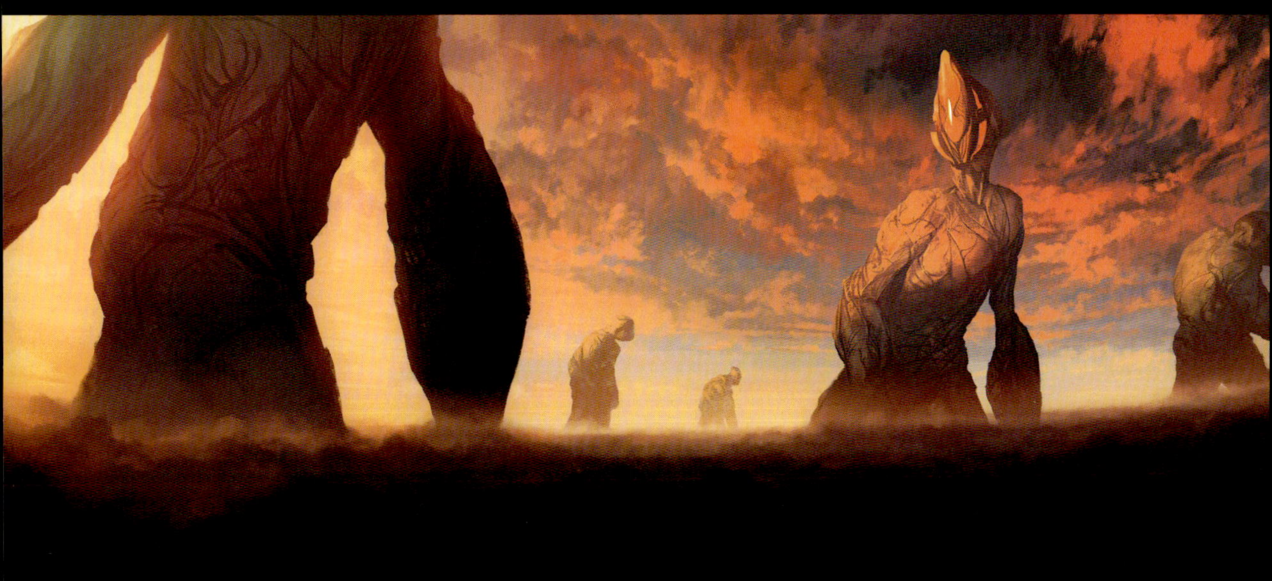

Till the Last Day
Photoshop
Vinh Pham, VIETNAM
[top]

Concentration Camp
SketchBook Pro,
Photoshop
Chuan Zhong, CHINA
[center]

Their Solemn Procession
Photoshop
Noah Bradley, USA
[bottom]

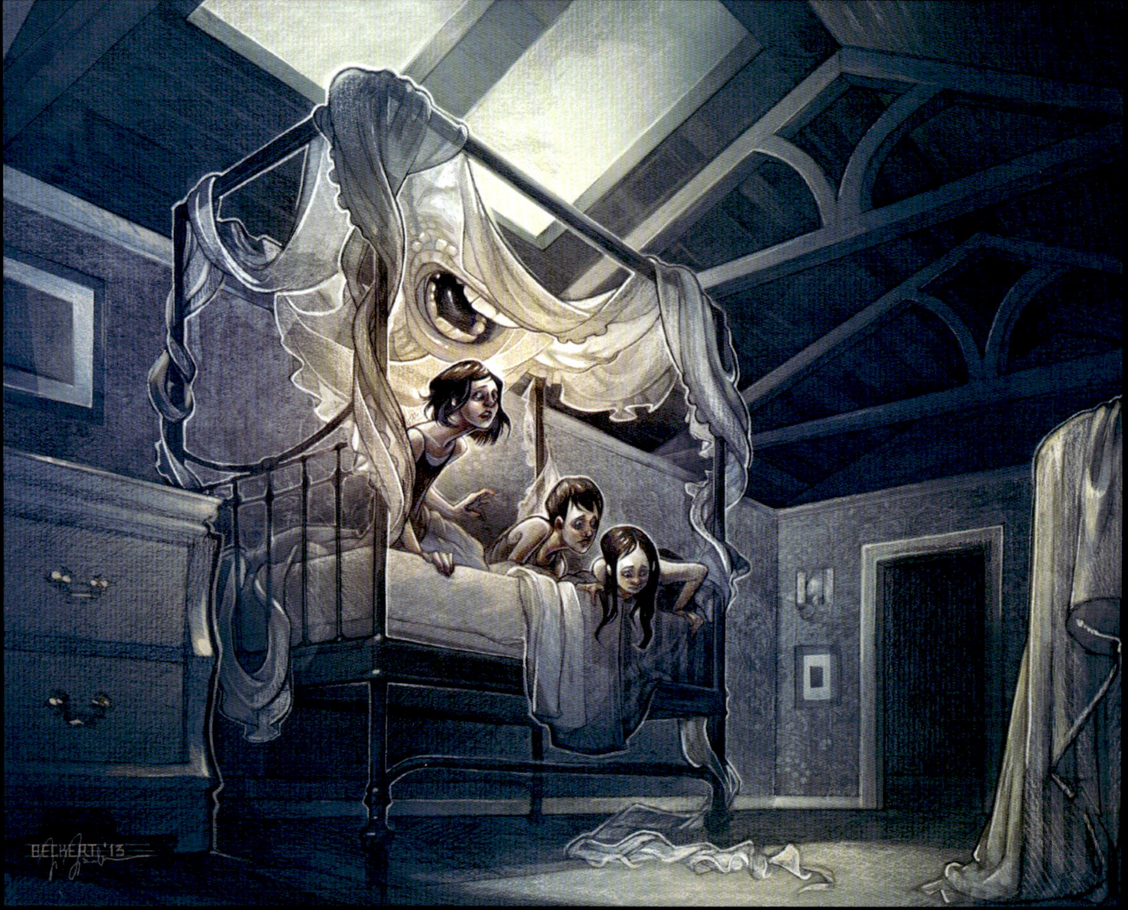

Nothing Under the Bed
Photoshop
Wylie Elise Beckert, USA
[right]

The Streets of Gateway: The Banner-bird Fiasco
Photoshop
Sean Andrew Murray, USA
[below]

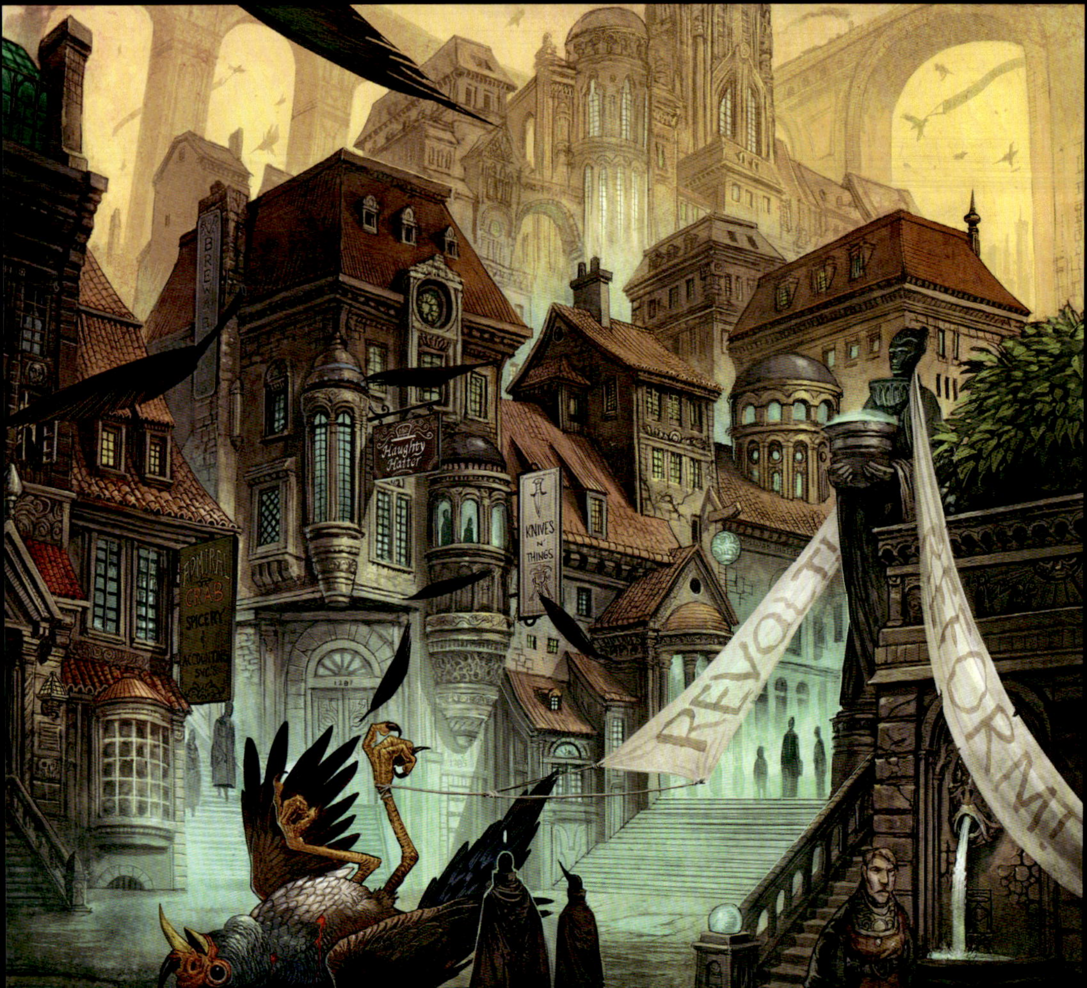

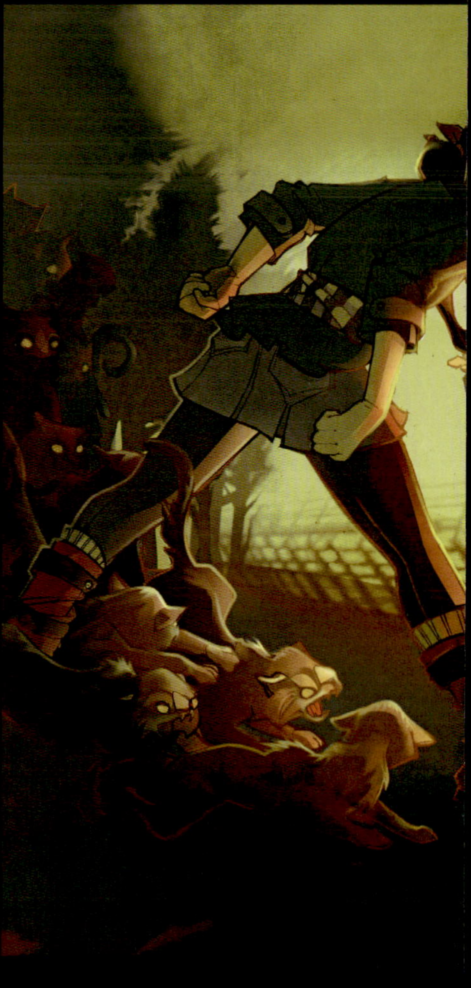

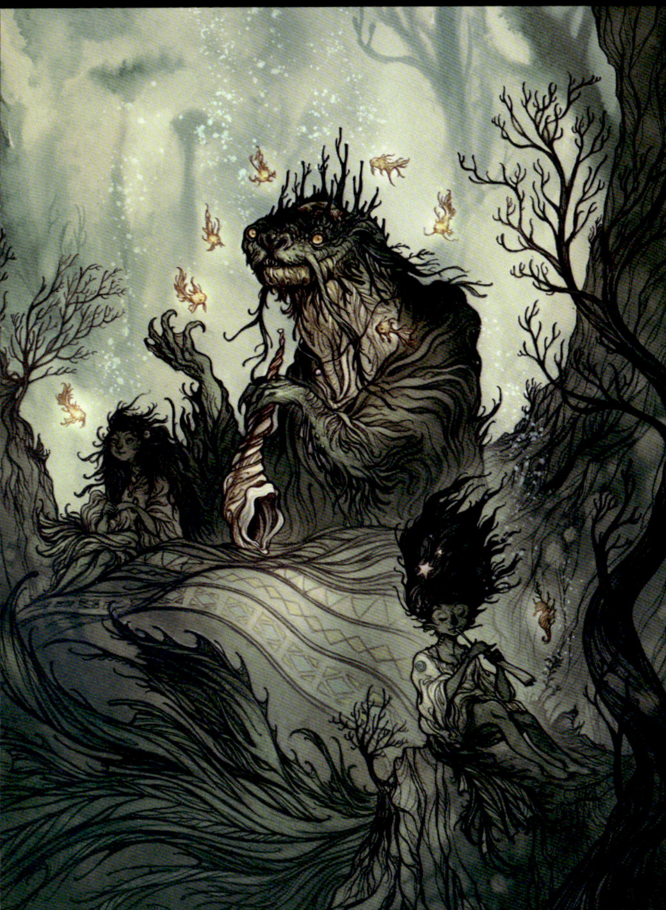

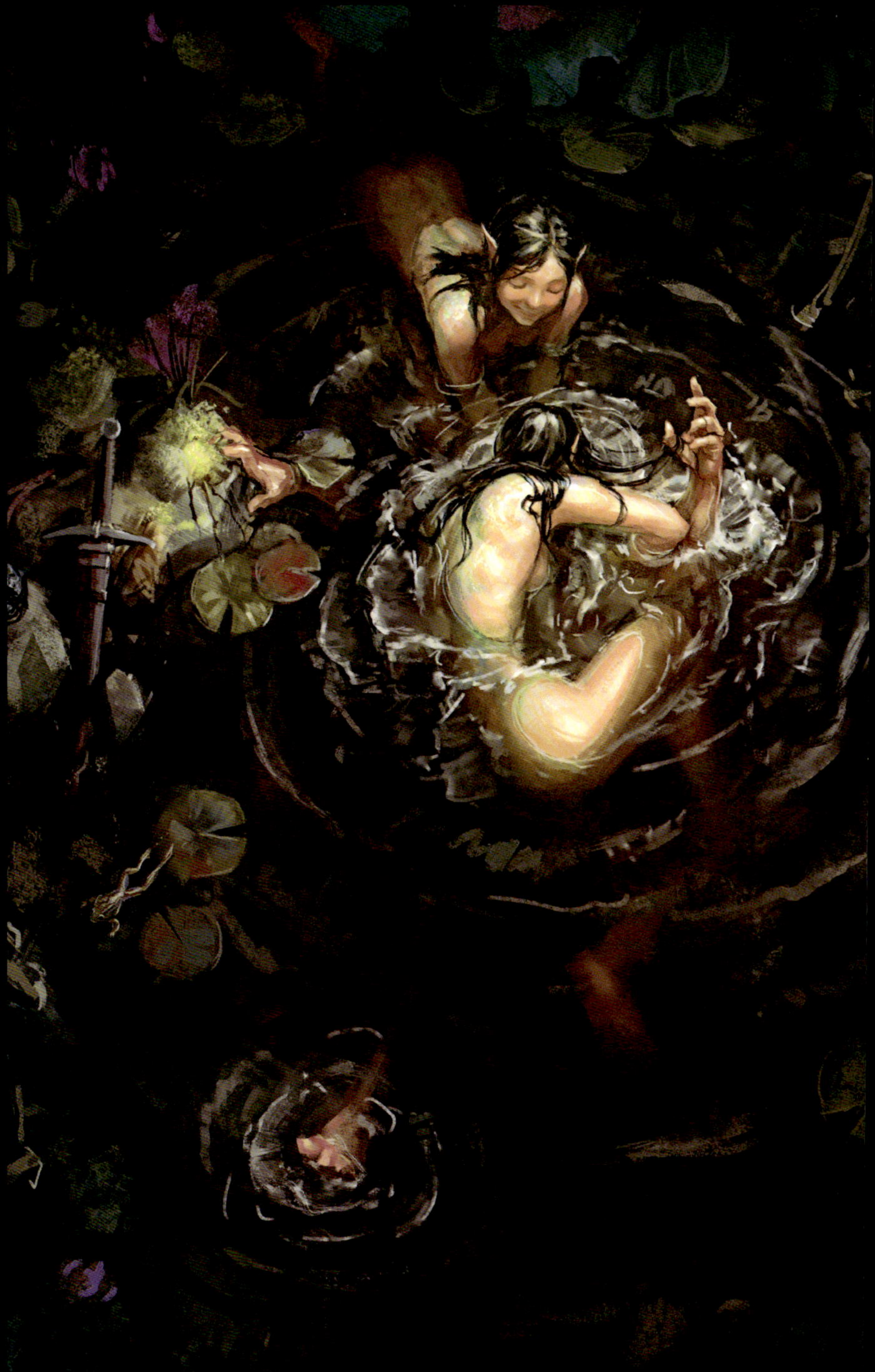

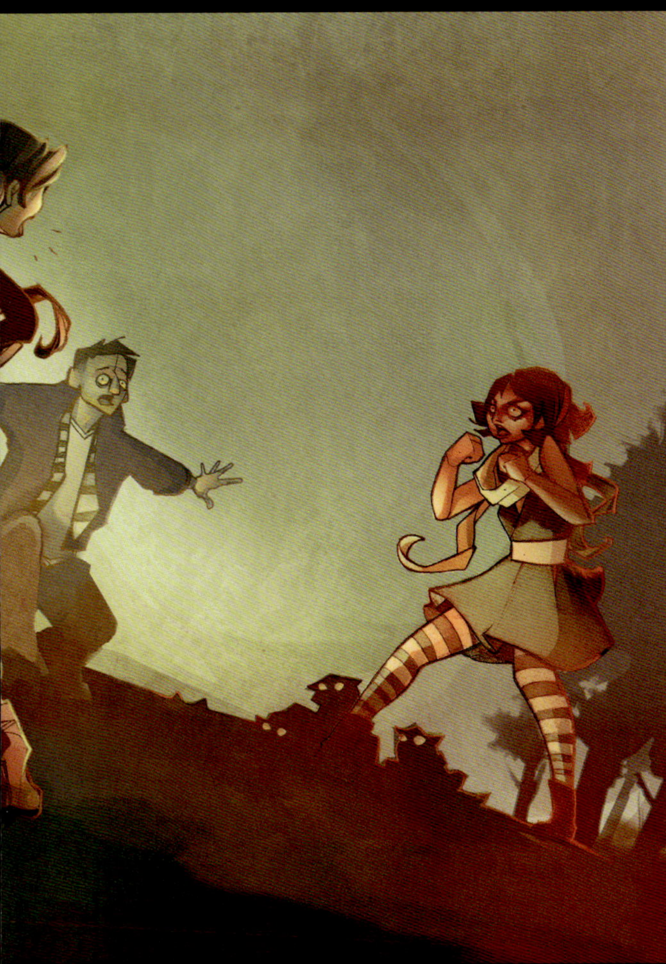

The Fish Master
Photoshop
Cory Godbey, USA
[above left]

The Toll of Temptation
Photoshop
Lane Brown, USA
[above]

Catfight
Photoshop
Wylie Elise Beckert, USA
[left]

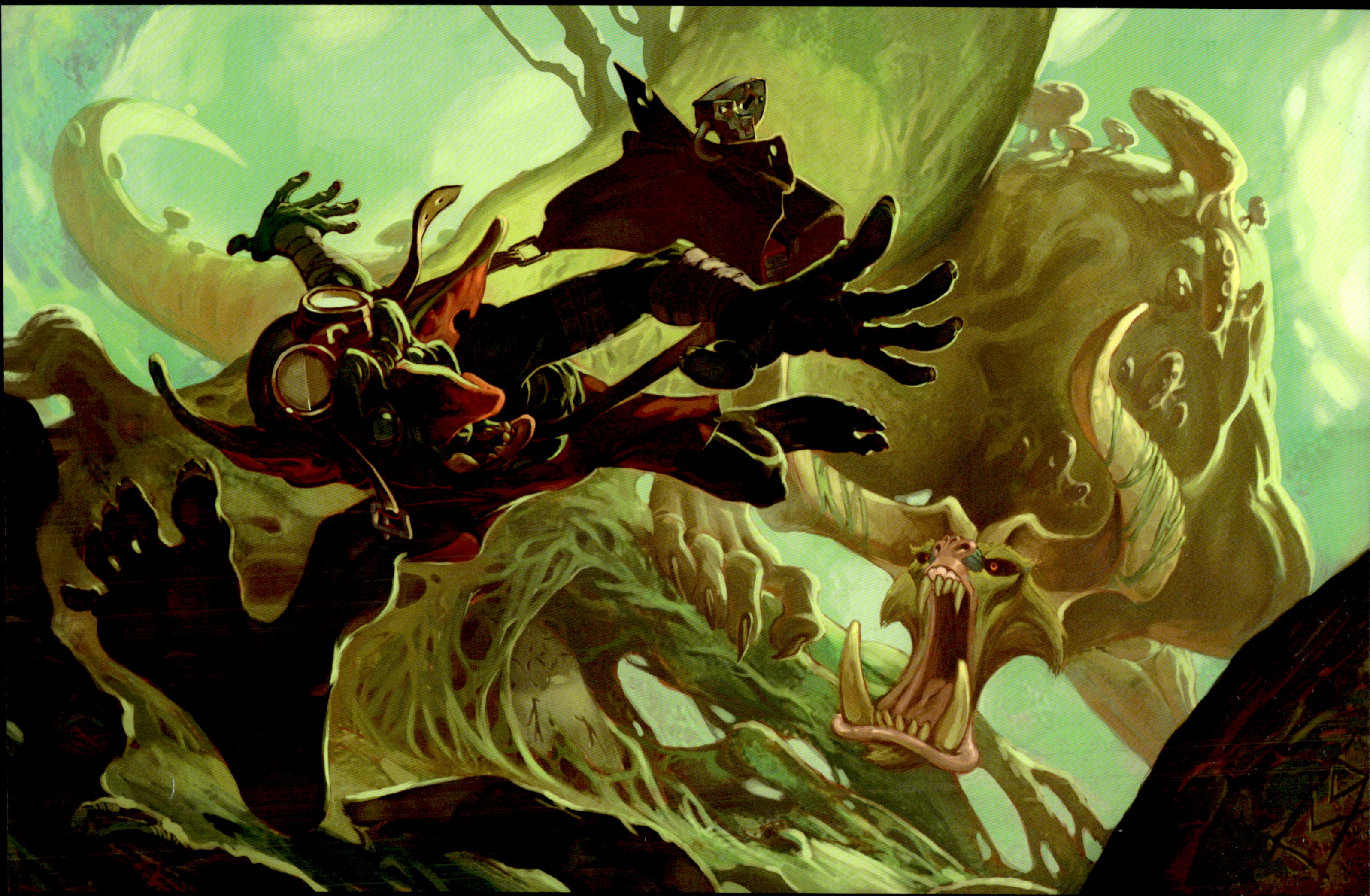

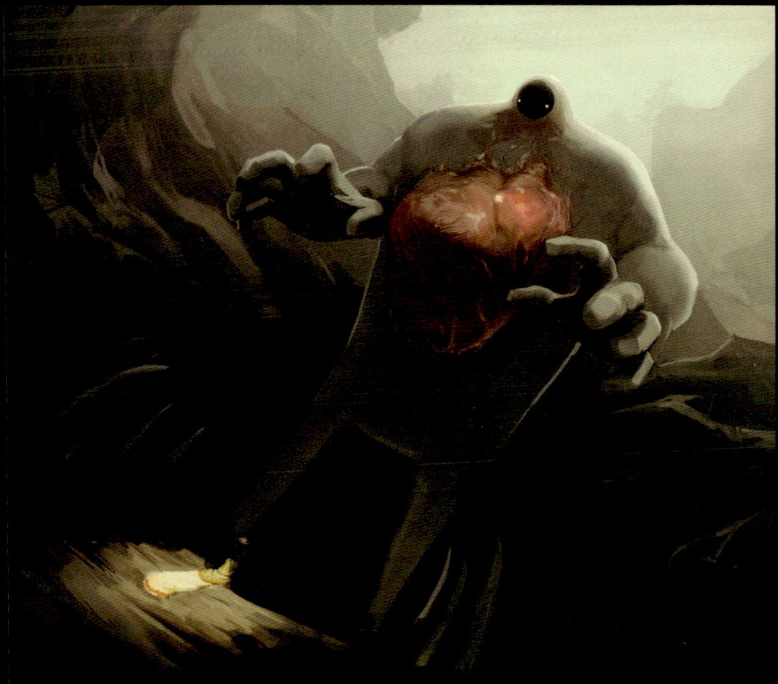

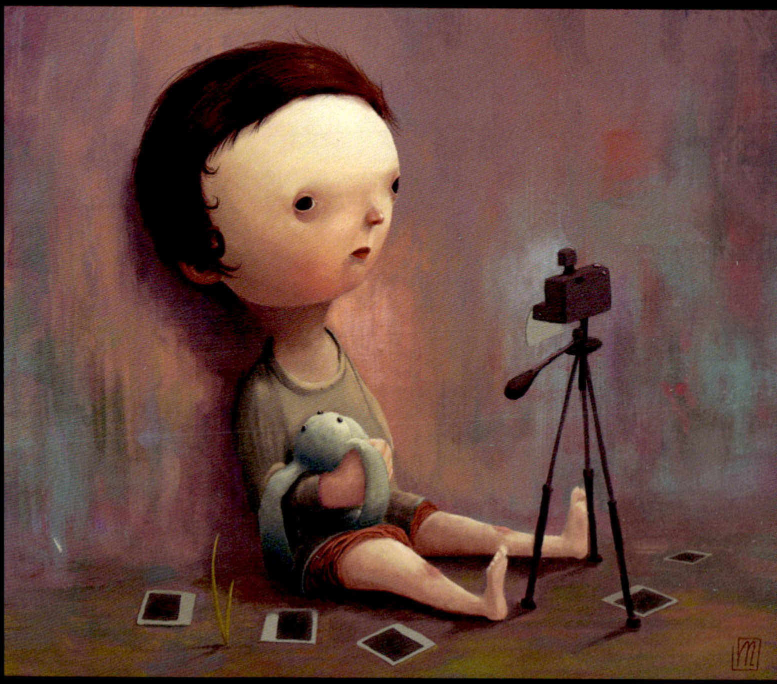

Run For Your Buns
Photoshop
Victor Maury, USA
[top]

The Sacrifice
Photoshop
Ulises Serrano, MEXICO
[above]

Polaroids
Photoshop
Marco Piunti, ITALY
[above]

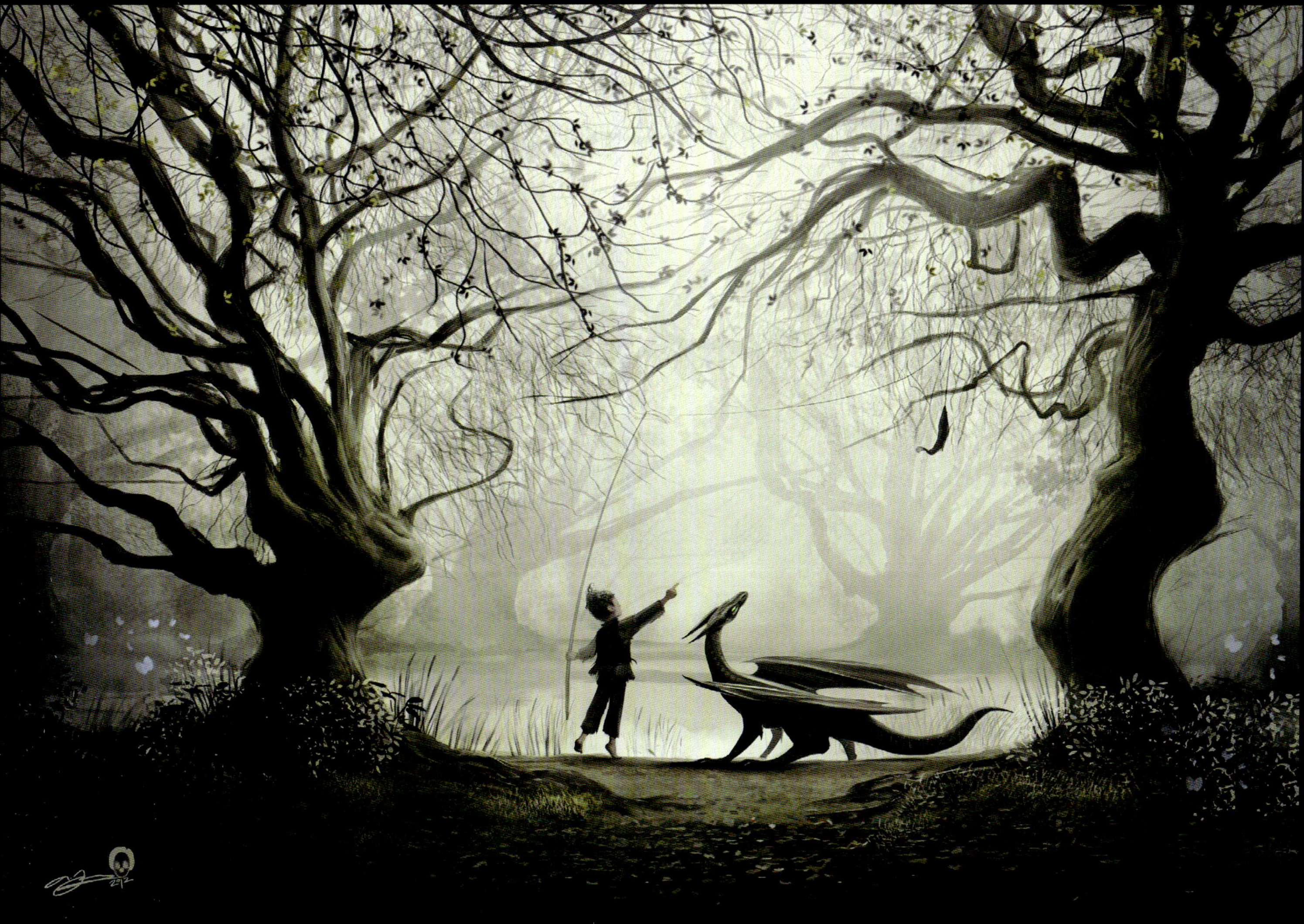

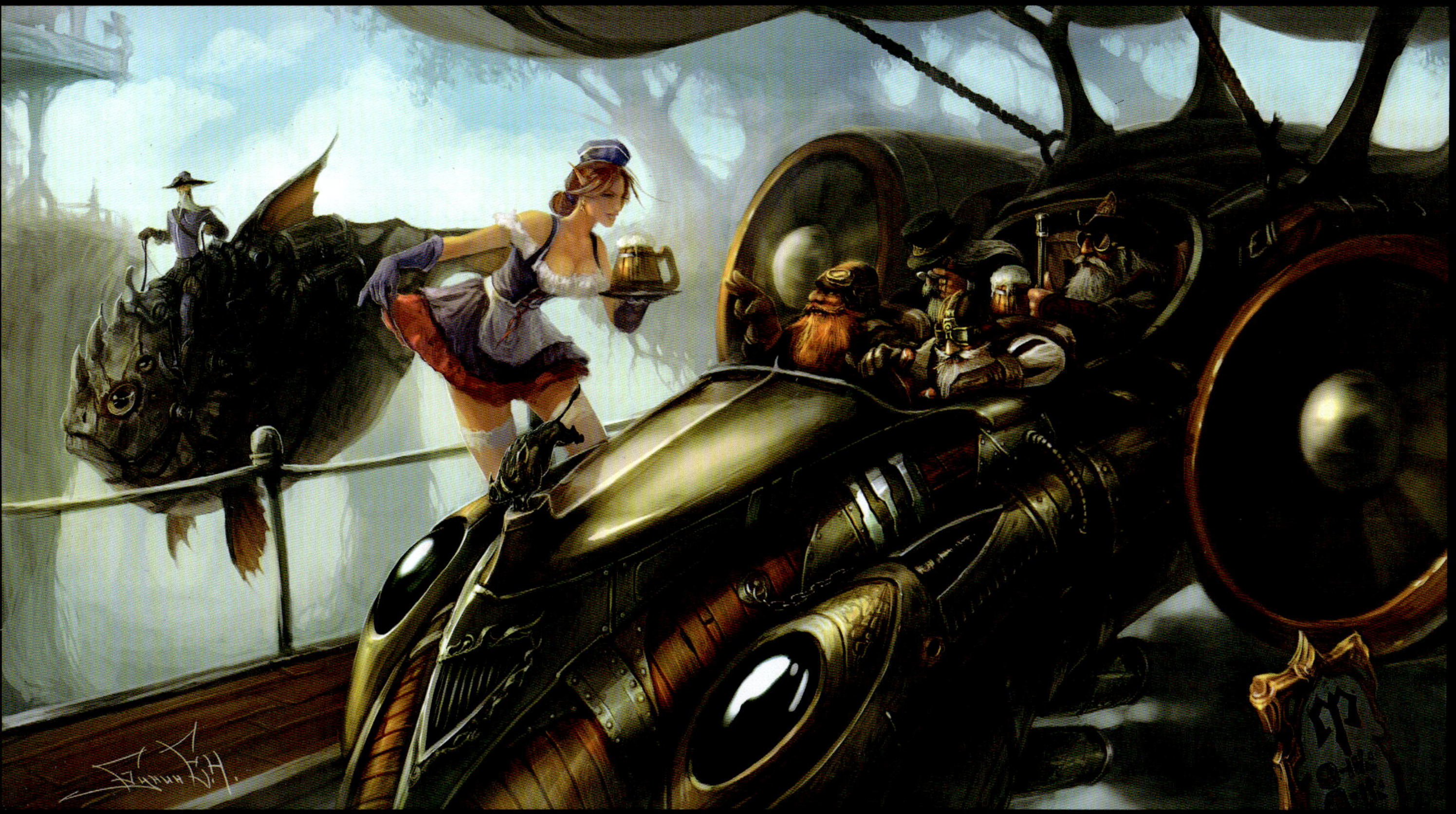

The Boy and His Dragon
Photoshop
Andy Fairhurst, GREAT BRITAIN
[top]

Two Beers
Photoshop
Evgeny Bunin, RUSSIA
[above]

Consumed
3ds Max, V-Ray,
ZBrush, Photoshop
Toni Bratincevic,
CROATIA

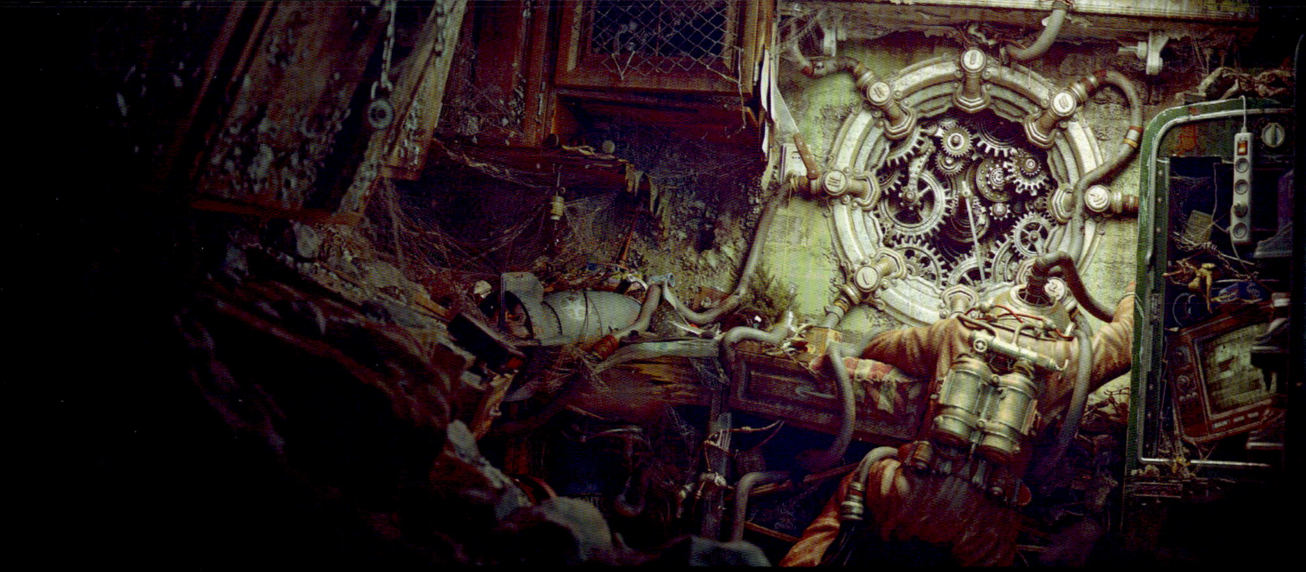

Crash
3ds Max, V-Ray,
ZBrush, Photoshop
Darko Vucenik,
CROATIA

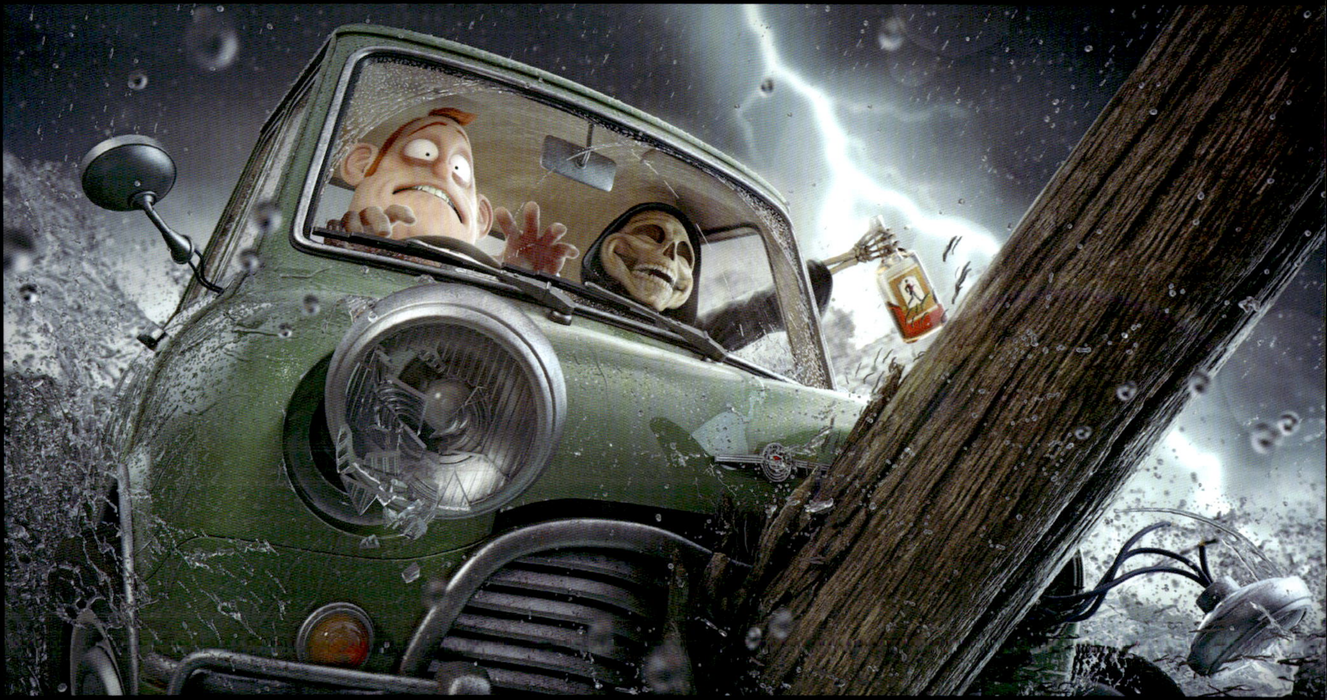

Moses: The Beginning
LightWave 3D,
ZBrush, Photoshop
Milivoj Popovic,
Lemonade3d,
CROATIA

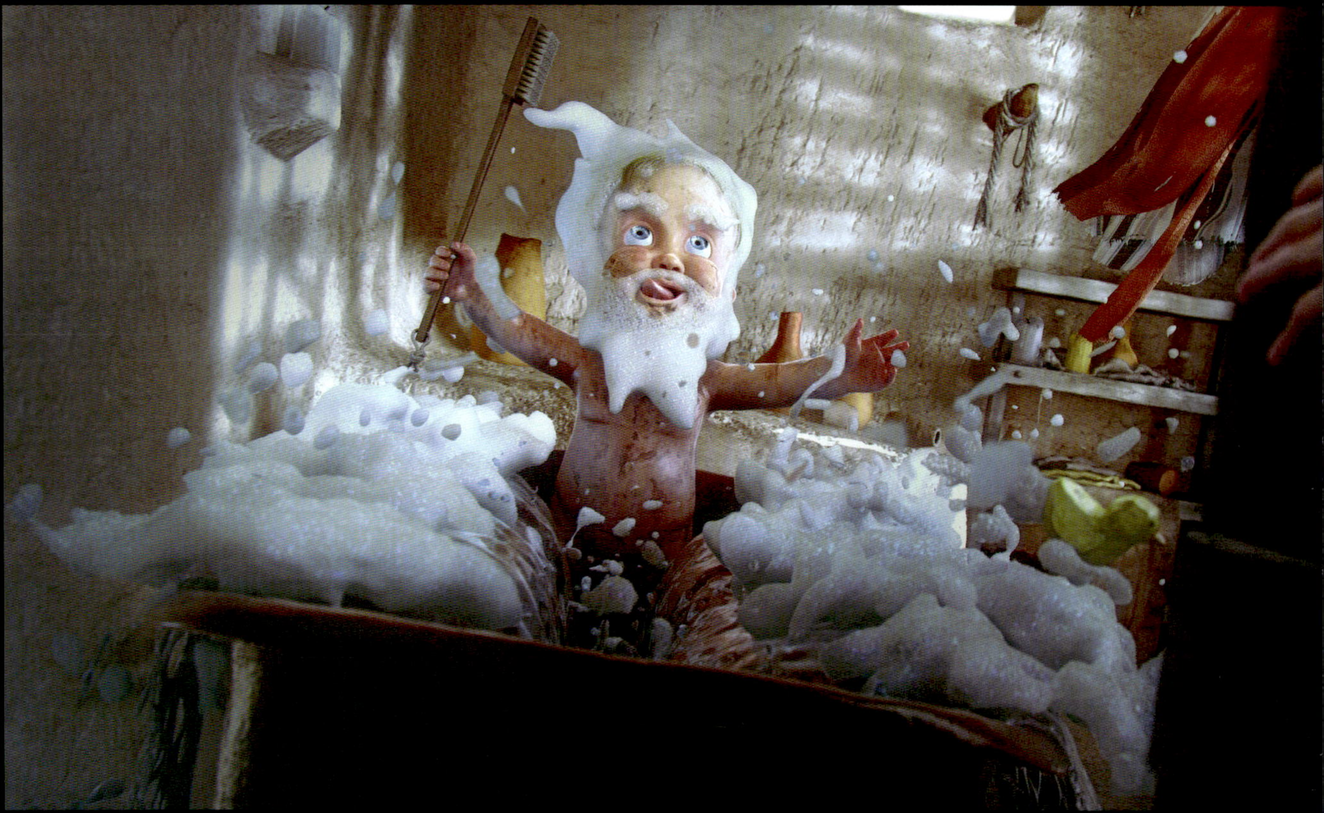

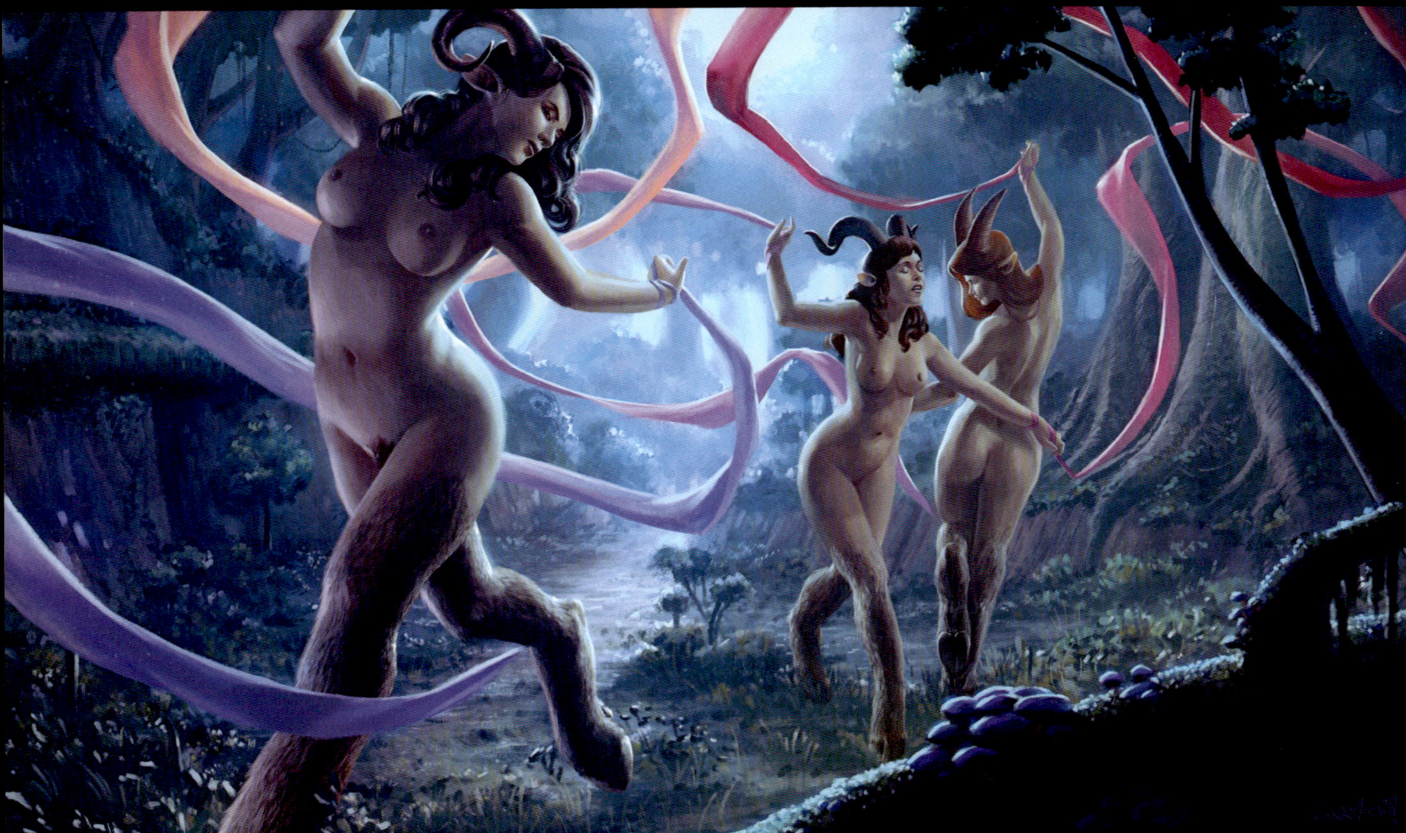

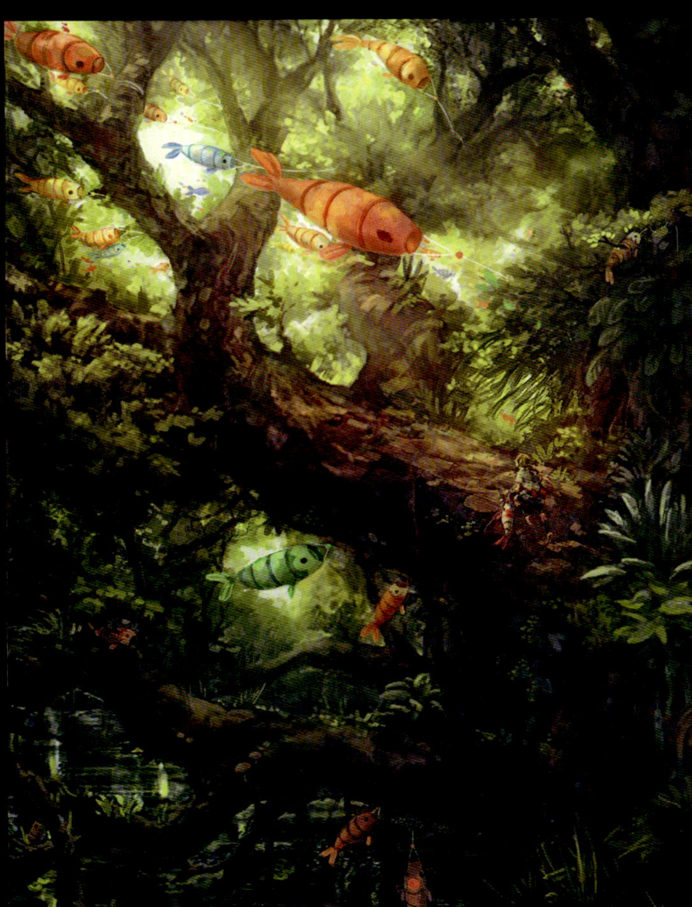

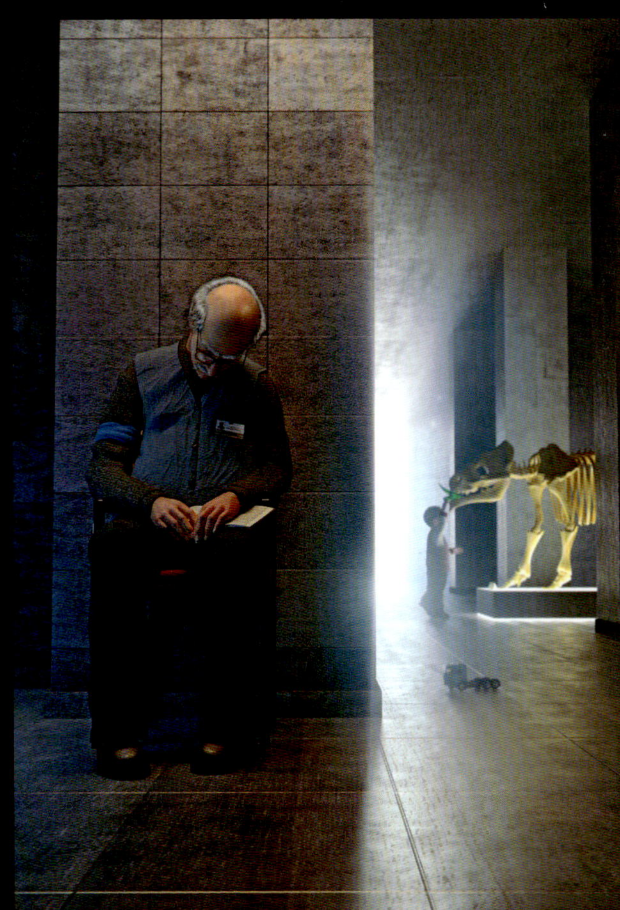

INDEX

Vadim Sverdlov
Haifa, ISRAEL
www.behance.net/tipa_graphic
55, 148

Raymond Swanland
Los Angeles, CA, USA
www.raymondswanland.com
69, 113, 126

Andrzej Sykut
Cracow, POLAND
azazel@platige.com
144

Syndrome
Los Angeles, CA, USA
www.syndromestudio.com
236

J Otto Szatmari
Budapest, HUNGARY
jottoszatmari-design.blogspot.com
137

Liran Szeiman
Sant Cugat del Valles, Barcelona, SPAIN
www.liransz.com
111, 113, 129, 262, 266

Bogdan Szot
Bydgoszcz, POLAND
www.bono35.iportfolio.pl
265, 267

T

Mohamed Taaeb
Faculty of Fine Arts
Cairo, EGYPT
www.taaeb.com
21

Renaud Taelemans
Gembloux, BELGIUM
eboladelit2fuite@gmail.com
53, 117, 232

Juraj Talcik
Bratislava, SLOVAKIA
jurajtalcik.com
196

Alben Tan
Davao, PHILIPPINES
albentan.blogspot.com
242

Darren Tan
Imaginary Friends Studios
SINGAPORE
wraithdt@gmail.com
75

Takashi Tan
Johor Bahru, Johor, MALAYSIA
bjiahao.deviantart.com
30, 56

Ivan Tao
Bandar Sunway, Selangor Darul Ehsan, MALAYSIA
ivantao.cghub.com
58

Teague
Seattle, WA, USA
www.teague.com
201

JP Targete
Cary, NC, USA
www.targeteart.com
220

Gareth Thatcher
Mi
Salford, GREAT BRITAIN
www.wearemi.com
249

Sarel Theron
Kommetjie, Western Cape, SOUTH AFRICA
www.sareltheron.com
181

Geoffroy Thoorens
FRANCE
www.djahalland.com
204, 208

Nguy Thuyngan
Saigon, VIETNAM
thuyngan.deviantart.com
53

Daniel Torres
Mexicali, Baja California, MEXICO
www.danieltorresdg.blogspot.com
73, 234

Cory Trego-Erdner
San Diego, CA, USA
corytregoerdner.daportfolio.com
116

Murat Turan
Malatya, TURKEY
designtu.deviantart.com
263

Seid Tursic
Sarajevo,
BOSNIA AND HERZEGOVINA
seidtursic@gmail.com
44

Mark Tuttle
San Diego, CA, USA
65, 71, 97, 131

U

Jan Urschel
Singapore, SINGAPORE
www.hendrix-design.com
135, 140, 169

V

Jody Valdes
Saint-Laurent, QC, CANADA
jvaldes.cgsociety.org
158

Corrado Vanelli
Casaletto Ceredano (CR), ITALY
www.landofsecretarts.com
121

Giorgio Vecchio
Absolute 2001
Pieve Ligure, Genova, ITALY
www.absolute2001.it
251

Nikita Veprikov
UKRAINE
www.veprikov.com
270

Gabriel Verdon
Ottawa, ON, CANADA
gabrielverdon.com
213

Sonia Verdu
Madrid, SPAIN
www.soniaverdu.es
130

Lennart Verhoeff
Utrecht, NETHERLANDS
www.lennartverhoeff.net
182

Jeremy Vickery
Emeryville, CA, USA
www.jermilex.com
183, 242

Nicolas Villeminot
Bordeaux, FRANCE
electronic0.deviantart.com
59

Darko Vucenik
Donji Laduc, CROATIA
dvucenik@yahoo.com
278

W

Bruno Wagner
Bourg en Bresse, FRANCE
www.yayashin.com
95

Crystal Wall Lancaster
Quispamsis, NB, CANADA
www.crystalwalllancaster.com
54, 264

Rokly Wang
Frankfurt, AUSTRIA
roklywang@gmail.com
37

Sarah Webb
Fairbanks, AK, USA
bonfireofstars.carbonmade.com
173, 179, 230, 232, 279

Fabien Weibel
Vich, VD, SWITZERLAND
www.fweibel.com
174-175

Tony Weinstock
Los Angeles, CA, USA
www.tonyweinstock.com
66, 86, 100, 240

Toni Weisskopf
Boston, MA, USA
www.baen.com
85, 120

Tom Winberg
Arendal, NORWAY
www.wide3d.no
246

Maciej Wojtala
Warsaw, Mazowieckie, POLAND
m@wojtala.com
www.wojtala.com
177

Ben Wootten
NEW ZEALAND
benwootten.com
71

Bayard Wu
Shenzhen, CHINA
bayardwu.cghub.com
127

Y

Guang Yang
Shanghai, CHINA
yg-cg@hotmail.com
37, 63, 270

Yongming Yang
Shanghai, CHINA
blog.sina.com.cn/u/1813524624
58, 271

Daniel Yaqub
twentyfourpixel
Geesthacht, GERMANY
danielyaqub@gmx.de
201

Xiao Yi
Nanning, CHINA
www.yixiaoart.com
239

Morgan Yon
Montpellier, FRANCE
morgan-yon.com
114, 136, 147, 178

Donglu Yu
Saint-Laurent, QC, CANADA
donglu-littlefish.blogspot.ca
50, 105, 132-133, 145, 175, 176, 179, 214

Qiu jian Yuan
Beijing, CHINA
ayuanqj@yahoo.com.cn
68, 125

Z

Gilberto 'Soren' Zaragoza
Metacube
Guadalajara, Jalisco, MEXICO
www.metacube.com.mx
33

Dmitry Zaviyalov
Tallinn, ESTONIA
dimms1@gmail.com
160-161

Richard Zela
Mexico City, MEXICO
www.richardzela.com
55, 56, 156

Apple Qingyang Zhang
Academy of Art University
San Francisco, CA, USA
www.appleqz.com
102

Zhangchendaxiao Zhang
Beijing, CHINA
zcwww--2030212@163.com
40

Guodong Zhao
Tianjin, CHINA
www.leewiart.com/space/8885
168

ZEZ Zhaoenze
Fuzhou, Fujian, CHINA
blog.sina.com.cn/zez0626
86, 99, 176

Hu Zheng
Shanghai, CHINA
376873746@qq.com
269

Chuan Zhong
Hangzhou, CHINA
zhongshouchuan@163.com
273

Galina Zhurkina
Moscow, RUSSIA
www.himera.be
100

Artur Zima
Orpington, GREAT BRITAIN
artur92@hotmail.co.uk
164

Loic Zimmermann
Santa Monica, CA, USA
www.e338.com
54

Egle Zioma
Vilnius, LITHUANIA
daywish.deviantart.com
59

Farkas Zsolt
Budapest, HUNGARY
mediadigital.hu/ekho
43

Products credited by popular name in this book are listed alphabetically here by company name:

Adobe After Effects, FreeHand, Illustrator, Photoshop
www.adobe.com

Ambient Design ArtRage
www.ambientdesign.com

Autodesk 3ds Max, AutoCAD, Maya, Mudbox, SketchBook Pro, Softimage
www.autodesk.com

Bjürn Gustavsson Wings3D
www.wings3d.com

Blender Blender
www.blender.org

Cebas GmbH finalRender
www.finalrender.com

Chaos Group V-Ray
www.chaosgroup.com

Corel PhotoPaint, Painter
www.corel.com

E-on Software Vue Esprit
www.e-onsoftware.com

Fred Slijkerman Ultra Fractal
www.ultrafractal.com

Graphisoft AutoCAD
www.graphisoft.com

GIMP GIMP
www.feversoft.com

Luxology MODO
www.luxology.com

Mandlebulb Mandelbulb3D
www.mandlebulb3d.com

MAXON BodyPaint 3D, CINEMA 4D
www.maxoncomputer.com

McNeel AccuRender, Rhino
en.na.mcneel.com

Mirve Software Shade
www.mirye.com

MyPaint MyPaint
mypaint.intilinux.com

NewTek LightWave 3D
www.newtek.com

Next Limit Technologies Maxwell Render
www.maxwellrender.com

NVIDIA mental ray
www.mentalimages.com

Pixologic ZBrush
www.pixologic.com

Solid Angle Arnold
www.solidangle.com

Trimble SketchUp
ww2.trimble.com

Virtual Fashion Marvelous Designer
www.marvelousdesigner.com

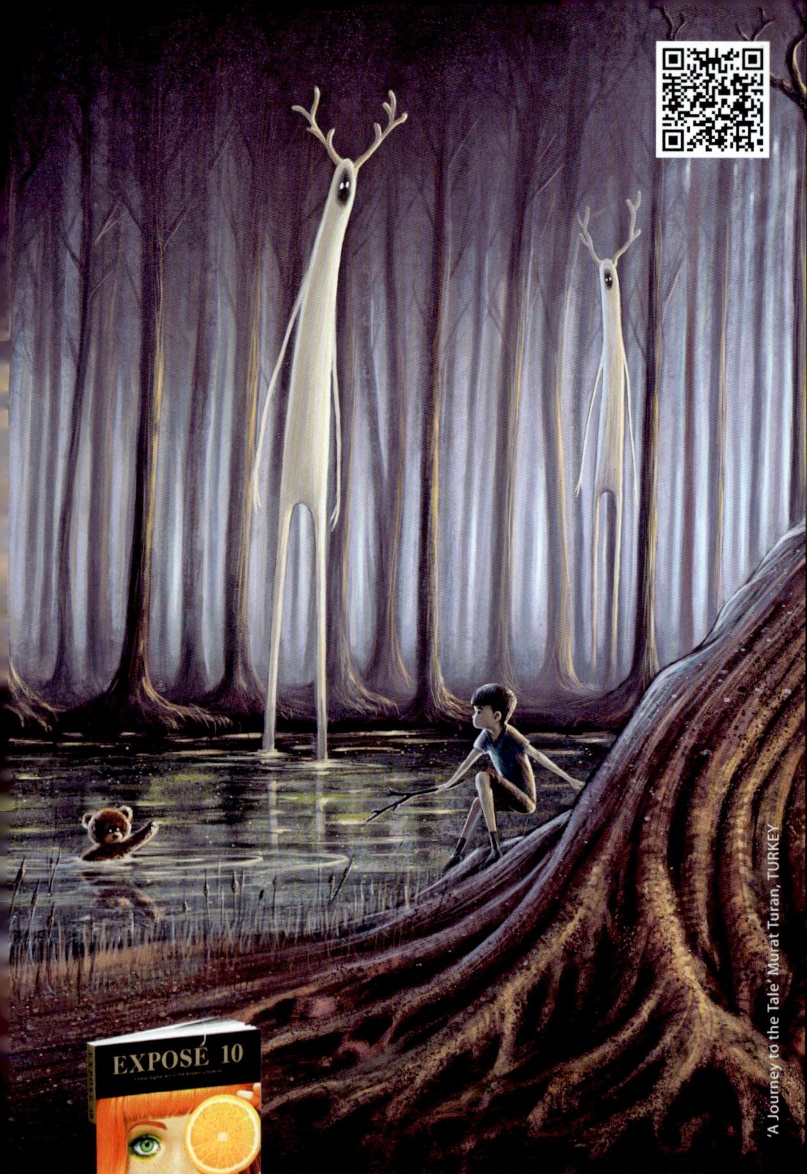

'A Journey to the Tale' Murat Turan, TURKEY

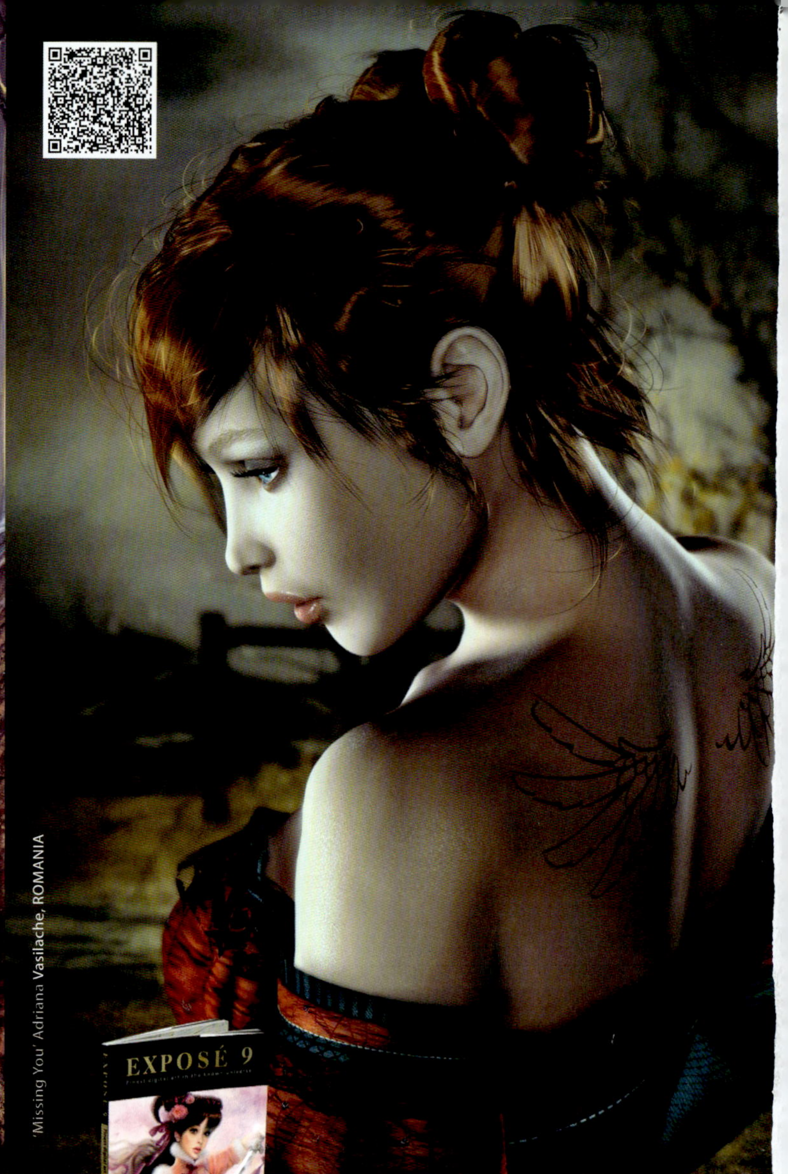

'Missing You' Adriana Vasilache, ROMANIA